Housing and Community Development

Housing and Community Development

Cases and Materials

Fourth Edition

James A. Kushner
Professor of Law at Southwestern Law School, and Adjunct Professor University of Southern California School of Policy, Planning and Development, Graduate Program of Urban Planning

Charles E. Daye
Henry P. Brandis Distinguished Professor at the University of North Carolina, Chapel Hill School of Law

Peter W. Salsich, Jr.
McDonnell Professor of Justice in American Society at St. Louis University School of Law

Henry W. McGee, Jr.
Professor of law at the Seattle University School of Law and Professor Emeritus UCLA School of Law

W. Dennis Keating
Professor in the College of Urban Affairs, Cleveland State University

Barbara L. Bezdek
Professor at University of Maryland School of Law

Otto J. Hetzel
Professor Emeritus at Wayne State University Law School

Daniel R. Mandelker
Howard A. Stamper Professor of Law at the Washington University School of Law

Robert M. Washburn
Professor of Law at the Rutgers University School of Law-Camden

Carolina Academic Press
Durham, North Carolina

ISBN: 978-1-59460-833-9
LCCN: 2010931479

Carolina Academic Press
700 Kent Street
Durham, North Carolina 27701
Telephone (919) 489-7486
Fax (919) 493-5668
www.cap-press.com

Printed in the United States of America

Dedication

We proudly dedicate this Fourth Edition of *Housing and Community Development* to our esteemed colleague, and friend Daniel R. Mandelker, Howard A. Stamper Professor, Washington University School of Law. His deep interest in the subject, extraordinary professional dedication, and outstanding scholarship have influenced all of us. He has inspired us as a role model and has served as our mentor.

Summary Table of Contents

Contents

Table of Cases

(Principal cases are listed in **bold**).

Preface to the First Edition (1981)

Housing and community development programs present fascinating and complex problems for lawyers concerned with the quality of urban life. This book, the first comprehensive treatment of this field in over a decade, presents a systematic overview of these programs and the policy issues they raise. Its authors have brought to these materials a wealth of personal and academic experience, which they hope will enliven its presentation and encourage their colleagues to consider this important area of public concern.

The core of the book is the central chapters on the key housing and community development programs. Chapter 3 considers housing subsidies, and concentrates on the federal housing programs. The chapter is organized by program type, and covers the extensive rental housing assistance programs and the more modest programs subsidizing home ownership. A subsidy matrix at the beginning of the chapter presents the basic policy choices any housing subsidy program must make, and provides an introduction and focus for the program material. A concluding section examines alternatives to existing subsidy programs, and points the way to reexamination and change. Chapter 7 continues and expands this examination of future policy alternatives.

Chapter 4 examines state landlord-tenant laws, state and local rent controls, and condominium conversion. It also considers the constitutional due process rights of tenants in subsidizing housing. The focus is on the lower income tenant in the housing market, and program strategies that can strengthen his bargaining position and improve his access to rental housing.

Chapter 5 is the key chapter on community development and revitalization. The opening section examines housing rehabilitation and housing maintenance programs undertaken under local housing codes. The next section considers the theoretical framework for community development. It includes discussion of urban blight as the urban redevelopment triggering concept and targeting issues in community development programs. Federal community development and Urban Development Action Grant programs next receive attention, and the chapter concludes with an examination of displacement problems and the federal Uniform Relocation Act.

Chapter 6 examines problems of race and class, focusing on equal opportunity issues arising under equal protection doctrine and the Federal Fair Housing Act. A concluding section considers growth management and environmental control problems as they affect the availability of housing for lower income groups.

Two introductory chapters raise policy and legal problems common to all of the housing and community development programs. Chapter 1 considers the housing deprivation problem, alternative strategies for a social response to this problem, and the "right to housing" as a constitutional and statutory protection of access to housing service.

Chapter 2 discusses the legislative and administrative process through which Congress and public agencies formulate housing and community development policy. This chapter also examines the role of the courts in implementing and reviewing housing and community development programs. A final section reviews intergovernmental relationships between federal and local governments.

The casebook makes numerous references to R. Montgomery & D. Mandelker, Housing in America: Problems and Perspectives (2d ed. Michie/Bobbs-Merrill, 1980). This book, a collection of essays and editorial comment on housing and community development policy and programs, provides necessary background material on the issues considered in the casebook. The authors recommend Housing in America for assignment along with the casebook materials. Material in Housing in America that supplements the casebook is indicated when appropriate.

Teachers faced with time limitations can consider a number of alternatives for assigning the materials in this book. The professor who focuses on the key programs will concentrate assignments in the program chapters. The teacher who wishes to provide a broader overview will concentrate on the first two and final chapters with selected assignments from the program material. Coverage of the principal federal programs is possible if the instructor concentrates on public housing, the subsidized rental housing programs, and the federal community development program.

Only selected footnotes from the cases and other reprinted material have been reproduced. These have not been renumbered. Insertions within reprinted materials have been placed in brackets.

References to statutes and federal regulations appear throughout the casebook. A pocket-part statutory supplement containing the major federal housing and community development legislation is also included. No dates are given for citations to federal and state statutes and to the Code of Federal Regulations. These citations are current as of the date of publication. The casebook authors regularly make assignments to the statutes so that students can explore the statutory detail of federal programs. The teacher whose time is limited may prefer to place less emphasis on the statutory material.

A word is in order on the problem of change in this fast-moving area of the law. While change is inevitable, the essential elements of federal housing and community development legislation enjoy remarkable public consensus. Program detail may change, but the critical issues remain and require resolution by any national administration, whatever the specifics of its program strategy. Program changes that require revision will be covered in supplements and in revisions to the statutory material.

The authors welcome you to this challenging area of social concern. It is filled with critical policy and legal issues which society must continue to resolve in the years ahead.

The Authors

Preface to the Second Edition (1989)

The authors have undertaken the challenge of revising and updating the Housing and Community Development casebook. In doing so the authors have drawn upon teaching experiences in using the First Edition. The book contains the same basic format of the First Edition. It may be surprising to many that the authors determined to shorten the book. Through teaching experiences the authors realized that in some cases the book had more detail than could be effectively handled and which made the book peculiarly susceptible to obsolescence.

The Second Edition is a "core" book. Much of the detail in programs, statutes and regulations—always in a state of flux—has been omitted. Users of the book may wish to supplement its text with handouts of the most recent program detail from the regulations, statutes, or reports from services that report on current developments in the field.

Chapter 1 continues to take a "perspectives approach" to housing and community development matters. It explores major policy issues that frame the consideration of housing and community development issues, problems, and programs.

Chapter 2 looks at the institutional setting in which housing and community development is played out. It considers the way national policy is determined and implemented. It examines the roles of the agencies that implement policy and programs. It analyzes the role of courts as protectors of individual rights and as forums for challenging the execution of programs in ways the advocate believes to be at odds with statutory mandates and constitutional prescriptions.

Chapter 3 continues coverage of major housing approaches, through a Matrix as a principal conceptual and organizing device, and through selected coverage of programs to illustrate attempted solutions. Chapter 3 has been expanded in its coverage of state activity and contains a new section on the role of non-profits in the housing arena. The authors also have included limited treatment of the changes wrought on housing investment and production incentives by the Tax Reform Act of 1986. A cautionary note is in order: the tax material is only introductory in nature.

In Chapter 4 the authors retain material that examines tenant protections and the "consumerism" issues in private, public, and quasi-private "assisted" housing.

The detail with which the Federal community development program is addressed in Chapter 5 has been reduced. Yet sufficient coverage is retained to provide a serious appreciation of the range of possibilities, issues, problems and shortcomings of the Federal programs.

Chapter 6 continues to explore the major problems of access to housing. It examines both governmental duties and limitations as well as protections against discrimination in the private market. It explores changes made by the 1988 amendments to the Federal Fair Housing Act and some of the intractable issues of attempting to maintain stable racially integrated living environments through various sorts of "managed occupancy" techniques.

Chapter 7, which was entitled: "Policy Alternatives for the Future: Out of the Maze," has been deleted from the Second Edition. That chapter, as the title suggested, was an attempt to marshal material on possible future directions. Instead, in the Second Edition, coverage throughout the book points to possible future directions—to correct problems in present programs, to make the housing and development effort more effective and complete, as well as, to address problems that are not addressed or not addressed adequately by ongoing programs.

Some of the authors teach the course in a seminar format which allows students to pursue additional depth on the topics covered through individual research papers. Others have taught from the casebook in a regular classroom format, sometimes with the option of student papers which explore specific topics in greater depth for extra credit. Indeed, one co-author teaches the course as a housing discrimination class commencing with Chapter 6, and proceeding through the chapters emphasizing social equity and discrimination issues and applications.

The materials in the casebook are edited for student use. Accordingly, state cases cite only unofficial reporters. United States Supreme Court cases cite only United States Reports. In reproducing cases and other matter, the authors have not noted with elisions when material has been deleted, except in instances when clarity requires elisions, for example, when part of a sentence has been deleted. Also, in reproducing cases and other material, many citations and all string citations have been deleted, except when, in our judgment, the citations were especially pertinent. In a similar vein, most footnotes in all materials have been deleted without notation. When footnotes are included, their original numbering has been retained.

The casebook does not contain reproduction of the statutory or regulatory materials which may be cited, except when a particular excerpt is being discussed. The authors found that it was necessary to reproduce pertinent current materials on a yearly basis at the time the courses were taught to be sure the most current materials were available. The authors commend that course to others. Current materials, both statutes and regulations, can generally be found in the four volume Housing and Development Reporter, published in loose leaf form and updated bi-weekly by Warren, Gorham & Lamont, Inc., 210 South Street, Boston, Massachusetts, 02111. Congressional, executive and other governmental developments are reported on a weekly basis in Housing Affairs Letter, published in newsletter format, by CD Publications, 8555 16th Street, Suite 100, Silver Spring, Maryland, 20910. Periodically, however, resort to current versions of the Code of Federal Regulations will be required. For new, pending or proposed regulatory changes the Federal Register may need to be consulted.

As with the First Edition, the authors continue to welcome you to this challenging area of social concern. The critical policy and legal issues continue to demand attention for the years ahead.

The Authors

Preface to the Third Edition (1999)

Again we have undertaken the challenge of revising and updating the Housing and Community Development text. This Third Edition continues the basic format of prior editions.

Although the exact content that should comprise "housing and community development" as a discipline might be regarded as unsettled, if not unstable, the concept of a "core" book has worked reasonably well for nearly two decades. We continue that concept in the Third Edition. We have continued to emphasize broad themes and to omit much of the detail in programs, statutes, and regulations—which are always in a state of flux. For users of the book who choose to focus on more specific aspects of a policy or program, we still recommend supplementing the text with handouts of the most recent program detail from the regulations, statutes, or reports from services that cover current developments in the housing and community development field.

Chapter 1 continues to take a "perspectives approach" to housing and community development issues, problems, policies, and programs. This chapter highlights some of the basic policy issues that frame the choices that are available to policy makers and advocates.

Chapter 2 examines the institutional setting in which housing and community development is played out. It considers the context in which national policy is determined and implemented. It explores the roles of the agencies that implement policy and programs. It analyzes the role—powers and limitations—of courts as protectors of individual rights and as forums for challenging the execution of programs in ways the advocate believes to be at odds with constitutional requirements or statutory mandates.

Chapter 3 continues coverage of major housing approaches, through a Matrix as a principal conceptual and organizing device, and through selected coverage of programs to illustrate attempted solutions. Chapter 3 has expanded coverage in this Third Edition by adding coverage of the Federal response to homelessness.

Chapter 4 continues to examine tenant protections and the "consumerism" issues in private, public, and quasi-private "assisted" housing. We have added coverage of the intractable and special problems of and response to drug activity in public housing.

Chapter 5 continues to cover the legal and policy origins and underpinnings of community revitalization. It continues to examine the broad outline of the Federal community development program.

Chapter 6 continues to explore the major problems of access to housing, although its title has been changed to "Fair Housing" to more clearly reflect the dominance of the statutory protections against housing discrimination and the concomitant demise of constitutional grounds in the most frequently occurring instances of discrimination. It has been reorganized to highlight themes of governmental duties, on the one hand, and protections in the marketplace, on the other. It expands the topics to include coverage of protections for families with children, persons with disabilities, and on the basis of sex. Coverage is added on discrimination in financing and lending.

We continue to believe that this "coursebook" is adaptable for diverse course formats: (a) seminars that allow consideration of selected topics through in-depth research papers; (b) writing courses that permit or require additional coverage through the preparation of papers that have varying characteristics; (c) "problem oriented" discussion and analysis small-section courses; (d) regular classroom courses with Socratic dialogue and discussion; (e) specialized courses focussing on a particular or limited set of topics, such as housing programs (emphasizing Chapters 1 and 3), community development (emphasizing Chapters 1 and 5), or fair housing (emphasizing Chapters 1 and 6); as well as (f) interdisciplinary courses, for example, law and planning or law and public policy.

The materials in the casebook are edited for student use. Accordingly, for state cases we cite only unofficial reporters. For United States Supreme Court cases we cite only United States Reports. In reproducing cases and other matter, we have not noted with elisions when material has been deleted, except in instances when clarity requires elisions (for example, when part of a sentence has been deleted). Also, in reproducing cases and other material, many citations and all string citations have been deleted, except when, in our judgment, the citations were especially pertinent. In a similar vein, most footnotes in all materials have been deleted without notation. When footnotes are included, their original numbering has been retained.

When we cite Federal statutes (especially those enacting programs discussed in the book), we have cited the current official reporter—United States Code (U.S.C.), except when otherwise noted. We do not normally include dates on statutory cites unless the date is pertinent to the discussion. For the Code of Federal Regulations we have noted the version that we have cited. Generally that will be the 1998 version, except when historical materials are cited, in which case the date of that regulation is cited. In reprinted cases, articles, and other materials, we have left the citation form as it appears in the original work.

We have not reproduced in the book statutory or regulatory material that we cite, except when a particular excerpt is being discussed. Statutory and regulatory materials change frequently (even when the substance in carried forward—as is frequently the case with the Code of Federal Regulations). We have found that annual preparation of supplements containing current statutes and regulations is advisable to assure that these materials are up-to-date. We recommend that course to others. Current materials—statutory, regulatory, and political developments—can be found in the multi-volume Housing and Development Reporter, published in loose leaf form and updated weekly by West Group, 610 Opperman Drive, Eagan, MN 55123-1396 (800-728-4880). Congressional, executive, and other governmental developments are reported weekly in Housing Affairs Letter, in newsletter format, by CD Publications, 8204 Fenton Street, Silver Spring, Maryland, 20910 (301-588-6380). Periodically, however, one must consult current versions of the Code of Federal Regulations for current program regulations. For new, pending or proposed regulatory changes the Federal Register will have to be consulted.

As with the First and Second Editions, we continue to welcome teachers and students to this challenging area of social concern and political activity. The critical policy questions and legal issues continue to demand attention for the years ahead.

The Authors

Preface to the Fourth Edition (2010)

The Fourth Edition presents a fresh and comprehensive look at housing and community development law and policy with full coverage of the foreclosure crisis and its aftermath, exploring housing policies and neighborhood revitalization strategies to address the new urban reality. It also discusses the issue of sustainability and the relationship between community development, housing, and climate change. The book contains materials covering housing policy and litigation; tenants rights in the private and public spheres; urban redevelopment, including a comprehensive look at *Kelo v. New London*, including its setting and aftermath; and a completely revised section of the book covering neighborhood investment and revitalization. The materials on fair housing and discrimination reflect many recent debates, including school desegregation, affirmative action, subprime and other variations of predatory lending, and other issues touching on race, class, national origin, gender, disability, and discrimination against families with children.

We believe the edition is being published at the perfect time to debate the exciting current urban, suburban, and rural issues of housing, transportation, and community design and development. The Fourth Edition continues the basic format of prior editions.

Chapter 1 continues to take a "perspectives approach" to housing and community development problems and programs. Special attention is paid to the 2007-2010 housing market collapse and resultant foreclosure crisis, as well as the persistent problem of homelessness and international perspectives on the "right to housing" debate. This chapter highlights some of the basic policy issues that frame the choices available to policy makers and advocates.

Chapter 2, discussing the legislative process, the administration of federal programs, the litigation of housing and community development issues, the intergovernmental workings in the field, including the relation of states, the federal government, and private developers and stakeholders.

Chapter 3 has been reorganized to focus greater attention on responses to the foreclosure crisis and on the distinguishing characteristics of demand side and supply side programs, as well as direct and indirect subsidies. The Matrix of Subsidy Alternatives, which remains the principal conceptual and organizing device for the chapter, has been modified by revising the examples to reflect representative 2010 cost estimates and by adding additional programs such as the Low Income Housing Tax Credit and the newly authorized National Affordable Housing Trust Fund. Major housing approaches are discussed, with special emphasis on federal initiatives. The HOPE VI program, which was introduced in the Third Edition, receives expanded coverage in this edition. State and local programs also are discussed. Emphasis is on current programs, housing policy after the mortgage crisis, and includes governmental policy responses.

Chapter 4 continues to examine tenant protections and the "consumerism" issues in private, public, and quasi-private "assisted" housing. Coverage reflects the intractable and special problems of and response to drug activity in public housing.

Chapter 5 has been substantially expanded in several respects, while retaining its focus on the federal, state and local legal mechanisms by which community development and revitalization activities may enhance and compromise the quality of life in U.S. communities. The chapter attends to two important themes: (1) the vigorous embrace by state and local governments for programs of tax incentives, direct financial assistance, and regulatory relief, by which to promote and capture economic growth, and (2) an equally vital and diverse movement of grass-roots and policy advocates engaged in development projects and policies to assure that low-wealth communities share in direction and resulting benefit from public expenditures for community development. New material in the chapter includes contemporary legal approaches to reclaim depopulated urban neighborhoods; the coordination of public and private investment in urban, rural, and disaster-stricken areas; and a new section on the powers, justifications and contested limits of governmental takings for economic development projects. Chapter 5 concludes with emerging issues in "sustainable community development," including transit policy, 'green' building, and community benefits/equitable development theory and practice. The chapter continues to cover the legal and policy origins and underpinnings of community revitalization. It continues to examine the broad outline of the Federal community development program. The Fourth Edition explores housing policies and neighborhood revitalization strategies to address the new urban reality. It also discusses the issue of sustainability and the relationship between community development, housing, and climate change. The new and extensive materials on urban redevelopment includes a comprehensive look at *Kelo v. New London*, including its setting and aftermath and the dilemma of utilizing redevelopment for economic development goals and its need for densification, brownfield redevelopment, infill development, and the need to modernize transportation. The chapter includes a completely revised section covering neighborhood investment and revitalization.

Chapter 6 continues to explore the major problems of fair housing, reflecting the dominance of the statutory protections against housing discrimination and the concomitant demise of constitutional grounds in the most frequently occurring instances of discrimination. It has been reorganized to highlight themes of governmental duties, on the one hand, and protections in the marketplace, on the other. It expands the topics to include coverage of protections for families with children, persons with disabilities, and on the basis of sex. Coverage is added on discrimination in financing and lending. The materials reflect many recent debates, including school desegregation, affirmative action, subprime and other variations of predatory lending, and other issues touching on race, class, national origin, gender, disability, and discrimination against families with children.

The Authors

Acknowledgments

Professor Kushner expresses appreciation to Bryant G. Garth, Dean, Southwestern Law School, for his support and encouragement. In addition, he would like to express appreciation to Martha A. Fink for her extraordinary support on this manuscript and the regular preparation of his Housing and Community Development course materials, and to his students who have provided stimulation, enthusiasm, and constructive feedback on these materials.

Professor Daye acknowledges with great appreciation the support of the University of North Carolina School of Law and the support and encouragement of deans who served during the preparation of the now four editions of this book. He thanks the students who, over nearly four decades, have taken the Housing course, who have demonstrated their interest in the housing policies and programs that assist those in need, who have evidenced their desires to keep working for social justice, and who have helped sustain his commitment to the pursuit of new levels of understanding and deeper insight.

Professor Salsich thanks Dean Jeffrey Lewis for his encouragement and support; Saint Louis University law students, William Holthaus, Chester Hutchinson and David Leipholtz, for their extremely helpful research assistance; Lynn Hartke and David Kullman, Assistant Professors of Legal Research, for their truly superb library support, and Lori Owens, Senior Secretary, for her patient and effective administrative and technical support.

Professor McGee is indebted to Andrew Ondrak, Seattle University School of Law class of 2010, for his invaluable research assistance, and to his wife, Victoria L. Kill, PhD, Seattle University English Department, for her editing suggestions.

Professor Bezdek warmly acknowledges University of Maryland law students Bernice Banks, Patrick Tyler, Greg Tinch, and Nancy Obedele, for their enthusiasm and research assistance, and a special thanks to Pamela Bluh and Kurt Meyer, librarians extraordinaire.

Professor Hetzel, in addition to thanking his wife, Bonnie, his former students, and members of the European Network for Housing Research, for their insights and support for his efforts in producing these materials, would also like to express his appreciation of Cliff Schrupp, Executive Director of the Fair Housing Center of Metropolitan Detroit, and Bill Maher, General Counsel of NAHRO, for their interest and dialogues relating to housing issues and policy that are incorporated in my contributions to this text.

Professor Keating acknowledges the assistance of Harold Jackson of the Cleveland-Marshall College of Law staff and Marie Rehmar of the library of Cleveland-Marshall College of Law.

The authors acknowledge the assistance of West Publishing Company for the use of Westlaw® in the preparation of this book.

List of Copyright Permissions

The authors gratefully acknowledge permission to reprint the following materials:

Academic Press, Inc. for permission to reprint from Joel F. Handler, Social Movements and the Legal System 22–25 (1978).

Agathon Press, Inc. for permission to reprint from William G. Grigsby & Louis Rosenburg, Urban Housing Policy 3–7 (1978).

Albany Government Law Review for permission to reprint from Vicki Been & Allegra Glashausser, Tenants: Innocent Victims of the Nation's Foreclosure Crisis, 2 Albany Government Law Review 1 (2009).

Albany Government Law Review for permission to reprint from Joseph Schilling, Enforcement and Community Stabilization: The Forgotten First Responders to Vacant and Foreclosed Homes, 2 Albany Government Law Review 101 (2009).

American Bar Association for permission to reprint from Roger A. Clay, Jr. & Susan R. Jones, Building Healthy Communities 4–5 (Roger A. Clay, Jr. & Susan R. Jones eds. 2009). Copyright © 2009 by the American Bar Association. Reprinted by permission.

American Bar Association Forum Committee on Affordable Housing and Community Development Law for permission to reprint from Charles L. Edson, *HUD's Interim Mark to Market Regulations: A Work in Progress*, 8 Journal of Affordable Housing & Community Development Law 15–25 (1998). Copyright © 1998 by the American Bar Association. Reprinted by permission.

American Bar Association Forum Committee on Affordable Housing and Community Development Law for permission to reprint from James J. Kelly, Refreshing the Heart of the City: Vacant Building Receivership as a Tool for Neighborhood Revitalization and Community Empowerment, 13 WTR-Journal of Affordable Housing and Community Development Law 215, 217 (2004).

American Bar Association Forum Committee on Affordable Housing and Community Development Law for permission to reprint from, Patricia E. Salkin & Amy Levine "Negotiating for Social Justice and the Promise of Community Benefits Agreements: Case Studies of Current and Developing Agreements, 17 WTR-Journal of Affordable Housing & Community Development Law 113, 114–15 (2008). Copyright © 1998 by the American Bar Association. Reprinted by permission.

American Bar Publications for permission to reprint from Otto J. Hetzel et al., Housing and Urban Development in Developments in Administrative Law and Regulatory Practice (Jeff F. Lubbers ed. 2010). Copyright © 2010 by the American Bar Association. Reprinted by permission.

American Bar Association Publications for permission to reprint from Peter W. Salsich, Jr. & Timothy J. Tryniecki, Land Use Regulation: A Legal Analysis and Practical Application of Land Use Law 336–341, 350–52, 356–358 (1998). Copyright © 1998 by the American Bar Association. Reprinted by permission.

American Bar Association Section of Local Government Law for permission to reprint from W. Dennis Keating, Judicial Approaches to Urban Housing Problems: A Study of the Cleveland Housing Court, 19 Urban Lawyer 345, 347–48, 351–57. Copyright © 1987 by the American Bar Association. Reprinted by permission.

American Bar Association Section of Local Government Law for permission to reprint from Edward H. Ziegler, The Case for Megapolitan Growth Management in the 21st Century: Regional Urban Planning and Sustainable Development in the United States, 41 Urban Lawyer 147, 148–152 (2009). Copyright © 2009 by the American Bar Association. Reprinted by permission.

APS Publications, Inc. and the Center for Urban Policy Research for permission to reprint from William G. Grigsby & Louis Rosenberg, Urban Housing Policy 235–236 (1975).

Bernan Press, Inc. for permission to reprint from Patrick A. Simmons, ed. Housing Statistics of the United States, 1st edition, xi–xiii, xvi–xvii, xix–xx (1997). Copyright © 1997 by Bernan Press, Inc.

Bobbs-Merrill for permission to reprint from Daniel R. Mandelker, Housing Subsidies in the United States and England 84–85, 88–94 (1973). Copyright © 1973 by Bobbs-Merrill. Reprinted by permission.

University of California at Los Angeles Journal of Environmental Law and Policy for permission to reprint from James A. Kushner, *The Reagan Urban Policy: Centrifugal Force in the Empire*, 2 U.C.L.A. Journal of Environmental Law & Policy 209, 211–213, 226–231 (1982).

Canarsie Courier for permission to reprint from Neil S. Friedman, Owners Cancel Starrett City Sale Amid Tough Real Estate Market, Canarsie Courier, Feb. 26, 2009.

Carolina Academic Press and James A. Kushner for permission to reprint from, James A. Kushner, Global Climate Change and the Road to Extinction 115–117, 141–143, 145–147, 181–182 (2009).

Carolina Academic Press and James A. Kushner for permission to reprint from, James A. Kushner, The Post Automobile City 61–62 (2004).

Cleveland State Law Review for permission to reprint from Matthew J. Samsa, Reclaiming Abandoned Properties: Using Public Nuisance Suits and Land Banks to Pursue Economic Redevelopment, 56 Cleveland State Law Review 189–190 (2008).

Columbia Law Review for permission to reprint from Special Project, *The Remedial Process in Institutional Reform Litigation*, 78 Columbia Law Review 784, 858–865 (1978).

Jean L. Cummings for permission to reprint from Jean L. Cummings & Denise DiPasquale, Building Affordable Rental Housing 36 (1998).

Economic Development Quarterly and George C. Galster for permission to reprint from George C. Galster, Consequences From the Redistribution of Urban Poverty During the 1990s: A Cautionary Tale, 19 Economic Development Quarterly 123–124 (2005), available at http://edq.sagepub.com/content/19/2/119.full.pdf+html.

Charles L. Edson for permission to reprint his Matrix of Governmental Housing Programs.

Fordham Urban Law Journal for permission to reprint from Colin Gordon, Blighting the Way: Urban Renewal, Economic Development, and the Elusive Definition of Blight, 31 Fordham Urban Law Journal 305, 306–319 (2004).

Professor Lawrence M. Friedman for permission to reprint from Government and Slum Housing 3–4, 7, 9–10, 104–106 (1968).

Georgetown Law Journal for permission to reprint from Note, *Blockbusting*, 59 Geo. L.J. 170–171 (1970). Reprinted with permission of the publisher, Georgetown Law Journal, copyright © 1970.

Professor Gerald Gunther and Harvard Law Review for permission to reprint from *Foreword: In Search of Evolving Doctrine on a Changing Court: A Model for a Newer Equal Protection*, 86 Harvard Law Review 1, 8, 10 (1972). Copyright © 1972 by Harvard Law Review Association.

Harvard Civil Rights—Civil Liberties Law Review for permission to reprint from Frank I. Michelman, *The Advent of a Right to Housing: A Current Appraisal*, 5 Harvard Civil Rights—Civil Liberties Law Review 207–16 (1970).

Hofstra Law Review for permission to reprint from Barbara L. Bezdek, To Attain "the Just Rewards of So Much Struggle": Local Resident Equity Participation in Urban Revitalization, 35 Hofstra Law Review 37 (2006)

Joint Center for Housing Subsidies for permission to reprint from The State of the Nation's Housing 2008 (2008).

Journal of the American Planning Association for permission to reprint from Peter Dreier, The New Politics of Housing, 63 Journal of the American Planning Association 5, 6–9, 18–22 (1997). Reprinted by permission of the Journal of the American Planning Association.

Lexington Books for permission to reprint Roger S. Ahlbrandt & Paul C. Brophy, Neighborhood Revitalization: Theory and Practice 152–53 (1975).

Lexis Law Publishing/MICHIE for permission to reprint from Daniel R. Mandelker, Land Use Law (4th Ed. 1997). Copyright © 1997, Lexis Law Publishing. Reprinted with permission from *Land Use Law* by Daniel R. Mandelker. Lexis Law Publishing Charlottesville, VA (800) 446-3410. All rights reserved.

McCormack, Baron, & Associates for permission to reprint from materials about the Murphy Park Development: Regulatory and Operating Agreement; Memorandum of Ground Lease; and the Declaration of Land Use Restriction Covenants for the State of Missouri Affordable Housing Tax Credits.

McGraw Hill for permission to reprint Michael Bernick & Robert Cervero, Transit Villages in the 21st century 112, 224–227 (1997).

Michigan Law Review for permission to reprint from Daniel R. Mandelker, Housing Codes, Building Demolition, and Just Compensation, 67 Michigan Law Review 635, 649–52 (1968).

Minnesota Law Review for permission to reprint from Ilya Somin, The Limits of Backlash: Assessing the Political Response to *Kelo*, 93 Minnesota Law Review 2100, 2120 (2009).

MIT Press for permission to reprint from Arthur P. Solomon, Housing the Urban Poor 16–17, 78–80, 89–90 (1974). Reprinted by permission for the MIT Press, Cambridge, Massachusetts. Copyright © 1974 by the Joint Center for Urban Studies of the Massachusetts Institute of Technology and the President and Fellows of Harvard University.

The National Housing Law Project for permission to reprint from 16 Housing Law Project Bulletin 6 (June–July 1979).

Nevada Law Journal for permission to reprint from Kristen David Adams, Do We Need a Right to Housing?, 9 Nevada Law Journal 275, 305, 314–319 (2009).

New York University Law Review for permission to reprint from Theodore Eisenberg, *Disproportionate Impact and Illicit Motive: Theories of Constitutional Adjudication*, 52 New York University Law Review 36, 46–47 (1977).

The Public Interest for permission to reprint from Peter Salins, *Toward a Permanent Housing Problem*, 85 Public Interest 22–33 (1986). Excerpted with permission of the author. Copyright © 1986 by National Affairs, Inc.

Rutgers, The State University of New Jersey, and the Center for Urban Policy Research, for permission to reprint from William G. Grigsby & Louis Rosenberg, Urban Housing Policy 235–236 (1975). Copyright © 1975 by Rutgers, The State University of New Jersey. Reproduced with permission

Rutgers, The State University of New Jersey, and the Center for Urban Policy Research, for permission to reprint from David Listokin & Stephen Casey, Mortgage Lending and Race: Conceptual and Analytical Perspectives of the Urban Financing Problem (1980). Copyright © 1980 by Rutgers, The State University of New Jersey. Reproduced with permission.

Rutgers, The State University of New Jersey, and the Center for Urban Policy Research, for permission to reprint from Eugene J. Meehan, Public Housing Policy: Convention Versus Reality 169–79 (1975). Copyright © 1975 by Rutgers, The State University of New Jersey. Reproduced with permission.

Saint Louis University Public Law Review and Louise A. Howells for permission to reprint from Louise A. Howells, *Looking for the Butterfly Effect: An Analysis of Urban Economic Development Block Grant Program*, 16 St. Louis U. Pub. L. Rev. 383, 385, 389–390, 391–398, 400–404, 406 (1997). Reprinted with permission of the Saint Louis University Public Law Review © 1997 St. Louis University, St. Louis, Missouri.

Saint Louis University Public Law Review for permission to reprint from Janet Ellen Stearns, *Voluntary Bonds: The Impact of Habitat II on United States Housing Policy*, 16 St. Louis University Public Law Review 419–420, 422–424, 426–429 (1997). Copyright 1997 by St. Louis University. Reprinted with permission of the Saint Louis University Public Law Review © 1997 St. Louis University, St. Louis, Missouri.

Seattle Journal for Social Justice for permission to reprint from Davida Finger, Stranded and squandered: Lost on Road Home, 7 Seattle Journal for Social Justice 59 (2008).

Stanford Law Review and Bruce L. Ackerman for permission to reprint from Bruce L. Ackerman, Integration for Subsidized Housing and the Question of Racial Occupancy Controls, 26 Stan. L. Rev., 245, 254–55 (1974). Copyright © 1974 by the Board of Trustees of the Leland Standford Junior University.

Stanford Law Review for permission to reprint from Thomas C. Grey, *Property and Need: The Welfare State and Theories of Distributive Justice*, 28 Stanford Law Review 877–886 (1976). Copyright © 1976 by the Board of Trustees of the Leland Standford Junior University.

Supreme Court Economic Review for permission to reprint from Ilya Somin, The Capture Problem Illustrated In Poletown "Controlling the Grasping Hand: Economic Development Takings after *Kelo*," 15 Supreme Court Economic Review 183, 185–187, 193–197 (2007).

The Supreme Court Review for permission to reprint from John S. Wiley, *The Berkeley Rent Control Case: Treating the Victims as Villains*, 1886 The Supreme Court Review 157–61; 163–66. Copyright © 1987 by the University of Chicago.

Temple University Press for permission to reprint from Peter Drier, Federal Housing Subsidies: Who Benefits and Why? in A Right to Housing: Foundation for a New Social Agenda (Rachel G. Bratt, Michael E. Stone & Chester Hartman eds. 2006).

Temple University Press for permission to reprint from Peter Marcuse & W. Dennis Keating, The Permanent Housing Crisis: The Failures of Conservatism and the Limitations of Liberalism in A Right to Housing: Foundation for a New Social Agenda (Rachel G. Bratt, Michael E. Stone & Chester Hartman eds. 2006).

UCLA Journal of Environmental Law & Policy for permission to reprint from James A. Kushner, The Reagan Urban Policy: Centrifugal Force in the Empire, 2 UCLA Journal of Environmental Law & Policy 209, 211–213 (1982).

University of Detroit Journal of Urban Law and Daniel R. Mandelker for permission to reprint from Daniel R. Mandelker, et al., *Differential Enforcement of Housing Codes—The Constitutional Dimension*, 55 University of Detroit Journal of Urban Law 517, 523–533, 555–556 (1978).

University of Miami School of Law for permission to reprint from James A. Kushner, *A Comparative Vision of the Convergence of Ecology, Empowerment, and the Quest for a Just Society*, 52 University of Miami Law Review 301, 309–315 (1998).

University of Pennsylvania Law Review for permission to reprint from Daniel R. Mandelker, The Comprehensive Planning Requirement in Urban Renewal, 116 University of Pennsylvania Law Review 25 (1967).

University of Pennsylvania Law Review for permission to reprint from Eduardo Moisés Peñalver & Sonia K. Katyal, Property Outlaws, 155 University of Pennsylvania Law Review 1122–29 (2007).

Wake Forest Law Review for permission to reprint from Peter W. Salsich, Jr., Toward a Policy of Heterogeneity: Overcoming a Long History of Socioeconomic Segregation in Housing, 42 Wake Forest L. Rev. 459–64 (2007).

Washington University Journal of Law & Policy for permission to reprint from Peter Salsich, Grassroots Consensus Building and Collaborative Planning, 3 Washington University Journal of Law & Policy 309 (2000).

Washington University Journal of Urban and Contemporary Law for permission to reprint from Donald C. Bryant & Henry W. McGee, Jr., *Gentrification and the Law*, 25 Wash. University Journal of Urban & Contemporary Law 43, 62–65; 75–81; 120–126 (1983). Copyright © 1983 Washington University.

Yale Law School for permission to reprint from T. Alexander Aleinikoff, Note, Racial Steering: The Real Estate Broker and Title VIII, 85 Yale L.J. 808, 809–12 (1976).

Yale Law School for permission to reprint from Sara C. Galvan, Rehabilitating Rehab Through State Building Codes, 115 Yale Law Journal 1744, 1746 (2006).

Yale Law School for permission to reprint from Maria Foscarinis, *Downward Spiral: Homelessness and Its Criminalization*, 14 Yale Law & Policy Review 1, 4–12 (1996).

Housing and Community Development

Chapter 1

Overview: The Social, Political, Economic, and Policy Matrix

The economic importance of the American housing market, and the traditional boom and bust cycle of that market, was nowhere more evident than during the first decade of the 21st Century. The almost total collapse of the housing market in 2007–2008 following several years of double-digit growth in both price and size of American houses triggered the greatest global recession since the Great Depression. After decades of progress towards achievement of the "American Dream" for successor generations, the crush of mortgage defaults, foreclosures and increasing homelessness resulting from job losses, savings and investment portfolio declines, and property value collapse raised the specter of necessary and fundamental change in the nation's housing and community development policies and practices.

As the Nation moves into the second decade of the 21st Century, it confronts major societal and policy forces that contribute to the complexity of the environment in which housing and community development problems must be addressed. These forces include the obsolescence of the industrial jobs base in the aftermath of the global "Great Recession," the growth of regions and even multi-state "mega"-regions fueled by waves of migration from central cities to increasingly distant suburbs that have grown outward in rings or tiers, as people seek safer communities, higher quality educational and social services. The emergence of slums in first tier suburbs (those nearest adjacent central cities) has resulted from many of the forces responsible for slums in central cities: the aging of the baby boomers, increased immigration, particularly from less developed countries, the search for a proper balance between market and regulatory policies, privatization of traditional public services, and "devolution" of federal social programs to state and local governments.

In urban centers, first-tier suburbs and rural communities, consumers often are unable to satisfy their housing needs with available income. Racial minorities and low-income people suffer from housing discrimination. Significant areas of our nation contain substandard and abandoned housing as urban and suburban neighborhoods decline and as rural areas decay.

The automobile-dependent, dispersed development pattern characteristic of the latter half of the 20th Century dominates metropolitan areas. Scores, even hundreds, of suburbs radiate outward from central cities like ripples from a rock dropped in a pond. Households increasingly gravitate to low density, homogeneous neighborhoods featuring people of like economic and social status. This pattern of development, termed "sprawl" by its detractors, has triggered concerns that carbon emissions from habitual reliance on automobiles may contribute to global warming through release of excessive amounts of carbon dioxide into the atmosphere. This concern is discussed in Chapter 5 *infra*. As the wealthier move out to the exurbs, or return to the central cities, first-tier suburbs may become the slums of the 21st Century. The 2010 census may find that more poor now live in the suburbs than in the central cities. The "smart growth" movement seeks to respond to these forces by encouraging greater density through mixed-use, transit-oriented development. But competition among jurisdictions chasing sales tax revenue makes it difficult, if not impossible, to reach agreement on regional approaches to economic and environmental problems.

Housing is a major capital resource that affects every aspect of national life. How people live and what they must pay for shelter significantly affect their personal well-being, while the condition of cities and their neighborhoods has a major influence on educational, employment, and social opportunities. Cities present a social problem because cities do not generate enough resources for their renewal and redevelopment and because housing markets do not always function effectively.

In rural areas housing problems can be less visible but an intensified version of city problems because of geographic isolation, economic neglect, lack of jobs, and sparse capital resources are often present. Credit may be unavailable. Pockets of substandard living conditions may abound in which fundamental facilities such as good water and inside toilets are absent.

The study of housing and community development law, policies and programs requires an examination of the relationship of housing to school, jobs, and social services. This course book examines programs that governments have adopted in response to housing and community development problems and the legal remedies available to overcome discrimination and other failures in housing markets. Government intervention is the social response to market failure problems. Government subsidies supplement personal income so that lower-income households can obtain adequate and affordable housing. Community development programs provide government assistance to reverse the decline of cities, suburbs, rural, and urban neighborhoods. Legislation prohibits racial and other forms of discrimination in the supply of housing, and regulates the development process to preserve the environment and encourage sustainable development practices.

This chapter provides a perspective on housing and community development problems. The first section reviews the social problems presented by housing market failure, city decline, and racial discrimination. The next section considers the strategy of social response to housing and community development problems. The chapter closes by examining the claim that society should recognize a "right to housing" through constitutional or statutory guarantees.

A. The Dimensions of the Housing Problem

The housing market collapse in 2007–2008 and the subsequent surge in foreclosures and homelessness cast doubt on the traditional claim that as a nation, we are better housed than ever before. The success of the building industry in providing new dwelling units over the past decades has substantially improved the quality of the housing stock. Abandonment and clearance have removed the worst slums in older cities. Despite these improvements in the quality of our housing, changes in housing markets have created a housing affordability and availability problem. A spike in foreclosures triggered by the housing market collapse and subsequent recession has caused widespread concern in affected neighborhoods, not to mention the stress placed on affected households. Rents have increased as a percentage of income among lower-income groups. The supply of low-cost rental housing continues to shrink. Racial, ethnic, and economic segregation are still widespread. Discrimination in housing and mortgage lending continue to exacerbate housing problems. Homelessness is a persistent and growing phenomenon. The next reading summarizes some of the significant changes in housing in the generation between 1990 and 2008.

Joint Center for Housing Studies, The State of the Nation's Housing 2008

6, 11, 13, 16, 27–28, 30–31 (2008)

The Unraveling Housing Market

During the expansion that started in the early 1990s, demand fundamentals kept household growth going strong, real incomes were up, and interest rates were favorable. But just prior to the 2001 recession, the Federal Reserve began to cut interest rates to avert deflation and a deeper contraction of the economy. Soon after, home sales began to take off ahead of production. By 2003, these conditions helped to create the tightest housing markets and the lowest interest rates in at least a generation.

A dramatic run-up in home prices ensued as buyers with access to low-cost mortgage credit competed in bidding wars. For the first time since records were kept, median prices across the nation increased multiple times faster than incomes for several years in a row. The relaxation of underwriting requirements and the advent of mortgage products that initially reduced borrowers' payments—together with the unprecedented availability of mortgage credit to speculators, investors, and homebuyers with past credit problems—helped to fuel the boom.

But even lax lending standards and innovative mortgage products could not keep housing markets going indefinitely. With interest rates on the rise starting in 2004, price appreciation showed signs of weakening in late 2005. Investors quickly exited markets and homebuyers lost their sense of urgency. But builders had ramped up to meet the higher level of demand from investors as well as buyers of first and second homes, pushing single-family starts from 1.3 million in 2001 to 1.7 million in 2005. Just as housing demand started to abate, record numbers of new single-family homes were coming on the market or were in the pipeline....

With excess supplies beginning to mount and the temporary lift from mortgage product innovations coming to an end, nominal house prices finally turned down on a year-over-year basis in the third quarter of 2006. Meanwhile, interest rates on some adjustable loans began to reset and mortgage performance deteriorated as poor risk management practices took their toll. Lenders responded by tightening credit in the second half of 2007, dragging the market down even more sharply and exacerbating the threat of a prolonged housing downturn....

Household Growth Trends

After averaging 1.15 million per year in 1995–2000, household growth notched up to 1.37 million annually in 2000–2006. While some of this increase may be due to the unusually favorable home buying conditions in the first half of the decade, much of it was expected as the echo boomers began to form independent households and immigration continued to climb. [The collapse of the housing market in 2007 triggered a sharp drop in the number of owner households.—Eds.]

Looking ahead, household growth should return to the path set by the changing age composition of the population, the strength of ongoing immigration, and social trends such as divorce and remarriage rates that influence the size of households. Indeed, if immigration remains near its current pace of 1.2 million per year, the combination of several years of high immigration, high divorce and low remarriage rates, and the aging of the echo boomers should push household growth to average more than 1.4 million per year in 2010–2020.... Even if immigration were to drop by about 30 percent, household growth should still exceed its 1995–2000 average annual level.... [The Harvard study notes that unmarried-partner, single-parent, and single-person households are an increasing share of independent households.—Eds.]

Minority Household Gains

Thanks to higher rates of immigration and natural increase (excess of births over deaths), minorities contributed over 60 percent of household growth in 2000–2006. Minorities now account for 29 percent of all households, up from 17 percent in 1980 and 25 percent in 2000. If immigration continues at its current pace, the minority share is likely to reach about 35 percent by 2020, with Hispanic households leading the gain.

Minorities are younger on average than whites. As a result, minority household growth among 35 to 64 year-olds should remain strong in 2010–2020. In contrast, the number of white middle-aged households will start to decline after 2010 as the baby boomers begin to turn 65. The number and share of white households under age 35 will also fall after 2015 as the children of the baby-bust generation begin to reach household-forming ages.

The Outlook

Once housing markets stabilize, household growth should return to levels consistent with long-term demographic trends. As the number of minority and foreign-born households grows, the housing industry will increasingly serve groups with lower homeownership rates, incomes, and wealth than native-born whites. Ethnic identification of some minorities and cultural preferences of recent immigrants will also challenge housing suppliers to tailor their marketing to a diverse population.

With unmarried-partner households increasing in number and share, the industry may also want to look past marital status to the housing preferences of this growing customer segment. Furthermore, the likely increase in the number of adult children living at home and of adults other than spouses or partners living together may create niche marketing opportunities for both the construction and remodeling industries.

While rising incomes and wealth have so far placed each generation on a path to higher housing consumption, the weak income performance earlier in this decade and the recent jump in energy costs have raised concerns that this upward trend may not continue. Adding to this risk is the very real prospect that some of the recent gains in household wealth—which came largely from rising homeownership rates and home price inflation—will erode. Housing demand will, however, pick up once the economy begins to recover, home prices reach bottom, and homeownership again becomes an attractive way to build wealth....

Eroding Affordability

Affordability problems are edging up the income scale.... While low-income renters make up the largest share of severely burdened households, a rising number of middle-income homeowners also face cost pressures. Between 2001 and 2006, the number of severely burdened renters in the bottom income quartile increased by 1.2 million, while the number of severely burdened homeowners in the two middle-income quartiles ballooned by 1.4 million.... By 2006, middle-income homeowners were twice as likely as middle-income renters to pay more than half their incomes for housing.

Owners who recently moved are especially likely to be severely cost burdened. While this in part reflects their younger average age, the share of recent movers with severe burdens has climbed sharply since 2001, due in part to the run-up in house prices, the increase in interest rates after 2004, and the interest-rate resets on many adjustable loans originated in 2004 and 2005.

Tapping home equity through second mortgages has apparently led to higher housing cost burdens as well. In 2006, approximately 20 percent of all middle-income homeowners with second mortgages paid more than half their incomes for housing. This is nearly twice the share among those with only a first mortgage. Among low-income homeowners, 90 percent of those with second mortgages are severely cost burdened compared with 70 percent of those with just a first mortgage.

For homeowners earning more than the median income, the likelihood of being housing cost burdened nearly doubled between 2001 and 2006. Some of this increase reflects the substitution of mortgage debt for unsecured consumer debt through either cash-out refinances or second mortgages. In the short run, this allows borrowers to reduce their monthly carrying costs on the same amount of debt. But consumer debt can be discharged in bankruptcy without the lender's consent, while mortgage debt cannot. As a result, debt substitution exposes homeowners to even greater foreclosure risk.... [The study notes that increases in energy costs are having significant impact on households, particularly those in the low- and middle-income ranges.—Eds.]

Local land use regulations are also contributing to the increase in housing cost burdens by skewing development toward more expensive homes and restricting the types and density of housing that can be built. One study concluded that land use restrictions slow building activity and inflate housing prices both during boom times and over the long term. House price appreciation in 2002–2005 averaged 45 percent in the most restrictive areas, compared with 24 percent in the least restrictive.... In addition, despite having higher average incomes as well as higher housing costs, the most restrictive metros have a greater incidence of severe housing cost burdens. In 2006, the aggregate share of severely cost-burdened renters was about three percentage points higher in these areas than in the least restrictive metros. The reason the gap is not larger is that severe burdens are concentrated among low-income households that have to stretch to afford housing even in the least restrictive metro areas....

Government Assistance

Despite the alarming scope of affordability problems, housing assistance represents a small and shrinking share of the federal budget. From 1997 to 2007, housing assistance programs fell from 10 percent to 8 percent of the nation's dwindling domestic discretionary outlays. And even though the number of households with severe burdens rose by more than 20 percent from 2001 to 2005, the share of renter households receiving assistance barely budged. While the Low Income Housing Tax Credit program [discussed in Chapter 3 *infra*—Eds.] has succeeded in expanding the supply of affordable units, losses from the inventory remain exceedingly high. With the number of low-income renter households continuing to rise and the number of affordable and available units continuing to fall, the need grows ever larger. [In 2008, there were] only about 6 million rentals affordable to the nearly 9 million households with incomes below 30 percent of the median for their Census division ($11,000 to $18,000). But nearly half of these affordable units are either inhabited by higher-income households or stand vacant. As a result, about 9 million lowest-income households must compete for just 3 million affordable and available rental units....

Heavily targeted toward renter households, federal housing assistance currently does next to nothing for owners that have severe housing cost burdens and are at risk of losing their homes. While federal and state governments have intervened to blunt the impending wave of foreclosures, the relief is temporary and in many cases relies on the voluntary efforts of lenders, servicers, and investors. The largest-scale program uses federal housing insurance to allow some homeowners to refinance their way out of trouble. As it is, however, many owners do not qualify for any of the forms of assistance being offered. Once the current storm passes, foreclosure rates may settle back down but the affordability problems of owners—and especially of former owners forced back into renting—will persist.

The Outlook

The weakness of the economy does not bode well for income growth in the short run. But even in the longer run, the housing cost pressures on working Americans are unlikely to lighten. Much of employment growth will continue to be in part-time and low-wage positions. This trend, together with the high operating costs of housing and the restrictions on building modest homes at higher densities, makes efforts to meet the nation's affordability challenges an uphill battle. Thus far, there has been little national outcry about the fact that growing numbers of low- and middle-income families are spending half or more of their incomes on housing, and that so many children are living in unhealthy, unsafe conditions—or, worse yet, forced to make their way on the streets. The grim plight of many veterans has also failed to rally a groundswell of support to tackle these urgent issues....

Notes and Questions

1. The Joint Center's 2009 report observes that the "housing sector provides a number of opportunities to address two urgent national goals—reducing greenhouse gasses and foreign oil dependence." The main strategies being advocated are "retrofitting the existing housing stock" with "green building practices and energy-efficient improvements" and reducing sprawl by "creating more densely settled, transit-served, mixed-use communities and ... encouraging businesses to expand in or relocate to these areas." JOINT CENTER FOR HOUSING STUDIES, THE STATE OF THE NATION'S HOUSING 2009 30–31 (2009). Does retrofitting the entire existing housing stock strike you as a realistic national goal? Who should be responsible to pay for that—current homeowners, the building industry, the government? What local land use regulations would have to change to accommodate more compact, transit-oriented development? These issues are discussed in Chapters 3 and 5 *infra*.

2. The Joint Center excerpt reproduced above notes that high levels of immigration have played an important role in changing housing demographics. During the last decade of the 20th Century and the first decade of the 21st Century, more legal and undocumented immigrants arrived in the United States than in any other similar period on record, with the total number of resident immigrants doubling between 1990 and 2007. Census data indicates that over twelve percent of the population in 2007 was foreign-born (about 38 million persons). Twenty-seven percent of those immigrants were undocumented (about 11.6 million), with over half of that number coming from Mexico. MIGRATION POLICY

INSTITUTE, MPI DATA HUB, STATES RANKED BY NUMBER OF FOREIGN BORN: 1990, 2000, and 2007, *available at* www.migrationinformation.org/datahub/acscensusus.cfm#rankings. Other studies estimate that minorities may make up more than 50% of the population by 2050. Sam Roberts, *Minorities Often a Majority of the Population Under 20,* N.Y. TIMES, Aug. 7, 2008, at A13.

Immigrants are having significant effects on housing and community development issues in a number of ways. According to James Andrews, associate editor of *Planning,* (the magazine of the American Planning Association), immigrants are settling in and helping to revitalize "neglected areas" in urban centers and inner ring suburbs. He notes that immigrants have been a "boon to depressed areas in New York and Los Angeles, bringing people, energy, and economic growth," as well as to other cities and suburbs. But differences in culture bring change and confusion. Immigrants don't necessarily share a common American consensus against residential crowding, and their housing may include illegal apartments, including garage units and "squatters living in shanty towns." Immigrants' culture "shapes preferences about density within dwelling units and the social use of outdoor space," which may conflict with local land use policies. James H. Andrews, *The Newest Americans,* 63 PLAN. 4, 6–7 (No. 9 1997).

The recent surge of immigrants, particularly undocumented persons after 9/11, has called attention to major shortcomings in federal immigration law and policy and prompted states and localities to respond with a variety of initiatives, some designed to assist persons attempting to assimilate, such as free photo identification cards made available to undocumented persons seeking to open bank accounts, and others designed to discourage businesses from employing or providing housing for undocumented persons. JoAnn Greco, *La Vida Local,* 74 PLAN. 14 (No. 3 2008). For an analysis of immigration trends and local policy responses, with special emphasis on "second tier" metropolitan areas, see TWENTY-FIRST CENTURY GATEWAYS: IMMIGRANT INCORPORATION IN SUBURBAN AMERICA (Audrey Singer, Susan W. Hardwick & Caroline B. Brettell eds. 2009) (Brookings Institution study presenting a series of case studies from newer, predominately suburban gateways for immigrants and recommending that greater attention be paid to the social, political and economic integration of immigrants into American society).

3. As the 2008 Harvard Joint Center study notes in its conclusion, little public attention has been paid in recent years to the housing problems of low- and middle-income Americans, particularly as those problems affect children and veterans. Why is that? If you were asked to make a list of the 10 most pressing concerns of the nation, your state and your city, would housing make the list?

4. Peter Dreier, a former housing and community development administrator in Boston, makes the following observation about the traditional approach to housing and community development concerns in the U.S.

> No other major industrial nation has allowed its cities to face the fiscal and social troubles confronting America's urban areas. Other industrial nations do not permit the level of sheer destitution and decay found in our cities....
>
> Among western democracies, the United States relies most heavily on private market forces to house its population. This doesn't mean that the government is not involved in housing matters, but rather that American policy emphasizes bolstering market forces and minimizing assistance for the poor.
>
> Government's role dates primarily from two major turning points in our housing history. First, at the turn of the [20th] century, tenement reform laws set the

> precedent that *local* government would set standards and regulate housing safety. Second, during the 1930s, the public housing program and banking reforms established the *federal* role in expanding home ownership and providing subsidies to the poor.

Peter Dreier, *The New Politics of Housing*, 63 J. Am. Plan. Ass'n 5, 6 (Winter 1997) (emphasis in original—Eds.).

5. The role of local housing and building standards is discussed in Chapter 5 *infra*. The traditional federal and state roles in housing law and policy are discussed in Chapter 3 *infra*. A third turning point, enactment of the Fair Housing Act in 1968, is discussed in Chapter 6 *infra*. As you explore these materials, consider whether private market forces can be expected to respond effectively to housing needs of low- and middle-income persons. If not, what should be the role of government, and at what level should government respond—national, state or local?

6. General treatments of housing policy questions include Housing Markets and the Economy: Risk, Regulation and Policy (Edward L. Glaeser & John M. Quigley eds. 2009); Revisiting Rental Housing: Policies, Programs and Priorities (Nicholas P. Retsinas & Eric S. Belsky eds. 2008); and A Right to Housing: Foundation for a New Social Agenda (Rachel G. Bratt, Michael E. Stone & Chester Hartman eds. 2006). An excellent source for discussion of housing policy questions is Housing Policy Debate, a quarterly journal originally published by the Fannie Mae Foundation and since 2007 by the Metropolitan Institute at Virginia Tech University.

The next selection examines different political perspectives influencing housing policies and programs.

Peter Marcuse and W. Dennis Keating, The Permanent Housing Crisis: The Failures of Conservatism and the Limitations of Liberalism

A Right to Housing: Foundation for a New Social Agenda 139, 156–158 (Rachel G. Bratt, Michael E. Stone & Chester Hartman eds. 2006)

Housing is both a necessity of life, and, in our society, a commodity provided for profit.... The tension between the two underlies the vagaries of housing policy in the United States. Liberals and conservatives agree that the market should be the expected provider of housing for all, with the government acting only where the for-profit market "fails." The only disagreement is on how serious that "failure" is and just what government should do about it.... Throughout this decades-long history both [the "housing is a necessity of life" and "housing is a commodity"] approaches were found to share a number of assumptions and in common mold their different policy stands around them. They include:

1. *The primacy of the profit-driven market as both the instrument for the provision of housing and the mechanism for its allocation.* In both approaches, government action has always been seen as being supplementary to what the private market accomplishes: a safety net to catch those not well served by the market. Both approaches fail to ... recognize that the market relies on the profit motive for supplying housing, and thus neither approach will ever provide an adequate supply for those not in a position to produce profit in the market. Both approaches fail to recognize the undesirable social consequences of permitting the market to allocate housing—its location, quality and type—by the in-

come and therefore by the profit-producing status of its users; both will always tend to produce segregation, ugliness and deterioration in large parts of the market and an unconscionable gap between the housing conditions of the rich and the poor. Both approaches refuse to acknowledge the defects of the housing market even in those areas where it does supply adequate housing, including the limitations on competition under circumstances of housing shortage and the inherently monopolistic commodity that is land, so neither will ever consistently provide housing at appropriate prices generally affordable to most users.

2. *A preference for demand-side as opposed to supply-side policies in those limited areas where government does act on housing issues.* This flows from the primacy accorded the market by both. In both approaches, the direct provision of housing by government, at whatever level ... whether in planning, construction, financing or management—is held to the minimum possible. Thus, both approaches surrender precisely those tools that would best enable them to overcome the weaknesses of profit-driven market domination of the housing supply, and both exclude even market-compatible steering mechanisms such as a yardstick function or a limitation on excess profits or speculation that might render the market more "social" in its results.

3. *Subservience to the private real estate and housing industry in the formulation of policy.* This is partial cause and partial consequence of the two approaches described, but in both approaches, it narrows the discussion of possible alternatives in dealing with housing to those acceptable to politically powerful interest groups. Neither can rationally examine the pros and cons of alternatives or logically draw conclusions from the experience of prior policies in shaping new ones. Only in times of severe stress—when opposing political and economic forces clash, whether from tenants and homeowners facing extreme hardship (as in the early New Deal) or from exigencies of a war (as in both world wars)—is the range of the possible expanded and open to consideration by either approach.

4. *Homeownership as a cardinal goal of housing policy.* In both approaches, it is taken as a matter of faith that homeownership is the preferable form of tenure over any other. Both approaches consider increasing the number of homeowners to be a major indicator of the success of housing policy, and both devote substantial policy attention to spreading that particular form of tenure to the broadest possible strata of the population. Both distribute considerable subsidies via tax policies, infrastructure and highway provision and financial aids in a highly regressive fashion among users of housing, and both support environmentally damaging and inefficient patterns of land use. Neither supports serious consideration of alternative forms of tenure as being positive goals of public policy, whether tenant-owned nonprofit cooperatives, mutual housing associations or social housing such as is common in many other countries.

5. *Ideological rigidities, prominently including opposition to government action as such and limitation of moral concern to the "worthy" poor.* In both approaches and increasingly since the end of World War II, government action in the social sphere is seen as something "undesirable." On ideological grounds, both approaches favor reduction of government expenditures, reduction of taxes, decentralization of federal government and reduction of regulation. Neither approach is willing to concede that it is an appropriate function of government permanently to act to secure the provision of housing for any underserved group, and neither is willing to confront the fact of a permanent housing crisis in the absence of adequate and sustained government action.

As a result of these shared assumptions, the following continuing failures are clear:

1. *Permanent exclusion at the bottom.* There has never been a time in the United States in which a substantial minority did not face a serious housing crisis. Whether we look at the one-third of a nation that President Roosevelt in 1937 acknowledged to be without adequate shelter; the 6.2 million households paying more than 50 percent of their incomes for rent or the 5.4 million households that the Department of Housing and Urban Development identified in 2000, in a period of unprecedented prosperity, as having "worst case housing needs" (including 10.9 million people, among them 3.6 million children, 1.4 million elderly and some 1.3 million disabled adults) ... the bottom rungs of the economic ladder in the United States have always been excluded from the benefits of adequate housing. While both liberal and conservative approaches claim concern for those who "through no fault of their own" (in the phrase accepted by both) are unable to obtain adequate housing, and liberals tend to be more generous in their response than conservatives, both cling to the importance of "self-help" (as in welfare-to-work programs) and bypass confrontation with the social causes of housing problems, thus leaving homelessness, for example, a permanent part of the housing scene.

2. *Insecurity in housing occupancy.* Housing policy in the United States has never been able to avoid sharp fluctuations in the housing circumstances of the majority of the population. In periods of economic depression or high unemployment, evictions have always grown in number, mortgage foreclosures have increased, affordability has dwindled, overcrowding has increased and quality (especially neighborhood quality) has deteriorated. Improvement has been sharpest in the periods of liberal Democratic government—for instance, the Roosevelt New Deal, the Truman postwar Administration and the Kennedy-Johnson years—but the improvement has been more through having to confront increasingly visible problems and efforts at their amelioration rather than through steps to achieve long-term solutions. In conservative periods, the tendency has been to deny the existence of problems and deal with them in partial, specialized segments, never recognizing any systemic difficulties.

3. *Segregation and discrimination based on race.* The problem of segregation and discrimination in housing has been ongoing in United States history since the founding of the Republic. Liberal Democrats have been more forthright in confronting the issue than have conservatives. There have been advances, but the high level of segregation and continued discrimination in housing sales, rentals and financing is demonstrable. Neither liberal nor conservative approaches have given hope for a real solution to either problem, and to many in the field, levels of segregation and inequality based on race seem to be unalterable....

4. *Environmental degradation.* Sprawl is not merely an issue of declining green spaces and natural habitat; it is wasteful of energy resources both in home heating and cooling and in transportation, increases air pollution from commuting and uses land and building resources inefficiently. Under both liberal and conservative administrations, sprawl has been encouraged through highway construction, tax policies and financing subsidies; neither has made a serious attempt to limit sprawl or provide for effective environmentally oriented national land use regulation.

5. *Increasing problems of affordability.* Much is made of the increasing quantity and quality of housing in the United States, for which each administration, whether Democratic or Republican, takes credit. However, primarily the progress has been made among those who have been in a position to obtain their housing through the private market. As a consequence and inevitably, problems of housing affordability have grown as problems of housing quality have declined. Housing affordability problems may be at the highest point today since the Great Depression.

Notes and Questions

1. Chapter 3 *infra* contains an analysis of the major federal and state housing programs which have been active since the 1930s, including public housing, supply-side and demand-side subsidies for privately-owned housing, mortgage insurance, tax exempt bond financing, and tax credits for low-income housing developments. As you study these programs, consider whether the "continuing failures" identified by Marcuse and Keating are being addressed or ignored by federal and state housing programs.

Professor Dreier has proposed a radical restructuring of federal housing policy by canceling most of the federal programs administered by the Department of Housing and Urban Development and substituting in their stead a $50 billion housing voucher program administered by the Department of Health and Human Services. In addition, he would substitute a refundable progressive homeowner tax credit for the current mortgage interest tax deduction. This credit would be available to all families, whether or not they itemize their deductions. He would also allocate about $6 billion for community development and empowerment through neighborhood and resident-based organizations and $7 billion for modernization and operating subsidies for existing public housing. Peter Dreier, *The New Politics of Housing, supra,* at 18–22. As you study the housing programs in Chapter 3 *infra*, compare those programs with Professor Dreier's proposals.

2. Although some housing analysts may not agree with his conclusions, Professor Peter Salins identifies major policy issues that housing programs must consider.

> We must recognize that sheltering today's poor—who have personal, social, and economic problems much more severe than yesterday's poor—according to contemporary housing standards that are considerably more demanding than those of the past poses a great challenge. Furthermore, this daunting task must be pursued with more slender resources. The public housing failures of the past, the retrenchment of the public sector, and the public refusal to engage so heavily in social amelioration or income redistribution all add up to an environment for housing reform which demands that we must rely primarily on the private market, and that we make sure that those housing subsidy dollars which are made available stretch further.
>
> Above all, a realistic view of the housing problems of the poor, especially the ubiquitous spectacle in the cities from coast to coast of neighborhood squalor, demands that we fit our policies and programs to a brutally honest assessment of the constraints posed by the social and behavioral characteristics of the families we wish to help. We must recognize the role these characteristics play in causing dwelling and neighborhood deterioration, and reject the simplistic charge that such recognition means we are thereby "blaming the victim." We must also recognize the legitimate wishes of the poor themselves, who may interpret their needs quite differently from the physical and aesthetic meliorism of middle-class planners. They may not even want their meager allotment of subsidy crumbs from the public banquet table to take the form of housing assistance at all.

Peter Salins, *Toward a Permanent Housing Problem*, 85 PUB. INT. 22, 33 (1986). You should compare Professor Salins' analysis with the discussion of policy "images" in the Grigsby and Rosenberg selection in the next section. One of the major issues Professor Salins identifies is the difference in perspective created by an emphasis on housing affordability rather than housing conditions. An earlier study by the Joint Center commented:

> Housing affordability is, of course, a relative concept. Whether housing is affordable or not ... depends on one's point of view. In the face of higher housing costs, households may choose to purchase a smaller home or one with fewer amenities.

JOINT CENTER FOR HOUSING STUDIES, HARVARD UNIVERSITY, THE STATE OF THE NATION'S HOUSING 10 (1988).

3. Whether there is a housing affordability crisis also depends on how an appropriate rent and housing cost burden is defined. For years, federal statutes limited rents in rental subsidy programs to 25% of income. Legislation sponsored by the Reagan administration and adopted by Congress in 1981 raised this percentage to 30%. How should this issue be decided as a policy matter? Is it important that the percentage of income paid for housing usually increases as incomes decline?

The 2008 Harvard study reported that "the nearly 9 million households with incomes below 30 percent of the median for their Census division ($11,000 to $18,000) ... must compete for just 3 million affordable and available rental units." JOINT CENTER FOR HOUSING STUDIES, HARVARD UNIVERSITY, THE STATE OF THE NATION'S HOUSING 2008 31 (2008). What do these statistics tell you about the use of numbers in housing policy analysis? Should there be a threshold at which the numbers become urgent enough for some form of government intervention. Are 9 million very low-income households competing for 3 million units enough?

4. Aggregate statistics mask important differences among the housing problems of racial groups. A 2008 Harvard study indicates that black and Hispanic families at lower-income levels have more serious housing affordability problems than white families. JOINT CENTER FOR HOUSING STUDIES, HARVARD UNIVERSITY, AMERICA'S RENTAL HOUSING: THE KEY TO A BALANCED NATIONAL POLICY 15 (2008). These findings suggest that racial and national minorities suffer a discrimination penalty in housing markets, a problem that adds another dimension to housing policy. Racial discrimination in housing markets is discussed in section C of this chapter, and in Chapter 6 *infra*.

A Note on Affordable Workforce Housing Concerns and the Foreclosure Crisis

a. Affordable Workforce Housing Issues

The rapid increase in housing prices noted by the Joint Center triggered increasing attention to housing problems of America's service workers—firefighters, janitors, nurses, paralegals, police officers, school teachers, social workers, etc. A study for the Center for Housing Policy, MAYA BRENNAN & BARBARA J. LIPMAN, THE HOUSING LANDSCAPE FOR AMERICA'S WORKING FAMILIES 2007, *available at* www.nhc.org/housing/landscape2007, examined housing conditions for this sector in 31 metropolitan areas. The study found that from 1997 to 2005 the number of working families paying more than 50% of their income for housing increased by 87%, from 2.4 million to 4.5 million. The number of renters paying more than 50% for housing grew from 1 million in 1997 to 2.1 million in 2005, an increase of 103%. Renters also were twice as likely as homeowners to live in inadequate housing or crowded conditions.

Peter Dreier, in *Housing the Working Poor*, 29 SHELTERFORCE 8, 10 (Fall No. 3 2007), *available at* www.nhi.org/online/issues/151/housingtheworkingpoor.html, concluded that "there are about 12 million 'working poor' families—owners as well as renters—who pay more [than 30% of their income, which is more] than they can reasonably afford for housing. Despite this great need, federal housing subsidies are not an entitlement, like food stamps, public education, or the EITC [earned income tax credit].... Only 3.2 million of the 9.7 million renter households with incomes below 30 percent of median income [approximately $20,000] received any form of federal housing assistance [in 2005]."

The National Low Income Housing Coalition (NLIHC), an advocacy organization, has concluded from its research that "*no rental market in America can offer Americans safe harbor from unaffordable housing.*" Using the concept of a "housing wage" (what one would need to earn to be able to afford the estimated local Fair Market Rent ("FMR"), spending no more than 30 percent of income for housing costs, NLIHC estimates that an income of $37,105 ($17.84/hour for a full-time worker) is necessary "in order to afford" the national average FMR of $928/month for a two bedroom rental unit. NATIONAL LOW INCOME HOUSING COALITION, OUT OF REACH 2009 Introduction, 3–4 (2009), *available at* www.nlihc.org/oor/oor2009/onlineguide.pdf (emphasis added). *See also* U.S. Dep't of Housing & Urban Development, *Housing: Critical For Working Families and Communities*, RES. WORKS 1, 2, n. 5 (No. 5 May 2008), *available at* www.huduser.org/periodicals/researchworks/ResearchWorks_may_08.pdf, for another dimension to the workforce housing issue:

> When the Brookings Institution analyzed the distribution of jobs and workers in the largest 150 U.S. metropolitan areas, analysts found that about 65 percent of the population and 60 percent of jobs are in the suburbs, but a spatial mismatch exists between where people work and live. During the 1990s, lower-income suburbs experienced slow job growth but sharp population increases. At the same time, higher-income suburbs saw strong job growth and a need for both skilled and service workers. As a result, residents of lower-income suburbs and central cities increasingly commute to jobs located in higher-income areas. Access to jobs often depends on the distance between home and work, car ownership, commuting costs, and the layout of roads, highways, and transit lines.

The $4.00/gallon gasoline price surge during the summer of 2008 highlights the impact of long commuting distances on working families. In a 2006 study prepared by the Center for Housing Policy and completed before the run-up in gas prices, BARBARA LIPMAN, A HEAVY LOAD: THE COMBINED HOUSING AND TRANSPORTATION BURDENS OF WORKING FAMILIES (2006), *available at* www.nhc.org/pdf_heavy_load_10_06.pdf, found that working families in the 28 metropolitan areas she examined were spending about 57 percent of their incomes on the combined costs of housing and transportation, split almost evenly between the two (28 percent for housing and 29 percent for transportation). But higher costs for one tended to result in families spending less on the other. For example, in their search for lower cost housing, working families often located far from their place of work, dramatically increasing their transportation costs and commute times. Ms. Lipman concluded that policy makers should consider housing and transportation together, a topic that the Obama Administration began addressing in the spring of 2009. NLIHC, *HUD, DOT, EPA Announce Joint Effort to Improve Community "Livability,"* 14 MEMO TO MEMBERS 1 n.24 (Jun. 19, 2009). *See also* CENTER FOR TRANSIT ORIENTED DEVELOPMENT and CENTER FOR NEIGHBORHOOD TECHNOLOGY, THE AFFORDABILITY INDEX: A NEW TOOL FOR MEASURING THE TRUE AFFORDABILITY OF A HOUSING CHOICE (2006) (Brookings Institution study describing an affordability index that combines the cost of housing with the cost of transportation associated with employment, education and household errands. When the index was applied to four neighborhoods in the seven-county Minneapolis-St. Paul metropolitan area, transportation costs as a percentage of income equaled or exceeded housing costs in three suburban locations, but were one percentage point less than housing costs in a near-downtown neighborhood of Minneapolis. *Id,* at 11). Affordability indices are discussed in Chapter 3 *infra.* The link between housing and transportation is discussed in Chapter 5 *infra.*

b. Subprime Mortgages and the Housing Market Collapse

As the Harvard Center's STATE OF THE NATION'S HOUSING report *supra* indicated, an overheated housing market virtually shut down in 2007–2008. A major factor in what became a full-blown crisis in 2008 and 2009 was the prevalence of *subprime* loans secured by *adjustable rate* mortgages ("ARMs"). The term, subprime, does not refer to a lower than prime interest rate. Rather, it refers to the fact that the borrowers are people "who, for a variety of reasons, would otherwise be denied credit." A loan is labeled subprime if the borrower is charged "a premium above the prevailing prime market rate." Souphala Chomsisemgphet & Anthony Pennington-Cross, *The Evolution of the Subprime Mortgage Market,* 88 FED. RES. BANK ST. LOUIS REV. 31, 36 (No. 1 Jan./Feb. 2006).

In a typical scenario, a mortgage broker arranges a subprime ARM loan to finance the purchase of a house or condominium. Once the transaction is completed, the loan would be sold by the lender to an intermediary on the secondary mortgage market who would package it with other mortgages into a pool of 100 to 10,000 such mortgages. Individual investors would then be invited to purchase interests in the pool of mortgages. This process became known as mortgage securitization. Between 2004 and 2006 "more than 2,500 banks, thrifts, credit unions and mortgage companies made a combined $1.5 trillion in high interest-rate loans ... in poorer communities [as well as] middle class and wealthier communities." Rich Brooks & Constance Mitchell Ford, *The United States of Subprime; Data Show Bad Loans Permeate the Nation; Pain Could Last Years,* WALL ST. J, Oct. 11, 2007, at A1.

c. The Foreclosure Crisis

Beginning in 2007, the housing foreclosure crisis attributable in large part to reckless and often fraudulent lending practices took on national dimensions (discussed *infra* chapters 3, 5, and 6). Its roots lay in a combination of factors, including the following:

- federal policies in the 1980s and 1990s deregulating mortgage lenders;
- a growing flow of capital into real estate in an era of low interest rates and the widespread use of refinancing by homeowners;
- a shift in mortgage lending to non-regulated mortgage firms that promoted subprime loans to financially marginal borrowers;
- the development of new and much riskier mortgage loan products (e.g., interest only, no down payment), the promotion of "teaser" adjustable rate mortgages (ARMs) with rapidly escalating interest rates after the initial period of the loan, and the "securitization" of loans through a complex secondary mortgage market that attracted investors in mortgage-backed securities that was based in part on very risky subprime mortgage loans;
- "predatory" lending practices (e.g., costly conditions and exorbitant fees) and outright fraud (e.g., "liar" loans, in which the borrower's income is fraudulent); subprime loans carry higher interest rates reflecting the borrower's poorer credit rating and income, in contrast to "conventional" loans at "prime" interest rates. "Predatory" lending is the practice of including excessive and hidden fees and draconian terms like severe penalties for pre-paying the loan.
- the promotion of home ownership for lower-income and minority homeowners by both the administrations of former presidents Bill Clinton and George W. Bush;

- borrowing by homebuyers who did or should have known that they could not afford to repay subprime mortgage loans, as well as speculative purchasing by "flippers" looking to resell for a quick profit.

Combined with a severe national recession that cost many homeowners their jobs and income, the reduction in consumer spending, personal financial problems, the collapse of the housing "bubble" of constantly escalating housing values, and the failure of major investment firms and banks requiring massive federal intervention and bailouts from the Federal Reserve Bank and the U.S. Treasury, led to the foreclosure of millions of homes and the loss of trillions of value for homeowners. The rapid decline in demand for both unsold over-constructed housing inventory and existing single-family homes and condominiums led as well to millions abandoning homes with mortgage payments far in excess of value in a previously escalating market in which many over-invested and bought homes that were too expensive or had speculated in the ostensible "sure thing" of real estate. All levels of government responded in an attempt to stabilize the housing market and housing construction industry. Homeowners lost an estimated $3.3 trillion in property values in 2008 alone. As of the third quarter of 2009, according to the Mortgage Bankers Association, about one in seven of 45 million home mortgage loans in the United States were either delinquent or in some stage of foreclosure. See Renae Merle, *Foreclosure, Delinquency Rates Spike Amid Growing Unemployment*, WASH. POST, Nov. 19, 2009. As of the end of 2009, more than one in five homeowners' mortgages were "under water," i.e., the outstanding mortgage principal exceeded the current market value of the house. This had led many homeowners with negative equity to abandon their homes without facing a foreclosure action by the lender. Analysts estimated that more than two million homeowners might lose their homes in 2010.

Mortgage delinquencies and foreclosure rates vary considerably by state and city, with some with much higher rates than many others. For current data, see Realty Trac: www.realtytrac.com. As the magnitude of the foreclosure crisis unfolded, debates over its causes became widespread. A particularly sharp debate took place over the role of the Community Reinvestment Act (CRA), 12 U.S.C. §§ 2901–2908, which has promoted homeownership for those borrowers in disinvested neighborhoods "redlined" by federally-regulated banks (see discussion *infra* chapter 6), and the government sponsored enterprises (GSEs)—"Fannie Mae" and "Freddie Mac" (see the discussion in this chapter and chapter 3 *infra*) which were mandated by Congress to help meet affordable housing and increased home ownership goals through assuring available capital by the purchase of mortgages. The conservative attack on CRA was led by critics like Peter J. Wallison, a fellow at the American Enterprise Institute (www.aei.org). *Contra* Warren W. Traiger, *The CRA: A Welcome Anomaly in the Foreclosure Crisis*, 53 N.Y.L. SCH. L. Rev. 227 (2008–2009). Ellen Harnick argued (2009), that victimized homeowners who received unfair and deceptive loans also could not be blamed. Ellen Harnick, *The Crisis in Housing and Housing Finance: What Caused It? What Didn't? What's Next?* 31 W. NEW. ENG. L. REV. 625 (2009).

Beginning in 2007, major federal legislation was enacted and anti-foreclosure policies initiated by various federal agencies. States and local governments also initiated their own programs. Events moved rapidly. This section discusses those developments.

Long before the federal government acknowledged the enormity of the foreclosure problem, states and local governments acted. For example, the state of North Carolina enacted legislation in 1999 to curb predatory lending. N.C. GEN. STAT. § 24-1.1A. When several Ohio cities attempted to regulate mortgage brokers' practices under their home rule power in 2002 in the absence of state regulation, the state legislature pre-empted their ordinances. *American Fin. Serv. v. City of Cleveland*, 858 N.E. 2d 776 (Ohio 2006). The Ohio legislature later reversed itself and adopted regulatory legislation in 2006. Ohio Rev. Code §§ 1349.25 *et seq*. Several State Attorneys General, led by California and Illinois, sued Countrywide Financial, then the largest private mortgage lender in the country, under their consumer fraud statutes for deceptive practices, leading to an $8.4 billion settlement in October, 2008 (although by that time a failed Countrywide had been acquired by Bank of America): *Countrywide Reaches $8.4B Fraud Settlement with 11 States*, Boston Globe, Oct. 7, 2008.

Cities and many of their neighborhoods have been hardest hit by the impact of this crisis, as the number of abandoned and vacant foreclosed houses mounted. Due to lack of a normal housing market and the often deteriorated condition of these foreclosed homes, cities and suburbs alike often had to spend considerable funds to board up what became a public nuisance. Trying to persuade absentee lenders to secure and maintain these buildings has proven very difficult. Many have been stripped of their fixtures by vandals, are used by drug dealers and are the site of other criminal activities, and present a danger to neighbors, whose property values have been hurt by their presence, driving more to abandon their homes and neighborhoods. The cities of Buffalo and Cleveland, both hard hit by foreclosures, have sued lenders for damages on the basis that this was a foreseeable result from subprime lending to lower-income homeowners in older neighborhoods. Cleveland's lawsuit, based upon a nuisance abatement theory, was transferred from state to federal court and was dismissed in May, 2009. *City of Cleveland v. Ameriquest Mortgage Sec., Inc.*, 621 F. Supp. 2d 513 (N.D. Ohio 2009). In dismissing Cleveland's suit, the judge gave three reasons: 1) Ohio law pre-empted such lawsuits by a municipality, 2) the city's failure to establish a nuisance due to the existing regulation of mortgages, and 3) the remoteness of the alleged harm to the city.

Lenders have denied their liability. Some disputed the foreseeability argument, while others holding title as trustees for investors were not the original lenders. Cleveland's Municipal Housing Court judge has also attempted to force lenders to comply with the city's housing code through fines, which proved difficult to enforce. *See* www.clevelandhousingcourt.org. Some lenders have decided to not proceed to foreclose, thereby avoiding any responsibility for the condition of homes abandoned by homeowners. They are also influenced by the costs of foreclosure and where there is a glut of abandoned houses the lack of arms length buyers. Bank "walk aways" leave the departed homeowner as still the legal owner, creating a "toxic title" (i.e., cities have no recourse to enforce their housing codes and if the owner cannot be located, trying to arrange a sale if the house is still habitable can be virtually impossible). Some lenders have engaged in large-scale "dumping" of foreclosed homes to wholesalers. In Cleveland, community organizations have sued to try to prevent sales of foreclosed substandard homes at bargain basement prices, leading to the purchasers then reselling them, often on the internet, to unsuspecting buyers, compounding the problem of deterioration. *See* Frank Ford, *Cleaning Up After the Foreclosure Tsunami: Tackling Bank Walk-Aways and Vulture Investors*, 159/160 Shelterforce 54 (Fall/Winter 2009).

State and local governments have created foreclosure prevention and mitigation programs, many federally funded by the National Foreclosure Mitigation Counseling program for HUD-approved agencies, primarily through NeighborhoodWorks America (www.nw.org/network/foreclosure/default). These foreclosure counseling agencies have attempted to convince lenders to modify mortgages, with mixed success. The Federal Deposit Insurance Corporation (FDIC), a Depression-era federal agency created to insure deposits in federally-chartered lenders and, when necessary, acquire and re-organize failed banks, led the way. It created a program under which it would attempt to save homeowners from foreclosure by lowering or postponing mortgage interest payments, deferring principal repayments, and lengthening the term of the mortgage. This assumes that the defaulting homeowner is still able to pay the modified mortgage (at least at a ratio of 31% to income). This policy was then adopted by the Obama Administration in March, 2009 under its "Making Homes Affordable" or the "Home Affordable Modification Program (HAMP)." Part of the economic stimulus program, it was funded for $75 billion, administered by the U.S. Treasury, and is to last through 2012. In addition, it made mortgage servicers eligible for a payment of $1,000 for each modified loan and another annual fee of $1,000 for up to three years if the borrowers stay current on the modified mortgage. See: www.MakingHomeAffordable.gov.

However, obtaining mortgage modifications proved difficult. In particular, mortgage servicers often proved to be a major obstacle, either claiming that they lacked authority on behalf of the lenders or because proceeding to foreclose was more profitable for them and their clients. As of January, 2010, only approximately 940,000 out of an estimated up to 3–4 million homeowners eligible for mortgage modifications under the Obama program had entered the program on a trial basis (three to five months), despite the administration pressuring the participating lenders. Worse, only 116,000 of these had their mortgages permanently modified. While all had their interest rate reduced, only a small number had the principal amount reduced. Renae Merle, *Administration Pushed to Expand Foreclosure-Prevention Program*, Wash. Post, Feb. 18, 2010, at A13.

Lenders claimed that the slow start was attributable to staffing shortages, participating borrowers failing to provide necessary paperwork, and the inability of many borrowers to pay even a reduced modified loan. One reaction to the latter problem was to change the eligibility requirement by increasing the loan-to-value ratio from 105% to 125%. A later change intended to address the paperwork issue was to require lenders to collect necessary information at the application stage rather than later. David Streitfeld, *Treasury Streamlines Its Mortgage Program*, N.Y. Times, Jan. 29, 2010, at B3.

Many homeowners seeking loan modifications have not been notified that their applications have been denied, resulting in unforeseen foreclosure actions. The Housing Preservation Project in Minnesota filed a class action lawsuit on their behalf against federal agencies responsible for implementing HAMP, claiming that HAMP is an entitlement program and these agencies' failure to promulgate rules requiring notice of a denial or an appeals process violated the Due Process rights of defaulting borrowers seeking relief. In *Williams v. Geithner*, Civ. No. 09-1959 ADM/JJG, 2009 WL 3757380 (D. Minn. Nov. 9, 2009), the court rejected the argument that HAMP created a protected property interest for its intended beneficiaries. It pointed to the discretionary powers given to the agencies and the voluntary participation of the mortgage servicers. *See* 40 Housing L. Bull. 12 (Jan. 2010).

In July, 2008, President Bush signed the Housing and Economic Recovery Act (HERA), Pub. L. No. 110-289, 122 Stat. 2654 (2008), designed to address the crisis. HERA has five governmental aims:

> 1) helping government-sponsored entities (GSEs) that regulate the mortgage industry; 2) providing relief for borrowers and lenders currently dealing with the effects of the housing crisis; 3) stabilizing the housing markets; 4) remedying the social consequences of foreclosures; and 5) preventing a future housing crisis.

Bruce Arthur, *Housing and Economic Recovery Act of 2008*, 46 Harv. J. on Legis. 585 (2009). To oversee the GSEs (*infra*), HERA created the Federal Housing Finance Agency

(FHFA). It contained a $4 billion aid program (first round) for state and local governments to address the housing abandonment problem. Funding is provided through the Neighborhood Stabilization Program (NSP), administered by HUD, and can be used for the purchase of foreclosed-upon homes to rehabilitate or demolish them. In 2009, a second round of NSP funding was authorized. *See* http://hud.gov/communitydevelopment/programs/neighborhoodspg/and www.hud.gov/recovery. HERA authorized a "HOPE for Homeowners" program, under which $300 billion was provided to cooperating lenders willing to modify voluntarily mortgages into conventional fixed rate, 30-year mortgages to be guaranteed by the Federal Housing Administration (FHA).The FHA, created in 1934, provides federal insurance for mortgages within prescribed eligibility limits. This program was limited to homeowners whose conventional mortgage loans originated prior to January 1, 2008, whose total monthly payments were more than 31 percent of their gross income, and whose loans did not exceed $550,440. Due to the demands on the FHA and a rising rate of mortgage defaults on its insured loans, its reserve fund was dangerously low by the fall of 2009. David Streitfeld & Louise Story, *F.H.A. Problems Raising Concern of Policy Makers*, N.Y. Times, Oct. 9, 2009, at A1.

The HOPE for Homeowners program took effect in September, 2008, just as the federal government was forced to rescue the two major government-sponsored enterprises that controlled approximately half of the mortgage lending in the United States through the secondary market: the Federal National Mortgage Association (FNMA) ("Fannie Mae"), created in 1938, and the Federal Home Loan Mortgage Corporation (FHLMC) ("Freddie Mac"), created in 1970. The secondary mortgage market is discussed in Chapter 3 *infra*. While not the major force in promoting subprime mortgages (which grew from 6 percent of all mortgage loans in 2000 to 25% by 2006), Fannie Mae and Freddie Mac also were caught short by the collapse of the housing bubble, which came after previous revelations of accounting manipulation exaggerating their profits and requiring the two agencies to reduce their prior profit claims. Binyamin Appelbaum, Carol D. Leonnig & David S. Hilzenrath, *How Washington Failed to Rein in Fannie, Freddie*, Wash. Post, Sept. 14, 2008, at A1.

Fannie Mae and Freddie Mac are privately-owned, government-sponsored enterprises ("GSE") originally created by the federal government to expand "liquidity" in the mortgage market by buying and selling loans originated by primary lenders (e.g., banks and savings and loan associations). The U.S. Treasury committed up to $400 billion (a cap later lifted) and took over majority control of both mortgage giants. Within a year, it had committed almost $100 billion to try to stabilize these two secondary mortgage giants. For a brief review of the history of these GSEs, their role in the financial crisis, and their possible future role, see Theresa DiVenti, *Fannie Mae and Freddie Mac: Past, Present, and Future*, 11 Cityscape 231 (2009).

Despite these emergency measures, foreclosures continued to mount. Relatively few mortgages were modified under the HOPE for Homeowners voluntary program. And there were signs that many of those whose mortgages were modified still fell into foreclosure. Temporary mortgage foreclosure moratoria declared by Fannie Mae, Freddie Mac, and several major banks at the end of 2008 through early 2009 did not last. The impact on tenants, innocent victims of their landlords' foreclosure, became a growing problem. They were typically subject to immediate eviction. Fannie Mae and Freddie Mac both adopted policies intended to keep them in the homes, at least until they were sold. The Emergency Economic Stabilization Act (EESA), Pub. L. No. 110-343, 122 Stat. 3765 (2008), enacted in October, 2008, also provided some limited eviction protection for federally-subsidized tenants. The Protecting Tenants at Foreclosure Act, Pub. L. No. 111-22, 123

Stat. 1632 (2009), enacted in May, 2009, provided a 90-day notice which would help those tenants with month-to-month tenancies.

Consumer advocates pushed for reform of U.S. bankruptcy law (11 U.S.C.§ 1322(b)(2)) to allow judges to modify delinquent mortgages for the primary residences of homeowners under Chapter 13 (the "strip down" or "cram down" process under which the debtor's mortgage loan payments would be reduced). The banking lobby strongly opposed this. The U.S. House of Representatives easily passed the amendment but it was defeated in the U.S. Senate in April, 2009 by a vote of 51–45. Renae Merle, *Senate Defeats Measure to Allow Bankruptcy Judges to Change Mortgage Terms*, WASH. POST, Apr. 30, 2008. The Obama administration then proposed in the summer of 2009 the creation of a new federal regulatory agency (a Consumer Financial Protection Agency) to protect borrowers against unfair and deceptive lender practices. This faced opposition not only from the banking industry but also from some federal regulatory agencies. Jackie Calmes & Sewell Chan, *Obama Pressing for Protections Against Lenders*, N.Y. TIMES, Jan. 20, 2010, at A1 and Robert G. Kaiser, *How a Crusade to Protect Consumers Lost its Steam.* WASH. POST, Jan. 31, at G1. One year later, compromise legislation creating the new agency was approved by Congress. Pub. L. No. 111–203 (July 21, 2010).

Other reforms aimed at preventing future predatory lending included new standards for real estate appraisers (a Home Valuation Code of Conduct), adopted by Fannie Mae and Freddie Mac, and a more transparent real estate settlement process announced by HUD. Meanwhile, yet another wave of fraudulent practices by so-called foreclosure rescue firms resulted in desperate homeowners not only failing to receive the services promised but also still losing their homes.

At the state level, many tried to assist homeowners threatened with foreclosure. Some reformed their foreclosure laws, which the National Consumer Law Center argued exacerbated the crisis. State responses were detailed by the Pew Center on the States *infra*.

In other legal developments in the federal courts, a Cleveland federal district court judge ruled in 2007 that lenders could not proceed in foreclosure unless they could produce proof of ownership by filing executed documents. *In re Foreclosure Cases*, Nos. 07-cv-166, 190, 226, 279, 423, 534, 536, 642, 706, 727, 731, 963, 1047, 1119, 1150, 2007 WL 4589765 (S.D. Ohio Dec. 27, 2007). Much of the securitization of mortgages was done electronically, without such documents. Other federal judges have dismissed foreclosure actions on similar grounds. Lenders turned to the federal courts where there were growing delays in state courts due to the massive increase in foreclosure actions. *Contra Hafiz v. Greenpoint Mortgage Funding, Inc.*, 652 F. Supp. 2d 1039 (N.D. Cal. 2009) (rejecting mortgage fraud and reverse redlining claims under the Equal Credit Opportunity Act and Title VIII arising from foreclosure upon adjustable rate mortgage; California does not require possession of the note as a precondition to non-judicial foreclosure under a deed of trust and the trustee has the right to initiate the foreclosure process).

In another innovative lawsuit, the city of Baltimore sued Wells Fargo under the Federal Fair Housing Act, alleging that it had illegally targeted African-American neighborhoods for subprime loans. *Mayor of Baltimore v. Wells Fargo Bank, N.A.*, 631 F. Supp. 2d 702 (D. Md. 2009). A federal judge dismissed the case because of the "implausibility" that such a practice could be held responsible for the deterioration of the inner city. Tricia Bishop, *Court Dismisses City's Discriminatory Lending Lawsuit Against Wells Fargo*, BALT. SUN, Jan. 6, 2010). In December, 2009, the city of Memphis also filed a similar lawsuit against Wells Fargo. Michael Powell, *Memphis Accuses Wells Fargo of Discriminating Against Blacks*, N.Y. TIMES, Dec. 31, 2009, at A17. (see discussion of discrimination in the foreclosure context *infra* chapter 6). Subsequently, the Civil Rights Division of the U.S. Department of Justice announced the creation of a new unit to focus exclusively on unfair lending practices. Charlie Savage, *Justice Department Opens Front Against Bias in Lending*, N.Y. Times, Jan. 14, 2010, at A18.

Despite all of these legislative and program initiatives at all governmental levels, the unprecedented intervention of the federal government in the housing field, and litigation, the foreclosure crisis showed no signs of ending very soon. While implementation of many reforms is still in the early stages, it is likely that much more will have to be done to reform the entire system of home ownership and housing finance. It is noteworthy that the banking and real estate lobbies have opposed many of these reforms, arguing that they would be counter-productive. While much attention was focused on the foreclosure crisis, the federal government was just as concerned about saving major mortgage lenders and rejuvenating the housing construction industry and real estate market.

For a history of the foreclosure crisis and a summary of responses by state governments, *see* The Pew Charitable Trusts, Defaulting on a Dream—States Respond to America's Foreclosure Crisis (2008), *available at* www.pewtrusts.org/uploadedFiles/wwwpewtrustsorg/Reports/Subprime_mortgages/defaulting_on_the_dream.pdf. *See also* John Atlas & Peter Dreier, *Stemming the Red Tide,* 30 Shelterforce, 8, 14 (No. 1 Spring 2008), *available at* www.shelterforce.org/article/210/stemming_the_red_tide (reviewing the foreclosure crisis and arguing the not-for-profit lenders, such as federally-chartered Neighborhood Housing Services of America ("NHS"), which has offices in urban areas around the country, have done a better job than for-profit lenders in "helping working-class families become homeowners without putting them at risk"); Bob Erlenbusch, Kelly O'Connor, Sherrie Downing and Sue Watlov Phillips, *Foreclosure to Homelessness: The Forgotten Victims of the Subprime Crisis: A National Call to Action* (2008), *available at* www.nationalhomeless.org/housing/foreclosure_report.pdf (a study by the National Coalition For The Homeless reporting that many victims of foreclosure, homeowners as well as renters whose landlords lost their rental units to foreclosure, have become homeless).

Notes and Questions

1. A major lesson of the foreclosure crisis is the importance of the concept of affordability. Granted, the loss of a job can play havoc with even the most responsible housing budget. But did too many people take too big a risk in buying homes with mortgages that, when measured against even the federal standard of affordability (paying no more than 30 percent of income for housing) clearly were not affordable? Did too many people lose sight of a fundamental question of financial responsibility, "How much can I afford to pay back?" in pursuit of the answer to a different question, "How much can I borrow?" The secondary mortgage market and mortgage securitization are discussed in Chapter 3 *infra*. Consider what roles those institutions and practices played in the foreclosure crisis.

2. Marcuse & Keating, *supra*, argue that affordability problems in the first decade of the 21st Century were at their highest levels since the Great Depression. Should the federal government intervene? If so, how? For an argument that support for the rental housing market should be part of any federal response, *see* Joint Center for Housing Studies of Harvard University, America's Rental Housing: The Key to a Balanced National Policy (2008), *available at* www.jchs.harvard.edu/publications/rental/rh08_americas

_rental_housing/index.html. Federal responses to the foreclosure crisis are discussed in Chapter 3 *infra.*

3. For the background to the programs aimed at increasing lower-income home ownership, see CHASING THE AMERICAN DREAM: NEW PERSPECTIVES ON HOME OWNERSHIP (William E. Rohe & Harry L. Watson eds. 2007). The federal government has promoted home ownership from Herbert Hoover's efforts in the 1920s culminating in his presidential conference on "Home Building and Home Ownership" in 1931 to George W. Bush's support for the 2003 American Dream Home Ownership Act providing assistance to first time homebuyers for down payments and settlement costs to the provision of tax credits in 2009 to first time homebuyers as part of the Obama economic stimulus program. This policy has long included tax incentives to homeowners (itemized deductions for payments for property taxes and mortgage interest) not available to tenants. This policy has been criticized for being inequitable to tenants and also for being regressive since it favors wealthier homeowners. Why is owning a home considered preferable to renting? Is the push for wider home ownership including lower income Americans well considered? Should first time homebuyers who are being subsidized by the government be required to attend counseling sessions intended to educate them about home buying and ownership?

4. For a more thorough understanding of the mortgage foreclosure crisis, see DAN IMMERGLUCK, FORECLOSED: HIGH-RISK LENDING, DEREGULATION, AND THE UNDERMINING OF AMERICA'S MORTGAGE MARKET (2009). For a detailed review of the causes of the impact and causes of the subprime mortgage crisis, see Peter W. Salsich, *National Affordable Housing Trust Fund Legislation: The Subprime Mortgage Crisis Also Hits Renters*, 16 GEO. J. ON POVERTY L. & POL'Y 11, 19–32 (2009). See also Ellen Harnick, *The Crisis in Housing and Housing Finance: What Caused It? What Didn't? What's Next?* 31 W. NEW. ENG. L. REV. 625 (2009). For rebuttal of the claim that the GSEs caused the crisis by overinvesting in subprime mortgages under pressure to increase low-income homeownership, see Christopher L. Peterson, *Fannie Mae, Freddie Mac, and the Home Mortgage Foreclosure Crisis*, LOY. J. PUB. INT. L. 149 (2009).

5. To understand the mortgage securitization process and its part in the crisis, see Kurt Eggert, *The Great Collapse: How Securitization Caused the Subprime Meltdown*, 41 CONN. L. REV. 1257 (2009). *See also* Kathleen C. Engel & Patricia A. McCoy, *Turning a Blind Eye: Wall Street Finance of Predatory Lending*, 75 FORDHAM L. REV. 2039 (2007); Christopher L. Peterson, *Predatory Structured Finance*, 28 CARDOZO L. REV. 2185 (2007).

6. For an analysis of the impact of the foreclosure crisis on cities, see A. Michele Dickerson, *Over-Indebtedness, the Subprime Mortgage Crisis, and the Effect on Cities*, 36 FORDHAM URB. L. J. 395 (2009). Cleveland, Ohio was one of the cities earliest hit hardest by the foreclosure crisis. For an account by the director of the Urban Development Law Clinic of the Cleveland-Marshall Law College of the foreclosure and abandonment crisis in Cleveland and its Slavic Village neighborhood, see Kermit Lind, *The Perfect Storm: An Eyewitness Report from Ground Zero In Cleveland's Neighborhoods*, 17 J. AFFORDABLE HOUSING & COMMUNITY DEV. L. 237 (2008). For a description of the impact of the crisis on Cleveland's Slavic Village neighborhood, see also Alex Kotlowitz, *All Boarded Up*, N.Y. TIMES, Mar. 8, 2009, Magazine, at 28.

7. For an analysis of North Carolina regulation's of predatory lending, see Roberto Quercia, Michael Stegman & Walter R. Davis, *Assessing the Impact of North Carolina's Predatory Lending Law*, 15 HOUSING POL'Y DEBATE 573 (2004). They concluded that the law did contribute to a reduction in subprime loan abuses. For other state responses, see

PEW CENTER FOR THE STATES, DEFAULTING ON THE DREAM: STATES RESPOND TO AMERICA'S FORECLOSURE CRISIS (2008).

8. For a comprehensive analysis of the foreclosure process, housing abandonment and neighborhood recovery strategies, see ALAN MALLACH, BRINGING BUILDINGS BACK: FROM ABANDONED PROPERTIES TO COMMUNITY ASSETS (2006). For a detailed review of state foreclosure laws and their shortcomings, see NATIONAL CONSUMER LAW CENTER, FORECLOSING A DREAM: STATE LAWS DEPRIVE HOMEOWNERS OF BASIC PROTECTIONS (2009). See generally CHERYL A. KELLY ET AL., FORECLOSURE LAWS AND RELATED REMEDIES (2d ed. 2009). Due to the virtual collapse of the housing market in many areas, some lenders decided not to foreclose on delinquent loans if there was little or no prospect of recouping at least part of the outstanding loan amount for lack of legitimate buyers and their liability and costs for maintaining the foreclosed house. This has aggravated the problem that cities have in recovering the costs of maintaining or demolishing abandoned, foreclosed homes where the homeowner has left but remains the legal owner.

9. HERA is described in detail in Bruce Arthur, *Housing and Economic Recovery Act of 2008*, 46 HARV. J. ON LEGIS. 585 (2009). For critiques of HERA and the Hope for Homeowners program, see Carole O. Heywood, *Hope for Homeowners: Too Little, Too Late*, 18 J. AFFORDABLE HOUSING & COMMUNITY DEV. L. 27 (2008); Alan M. White, *Deleveraging the American Homeowner: The Failure of the 2008 Voluntary Mortgage Contract Modifications*, 41 CONN. L. REV. 1107 (2009). Consider the voluntary approach versus stricter remedial approaches to mortgage modification. For an analysis of the mediation approach to avoiding foreclosures, see NATIONAL CONSUMER LAW CENTER. STATE AND LOCAL FORECLOSURE MEDIATION PROGRAMS: CAN THEY SAVE HOMES? (2009). It concludes that mediation can only be more successful if the mortgage "servicers" are more strictly regulated and that mediation is not an effective substitute for federal legislation mandating loan modification by lenders. See White, *supra* at 1127–1129, for an analysis of the servicers' situation. For additional analysis of the problems with federal mortgage loan regulatory programs, see Arielle L. Katzman, *A Round Peg for a Square Hole: The Mismatch Between Subprime Borrowers and Federal Mortgage Remedies*, 31 CARDOZO L. REV. 497 (2009).

10. For an argument for reforming the Chapter 13 bankruptcy process, see Adam J. Levitin, *Resolving the Foreclosure Crisis: Modification of Mortgages in Bankruptcy*, WIS. L. REV. 565, 647 (2009). Levitin concludes:

> Permitting modification of all mortgages in bankruptcy would not have prevented the economic situation leading to a foreclosure crisis, although it would have encouraged more prudent and sustainable underwriting and limited some of the systematic risk involved. Bankruptcy modification is not a magic-bullet solution, but it is quick, fair, efficient, and administrable response that would be far more effective at stabilizing the housing market and preventing the deadweight social and economic losses of foreclosure than any other proposed solution.

See also John Eggum, Katherine Porter & Tara Twomey, *Saving Homes in Bankruptcy: Housing Affordability and Loan Modification*, 2008 UTAH L. REV. 1123. Why would Congress exempt the primary residence of homeowners from bankruptcy protection? See Harnick, *supra* note 4. *See* also Michelle Garfinkle, *State and Local Measures Safeguard Tenants' Rights During Foreclosure*, 40 HOUSING L. BULL. 87–91 (Mar. 2010) (survey of state and local protections for tenants).

11. For a review of local government lawsuits against lenders, see Creola Johnson, *Fight Blight: Cities Sue to Hold Lenders Responsible for the Rise in Foreclosure and Aban-*

doned Properties, 2008 UTAH L. REV. 1169. For an analysis of the Cleveland and Baltimore lawsuits, see *Cities' Suits Seek Foreclosure-Related Damages*, 39 Housing L. Bull. 235 (Sept. 2009). For an analysis of cities suing lenders under the federal Fair Housing Act, see Ngai Pindell, *The Fair Housing Act at Forty: Predatory Lending and the City as Plaintiff*, 17 J. AFFORDABLE HOUSING & COMMUNITY DEV. L. 169 (2009). If cities should prevail in these types of lawsuits against lenders, how would the courts calculate the damages to be awarded to these cities from the impact of vacant and abandoned housing?

12. For the plight of tenants, see generally NATIONAL LOW INCOME HOUSING COALITION, RENTERS IN FORECLOSURE: DEFINING THE PROBLEM, IDENTIFYING SOLUTIONS (2009). Under the Oakland, California just cause eviction ordinance, lenders were prevented from arbitrarily evicting tenants in violation of the requirement for explaining the cause, with tenants having the right to appeal to the city's rent control board. See *California Cities Take Steps to Protect Tenants in Foreclosed Properties*, 39 HOUSING L. BULL. 234 (Sept. 2009). See also *HUD, States Take Additional Steps to Protect Tenants in Foreclosed Properties*, 40 HOUSING L. BULL. 43 (Feb. 2010).

13. For the chief arguments behind legislation enacted in 2010 creating new federal protections for mortgage borrowers and other consumers through a new agency, see Elizabeth Warren & Oren Bar-Gill, *Making Credit Safer*, 157 U. PA. L. REV.1 (2009).

14. If the federal or state governments should declare a temporary mortgage foreclosure moratorium, what legal obstacles would this face if challenged by lenders? For the constitutional fate of Depression-era state mortgage foreclosure moratoria, see *Home Building & Loan Assn. v. Blaisdell*, 290 U.S. 398 (1934) (upholding state moratorium in the face of the depression crisis over the contract clause that only limits the states). Congress enjoys broader powers, compare *Allied Structural Steel v. Spannaus*, 438 U.S. 234 (1978) (invalidating state pension protection legislation under the contract clause) with *Connolly v. Pension Benefit Guaranty Corp.*, 475 U.S. 211 (1986) (upholding constitutionality of withdrawal liability provisions of Multiemployer Pension Plan Amendments Act of 1980).

15. Mortgage counseling and foreclosure rescue fraud has become yet another aspect of this crisis. *See* NATIONAL CONSUMER LAW CENTER DESPERATE HOMEOWNERS: LOAN MOD SCAMMERS STEP IN WHEN LOAN SERVICERS REFUSE TO PROVIDE RELIEF (2009).

Of course, housing is but one facet of a modern community. People also need jobs, schools, services and infrastructure. The planning and growth management disciplines have the general responsibility of managing the relationships and consistency between these elements. The following excerpt raises questions about the United States' traditional emphasis on low density development.

Edward H. Ziegler, The Case for Megapolitan Growth Management in the 21st Century: Regional Urban Planning and Sustainable Development in the United States

41 Urban Lawyer 147, 148–152 (2009)

Most people in the United States do not live in major cities. Most Americans live, work, shop, and play in suburban areas, scattered about metropolitan landscapes far from any downtown urban core. We have become, as other affluent countries in Europe and Asia are becoming, a metropolitan (and increasingly megapolitan) nation. In the United States, the top 100 metropolitan areas are home to 65% of the nation's population (including 85% of the nation's immigrants and 77% of the nation's minorities) and those 100 regions generate two-thirds of the nation's jobs and three-quarters of the nation's economic GDP.

Those largest 100 metro areas also contain over 9000 local governments and one-third of these metropolitan areas span state jurisdictional boundaries. Nearly all the growth in the years ahead in this country (perhaps 200 million additional people in the next 50 years) will be located in just 20 mega regions of the United States. Two out of three people in this country will live in these 20 mega regions by 2040. While we have become an increasingly megapolitan nation, we are just beginning to focus on addressing a number of serious, complex, and regional sustainable development problems....

As city, state, and national governments, both in the United States and throughout the world, begin to address an array of problematic sustainable development issues, a paradigm shift in the framework of governing responsibilities seems likely to occur. Local urban planning and zoning controls, as well as related public and private infrastructure and transportation investments, are all likely to operate, in the years ahead, within, and in support of, an overriding larger state and national sustainable development policy framework. Attempts at systemic and structural urban planning policy reform at the metropolitan and megapolitan levels seem inevitable. Given the enormous future growth projected for the United States, both in the country's population and in its built environment, questions about broader regional governing arrangements may really be more of merely timing and degree, of the devising and analysis of potential metropolitan institutional forms and arrangements, not if, but simply when and how this transformation occurs.

Questions related to the competence and efficacy of existing institutions and governing arrangements are at the heart of any analysis of sustainable development problems. Adjustments in institutional governing arrangements related to urban planning, housing, energy, and supporting transit and infrastructure development are now increasingly advocated as an antidote to the problems of automobile-dependent regional sprawl. Proposals for metropolitan regionally-coordinated (even megaregionally-coordinated) approaches to urban planning policy, both in the United States and elsewhere in the world, appear to be based on the following perceptions: (1) the increasing recognition of the unsustainability of low-density, automobile-dependent regional sprawl; (2) the increasing recognition that local individual low-density zoning, parking, and growth management programs are a significant cause of regional automobile-dependent sprawl, dominated as they are, especially in the United States, by local parochial NIMBY (not in my back yard) and city fiscal concerns; and (3) an increasing awareness of the critical importance of urban planning and related public and private built environment, transportation, and infrastructure investment decisions to resource and energy consumption.

There also is a growing awareness that better designed and higher-density residential development can have enormous economic benefits in this country. This relates to the emerging role of urban planning as an ever increasing "efficiency link" to the future economic prosperity of the country's metropolitan areas. As Richard Florida has pointed out in his recent work:

> [O]ur public policy must work toward, not against, density. Nearly every expert on the subject agrees that innovation and productivity are driven by density. For the better part of a century, we've subsidized suburbanization. That stimulated consumption of cars and appliances, which drove the industrial economy and allowed families to buy affordable homes. But it also diffused the density that is increasingly required for innovation and growth. Of course, every place does

> not have to be like Tokyo or Manhattan. Silicon Valley-style density would probably be sufficient. We can still have suburbs, but our economic policy has to start to encourage density, not sprawl. [Richard Florida, Opinion, *The Rise of the Mega Region*, Wall St. J., Apr. 12, 2008, at A8]

In short, there is growing awareness of the important role that coordinated urban planning policy at the metropolitan level can play in creating higher-density and prosperous urban core areas as a path to building sustainable communities in the twenty-first century.

Notes and Questions

1. *The decline of the "first tier" suburb.* The first suburbs, those located adjacent central cities, are showing clear signs of stress. Much of the housing in those communities, both owner-occupied and rental, was built before 1960—at a time when expectations regarding size and amenities were far different from 21st century expectations. An emerging challenge for policy makers, highlighted by the subprime mortgage foreclosure crisis, is what to do with a typical two- or three-bedroom, 900–1,200 square foot unit built in the early 1950s and currently vacant because of foreclosure. Would you recommend rehabbing it and attempting to sell or rent it to a low-income family? Tearing it down and building a new, larger unit that could be marketed to a middle- or upper-income family? For discussion of the plight of the "first tier" suburbs, also known as "older, inner" suburbs, see Bernadette Hanlon, *The Decline of Older, Inner Suburbs in Metropolitan America,* 19 Housing Pol'y Debate 423 (2008); W. Dennis Keating & Thomas Bier, *Greater Cleveland's First Suburbs Consortium: Fighting Sprawl and Suburban Decline,* 19 Housing Pol'y Debate 457 (2008).

2. *Unincorporated pockets of suburbia.* In addition to the problems of first tier suburbs, many metropolitan areas have unincorporated zones on the borders of the center city and/or in scattered portions of the urban fringe. These unincorporated zones often are populated by low-income families who have moved from ghettos in the center city to suburbia in search of jobs, affordable housing and better schools. While the inhabitants of these unincorporated areas may create close-knit communities, they face serious challenges occasioned by poor or nonexistent infrastructure and public services, as well as the aftereffects of the 2007–2009 economic crisis. For an analysis of this phenomenon, see Michelle Wilde Anderson, *Cities Inside Out: Race, Poverty, and Exclusion at the Urban Fringe,* 55 UCLA L. Rev. 1095 (2008).

Anderson argues that "economic gravity" pulls households toward jobs and affordable housing. The urban fringe is "more likely to provide access to single-family homes and the opportunity for land ownership" for low-income households, *Id,* at 1129–30, but in unincorporated fringe areas public services may be less than adequate. Examining unincorporated urban neighborhoods in California, Florida, North Carolina and Texas, Anderson notes that low-income communities in such neighborhoods often lack basic public services or are sited on environmentally-damaged land ("brownfields") or near undesirable land uses such as land fills or toxic waste dumps. She argues that in such cases, the traditional role of county government to administer state functions and services, such as elections, public health programs and the state judicial system, deserves greater attention than it has received to date. *Id.* at 1159–60. *See also* Jennifer Steinhauer, *A Cul-de-Sac of Lost Dreams, and New Ones,* N.Y. Times, Aug. 23, 2009, at 1 (reporting on the trials of families residing on Beth Court, a cul-de-sac in the Los Angeles suburb of Moreno Valley that was hit hard by foreclosures in 2007–2009).

3. *The rise of the megapolitan area.* What are the implications of Professor Ziegler's forecasts that growth during the first half of the 21st Century will be concentrated in 20 multi-state mega regions and that two-thirds of the U.S. population will live in those 20 mega regions by 2040? Is this likely to increase or reduce the supply of, or barriers to, affordable housing for low-income households?

For a theoretical analysis of the impact that a unified regional government structure might have on the supply of, and barriers to, affordable housing, see Andrew Aurand, *The Impact of Regional Government Structure on the Concentration and Supply of Affordable Housing,* 18 HOUSING POL'Y DEBATE 393 (2007), who applies the Tieboutian public choice theory that "people vote with their feet by choosing a municipality that offers a preferable mix of public goods and services," *Id.* at 395, citing Charles Tiebout, *A Pure Theory of Local Expenditures,* 64 J. POL. ECON. 416, 419 (1956). Aurand concludes that

> the concentration and supply of affordable housing cannot be adequately explained by public choice theory.... The results [of his theoretical analysis] indicate a positive relationship between a more disbursed distribution of power among small municipalities and the supply of affordable housing.... However, these results should not lead to the conclusion that encouraging a more fragmented metropolitan government structure is an effective affordable housing policy.... [R]educing fragmentation may have other regional nonhousing benefits, such as reduction in tax-base disparities, improved comprehensive planning, and a more efficient coordination of services.

As you study the materials in this book, consider who should make decisions about the appropriate amount of public investment in housing and community development initiatives—the Federal government, state governments, mega-regional governments, if such exist or are created, or traditional local governments (cities and counties). What factors influence your analysis? If you conclude that all levels of governments have roles to play, how should their roles be coordinated?

4. *Sustainable development.* Increasing concerns about the environmental cost of the half-century pattern of development sprawl, as reflected in the loss of open land and forests as well as the polluting effects of automobile dependency, have given rise to a "sustainable development" movement. What do you understand sustainable development to mean? High density development? Low density development? What type of development patterns might accommodate the growth forecasts for the U.S., yet be "sustainable?" *See e.g.,* WILLIAM R. BLACKBURN, THE SUSTAINABILITY HANDBOOK (2007) (publication of the Environmental Law Institute); COMPENDIUM OF LAND USE LAWS FOR SUSTAINABLE DEVELOPMENT (John R. Nolon ed. 2006); TOWARD A VISION OF LAND IN 2015 (Gary C. Cornia & Jim Riddell eds. 2008); John R. Nolon, *Comparative Land Use Law: Patterns of Sustainability,* 37 URB. LAW. 807, 815 (2005) (identifying "economic efficiency, environmental protection, and equity [as the] three pillars of sustainability"). Sustainable development concerns are discussed in Chapter 5 *infra.*

A Note on Homelessness

Homelessness presents an urgent housing problem in American cities. Estimates of the number of homeless vary widely, but they are visible everywhere. The 2008 Annual Homeless Assessment Report ("AHAR") estimated that 664,000 persons were homeless on a single night in January 2008, and that "[a]bout 1.6 million people were homeless in emergency shelters or transitional housing at some point during the year between October 1, 2007 and September 30, 2008." U.S. DEP'T OF HOUS. AND URB. DEV., THE 2008 ANNUAL HOMELESS ASSESSMENT REPORT TO CONGRESS 3 (2009). Of the persons counted on a single night in January, 2008, 58% were living in shelters and 42% were "unsheltered" (living on the streets or with other family members). Single adults made up approximately 60% of the total while homeless families were about 40% of the total counted. Slightly over 20% of the total homeless counted in January 2008 were reported as "chronically homeless," meaning according to HUD's definition that they were homeless for long periods of time or repeatedly and had a disability. *Id.* at 15. *See also* NATIONAL ALLIANCE TO END HOMELESSNESS, RESEARCH REPORTS—HOMELESSNESS COUNTS (2007), *available at* www.endhomelessness.org/content/article/detail/1440; U.S. CONFERENCE OF MAYORS, HUNGER AND HOMELESSNESS SURVEY (2008) (an annual survey reporting that 19 of 25 cities surveyed experienced an increase in homelessness in 2008). Significant increases in homelessness were triggered by the wave of foreclosures that resulted from the subprime mortgage crisis and related economic collapse in 2007–2008. Homeless service providers reported that, on average, 19% of the persons who became homeless did so as a result of foreclosure, with renters outnumbering owner-occupiers. NATIONAL COALITION FOR THE HOMELESS ET AL., FORECLOSURE TO HOMELESSNESS 2009: THE FORGOTTEN VICTIMS OF THE SUBPRIME CRISIS 5 (2009).

Who are the homeless and what causes the homeless problem? Many causes of homelessness have been identified. Cities responding to the U.S. Conference of Mayors' annual survey in 2008 listed lack of affordable housing, poverty, and unemployment as the most common causes of homelessness for persons in families, with unemployment replacing domestic violence from the previous year's survey. Causes of homelessness among singles were substance abuse, lack of affordable housing, and mental illness. HUNGER AND HOMELESSNESS SURVEY, *supra* at 19. While analysts and policy makers generally agree that lack of sufficient affordable housing is one of the most, if not *the* most important cause of homelessness, they have disagreed on the proper responses. As you study the government programs in this book, consider their potential for responding to homelessness.

Do people choose to be homeless? Maria Foscarinis, Executive Director of the advocacy group, National Law Center on Homelessness and Poverty, answered that question as follows: "In general, 'structural' causes—such as insufficient housing affordable by the poor, poverty, unemployment, insufficient income assistance, and insufficient treatment facilities—determine that some number of the poor will become homeless. Specific 'personal' characteristics—such as disabilities, substance abuse, and social isolation—place individuals at risk for being members of that group. In neither case, however, can homelessness be considered a choice." Maria Foscarinis, *Downward Spiral: Homelessness and Its Criminalization*, 14 YALE L. & POL'Y REV. 1, 12 (1996).

Ms. Foscarinis' article reviews what she terms the "criminalization" of homelessness through enactment of restrictive local ordinances "penalizing activities associated with homelessness, such as sleeping, sitting, and begging in public places ... and [use of] rarely enforced laws, such as prohibitions on vagrancy and loitering, to conduct 'sweeps' aimed at homeless people." *Id.* at 2. Her organization began tracking such ordinances in 1991 and has published several reports, including some in collaboration with another advocacy group, the National Coalition for the Homeless, analyzing local ordinances. *See, e.g.*, NATIONAL LAW CENTER ON HOMELESSNESS & POVERTY AND THE NATIONAL COALITION FOR THE HOMELESS, HOMES NOT HANDCUFFS: THE CRIMINALIZATION OF HOMELESSNESS IN U.S. CITIES (2009) (analyzing ordinances and practices in 273 cities, and describing lawsuits challenging criminalization measures); Jamie Michael Charles, Note, *"America's Lost*

Cause": The Unconstitutionality of Criminalizing Our Country's Homeless Population, 18 B.U. PUB. INT. L.J. 315 (2009).

Jones v. City of Los Angeles, 444 F.3d 1118 (9th Cir. 2006), illustrates a typical criminalization ordinance and litigation strategy in response. A Los Angeles ordinance made it illegal to sit or lay on public sidewalks. A divided panel of the Ninth Circuit held that "the Eighth Amendment prohibits the City from punishing involuntary sitting, lying, or sleeping on public sidewalks that is an unavoidable consequence of being human and homeless without shelter in the city of Los Angeles." *Id.* at 1138. A key factor in the court's conclusion that violation of the ordinance was not voluntary was the widespread disparity between the number of homeless in Los Angeles and the number of available beds in shelters. *Id.* at 1122 ("more than 1000 people unable to find shelter each night [in Skid Row, where the city's shelters were concentrated] ... and almost 50,000 more homeless people than available beds [in Los Angeles County]"). The case was vacated upon settlement, 505 F.3d 1006 (9th Cir. 2007), after the city "agreed not to enforce the law between the hours of 9 p.m. and 6 a.m. until it builds 1,250 units of supportive housing," HOMES, NOT HANDCUFFS, *supra* at 35. For discussion of the case, see Mary Boatright, Jones v. City of Los Angeles: *In Search of a Judicial Test of Anti-Homeless Ordinances,* 25 L. & INEQ. 515 (2007); Sarah Gerry, Jones v. City of Los Angeles: *A Moral Response to One's City's Attempt to Criminalize, Rather than Confront, Its Homelessness Crisis,* 42 HARV. C.R.-C.L. L. Rev. 239 (2007); Casey Garth Jarvis, *Homelessness: Critical Solutions to a Dire Problem; Escaping Punitive Approaches by Using A Human Rights Foundation in the Construction and Enactment of Comprehensive Legislation,* 35 W. ST. U. L. REV. 407 (2008).

In addition to the problem of criminalization, efforts by religious and charitable organizations to provide temporary responses to homelessness such as soup kitchens and tent cities can trigger other legal problems, as the following case illustrates.

City of Woodinville v. Northshore United Church of Christ

Supreme Court of Washington
211 P.3d 406 (2009)

J.M. JOHNSON, J.

Tent City 4 is a movable encampment of homeless people in the Puget Sound area sponsored by nonprofit Seattle Housing and Resource Effort/Women's Housing Equality and Enhancement Project (Share/Wheel). The encampment houses approximately 60–100 people and moves from place to place every 90 days. It relies on property owners to volunteer sites and in 2006 asked Northshore United Church of Christ (the Church) to host. The Church agreed to allow use of its property in the R-1 residential area around the church buildings in the city of Woodinville (City) and applied for a temporary use permit from the City. Several months before the application, the City had passed a six-month moratorium [later extended to one year—Eds.] on all land use permit applications in the R-1 zone, pending completion of a study on sustainable development. Relying on the moratorium, the City declined to process the Church's permit application.

The Church argues the City's (in)action conflicts with our cases considering article I, section 11 of Washington's constitution. That provision guarantees, "[a]bsolute freedom of conscience in all matters of religious sentiment, belief and worship, ..." but also provides the provision, "shall not be so construed as to ... justify practices inconsistent with the peace and safety of the state."

Concerned that the encampment would go forward, the City sought, and the trial court entered, an injunction against the Church and Share/Wheel, prohibiting Tent City 4 from proceeding without the necessary permits. The Court of Appeals upheld the City's denial of the permit based on the moratorium.... Based on our precedent construing article I, section 11 of the Washington Constitution, we hold that the City cannot apply a moratorium to refuse to consider a permit request from the Church and therefore reverse....

The main facts underlying this case occurred in 2006, but several important events occurred two years earlier. In 2004, Share/Wheel and Tent City, working with the Church, also sought a location in the City as a temporary home. The City offered to allow Tent City free use of a site on city property intended for a public park. The City, Share/Wheel, and the Church executed a contract spelling out conditions for the temporary use and the parties' rights and duties. In a relevant provision, the 2004 contract provides for Share/Wheel and the Church to "submit an application to locate a future Tent City at some other church-owned location, but ... must agree not to establish ... any homeless encampment within the City of Woodinville without a valid temporary use permit.... In 2004, Tent City spent three months on the city property pursuant to this contract and then moved on to other areas of King County.

Two years later, with the Church again as host, Tent City 4 sought to move back to the city. In the meantime, the City had adopted a moratorium on all temporary use permits in the R-1 residential zone where the Church is located....

Washington's constitution guarantees, "[a]bsolute freedom of conscience in all matters of religious sentiment, belief and worship" and also provides that this "shall not be so construed as to ... justify practices inconsistent with the peace and safety of the state." Wash. Const. art. I, § 11....

Proceeding under article I, section 11, a party challenging government action must show two things: that the belief is sincere and that the government action burdens the exercise of religion. The government must then show it has a narrow means for achieving a compelling goal....

There is no issue raised here of whether hosting Tent City is important or central to the Church's exercise (though the Church has never before engaged in such practice around or in its church). The City conceded in its briefing in this case the Church's sincerity of belief. The City has also not argued in its briefing that the moratorium fulfills a compelling goal and only offered argument that the moratorium did not substantially burden the Church's free exercise of religion. Thus, the only issue presented is whether the City's actions substantially burden the free exercise of the Church's religious "sentiment, belief [or] worship."

Government burdens religious exercise "[i]f the 'coercive effect of [an] enactment' operates against a party 'in the practice of his religion....'" This does not mean any slight burden is invalid, however.[1] If the constitution forbade all government actions that worked *some* burden by minimally affecting "sentiment, belief [or] worship," then any church actions argued to be part of religious exercise would be totally free from government regulation. Our constitution expressly provides to the contrary. The argued burden on religious exercise must be more, it must be substantial. Here, the total refusal to process a permit application is such a burden.

---

1. When deciding if a government regulation is a substantial burden, courts should look at any alternatives the regulation leaves open. For example, at oral argument, the Church conceded it would be possible to house Tent City inside the Church. Worship traditionally takes place inside a church and this alternative would obviate many of neighbor/city legitimate concerns. We make no decision on such a regulation because the City did not allow such alternative....

Any state burden must be evaluated in the context in which it arises. The City properly did not dispute in court the sincerity of the beliefs nor their importance to believers. Housing the homeless may be a part of religious belief or practice, but it is different from prayer or services, for example, which are at the core of protected worship. The Church has never before hosted the homeless on or in its property but has long continued to worship in a manner preferred by its congregation.

The context for the constitutional evaluation of any burden necessarily encompasses impact on others in the city. Housing the homeless affects those outside the church in a way that private prayer or religious services inside the church buildings do not. Indeed, a homeless encampment likely affects the neighbors who live nearby far more than it impacts most parishioners who spend only hours in church weekly while neighbors must live continuously with the encampment. Cities may mediate these externalities reflecting concerns for safety, noise, and crime but may not outright deny consideration of permitting. By way of analogy, while healing the sick is similarly connected to worship, a church must still comply with reasonable permitting processes if it wants to operate a hospital or clinic. This notion is expressly reflected in article I, section 11 providing, "the liberty of conscience hereby secured shall not be so construed as to ... justify practices inconsistent with the peace and safety of the state."

Applying these principles, the City's total moratorium placed a substantial burden on the Church. It prevented the Church from even applying for a permit. It gave the Church no alternatives.... The City failed to show that the moratorium was a narrow means for achieving a compelling goal. Therefore, the City's action constituted a violation of article I, section 11 of our constitution.

Since we hold for the Church on state constitutional grounds, we need not, and therefore do not, decide whether there is violation of [the Religious Land Use and Institutionalized Persons Act of 2000] RLUIPA. Our decision rests solely on our state constitution.... [The court also held that the city breached the 2004 contract by refusing to consider the church's permit application, thereby excusing the Church from full compliance with the contract—Eds.]

Conclusion

The City violated the Church's constitutional rights under article I, section 11 when it refused to process the Church's permit application based on a total moratorium on temporary use permits in the area. Rather than seeking to impose reasonable conditions on the Church's project to protect the safety and peace of the neighborhood, the City categorically prevented the Church from exercising what the City concedes is religious practice. We therefore reverse the Court of Appeals.

Notes and Questions

1. As the *Woodinville* court noted, homeless shelters and encampments, as well as concentrations of homeless persons on public sidewalks, can and do have significant impact on business and residential neighbors. What alternatives may be available for responding to tensions that may flare up between homelessness service providers and residents and businesses in the area where the services are made available? Is the element of choice, or lack thereof, as emphasized by the court in *Jones v. City of Los Angeles*, a reasonable basis for line drawing? Should the motivation of the provider, which was perhaps the key factor in *Woodinville*, carry such weight? What responsibilities do providers have to neighboring residents and businesses? *See Armory Park Neighborhood Ass'n v. Episcopal*

Community Serv. in Arizona, 712 P.2d 914 (Ariz. 1985) (failure of church-affiliated service center to prevent recipients of free meals from littering neighboring residents' yards and otherwise disturbing the peace constituted public nuisance, despite fact that center complied with applicable zoning and public health ordinances).

2. In addition to the fundamental problem of shelter, homeless persons often have great difficulty in obtaining access to public services that other persons may take for granted. How, for example, does a homeless person gain access to mail service? *See, e.g., Currier v. Zinser*, 379 F.3d 716 (9th Cir. 2004) (Postal Service's decision to offer general delivery service to homeless persons only at the downtown Seattle post office, and not also at branch offices, and its refusal to provide no-fee lock box service to homeless persons, upheld as rational, content- and viewpoint-neutral regulations).

3. For discussion of the federal programs that specifically address homelessness and additional dimensions of the phenomenon, see Chapter 3, Section I *infra*. Maria Foscarinis and other advocates have long pressed for a "proactive" approach, one aimed at the causes of homelessness, HOMES NOT HANDCUFFS, *supra* at 12–13; 14 YALE L & POL'Y REV., at 60–63. As you study the housing and community development materials in this book, consider how these programs might be used to develop and implement an effective strategy. Do the programs in place have the potential to help low-income families avoid homelessness while their children are growing up, and to help "dysfunctional" individuals find decent housing.

4. Welfare reform may have a significant impact on homelessness. The Personal Responsibility and Work Opportunity Reconciliation Act of 1996, Pub. L. No. 104-193, 110 Stat. 2105, substituted a new block grant, Temporary Assistance for Needy Families (TANF), for the 60-year-old federal entitlement program, Aid to Families with Dependent Children (AFDC), 42 U.S.C. §§601–617. Following four years of contentious debate, TANF was reauthorized in 2006 through 2010, The Deficit Reduction Act of 2005, Pub. L. 109-171, Title VII—Human Resources and Other Provisions, Subtitle A, 120 Stat. 135. Under TANF, parents and caretakers of children receiving assistance must "engage in work" within 24 months of receiving assistance, and may only receive such assistance for a total of five years, 42 U.S.C. §602(a)(1)(4)(ii). Under the reauthorization act, state work participation rate requirements increase in 5% increments from 50% in 2006 to 70% in 2010. Consider the implications for a single mother with small children. If she gets a job, will it be for much more than minimum wage? The federal minimum wage went to $7.25/hour in July, 2009. A person working full time at that rate can expect to make approximately $14,500/year. NATIONAL LOW INCOME HOUSING COALITION, OUT OF REACH (2009), concluded that persons making minimum wage would have to pay over 80% of their income to obtain a two bedroom apartment in good condition at the national median fair market rent for such units ($928/month in 2009). What if the new job turns out to be temporary, but the five-year TANF period has expired? As you study the housing and community development programs discussed in this book, consider the plight of the minimum wage worker—and the TANF recipient. Can the programs discussed prevent those individuals from experiencing homelessness?

For an analysis of the U.S. experience, both before and after welfare reform, see ROBERT MOFFITT, WELFARE REFORM: THE U.S. EXPERIENCE (2008) (Institute for Research on Poverty, Discussion Paper No. 1334-08), *available at* http://www.irp.wisc.edu. The author notes that welfare reform through TANF has reduced program caseload and governmental expenditures. In addition, the reform has had generally positive average effects on employment, earnings, and income.

For an analysis of welfare-to-work programs spawned by TANF, see DAVID GREENBURG, VICTORIA DEITCH & GAYLE HAMILTON, WELFARE TO WORK PROGRAMS: BENEFITS

AND COSTS, A SYNTHESIS OF RESEARCH (2009). The authors examined cost-benefit studies of 28 welfare-to-work programs in eleven states and two Canadian provinces in which over 100,000 persons participated. Six different types of programs were analyzed: mandatory work experience, mandatory job-search, mandatory education, mandatory mixed-initial-activity, earnings supplements, and time-limit mix. The study found that some programs placed more emphasis on reducing government expenditures, while others focused more on increasing incomes of participants.

Earnings supplement programs realized the "largest participant net gains," while mandatory education programs were the "least successful program type." Mandatory-mixed-initial-activity programs generally were successful in "balanc[ing] reducing welfare costs and increasing participant income," and mandatory job-search programs were successful in reducing government expenditures, study directors concluded. *Id.* at 33 (ES-11). For an argument that the federal government's housing and welfare systems should develop "more collaborative relationships" in order to minimize any negative impact of welfare reform on the public and assisted housing programs, see Rachel G. Bratt, *Housing and Economic Security, in* A RIGHT TO HOUSING 399, 405–408 (Rachel G. Bratt, Michael E. Stone & Chester Hartman eds. 2006).

5. Advocates for the homeless and service providers developed a phased strategy to respond to homelessness, called the Continuum of Care, which was adopted by HUD in 1994 as a "planning process to encourage communities to address the problems of housing and homelessness in a more coordinated and strategic fashion." HUD, COORDINATING COMMUNITY PLANS 14 (2008), *available at* www.hudhre.info/index.cfm?do=viewResourcesByTopic. HUD's competitively awarded funding programs under the McKinney-Vento Homeless Assistance Act, 42 U.S.C. § 11301 & ff, discussed in Chapter 3 *infra*, require grant applicants to develop a Continuum of Care plan, including a coordinated community-based process of identifying needs and building a system to address those needs." HUD, HOMELESS ASSISTANCE PROGRAMS, *available at* www.hud.gov/offices/cpd/homeless/programs/index.cfm. The elements of the strategy include providing emergency shelters, transitional housing, and permanent housing, as well as social services, health care and job training. Homeless persons are supposed to move through this continuum with a case manager, a staff person "who is responsible for determining what services a client needs and for ensuring that services are made available." GAO, HOMELESSNESS: MCKINNEY ACT PROGRAMS PROVIDE ASSISTANCE BUT ARE NOT DESIGNED TO BE THE SOLUTION 13 (1994). *See also* ESTER FUCHS & WILLIAM MCALLISTER, THE CONTINUUM OF CARE: A REPORT ON THE NEW FEDERAL POLICY TO ADDRESS HOMELESSNESS (1996) (report prepared by the Barnard-Columbia Center for Urban Policy, Columbia University, and issued by HUD).

Communities initially responded to homelessness by establishing soup kitchens, shelters and transitional housing, all designed primarily to get homeless people "off the street." The federal government helped establish this system with a $2 billion investment. While responding to immediate needs, such programs did little or nothing to decrease homelessness, "leaving communities frustrated and hopeless." NATIONAL ALLIANCE TO END HOMELESSNESS, A NEW VISION: WHAT IS IN COMMUNITY PLANS TO END HOMELESSNESS? 3, 6 (2006). *See also* MARTHA BURT, WHAT WILL IT TAKE TO END HOMELESSNESS? (2001) (Urban Institute report); HELPING AMERICA'S HOMELESS: EMERGENCY SHELTER OR AFFORDABLE HOUSING? (2001) (Urban Institute report includes a history of homelessness policy). Specific aspects of these approachs are discussed in Chapter 3. For a description of the Continuum of Care collaborative planning process, see HUD, BUILDING EFFECTIVE COALITIONS (2009), *available at* www.hudhre.info/index.cfm?do=viewResourcesByTopic.

See also NATIONAL ALLIANCE TO END HOMELESSNESS, A PLAN, NOT A DREAM: HOW TO END HOMELESSNESS IN TEN YEARS (2000), available at www.endhomelessness.org (to encourage communities to adopt comprehensive strategies to end homelessness; The Alliance's approach "focuses on using data to plan for outcomes, closing the front door to homelessness through prevention programs, and opening the back door out of homelessness by rapidly re-housing individuals and families." *Id.* at 6. By 2006, the Alliance's planning process had been endorsed by over 200 cities, counties and states and 90 plans had been completed.

6. For an argument that "reallocating resources to community programs that provide services regardless of housing status, rather than through residential institutions such as shelters" will reach more people than do shelter programs, see Dennis P. Culhane & Stephen Metraux, *Rearranging the Deck Chairs or Reallocating the Lifeboats? Homelessness Assistance and Its Alternatives,* 74 J. AM. PLAN. ASS'N 111 (No. 1 2008). The authors concede that their proposal will not solve the "housing affordability problem," but argue that providing temporary services such as rental assistance for a year or two "promises to be a more direct and more efficient means to house families than emergency and transitional shelters." *Id.* at 119.

7. For additional discussion of aspects of the homelessness problem, see HOMELESSNESS IN AMERICA (Robert Hartmann McNamara ed. 2008) (three volume work); THE HOMELESS: OPPOSING VIEWPOINTS (Louise I. Gerdes ed. 2007); KIM HOPPER, RECKONING WITH HOMELESSNESS (2003) (an anthropological, ethnographical and historical examination of homelessness); PAUL A. ROLLINSON & JOHN T. PARDECK, HOMELESS IN RURAL AMERICA: POLICY AND PRACTICE (2005); Tulin Ozdeger, *Targeting the Homeless: Constructive Alternatives to Criminalization Measures in U.S. Cities,* 41 CLEARINGHOUSE REV. 202 (2007); Patricia Salkin, *A Quiet Crisis in America: Meeting the Affordable Housing Needs of the Invisible Low-Income Healthy Seniors,* 16 GEO J. ON POVERTY L. & POL'Y 285 (2009); John H. Wong et al., *McKinney-Vento Homeless Assistance Act Subtitle B—Education for Homeless Children and Youths Program: Turning Good Law into Effective Education,* 16 GEO. J. ON POVERTY L. & POL'Y 53 (2009).

B. The Strategy of Social Response

The many dimensions of the housing and community development problem explored in the last section provide a starting point for the social response to these problems. In the selection that follows, Grigsby and Rosenburg describe a number of housing policy "images" that provide a rationale for social intervention. Note that the "images" conflict. Is it possible to develop a social policy responsive to one of the "images" without producing a conflict with a social policy necessary to respond to one of the other images?

William G. Grigsby and Louis Rosenburg, Urban Housing Policy

196–206 (1975)

Filtering Image

According to this traditional view of the problem, low-income families occupy unsatisfactory living accommodations primarily because of an inherent defect in the functioning of the housing market. Nearly all of them acquire homes through the filtering process, inheriting structures that no longer meet the needs of upper-income households. By itself, there is nothing necessarily wrong with this system of rationing shelter. Most of us live in used housing. However, because of the slow rate at which the residential inventory depreciates in value, by the time dwelling units come within the financial reach of poor families, most of the units, it is alleged, are in unsatisfactory condition. Although direct subsidies to the poor would be one way to solve this problem, a central assumption of the filtering image is that a cheaper and more politically acceptable alternative would be to make filtering "work"—to accelerate the process so as to free-up housing for low-income households much sooner than is now possible. According to the image, this could best be accomplished by subsidizing new construction for middle-income families. Such a strategy would be superior to direct subsidies to the poor, because at any given subsidy level it could induce a greater amount of new construction than could low-income subsidies, and thereby could serve, indirectly through the filtering process, more of the low-income population. If the same total subsidy were distributed to the same number of low-income families, it would not be sufficient to enable them to compete in the new construction market.

There are several problems with the filtering image, aside from the fact that it seems to be based on inadequate understanding of the filtering process. First, it looks at only one-half of the picture—low-income families improving themselves as they move upward in the stock. It does not examine what happens to the homes and neighborhoods these families leave behind. It ignores evidence suggesting that accelerated filtering, unaccompanied by market support mechanisms for the inner city, accelerates decay. Implicitly, it makes the incorrect assumption that these vacated neighborhoods are all bad, would be entirely vacated in short order, and could be quickly demolished. Second, it assumes that if low-income families did manage to obtain homes in good condition, they would have the necessary resources to keep them in adequate repair. Third, it fails to recognize that demand-side subsidies to the poor would, as have rising incomes for the population generally, precipitate an upward filtering of families which would ultimately play itself out in the form of increased demand for new homes and apartments by many of the same middle-income families whom filtering strategies seek to subsidize....

Obsolescence Image

This image pictures the inner-city housing problem as stemming in large part from the market consequence of preferences for suburban living and the rise in incomes which permits these preferences to be satisfied. As families who can afford to do so move outward to new homes, they initiate a filtering process which initially makes better structures available to low-income families and ultimately results in the abandonment of the worst sectors of the inner-city stock. As values decline, however, home purchases become impossible, landlords' attitudes about upkeep shift, responsible ownership gradually disappears, institutional lenders withdraw from the market, the upgrading activities that occur on a regular basis in stable neighborhoods in order to combat obsolescence cease, and even the city reduces its level of services. Thus, several forms of neighborhood abandonment occur even while the structures are occupied. In contrast to what is assumed in the filtering image, the filtering process is seen here as being partially perverse in its effects; the poor are in a real sense the victims as well as the beneficiaries of housing progress. They get less housing for their money than they would in a stable market. Demand-side subsidies do nothing to ameliorate the problem, because there is no way for individual owners to prevent site and locational obsolescence; they cannot alter either lot sizes or street patterns or surrounding land uses....

Low-Income Image

This image, which is the most commonly held of all, emphasizes the lack of resources of the poor. As the outward movement of upper-income families occurs, the structures which are left behind for occupancy by low-income households are, contrary to what is assumed in the filtering image, in reasonably good condition. However, the costs of financing and operating these structures do not decline sufficiently to permit rents which the poor can afford unless adequate maintenance is sacrificed. Conversions to multifamily occupancy may raise rental incomes sufficiently to forestall decay for a time, but they also lead to increased wear and tear, so eventually deterioration wins the day anyway. The process is hastened by the competitive disadvantage of low-income families in dealing with a class of landlords who enjoy a partial monopoly in the market and who demonstrate less concern for the well-being of their tenants, structures, and neighborhoods than do landlords generally. It also is hastened by the powerlessness of the poor to prevent their neighborhoods from being inundated by bars, junkies, abandoned cars and other unpleasant accouterments. Thus, as long as there are poor families, so the reasoning goes, there will be substandard housing, overcrowding, and an unsuitable living environment. Housing preferences and market dynamics may also play a part, but they are secondary to low income. What is needed to correct the situation, therefore, are either employment and income-maintenance programs or, if these are not possible, some form of housing subsidy....

Low-Income Concentration Image

This view of the problem ... argues that although low income by itself may be less important in explaining blight and decay than is commonly alleged, the concentration of disadvantaged populations into separate geographic areas greatly aggravates housing and neighborhood problems, not only for these populations but also for those around them, and leads to other difficulties as well. In addition to the social dysfunctioning which is associated with large clusters of poor families, market failure, particularly in the area of housing, can be traced to these agglomerations. In growing urban areas, for example, low-income neighborhoods pose a constant threat to adjacent blocks and sometimes seem to precipitate withdrawal of investment funds from these blocks and their premature deterioration, just by being nearby. Although the precise way in which this happens is a matter of speculation, it is clear that the dynamics of decay in large metropolitan areas where the poor collect in massive numbers are quite different from what obtains in smaller communities which have a similar proportion of low-income families but few low-income neighborhoods. It does not necessarily follow from this observation, however, that the most cost-effective way to alter negative market dynamics or to create decent neighborhoods or to reduce poverty is to disperse the poor.

[Dispersal of racial as well as low-income minorities has become an important catechism of national housing policy. National housing legislation contains a strong dispersal policy implemented through federally subsidized housing and community development programs. The attack on suburban exclusionary zoning also reflects the commitment to a dispersal policy.—Eds.]

The Problem-Family Image

Attempts to explain why so many low-income families do not live in substandard housing have led many persons to this image. It presumes and stresses a lack of middle-class norms of cleanliness and responsibility among the poor. As filtering enables low-income families to move into better housing, many of these families create the forces of decline, not because the rents which they pay are too low to permit adequate maintenance, but because their behavior raises the cost of maintenance and management. Investors, faced with vanishing cash-flows and perceiving surrounding owners in the same situation, eventually cease to try very hard to maintain their stock. So the ring of blight spreads, not because of a collapse of market supports and investor greed, as in several of the other images, but because of bad tenantry.

The problem-family image, insofar as it refers only to behavior toward housing and not to social pathology generally, can probably be rejected on factual grounds. As mentioned earlier, according to inner-city landlords themselves, problem families comprise a very small proportion of the tenantry, on the average. Over a period of time, however, a bad tenant may abuse a number of different dwellings and adversely affect entire structures. In some neighborhoods, moreover, such tenants, even though few in number, could conceivably constitute a critical mass, and in both their housing and non-housing behavior reduce the attractiveness of the neighborhoods to the point where not all of the dwelling units could be rented and would have to be abandoned. It is equally possible, therefore, that identifying and concentrating on the small minority of troublemakers would have a much more favorable impact on the market than the numbers themselves would suggest. To ascribe a major part of blight and decay to problem families, however, is to overlook too many other variables.

Greedy-Investor Image

[It is widely held] ... that slums are caused primarily by slumlords—owners who seek a quick dollar by crowding their structures and charging monopoly rents to families who have nowhere else to go. The image usually assumes as well that the slumlord, in order to extract even greater income from his inventory pursues a deliberate policy of under maintenance. The fact that his structures eventually become uninhabitable does not matter to him, because by then he has long since had his initial investment returned together with an exorbitant profit. It does matter to the community at large, however. Not only do neighborhoods which became accessible to poor households quickly deteriorate, but their decline weakens the market in adjacent areas, making it possible for the slumlord to extend his insidious practices into previously sound blocks. Thus, as he befouls one nest he moves on to another. Illustrative of the greedy-investor image is the frequently heard cry to "tax the profits out of slums," the hope being that this would force the avaricious speculator out of the slum business and replace him with more responsible entrepreneurs. Such persons would be in the business now, were it not for the stigma that the slumlord has brought to the ownership of low-rent property....

The policy implications of the image are more in the realm of what not to do rather than what should be done. Persons who hold the image resist any proposal which appears to either bail out the investor-owner or help improve his ability to continue operating. Better to drive him out of business by strict code enforcement and by various measures to eliminate his monopoly situation where it still exists. To help him liquidate his assets even at currently depressed market values is to pay him for socially valueless property and for property which has already been fully amortized. Moreover, if help were given, slumlords would simply use the proceeds to infect other neighborhoods....

[The slum landlord has long been a commanding image in housing policy. Housing code enforcement strategies and tenant self-help activities often assume that the slums contain slumlords whose profits can finance needed housing improvements. landmark study of the Newark, New Jersey, slums. George Sternlieb, in his landmark study, The Tenement Landlord (1966), undercut the "greedy investor" image. It found that slum housing was not profitable and that many landlords were as poor as their tenants—Eds.]

Racial Image

[N]one of the above ... images incorporates the element of race as an explanatory variable. Race, however, is frequently seen not only as an embellishment of all the images but also a separate theme. As an embellishment, it appears in the form of a belief, which is widely shared among blacks as well as whites, but for quite different reasons, that racial change generally triggers neighborhood deterioration. On one side, it is alleged that low-income black tenants behave less responsibly than do low-income white tenants, especially in failing to exercise control over their children; and in reverse, it is alleged that housing discrimination, which most observers agree is still widespread, explains more of the deterioration of housing in the inner city than do either low income or market forces generally. As neighborhoods change racially, landlords gouge tenants and milk properties, while the city not only ignores such practices as long as possible, but allows its own services in these areas to deteriorate. In a more benign context, race is also used as the variable to explain an apparent communication gap between reasonably responsible landlords and reasonably responsible tenants, a gap which adds to the basic difficulties. It is used, too, as a partial explanation of the exodus of white families to the suburbs.

The various racial images that serve to embellish the other images need not be evaluated, since they do not have any special policy significance by themselves. They emphasize the importance of exploring the racial implications of any program, but they do not either suggest or indict specific proposals of major importance. Not so in the case of the forced-confinement image. If solutions to the housing problems of the inner city are not possible until the residential market generally is desegregated, priorities must be reordered and the scale of existing desegregation efforts greatly expanded. Not only the barrier of discrimination, but also the reluctance of most blacks to attempt to exercise their rights must be overcome. This will take a number of years, even assuming acceleration in the current rate of progress. In the meantime, programs for the inner city are stalled or ineffective....

Social Fabric Image

All of the above images focus on housing. No matter which one is selected, the centerpiece is some aspect of either behavior toward housing or market forces. The ... final image explains the problems almost completely in non-housing terms. It suggests that crime, poor schools, unemployment, family instability, and related social maladies turn inner-city neighborhoods into places to get out of. As families who can exercise this option do so, and as leadership in the city mentally makes a similar move, those who must remain behind are gradually overcome by a sense of impotence, and the deterioration of the social fabric becomes irreversible. With so many other concerns for families to worry about, much of the housing stock is badly neglected. The malaise is pervasive. It is not one of a few problem families, but of many families confronted by many problems. This image differs from the housing obsolescence concept in its emphasis on serious disabilities of inner-city areas, rather than on positive amenities of suburbia. It leads, however, to a similar conclusion that only drastic surgery—dispersal of the inner-city population and elimination of social ills—will solve the various dimensions of the housing problems. In some respects it is an even more disturbing view of the problem, because it implies that inner-city housing interventions deal only with symptoms and, consequently, are largely ineffective....

[This last image reminds us that the ills of the cities cannot be traced solely to slums and poor housing. Housing programs can only deal with housing problems. Critics of housing policy who fault housing programs because they do not remedy poor schools, unemployment, crime, and other urban ills do not keep this important limitation in mind.—Eds.]

Notes and Questions

1. This constellation of housing policy "images" makes it difficult to know where to start in fashioning programs of social intervention in the housing market. In fact, housing reform programs began in New York City in the nineteenth century, a response to the terrible living conditions then common in the tenement slums of that metropolis. A review of the motivations that dominated this early housing reform movement provides insight into the problems of developing a social strategy for housing and community development programs.

The New York State legislature attempted to remedy tenement housing conditions in a state building code enacted in 1867 that imposed minimum housing standards. The state code failed. As Professor Lawrence Friedman points out in his brilliant history of American housing policy, by 1900, New York City "was more crowded, the poor suffered more, and the moral and physical stench from the slums was more offensive than ever to the respectable members of the community." LAWRENCE M. FRIEDMAN, GOVERNMENT AND SLUM HOUSING 29 (1968).

2. Reformers like Jacob Riis and Lawrence Veiller then took up the housing reform movement in New York City. Through their efforts the tenement code was strengthened, and their leadership stimulated the enactment of similar codes throughout the country. These early housing reformers saw the improvement of living conditions as the major housing issue. They achieved this goal by using the regulatory "police" powers of the state to compel private owners, without compensation, to improve their dwelling units. The modern housing code is the successor to the early tenement code approach to substandard housing conditions.

The housing reform movement led by Veiller and others died out after World War I, but the motivations for their interest in tenement house reform still influence housing policy. Professor Friedman provides a good description of these motivations.

Lawrence M. Friedman,
Government and Slum Housing

3–4, 7, 9–10 (1968)

Definitions of slums and bad housing can be divided, however, into two broad classes. Housing can be described as meeting or not meeting certain physical standards: Does it have plumbing? How many people to the room? A slum would then simply be a neighborhood of substandard houses. A slum can also be defined in social terms as an area where people of a certain class live. One authority has succinctly described the slum as "the home of the poor and the stranger." Common sense tells us that the slum is both a social and a physical fact. It is the home of the poor, and the poor live badly. The two elements—physical and social—of a definition of the slum are related to two key ways of analyzing the problem of the slum. These are: (a) in terms of the costs imposed by the slums on society at large, and (b) in terms of the costs imposed by the slums on the people who live in them. We can call these, respectively, the social-cost approach and the welfare approach. They are not unique to the housing problem. Social legislation in general is proposed and defended on one or both of these bases, either that it helps the poor or some worthy class or that by helping the poor it helps us all. Most frequently, perhaps, both justifications are used.

Since the dawn of American consciousness of the problem of slum housing, the social-cost approach has been heavily emphasized by those eager for reform. The whole community, we are told, bears the scars of the slums. Jacob Riis, in 1890, labeled the tenements as sources of crime, disease, fire and corruption. [JACOB A. RIIS, HOW THE OTHER HALF LIVES: STUDIES AMONG THE TENEMENTS OF NEW YORK (Penguin Books 1997) (1890).] They were "the hot-beds of the epidemics that carry death to rich and poor alike; the nurseries of pauperism and crime," they bred "a scum of forty thousand human wrecks to the island asylums and workhouses year by year." The tenements "turned out in the last eight years around a half million beggars to prey upon our charities"; they maintained "a standing army of ten thousand tramps"; and above all, they touched family life "with deadly moral contagion." In slum districts, masses of ignorant foreigners voted as they were told by their bosses—at least so it appeared to reformers. A Boston settlement study of 1898 warned that the slums had no "neighborhood life ... no watchfulness over common interest"; as a result, "political corruption" flourished and money was "laid out at election time." Jacob Riis darkly reminded his readers that Boss Tweed "was born and bred in a Fourth Ward tenement...."

Social-cost arguments have legal usefulness as well as political usefulness. American social legislation operates necessarily in a constitutional context. Under the American system of government, the courts have the power to review legislation to determine if it meets constitutional standards. In the late nineteenth century, the federal and state courts developed the concept of substantive due process which they then used to limit the right of legislative bodies to enact social and economic legislation. Both the limits of the courts' powers of judicial review and the corresponding limits of the states' rights to enact new forms of law were vague and controversial. Though the federal courts have virtually abandoned use of the doctrine of substantive due process, the concept retains some measure of vitality in the states. A major piece of economic or social legislation must prove its validity by fitting itself within some historically recognized branch of governmental power (the "police power" of government) or find some other conceptual means to defend itself against legal attack. The limits of the police power roughly correspond—in verbal formula at least—to the limits of the concept of social cost. Indeed, roughly speaking, the concept of police power is a concept of social cost; it validates legislation designed to limit or alleviate the burden of social costs. On the basis of the police-power concept, it becomes possible to reconcile strict free-enterprise economics with regulation by the state in the name of public health, safety, or welfare....

Of course, computing the social costs of the slums raises empirical questions of ferocious difficulty. Few of these questions have been resolved. Do slums really breed crime, so that the elimination of slums would eliminate organized crime, criminal gangs, and juvenile delinquency? It is difficult to investigate this question. Classically, the answer was believed to be "Yes"; but some modern sociologists (perhaps wrongly) are dubious and indeed speak of the "demoralizing effect of the massive slum-clearance programs which have recently been undertaken" and of the "divisive influence of public-housing programs." It is even more difficult to approach some of the more value-loaded counts in the indictment of the slums. Have the slums corrupted local government by breeding boss-rule? To this question no scientific answer is possible. There are even defenders of the bosses. Yet the logic of the social-cost approach seems to demand an accounting. It seems to demand that we ask: Is reform worth the price?

Quite a different kind of cost-benefit analysis is required by a welfare approach to the slums. Under this approach, the problem of the slums is perceived as a problem of the suffering people who live there, whether or not the slums hurt society at large. Relieving their pain is worthwhile in itself, unless the mode of doing so is inordinately harmful to other social values.... [L]egal-constitutional barriers do not seriously inhibit or imperil the major aspects of a war against poverty and slums. This means that direct slum action by government is not deemed to endanger social, economic, or political values insofar as they are constitutionally protected. Most people would probably agree that the government can and should increase economic and social opportunities for the poor, at least as an abstract proposition. Indeed, even in the palmiest days of the Fourteenth Amendment, when the concept of substantive due process terrorized social legislation, few people seriously questioned the right of government to help the poor and helpless. Public aid to the destitute poor was acceptable to Queen Elizabeth I and to Cotton Mather; it was also constitutionally acceptable to nineteenth century America. Constitutional and political problems were raised, however, by considerations of the level of government at which poor relief should be administered and financed....

Notes and Questions

1. Note that Professor Friedman links the justification for public intervention to eliminate slum conditions with the legal justification for government programs that accomplish this objective. There is even a suggestion in the quotation from Jacob Riis that "bad slums make bad people," an echo of the causality theory of slums and social disorder discussed *supra*. The attack on urban blight through slum clearance and similar programs is to some extent a contemporary example of the causality theory.

2. The early tenement reform movement and the motivations of the tenement house reformers reflect an important characteristic of interventionist social programs that remedy housing deprivation: these programs are likely to emerge from the special perspective of pressure groups rather than the rational consideration of policy alternatives. Roger Montgomery and Martin Gellen make this critical observation in their review of housing policy issues. They also note that no single private interest has the political influence on housing policy which is typical in other areas of public concern. Housing in this regard offers a somewhat curious picture because the key lobbies do not represent highly concentrated industries. Rather, the fragmentation among housing suppliers supports a continuous debate over policy directions which in other sectors have already been largely determined. Housing policy often gives the appearance of an ongoing social dialogue. Roger Montgomery & Martin Gellen, *Emerging Issues in American Housing Policy, in* A Decent Home and Environment 157 (Donald Phares ed. 1977).

Students of housing and community development programs should not expect to find a rationalized, integrated set of governmental interventions. These programs are an accumulation of decades of experimentation, often taking contradictory directions.

3. The conservative reaction that swept the country at the end of World War I saw the temporary decline and disappearance of the housing reform movement. New York's tenement codes survived, but elsewhere the housing reform movement lost its momentum.

The next innovation in governmental housing policy took a very different turn. Although the federal government built some public housing during World War I, private ownership of housing has always characterized the American housing market. With the coming of the New Deal, government again entered the housing market. Congress authorized a public housing program in 1937 which has left a permanent imprint on American housing policy. In this program, the federal government made subsidies available to local public housing authorities that built, owned, and managed rental housing for lower-income groups.

The following excerpt from Professor Friedman's book explains the origins of the public housing program. It is included here to illustrate the ongoing "social dialogue" that produces government housing programs in response to pressures from fragmented interest groups.

Lawrence M. Friedman, Government and Slum Housing

104–06 (1968)

[P]ublic housing in the United States is virtually synonymous with housing built under the great Housing Act of 1937. This law was the culmination of a long legislative struggle. That it was passed in 1937, rather than in 1933, is not without meaning. A major program of public housing was not part of the first phase of the Roosevelt New Deal. The precursors, as we have seen, were outgrowths of a public-works campaign. Roosevelt himself was lukewarm toward the Housing Act. Ultimately he embraced it, but with a certain touch of reluctance. Public housing for low-income groups was not one of his "musts," at least initially. He had to be coaxed.

The coaxing came from a number of sources. Labor—in particular the building trades—showed great enthusiasm, for obvious reasons. In 1936, Senator Wagner read into the Congressional Record a resolution of the American Federation of Hosiery Workers which pointedly mentioned labor's "double interest in the construction of low rent dwellings." Labor was the "representative both of the unemployed building and material workers and of low-income families in need of better housing." In addition, the New Deal had opened the doors of government to a class of reformers naturally sympathetic to the general principles of public housing. Economic and social planning was regarded with more understanding than in the 1920's. Reform-minded men and women had more influence in Washington than before. Liberal pressure groups lobbied for the act. The key legislative figure in the passage of the housing act was Senator Wagner of New York. But he had wide and powerful help.

Passage of the bill was perhaps delayed less by concrete opposition than by problems of administration (Would Ickes or Hopkins be the new czar of housing?) and by considerations of legislative tactics; but concrete opposition was also manifested. The National Lumber Dealers' Association wrote to Senator Vandenberg complaining of government interference with the business of house-building; the mere threat of public housing, they claimed, retarded construction. Many members of Congress were conservative and reluctant to vote for a measure that would so emphatically put Congress and the country in the business of building and operating housing. The usual cries of socialism went up. The law was denounced as "a scheme whereby a preferred few may live at the expense of the taxpayers of the Nation through the instrumentality of Government paternalism." More to the point was the concept, as expressed by Senator Walsh, for example, that government ought not to compete with "private property." This was a period when business was struggling to survive the stagnation and low profits of the depression. The National Association of Real Estate Boards (NAREB) favored federal support for mortgage insurance in order to stimulate homeownership and home sales; but they bitterly opposed public housing. Public housing would "discourage ownership by setting up competition which individuals cannot meet," or it might make "tenement occupancy so attractive that the urge to buy one's home will be diminished." Whatever one may think of this argument as fact or logic, the voice of NAREB was loud, and it echoed in Congress. The New Deal's huge legislative majorities did not mean that opposition could be utterly ignored. In order to pass the bill, it was necessary, or felt to be necessary, to confine the program to the construction of housing only for those who could not afford what private enterprise was willing and able to build. Yet insofar as we can speak of the potential tenants of public housing as at least an indirect pressure group, influence flowed not from the destitute, the descendants of the destitute, the children of Five Pointers, the Negro ghetto dwellers, or the abject poor; it flowed from the submerged and potential middle class. The ideal housing act, then, would be one which would accept the new and reject the old poor; it would shut the doors on those with the ability to get housing privately, but would not open the doors to people on the dole and likely to stay there. It would also provide employment for workers. For legal and political reasons and to disarm conservative opposition, a decentralized program was desirable. Local initiative would govern as much as possible; states and communities would be allowed to opt out if they wished.

Notes and Questions

1. The public housing program was not a rational governmental response to lower-income housing problems. It illustrates a housing program that responded to pressures from interest groups which had much narrower objectives. There is clear evidence that the public housing program was one of several governmental initiatives intended to stimulate the construction industry and relieve the high unemployment rate prevailing at the time. Housing concerns were secondary. Professor Friedman also suggests that public housing was intended for a submerged middle class which found itself temporarily unable to afford rental accommodation during the Great Depression.

2. In a provocative article, Professor Peter Marcuse relies on the motivations for the early tenement housing reform movement, the public housing program and other examples to dispute the myth that governmental intervention in housing is a benevolent attempt to remedy the housing conditions of the poor. He argues that these programs reflect upper class fears of public health menace and public disturbance and a tendency to make subsidized housing programs profitable to make them attractive to private capital. Peter Marcuse, *Housing Policy and the Myth of the Benevolent State*, Soc. Pol'y, Jan./Feb. 1978, at 21. This view of housing policy is also reflected in the earlier excerpt from Professor Friedman's book, *supra*. It is well to keep these alternative views of housing policy motivation in mind when studying the programs discussed in the chapters that follow.

3. Housing and community development policy makers have long debated the merits of policies focusing on responding to market problems in specific places, so-called "placed-based" or "supply-side" policies, and policies centered on improving the lives of individuals wherever they may be or go, so-called "people-based" or "demand-side" policies. Peter Dreier, John Mollenkopf & Todd Swanstrom, Place Matters (2d ed. 2004); Nestor Davidson, *Reconciling People and Place in Housing and Community Development Policy*, 16 Geo. J. on Poverty L. & Pol'y 1, 1–2, 10 (2009) (arguing that the dichotomy of people and place "is much more illusory than the traditional debate assumes, or at the very least, it is more complicated," and advocating that all programs be "designed carefully to address holistically individual incentives, market forces, the nature of community, and the importance of context").

4. The historic view of the development of government housing programs will not be continued here. A detailed account can be found in U.S. Dept. of Hous. & Urb. Dev., Housing in the Seventies: A Report of the National Policy Review 7–21 (1974).

The report covers the period up to the major reforms introduced by the 1974 federal housing legislation. Federal housing and community development programs now in effect are based on this legislation. For a description of active and inactive federal housing and community development programs, *see* U.S. Dept. of Housing & Urb. Dev., Programs of HUD (2005). Other references include The Encyclopedia of Housing (Willem Van Vliet, ed. 1998); Barry G. Jacobs, HDR Handbook of Housing and Development Law 2008–2009 (2008) (revised annually); The Legal Guide to Affordable Housing Development (Tim Iglesias & Rochelle E. Lento eds. 2005); Housing & Development Reporter, edited by Charles L. Edson, Bruce S. Lane & Barry G. Jacobs and presented in a multi-volume treatise with a companion bi-weekly Current Developments newsletter and published by Thomson-West Publishing Co. For an advocacy guide, see National Housing Law Project, HUD Housing Programs: Tenants Rights (3d ed. 2004 & Supp. 2006–2007).

A Note on the Role of Lawyers, Planners, and Other Professionals in Housing and Community Development Programs

The inquiring student may ask: All of this policy discussion is interesting, but what role do lawyers, planners, and other professionals who are not high level governmental officials have in the formulation and implementation of housing policy? The question deserves an answer.

First, and perhaps foremost, lawyers, planners, and other professionals are citizens who, based on their specialized training, may play important roles as informed citizens about matters of public policy.

Second, they may participate in a variety of ways in housing and community development programs. Often they are found as aides to the private sector. Government-assisted housing programs provide considerable scope for private initiative in the development of subsidized housing projects and their management. Lawyers and planners, in particular, assist developers in packaging applications for governmental assistance to housing projects, in carrying these projects through the application and approval process, and in seeing the project through to its conclusion. Lawyers and planners have a similar assistance role in private development projects undertaken in community development and related programs. These programs feature a public-private partnership in the development of commercial and industrial projects in part assisted with public subsidy.

Third, lawyers, planners, and a host of professionals are also found, of course, on the government side. Federal, state, and local legislative bodies employ a vast array of professionals to assist with laws. At all levels, governments have agencies responsible for aspects housing and community development. They employ lawyers on their staffs and as outside counsel. They also employ planners as staff members or consultants on the varied legal and implementation questions that arise in the administration of their programs. Lawyers provide important advice, ranging from counsel on the legality of private and public housing and development projects to the usual kind of legal advice necessary in the management of public enterprises like public housing projects. Planners and others develop data, organize issues, study zoning and other issues, and advise and make recommendations on a broad range of questions.

Fourth, lawyers, planners and others also serve private pressure groups in the housing field. These groups frequently resort to litigation to establish and enforce private rights in government programs. These rights include the rights of private developers arising out of federal grants and subsidies, the rights of people displaced by government programs, and the rights of tenants in public and private housing assisted by government subsidies. Legal service agencies have been in the forefront in litigation challenging government programs. They often serve as a catalyst for "reform" litigation intended to establish new legal principles in these programs. An important public interest group, the National Housing Law Project in Berkeley, California provides major backup and other legal support to these reform movements in housing. Lawyers also assist tenant and other housing consumer groups which have been organized in many cities. Lawyers serving these private reform groups play an important lobbying role in national and state legislatures and local governing bodies. All of these professionals may serve as leaders in organizations, on boards of directors of advocacy groups, and as advocates before public and private entities.

Fifth, sometimes litigation must be undertaken. Here the role of lawyers is clear. But lawyers rely on planners and other professionals for support and analysis of statistics, for data on policy implications, and for the substantive competence to shape the contours of litigated cases and to inform the lawyer on policy matters. But litigation, though important, does not necessarily comprise the most effective strategy in many instances. Lawyers, planners, and others may be catalysts for organizing communities and political groups to advocate the interests of citizens and communities.

In sum, lawyers, planners, and other professionals are informed citizens with special competencies. These professionals play a wide variety of roles in housing and community development matters. They serve in professional capacities as counselors and advisors to private clients on their proposals and activities and to public agencies. They will be found assisting the development of publicly assisted projects to take the best advantage of government subsidy and assistance. They assist in developing and carrying out polices that govern programs and activities. They engage in monitoring and enforcing rights through advocacy and litigation. They help advocacy groups and interested citizens shape public policies and programs. For discussions of roles that lawyers play in housing and community development matters, see PETER W. SALSICH, JR. & TIMOTHY J. TRYNIECKI, LAND USE REGULATION 401–403 (2d ed. 2003); Lisa Alexander, *Stakeholder Participation in New Governance: Lessons from Chicago's Public Housing Reform Experiment*, 16 GEO. J. ON POVERTY L. & POL'Y 117, 183–184 (2009) (describing collaborative efforts of litigation-skilled and transaction-skilled lawyers); Nestor Davidson, *Values and Value Creation in Public-Private Transactions*, 94 IOWA L. REV. 937 (2009) (engaging private sector in public development creates special challenges for lawyers); Shelia R. Foster & Brian Glick, *Integrative Lawyering: Navigating the Political Economy of Urban Redevelopment*, 95 CAL. L. REV. 1999 (2007) (arguing that "integrative lawyering" requires transactional, litigation and facilitative legal skills); Susan R. Jones & Dorcas Gilmore, *Community Lawyering*, *in* BUILDING HEALTHY COMMUNITIES: A GUIDE TO COMMUNITY ECONOMIC DEVELOPMENT FOR ADVOCATES, LAWYERS, AND POLICYMAKERS 235 (Roger A. Clay, Jr. & Susan R. Jones eds. 2009).

C. A Right to Housing

1. Toward Recognition of a Right to Housing

In a market economy such as that of the United States, housing deprivation can be viewed as a market failure and government programs, such as the public housing program, can be considered optional public responses to that market failure. But at least since the end of World War II and the creation of the United Nations, advocates and social critics across the globe have called for recognition of a right to housing as the basis for correcting housing deprivations suffered in housing markets. President Franklin Delano Roosevelt set the tone for such advocacy in his 1944 State of the Union address: "We have adopted a ... second Bill of Rights.... Among those are ... the right of every family to a decent home." President Franklin Delano Roosevelt, State of the Union Address (Jan.11, 1944), *available at* http://www.fdrlibrary.marist.edu/011144.html. Four years later, the United Nations Universal Declaration of Human Rights recognized "the right to a standard of living adequate for the health and well-being of himself and his family, including ... housing." Universal Declaration of Human Rights, G.A. Res. 217A(III) at art. 25(1), U.N. Doc A/810 (Dec. 12, 1948). Advocates point to the landmark Federal Housing Act of 1949 that recognized "the goal of a decent home ... for every American family" as a basis for a right to housing, Katherine E. Walz & Judith Levey, *Keeping an American Promise: Safe, Decent, and Affordable Housing for Everyone in Need*, 42 Clearinghouse Rev. 365 (2008). Others note that the word *goal* represents an aspiration, not an enforceable right. Eric S. Tars & Caitlin Egleson, *Great Scot!: The Scottish Plan to End Homelessness and Lessons for the Housing Rights Movement in the United States,* 16 Geo. J. on Poverty L. & Pol'y 187, 188 (2009). Even more fundamentally, a right to housing can also be based on constitutional guarantees, such as the guarantee of due process and equal protection of the laws.

Read the materials in this section with the following questions in mind. What are advocates of a right to housing seeking to accomplish? What would be the significance of constitutional or legislative establishment of a right to housing? Is a right to housing compatible with a market economy? Does talk of a right to housing so politicize the discussion as to render progress in responding to housing deprivation much more difficult?

The seminal article on the right to housing is by Professor Frank I. Michelman. An excerpt follows. When Professor Michelman wrote, the U.S. Supreme Court had recognized some fundamental rights, such as the right to vote. It had also recognized some suspect classifications, such as classifications based on racial discrimination. Legislation affecting fundamental constitutional rights and suspect classifications is reviewed more rigorously under the due process and equal protection clauses. The Court applies a strict scrutiny judicial review standard that requires a compelling governmental interest for suspect classifications and classifications substantially burdening fundamental rights. Professor Michelman's article, in part, is an argument that the Court should hold that the right to housing is a fundamental constitutional right and that legislative classifications affecting low-income housing are suspect. As the cases that follow his article indicate, the Court did not adopt this position, but Professor Michelman's article still provides a critical analysis of what a right to housing might include.

Frank L. Michelman, The Advent of a Right to Housing: A Current Appraisal

5 Harvard Civil Rights & Civil Liberties Law Review 207, 207–208, 211–212 (1970)

Is there, or is there developing a "right to housing"? Most simply and fundamentally, the notion of a right to housing might mean a claim upon organized society, on behalf of each individual or household unit, to be assured of access to minimally adequate housing. I shall refer to this as "the right to be housed." Even such a broad statement, of course, leaves open a number of crucial issues. If the statement were accepted as positing a social ideal (it plainly is not accurate as a description of actual practice), further discussion would be required of at least the following questions:

(1) *How absolute an "assurance"?* At one extreme, we might intend merely an assurance that housing will be available without arbitrary interference or deprivation and according to the rules which normally govern access to goods. In our present society this perhaps suggests nothing much more than a kind of Horatio Alger guaranty that ability, prudence, industry, and thrift will bring rewards. At the other extreme, we might intend an ironclad assurance that no one, no matter his profligacy or obstinacy, shall ever be deprived of decent shelter. Reference to a right to be housed suggests something closer to the latter extreme—an assurance that acceptable housing will be available irrespective of the market returns commanded by one's endowments of talent, influence, or capital; and irrespective, even, of voluntary choices in one's remote past which result in present inability to pay the true costs of acceptable housing. The principal qualification might be that a person should bear the consequences of unambiguous voluntary choices which involve, for example, deliberate and culpable waste of socially provided housing resources.

(2) *"Access" in how inflexible a form?* Again, the question can be stated in terms of extremes. At one extreme, society would fulfill its obligation by tendering a particular housing accommodation on a take-it-or-leave-it basis—a conventional public housing program. At the other extreme, society would simply undertake to amplify the claimant's income to the point where he was autonomously allocating to shelter needs as much as acceptable housing really costs. This would be a fully implemented program of income maintenance. An intermediate undertaking might be to transfer income in a form prohibiting diversion from the claimant's specific housing needs, but at the same time allowing the claimant a range of housing choice. This would be a rent-supplement program. A *right to be housed*—as distinguished from, say, a "right to life" or a "right to a decent income"—probably envisions something which ranges between provision of specific housing in kind and provision of rent supplements.

(3) *"Adequate" by how relative a standard?* Do we have in mind a kind of absolute standard of minimum performance to preserve basic health, privacy, and sanity? Or do we mean something more relative, more emulative, more informed by "equality" impulses? The right to be housed notion itself does not seem to point particularly in either direction; but it seems likely that the suggested duality is not a true one, since resort to such locutions as "minimum" and "basic" will never purge our housing quality judgments of knowledge about what others in the community or society enjoy.

(4) *"Adequate" by how idiosyncratic a standard?* It is possible to regard housing as a well-understood, staple commodity, the relative adequacy of each person's portion of which can be judged according to common, objective standards. While this approach is doubtless valid for some purposes, it is not the only possible one. Some students of housing insist that at least as important as the physiological need for shelter is a broader need for family living space—for private environment—compatible with a household's particular composition, relationships, and current strivings. A "suitable home" may be taken to mean not just a sound, sanitary, and ample structure, but a home truly suited to the occupants. If, for example, a family's background and culture stresses a great deal of community elbow-rubbing in busy streets, neither a room at the top of a high-rise project nor a suburban tract house would seem quite suitable. Whether it is helpful to conceive of a right to be adequately housed as encompassing individual and subcultural idiosyncrasies is a question better discussed at a later point.

Is there, then, a "right to be housed" in some sense generally corresponding to the foregoing sketch? The answer may depend on which of our several normative systems we choose to address. Are we asking a question of common morality, of philosophical ethics, or of law? In common morality, it would seem that acknowledgment of a right to be housed is closely linked with acceptance of the welfare state, and that the "right" is—at least at a rhetorical level—fairly well established. It seems likely for example, that in declaring the famous ideal of a "decent home and a suitable living environment for every American family" Congress meant to convey more than a mere Alger-ism. Yet in formal, systematic, philosophical discussions of social justice (limiting ourselves now to those proceeding within a "liberal," individualistic, and market-oriented framework) a right to be housed is much more problematical. In recent years there has emerged among analysts of justice some interest in "social" or "just" minimums, but the discussion so far remains tentative and general, suggesting no very rigorous approaches to defining the minimum or specifying its contents.

[These issues are discussed in more detail in the article by Grey at the end of this section.—Eds.]

A Constitutional Right to Be Housed?

A constitutional right to be housed is necessarily even more problematical. The perfection of such a right seemingly would require first, a commanding and coherent ethical theory capable of informing such general constitutional locutions as Due Process and Equal Protection (since we lack a specific constitutional text on the subject); second, actual (even if inexplicit) adoption of the theory by the courts, and especially the Supreme Court; and third, practical enforcement of the theoretical right in the face of inaction or resistance on the part of legislative and executive agencies. Since no such ethical theory seems now available, it is unsurprising that there are few clear signs yet of a legal right to be housed under the Fourteenth Amendment. When and if such an ethical argument does appear, the problems of judicially enforcing the-full-blown right may themselves be baffling enough to prevent its outright espousal by the courts.

[At this point, Professor Michelman discusses the constitutional developments noted above, which suggested that the Supreme Court might recognize a right to housing.—Eds.]

A Statutory Right to Be Housed?

Lack of a perfected constitutional right to be housed would be immaterial during any period when a like right prevailed by force of statute. But despite the great volume of housing subsidy legislation, it probably cannot now be said that there is a statutory right to be housed. If a "decent home for every American family" is not merely a commitment to freedom of economic opportunity, neither is it yet the declaration of an enforceable legal claim. It remains the statement of a welfare ideal, a general guide to administration and interpretation of the housing statutes—but not an enforceable promise by the government to the public to tax and appropriate as heavily as would be required to satisfy the ideal. Nor, indeed, are the more specific authorizations of the several Housing Acts now being interpreted, or judicially enforced, as such promises. They are understood, rather, as the public talking to itself and its agents—ordering, guiding, legitimating, and to some extent predicting the conduct of public affairs. But when the duly appropriated rent-supplement or public housing money runs out, lawsuits do not pry loose more money—despite unappropriated authorizations or unfilled need....

[In the remainder of his article, Professor Michelman discusses the right not to be tendered substandard housing; free choice in the location and use of housing; the right not to be uprooted, either through compulsory acquisition or eviction; the right to own one's home; and the right to exercise control over one's environment. As an example of the last "right," Michelman cites the right of tenants to organize and bargain collectively with their landlord.—Eds.]

Notes and Questions

1. Are all of the "rights to housing" discussed by Professor Michelman of equal importance? Are they commensurate? That is, do all of the "rights" reflect comparable problems of housing deprivation? Does Michelman recognize the conflicts likely to exist among the "rights" to housing he identifies? Which of these rights are most likely to be recognized constitutionally? By statute? Which are least likely to be recognized? See also Frank I. Michelman, *Welfare Rights in a Constitutional Democracy*, 1979 Wash. U.L.Q. 659 and a critique. Susan F. Appleton, *Professor Michelman's Quest for a Constitutional Welfare Right. Id.* at 715.

2. At the time Professor Michelman's article was published, housing activists thought they saw an opportunity to merge the cases that required rigorous equal protection review of racial discrimination and the cases that required rigorous equal protection review of discrimination against lower-income groups, such as the cases dealing with the legal representation of indigent criminal defendants. Local governments often prohibit lower-income housing in order to exclude racial minorities or the non-affluent and maintain racial and/or class segregation. Housing activists believed the Supreme Court might invalidate lower-income housing discrimination when it had racially discriminatory effects. Although the Court had not definitely settled the issue at that time, litigants hoped that the Supreme Court would apply rigorous strict scrutiny review to legislative classifications that had a racially discriminatory effect even though a racially discriminatory intent could not be shown. The Court's answer came shortly thereafter in the *Valtierra* and *Normet* cases *infra*, as well as *Arlington Heights,* excerpted in Chapter 6 *infra.*

The case that came before the Supreme Court that raised the "right to housing" issue arose in an unusual substantive and litigation setting that contributed to the result. The Court's opinion in this case is reproduced next.

James v. Valtierra

United States Supreme Court
402 U.S. 137 (1971)

Mr. Justice BLACK delivered the opinion of the Court.

These cases raise but a single issue. It grows out of the United States Housing Act of 1937, 50 Stat. 888, as amended, 42 U.S.C. § 1401 *et seq.*, which established a federal housing agency authorized to make loans and grants to state agencies for slum clearance and low-rent housing projects. In response, the California Legislature created in each county and city a public housing authority to take advantage of the financing made available by the federal Housing Act. *See* Cal. Health & Safety Code § 34240. At the time the federal legislation was passed, the California Constitution had for many years reserved to the State's people the power to initiate legislation and to reject or approve by referendum any Act passed by the state legislature, Cal. Const. Art. IV § 1. The same section reserved to the electors of counties and cities the power of initiative and referendum over acts of local government bodies. In 1950, however, the State Supreme Court held that local authorities' decisions on seeking federal aid for public housing projects were "executive" and "administrative," not "legislative," and therefore the state constitution's referendum provisions did not apply to these actions. Within six months of that decision the California voters adopted Article XXXIV of the state constitution to bring public housing decisions under the State's referendum policy. The Article provided that no low-rent housing project should be developed, constructed, or acquired in any manner by a state public body until the project was approved by a majority of those voting at a community election.

The present suits were brought by citizens of San Jose, California, and San Mateo County, localities where housing authorities could not apply for federal funds because low-cost housing proposals had been defeated in referendums. The plaintiffs, who are eligible for low-cost public housing, sought a declaration that Article XXXIV was unconstitutional because its referendum requirement violated: (1) the Supremacy Clause of the United States Constitution; (2) the Privileges and Immunities Clause; and (3) the Equal Protection Clause. A three-judge court held that Article XXXIV denied the plaintiffs equal protection of the laws and it enjoined its enforcement. 313 F. Supp. 1 (N.D. Cal. 1970). Two appeals were taken from the judgment, one by the San Jose City Council, and the other by a single member of the council. We noted probable jurisdiction of both appeals. For the reasons that follow, we reverse.

The three-judge court found the Supremacy Clause argument unpersuasive, and we agree. By the Housing Act of 1937 the Federal Government has offered aid to state and local governments for the creation of low-rent public housing. However, the federal legislation does not purport to require that local governments accept this or to outlaw local referendums on whether the aid should be accepted. We also find the privileges and immunities argument without merit.

While the District Court cited several cases of this Court, its chief reliance plainly rested on *Hunter v. Erickson*, 393 U.S. 385 (1969). The first paragraph in the District Court's decision stated simply: "We hold Article XXXIV to be unconstitutional. *See Hunter v. Erickson....*" The court below erred in relying on *Hunter* to invalidate Article XXXIV. Unlike the case before us, *Hunter* rested on the conclusion that Akron's referendum law denied equal protection by placing "special burdens on racial minorities within the governmental process. *Id.*, at 391. In *Hunter* the citizens of Akron had amended the city charter to require that any ordinance regulating real estate on the basis of race, color, religion, or national origin could not take effect without approval by a majority of those voting in a city election. The Court held that the amendment created a classification based upon race because it required that laws dealing with racial housing matters could take effect only if they survived a mandatory referendum while other housing ordinances took effect without any such special election. The opinion noted:

> Because the core of the Fourteenth Amendment is the prevention of meaningful and unjustified official distinctions based on race, [citing a group of racial discrimination cases] racial classifications are 'constitutionally suspect'... and subject to the 'most rigid scrutiny....' They 'bear a far heavier burden of justification' than other classifications. *Id.* at 391–392.

The Court concluded that Akron had advanced no sufficient reasons to justify this racial classification and hence that it was unconstitutional under the Fourteenth Amendment.

Unlike the Akron referendum provision, it cannot be said that California's Article XXXIV rests on "distinctions based on race." *Id.* at 391. The Article requires referendum approval for any low-rent public housing project, not only for projects which will be occupied by a racial minority. And the record here would not support any claim that a law seemingly neutral on its face is in fact aimed at a racial minority. *Cf. Gomillion v. Light-*

foot, 364 U.S. 339 (1960). The present case could be affirmed only by extending *Hunter*, and this we decline to do.

California's entire history demonstrates the repeated use of referendums to give citizens a voice on questions of public policy. A referendum provision was included in the first state constitution, Cal. Const. of 1849, Art. VIII, and referendums have been a commonplace occurrence in the State's active political life. Provisions for referendums demonstrate devotion to democracy, not to bias, discrimination, or prejudice. Nonetheless, appellees contend that Article XXXIV denies them equal protection because it demands a mandatory referendum while many other referendums only take place upon citizen initiative. They suggest that the mandatory nature of the Article XXXIV referendum constitutes unconstitutional discrimination because it hampers persons desiring public housing from achieving their objective when no such roadblock faces other groups seeking to influence other public decisions to their advantage. But of course a lawmaking procedure that "disadvantages" a particular group does not always deny equal protection. Under any such holding, presumably a State would not be able to require referendums on any subject unless referendums were required on all, because they would always disadvantage some group. And this Court would be required to analyze governmental structures to determine whether a gubernatorial veto provision or a filibuster rule is likely to "disadvantage" any of the diverse and shifting groups that make up the American people.

Furthermore, an examination of California law reveals that persons advocating low-income housing have not been singled out for mandatory referendums while no other group must face that obstacle. Mandatory referendums are required for approval of state constitutional amendments, and for certain municipal territorial annexations. *See* Cal. Const., Art. XVIII; Art. XIII, § 40; Art. XI, § 2(b). California statute books contain much legislation first enacted by voter initiative, and no such law can be repealed or amended except by referendum. Cal. Const., Art. IV, § 24(c). Some California cities have wisely provided that their public parks may not be alienated without mandatory referendums, *see, e.g.*, San Jose Charter § 1700.

The people of California have also decided by their own vote to require referendum approval of low-rent public housing projects. This procedure ensures that all the people of a community will have a voice in a decision which may lead to large expenditures of local governmental funds for increased public services and to lower tax revenues. It gives them a voice in decisions that will affect the future development of their own community. This procedure for democratic decision-making does not violate the constitutional command that no State shall deny to any person "the equal protection of the laws."

The judgment of the three-judge court is reversed and the cases are remanded for dismissal of the complaint.

Mr. Justice DOUGLAS took no part in the consideration or decision of these cases.

Mr. Justice MARSHALL, whom Mr. Justice BRENNAN and Mr. Justice BLACKMUN join, dissenting. [Omitted.]

Notes and Questions

1. *Valtierra* is a transitional case in the development of Supreme Court equal protection doctrine, although it clearly foreshadowed later Supreme Court decisions eventually holding that proof of discriminatory intent is essential in racial discrimination cases. *Valtierra* also marked a turning point in attempts to convince the court that discrimination against lower-income groups is suspect and entitled to strict scrutiny review. For

further discussion, see Fred P. Bosselman, *Commentary on* James v. Valtierra, 23 Zoning Dig. 117 (1971); Donna M. Murasky, Comment, James v. Valtierra, *Housing Discrimination by Referendum?*, 39 U. Chi. L. Rev. 115 (1971).

2. What "right to housing" did the plaintiffs assert in the *Valtierra* case? The right to freedom of location? Note that Justice Black summarily dismissed a federal supremacy argument. What might have been the basis for this argument? If Justice Black did not apply strict scrutiny judicial review, what standard of judicial review did he apply? The Court applies a deferential "rational relationship" standard of judicial review in equal protection cases when it does not consider a fundamental right or suspect or quasi-suspect classification. Did Justice Black apply this judicial review standard?

3. *Valtierra* raises another problem facing litigants who attempt to establish a right to housing based on constitutional command. A plaintiff can attack a single public action, such as an attack on a public housing referendum in which the voters decided not to approve a public housing project. *Compare United States v. City of Birmingham*, 727 F.2d 560 (6th Cir.) (city actions that blocked low-income housing project, including advisory referendum, held to violate Federal Fair Housing Act), cert. denied, 469 U.S. 821 (1984), *with Ranjel v. City of Lansing*, 417 F.2d 321 (6th Cir. 1969), cert. denied, 397 U.S. 980 (1970) (court refused to enjoin referendum on municipal approval of a federally subsidized low-income housing project).

4. Litigation that challenges a single governmental action may not only be expensive and time-consuming but may produce only limited results. A court will invalidate the governmental action if plaintiffs are successful, but the decision may have limited precedential value. Perhaps for this reason, plaintiffs in *Valtierra* brought a facial attack on the California constitutional provision which, if successful, would have removed an institutional obstacle to public housing throughout the entire state. The case never came to trial because the three-judge lower court granted plaintiff's motion for summary judgment on the pleadings. *Valtierra v. Housing Auth.*, 313 F. Supp. 1 (N.D. Cal. 1970). The lower court relied heavily on *Hunter v. Erickson*. Was this reliance justified, or did the Supreme Court properly distinguish this case?

5. Since the case did not go to trial, plaintiffs were unable to develop factual support for their constitutional claim but did introduce affidavits in support of their summary judgment motion. These affidavits, on which the lower court relied, showed that areas of lower-income population concentration were also areas of black concentration and supported the racial discrimination claim. Plaintiff's affidavits also indicated that public housing was rejected in a referendum in one of the counties that was a defendant, and that voters approved only 52% of public housing referenda statewide. Note that Justice Black did not refer to the evidence contained in these affidavits. He might not so successfully have avoided evidence of comparable facts proved at a trial. For discussion of the racial and related dimensions of the *Valtierra* case, see George Lefcoe, *The Public Housing Referendum Case, Zoning, and the Supreme Court*, 59 Cal. L. Rev. 1384 (1971).

6. Michelman does not fully distinguish between right to housing litigation that challenges institutional barriers, as in *Valtierra*, and litigation that attacks individual right to housing violations in a detailed factual setting. This distinction is important and should be kept in mind as you study the right to housing issues raised by the cases included in this book. What do you think of the litigation strategy in *Valtierra*? Would you have moved for summary judgment or would you have gone to trial?

7. *Valtierra* introduces another element in "right to housing" analysis—the popular referendum. Does *Valtierra* hold constitutional a requirement that the right to housing re-

quires popular approval? Is this holding consistent with the analysis in the Michelman article? Is it consistent with the holding in the *Hunter* case, which is discussed in *Valtierra*?

8. In *City of Eastlake v. Forest City Enterprises, Inc.*, 426 U.S. 668 (1976), the Supreme Court held constitutional a local charter that required any changes in land use by the city council to be approved by a 55% vote in a referendum. The Court again believed that judicial deference to popular lawmaking justified the requirement. Note that local referenda on zoning changes and public housing can effectively block lower-income housing projects in a community. These projects are often built at high densities that require changes in local zoning regulations.

9. The Supreme Court returned to the *Valtierra/Eastlake* issue in *City of Cuyahoga Falls v. Buckeye Community Hope Foundation*, 538 U.S. 188 (2003). After the City had approved a site plan for a low-income housing development, a citizen-initiated referendum petition was placed on the ballot to repeal the site plan approval. During the pendency of the referendum election, which voters later approved, the city refused to issue building permits. The Ohio Supreme Court ruled that the referendum was unconstitutional on the grounds that the Ohio Constitution permitted referendum powers only on those matters constituting legislative action, not on administrative action, and the City council's act of passing an ordinance that approved the developer's project was an administrative action. *Buckeye Community Hope Foundation v. Cuyahoga Falls*, 697 N.E.2d 181 (Ohio 1998). The City issued the building permits and construction proceeded. The developers also had filed suit in federal court and subsequently reduced that action to a claim for damages for the delay in construction, i.e. they claimed injury from the referendum petitioning process, not from the referendum itself—which never went into effect. The developers claimed that by submitting the petition to the voters and refusing to issue building permits while the petition was pending, the City and its officials violated both the Equal Protection and Due Process Clauses. The Supreme Court rejected these arguments, ruling that provisions for referendums demonstrate devotion to democracy, not discrimination, and thus referendums should be given deference as the people retain power to govern, citing *Eastlake* and *Valtierra*, 538 U.S. at 196–199.

10. Professor Lawrence Gene Sager has presented one view on the constitutional status of the popular referendum as opposed to other constitutional values:

> The institution of legislation by the electorate, whether by initiative or referendum, presents a sharp clash of constitutional entitlement to the mediation of a deliberative tribunal between the public will and individuals who stand to suffer unjustly from legislative enactments on the one hand, and the democratic virtues of direct majority rule on the other. The issues presented by this clash of values have never enjoyed a full airing in the federal courts, and it is likely that they will continue for some time to elude definitive resolution.

Lawrence Gene Sager, *Insular Majorities Unabated:* Warth v. Seldin *and* City of Eastlake v. Forest City Enterprises, Inc., 91 Harv. L. Rev. 1373, 1403 (1978). *See generally,* Marcilynn A. Burke, *The Emperor's New Clothes: Exposing the Failures of Regulating Land Use Through the Ballot Box,* 84 Notre Dame L. Rev. 1453 (2009) (arguing that ballot box land use regulation results in deliberative and planning failures).

After Sager wrote, the Court resurrected *Hunter* to invalidate a state statute adopted by initiative that prohibited school boards from requiring any student to attend a school not geographically nearest or next to his place of residence. Exceptions in the statute indicated it prohibited only busing to achieve racial integration. *Washington v. Seattle School Dist. No. 1,* 458 U.S. 457 (1982). The Court held that the *Hunter* rule does not apply to "legislation intended to benefit some larger group of under-privileged citizens among whom minorities were disproportionately represented." What effect does this holding have on *Valtierra*? *Compare Birkenfeld v. City of Berkeley*, 550 P.2d 1001 (Cal. 1976), holding that the city could use the initiative process to amend its charter to provide for rent control. Does this case somewhat undercut Professor Sager's criticism of the initiative and referendum in housing? *Birkenfeld* is excerpted in Chapter 4 where rent control is discussed. *See also Committee of Petitioners for Referendum v. City of Norfolk*, 645 S.E. 2d 464 (Va. 2007) (referendum to repeal four ordinances rezoning redevelopment area to permit a single family planned unit development upheld).

Shortly after the decision in the *Valtierra* case, the Supreme Court again had occasion to consider a right to housing question, again in a legal setting in which the right to housing was raised indirectly:

Lindsey v. Normet

United States Supreme Court
405 U.S. 56 (1972)

Mr. Justice WHITE delivered the opinion of the Court.

This case presents the question of whether Oregon's judicial procedure for eviction of tenants after nonpayment of rent violates either the Equal Protection Clause or the Due Process Clause of the Fourteenth Amendment.

The material facts were stipulated. Appellants were the month-to-month tenants of appellee Normet and paid $100 a month for the use of a single-family residence in Portland, Oregon. On November 10, 1969, the City Bureau of Buildings declared the dwelling unfit for habitation due to substandard conditions on the premises. Appellants requested appellee to make certain repairs which, with one minor exception, appellee refused to do. Appellants, who had paid the November rent, refused to pay the December rent until the requested improvements had been made. Appellee's attorney wrote a letter on December 15 threatening to "get a Court Order out on this matter" unless the accrued rent was immediately paid.

On January 7, 1970, however, before statutory eviction procedures were begun in the Oregon courts, appellants filed suit in federal district court under 42 U.S.C. § 1983 seeking a declaratory judgment that the Oregon Forcible Entry and Wrongful Detainer (hereinafter sometimes FED) Statute, Or. Rev. Stat. (ORS) §§ 105.105—105.160, was unconstitutional on its face, and an injunction against its continued enforcement. A three-judge court was convened under 28 U.S.C. § 2281, a temporary restraining order was issued against the enforcement of the FED Statute, and appellants were ordered to make their rent payments into an escrow account during the pendency of the District Court proceeding. A lengthy stipulation of facts was agreed upon, a number of exhibits and depositions were submitted, and the District Court then granted appellee's motion to dismiss the complaint, after concluding that the statute was not unconstitutional under either the Due Process Clause or the Equal Protection Clause of the Fourteenth Amendment. Appellants promptly appealed, and we noted probable jurisdiction.

The Oregon Forcible Entry and Wrongful Detainer Statute establishes a procedure intended to insure that any entry upon real property "shall be made in a peaceable manner and without force." § 105.105. A landlord may bring an action for possession whenever the tenant has failed to pay rent within 10 days of its due date, when the tenant is holding contrary to some other covenant in a lease, and whenever the landlord has terminated the rental arrangement by proper notice and the tenant remains in possession after the expiration date specified in the notice. § 105.115. Service of the complaint on the tenant must be not less than two nor more than four days before the trial date, § 105.135; a tenant may obtain a two-day continuance, but grant of a longer continuance is conditioned on the tenant's posting security for the payment of any rent that may accrue, if the plaintiff ultimately prevails, during the period of the continuance. § 105.140. The suit may be tried to either a judge or a jury, and the only issue is whether the allegations of the complaint are true. § 105.145, 105.150. The only award that a plaintiff may recover is restitution of possession. § 105.155. A defendant who loses such a suit may appeal only if he obtains two sureties who will provide security for the payment to the plaintiff, if the defendant ultimately loses on appeal, of twice the rental value of the property from the time of commencement of the action to final judgment. § 105.160.

Appellants' principal attacks are leveled at three characteristics of the Oregon FED Statute: the requirement of a trial no later than six days after service of the complaint unless security for accruing rent is provided; the provisions of § 105.145 which, either on their face or as construed, are said to limit the triable issues in a FED suit to the tenant's default and to preclude consideration of defenses based on the landlord's breach of a duty to maintain the premises; and the requirement of posting bond on appeal from an adverse decision in twice the amount of the rent expected to accrue pending appellate decision. These provisions are asserted to violate both the Equal Protection and Due Process Clauses of the Fourteenth Amendment. Except for the appeal bond requirement ... we reject these claims.

[The Court dismissed the due process challenge to the statute. It noted that "[a] requirement that the tenant pay or provide for the payment of rent during the continuance of the action is hardly irrational or oppressive." It also found no due process violation in the failure of the Oregon statute to allow the tenant to raise the claim that the landlord had failed to maintain the premises. This claim could be raised in another action. Moreover, the Court had earlier held that actions for the possession of property could be segregated from other actions arising out of the same factual situation. The Court's concluding observations on the due process claim are of interest.—Eds.]

Underlying appellants' claim is the assumption that they are denied due process of law unless Oregon recognizes the failure of the landlord to maintain the premises as an operative defense to the possessory FED action and as an adequate excuse for nonpayment of rent. The Constitution has not federalized the substantive law of landlord-tenant relations, however, and we see nothing to forbid Oregon from treating the undertakings of the tenant and those of the landlord as independent rather than dependent covenants. Likewise, the Constitution does not authorize us to require that the term of an otherwise expired tenancy be extended while the tenant's damage claims against the landlord are litigated. The substantive law of landlord-tenant relations differs widely in the various States. In some jurisdictions, a tenant may argue as a defense to eviction for nonpayment of rent such claims as unrepaired building code violations, breach of an implied warranty of habitability, or the fact that the landlord is evicting him from reporting building code violations or for exercising constitutional rights. Some States have enacted statutes authorizing rent withholding in certain situations. In other jurisdictions, these claims, if cognizable at all, must be litigated in separate tort, contract, or civil rights suits. There is no showing that Oregon excludes any defenses it recognizes as "available" on the three questions (physical possession, forcible withholding, legal right to possession) at issue in an FED suit.

III

We also cannot agree that the FED Statute is invalid on its face under the Equal Protection Clause. It is true that Oregon FED suits differ substantially from other litigation, where the time between complaint and trial is substantially longer, and where a broader range of issues may be considered. But it does not follow that the Oregon statute invidiously discriminates against defendants in FED actions.

The statute potentially applies to all tenants, rich and poor, commercial and non-commercial; it cannot be faulted for over-exclusiveness or under-exclusiveness. And classifying tenants of real property differently from other tenants for purposes of possessory actions will offend the equal protection safeguard "only if the classification rests on grounds wholly irrelevant to the achievement of the State's objective." *McGowan v. Maryland*, 366 U.S. 420, 425 (1961), or if the objective itself is beyond the State's power to achieve.... It is readily apparent that prompt as well as peaceful resolution of disputes over the right to possession of real property is the end sought by the Oregon statute. It is also clear that the provisions for early trial and simplification of issues are closely related to that purpose. The equal protection claim with respect to these provisions thus depends on whether the State may validly single out possessory disputes between landlord and tenant for especially prompt judicial settlement. In making such an inquiry a State is "presumed to have acted within [its] constitutional power despite the fact that, in practice, [its] laws result in some inequality." *McGowan, supra* at 425–426.

At common law, one with the right to possession could bring an action for ejectment, a "relatively slow, fairly complex, and substantially expensive procedure." But, as Oregon cases have recognized, the common law also permitted the landlord to "enter and expel the tenant by force, without being liable to an action of tort for damages, either for his entry upon the premises, or for an assault in expelling the tenant, provided he uses no more force than is necessary, and do[es] no wanton damage." *Smith v. Reeder*, 28 P. 890, 891 (Or. 1892). The landlord-tenant relationship was one of the few areas where the right to self-help was recognized by the common law of most states, and the implementation of this right has been fraught with "violence and quarrels and bloodshed." *Entelman v. Hagood*, 22 S.E. 545 (Ga. 1895). An alternative legal remedy to prevent such breaches of the peace has appeared to be an overriding necessity to many legislators and judges.

Hence, the Oregon statute was enacted in 1866 to alter the common law and obviate resort to self-help and violence. The statute, intended to protect tenants as well as landlords, provided a speedy, judicially supervised proceeding to settle the possessory issue in a peaceful manner.... The objective of achieving rapid and peaceful settlement of possessory disputes between landlord and tenant has ample historical explanation and support. It is not beyond the State's power to implement that purpose by enacting special provisions applicable only to possessory disputes between landlord and tenant.

There are unique factual and legal characteristics of the landlord-tenant relationship that justify special statutory treatment inapplicable to other litigants. The tenant is, by definition, in possession of the property of the landlord; unless a judicially supervised mechanism is provided for what would otherwise be swift repossession by the landlord himself, the tenant would be able to deny the landlord the rights of income incident to ownership by refusing to pay rent and by preventing sale or rental to someone else. Many expenses of the landlord continue to accrue whether a tenant pays his rent or not. Speedy adjudication is desirable to prevent subjecting the landlord to undeserved economic loss and the tenant to unmerited harassment and dispossession when his lease or rental agreement gives him the right to peaceful and undisturbed possession of the property. Holding over by the tenant beyond the term of his agreement or holding without payment of rent has proved a virulent source of friction and dispute. We think Oregon was well within its constitutional powers in providing for rapid and peaceful settlement of these disputes.

Appellants argue, however, that a more stringent standard than mere rationality should be applied both to the challenged classification and its stated purpose. They contend that the "need for decent shelter" and the "right to retain peaceful possession of one's home" are fundamental interests which are particularly important to the poor and which may be trenched upon only after the State demonstrates some superior interest. They invoke those cases holding that certain classifications based on unalterable traits such as race and lineage are inherently suspect and must be justified by some "overriding statutory purpose." They also rely on cases where classifications burdening or infringing constitutionally protected rights were required to be justified as "necessary to promote a compelling governmental interest."

We do not denigrate the importance of decent, safe, and sanitary housing. But the Constitution does not provide judicial remedies for every social and economic ill. We are unable to perceive in that document any constitutional guarantee of access to dwellings of a particular quality, or any recognition of the right of a tenant to occupy the real property of his landlord beyond the term of his lease without the payment of rent or otherwise contrary to the terms of the relevant agreement. Absent constitutional mandate, the assurance of adequate housing and the definition of landlord-tenant relationships are legislative, not judicial functions. Nor should we forget that the Constitution expressly protects against confiscation of private property or the income there from.

Since the purpose of the Oregon Forcible Entry and Wrongful Detainer Statute is constitutionally permissible and since the classification under attack is rationally related to that purpose, the statute is not repugnant to the Equal Protection Clause of the Fourteenth Amendment.

IV

We agree with appellants, however, that the double-bond prerequisite for appealing an FED action violates their right to the equal protection of the laws.... [The double bond requirement applied only to FED litigants, and the Court's holding on the constitutionality of this provision is captured in the final paragraph of the opinion.—Eds.]

We do not question here reasonable procedural provisions to safeguard litigated property ... or to discourage patently insubstantial appeals, if these rules are reasonably tailored to achieve these ends and if they are uniformly and non-discriminatorily applied. Moreover, a State has broad authority to provide for the recovery of double or treble damages in cases of illegal conduct that it regards as particularly reprehensible, even though posting an appeal bond by an appellant will be doubly or triply more difficult than it otherwise would be. In the case before us, however, the State has not sought to protect a damage award or property an appellee is rightfully entitled to because of a lower court judgment. Instead, it has automatically doubled the stakes when a tenant seeks to appeal an adverse judgment in an FED action. The discrimination against the poor, who could pay their rent pending an appeal but cannot post the double bond, is particularly obvious. For them, as a practical matter, appeal is foreclosed, no matter how meritorious their case may be. The nonindigent FED appellant also is confronted by a substantial barrier to appeal faced by no other civil litigant in Oregon. The discrimination against the class of FED appellants is arbitrary and irrational, and the double-bond requirement of ORS § 105.160 violates the Equal Protection Clause.

The judgment of the District Court is *affirmed in part and reversed in part.*

Mr. Justice POWELL and Mr. Justice REHNQUIST took no part in the consideration or decision of this case.

Mr. Justice DOUGLAS, dissenting in part. [Omitted.]

Notes and Questions

1. Just as the *Valtierra* case implies that discrimination against lower-income groups is not suspect, *Lindsey* holds that housing is not a fundamental right under the federal Constitution. Strict scrutiny in equal protection housing cases is now apparently available only when racial discrimination is claimed. To what extent does this outcome undercut the right to housing as outlined in Michelman's article?

Note that the Supreme Court in *Lindsey* invalidated the double bond requirement. Does the Court say which equal protection test it applied in reaching this result? What right to housing does this part of the opinion implement?

2. *Lindsey* must be placed in the context of other contemporaneous Supreme Court opinions diminishing the stringency of equal protection review in housing and social welfare cases. The case in which the Court refused to invalidate the Texas state school finance system is one example. *San Antonio Indep. School Dist. v. Rodriguez*, 411 U.S. 1 (1973). Another is *Dandridge v. Williams*, 397 U.S. 471 (1970), which upheld a Maryland law mandating percentage reductions in welfare payments and imposing heavier relative deprivations on large welfare families by setting a maximum grant cap. To some extent, then, cases like *Lindsey* can be explained by the gradual withdrawal of the Supreme Court from an activist role in public interest litigation in which litigants ask the courts to undertake major institutional reform. Note the comment in *Lindsey* that there is no "federal" law of landlord and tenant. For a review of *Valtierra* and *Lindsey* and a discussion of zoning's role in economic segregation, *see* David Ray Papke, *Keeping the Underclass in Its Place: Zoning, the Poor, and Residential Segregation*, 41 URB. LAW. 787 (2009).

3. The Fourteenth Amendment prohibits state action. It reaches local governmental action because local governments are instrumentalities of the state. It will be found to apply to the conduct of private entities if the private entities carry out public functions or become so involved with the state that private conduct will be deemed to be "state action." The Constitution does not reach actions by purely private parties.

To the extent that the right to housing is protected by constitutional guarantees, that protection is attenuated by the state action doctrine. The plaintiffs in *Lindsey* avoided the state action requirement by attacking discrimination claimed to exist in the statutory judicial procedures for the eviction of tenants. Compare *Brentwood Academy v. Tennessee Secondary School Athletic Ass'n*, 531 U.S. 288 (2001) (operations of a not-for-profit athletic association that regulated interscholastic sports among Tennessee public and private high schools constituted state action, even though the association's staff were not state employees, the Court ruling that as most of the members were public school officials, that there was sufficient entwinement with the state resulting in a finding of state action) with *American Manufacturers Mutual Ins. Co. v. Sullivan*, 526 U.S. 40 (1999) (private insurers' decisions to withhold payment for disputed medical treatment was not state action, even though insurers were subject to extensive government regulation as well as authorization).

In many instances, right to housing problems arise from private action taken by private landlords against private tenants. A landlord may notify a tenant, for example, that he does not intend to renew a lease. If this action is racially correlated, it will raise problems under the Federal Fair Housing Act and other civil rights statutes discussed in Chapter 6 *infra*. Constitutional claims cannot be asserted because the action is taken by a private party. The state action problem may change when private housing is federally subsidized.

An example is a case in which a private landlord evicts tenants from federally subsidized housing, and the tenants make procedural due process objections. *But cf. Rendell-Baker v. Kohn*, 457 U.S. 830 (1982) (no state action despite extensive government regulation and government funding of private school receiving students expelled or referred by the board of education). This issue is explored in Chapter 4.

4. *Lindsey* did indicate that the states, through legislative reform, could take steps to protect tenant interests. Chapter 4 also traces the evolution of state legislative reform and judicial innovation in this field. Does *Lindsey* suggest a sympathetic view toward state efforts to recognize a "right to housing"? *See DePaul v. Kauffman*, 272 A.2d 500 (Pa. 1971), [reprinted in Chapter 5 *infra*—Eds.] decided about the same time as *Lindsey*, which upheld the constitutionality of the state Rent Withholding Act.

5. The courts have often relied on the presence of severe housing conditions or conditions of urban blight to uphold rent control and other laws affecting ownership rights in housing. *See e.g.*, Note, *Preference Liens for the Costs of Repairing Slum Property*, 1967 WASH. U.L.Q. 141, discussing a New York case upholding a housing receivership law displacing prior mortgage liens on residential property. Courts have dropped the "emergency" doctrine when sustaining housing legislation. *See Birkenfeld v. City of Berkeley*, 550 P.2d 1001 (Cal. 1976) (rejecting the requirement of an emergency) (excerpted and discussed in Chapter 4 *infra*); Kenneth K. Baar & W. Dennis Keating, *The Last Stand of Economic Substantive Due Process—The Housing Emergency Requirement for Rent Control*, 7 URB. LAW. 447 (1975); Karl Manheim, *Tenant Eviction Protection and the Takings Clause*, 1989 WIS. L. REV. 925. For further analysis of this topic, *see* W. DENNIS KEATING, MICHAEL B. TEITZ & ANDREJS SKABURSKIS, RENT CONTROL: REGULATION AND THE RENTAL HOUSING MARKET (1998); Karl Manheim, *Rent Control in the New* Lochner *Era*, 23 UCLA J. ENVTL. L. & POL'Y 211 (2005).

The emergency doctrine probably arose as an escape around earlier due process doctrine, which was not tolerant of legislation interfering with property rights. The disappearance of the emergency doctrine may simply reflect the present tolerant judicial attitude toward economic regulation. Is there any suggestion in the Michelman article that the right to housing requires the existence of an emergency?

A Right to Housing and the Challenge of Homelessness

The almost total collapse of the housing market in 2007–2008, the increase in homelessness resulting from that collapse, and the severe recession that followed has prompted additional discussion of a right to housing. One of the key questions is why focus on housing? The following excerpt explores that question.

Kristen David Adams, Do We Need a Right to Housing?

9 Nevada Law Journal 275, 305, 314–319 (2009)....

Why Housing?

If, as a society, we determine that rights are the most appropriate means of protecting the interests of disadvantaged persons, and if we determine that a right to housing is sensible and consistent with public values, it remains necessary to determine whether housing, as opposed to other important needs such as health care and employment, merits particular priority.

A. Attributes Associated with Home

Belonging, Comfort, and Security

Many have argued that the concept of "home" is special, and it is important to understand why this might be so ... [The author reviews the relationship of "home" and the concepts of security, belonging, control, privacy, continuity, and family life—Eds.] ...

Is Housing the Best Point of Emphasis?

If providing housing for low-income persons is an effective means of supporting other important goals as well, then it may make sense to give primacy to housing rather than the other supported goals. As one example, affordable housing plays an important role in the provision of supportive services. In addition, high-quality housing may tend to promote health and safety.... Housing quality and location may also affect the availability of employment, education, and other opportunities. Stated another way, failing to provide affordable housing can have far-reaching negative effects at the individual level, as well as the community level.

At the same time, establishing a causal relationship between housing quality and the quality of family life with any certainty can be difficult. Chester Hartman notes that, even though prevention of disease was one early justification for subsidized housing, studies have not necessarily proven a connection between housing quality and health. Hartman admits that what he calls the "social pathology case"—that is, the argument that bad housing leads to delinquency, poor performance at school and in the workplace, and a decline in family life, is even more difficult to prove. Thus, there is no consensus that improving the supply and quality of low-income housing will improve residents' lives in other ways as well....

Furthermore, simply improving the supply and quality of low-income housing will not ensure that the housing will be a success. Instead, as architecture critic Blair Kamin notes, thoughtfully designed housing can be most effective in improving the lives of low-income persons when coupled with social services, job training, and other programs. In other words, success demands an emphasis on people, not just buildings, and the poverty problem is too complex to be solved by merely addressing any single area, such as housing.

Even so, housing may be the most effective single point of emphasis in attacking the larger problem of poverty. First, even though housing obviously cannot solve every problem that contributes to poverty, it can help to address at least some of those problems in significant ways.... [A]ddressing the housing problem would make a significant difference in the lives of low-income persons. In addition, housing does have some unique attributes, most notably its positive effect on certain important personal, interpersonal, and societal dynamics. As Blair Kamin has noted, the built environment has the potential to either lift or crush the spirit. Others, too, have noted the powerful role of a very bad—or very good—built environment in affecting the lives of those who reside there....

D. Home, House, or Housing?

If the United States were to recognize a right to housing, should it more properly be termed a right to "a home" or even "a house?" Starting first with the second possibility—a "right to a house"—single-family housing for low-income persons presents a complex set of issues. On the one hand, the expense associated with single-family housing makes multi-family housing much more attractive financially. On the other hand, homeownership remains the ideal in American life, a preference that can perhaps be traced back to the country's history of homesteading. Even when renting, tenants often prefer single-family housing to apartments. Like residents, policymakers often prefer single-family housing to apartments. One reason both policymakers and residents sometimes prefer homeownership to tenancy is that owning a home is an empowering experience. Ownership may also be associated with a greater sense of belonging on the property and control over the property than tenancy provides. These benefits—empowerment, belonging, and control—are all personal in nature; homeownership has been credited with benefits to the larger society, as well. For example, homeownership has been described as a source of civic virtue and social esteem.

The federal government, perhaps in response to the widespread preference for homeownership over renting, has increasingly shifted its focus from the provision of subsidized rental housing to the promotion of homeownership. Not every person, however, is a good fit for homeownership, and thus the emphasis on homeownership can have very negative consequences for certain persons who are most vulnerable—and thus most in need of housing rental assistance. One negative consequence that has received considerable attention in recent times is the rise in default rates for subprime mortgages. Fairly widespread default rates have suggested that homeownership, although very attractive for persons who can afford it, cannot on its own provide a comprehensive solution to the need for affordable housing. Thus, if the United States should decide to create a right to housing, this right should not be equated with "a right to own a house" or even "a right to rent a house." Instead, multi-family housing and rental housing should be considered important components of any such right....

Who decides whether housing is sufficient? In addition to policymakers and code enforcement agencies, resident involvement is exceedingly important. Sometimes, the interaction between third parties and residents is controversial. For example, a resident may feel as though his or her housing is entirely sufficient, even though it may not be up to housing-code standards. Noting the potential for conflict between resident preferences and external standards, Ezra Rosser would take the concept of resident empowerment ... one step further, giving residents the right to trump code-enforcement agencies. He argues that housing codes, rather than improving housing conditions for low-income persons, are actually destructive when they impose standards that individuals whom society intends to protect cannot afford. Nathan Glazer has made a similar point, acknowledging the danger inherent in purporting to declare with certainty what good or bad housing is. Thus, if the United States were to create a right to housing, it would be important to allow the residents to have a significant voice—perhaps even the deciding vote—in determining what kind of housing is sufficient to meet their needs....

Notes and Questions

1. Assuming, as Adams does, that a right to housing "is a cogent notion," *Id.* at 320, what might it look like? Should, for example, the beneficiary of such a right—low-income family, homeless person, etc.—have any legal obligations? What might they be? Against whom should a right to housing be enforceable—the government (federal, state, or local), private housing providers, lenders? Adams proposes a Promise Enforcement model—an enforceable bilateral contract—as the implementation mechanism for a right to housing. *Id.* at 320–324.

2. Would it surprise you that "[s]ome of the strongest arguments against a right to housing are made by public housing authorities and other providers of low-income housing"? *Id.* at 321. Is their argument that a right to housing would make it difficult, if not impossible, to protect their residents persuasive?

3. Given the importance of housing to individual and societal well being, why does a "right to housing" elicit opposition? For an argument that "the common experience of a dwelling as a 'home' generates a wide range of human meanings, expectations, and interests related to liberty, privacy, security, and possession," *see* Tim Iglesias, *A Place to Call Home? Affordable Housing Issues in America: Our Pluralist Ethics and the Struggle for Affordability,* 42 WAKE FOREST L. REV. 511, 514–515 (2007). Iglesias identifies five housing ethics: (1) housing as an economic good, (2) housing as home, (3) housing as a human right, (4) housing as providing social order, and (5) housing as one land use in a functional system," and discusses how different housing ethics combine and conflict with one another and how they influence the availability of affordable housing. *Id.* at 518–577. He sees "twin challenges" confronting affordable housing advocates: "surviving our housing ethics' pluralism and resisting the threatened hegemony of versions of two housing ethics: the deregulation (or 'free market') version of the 'housing as an economic good' ethic and the exclusionary version of the 'housing as providing social order' ethic. He notes that "[w]hile affordability is not one of our housing ethics, it is not a permanent minority interest either." *Id.* at 590. After identifying widespread support for affordable housing, "at least in principle," he concludes with the observation that the "housing as one land use in a functional system" ethic appears to offer the "most fruitful opportunities to promote affordability in the current and near future" because it "supports the growing view of affordability as a necessary element of a healthy community.... [and] "can help neutralize affordability's historical association with divisive poverty and race issues." *Id.* at 591. As you study the materials in this book, consider whether Professor Iglesias' concluding observation is persuasive

4. *Statutory Right to Housing.* Although judicial recognition of a right to housing appeared difficult after cases like *Lindsey* and *Valtierra*, more recent cases suggest the courts may find a right to housing based on specific statutory requirements. For example, the D.C. Circuit concluded that a landlord's refusal to accept enhanced Section 8 vouchers, discussed in Chapter 3 *infra*, as rent violated the Human Rights Act of the District of Columbia. *Feemster v. BSA Ltd. Partnership*, 548 F.3d 1063 (D.C. Cir. 2008). The D.C. statute banned discrimination in "any transaction in real property ... based on [an individual's] source of income," and identified section 8 vouchers specifically as a source of income. D.C. Code §2-1402.21(e). "Permitting [the landlord] to refuse to accept Section 8 vouchers on the ground that it does not wish to comply with Section 8 requirements would vitiate [the source of income] definition and the legal safeguard it was intended to provide," the court concluded. 548 F.3d at 1070–71.

See also Hodge v. Ginsberg, 303 S.E.2d 245 (W. Va. 1983), in which the court found a state statutory entitlement to housing for homeless persons as incapacitated adults. A statute authorized the state department of welfare to "develop a plan for a comprehensive system of adult protective services." The department was to "offer such services as are available and appropriate in the circumstances to ... such incapacitated adults or to adults who may request and be entitled to such protective services." An "incapacitated adult" was defined as "any person who by reason of physical, mental or other infirmity is unable to independently carry on the daily activities of life necessary to sustaining life and reasonable health."

The petitioners were homeless persons unable to provide adequate shelter for themselves and sought adult protective services in the form of shelter, food and medical care as incapacitated adults. The department had adopted regulations limiting adult protective services to persons who were incapacitated due to physical or mental infirmity and claimed the petitioners were not qualified to receive these services. The court held that the regulations did not comply with the law, which extended such services to "any person who by reason of physical, mental or other infirmity" is in need of aid. It relied on the remedial nature of the legislation and a dictionary definition of "infirmity." The court also held that the department lacked the discretion to exclude the homeless from the scope of its services.

The dissenting opinion, after noting that "[w]e are asked by the petitioners to dream," commented:

> [T]he word "housing" does not appear in the statute, whose entire thrust is toward the provision of temporary emergency care. In fact, the stated purposes of the statute ... [are] to wean its beneficiaries of dependency on the state.... [T]hat stated purpose ... conflict[s] directly with the new entitlement the majority has read into the statute.

Id. at 252. Is the dissent suggesting it is wrong to read a permanent entitlement to housing into a statute that provides only for emergency care? If so, do you agree?

Compare Boehm v. Superior Court, 223 Cal. Rptr. 716 (Ct. App. 1986) (court held that county general assistance grant must include appropriate allowance of necessities, including housing). *See generally* Gary L. Blasi, *Litigation on Behalf of the Homeless: Systematic Approaches*, 31 Wash. U. J. Urb. & Contemp. L. 137 (1987); Kenneth M. Chackes, *Sheltering the Homeless: Judicial Enforcement of Government Duties to the Poor*, *Id.* at 31; Robert C. Coates, *Ending Chronic Homelessness in America's Major Cities—The Justice Systems' Duty*, 42 U.S.F. L. Rev. 427 (2007).

Whether there exists a statutory right to housing at the federal level depends on provisions in the federal housing legislation. *See Wright v. Roanoke Redev. & Hous. Auth.*, 479 U.S. 418 (1987), holding that tenants in public housing have an implied cause of action in federal court to enforce a provision of the public housing statute limiting the rents of tenants. The *Wright* case is excerpted in Chapter 2 *infra* and the issue of access to the courts is also analyzed. Two federal courts post-*Wright* disagree on whether tenants have a statutory right to prevent the constructive demolition of public housing through lack of maintenance by the housing authority. *See* 42 U.S.C. § 1437p. *Compare Concerned Tenants Ass'n v. Pierce*, 685 F. Supp. 316 (D. Conn. 1988) (recognizing right) *with Edwards v. District of Columbia*, 821 F.2d 651 (D.C. Cir. 1987) (contra). The Fifth Circuit, in *Johnson v. Housing Auth. of Jefferson Parish*, 442 F.3d 356 (5th Cir. 2006), applied *Wright* in holding that low-income recipients of housing subsidies under the Section 8 Housing Choice Voucher program had a right to bring a private action under 42 U.S.C. § 1983 (federal civil rights statute) to challenge the calculation of their utility allowances by public housing authorities. Noting that the Supreme Court limits statutory-based private causes of action under § 1983 to statutes that "unambiguously conferred" such rights, 442 F.3d at 360, quoting *Gonzaga University v. Doe*, 536 U.S. 273, 283 (2002), the court held that Congress impliedly granted a private right of action when it enacted the Housing Choice Voucher law. Three years later, that same court held that public housing residents in New Orleans displaced in the aftermath of Hurricane Katrina did not have a statutory private right of action to block demolition of public housing complexes in that city. *Anderson v. Jackson*, 556 F. 3d 351 (5th Cir. 2009). Again citing *Gonzaga University*, the court held that a statutory requirement that the Housing Authority of New Orleans notify residents ninety days prior to displacement and offer displaced residents comparable housing did not amount to an "unambiguously conferred right" to prevent demolition of the public housing units. The public housing and Section 8 programs are discussed in Chapter 3 *infra.*

For a discussion of state court litigation on the right to housing, see David B. Bryson, *The Role of the Courts and a Right to Housing, in* A RIGHT TO HOUSING: FOUNDATION FOR A NEW SOCIAL AGENDA 193 (Rachel G. Bratt, Michael E. Stone & Chester Hartman eds. 2006) (discussing litigation seeking recognition of housing rights and arguing that "courts have played an important role in laying the groundwork for elements of a Right to Housing" such as housing in decent physical condition, security of tenure, right to fair treatment, and freedom from race, ethnic and other forms of discrimination). Bryson concludes that "it is not unreasonable to anticipate that eventually the United States will make the judgment that everyone is entitled to a decent home and that the societal judgment will become embodied in a constitutional amendment or a statutory enactment. Should that happen, "courts will have extensive responsibility to work out the details of what such a right means," he noted. *Id.* at 2

5. *Constitutional Right to Housing.* Professor Peter Edelman's arguments for a constitutional right to a minimum income, published during the constitutional bicentennial in 1987, also provide a theoretical basis for a constitutional right to housing:

> There are two lines of theoretical justification for this: one, that it is an obligation which has been implicit in our constitutional structure all along, or at least since American polity has had enough resources to share its wealth more equitably; and two, that it is an obligation which has been acquired as a consequence of government's historic and continuing complicity in economic arrangements that foreseeably resulted in the current maldistribution. The first is a substantive due process argument; the second is an equal protection theory.

Peter Edelman, *The Next Century of Our Constitution: Rethinking Our Duty to the Poor,* 39 HASTINGS L.J. 1, 5 (1987).

Important cases establishing a state constitutional right to housing have been brought on behalf of the homeless. *Callahan v. Carey*, N.Y.L.J., Dec. 11, 1979, at 10, Col. 4 (N.Y. Sup. Ct. Dec. 5, 1979), brought on behalf of the 10,000 homeless men of New York City, is the seminal case. The plaintiffs claimed not only that housing was critically scarce, but that what little shelter existed was unhealthy and dangerous. They further claimed the city failed to provide showers or laundry facilities, information regarding public assistance, and other relevant services to which they may have been entitled. The court granted the plaintiffs a temporary injunction based on a state constitutional provision requiring the state to provide "aid, care and support to the needy."

The parties eventually agreed to a consent degree. It obligated the city to provide shelter and board to each homeless man who applied if he met all the requirements for relief or was in need of temporary shelter because of physical, mental or social dysfunction. *See also Elridge v. Koch*, Index 41494/82 (N.Y. Sup. Ct. Dec. 13, 1982) (similar decree for homeless women).

6. Housing activists continue to press for recognition of a right to housing, believing that "[i]t is unconscionable that in the 21st century, upwards of 100 million people in the United States live in housing that is physically inadequate, in unsafe neighborhoods, overcrowded or way beyond what they realistically can afford. Yet it could be quite different." A RIGHT TO HOUSING: FOUNDATION FOR A NEW SOCIAL AGENDA 1 (Rachel G.

Bratt, Michael E. Stone & Chester Hartman eds. 2006). *See also* National Perspectives on Housing Rights (Scott Leckie ed. 2003); Raymond H. Brescia, *Sheltering Counsel: Towards a Right to a Lawyer in Eviction Proceedings*, 25 Touro L. Rev. 187 (2009); Maria Foscarinis, *Advocating for the Human Right to Housing: Notes from the United States,* 30 N.Y.U. Rev. L. & Soc. Change 447 (2006) (discussing the impact of testimony before the Inter-American Commission on Human Rights concerning the "right to adequate housing in the Americas"); Chester Hartman, *The Case for A Right To Housing,* 9 Housing Pol'y Debate 223, 229–230, 237–238 (1998), reprinted with changes in A Right to Housing: Foundation for a New Social Order 177 (Rachel G. Bratt, Michael E. Stone & Chester Hartman eds. 2006); Rachel Bratt, *Why CDCs Should Advocate for a Right to Housing* (2006) (published by the National Housing Institute, *available at* www.nhi.org/online/issues/148/whycdcs.html. *Compare* Robert E. Land, Katrin B. Anacker & Steven Hornburg, *The New Politics of Affordable Housing,* 19 Housing Pol'y Debate 231 (2008), with comments by Chester Hartman, *Id. at* 249, and Ronald D. Utt, *Id. at* 255. Land, Anacker and Hornburg examined survey data gathered by the National Association of Realtors concerning public attitudes, noting how housing program labels have evolved over the years from "public housing to ["subsidized housing"] to "assisted housing" to "affordable housing" to "housing that is affordable" in the hopes of garnering more favorable public reaction. Land et al., *supra* at 243.

International Perspectives on a Right to Housing

The Habitat Agenda

The United Nations-sponsored Conferences, Habitat I, held in Vancouver, Canada in 1976 and Habitat II, held in Istanbul, Turkey in 1996, gave new impetus to the right to housing debate. For an in-depth discussion of Habitat II, *see* Janet Ellen Stearns, *Voluntary Bonds: The Impact of Habitat II on U.S. Housing Policy*, 16 St. Louis U. Pub. L. Rev. 419 (1997). Among the many documents and statements issued at the conference that was attended by over 16,000 persons from 171 countries was the following declaration:

> We affirm our commitment to the full and progressive realization of the right to adequate housing as provided for in international instruments. To that end, we shall seek the active participation of our public, private and nongovernmental partners at all levels to ensure legal security of tenure, protection from discrimination and equal access to affordable, adequate housing for all persons and their families.
>
> We shall work to expand the supply of affordable housing by enabling markets to perform efficiently and in a socially and environmentally responsible manner, enhancing access to land and credit and assisting those who are unable to participate in housing markets.

Id. at 426, quoting *Istanbul Declaration on Human Settlements* ¶¶ 8–9 (1996), *available at* http://www.undp.org/un/habitat/agenda/ist-dec.html. A set of fourteen *Commitments*, or objectives, dedicated to "adequate shelter for all" were issued. These commitments included legal, financial, housing development and social objectives that signatory nations undertook to pursue. *Habitat Agenda,* ch. III, ¶¶ 39–41 (1996), *available at* http://www.undp.org/un/habitat/agenda/ch-3.htm/. A *Global Plan of Action* also was adopted, including a statement urging all signatory nations to:

> striv[e] to fulfill the agreed target of 0.7 per cent of the gross national product

> ner, enhancing access to land and credit and assisting those who are unable to participate in housing markets.

Id. at 426, quoting *Istanbul Declaration on Human Settlements* ¶¶ 8–9 (1996), *available at* http://www.undp.org/un/habitat/agenda/ist-dec.html. A set of fourteen *Commitments*, or objectives, dedicated to "adequate shelter for all" were issued. These commitments included legal, financial, housing development and social objectives that signatory nations undertook to pursue. *Habitat Agenda*, ch. III, ¶¶ 39–41 (1996), *available at* http://www.undp.org/un/habitat/agenda/ch-3.htm/. A *Global Plan of Action* also was adopted, including a statement urging all signatory nations to:

> striv[e] to fulfill the agreed target of 0.7 per cent of the gross national product of the developed countries for official development assistance as soon as possible and to increase, as necessary, the share of funding for adequate shelter and human settlements development programmes commensurate with the scope and scale of activities required to achieve the objectives and goals of the Habitat Agenda.

Stearns, *supra* at 428–29, quoting *Habitat Agenda*, ch. IV, ¶ 204(b).

The *Habitat Agenda* was preceded by a seven criteria definition of the "human right to adequate housing" promulgated by the United Nations Committee on Economic, Social, and Cultural Rights: "(a) Legal security of tenure, (b) Availability of services, materials, facilities and infrastructure, (c) Affordability, (d) Habitability, (e) Accessibility, (f) Location, and (g) Cultural adequacy." Eric S. Tars & Caitlin Egleson, *Great Scot!: The Scottish Plan to End Homelessness and Lessons for the Housing Rights Movement in the United States*, 16 GEO. J. ON POVERTY L & POL'Y 187, 188–189 (2009), quoting COMMITTEE ON ECON., SOC. AND CULTURAL RIGHTS, *General Comment 4, The right to adequate housing*, at 114 U.N. Doc. E/1992/23, annex III (1991), *reprinted in* Compilation of General Comments and General Recommendations Adopted by Human Rights Treaty Bodies, at ¶ 8, U.N. Doc. HRI/GEN/1/Rev.6 at 18 (2003).

Within ten years of its promulgation, the *Habitat Agenda* had been adopted by 171 countries. The *Millennium Declaration*, the UN development agenda for the first 15–20 years of the 21st Century, was approved in 2000, and a United Nations agency, UN-HABITAT, was elevated to full UN programme status in 2002. The *Millennium Declaration* includes the following commitment:

> We will spare no effort to free our fellow men, women and children from the abject and dehumanizing conditions of extreme poverty, to which more than a billion of them are currently subjected. We are committed to making the right to development a reality for everyone and to freeing the entire human race from want.

United Nations General Assembly, *United Nations Millennium Declaration*, A/RES/55/2, Sept. 18, 2000. The Third Session of UN-HABITAT's World Urban Forum reached the "general consensus that governments should respect the right to adequate housing and that forced evictions run counter to … the Habitat Agenda." Report of the Third Session of the World Urban Forum, at 32 (Vancouver, Canada, June 19–23, 2006), *available at* www.unhabitat.org.

The Scottish Experience

To the question whether any country has come close to establishing a right to housing, the answer increasingly is Scotland. With the enactment of the Homelessness, Etc.

(Scotland) Act of 2003, a movement that began with the Housing (Homelessness) Act 1977 and built on the Housing (Scotland) Act 1987 and the Housing (Scotland) Act 2001, created "the closest thing to the practical implementation of the right to housing the world has yet seen." Tars and Egleson, *supra* at 190. A Homeless Task Force ("HTF"), created by the Scottish Executive in 1999, presented a series of recommendations based on "the perspective that housing is a right that should be available to all." *Id.* at 192, *citing* SCOTTISH EXECUTIVE, HELPING HOMELESS PEOPLE: LEGISLATIVE PROPOSALS FOR HOMELESSNESS (2000) and HELPING HOMELESS PEOPLE: AN ACTION PLAN FOR PREVENTION AND EFFECTIVE RESPONSE (2003), and noting that Scotland joined India, South Africa and France as the only nations that "have created similar legal duties regarding the right to housing." The Scottish approach is based on an "inclusive definition of 'homelessness'" that is "significantly broader" than definitions employed in the U.S.

> The comprehensive features of Scotland's housing plan include the right to be immediately housed for all homeless persons and the right to long-term, supportive housing as long as is needed for priority groups—a category that will be progressively abolished by 2012, at which point the right will extend to all. Crucially, this includes an individual right to sue if one believes one's rights are not being respected. Complementary policy includes a number of other rights, including the right to purchase public housing units and the ability to sell one's house to the government to avoid foreclosure, but rent it back to allow one to maintain one's residence through financial difficulty, perhaps ultimately repurchasing the home. All of these policies work together to ensure the right to housing is upheld.

Tars and Egleson, *supra* at 190. The Scottish definition of homelessness adds to traditional definitions two groups of people, "those whose housing presents unreasonable risks to their safety or health, and those at risk of imminent housing loss." *Id.* at 208

> This definition is noteworthy in that it demands assistance be given not only to those who are literally without shelter, but rather to many people under a wide range of circumstance, including those living in intolerable conditions and those who are threatened with homelessness but are presently housed. In addition to covering a wide range of circumstances, it lays out specific factors that raise the risk of homelessness, such as domestic violence.... [and] is significantly broader than those used in the U.S.

Id. at 193–94. Tars and Egleson note that four "gate keeping tools" were included in the original 1977 legislation. To be eligible for assistance, applicants had to (1) meet the definition of homelessness; (2) be in a "priority need" category, such as pregnancy, dependent children in the household, old age, illness, disability, or homeless as the result of fire or flood; (3) not be homeless intentionally; and (4) have a local connection (residence or employment) to the jurisdiction from which assistance is being sought. These inquiries originally were "used exclusively—with a view toward minimizing the burden—rather than inclusively—with a view toward ensuring a right to housing." Amendments in 2003 "fundamentally shifted" the approach to an inclusive one by expanding the categories of "priority need" to include teen age youth, adults with personality disorders, "people who are discharged from prisons, hospitals, and the armed forces, and those at risk of violence or harassment;" requiring that homeless people who are in a "priority need" category be provided permanent housing with "security of tenure," imposing a duty to provide social services and short term housing for persons who intentionally are homeless, and modification of the local connection requirement for services to recognize the fact that "some people may be requesting assistance in a specific location for good reason, such as the desire to leave an abusive partner."

Id. at 195–198. Tars and Egleson acknowledge that "the Scottish situation is not identical to that of the U.S.," *Id.* at 191, but believe that by expanding the definition of homelessness, requiring comprehensive affordable housing planning for all income levels, and creating legally enforceable duties to meet housing needs, a right to housing could be implemented in the U.S. *Id.* at 191, 207–216....

Notes and Questions

1. Janet Stearns criticizes the Habitat II Conference for its failure to articulate a clear standard of housing rights and a clear basis for implementation of such rights. She argues that:

> a right to housing can be seen as including four governmental 'layers of obligation'—the duty to respect, to promote, to protect and to fulfill." The duty to respect requires governments to refrain from sponsoring or tolerating policies which violate individuals' rights to use available resources for housing. The duty to promote includes taking steps to ensure that no governmental action deliberately erodes housing rights, including repealing or altering legislation or policies. The duty to protect requires the state to prevent violations of individual housing rights by other individuals or private organizations such as abuse by landlords and developers and to create legal remedies for abuses. The duty to fulfill, described as the "most aggressive of these rights, requires states to make budgetary allocations and regulate the housing market to guarantee housing for those persons who cannot obtain it through personal efforts.

Janet Ellen Stearns, *Voluntary Bonds: The Impact of Habitat II on U.S. Housing Policy*, 16 St. Louis U. Pub. L. Rev. 419, 430–32 (1997). Do the subsequent developments noted above respond to Janet Stearns' criticism of the Habitat II Conference? *See* Maria Foscarinis, *Advocating for the Human Right to Housing: Notes from the United States*, 30 N.Y.U. Rev. L. & Soc. Change 447 (2006) (discussing use of international human rights norms as a basis for overcoming the traditional "negative rights" interpretation of U.S. law in favor of a more positive human right to housing), *contra* Robert Ellickson, *The Untenable Case for an Unconditional Right to Shelter*, 15 Harv. J. L. & Pub. Pol'y 17 (1992).

2. Compare the Scottish definition of homelessness with the new and more comprehensive definition of homeless people that was adopted in the 2009 reauthorization of the McKinney-Vento Homeless Assistance Act as part of the Helping Families Save Their Homes Act, Pub. L. No. 111-22, Div. B, § 1003(a), 123 Stat. 1632 (*amending* 42 U.S.C. § 11301 and ff and *codified at* 42 U.S.C. §§ 11301–472, and discussed in Chapter 3 *supra*).

The new U.S. definition contained in 42 U.S.C. § 11302 includes six categories of homeless people:

(1) persons lacking "a fixed, regular, and adequate nighttime residence;"

(2) persons whose regular nighttime residence is a car, abandoned building or other "public or private place" not designed for regular sleeping accommodations;

(3) persons living in shelters, hotels and motels or other "temporary living arrangements;"

(4) persons "exiting an institution where he or she temporarily resided;"

(5) persons (A) facing imminent loss of housing because of (i) an eviction notice, (ii) lacking resources to stay more than 14 days in a hotel or motel, or (iii) having "credible evidence" that the owner will not allow the household to stay in the housing for more than 14 days, (B) having "no subsequent residence identified," and (C) lacking the "resources or support networks needed to obtain other permanent housing;" and

(6) unaccompanied youth and families with children who have experienced "a long term period without living independently in permanent housing, who have moved frequently, and who have chronic disabilities and other conditions contributing to housing instability. In addition to these six categories, persons fleeing domestic violence and other dangerous situations, "including where the health and safety of children are jeopardized" and who do not have the resources to obtain permanent housing are considered homeless.

How do the two statutes treat persons who are living in dangerous, insanitary or overcrowded housing? Short term tenants? Do the 2009 amendments to the U.S. definition create a basis for a Scottish "right to housing" argument? For additional discussion of the Scottish approach to homelessness, see Isobel Anderson, *Sustainable Solutions to Homelessness: the Scottish Case,* 1 EUR. J. HOMELESSNESS 163 (2007).

3. The right to housing debate has gained greater attention in the first decade of the 21st Century as the forces of population growth, globalization and worldwide recession have collided. At some point in 2007 more people in the world were living in cities than elsewhere, and more than one billion of the world's population was living in slums. UN-HABITAT, THE STATE OF THE WORLD'S CITIES REPORT 2006/2007 viii (2006). How significant are these trends? Do they suggest particular responses by individual nations such as the United States?

Philosophic Attitudes Influencing the Right to Housing Debate

So far, you've read enough about the right to housing to know that the nature of this right and the measures required for its recognition remain nebulous and undefined. In the hope of providing some clarity and guidance, the following excerpt from Professor Thomas C. Grey's article suggests that philosophic attitudes may affect the social acceptance of housing rights. Grey distinguishes the philosophies of two leading exponents who hold widely different views on the state's role in social programs.

Thomas C. Grey, Property and Need: The Welfare State and Theories of Distributive Justice

28 Stanford Law Review 877, 877–86 (1976)

Perhaps the most fundamental of all public issues are those concerning the proper distribution of wealth and income. Risking oversimplification, let me suggest that the standard positions taken in the unending debate over these issues can usefully be classified as either egalitarian or libertarian. Egalitarians hold that economic assets should be distributed equally—allowing various exceptions. Libertarians hold that economic assets should be left in whatever hands they reach through free and fair individual transactions—again, allowing various exceptions.

In recent years, there has been a virtual explosion of serious writing on questions of economic justice. Certainly the best known of these works is John Rawls' massive A Theory of Justice, which advances a theory of qualified egalitarianism. On the other side is Robert Nozick's Anarchy, State and Utopia, which expresses a less qualified and more radical libertarian view. They are superficially very different books—Rawls' is sober, earnest and relentlessly abstract, while Nozick's is flashy, funny and filled with examples. But both seem to me at core extraordinarily serious, honest and able expositions of their respective doctrines. What follows is a brief outline of some significant contrasts between their positions and a tentative argument for an alternate and intermediate theory—one which moves from a libertarian starting point toward guarantees of basic material needs....

II. Rawls' Theory

Let me now describe, in rough outline, the substance of Rawls' conception of social justice. Rawls argues that an observer of human affairs who was knowledgeable and rational but impartial—that is, one who knew he would live in society but did not know his place either in that society or in the distribution of natural talents—would establish the following hierarchy of three basic principles as constraints on the design and working of political and social institutions. The three are ordered "lexically," so that when they conflict the first overrides the second and the second overrides the third.

First is the principle of liberty, which protects basic substantive freedoms such as the freedoms of speech, religion and occupational choice. Also covered are the basic procedural rights implicit in the concept of the rule of law and the political rights necessary for republican government such as the right to vote under a fair system of representation.

Second is the principle of equal opportunity, which not only forbids formal caste or class barriers but also requires affirmative action by government to give persons of unequal background a reasonably equal chance to compete for the rewards of life insofar as their talents allow. It might require, for example, government subsidy or direct provision of education to those who could not afford it.

It is Rawls' third principle—the "difference" principle—that deals directly with economic distribution. On this principle rests my characterization of Rawls as an egalitarian, and with it I shall be mainly concerned. Under this third principle economic assets must be distributed so as to maximize the position of the worst-off segment or poorest class in society. To put the point in another way, income and wealth are to be distributed equally except insofar as unequal distribution will give the poorest group more in the long run than they would have under complete equality, by virtue of the effect of incentives on overall economic prosperity.

III. The Problem of Property Rights

How much actual economic redistribution does Rawls' theory require? It is difficult to give a concrete answer because of his almost total failure to confront the question of the place of property in his system. Rawls makes clear that the implementation of the difference principle requires an extensive system of taxation and transfer payments. On the other hand, he makes casual reference to the "right to hold ... property" as one of the liberties protected by his first principle, which, it will be recalled, takes priority over the difference principle whenever the two conflict. This may mean that taxation for purposes of maximizing the economic position of the worst-off group is somehow not regarded as in conflict with property rights. But then what are the property rights protected by the first principle? Perhaps Rawls is implicitly relying on a distinction between protection of property against infringement by taxation on the one hand and by condemnation or trespass on the other. If so, it is a distinction which needs clarification and defense. It has been part of the liberal tradition that taxation infringes upon the rights of property and thus requires substantial justification.

By contrast to Rawls' virtual silence on the status and extent of property rights, Nozick makes the statement and defense of those rights his central theme in Anarchy, State and Utopia. The book states and defends a classical minimal-state liberalism, with a strong stress on property and economic freedom. The unusual interest of Nozick's work lies not in its restatement of this doctrine, which it shares with Spencer and to a lesser extent with Locke, but in its arguments against the positions of Rawls and other contemporary egalitarians.

Nozick begins by arguing that the very term "distributive justice" begs important questions. It carries with it the implication that "some thing or mechanism uses some principle or criterion to give out a supply of things." On the contrary, he says, "there is no central distribution, no person or group entitled to control all the resources, jointly deciding how they are to be doled out." He points out that most economic assets do not fall like manna from heaven; they come into being with individual claims of ownership attached to them. Those claims are claims of moral right; coercive dispossession of assets owned by another is theft. Theft is a fundamental moral conception just as is murder or assault; it is no more a creature of convention or positive law than they are. Property rights, like rights of personal liberty and security, exist and have moral force in a state of nature.

Nozick proposes an "entitlement theory" of what he calls "justice in holdings." Holdings of economic assets are justified if they result from legitimate original acquisition from nature or from a free and fair transfer from a person who is entitled to them. Such a conception of justice is entirely historical; the amounts of assets held by persons are not justified or condemned by their size relative to the amounts held by others but by their pedigree, their chain of title.

By contrast, Nozick says, Rawls holds an "end-state" theory of justice in holdings. The question whether the economic holdings of different individuals are just under Rawls' difference principle depends entirely on their size relative to each other. If the holdings are equal, they are just. If they are unequal, they are just only if the smallest of them is as large as it could possibly be, taking into account the long-run.

Rawls' exclusive focus on the relative sizes of holdings and total disregard of how those holdings come about is powerfully counter to ordinary intuitive judgments of justice in holdings. Perhaps Mafia chieftains and brain surgeons are about equally rich; surely their wealth is not equally suspect. Perhaps nuns or commune-dwellers on the one hand and the helpless aged on the other are about equally poor; surely their poverty is not of equal moral significance.

Unlike Rawls' difference principle, the egalitarian arguments that have actually animated political movements and shaped events have been based on a historical conception of distributive justice and on claims of moral entitlement to property.

Rawls' difference principle, in contrast to these popular egalitarian arguments, is based on the premise that corrective justice has been achieved so that existing property holdings are legitimate. It is the striking and radical feature of the principle that it requires further redistribution of these legitimately acquired holdings until the economic position of those worst-off is maximized. This goes beyond the widely accepted notion that the state may, in pursuit of the public good, engage in some redistribution away from the relatively rich toward the relatively poor. Rawls makes maximization of the income of the poor the most stringent sort of obligation of government, an obligation of justice conferring correlative rights on the beneficiaries.

Rawls' main ethical argument for requiring as a matter of justice the kind of redistribution apparently contemplated by the difference principle is that the qualities which tend to produce wealth even in an entirely fair market economy—one in which all transactions are entirely voluntary, untainted by any fraud, trickery or artificial monopoly power—are "arbitrary from a moral point of view." That is, people have the scarce talents or skills which attract high incomes through accidents of nature or social circumstance, and it is unjust to let accident produce unequal rewards, at least where such inequality can be corrected without infringing basic liberty or equal opportunity.

There are, as Nozick suggests, two decisive responses to this line of argument. First and most important, it suggests a kind of determinism which is incompatible with the liberal tradition generally and with the larger body of Rawls' own work specifically. While it is true that people deserve no credit for the talents with which they are born or the family and circumstances into which they are born, what they do to develop or waste their talents and social advantages is in part the result of their own choices. It might be said that the choices they make are determined by their character, which in turn is determined by their heredity and external environment—for which, again, they deserve no credit. But on this view, human beings are never free to choose and are never responsible for their choices. This view sits uneasily with a conception of justice that proclaims liberty as a fundamental value. And it is flatly inconsistent with liberalism based on a Kantian ethical position, which exalts human autonomy and responsibility—a position that Rawls eloquently avows.

Nozick's second response is that even assuming that people have in no way earned or deserved the material rewards they acquire or that rewards traceable to natural gifts can be segregated from those traceable to effort, not all moral rights or entitlements are based on desert. To use Nozick's own characteristically vivid example, people may have done nothing to earn their healthy bodies, yet still be entitled to keep them. Would not a program to redistribute eyes or kidneys to those who need them more be a morally intolerable infringement of a basic right to bodily integrity? Indeed, one need not resort to this kind of science fiction to make the point. Children have rights of support against their parents which they have not earned and have done nothing to deserve. The very right to life itself protects an "asset" that none of us has earned.

One could retain a weak but coherent conception of property rights providing that redistribution way from the natural pattern of holdings produced by free and fair transactions was justified as long as it tended in the direction of equality of wealth or income. Such a general proposition would be plausible though debatable; it might be supported by a showing of a consensus approaching unanimity in favor of greater economic equality. Such a consensus could arise from pursuit of a policy of social cohesion or, indeed, from simple generosity. Coercive implementation of such a consensus would then arguably be justified to deal with the problem of the free rider under a regime of voluntary redistribution—the asset holder who enjoys the fruits of the improved social climate resulting from redistribution without making his fair contribution to that climate.

Rawls' position goes well beyond this. On his view, the failure to redistribute until the position of the worst-off group is maximized is itself unjust, a violation of human rights. It is unjust whatever the views of the rest of society concerning the desirability of redistribution and hence does not depend on the extent to which equality can be regarded as a public good.

Further, the difference principle carries well beyond arguments for redistribution that are founded on a notion of a right to life or on a right to have basic material needs met or on the evil and degradation of poverty. For Rawls, even if the worst-off group is not suffering poverty in any recognizable form, it is still entitled to have the otherwise rightful holdings of others redistributed to it as long as that process does not impair its own long run prospects. That entitlement is ultimately founded, it seems, on the supposed moral ideal of an abstract pattern of equality of holdings—an ideal that seems to have little intuitive appeal as an ultimate value and that has not been supported by plausible arguments from other values.

Notes and Questions

1. Later in his article, Professor Grey illustrates his arguments with a number of constitutional analogies. He then makes the following comment on the role of courts and legislatures in making distributive social judgment:

> My use of generally recognized constitutional rights as analogies does not necessarily suggest that the right to have basic material needs met is, or soon will be or even should be, a judicially enforceable constitutional right in this country. That is not an unimaginable development, but it may be that institutional considerations governing the relations between the judiciary and the legislative branch of government will forever preclude it. It has not been part of our tradition that the judiciary should enforce rights that by their very nature require large expenditures of public money raised by taxation, while it is part of our quasi constitutional tradition that there should be no taxation without representation.

Id. at 900–901. Do you agree or disagree with this statement? Did the Court hold as it did in *Valtierra* to avoid the necessity of local expenditures for public housing without voter approval by the local electorate? Did the Court mandate the expenditure of public funds in some of the cases recognizing a right to housing discussed earlier in the note in this section? Would Grey agree with these decisions? *See also* John Stick, *Turning Rawls into Nozick and Back Again*, 81 Nw. U. L. Rev. 363 (1987). *Cf. United States v. Yonkers Bd. of Educ.*, 837 F.2d 1181 (2d Cir. 1987), *cert. denied*, 486 U.S. 1055 (1988) (upholding decree mandating construction of subsidized housing in white neighborhoods to achieve residential integration).

2. Note the extent to which a recognition of a right to housing requires an interference with property rights to which Nozick might object and the extent to which it requires a redistribution of wealth to improve the housing conditions of lower-income groups. If the housing problem is now primarily a problem of housing affordability, does the property rights interference objection still have much force? Are the cases recognizing the rights of tenants in public housing projects an interference with property rights, or does the governmental status of the housing agency make a difference?

3. Grey quotes Nozick as holding that "economic assets are justified if they result from legitimate original acquisition or from a free and fair transfer from a person who is entitled to them." Most housing is acquired by its owners in free and fair transactions. If so, can the housing deprivation that flows from these acquisitions be disregarded by society under the Nozick view?

4. The articulation of Rawls' views in the Grey article makes explicit the distributive assumptions contained in Michelman's analysis of a right to housing. Housing deprivation appears as one type of inequitable distribution. The difficulty is that judgmental criteria to correct this distribution appear arbitrary and difficult to formulate. Michelman's article contains implicit distributive criteria in its arguments for augmenting the rights of tenants and other consumers of housing. Note how this issue is presented in *Lindsey*. Would a contrary opinion in *Lindsey* be consistent with the Rawls view as elaborated by Michelman? An affirmative answer to this question assumes that all tenants are poor and all landlords are rich. Empirical studies of housing ownership in some cities dispute this conclusion. Low-income minority group members own and manage rental housing in many cities.

Consider the following comment on the role of the courts in income redistribution:

> This topic lies at the core of social decision-making and arises in virtually every substantive setting. Where legislation (or legislative inaction) directly confronts income redistribution, the courts are competing with the political process for some of the most pervasive and controversial social issues.... It is very difficult to imagine that serious review could take the form of sweeping solutions. Without a confining strategy, the judicial roles could easily exceed its physical capacity and substantive competence.

Neil K. Komesar, *A Job for the Judges: The Judiciary and the Constitution in a Massive and Complex Society*, 86 MICH. L. REV. 657, 717 (1988). *See also* Richard F. Muth, *Redistribution of Income Through Regulation of Housing*, 32 EMORY L.J. 691 (1983); David A. Weisbach, *Should Legal Rules Be Used to Redistribute Income?* 70 U. CHI. L. REV. 439 (2003) (arguing that the tax system is a more efficient and thus better way to redistribute income than are legal rules).

5. Does Adams' Promise Enforcement model, *supra*, respond to Nozick's concern about property rights? Is it consistent with Rawls' difference principle? Could Congress create (or mandate) an exchange of promises between the provider and the recipient of housing support? What implications does the Scottish approach to homelessness have for property rights?

6.Two examples of social intervention in housing problems illustrate the complexity of making distributive choices to alleviate housing deprivation:

Case 1: Metro City is a large metropolis with some substandard housing areas and a significant low-income and minority population. The city is considering a program of municipal loans for housing renovation. The loans would be funded by proceeds from the municipal income tax, a flat 1% tax levied against all city residents and all commuters who work in the city. The loans would be made available only to homeowners in "stable" residential neighborhoods capable of revitalization through housing improvement, and only to homeowners earning less than 150% of the median income in the city. The loans carry a low interest rate substantially below the interest rate charged on mortgages for single family homes. Blacks in the city generally live in rental housing. Sixty-five percent of all whites in the city own their own homes. The figure for blacks is 20%.

Note that public funds for the loans will come from a flat municipal income tax, which is usually considered regressive. That is, it falls more heavily on low-income groups. Note the recipients of the loans. Note also that the loans may impede the filtering process by providing for the upgrading of housing within selected neighborhoods within the city. Would you support the loan program if you agreed with Michelman's views? Rawls? Nozick?

Case 2: Metro City is considering a tax abatement program for office development. Prospective developers would be required to file a development plan for approval by the city council. Council approval carries with it an abatement on property taxes for twenty years, which would be frozen at the pre-development level. The city is considering the program because of the continuing decline in the city's commercial activity. Many new office buildings have been built in the suburbs in recent years, and office employment in the city has decreased substantially.

Studies by the city indicate that new office development aided by the property tax abatement would remove blight, create new jobs, stimulate related economic activity, and increase taxes from the municipal income tax (see Case 1). The unemployment rate in the city is substantially above the national average, especially for blacks. It is also true that blacks are under-represented in office employment, and that one-third of all office workers in

Chapter 2

The Intergovernmental Framework and Legal Process for Various Governmental Housing and Development Programs

Housing and community development programs involve allocation of defined roles to different levels of government—federal, state, and local—and, increasingly, to private sector entities involved in providing housing services. This Chapter describes and analyzes the various governmental roles in providing assistance to housing and community development activities and their interrelationships in operation of governmental financial assistance. Later chapters of this course book examine selected federal programs designed to alleviate some of the housing and community development problems considered in Chapter 1 *supra*.

We have previously examined the conflicting interests and pressures that lead to the adoption of federal housing programs and we have noted the role of Congress in formulating housing policy. Now it is necessary to look more closely at the different legal entities that participate in the adoption of federal housing and community development programs and at the structures through which these programs are implemented. Both the federal government and the fifty state governmental systems require separation of powers among the branches within each system, respectively. The federal system, moreover, recognizes role differentiation between the national, state, and local governments. Further, private sector entities are frequently used to implement government programs, especially at the state and local levels, and the private role is often encouraged or required by federal legislation. This represents a complicated arrangement, both as to allocation of roles and for their coordination.

This intergovernmental framework for program administration is a significant dimension in the implementation of federal housing programs. The federal government provides financial support in varying degrees for the housing programs it authorizes. It rarely administers these programs directly, for example as a landlord. Rather, Congress usually delegates program administration to the local government level or through local governments to private, profit and non-profit sub-recipients. It largely bypasses the states whose main role is in enacting the necessary legislation that allows local governments and their agencies to carry out their program responsibilities, unless state constitutions applicable in some states have specifically provided powers to local jurisdictions. States also administer a portion of Community Development Block Grant (CDBG) funds aside from funds that are sent directly by HUD to local governments that are entitled to funds under formula grants under the 1974 legislation that created the program.

While local agencies administer federal programs and carry out local policies, Congress also legislates national policies that these agencies must follow. Congress has a number of opportunities to influence local compliance with national program policies. It can adopt formulas for federal financial assistance that respond to local needs it considers critical. Congress can also delegate to federal agencies, most often HUD, the responsibility to implement federal policy through monitoring the administration of the program carried out locally, frequently communicated through regulations which are adopted by the federal government pursuant to rule-making requirements set up by the Administrative Procedures Act. These federal-local and state intergovernmental relationships are delicate, however. Most funds flow *from* the federal *to* local governments. The purse strings are generally given to the federal administrator—HUD—to oversee the local administration. Failure to adhere to program requirements can result in loss of federal funds for specific violations of federal requirements. Generally, sanctions do not include more than monetary ones. Occasionally, HUD has acted to debar recipients of federal funds and individuals in them. Debarment can result in restrictions on further participation in the administration of any federal program. A ban on participation generally is time limited, usually to three years, but it can be government wide. A limited denial of participation is limited to one year and relates only to the area served by a HUD regional office.

Thus, through the funding power, HUD sets the limitations and requirements that determine the propriety of the use of its funds. In some cases, when it enacts programs, Congress has not only mandated the allocation of program funds to local government recipients but also has specified the manner in which HUD (as the distributor and monitor of their use) is to carry out its responsibilities. One example of this phenomenon is the community development block grant program in which Congress specified that designated recipients would receive allocations from appropriated funds based upon a distributional formula. Essentially, HUD was denied administrative discretion to determine local use of these funds. In fact, given some history of delay on HUD's part in making determinations regarding permissible activities, Congress has required that HUD provide approval of local plans for use, e.g. for CDBG funds, within a set time period (originally 75 days) to prevent the federal government from continuing to impose long delays in deciding whether it agreed with the local governments' proposed use of federal funds.

The executive branch agency, the Office of Management and Budget (OMB), facilitates management policies of the executive branch and, contributes to determining program policies and requirements through a series of OMB formal issuances or guidance documents. In particular, with relevance to housing and development programs are the guidance documents relating to the use of federal funds, such as OMB Circular A-87 (and its attachments), "Cost Principles for State, Local, and Indian Tribal Governments," that are applicable to activities and use of funds by local governments, and OMB Circular A-122, "Cost Principles for Non-Profit Organizations," pertaining to the role of private non-profit organizations in administering federal programs. These issuances are occasionally updated, and have been subject to formal rule-making with opportunities for notice and comment, making them binding on recipients of federal funds. Other actors with regard to use of federal funds are the various Offices of Inspector General with responsibilities for the particular federal department or agency for which they are given jurisdiction. Along with the Government Accountability Office (previously named "General Accounting Office"), which frequently reviews federal agency actions and adherence to applicable Congressional policies, the various Offices of Inspector General provide continuing oversight on behalf of Congress of federal agency actions and use of funds by recipients of federal monies. They report to Congress and the Secretary of the Department.

The exact scope of program policy that is subject to federal control is not always clear. Advocates of local autonomy often resist federal efforts to implement federal objectives and often cite concepts of federalism as justification of "letting a thousand flowers grow" so as to discover alternative options for effectively delivering and formulating federal housing and development programs. At the same time, while efforts to force adherence to federal requirements is a major consideration for agencies involved in formulating procedures and administrating use of federal funds, particularly to limit problems of "fraud, waste, and abuse" in operation of federal programs, there has been an increasing tendency to leave more discretion to state and local governments in operational decisions regarding use of federal funds since they are generally considered to be closer to the ultimate beneficiaries of the programs and should be more informed on and responsive to local conditions and needs.

A. The Intergovernmental Roles of Federal, State, and Local Governments as Well as Private Sector Participants in Housing and Development Programs

This section of this Chapter describes federal, state, and local roles in the distribution and administration of federal financial assistance.

The cases set forth in the following section include access to the courts and also serve to indicate the dual governmental nature of federal housing programs. The federal government makes financial assistance available subject to conditions that it believes will implement federal policies. Local agencies administer the programs. In litigation challenging actions taken in federal housing programs, sorting out the responsibilities of federal and local agencies can prove to be a difficult task. This section of this Chapter looks more closely at the intergovernmental framework for federal housing programs. First, we will examine the federal grant and subsidy system and its structure that can influence congressional decisions to distribute federal financial assistance.

1. The Federal Grant and Subsidy Structure

The number of federal grants for state and local governments has increased enormously over the years, and the contribution of federal assistance to state and local government budgets has increased concurrently. For instance, the recent $787 billion economic stimulus legislation enacted in February, 2009, HR-1, the American Recovery and Reinvestment Act (ARRA) of 2009, Pub. L. No. 111-5, 123 Stat. 115 (to be *codified at* 26 U.S.C. § 1). It has been critical in helping states and local governments retain much of their workforce. Over the years in some cities, federal grants per capita of population have increased from less than $1 to almost $300. While the rate of increase in federal assistance to state and local governments slowed somewhat during the Bush Administrations, federal aid continues to make a significant contribution to state and local expenditure levels. Federal assistance is an absolutely critical factor in housing and community development programs. The importance of the federal funds can be seen in the ARRA program that used state and local governments to provide "shovel ready" projects that could be put into effect quickly and would result either in new employment or retention of state and local workers. Significant increases in housing and development funding was an integral part of the Act.

Historically, federal assistance has been targeted for specific projects and purposes, a form of federal aid known as a "categorical" grant. Federal public housing subsidies are in this category. So were the original federal grants for local slum clearance and urban renewal programs. Federal categorical grants may require a local project application and federal project approval for each project that receives federal assistance.

Starting in the 1970s, Congress began enacting consolidated block grants which recipient local governments may use in their discretion for any of the purposes designated in the federal block grant legislation. Federal block grants are distributed to recipient governments usually under a statutory formula intended to target the grant to communities where it is most needed. As distinguished from the special purpose categorical grants, these block grants confer considerable autonomy on recipient governments in the use of grant funds. Advance federal approval of individual projects is not required. The federal agency usually approves a local program indicating how the block grant is to be used for the designated grant purposes. The federal block grant community development program, which replaced the original federal slum clearance and related programs and the subsequent Model Cities program, is an important example of a federal block grant. This program is described in the *Kansas City* case, *supra,* and is examined in Chapter 5 *infra.*

The following selection is from a major study of the federal financial assistance system. The author of the study, the Advisory Commission on Intergovernmental Relations (ACIR), was an influential quasi-governmental organization devoted to the study of intergovernmental relations and governmental fiscal problems. The study explains the nature of the different federal grants, the elements that enter into their design, and some of the conditions attached to federal grants to implement national policy objectives. It still provides a good description of the federal grant system and contains insights for the development of future grant and subsidy programs.

Advisory Commission on Intergovernmental Relations Categorical Grants: Their Role and Design

5–6, 31–33, 100–09, 246–47, 249–53 (1978)

A Typology of Federal Grants

Categorical grants can be used only for a specifically aided program and usually are limited to narrowly defined activities. Legislation generally details the parameters of the program and specifies the types of funded activities. However, in some cases ... the specific activities may be determined by administrators.

This study identifies four types of categorical grants: formula grants, project grants, formula-project grants (combining various aspects of both grant types), and open-end reimbursement grants. This classification is based chiefly on an analysis of the means of distributing the funds available to carry out approved activities and focuses on the degree to which the process fosters competition among potential recipients and vests discretion in federal administrators.

When grant funds are allocated among recipients according to factors specified within enabling legislation or administrative regulations, the grant is considered a formula grant. Project grants are non-formula in nature—potential recipients submit specific, individual applications in the form and at the times indicated by the grantor. The formula-project categorical grant uses a mixture of fund allocation means; distribution takes place in two stages—the first involves state area allocations governed by a statute or a regulation formula, and the second entails project applications and discretionary awards. Open-end reimbursement grants—often regarded as formula grants—are characterized by an arrangement wherein the federal government is committed to reimbursing a specified proportion of state-local program costs, thus eliminating competition among recipients as well as the need for an allocation formula.

[T]he block grant ... [is] a grant that is given chiefly to general purpose governmental units in accordance with a statutory formula for use, largely at the recipient's discretion, in a variety of activities within a broad functional area. Fundable activities are more numerous than for a categorical grant and fewer conditions constraining recipient's discretion in funds spending are attached. [Grants reflect] varying combinations of three characteristics:

1. *The range of federal administrator's funding discretion.* At one extreme no such discretion exists because grant funds are distributed by an entitlement formula with a legislative prescribed matching ratio. At the opposite extreme, the federal administrator has wide latitude in awarding project grants among many competing eligible recipients.

2. *The range of recipient discretion concerning aided activities.* Such discretion is ... most constrained in certain project grants, wherein the scope of permitted activities is narrowly specified, sometimes to a particular facility or experimental program.

3. *The type, number, detail, and scope of grant program conditions.* These conditions, such as planning, fiscal management, administrative organization, and performance standards requirements, determine the degree of federal intrusiveness in the recipient's conduct of the grant-aided activity.

The Nixon Administration, coming to power in 1969, moved forward in the search (initiated toward the end of the Johnson presidency) for alternatives to and improvements of the categorical grant system. Emphasis was placed on broader, more flexible grant forms.... Compromise block grants emerged from the Congress with programs established in the manpower field (1973), community development (1974), and social services (1974). These were added to the previous block grant programs for public health and criminal justice created in the 1960s. [Additional block grants were added early in the Reagan administration, and Congress also made substantial cuts in program funding. The use of the CDBG program as a primary conduit for providing funding for local jurisdictions continued through the administrations of Presidents, Bush (1), Clinton, Bush (2) and into the Obama administration—Eds.]

Commonly Used Allocation Factors

Special formulas vary from one program to another because of the varying types of activities covered. Yet definite patterns emerge when considering formula grants as a group. Some programs' formulas include the distribution of an equal amount of assistance for each eligible recipient in addition to any amounts allocated by factors that are designed to indicate program need.

[Some formulas provide] for an adjustment of the amounts derived for each state to guarantee a stated basic minimum entitlement. At the other end of the spectrum are programs that include a cap or maximum amount to be made available for grants in any eligible jurisdictions.

Congress has [also provided for grant reductions] if the grantee does not meet standards and conditions under other related but separate programs. For instance, amounts allocated to a state for specified major highways programs are to be reduced by amounts equal to 10% of what otherwise would be allotted if the state has not made provisions for the effective control of outdoor junkyards.

Population

The most commonly used formula clearly is population, either the total or that for some segment of the population....

Financial Need

This factor is based on the concept that income is a proxy measurement of a governmental unit's ability to raise revenues to pay for activities financed by a grant as well as for other governmental services. Where a distributional factor is a state's per capita income in relation to the national average per capita income, equalization is probably the reason for its inclusion. Use of the factor tends to equalize the tax burden directly arising from matching and other cost-sharing requirements. This factor also impacts indirectly on the financing of other activities, because those nonfederal funds that would have been spent on the aided activity in the absence of a federal grant program become available for other governmental activities. Thus equalization provisions help bring about a certain measure of income redistribution.

Although the personal income of residents of a state typically is used as the proxy indicator of fiscal capacity in a distribution formula, it is only a partial indicator of a state's fiscal capacity. It fails to reflect closely the potential of certain other revenue resources, such as severance taxes in states like Louisiana, New Mexico, Texas, and Wyoming; motor fuel taxes in tourist-oriented states like Maine and Vermont; or gambling taxes in Nevada.

Program Need

Besides fiscal equalization, an income factor sometimes is used to indicate program need, especially when income directly pertains to the group benefiting from the aid. Generally when the income factor is used in a formula to help describe a segment of the population (e.g., number living in poverty, number of children aged three to 17 in families with incomes below a certain level), it should be considered as an indicator of program need rather than as a device for fiscal equalization.

Formula factors other than population or income sometimes are considered as indicators of program need. For some programs pinpointing is possible for those statistical indicators that are related directly to the volume and distribution of the service needed. The distribution formula for the state boating safety program, for instance, provides that one-third of the funds are allocated among the states according to the number of vessels registered in each state. For this formula approach to be effective, clear understanding is required concerning the program objectives and a selection of data most relevant to these objectives.

Project Grants: The Nonformula Approach

This chapter has dealt with formula grants, including project grants that are subject to formula distributions to determine state-area amounts. This section examines some basic features of the main body of project grants—nonformula grants for which potential recipients submit specific, individual applications in the form and at the times indicated by the grantor agency and which are not subject to state-area formula distributions.

Project grants, as a group, have extended the types of activities for which state and local governments receive financial aid from the federal government. Early grants were mainly formula grants for a limited range of activities, such as highways, agricultural enhancements and agricultural extension work. Even during the 1930s when many additional federal aid programs were enacted, aid generally took the form of formula grants. Project grants are largely a recent phenomenon, gaining importance as a grant mechanism in the 1960s and continuing to do so in the 1970s.

The reasons for the sudden popularity of project grants in the 1960s were manifest and complex—a heightened concern over critical urban needs; the widespread view that state governments were constitutionally and philosophically unwilling or incapable of dealing with these needs; the difficulty of using the traditional state plan approach under formula grants to target on social problems at the community level; the absence of reliable substate allocation data; a growing interest in employing nongovernmental as well as governmental agencies as grant recipients; and the desire to stimulate innovative approaches to the solution of particular problems.

[The public housing program requires federal agency approval of individual local public housing projects. The federal legislation also includes a formula for the distribution of housing subsidies.—Eds.]

Competition for Grants

Formula-based grants minimize administrative discretion and grantsmanship, inasmuch as funds are distributed largely on the basis of a legal entitlement rather than administrative judgment and the relative ability of potential recipients to press their claims for funds. In general, formula-based grants tend to restrict competition while project grants tend to encourage competition among potential recipients. The degree of competition also may be constrained by the fund amounts available relative to the number of eligible potential recipients.

Nondiscrimination Requirements

[At this point, the ACIR Report discusses a number of conditions generally attached to all federal grants to implement a number of important national policy objectives. Chief among these conditions is the requirement of Title VI of the federal Civil Rights Act of 1964, which prohibits discrimination in federal financial assistance programs. This title, and related federal civil rights statutes, play an important role in housing and community development programs.—Eds.]

The most general set of nondiscrimination requirements attached to the grant system arises under Title VI of the *Civil Rights Act of 1964*, [as amended]. This title provides that "no person in the United States shall, on the ground of race, color, or national origin, be excluded from participation in, be denied the benefits of, or be subjected to discrimination under any program or activity receiving federal financial assistance." Although Title VI does not cover sex discrimination, that ban has been attached individually by Congress to a number of specific program statutes, and granting agencies generally have adopted Title VI enforcement procedures for this additional dimension of discrimination.

The *Civil Rights Act* [of 1964—Eds.] places responsibility on each federal agency to assure that its grant programs are subject to nondiscrimination regulations. Although voluntary compliance is emphasized, recalcitrant grantees are subject to termination of their grants and/or ineligibility for extensions or future funding.

Executive Order 11247, issued in 1965, gave the Attorney General responsibility for assisting agencies to coordinate their Title VI activities. This was superseded by Executive Order 11764 on January 21, 1974, when the Attorney General was given authority to prescribe Title VI procedures and to require federal granting agencies to act in accordance with them. Under this authority, the Attorney General has developed uniform provisions for (a) nondiscrimination in site selection, (b) affirmative action to compensate for past discrimination, and (c) equal employment opportunities under grant programs required to avoid discrimination in resulting facilities and services.

Notes and Questions

1. Just as further devolution of responsibility for program administration from federal to state and local governments started to accelerate, ACIR was dismantled. The ACIR closed in April 1996. The University of North Texas Libraries and the Government Printing Office, in a Federal Depository Library Program partnership, established a web site to provide permanent public access to the electronic publications that were available on the World Wide Web site of the Advisory Commission on Intergovernmental Relations when the agency closed. *See* http://www.library.unt.edu/gpo/acir/acir.html (last visited Feb. 12, 2010).

2. The large number and variety of federal grants has created problems of coordination at state, regional, and local government levels. Lines of authority in federal grant programs are vertical. Continuing relationships are established between the federal grant agency and its recipient agency at a lower governmental level. Measures for coordinating federal grant programs at state, regional, and local levels are practically nonexistent in state legislation. The federal government remedied this deficiency by initiating administrative procedures through the Office of Management and Budget circulars that required federal agencies to ensure the review and coordination of federal grant programs by state and regional agencies.

3. For a critique differentiating between federal categorical programs and single block grants, see Duane A. Martin, *The President and the Cities: Clinton's Urban Aid Agenda*, 26 URB. LAW. 99 (1994).

4. Categorical programs, such as the original federal urban renewal program, often delegate substantial discretion to the federal agency to review local projects. The following excerpt, which describes the plan which was required for federally assisted urban renewal projects, indicates the level of detail at which federal review operated.

> When the LPA [Local Public Agency] is ready with a plan, it then submits to HUD the Final Project Report, Part I of the Application for Loan and Grant. This is a most elaborate submission. It contains the proposed Urban Renewal Plan and supporting documentation in great detail—for example, project boundaries, designation and description of buildings to be cleared or rehabilitated, plan objectives, reuse intentions and controls, relocation arrangements, acquisition cost and disposal price estimates, and the city's anticipated non-cash grants-in-aid. It must also contain a report on "minority group considerations." With this application, the LPA solicits HUD's tentative approval of the project pending ratification of the plan by the local governing body and submission of the Part 11 application. In reviewing the Final Project Report, HUD will often issue comments detailing the revisions necessary to achieve an acceptable plan

Curtis J. Berger & Joel T. Cogen, *Responsive Urban Renewal: The Neighborhood Shapes the Plan*, 1968 URB. L. ANN. 75, 85.

In theory, all of the substantive issues covered by the urban renewal plan are now determined by local governments undertaking activities equivalent to those under urban renewal projects, by using the community development block grant program. The extent to which HUD and Congress have acquiesced in this program to the delegation of local policy-making authority is considered in Chapter 5 *infra*. For a review of block grant programs, see PAUL E. PETERSON, BARRY RABE & KENNETH WONG, WHEN FEDERALISM WORKS (1986).

5. Curiously, in the 1998 Act, HUD has been allocated a somewhat more limited policy-making authority in the public housing program, although the public housing subsidy is categorical. Local administrative responsibility in this program is delegated to a state-created, locally, independently organized Public Housing Authority (PHA). The municipality in which the PHA is organized also has some voice over program operations. It can exercise some control, for example, through the cooperation agreement it is required by federal law to execute with the PHA covering zoning, municipal services, and the like. In limited circumstances, it can request of HUD that the City take over directly management of the Low Rent Public Housing program. *See* Quality Housing and Work Responsibility Act of 1998, Pub. L. No. 105-276, § 561, 112 Stat. 2616 (1998) (*amending* the Housing Act of 1937, by adding a new Title IV—Home Rule Flexible Grant Demonstration, codified at various sections of 42 U.S.C).

The following excerpt indicates the role played in this program by HUD, the federal agency, the PHA, and the municipality:

> The program created by the 1937 Housing Act was built on a local-federal arrangement from which the state was virtually excluded once enabling legislation was passed. Over time, Congress tended to concentrate on four basic areas of housing policy, leaving most other matters for administrative decision: first, the amount of housing authorized for addition to the public housing stock; second the cost of developing the facilities; third, the fiscal arrangements that controlled program operations; fourth, the conditions of tenancy. Federal administrators exercised a great deal of control over the program through budgetary oversight allocating resources for new development, auditing, and monitoring everyday operations. Local governments could influence the program in their areas through the formal cooperative agreement required by statute and, less formally, through appointment of the governing body that directed the program. In practice, local governments had veto power over certain critical aspects of development, notably the size, location, design, and staffing of the facilities. The local housing authority under the overall direction of the governing body had a voice in site selection choice of architect, design, and so on; it also controlled such aspects of daily operations as tenant selection, maintenance and repairs, legal actions against tenants, staffing, and general administration. Until the 1970s, the LHAs [now PHAs—Eds.] were given wide latitude in operations by the federal Administration; central control over details of day-to-day operations increased substantially after 1969. [With the advent of HUD's Asset Management (*See* Implementation of the Final Rule to the Public Housing Operating Fund Program, 24 C.F.R. Pt. 990; PIH Notice 2005-34 (Nov. 2, 2005)] PHAs were to transfer most of the decision-making and operational activities from a centralized office at the PHA to the managers of individual buildings or project areas within the PHA housing stock. Thus, considerable management responsibility was transferred back to those responsible for operations in each building or complex, modeling these efforts on the Federal Housing Administration model for operation of its funded housing units.—Eds.]

> There were two curious lacunae in the development policies generated within the federal government: first, little effort was made to control the quality of the housing produced; second, the cost of the site was not limited by any of the statutes. The 1937 Housing Act placed a ceiling on the overall cost of each dwelling unit and on the cost per room; established limits could be adjusted upward 25 percent in "high construction cost" areas—usually the larger cities where powerful construction unions operated. In 1949, limits on overall cost per unit were eliminated leaving cost per room as the sole criterion available for controlling development cost. Since room cost limits were included in the legislation, they applied to the country as a whole. In 1970, Congress adopted a "prototype" cost base for dwelling units of various sizes and types of construction and HUD was charged with establishing suitable limits and revising them annually. Again, the limits could be exceeded by 10 percent without waiver and by another 10 percent with federal approval. Land costs remained uncontrolled and no qualitative construction controls were specified in the statutes.
>
> The effect of weak control over development costs and construction quality is readily foreseen. Site costs were often unconscionable, particularly in the 1950s when the rate of development was high and projects were deliberately located in cleared slum areas—and forced to absorb clearing costs. In the long run, the economic inefficiencies generated by land speculation were probably less important than the common practice of paying premium prices for apartments so shoddily built that a choir of angels could not have resided in them regularly without producing serious disrepair. Poor quality cannot be ascribed to federal miserliness. In St. Louis, the Housing Authority paid for its projects at costs equal to or greater than the cost of luxury housing in the suburbs. It did not receive value for money from the housing industry.

EUGENE J. MEEHAN, THE QUALITY OF FEDERAL POLICY MAKING 20–22 (1979).

6. For more information on the current direction of HUD's public housing program, HUD's proposed 2011 Budget provides some guidance. Released February 1, 2010, it announces HUD's proposal to make a potentially fundamental change in its existing public housing program. The Budget "proposes long term fundamental reforms including launching a new initiative called Transforming Rental Assistance (TRA) to bring HUD's twentieth century rental assistance programs into the twenty first century. TRA will preserve public housing by enabling its owners to address the current and future capital needs of their properties, especially by leveraging private capital, provide more choice to residents and begin to streamline the thirteen separate rental assistance programs run by HUD." The Proposed Budget of HUD identifies $350 million for this purpose. See HUD Press Release, No. 10-026, Feb. 1, 2010, For further discussion of issues raised by TRA see Chapter 3 *infra*.

7. Determining criteria to reflect city needs in formula grant programs is not an easy task. Recall the discussion of inner city decline in Chapter 1. It can be argued that the continuing decline of older cities reflects long-term structural trends in the economy which may be irreversible:

> Many of America's cities grew and became prosperous as a result of the industrial revolution, but changes in the technologies or production, transportation, and communication, as well as changes in real income and consumer tastes, have made many older cities less desirable locations for businesses or residences. Certain characteristics of cities that were once important determinants of business

> location—for example, access to rail or port facilities—are either less important, or like high density, are now a liability. As a result of these changes, economic activity has decentralized in two ways. Initially economic growth and development shifted outward to undeveloped fringe—now suburban—locations. More recently a regional shift has occurred: growth rates in the South and in the West exceed those in the northeast and north central regions.

Report, *City Need and the Responsiveness of Federal Grants Programs, Subcomm. of the City of the House Comm. on Banking, Finance and Urban Affairs*, 95th Cong., 1st Sess. 5 (1978).

This congressional report identified social, economic, and fiscal factors that could identify urban need and provide a basis for the distribution of federal financial assistance to cities. As measured by these indicators, the report found that federal grants are generally responsive to city needs. Is there an argument that the structural economic changes identified in the report argue for less emphasis on federal programs directed to distressed cities or federally assisted housing to be located in these cities? What other factors should be considered in developing a formula grant for distressed cities, such as housing abandonment, substandard housing, and the extent of substandard housing areas? What weight should be given to each of these factors?

8. While HUD's authority is still limited and local flexibility has now become an important matter, the 1998 legislation expand HUD's powers in dealing with PHAs that are in "substantial default" of obligations or otherwise are designated as "troubled." *See* Quality Housing and Work Responsibility Act of 1998, Pub. L. No. 105-276, § 565, 112 Stat. 2628 (*codified at* 42 U.S.C. § 1437d(j)(3)) and Pub. L. No. 105-276, § 568, 112 Stat. 2628, 2634 (*codified at* 42 U.S.C. § 12705).

2. Intergovernmental Relationships

Federal housing and community development programs are unusual in federal assistance programs because federal assistance goes directly to the recipient local government authority. The state role is mostly passive, although the state must authorize local participation in the federal public housing program through enabling legislation. The need for state legislative authority is especially critical in these programs because they rely heavily on specially created local authorities to implement federal program objectives at the local level. The local public housing authority illustrates a special authority created to administer public housing programs. Urban renewal programs were usually administered either by the PHA or by a separately created urban renewal authority. The emphasis on special purpose authorities, however, changed somewhat in the 1970s with first the Model Cities program and then with its successor the Community Development Block Grant program. Policies changed to provide funds and authority to municipal and county governments for major population centers.

Initially, there were a number of reasons for creating independent local authorities to administer federal assistance programs, and fiscal reasons were prominent among them. Local housing and urban renewal projects require the issuance of local bonded debt to finance these projects. Local housing authorities, for example, must issue bonds to finance the construction of low-income housing. Cities in many states have very low debt limits and may not be able to issue bonds to cover these projects. The independent public housing and urban renewal authorities created by statute at the local level were given bonding authority sufficient to cover the projects they carried out. To the extent the subsequent block grant program emphasized grants, this problem was avoided.

There were several consequences of this tendency to create independent local authorities to carry out federally assisted housing and community development programs. In most states, these authorities have a territorial jurisdiction coterminous with the boundaries of the city that creates them. This limitation means, for example, that public housing authorities may only build projects within the city or county limits where they are sited, a limitation that affects the ability of this program to disperse lower-income families to suburban areas.

Another result of the independent authority strategy was to fragment political responsibility for federally assisted programs at the local level. This fragmentation of authority has several consequences. Often political responsibility for local public housing and renewal projects is outside the control of the elected mayor and city council. Coordination is another problem. Local public housing authorities, for example, may build and manage public housing projects but they need the assistance of the municipality to make their projects possible. City action on local zoning is one illustration. In some communities, city council opposition to public housing projects has frustrated local housing authority programs.

In public housing, the federal agency had always delegated considerable decision-making authority to public housing authorities. This delegation of federal authority was not impeded by state enabling legislation for public housing programs. Most state legislation contains very little in the way of substantive requirements that affect the management of public housing projects. Local authorities remain relatively free to determine tenant selection and other policies that affect project management.

Thus, the community development program represented an attempt to return political authority over program planning and administration to the elected council and city executive. This program places political responsibility for program planning on the mayor and council. Along with the elimination of highly specific federal controls on program planning, the community development program provides a substantial delegation of autonomy for program direction to the local political process.

Notes and Questions

1. Can you articulate some of the policies that the current admixture of federal-state-local responsibilities in housing and community development serves? Why did that become the prevailing model for the pursuit of housing and community development goals? Are there trade-offs here? Can you list some?

The following Table of Federal Housing and Development Programs provides a structured basis for examining the relative roles of federal, state, and local governments and that of the private sector with regard to the provision of governmentally subsidized housing and development programs.

Table of Governmental Housing and Development Programs*

	Subsidize Public or Private Owners	Make Direct Loans	Guarantee Loans	Secondary Mortgage Purchase	Own and Manage Housing	Tax Subsidies	Land Use Requirements
Federal Government	•Sec. 235: Home Ownership Interest Subsidy (Inactive) •Sec. 221(d)(3) and Sec. 236: Multifamily Assistance (Inactive but subject to LIHPRHA) •Sec. 8: Subsidize Rentals. New construction and substantial rehab (inactive). Existing Sec. 8 still active •Low Rent Public Housing and HOPE VI: Pay debt service, operating and modernization expenses and capital grants to local housing authorities •HOME: Make funds available to state or localities to subsidize single or multifamily owners •CDBG funds for rehab; Special CDBG funds useable for new construction as well •McKinney Act: Grants to localities to provide for homeless •Deduction of costs of land assembly and write down of acquisition costs to private developers under former Urban Renewal and current CDBG programs •Grants to First Time Homebuyers •Sometimes waive mortgage insurance requirements •Neighborhood Stabilization Program grants & technical assist.	•HUD: Section 202 (Elderly) and Section 811 (handicapped); converted to grant program in 1990 •FmHA: Section 502 (Single Family); •Section 515 (Rental)	•HUD FHA: •203 (Single) •234 (Condominium) • 213 (Cooperative) • 207 (Multifamily) •220 (Multifamily) •221 (Multifamily) •Lower interest and reduced down payment Veterans Administration loans and mortgages	•Federal National Mortgage Association (Fannie Mae) •Federal Home Loan Mortgage Corporation (Freddie Mac) •GNMA subsidized purchases under Tandem Plan •GNMA Mortgage Backed Securities	•Owned and managed "war housing" during WWII. Projects sold after war mainly to PHAs •DOD presently owns and manages housing for military families	•Deduction of mortgage interest, points, and state property taxes for taxpayers who itemize •Low Income Housing Tax Credit (LIHTC), including exchange program enacted as part of stimulus bill •Deductions for Second Homes •Deduction from income from vacation homes primarily leased out for all but two weeks •$8,000 Tax Credit for limited periods available to first-time homebuyers •Like-kind exchanges to delay tax on gains available for multi-family affordable housing •The income for Housing costs for ministers not subject to federal income tax	•Provide surplus federal property not subject to state land use restrictions, and write-down value

State Governments	•3 states had public housing programs. Now states subsidize owners through HOME Funds or state funds.	•State Housing Finance Agencies issue bonds to finance single and multi-family rental housing. •Housing Trust Funds	•Several states have mortgage insuring agencies.	•Several states and some counties in them have mortgage purchase assistance or loans to lenders programs.	•Create state entities authorized to own and manage low rent public housing.	•State Tax Credit Programs (i.e., California and Missouri) to complement federal programs.	•Provide Zoning categories allowing for lowering requirements and costs for affordable housing.
Local Government	•Utilize HOME funds or local funds to subsidize rentals and homeowners. •Grants to non-profit developers for construction or rehab of affordable housing.	•Local housing finance agencies, similar to state. •Housing Trust Funds			•Low Rent Public Housing: roughly 3,000 PHAs own and manage over 1,000,000 public housing units.	•Tax abatement for low income projects. •Reduced "Payments in Lieu of Taxes" for city services for PHAs. •Tax Increment Financing	• Inclusionary Zoning bonuses and set asides, both mandated and negotiated.
Private Entities such as Lenders, Insurers, Developers, and Syndicators		•Loans to developers of tax credit projects and homeowners; some loans insured by HUD-FHA or VA; lenders sell loans to FNMA, Freddie Mac and private conduits.	•Private mortgage insurance companies insure loans.	•Private secondary market by issuers of mortgage backed securities. (Unwise purchase of unsound mortgages led to our current recession.)	•Provide subsidized mortgages and write downs for housing for university employees, e.g. Stanford Univ.	•Lender provides debt financing for LIHTC projects; syndicator raises equity from investors.	
Private Sector	•Organize non-profit developers. •Develop affordable projects using grants, loans and set asides available to certain non-profit developers. •Own/manage Sec. 236, 221(d)(3), Sec. 8 and tax credit housing. Provide equity capital. •Own and manage LIHTC Projects.						

* This Index was adapted from a matrix of governmental housing programs created by Charles L. Edson, Adjunct Professor of Law, Georgetown University Law School, Co-Editor of the Housing Development Reporter, and a principal legal practitioner relating to federal housing programs. His original chart has been expanded with regard to the federal role in housing, and for purposes of this Chapter to cover federal development programs as well.

Notes and Questions

1. An interesting cross-cutting analysis can be made for the rationale for the various housing assistance programs listed in the Table. Can you identify the political, budget, and effectiveness of the various programs listed? Consider the interests of the various actors and governmental levels involved and how each is affected, both financially and politically. Note the interrelationships between tax policy as a form of housing subsidy (the largest of all housing subsidies provided by the federal government and affecting the most beneficiaries) and the influence of such values as homeownership in our society. Are there considerations regarding the beneficiaries of these programs that may influence the federal support for them? Few lower income persons benefit from these tax reduction policies. Similarly, consider the recent housing credit subsidy provided as a stimulus. Who benefits from the $8,000 and $6,500 credits that were provided? Were there other values to the economy?

2. What advantages do states enjoy when they provide supplements to federal programs, such as add-ons to the federal HOME program. Is it relevant that the HOME program, while funded federally in large part, is actually administered by local governments? What advantages does this have? When funding for specific projects are provided, often all levels of government attend the ceremony. Are there political dimensions regarding which projects are funded and who may claim credit for accomplishing them? How important is it as to which income levels benefit from these projects? On the other hand, when housing programs cause problems or corruption has occurred, which governmental level is likely to be blamed?

3. What is the significance of the role that state housing finance agencies play in providing financial support for housing projects? If it is duplicative of federal efforts, how does their role differ from that of the federal participants? Is there potential for excessive use of governmental subsidies? Which governmental level should be responsible for controlling potential excesses? Is the availability of state bonding authority relevant? What is the role that investments in state government bonds can play? For instance, what is the significance of avoidance of state taxes when investing in state securities? Avoidance of federal taxes on income from state investments is also possible. What is the significance of these considerations? What problems can arise?

4. One of the new initiatives of both the federal and state governments is the concept of Housing Trust Funds. These are described in some detail in Chapter 3. The design of these programs cuts across governmental lines and involves various levels of government. What advantages does this have? How are the policy objectives of the Trust Fund concept of interest to each involved level of government?

5. Note that local governments almost always run public housing programs, both Low Income Rent and Section 8 Voucher programs. What considerations may have encouraged Congress to get local governments involved in administering these programs?

6. How do zoning laws, both state and local, impact decisions where to site housing projects and who benefits from those decisions? What are the various interests of the different actors: private developers, and other residents, local, state, and federal officials, including both appointed and elected officials?

7. What are the interrelationships between governmental levels that can be observed in the various programs? What values are at work? To what extent do the programs utilize the different competencies through the assignment of roles to the various governmental levels? Often the more effective taxing and generation of revenues for operation

of government and government programs at the federal level are cited to justify the federal role. What are the state interests and how do they relate to effectuating the federal program objectives. Which of these programs are likely to attract continuing support from Congress for the budgeting of program funds. Who are likely to be the beneficiaries of various programs? For instance, who is most likely to benefit from federal tax subsidies through the deductibility from income that are provided for mortgage interest and state and local government property taxes?

8. What are the administrative costs of providing the various housing and development assistance funds? Which approaches are likely to be the most efficient? Often, the relative minimal cost of providing social security assistance is cited as one of the most efficient distribution approaches for federal assistance. How do the other various housing assistance programs match up? That there are considerations regarding costs of administration is clear by the CDBG statute that sets a 10% cost limit for program administration costs. In addition, the later reference in this chapter to OMB Circulars clearly relates to the interest of the federal funders to ensuring efficient administration and thereby getting most of the funds to the intended beneficiaries, rather than the local government administrators. What interest do the states have in deductibility of their taxes by homeowners? Does it make such costs more palatable? Do states benefit when their taxes are deductible from federal taxes? Funding for state and local governments are frequently reliant on property taxes. Some commentators have noted that California's Proposition 13 a number of years ago, which limited those real estate taxes, has significantly exacerbated California and its local jurisdiction's current financial distress.

A Note on Creating and Resolving Conflicts Arising out of the Delivery Structure of Federal Housing and Development Programs

The second section of this chapter considers the legislative, administrative, and judicial process under which the intergovernmental relationships operate as well as, the processes through which conflicts between various levels of government, private sector participants, and the ultimate beneficiaries of these programs have been resolved. Thus, this chapter initially examined the roles of the various actors in federal assistance programs and the structure of the delivery system through which they are provided. Now the focus moves to the manner by which federal policies for housing and development are formulated, implemented, and controlled. This is accomplished by reviewing the legislative, administrative, and judicial processes through which federal housing and development programs are adopted, implemented, and conflicts resolved. In doing so, the objective is to understand how we maintain a proper balance among the interests of the different entities that are involved in the system, and to discern some of the ways in which these processes influence basic housing and development policies.

More specifically, we look at the procedure for congressional enactment of housing policy and how it may affect the programs that Congress enacts. We also explore the administrative and monitoring role of the primary federal department that carries out housing policy—the U.S. Department of Housing and Urban Development (HUD)—as another dimension in policy implementation. This also includes the role that the HUD Office of Inspector General plays in its monitoring of federal program expenditures. Other federal agencies also have housing-related roles. These include the Treasury Department (which administers the tax code), the Department of Agriculture (which administers farm and rural housing programs), the Justice Department (which administers certain fair housing provisions) and prosecutes criminal actions arising from abuses of the program funds, and the Departments of Veterans' Affairs and Defense (which administer certain housing-related responsibilities for military personnel, their dependents, and veterans).

Courts play a role in implementing federal housing programs when they determine constitutional and legislative rights for claims involving housing. Thus, the second part of this chapter examines the extent to which federal housing programs provide opportunities to recipients of federal funds and program beneficiaries to assert their rights and make claims arising under these programs against the agencies that administer housing and community development programs. The emphasis in this chapter is on access to the courts—mostly federal—to assert claims. Later chapters examine particular programs in more detail, and judicial access and judicial review available in specific program settings and consider in more detail the role of the courts in implementing constitutional guarantees of fairness and due process in the administration of housing programs.

B. The Legislative, Administrative, and Judicial Process

1. The Legislative Process

The Committee Structure of Congress and Applicable Procedures. The legislative process begins, of course, in the congressional committees. In one sense it starts with the President's proposed budget which is released shortly after his State of the Union speech. Technically, the President's Proposed Budget is sent to Congress for its consideration. In fact, the relevant committees in both houses have been working on their own versions well before then. Both the Senate and the House of Representatives have authorizing committees that consider substantive policies related to HUD-administered housing and development programs. In the Senate, it is the Banking, Housing and Urban Affairs Committee. Its counterpart in the House is the Financial Services Committee. Each of these committees has a subcommittee responsible for housing and community development authorizing legislation. In the House, the subcommittee is Housing and Community Opportunity; in the Senate, the subcommittee is Housing, Transportation, and Community Development.

At the same time, both houses have Appropriations Committees that determine the funding that will be available for these programs. In the Senate, the sub-committee is Transportation, Housing and Urban Development, and Related Agencies. In the House, the subcommittee is also Transportation, Housing and Urban Development, and Related Agencies. In the end, unless appropriations are provided for a program, it rarely has any significance, so that obtaining appropriations for any program is ultimately the critical element.

Some legislation affecting HUD programs does not originate in these committees or subcommittees. Fair housing legislation, for example, usually originates in the Senate and House Judiciary Committees. Similarly, for example, housing policies carried out through the tax code originate in the House Ways and Means Committee and the Senate Finance Committee.

The legislative process is initiated by proposed bills. Usually a bill will be introduced by one or more members containing the President's proposed housing and development programs and another bill will be produced for the related appropriations for it. These measures are then subjected to hearings and are acted upon in committee proceedings that consider various pending housing and community development bills. A "markup" session is held for the bill that the committee has determined (usually by the Chair of the committee or subcommittee) will be voted on and sent to the house for its consideration after a majority vote of the committee. Proposed bills other than those requested by the Administration, can also emanate from individual committee members or from even outside interest groups who have obtained a member to sponsor it.

Generally, Congress will consider one or more housing bills each session, but it does not necessarily enact any. Often bills enacted contain only minor amendments or reauthorizations for existing programs. But, Congress from time to time considers and enacts legislation containing major new programs. As a result of the sub-prime market scandals leading to foreclosures and various financial problems experienced in 2008 and 2009, a number of bills were introduced on these issues and a number of them were enacted, such as the various programs and topics handled in the 2008 Housing And Economic Recovery Act, (HERA).

Hearings in sub-committees are followed by publication of sub-committee reports to accompany the bill for consideration of the full committee. The full committee then reports out approved bills for which committee reports are provided and both go to the full house which considers and votes on them. Conference Committees resolve differences that arise between the two chambers by fashioning an amended bill and a Conference Committee Report to the respective houses. In some instances, rather than use a conference committee, one house may decide simply to adopt the bill from the other house so that both houses have approved the same language and then the bill is sent to the President. Otherwise, each house will enact an identical Conference version and the bill is presented for presidential signature. Congress has taken an increasingly active role in the legislative development of housing and community development policy.

It is typical in the congressional legislative process, in both houses, that key senators and representatives have dominating influence. Frequently the most influential persons chair the full committee or the relevant subcommittee; in part this is because committee leadership almost always determine the actions of a committee. The process for housing and community development legislation is not fundamentally different. A strong congressional personality may also dominate and even carry major legislative proposals through the Congress. A strong senator, for example, can carry a subcommittee, the committee, and the entire Senate. If that key person is a member of the Conference Committee on a disputed bill, that person can often carry the day against the objections of the other chamber. There are other actors in the congressional process. The HUD Secretary usually speaks for the Administration and supports passage through its views. Interest groups of all kinds make themselves heard.

The Congressional Development of Tenant-Based Public Housing Subsidies

The previous chapter introduced the federal public housing program and noted the nature of its origins. Chapter 3 *infra* considers the details of this program (including many ways the provisions discussed below have been changed), but the following description is used here to illustrate the congressional process through which housing programs are formulated.

The federal subsidy structure for public housing was initially quite simple. This subsidy paid the principal and interest on federally guaranteed and locally-issued debt obligations. Proceeds of these obligations were used by the local entities to finance the construction of local public housing developments. Tenant rents covered operating expenses and a payment in lieu of local property taxes, since federal public housing projects are exempt from taxes of the local government.

This subsidy mechanism worked well from the 1930s until the 1960s, when increases in local operating costs forced rent increases. Since the incomes of public housing tenants did not increase comparatively, public housing rents as a proportion of income often rose to very high levels. Congress responded to local public housing rent increases in 1969 by enacting a limitation on public housing rents introduced as an amendment to the Housing Act of 1969 by then Senator Edward Brooke of Massachusetts. Brooke's amendment limited public housing rents to 25% of tenant income. While a percentage limit is still in the statute, it has been increased to limit tenants to pay 30% of their income after certain mandated adjustments for calculation of their income.

The Brooke Amendment naturally created operating deficits for local public housing authorities whose income could not cover escalating operating costs, especially when rental income is limited to a percentage of a very low income family's income. To meet these deficits, a new subsidy for operating expenses was created. The following excerpt outlines the congressional and political process through which the operating subsidy portion of the Brooke Amendment was enacted and conveys an idea of how Congress makes housing policy. The technical features of these statutory changes are less important than the process through which they were adopted and the roles of the different actors in that process.

Daniel R. Mandelker, Housing Subsidies in the United States and England

84–85, 88–91 (1973)

When Senator Edward Brooke of Massachusetts was first elected to the Senate in 1966, and assigned to the subcommittee of the Senate ... Committee that has jurisdiction over housing matters, he did not show a strong interest in the housing field. Events, however, conspired to motivate his interest, and to catapult him into a leadership position on housing, and especially on public housing legislation.

Brooke had gone on a routine tour of his state early in 1969, and returned from visits to local public housing projects shocked by what he had seen; maintenance was bad, and recreational facilities were nonexistent. His impressions from this tour led Brooke to question the federal financial base for the public housing program, and these impressions were reinforced by another development of national importance the first successful rent strike in a public housing project in St. Louis, Missouri. In the notorious and ill-fated Pruitt-Igoe public housing project, a series of high-rise structures had been increasingly abandoned and vandalized by their tenants. In spite of the deteriorating condition of its buildings, however, rents in this project had risen dramatically; welfare tenants were paying sixty to seventy-five percent of their grant for rent. Low welfare budgets in Missouri contributed to this high rent/income ratio but the tenants found it easier to strike the public housing agency for lower rents than to strike the welfare agency for higher grants.

The Pruitt-Igoe strike ended successfully in 1969 with substantial changes in management of the St. Louis public housing agency. But the management and financial problems exposed by the strike led the only black congressman from St. Louis to approach HUD for financial assistance for St. Louis and other stricken public housing programs. HUD, the federal Department of Housing and Urban Development, was the agency then responsible for the public housing program at the national level. As HUD was cool to St. Louis' pleas for more financial help, the St. Louis group decided to act legislatively.

All of these problems in St. Louis surfaced just at the time the Housing Act of 1969 was making its way through Congress, an act which contained the usual group of annual technical and other minor modifications to the national housing legislation. Senator Brooke was persuaded to draft an amendment to the 1969 act that would provide the financial assistance which the St. Louis and similar situations elsewhere seemed to require. He was influential enough with his committee to have the amendment attached to the housing act when it was reported to the Senate floor. It was changed substantially, however, before it was finally enacted.

Brooke's Amendment was quickly drafted, and he did not attempt to deal systematically with the complex system of federal subsidies and local public housing rents.... Instead, he simply added a new section to the federal public housing title which covered both the problem of excessive rents and additional federal subsidies.

Sponsors of the Brooke Amendment were aware of the limitations of the Amendment, and also of the fact that intensive lobbying before Congress was necessary if its enactment was to be assured. Brooke himself was a Republican, but party affiliation did not prevent leading figures in the national housing Department of a Republican administration from opposing him. Opposition inside HUD was led by [the] then General Counsel to the agency, and [the] then assistant secretary for housing assistance. [The General Counsel] had had no previous housing experience, but [the Assistant Secretary] had been housing and renewal director in Norfolk, Virginia. Just what the opposition of HUD officials to Brooke's Amendment was based on is not clear. Supposedly, [they] were worried about the effect that operating subsidies would have on local public housing agencies, and also about lax management and improper tenant selection practices at the local agency level. They were also concerned that making operating subsidies available to local public housing agencies would aggravate and not improve these problems. Some would also argue that [they] were simply hostile to the public housing program, deplored the change in tenants which came about when large numbers of welfare recipients were admitted, and wished to avoid any step which would increase the number of so-called problem families in the projects. The Senate Report, in commenting on Brooke's Amendment, had indicated that the amendment was intended to apply to "all families who otherwise ... would be barred from public housing because their income was inadequate." A large family needing a four or five bedroom unit was cited as an example, apparently on the basis that large families often find themselves with inadequate resources for decent housing.

As a result of HUD opposition, behind-the-scenes pressure was put on the congressional committees to make substantial changes in the Brooke proposal. This conflict, though not reflected in the written record, was a critical influence in determining the final shape of the new subsidy. Indeed, differences between the Senate and House of Representatives version of the Brooke Amendment were one factor which finally sent the entire 1969 housing act to a Conference Committee. What finally emerged was a compromise which included substantial changes in the Brooke Amendment.

[M]ajor surgery was carried out on those provisions of the Brooke Amendment which had specifically authorized additional public housing subsidies.... [T]he new [separate] appropriation for an operating subsidy which had been authorized by Brooke's Amendment was transferred to and made a part of the budget item from which all annual contributions to local public housing agencies are paid, and the language explaining the purposes for which the operating subsidy was to be used was deleted from the bill. Instead, the report of the Conference Committee which handled the 1969 housing act explained in detail the purposes for which the new subsidy could be used. This explanation was inserted into the Conference Committee report at the insistence of HUD officials who had opposed the Brooke Amendment initially, and became the basis for the HUD regulations under which the subsidy was ultimately distributed.

Notes and Questions

1. Implementation of virtually all housing legislation calls for the expenditure of money, but the enactment of legislation like the Brooke Amendment does not necessarily mean that the money will be forthcoming. The Brooke Amendment, like most substantive legislation directing the expenditure of federal funds for housing programs, was interpreted to be an authorization. An authorization states the federal authority to make an expenditure of funds, sets forth the requirements for distribution of funds, and may set a ceiling on the amount that can be spent during a given time period. It does not actually appropriate any funds to be expended or direct the appropriation of funds. Only an appropriation can do that.

Appropriations are the province of the Senate and House appropriations committees, and specific subcommittees in each house for HUD appropriations as noted above. These appropriation committees may or may not agree with programs adopted by Congress and authorized in substantive legislation. Since Congress processes the federal budget annually, it has periodic opportunities to review federal spending priorities. At times, moreover, the appropriations committees can reflect different priorities than their counterpart substantive housing committees. Programs authorized by a housing act may not be funded or may be funded at lower levels or with restrictions that change their substantive content. The effect of deficit reduction efforts such as the Gramm-Rudman-Hollings Act (Balanced Budget and Emergency Deficit Control Act of 1985, 2 U.S.C. §§ 901–922) have increased the negative role on the availability and extent of funding for operational programs played by appropriations committees. Each house also has a budget committee whose actions can also impact the extent of funds generally available for Congress to spend.

2. Appropriations committees may also attach substantive restrictions to federal programs through appropriation act language. This technique provides a somewhat covert method for changing the substantive content of federal legislation, including housing legislation. In recent years, for example, housing appropriation bills have made significant changes in the allocation of funds for the numerous federal housing programs.

In 1998, Congress procrastinated on enacting a good deal of the legislation then pending and towards the end of the term, heading into the November elections, the Republican-dominated Congress had limited time to consider all pending legislation. In that there was substantial agreement on a new housing act on the part of Congress, HUD, and relevant interest groups representing actors in the housing and development industry, but only limited time remaining in the Congressional term, the entire 1998 Housing Act was at the last minute incorporated in the pending HUD appropriations measure that was sure to be enacted before Congress adjourned. For only the second time in decades, authorization and appropriation measures were incorporated in the same legislation.

A Note on Complexities in the Appropriations and Legislative Process

The Appropriations Process

In 1974, Congress substantially revised the formal appropriations process which had been last overhauled in 1921. The basic elements of that process are still followed to this date. Full adherence to the dates by which action was to be accomplished, however, have not been uniformly observed. That revision set out procedures to be used in adopting both the national budget and the individualized appropriation measures which make it up. The procedure specified that a concurrent budget resolution for the upcoming fiscal year (starting on October first of each year) was to be adopted by the full Congress by April 15th. This was to give the various appropriations and substantive committees some target dates and procedures for the appropriations legislation to be considered and enacted for that year. In these procedures, Congress was responding to what was, up until then, the President's clear advantage in the battle to determine allocations to various agencies and the programs of those agencies. The President could mandate his policies and override Congressional priorities, through the threat and occasionally the use, of the veto.

That Presidential power was often justified on the basis that only the President could exercise an overall perspective on government expenditures. To offset Presidential power and to retain Congressional ability to allocate overall amounts available for the fiscal year, Congress set up a series of budget resolutions controlling expenditures and binding on the various committees within Congress. An initial budget resolution gives each area of the budget its targeted amount. A later budget reconciliation measure considers the final appropriations amount overall. The reconciliation may make reallocations of funds to balance the individualized programmatic interests of the several committees that considered appropriation measures for the various departments and agencies of the federal government (and the financial and regulatory programs the agencies administer). In the case of housing and development, this agency was HUD.

Disagreement on allocation of funds for various programs was so rampant in Congress in 1998, however, that for the first time since the 1974 legislation was implemented, neither an initial nor a reconciliation resolution was ever enacted. Only the need to come up with budget measures before elections to avoid criticism of the lack of action by a Republican-controlled Congress (as occurred when Congress delayed passing appropriation measures in 1995), forced Congress finally to act. In some instances, separate bills were merged in order to get all agencies of government funded so that government would not close down. One approach to solving the need for detailed provisions under such circumstances has been the use of "continuing resolutions" that allow agencies to continue to expend funds consistent with amounts used the prior year. That procedure, however, does not allow for new initiatives. Further, given even limited inflationary factors, holding budgets static can result in a real loss of funding to the extent of inflation or for entities that are not annual recipients of funds. When this happens, Congress has failed to exercise its oversight responsibilities on effective use of federal financial resources through these agencies and the exercise of these policy functions.

The House Appropriation subcommittees, generally using thirteen separate bills for agencies within their jurisdiction, start the appropriations process. Once they complete action, and the House acts, the bills go to the Senate. If delays occur in the House, however, the Senate Appropriation subcommittees have at times initiated their own version of the appropriations legislation to avoid having to make last minute consideration of programs and activities when finally approved in the House.

During the decade of the 1990s, the various bills from each house have differed sufficiently to require reconciliation of programs and amounts appropriated through conference committee action. Thus, sequential appropriations legislation that could limit disagreements, is less of a consideration. It is in conference discussions that the resolution of differences usually occurs. While technically the conference committee is only to choose between one house's version or the other, increasingly the conference committees' product can significantly differ from either house's version as conferees come up with negotiated provisions to resolve differences between the measures in each house.

Other consequences occur because of the increased use of conference committees to resolve gross differences in policy. Once the conference committee reaches an agreement on the final version of the bill, it must be resubmitted to each house for its approval of this new version; identical versions are presented by the Conference Committee to each Chamber for approval. At times, moreover, little advance time is provided for most Members of Congress to brief themselves on the details, as legislation piles up towards the end of the term. This means that frequently only conference committee members are likely to have even seen the draft legislation before the vote is taken. At best, only one copy is provided for examination which is held in the Clerk's office. The impact of this limited knowledge of those who are voting on legislation on traditional concepts of legislative intent used for statutory interpretation have not been adequately considered to date.

Notes and Questions

1. Consider that you are representing an interest group seeking to influence the development and implementation of the legislation described below. How might you attempt to go about that? What considerations should go into your decisions as to how to influence the legislative result?

Assume that $100 million has been authorized in the House version of an annual HUD authorization bill for a new development program, but it is not in the Senate's bill. In the subsequent conference committee, the Senate acquiesces to the House version. The specific development program is to be administered by local government community development program administrators pursuant to an allocation formula based on population and other factors. That bill becomes law when both houses of Congress vote for it and it is signed into law by the President. (For a brief time in 1997–98, Congress allowed the President to exercise a line-item veto upon signing the bill, but the Supreme Court struck down that delegation of legislative power to the executive. *Clinton v. City of New York*, 524 U.S. 417 (1998)). That authorization must then be followed by an appropriation measure to provide the funds called for.

2. How would the considerations for your strategy in achieving appropriations for the authorization provision differ from those applicable to the authorization efforts to get substantial funds allocated to this program?

The Appropriations Committees in each house may individually differ on that amount, depending upon the interests of those on the committee in each house, and thus the program may be underfunded by a lesser or greater amount. In fact, no appropriations may be provided. The authorization bill, however, does act as a ceiling on the funds that may be appropriated, since the authorization specification of the amount of funds normally controls. This limitation can be adjusted by amendments to the authorization act or through a new provision, but that process can be complex because of the separate committee jurisdictions within Congress of substantive authorization committees and those committees dealing with appropriations. Sometimes the problem is solved simply by not specifying a ceiling but simply authorizing "such sums as may be" appropriated.

The length of time that an appropriation is made available for use is usually limited. Some measures require "obligation of funds," a technical term calling for a legal commitment of the funds to specified recipients, within the current fiscal year, such as by execution of a contract with the recipient and the federal agency. Other measures provide a somewhat longer period for obligation of funds, say for 2 or 3 years. Once obligated, however, funds generally remain available until expended, i.e. drawn down by the recipient, for a period of 5 years in addition to the enacted period of availability. *See,* 31 U.S.C. §§ 1535–1557.

The time period for obligation and expenditure of funds is used by Congress as a form of oversight on the administration of federal programs. Requiring frequent appropriations to fund programs allows the appropriation committees in each house to review the effectiveness of the programs and to determine whether to increase, decrease, or even terminate programs based on its perceived effectiveness or the changing policy predilections of the committees' members. Where amounts provided are determined to be insufficient, either because of intervening events or because additional amounts become available as occurred in 1998 with an unanticipated surplus, the amounts can be increased. The use of that surplus, which if continued would have provided over $4 trillion over the next 15 years, became the major game in town for 1999 with over 70% of that amount reserved for social security reform and to stabilize Medicare. The battle was primarily over the remaining portion. Republicans pushed for tax cuts and Democrats, led by the President, argued for specific programmatic priorities.

When changes in committee leadership occur, policy changes frequently accompany the new leadership who may have different perceptions on priorities for their committee's funds. For instance, in 2010, with the death of John Murtha (D-Pa), Chair of the Defense Appropriations Sub-Committee in the House, a new Chair of that committee took over with their own set of priorities, meaning legislation and projects that had gone to Murtha's district were likely no longer to be given the same priorities. The personal nature of the legislative process that relates to the individuals in leadership positions occurs both for the authorization and appropriation committees. When control of Congress came to Republicans following the 1994 elections, considerable revisions in policies occurred. The former committee chairmen became "ranking minority members" but with considerably reduced staff resources and with limited negotiating opportunities to continue and support policies they had previously implemented. Changes in the rules of the House and Senate further reduced the "minority" members' powers. Often decisions in the House were taken by the majority without even informing or inviting minority committee members to participate. In the Senate, because the majority status of the parties has changed more frequently, and because of the more intimate nature of the body, both political parties tend to be more respectful of the rights of the minority party in order to engender mutual consideration when a party goes out of power.

2. The Administrative Process

A Note on Practical Issues in Implementing Federal Programs for Housing and Development

Implementation of Legislation and Utilization of Funds Occurs Relatively Slowly

Don't expect a new program to take place immediately even once its legislation is enacted. Once a policy change incorporated by legislation is enacted, there is still the need for the relevant federal agency to gear up for administration of the program. It is likely that personnel need to be hired or assigned from other responsibilities to administer the program. It would be rare for new programs to be capable of implementation for at least several months. In addition, creation of regulations and other program decisions will also take time. So, while policy changes will occur, they are unlikely to occur quickly. In addition, even after the necessary funds have been appropriated, they still must be allocated. Depending upon the whether the program permits discretionary selection of grant recipients or is pre-determined in amounts for designated recipients (as in most block grant programs), putting together the necessary requirements for allocation of formula grants (including obtaining the relevant data on which allocations will be based) are likely to take more time. Further, procedures for applying for and choosing recipients after competitive applications must first be established for competitive programs. Notices of Funding Availability (NOFAs) have generally become the means to announce criteria and allocate funds once appropriation measures have been enacted. These notices set the programmatic parameters. Not only is lead time required to establish the application process, but further time is required to evaluate the competitive proposals.

The gearing up and distribution of funds under the 2009 stimulus program (ARRA) was perhaps the most rapid mobilization of resources and promulgation of program requirements by HUD ever. The importance of getting funds into recipients hands to stimulate the economy was a primary objective of the program. Whether the selection of recipients and projects were adequately considered given the haste with which the funds were sent out is likely to be a potential source of criticism or embarrassment for the program. As sometimes said, "haste makes waste."

An earlier major program initiative in a prior administration was the Empowerment Zone program that allocated $100 million each to selected cities and rural areas nationally, totaling over $1 billion. In this case, the entire amount of the funds to be provided had been authorized and appropriated when the legislation was enacted as in the case of the stimulus funds. In some EZ jurisdictions, almost a year was required before funds would flow for specific activities under the program. HUD had to establish program guidelines for submissions, set time for cities to develop proposals, and then allow time to evaluate the proposals. A subsequent review of the selection process by HUD's Inspector General suggested, not surprisingly, that political considerations may have influenced the selections made.

The second round of Empowerment Zones provides an interesting example of using recipient demands to force appropriations actions. Despite the fact that Congress had failed to provide budgetary authority in its initial appropriations and authorizing authority in fiscal year 1999 for a new round of grants, HUD and the Department of Agriculture (involved in selection of rural zones) nevertheless solicited competitive proposals from various cities, counties, and rural areas for new zones. The competitors became a potent force in helping HUD obtain at least initial funding of the first year of that program as part of the last minute compromise on HUD funding for that year. Actual selection of those to be designated did not occur until after the necessary legislation was enacted. Therefore, all applicants supported the efforts to get the program enacted. After recipients had been identified—15 urban and 5 rural zones—however, it meant broad support for continuing appropriations to the selected cities was less likely, and that was the case. A competition for a further 15 strategic Planning Communities were also designated to bolster additional support for new funding. But, that was the last of the possible participants selected, and thus further financial assistance for this particular program did not receive adequate support for it to continue, since the possible recipients were by then limited.

An earlier development program, the Model Cities program in 1974 confronted this issue of obtaining sufficient Congressional interest and thus support with the result that three rounds of competition for selection in the program occurred, meaning that potential applicants for additional designations in the future joined the lobbying effort for creation and funding of the second and third rounds. Finally, once a reasonable number of jurisdictions were selected, they became a potent force for limiting further applicants for the program since appropriations for this program were essentially capped as a practical matter in light of competing interests for the available funding. When the next Administration came into power after Nixon took office, there was little interest in carrying on an initiative that a prior Administration had put in place. In this case, the new Administration decided to continue to fund local governments, but did so by renaming the program and thus, the Community Development Block Grant Program became the succeeding administration's favored program.

To conserve the impact on the Treasury's resources or the need for it to borrow funds, recipients of funds are expected to obtain the actual funds generally only a few days before they will be needed for expenditure by the local government recipient. HUD uses a "LOCCS" (a Line of Credit and Control System) activated by telephone and/or email. It is a computerized application system through which grant recipients set forth their specific need for appropriated and allocated funds. HUD controls release of funds to the recipient's account by the Treasury by a having to countersign the request for funds. This means that funds from the Treasury, even after they are obligated for use with a particular recipient, are unlikely to be actually drawn down until some time in the future. Funds will be drawn down after local organizational efforts to administer the program are determined and, then, only after specific projects there are selected, the relevant participating actors are designated, and the planning process is completed. In the various programs, reports on use of funds after-the-fact have replaced earlier requirements for advanced HUD approval before projects can be initiated on the local level. The LOCCS apparatus also allows HUD to refuse to release funds for projects it objects to, creating potential conflicts that sometimes are resolved only by the recipient invoking options for judicial review of HUD's actions as described below.

Use of Set Asides

Where major programs have been established for a number of years, Congress has often used a small portion of these large allocations as the vehicle to fund unrelated programs through use of "set-asides." One example of this in the 1990s was that an increasing amount of funds annually was designated for specific and unrelated purposes as a part of the general allocation by Congress for the Community Development Block Grant program (CDBG) with its multi-billion dollar appropriations. It is easier to append a new policy approach to an existing source of funding that is widely supported, and then allocate a fairly small amount, out of the large total provided, for a new program than to obtain separate appropriations for a new initiative. Obviously there are limits to this approach as the amount of set asides increases and starts to impact the total amount received by recipients who are expecting to receive their usual annual allocation. At this point, the various affected interest groups will lobby on behalf of their respective interests, with the more appealing and powerful of these groups generally succeeding.

This set-aside tactic has continued through 2010, with significant amounts set aside in the CDBG program funding through fiscal year 2011. See The President's Budget for 2011, OMB 2-2-1010. It proposes that of the $4.45 billion (out of a total HUD budget of $41 billion) that $3.99 billion (same as the 2010 actual budget) go for CDBG funding. The set asides under CDBG proposed are: $150 million for Sustainable Communities; $150 million for Catalytic Investment Competition Grants (gap funding for innovative and targeted economic investment), and $25 million for a University Community Fund (to stimulate revitalization of communities surrounding universities)

Budget Considerations and Policies Affect Program Design

The effect of budget considerations has a significant impact on what type of housing program is crafted by Congress. For instance, at times when government spending needs to be reduced, Congress and the Administration may emphasize existing housing in subsidy programs. If the need is to jump-start the economy and increase employment, new construction or rehabilitation projects is often used for this purpose. It usually has a direct effect by increasing the number of jobs available. The specific design elements in a program can also be important. If funding is generally in short supply for housing purposes versus other objectives, subsidy programs that provide a limited subsidy to supplement tenant incomes or make limited payments of interest sufficient only to cover the gap between lower interest rates under a program and the actual cost of borrowing funds are more likely to be included in the design. Such budget considerations in many cases essentially dictate how a program will be designed.

Budget Rules For Calculating Costs Affect Program Design

Setting out how a particular program's expenditures are calculated for budget purposes can enormously affect the budgetary impact. Annual payments for rent involving only an annual term before renewal is required will have a lesser immediate budgetary impact than a program where the amount involved is provided for a ten or even 30 year period. Under budget rules, the subsidy payments authorized by the subsidy contract in any one year have generally had to be multiplied by the contract term to get the amount charged to the budget. Housing is one of the few government programs that experiences this kind of budgetary situation. In the case of interest subsidies, however, if properly designed to meet budget rules, only the amount applied in the current year will be counted for budget purposes. Thus, the same amount of budget authority and appropriations can be leveraged to affect a far greater number of housing units that will be subsidized. The result of budget rules has meant that shorter periods for subsidies are now frequently utilized and the costs are allocated to annually accounted items, such as annual interest reductions. This avoids having to allocate the full cost of something like a construction program to the current budget year that, under the budgetary rules, would be required otherwise.

There's nothing wrong about concern for spending levels for the current year. Nevertheless, a true estimate of future costs would require considerably more sophistication, both economically and politically, than the present budget system provides. This is among the issues that the present budget system does not handle well. A related but different consideration arises from other budget rules. For instance, currently an estimate is required from the Congressional Budget Office whenever a new program is proposed so that its budget impact may be evaluated. Congress has frequently required that new programs need to "pay as they go." Many HUD-funded programs other than CDBG and some low rent public housing operating expenses have generally used "discretionary" funding (as distinct from "mandatory" funding, as in entitlement programs). In order for a new program to be considered, an equivalent amount of funds currently designated by Congress for other purposes must be deleted or reduced to free up the funds for the new use. When program funds are either increased or reduced, if the estimating process for costs to be incurred is deficient, particularly as to secondary consequences on other budget expenditures that may be felt (such as welfare costs), the scoring of expected potential budget impact of such new initiatives can be extremely arbitrary. For instance, in discussions about the costs of Health Care Reform, proponents and opponents of different provisions anxiously awaited the determinations of the Congressional Budget Office estimates of the financial and budgetary impact such proposals would involve.

Susceptibility of Reserved Funds

In order to safeguard its programs that involve subsidies of units rather than of individuals, HUD has frequently been able to obtain what are essentially reserves of funds to handle changes in tenant income and increases in rental costs that must be met in subsidy amounts to ensure the continuing affordability of the unit. In advance, no one can accurately predict these considerations since they depend upon employment potential, welfare benefits, and rental costs. Setting aside such reserves ensures that funds will be available to meet contractual commitments even though they cannot be fully determined in advance.

Congress criticized HUD for reserving too much funding for housing authorities for these purposes in 1997, and raided the reserved funds for other federal programs, providing an unenforceable promise to later make-up funds if more reserves seemed necessary. Whether the necessary funds will be forthcoming at that time is problematic. If they are not appropriated in a timely fashion, recipients of funds who rely upon the federal financial assistance are likely to be put in some legal jeopardy. These funds were being held in accounts by Treasury that were not normally subject to annual oversight review for the new budget year. The extent of draw downs of a program's funds are normally reported as part of the re-authorization process. In the case of the 1997 reserves that had not been required to meet program needs to that point—funds that totaled roughly $6 billion—although a matter of public record, the existence of such funds was not disclosed initially to Congress for its consideration in making that year's overall HUD budget. Once Congress considered these funds during its annual budget deliberations, however, these amounts were quickly committed for other priorities set by Congress which priorities had limited funds available to them and were otherwise constrained by complicated restrictions on reallocation of funds. That, of course, meant any increase in an allocation for one purpose would require a reduced allocation for another use.

Notes and Questions

1. The above descriptions note the difficulty of estimating future housing subsidies in light of inflation in housing costs. In 2009, inflation has been held to roughly about two percent, but when inflationary trends in housing costs return because of increased demand for housing by a greater number of employed workers, how do you think this would affect budgetary estimates for housing subsidies? Budgetary considerations in housing programs and related problems like the choice between new and existing housing are further considered in Chapter 3 *infra*.

2. The interaction over policy conflicts between the executive and legislative branches is often acute in the area of budget and appropriations matters. The Federal Budget and Impoundment Control Act of 1974, which created a process by which the legislative branch could be better informed in processing its budget authority and related legislation, had a secondary objective: that of controlling past practices of the President to assert "policy" impoundments of money to frustrate legislative policy, expenditures, and priorities, by substituting uses of funds he might choose to make. The legislative/executive conflict came to a head in 1986 and resulted in litigation in *City of New Haven v. United States*, 809 F.2d 900 (D.C. Cir. 1987). The court held that a provision in the 1974 Act authorizing the President to "defer" expenditures, which in this instance had been exercised to defer use of monies for certain housing programs, was invalid because it was not severable from an invalid section in the provision authorizing a legislative veto of any deferrals.

The Supreme Court had previously determined such vetoes to be unconstitutional in *Immigration & Naturalization Serv. v. Chadha,* 462 U.S. 919 (1983).

As this discussion of the congressional process has indicated, housing and community development legislation is complex. The statutes cannot cover in detail all of the issues that must be resolved before housing subsidy and community development grants are actually made to local government entities. Detailed regulations are necessary to give content to the program outline contained in the federal statutory code.

HUD is now the federal department given the primary responsibility for almost all urban housing and community development programs. HUD provides the federal administration and regulation for Congressionally-authorized and funded housing programs. The Department was created by Congress in 1965 during President Johnson's administration after a long struggle with the various and often disparate interests constituting the recipients of its financial assistance and subsidies. Federal housing programs had previously been distributed among several independent federal agencies that were consolidated into one department to form HUD.

3. *HUD Management Criticized.* Consolidation in 1965, however, came under attack by Congress several decades later in the 1990s after political scandals in the allocation of funds and considerable evidence of lack of enforcement of program requirements. While problems were highlighted due to publicity generated by an Inspector General's staff anxious to justify their role, the antipathy to HUD's management was also stimulated by perceptions that HUD was the principal representative of the interests of residents of cities and urban areas, who were often minorities. Criticism of HUD's administration of its programs brought considerable pressure on the Department to reform its efforts. In the mid-1990s, calls for abolishment of HUD were heard, and distribution of its various programs to other agencies was frequently threatened by Congress. Matters even went so far as the introduction of legislation (that died only in Conference Committee deliberations) transferring all housing-related civil rights enforcement out of HUD to the Justice Department in 1996, which had neither sought nor wanted the responsibility.

That transfer was delayed and in 2010, civil rights enforcement, except for pattern and practice cases, still remains with HUD which handles matters in large part through negotiations and administrative proceedings. In some instances, HUD refers matters for judicial enforcement to the Department of Justice. As discussed in Chapter 6, a substantial part of the enforcement of housing rights of individuals claiming discrimination has been taken over by private enforcement through non-profit organizations which generally receive funds from HUD to carry out their activities under HUD grants under its Fair Housing Initiatives Program (FHIP).

In addition to seeking HUD assistance in redress of discrimination, claimants under the Fair Housing Act may also seek recourse to private civil actions for damages in federal court. Successful actions can result in recovery of attorney fees for the claimant, providing a contingent source of compensation for the private attorneys that handle most of these cases, encouraging attorneys to take on these complaints. They have been remarkably successful. (See "$275 million and Counting" prepared by the Fair Housing Center of Metropolitan Detroit (2009), which details actual amounts recovered in such private suits nationally over the last 18 years by fair housing organizations and their cooperating attorneys. As discussed in Chapter 6 in more detail, the availability of "testing" to obtain evidence of discrimination is really feasible only if such evidence is obtained before the matter is submitted to HUD which must notify defendants almost immediately of the pendency of a complaint. The availability of the relatively conclusive testing evidence provides a significant advantage to using federal courts rather than HUD administrative actions to obtain damages.

In 1994, the U.S. General Accounting Office, now named the Government Accountability Office (GAO)—a monitoring agency of Congress—reported that HUD had major management deficiencies. In 1997–98, in response to such criticism, HUD instituted major reforms in its management, through the Secretary's 2020 Management Reform Plan. This plan created different cross-cutting organizational units to oversee various aspects of its programs and an enforcement unit to carry out oversight on its own of problems experienced in use of HUD funds. Owners that failed to maintain conditions for rental units who had siphoned off funds for their own benefit became a major target. Disbarment of such owners from participation in HUD programs was increasingly utilized to prevent continued involvement in federal programs.

In 1999, however, although giving HUD's leadership credit for "significant changes" and "credible progress," the GAO still listed HUD as having significant management deficiencies that placed "the integrity and accountability of HUD's programs at risk." Finally, in January 2007, HUD announced that GAO had recognized HUD's management reforms and for the first time in 13 years that HUD programs were not on GAO's "High-Risk" list. Citing significant financial and management reforms put in place at HUD, GAO announced that two of HUD's critical housing programs have been removed from its "high-risk" list, recognizing HUD's progress in implementing management controls that have led to significant improvements in HUD's managing its Single-Family Mortgage Insurance and Rental Housing Assistance Programs. This action marked the first time since 1994 that no HUD programs had been on GAO's "high-risk" list. Indicative of the continuing oversight carried out by GAO of various federal programs, GAO in June 2009, counseled HUD to improve its oversight of its Public Housing program and ensure that those funds were being used as intended and were properly managed by PHAs. See GAO Report 09-33, June 2009.

HUD's administration of its various housing and development programs is also audited by HUD's Office of Inspector General to disclose waste, fraud, and abuse. The OIG is part of the federal effort to ensure federal government programs, such as HUD programs, are properly managed and administered by HUD and the recipients of its funds. The Office of Inspector General's mission "is independent and objective reporting to the Secretary and the Congress for the purpose of bringing about positive change in the integrity, efficiency, and effectiveness of HUD operations." The OIG produces a Semi-Annual Report to Congress. *See, e.g.*, U.S. Dep't of Housing and Urban Development, Office of Inspector General, Semiannual Report to Congress for April 1, 2009, through September 30, 2009.

4. *Origins of Executive Branch Policy*. Aside from the applicable legislative committees as a source of housing and development policy, executive branch policy may evolve from HUD, the Treasury Department, the Council of Economic Advisors, and the President's Domestic Policy advisor in the White House, This advisor has policy-making functions and provides presidential direction for HUD secretaries who occasionally take a political viewpoint opposed to a presidential position. The President's Office of Management and Budget (OMB) also has a housing section which works with HUD in developing legislative policy and then reviews HUD's budget requests. In some years, OMB was instrumental in paring down housing expenditures in the federal budget by over 75%. Thus, OMB acts as the President's agent to set federal budget priorities.

OMB can be at odds with HUD policy makers. One of HUD's roles is as a representative of the interests for the various parts of the housing and development industry interested in its programs, including developers and city officials, although in the end, the Administration expects HUD to follow "the party line." As to the process, HUD submits its proposed budget items to OMB which reviews and vets them for consistency with Administration policy and then incorporates them in the Administration's total budget that is publicly released in February each year. At times OMB has had HUD and the entire housing industry up in arms over reductions in funding. At one time, OMB even proposed that housing subsidies be abolished entirely, suggesting they be consolidated with welfare assistance payments. OMB has historically been particularly cautious in the use of federal credit resources, and HUD is a major user of federally-backed credit subsidies. After OMB comes up with its critique of the HUD proposals, HUD is given an opportunity to respond to ask for restoration of the funds rejected. This pass back dance is finally resolved by the President. Fighting the President's agent's, i.e. OMB's, position is politically risky within an Administration. In the end, considerable problems will be encountered if the Administration does not have a consistent position. At times, however, HUD Secretaries have almost openly lobbied Congress to restore budget reductions imposed by OMB speaking on behalf of the President after the President has sent his proposals to the Hill.

The combination of tax cuts and ensuing deficits in the Reagan years effectively transferred policy powers to the budget cutters. OMB currently plays a continuing role in formulating executive branch policies. It coordinates legislative positions and recommends Presidential positions on legislation presented to him for his signature after consulting affected federal agencies. OMB's decisions are facilitated through its role of review and approval of departmental legislative proposals and departmental program and administrative budgets.

5. *Federal Agency Regulations Guide Federal Programs.* Regulations appear initially in the Federal Register when promulgated by a federal agency and are subject to an Administrative Procedure Act notice and comment process for such rulemaking. When finally issued, they are codified in the Code of Federal Regulations (C.F.R.). Until the 1970s, HUD resisted this method of publishing its rules. Advice for its programs was issued in the form of circulars and handbooks, and in letters to HUD regional and area offices, not always even circulated to grant recipients or recipients of federal assistance. The informal policies constantly changed and were difficult for outsiders to obtain. HUD now publishes the core of its regulations in the Federal Register, but continues to issue handbooks, circulars, notices, and the like which give additional content to its program guidance. These are primarily for guidance of its own employees. Conflicts can arise when these legally unenforceable Notices and Guidances are imposed on grant recipients. Recently, HUD has improperly even used its NOFAs as a source of program requirements to which it refers applicants.

Only those matters which are subject to rulemaking can legally bind recipients, however. At best, the other HUD issuances constitute essentially "safe harbors" ensuring that recipients of funds who comply with them will not be subject to sanctions for improper or ineligible use of funds.

To build on the example of development of the public housing program and its revision through the Brooke Amendment, how HUD makes housing policy through the regulatory process can be illustrated by HUD's initial interpretations of the operating subsidies for public housing authorized by the Brooke Amendment. The nature and purpose of this subsidy was outlined in the Conference Report. The report described the subsidies as:

> (1) [P]ayments to cover existing operating deficits of public housing authorities and enable them to maintain adequate operating and maintenance services and reserve funds, and

(2) Additional payments to make up the amount by which the proportionate share of operating and maintenance expenses attributable to a public housing tenant's dwelling unit exceeds 25 percent of the tenant's income.

What happened next in the administrative process with the promulgation of regulations is reflected in the following excerpt:

Daniel R. Mandelker, Housing Subsidies in the United States and England

92–94 (1973)

Though they were dismayed by the Conference Report, supporters of the Brooke Amendment were encouraged by the new legislation and viewed it as an important breakthrough. They turned with anticipation to the drafting of the HUD regulations for the new subsidies. This task was made all the more critical because the language of the Conference Report had not sufficiently clarified the purpose of the new subsidies, and the resolution of ambiguities in the Report was now left to HUD to interpret.

Responsibility for drafting the necessary regulations was delegated to officials in HUD's housing assistance branch, and they took a step which has increasingly become part of HUD's operating policies by bringing several organizations active in the housing field directly into the drafting process. The oldest and best established of these organizations was the National Association of Housing and Redevelopment Officials (NAHRO). Dating back to the resurgence of interest in housing in the mid-1930's, this national organization represents the interests of professional administrators in the housing and redevelopment field, and tended to take a liberal view of the newly enacted legislation. Similar views were expressed even more actively by three other organizations, all of which had been organized in recent years to serve a newly emerging advocacy role in the administration of social benefit programs. These outside organizations were not very successful in advocating a liberal interpretation of the new subsidy. What HUD officials could not entirely accomplish through congressional influence they accomplished by placing limitations on the new subsidy program.

[The three outside organizations were the National Tenants Organization, the National Welfare Rights Organization, and the National Housing and Development Law Project, a backup research center for legal service attorneys engaged in housing litigation and activities.—Eds.]

Just how these provisions were to be interpreted was something of a puzzle, and most of the controversy centered on the new subsidies which the Conference Report had authorized. HUD's solution, hotly contested by its outside advisers, was to break the new subsidies into two types. The first type of subsidy was to be a one-time payment to cover "existing operating deficits" of public housing agencies, was payable in HUD's discretion, and was conditioned on a demonstration by the public housing agency that "satisfactory standards of management and tenant responsibility have been or will be achieved." The second type of subsidy was to be made available "To make up the amount by which the proportionate share of operating and maintenance expenses attributable to a dwelling unit exceeds 25 percent of the tenant's income."

HUD argued that limiting the first type of subsidy to existing deficits was justified by the Conference Report which had authorized "payments to cover existing operating deficits of public housing ... [agencies] and enable *them*" to maintain adequate services and reserves. [emphasis supplied] HUD lawyers interpreted the word "them" in this quotation to refer to the deficits and not to the agencies; thus the decision to limit the subsidy to the one-time removal of existing deficits. This interpretation was bitterly contested by the organizations advising HUD, who argued that HUD's interpretation strained the Report's language. They pointed to other language in the Conference Report which indicated that operating costs of public housing agencies were to be "covered" on a permanent basis, without regard to deficits existing when the bill was enacted.

Notes and Questions

1. Is HUD's solution to the subsidy problem a reasonable interpretation within its area of expertise? Was it within the scope of the statutory language and consistent with the Conference Report language? The issue of operating subsidies for public housing was dealt with in the Housing and Community Development Act of 1974. The subsidy does not make up deficits incurred because of the Brooke Amendment rent limitation and is based on a formula reflecting good housing authority management practices.

2. While HUD previously issued its policy for operating subsidies in the form of circulars, today it would be expected to go through the formal rule-making process in most instances. This process is not adjudicatory, nor is it very complicated. (Its ease of reading is another matter, since its actual content is provided in small fonts of dense text.) It requires the formulation and publication of a proposed rule for comment in the Federal Register followed by adoption of a final rule once the agency has received and considered all of the comments filed with it. The agency need not formally accept or reject comments submitted to it, although it is sensitive to political pressure from housing advocates and other groups, frequently expressed through influential Congressional sources. Informal consultation still continues, as program rules are in progress, providing opportunities for both HUD and recipients to better tune program operations. OMB also reviews proposed HUD regulations and other significant documents. As noted earlier, HUD regulations must adhere to OMB guidance in the form of OMB Circulars generally applicable to all government agencies. These Circulars, however, are developed only after OMB's self-imposed compliance with rule-making requirements under the APA.

3. Consider and evaluate the following commentary on the federal agency rule-making process in light of the Brooke Amendment's operating subsidy experience:

> One widely accepted reason for preferring rulemaking as a technique of policymaking is that the usual rulemaking procedures accord greater procedural freedom to the agency than does adjudication. In adjudication, it is said, the ability of the decision-makers to rely on their "expertise" is limited by the formal requirements of adjudicatory hearings and by the restrictions imposed. No doubt it is. Such is typically the consequence of all legal requirements. While not all restraints can be justified, it is questionable whether the constraints imposed by adjudicative proceedings have unduly or unwisely hampered administrative process. Certainly there are instances when it is desirable to place greater reliance on experience and expert judgment than is now done in some areas of the administrative process, but we have not suffered from too little faith in and reliance on expert wisdom. Professor Louis Schwartz's judgment "[e]xpertness has been oversold in this country," seems accurate. Intensive work in an agency may reward the individual with an accumulation of knowledge and experience about particular problems with which the agency deals. But processes by which agency personnel acquire intensive knowledge and experience about a particular industry, program, or set of problems tends to isolate them from other considerations and broader concerns.

> Expertise can also mean narrow-mindedness. This obviously does not mean that expert judgment and experience is not to be used and never to be trusted. It does mean that it should neither be trusted implicitly, nor be left subject to no greater discipline than its own conscience. Removing procedural restrictions, eliminating the requirement of a record hearing, and denying the use of cross-examination and other requirements of the adjudicative process results, in some cases, in the removal of a significant and salutary discipline from the process.

Glen O. Robinson, *The Making of Administrative Policy: Another Look at Rulemaking and Adjudication and Administration Procedure Reform,* 118 U. Pa. L. Rev. 485, 519–20 (1970).

4. Would HUD's policy-making process in developing regulations for Brooke Amendment operating subsidies have been improved through the use of adjudicatory procedures allowing, for example, preservation of testimony and cross-examination of those testifying, including HUD officials? What purpose would cross-examination accomplish?

5. HUD's regulatory treatment of the Brooke Amendment operating subsidies illustrates the difficulty of translating often vague statutory language into program administration. Often the lack of direction in the statute reflects the controversy that surrounded enactment of the legislation. The Brooke Amendment's history illustrates this point. Congress often delegates the policy-making controversy to the administrative agency, here HUD. Does the United States Supreme Court's refusal since the 1930s to invalidate federal legislation on grounds of improper delegation of power mean that there is no judicial check on administrative agency discretion in implementing vague and ambiguous federal legislation?

6. Congress did not attempt to intervene in the administrative rulemaking until the late 1970s, when controversial rulings by HUD and other federal agencies provoked a congressional response. For HUD, the controversy that drew congressional attention arose in the community development, not the public housing program. *See* Chapter 5 *infra.*

7. Congress has not responded to excessive agency policymaking in the rulemaking process by tightening legislative language. Instead, it has considered a number of measures for congressional review of agency regulations. These measures included the legislative veto of agency regulations, a measure which was challenged on constitutional grounds. As noted earlier, the legislative veto was invalidated by the Court in *Immigration & Naturalization Serv. v. Chadha,* 462 U.S. 919 (1983), which held that Congress could not veto executive agencies' formulation of policy by regulation, but could only do so through legislation signed by the President.

The legislative veto that Congress had imposed on HUD required HUD to provide the Banking Committee in each house with an agenda of regulations under development or review. Either committee could then notify HUD that it intended to review any proposed rule or regulation. HUD then had to submit to both committees a copy of any such rule or regulation at least 15 days before it was published for comment in the Federal Register.

No rule or regulation could become effective within 20 days of the date of final publication. Within this period either committee could report out a resolution disapproving, modifying, or invalidating the rule, which could not become effective for another 90 days unless the house to which the rule was reported rejected the resolution.

The Conference Report that adopted this procedure claimed it was not a legislative veto, but rather was intended to formalize a procedure "to assure a constructive consultative relationship between Congress and the executive branch. The intent is to encourage cooperation and to develop a spirit of comity." The formality of the procedure was intended to increase cooperation and the Conference Report stated that the deferral provision would only be followed where either committee believes that the proposed regulations violate the intent of Congress. Obviously, even today, if a committee asks for advance notification of an agency's proposed regulations before it is published in the Federal Register, an agency would comply.

8. What are the effects of such a legislative review of agency regulations? Does it tend to make legislation less precise? Does it shift policy development to the committee rather than the whole Congress? Given that legislation starts with a committee, is that inappropriate? In what ways could it affect the policy-making process in federal housing and community development programs? For a member of one of the congressional housing committees who disagrees with newly issued HUD regulations, what options are available today? Consider that the committee can always hold oversight hearings and has leverage over HUD when it requests new legislation or appropriations.

9. The Quality Housing and Work Responsibility Act of 1998 consolidated all Federal assistance for local public housing authorities into two basic funds: a capital fund and an operating fund. The operating fund may be used for management procedures and systems, routine preventive maintenance, anti-crime and anti-drug activities, social service provisions, participation in management and policy making by public housing residents, insurance, energy conservation and costs, administering public housing work programs, repayment of debt incurred in financing rehabilitation and development of units, and management of mixed projects "to the extent appropriate." Quality Housing and Work Responsibility Act of 1998, Pub. L. No. 105-276, §519, 112 Stat. 2551 (*amending* §9 of the Housing Act of 1937, *codified at* 42 U.S.C. §1437g). A considerable effort was required by HUD to reissue and conform its existing regulations in the programs, primarily applicable to public housing, affected by this legislation. At times, HUD has utilized the justification that it must initially abandon the rulemaking process in order to meet Congressional timetables, presumably with a subsequent reevaluation of the initial promulgations after programs have become operational and Congressional deadlines have been met.

10. As noted earlier, HUD and its Office of Inspector General, are continually involved in attempting to police operation and administration of the programs for which the Department is responsible. The Inspector General reports to Congress and furnishes it Semi-Annual Reports while also reporting to the HUD Secretary. The Inspector General provides an audit function and also investigates possible criminal violations associated with these programs, many of which involve considerable sums of monies that can and at time have been diverted to inappropriate uses. In addition to fraud and direct pocketing of federal funds being administered by recipients of these funds, other possible criminal violations are also investigated by the Inspector General.

Indicative of the scope of the OIG's activities are the profile of its performance in its September 30, 2009 report (covering 9 months of 2009). The HUD OIG states that based upon its audits it had recommended that $1,948,438,436 of the use of funds it examined could have been "put to better use,; that it had "questioned costs" of $371,368,053 of funded recipients expenses it examined; and that it had collected repayments of $165,766,317 in improperly expended funds. In its companion investigative efforts, it had recommended that $116,438,222 could have been "put to better use," and that $219,778,868 were either receivables or recovered as a result of its investigations. Its investigations had resulted in 1,182 grand jury indictments or filing of criminal informations by U.S. Attorneys and in 847 convictions, pleas, or pretrial diversions. It also had been responsible for the filing of 92 civil actions and 1,018 administrative sanctions against fund recipients, as well as 82 personnel actions against federal employees for improper handling of their responsibilities, or through actions by Federal agencies to suspend, debar, or exclude parties from contracts, grants, loans, etc. Their work, it reported, also resulted in 1,554 criminal arrests, the issuance of 136 search warrants, and 1,031 subpoenas. The OIG also provides a "hotline" to take anonymous complaints which resulted in determining $4,370,166 in funds that could have been put to better use, and recoveries or receivables of $506,649.

11. The category of recommendation of "funds be put to better use" amounting to roughly $2 billion raises questions about on what basis that assessment can accurately be made after-the-fact and on what policy grounds such amounts can be determined. The Inspector General Act under which all IGs operate defines the term: "recommendation that funds be put to better use," as funds that "could be used more efficiently through, among other actions, reductions in outlays, deobligations, costs avoidance, and other savings which are specifically identified ..." and that care and sound judgment must be exercised to ensure that only reasonable and defensible estimates and factual data are used." Report of the Inspector General of the U.S. Department of Labor, March 21, 2007, as part of an "external peer review" of the HUD OIG. That Peer Review Report also indicated: "we also noted that questioned costs totaling $1.5 million were reported. However, we also noted [HUD] OIG subsequently reported in its Semiannual Report to Congress (SAR) an additional $72.9 million of monetary impact associated with the audit." The Peer Review went on to comment: "HUD OIG indicated that the $72.9 million was the best estimate at the time the HUD program office wanted to close this audit. However, we believe this is contrary to HUD OIG's AOM which required that no monetary benefit be claimed if there was any uncertainty as to the dollar amount involved. Neither Government Auditing Standards, the Inspector General Act, nor HUD OIG policy requires quantification of a monetary impact."

When the OIG performs an audit, it issues proposed audit reports that detail its findings and then final reports. Those being audited have an opportunity to respond before the final report, although in practice persuading the OIG to revise its findings is extremely difficult at that stage. The major impact of the findings is that they are made public, often released to the local press and always distributed to the relevant members of Congress with interest in the matters. For local government or developers, the real sanction is the impact on the recipient's reputation. In addition, as the HUD OIG's SAR notes, criminal and administrative sanctions can result.

12. There is an administrative legal process applicable for allegations of certain violations in handling of federal funds by fund recipients. Such proceedings are initiated by HUD's Enforcement Office. The following description raises several questions about the propriety of such proceedings when initiated against the volunteer Public Housing Commissioners in Harrisburg, Pennsylvania. In theory, debarment proceedings are based upon violations of the contract between HUD and recipients of its funds. The following materials raise fundamental questions whether actions of officers or directors of PHAs are subject to debarment, as well as the legal process and standards that should be used in such proceedings which have been described by some lawyers as essentially kangaroo court proceedings. You will need to judge the appropriateness of these criticisms of this administrative process.

Otto J. Hetzel et al., Housing and Urban Development

Developments In Administrative Law and Regulatory Practice
(Jeff F. Lubbers ed. 2010)

In *Feinerman v. Bernardi*, 558 F. Supp. 2d 36 (D.D.C. 2008), three housing authority commissioners challenged their HUD debarments under the Administrative Procedures

Act (APA). The commissioners alleged that HUD's debarment was an arbitrary and capricious action and was contrary to HUD's own regulations. In June 2008, the district court granted a preliminary injunction against HUD's enforcement of the debarments against one of the three commissioners, the one who provided a showing of immediate harm in light of the court's determination that the commissioners had demonstrated a great likelihood of success on the merits of their challenge to HUD.

In 1998, in order to provide financial services needed by its residents, the Harrisburg Housing Authority (HHA) in Harrisburg, Pennsylvania, became involved in the planning for a low-income community credit union, which later became the Greater Harrisburg Community Credit Union (the Credit Union). In 1999, HHA's Board of Commissioners were informed by the Authority's Executive Director that HHA's Five Year Plan (which HHA was required to submit to HUD) expressly identified that $100,000 per year for next five years had been set aside to support the Credit Union. The HHA board members understood that the expenditures for the Credit Union were detailed in the Plan that HUD subsequently approved. However, the Plan actually submitted to HUD by HHA inadvertently failed to include the information relating to the support for the Credit Union.

HHA continued to financially support the Credit Union through 2006 when it was closed by the National Credit Union Association for an inability to meet net worth requirements. During this period of time, at each HHA Board meeting during which the Credit Union was discussed and expenditures for it were authorized, HHA's Executive Director, other members of its senior management, and HHA's General Counsel were in attendance and were supportive of the action proposed and undertaken. None of those professionals ever advised HHA's Board of Commissioners not to provide financial support to the Credit Union, and the Commissioners were never informed that HUD had not been notified of, and had not authorized, that support.

In 2006, the HUD Office of Inspector General (OIG) began an audit of HHA and its activities. In the course of the audit, the auditor decided that the support of the credit union was an ineligible use of funds, in part based upon the fact that their use had not actually been approved by HUD. HHA objected to the findings of the auditor and contested those findings through the audit process and in the initial stages of the subsequent debarment proceedings. The eligibility of those funds, however, was not an issue in the case brought in the District Court.

After the OIG had published its draft audit findings, in July 2007 HUD separately notified three of HHA's commissioners (the "plaintiffs") that it was proposing their debarments from future participation in transactions with the executive branch of the federal government for three years. (See Letter to L. Feinerman from HUD, RE: Notice of Proposed Debarment, July 30, 2007. This letter was included as Exhibit 1 in the Government's Brief in Support of Three Year Debarment, which is part of the administrative record.) The HUD Notices charged the plaintiffs with "allowing large sums of HHA's operating subsidy funds, which it receives annually from HUD for the purpose of developing and operating the HHA, to be used to fund ... the Greater Harrisburg Community Credit Union (GHCCU) without obtaining HUD's authorization for such expenditures" in violation of the Annual Contributions Contract (ACC) between HUD and HHA. HUD charged that under its debarment regulations, the votes by the directors to provide support to GHCCU were grounds for "imputation" of the HHA's violations against the directors and therefore constituted a willful violation of the ACC, and doing so for several years also meant they had a history of willful violations of the ACC, and of the statutory and regulatory provisions applicable to the ACC. HUD also charged that the approval votes by the directors were a cause so serious or compelling that it affected the directors' "present responsibility" so as to justify their debarment. (See the debarment regulations at 2 C.F.R. § 180.800(b) and (d).)

The three debarment actions were subsequently consolidated and HUD filed its brief and evidence in support of the debarments. Plaintiffs filed their oppositions to their debarments in HUD's informal proceedings as provided under HUD's debarment regulations. Among other facts and arguments, the plaintiffs presented undisputed evidence that they had not participated in, had no knowledge of, and had no reason to know of, the lack of HUD authorization for HHA's expenditures for the Credit Union. Plaintiffs also presented evidence concerning the various factors that mitigated against their debarment, including the steps which HHA and they had taken to avoid a recurrence of the conduct cited in the OIG audit, and requested dismissal of the actions or a fact-finding hearing before an administrative law judge. HUD, however, instead provided an informal hearing on January 30, 2008, before its Debarring Official's designee (a HUD employee) who heard arguments from both HUD's and plaintiffs' counsel.

On March 31, 2008, HUD's Debarring Official, Henry S. Czauski, *who did not attend the January 30 informal hearing,* issued a determination debarring two of the three plaintiffs for three years and the third for eighteen months. (See Debarring Official's Determination, issued by Henry S. Czauski on March 31, 2008, and included as Exhibit 10 of the Plaintiffs' Amended Application for Preliminary Injunction and Request for Expedited Ruling.) Czauski found that "[t]he HHA Board did not solicit, make inquiry, or receive any legal opinion or professional advice from legal counsel, professional staff, or HUD as to whether the use of HUD funds for the establishment or support of the credit union was an eligible expense under section 9 of the ACC." Based on that finding, Czauski concluded that "[t]he HHA Board actions in failing to comply with the specific terms of the ACC on more than one occasion and its failure to solicit or make affirmative inquiry to determine whether funding of the GHCCU was appropriate under the ACC, and if not, to obtain approval, constitutes a willful failure to perform, a history of failure to perform and unsatisfactory performance in accordance with the ACC so serious as to affect the integrity of the program."

Mr. Czauski's Determination made no reference to any disputes about material facts, or lack thereof. Nonetheless, he concluded that "[t]he improper conduct of the HHA is imputable to Respondents ... who participated in, had knowledge of, or had reason to know of the improper conduct." Mr. Czauski's Determination similarly made no reference to the plaintiffs' contention that, if the debarment action was not dismissed, they were entitled to an adjudicative fact-finding proceeding. Further, in reference to the factors mitigating against debarment, Mr. Czauski concluded that "[a]lthough Respondents allege that they have taking *(sic)* certain steps to put procedures and controls in place, including the creation of a governance committee and an audit committee to avoid a repetition of a similar problem and a proposal to repay all the funds contributed to GHCCU with non-federal funds, no affirmative action has been taken by any of the respondents or the HHA Board to implement the steps, controls or repayment suggested and to avoid a recurrence."

Plaintiffs argued that the Debarring Official's decision did not address long-standing legal doctrines providing certain protections to actions of directors and commissioners of corporations exercising due care and that well established common law exists in most states that in carrying out fiduciary responsibilities, directors of corporations—including directors or commissioners of public corporations such as public housing agencies—will not be found liable for their actions if they have exercised diligence and due care. Plaintiffs asserted that common law doctrine, and in this instance specific Pennsylvania statutory law, permits directors to reasonably rely on the expertise of management, consultants, and legal counsel in reaching decisions, and in circumstances where those decisions subsequently are proven wrong, if originally made in reliance upon such expert's advice, directors will not be held liable.

In contrast, plaintiffs pointed out the Debarring official had attempted to fashion a standard for the conduct of housing authority commissioners—the duty to inquire—that is wholly absent from the debarment regulations or traditional fiduciary duties. Rather, they noted, debarment regulations as well as the District of Columbia Circuit Court of Appeal have adopted a "reason to know" standard with regard to whether the liability of the organization can be imputed to the commissioners. (*See* 68 Fed. Reg. 66533, 66539 (Nov. 26, 2003); *Novicki v. Cook*, 946 F.2d 938, 941 (D.C. Cir. 1991))

The "reason to know" standard, as adopted, does not include any duty to inquire. Instead, it simply requires that such persons draw reasonable inferences from information already known to them. *Id.* Had the Debarring Official's proposed standard not been rejected subsequently by the District Court, it would have imposed a much broader scope of responsibility and liability on housing authority commissioners than current law and HUD regulations.

On May 1, 2008, the commissioners filed a complaint in the United States District Court for the District of Columbia seeking review of HUD's debarments under the APA. Plaintiffs asserted that HUD's determination was factually and legally flawed and was based on findings that were arbitrary, capricious, an abuse of discretion, and not otherwise in accordance with law because the Debarring Official relied upon the wrong legal standard and erroneous factual findings as the basis for his determination to debar the plaintiffs.

Plaintiffs also sought a preliminary injunction to stay the enforcement of the debarments because the debarments would cause the plaintiffs irreparable harm. Following a hearing on plaintiffs' motion for a preliminary injunction, the district court ruled from the bench that one plaintiff was likely to succeed on the merits of his APA claims because the Debarring Official employed the wrong standard in imputing any misconduct by the HHA to the plaintiffs and erred in failing to explain why he did not consider the mitigating evidence presented by the plaintiffs. The failure to consider mitigation itself was enough for the plaintiff to establish his likelihood of success on the merits. *Feinerman v. Bernardi*, 558 F. Supp. 2d 36, 43–44 (D.D.C 2008). The court made an important distinction relating to the "imputation" standard HUD had used to justify its debarment proceedings against the plaintiffs and the extent to which housing authority commissioners have a contractual relationship with HUD through the ACC. Judge Walton stated the Debarring Official erred in his conclusion that the plaintiffs should be debarred because the Debarring Official improperly conflated the plaintiffs with the HHA itself. Judge Walton pointed out that "Although the plaintiffs are subject to HUD's regulation by virtue of their status as "participants in a 'covered transaction'" that does not mean, as the debarring official apparently assumed, that they owed any contractual duties to HUD under the ACC."

Accordingly, Judge Walton held the Debarring Official was incorrect as a matter of law to have determined that the plaintiffs' actions constituted a willful failure to comply with the ACC. Further, the Judge explained that even if the Debarring Official had properly considered the conduct of HHA to constitute a willful violation of the ACC, that conduct could not have been imputed to the plaintiffs because the administrative record demonstrated that the plaintiffs did not have any knowledge of HHA's failure to obtain HUD approval or any reason to know of it. Finally, Judge Walton found that the Debarring Official had also erred by failing to provide any explanation as to why he did not consider the mitigating evidence presented by the plaintiffs.

Following the issuance of the Memorandum Opinion, the parties undertook settlement negotiations, but were unable to reach any agreement. On August 28, 2008, however, the evening before Motions for Summary Judgment were due, HUD issued letters to each of the plaintiffs voluntarily withdrawing its debarments. After issuing the letters, HUD also filed a Motion to Dismiss, claiming that because it had withdrawn the debarments, the case was moot and the Court no longer had subject matter jurisdiction. On October 30, 2008, the District Court dismissed the case. Following dismissal, Plaintiffs petitioned for an award of attorney's fees under the Equal Access to Justice Act (28 U.S.C. 2412(d)). While HUD did not oppose the motion on grounds that plaintiffs were not the prevailing party or HUD's position was substantially justified, its opposition was based solely on objections to the amount of the fee in that some of the work was duplicative, not adequately documented, and was for clerical services. Plaintiff received payment for its reasonable attorney's fees based upon a settlement agreement reached with HUD prior to a ruling by the Court.

Notes and Questions

1. How did HUD's version of an administrative proceeding compare as a tribunal with that available to a litigant in a judicial proceeding, such as in federal court? For whose benefit does the informal nature of the proceeding favor. If the hearing officer is a HUD employee, does this provide even the appearance of detachment one would expect from a hearing officer? Should the hearing officer at least been present for the hearing rather than gaining an understanding of the facts and credibility of witnesses from a written record? What legal safeguards should apply to such proceedings? The HUD process as currently practiced has not been challenged in court to date. Why do you think that has not occurred?

2. What is the significance of the "imputation" standard that the HUD hearing officer used in presenting a case against individuals who have not signed the contractual agreement between HUD and the Authority for whom they are employed or provide services, compensated or not?

What appears to be the basis for the government debarment proceedings? What is the effect on the person or entity debarred? What is the government's interest to be served. What reasonable limitations should be applicable to its exercise?

3. The Judicial Process: The Problem of Access to Federal Courts

Litigation arises in government housing programs in a number of ways. Government agencies must often resort to compulsory land acquisition proceedings for housing under their eminent domain power to acquire land necessary for government projects. Disputes between federal and local government agencies and between private contractors and developers and state and local governments can also lead to litigation, as can disputes between private participants in government programs.

Litigation can also arise over HUD interpretations of federal housing statutes with regard to its programs. Federal housing legislation often confers considerable discretion on federal and local agencies in the interpretation of legislative requirements and in program administration. The Brooke Amendment experience makes this point. Program beneficiaries and local agencies who objected to HUD interpretations of federal statutory requirements or to local program administration have as a final recourse that they can go to court. In the face of HUD or local refusals to make program modifications, judicial review becomes the avenue of last resort. The legal cost of doing so can be a major consideration. Where are funds to support such actions to be found?

This section considers the problem of access to court by cities and by consumer beneficiaries of housing programs who challenge statutory interpretations and program administration decisions by HUD. Consumers and suppliers often wish to challenge local housing agencies funding decisions as well as those of HUD.

Judicial review of federal programs lies in the federal courts and is primarily governed by the federal Administrative Procedure Act (APA). The APA places substantial obstacles in the way of successful litigation in its provision that action "committed to agency discretion" is not subject to judicial review. Because federal housing legislation on occasion confers a substantial amount of discretion on federal and local agencies, judicial challenges to agency action in those cases may not be successful, unless clearly "arbitrary and capricious."

Litigants may achieve more success in court when they challenge federal or local agency action on racial discrimination grounds. Federal anti-discrimination statutes as well as the constitutional equal protection clause provide a basis for litigation in these cases. The federal courts are more sensitive to racial discrimination issues than they are to questions of agency misconduct under discretionary grant programs.

A distinction must also be made between litigation that challenges decisions about programs and litigation that challenges decisions about specific projects within programs. Courts are likely to find program decisions discretionary and not subject to judicial review. A decision by a local housing authority not to apply for federal funding for its public housing program in any one year is discretionary and not subject to judicial review. Courts have more leverage over project decisions, which often must meet more specific statutory requirements. Project decisions may also present more concrete instances of differential decision making that have a negative impact on racial and other minority groups. To take an extreme case, a decision by a public housing authority to exclude African Americans from its public housing developments would present a clear case of racial discrimination.

Conflicts between HUD and local governments in program administration and use of funds presents one set of issues. A more difficult problem involves the legal position of third party beneficiaries in housing and community development litigation. Note that federal legislation authorizing housing programs creates legal relationships only between HUD, which is the federal funding agency, and the federal grant recipient, such as a city or local public housing authority. This legislation does not explicitly create legal rights in persons who benefit from these programs, such as persons who are eligible for admission to public housing.

Local public agencies which are the recipients of federal assistance are not likely to challenge federal agency program decisions unless HUD denies their program application or challenges their use of funds. Even then, the need to maintain good working relationships with federal policy makers usually inhibits local agencies from challenging HUD decisions.

The Kansas City litigation that follows is an example of a direct conflict between a local government administering a federal community development program and HUD.

The effect of HUD's interpretation of its powers and its regulatory authority were an important element in this dispute.

City of Kansas City v. United States Department of Housing and Urban Development

United States Court of Appeals
861 F.2d 739 (D.C. Cir. 1988)

Before: EDWARDS, BUCKLEY, and SENTELLE, Circuit Judges.

EDWARDS, Circuit Judge:

Under the Community Development Block Grant ("CDBG") program, the Secretary of the Department of Housing and Urban Development ("the Secretary" or "HUD") makes grants to units of state and local government. The appellee, the City of Kansas City ("the City"), is a recipient of annual CDBG grants. After a dispute arose over the City's use of CDBG funds from 1978 to 1985, the Secretary, proceeding under section 104(d) of the Housing and Community Development Act of 1974 ("CDBG Act" or "the Act"), 42 U.S.C. § 5304(d) (1982 & Supp. IV 1986), conditioned part of the City's 1987 grant on certain actions to be taken by the City. The City filed suit, arguing both that it was entitled to the funds unconditionally and that HUD had violated the CDBG Act by proceeding under section 104(d) of the Act, rather than under section 111, 42 U.S.C. § 5311 (1982), which requires notice and an opportunity for a hearing. The district court granted summary judgment in favor of the City on the procedural claim, and the Secretary appealed. Because we find that the Secretary has adopted an interpretation of the CDBG Act that violates Congress' clear intent to provide cities with procedural protections, we affirm.

I. BACKGROUND

A. Statutory Background

The CDBG Act distinguishes between two types of grantees: those entitled to receive grants every year ("entitlement cities") and grantees that receive funding only on a discretionary, case-by-case basis ("nonentitlement areas"). Kansas City is an entitlement city.

Once a grant to an entitlement city is approved, it is normally provided in the form of a letter of credit, which is increased annually by the amount of the grant. The grantee draws on the letter of credit as it makes obligations throughout the year, and funds not used in one year may be carried over to the next.

The Act contains two monitoring provisions. Section 104(d) requires the Secretary, on at least an annual basis, to make reviews and audits of a grantee's activities, and allows him to "make appropriate adjustments in the amount of the annual grants" in accordance with his findings. 42 U.S.C. § 5304(d) (Supp. IV 1986). The second monitoring provision is found in section 111 of the Act, 42 U.S.C. § 5311 (1982). Under the provision,

> If the Secretary finds *after reasonable notice and opportunity for hearing* that a recipient of assistance under this chapter has failed to comply substantially with any provision of this chapter, the Secretary, until he is satisfied that there is no longer any such failure to comply, shall:

> (1) terminate payments to the recipient under this chapter, or
>
> (2) reduce payments to the recipient under this chapter by an amount equal to the amount of such payments which were not expended in accordance with this chapter, or
>
> (3) limit the availability of payments under this chapter to programs, projects, or activities not affected by such failure to comply.

Id. §5311 (a) (emphasis added). Thus, under section 111, a grantee must be given notice and opportunity for a hearing when charged with a failure to comply substantially with any provision of the CDBG program. The Secretary has promulgated regulations detailing the procedures to be followed when section 111 is to be invoked. *See* 24 C.F.R. §570.913 (1988). Actions taken under section 111 are directly reviewable in the courts of appeals. 42 U.S.C. §5311(c).

B. The Proceedings Below

In 1975, Kansas City used CDBG monies to establish a fund (Fund 225) to improve streets, gutters and sidewalks in certain areas of the City. The City assessed property owners for the cost of sidewalks constructed in front of their homes, and these assessments went back into the Fund to be used for further improvements.

In 1978, HUD adopted a regulation that prohibited this type of assessment. 24 C.F.R. §570.200(c) (1988). The City asked that it be allowed to continue Fund 225, and in May 1978 HUD informed the City by letter that "no additional block grant funds may be provided for the project through an amendment or approval of a new program year component. However, funds approved for the project prior to March 1, 1978, may continue to be used by the recipient." The City subsequently transferred into the Fund unspent CDBG monies from the 1975, 1976 and 1977 grants.

In 1983, HUD's Regional Inspector General audited Kansas City's use of CDBG monies and concluded that the City's transfer of the earlier grants into Fund 225 had violated the 1978 regulation. HUD therefore ordered the City to reimburse property owners who were assessed for improvements financed by those grants. On March 5, 1986, on reconsideration at the City's request, HUD partially reversed itself and found that the transfers of pre-1978 CDBG grants were not subject to the 1978 regulation. However, HUD determined that assessments made after 1978 for the costs of improvements financed by the transfers constituted CDBG "program income" and were subject to the regulation. Therefore, HUD ordered the City to refund any further assessments made for improvements financed by that income. HUD did not object to any of the City's ongoing activities, nor has it done so since.

On December 23, 1986, fearing that HUD planned to withhold the City's 1987 CDBG entitlement, Kansas City filed an action in federal district court. The City sought declaratory and injunctive relief to compel HUD to distribute the City's full 1987 entitlement prior to the beginning of the City's fiscal year on March 1, 1987, and to require HUD to follow the procedures of section 111 before attempting to terminate or reduce the City's annual grant.

On April 27, 1987, when, contrary to its normal procedure, HUD still had not acted on the City's 1987 grant, the City moved for partial summary judgment. Four days later, on May 1, 1987, HUD proposed a Grant Agreement and Funding Approval, which it required the City to sign before it would release any of the $6.5 million in CDBG funds for 1987. The agreement contained two "special conditions" on $3.7 million of the grant. The Secretary conditioned $500,000 on the City's repayment of the allegedly improper assessments. HUD withheld the remaining $3.2 million until the City submitted revised "Grantee Performance Reports" (GPRs) listing certain loan repayments as CDBG program income. In late May 1987, after an agreement was worked out allowing the City to sign the Grant Agreement and to submit revised GPRs without waiving its right to contest the special conditions and the proper characterization of the loan repayments, respectively, HUD released all of the City's 1987 grant except the $500,000.

On August 6, 1987, the district court granted partial summary judgment for the City and declared the special conditions invalid. 669 F. Supp. 525 (D.D.C. 1987). The court found that the statutory framework made clear that section 111, and not section 104(d), applied to the dispute in this case. HUD's reading of the statute, the court found, would make section 111 a "nullity." In fact, the court pointed out, "the Secretary does not seem adverse to making Section 111 a nullity—in the 13 years this statute has been in existence, the Secretary has *never* initiated Section 111 procedures against any grant recipient." (emphasis in original).

After the court issued its opinion, HUD continued to refuse to release the $500,000 until the court ordered it to do so on October 2, 1987. HUD has appealed both the August 6 and October *2* orders.

II. ANALYSIS

A. The Applicable Standard of Review

The narrow question before this court is whether HUD must provide notice and an opportunity for a hearing when it proposes to condition, reduce or terminate an entitlement city's annual CDBG grant because of alleged past noncompliance that does not affect current or future performance. Since this case presents "a pure question of statutory construction, our first job is to try to determine congressional intent, using 'traditional tools of statutory construction.' If we can do so, then that interpretation must be given effect...." *NLRB v. United Food Commercial Workers Union,* 108 S. Ct. 413, 421 (1987) (quoting *INS v. Cardoza-Fonesca,* 480 U.S. 421, 446 (1987)). If, on the other hand, "the statute is silent or ambiguous with respect to the specific issue," *Chevron U.S.A., Inc. v. Natural Resources Defense Council, Inc.,* 467 U.S. 837, 843 (1984), then the question for the court becomes whether the agency's construction of the statute is "permissible," that is, one that is "rational and consistent with the statute." In the present case, the agency's construction of the statute cannot survive scrutiny under *Chevron United Food.* Our review of the CDBG Act convinces us that congressional intent is absolutely clear and totally at odds with the agency's position in this case: Section 111, and not section 104(d), governs the Secretary's actions in the case and requires the Secretary to provide the City with reasonable notice and an opportunity for a hearing.

B. The Clear Terms of Section 111

Section 111 of the CDBG Act specifically addresses the present situation. The very title of the section, "Remedies for Noncompliance," indicates that the section covers the Secretary's "special conditions" on the City's 1987 grant: the Secretary imposed those conditions as a remedy for the City's refusal to comply with HUD's order to refund the disputed assessments. More importantly, the language of section 111 provides for precisely this type of remedy.

The sanctions specified in section 111 are available—indeed, mandated—when the Secretary determines that a receipt "has failed to comply substantially with any provision of this chapter." 42 U.S.C. § 5311(a). Under the terms of the statute, that determination is made after the notice and opportunity for hearing contemplated in section 111. Thus, a recipient like Kansas City is entitled to a formal opportunity to contest the Secretary's allegations before being subject to sanctions.

If the Secretary determines that a grantee has substantially failed to comply with the rules governing the CDBG program, section 111 requires the Secretary to take one of three actions. One of the available sanctions is a reduction in "payments to the recipient under this chapter by an amount equal to the amount of such payments which were not expended in accordance with this chapter." *Id.* § 5311(a)(2). The sanction sought by the reduction, and the fact that the reduction was conditional does not remove it from the strictures of section 111. In fact, section 111 specifically provides for conditional sanctions, by authorizing the Secretary to reduce or terminate funding "until he is satisfied that there is no longer any such failure to comply" with the Act. *Id.* § 5311(a). Moreover, the net effect of the "special conditions" that HUD imposed on Kansas City's 1987 grant was to reduce immediately the amount of funds available to the City. If the district court had not intervened, those reductions would have been permanent unless the city, without any opportunity for a hearing, had acquiesced in HUD's interpretations of the disputed issues.

The clear language of section 111 thus controls this case. Kansas City is alleged to have substantially failed to comply with the CDBG Act, and the Secretary has attempted to impose a section 111 sanction. The problem is that the Secretary acted without first affording Kansas City notice and opportunity for a hearing as required under section 111 and its accompanying regulations. *See id.;* 24 C.F.R. § 570.913(b), (c) (1988). The Secretary therefore violated the CDBG Act by failing to follow procedures mandated by the statute before reducing Kansas City's 1987 grant.

C. The Inapplicability of Section 104(d)

The Secretary contends that notice and an opportunity for a hearing were not required because the Act gives the Secretary the choice of whether to proceed under section 111 or section 104(d). He claims that the action against Kansas City was permissible because section 104(d) authorizes the Secretary to review a grantee's past performance and to make "appropriate adjustments in the amount of the annual grants." 42 U.S.C. § 5304(d). We reject this argument because it is flatly at odds with the terms of the statute.

Nothing in section 104(d) suggests that it covers sanctions sought for past substantial noncompliance or that it carves out an exception to section 111. The Secretary has not charged that the City's current use of CDBG funds is improper, but rather seeks to impose sanctions to remedy the City's alleged past noncompliance. Section 104(d) is therefore inapplicable, and the Secretary may not avoid the procedural requirements of section 111 by invoking the adjustment authority of section 104(d).

Our conclusion that section 104(d) does not authorize the Secretary's actions against Kansas City also follows from a review of the 1977 amendments to the CDBG Act. In 1977, Congress amended the "appropriate adjustment" provision of section 104(d) to add the following language:

> With respect to assistance made available to [nonentitlement areas], the Secretary may adjust, reduce, or withdraw such assistance, or take other action as appropriate in accordance with the Secretary's reviews and audits under this subsection, except that funds already expended on eligible activities under this chapter shall not be recaptured or deducted from future assistance to such [nonentitlement areas].

Pub. L. No. 95-128, § 104(e)(2), 91 Stat. 1111, 1115 (1977), *codified at* 42 U.S.C. § 5304(d) (Supp. IV 1986).

This provision does not affect entitlement cities such as Kansas City. However, Congress would not have amended the Act to specify that HUD may "adjust, reduce, or withdraw" a nonentitlement area's assistance in connection with the review and audit procedures if section 104(d) already gave HUD that authority. HUD argues, to the contrary, that the fact that Congress specifically prevented HUD from using section 104(d) to recapture expended funds from a nonentitlement area's future assistance indicates that HUD has that power with respect to entitlement cities. Yet, it would be anomalous for Congress to give recipients of discretionary grants greater protection than cities that are legally entitled to receive annual funding. Rather, we believe that Congress specifically prevented HUD from recapturing expended funds from a nonentitlement area's future grant in order to ensure that HUD did not read the language in the first half of 1977 amendment to give it that power. The fact that Congress took pains to limit the Secretary's power in this respect further indicates that the Secretary's actions against Kansas City were not authorized by section 104(d).

We need not delineate here the precise scope of the authority available under section 104(d), because there is no conflict between section 104(d) and section 111 on the facts of this case. When, as here, a recipient's current use of grant funds is not in question, nothing in section 104(d) gives the Secretary the authority to condition or reduce current funding as a sanction for past noncompliance with the CDBG Act. Section 111 specifically provides the sanction for past noncompliance, and the Secretary must comply with the requirements of that section when he wishes to invoke those sanctions.

The Secretary cannot ignore the notice and hearing provisions of section 111 simply because he prefers the more informal procedures of section 104(d). HUD's own report admits that HUD has used section 104 in order to "avoid the more detailed and rigorous procedural standards of Section 111." HUD, Office of Community Planning & Dev., Consolidated Annual Report to Congress on Community Development Programs 33 (1983). This application of the statute plainly violates congressional intent. As we have previously noted, "[w]hen a statute dictates that parties receive notice and a hearing ... the provision of those basic procedural rights is not left to be decided by administrative 'flexibility' or 'discretion.'" In the district court's words, section 111 would be a "nullity" if the Secretary could avoid it whenever he chose, as he has for fourteen years, by using section 104(d) instead. *See* 699 F. Supp. at 528.

D. The Importance of Section 111 Procedural Protections

One of the principal purposes of the CDBG Act was to develop "a consistent system of Federal aid which ... provides assistance on an annual basis, with maximum certainty and minimum delay, upon which communities can rely in their planning." 42 U.S.C. § 5301(d)(1) (1982). Statutory procedural protections play a critical role in this scheme, because they ensure that a city legally entitled to an annual CDBG grant will not be "precipitously deprived of funding" pursuant to arbitrary action by HUD. *East Ark. Legal Servs. v. Legal Servs. Corp.,* 742 F.2d 1472, 1480 (D.C. Cir. 1984), *cert. denied,* 470 U.S. 1028 (1985). In the present case, for example, HUD subjected Kansas City to a potential loss of $3.2 million simply for refusing to record certain income in a particular column and thus to acquiesce in HUD's interpretation of that income. The remaining $500,000 was related to assessments that the City believes both were properly made and involved an amount closer to $197,000. The City thus risked losing over half of its annual grant without being given its rightful opportunity to dispute HUD's contentions in a hearing.

We are particularly mindful of the importance of giving effect to section 111 in light of the due process rights involved. As this court has noted, "[I]n most cases, Congress has been silent on the question of a grantee's procedural rights when an agency decides to terminate some or all of its federal grant." When, as in this case, Congress has not been silent, a court has a special obligation to ensure that the agency does not "end-run the clear procedural protections which Congress provided." *Id.* at 1480; *accord Conecuh-Monroe Community Action Agency v. Bowen,* 852 F.2d 581, 589 (D.C. Cir. 1988) (refusing to adopt an agency's statutory interpretation that would destroy the protection Congress provided to grant recipients).

III. CONCLUSION

Congress specifically required the Secretary to provide CDBG entitlement cities with reasonable notice and an opportunity for a hearing before conditioning, reducing or terminating their current grants as a sanction for past noncompliance. The Secretary did not follow those procedures when it conditioned Kansas City's 1987 grant. The judgment of the district court is therefore affirmed.

Notes and Questions

1. How significant a right is the hearing process provided under section 111 of the Act? Is a local government likely to accept the offer of a hearing if that government is clearly not in compliance with applicable statutory or regulatory requirements? The cost of litigation challenging HUD in court must be shouldered by the local government from its own funds; unless defending against HUD litigation. In the latter case, costs of litigation either in court or in an administrative hearing can be reimbursed out of available grant funds. Doing so, however, reduces the funds available for programmatic objectives of the local government. Is there any advantage, given that disincentive, for a recipient to use an administrative hearing as a delaying tactic? Can local political considerations affect the local judgment about seeking a hearing? Can federal program funds provided recipients be used to cover legal expenses to resolve disputes with HUD concerning administration of the federal program. See OMB Circular A-87, 10. "Defense and prosecution of criminal and civil proceedings, and claims.... b. Legal expenses required in the administration of Federal programs are allowable. Legal expenses for prosecution of claims against the Federal Government are unallowable."

2. Given the general philosophy of block grants for post-review of expenditures, the use of preestablished formulas to allocate appropriations, and creation of an "entitlement" status for recipients of CDBG funds, what expectations would Congress reasonably have had regarding HUD monitoring of a local government's use of CDBG funds? What function is served by having a local government submit an annual statement of *proposed* use of funds? Of what significance is it that at HUD's request, Congress deleted formal CDBG application procedures in 1983? What function does section 104(d) serve after that change? Is it reasonable to expect HUD to audit use of funds during the program year so as to be able to react under section 104(d) by year's end, before approving the new proposed use of the year's funds in the annual statement?

3. Originally a 75-day limit was imposed on HUD within which it had to act on the annual application for funding by an entitlement justification. Congress eliminated that requirement in 1981 and HUD substituted a regulation that promises only that funds generally will be provided within 30 days. In fact, HUD has taken more than three or four months to act in some instances, causing significant disruption in funding for personnel and activities of local organizations that carry out many CDBG projects. Since reduction of federal nit-picking with local decisions was a major objective of the block grant

concept, is more than 30 days processing time ever justified? Since adverse audit findings should require that notice of the alleged violation be provided and a hearing offered, is it realistic for HUD to try to deal with audit issues as part of its annual review of entitlement funds?

4. Section 106(d) provides for reallocation of amounts withheld under section 104(d) and section 111. The funds, however, are to be kept within the same geographical area as that of the recipient from whom the funds were taken. What policy objectives are served by this provision?

5. Equivalent issues would seem equally applicable to funding for public housing given the greater discretion and freedom provided in HUD's 1998 housing legislation. What protections should be provided for recipients of these funds against arbitrary HUD actions in disregard of local decision making? To what extent should considerations related to the local housing authority's competence in handling its operations be considered? Can you conceive of circumstances that would impel a local community to request of HUD that it be allowed to take over the program pursuant to provisions of the 1998 legislation? *See* Quality Housing and Work Responsibility Act of 1998, Pub. L. No. 105-276, §561, 112 Stat. 2616 (*amending* the Housing Act of 1937, by adding a new Title IV—Home Rule Flexible Grant Demonstration, *codified at* selected sections of 42 U.S.C.). Since the city must still deal with HUD will it have achieved any advantages in dealing directly with what has been characterized by some as a paternal and plodding public housing bureaucracy at HUD? What are the considerations applicable to a local government in circumstances where HUD threatens to take over a housing authority and bring in HUD-selected consultants to administer the program? *See* Cranston-Gonzales National Affordable Housing Act, §105, 42 U.S.C. §12705 (setting forth extensive criteria governing required state and local housing strategies).

6. Grant funds are credited to a letter of credit. This enables the Treasury to retain funds for the government's own use until they are actually needed by the local government recipient for a specified, permissible use. This means that significant backlogs of funds are held in these accounts pending the recipient's requests for payment. Several years may be required before certain brick and mortar activities actually need the funds. What impact does the accumulation of funds have on federal program objectives, especially as contrasted to earlier categorical program requirements that often mandated that funds be obligated to recipients within relatively limited time periods?

A Note on the Chevron *Defense*

As part of the court's decision in *Kansas City,* above, it makes reference to and rejects the government's reliance on the decision in *Chevron, U.S.A., Inc. v. National Resources Defense Council, Inc.,* 467 U.S. 837 (1984) in support of its interpretation of the two sections of the statute. Several theories have evolved over the years regarding the weight and deference to be accorded federal administrative agencies' interpretations of their statutory authority. The more traditional approach has been that the interpretive authority is primarily that of the courts. The agency interpretation is treated as that of an expert but is still simply a factor in the court's analysis of the statute. The other treatment of administrative interpretation has been to have courts defer to the agency's expertise and involvement with the legislation it is to enforce. This was the position taken by the Court in *Chevron.*

What is significant is that in most any litigation in which the government's action is challenged, a *Chevron* defense of deference to the agency's decision is likely to be presented. In most cases this deference is claimed for agency rulemaking and was not based on a claim that whatever administrative action was taken must be given deference. In the *Kansas City* situation, there was not only an asserted conflict of statutes that needed to be resolved, but there was also a conflict between regulations issued by the agency that mirrored the statutory conflict. In those circumstances, should reliance be given to what the agency now says should be the interpretation given to the statute.

In *Kansas City,* in fact, the only source for the interpretation HUD was asserting was provided by the affidavit, attached to a pleading in the case, of an assistant general counsel of the department as to what its practice had been. The informal nature of these circumstances presents vivid evidence of why deference to an administrative agency's interpretation of its own authority from the statutes governing its actions that has not been formally subject to notice and hearing requirements under the APA is suspect.

When the federal agency approves a local program or project, the local agency is normally satisfied with the federal decision. Objection may come, however, from private interests affected by the federal funding decision who were not part of the decision-making process. Note, for example, the litigation possibilities in HUD's regulation of the Brooke Amendment's public housing subsidies. A local housing authority could conceivably have challenged HUD's interpretation of the statute. Otherwise, the challenge would have to be brought by private litigants such as project residents, tenant organizations, or a housing advocacy group. Whether such groups can mount a challenge is discussed below.

a. Implied Rights of Actions

One way in which agency actions in housing programs has been challenged is on the basis of a claim that the federal statute includes an implied right of action in federal court that allows the plaintiff beneficiary to sue. The next two cases consider the availability of implied causes of action in cases brought against HUD and local housing and community development agencies by program beneficiaries or their representatives. The first was written by current Supreme Court Justice Breyer when on the First Circuit.

N.A.A.C.P., Boston Chapter v. Secretary of Housing and Community Development

United States Court of Appeals
817 F.2d 149 (1st Cir. 1987)

Before BOWNES, BREYER, and TORRUELLA, Circuit Judges.

BREYER, Circuit Judge....

[Plaintiffs filed an action seeking interpretation and enforcement of § 808 of the Fair Housing Act, which requires HUD "to affirmatively further" the policies of the act The plaintiff claimed that HUD had not complied with this provision in its administration of Community Development Block Grant funds and Urban Development Action Grants it awarded to the City of Boston. The court first had to determine whether the statute included an implied cause of action to bring suit against HUD. The part of the Court's opinion discussing that issue is set forth:—Eds.]

II *Private Right of Action*

The NAACP argues that the district court's dismissal of its case is wrong because Congress, in enacting Title VIII, implicitly created a "private right of action" allowing it to enforce "directly" the obligations that Title VIII imposes upon the federal government. *See Cort v. Ash,* 422 U.S. 66 (1975). The short, conclusive answer to this argument, however, is that this court has recently held that Congress did not create any such direct private cause of action under Title VIII. *Latinos Unidos de Chelsea en Accion v. Secretary of Housing and Urban Development,* 799 F.2d 774, 791–93 (1st Cir. 1986).

In fact, it is difficult to understand why a court would ever hold that Congress, in enacting a statute that creates federal obligations, has implicitly created a private right of action against the *federal* government, for there is hardly ever any need for Congress to do so. That is because federal action is nearly always reviewable for conformity with statutory obligations without any such "private right of action." *See Abbott Laboratories v. Gardner,* 387 U.S. 136, 140 (1967) ("judicial review of a final agency action ... will not be cut off unless there is persuasive reason to believe that such was the purpose of Congress"); *American School of Magnetic Healing v. McAnnulty,* 187 U.S. 94, 110 (1902) (where agency makes "a clear mistake of law ... the courts ... must have power in a proper proceeding to grant relief"); 5 Davis, *Administrative Law Treatise* § 28.1, at 254–56 (1984); Jaffe, *Judicial Control of Administrative Action* 339–53 (1965). This "presumption" of judicial reviewability, now codified in the Administrative Procedure Act, 5 U.S.C. § 701 *et seq.*, applies not only to "[a]gency action made reviewable by statute," but also to any other "final agency action for which there is no other adequate remedy in a court," 5 U.S.C. § 704. Any person "adversely affected or aggrieved by agency action," 5 U.S.C. § 702, may ask a court to "set aside agency action ... not in accordance with law" or to "compel agency action unlawfully withheld," 5 U.S.C. § 706.

Given these (and related) principles of administrative law, as set forth in the APA, it is not surprising that cases discussing a "private right of action" implied from a federal statute do not involve a right of action against the federal government. Rather, they typically involve statutes that impose obligations upon a *nonfederal person* (a private entity or a nonfederal agency of government). The statute typically provides that the federal government will enforce the obligations against the nonfederal person. The "private right of action" issue is whether Congress meant to give an injured person a right himself to enforce the federal statute directly against the nonfederal person or whether the injured person can do no more than ask the federal government to enforce the statute. *Cort v. Ash,* the leading case on the subject, simply lays down a set of rules to help the courts determine what Congress intended when the statute itself is silent.

One can imagine a few instances in which a court might, notwithstanding the APA, wonder whether Congress meant to create a private right of action against the federal government. The APA, for example, does not award attorney's fees to a successful litigant. *But see* 28 U.S.C. § 2412(b) (authorizing award of attorney's fees against the United States "to the same extent that any other party would be liable under the common law or under the terms of any statute which specifically provides for such an award"). Yet, a particular statute might provide for attorney's fees for successful private enforcement of its obligations. A court might then have to decide whether a private party who enforces the statute against the federal government also is entitled to attorney's fees, thus requiring the court to determine whether the action arises under the *particular* act or whether it is simply a general APA-based request for judicial review.... Alternatively, a court might have to decide whether Congress implicitly means a statute to provide a party with a "private right of action" against one of the few federal bodies exempted from the APA's coverage. *See* 5 U.S.C. § 701(b)(1) (exempting, *inter alia,* Congress, federal courts, territorial and District of Columbia governments, and certain military bodies). In other special circumstances it might have to decide whether Congress implicitly means a statute to confer a private right of action that differs in its procedural contours from the review that the APA typically provides. *See* 5 U.S.C. § 704 (ordinarily requiring exhaustion of administrative remedies before invoking APA). One would ordinarily expect, however, that when Congress means to permit a private party to ask a court to review the legality of federal actions in a manner that differs from APA review, Congress will say so explicitly in the statute.... Otherwise, it is reasonable to assume that Congress meant the APA to govern.

Of course, we recognize that to apply the APA will mean no review if (to use the APA's language) "statutes preclude judicial review" or "agency action is committed to agency discretion by law." 5 U.S.C. § 701(a). But this fact creates no anomaly, for it would be a self-contradiction for a court to find both (1) that one of these exceptions applies and (2) that Congress nonetheless intended to grant a private right of action permitting review.

We note that in those few cases in which courts have spoken of inferring a "private right of action" against the federal government, the courts have not considered the role of the Administrative Procedure Act. *See, e.g., Young v. Pierce*, 544 F. Supp. 1010, 1017–19 (E.D. Tex. 1982) (finding a private right of action under Title VIII). Had they done so, they might have found the discussion of "private right of action" unnecessary. *See Munoz-Mendoza v. Pierce,* 711 F.2d 421, 429 (1st Cir. 1983). (suggesting that district court on remand consider civil rights action as arising under APA rather than under direct private right of action). Regardless, no special circumstances exists in this case, or under Title VIII, that would call for other than APA review. Hence, we affirm our holding that Congress intended no special private right of action against the federal government.

Notes and Questions

1. The part of this opinion dealing with the substantive issue raised under the Fair Housing Act regarding HUD's duty to "affirmatively further" is reprinted in Chapter 6 *infra*. At this point we need to note that the failure to succeed on the assertion of a private right of action was not fatal to seeking review. But there are other issues that the agency can raise on the substantive question which are discussed in Chapter 6.

2. Generally, it might be said that the structures for the administration of housing and community development programs stand as obstacles to effective court review or action. Sometimes that is not the case. Consider how the Court review was obtained in the following case and the way in which the Court viewed the claim that the HUD was the only forum in which review could be obtained for the issue the plaintiffs sought to raise.

3. Note that the Court mentioned the possible need to enforce federally-created rights against third parties. Recall that the Brooke Amendment placed a limit on the proportion of a family's income to be devoted to rent for public housing tenants. If tenants claim that a PHA is not complying with the Brooke Amendment limits can the tenant sue the PHA directly to seek adjudication of the issue or is the matter exclusively committed to enforcement by HUD?

The next case addresses this issue.

Wright v. Roanoke Redevelopment and Housing Authority

United States Supreme Court
479 U.S. 418 (1987)

Justice WHITE delivered the opinion of the Court.

Petitioners in this case, tenants living in low-income housing projects owned by respondent, brought suit under 42 U.S.C. § 1983, alleging that respondent overbilled them for their utilities and thereby violated the rent ceiling imposed by the Brooke Amendment to the Housing Act of 1937, and the implementing regulations of the Department of Housing and Urban Development (HUD). The District Court, 605 F. Supp. 532 (W.D. Va. 1984), and the Court of Appeals for the Fourth Circuit, 771 F.2d 833 (4th Cir. 1985), concluded that petitioners did not have a cause of action under § 1983. We granted certiorari and now reverse.

I

Respondent is one of many public housing authorities (PHAs) established throughout the country under the United States Housing Act of 1937 to provide affordable housing for low-income people. In 1969, the Housing Act was amended in a fundamental respect: the Brooke Amendment imposed a ceiling for rents charged to low-income people living in public housing projects, and, as later amended, provides that a low-income family "shall pay as rent" a specified percentage of its income. HUD has consistently considered "rent" to include a reasonable amount for the use of utilities which is defined by regulation as that amount equal to or less than an amount determined by the PHA to be a reasonable part of the rent paid by low-income tenants.

In their suit against respondent, petitioners alleged that respondent had overcharged them for their utilities by failing to comply with the applicable HUD regulations in establishing the amount of utility service to which petitioners were entitled. Thus, according to petitioners, respondent imposed a surcharge for "excess" utility consumption that should have been part of petitioners' rent and deprived them of their statutory right to pay only the prescribed maximum portion of their income as rent. The District Court granted summary judgment for respondent on petitioners' § 1983 claim, holding that a private cause of action was unavailable to enforce the Brooke Amendment. The Court of Appeals for the Fourth Circuit affirmed. Relying on two of its earlier decisions, the Court of Appeals held that while the Brooke Amendment confers certain rights on tenants, these rights are enforceable only by HUD, not by the individual tenant: "the situation is very analogous to the one in which a trustee [that is HUD], not *the cestui que trust,* must bring suit."

II

Maine v. Thiboutot, 448 U.S. 1 (1980), held that § 1983 was available to enforce violations of federal statutes by agents of the State. *Pennhurst State School and Hospital v. Halderman,* 451 U.S. 1 (1981) and *Middlesex County Sewerage Auth. v. National Sea Clammers Assn.,* 453 U.S. 1 (1981), however, recognized two exceptions to the application of 1983 to remedy statutory violations: where Congress has foreclosed such enforcement of the statute in the enactment itself and where the statute did not create enforceable rights, privileges, or immunities within the meaning of § 1983. Similarly, *Smith v. Robinson,* 468 U.S. 992 (1984), held that allowing a plaintiff to circumvent the Education of the Handicapped Act's administrative remedies would be inconsistent with Congress' carefully tailored scheme, which itself allowed private parties to seek remedies for violating federal law. Under these cases, if there is a state deprivation of a "right" secured by a federal statute, section 1983 provides a remedial cause of action unless the state actor demonstrates by express provision or other specific evidence from the statute itself that Congress intended to foreclose such private enforcement. "We do not lightly conclude that Congress intended to preclude reliance on § 1983 as a remedy" for the deprivation of a federally secured right.

Here, the Court of Appeals held that the statute and the Brooke Amendment clearly manifested congressional intention to vest in HUD the exclusive power to enforce the benefits due housing project tenants and hence the intention to foreclose both a private cause of action under the Housing Act and any private enforcement under § 1983. For the Court of Appeals, the barrier was not the lack of statutory right or its quality or enforceability—"the plaintiffs under 42 U.S.C. § 1437a [the Brooke Amendment] have certain rights,"—but the fact that Congress had not intended tenants to have the authority themselves to sue: "HUD alone may, as quasi trustee, take legal action, for the right is explicitly tailored not to allow the beneficiaries, the low cost housing tenants, to do so."

We disagree with the Court of Appeals' rather summary conclusion that the administrative scheme of enforcement foreclosed private enforcement.... Not only are the Brooke Amendment and its legislative history devoid of any express indication that exclusive enforcement authority was vested in HUD, but there have also been both congressional and agency actions indicating that enforcement authority is not centralized and that private actions were anticipated. Neither, in our view, are the remedial mechanisms provided sufficiently comprehensive and effective to raise a clear inference that Congress intended to foreclose a § 1983 cause of action for the enforcement of tenants' rights secured by federal law.

HUD itself has never provided a procedure by which tenants could complain to it about the alleged failures of PHAs to abide by their annual contribution contracts, the Brooke Amendment or HUD regulations; nor has it taken unto itself the task of reviewing PHA grievance procedure decisions. Moreover, § 966.57(c) of HUD's grievance procedure regulations provides that a decision terminating a grievance proceeding shall in no way affect the rights of a tenant either to seek "trial *de novo* or judicial review in any judicial proceedings, which may thereafter be brought in the matter." HUD thus had no thought that its own supervisory powers or the grievance system that it had established foreclosed resort to the courts by tenants who claimed that a PHA was not observing the commands of the Brooke Amendment.

There is other evidence clearly indicating that in HUD's view tenants have the right to bring suit in federal court to challenge housing authorities' calculations of utility allowances. Among HUD's 1982 proposed regulations was § 865.476(d), 47 Fed. Reg. 35249, 35254 (1982), which would have confined tenant utility allowance challenges to the procedures available in state court. The final regulation, however, contained no such limitation and contemplated that tenants could challenge PHA actions in federal as well as state courts. 24 C.F.R. § 965 473(e) (1985). As the comment accompanying the final regulation explained, the proposal to limit challenges to state court actions had been abandoned. The final "provision does not preclude Federal court review." 49 Fed. Reg. at 31403 (1984). HUD's opinion as to available tenant remedies under the Housing Act is entitled to some deference by this Court.

In both *Sea Clammers* and *Smith v. Robinson,* the statutes at issue themselves provided for private judicial remedies, thereby evidencing congressional intent to supplant the § 1983 remedy. There is nothing of the kind found in the Brooke Amendment or elsewhere in the Housing Act. Indeed, the only private remedy provided for is the local grievance procedures which the Act now requires. These procedures are not open to class grievances, and even if tenants may grieve about a PHA's utility allowance schedule, which petitioners dispute, the existence of a state administrative remedy does not ordinarily foreclose resort to § 1983.

The Court of Appeals and respondents rely on HUD's authority to audit, enforce annual contributions contracts, and cut off federal funds. But these generalized powers are insufficient to indicate a congressional intention to foreclose § 1983 remedies.... HUD has the authority to audit, but it does not do so frequently and its own Handbook requires audits only every eight years. There are no other mechanisms provided to enable HUD to effectively oversee the performance of the some 3,000 local PHAs across the country. The statute does not require and HUD has not provided any formal procedure for tenants to bring to HUD's attention alleged PHA failures to abide by the Brooke Amendment and HUD regulations. Hence, there will be little occasion to exercise HUD's power to sue PHAs to enforce the provisions of the annual contributions contracts. Respondent asserts PHAs must annually file their utility allowance schedules with HUD and that HUD must approve them, but the final regulations eliminated HUD's duty to approve these schedules before their effective date. 24 C.F.R. § 965.473(d) (1986). Review of the schedules would be done in the course of audits or reviews of PHA operations.

Lastly, it is said that tenants may sue on their lease in state courts and enforce their Brooke Amendment rights in that litigation. Perhaps they could, but the state court remedy is hardly a reason to bar an action under § 1983, which was adopted to provide a federal remedy for the enforcement of federal rights.

In sum, we conclude that nothing in the Housing Act or the Brooke Amendment evidences that Congress intended to preclude petitioners' § 1983 claim against respondent.

III

Although the Court of Appeals read the Brooke Amendment as extending to housing project tenants certain rights enforceable only by HUD, respondent asserts that neither the Brooke Amendment nor the interim regulations gave the tenants any specific or definable rights to utilities, that is, no enforceable rights within the meaning of 1983. We perceive little substance in this claim. The Brooke Amendment could not be clearer: as further amended in 1981, tenants could be charged as rent no more and no less than 30 percent of their income. This was a mandatory limitation focusing on the individual family and its income. The intent to benefit tenants is undeniable. Nor is there any question HUD interim regulations, in effect when this suit began, expressly required that a "reasonable" amount for utilities be included in rent that a PHA was allowed to charge, an interpretation to which HUD has adhered both before and after the adoption of the Brooke Amendment. HUD's view is entitled to deference as a valid interpretation of the statute, and Congress in the course of amending that provision has not disagreed with it.

Respondent nevertheless asserts that the provision for a "reasonable" allowance for utilities is too vague and amorphous to confer on tenants an enforceable "right" within the meaning of 1983 and that the whole matter of utility allowances must be left to the discretion of the PHA, subject to supervision by HUD. The regulations, however, defining the statutory concept of "rent" as including utilities, have the force of law, they specifically set out guidelines that the PHAs were to follow in establishing utility allowances, and they require notice to tenants and an opportunity to comment on proposed allowances. In our view, the benefits Congress intended to confer on tenants are sufficiently specific and definite to qualify as enforceable rights under *Pennhurst* and § 1983, rights that are not, as respondent suggests, beyond the competence of the judiciary to enforce.

The judgment of the Court of Appeals is accordingly reversed.

Justice O'CONNOR, with whom the Chief Justice, Justice POWELL, and Justice SCALIA join, dissenting.

[Justice O'Connor argued in dissent that there was no basis in the statutory language or legislative history to support the conclusion that Congress intended to create a statutory right to reasonable utilities, that HUD had consistently viewed the question whether utilities should be included in the definition of rent as a matter of agency discretion rather than statutory entitlement, and that tenants have an adequate remedy without resort to § 1983 because they can sue on their leases under a clause that obligates the housing authority to provide utilities. She was also concerned that agency regulations were relied upon by the majority in arriving at their formulation of congressional intent.—Eds.]

Notes and Questions

1. What is the difference between the use of the implied right of action in *NAACP* and the § 1983 remedy in *Wright*? Why not use the APA in *Wright*? For a pre-*Wright* case refusing to imply a cause of action against a private landlord under a regulatory agreement required for federally subsidized housing under a federal housing statute, see *Falzarano v. United States,* 607 F.2d 506 (1st Cir. 1979).

2. The implied cause of action doctrine derives from *Cort v. Ash,* discussed in *NAACP*. The doctrine has had a varied history in the federal courts. *Cort* delineated four factors as relevant in determining whether a private remedy is implicit in a statute that does not expressly provide for one: (1) is plaintiff one of the class for whose especial benefit the statute was enacted? (2) is there any indication of legislative intent, explicit or implicit, either to create such a remedy or deny one? (3) is it consistent with the underlying purposes of the legislative scheme to imply such a remedy for plaintiff? and (4) is the cause of action one traditionally relegated to state law so that it would be inappropriate to infer a cause of action based solely on federal law?

Later Supreme Court cases have tended to find against implied causes of action outside the housing field, as in *Thompson v. Thompson,* 484 U.S. 174 (1988), where Justice Scalia suggested in dissent that *Cort v. Ash* has been overruled. For discussion of this case, see David Bryson, *Implied Private Rights of Action: Progress on the Road Back from Chaos,* 22 Clearinghouse Rev. 143 (1988).

In *Wilder v. Virginia Hospital Association*, 496 U.S. 498 (1990), the Court consolidated the four-factor *Cort* test used since 1975 into a question of whether there is a separation of powers violation in the judiciary's review of congressional intent and set forth a three-factor test:

(1) Whether the plaintiffs are the intended beneficiaries of the federal statute;

(2) Whether the statute is vague; and

(3) Whether the judiciary has the power to enforce the statute.

Subsequently, in *Suter v. Artist M.*, 503 U.S. 347 (1992), the Court did not use this test and departed from its previous presumption of the validity of the statute. For a critique of this decision, see Lisa L. Frye, Suter v. Artist M. *and Statutory Remedies Under Section 1983: Alteration Without Justification*, 71 N.C. L. Rev. 1171 (1993). *See also* Carol Schwetschenau Wood, Note, *Section 1983 and the Brooke Amendment to the 1937 Housing Act:* Wright v. Roanoke Redevelopment and Housing Authority, 56 U. Cin. L. Rev. 1141 (1988).

3. For a general critique of how the Supreme Court handles the separation of powers doctrine in contemplating *Wright*, see Lisa E. Key, *Private Enforcement of Federal Funding Conditions Under § 1983: The Supreme Court's Failure to Adhere to the Doctrine of Separation of Powers*, 29 U.C. Davis L. Rev. 283 (1996).

4. *Wright* actually combined an analysis of whether an implied right of action was available with an analysis of whether a similar private right of action is available under

§ 1983 of the Federal Civil Rights Act. The analysis under § 1983 is similar but there are subtle differences. Is it apparent from *Wright* what these differences are? To answer this question re-read especially the discussion of the *Pennhurst, Sea Clammers,* and *Robinson* cases. These cases deal with the availability of a private right of action under § 1983.

A student Note has concluded that the Court's analysis under § 1983 parallels the analysis it would have undertaken to determine whether an implied cause of action was available, although the Court did not sufficiently clarify the distinction. Paul E. Harner, Note, *Implied Private Rights of Action Under the United States Housing Act of 1937,* 1987 Duke L.J. 915.

5. *Wright* left open the extent to which courts will imply a cause of action under federal housing statutes. For a post-*Wright* case implying a cause of action under § 1983 to enforce statutory admission procedures in a federally subsidized housing program, see *Drake v. Pierce,* 691 F. Supp. 264 (W.D. Wash. 1988).

6. A theory sometimes used to challenge HUD or local administrators of federal programs has been the contention that the sub-recipients or individuals for whom the benefits are targeted are "third party beneficiaries" of the program entitled to enforce program requirements or agreements against either HUD or the local administrators. *See Price v. Pierce,* 823 F.2d 1114 (7th Cir. 1987) (rejecting contention by low-income applicants denied Section 8 units that they are the beneficiaries of the agreement between HUD, the state developmental authority and the developers of the project).

A Note on Standing in Federal Court to Challenge Housing and Community Development Programs

Standing to sue is another judicial hurdle that faces third party plaintiffs who challenge federal housing programs in federal court. The standing problem raises issues similar to the implied right of action problem, but has a constitutional rather than a statutory basis. It arises because third party beneficiaries are not part of the process through which federal program grants are awarded. That process only includes HUD and the recipient local agency. Third parties must allege some interest conferred on them by the program that allows them to challenge the program in federal court.

Standing problems permeate federal litigation over federal housing programs. The concept of standing is a "door closing" device that allows or requires a court to refuse to hear a case on the merits. Beyond that rather simple concept, lie doctrine and explication that make standing law, at best, difficult to understand, and at worst, incomprehensible.

Federal standing rules seem to have three "elements:" (1) an "injury in fact" requirement; (2) a "causality" test; and, (3) a later added "redressability" component.

Injury-in-fact. Litigants must satisfy a constitutional "injury in fact" test to meet the federal constitutional requirement that federal courts may only hear actual "cases and controversies." A case or controversy is present only when the litigant can show actual injury.

Baker v. Carr, 369 U.S. 186 (1962), the legislative reapportionment case welcomed in a liberalizing of justiciability problems that signaled the trend of development by the Warren Court. It appeared that "injury in fact" was the requirement for a citizen to seek judicial review. The Court subsequently decided *Flast v. Cohen,* 392 U.S. 83 (1968), which liberalized taxpayer suits in the field of establishment clause interpretation, suits which had been barred under *Frothingham v. Mellon,* 262 U.S. 447 (1923).

The federal courts have since adopted "prudential" standing rules that place discretionary limits on the cases they agree to take. One of these rules requires that the litigant be within the "zone of interest" of the statute or constitutional provision on which the litigation is based. This rule—which may have lost favor with the United States Supreme Court—is troublesome in litigation under housing and community development legislation. This legislation arguably is enacted to provide benefits to the general public. Community development legislation, for example, is intended to improve the condition of substandard urban neighborhoods. Recall again the discussion of the social costs and social welfare theories of governmental intervention discussed at the beginning of this chapter.

In *Massachusetts v. E.P.A*, 549 U.S. 497, 516–18 (2007), Justice Stevens, speaking for the Supreme Court majority, reviewed the injury issue as a basis for standing stating:

> EPA maintains that because greenhouse gas emissions inflict widespread harm, the doctrine of standing presents an insuperable jurisdictional obstacle. We do not agree. At bottom, "the gist of the question of standing" is whether petitioners have "such a personal stake in the outcome of the controversy as to assure that concrete adverseness which sharpens the presentation of issues upon which the court so largely depends for illumination." *Baker* v. *Carr*, 369 U. S. 186, 204 (1962). As Justice Kennedy explained in his *Lujan* concurrence:
>
>> While it does not matter how many persons have been injured by the challenged action, the party bringing suit must show that the action injures him in a concrete and personal way. This requirement is not just an empty formality. It preserves the vitality of the adversarial process by assuring both that the parties before the court have an actual, as opposed to professed, stake in the outcome, and that the legal questions presented ... will be resolved, not in the rarified atmosphere of a debating society, but in a concrete factual context conducive to a realistic appreciation of the consequences of judicial action. 504 U.S. at 581.
>
> To ensure the proper adversarial presentation, *Lujan* holds that a litigant must demonstrate that it has suffered a concrete and particularized injury that is either actual or imminent, that the injury is fairly traceable to the defendant, and that it is likely that a favorable decision will redress that injury. However, a litigant to whom Congress has "accorded a procedural right to protect his concrete interests,"—here, the right to challenge agency action unlawfully withheld, §7607(b)(1)—"can assert that right without meeting all the normal standards for redressability and immediacy." When a litigant is vested with a procedural right, that litigant has standing if there is some possibility that the requested relief will prompt the injury-causing party to reconsider the decision that allegedly harmed the litigant. See also *Sugar Cane Growers Cooperative of Fla.* v. *Veneman*, 289 F. 3d 89, 94–95 (D.C. Cir. 2002) ("A [litigant] who alleges a deprivation of a procedural protection to which he is entitled never has to prove that if he had received the procedure the substantive result would have been altered. All that is necessary is to show that the procedural step was connected to the substantive result").
>
> Only one of the petitioners needs to have standing to permit us to consider the petition for review. See *Rumsfeld v. Forum for Academic and Institutional Rights, Inc.*, 547 U.S. 47 n.2 (2006). We stress here, as did Judge Tatel below, the special position and interest of Massachusetts. It is of considerable relevance that the party seeking review here is a sovereign State and not, as it was in *Lujan*, a private individual.

The causality rule. The constitutional standing rule also requires the litigant to show that the injury was caused by the defendant. This can be shown by showing that the "injury in fact" is indeed being caused by the conduct complained of and that there exists some relief the court can grant that will provide a remedy for that injury. This rule is troublesome in housing and community development litigation. In many cases, the litigant attacks a funding decision in a federal assistance program. A successful showing in court that the funding decision was incorrect does not necessarily mean that the agency will make another funding decision that will meet the litigant's demands.

The causality rule was applied by the Burger Court, in *Warth v. Seldin,* 422 U.S. 490 (1975), to deny standing to third parties challenging an exclusionary zoning ordinance of a suburb near Rochester, New York. Among the plaintiffs in this case were minority residents of Rochester who alleged that the suburb's exclusionary zoning made it impossible for them to find housing at prices they could afford. One of the other plaintiffs was a nonprofit corporation working to remedy the housing shortage in the Rochester area. The plaintiffs claimed that the purpose and effect of the suburban zoning ordinance was the exclusion of lower income and racial minorities, but the Supreme Court did not treat the case as a racial discrimination claim. It was simply not demonstrated that but for the suburb's zoning that affordable subsidized housing would have been developed. The injury to taxpayers of the central city of Rochester forced to house a disproportionate number of the poor was ruled to be the city's fault and not that of suburban Penfield.

Redressability. The constitutional standing rule also requires the litigant to show that if the litigant succeeds in the case that the court can fashion judicial relief that will remedy the harm complained of. The Supreme Court reaffirmed the causality and redressability elements of the *Warth* doctrine in *Simon v. Eastern Kentucky Welfare Rights Organization,* 426 U.S. 26 (1977). *Simon* rejected an attack on the granting of a charitable exemption by the federal Internal Revenue Service (IRS) to a hospital that failed adequately to serve the poor in compliance with IRS regulations. The Court found that denying the exemption would not guarantee that the hospital would serve the poor. In *Warth v. Seldin,* in a complex opinion, the Supreme Court in part based its decision on the premise that invalidation of the exclusionary suburban zoning ordinance did not carry with it a "substantial probability" that construction of housing affordable by lower-income groups would follow.

One perspective on the decision is that no "injury in fact" could be shown because plaintiffs were unable to identify particular projects that had been blocked. Another is that "causality" was lacking because plaintiffs did not claim that they wanted to and could afford to live in any particular project. Professor Sager has roundly criticized the *Warth* decision:

> The bare requirement that there be a causal link between the injury upon which a claim of standing is based and the practices against which the litigation is levied is hardly objectionable. Without such a requirement, the notion of a personal injury as the *sine qua non* of judicial attention would be nonsensical. But the requirement of a "substantial probability" showing, however, badly confuses the idea of what constitutes an injury. An injury can consist of the deprivation of an opportunity to secure some ultimate benefit; it does not have to be the deprivation of the ultimate benefit itself. By the majority's reasoning, the loss or theft of a lottery ticket would not be an injury.

Lawrence Gene Sager, *Questions I Wish I Had Never Asked: The Burger Court in Exclusionary Zoning,* 11 Sw. U.L. Rev. 509, 516 (1979).

Generalized Grievance. In order to have standing, plaintiffs must allege that they have been injured in some unique way, for injury to all in society is a nonjusticiable generalized grievance. *Schlesinger v. Reservists Committee to Stop the War,* 418 U.S. 208 (1974); *United States v. Richardson,* 418 U.S. 166 (1974).

Whither Standing Now? Did subsequent Supreme Court cases relax the strict "substantial probability" test adopted in *Warth? See Duke Power Co. v. Carolina Environmental Study Group,* 438 U.S. 59 (1978). In that case, the Court accepted the somewhat improbable finding by the federal district court that construction and operation of nuclear power plants would cease without a federal limitation on nuclear power plant liability.

In *Gladstone Realtors v. Village of Bellwood,* 441 U.S. 91 (1979), residents of a racially integrated neighborhood, to which black home buyers were selectively steered by real estate agents, were granted standing under the Federal Fair Housing Act to attack this racial steering. The Court granted standing even though the facts raised an obvious causality issue. It certainly is not clear that a complex social phenomenon such as neighborhood racial integration is governed solely by one set of practices, such as racial steering. Justice Powell, who also wrote the *Warth* opinion, held in *Gladstone* that the plaintiff need only have suffered "a distinct and palpable injury" that is "likely to be redressed if the requested relief is granted."

Echoing the program versus project distinction, the Court in *Warth* had also indicated that it would be more likely to confer standing when a plaintiff challenged the denial of a specific housing project on exclusionary grounds. This suggestion bore fruit in *Village of Arlington Heights v. Metropolitan Housing Development Corporation,* 429 U.S. 252 (1977), an action brought by a developer of a federally subsidized housing project. It challenged on racial discrimination and equal protection grounds the refusal of the village to grant a rezoning which would allow the project to be built. A black plaintiff also alleged that he had sought and would qualify for residence in the project. The Court, again in an opinion by Justice Powell, granted standing. Professor Sager notes that *Arlington Heights* adopted a more generous view of standing than the Court had adopted in *Warth:*

> In adjudging [the private plaintiff's] injury to be sufficient under the *Warth* test, the Court ignored both the possibility that the housing might not in fact be constructed and the remoteness of the likelihood that any one applicant would obtain housing amid the brisk competition for the units which would develop if they were completed. The individual plaintiffs in *Arlington Heights* could thus lay claim only to an intermediate state of affairs pursuant to which their opportunity to obtain housing was marginally enhanced.

Sager, *supra,* at 517 n.25. *See also* Lawrence Gene Sager, *Insular Majorities Unabated:* Warth v. Seldin *and* City of Eastlake v. Forest City Enterprises, Inc., 91 Harv. L. Rev. 1373 (1978).

Warth has become a dubious precedent, and its applicability to litigation under federal housing legislation is not clear. The decision may be explained by its context. The Supreme Court may have been unwilling to authorize the broad inquiry into exclusionary local zoning practices which the plaintiffs in that case demanded. Federal judicial experience in the school segregation cases may have taught the Supreme Court that federal court management of wide-sweeping reform of institutional governmental practices is unwise. Sager also suggests in his article that principles of federalism may underlie the *Warth* decision. The Supreme Court may be unwilling to allow federal court intrusion into areas of concern, such as zoning, which are strictly a matter of state and local competence unless the claim is based upon racial bias. *Arlington Heights* is examined further on the merits of the exclusionary zoning issue in Chapter 6 *infra.* We may note for now, however, that the Court adopted a highly restrictive view of racial discrimination in zoning under the equal protection clause that all but forecloses a racial discrimination claim against local zoning practices.

Principles of federalism do not inhibit the federal courts in granting standing to third party plaintiffs who challenge the administration of federal housing programs on grounds of violation of rights protected under federal law. This is the case even when a state or local actor is involved. The case that follows is representative of this kind of litigation.

Jackson v. Okaloosa County, Florida

United States Court of Appeals
21 F.3d 1531 (11th Cir. 1994)

ANDERSON, Circuit Judge:

Appellants Jackson and Musgrove appeal the dismissal of their class action complaint against Okaloosa County, Florida and its Commissioners, (the "County"), and the Fort Walton Beach Housing Authority and its members, (the "authority"), regarding the siting process for a new public housing project. All defendants were sued under the Fair Housing Act, 42 U.S.C. §§3601 *et seq.*, and the County was also sued under 42 U.S.C. §§1982 and 1983. Both defendants made motions to dismiss the complaint pursuant to Fed. R. Civ. P. 12(b)(6) that were granted. For the following reasons we reverse the decision of the district court and remand for further proceedings....

I. FACTS AND PROCEEDINGS BELOW

For the purpose of this appeal we accept the facts that follow as true. Plaintiff Jackson is an African-American woman who receives public benefits, lives in a racially impacted area of Fort Walton Beach, Florida, is eligible for public housing, and whose name is on the Authority's wait-list for public housing. She expects to move into a new project that will be built by the Authority, and she wants this facility to be located in an area without a concentrated minority population. Plaintiff Musgrove presently resides in public housing provided by the Authority, in the facility located at Third Street and Methodist Avenue. The census tract containing this unit is 38% African-American, the highest proportion within the territorial limit of the Authority. Because she does not want her racially impacted neighborhood to become further segregated, Musgrove does not want the new housing project to be constructed in her neighborhood. These two plaintiffs filed a class action against the defendants on behalf of themselves and all others similarly situated. The class has not yet been certified under Fed. R. Civ. P. 23(c).

The Authority was established under Fla. Stat. §421.04 to provide public low-income housing and housing assistance. It operates all public housing in the Fort Walton Beach area, which is a city with a population under 25,000. Current public housing facilities, which contain a total of 186 units, are located at Third Street and Methodist Avenue, and on Ed Brown Street. Under Florida law, the territorial area of operation of housing authorities in cities having a population of less than 25,000 includes the area within 5 miles of the territorial boundaries of that city. Fla. Stat. §421.03(6)(a). The area within five miles of Fort Walton Beach, Florida, includes areas that are unincorporated and lie within the boundaries of Okaloosa County....

The plaintiffs allege that the defendants have maintained racially segregated public housing in the Fort Walton Beach area. Although the Okaloosa County population is 8% African-American, all of the public housing units built within the Authority's territory have been built in one predominantly African-American neighborhood, within the city limits of Fort Walton Beach; and this neighborhood lies within the racially impacted census tract. Ninety-two percent of the residents in the Authority's existing housing are African-American, and eighty-six percent of the persons on the Authority's waiting list are African-American.

In July 1988, the Authority applied to HUD for $2,500,000 to construct 50 units of multi-family housing. In its application, the Authority identified a site on Bass Street that is adjacent to existing public housing as the proposed construction site, although there were several sites within the Authority's territorial limit that met HUD's selection criteria and were not in areas impacted by race. This proposed site also was located in the racially impacted census tract. HUD approved the Authority's application for the construction funds in September 1988.

HUD rules require a housing authority to obtain a cooperation agreement with pertinent local governments to build housing. Therefore, the Authority sought permission to build public housing in the unincorporated five-mile area from the Okaloosa County Board of County Commissioners. HUD procedure requires a housing authority to identify a potential site within the local government's jurisdiction when the authority seeks a cooperation agreement with that government. Thus, the Authority identified for discussion purposes a potential construction site within the unincorporated five-mile area when it approached the County. Several white residents living near this potential site expressed objections to the Authority's request. The County initially rejected the Authority's request. Later, the County agreed, in theory, to cooperate with the Authority. However, the County unilaterally enacted a policy (the "Policy") pursuant to which the County would permit the construction of public housing. The County tendered the Policy to the Authority in a unilaterally designated "Cooperative Agreement."

The Policy adopts several requirements for the approval of a site for public housing. No project can be sited in the unincorporated five-mile area unless approved by a majority vote of the Board of County Commissioners. Actual notice of the scheduled vote must be given to property owners in the affected area of the project. If the vote of the Board fails, project sponsors can only obtain approval by majority vote in a referendum of the residents in the voting precinct where the project would be located. The Policy also requires the Authority to pay the cost of notice to property owners of upcoming votes and referendums.

In January 1992, the Authority solicited bids for proposed sites for the construction of its 50 unit project. Although the Authority had proposed the Bass Street site, the bidding was open to other sites. However, the bidding procedure required than any site in the unincorporated five-mile area have site-specific approval of the County, thus in effect incorporating the requirement's of the County's Policy. One bidder submitted a site zoned for multi-family housing in the unincorporated five-mile area. That bidder sought site-specific approval of this site from the County, but requested that the site be approved without the procedural requirements of the Policy. The County informed the bidder that it would maintain adherence to the Policy, and the bidder did not complete the process for approval mandated by the Policy.

On February 26, 1992, the Authority ranked the bids for the project, but it did not consider the bid submitted in the unincorporated five-mile area, because that bidder had not obtained site-specific approval. The bid submitted for the unincorporated five-mile area was the only bid submitted that would have allowed the new facility to be sited in an area that was not racially impacted. The Authority ranked first a bid site submitted by Barber Construction, Inc. This site, located at Third Street and Shell Avenue, is located within the racially impacted census tract and is immediately adjacent to existing public housing, where 92% of the residents are African-American, including plaintiff Musgrove. HUD had not given final approval to the site at the time the plaintiffs filed their complaint.

On May 22, 1992, the appellants filed their complaint in the district court. The complaint claimed that the Authority had violated the Fair Housing Act by incorporating the Policy in the bidding process and maintaining a pattern of segregated residential public housing within the territorial limit of the Authority. The appellants made the same segregation claim against the County and alleged that by enacting the Policy the County had violated the Fair Housing Act, through intent and effect, by excluding African-American tenants of public housing from the unincorporated five-mile area. The complaint also alleged that the County, by enacting its Policy, had violated 42 U.S.C. §§ 1982–83. The appellants sought, *inter alia,* the following relief: a declaratory judgment and an injunction requiring the County to strike the Policy and requiring the Authority to strike the portions of the bidding process which violate federal law, i.e. the incorporation of the Policy through the "Cooperative Agreement."

The district court stated, in an oral judgment, that it was granting the motion to dismiss because, in its view, no case or controversy was presented. Article III § 2 of the U.S. Constitution limits federal jurisdiction to certain cases or controversies. The principles of standing, ripeness and mootness derive from the Article III limits on the jurisdiction of federal courts. *See, e.g., Warth v. Seldin,* 422 U.S. 490, 498–99 (1975) (standing); *Flowers Industries v. F.T.C.,* 849 F.2d 551 (11th Cir. 1988) (ripeness); *Church of Scientology Flag Service Org., Inc. v. City of Clearwater,* 777 F.2d 598 (11th Cir. 1985) (mootness). The defendants argue that the instant action failed to establish a case or controversy because the plaintiffs do not have standing and the case is not ripe. We find that the present action satisfies the requirements for standing and ripeness, and thus presents a live case or controversy.

A. *Case or Controversy*

1. Standing

This lawsuit presents claims against both the Authority and the County for violations of the Fair Housing Act, and claims against the County under 42 U.S.C. §§ 1982 and 1983. In order for this court to have jurisdiction over the claims before us, at lease one named plaintiff must have standing for each of the claims....

a. Jackson

Jackson is an African-American woman who is eligible for public housing and whose name is on the Authority's wait-list for public housing. She states that she intends to live in the new facility. Assuming the truth of her complaint, we determine that she has standing to bring all of the claims the she asserts....

There are three minimum constitutional requirements for standing: (1) the plaintiff must allege an actual or imminent injury; (2) the injury must be traceable to the alleged unlawful conduct; and (3) the relief requested must be likely to remedy the plaintiff's injury. Thus, Jackson must plead injury in fact, causation and redressability in order to have standing to assert her claims.

We find that Jackson has properly alleged a redressable injury caused by the defendants. The record before us shows that Jackson claims two distinct injuries—exclusion from the unincorporated five-mile area and, as a result of this exclusion, imminent segregation....

b. Musgrove

Plaintiff Musgrove asserts claims similar to those of plaintiff Jackson. However, based on the record before us it is clear that she derives standing in a manner different from plaintiff Jackson. Although Musgrove lives in public housing now, she has not asserted any intent to relocate into the new project. Rather, she asserts that she will be injured because the site currently ranked first for the new project is located next door to the public facility where she resides. Since 86% of the persons on the waiting list for the new facility are African-American, she argues that the defendants' actions with regard to the siting process will exacerbate segregation in her neighborhood. We hold that she does have standing to pursue her Fair Housing Act claim, but do not decide the issue of her standing under §§ 1982–83.

The Supreme Court has held that "the loss of important benefits from interracial associations" is an injury in fact sufficient for standing under § 804, (42 U.S.C. § 3604) of the Fair Housing Act. *Trafficante v. Metro. Life Insurance Co.*, 409 U.S. 205, 210 (1972); *Gladstone,* 441 U.S. at 112. Thus, a plaintiff may have "neighborhood" standing to challenge violations of the Fair Housing Act even if the discriminatory acts are not directed at that person. In order to establish neighborhood standing, the plaintiff must show that the racially discriminatory practice at issue affected the neighborhood where the plaintiff resides. The neighborhood in question must be relatively compact. In this case the effect on Musgrove's neighborhood is clear. There is a substantial probability that a facility almost entirely African-American in population will be placed right next door to Musgrove's complex, which is itself almost entirely African-American. The segregative effect of this process on a compact area is distinct and palpable. Musgrove has standing under the Fair Housing Act.

c. Other Arguments on Standing

The County argues that the plaintiffs have no standing because they are not entitled to select the site for the public housing themselves. *See Jaimes v. Toledo Metro. Hous. Auth.*, 758 F.2d at 1093–94. The relief that the plaintiffs request, however, does not purport to select a certain site, it merely requests a remedy that eliminates the Policy. Courts have observed that "governmental bodies are bound to uphold and obey the provisions of the Fair Housing Act ... and cannot seek refuge in broad generalizations regarding the absence of a constitutional guarantee of adequate housing." *Smith v. Town of Clarkton,* 682 F.2d 1055, 1067 (4th Cir. 1982). If the district court finds that the allegations in the complaint are true, then "the district court has broad and flexible powers to fashion a remedy to fully correct past wrongs."

The County argues that neither Jackson's nor Musgrove's claims are redressable because striking down the Policy will not guarantee that the facility will be constructed in the unincorporated five-mile area or even that it will be built in an integrated area. Additionally, the County contends that Jackson cannot prove that she would live in the project. The plaintiffs need not reach either level of certainty in order to show redressability. The requirement of redressability is not a demand for complete certainty in results, for requiring absolute certainty "would be to close our eyes to the uncertainties which shroud human affairs." *Huntington Branch, NAACP v. Town of Huntington,* 844 F.2d 926 at 394 (2d Cir.), [*aff'd per curiam,* 488 U.S. 15 (1988)—Eds.] (granting standing to plaintiffs challenging a refusal to amend zoning ordinances even though HUD funding had not been secured for the proposed project). [*Huntington Branch* is reproduced in Chapter 6 *supra*—Eds.] Jackson has shown a substantial probability that she would live in the new public housing facility and that, but for the acts of the defendants, the new facility would be built at the specific proposed site in a racially integrated location. Musgrove has shown a substantial probability that the facility would not be built next door to her if the courts intervened. That is sufficient for standing....

[The discussion of ripeness and failure to state a claim issues is omitted.—Eds.]

III. CONCLUSION

In sum, we hold that the complaint was improperly dismissed. Construing the complaint in the light most favorable for the plaintiffs, we can conceive of facts under which the plaintiffs have standing and state a claim under which relief may be granted. Furthermore, we find that the claims are ripe for adjudication. Thus, it is clear that this action should not have been dismissed on the pleadings.

Notes and Questions

1. Some of the most interesting standing questions in housing and community development cases arise when plaintiffs challenge an "injury" to an entire community, such as the perpetuation or creation of racial discrimination. These cases present important injury in fact and causality questions, as the principal case indicates. For an earlier standing case raising similar questions concerning HUD grants to Boston, see *NAACP Boston Chapter v. Harris*, 607 F.2d 514 (1st Cir. 1979); *Munoz-Mendoza v. Pierce*, 711 F.2d. 421 (1st Cir. 1983); and *Latinos Unidos de Chelsea En Accion (LUCHA) v. Secretary of Housing and Urban Development*, 799 F.2d 774 (1st Cir. 1986). Chapter 6 *infra* covers related standing questions of this type that arise when plaintiffs challenge racial steering under Title VIII.

2. Note that the *Jackson* court pointed out the "the injury must be traceable to the alleged unlawful conduct." This is referred to as the "causality" requirement. The Supreme Court spoke again on the causality issue in *Allen v. Wright*, 468 U.S. 737 (1984) and denied standing to parents of black children seeking to challenge the failure of the Internal Revenue Service to adequately implement its obligation to deny tax exempt status to racially discriminatory schools. The Court noted that the stigmatizing injury caused by racial discrimination is the "sort of noneconomic injury [that] is one of the most serious consequences of discriminatory government action and is sufficient in some circumstances to support standing." *Id.* at 755. Yet the Court relied on the *Simon* decision [discussed in A Note on Standing *supra*] to deny standing.

> The chain of causation is even weaker in this case. It involves numerous third parties (officials of racially discriminatory schools receiving tax exemptions and the parents of children attending such schools) who may not even exist in [plaintiffs'] communities and whose independent decisions may not collectively have a significant effect on the ability of public school students to receive a desegregated education.

Id. at 759.

What if a group of plaintiffs brought an action claiming that federal loans and subsidies for housing in their neighborhood had caused its segregation? Would they have standing? For a case denying standing based on a claim of this type, see *Jorman v. Veterans Admin.*, 830 F.2d 1420 (7th Cir. 1987) (residents of all-black neighborhoods lacked standing to challenge alleged segregative effect of Federal Housing Administration's and Veterans' Administration's mortgage insurance practices.)

3. For a discussion of standing under the Fair Housing Act, including third-party standing versus first-party standing, see Michael E. Rosman, *Standing Alone: Standing Under the Fair Housing Act*, 60 Mo. L. Rev. 547 (1995), which comments on William A. Fletcher, *The Structure of Standing*, 98 Yale L. J. 221 (1988).

4. An important "prudential" standing requirement is that the plaintiff must be within the "zone of interest" protected by the statute. How does the principal case decide this question? A Supreme Court statement on this problem can be found in *Clarke v. Securities Industry Association*, 479 U.S. 388 (1987) (association had standing to challenge sections of the National Bank Act's application to "branch banking" as falling

within zone of interest protected under the statute). The Court has held that the zone of interest test is not a limitation on standing to bring actions under Title VIII. *See* Chapter 6 *infra.*

Another hurdle for litigants desiring to challenge federal housing and community development program decisions is the doctrine of "exhaustion of administrative remedies" before a statute or ordinance can be challenged. The following case illustrates the application of the rule in a housing context.

Darby v. Cisneros

United States Supreme Court
509 U.S. 137 (1993)

JUSTICE BLACKMUN delivered the opinion of the Court.

This case presents the question whether federal courts have the authority to require that a plaintiff exhaust available administrative remedies before seeking judicial review under the Administrative Procedure Act (APA), 5 U. S. C. § 701 *et seq.*, where neither the statute nor agency rules specifically mandate exhaustion as a prerequisite to judicial review. At issue is the relationship between the judicially created doctrine of exhaustion of administrative remedies and the statutory requirements of § 10(c) of the APA.

Petitioner R. Gordon Darby is a self-employed South Carolina real estate developer who specializes in the development and management of multifamily rental projects. In the early 1980's, he began working with Lonnie Garvin, Jr., a mortgage banker, who had developed a plan to enable multifamily developers to obtain single-family mortgage insurance from respondent Department of Housing and Urban Development (HUD). Respondent Secretary of HUD (Secretary) is authorized to provide single-family mortgage insurance under § 203(b) of the National Housing Act, 48 Stat. 1249, as amended, 12 U.S.C. § 1709(b). Although HUD also provides mortgage insurance for multifamily projects under § 207 of the National Housing Act, 12 U.S.C. § 1713, the greater degree of oversight and control over such projects makes it less attractive for investors than the single-family mortgage insurance option.

The principal advantage of Garvin's plan was that it promised to avoid HUD's "Rule of Seven." This rule prevented rental properties from receiving single-family mortgage insurance if the mortgagor already had financial interests in seven or more similar rental properties in the same project or subdivision. *See* 24 C.F.R. § 203.42(a) (1992). Under Garvin's plan, a person seeking financing would use straw purchasers as mortgage insurance applicants. Once the loans were closed, the straw purchasers would transfer title back to the development company. Because no single purchaser at the time of purchase would own more than seven rental properties within the same project, the Rule of Seven appeared not to be violated. HUD employees in South Carolina apparently assured Garvin that his plan was lawful and that he thereby would avoid the limitation of the Rule of Seven.

Darby obtained financing for three separate multiunit projects, and, through Garvin's plan, Darby obtained single-family mortgage insurance from HUD. Although Darby successfully rented the units, a combination of low rents, falling interest rates, and a generally depressed rental market forced him into default in 1988. HUD became responsible for the payment of over $6.6 million in insurance claims.

HUD had become suspicious of Garvin's financing plan as far back as 1983. In 1986, HUD initiated an audit but concluded that neither Darby nor Garvin had done anything wrong or misled HUD personnel. Nevertheless, in June 1989, HUD issued a limited denial of participation (LDP) that prohibited petitioners for one year from participating in any program in South Carolina administered by respondent. The Assistant Secretary notified petitioners that HUD was also proposing to debar them from further participation in all HUD procurement contracts and in any non-procurement transaction with any federal agency. See 24 C.F.R. § 24.200 (1992).

Petitioners' appeals of the LDP and of the proposed debarment were consolidated, and an Administrative Law Judge (ALJ) conducted a hearing on the consolidated appeals in December 1989. The judge issued an "Initial Decision and Order" in April 1990, finding that the financing method use by petitioners was "a sham which improperly circumvented the Rule of Seven." The ALJ concluded, however, that most of the relevant facts had been disclosed to local HUD employees, that petitioners lacked criminal intent, and that Darby himself "genuinely cooperated with HUD to try [to] work out his financial dilemma and avoid foreclosure." In light of these mitigating factors, the ALJ concluded that an indefinite debarment would be punitive and that it would serve no legitimate purpose; good cause existed, however, to debar petitioners for a period of 18 months.

Under HUD regulations,

> The hearing officer's determination shall be final unless, pursuant to 24 C.F.R. part 26, the Secretary or the Secretary's designee, within 30 days of receipt of a request decides as a matter of discretion to review the finding of the hearing officer. The 30 day period for deciding whether to review a determination may be extended upon written notice of such extension by the Secretary or his designee. Any party may request such a review in writing within 15 days of receipt of the hearing officer's determination.

24 C.F.R. § 24.314(c) (1992).

Neither petitioners nor respondents sought further administrative review of the ALJ's "Initial Decision and Order."

On May 31, 1990, petitioners filed suit in the United States District Court for the District of South Carolina. They sought an injunction and a declaration that the administrative sanctions were imposed for purposes of punishment, in violation of HUD's own debarment regulations, and therefore were "not in accordance with law" within the meaning of § 10(e)(B)(1) of the APA, 5 U.S.C. § 706(2)(A).

Respondents moved to dismiss the complaint on the ground that petitioners, by forgoing the option to seek review by the Secretary, had failed to exhaust administrative remedies. The District Court denied respondents' motion to dismiss, reasoning that the administrative remedy was inadequate and that resort to that remedy would have been futile. In a subsequent opinion, the District Court granted petitioners' motion for summary judgment, concluding that the "imposition of debarment in this case encroached too heavily on the punitive side of the line, and for those reasons was an abuse of discretion and not in accordance with the law."

The Court of Appeals for the Fourth Circuit reversed. It recognized that neither the National Housing Act nor HUD regulations expressly mandate exhaustion of administrative remedies prior to filing suit. The court concluded, however, that the District Court had erred in denying respondents' motion to dismiss, because there was no evidence to suggest that further review would have been futile or that the Secretary would abuse his discretion by indefinitely extending the time limitations for review.

The court denied petitioners' petition for rehearing with suggestion for rehearing en banc. In order to resolve the tension between this and the APA, as well as to settle a perceived conflict among the Courts of Appeals, we granted certiorari.

Section 10(c) of the APA bears the caption "Actions reviewable." It provides in its first two sentences that judicial review is available for "final agency action for which there is no other adequate remedy in a court," and that "preliminary, procedural, or intermediate agency action ... is subject to review on the review of the final agency action." The last sentence of § 10(c) reads:

> Except as otherwise expressly required by statute, agency action otherwise final is final for the purposes of this section whether or not there has been presented or determined an application for a declaratory order, for any form of reconsideration ... or, unless the agency otherwise requires by rule and provides that the action meanwhile is inoperative, for an appeal to superior agency authority.

80 Stat. 392–393, 5 U.S.C. § 704.

Petitioners argue that this provision means that a litigant seeking judicial review of a final agency action under the APA need not exhaust available administrative remedies unless such exhaustion is expressly required by statute or agency rule. According to petitioners, since § 10(c) contains an explicit exhaustion provision, federal courts are not free to require further exhaustion as a matter of judicial discretion.

Respondents contend that § 10(c) is concerned solely with timing, that is, when agency actions become "final," and that Congress had no intention to interfere with the courts' ability to impose conditions on the timing of their exercise of jurisdiction to review final agency actions. Respondents concede that petitioners' claim is "final" under § 10(c), for neither the National Housing Act nor applicable HUD regulations require that a litigant pursue further administrative appeals prior to seeking judicial review. However, even though nothing in § 10(c) precludes judicial review of petitioners' claim, respondents argue that federal courts remain free under the APA to impose appropriate exhaustion requirements.

We have recognized that the judicial doctrine of exhaustion of administrative remedies is conceptually distinct from the doctrine of finality:

> [T]he finality requirement is concerned with whether the initial decisionmaker has arrived at a definitive position on the issue that inflicts an actual, concrete injury; the exhaustion requirement generally refers to administrative and judicial procedures by which an injured party may seek review of an adverse decision and obtain a remedy if the decision is found to be unlawful or otherwise inappropriate.

Williamson County Regional Planning Comm'n v. Hamilton Bank of Johnson City, 473 U.S. 172, 193 (1985).

Whether courts are free to impose an exhaustion requirement as a matter of judicial discretion depends, at least in part, on whether Congress has provided otherwise, for "[o]f 'paramount importance' to any exhaustion inquiry is congressional intent," *McCarthy v. Madigan*, 503 U.S. 140, 144 (1992), quoting *Patsy v. Board of Regents of Florida*, 457 U.S. 496, 501 (1982). We therefore must consider whether § 10(c), by providing the conditions under which agency action becomes "final for the purposes of" judicial review, limits the authority of courts to impose additional exhaustion requirements as a prerequisite to judicial review.

It perhaps is surprising that it has taken over 45 years since the passage of the APA for this Court definitively to address this question....

While some dicta ... might be claimed to lend support to respondents' interpretation of 10(c), the text of the APA leaves little doubt that petitioners are correct.... Although § 10(a) provides the general right to judicial review of agency actions under the APA, § 10(c) establishes when such review is available. When an aggrieved party has exhausted all administrative remedies expressly prescribed by statute or agency rule, the agency action is "final for the purposes of this section" and therefore "subject to judicial review" under the first sentence. While federal courts may be free to apply, where appropriate, other prudential doctrines of judicial administration to limit the scope and timing of judicial review, § 10(c), by its very terms has limited the availability of the doctrine of exhaustion of administrative remedies to that which the statute or rule clearly mandates.

The last sentence of § 10(c) refers explicitly to "any form of reconsideration" and "an appeal to superior agency authority." Congress clearly was concerned with making the exhaustion requirement unambiguous so that aggrieved parties would know precisely what administrative steps were required before judicial review would be available. If courts were able to impose additional exhaustion requirements beyond those provided by Congress or the agency, the last sentence of § 10(c) would make no sense. To adopt respondents' reading would transform § 10(c) from a provision designed to "'remove obstacles to judicial review of agency action,'" *Bowen v. Massachusetts,* 487 U.S. at 904, quoting *Shaughnessy v. Pedreiro,* 349 U.S. 48, 51 (1955), into a trap for unwary litigants. Section 10(c) explicitly requires exhaustion of all intra-agency appeals mandated either by statute or by agency rule; it would be inconsistent with the plain language of § 10(c) for courts to require litigants to exhaust optional appeals as well....

IV

We noted just last Term in a non-APA case that

> appropriate deference to Congress' power to prescribe the basic procedural scheme under which a claim may be heard in a federal court requires fashioning of exhaustion principles in a manner consistent with congressional intent and any applicable statutory scheme.

McCarthy v. Madigan, 503 U.S. at 144.

Appropriate deference in this case requires the recognition that, with respect to actions brought under the APA, Congress effectively codified the doctrine of exhaustion of administrative remedies in § 10(c). Of course, the exhaustion doctrine continues to apply as a matter of judicial discretion in cases not governed by the APA. But where the APA applies, an appeal to "superior agency authority" is a prerequisite to judicial review *only* when expressly required by statute or when an agency rule requires appeal before review and the administrative action is made inoperative pending that review. Courts are not free to impose an exhaustion requirement as a rule of judicial administration where the agency action has already become "final" under § 10(c).

The judgment of the Court of Appeals is reversed, and the case is remanded for further proceeding consistent with this opinion.

Notes and Questions

1. There is another important context in which Congress has specifically dispensed with any requirement of exhaustion of administrative remedies. When no administra-

tive proceeding has been filed or even when an administrative proceeding is underway, a plaintiff alleging a violation of Title VIII may file a civil action nevertheless. *See* Enforcement Procedures, Options, Damages, and Remedies in Chapter 6 *infra,* for further discussion.

2. Does the exhaustion requirement serve a good purpose? If so, why does Congress choose to dispense with it in certain circumstances?

A Note on Breach of Contract Claims against the Federal Government

What can a party who enters into a relationship with the government do to assure that the government (in the form of legislation or executive action) will not change the rules in a way that disadvantages, or dashes reasonable expectations of, the party? If an agency makes a contract with a party, for example, as HUD does in many housing and development contexts, and then does not carry through with the contractual promise, what can the party do?

In *United States v. Winstar Corporation*, 518 U.S. 839 (1996), the Supreme Court determined that breach of contract suits against the federal government were justiciable and within the jurisdiction of the United States Court of Federal Claims. In *Winstar,* the plaintiffs—certain stronger financial institutions—claimed that the federal government had breached express contracts that provided incentives for the plaintiffs to purchase "financially troubled" savings and loans institutions. These stronger savings and loans institutions, entered into contracts with an agency of the government and purchased failing S&Ls. As incentives, the agency granted the acquiring institutions (1) exceptions to certain minimum capital assets required for their loan portfolios and (2) the right to amortize the institution's goodwill to improve its debt equity ratio.

When Congress enacted the Financial Institutions Reform, Recovery, and Enforcement Act of 1989 [FIRREA] it breached these commitments by setting more rigorous standards to determine the fiscal condition of savings and loans. As a result, the very institutions that government regulators had enlisted to prevent the worsening of the savings and loan crisis were determined themselves to now have insufficient capital assets following the performance of the contracts. Ultimately, these acquiring institutions were themselves closed down by the government since they could not meet FIRREA capital asset requirements.

The agreement to take over the failing S&Ls, on the one hand, and the regulatory agency's approval of exceptions to the generally-applicable government requirements, on the other, both contained specific "integration" clauses tying the two documents together. The Court held in *Winstar* that the breach of these integrated contracts between the government and the acquiring S&Ls created valid grounds for a breach of contract claim and that the cause of action could be heard in the Court of Federal Claims. The result was a very substantial recovery for the stockholders of these former savings and loans.

Housing Cases Based on Breach of Contract

After *Winstar,* litigants in housing contexts have filed breach of contract claims against the federal government. These suits include claims by some 600 housing developers alleging breach of contracts entered into with HUD providing for mortgage insurance and housing subsidies for construction or renovation of assisted housing units. See discussion in Chapter 3, *infra* regarding this program. The first of these cases to reach appellate review was *Cienega Gardens v. United States,* 194 F.3d 1231 (Fed. Cir. 1998), *cert. denied,* 528 U.S. 820 (1999).

The *Cienega* litigation arose out of federal efforts to encourage private developers to construct, own, and manage low- and moderate-income housing. Commitments of financial incentives, such as below-market interest financing and the opportunity for the owner to privatize the units after 20 years, were made to obtain developer participation. HUD-insured mortgages were reflected in a deed of trust note payable to the lender that contemplated advances to the owner. HUD dictated the form of the notes and deeds of trust which generally contemplated a 40-year repayment period and specifically endorsed them as part of its provision of mortgage insurance necessary to entice financial institutions to undertake these loans. Consistent with HUD regulations at the time, the developer was obligated under a regulatory agreement with HUD to accept restrictions on tenant income, allowable rents, and rates of return, so long as federally-assisted financing applied.

A rider to the deed of trust note contained a provision permitting the owner to prepay the loan in full after twenty years. By prepaying, the owner could terminate HUD's affordability restrictions and could convert the property into a conventional rental property and charge market rents, increasing the return on the investment.

Congress, concerned that a large number of owners might exercise their prepayment option, enacted legislation in 1989 imposing a temporary moratorium on mortgage prepayments except with HUD's approval. In 1990, Congress made the moratorium and HUD approval requirements permanent while authorizing HUD to offer incentives to owners to forebear selling and retain the restrictions on rentals and tenant incomes. HUD established procedures resulting in a lengthy process for developers wishing to exercise their prepayment option. In 1996, Congress eliminated requirements for prior HUD approval for prepayment. See Chapter 3 for further discussion of low-income housing preservation efforts.

Ruling in *Cienega*, the Court of Federal Claims upheld the owners' breach of contract claims rejecting HUD's contentions that there was no privity of contract between HUD and the owners because the prepayment provisions were in the deed of trust notes between the owners and their lenders, and were not in regulatory agreements between HUD and owners. The court interpreted all of the contract documents together that were signed contemporaneously in determining the full extent of the privity relationship.

The Court of Federal Claims also rejected HUD arguments (1) that HUD was protected from suit by the "sovereign acts" doctrine *(see, Bowen v. Agencies Opposed to Soc. Sec. Entrapment*, 477 U.S. 41, 52–53 (1986)); (2) that the transaction exceeded the "unmistakability" doctrine (*Winstar* 518 U.S. at pp. 871–87); and, (3) that HUD lacked contracting authority (on the ground that the HUD promise of prepayment lacked express authority from Congress).

The Court of Appeals for the Federal Circuit in what ultimately involved additional years of litigation, determined that the plaintiff Owners did have vested property interests at the time of the passage of the federal legislation, ELIHPA and LIHPRHA. [discussed in Chapter 3 *infra*—Eds.). Specifically, in abrogating the Owners' contractual prepayment rights, the statutes intentionally defeated the Owners' real property rights to sole and exclusive possession after twenty years and to convey or encumber their properties after twenty years. The Owners thus had property interests and these were based on the interaction of both real property rights and contractual rights. They were entitled to compensation for the regulatory taking that took place with the enactment of the federal housing preservation statutes and the effects on the owner's property rights.

Selected Related Issues

Jurisdiction and Forum for Suits. Suits against the federal government for contract breach or for taking of property without due process can be brought in the Court of Federal Claims, with appellate review in the Federal Circuit Court of Appeals. District courts have jurisdiction for Tucker Act claims under $10,000 or over declaratory judgment actions to enforce the terms of existing contracts, such as, the obligation to release contract payments. Declaratory judgment actions are within the district court's jurisdiction so long as the suit does not request money damages from the government. In effect, the claims would be for specific performance. Otherwise, claims for money damages must be submitted to the Court of Federal Claims. The latter court does not have equitable jurisdiction, however.

Legal Fees. In federal grants and contracts to local governments and private entities, the government accepts as a legitimate the cost of legal representation for defending against government attempts to assert claims or withhold funds where the government is the plaintiff. The defendant is entitled to defend itself when disputes arise concerning the administration of federal grants and programs. As noted above, OMB Circular A-87, Section 10(b) provides for use of federal funds: "b. Legal expenses required in the administration of Federal programs are allowable. Legal expenses for prosecution of claims against the Federal Government are unallowable." The latter clause implies that defending against HUD action against a recipient are allowable. Exactly what "prosecution of claims" implies has not been tested. Another alternative for federal fund recipients who qualify under that Act which have successfully challenged HUD's actions against them, is to seek legal fees through the federal Equal Access to Justice Act in successful cases. The attorney fees, however, are only available at a relatively low rate of $125 per hour. Note that in the Harrisburg Housing Authority case, such fees were obtained.

Sources of Appropriated Funds for Redress. Federal funding commitments require that sufficient funds have been appropriated and remain available to satisfy a claim against the government. The period for which appropriated funds remain available, therefore, can impose a *de facto* statute of limitations, significantly limiting the time in which an action can be brought. Thus, an action calling for payments from a three-year appropriation would have to be brought prior to the expiration of that period. In doing so, moreover, the federal court must be asked to enjoin the government's other use of the funds available to remedy the claim, pending the litigation, and to issue an injunction preventing their lapse. In *Houston v. HUD*, 24 F.3d 1421 (1994), the Court held that only the specific funds for the year in question that were reserved for an entitlement grantee could be used to satisfy a judgment against HUD, and not subsequent year CDBG appropriations or the federal "judgment fund" providing funds to satisfy judgments against the government. In that case, HUD claimed it had paid out the grantee's funds to other recipients once HUD decided to reduce the City's funds even if it did so improperly without providing for a prior hearing. Thus, the court found the City's claim was moot, since no funds were available from which to provide a remedy. In that instance, however, Congress immediately responded to a request by the City to make it whole with a special appropriation to cover the amount of the City's CDBG funds that had been improperly reduced.

A Congressional Bar on HUD's Attempts to Reduce Rent Subsidy Commitments. Other litigation has involved efforts by HUD to reduce previously established rent subsidies provided to developers for Section 8-assisted rentals. These subsidies are usually crucial to the developer undertaking new assisted development or rehabilitation. HUD attempted, years after the fact, to reduce subsidies established prior to the construction upon which the developers had relied in proceeding with the construction. Justifying its actions on asserted "mistakes" in its earlier approval of the initial subsidy level, HUD attempted to reduce retroactively current subsidy levels established at the project's inception. Congress, in 1987, passed a statute, 42 U.S.C. 1437(f)(c)(2)(C), that prevented HUD from reducing such rental subsidies, stating: "The Secretary may not reduce the contract rents in effect ..." under the Section 8 Moderate Rehabilitation Program. Notwithstanding that language, HUD attempted to retroactively "correct" the rents previously approved. Three U.S. Courts of Appeal ruled that the statutory prohibition on reducing subsidies was clear and that HUD could not reduce previously established subsidy commitments, after the fact. *2225 New York Avenue Ltd. v. Cisneros,* 38 F.3d 210 (5th Cir. 1994); *Foxglenn Investors Ltd. Partnership v. Cisneros,* 35 F.3d 210 (4th Cir. 1994); *Terrace Hous. Assocs., Ltd.,* 32 F.3d 461 (10th Cir. 1994).

Liability of Federal Government Officials. In selecting defendants to name, in addition to naming the Secretary of the federal department, an action can also be maintained against federal officials in their individual as well as their official capacity where a violation of constitutional rights has occurred. In a recent case in California, individual HUD Fair Housing staff were personally sued on the grounds that they attempted to deprive residents from the surrounding community where a assisted project was to be constructed from expressing their first amendment rights opposing the construction. *See White v. Julian,* No. C95-1757 MHP, (N.D. Cal., Dec. 18, 1998). For a discussion of the *White* case and potential individual liability, see Chapter 6 *infra* discussing *White v. Lee,* 227 F.3d 1214 (9th Cir. 2000) (rejecting immunity).

Notes and Questions

1. How can one distinguish a request for payment under a contract with the federal government for an improperly withheld commitment and a request for money damages for breach of a contract, given that the difference may determine the appropriate forum?

2. The extent of transferability of the case from one federal forum to another if the wrong forum is utilized can be important. Otherwise the forum issue can present a trap for the unwary.

3. Is filing a declaratory judgment action actually prosecution of claims against the federal government if it entails a challenge to an anticipated government action or threat of such action, for instance in challenging a government denial of eligibility for certain costs? Normally declaratory judgment actions simply allow those who anticipate being harmed by a defendant's action to obtain a ruling in advance on the validity of the threatened action.

4. Should the government acting through Congress be able to abrogate the terms of contracts providing government incentives and benefits to which it has committed itself, especially in that the incentives induced reliance by third parties? What policy issues are raised by Congressional action to limit administrative agency corrections of such "errors?"

5. What is the likely result of destabilizing the contractual relationships through unilateral government-imposed revisions in contracts between the federal government and developers that were designed to encourage low- and moderate-income housing development and rehabilitation?

6. Note how the use of inducements for private investment in low-income housing creates a Catch-22 situation: As an inducement, the government promises a right to pay off the loan in 20 years and then to convert to market rates. But the subsidized tenants cannot afford market rates. So in order to preserve the units for low-income tenants, the government withdraws the right to convert to market rates because that would lead to reduction in the number of subsidized units in general and the eviction of the tenants

from the particular units. Then the government gets sued for breach of contract by the private investor.

7. In some instances, private parties are entitled to initiate legal actions against recipients of federal funds where a false claim has occurred in obtaining the federal funds. The following material from Otto J. Hetzel *et al.*, Housing and Urban Development, *in* Developments in Administrative Law and Regulatory Practice, 2008–2009 (Jeff F. Lubbers ed. forthcoming Spring 2010) (published by ABA Press), describes such a case. An interesting aspect of this case is the potential it suggests for HUD to have the U.S. Attorney bring such civil actions where false statements of compliance with applicable civil rights laws or other HUD requirements can be raised.

> The Anti-Discrimination Center of Metro New York, Inc. (ADC) filed a Federal False Claims Act *qui tam* proceeding as Relator accusing Westchester County of obtaining funds from the United States by making false statements about the County's efforts to integrate housing on its applications for federal Community Development Block Grant funding, i.e. that County officials knowingly and falsely certified that they were affirmatively furthering fair housing. Federal False Claims Act *qui tam* cases are essentially brought by a private party to enforce false claims for funds made to the United States, with the private party suing on behalf of the United States. HUD, and the Dept. of Justice, can intervene and take over the case, in their discretion, as occurred in this case. If the plaintiff is successful, the United States awards it substantial amounts of the funds that were falsely claimed, as an incentive to bring such actions that ultimately benefit the United States. Attorneys for the Relator also are entitled to receive their attorney fees for prosecuting the action.
>
> Here, the United States intervened in the False Claims Act proceeding and all three parties entered into a two settlements. In one, the County agreed to pay the United States $30,000,000 in satisfaction of the allegations in the False Claims Act. The ADC was allocated $7,500,000 of this recovery by the United States in ADC's capacity of Relator in initiation of this action. In addition, its attorneys were paid an additional $2,500,000 as reasonable expenses for its attorney fees, expenses and costs by the County.
>
> In the second settlement, the County agreed to submit to the oversight of a court-appointed monitor who will oversee expenditures of $50 million by the County over seven years for the purpose of building 750 homes in areas with low racial and ethnic diversity, i.e., in areas that are overwhelmingly white and affluent. The County also agreed to enact a (Bond) Act authorizing it to issue up to Thirty-Six Million Dollars ($36,000,000) in bonds to fund costs related to the settlement of the litigation and an additional Act setting forth policies and procedures which must be utilized in furtherance of the commitments established by the Stipulation and Order. *See United States ex rel. Anti-Discrimination Center of Metro New York v. Westchester County*, Stipulation and Order of Settlement and Dismissal, No. 6 Civ. 2860 (August 10, 2009).

4. Legal Strategies for Challenging Housing and Community Development Programs

The cases reproduced above illustrate the tendency of lawyers, representative tenants, or community residents to politicize the judicial process by challenging housing and community development programs viewed as hostile to their interests. Their reliance on judicial relief reflects similar tendencies in other social, programs. such as welfare assistance. The truth is that many interest groups, especially minority interest groups, often have been locked out of the political and regulatory process in which major policy decisions are made. Even when they are consulted, as in the Brooke Amendment example, their demands may go unsatisfied.

HUD may entertain "administrative complaints," but it does not conduct adversary proceedings to resolve these complaints, and naturally reserves the final decision. Ultimately, as in that case, the final recourse is to the courts.

The *NAACP* and *Jackson v. Okaloosa County, Fla.* cases, in particular, are examples of public interest litigation that differs substantially from ordinary private litigation in judicial forums. Professor Chayes has summarized these differences in a seminal article:

The public law litigation model portrayed in this paper reverses many of the crucial characteristics and assumptions of the traditional concept of adjudication:

(1) The scope of the lawsuit is not exogenously given but is shaped primarily by the court and parties.

(2) The party structure is not rigidly bilateral but sprawling and amorphous.

(3) The fact inquiry is not historical and adjudicative but predictive and legislative.

(4) Relief is not conceived as compensation for past wrong in a form logically derived from the substantive liability and confined in its impact to the immediate parties; instead, it is forward looking, fashioned ad hoc on flexible and broadly remedial lines, often having important consequences for many persons including absentees.

(5) The remedy is not imposed but negotiated.

(6) The decree does not terminate judicial involvement in the affair: its administration requires the continuing participation of the court.

(7) The judge is not passive, his function limited to analysis and statement of governing legal rules; he is active, with responsibility not only for credible fact evaluation but for organizing and shaping the litigation to ensure a just and viable outcome.

(8) The subject matter of the lawsuit is not a dispute between private individuals about private rights, but a grievance about the operation of public policy.

Abram Chayes, *The Role of the Judge in Public Law Litigation,* 89 HARV. L. REV. 1281,1302 (1976). *See also* DONALD L. HOROWITZ, THE COURTS AND SOCIAL POLICY chs. 1, 2 (1977).

The question that remains is whether and to what extent the courts should grant relief in public interest litigation of this kind. Professor Charles Daye has summarized the major issues:

1. Whether the judiciary possesses, or has the capacity to acquire the competence to evaluate the basis, and determine the validity, of the claim presented for resolution. ("The Competence Issue").

2. Whether, in the absence of relief in the judicial forum, any other forum offers a reasonable prospect of timely effective resolution of the claims, and relief. ("The Forums Issue").

3. Whether assuming judicial relief is necessary (and of course, possible) based on analysis of the Competence and Forums Issues, what form of relief, among the alternatives available, holds

(a) the best prospect of being effective, and

(b) the *least* prospect of involving the court in matters

i. as to which its competence is limited,

ii. which it lacks capacity to manage (or implement) effectively, and

iii. which risk causing unreasonable judicial intrusion into areas best left to other organs of government. ("The Relief Issue").

4. Assuming some form of relief is selected (under the Relief Issue), whether the court has power to grant it. ("The Power Issue").

5. Assuming power, whether other factors exist which nevertheless ought to prevent the court in the particular case from granting that relief selected. ("The Propriety Issue").

Charles E. Daye, *Role of the Judiciary in Community Development and Housing-A Suggested Analytical Method,* 52 J. Urb. L. 689, 700 (1975).

In the following excerpt, one commentator presents a view of the effectiveness of judicial relief in public interest litigation:

Joel F. Handler, Social Movements and the Legal System

22–25 (1978)

It is because social-reform groups lack the power to seek their demands through the normal political processes or through direct action that they turn to the legal system for help. Courts have always been used by those who find the balance of political forces against them. The powerless seek to neutralize inequities in bargaining power or at least to extract some concessions from their opponents. The use of the courts often appears to be a less dangerous and less costly means than nonlegal struggles against formidable opponents.

But how much can litigation accomplish? ... [T]he judicial system helped social reform groups press for their demands. The legal rules opening courts to reformers expanded greatly. There were new statutory rights, but courts also made use of constitutional doctrines. The due process clause, for example, helped people who claimed welfare benefits, or who wanted employment tenure, or security of tenancy in low-income housing. Courts held that government could not take rights away or revoke privileges without holding hearings. In reviewing administrative agency decisions courts were less willing to defer to claims of agency expertise and discretion; they scrutinized the decision-making processes of the agencies. Courts also expanded the doctrine of standing that comprises the rules governing what persons or groups can challenge government decisions either before the agencies or in court. In the 1970s, the Supreme Court has retreated somewhat from the doctrines created during the activist period, but the pendulum has not swung back very far. Compared with the situation before the 1950s, courts now are available to hear many social-reform claims that previously would have had no forum.

Nevertheless, agencies can still thwart the will of the courts, and hence, that of social-reform groups.... [The] premise is that agencies are usually hostile to the claims of social-reform groups. Agencies become sponsors and developers in partnership with their regulated clients; they want to carry out their programs without interference from outsiders. When ordered to do otherwise, an agency will often do the absolute minimum needed to comply with the letter of the order.

Bureaucratic hostility is important because, despite the availability of judicial remedies, social-reform groups are still forced to seek relief first and foremost from the agencies. Only rarely can a claimant persuade a court to act against an agency before the claimant has first gone to the agency. At its core, this attitude makes sense; agencies have primary responsibility for making and maintaining policy and it is disruptive for courts to intervene in matters that are committed to agency discretion, especially before the agency has had a chance to consider the matter. Therefore, unless the claimant can show that it will suffer irreparable harm and that it is hopeless (or virtually so) to go to the agency, the court will usually tell the claimant to go to the agency first. This deference has enormous practical consequences for social-reform groups. They are subject to delays, complex administrative procedures, problems of moot arguments, and other difficulties in fighting their way through the decisionmaking processes of the agencies.

After the agency has acted (or refused to act), judicial review is usually available. Yet, for a variety of reasons, judicial review may be an inadequate remedy. Many cases involving social-reform groups ... focus on procedures; they ask for a hearing or for the agency to consider additional factors in reaching its decision. "Victory," then, means that the claimants must return to the agency for a hearing. Even though a claimant can persuade an appellate court to overturn an administrative decision on the ground that it was arbitrary and capricious, the court will rarely make a substantive decision. In matters committed to agency discretion, reviewing courts are very reluctant to substitute their judgments for the agencies.... Courts also consider themselves overburdened and, especially in technical and complex areas, would rather delegate substantive responsibility than handle such matters.

Perhaps the most serious problem with judicial remedies has to do with enforcement. Traditionally, courts tend to avoid regulatory or structural injunctions, which are those seeking to control or direct behavior over a long period of time or alter the relationship between people, groups, or institutions. Under extreme situations, activist courts have reorganized voting districts, supervised the formulation and implementation of school desegregation and busing plans, and framed programs for patients in mental hospitals. But these are extraordinary situations. In the usual case, the court will not set up elaborate machinery to enforce its orders. Lawyers and judges have great faith in the propensity of court orders (as well as other rule changes) to change behavior and compliance is usually taken for granted ... This is an unfortunate assumption as far as social-reform groups are concerned. Many of the things that the groups want are either technically complex or require behavior changes in decentralized bureaucracies where ... supervisors even experience great difficulty in implementing lower-level change. With court orders, as with administrative rules, as the number of units whose behavior must change expands, so do the occasions to evade the orders. Courts become almost impotent when confronted with supervising difficult problems of enforcement. They lack the machinery or the will to engage in these tasks; often judges express irritation or weariness when litigation becomes protracted. Reliance, then, is usually placed on the original parties. This not only makes enforcement sporadic, but, more importantly for our purposes, it places great strain on the staying power of the social-reform groups.

The judicial remedy is most effective if the court can substitute its decision for the agency's, that is, if it need not defer to agency discretion, or can solve the matter for the social-reform group by a preventive injunction, or, otherwise render a decision that is readily monitored (monetary orders, for example). A permanent injunction against a construction program satisfies all three tests. But this is not typical. Social reform groups usually will need remedies that call for administrative discretion, are long term, technically complex, and require lower-level implementation.

Notes and Questions

1. The remedial problem in public interest litigation is especially serious, as Professor Handler points out. If judicial remedies are problematic, is there any effective avenue for seeking resolution of the problem? Consider the options: Congress, the administrative agency, a local agency, political pressure? Is there some other mechanism that you can think of?

2. The remedial complexities of public interest litigation have beer explored in a Columbia Law Review student project. The following excerpt from that article discusses the intrinsic limitations on judicial relief critical to public interest litigation involving the housing and community development programs covered in this book as well as in litigation based on constitutional guarantees relied upon to enforce rights to housing. *See also* Note, *Implementation Problems in Institutional Reform Litigation,* 91 HARV. L. REV. 428 (1977).

Special Project, The Remedial Process in Institutional Reform Litigation

78 Columbia Law Review 784, 858–65 (1978)

a. "Judicial" Nature of Remedial Powers. The court's remedial power is an aspect of its judicial power, which is conferred upon it by statutory grant under article III of the Constitution. However, in undertaking the remedial activities required in institutional reform litigation, the trial court must often perform quasi-legislative an quasi-administrative tasks. The questions have been raised, most recently by the Supreme Court in *Milliken v. Bradley,* [418 U.S. 717 (1974)], whether the judicial derivation of the remedial power precludes its exertion in legislative or executive task and whether certain kinds of reforms are beyond the competence of the courts because their accomplishment requires skills and activities that are not judicial in nature [Plaintiffs in this case sought a metropolitan, area-wide remedy for school segregation which the Court denied. This issue has arisen in housing cases.—Eds.]

Justice Marshall, dissenting in *Milliken,* wrote that at the remedial stage trial court powers are not limited to activities traditionally "judicial" in nature, but that the remedial power extended to activities necessary to devise and enforce an effective remedy. This assertion that the inherently "judicial" nature of the court's remedial; power offers no practical limitation on it has been echoed on other occasions.

Although the courts do not have plenary authority to run school systems, or manage any other institution, the exercise of the judicial power is vested in them. From that power flows a duty to provide an adequate remedy upon the adjudication of dispute brought before them. Just as the power to interpret the Constitution finally was derive from that judicial power, so too must an adequate remedial power. Nevertheless, to conclude that the inherently judicial quality of the remedial power puts no constraint on those powers is not, obviously, to conclude that remedial powers are without practical limitation. They remain subject to limitation by considerations of equitable discretion, federalism, and congressional policy....

b. Equitable Discretion—Constraints and Guidelines. A federal district court sitting in equity must exercise its powers with discretion. To do otherwise is to abuse the grant of discretion and commit reversible error. Therefore, the concept of discretion serves as a constraint on a trial court's use of its power as well as a source of that power. Discretion is an equitable consideration, rather than a constraint of constitutional magnitude.

Discretion however defined ... is a product of appellate review, reflected in the standard of review applied by the courts of appeals to district court activities, and the more relaxed the standard of review, the greater the trial court's latitude and power.

The standard of review is seldom so strict as to compel the choice of a single remedy. Requiring, in the name of reasonableness, that the trial court balance equities before ordering relief is one approach.

Effectiveness. Courts have a duty to devise effective remedies. The remedies must be effective in two senses. First, they must be sufficiently extensive to correct the substantive violation. Second, they must be enforceable against the parties. Although courts have generally overcome their resistance to ordering defendants to undertake affirmative activity, a resistance grounded in the difficulty in enforcing such an order, courts remain sensitive to enforcement problems.

This latter concern, that of administrative effectiveness, compels judicial focus on the particular factual context of each case. Two considerations are particularly important. If the defendant institution is exceptionally recalcitrant in implementing the ordered relief, the district court will be compelled to take exceptionally intrusive steps to force effective compliance. And, if the plaintiffs are less cohesive and poorer in institutional resources than are the defendants, the court may be compelled again to take a more active, or more intrusive, role in the remedial regime to ensure that its decree is implement and, when implemented, is a sufficient remedy.

The more important side of remedial effectiveness is the sufficiency of the decree to correct the substantive violation. The importance of the factual context of the case in measuring this substantive effectiveness depends on the kind of institutional reform being ordered.

Intrusiveness. Courts properly seek to minimize the intrusiveness of their involvement in the situations for which they must fashion and enforce relief. This goal of minimizing intrusion while maintaining an effective remedial regime operates in conjunction with, but independently of, other constraints on trial court activity. In particular, considerations of federalism have a parallel and independent limiting effect on federal court involvement in the affairs of local institutions.

Judicial involvement is intrusive to the extent that the court intervenes in the affairs of the parties and non-parties affected by the litigation. Although judicial activism in forming and controlling the shape of litigation is usually not considered intrusive, similar activism may be intrusive when it takes place during the design and enforcement of the remedy.

Judicial intervention, to be effective, must be to some degree intrusive. This intrusiveness is measured both by the administrative and enforcement characteristics of the remedy and by the process employed to formulate it. There is an obvious tradeoff between administrative and substantive intrusiveness. A more detailed, more substantively intrusive remedy may be more easily administered, and result in less interference with the defendant institution's unrelated activities, than a less detailed remedy that requires repeated returns to court and close supervision of institutional practices to ensure compliance with the general spirit of the decree. The intrusiveness of a remedial regime depends, consequently, on the entire canvas of judicial involvement in the formulation, terms, and enforcement of the decree.

Success at attaining effectiveness with minimal intrusiveness is a measure of a kind of judicial efficiency. Courts frequently, therefore, give the management of the defendant institution the first chance at formulating relief. Similarly, in reapportionment cases the court will sometimes deny relief until the legislature has had the opportunity to correct the malapportionment. In cases involving the funding of constitutionally mandated state functions, courts have also deferred to state legislatures in the first instance, to offer them the chance to remedy the violation. Complete remedial abstention is not, however, the best approach to remedy formulation, precisely because it so frequently leads to an ineffective remedy.

Courts also seek to reduce their intrusiveness by minimizing the negative consequences on non-participating parties and institutions of the remedial measures that they order. However, non-parties are invariably affected by the relief ordered in institutional reform cases. When judicially-ordered reform results in the reallocation of limited institutional resources, the diversion of those resources from their previous use will usually cause some harm to the previous beneficiaries. Although cognizant of their external impact, courts have not, to date, refused to order such remedies.

Notes and Questions

1. Control of public interest litigation also presents special problems. Usually this litigation is brought by a public interest litigator who represents an amorphous class of plaintiffs. The public interest litigator is often independently supported by a civil rights or housing organization and takes on the role of coordinating and conducting the litigation for the class of plaintiffs that brings the litigation.

A number of problems arise in public interest class actions of this kind. Differences may arise among members of the plaintiff class, due in part to difference in their strategies, their view of the purpose of the litigation, and their relationship to the defendant public agency. Differences may also arise between the public interest litigator and his client group. The plaintiff class in a housing case may be interested in quite specific remedies, such as a reallocation of housing units by a public housing agency, or a reallocation of expenditures in a local community development program. The public interest litigator may have a much broader view of the litigation, and may see it as an opportunity to establish more general constitutional and statutory principles. As the Columbia Student Project points out:

> More frequently, subordination of class members' interests occurs not because of any explicit choice or intent on the part of the litigator, but inadvertently because of his inattentiveness to the possibility of attorney-class conflicts of interests. Often, this inattentiveness is caused by a failure on the part of the litigator to discuss the lawsuit with his class clients, possibly because of an "I know what's best" attitude that is reinforced by his expertise and the clients' inability to pay for his services. In addition, the professional group rights litigator may be so sure of his idealistic motivations that he fails to see that the sort of remedy he considers most beneficial may not in fact be the one most desired by the class members. In the Boston and Atlanta school cases, for example, the attorneys' assumptions that their clients would accept a radical desegregation plan stemmed in large part from the attorney's strong commitment to an integrated society.

Id. at 886.

2. What possible differences in strategy can be anticipated between class members in school integration suits and the public interest litigator who brought the case? Might the

class of plaintiffs have been selected with a view toward advancing the purposes of the litigation as conceived by the plaintiffs' attorney? If so, is this desirable? *See, e.g.*, Derrick A. Bell, *Serving Two Masters: Integration Ideals and Client Interests in School Desegregation Litigation*, 85 YALE L.J. 470 (1976).

3. For a detailed study of the problems of providing a remedy in a complicated desegregation case, see W. Dennis Keating, *The Parma Racial Discrimination Remedy Revisited*, 45 CLEV. ST. L. REV. 235 (1997) (pointing out that in the case started in 1973 as *United States v. City of Parma*, 494 F. Supp. 1049 (N.D. Ohio 1980), "the results of twenty-four years of litigation and implementation of remedial orders ... suggest the limits of judicial intervention." *Id.* at 248.

4. This entire topic of desegregation and remedies is analyzed further in Chapter 6 *infra*.

Chapter 3

Governmental Housing Policies and Programs

The federal government, and state and local governments to a lesser extent, have been involved in housing programs since the 1930s. With the exception of the mortgage interest and property tax deductions available to homeowners, the original, and still the most comprehensive, federal programs are the FHA mortgage insurance program, begun in 1934, and the public housing program, begun in 1937. The FHA mortgage insurance program, discussed in section B of this chapter, fundamentally altered residential mortgage finance by encouraging use of long-term (30 year) mortgages that are self-amortizing through equal monthly payments, have lower interest rates that are fixed for the term of the loan, and permit low down payments (originally 10%, reduced over the years to "not less than 3.5% of the appraised value of the property" in 2009. 12 U.S.C. § 1709. FHA-insured mortgages, supported by the growth of the secondary mortgage market, discussed in section A, played a major role in the post-World War II growth of suburban America.

From its inception, the public housing program, discussed in section C, was controversial. In the decades after World War II, dissatisfaction with the public housing program led an impatient Congress to experiment with alternative forms of subsidy. These subsidies included, for example, direct loans at below market interest rates; subsidies to reduce interest rates on private mortgage loans; housing assistance payments to housing developers who would rent newly constructed, rehabilitated, or decent existing housing to low-income families; capital grants and low-interest loans to reduce the development costs of housing; rental assistance payments on behalf of individuals or families who obtained certificates or vouchers attesting to their eligibility for federal assistance, and tax credits for investors in the construction or substantial rehabilitation of housing for low-income households. Most of these programs were aimed at encouraging private developers and lenders to provide decent housing at prices that low- and moderate-income persons could afford. The subsidy programs generally suffered from a lack of clarity of purpose and shallow political support, and all proved to be considerably expensive.

Over the years, economists, housing specialists, academics, politicians, and trade associations have debated the appropriate focus of governmentally assisted housing programs. Should such programs increase the supply of affordable housing, or help create effective demand for housing supplied by the private housing market? Should housing programs be directed by the federal government, or administered by state and local governments? What role should private developers and lenders play? Can nonprofit organizations be effective participants? What about social service providers, including administrators of homeless shelters and programs for persons with disabilities?

These questions assume even greater importance in the aftermath of the 2007–2010 collapse of the housing market. As noted in Chapter 1, during the first decade of the 21st Century an enormous housing bubble, fed by cheap money, extremely relaxed lending and regulatory standards, along with public policies emphasizing home ownership with little regard for ability to pay, led to an attitude that "bigger is better" and mortgage risk is insignificant because "property values always will rise." The subsequent collapse of the housing market triggered massive foreclosures and the deepest recession since the Great Depression of the 1930s. The subprime mortgage crisis that precipitated the collapse called attention to the risks of homeownership for people with marginal resources, as well as the cumulative impact of years of reductions in the housing assistance programs and limitations in other social programs (such as welfare reform). As a result the housing choices of low-income renters have been increasingly and severely constrained, with a resultant negative effect on distressed communities. Policy makers at all levels of government, as well as in the private sector, have been forced to re-think the appropriate roles of the public and private sectors in housing.

This chapter will consider the major federal housing programs, with particular attention given to the different approaches of demand-side and supply-side programs. In addition, state and local housing programs will be examined, as well as the special roles played by nonprofit organizations.

The following problem is designed to direct the discussion.

Problem: Transforming Metro City Public Housing

In the 1940s and 1950s, Metro City Housing Authority constructed 1000 apartments for low income families in a concentrated area of the inner city with the support of the Federal government's public housing program. Grand Square, a 400-unit development of two- and three-story townhouse and garden apartments, was built during and shortly after World War II for working class families squeezed by war time housing shortages. In the 1950s, urban renewal came to Metro City in a big way. Large tracts of land surrounding downtown were cleared of derelict buildings. The Laclede Family Apartments, a 600-unit development of four twelve-story towers, was built in 1958 by the housing authority on one such tract adjacent to Grand Square for families forced to move because of the land clearance activities.

Over the next 40 years, the devastating forces that swept American cities have left Grand Square and Laclede Apartments as isolated ghettos of low-income, predominately minority, single-parent families and elderly individuals. Grand Square remains almost fully-occupied, but its units are obsolete in design and in bad need of major repairs and renovation. More than 450 of the 600 units in Laclede have been vacant for years because the high density, high rise environment is not conducive to raising children. All but a handful of the current tenants in Laclede are single elderly and persons with disabilities.

Despite their troubled history, Grand Square and Laclede have provided housing for one and sometimes two generations of low-income families. The 1000 units are a potential housing asset for the city. A major effort has been organized by the mayor's office to revitalize city neighborhoods. An important component is the development of mixed-income communities offering ownership and rental opportunities across the income spectrum from very-low to middle- and upper-income households. The mayor hopes that interaction among the differing economic classes will not only generate stability in the neighborhoods, but also encourage persons in public housing to "move up" and off of government assistance. The housing authority, as part of that effort, plans to issue requests for proposals (RFPs) to:

1) Reduce Grand Square to 300 completely renovated, two- to four-bedroom units, and reorganize it as a housing cooperative for low- and moderate-income families, including families containing persons with disabilities.

2) Demolish 500 of the 600 units in Laclede and replace them with 200 new town homes for families with a range of incomes from very low- to middle-income, 50 one-bedroom units for single, non-elderly persons accessible to persons with disabilities as well as others, and 50 single family homes affordable to persons in the workforce (fire-fighters, nurses, police officers, school teachers, etc.). One tower containing 100 units would be retained and renovated as apartments for elderly persons.

3) Provide 200 Section 8 certificates and vouchers that can be used in other parts of the city by persons choosing to leave Grand Square and Laclede.

In both the renovation of Grand Square and the construction of new units at Laclede, the housing authority wishes to create a mix of 2, 3, 4, 5, and 6 bedroom units to accommodate families of varying size. At least 50% of the units will be operated as public housing, with the balance split between low-income units operated in accordance with Low Income Housing Tax Credit (LIHTC) provisions and unrestricted market-rate units.

The density of the new developments at Laclede will be 14 units per acre, approximately one-third the density of the units to be demolished. Grand Square's density will be reduced by 25%. The new townhouses will be in two-to-five unit buildings, although the five- and six-bedroom units will be designed as single unit, detached homes. Individual front entrances, some with porches, and rear patios will provide private space for families.

Total development costs are estimated to be $97 million for the 650 unit, new construction/substantial rehabilitation project, or approximately $150,000 per unit. This figure includes about $10 million for lead-based paint, asbestos, and other environmental abatement, demolition of existing structures, preparation of the site for new construction and substantial rehabilitation, construction of new streets, sidewalks, sewers and a community center, and relocation of residents. Metro City and the Housing Authority will share the $10 million cost, using community development block grant funds, discussed in Chapter 5 *infra*, and public housing modernization funds. The $87 million cost to construct and rehabilitate the housing units will be raised through a combination of public housing capital contributions, debt, and equity financing reflecting the relative proportion of public housing, LIHTC, and market-rate housing planned for the developments.

Average incomes for the residents of the completed developments are estimated to be as follows: $15,000 (public housing), $30,000 (LIHTC), $60,000 (market rate).

The housing authority desires to enter into partnerships with professional developers, neighborhood corporations, tenant organizations, city, state and federal agencies, as well as the business and social service communities. As consultant to the housing authority, review the available programs and suggest a strategy for accomplishing the goals announced in the RFPs. Pay particular attention to the legal requirements of available federal and state housing assistance programs, as well as the potential for combining such programs in an integrated financing strategy.

A. Theoretical Framework

1. Nature of the Affordability/Subsidy Gap

When the cost of a product, such as housing, exceeds a person's ability to pay for that product, an income/cost gap occurs. From an individual's perspective, the gap is an "affordability" gap; from a government official's perspective, the gap is a "subsidy" gap. Such gaps are formed by the rapidly increasing costs of housing construction, financing, and operation on the one hand, and less rapidly increasing, indeed stagnant, incomes of lower-income persons on the other. Land, construction, financing, operating and maintenance, real estate tax costs, and the cost of government regulation have risen to the point that even middle-income persons experience difficulty in affording suitable housing at a reasonable cost. Housing professionals typically define reasonable cost as a shelter payment amount that does not exceed a stated percentage of a household's income, such as 25 or 30%. The affordability/subsidy gap can be defined as the amount by which this reasonable percentage of household income falls short of the cost of occupying suitable, standard housing, appropriate in amenity and size to the household's needs. It is not unusual for moderate- and lower-income families to pay 35% or more of income for shelter, and if very low-income families are to live in standard housing without benefit of subsidy, they may pay in excess of 50% of income on shelter.

The purpose of a housing subsidy is to fill this gap and allow households to afford standard housing with the defined reasonable proportion of their income. A subsidy designed to fill the gap will solve the high-cost/low-income problem.

A second problem to which programmatic intervention has been directed is providing housing for poor persons and families that is in good condition. At present, many low- and moderate-income families pay unreasonable proportions of income for substandard and overcrowded housing. A policy to provide a subsidy which simply permitted these families to more easily afford their substandard housing would be misguided. The second purpose of a subsidy program should be to upgrade existing substandard housing or to produce newly constructed standard housing for program beneficiaries. A program that attempts both to fill the subsidy gap and improve housing conditions is a very expensive program. The cost of upgrading or constructing new housing will push monthly housing expenses even higher, and the government program must fund housing improvement and the increased subsidy gap caused by that improvement. These factors have contributed to criticisms of federal housing subsidies based on their cost to the federal treasury.

Notes and Questions

1. Economic trends, housing, and the affordability/subsidy gap are discussed in two influential housing reports: National Housing Task Force, A Decent Place to Live (1988) and Report of the President's Commission on Privatization: Toward More Effective Government (1988). The two reports, which adopted radically different views of the role government should play in housing, agreed on at least one fact: the affordability/subsidy gap continued to plague low-income households in America. While the President's Commission on Privatization began its section on low-income housing with the observation that the history of U.S. housing was a "success story," it notes that "in 1983

about 47% of very low-income renters were paying over half their incomes for housing." Similarly, the National Housing Task Force reports that, "[i]n 1975, 3.7 million low-income renter households paid more than 50% of their incomes for rent. By 1983, that number had grown to 6 million, or almost half of the universe of low-income renters, paying more than half of their incomes for rent." The two reports differed widely in their approach to the housing affordability/subsidy gap, with the housing task force report recommending a return to housing production subsidies to increase the available housing stock, and the privatization study advocating housing demand subsidies to help low-income persons afford housing that the private market produces.

Ten years after these two reports were issued, the National Low Income Housing Coalition reported that between a quarter and a half of all renters would have to pay more than 30% of their monthly income to be able to afford to rent a two-bedroom apartment at the Section 8 fair market rental (FMR) range (discussed *infra*). The report also indicated that persons making minimum wage ($5.15 in 1998) would have to work at least 65 hours per week to be able to afford units at the FMR rate. NATIONAL LOW INCOME HOUSING COALITION, OUT OF REACH: RENTAL HOUSING AT WHAT COST? (1998). By 2009, while the minimum wage had increased to $7.25 per hour, persons making that amount still would have to work at least 68 hours per week to be able to afford FMR rates. NATIONAL LOW INCOME HOUSING COALITION, OUT OF REACH 2009: PERSISTENT PROBLEMS, NEW CHALLENGES FOR RENTERS 203 (2009). Another way to state the problem is through the concept of an "affordable housing wage," the amount said to be needed to afford average two-bedroom rental rates. In 2009, with a national average FMR, the national average affordable housing wage was said to be $17.84 per hour. *Id.* at Introduction.

Is the problem one of a shortage of housing on the supply side, resulting in a demand/supply inflation? Or is there enough housing stock which is too costly for low-income families to afford? If there is too little available housing, should the private sector or the government be responsible for addressing the shortage? If there is enough housing, but it is too costly for low-income people to afford, would direct subsidies such as housing vouchers paid to eligible low-income persons solve the problem? Or is the affordability gap a result of both phenomena?

2. Other recent research confirms the income/cost gap problem. As incomes decline, the affordability gap expands. Recent studies show that low-income families spend between 35% and 50% of their income on housing. JOINT CENTER FOR HOUSING STUDIES OF HARVARD UNIVERSITY, THE STATE OF THE NATION'S HOUSING 2009 at 26 (2009) (In 2007, fully 51% of low-income renters and 43% of low-income owners paid more than half their incomes for housing); JOINT CENTER FOR HOUSING STUDIES OF HARVARD UNIVERSITY, AMERICA'S RENTAL HOUSING: THE KEY TO A BALANCED NATIONAL POLICY 15 (2008) (nearly half of all renters paid more than 30% of their incomes for housing in 2006, and about a quarter—nearly nine million households—spent more than 50%).

3. The "housing affordability index" developed by the National Association of Realtors and the U.S. League of Savings Institutions measures housing affordability by comparing the median family income with median-priced existing homes. Assuming a 20% down payment, an "affordable house" is one for which monthly housing expenses do not exceed 25% of gross monthly income. (Other organizations use higher affordability ratios, such as CNNMoney.com, which uses ratios of 28 and 33% of gross monthly income, *available at* http://cgi.money.cnn.com/tools/houseafford/houseafford.html (last visited Jan. 18, 2010). Most housing assistance programs now use 30% of income as the standard bench mark of affordability. If median income is sufficiently high that median monthly housing expenses are less than 25% of income, the house is said to be affordable; if payments ex-

ceed 25% of income, there is an "affordability gap" that must be accounted for, either by reallocating funds from other portions of the family budget, by seeking additional income through a second job, by selecting less expensive housing, or by seeking governmental assistance of some type.

Changing interest rates have a sharp effect on the affordability index. For example, when the index was first used in 1971, interest rates adjusted for inflation were still in a 30-year stable pattern of 3% to 4%. The affordability index was 151.9, meaning that the median family had 151.9% of the income needed to afford a median priced house. Median income was $10,300, but only $6,700 was needed to afford the median priced house of $24,800. When interest rates reached the 9% to 9.5% range in 1977–1978, the affordability index dropped to 111–120. When interest rates soared, reaching the 14% to 16% range during 1982, the affordability index dropped below 70, meaning that a family earning a median income of $23,000 had only 70% of the money needed to afford the median-priced home of $67,300. In the spring of 1986, when interest rates had dropped below 10% for the first time in almost a decade, the affordability index on a $80,000 home had climbed back above 100. *See* NATIONAL ASSOCIATION OF REALTORS, EXISTING HOME SALES (1986).

Housing price change has a similar effect on the index, as illustrated by the spike in housing prices from 2001–2005 and subsequent collapse in 2006–2008. By 2006, the affordability index had dropped to 106.1 as median priced existing houses cost $221,900. The index rose in 2007 to a yearly average of 111.7 as median housing prices dropped to $217,900 but by December, 2007, median housing prices were down to $205,000 and the index was up to 123.0. In January, 2008, the median housing price was $197,000 and the index was 131.3, but by December, 2008, median housing prices had plummeted to $174,700 and the affordability index had climbed to a record 158.8. Catherine Rampell, *Housing Affordability at Record High,* N.Y. TIMES, Jan. 30, 2009, *available at* http://economix.blogs.nytimes.com/2009/01/30/housing-affordability-at-record-high/ (citing National Association of Realtors, Housing Affordability Index).

A more comprehensive approach to affordability factors in the cost of transportation to and from jobs and services. As noted in Chapter 1, *supra.* The Center for Neighborhood Technology (CNT) has developed a Housing + Transportation Affordability Index, which assumes that a house is affordable if housing and transportation costs do not exceed 48% of a household's income, available at http://htaindex.cnt.org. The Index was developed from earlier research by CNT on Location Efficiency, which included the development of Location Efficient Mortgages (LEMs), "reinforcing the relationship between urban form, housing site selection and transportation costs. CENTER FOR NEIGHBORHOOD TECHNOLOGY, HOUSING + TRANSPORTATION AFFORDABILITY INDEX, *available at* www.cnt.org. *See also* CENTER FOR HOUSING POLICY, A HEAVY LOAD: THE COMBINED HOUSING AND TRANSPORTATION BURDENS OF WORKING FAMILIES 5 (2006) ("At some distance, generally 12 to 15 miles, the increase in transportation costs outweighs the savings on housing—and the share of household income required to meet these combined expenditures rises"). Note the link between location and affordability. Does this link suggest that housing policy should take into account factors in addition to housing affordability, such as location of jobs and availability of public transportation?

4. Critics of the "affordability approach" contend that housing affordability problems are overstated by too much emphasis on increases in housing costs and not enough on the after-tax costs of owning a home. For example, a study of the first decade that the affordability index was used (the 1970s) concluded that when the effects of the tax

code (primarily the deductibility of home mortgage interest and property taxes) were factored in with an average eight year actual occupancy duration during that period and buyers' expectations about inflation, homeownership costs declined steadily since 1970, except for the period of high inflation between 1979 and 1982. John F. Kain, *America's Persistent Housing Crises: Errors in Analysis and Policy*, 465 ANNALS 136 (1983). Mortgage interest deductibility would apply to upper income homeowners, but not to those who do not itemize deductions or itemize but a modest amount and those who rent. *See also* John M. Quigley & Steven Raphael, *Is Housing Unaffordable? Why Isn't It More Affordable?* 18 J. ECON. PERS. 191 (2004) (finding little evidence of affordability problems for homeowners, but substantial evidence of affordability problems for low-income renters). On the question of occupancy duration, a 2009 study for the National Association of Home Builders concluded that "the average length of stay in a single family home is a little over 12 years for all home buyers, 11 years for first-time home buyers, and a little under 14 years if the analysis is confined to trade-up buyers." PAUL EMRATH, HOW LONG BUYERS REMAIN IN THEIR HOMES (2009), *available* at www.nahb.org.

5. Of course, the housing affordability index assumes a household has a median income, which in December, 2008, was above $61,000. As discussed in Chapter 1 *supra*, households in the lower quartiles have considerably less income and considerably greater difficulties in obtaining decent housing at an affordable price, whether they seek to buy or rent. As you review the material that follows in this chapter, what strategy or combination of strategies would you advocate to address these problems? How would you provide assistance to the "worst case" needs: persons whose incomes are below 30% of area median income—less than $20,000 and/or who are homeless? Will economic growth and an improving economy provide a cure? Can we rely upon the private market to respond? Are public/private partnerships or the non-profit sector the answer? Would you advocate governmental assistance? If so, in what form? At what level of government?

6. What role, if any, should the government play in encouraging homeownership? Should the government take direct action through subsidy programs or tax preferences, or should the government limit its attention to macroeconomic conditions such as interest rates, inflation, and employment through monetary and fiscal policy?

Peter Dreier, Federal Housing Subsidies: Who Benefits and Why?

A RIGHT TO HOUSING 105–107, 110, 113
(Rachel G. Bratt, Michael E. Stone & Chester Hartman eds. 2006)

Most Americans think that federal housing assistance is a poor people's program. In fact, relatively few low-income Americans receive federal housing subsidies. In contrast, about three-fourths of wealthy Americans—many living in very large homes—get housing subsidies from Washington in the form of tax breaks. These tax breaks subsidize many households who can afford to buy homes without it. Our policymakers and opinion leaders, however, focus more attention on federal aid to the poor. These programs—such as public housing and rent subsidies—are much more visible than hidden tax subsidies to the affluent. For example, a Lexis/Nexis search of major daily newspapers for 1999 found 4,822 articles that mentioned "public housing"; 164 references to "Section 8"; and a scant 37 stories with a combination of "mortgage interest" and "deduction."

As a result of housing's weak constituency, Congress has not put low-income housing programs high on its priority list. Despite slight increases in the late 1990s, federal funding for low-income housing has declined dramatically since the late 1970s. And during the 1990s, some members of Congress even proposed eliminating the U.S. Department of Housing and Urban Development (HUD) altogether....

The Magnitude Of Federal Housing Subsidies

In 2000, the federal government spent some $148.9 billion (in 2001 dollars) for various housing subsidies. [In 2008, the figure was $228.4 billion—Eds.] Americans typically associate the phrase "housing subsidy" with the poor. They think of public housing projects, homeless shelters or perhaps rent vouchers, most of which are administered by HUD. But the largest housing subsidies are much more invisible. These are subsidies that come through the tax code in the form of tax breaks or tax expenditures.

There are basically two kinds of housing subsidies—direct expenditures (administered by government agencies) and indirect expenditures—"tax expenditures" (which are incorporated in the federal tax code).... [V]arious tax expenditures for housing comprise the largest tax expenditures in terms of revenue loss to the federal government. These tax subsidies for housing go either to homeowners or to investors.... [T]ax expenditures account for over $118 billion—over three-fourths (79.2%) of the federal government's housing subsidies. Put another way, tax expenditures cost almost four times as much as direct housing subsidies. The Treasury Department—not HUD—is the largest government housing subsidy agency. Moreover, the gap between direct housing subsidies and tax expenditures has been widening since 1976.

These figures do not include the direct housing subsidies provided by the U.S. Department of Defense for military members and their families who live on and off military bases. In FY2001, the Department of Defense spent more than $10 billion in housing subsidy. These figures also do not include the proportion of social welfare subsidies—such as Temporary Assistance to Needy Families (TANF), cash assistance (formerly Aid to Families with Dependent Children) and the Earned Income Tax Credit—that families spend on housing.

Whether the federal government uses direct expenditures or tax breaks to subsidize housing is not important on its own terms. But the reality is that most of the direct subsidy programs go to low- and moderate-income people, while most of the tax subsidies go to middle- and upper-class people.

Homeowner Tax Expenditures

By far, the largest federal housing subsidies are the tax breaks for homeowners, totaling $103.1 billion in 2000 (in 2001 dollars). [The 2008 figure was $179.3 billion—Eds.] These include the deductions on mortgage interest payments ($61.5 billion), deductions on property tax payments ($22.6 billion) and the deferral of capital gains on home sales ($18.9 billion). About 31.8 million homeowners received at least one of these deductions.... [T]hese tax breaks are quite regressive. The highest income taxpayers with the largest houses and biggest mortgages get a disproportionate share of these federal tax expenditures. Over one-half (59%) of the mortgage interest deduction subsidy goes to the richest 10.2% of taxpayers, those with incomes over $100,000. The 2.2% of taxpayers with incomes over $200,000 received 22.4% of the entire amount.

Only 22.6% of all 140 million taxpayers took the mortgage interest deduction, but this varies significantly with income. For example, 69.8% of taxpayers with incomes over $200,000 took the mortgage interest deduction, with an average benefit of $6,293. In contrast, less than one-fourth (23.1%) of those in the $40,000 to $50,000 bracket took the deduction; those who did so saved an average of $859 on their taxes. Among those in the $20,000 to $30,000 income category, only 4.6% took the deduction; those who did so received an average benefit of only $426.

Consider that among households with incomes under $20,000, slightly more than half own their homes. Of those who own their homes, only 28.5% have mortgages. Of those who have mortgages, only 6.8% itemize. Among households in the $60,000 to $100,000 income bracket, more than 80% own their homes. Of those who own their homes, about 78% have mortgages. Of those who have mortgages, about 66% itemize. Among households in the $120,000 to $140,000 income bracket, almost 91% own their homes. Of those, about 82% have mortgages. Among this group, about 92% itemize).

For many low- and middle-income taxpayers, the mortgage interest deduction offers little or no incentive to own rather than rent. For many of these taxpayers—who can only afford a modestly priced house and are in a low tax bracket—the mortgage interest deduction (on its own and in combination with other itemized deductions) is likely to be lower than the standard deduction.

These tax breaks have significant social consequences. The mortgage interest deduction artificially inflates home prices, since both owners and sellers impute the subsidy into their calculations. This is especially the case at the upper end, but it has ripple effects throughout the housing market. Since the mortgage interest deduction is proportional to the cost of housing, it encourages homebuyers to buy larger homes in outlying areas rather than more modest homes in central cities and older suburbs ... thus promoting suburbanization and sprawl. Moderate-income homeowners, who cannot take advantage of the deduction, are concentrated in older suburbs and central cities. The tax code provision (eliminated in 1997) that allowed homeowners to defer capital gains taxes if they purchase a more expensive home, but not a smaller one, exacerbated this tendency, encouraging the purchase of larger homes, typically in suburbs farther from the central city.... And so by encouraging the suburbanization of housing, the tax code contributes to the well-known costs of metropolitan sprawl—transportation gridlock, pollution, costly infrastructure and related dilemmas. In other words, the "cost" of these housing tax breaks exceeds the amount that appears in the federal budget each year. There are related "external" costs to the environment, public health and other factors that do not show up when policymakers itemize the list of tax expenditures....

Who Benefits?

What is the "bottom line" concerning who benefits most from federal housing subsidies? First, federal spending for low-income housing has not kept pace with growing needs. While overall funding has grown, mainly (since the 1980s) to pay for prior commitments, new budget authority—capturing the rate of which new assisted units are added—has fallen dramatically.

Second, tax expenditures for housing, particularly those benefiting higher-income groups, far outweigh direct expenditures for housing. Measured in constant (2001) dollars, tax expenditures for homeowner subsidies and investor subsidies increased almost 300% between 1976 and 2000, from $29.4 billion to $117.6 billion. In contrast, federal funds for low income housing—through HUD, the USDA and the Low Income Housing Tax Credit—increased only 135% during that period. More telling, the HUD budget authority for additional housing units declined by 68%, from $76.9 billion to $24.3 billion....

Notes and Questions

1. The dichotomy between direct federal housing assistance and federal tax expenditures for housing continued in the first decade of the new millennium. While direct support of low-income households through the section 8 rental assistance and public housing programs totaled $42 billion in 2006, "tax subsidy programs that support homeownership, such as the mortgage interest deduction, the real estate property tax deduction, the exclusion of net imputed rental income on owner-occupied housing, and the capital gains exclusion on home sales" came to $154.8 billion. ADAM CARASSO, GILLIAN REYNOLDS & C. EUGENE STEURELE, HOW MUCH DOES THE FEDERAL GOVERNMENT SPEND TO PROMOTE ECONOMIC MOBILITY AND FOR WHOM? 14 (2008) (published by the Economic Mobility Project of the Pew Charitable Trusts), *available at* www.economicmobility.org/. The Economic Mobility study also noted that "more that 80% of the benefits from the home mortgage interest deduction accrue to families in the top fifth of the income scale—families that would likely purchase a home in any case...." *Id.*

2. Professor Dreier appears to shrug off a major policy debate with his comment that the government's choice to use direct expenditures or tax breaks as its housing subsidy vehicle is not particularly important. Do you agree? What implications are raised by this choice? Is one approach more visible than the other? Examine the programs being studied from this perspective. Is it possible to generalize that one approach is the better one, or will the results be better if both approaches are reflected in the programs?

3. Federal housing subsidies have been criticized for "perpetuat[ing] serious inequities" in two dimensions—vertically and horizontally.

> The first of these, the issue of vertical equity, refers to the fact that a disproportionate share of program benefits actually finds its way into the pockets of individuals above the poverty level, rather than the poor themselves. This diversion of subsidy dollars is inherent in the structure of the federal government programs.... Syndication of ... tax shelters is an exceedingly costly method of raising development capital. Altogether, the use of intermediaries and high capital costs consume 35% of every subsidy dollar, seriously reducing the actual expenditure on bricks and mortar to house the poor.
>
> The second, and potentially more explosive, aspect of the equity issue centers on the problem of horizontal, as opposed to vertical, equity: the fact that persons in essentially the same circumstances receive widely varying treatment. Given the current structure of federal housing programs, and their levels of funding, only a small fraction of those eligible for assistance receive any government aid at all. In addition, many households whose incomes hover just beyond eligibility requirements pay market prices to occupy substandard housing, while other families with only marginally lower incomes are provided new standard housing at below-market rents.

ARTHUR P. SOLOMON, HOUSING THE URBAN POOR 16–17 (1974).

4. Can the apparent inequities in the federal housing programs be remedied, or are they inherent in the type of programs involved? If you conclude that housing subsidy programs will always produce some inequities, what legal, practical, and political problems does this raise? What remedial suggestions would you make?

To what extent does horizontal inequity result from the traditional emphasis on new construction in the federal subsidy programs? Would the problem be measurably reduced by a shift in program design to use of existing housing with substantial rehabilitation?

Solomon takes the position that a less expensive and more equitable way to subsidize families is to place greater reliance on existing housing not in need of rehabilitation. But might the same horizontal inequity occur if insufficient funds were appropriated for a demand side subsidy? The Section 8 voucher program, discussed *infra,* has been plagued by extremely long waiting lists. If our housing program depended solely on the use of the existing stock, what additional problems might be created? Many economists believe that sole reliance on the existing stock (or a demand side subsidy), without increasing the supply, would simply drive up the cost of existing housing, worsen financial housing needs, and increase subsidy costs.

An argument can also be made that any federal program must include at least some new construction to increase the supply of housing, increase opportunity that new construction presents to encourage integration by placing subsidized housing in un-impacted areas and suburban jurisdictions, the potential new construction offers urban redevelopment efforts to improve slum areas, and the likelihood that new construction will provide jobs to the construction industry, especially during periods of building recession such as the 2007–2010 recession.

How would you evaluate these factors and policies in determining the proper program balance between new construction and the use of existing housing? How would you answer the complaint of Family A, living in a modest home, whose income is just above the subsidy eligibility line, when Family B, earning just a few thousand dollars less, moves into an expensive, new home at a much lower rent in the same neighborhood? Would it materially improve our national perception of housing subsidies if Family B moved into a modest, existing house, even though its housing payments were still substantially less than Family A?

5. One form of intermediary involvement identified by Solomon, *supra*, is the process of raising development capital through the favorable tax treatment of private investors. Do you agree with Solomon that these costs are "inherent in the structure of the federal government programs?" Is favorable tax treatment necessary or desirable to assure an acceptable level of production under the programs, or is it an inequitable tax loophole of benefit only to the wealthy? Can you propose alternatives to either (1) raise development capital without tax benefits to intermediaries, or (2) convert some of the investor benefits for use in the programs or to aid low-income tenants? To what extent does the favorable tax treatment of homeowners contribute to the vertical equity problem?

A second form of intermediary is the public intermediary. Can the cost of administration of the subsidy programs by HUD, local housing authorities, and other local government agencies be fairly characterized as siphoning off benefits that should go to the poor? Or, is the real complaint that governmental costs should be reduced by improvements in bureaucratic efficiency? Do you agree that a direct consumer subsidy would substantially reduce the cost of public intermediary involvement? Would a block grant approach for housing subsidies solve or reduce the problem?

The third form of intermediary involvement is the myriad of outside professions required for construction and operation of housing. These include financial institutions, lawyers, title insurers, architects, engineers, and management agents. Although the housing production mechanism works through such intermediaries, an argument can be made that the higher program costs engendered by these intermediaries reduce the actual benefits to the poor from the limited amount of subsidy funds. Are these intermediary costs necessary to achieve the other goals of the programs (e.g., stimulation of private industry)?

To what extent would a direct consumer subsidy reduce these types of intermediary costs? Besides increasing cost, public and private intermediaries influence the location of subsidized housing, thus restricting consumer choice.

6. Federal housing programs do not operate in a vacuum; they may have an effect on the housing market in which the subsidy is provided. This effect reflects the market equilibrium between supply and demand relative to the nature of the subsidy involved. An income supplement or consumer housing subsidy contributes to demand, by making more money available to purchase housing resources. A subsidy connected to new construction, as most of our national programs were until the 1980s, contributes to supply, by producing new dwelling units.

The ultimate effect of either type of subsidy (or a combination of demand and supply subsidies) depends on the state of the local housing market. A vacancy rate of 3–4% is normal, and a subsidy of either type would have a minimal effect unless massive in size. A low vacancy rate (say, 1%) argues for a supply subsidy. Many economists believe a demand subsidy would only increase prices and rents until the market could respond with new production, since an increased number of families would have sufficient resources to compete for a small number of available units. Increases in market costs due to the program can result in higher program costs as well as increased housing expense for nonparticipants. A high vacancy rate would only be aggravated by a supply subsidy and therefore argues for a demand subsidy in order to absorb the excess supply. A supply subsidy in a loose housing market would reduce the already low demand for lower cost private housing. When policy makers evaluate alternate subsidy approaches, should they be equally concerned with market impacts as with direct effects on the poor?

7. Housing subsidy programs also raise questions of consumer choice, location of housing, and the mobility of low-income families. Historically, from inception in the 1930s through perhaps the early 1980s, federal subsidy programs emphasized construction of new dwelling units. A construction subsidy has the disadvantage of being tied to the dwelling unit rather than the consumer. This means that the consumer must live where builders and developers choose to build, another dimension of the intermediaries problem. The implications of locational choice on issues of racial discrimination and concentration are discussed in Chapter 6 *infra*. Another effect of tying the subsidy to a newly constructed unit is that it deprives the consumer of mobility. If the tenant of subsidized housing wishes to move to a new jurisdiction, in search of new employment or better educational opportunities, the tenant family cannot take the subsidy with it. It must gamble on the existence of subsidized housing in the new jurisdiction. Even if subsidized units are available in the new jurisdiction, chances are there is a substantial waiting list. The immigrant tenant family receives no priority for subsidized housing in the new jurisdiction by reason of its prior occupancy of such housing. Tying the subsidy to the dwelling unit and to new construction thus greatly discourages low-income families from moving from one neighborhood or jurisdiction to another within metropolitan areas and from one metropolitan area to another. In addition, the consumer is greatly limited in type and size of housing available to what private developers choose to build.

What remedies to this problem can you suggest? Granting the subsidy to the tenant rather than the dwelling units is an obvious choice. What administrative difficulties would this entail? *See, e.g.*, 24 C.F.R. §§ 982.201 to 982.401 (establishing policies in the tenant-based program governing, *inter alia*, admission to the program, finding a suitable unit in a suitable location, executing a lease, setting dwelling quality standards, portability of the assistance upon moving, and tenant and owner duties in the Section 8 program). The Section 8 program is discussed *infra*. Would greater emphasis on existing housing ameliorate the problem, even if the subsidy continued to be tied to the dwelling unit?

A secondary problem caused by the new construction emphasis is that subsidized units are more identifiable, especially when large numbers are concentrated at a single location. This causes subsidized housing (particularly public housing) to be referred to as "the projects." The higher visibility of subsidized housing due to concentration creates a visible target for neighborhood objection, and has frequently prevented subsidized developments from being built.

Could this problem be solved by placing smaller groups of newly constructed subsidized housing on scattered sites, or would the same opposition result? If a scattered-site strategy is used, would it increase public costs by making construction and management more expensive? Would use of existing housing or a consumer subsidy solve this problem? *See* Report of the President's Comm. on Urban Housing: A Decent Home 68–73 (1968) (Kaiser Committee).

8. During the Reagan administration, HUD's budget suffered the most drastic reductions of any cabinet level agency. Appropriations for HUD's subsidized programs declined from $26.9 billion in 1981 to only $9.7 billion in 1988. In 1980, HUD provided rental housing assistance to 316,000 additional low-income households. Between 1981 and 1988 annual increases in households receiving assistance averaged only 82,000. The trend continued during the Bush and Clinton administrations, reaching a low point in the 1996 housing appropriations bill which allocated no money for new recipients of Section 8 assistance, discussed *infra*. Pub. L. No. 104-204, 110 Stat. 2874 (1996). In 1979, approximately 4 million poor-renter households received no federal assistance. By 1995, this group had increased to 5.3 million households, an increase of more than one third. Rental Housing Assistance At A Crossroads: A Report To Congress On Worst Case Housing Needs (1996), *available at* http://www.huduser.org/publications/affhsg/rental2.html. Ten years later, following a dip to 5.18 million households in 2003, the number of worst case housing needs had climbed to 5.99 million in 2005. "Households with 'worst case needs' are defined as unassisted renters with very low incomes who have one or two 'priority problems' either paying more than half of their income for housing or living in severely substandard housing." U.S. Dep't of Housing &Urban Development, Affordable Housing Needs 2005: A Report To Congress 1 (2007), *available at* www.huduser.org/publications/affhsg/affHsgNeeds.html.

In contrast to the drastic reduction in direct federal housing assistance to the poor, federal tax expenditures on housing (revenue loss estimates from the deductibility of mortgage interest and state and local property taxes on owner-occupied homes), which primarily benefit middle- and upper-income homeowners, rose steadily during this period. In 1981 federal housing tax expenditures were $33.4 billion; by 1997, they had risen to an estimated $70 billion and were projected to rise to $85 billion in 2001. Office of Management and Budget, Analytical Perspectives, Budget of the United States, Fiscal Year 1997 at 61–62 (1997). For a short history on how housing related tax expenditures increased in comparison to outlays, *see* National Low Income Housing Coalition, Changing Priorities: The Federal Budget and Housing Assistance (2004), *available at* www.nlihc.org/doc/cp04.pdf.

The dichotomy between direct federal housing assistance and federal tax expenditures on housing continues into the second decade of the new millennium. While direct federal support for low-income households through the public housing and section 8 rental assistance programs had climbed to $42 billion in 2006, tax expenditures (home mortgage interest and property tax deductions, along with exclusions of capital gains on home sales and exclusion of new imputed rental income on owner-occupied housing) rose to $154.8 billion. ADAM CARASSO, GILLIAM REYNOLDS & C. EUGENE STEURELE, HOW MUCH DOES THE FEDERAL GOVERNMENT SPEND TO PROMOTE ECONOMIC MOBILITY AND FOR WHOM? 14 (2008) (a publication of the Economic Mobility Project of the The Pew Charitable Trusts), *available at* www.economicmobility.org. The authors of the Economic Mobility study also noted that "more than 80% of the benefits from the home mortgage interest deduction accrue to families in the top fifth of the income scale-families that would likely purchase a home in any case...." *Id.* Outlays for 2010 are expected to be $51.5 billion for HUD direct assistance programs and $168,530 billion for major housing tax expenditures ($107,980—mortgage interest deduction, $14,980—state property tax deduction, $30,460—capital gains exclusion on home sales, $4,340—credit for housing investments, and $10,770—accelerated depreciation on rental housing (normal tax method)). OFFICE OF MANAGEMENT AND BUDGET, ANALYTICAL PERSPECTIVES, FISCAL YEAR 2010 at 300, 390 (2010).

2. Matrix of Subsidy Alternatives

As noted in the introduction to this chapter, a wide variety of subsidies have been used to make housing more accessible and more affordable to low- and moderate-income households. The type or types of subsidy employed will determine how the cost of housing is affected. Fixed housing costs which must be covered by tenant rent payments include construction costs, financing costs, operating expenses and developer profit. A governmental subsidy can be designed to directly (or indirectly) affect one or more of these individual costs.

Capital costs associated with a housing unit include land acquisition and improvement, construction materials, labor costs, construction loan financing charges and fees, governmental approvals, fees and permits, and charges for permanent mortgage financing. All of these costs equal the total development cost of the housing unit. With no government subsidy, these costs represent approximately 45% of the total rental payments of the unit. A capital subsidy eliminates these costs as part of tenant payment. In essence, the government buys the unit, paying all capital costs. In practice, a capital subsidy is funded through the issuance of low interest, tax exempt bonds. The government pays the bond amortization payments, leaving the tenant to pay only operating expenses.

Operating expenses for a housing unit include management fees, utilities, maintenance, insurance, payroll, and real estate taxes. An operating expense subsidy can be designed to reduce expenses that must be covered by tenant payment by a fixed percentage of the total.

The total development cost of the housing unit determines the amount of the permanent mortgage loan needed to finance it. The interest rate, maturity, and amortization plan of the mortgage determine the amount of the monthly payment (debt service) required to amortize the loan over its term. A reduction in the interest rate charged results in lower rent. An interest subsidy can reduce the debt service on the loan that must be supported by tenant rent. The government subsidy would be in the form of a payment to the lender of the difference between the face interest rate of the mortgage and the rate at which the tenant pays, or a direct government loan at an interest rate below that charged in the private market.

Each of these subsidies reduces a particular fixed cost of housing. A different type of subsidy, a rental subsidy, is not based on housing costs. The tenant payment is fixed at an arbitrarily chosen percentage of tenant income. The subsidy is the difference between that amount and the tenant's monthly housing expense. A rise in expenses or interest rate does not affect tenant payment, but does increase the subsidy. Tenant payment increases only if there is increased income.

The subsidies discussed above are direct subsidies, operating within the housing process. They represent the difference between the market cost or rental of the unit and what the tenant actually pays. Indirect subsidies are benefits associated with housing which provide incentives for lenders or developers.

All rental housing provides tax deductions which offset operating income, resulting in lower taxes for the developer/investor. Low-income rental housing historically provided higher benefits in early years due to accelerated depreciation deductions. Prior to the 1986 Tax Reform Act, and still to a limited extent, the resulting higher losses shelter other income of the taxpayer. The taxpayer's savings can be expressed as federal taxes forgone to the Treasury, as an indirect subsidy for investors in low-income housing. (*See* Note 3 and Note on Tax Policy *infra.*)

The indirect subsidy of forgone federal taxes associated with a direct capital subsidy is due to the method of financing the capital costs. The bonds issued to finance capital costs typically are tax exempt, thereby producing a tax loss to the Treasury, although taxable bonds, discussed *infra,* are gaining popularity. The bonds are also issued at a lower than market interest rate. Investment of these funds in taxable bonds at market interest rates would produce even higher taxes. The impact on the Treasury is therefore larger than simply taxes forgone on 6% tax exempt bonds.

Another form of indirect subsidy is produced by secondary mortgage market financing. In order to reduce the debt service amount, lenders write mortgages below the market interest rate, with the guarantee that they will be purchased by a governmental secondary mortgage market entity at face value immediately. The lender can still service the mortgage, for a fee, and has full use of the loan amount to write another mortgage. The cost to the budget occurs when the governmental entity resells the mortgage at a loss, which enables the purchaser of the mortgage to obtain a market rate yield on the investment. This is popularly known as the Tandem Plan. (*See* Format XIV and the Note on the Secondary Market *infra.*)

Tax shelter benefits and tax-free bonds produce tax losses for the entire term of the loan or the owner's holding period of the property. The indirect subsidy from the secondary mortgage market has a one-time budget impact that occurs in the year the mortgage is made.

Illustration of subsidy choices: a prototype apartment unit

In order to illustrate the choices policy makers have in designing housing programs, estimated housing cost and subsidy effects are applied to a prototype three-bedroom, two-bathroom garden apartment of about 1,200 sq. ft. occupied by a family of four. It is located in an apartment development of 100 units, with 15 efficiency, 25 one-bedroom, 30 two-bedroom, and 30 three-bedroom units. The estimates used are based on representative housing costs in the Midwest in 2008–2009. Figures are rounded off for ease of calculation and presentation, and are intended only as examples. Development costs and interest rates can vary considerably in different parts of the country.

The total development cost of the three-bedroom unit is estimated to be $145,000. This includes approximately $90 per square foot for construction costs ($108,000), roughly $20,000 for soft costs (construction loan interest, legal and architectural fees, etc.), about $10,000 for a development fee and about $7,000 for land costs. Except where noted, the unit is financed with a mortgage loan of 85% of the total development cost (approximately $125,000). The standard mortgage is for a term of twenty years at the interest rate obtainable by the developer on the commercial mortgage market, although the term is extended to thirty years to illustrate the impact of some of the programs noted. (The 7% market interest rate used in the example is about half-way between quoted commercial loan rates of 6.50% for 10 year loans and 8.25% for 30 year loans by a commercial lender in San Francisco on February 1, 2010, Steelhead Capital, Inc., Multi-Family Commercial Mortgage Rates, Feb. 2, 2010, *available at* www.steelheadcapital.com/rates.asp). The mortgage is a standard level payment, self-amortizing loan. The developer invests the remaining 15% of the total development cost. The return on this investment is estimated at 10% yearly, adding $125 to the monthly rent. Real estate taxes attributable to the three-bedroom unit have been estimated at 1.50% of the total development cost. Total operating expenses for this unit have been estimated at $460 per month (including real estate taxes). There is an additional adjustment which must be made to the operating expenses. With a predicted vacancy rate of 5%, there will be no rental income (to defray costs) one month out of every twenty months. Therefore, operating expenses are increased to $500 per month to absorb the losses when the unit is unoccupied.

The chart titled "Matrix of Subsidy Alternatives" is intended to demonstrate the various direct and indirect subsidy mechanisms.

The chart sets out rentals associated with the prototype housing unit, population served, and subsidy amounts. The costs and operating expense of the unit are established as described above. The interest rate column (Column A1) gives the percentage interest charged by the lender on the permanent mortgage loan. This rate determines monthly debt service payments needed to amortize the mortgage loan in equal monthly installments over the life of the mortgage. Column A2 sets forth the length of the mortgage as twenty years or thirty years, or bond financing of forty years. In formats with two numbers in Column A2, the first is the rate charged by the lender and the second is the subsidized, reduced rate at which debt service is calculated for rental purposes.

The monthly rent column (Column B) is the monthly rent needed to cover debt service payments at the lender's interest rate, operating expenses, developer-investor profit, and vacancy loss. This figure is what a tenant must pay if there is no direct subsidy. Tenant payment (Column C) states market rent less any direct subsidy, or the subsidized rent that the tenant must pay.

Assuming 30% of family income is used to meet rental payments, Column D gives the annual income needed to afford the dwelling unit at the rent specified in Column C. Columns E and F express tenant rent as a percentage of annual income at two selected income levels, a moderate-income level and a poverty-income level. The assumed area median annual income for the hypothetical family of four is $50,000. (Source: U.S. Bureau of the Census, Income, Poverty and Health Insurance Coverage in the United States: 2008, at 5 (2009)). In Column E, rent is expressed as a percentage of income for the family if its income is 80% of the area median ($40,000, referred to as a moderate-income family). Households in the lowest quintile had incomes of $20,712 or less in 2008. *Id.* at 9. Column F expresses rent as a percentage of annual income for households at this level of income.

Column G is divided into direct subsidies (Column G1) and indirect subsidies (Column G2). The direct subsidy may reduce specific fixed costs of the housing unit or reduce rent to a fixed percentage of tenant income. The direct subsidy amount shown is the

Matrix of Subsidy Alternatives

	A	A 1	B	C	C 1	D	E	F	G 1	G 2
Format	Interest Rate on Mortgage	Years Term of Financing	Monthly Rent (Market)	Tenant Portion of Monthly Rent	Monthly Rent x 12 = Annual Rent	Annual Income to Pay Rent with 30% of Income	Rent as % of 80% Median Income (40,000)	Rent as % of Low Income (20,712)	Direct Subsidy	Monthly Indirect Subsidy
I	7.0%	20	$1,636.50	$1,636.50	$19,638.00	$65,460.00	49%	95%	0	70 + 315 = 385
II	7.0%	30	1,501.24	1,501.24	18,014.88	60,050.00	45%	87%	0	70 + 315 = 385
III	7.0%	30	1,501.24	1,251.24	15,014.88	50,046.60	37%	72%	250	70 + 315 = 385
IV	6.0%	40	1,359.39	1,359.39	16,312.68	54,255.60	41%	78%	0	605
V	7% / 3%	30	1,501.24	1,200.88	14,410.56	48,035.00	36%	70%	300	70 + 315 = 385
VI	7% / 1%	30	1,501.24	1,077.67	12,932.04	43,107.00	32%	62%	424	70 + 315 = 385
VII	7% / 1%	30	1,501.24	827.67	9,932.04	33,106.80	25%	48%	674	70 + 315 = 385
VIII	6.0%	40	1,178.14	500.00	6,000.00	20,000.00	15%	28%	678	605
IX	6.0%	40	1,178.14	250.00	3,000.00	10,000.00	7.5%	14%	928	605
X	7.0%	20	1,636.50	1,000.00	12,000.00	40,000.00	30%	58%	637	70 + 315 = 385
XI	7.0%	20	1,636.50	517.80	6,213.60	20,712.00	16%	30%	1,119	70 + 315 = 385
XII	6.0%	40	1,359.39	1,000.00	12,000.00	40,000.00	30%	58%	359	605
XIII	7.0%	30	1,501.24	750.00	9,000.00	30,000.00	30%	x	x	435
XIV	5.5%	30	1,381.05	1,381.05	16,572.60	55,242.00	41%	76%	17,255	70 + 315 = 385
XV	7.0%	30	1,636.50	375/625	4,500/7,500	15,000/25,000	11%/19%	22%/28%	261/1,011	70 + 315 = 385

monthly cost of the subsidy used for each format. Generally, this is a sum that must be covered by an annual congressional appropriation

There are four distinct indirect subsidies illustrated in Column G2. Except for the Tandem Plan illustration, figures used illustrate monthly indirect subsidies. The housing finance agency ("HFA") bonds and the capital subsidy formats illustrate monthly indirect subsidies representing federal taxes forgone because of the use of tax exempt bond financing, which results in a lower rate of interest because of the fact that bond purchasers do not have to pay income taxes on their investment income. The indirect subsidy continues over the life of the bond. The capital subsidy format also contains a direct subsidy because the federal government uses the bond proceeds to fund the capital costs of the housing unit. The indirect subsidy shown in the interest subsidy and rent subsidy formats also represents federal taxes forgone. In these formats the tax loss is the result of tax shelter benefits which accrue to developers-investors of low-income rental housing. The figure represents taxes forgone in the first year of project occupancy. This indirect subsidy continues over the life of the mortgage, but declines in subsequent years. Finally, the indirect subsidy in the tax credit format illustrates federal taxes foregone through the use of a tax credit, and represents a monthly figure for the life of the tax credit. Generally speaking, except for the Tandem Plan illustration, the indirect subsidy is not subject to any appropriation.

Format I: Market Rate. This format illustrates the required rental ($1,636.50 per month) for the prototype housing unit with no direct subsidy at a market interest rate of 7%. (Earlier editions used an interest rate of 9% for this illustration. In recent years interest rates dropped to historic lows, but began to trend upward again in 2010. A one percent change in interest rates would add or subtract approximately $75 to or from the monthly payment on a 20-year, $125,000 loan.) Conventional multifamily housing of this type serves middle- to upper-income families. If the hypothetical family of four did not want to spend more than 30 percent of their income on rent, a currently popular measure of housing affordability, the family would need a minimum annual family income of $65,460 (Column D). Moderate-income families would have to spend 49 percent of their income for rent to occupy this unit (Column E), while poverty-level families would have to spend 95 percent of their income (Column F).

The indirect subsidy of this format (Column G2) represents federal taxes forgone for the first year of occupancy. In the early years of operation, depreciation, interest, and expense deductions exceed operating income. The developer-investor has losses which can be used to shelter other income under certain circumstances. If a taxpayer in the 2010 maximum 35% tax bracket incurred losses of $200 in the first year of operation, and used those losses to shelter other income under this format, approximately $70 in taxes would be lost to the Treasury.

A second sum of $315, represents the monthly cost of the mortgage interest deduction taken by a taxpayer in the 35% bracket. Total indirect subsidy is $385 lost to the Treasury in the first year of the development.

Format II: FHA Insurance. This second format illustrates a program that simply places an upper limit on the permanent loan interest rate. Because this would be an insured program under the Federal Housing Administration (FHA-insured), the mortgage term has been increased to 30 years. The developer obtains a mortgage which has a maximum interest rate of 7%. Although for many years the FHA insurance program placed a cap on interest rates to keep them slightly below market rates, Congress removed that cap in 1983 and FHA rates have been at or slightly above market rates since then. Thus the main impacts FHA insurance has on affordability are a low down payment (3.5% in 2010) and a longer term loan (30 years) The resulting reduction in rent, $135 per month, is insufficient to effect a change in the population served. The unit remains out of reach for moderate-income and poverty-level families.

Format III: Operating Subsidy. First used in conjunction with the Public Housing program discussed *infra,* an operating cost subsidy is a direct governmental subsidy that is paid monthly to the owner of the unit. In our hypothetical it is established at 50% of total operating expenses associated with the unit. The direct subsidy is estimated to be $250 per month (Column G) and will increase or decrease in direct proportion to any increases or decreases in operating expenses since the subsidy is fixed at 50% of those expenses. Because operating expenses account for less that half of the total rent of the unit, this subsidy alone does not have a substantial impact on tenant rent. The rent is reduced less than 10% from that of the Market Rate Format. Moderate-income families are served by this subsidy with 37% of their income, but poverty-level families are not reached. Columns E and F).

*Format IV: HFA Bonds.*Tax exempt bonds issued by state and local housing finance agencies can produce lower rents because the investors generally are willing to accept a lower interest rate in return for not having to pay income tax on their investment income. The difference of 1% in the interest rate over the Market Rate Format reduces rent by only an additional $276. This reduction does not help a poverty-level family (Column F), although a moderate-income family could occupy the unit if willing to bear a larger rent burden of 41% of income (Column E). Taxes foregone on bond investor income constitute an indirect subsidy (Column G).When HFA bonds are used to support first-time homebuyer mortgages, an additional indirect subsidy is the deductibility of mortgage interest by the homebuyer borrower.

Format V: Interest Subsidy (3%). This example shows the operation of an interest subsidy. Column A shows the lender's interest rate at 7%, resulting in a market rent of $1501 per month, on a thirty year mortgage as in Format II. The subsidy is designed to reduce one of the fixed costs of the unit, the debt service payment. The effective interest rate on the mortgage which must be covered by tenant payments is reduced to 3%, resulting in a monthly cost to the tenant of $1,200. The government pays the difference between rates to the lender, a direct subsidy of $300 each month for the prototype three-bedroom dwelling unit (Column G1). The income required to afford the unit spending just 30% of family income has been reduced to $48,035 (or about 20%) from the $60,050 required in Format II (Column D). This subsidy format has reduced rent to a more reasonable, but still burdensome level of 36% for the moderate-income family (Column E), but, at 70% of income, the rent remains out of reach for a poverty-level family (Column F). The indirect subsidy (Column G) represents federal taxes forgone monthly in the first year of occupancy.

Format VI: Interest Subsidy (1%). This subsidy format is the same type of interest reduction payment as used in Format V. The interest rate supported by tenant payment has been further reduced to 1%, resulting in a rent of $1,078 per month. The direct subsidy, paid to the lender, has increased to $424 per month (Column G). The moderate-income family is helped by this format, but still faces a burdensome rent-income ratio of approximately 32% of income (Column E). However, this subsidy format does not serve the poverty-level family, whose rent-income ratio is 62%. (Column F). The indirect subsidy (Column G) represents federal taxes forgone monthly in the first year of occupancy, as above.

Format VII: Interest and Operating Subsidies. In this example, two direct subsidies are combined: the debt service subsidy (1% interest) and the operating subsidy described in

Format VI. The $1,078 monthly tenant payment of the 1% interest subsidy is reduced by an additional $250 by adding the 50% operating expense subsidy. The direct monthly subsidy of $674 (Column G1) consists of two payments. The operating subsidy of $250 is paid to the owner of the project and the debt service subsidy of $424 is paid to the lender. The income required to occupy this unit at a 30% rent-income ratio has been reduced over 40% from that required in Format II (Column D). Although this format reduces rent to a reasonable level, 25% for the hypothetical moderate-income family (Column E), it would still require 48% of the income of a poverty-level family (Column F). The addition of the direct operating expense subsidy has no effect on the indirect subsidy cost (Column G).

Format VIII: Capital Cost Subsidy. Previous formats illustrate the effect on tenant rent payment obligations of reducing the interest rate on the permanent mortgage loan, thereby reducing debt service covered by rent. In this format, debt service has been eliminated from tenant payment, leaving only operating costs to be paid by the tenant. The capital costs and permanent financing expenses associated with the prototype housing unit are funded by direct government payment to amortize the loan. If tenant payment had to support debt service (at a 6% bond rate), rent would be $1,178 per month (Column B). However, due to the direct capital subsidy of $678.14 per month (Column G), tenant payment has been reduced to $500 per month (Column C) to cover operating expenses. This format is the first one that even approaches a reasonable rental for the poverty-level family at 28% of income. (Column F). The indirect subsidy associated with the direct capital subsidy is expressed in terms of federal taxes forgone monthly because of the use of tax exempt bonds to fund the capital costs (Column G2).

Format IX: Capital Cost and Operating Subsidies. This format combines two direct subsidies: a capital cost subsidy and an operating expense subsidy. With no debt service payment included in tenant payment, rent was $500 per month in the Capital Cost Format. Reducing operating expenses covered by tenant payment by 50% lowers rent to $250 per month (Column C). The total direct subsidy has increased to $928 per month (Column G1). This format has the deepest subsidy, serving the lowest-income families (Column D). It reduces rent to well within a reasonable expenditure for the poverty-level family (Column F). The addition of the second direct subsidy to the capital cost subsidy has no effect on the indirect subsidy (Column G2).

Format X: Rent Subsidy. Each government subsidy illustrated has been directed at reducing a particular fixed cost associated with the prototype housing unit. A rental subsidy is not based on housing costs or expenses. The subsidy is based on the income of the family served. Rent is set at 30% of family income, without regard to fixed costs and expenses. The amount of the subsidy varies directly with the income of the population served. The family served in this format is at 80% of the area median income (Columns D) and pays 30% of income for rent (Column E). Market rent is set as shown in Format I and remains at $1,636.50 per month (Column B), but tenant payment, fixed at 30% of income, is reduced to $1000 per month (Column C). The direct subsidy is $636.50 per month (Column G1), paid to the owner of the housing unit. This direct subsidy varies with both housing cost and tenant income. Changes in housing costs and expenses do not affect tenant payment. Since the subsidy covers the gap between market rent and 30% of income, it in effect covers production, financing and operating costs. As costs increase, rents can be raised without financially burdening tenants; the only effect is on the amount of the subsidy. This type of subsidy results in a financially strong project, but is an expensive approach. The indirect subsidy (Column G2) is a combination of the amount of federal taxes forgone in the first year of occupancy through tax sheltering, and the deductibility of mortgage interest.

Format XI: Rent Subsidy (2). This rental subsidy format shows costs when serving a poverty-level family (Columns D and F) in contrast to the previous format, which was designed to serve a moderate-income family. Since tenant payment is reduced to the selected level of 30% of family income, the hypothetical poverty-level family must pay just $500 per month in rent (Column C). This is only the third format under which a poverty-level family can afford to occupy the prototype unit with the assumed reasonable percentage of income. The direct subsidy paid to the unit owner has increased to $1,119 per month (Column G). The indirect subsidy is unaffected, since operating income and deductions are the same as in the moderate income format.

Format XII: Rent Subsidy and HFA Bonds. This format shows the effects of combining two subsidies: the rental subsidy and tax-exempt bond financing. A moderate-income family is served, and tenant payment is fixed at 30% of income. Therefore, the rent is the same as in the rent subsidy in Format X. (Column C). Tenant payment is unaffected by the addition of the second subsidy. The major affect of adding the financing subsidy is budgetary. The direct subsidy has been reduced to $359.30 per month (Column G), because the lower interest charged has reduced housing expenses, thereby reducing market rent (Column B). Likewise, if bonds were used with a rent subsidy for low-income households, the $950 direct subsidy previously noted would be reduced to $720. The indirect subsidy (Column G) represents a combination of taxes foregone monthly on bond investor income and the deductibility of mortgage interest by the borrower

Format XIII: Tax Credit. This format shows the effect of an indirect subsidy only, the use of a tax credit for the owner of low-income housing. (See Section J *infra*, for further discussion.) The project is financed with a commercial loan (Column A). This format assumes that 40% of the prototype housing development is occupied by families at 60% of area median income ($30,000, Column D), paying $750 per month (30% of income) (Column C). There is no direct subsidy. The tax credit results in taxes forgone by the Treasury, for the prototype dwelling unit, in the approximate amount of $435 per month for the life of the tax credit.

Format XIV: Tandem Plan. Tandem Plan financing, discussed in the Note on the Secondary Market, *infra,* is used to provide rent reduction. As in several other formats discussed above, lower rent is obtained by reducing the interest rate on the mortgage loan. The difference of 1.5% in the interest rate over the FHA-insured rate in Format II reduces rent by only an additional $120. This reduction does not help either family in our hypothetical, although the moderate-income family might be able to stretch its budget to afford the 41% rent-income ratio. This form of financing causes a substantial one-time budget cost when the mortgage is closed, and is likely to be used only when FHA-insured mortgage rates are higher than the target population can afford.

Format XV: National Housing Trust Fund. The National Housing Trust Fund ("NHTF") was created in 2008 as a direct subsidy for "production, preservation, and rehabilitation" of housing for extremely low-income (30% of area median income—$15,000 in our hypothetical) and very low-income (50% of area median income—$25,000) households. The fund's basic purpose is to provide grants to states for redistribution to local entities to support housing development activities. The direct subsidy estimates in the Matrix are designed to illustrate the potential impact (and cost) of a fully funded NHTF. In a bow to the realities of the foreclosure crisis and the severe recession, any funds appropriated for the first three years are to go to foreclosure efforts. The NHTF is discussed in Section M *infra.*

A Note on the Secondary Market

The operation of secondary mortgage markets is a complex topic. Detailed consideration of secondary markets is beyond the scope of this book. But it is necessary to present a brief description of the secondary mortgage market because of its impact on financing for unsubsidized as well as subsidized housing.

Any discussion of the secondary mortgage market must begin with an introduction to the three entities which comprise it. The primary entity is the Federal National Mortgage Association (FNMA, also known as "Fannie Mae"), a quasi-private entity that receives no governmental financing but is subject to some governmental regulation. Fannie Mae was created in 1938. It was chartered by statute in 1968 and one-third of its board of directors is appointed by the President of the United States. Fannie Mae must comply with certain statutory objectives in administering its programs. 12 U.S.C. §§ 1716–1723. Another federal secondary mortgage market entity is the Federal Home Loan Mortgage Corporation (FHLMC, also known as "Freddie Mac"), created by statute in 1970, which originally operated as an arm of the Federal Home Loan Bank System. 12 U.S.C. §§ 1451–1459. While Fannie Mae was chartered to deal primarily in government-insured mortgages (both single-family and multifamily), Freddie Mac's mandate was to trade primarily in conventional (non-insured) mortgages. Although both entities have statutory authority to deal in both types of mortgages, Fannie Mae traditionally purchased primarily from mortgage bankers and other FHA loan originators. Today, most Fannie Mae purchases are conventional mortgages. Freddie Mac deals primarily with savings and loan associations, which are regulated by its parent, the Office of Thrift Supervision. Fannie Mae and Freddie Mac are financed by the sale of common stock (they are listed on the New York Stock Exchange), bonds, and other obligations in the private capital markets. Fannie Mae and Freddie Mac have a $2.25 billion line of credit with the United States Treasury for use in case of emergency.

The third entity is the Government National Mortgage Association (GNMA, also known as "Ginnie Mae"). Ginnie Mae is a government agency created in 1968, located within HUD, and funded by the federal Treasury. 12 U.S.C §§ 1716b–1723. Ginnie Mae's role is to purchase mortgages that have been subsidized by the federal government pursuant to the HUD subsidy programs discussed *infra.*

Fannie Mae and Freddie Mac, are also known as Government-Sponsored Enterprises ("GSEs") because they are chartered by the federal government but owned by private investors who hold their stock, were created to establish a national secondary mortgage market, the purpose of which is to assure a constant and sufficient flow of mortgage funds for residential construction and purchases. Mortgages in the United States are originated by commercial banks, savings and loan associations, mutual savings banks, and mortgage companies, which are collectively referred to as the primary mortgage market. The traditional role of the secondary market is to channel mortgage funds from areas of the country with a credit surplus to areas that are credit deficient, and to provide a source of funds when mortgage money is in short supply due to adverse economic conditions. Today, the primary role of the secondary market is to aid primary lenders in maintaining their liquidity by providing a market in which they can sell mortgages to obtain new money with which to make additional loans. Fannie Mae and Freddie Mac fulfill their functions by purchasing mortgages from these primary lenders, especially when the primary lenders are short of funds to loan, holding the mortgages in their portfolios, and ultimately selling them. The Fannie Mae and Freddie Mac sales function is just as important as the purchase function. When there is a surplus of funds in the private mortgage market, Fannie Mae and Freddie Mac sell mortgages, just as they buy when funds are short. In addition, Fannie Mae and Freddie Mac tap nontraditional sources of mortgage funds by selling large blocks of mortgages and mortgage-backed securities as investments to pension funds, credit unions, insurance companies, and others, thus increasing sources of funds for mortgages. Banks and other commercial lenders also purchase these securities. Fannie Mae and Freddie Mac fundamentally changed the market by converting residential mortgages into marketable securities, and have fostered the development of an active private secondary mortgage market.

The secondary mortgage market also aids in the production of subsidized housing by purchasing subsidized mortgages from lenders as a method of assuring that such mortgages will be made. In addition to the normal operation of the mortgage market with regard to subsidized mortgages, the secondary mortgage market entities have employed several programs which subsidized the interest rate as an aid to production.

Federal multifamily housing subsidy programs employ mortgages insured by the Federal Housing Administration. Until 1983, the FHA mortgage interest rate was established by the Secretary of Housing and Urban Development, who normally set it 1/4% to 3/4% below market interest rates. The FHA rate was set lower than the market rate to reflect the lenders' lower risk on FHA mortgages, which are insured against loss from default and foreclosure. Developers of housing with insured mortgages obtain permanent mortgages from private mortgage market primary lenders. A mortgage at the FHA rate was not competitive with market interest rate mortgages and thus unattractive to lenders. The existence of the secondary mortgage market enabled the private lender to sell the mortgage to Fannie Mae immediately upon the permanent closing of the project. The private lender still had an incentive to make the mortgage since it obtained the origination fee (usually 1% of the mortgage amount), fees for other services, and retained servicing of the mortgage for the purchaser, for which it received a servicing fee. In the case of FHA mortgages, both single-family and multifamily, the secondary mortgage market essentially converted a low interest mortgage in the hands of the primary lender into a mortgage with a competitive rate in the secondary mortgage market. The 1983 Housing Act deregulated the FHA rate; it is now set competitively in the market rather than by HUD.

Historically, when interest rates rose, money for making insured loans dried up because the HUD-established interest rate fell too far below the market level. The normal operation of the secondary market could not ameliorate the situation because the difference was too great. For Fannie Mae to purchase mortgages during such periods, it would either have to sustain a large loss or charge such a high discount that the mortgage would be uneconomic to the private lenders, project developers, and owner-sellers of the property. At such times the government, through Ginnie Mae, supplemented the secondary mortgage market by means of the special assistance function, known as the Tandem Plan. The Tandem Plan thus provided an additional, indirect subsidy when discounts on insured loans in the secondary mortgage market became excessive.

The Tandem Plan worked as follows. Immediately following the final closing of the project mortgage, the private lender sold the mortgage to Ginnie Mae at 100% of its face value. Ginnie Mae then sold the mortgage to Fannie Mae at a reduced price calculated to make the yield on the mortgage equivalent to the yield on mortgages with market interest rates. Fannie Mae took the discounted mortgage into its portfolio and retained it as an investment, or resold it to private mortgage holders (such as insurance companies). The difference between the face amount of the mortgage and the discounted price received upon sale was absorbed as a loss by Ginnie Mae and was funded by congressional appropriation from the federal Treasury. While the Tandem Plan assisted a large volume of subsidized housing, Congress repealed Ginnie Mae's mortgage purchase authority in 1983. The loss sustained by Ginnie Mae is an indirect subsidy for low-income housing, and is reflected in Column G of the Matrix. This subsidy is one-time payment in the form of a loss to Ginnie Mae sustained in the year the mortgage is closed. It is not spread out over the life of the mortgage as is the basic interest subsidy format.

The Tandem Plan indirect subsidy is a trade-off for increased direct subsidies. Since lenders would not make below market interest rate mortgages, even though the risk of loss is insured, subsidy programs dependent on FHA mortgages could not work without the Tandem Plan. If the mortgage were required to be at the FHA rate, lenders would make such mortgages only if they were subject to large discounts to compensate for the low rate. (The discount points would be paid by the builder, developer, or seller, and increase the lender's yield above the HUD regulated interest rate.) These discounts would have to be included in the mortgage amount, thus increasing monthly mortgage debt service and increasing tenant payments. If tenant payments were kept the same, the discount mechanism would increase the amount of the direct subsidy. The Tandem Plan provided an initial subsidy of the discount and resulted in a reduction of direct subsidy costs over the term of the mortgage.

Ginnie Mae performs another important function in the operation of the secondary mortgage market by guaranteeing mortgage-backed securities. Fannie Mae and Freddie Mac finance their activities, and keep the mortgage market liquid, by issuing securities backed by pools of mortgages in their portfolios. Ginnie Mae enhances the marketability of these securities by guaranteeing repayment, and the guarantee is backed by the full faith and credit of the government. 12 U.S.C. §1721(g). Private companies, such as mortgage banking firms, also issue mortgage-backed securities under the Ginnie Mae guaranty program. The mortgages behind these securities consist of FHA insured mortgages, both single-family and multi-family. The existence of this program is a major stimulus to the FHA multi-family market. The sale of these securities is another way of obtaining nontraditional funds for the mortgage market. In 2008, Congress authorized Ginnie Mae to guarantee securities backed by mortgages insured by FHA to enable qualified homeowners to refinance their mortgages to avoid foreclosure. HOPE for Homeowners Program, contained in the Housing and Economic Recovery Act of 2008 ("HERA"), Pub. L. No. 110-289, §257 to title II of the National Housing Act, 106 Stat. 3956–3964 (*codified at* 12 U.S.C. §§1401–1404).

Finally, Fannie Mae has a Targeted Affordable Housing initiative, through which it offers favorable underwriting terms and interest rates for apartment buildings targeted to lower-income households. Fannie Mae's initiative can be coupled with other public sector subsidies, such as Section 8 assistance, tax credits, and tax-exempt bond financing.

As noted in Chapter 1, the mortgage foreclosure crisis of 2007–2010 was influenced by and had a significant impact on the secondary mortgage market. A fast-track, home purchase process featuring a combination of 1) adjustable-rate or interest-only adjustable mortgage loans, 2) made to households with poor credit or little financial history (the subprime market), and 3) sold and re-sold on the secondary mortgage market as interests in pools of mortgages (mortgage securitization) degenerated into chaos as the housing bubble burst in 2008. The housing bubble that burst in 2008 was fueled in part by aggressive efforts of the federal government to encourage more home ownership mandated in 1992 by a Congressional directive to HUD to establish annual housing goals for the GSEs. Federal Housing Enterprises Financial Safety and Soundness Act of 1992, Subpart B, Pub. L. 102-550, §§1331–1338, 106 Stat. 3956–3964 (*codified at* 12 U.S.C. §§4561–67). In furtherance of the goals established by HUD, the GSEs increased their purchases of subprime mortgage-backed securities-pools of mortgages that were offered to borrowers with less than stellar credit ratings at higher than normal interest rates. Carol D. Leonnig, *How HUD Mortgage Policy Fed the Crisis,* WASH. POST, June 10, 2008, at A1. Mortgage refinancing was also widely available during the run up to the bubble, allowing debtors to withdraw and spend or invest highly inflated home equity that significantly disappeared when the bubble was deflated.

With the threat of a collapse of the housing market and perhaps of the overall U.S. economy looming, Congress, after seven months of debate, approved a compromise bill, the Housing and Economic Recovery Act of 2008, Pub. L. No. 110-289, 122 Stat. 2654, (H.R. 3221) on July 26, 2008, which the President signed on July 30, 2008. The 2008 legislation created a new independent agency, the Federal Housing Finance Agency (FHFA), which replaced HUD as the supervising agency of the GSEs. The director of the new agency is responsible for establishing "prudent management and operations standards" for Fannie Mae and Freddie Mac and the Home Loan Banks, as well as setting standards for holdings in the entities' portfolios, establishing capital requirements to manage risks and determining when minimum capital levels should be increased, HERA, *supra* §§1101–1111 (*amending* §1313 of the Federal Housing Enterprises Financial Safety and Soundness Act of 1992, *codified* at 12 U.S.C., §4513). Shortly after FHFA was organized, the new agency placed Fannie Mae and Freddie Mac into conservatorship until they could be stabilized and then returned to normal operation, Federal Housing Finance Agency, Statement of FHFA Director James B. Lockhart, Sept. 7, 2008, *available at* http://www.ofheo.gov/media/statements/FHFAStatement9708.pdf.

HERA made explicit an implicit commitment by the Federal government to honor commitments of Fannie Mae and Freddie Mac which, by the time Congress acted, had purchased or guaranteed \$5.2 trillion of the nation's \$12 trillion in outstanding residential mortgage loans, David M. Herszenhorn, *House Approves Sweeping Effort to Help Housing,* N.Y. TIMES, July 24, 2008, *available at* www.nytimes.com/2008/07/24/business/24housing.html?. The two agencies had become, along with the FHA, the dominant players in the residential mortgage market. Damian Paletta & James R. Hagerty, *Housing Bill Will Extend Federal Role in Markets,* WALL ST. J., July 24, 2008, at A1. The legislation gave temporary authority, until December 31, 2009, enabling the Secretary of the Treasury to expand the Federal Government's \$2.5 billion line of credit to the two agencies and to buy equity shares in the agencies if deemed necessary—a move estimated to cost \$25 billion if it occurred. *Id.* The Housing and Economic Recovery Act of 2008, *supra,* in §§1117 and 3083 raised the federal debt limit from \$9.8 trillion to \$10.615 trillion to accommodate the temporary authority. In addition, the 2008 legislation makes a number of other changes to housing programs which are discussed later in the chapter.

Notes and Questions

1. For discussion of the subprime and mortgage financing crisis, *see* Symposium, *1.9 Kids and a Foreclosure: Subprime Mortgages, the Credit Crisis and Restoring the American Dream,* 60 S.C. L. REV. 549 (2009). Reform options for the GSEs are discussed in two articles in the South Carolina symposium, Gerald Korngold, *Legal and Policy Choices in the Aftermath of the Subprime and Mortgage Financing Crisis, Id.* at 727, 737–739 (suggesting that federal preemption of state mortgage law "might be better accomplished more transparently through congressional study and action" than by the indirect process of standard note and mortgage forms promulgated by the GSE's); Thomas E. Plank, *Regulation and Reform of the Mortgage Market and the Nature of Mortgage Loans: Lessons from Fannie Mae and Freddie Mac, Id.* at 779, 794–804 (reviewing the history of GSE involvement in the mortgage market). For a discussion of the GSEs' first months under conservatorship, see Win-

ston Sale, *Effect of the Conservatorship of Fannie Mae and Freddie Mac on Affordable Housing*, 18 J. Affordable Housing & Community Dev. L. 287 (2009).

2. The housing crash in 2007–2009 exposed the inherent conflict between the GSEs' mission to foster affordable housing and produce profits for their shareholders. How should that conflict be resolved? Should the GSE's be nationalized (taken over by the Federal government)? Should the affordable housing mission be spun off to a new entity created for that purpose—"a nonprofit National Affordable Housing Mortgage Association, 'Addie Mae,'" as suggested by Winston Sale, *supra*, at 308?

3. For further study of the secondary market, see generally, Richard Williams, Alternative Assessments of GSE Performance, Influence, and Impact, 1993–2003 (2006); Richard S. Carnell, *Handling the Failure of a Government-Sponsored Enterprise*, 80 Wash. L. Rev. 565 (2005); David Reiss, *The Federal Government's Implied Guarantee of Fannie Mae and Freddie Mac's Obligations: Uncle Sam Will Pick Up the Tab*, 42 Ga. L. Rev. 1019 (2008); Lawrence J. White, *Fannie Mae, Freddie Mac, and Housing: Good Intentions Gone Awry*, *in* Housing America: Building Out of a Crisis 263 (Randall G. Holcombe & Benjamin Powell eds. 2009).

4. The second form of indirect subsidy identified on the Matrix occurs through the federal income tax system. This includes the ability to invest in tax exempt bonds used to finance construction of subsidized housing, and the use of equity syndication to provide tax shelter to high-income investors. In the tax exempt bond format, the indirect subsidy in Column G is the estimated federal taxes forgone each year for the life of the bond; it is an annual number. The Column G figure for the syndication examples is also an annual number, but it represents federal taxes forgone only for the first year of occupancy; the number declines in subsequent years as the mortgage interest deductions decrease.

5. For an analytic framework similar to that employed in the Matrix, dealing with homeownership subsidies, see Philip Halpern, *Creating Fair and Efficient Subsidies for Home Ownership*, 4 J. Affordable Housing & Community Dev. L. 125 (1995). For all of the housing programs discussed later in this chapter, comparison with the various formats set forth in the Matrix will help in identifying and analyzing the subsidy mechanism involved, the structure of the program, and the budgetary impacts of the program. Before we turn to that we need to take a look at two matters: tax policy and the related question of real estate syndication.

A Note on Tax Policy and Illustrations on the Matrix

The 1986 Tax Reform Act (TRA) amended the Internal Revenue Code in a number of ways designed to reduce the attractiveness of real estate investment syndications. The benefits illustrated on the Matrix may no longer be available to some taxpayers.

First, the TRA imposed a limitation on the use of tax losses generated by passive activities, which are specifically defined to include rental real estate activities. An investor cannot use losses from passive activities to offset active or portfolio income; such losses can offset project income or income from other passive investments. There are several exceptions: (1) an investor can still deduct losses if the investor is a "material participant" in the enterprise, but rental real estate is specifically excluded from this definition, and limited partners in partnerships cannot qualify; (2) an individual who qualifies as a "real estate professional" under the Tax Code can also deduct losses, but, again, mere investors cannot qualify; and (3) there is a special deduction, available to investors in rental real estate who "actively participate" in operation of the property.

Those meeting the terms of this special deduction can deduct up to $25,000 in passive losses from ordinary income, provided that their adjusted gross income is below $100,000. The $25,000 allowance is phased out for taxpayers with adjusted gross income between $100,000 and $150,000; there is no deduction for taxpayers above $150,000. Passive losses which cannot be used to offset passive income or which do not fall under the $25,000 allowance can be carried forward and used to offset passive income in subsequent years. The excess losses are also suspended until the taxpayer's interest in the passive investment is disposed of, at which time the suspended losses offset gain from the transaction, and can also be applied against the taxpayer's other income. These limitations on passive activity losses greatly restrict the benefit from tax shelter syndications, since investors can no longer offset tax losses against their other income. One of the few ways that a taxpayer can generate tax losses to offset active income is the low-income housing tax credit, which is discussed in Section J *infra* this chapter.

Second, the TRA extended the at-risk rules to real estate. The at-risk rules limit deductions to the amount that the taxpayer can actually lose in the investment, unless the real estate acquisition is financed with qualified nonrecourse financing.

Third, the TRA amended the Accelerated Cost Recovery System by prohibiting accelerated depreciation for real estate; investors can only use straight-line depreciation. Depreciation deductions are also reduced by extending useful lives of real estate. In the case of residential rental real estate, taxpayers must employ a useful life of 27.5 years.

Fourth, the 1986 Act eliminated the preferential tax treatment for long term capital gains. Under the Act, it was no longer possible for real estate investors to convert ordinary income into capital gains, a classic tax technique in syndications. However, the Taxpayer Relief Act of 1997 restored a preferential capital gains tax rate at 20% (18% for assets acquired after 31 December 2000).

Finally, the TRA made a number of smaller changes which also reduced the attractiveness of real estate as a tax shelter mechanism. The Act limits investor interest deductions by disallowing the $10,000 deduction. The provision, formerly contained in Internal Revenue Code Section 167(k), allowing rehabilitation expenses to be amortized over five years has been repealed. Under prior law, construction period interest and taxes were currently deductible for low-income housing. The Act now requires that these expenses be capitalized and amortized over a ten-year period.

Notes and Questions

1. Concerning the traditional role of tax syndications in low-income housing, *see generally* Novogradac & Co. LLP, Low Income Housing Tax Credit Handbook (2007); Sharon Hom, *Does Real Estate Syndication Provide a Viable Financing Strategy for Low-Income Housing*, 50 Brook. L. Rev. 913 (1984); Tracy A. Kaye, *Sheltering Social Policy in the Tax Code: The Low-Income Housing Credit*, 38 Vill. L. Rev. 871 (1993); Rochelle E. Lento, *Federal Sources of Financing, in* The Legal Guide to Affordable Housing Development 215, 217–235 (Tim Iglesias & Rochelle E. Lento eds. 2006); Robert M. Washburn, *The Role of Tax Syndications in Housing: A Policy Perspective*, 5 Urb. L. & Pol'y 1 (1982). For an analysis of the role of syndication and the New Markets Tax Credit program in fostering community economic development, including affordable housing, see Sarah Vallim, *The New Markets Tax Credit and the Community Economic Development Movement: A Los Angeles Case Study*, 16 J. Affordable Housing & Community Dev. L. 117 (2007).

2. The changes wrought by the 1986 Tax Reform Act are discussed in Alan J. Auerbach & Joel Slemrod, *The Economic Effects of the Tax Reform Act of 1986*, 35 J. ECON. LITERATURE 589 (1997); Stuart Becker, *The Effect of the Tax Reform Act of 1986 on Present and Future Tax Motivated Investments*, 45 INST. ON FED. TAX'N § 43.01 (1987); Gerald J. Mehlman et al., *Syndications Under the Internal Revenue Code of 1986*, 39 MAJOR TAX PLAN. 21.1 (1987); Cherie J. O'Neil & Clarence C. Rose, *Real Estate Tax Shelters Under the Tax Reform Act of 1986*, 14 J. REAL EST. TAX'N 115 (1987).

3. For further discussion of the implications of tax policy for housing programs, including specific discussion of the tax reform measures enacted in 1986, see Section J, Tax Policy and Housing *infra* this chapter.

A Note on Real Estate Syndication

An operational definition of a real estate syndication is that high-income persons will pay a developer a sum of money (usually based on a percentage of the mortgage amount) in return for a share of the profits and losses of the partnership. Since newly constructed multifamily rental housing employs depreciation, investors realize only losses in the early years. The 1986 Tax Reform Act restricted use of depreciation to a straight-line basis; prior law permitted accelerated depreciation. Depreciation periods were as short as 15 years under prior law; under the TRA, residential real estate must use a 27.5 year useful life. Investors can depreciate in excess of their contributions to the partnership because a partner's tax basis includes his *pro rata* share of the project mortgage, assuming no partner is personally liable on the mortgage. The partnership can take depreciation deductions based on the entire cost of the project, even though it is financed largely with borrowed money. However, the extension of the at-risk rules to real estate has limited this ability somewhat.

In addition to depreciation, interest, real estate taxes, and other operating expenses are deductible and contribute to the losses. These losses exceed project income and, prior to the 1986 Tax Reform Act, could be reported on the investors' personal income tax returns, offsetting the investors' other income and sheltering it from federal and state income taxes. Equity syndication was therefore a technique to market tax shelter to those who can best use it. By syndicating the equity in a subsidized development, the developer converts tax losses that he probably would not be able to use fully into immediate cash. As discussed above, the 1986 Tax Reform Act placed severe limitations on the use of the excess losses. While investors can obtain tax free income from real estate syndications, they cannot, for the most part, use those losses to offset other income.

The other benefits flowing from a tax shelter are the normal benefits in any real estate development. First, cash flow is the profit from operating the property, the difference between rentals received and operating costs, maintenance, and debt service. Second, the investors receive benefits from the property's residual value, the profit from sale of the property at some time in the future. The expectation is that the investors will recover their entire equity investment after retiring the outstanding indebtedness and paying taxes and other costs of sale, plus an additional profit by reason of appreciation in the value of the property. The tax law grants owners of real estate an additional benefit upon sale, by taxing the sale profit at capital gains rates (exclusive of any depreciation), which is taxed at a maximum 25% rate. Under the Taxpayer Relief Act of 1997, Pub. L. No. 105-34, 111 Stat. 788, appreciated property is subject to a maximum capital gains tax rate of 18% or 20% depending on the acquisition date. The capital gains rate was reduced to 15% by the Jobs and Growth Tax Relief Reconciliation Act of 2003, Pub. L. No. 108-27, 117 Stat.

752 (*amending* 26 U.S.C. § 1(h)(1)(C)). Under a sunset provision, the 15% rate, and other rates that were cut in 2001 and 2003, will return to the previous rates on January 1, 2011, unless Congress rescinds the sunset provision. Economic Growth and Tax Relief Reconciliation Act of 2001, Pub. L. No. 107-16, § 901(a)-(b), 115 Stat. 38. Under the former tax law, the tax savings were so substantial that the investors were usually repaid their initial cash investment through tax savings by the fourth or fifth year of project operation. Equity syndications still exist, but they now largely rely on the income from the project since the tax benefits have been greatly restricted.

The vehicle for syndicating real estate is usually the limited partnership. The developer serves as general partner, with full operational authority, and the investors buy in as limited partners. As limited partners, the investors are not liable for the project's debts and obligations and risk only their initial capital investment. Since the partnership is not a taxable entity (assuming it meets the tests for avoiding corporate tax status), the gains and losses pass through to the investors.

The investors' contribution is usually paid in over a three- to five-year period. These payments serve to fund the project's equity requirement and produce an immediate cash profit to the developer. The investment funds are normally not contributed to the project to increase amenities or reduce tenant payments.

Since the formerly available accelerated depreciation and interest deductions declined during the life of the development, the tax losses ran out at some point. The result was that the development would yield taxable income, often in excess of the cash flow from normal operations. Since the investors' interest was always in the tax shelter, they had no incentive to retain ownership of the project once the shelter ran out, especially after the recapture period expired. The tax laws thus worked against investors' long-term involvement with the development and a commitment to maintaining the benefits for low-income tenants, one reason Congress amended the Internal Revenue Code to eliminate most of the tax benefits.

The ability to syndicate functioned as an inducement for private developers to develop and own subsidized projects. Since Congress believed that the availability of these benefits was essential to attracting adequate amounts of private equity capital to achieve high levels of subsidized housing production, it maintained special tax benefits for subsidized housing for many years. Only during the massive tax overhaul of 1986 did Congress finally restrict the benefits and deprive subsidized housing of its favored position. Even then, Congress sought to maintain a tax incentive for subsidized housing by providing tax credits through the Low Income Housing Tax Credit ("LIHTC") program discussed *infra*.

The following excerpt will serve to bridge this Section's consideration of subsidy policies, issues, and frameworks with the discussion of the specific programs that follows.

Bruce Katz and Margery Austin Turner, Rethinking US Rental Housing Policy: A New Blueprint for Federal, State, and Local Action

REVISITING RENTAL HOUSING 328–332
(Nicholas P. Retsinas & Eric S. Belsky eds. 2008)

The Federal Response to the Affordable Housing Challenge

Over the past seven decades, the federal government has created a complex web of spending, tax, and regulatory programs for financing and subsidizing the production of affordable rental housing, providing rental assistance for tenants to use in the private market, and revitalizing distressed neighborhoods by demolishing public housing and constructing economically integrated housing in its place. These policies have a substantial record of achievement and accomplishment. Yet current and past programs also suffer from serious deficiencies of scale, design, and implementation....

What Federal Housing Policies Have Achieved

Federal housing policies have three central accomplishments. Since the 1930s, federal production programs have stimulated the construction of millions of affordable rental housing units and built networks of private and public practitioners, skilled in the financing and development of affordable housing. Since the 1970s, federal demand-side rental assistance has helped millions of renters afford privately owned housing, often in neighborhoods with quality schools, safe streets, and functioning local markets. And since the mid-1990s, the demolition of distressed public housing and its replacement with economically integrated rental housing is transforming the economic and physical landscape of some of the most distressed neighborhoods in the United States.

Rental Production Programs. Federal rental production policy has gone through three distinct phases. During the first phase, dominant from the 1930s through the 1960s, the federal government financed the construction of more than a million units of public housing. The federal government contracted with local public housing agencies to produce and manage these units. In effect, these contracts required the agencies to maintain the affordability of public housing units in perpetuity.

During the second phase of rental production policy, dominant from the 1960s to the early l980s, the federal government subsidized the construction of more than 1.3 million units of privately owned affordable housing through a combination of below-market financing, income tax preferences, and operating support. The focus on private sector delivery altered both the means of production and the management of the built product. Under these programs, the federal government executed contracts directly with for-profit and nonprofit developers of affordable housing, rather than with local public housing agencies. The terms of contracts generally limited the period during which affordability restrictions needed to be maintained.

The current phase of federal production policy, dominant since the mid-1980s, has delegated key decisions to state and local governments. These governments are vested with responsibility for allocating federal tax credits and block grant finding in accordance with federally mandated affordability plans. In general, these federal resources have been used to produce quality affordable housing in low-income neighborhoods of distress, often through community-based housing providers. The key subsidy programs of this period (which are still in use) are the [Low Income Housing Tax Credit] LIHTC program, the Community Development Block Grant [CDBG] program, and the HOME Investment Partnerships program. These programs have been complemented by federal regulatory efforts under the Community Reinvestment Act and by government-sponsored enterprises to encourage the provision of private debt capital. In addition, the National Community Development Initiative, a joint effort involving large philanthropic foundations, major financial institutions, and the federal government, builds the capacity of community development corporations and the national housing intermediaries—the Local Initiatives Support Corporation and the Enterprise Foundation—that support them....

Demand-Side Rental Assistance Programs. Beginning in the mid-1970s, rental housing vouchers emerged as the most substantial form of subsidized housing in the United States.

They now serve some 2.1 million households. In general, housing vouchers pay the difference between 30% of a recipient's income and the rent of a qualifying, moderately priced house or apartment. Vouchers are the most direct way of meeting the principal housing challenge facing very low-income renters: affordability. Unlike production programs, vouchers can be delivered quickly to families who need assistance. They also enable their users to adjust rapidly to changes in local and metropolitan housing and job markets....

Public Housing Transformation. Over the past decade, the federal government has embarked on an ambitious effort to demolish the worst public housing projects in the country and replace them with housing that is economically mixed, better designed, less dense, and fundamentally integrated into the fabric of local neighborhoods and local economies. Called the Housing Opportunities for People Everywhere (HOPE VI) program, this transformation effort includes funding for supportive services to help former public housing residents make the transition to work. Congress also appropriated funds for a separate pool of housing vouchers to aid the relocation of residents who choose to move out of the neighborhood....

Socioeconomic integration has become a central feature at many HOPE VI sites across the country.... Some developments are even experimenting with mixed-tenure approaches, with a portion of the new housing reserved for homeowners rather than renters.

The new developments are leveraging substantial resources from the public, private, and philanthropic sectors—resources that were virtually absent (and, in some cases, prohibited) from former public housing developments. They are also experimenting with a range of management approaches: many have employed private sector property management firms on-site (and at risk) rather than relying on remote public agencies. Such firms are using basic management techniques—lease enforcement, enhanced screening procedures, improved amenities—to attract and retain a broad spectrum of residents....

The quality of many of the new HOPE VI developments is sparking significant improvements in the surrounding neighborhoods. Case studies almost uniformly show substantial declines in neighborhood crime and unemployment and substantial increases in income, property values, and market investment. In several high-profile developments, HOPE VI investments have been accompanied by significant improvements in the quality of the local schools and the educational performance of low-income children.... With some of these findings, of course, cause-and-effect is not entirely clear. It is as yet hard to tell how much of the steep decline in crime, for example, derives primarily from the demolition of the dilapidated public housing projects rather than the construction of the new, economically integrated developments. Only the passage of time will enable these more nuanced questions to be fully answered.

Notes and Questions

1. The federal housing glass is not completely full, though. Katz and Turner also point out a number of serious policy issues:

a) a steadily widening gap between housing needs and resources to meet those needs;

b) deterioration and threatened loss of large portions of the existing federally subsidized affordable housing inventory;

c) concentration of assisted rental units in inner city neighborhoods, exacerbating concentration of poverty problems in many cities;

d) continued failure to address problems stemming from exclusionary and cost-enhancing state and local building and land use regulations;

e) challenges to the voucher system occasioned by exclusionary rental markets, lack of counseling services and fragmented local administrative systems;

f) uncertainty about the impact of HOPE VI on the original residents of the public housing HOPE VI replaced, and

g) a compartmentalized and inefficient assisted housing administrative system. *Id.* at 332–339. As you study the programs discussed in this chapter, consider how these issues might be resolved.

2. As discussed in Chapter 1 *supra*, housing programs can be thought of as market interventions designed to respond to market failures. Traditionally, such interventions have been viewed as favoring the supply side (funds to encourage production of additional housing units) or the demand side (funds to create effective demand for existing private market-supplied housing units). Does one approach appear to be better able to respond to the issues identified above?

3. Do some of these issues require a regulatory, rather than a spending, response? If so, which level of government is the most appropriate responder? Or will the market respond appropriately if more effective demand is created?

B. Mortgage Insurance Programs

The mortgage insurance programs authorized by the National Housing Act, Pub. L. No. 479, 48 Stat. 1246 (1934) (codified and amended in various sections of 12 U.S.C. §§ 1707 to 1715z), brought about profound changes in housing finance by inducing mortgage lenders to make credit available on more liberal terms. Congress enacted this legislation to improve the flow of mortgage credit to the housing industry, thereby creating more jobs which people badly needed during the Depression.

1. Insurance for Single-Family Units (Section 203)

The basic homeownership mortgage insurance program, 203(b), is the oldest continuing federal housing effort. Section 203 has been the most popular of the several insurance programs established by the Act, and it has permitted millions of people to obtain their "dream home," usually in the suburbs. FHA has insured over 37 million single-family home loans since 1934 and had 5.8 million insured single family home loans totaling $750 billion in its portfolio in January 2010. Section 203 and the Section 221(d) program provide mortgage insurance but do not directly subsidize homeowners.

The unsubsidized ownership programs involve mortgage insurance, which has generally been a self-supporting mechanism not requiring federal subsidy. The 203(b) program is an insurance program. HUD (through the Federal Housing Administration) insures the mortgage lender against loss because of nonpayment of the indebtedness on mortgages made on qualified homes purchased by qualified mortgagors. Over the years, the FHA Section 203 mortgage insurance program catered primarily to moderate income, first-time home buyers and was an important, but relatively minor, part of the total single family mortgage market. However, during the overheated housing market and subsequent market collapse in 2008, a surge in FHA-insured loans caused its market share to climb from 2% in 2006 to about 25% at the end of 2009. As a result, reserves for "unexpected loan losses" fell to slightly over one-half of one-percent of FHA's portfolio, well below the required 2% of its portfolio. As a result, with more than half a million of those loans threatened with foreclosure, the possibility that the government may need to subsidize FHA became a topic of conversation in 2009 and 2010. Nick Timiraos, *Housing Agency's Reserves Fall Far Below Minimum,* Wall St. J., Nov. 13, 2009, at A6; David Streitfeld, *F.H.A. to Raise Standards for Mortgage Insurance,* N.Y. Times, Jan. 20, 2010.

A subsidized ownership program on the supply side, Section 235, discussed *infra*, in which housing need is met in-kind by an interest rate subsidy was in effect from 1968 through 1989. All of the homeownership programs make use of the indirect subsidy produced by favorable federal income taxation of homeowners. All of the programs make use of both newly constructed and existing housing, with the exception of the revised Section 235 program, which was restricted to new construction. For further comparisons, *see* the matrix of subsidy alternatives, *supra.*

The primary impact of Section 203(b) was to standardize mortgage lending and liberalize loan terms. This was accomplished by increasing loan-to-value ratios (thereby decreasing down payments), lengthening the mortgage term to reduce monthly payments, standardizing the self-liquidating level payment mortgage, and reducing interest rates. Prior to the 203(b) program, loans averaged 50–60% of value for single-family houses. FHA loan-to-value ratios are in excess of 95%, making home purchases easier by greatly reducing down payments. Loan terms were ten to fifteen years prior to FHA. By extending maturities to thirty years, the program dramatically reduced monthly payments. Since loan terms were relatively short before 1934, many loans were not fully amortized; there was a large balance (called "balloon mortgage") left at maturity which had to be paid off or refinanced. The inability to do so during the Depression was one reason there were widespread defaults and foreclosures on home loans. The advent of the mortgage insurance program standardized the level payment, self-liquidating mortgage, which is paid off in full by equal monthly payments over the life of the loan, leaving no "balloon" at the end of the term.

The Section 203(b) program does not involve a direct subsidy to homeowners. However, the indirect subsidy provided by the federal income tax deductibility of mortgage interest payments and real estate taxes applies to 203(b) purchasers as it does to all homeowners. This tax benefit has been called the largest housing subsidy. Because Section 203(b) is an insurance program and not a subsidy program, the only effect on the purchaser's housing expense is a slight reduction in debt service since the HUD-established interest rate is set slightly below market interest rates. The major advantage of FHA insurance to home buyers is that it makes homes easier to purchase by drastically reducing down payments.

HUD charges a premium for the insurance, as do all insurers. Subsequent amendments require the collection of a mortgage insurance premium not to exceed 3.0% (2.75% for first-time homebuyers who complete HUD counseling) of the original mortgage amount at the time the loan is insured, along with an annual premium not to exceed 0.5% of the remaining principal balance. In recent years, the premium had been only 1.75%, but as one of the steps to shore up its portfolio, HUD announced an increase in premium to 2.25% in February, 2010 and proposed legislation authorizing an increase in the 3% maximum rate. U.S. Dep't of Housing and Urban Dev., *FHA Announces Policy Changes to Address Risk and Strengthen Finances*, HUD No. 10-016 (Jan. 20, 2010), *avail-*

able at http://portal.hud.gov. The entire premium is refundable if payment is made in full prior to the maturity date of the mortgage. The annual premium is to be collected for the first 30 years of 90% or higher mortgages but only the first 11 years of mortgages of lower amounts. 12 U.S.C. § 1709(c)(2)(A) and (B). The premium is paid by the lender, but is passed through and is actually paid by the purchaser as part of the monthly debt service payment. The lender is permitted to charge the purchaser a loan origination fee not in excess of 1% of the loan amount. The interest rate on the mortgage is administratively established by HUD and changed periodically to adjust to fluctuations in the mortgage market. The mortgage and note must be on approved HUD forms. The loan must be a first lien on real estate or on a ground lease with not less than fifty years remaining term.

In order to be eligible, the mortgage must be secured by a one- to four-family house, which can be newly constructed or existing, previously occupied housing. The mortgagor must live in the unit as a primary residence; mortgage insurance is not available for investment property. The mortgage must be approved by HUD. As an indication of the basically conservative nature of the program, the statutory underwriting standard provides that "no mortgage shall be accepted for insurance ... unless the Secretary finds that the project with respect to which the mortgage is executed is economically sound." 12 U.S.C. § 1709(c).

In response to the collapse of the housing market in 2007–2008, Congress in 2008 enacted comprehensive legislation, the Housing and Economic Recovery Act of 2008 ("HERA"), Pub. L. No. 110-289, 106 Stat. 3956–3964. Among other changes, HERA increased the maximum mortgage limit and now permits the FHA to insure, and the government sponsored enterprises (Federal National Mortgage Association and Federal Home Loan Mortgage Corporation) to purchase, mortgages for up to 115% of the median house price in the area for a single family residence or 150% of the dollar amount limitation under the Federal Home Loan Mortgage Corporation Act (FHLMCA) for a residence of applicable size, so long as the mortgage does not exceed 100 per cent of the appraised value of the property. For 2–4 family residences HERA permits the FHA to insure the median price that bears the same ratio to such median price as the dollar amount limitation of the FHLMCA for a 2-, 3-, or 4-family residence, respectively, bears to the dollar amount limitation determined under such section for a 1-family residence, again so long as the mortgage does not exceed 100% of the appraised value of the property. Pub. L. No. 110-289, § 2112(a), 106 Stat. 3956–3964 (HERA, *amending* 12 U.S.C. § 1709(b)(2)(A). The dollar amount limitations were increased by HERA to $417,000 for single-family mortgages, $533,850 for 2-family mortgages, $645,000 for 3-family mortgages, and $801,950 for 4-family mortgages. In future years, maximum limitations are to be adjusted annually on January 1, based on changes in a housing price index maintained by the Federal Housing Finance Agency, a new agency created by the same legislation to supervise the government's role in the secondary mortgage market. Pub. L. No. 110-289, § 1124, 106 Stat. 3956 (HERA, *amending* 12 U.S.C. § 1717(b)(2). *See, e.g.*, Mortgagee Letter 2009-50, *2010 FHA Maximum Loan Limits* (Nov. 25, 2009), *available at* www.hud.gov.

Under this statute, "area" is defined as a standard metropolitan statistical area, and "median 1-family house price for an area" is that of the county with the highest median price. Sec. 228, amending 12 U.S.C. at 1709 (b)(2)(B)(ii). Previous amendments eliminated the disparities within metropolitan areas that had been hampering city revitalization efforts. For example, in the spring of 1998, the maximum insurable loan in the City of St. Louis was $95,000 while in St. Louis County it was $145,000. Supporters of city revitalization efforts had argued that this disparity made it difficult to encourage prospective middle income home buyers to consider residing in the city.

Mortgages may be for thirty-five years on new houses and thirty-years on existing houses. 12 U.S.C. § 1709(b) (3). There are no income limits for eligible buyers. Any family that can make the required down payment, increased in 2008 to 3.5% of the appraised value "or such larger amount as the Secretary may determine" and has sufficient income to carry the mortgage can qualify. 12 U.S.C. § 1709(b)(9)(A). Beginning in 2010, new buyers with FICO credit scores under 580 were required to make a 10% down payment. HUD No. 10-016 *supra.*

An individual home purchaser can seek an FHA-insured mortgage by applying to a HUD-approved bank, savings and loan association, or mortgage company. The financial institution processes the insurance request and receives an insurance commitment from HUD. Before issuing a commitment, HUD inspects and appraises the property and verifies the borrower's credit history and ability to carry the loan. When the terms of the commitment are fulfilled, HUD endorses the mortgage note as evidence that it has been insured. Developers of new subdivisions often seek to have the entire subdivision qualified for insurance. The builder will obtain, through an approved mortgagee, an FHA blanket commitment on the development prior to construction. This process makes it easier for potential purchasers to obtain insured loans.

HERA also created a temporary program, *HOPE for Homeowners Program*, 12 U.S.C. § 1715z-23, which authorizes the FHA to give distressed homeowners struggling to meet their mortgage payments the opportunity to reduce their monthly payments by modifying their home loans or refinancing them with new FHA-insured mortgages. Qualified borrowers must have mortgage debt greater than 31% of their income, must not have intentionally defaulted on their existing loan, and must have the "reasonable" ability to make the new mortgage payments. In the refinancing program, the new loan must not exceed 90% of the appraised value of the property, which proved to be a difficult standard to meet because of the severe drop in home values that occurred following the collapse of the housing market. As enacted, the program was voluntary on the part of both borrowers and lenders. As an incentive to lenders to accept less than full payment of loans being refinanced, the statute provides that any appreciation in value occasioned by the refinancing will be shared by the mortgagor and HUD.

Amendments to 12 U.S.C. § 1715u(b), enacted in 2009 as part of the Helping Families Save Their Homes Act of 2009, Pub. L. No. 111-22, 123 Stat. 1632, authorize payments to loan servicers to encourage them to cooperate in the *FHA-Home Affordable Modification Program (FHA-HAMP)* loan modification and HOPE for Homeowners refinance programs. A HUD announcement states that HAMP "permanently reduces a family's monthly mortgage payment through the use of a partial claim" of up to 30% of the unpaid principal balance as of the date of default. This partial claim "defers the repayment of mortgage principal through an interest-free subordinate mortgage that is not due until the first mortgage is paid off.

FHA has used the partial claim option in the past, which allows a lender to advance funds on behalf of a borrower, to reinstate a delinquent loan that was up to 12 months delinquent. Now, this program will allow HUD to bring the borrower's payment down to an affordable level. This will be accomplished by bringing the mortgage current, buying down the loan by up to 30% of the unpaid principal balance and deferring these amounts in a partial claim. FHA will pay an incentive to loan servicers for each FHA loan modified under this program. HUD Announcement No. 09-137, *available at* www.hud.gov/content/releases/pr09-137.cfm. The programs got off to a slow start. *See, e.g.*, John Collins Rudolf, *Judges' Frustration Grows With Mortgage Servicers,* N.Y. Times, Sept. 4, 2009, at B1; Nick Timiraos, *Confusion Roils HARP Program for Refinancing,* Wall

St. J., Sept. 2, 2009, at B7. The loan modification and refinancing programs are discussed in Chapter 1 *supra* as part of a review of the home mortgage foreclosure crisis and its effect on communities.

2. Insurance for Multifamily Units (Section 207)

Section 207 of the National Housing Act, codified at 12 U.S.C. § 1713, is a program of mortgage insurance for multifamily housing development without a direct subsidy. HUD insures the private mortgage lender against loss from default and foreclosure on the loan. In consideration of the risk reduction, HUD sets the maximum interest rate that the lender can charge. The effect on tenants is simply to reduce the rent since the debt service is based on a mortgage interest rate set below the market.

Section 207 is a middle-income program, although projects are regulated by HUD in order to produce reasonable rentals and an acceptable return on the owner's investment. To be eligible for insurance under Section 207, the principal obligation must not exceed 90% of the "estimated value" of the project. Nor may the principal obligation exceed 90% of the replacement cost of the project when the proposed improvements are made. 12 U.S.C. § 1713(c)(2). The statute contains mortgage limits per dwelling unit, which can be increased by 215% in high-cost areas. 12 U.S.C. § 1713(c)(3). The mortgage, as in all HUD multifamily programs, is a level payment, self-liquidating mortgage with "such term as the Secretary [of HUD] shall prescribe." Default is defined as failure to make any payment on a mortgage insured under this section, and if this failure of payment continues for thirty days, the mortgage is entitled to receive the benefits of the insurance provided under Section 207. Section 207 can insure mortgages on newly constructed or substantially rehabilitated developments. The mortgage insurance premium (MIP) may range between .25% and 1% per year of the mortgage amount. 24 C.F.R. § 207.252. The maximum mortgage amount that can be insured is 90% of appraised value, which is more conservative than the replacement cost standard used in the other multifamily programs.

Sponsorship of a Section 207 development is restricted to profit-motivated entities. Nonprofit sponsors are not eligible. Since there is no direct subsidy involved, the program imposes no income limits on tenants.

3. Mortgage Insurance for Moderate-Income Persons (Section 221)

During the 1950s, Congress began giving serious attention to the housing problems of the large number of persons whose incomes were sufficiently high to deny them admission to public housing and yet too low to enable them to take advantage of the normal housing market, even as modified by the FHA 203 (homeownership) and 207 (rental) programs. The format adopted, beginning with the 221 programs of the 1950s and early 1960s and culminating in the 235 and 236 programs of the 1968 Housing Act, continued the indirect cost reduction policy of the FHA programs by stressing insurance and interest subsidies for lenders and tax incentives for investors, rather than the direct reduction approach of the low rent public housing program. The statutory purpose of the Section 221 programs is "to assist private industry" in providing housing for low- and moderate-income families and displaced families. § 221(a). This purpose is to be accomplished by the provision of insurance to qualified lenders. § 221(b). Section 221 programs are codified at 12 U.S.C.§ 1715*l*.

Section 221 contains five separate programs:

(1) 221(d)(2). *Insurance for Mortgages on Individual Homes.* This program was designed to reach persons with lower incomes than those typically qualifying for Section 203 homeownership insurance. The reach was accomplished by limitations on the down payment requirement and the amount of the principal obligation that may be insured, as well as by authorization for longer term mortgages. The down payment required of a "displaced family" is $200 for a single-family dwelling; $400 for a two-family dwelling; $600 for a three-family dwelling; and $800 for a four-family dwelling. For other families, this section requires a down payment of only 3% of HUD's estimated "acquisition cost" of the property. The statute also provides that "the mortgagor shall to the maximum extent feasible be given the opportunity to contribute the value of his labor as equity in such dwelling." Section 221(d)(2) authorizes insurance on mortgages secured by existing, as opposed to newly constructed, property, and in such cases, HUD is responsible for estimating the property's value prior to the rehabilitation. The amount of the insured mortgage may not exceed the cost of the repairs plus the amount required to refinance the existing indebtedness secured by the property. While the program remains on the statute books, it has not been active since a scandal in the 1970s involving the sale of homes in bad need of repairs to inexperienced low-income home buyers. *See Jackson v. Romney*, 355 F. Supp. 737 (D.D.C. 1973), *aff'd sub nom. Jackson v. Lynn*, 506 F.2d 233 (D.C. Cir. 1974) (allegations that District of Columbia real estate brokers led 221(d)(2) buyers to believe that homes complied with FHA quality standards and that promised repairs never were made did not state private cause of action nor constitute waiver of sovereign immunity). For a case study of the St. Louis portion of the scandal and a reminder of the maxim that persons who don't know history are likely to repeat it, *see* Harry Wilson, Comment, *Exploiting the Home Buying Poor: A Case Study of Abuse Under the National Housing Act*, 17 St. Louis U. L.J. 525 (1973).

(2) 221(d)(3). *Insurance for Mortgages on Multifamily Developments.* This program is designed for persons with incomes lower than those required to be able to afford the rents in a 207-insured project. The lower range is reached primarily by the statutory imposition of cost limitations on the units constructed. The scope of the program proved too narrow for effective implementation, except when combined with the Rent Supplement Program. Housing and Urban Development Act of 1965, 12 U.S.C. § 1701s (§ 101), a forerunner of the Section 8 program.

(3) 221(d)(3). *Below Market Interest Rates.* The 221(d)(3) Below Market Interest Rate (BMIR) Program was enacted by the 1961 Housing Act, and is codified at 12 U.S.C. § 1715*l*(d)(5). The purpose of the program, which has been inactive since 1968, was to assist private enterprise to provide rental housing for moderate-income families, with a preference for persons displaced by government action. Section 221 (d)(3) mortgages are insured by FHA. The subsidy was an in-kind subsidy paid through a direct government loan at a reduced interest rate. A private lender made a permanent mortgage at a reduced interest rate of 3%; this mortgage was immediately purchased by the Government National Mortgage Association (GNMA) at par (100% of face value). In effect, the federal government made the loan at the below market interest rate. The sponsor based rentals on the 3% mortgage. The amount of the direct subsidy depended upon the cost of Treasury borrowing, since the GNMA funds used to purchase the mortgage were obtained at a higher rate than the 3% interest paid to GNMA by the mortgagor. The direct subsidy to the tenants depended upon the FHA interest rate at which the permanent mortgage would

otherwise be made. For example, the difference between the 3% BMIR mortgage and an FHA rate of 6% would reduce tenant rents by about 27%; if the FHA rate were 9%, the rent reduction would be about 37%.

The funding difficulty with the 221(d)(3) program was that the entire direct subsidy (the difference between 3% and GNMA's borrowing costs) was paid in the year the project was completed, creating a heavy budgetary impact. For this reason, the BMIR program was phased out and replaced by the 236 program. Although the direct subsidy in the 236 program is greater than in the BMIR program, the budgetary impact is reduced; since subsidy payments are made with the monthly mortgage payments, the subsidy is spread out over the forty-year life of the mortgage and only the subsidy falling due in a given year is included in that year's budget.

(4) 221(d)(4). *Insurance for Mortgages on Multifamily Projects for Persons of Moderate Income.* This section is similar to Section 207 in many respects. Sponsorship and tenant eligibility are the same, as are mortgage terms (interest rate, amortization, loan-to-value ratio, maturity, and insurance premium), except for use of the more liberal replacement loan-to-value ratio standard. This section is designed to aid moderate-income families and the per-unit mortgage limits are lower than those of Section 207. HUD insists on more modest design, and there is a statutory occupancy preference for families displaced by urban renewal or other federal action. Section 221(d) (4) served as the insurance program for Section 8 developments that were financed with insured mortgages. Both the 221(d)(3) and 221(d)(4) market interest rate programs remain active and often are used in conjunction with the Low Income Housing Tax Credit ("LIHTC"), tax-exempt bond and Section 8 rental subsidy programs, all of which are discussed *infra*. FHA ANNUAL MANAGEMENT REPORT, FISCAL YEAR 2009 at 12–16, *available at* www.hud.gov.

(5) 221(h). *Insurance for Nonprofit Rehabilitation and Resale.* This section provided insurance of mortgages to finance purchase and rehabilitation by not-for-profit organizations of housing for resale to low-income purchasers, and for insurance of mortgages executed for the purpose of financing rehabilitation or improvements of dwellings owned and occupied by mortgagors who purchased from not-for-profit organizations. The statute requires that the mortgagor pay $200 on account toward the purchase price of the property. The statute refers only to single-family dwellings, and stipulates that, if the family's income increases, their interest rate payment obligation shall increase correspondingly. While the program remains on the statute books, it has not been active for a number of years.

Notes and Questions

1. The FHA mortgage insurance programs have been an important part of the financing structure designed to encourage production and continued availability of both single family homes and apartments for persons of moderate income. The often confusing array of programs under the insurance rubric represents governmental attempts to tailor mortgage insurance programs to different slices of the moderate income range and different methods of organizing the legal relations of the participating parties. Does the FHA insurance mechanism amount to a subsidy? If so, is it a direct subsidy or an indirect one? If not, does it represent governmental intervention in the private housing market?

2. The fallout from the 2007–2008 housing market collapse put a significant strain on the government resources behind the mortgage insurance programs. In addition to the

new Hope for Homeowners loan modification/refinancing program, FHA's ability to insure loans with down payments as low as 3.5% made it an extremely popular actor in the effort to restart the housing economy. In the second quarter of 2009, FHA insured loans amounted to 23% of the market, compared to just 2.7% of the market in 2006. But loan losses continued to increase, both for FHA insured mortgages as well as traditional, non-FHA insured mortgages, raising fears that recovery from the housing meltdown may take longer and be less satisfactory than in previous downturns. Robin Sidel, *Troubles for 'Prime' Borrowers Intensify*, WALL ST. J., Sept. 4, 2009, at C1; Nick Timiraos & Deborah Solomon, *Loan Losses Spark Concern Over FHA*, WALL ST. J., Sept. 4, 2009, at A1. As you study the housing programs in this chapter, consider the following questions. What is the appropriate role of the government with respect to housing, particularly for persons whose incomes are below median income levels? Should the government assume an aggressive provider role, as the public housing program did in the 1940s and 1950s? Should it focus on filling gaps in private market transactions through interest subsidies or rent supplements? Should the housing market be federalized or are local variations in housing supply and demand best met by state and local programs?

C. Public Housing

Metro City Problem (cont.)

In considering the Metro City problem *supra*, the first step would be to review the federal public housing program. Grand Square and Laclede Family Apartments were constructed and managed under the auspices of the public housing program. Any modifications to those developments will have to be accomplished in accordance with the public housing laws and regulations.

Public housing—the governmental landlord—is unique among America's national programs for several reasons. First, it is the only national housing program (excluding military housing on defense installations) in which families enter into a landlord-tenant relationship with a governmental unit. Although the program is federally funded, the landlord is not the federal government. Rather, the landlord is a public instrumentality created by and responsible to local government under a state-enabling statute.

Second, public housing is a classic supply-side program where the housing need is met in-kind with governmentally supplied housing. The program is based on two direct subsides (capital cost and operating expenses) and an indirect subsidy (federal taxes forgone). Public housing is a rental program and has predominantly made use of newly constructed dwelling units.

Third, public housing, with more than 3,000 public housing authorities managing over 1.4 million units for more than three million residents, has been for decades the largest and perhaps most significant housing subsidy program (excluding the functional subsidy of the real estate property tax and interest deductions allowed by the Internal Revenue Code).

Fourth, public housing provides the deepest subsidy of the housing programs.

Fifth, public housing is the oldest assisted housing program and the one that has been most consistently in use from the date of its enactment in 1937.

The following section presents a brief description of the public housing program. The description presents the legal and operational parameters of the program, income limits and program beneficiaries, subsidy mechanism, and program processing and procedures. The description is based on the statute and administrative regulations, program handbooks, and actual practice. So as not to overburden the student, many program details are omitted; the description presents an overview. The major purpose of the program description is to present the general concept and parameters, knowledge of which is essential to anyone interested in our national housing effort.

1. Program Description

The public housing program was enacted by the United States Housing Act of 1937 and was codified at 42 U.S.C. §§ 1401 to 1436. In the Housing and Community Development Act of 1974, Congress completely revised the original act and added the Section 8 program discussed *infra*. The revised act is now codified beginning at 42 U.S.C. § 1437. While the program was created as a housing development program, authorization for construction of additional public housing units was reduced drastically during the 1980s. In 1998, Congress substantially revised the program again, placing greater emphasis on property and asset management and encouraging local public housing authorities to enter into public-private partnerships to transform public housing into mixed income communities. Quality Housing and Work Responsibility Act of 1998, Pub. L. No. 105-276, Title V, Departments of Veterans Affairs and Housing and Urban Development, and Independent Agencies Appropriations Act, 112 Stat. 2518.

The public housing program has a tripartite legal structure. Public housing is constructed, financed, and operated by local municipal corporations known as local housing authorities (LHA) or public housing agencies (PHA). State enabling legislation authorizes these local entities to be created and delegates governmental power to them. Federal legislation determines the basis on which the capital subsidies, and by later amendment the operating subsidies, are distributed. In addition, federal legislation contains additional requirements binding on PHAs. However, the basic legal authority is found in the state statute enabling the formation of the PHA. The enabling legislation will generally specify the powers, composition, mode of operation, and limitations governing the PHA. Since there is no state administrative agency that participates in the regulation of the public housing program, actual operation remains with the individual PHA with guidance from HUD. For example, tenant eligibility, selection and admissions policies are established by the PHA but subject to HUD approval. 42 U.S.C. § 1437c-1(d)(3).

Annual Contributions Contract

The PHA builds, owns, and manages public housing, but the statute contains the legal method by which the federal subsidy is distributed to the PHA. This is called the Annual Contributions Contract (ACC) and is authorized in § 1437c(a). The amount, scope, and conditions of the subsidy are established by the ACC, which obligates HUD to pay the capital costs of the development. The ACC system was a compromise in the original legislation. The program's sponsors advocated a one-time federal grant for the construction cost, but the budget impact was too great since the full amount of project cost would have had to be advanced in the year of construction. Instead, the PHA issues long-term bonds (forty years), payable in annual installments, which are purchased by private investors. The ACC obligates the federal government to pay the annual principal and interest costs over the life of the bonds. The annual contributions carry the full faith and credit of the United States and are pledged by the PHA to bond repayment. The bonds are tax exempt and carry a lower interest rate than a taxable bond. 42 U.S.C.§ 1437i(b). The federal government grants an additional indirect subsidy to public housing in the form of tax revenue forgone, since the interest on the bonds is tax free. However, this device allows the government to reduce its direct subsidy cost since it is amortizing the bonds at the lower, tax-free interest rate rather than at the higher rate required if the interest on the bonds were taxable.

In 1987, Congress authorized HUD to substitute one-time federal development grants for the long-term ACC process, retaining a forty-year period for terms and conditions of assistance under either approach. 42 U.S.C. § 1437c(a)(2). As a result of this authorization, direct grants became the primary means of funding public housing. The reasons for the shift to direct grants include the revenue loss from tax-exempt financing and the fact that the government's obligation to pay the debt service on the bonds over a 40-year period turned out to be greater than the cost of development. Barry G. Jacobs, HDR Handbook of Housing and Development Law 42 (2008).

In addition to payment of the development's capital cost through bond amortization or direct grant, the ACC may obligate HUD to pay an amount for operating and maintenance costs to provide adequate maintenance and reserve funds for the PHA. 42 U.S.C. § 1437g. HUD may, but need not entirely, pay the difference between the amount the tenant pays and the rental amount necessary to make income equal to operating and management costs.

In 1998, Congress ordered the consolidation of all federal assistance to local PHAs into two basic funds, a capital fund and an operating fund. Mixed-finance projects were added to the list of eligible expenditures from the capital fund. Social services provisions, anticrime and anti-drug activities, resident participation in management and policy development, and management of mixed finance projects "to the extent appropriate" are among the eligible expenditures from the operating fund. Pub. L. No. 105-276, § 519, 112 Stat. 2551 (1998) (*amending* 42 U.S.C. § 1437g (a)-(e)).

Cooperation Agreement

The main instrument for the protection of federalism in the public housing program is the requirement that the PHA and the local jurisdiction sign what is known as a Cooperation Agreement prior to the PHA undertaking the project. 42 U.S.C. § 1437c(e). In the Cooperation Agreement, the local jurisdiction waives normal real estate taxes, but requires the authority to make a payment in lieu of taxes (known as PILOT), which is an amount equal to 10% of the annual rentals received. 42 U.S.C. § 1437d(d). Since PILOT is less than the amount of taxes a similar taxable structure would generate, the locality is providing an indirect subsidy. The Cooperation Agreement also obligates the locality to provide usual municipal services (*e.g.*, police and fire protection) and utilities (*e.g.*, water and sewer) to a public housing development on the same basis as provided to private users. If local users pay separately, the PHA must pay separately; but the municipality must provide those services paid by property taxes in return for the PILOT payment.

Turnkey Development Process

Although local PHAs built their own developments for the first thirty years of the public housing program, since the mid-1960s the main format for housing production has been the turnkey format through which a PHA agrees to buy a finished product, including land and buildings, from a private developer, who "turns the keys over" to the PHA.

Under the turnkey model, the PHA, after receiving a reservation of program funds from HUD, advertises for proposals from private developers. The PHA, with HUD's concurrence, selects the best proposal, judged by cost, design, site location, equal opportunity, environmental factors, experience of the developer, and other factors. The PHA is not obligated to accept the lowest bid. Once the private developer is selected, it must obtain all land use, utility, building code, and other local approvals. Negotiation for and purchase of the site is the developer's responsibility. Once the site, plans, costs, and development program are approved, HUD and the PHA sign the ACC, and the PHA and the developer sign the turnkey contract of sale which obligates the PHA to purchase the development upon satisfactory completion by the developer.

The PHA does not make progress payments to the developer during the course of construction. Construction costs must be funded by the developer from commercial lending sources. As an aid in obtaining private construction financing, the developer is permitted to pledge the turnkey contract of sale. This pledge assures the lender of project eligibility under the ACC and establishes that funds are reserved for the PHA to purchase the development upon completion.

The developer constructs the development subject to inspection and final acceptance by the PHA and HUD. The developer must pay prevailing wages under the Davis-Bacon Act. 42 U.S.C. § 1437j. Once construction is completed, the developer transfers title to the entire development to the PHA. The PHA pays the cost of the project from the funds received from its bond sale.

Project Management

All management and operating functions are vested in the PHA. However, HUD has employed a turnkey management process, called Turnkey II, under which the PHA may enter into a management contract with a private corporation, a nonprofit community corporation, or a tenant organization. The PHA delegates project management to the management entity in return for a fee. In 1987 Congress added two new programs designed to encourage resident management and homeownership through gradual transfer of control over local public housing developments to resident management corporations approved by elected resident councils. 42 U.S.C. §§ 1437r, 1437s.

The public housing program serves the lowest income families of any assisted housing program. Within statutory and HUD limitations, the PHA sets income limits by determining, based on tenant income, how much the tenant can afford to pay. The rental may not exceed 30% of the tenant family's adjusted income. Adjusted income is determined by subtracting from the combined gross income of all family members amounts to reflect family size, presence of disabled, handicapped, elderly, or full-time students, and medical and child care expenses. 42 § 1437a(b)(5).

Notes and Questions

1. If one were starting anew to consider a housing program, can a less complicated program model be designed to achieve the purposes of the public housing program? What problems would you anticipate with any proposal you devise?

2. Looking again at the program model, can you determine a particular factor which seems to have influenced the public housing program? Consider concepts of federalism, confusion as to an overriding goal to be achieved, accommodation of differing interests (banking, investors, social reformers, state and local governments, real estate interests, clients of the program), and conceptions of the nature of the federal housing role.

3. Some scholars, after reviewing the complicated history of public housing, believe that public housing is necessary to protect low-income families from being exploited by the private housing market sector. *See* Lynn E. Cunningham, *A Structural Analysis of Housing Subsidy Delivery Systems: Public Housing Authorities' Part in Solving the Housing Crisis,* 13 J. Affordable Housing. & Community Dev. L. 95 (2003); Nestor M. Davidson, *Relational Contracts in the Privatization of Social Welfare,* 24 Yale L. & Pol'y Rev. 263 (2006); Shelby D. Green, *The Public Housing Tenancy: Variations on the Common Law that Give Security of Tenure and Control,* 43 Cath. U. L. Rev. 681 (1994). Private market landlord-tenant relationships are discussed in Chapter 4 *infra.*

Relationships between PHAs and their parent municipalities, governed by the Cooperation Agreement discussed above, can become quite complicated. Questions that can arise include the extent of changes that may be made in project concept, such as shift from "project location" to "scattered site" housing, extent of public services to be supplied by the city, the nature and amount of the PILOT payments, and whether one party to the Cooperation Agreement may unilaterally rescind the agreement. The following case discusses the rescission issue.

Cuyahoga Metropolitan Housing Authority v. City of Cleveland

United States District Court
342 F. Supp 250 (N.D.Ohio, E. D. 1972)
aff'd, 474 F.2d 1102 (6th Cir. 1973)

MEMORANDUM OPINION AND ORDER

BATTISTI, Chief Judge:

Cuyahoga Metropolitan Housing Authority (CMHA) has brought this action against the City of Cleveland and the members of the City Council of the City of Cleveland pursuant to 28 U.S.C.§ 1331 (a) to declare invalid the action of the City Council in adopting Ordinance No. 392-72 purporting to cancel its 1971 Cooperation Agreement with CMHA. In addition, CMHA seeks to have this court order the City to comply with said agreement.

On May 10, 1971, the Council of the City of Cleveland passed Ordinance No. 836-71 entitled "An Emergency Ordinance authorizing the execution of a Cooperation Agreement with the Cuyahoga Metropolitan Housing Authority for the development of and administration of 2,500 dwelling units for low income persons." Pursuant to the authorization granted him by Ordinance No. 836-71, the Mayor of the City of Cleveland, on May 21, 1971, on behalf of the City of Cleveland, entered into a Cooperation Agreement with CMHA. The City of Cleveland has received the substantial benefit of certification of its "Workable Program" by HUD because it executed the Cooperation Agreement. Such benefits accrued under other programs.

After execution of the Cooperation Agreement in May of 1971, CMHA in performance thereunder and in reliance upon this agreement instituted and engaged in the following activities.

General plans for the development of the 2,500 units over a 2-year period under the Cooperation Agreement were conceived. It was decided that construction under the new agreement was to proceed in five separate phases which would result in the development of 2,000 family units and 500 elderly units.

For the first phase of development, CMHA requested a program reservation for 500 units from the Department of Housing and Urban Development (HUD), which was approved and granted. All of the 500 units in the first phase were designated for single family scattered site housing to be developed under the traditional Turnkey method of construction. However, the plans and approvals have been recently changed so that now 150 units are to be constructed under a Turnkey acquisition program.

CMHA hired an additional planner and real estate officer, and also created a new position of Deputy Director, in order to meet the new demands for the development of the 2,500 units and the various development programs thereunder and assigned additional staff to the development program. The CMHA staff developed a letter inviting proposals and containing criteria to be sent to proposed Turnkey developers which were approved by HUD. CMHA placed legal advertisements inviting proposals from developers for the development of 500 Turnkey units.

Pursuant to said advertised invitation, proposals from ten developers were received by CMHA for a total of 509 units, and thereafter the CMHA staff devoted considerable time and money to the evaluation of said proposals. After the CMHA staff and the CMHA Board tentatively approved over 100 proposed sites, the HUD staff spent considerable time and effort in evaluating and studying same.

After the proposed sites had been approved by the CMHA staff, the CMHA Board and HUD, the CMHA staff and Board also spent considerable time in evaluating the financial and construction aspects of the various Turnkey proposals. To date, the CMHA Board has approved plans for approximately 71 sites in all respects and has agreed to enter into development programs therefore. These proposed development programs have all been sent to HUD for funding by amendments to existing Annual Contributions Contracts but the City of Cleveland's actions have created a cloud and have resulted in delays in HUD's approval.

To date, CMHA has expended approximately $45,000 in the development and planning of the 500 scattered site units as the first stage of construction under the 1971 Cooperation Agreement. This development money will not be reimbursed by HUD unless and until the proposed units are approved by HUD for construction by the execution of a development program.

This latter action is dependent upon the existence of a Cooperation Agreement. Federal funds amounting to approximately 62.5 Million Dollars will be lost by CMHA, which loss will prevent CMHA from carrying out its statutorily mandated purpose of providing persons of low income with decent, safe, and sanitary housing. The Council of the City of Cleveland on March 27, 1972, passed Ordinance No. 392-72 which purports to repeal Ordinance No. 836-71 and to cancel the Cooperation Agreement authorized and executed thereunder.

The question before this court is whether the City may rescind the Cooperation Agreement under which it and CMHA have pursued their obligations for almost one year. This issue has been presented to at least three State courts, and all three have overturned or enjoined the municipality from repudiating or canceling a valid Cooperation Agreement....

The City contends that a legislative body cannot bind its successor and that any law passed by one City Council is repealable.... This proposition, while generally valid, simply ignores the realities of the situation. Legislative bodies regularly enact statutes and enter into contracts which are, for all intents and purposes, unrepealable. Contracts or statutes entered into to build a building or a bridge or a dam can not be repealed at the next session of the legislative body, when certain parties have relied on that agreement, as CMHA has in this case. Statutes such as this ordinance are particularly immune from repeal when it is impossible to make one party to the contract whole by the payment of money damages. This issue will be dealt with more fully later in this opinion.

In order to determine if City Council's action has violated the contract clause, the equities must now be balanced. CMHA is in the business of building public housing and was established as a body corporate and politic in 1937. It has expended more than $40,000 pursuant to this agreement. If it is unable to build the 2500 homes which it plans to build, it will lose approximately $62,500,000 in federal funds. In addition, it will be effectively precluded from carrying out its mandate of providing persons of low income with decent, safe and sanitary housing. Although CMHA will lose $62,500,000, the real losers will be the persons of low-income residing in the City of Cleveland. These people are the true parties in interest here. Without the efforts of CMHA, with federal funds, many persons of low-income can never hope to live in a decent, safe and sanitary home in Cleveland.

When examined against these considerations, the City offers little. In fact, the City may suffer a greater loss than CMHA.

If the City's "workable program" is uncertified, when next it comes up for review, HUD may refuse to authorize any funds for Cleveland. These at present are far in excess of the $62,500,000 which CMHA will receive. These include Model Cities, Urban Renewal, Open Spaces and other moneys. On their side of the scale the City offers only an argument that they can repeal any ordinance any time it deems appropriate. According to the terms of the Cooperation Agreement, it could be cancelled only if one circumstance occurred and it has not. Section 10 of the Cooperation Agreement between the City and CMHA provides:

> The Local Authority in the planning, construction, purchase or occupancy of any low-cost housing Project shall comply with all valid charter and ordinance provisions of the Municipality including but not limited to those relating to planning, platting, subdividing, zoning and sanitation. A breach of this subdivision by the Local Authority shall be grounds for cancellation by the Municipality of the within agreement as to units authorized herein which have not been approved in writing by the Government for processing by the Local Authority prior to such cancellation. Cancellation shall be by ordinance of Council passed and made effective pursuant to the charter of the Municipality [Provided, however, that nothing herein shall in any way modify or change the obligations of the Municipality as set forth in subdivisions 1 through 9 hereof as the same are referable to obligations arising as to any units approved in writing by the Government for processing by the Local Authority prior to the effective date of such cancellation.

Under the time-honored rule of construction of *expressio unius est exclusio alterius,* the fact that the parties saw fit to provide this one specific situation in which the Cooperation Agreement could be cancelled demonstrated that all other situations are excluded. The defendant City and the defendant Councilmen proffer no reason for their purported cancellation of the Cooperation Agreement and thus the purported cancellation was an unjustified act.

Section 10 of the Cooperation Agreement only binds CMHA to comply with valid municipal ordinances. Ordinance No. 2092-52 referred to by *amici* which purports to require the approval of the Cleveland City Council (before) the establishment of any new low rent housing project in the City of Cleveland is clearly not a valid ordinance for the following reasons.

Ordinance No. 2092-52 is an attempt by one political subdivision of the State of Ohio without statutory authority to interfere with the statutory power of another political subdivision which is carrying out a state public purpose. It is a fundamental principle of law that a municipal legislative authority cannot subject the state, or any of its agencies, to the municipality's laws in the absence of express statutory authority granted by the state legislature....

Like a park district, a metropolitan housing authority is a political subdivision of the State of Ohio which by delegation performs state functions which are governmental in character.

That there is no statutory authority for the City of Cleveland's attempted interference is clear. Ohio Revised Code, § 3735.44 in fact requires that local planning, zoning, and sanitary laws apply to housing projects of a metropolitan housing authority to the same extent as if said projects were planned, constructed, owned, or operated by private persons; however, Ordinance No. 2092-52 applies solely to housing projects within the meaning of the 1937 Housing Act.

Ordinance No. 2092-52 was an attempt by the City unilaterally to modify a Cooperation Agreement. In a memorandum opinion in the recent case of *Davis v. City of Toledo*, 54 F.R.D. 386 (N.D. Ohio W.D.), Judge Young held that where a Cooperation Agreement does not contain a provision giving City Council site selection veto power, the same cannot be exercised even if subsequently agreed to by the housing authority. In *Davis*, the Toledo Metropolitan Housing Authority (TMHA) proposed sites for low income housing and submitted them to the City Council for approval. The Council disapproved and TMHA acquiesced in the Council's action although it was clear that the Cooperation Agreement between the City and TMHA contained "no provision which in any way gives the City of Toledo power to approve or disapprove sites selected for low rent housing". The court specifically held that the TMHA was under no obligation to submit the proposed sites to the City Council and that it was equally clear that Council was acting without authority in vetoing the proposal. The court in *Davis* also reviewed the federal law that requires a Cooperation Agreement between a housing authority and a local legislative body, 42 U.S.C. Section 1415(7)(a), and the state law requiring local compliance with planning and zoning laws, Ohio Revised Code Section 3735.44, and held: "None of these [laws] gives City Council the power exercised here." The Cooperation Agreement between the City of Cleveland and CMHA likewise contain no provision for site approval....

For the reasons that Ordinance No. 2092-52 is an invalid exercise of municipal power contrary to state law, and in direct conflict with the Cooperation Agreement between CMHA and the City of Cleveland, it is clear that CMHA's failure to submit projects for approval of the City Council is not in violation of a valid ordinance of the City of Cleveland and therefore may not serve as justification for cancellation of the Cooperation Agreement.

When one balances the equities in this case and applies the test of reasonableness, the action of the City Council must be held to be an impairment of the obligation of contract in violation of Article I, § 10. Plaintiff and amici curiae raise additional matters which merit discussion.

The plaintiff contends that the Cooperation Agreement may not be cancelled without the consent of the federal government. The Cooperation Agreement provides in Section 9 *inter alia:*

> So long as any contract between the Local Authority and the Government for loans (including preliminary loans) or annual contribution, or both, in connection with any Project remains in force and effect, or so long as any bonds issued in connection with any Project remain unpaid, *this Agreement shall not be abrogated, changed, or modified without the consent of the Government.* (emphasis added)

This section of the Cooperation Agreement is required by the government as a matter of Federal law in order to protect the government because of the obligations which it assumes based upon the existence of a Cooperation Agreement. Thus, the parties to the Cooperation Agreement, in this case CMHA and the City of Cleveland, must agree to give the government a beneficial interest in the Cooperation Agreement so that said Agreement may not be cancelled by the parties even should they mutually agree to do so unless the prior consent of the government is obtained.

Pursuant to its general rule-making power under § 8 of the United States Housing Act of 1937, 42 U.S.C. Section 1408, HUD has issued a Low-Rent Housing Application and Preliminary Loans Guide. This Guide, HPMC-FHA G 7404.1, provides that HUD requires as a prerequisite to approving an Application for a Low-Rent Housing Program that the Local Authority submit to the Area Office of HUD an executed Cooperation Agreement. This Agreement must be approved by the Area Office Legal Counsel and the proper forms for it are available from HUD. These forms provide without exception that a Cooperation Agreement may not be abrogated, changed, or modified without the consent of the government so long as there exists an Annual Contributions Contract between the government and the local authority. This HUD manual and this provision of the Cooperation Agreement preventing abrogation, change or modification are mandated under HUD's rulemaking power as federal law, pursuant to the Supremacy Clause of The United States Constitution (Article VI, Cl. 2). *See Thorpe v. Hous. Auth. of City of Durham*, 393 U.S. 268 (1969). Thus, the Cooperation Agreement, which has the status of federal law, in itself is effective in eliminating any possibility that a municipality can rescind such an Agreement in the manner in which the defendants have purported to do in the instant case.

The Congress of the United States has established a clear national policy of remedying the shortage of decent, safe and sanitary housing. The United States Housing Act of 1937 provides *inter alia:*

> it is ... the policy of the United States to promote the general welfare of the Nation by employing its funds and credit ... to assist the several States and their political subdivisions ... to remedy the unsafe and unsanitary housing conditions and acute shortage of decent, safe, and sanitary dwellings for families of low income ... that are injurious to the health, safety, and morals of the citizens of the Nation,"

United States Housing Act of 1937, § 1, 42 U.S.C. § 1401. In order to implement this national policy, Congress established the Low-Rent Public Housing Program and had continued to fund this program at increasing levels since 1937....

The federal housing law establishes a comprehensive scheme for federal involvement in the development of low rent public housing. For this involvement to be triggered, it is required that an initial local determination of need be made and that based on that determination a Cooperation Agreement be entered into. 42 U.S.C. Section 1415(7)(b). Once a municipality has made such an initial determination of need and entered into a Cooperation Agreement based thereon, commitment of federal government resources to further implement the national housing policy within that municipality is assured and authorized. The federal laws regulating the federal commitment, being triggered by the municipality's initial determination, via a Cooperation Agreement, must be read so as to prohibit repudiation of said Agreement. Otherwise, the federal scheme and national policy could be impeded and completely abrogated by municipal action. Clearly, 42 U.S.C. Section 1415(7) (b) cannot be read so as to authorize such result. *See Housing Auth. of City of Los Angeles v. City of Los Angeles*, 243 P.2d 515, 521 (Cal. 1952).

Therefore, having violated the national housing policy as set forth in the Housing Act of 1937, the action of the defendants is in violation of the Supremacy Clause of the United States Constitution. The plaintiff herein does not question the requirement of 42 U.S.C. Section 1415(7) (b) that an initial local determination of need be made and a Cooperation Agreement executed, because in the instant case the determination has been made and the Agreement entered into.

Amici curiae have suggested that a fiscal officer's certificate of availability of funds should have been attached to the Cooperation Agreement. The provisions of Section 5705.41 of the Revised Code, however, clearly have no application to the Cooperation Agreement. Section 5705.41 provides *inter alia:*

> No subdivision or taxing unit shall: ... D. Make any contract or give any order involving the expenditure of money unless there is attached thereto a certificate of the fiscal officer of the subdivision that the amount required to meet the same, or in the case of a continuing contract to be performed in whole, or in part, in an ensuing fiscal year, the amount required to meet the same in the fiscal year in which the contract is made, has been lawfully appropriated for such purpose and is in the treasury or in process of collection to the credit of an appropriate fund free from any previous encumbrances.

The Cooperation Agreement of 1971 is not a contract which involves the expenditure of money by the City of Cleveland. Under said Agreement, the defendant City binds itself only to cooperate with the plaintiff and generally to furnish the same municipal services to the plaintiff that are furnished to other property owners. All of the specific expenditures of money which are incurred as a result of the Cooperation Agreement involve the expenditure of funds by the plaintiff and HUD. Thus, clearly Section 5705.41 of the Revised Code of Ohio has no application to a contract of such a nature, for to require a fiscal officer to certify the availability of funds where specific funds need not be employed is a vain act....

Amici curiae represent individuals who were leaders of the initiative movement to repeal the Cooperation Agreement. These groups consist largely of homeowners on the West Side of the City of Cleveland, where much of the scattered-site housing is to be built. Their opposition to public housing has been very vocal. While these people will not admit publicly that they entertain any bias or prejudice against members of the Negro race or other minorities, these considerations clearly, in part, influence their thinking. They clearly object to having large numbers of low-income Negroes move into their all-White neighborhoods. They fear, among other things, a depreciation in the property values in the district and an increase in violence which they feel will follow the movement of public housing. In keeping with these views, amici curiae have appended to their brief numerous newspaper articles which indicate, in their view, ample evidence of danger to the general public to warrant cancellation of the Cooperation Agreement pursuant to the police power granted to the Cleveland City Council pursuant to Article XVIII, § 3 of the Ohio Constitution. This argument is most unfortunate because it appeals only to the basest of emotions and fears. Neither CMHA nor the concept of dispersed public housing represent a panacea for the ills of this society. Yet were it not for CMHA and those who have striven mightily for more than a century to bring equal rights to all, this country might not be as integrated as it is. The assumptions implicit in this argument is that tax dollars should not be used to promote integration in our society. It is unbelievable that 18 years after *Brown v. Board of Education*, 347 U.S. 483 (1954), such arguments can be made by intelligent people. This nation is committed to a policy of equal rights and opportunities for all its citizens. It is too late in the day to attempt to change this country's wise decision to move toward this goal.

In reliance upon the Cooperation Agreement, CMHA has obtained a Program Reservation from the Department of Housing and Urban Development, obtained the approval of HUD to invite bids for the development of projects authorized in said Cooperation Agreement, invited bids for such projects, and devoted considerable staff time to the planning and development of low rent public housing units authorized by said Cooperation Agreement. Additionally, HUD, at CMHA's request, has reviewed sites and caused appraisals of same to be made. Also in reliance on the Cooperation Agreement and CMHA's invitations to bid, numerous developers and builders have expended considerable time and money in submitting bids to CMHA. In total, CMHA has expended approximately $45,000.00 in funds in reliance upon the Cooperation Agreement.

Public corporations like the plaintiff CMHA are created for the sole purpose of carrying out their assigned public purposes. The plaintiff's public purpose is to provide decent, safe and sanitary housing for persons of low income. (*See* Ohio Revised Code, Section 3735.-31.) In carrying out this statutorily mandated public purpose, the plaintiff becomes of necessity a trustee of the rights of the persons of low income that it serves. These low income persons that CMHA by law is to serve will be damaged irreparably should CMHA's ability to provide decent, safe and sanitary low rent public housing for them be jeopardized. CMHA, both directly and through the beneficiaries of its public purposes, will be injured to the extent of approximately $62,500,000.00 in federal subsidies which will not be provided should the defendants City and Councilmen be permitted to carry forth the purported cancellation of the Cooperation Agreement. This sum of money represents the average cost of one unit of housing ($25,000.00) multiplied by the number of units contemplated by the Cooperation Agreement (2,500). In addition, the beneficiaries of public housing including residents and potential residents will be denied access to and availability of these 2,500 units at federally subsidized rental amounts. The average monthly rental in the City of Cleveland being $100.00 and the average rent charged by CMHA to elderly being $41.00 and to families being $60.00, low income persons will be denied substantial benefits of the public housing program.

It is also important to note the racially discriminatory effect of the purported cancellation of the Cooperation Agreement. As testified to by Director Fitzgerald, CMHA has a waiting list of approximately 5,600 persons. Of these persons, 4,200 or 75% are Black and 1,400 or 25% are White. In addition the proportion of Black persons on the waiting list for family units, as opposed to elderly units, is greater than the proportion of Blacks on the overall waiting list. The 500 scattered site units, the development of which marks the commencement of development under the Cooperation Agreement for 2,500 units, are all for family use. Thus, the cancellation of this Cooperation Agreement would have the effect of deprivation and discrimination primarily against Blacks.

In carrying forward with its statutorily imposed duties under state and federal law, CMHA must continue to pursue the development of low rent public housing projects within its jurisdictional area. The actions of the defendants in harassing CMHA have a ripple-like effect on all of CMHA's contractual, quasi-contractual, and statutorily mandated relationships. Developers and builders will refuse to deal further with CMHA since the binding effect of the Cooperation Agreement with the City of Cleveland has been called into question. HUD has refused to approve development programs and execute any further Amendments to its Annual Contributions Contract with CMHA, which contract is the very life-blood of public housing because its serves to channel the necessary federal subsidy to such housing. HUD has refused to continue to pursue the procedures which lead to development of a low rent public housing project since these procedures require the devotion of considerable HUD staff time and money.

It is obvious that CMHA and the people of Cleveland cannot be made whole by money damages. One cannot evaluate a decent, safe and sanitary home, the demise of racial divisions in a city, nor place a price on human dignity. The cost to the society of the continuation of racial segregation, de facto or de jure, may only be fairly judged when one considers the loss that this country suffered in men and material between 1861 and 1865.

Therefore, it is hereby ordered that the 1971 Cooperation Agreement between the City of Cleveland and CMHA is declared to be a valid and subsisting contract between the parties; that it has not been nor will be cancelled by virtue of Ordinance No. 392-72, which is declared to be unlawful, null and void; that the defendants are permanently enjoined from any further proceedings or actions in violation of or interference with plaintiff's rights under the 1971 Cooperation Agreement; and that the defendants are ordered to comply with said contract and perform all provisions thereof.

Notes and Questions

1. The *Cuyahoga* case raises the issue of local opposition to low-income housing, a topic discussed in detail in Chapter 6. For accounts of the battles over public housing at the local level, see LEONARD FREEDMAN, PUBLIC HOUSING: THE POLITICS OF POVERTY (1969); MARTIN MEYERSON & EDWARD BANFIELD, POLITICS, PLANNING AND THE PUBLIC INTEREST (1955); LAWRENCE J. VALE, FROM THE PURITANS TO THE PROJECTS: PUBLIC HOUSING AND PUBLIC NEIGHBORS (2000); LAWRENCE J. VALE, RECLAIMING PUBLIC HOUSING: A HALF CENTURY OF STRUGGLE IN THREE PUBLIC NEIGHBORHOODS (2002); Henry J. Schmandt & George D. Wendel, *The Pruitt-Igoe Public Housing Complex, 1954–1976*, 5 WERK-ARCHITHESE 3 (May 1977) (analyzing the factors leading to the demolition of the 33-building, high-rise Pruitt-Igoe public housing complex in St. Louis, which went from national architectural praise for "innovative cost-saving and community-building design features" to "an embarrassment to all concerned" in little over a decade). In 1998, Congress amended the local cooperation agreement provision by adding a requirement that public housing authorities agree to give advance notice and information upon reasonable request to local municipal officials before any funds are made available for "development of any housing or other property not previously used as public housing." 42 U.S.C. § 1437c(e)(2).

2. What is the legislative purpose in exempting public housing developments from local real estate taxes and other municipal charges? If this purpose is an important and valid one, why, then, does the housing statute require a payment in lieu of taxes?

3. If the tax exemption provision is a method of reducing federal subsidy costs, would you favor a requirement that local jurisdictions help defer the subsidy costs by contributing funds or services to subsidized housing developments? What policy and practical problems do you see with this suggestion? *See* Barbara O. Maffei, Should Local Governments Be Required to Contribute a Portion of the Total Costs of Federal Housing Programs?, *in Hearings Before the Subcomm. on HUD—Independent Agencies, House Comm. on Appropriations*, 95th Cong., 1st Sess. 65 (1977).

4. Major changes in public housing policy were authorized in 1990 and in 1998. Title IV of the 1990 Act provides for homeownership opportunities to permit qualified residents to buy their public housing units; this program is known as the "Homeownership and Opportunity for People Everywhere Program (HOPE)," 42 U.S.C. § 1437aaa-3. The program was slow to catch on, although it was reauthorized in the 1998 Act. Pub. L. No. 105-276, § 536, 112 Stat. 2586 (1998). However, an amendment to the 1937 Housing Act

authorizing a demonstration program to develop public housing units within a mixed income community led to a major policy change called HOPE VI, described *infra*. 42 U.S.C. § 1437v.

These changes reflect an attempt by Congress to address a nationwide concern that large, isolated public housing complexes have become social and operational white elephants, segregating predominately minority, low-income people in large masses. A general theme of the 1990 and the 1998 Acts is that housing solutions for low- and moderate-income families, as well as the disabled, elderly and the homeless, should provide individuals and families with the opportunity to live with the maximum amount of independence and dignity.

2. Program Relations and Coordination

The public housing program is a mixture of federal dollars and local production and operational authority. In order to protect the national interest in the program, and the investment of the purchasers of the PHA's—bonds, the statute provides the basis on which HUD can regulate PHA affairs. *See, e.g.*, 42 U.S.C. § 1437a(a)(1) (HUD approval of PHA established income limits and rents); § 1437(b) (HUD determination of bond terms); § 1437d(a) (HUD may set contract conditions); § 1437d(c)(1) (HUD may require PHA revision of income limits). In general, 42 U.S.C. § 1437d(c)(4) allows HUD to establish procedures and requirements to assure sound management practices including, but not limited to, tenant selection criteria, rent collections, tenant evictions, tenant-management relationships, and security and maintenance. On the other hand, 42 U.S.C. § 1437 states that "[i]t is the policy of the United States ... to vest in public housing agencies that perform well the maximum amount of responsibility and flexibility in program administration, with appropriate accountability to public housing residents, localities, and the general public...." This is the so-called "local autonomy" provision. Thus, there exists a tension between the initiative and responsibility of the PHA and HUD's administrative oversight and rule-making authority. The tension becomes even more pronounced in the turnkey program model in which the HUD-PHA relationship is complicated by the presence of a private developer. In the turnkey program, the developer contracts directly with the PHA, which in turn processes the development with HUD. However, since the developer requires HUD concurrence on many important program items, the developer frequently deals directly with HUD, sometimes to the exclusion of the PHA. Legal disputes among the three parties become complicated and difficult to resolve. The same complexity exists in HUD-PHA-tenant relationships, a topic examined in Chapter 4, section B.

HUD's authority to oversee and regulate PHAs was litigated in *Silva v. East Providence Hous. Auth.*, 565 F.2d 1217 (1st Cir. 1977) in which HUD terminated an Annual Contributions Contract for 100 units of public housing because of lack of diligent prosecution by the PHA (no units were constructed in five years). In upholding HUD's power to terminate under the statute, but remanding for a determination whether less restrictive alternatives, such as suspension, temporary takeover, or litigation might have been utilized, the court observed:

> We come down to the question whether, in the light of the strong policy directive of the statutes, the demonstrated need for public housing in the community, the existence of a binding Annual Contributions Contract between HUD and EPHA, and HUD's "last resort" guideline in its Handbook, HUD may terminate a public housing project without considering the appropriateness of three

> remedies less severe than termination. If it may, then it seems to us that the utility of a contract so easily discarded may be questioned, as well as whether a decision so made can truthfully be said to be "in the interest of the government."

Id. at 1224.

Notes and Questions

1. In *Housing Authority of Passaic v. Torres,* 362 A.2d 1254 (N.J. Super. Ct. App. Div. 1976), the tenant became disabled and unemployed. His rental, based on 25% of income, had been $124 per month; following the disability, he could afford only $74 with 25% of income. The tenant requested an immediate reduction in rental; the authority (PHA) sought to apply its regular procedure of annual income reexamination. The court denied the PHA's summary dispossess action for nonpayment of rent, holding, as binding on the PHA, a HUD circular requiring interim rent adjustments to maintain rental payments at 25% of income. The court stated that the circular was binding as a supplement to the Annual Contributions Contract. *See also National Tenants Organization, Inc. v. HUD,* 358 F. Supp. 312 (D.D.C. 1973), *remanded mem.,* 505 F.2d 476 (D.C. Cir. 1974); *Bloom v. Niagara Falls Hous. Auth.,* 430 F. Supp. 1183 (W.D.N.Y. 1977). For further development of tenants' rights issues, see Chapter 4 *infra,* section B.

2. One of the options discussed in the *Silva* opinion, federal takeover, was litigated in *United States v. Barrett,* 442 F.2d 642 (4th Cir. 1971), *aff'g* 315 F. Supp. 941 (N.D. W.Va. 1970). Local citizens filed a state court action challenging the legal existence of the PHA, after the ACC and the Turnkey Contract of Sale had been executed. A legal challenge to the PHA's right to enter into the Turnkey Contract constituted a "substantial default" under the terms of the ACC. The statute permits federal takeover in the event of a substantial default by the PHA. 42 U.S.C. § 1437d(g). The *Barrett* opinion upheld HUD's authority to require an assignment of the Turnkey Contract, based on the contractual and statutory provisions. (The district court had balanced the statutory requirement of federal-local cooperation against HUD's statutory right to take over a project in default, and concluded that the congressional intent that projects already begun should be completed had priority. The opinion also upheld HUD's discretion under the statute to define conditions which constitute a substantial default.) In addition, the circuit court reasoned that the state court litigation impaired the PHA's financial responsibility in the eyes of creditors (including bond purchasers) and subcontractors, thus thwarting the policy of the public housing program. The court enjoined the local residents from proceeding with the state court action.

3. During the 1980s, administration and congressional support for public housing shifted from construction of additional units to improvement and modernization of units already in the public housing inventory. The Comprehensive Improvement Assistance Program (CIAP) authorized grants to local public housing agencies based on five-year comprehensive plans prepared by the PHAs and approved by HUD which describe the conditions of public housing units, improvements needed, and specific plans for making improvements. Funds were made available to PHAs that own or operate 250 or more units under contracts that remained in effect for a twenty-year period. PHAs had wide discretion in choosing how to spend CIAP funds, so long as the expenditures were consistent with the approved plan.

The CIAP program was repealed in 1998 as part of a move to consolidate all public housing assistance into two funds, a capital fund and an operating fund (42 U.S.C. § 1437g), and to deregulate public housing authorities so that they can "perform as property and asset managers," including "facilitating mixed income communities and decreasing concentrations of poverty in public housing." Pub. L. No. 105-276, § 502(b), 112 Stat. 2521 (1998).

4. Responsibility for living conditions in public housing is placed on the local PHA as public landlord. When things go bad, can tenants enforce the PHA's responsibility in the federal courts? Lower courts initially declined relief to tenants, see, e.g., *Boston Public Housing Tenants' Policy Council v. Lynn*, 388 F. Supp. 493 (D. Mass. 1974), but the Supreme Court's decision in *Wright v. City of Roanoke Redevelopment & Housing Authority*, 479 U.S. 418 (1987) (reprinted in Chapter 2 *supra*) provides a basis for federal courts to grant relief. *See Concerned Tenants Ass'n of Father Panik Village v. Pierce*, 685 F. Supp. 316 (D. Conn. 1988).

5. Following their loss in federal court in *Boston Public Housing Tenants' Policy Council*, the public housing tenants turned to an often overlooked remedy in disputes involving federal housing: state and municipal habitability laws. After four additional years of litigation, the housing authority was placed in receivership. *See* N.Y. TIMES, July 26, 1979, at 8. *See also* 7 [Current Developments] Hous. & Dev. Rep. (BNA) 228 (1979). On the housing authority's appeal, the Massachusetts Supreme Court affirmed the trial court opinion. *Perez v. Boston Hous. Auth.*, 400 N.E.2d 1231 (Mass. 1980). Receivership powers were transferred in 1984 to the Mayor of Boston under court supervision. Available federal funds proved insufficient to pay for all needed renovations, so the authority sought and received a $13 million state grant funded by a general obligation bond issue. This grant, coupled with $27 million in unspent public housing development funds previously awarded the authority, was used in 1988 to pay for a turnkey renovation and new construction of 293 units in two of Boston's oldest public housing projects. A small number of public housing tenants were scheduled to receive up to 2,000 hours each of employment in the renovation effort. 15 [Current Developments] Hous. & Dev. Rep. (WGL) 943 (1988). The story of the Boston public housing controversies is told by Lawrence J. Vale. LAWRENCE J. VALE, RECLAIMING PUBLIC HOUSING: A HALF CENTURY OF STRUGGLE IN THREE PUBLIC NEIGHBORHOODS (2002).

Does this resolution of the Boston public housing problem suggest that the public housing program should be altered to vest greater authority in state or local administrative bodies? Would program coordination be improved if carried out by a state or local rather than a national governmental entity? Would a state or local administrative agency be more responsive to local problems than is HUD, which has national responsibilities? It is notable that the New York Times article cited above makes no mention of HUD; both the BHA's problems and their solution are discussed in purely local terms.

A Note on Public Housing Rental Policies

Rental policies have been a constant source of tension between HUD, PHAs, and tenants. For general background, see DANIEL R. MANDELKER, HOUSING SUBSIDIES IN THE UNITED STATES AND ENGLAND (1973).

While the initial scheme of public housing provided an extremely generous subsidy that funded capital and financing costs, tenants were required to make rental payment sufficient to cover operating expenses and administrative costs. Thus, even though the public housing program provides the deepest subsidy of all the federal housing programs, tenants must have enough income to make the established rental payments. A series of interrelated events, including a rapid shift in tenant population from predominantly moderate-income persons temporarily "down on their luck" to low-income persons in a "permanent" state of dependency through unemployment, single parent family status and little or no education, coupled with deferred maintenance of buildings and rent increases imposed by PHAs and approved by HUD, 42 U.S.C. § 1437a(a)(1), produced a crisis in public housing resulting in enactment of the Brooke Amendments, which placed a ceiling on rental and utility charges. (See the discussion of the history of Brooke I in Chapter 2, *supra*) Brooke I (1969) limited tenant rent payments to 25% of income, later increased to 30%. Brooke II (1970) refined and narrowed the definition of income to exclude certain items. Brooke III (1971) clarified that the percent of income limitation applied to families receiving public assistance. 42 U.S.C. § 1437a(1). By restricting tenant payments to a percentage of a narrowly defined income base, the Brooke Amendments led to increased deficits for PHAs. In order to avoid this result, Congress authorized HUD to make operating subsidy payments, in addition to the traditional capital subsidy. 42 U.S.C. § 1437g(a).

The operating subsidy program did not bring immediate relief to hard-pressed PHAs. First, Congress did not authorize sufficient funds to cover Brooke Amendment income losses. Even if Congress had done so, PHAs had large accrued deficits, and expenses were increasing; merely making up lost revenue was insufficient. In addition, HUD resisted full implementation of the operating subsides, requesting insufficient funding from Congress and refusing to spend what was appropriated. *See* Robert Pozen, *The Financing of Local Housing Authorities: A Contract Approach for Public Corporations,* 82 YALE L.J. 1208 (1973).

Faced with increasing costs, large deficits, and a limit on tenant rent payments, PHAs were encouraged by HUD to grant an occupancy preference to "wealthier" low-income families. This attempt to achieve solvency by giving consideration to a tenant's ability to pay is known as a rent range policy. A PHA will simply refuse to rent to tenants in the lower rental ranges until it has attracted sufficient tenants in the higher rental ranges to achieve solvency. Eligible applicants with lower incomes are required to remain on waiting lists for long periods for no reason other than inability to pay the higher rent. HUD, through its power to approve PHA rentals, encouraged rent range policies since they would require lower operating subsidy expenditures.

Congress responded to litigation invalidating rent range policies, *Fletcher v. Housing Authority of Louisville,* 491 F.2d 793 (6th Cir. 1974), *vacated & remanded,* 419 U.S. 812 (1974), *reinstated,* 525 F.2d 532 (6th Cir. 1975), by amending the statute in 1974 to legitimate rent range policies. In 1979 and 1983, Congress added admissions preferences for families occupying substandard housing, displaced families, and families paying more than 50% of their income for rent to the requirement that an economic mix of tenants be sought by local housing authorities. 42 U.S.C. § 1437(c)(4)(A). HUD failed to promulgate regulations concerning the three preferences. Holding that the statutory language providing that local housing authorities "shall comply with such procedures and requirements as the Secretary may prescribe," was not self-executing, the Court of Appeals for the Eleventh Circuit refused to require a local housing authority to grant such preferences in admission to housing units under its control. *Gholston v. Housing Auth. of City of Montgomery,* 818 F.2d 776 (11th Cir. 1987). Congressional impatience with HUD's response to such legislative changes led Congress in 1987 to order HUD to issue implementing regulations for another statutory preference (families with incomes less than 50% of area median family incomes) within sixty days of February 5, 1988, the effective date of the 1987 Act. In 1998, Congress revised the public housing rental policies in several important ways:

(1) Federal admissions preference were repealed and local housing authorities are given authority to establish their own preferences "based upon local housing needs and priorities" 42 U.S.C. § 1437d (c)(4).

(2) Public housing tenants may choose to pay a flat rent based on the rental value of the unit or one based on family income, established as the highest of 30% of adjusted monthly income, 10% of monthly income, or that portion of welfare assistance designated for housing costs. 42 U.S.C. § 1437a (a)(2).

(3) A minimum rent not to exceed $50 per month is required to be paid by each family residing in public housing, as well as those receiving tenant-based assistance under Section 8, discussed *infra*, subject to hardship exceptions 42 U.S.C.§ 1437a (a)(3).

(4) Rent payable by a public housing family may not be increased for 12 months after a previously-unemployed member of the family becomes employed or the family's earned income increases through participation in a family self-sufficiency or other job training program or while receiving assistance through the temporary assistance for needy families (TANF) program (welfare-to-work). 42 U.S.C. § 1437a(b)(5)(d).

(5) Families qualifying for the earned income disallowance noted above may request the housing authority to establish an individual savings account (ISA) in lieu of the disallowance into which would be deposited that portion of the rent payment attributable to employment. Withdrawals from ISAs are permitted only for purchasing a home, paying education costs of family members, moving out of public or assisted housing, or paying any other expense authorized by the housing authority to promote economic self sufficiency. 42 U.S.C. § 1437a (b)(5)(e).

(6) All adult residents, except the elderly, disabled, and those engaged in work activities or participating in welfare-to-work programs, are required to contribute at least eight hours per month of community service other than political activity, or participate in an economic self sufficiency program for eight hours per month. 42 U.S.C § 1437j(c). No reduction in rent is permitted if welfare or public assistance is reduced because of a failure to comply with economic self sufficiency program conditions or work activities requirements. 42 U.S.C. § 1437j (d).

(7) Housing authorities may permit otherwise ineligible police officers to reside in public housing units in order to increase security in the housing development, and small authorities (owning or operating less than 250 units) may lease units on a month-to-month basis to over-income families if there are no income-eligible families seeking assistance following 30 days notice of the availability of such assistance Pub. L. No. 105-276, § 524, 112 Stat. 2567 (1998).

(8) Site-based waiting lists may be established "under which applicants may apply directly at or otherwise designate the project or projects in which they seek to reside," provided such waiting lists comply with applicable civil rights laws. 42 U.S.C. § 1437d(s).

(9) Public housing residents may own one or more "common household pets" subject to reasonable regulations provided the resident "maintains each pet responsibly" and in accordance with applicable laws. Pub. L. No. 105-276, § 526, 112 Stat. 2568 (1998) (*amending* 42 U.S.C. § 1437).

Notes and Questions

1. Review the 1998 amendments to public housing rental policies. What do they tell you about changes in the philosophy of public housing? Do the 1998 amendments help maintain public housing as housing of last resort for extremely-low and very-low income households, a role it has played at least since the 1950s? Or do they provide evidence of the intent to shift the focus of public housing to households with greater stability and more optimistic prospects for the future?

2. Recall that the public housing program is an amalgam of federal, state and local law. Given that housing authorities are local public agencies governed by state law, can the state authorize a housing authority to impose late charges and attorneys' fees as "additional rent" in cases where tenants fall behind in their rent payments? *See Housing Auth. & Urban Redev. Agency of the City of Atlantic City v. Taylor*, 796 A.2d 193, 201 (N.J. 2002) (concluding that the Brooke Amendment's limit on public housing rent preempted state law).

3. Program Evaluation

Eugene Meehan, Public Housing Policy

169–79 (1975)

By 1970, the application of conventional public housing policy to the City of St. Louis had produced an internationally famous disaster. In all of the projects, the physical facilities were inadequately maintained and repaired; some areas were vandalized and ravaged beyond all possibility of rehabilitation. Apartments, buildings, and even whole projects, stood empty and abandoned; occupancy in the remaining facilities was low and falling steadily. The areas surrounding the projects were typically decaying, consisting for the most part of abandoned houses and empty lots, or, in some cases, rough commercial and industrial facilities. The areas on which the buildings stood were littered and neglected. The characteristics of the tenants had altered drastically in two decades. The working poor had been replaced by welfare recipients and the elderly; the two-parent family had given way to the female head of household; biracial occupancy, segregated by project, had been superseded by black occupancy, segregated as a whole from the remaining community both by race and by social stigma attached to project residence; the working-age population had left the area, leaving behind the very old and the very young; families of low income had been replaced by the abject, dependent poor. The social environment was increasingly characterized by extensive and varied criminal activity, by commonplace promiscuity and illegitimacy, by truancy among the school-age children, by gang activity among the youth, and by fear and insecurity among the elderly. And in the external community, public housing had come to be regarded with fear, with hatred, and with outrage—an antipathy extended without much discrimination to the buildings, their occupants, and the whole institution of public housing, symbolized, for most, as "Pruitt-Igoe."

Unfortunately, public housing policy as it developed in the 1930s was ambiguous with respect to both purposes and target population. The major concern built into the legislation had to do with the construction of housing and not the provision of housing-in-use, with the latent function of construction in eliminating slums and providing employment and not the satisfaction of the need for shelter.

The socioeconomic changes that disrupted the operation of public housing policy and thus contributed to the shambles of the 1970s are well known. Increasingly, the inner city was occupied by the poor, the black, the transient—a pattern reflected in public housing occupancy. Inner-city economic stagnation ... was the real key to the events of the fifties and sixties. Lack of adequate employment, particularly for the youth and the black population, increased outmigration of the able-bodied population of working age and left behind a community increasingly a prisoner of circumstances, unable to help itself in any significant way. Understandably, public housing ceased to be a way station on the road to a single-family dwelling, whether owned or rented, and became a permanent place of residence for a population that was essentially helpless and likely to remain so indefinitely.

In the production stage of public housing development, serious mistakes were made in all phases of the work: selection of sites, design of projects, and, of course, in construction. The projects were clustered together in the heart of deteriorated slum regions, without regard to the quality of the surrounding environment and its effect on the tenants, including such indirect effects as ready access to project grounds by inhabitants of the surrounding area. The sites were deficient in a number of important respects: access to work, shopping, transportation, and schools; area available for recreational and other facilities; lack of trees, grass, and shrubbery to break the monotony of the landscape and reduce the amount of loose dirt and grime in the projects. Design and construction were most grossly inadequate with respect to such factors as: (1) the number of apartments of different sizes actually constructed, and in particular the shortage of large units; (2) the amenities provided for the tenant, particularly the amount of living space in the apartments, elevator service in the high-rise buildings, kitchen equipment, ventilation, and playground areas for children; (3) the quality of the materials used in construction, particularly at the point of contact between tenant and building-doors and locks, windows, elevators, finishing materials, and so on; (4) the esthetic dimensions of the projects and buildings. Beyond such particulars, there is some question whether housing projects should be clustered or dispersed, how large any individual project should be, and what elevation the buildings should have.

Could those who framed program and policies have done more? That brings us to the second point relating to design and construction of public housing: Even if the economic interests involved are ignored, or if those with houses to sell or rent were compensated and those intending to invest in housing provided with alternative sources of profit, any serious effort to cope with the problem of need would almost certainly have foundered on the hard rock of public opposition—the underlying value system in the society would not have supported the effort. The fact is that American society has not yet come to grips with the question of public responsibility for the condition of life of the poor, the unfortunate, or the disadvantaged. If a study of need suggested that some elements of the population would have to be housed largely at public expense and more or less permanently, the sensible procedure to follow is to determine the most efficient form of public housing and build it. But if that housing, intended for the dependent poor, was significantly better in quality and available amenities than the housing which the working poor purchased in the private market, the latter would surely object, and given the social norms of the time, they would be right to do so.

Two aspects of the operation of public housing after design and construction were completed stand out as the major causes of project debilitation and failure: the fiscal arrangements created by Congress and the managerial control of operations exercised by national and local housing authorities. The fiscal policies imposed by the Congress in an effort to limit short-run costs and long-run responsibility were probably the most important single cause of the failure in conventional public housing. It was both humane and reasonable to link rental charges to the tenant's ability to pay rather than to the amount of space occupied or its location. It was not unreasonable to expect local housing authorities to operate their projects on the income obtained from rentals, leaving the federal government to pay capital costs as they came due. Imposing both requirements concurrently was an act of folly, given the known periodicity of the economic system.... [I]t is truistic in economics that increases in income for those at the bottom of the economic ladder do not keep pace with changes in income for the rest of society or with increases in costs. The logic of the fiscal policy that Congress adopted guarantees an income-cost squeeze for the local housing authority in any period in which wages and/or prices change rapidly, roughly in any period that is either inflationary or recessionary.

Inadequate managerial control over the operation of the housing program was characteristic of both national and local administrations, particularly in the post-1950 period.... [T]he national administration had too little control over the local authority; the system was too decentralized. The [HUD] regional office, for example, was unable to force compliance with requests to develop a regular maintenance program and an inventory of nonexpendable items of equipment despite frequent protests by the auditors. The weakness of managerial control over housing was augmented by the policy of depending mainly on traditional budget-audit procedures to control operations. That is, the major focus of concern down to the late 1960s tended to be the relation between actual and budgeted expenditures, the size of reserves, collection losses, and other fiscal matters.... To put the matter succinctly, though with due regard for exceptions, the public housing program operated from top to bottom as a fairly strict business enterprise with limited responsibilities toward its customers rather than a social service.

Notes and Questions

1. Analyze the above excerpt, and the evidence of program difficulty explored in the cases discussed in this section, in light of the material on subsidy need and policy in section A of this chapter. Can the problems be solved? Would it require legislative changes, administrative changes, or both? What program changes would you suggest?

2. Could a local housing network made up of representatives from the PHA, state and local officials, private developers, and nonprofit organizations solve the problem of an inadequate affordable housing supply? The 1990 Act, as a prerequisite to receipt of federal housing block grant funds, requires each jurisdiction to develop a five year housing strategy in conjunction with all interested parties and to review the strategy annually. 42 U.S.C. § 12705. The 1998 Act requires public housing agencies to engage in a similar five year and annual planning program. Pub. L. No. 105-276, § 511, 112 Stat. 2531 (1998). The planning requirements now are part of the Consolidated Plan requirement that is a prerequisite to receipt of federal community development block grants, as well as other federal housing and community development funds. Block grants and the Consolidated Plan requirement are discussed in Chapter 5 *infra*.

The 1998 Act also makes major changes in income eligibility targeting (reducing from 75 to 40% the number of dwelling units that must be made available to very-low-income families) and prohibits the concentrations of low income families in public housing. These changes must be reflected in the annual plans and accompanying admissions policies to bring "higher income tenants into lower income projects and lower income tenants into higher income projects." Pub. L. No. 105-276, § 513, 112 Stat. 2543 (1998) (*amending* 42 U.S.C. § 1437n).

3. Spectacular failures of high rise, urban public housing ghettos in the 1970s and 1980s raised serious questions about the future of public housing. But despite these failures, a national study of public housing emphasized that 94% of the approximately 1.4 million public housing units were providing "an important rental housing resource" for low-income families throughout the country. An estimated 86,000 units of "severely distressed" public housing generally were concentrated in the urban cores of large metropolitan areas. THE FINAL REPORT OF THE NATIONAL COMM'N ON SEVERELY DISTRESSED PUBLIC HOUSING 10–31 (1992).

D. Assisted Housing — Alternatives to Public Housing

Public housing changed after the Second World War from a place of temporary residence for working-class families laid low by the Depression to a place of permanent housing for low-income households. This change was occasioned by controversial site location and tenant selection policies discussed in Chapters 5 and 6 *infra*, as well as twin migration patterns from the rural South to the urban North, and from the city to the suburb. Seeking an alternative to the isolation and controversies of public housing, Congress and the U.S. Department of Housing and Urban Development ("HUD") which was created in 1965, experimented with a plethora of insurance and subsidy programs for privately-financed and privately-owned rental housing to serve households with incomes above the eligibility range for public housing, and later expanded to include persons with incomes low enough to be eligible for public housing. The most important of these programs, known primarily by National Housing Act section number, include 221(d)(3) (below market interest rate, insured mortgage), 236 (below market interest rate, insured mortgage), rent supplements (subsidized rental and insured mortgage), and Section 23 leased housing (sublet by PHA's at below-market rents to eligible households). For a variety of reasons, these programs proved unsatisfactory and were replaced in 1974 with the Section 8 rental assistance programs. Because of long term subsidy commitments made while the programs were active, they remain on the books. But no new commitments have been made since 1973. GENERAL ACCOUNTING OFFICE, FEDERAL HOUSING ASSISTANCE: COMPARING THE CHARACTERISTICS AND COSTS OF HOUSING PROGRAMS 73 (2002).

A key distinction between the federally assisted rental housing programs and public housing is that the landlord is a private person or corporation rather than a governmental entity. The federal-local PHA tension reviewed in section C of this chapter is mirrored by federal-private owner tension. Most of the programs involve supply-side subsidies in which housing need is met in-kind by a payment in the housing production system. The programs involve direct subsidies (typically an interest rate subsidy or a rent subsidy) and indirect subsidies (federal taxes forgone, mortgage insurance, and secondary mortgage market financing).

The original Section 8 new construction, substantial rehabilitation and moderate rehabilitation programs were combination supply- and demand-side programs. The subsidy went to the project owner in return for the owner's willingness to increase the supply of housing available to low-income households, but the amount of the subsidy was measured by the difference between an established market rent and what the low-income household could afford when paying no more than 30% of monthly income for housing expenses. Because of the severe budgetary impact of long term Section 8 commitments and a shift in policy to favor demand-side programs, no new commitments were made after 1983. *Id.* at 74. The current housing vouchers program is a demand subsidy, although the assistance payment is made to the landlord and not the tenant.

Comparison of the programs discussed with the formats of the Matrix, *supra*, will be helpful in delineating the subsidy, structure, and costs of the programs tenant and management issues in these programs are considered in Chapter 4 *infra*.

1. Program Descriptions—Section 8

The Section 8 Housing Assistance Payments (HAP) program was designed to accomplish a subsidy level comparable to that of public housing but available for privately financed, constructed, and owned housing. Direct subsidy payments are made to private landlords to make up the portion of the rent and utility costs that the tenant does not pay with 25% of income, later increased to 30%. The subsidy payment is based on tenant income. The Section 8 program is codified at 42 U.S.C. § 1437f. Extensive regulations to administer the program are promulgated periodically by HUD and published in 24 C.F.R. §§ 800 to 999.

As originally enacted in the Housing and Community Development Act of 1974, the Section 8 program had four subprograms: new construction, substantial rehabilitation, moderate rehabilitation, and existing housing. The new construction and substantial rehabilitation subprograms were repealed in 1983 and the moderate rehabilitation program was curtailed substantially because of Congressional concern over the costs of the subprograms. The subsidy payments in those programs are made by HUD to private landlords by means of housing assistance payments (HAP) contracts lasting from twenty to forty years. Thousands of units were built or rehabilitated under those programs, providing a critical housing resource for low-income households well into the 21st Century.

a. New Construction Program (repealed in 1983)

Although no new units have been built under this program since 1983, thousands of units were built in the program's nine year life and remain under contract. In addition, the basic parameters of the active Housing Choice Voucher program were established in the new construction program. Housing owners rent directly to low- or moderate-income tenants. The owner receives a contract rent that cannot exceed the HUD-established fair market rent for the area. The owner receives the contract rent in two parts. The tenant pays a rental charge, which includes an allowance for utilities, in an amount equal to the highest of 30% of monthly adjusted family income, 10% of such income, or housing cost portion of any welfare assistance the family may receive. The difference between the tenant payment and the contract rent is paid by HUD as the direct subsidy. The payment is made by HUD to the landlord under an agreement known as the Housing Assistance Payments Contract. 24 C.F.R. § 880.501.

A Section 8 new construction development can be 100% assisted. However, for family (non-elderly) developments in excess of fifty units, there is a statutory preference for buildings that are only 20% assisted. 42 U.S.C. § 1437f(c)(5). This preference is designed to achieve an economic mix in the housing development. An amendment in 1981 required developers to fulfill any commitments they may make to HUD regarding the number of units that will be assisted. Prior to that time, the only sanction for renting to a smaller number of low-income persons than originally committed was loss of the Section 8 subsidy. *See Price v. Pierce*, 823 F.2d 1114 (7th Cir. 1987) (applicants to Section 8 housing are not third-party beneficiaries of contracts between HUD and developers, distinguishing *Holbrook v. Pitt*, 643 F.2d 1261 (7th Cir. 1981) (Section 8 tenants are third-party beneficiaries).

The sponsor of a Section 8 new construction development planned and financed the building on a private basis. Although there was no construction or financing subsidy, the mortgages on Section 8 buildings could be insured under one of the HUD mortgage insurance programs, could be subsidized by use of the Tandem Plan, and could be financed through a state housing finance agency. In addition to private sponsors, PHAs could act as Section 8 developers and contract directly with HUD.

Tenant eligibility

The public housing admission procedure regulations and the lease and grievance procedure regulations are inapplicable to Section 8 new construction. The owner has sole management and operating responsibility, including tenant selection, eviction, and income verification and recertification. The owner must, however, have good cause for eviction and follow specified notice procedures. 42 U.S.C. § 1437(d)(1). HUD annually inspects units under Section 8 HAP contracts to insure that they are properly maintained. In addition, HUD requires periodic audits of the owner's financial records. 24 C.F.R. § 880.601(d). An owner of a Section 8 development can contract with a local housing authority for management and maintenance of the development. This is important because PHAs are one of the few entities in the housing sector which have experience in managing low-income housing.

Tenants are eligible if they are "lower income" (80% of the area median income as established by HUD). 42 U.S.C. §§ 1437a(b)(2), 1437f(a). As noted above, tenants pay the highest of 30% of monthly adjusted family income, 10% of such income, or the housing cost portion of any welfare assistance the family may receive. Adjusted income is determined by subtracting from the combined gross income of all family members statutorily established amounts to take into account minor children, elderly, disabled, handicapped, or full-time student members of the family, as well as a portion of medical and child care expenses. 42 U.S.C. § 1437a(b)(5).

Rental rates

The owner's construction cost, financing, and maintenance and operating budget yield a rental. This rental, if approved by HUD, becomes the contract rent for the Housing Assistance Payments contract. The upper limit on the contract rent is 10% above the fair market rent required by statute (20% if approved by HUD). 42 U.S.C. § 1437f(c)(1). HUD administratively establishes fair market rent (FMRs) for various size units and classes of construction and different housing market areas. The FMRs are revised annually and published in the Federal Register. Fair market rents are based on surveys of the comparable rents in the area for modest, non-luxury housing units. The fair market rents are trended for a two-year period to allow processing and construction time. Terms of new construction HAP contracts could range from twenty years for projects financed with HUD-insured mortgages to forty years for developments financed through state or local lending programs. The maximum term for projects without either type of financing was thirty years. 42 U.S.C. § 1437f(e)(3) (*repealed by* Pub. L. No. 98-181, § 209(a)(3), 97 Stat. 1183 (1983)).

The long term nature of the Section 8 subsidy and its relationship to market rents has produced a recurring controversy regarding the appropriate method for evaluating rental increase requests. The following case discusses the problem.

Cisneros v. Alpine Ridge Group

United States Supreme Court
508 U.S. 10 (1993)

JUSTICE WHITE delivered the opinion of the Court.

The question presented in this case is whether § 801 of the Department of Housing and Urban Development Reform Act of 1989, 103 Stat. 2057, violates the Due Process Clause of the Fifth Amendment by abrogating respondents' contract rights to certain rental subsidies.

I(A)

In 1974, Congress amended the United States Housing Act of 1937 (Housing Act) to create what is known as the Section 8 housing program. Through the Section 8 program, Congress hoped to "aid low-income families in obtaining a decent place to live," 42 U.S.C. § 1437f(a) (1988 ed., Supp. III), by subsidizing private landlords who would rent to low-income tenants. Under the program, tenants make rental payments based on their income and ability to pay; the Department of Housing and Urban Development (HUD) then makes "assistance payments" to the private landlords in an amount calculated to make up the difference between the tenant's contribution and a "contract rent" agreed upon by the landlord and HUD. As required by the statute, this contract rent is, in turn, to be based upon "the fair market rental" value of the dwelling, allowing for some modest increase over market rates to account for the additional expense of participating in the Section 8 program. *See* § 1437f(c)(1).

The statute, as originally enacted, further provided that monthly rents for Section 8 housing would be adjusted at least annually as follows:

> (A) The assistance contract shall provide for adjustment annually or more frequently in 'the maximum monthly rents for units covered by the contract to reflect changes in the fair market rentals established in the housing area for similar types and sizes of dwelling units or, if the Secretary determines the basis of a reasonable formula....
>
> (C) Adjustments in the maximum rents as hereinbefore provided shall not result in material differences between the rents charged for assisted and comparable unassisted units, as determined by the Secretary." 42 U.S.C. §§ 1437f(c)(2)(A) and (C) (1982 ed.).

The respondents in this case are private developers who entered into long-term contracts with HUD—known as Housing Assistance Payments (HAP) Contracts or "assistance contracts"—to lease newly constructed apartment units to Section 8 tenants. Their contracts established initial contract rents for each unit and provided, consistent with the statutory authorization, that these rents would be adjusted regularly, on the basis of a reasonable formula, to keep pace with changes in rental values in the private housing market....

In the early 1980's, HUD began to suspect that the assistance payments it was making to some landlords under the Section 8 program were well above prevailing market rates for comparable housing. Accordingly, the agency began to conduct independent "comparability studies" in certain real estate markets where it believed that contract rents, adjusted upward by the automatic adjustment factors, were materially out of line with market rents. Under these studies, HUD personnel would select between three and five other apartment buildings they considered comparable to the Section 8 building and compare their rents. The private market rents would then serve as an independent cap limiting the rent payments HUD would make under the Section 8 contracts.

After several landlords brought suit, the Court of Appeals for the Ninth Circuit ruled in 1988 that the standard assistance contracts described above prohibited the use of comparability studies as an independent cap on rents. In *Rainier View Associates v. United States*, 848 F.2d 988 [(9th Cir. 1988)—Eds.], the Court of Appeals reasoned that HUD, having contracted to increase rents automatically each year based upon a reasonable formula (the second of the two alternative approaches permitted by § 8(c)(2)(A) of the Housing Act, *see supra*), could not thereafter limit those increases by means of a market survey (the first of the two statutory alternatives). "Having made its choice," the court wrote, "HUD cannot now change its mind." 848 F.2d at 991.

After this Court denied certiorari to review the *Rainier View* decision, 490 U.S. 1066 (1989), HUD made clear its intention not to adhere to that decision's interpretation of its contracts outside the Ninth Circuit. Faced with the prospect of inconsistent application of Government contracts depending solely upon geography, Congress attempted to resolve the matter through amendments to the Housing Act in late 1989. Section 801 of the Department of Housing and Urban Development Reform Act (Reform Act), 103 Stat. 2057, amended § 8(c)(2)(C) of the Housing Act to provide explicitly that HUD may limit automatic rent adjustments in the future through the use of independent comparability studies. In an apparent compromise, however, the same section also sought to restore to Section 8 project owners a portion of the automatic rent adjustments they had been denied through the use of comparability studies prior to the enactment of the 1989 amendments. The amendments thus offered Section 8 project owners a partial retroactive remedy for lost rent attributable to comparability studies while at the same time affirming HUD's authorization to employ such studies to cap future rent adjustments....

In this litigation, respondents have alleged that § 801 of the Reform Act violates the Due Process Clause of the Fifth Amendment by stripping them of their vested rights under the assistance contracts to annual rent increases based on the automatic adjustment factors alone. In separate lawsuits, the United States District Courts for the Western District of Washington and the Central District of California each granted summary judgment for respondents. The Court of Appeals for the Ninth Circuit, in a consolidated appeal, affirmed both judgments. *Alpine Ridge Group* v. *Kemp*, 955 F.2d 1382 (1992). Refusing to reconsider its earlier holding in *Rainier View, supra*, the court first reaffirmed that the assistance contracts prohibited HUD from capping rents based on independent comparability studies. The court then held that Congress' attempt to authorize such caps through the Reform Act unconstitutionally deprived respondents of their "vested property interest in formula-based rent adjustments pursuant to their Section 8 contracts."

We granted certiorari, 506 U.S. 984 (1992), and now reverse.

II

We begin our analysis of respondents' due process claim with the assistance contracts. Because we find that those contracts do not prohibit the use of comparability studies to impose an independent cap on the formula-based rent adjustments, our analysis ends there as well. In our view, respondents' claimed entitlement to formula based rent adjustments without regard to independent comparisons to private-market rents is precluded by the plain language of the assistance contracts. To be sure, § 1.9b(2) of those contracts provides that the contract rents "shall be adjusted [annually] by applying the applicable Automatic Annual Adjustment Factor most recently published by the Government." Section 1.9d of the contracts, however, imposes what is labeled an "overall limitation" on the formula-based adjustments provided by § 1.9b. It provides that "notwithstanding any other provisions of this Contract, adjustments as provided in this Section shall not result in material differences between the rents charged for assisted and comparable unassisted units, as determined by the Government" (emphasis added). As we have noted previously in construing statutes, the use of such a "notwithstanding" clause clearly signals the drafter's intention that the provisions of the "notwithstanding" section override conflicting provisions of any other section.... Thus, we think it clear beyond peradventure that § 1.9d provides that contract rents "shall not" be adjusted so as to exceed materially the rents charged for "comparable unassisted units" on the private rental market—even if other provisions of the contracts might seem to require such a result. This limitation is plainly consistent with the Housing Act itself, which provides that "adjustments in the maximum rents," whether based on market surveys or on a reasonable formula, "shall not result in material differences" between Section 8 rents and the rents for comparable housing on the private market. 42 U.S.C. § 1437f(c)(2)(C) (1988 ed., Supp. III).

In its *Rainier View* decision, the Court of Appeals read § 1.9d's "overall limitation" as empowering HUD only to make prospective changes in the automatic adjustment factors where it discovered that those factors were producing materially inflated rents; under the court's view, § 1.9d would not permit "abandonment of the formula method whenever application of the formula would result in a disparity between Section 8 and other rents." 848 F.2d at 991. But this reading of the contract—under which Section 8 project owners could demand payment of materially inflated rents until the Secretary could publish revised automatic adjustment factors aimed at curing the overpayment—is almost precisely backwards. It would entitle project owners to collect the formula-based adjustments promised by § 1.9b notwithstanding that those adjustments were resulting in the sort of material differences in rents prohibited by § 1.9d.

Reading § 1.9d's "overall limitation" as allowing rent caps based on comparability studies does not, as the *Rainier View* court supposed, "render the formula method authorized by the statute and elected in the contract a nullity." *Ibid.* The rent adjustments indicated by the automatic adjustment factors remain the presumptive adjustment called for under the contract. It is only in those presumably exceptional cases where the Secretary has reason to suspect that the adjustment factors are resulting in materially inflated rents that a comparability study would ensue. Because the automatic adjustment factors are themselves geared to reflect trends in the local or regional housing market, theoretically it should not be often that the comparability studies would suggest material differences between Section 8 and private market rents.

Respondents assert that "the automatic adjustment provision was a central provision of the HAP Contracts and that the owners would not have signed contracts that expressly contained the [comparability] provision HUD asks the Court to imply." Brief for Respondents Acacia Village *et al.* 22. They urge us to eschew any interpretation of the contracts that would allow the displacement of the "automatic" adjustments for which they bargained by a "project-by-project comparability process" that "would leave [project owners] at the mercy of minor HUD officials." Brief for Respondent Alpine Ridge Group 30–31. At bottom, many of respondents' arguments in support of the decision below seem to circle back to their vigorous contention that HUD's comparability studies have been poorly conceived and executed, resulting in faulty and misleading comparisons. But the integrity with which the agency has carried out its comparability studies is an entirely separate matter from its contractual authority to employ such studies at all. Even if it could be demonstrated that HUD's studies have been unreliable, this would in no way suggest that the contract forbids HUD to cap rents based on accurate and fair comparability studies. If respondents have been denied formula-based rent increases based on shoddy comparisons, their remedy is to challenge the particular study, not to deny HUD's authority to make comparisons.

In sum, we think that the contract language is plain that no project owner may claim entitlement to formula based rent adjustments that materially exceed market rents for comparable units.... *Reversed.*

Notes and Questions

1. HUD's practice of using comparability studies remained controversial after *Alpine Ridge.* Could, for example, owners of Section 8 housing establish a property right to automatic rent increases under their HAP contracts that could not be capped as a result of comparability studies? Could owners prevent current rents from being reduced as a result of such studies? In *National Leased Housing Association v. United States*, 105 F.3d 1425 (Fed. Cir. 1997), the court answered both questions in the negative, stressing that the HAP contracts specifically authorize comparability studies and that the statute prohibits rents that are materially different from rents in unassisted units. Quoting *Alpine Ridge*, the court noted that plaintiff could challenge particular studies on the basis of poor quality.

2. In *Alpine Ridge*, the statute that was the source of the contractual relationship between the parties placed responsibility for determining whether rents were comparable on HUD. In 1994, Congress amended the statute to switch the burden concerning comparability of rents from HUD to the private owner by requiring the owner to "demonstrate that the adjusted rent would not exceed the rent for [a similar] unassisted unit...." Pub. L. No. 103-327, 108 Stat. 2298, 2315 (*amending* U.S.C. § 1437f(c) (2)(A)). To implement that shift, HUD required owners to engage a state-certified, general appraiser and submit at least three examples of comparable rents for unassisted housing at least 60 days prior to the HAP contract anniversary date as a condition to receipt of a rent adjustment. What impact does that shift in responsibility have on section 8 owners' contract rights? *See Statesman II Apartments, Inc. v. United States,* 66 Fed. Cl. 608, 620 (2005) (1994 amendments "abrogate[d] the provisions of the contracts regarding automatic annual adjustment of rents and ... breach[ed] the contracts").

3. In addition to the annual adjustment procedure construed in *Alpine Ridge*, HUD has statutory authority to grant special adjustments on applications by landlords. Special adjustments are to fund increases in taxes, utilities, or other charges not compensated by the annual adjustment. 42 U.S.C. § 1437f(c)(2)(B).

4. The importance of the subsidy to the feasibility of a newly-constructed or substantially-rehabilitated development was recognized in the statutory provision for vacancies. While Section 8 is intended to provide housing for low-income households, assistance payments may continue for a sixty day period when vacancies occur provided the owner is taking all necessary steps to fill the vacancy. 42 U.S.C. § 1437f(c)(4).

b. Existing Housing Program (Housing Choice Vouchers and Section 8 Certificates)

Federal regulations summarize the Section 8 tenant-based assistance programs as follows:

> (a) *General description.* (1) In the HUD Housing Choice Voucher Program (Voucher Program) and the HUD certificate program, HUD pays rental subsi-

dies so eligible families can afford decent, safe and sanitary housing. Both programs are generally administered by State or local governmental entities called public housing agencies (PHAs). HUD provides housing assistance funds to the PHA. HUD also provides funds for PHA administration of the programs. PHAs are no longer allowed to enter into contracts for assistance in the certificate program.

(2) Families select and rent units that meet program housing quality standards. If the PHA approves a family's unit and tenancy, the PHA contracts with the owner to make rent subsidy payments on behalf of the family. A PHA may not approve a tenancy unless the rents (*sic*) is reasonable.

(3) In the certificate program, the rental subsidy is generally based on the actual rent of a unit leased by the assisted family. In the voucher program, the rental subsidy is determined by a formula.

(4)(i) In the certificate program, the subsidy for most families is the difference between the rent and 30% of adjusted monthly income.

(ii) In the voucher program, the subsidy is based on a local "payment standard" that reflects the cost to lease a unit in the local housing market. If the rent is less than the payment standard, the family generally pays 30% of adjusted monthly income for rent. If the rent is more than the payment standard, the family pays a larger share of the rent.

(b) *Tenant-based and project-based assistance.* (1) Section 8 assistance may be "tenant-based" or "project-based." In project-based programs, rental assistance is paid for families who live in specific housing developments or units. With tenant-based assistance, the assisted unit is selected by the family. The family may rent a unit anywhere in the United States in the jurisdiction of a PHA that runs a voucher program.

(2) To receive tenant-based assistance, the family selects a suitable unit. After approving the tenancy, the PHA enters into a contract to make rental subsidy payments to the owner to subsidize occupancy by the family. The PHA contract with the owner only covers a single unit and a specific assisted family. If the family moves out of the leased unit, the contract with the owner terminates. The family may move to another unit with continued assistance so long as the family is complying with program requirements....

24 C. F. R. §982.1.

The Section 8 Housing Choice Voucher program is administered by public housing authorities that find and qualify tenants and pay the subsidy directly to landlords willing to lease units to Section 8-qualified tenants. 42 U.S.C. §1437f(b)(1). The subsidy payment from HUD to the PHA is financed through an Annual Contributions Contract, similar to the traditional public housing format. The PHA has substantial responsibility, including inspecting the dwelling units, advertising the availability of assistance, qualifying the tenants, approving the leases, and administering all aspects of the program. 24 C.F.R. §982.54. The Housing Choice Voucher program was created in 1998 by the merger of the original Section 8 certificate program, in which the certificate authorizing the subsidy payment was attached to an existing unit owned by a private landlord, and the voucher program created in 1983, in which the voucher authorizing the subsidy payment was held by a qualified household who then negotiated a lease with a private landlord. While the term of a Section 8 existing housing assistance (certificate) contract between the PHA and the landlord cannot exceed fifteen years. 42 U.S.C. § 1437f(d)(2), the term for housing choice voucher contracts typically is five years.

The basic parameters (tenant income limits and subsidy system) of the Section 8 existing housing program are the same as the new construction program. However, there is a separate set of fair market rents. The existing housing program is close to a cash subsidy since the payment is tied to the consumer to a greater extent than to the dwelling unit. The program starts with an eligible tenant rather than an eligible dwelling unit. However, the subsidy payment is still made to the landlord, rather than to the consumer.

Legislation enacted in October, 1998 establishes a single tenant-based rental assistance program with a uniform rent payment standard of between 90 and 110% of local fair market rents. Rent payment standards are established for each unit size (measured by number of bedrooms), and PHAs may choose "any level between 90 and 110%" without seeking HUD approval. 24 C.F.R. § 982.503(b). In exceptional cases, HUD may approve rent payment standards above 110% of local FMR when necessary to "prevent financial hardship for families, help families find housing outside areas of high poverty, or because voucher holders are having difficulty finding housing for lease under the terms of the voucher." 24 C.F.R. § 982.503(c)(2)&(3). Assistance is based on the difference between the rent charged and the tenant's statutory share (30% of monthly adjusted income, 10% of monthly income, or the housing portion of welfare payments). For rents exceeding the payment standard, tenant assistance is based on the difference between the payment standard and the tenant's statutory share, subject to the limitation that the family is not required to pay more than 40% of its monthly adjusted income for rent. Pub. L. No. 105-276, § 545, 112 Stat. 2596 (1998) (*amending* 42 U.S.C. § 1437f(o)).

Notes and Questions

1. Is the voucher program an improvement over the certificate program? While it gives voucher-holders more choice in locating housing, is the expansion in choice realistic, or is it likely to result in low-income families paying more for their housing than they can afford? Are choice and affordability in housing both achievable, or is one accomplished at the expense of the other? Vouchers have played a key role in the resolution of Fair Housing Act complaints against public housing authorities, discussed in Chapter 6 *infra*, and in the HOPE VI program, *infra*.

2. In response to the continuing national problem of substandard and abandoned structures in urban areas, Congress provided two rehabilitation programs within the Section 8 program. The substantial rehabilitation program is codified at 42 U.S.C. § 1437f(a); the regulations are at 24 C.F.R. §§ 881.101 to 881.709. The moderate rehabilitation program, added in 1978, is codified at 42 U.S.C. § 1437f(e)(5); the program regulations were added to the existing housing program regulations, 24 C.F.R. §§ 882.401 to 882.506.

The statutory provisions and regulations for the substantial rehabilitation program were similar to those of the new construction program. Although both the new construction and substantial rehabilitation programs were repealed in 1983, many units remain subsidized under twenty-, thirty- or forty-year annual contributions contracts authorized by those programs. HUD regulations define substantial rehabilitation to include gutting and extensive reconstructive, as well as cosmetic improvements if coupled with cure of substantial accumulation of deferred maintenance. 24 C.F.R. § 881.201.

The moderate rehabilitation program, which is administered by PHAs as part of the existing housing program, provides a subsidy to tenants in dwelling units which the owner agrees to upgrade to a decent, safe, and sanitary condition, in accordance with HUD standards, but which require less than substantial rehabilitation. Moderate rehabilitation is defined as rehabilitation involving a minimum expenditure of $1,000 per unit necessary to correct significant deficiencies, including repair or replacement of major building systems or components in danger of failure, but excluding routine maintenance. A building may be partially assisted, provided that the unassisted units do not adversely affect the assisted units.

The fair market rent limitation is set at 120% of the existing housing fair market rents, subject to an additional 20% increase in appropriate cases. However, the amount of the contract rent can be established based upon the amount of the rehabilitation expenditure and the term of the rehabilitation loan in order to enable the owner to amortize a short-term loan. In order to prevent owners from using the program to obtain financing and then withdrawing, the HAP (Housing Assistance Payment) contract is required to be for a fifteen-year term.

3. The Section 8 rehabilitation programs were attractive to owners because of the availability of an indirect subsidy contained in the Internal Revenue Code prior to the Tax Reform Act for 1986. Section 167(k), repealed in 1990 (Pub. L. No. 101-508, § 11812(a)(1), 104 Stat. 1388-1534 (1990)), provided that taxpayers could elect to compute depreciation on a straight-line basis over a period of five years for expenditures incurred in rehabilitating low-income rental housing. The maximum amount that could be depreciated was $20,000 per dwelling unit, and the improvements must have had a useful life of five or more years. The sum of rehabilitation expenditures for two consecutive tax years were required to exceed $3,000 per dwelling unit. The income test for tenant eligibility necessary for developments to qualify under Section 167(k) was 80% of area median income, the same as the Section 8 income limit. The rapid write-off provision applied only to rehabilitation expenditures. Other capital costs, such as the costs of acquiring the existing building, could be depreciated only in accordance with normal depreciation rules. *See* Janet Spragens, *The Rehabilitation of Low Income Rental Housing: A Look at the Section 167(k) Program and the Direct Subsidy Alternative*, 28 Case W. Res. L. Rev. 682 (1978); Michael Kohn, Comment, *Accelerated Depreciation: Rehabilitation of Low-Income Neighborhoods Through Appropriate Allocation of Capital Toward Obsolescence and Exhaustion*, 21 St. Louis U. L.J. 726 (1978). The rapid write-off of rehabilitation expenditures provision, along with numerous other tax preferences, was replaced in 1986 by the low-income housing tax credit, discussed in Section J *infra*.

4. It might be helpful to draw some comparisons between the Section 8 program and public housing. What is the relationship, if any, between the two programs? How do the obligations, responsibilities, and authority of HUD, the PHA, and the municipal government differ in the two programs? Are there significant differences in the role of private developers? What are the major differences in the subsidy policy and mechanisms in the two programs? Would a municipality prefer Section 8 over traditional public housing? Which program better serves tenants?

Identify the improvements in policy, program design, and procedures that Section 8 makes over public housing. What constraints or drawbacks in the public housing program are cured by Section 8? Which are not solved? What additional constraints does Section 8 involve?

5. For a review of Section 8 Housing programs, a short history behind these programs, and an exploration of the reasons behind the programs growth from serving 30,000 households in 1970 to serving 1.4 million in 2000, see U.S. Dep't of Hous. & Urb. Dev, Sec-

TION 8 TENANT-BASED HOUSING ASSISTANCE: A LOOK BACK AFTER 30 YEARS (2000) *available at* http://www.huduser.org/publications/pubasst/look.html.

Metro City Problem (cont.)

As adviser to Metro City Housing Authority in the problem, would you recommend the proposed plan with its retention of public housing units, or should the low-income portions of Grand Square and Laclede be recast entirely as Section 8 housing?

---

2. Program Participants and Relationships

Recipients of Housing Choice Vouchers receive something of great value to them—the wherewithal to obtain decent housing at a price they can afford. This becomes a property interest that receives procedural protections, as the following case illustrates. A more complete discussion of landlord and tenant relationships in Section 8-assisted developments is found in chapter 4 *infra.*

Basco v. Mach

United States Court of Appeals
514 F.3d 1177 (11th. Cir. 2008)

Barkett, Circuit Judge:

Teresa and Joseph Basco appeal from summary judgment granted in favor of Gil Machin, Director of Section 8 Housing of Hillsborough County, Florida, and Patricia G. Bean, Administrator of Hillsborough County, Florida, on their complaint asserting violations of due process pursuant to 42 U.S.C. § 1983 when their housing subsidy was terminated for the presence of an "unauthorized resident." We reverse.

Teresa Basco was a qualified participant in the Section 8 Program of her local public housing authority, the Health and Social Services Department of Hillsborough County, Florida ("PHA"). The PHA administers the Housing Choice Voucher rental-assistance program for the U.S. Department for Housing and Urban Development ("HUD"). That program provides monetary and rental assistance to lower-income families. As a Section 8 participant, Teresa Basco entered into a lease for a single-family residence in Tampa, Florida with her mother and landlord, Donna VanDerLaan. In the lease, Ms. Basco indicated that only she, her husband, and five minor children would reside in the assisted unit. The PHA and VanDerLaan entered into a Housing Assistance Payments Contract ("HAP Contract"), which provided that the PHA would pay a specific amount each month to VanDerLaan on behalf of Ms. Basco. The HAP Contract restricted the residents of the assisted unit to those listed in the lease. In connection with receiving Section 8 assistance, Ms. Basco signed a form acknowledging that her benefits could be terminated for any violation of the terms of the HAP Contract, including allowing disturbances at her unit and failing to notify the PHA of any changes in family composition.

HUD regulations prohibit the presence of an unauthorized resident in assisted units, but do not prohibit a participant from having house guests. *See* 24 C.F.R. § 982.551(h)(2). At the relevant time, the PHA interpreted these regulations in its Administrative Plan for the 2004–2005 period by establishing particular rules regarding visitors:

> Any person not included on the HUD 50058 who has been in the unit more than 15 consecutive days without PHA approval, or a total of 30 days in a 12 month period, will be considered to be living in the unit as an unauthorized household member.
>
> Absence of evidence of any other address will be considered verification that the visitor is a member of the household.
>
> Statements from neighbors and/or the landlord will be considered in making the determination.
>
> Use of the unit address as the visitor's current residence for any purpose that is not explicitly temporary shall be construed as permanent residence.
>
> The burden of proof that the individual is a visitor rests on the family. In the absence of such proof the individual will be considered an unauthorized member of the household and the PHA will terminate assistance since prior approval was not requested for the addition.

In November 2005, an anonymous person who identified himself as a neighbor of Ms. Basco telephoned the PHA to provide information regarding disturbances at Ms. Basco's assisted unit, multiple police calls to the unit, and the arrest of a member of Ms. Basco's household. The PHA assigned the matter to Section 8 Housing Counselor Sarah J. Matalon, who obtained from the Tampa Police Department copies of two police reports involving Ms. Basco's assisted unit.

The first report, dated February 28, 2005, stated that Joseph Basco gave a sworn statement to the police indicating that his stepdaughter had run away with a man named "Emanuel Jones," "who's staying at the house." The alleged sworn statement was not contained in or attached to the report. The February report further noted that Mr. Basco said he called Emanuel's stepfather to come and collect Emanuel's belongings. The report noted that Emanuel's address was the same as that of Ms. Basco's unit. The second report, dated July 18, 2005, listed "Elonzel Jones" as an eyewitness to an alleged battery on Mr. Basco by his stepdaughter, and listed Elonzel's address as that of the assisted unit.

Based on these two police reports, Section 8 Senior Housing Counselor Sherry Hanson sent Ms. Basco a Notice of Intent to Terminate along with copies of the reports. The termination notice advised Ms. Basco that the PHA intended to terminate her housing assistance based the presence of on an unauthorized resident in her unit in violation of 24 C.F.R. §§ 982.551 and .516. Although not expressly stated, the implication from the notice was that the PHA believed that Elonzel Jones and Emanuel Jones were the same person; that "Jones" had been living in Ms. Basco's assisted unit between February and July 2005; that this totaled more than fifteen days; and that Jones was therefore an "unauthorized resident." Indeed, in its brief on appeal, the PHA avers that the police reports "reflected Jones' address over a five month period."

In response to the termination notice, Ms. Basco requested a hearing. Section 8 participants are entitled to a "pretermination [of benefits] hearing" before an impartial Hearing Officer who is appointed by the Tampa Housing Authority, an entity distinct from the PHA. The PHA sent Ms. Basco a letter scheduling the hearing and advising her of her rights and also provided her with copies of the February and July police reports.

At the hearing and on behalf of the PHA, Matalon presented, as the only evidence, copies of the February and July police reports she had obtained. In her defense, both Ms. Basco and her landlord testified that Jones did not live at the assisted unit. Ms. Basco also submitted a December 7, 2005 notarized letter from Jones's mother stating that Jones had only ever lived at two addresses, neither of which was Ms. Basco's. To rebut the alleged statement by Mr. Basco contained in the February 2005 police report, Ms. Basco asked to have her husband directly testify by telephone.[5] The Hearing Officer denied the request and upheld the PHA's decision to terminate Ms. Basco's benefits, stating:

> Mrs. Basco could not provide information regarding [the] unauthorized resident. Mr. Basco gave a statement to police that states that Mr. Jones stay [sic] in assist [sic] unit. Landlord who is also Mrs. Basco [sic] mother became upset and demand [sic] extra time to gather more information (records on Mr. Jones). Her request were [sic] denied. Decision is upheld.

The Bascos twice sought to have the Hearing Officer's decision overturned. They met with Gil Machin, the Acting Operations Manager of the PHA, and presented new evidence, including a January 10, 2006 notarized letter from Jones stating that he had only lived with his grandmother and mother, and that he had never lived in Ms. Basco's unit. After reviewing the new evidence, Machin concluded that there was not a sufficient basis under HUD regulations to overturn the Hearing Officer's decision or to provide Ms. Basco with a new hearing. The Bascos also retained a legal services attorney, who again requested that Machin reject the decision of the Hearing Officer. After reviewing the file a second time, Machin again denied the request. In a letter to the Bascos' attorney, Machin cited the PHA's Administrative Plan provision stating that "[t]he burden of proof that the individual is a visitor rests on the family. In the absence of such proof the individual will be considered an unauthorized member of the household and the PHA will terminate assistance...."

The Bascos then filed this suit, alleging deprivations of their right to procedural due process under 24 C.F.R. § 982.555(e)(5) and (6), and 42 U.S.C. § 1983. In particular, the Bascos asserted that the PHA denied them the opportunity to confront and cross-examine witnesses against them, and improperly placed the burden of proof on them rather than on the PHA, which sought to terminate their housing assistance.

The district court granted summary judgment in favor of the PHA, finding no violation of due process. We review the district court's grant of summary judgment *de novo*, applying the same legal standards as the district court.

II. DISCUSSION

The Bascos ask us to resolve two issues in appealing the district court's grant of summary judgment. We must first decide if the PHA or the Section 8 participant bears the burden of persuasion[6] in an administrative hearing held under HUD regulations to determine whether a participant's housing subsidy should be terminated. If the PHA bears that burden, we must then decide whether due process allows the burden to be met in this case by Matalon's submission of copies of the police reports.

---

5. According to the Bascos, Mr. Basco was unable to attend the hearing because he had to care for the couple's disabled son at home.

6. A brief cautionary note on our terminology is warranted. The Supreme Court has recognized that the phrase "burden of proof" has a history of ambiguous usage despite the now-apparent consensus that it refers only to the burden of persuasion, and not to *both* the burdens of persuasion and production. *Dir., Office of Workers' Comp. Programs v. Greenwich Collieries,* 512 U.S. 267, 272–76 (1994).

In this case, the PHA's Administrative Plan uses the phrase "burden of proof." To prevent confusion, we limit our use of that phrase to references to the Administrative Plan and otherwise refer to the "burden of persuasion."

HUD regulations establish the substantive rights at issue and the basic procedures to be followed in an informal Section 8 termination hearing, but do not expressly address which party bears the burden of persuasion at such a hearing.... However, contrary to Machin's declaration that the "burden of proof that the individual is a visitor rests on the family," and as the PHA conceded at oral argument, the PHA has the burden of persuasion and must initially present sufficient evidence to establish a prima facie case that an unauthorized individual "has been in the unit more than 15 consecutive days without PHA approval, or a total of 30 days in a 12 month period." Thereafter, the Section 8 participant has the burden of production to show "that the individual is a visitor."[7]

Thus, the question here is whether the Hearing Officer's determination that the PHA met its burden of persuasion through Matalon's submission of the unauthenticated copies of the two police reports comports with due process.

Although the rules of evidence are not strictly applied in administrative hearings, there are due process limits on the extent to which an adverse administrative determination may be based on hearsay evidence. As was held in *U.S. Pipe and Foundry Company v. Webb,* "hearsay may constitute substantial evidence in administrative proceedings as long as factors that assure the 'underlying reliability and probative value' of the evidence are present." 595 F.2d 264, 270 (5th Cir. 1979). The reliability and probative force of such evidence depend on "whether (1) the out-of-court declarant was not biased and had no interest in the result of the case; (2) the opposing party could have obtained the information contained in the hearsay before the hearing and could have subpoenaed the declarant; (3) the information was not inconsistent on its face; and (4) the information has been recognized by courts as inherently reliable." *J.A.M. Builders, Inc. v. Herman,* 233 F.3d 1350, 1354 (11th Cir. 2000) (citing *U.S. Pipe & Foundry Co.,* 595 F.2d at 270 (citing *Richardson v. Perales,* 402 U.S. 389, 402–06 (1971)).

In *Perales,* the Court examined the admissibility of physicians' reports in a social security disability claim hearing and found that the reports were admissible despite their hearsay character and "may constitute substantial evidence supportive of a finding by the hearing examiner adverse to the claimant." The dispute in *Perales* involved the physicians' diagnoses and medical conclusions, and the parties did not contest or dispute the underlying facts in the reports. The *Perales* court was careful to note that it was applying a lesser standard than would apply to the consideration of hearsay in hearings initiated to terminate benefits, where the concerns of *Goldberg* might attach:

The Perales proceeding is not the same. We are not concerned with *termination* of disability benefits once granted. Neither are we concerned with a change of status without notice. Notice was given to claimant Perales. The physicians' reports were on file and available for inspection by the claimant and his counsel. And the authors of those reports

7. This reading of the Administrative Plan is consistent with *Goldberg v. Kelly,* wherein the Supreme Court held that the Due Process Clause of the U.S. Constitution requires that welfare recipients be afforded an evidentiary hearing with minimum procedural safeguards before their benefits may be terminated. 397 U.S. 254, 266 (1970). The Supreme Court reasoned that the interests of the recipient in the uninterrupted provision of benefits and of the State in not wrongly terminating benefits outweighed the State's competing interest in summary adjudication. This reasoning applies with equal force to public housing assistance provided pursuant to Section 8, where eligible participants rely on subsidies to meet their basic need for housing. *See Davis v. Mansfield Metro. Hous. Auth.,* 751 F.2d 180, 185 (6th Cir. 1984); *Escalera v. N.Y. City Hous. Auth.,* 425 F.2d 853, 861 (2d Cir. 1970); *see also Goldberg,* 397 U.S. at 262 ("Relevant constitutional restraints apply as much to the withdrawal of public assistance benefits as to disqualification for unemployment compensation; or to denial of a tax exemption; or to discharge from public employment").

were known and were *subject to subpoena and to the very cross-examination* that the claimant asserts he has not enjoyed. Further, the specter of questionable credibility and veracity is not present; there is professional disagreement with the medical conclusions, to be sure, but there is no attack here upon the doctors' credibility or veracity. [*Goldberg v.*] *Kelly* affords little comfort to the claimant. Ultimately, the Court rested its holding on its analysis of the four factors that we later enumerated in *J.A.M. Builders, supra* at 402–06.

Initially, we need not consider the description, in the first police report, of Mr. Basco's alleged written statement.... The statement was not attached to the police report, and although it is not hearsay, *see* Fed. R. Evid. 801(d)(2)(A), it is insufficient alone to establish that Jones was an unauthorized resident. It merely establishes that Jones stayed with the Bascos, but it does not speak to the length of his stay, which, according to the PHA's Administrative Plan, must be at least fifteen consecutive days or thirty days in a twelve-month period in order for Jones to be an unauthorized resident....

Therefore, we consider only the police reports as to the statements allegedly made to the police officers by Emanuel and Elonzel. The primary *J.A.M. Builders* factor that counsels against basing an adverse administrative determination on those hearsay statements is the second factor, as the Bascos could not subpoena the officers, Emanuel, or Elonzel for cross-examination. However, we need not decide whether that deficiency renders the Hearing Officer's reliance on the reports and the statements described therein a violation of due process. Even assuming arguendo that the reports and statements were properly admitted, they do not establish that Emanuel and Elonzel are the same individual and therefore, as with Mr. Basco's alleged statement, do not speak to the length of the stay at the Bascos' residence. Although the PHA argues that the two individuals are one and the same, absolutely no evidence substantiates that claim. Therefore, the police reports presented by the PHA were legally insufficient to establish a prima facie case that either Emanuel or Elonzel had resided at the Bascos' residence for fifteen consecutive days or for thirty days in a twelve-month period.

III. CONCLUSION

We conclude that the PHA bears the burden of persuasion at an informal administrative hearing held pursuant to HUD regulations to determine whether a Section 8 participant's housing subsidy should be terminated. For the reasons expressed above, we further find that the Hearing Officer erred in this case in relying upon legally insufficient evidence to terminate Ms. Basco's Section 8 assistance. Accordingly, we REVERSE the district court's grant of summary judgment, and REMAND for further proceedings consistent with this opinion....

Notes and Questions

1. What does *Basco* have to say about the complexities of the Section 8 Housing Choice Voucher program? In their zeal to guard the public purse, have Congress and HUD devised a program that requires low-income families to jump through too many hoops in order to receive housing benefits? How realistic is it to expect families who may be in desperate financial and social straits to find suitable housing and landlords who will rent to them in the relatively short time allowed after receipt of a Housing Choice Voucher?

2. What purpose is served by terminating a household's Housing Choice Voucher for rule violations such as occurred in *Basco*? Would eviction from the unit be a sufficient sanction, or would that allow voucher recipients to continue to flout the rules by moving from apartment to apartment.

3. Preservation of Assisted Rental Housing

Federal housing policy directed toward the private sector is a blend of direct and indirect subsidies on both the supply and demand sides, none of which are designed to be permanent. Once the subsidies end, private owners who have depended on the subsidies face the choice of raising rents to fill gaps in their budgets left by the departure of the subsidies, or trying to find buyers for their developments. Either way, low-income tenants who cannot afford higher rents face the loss of affordable housing when the subsidies end. This lack of permanency creates a continuing need to consider mechanisms for preserving the inventory of affordable housing that has been developed by the private sector.

For a variety of reasons, the maximum terms for the various subsidies are not the same, e.g., twenty to forty-year federally-insured mortgages, five to twenty-year Section 8 contracts, and ten to fifteen-year tax credit recapture periods, discussed *infra*. As subsidized housing built by the private sector in the 1960s, 1970s and 1980s matured and the tax shelter potential of such developments was exhausted (usually somewhere between the eighth and sixteenth year), owners began to consider prepaying thirty-and forty-year mortgages. Such prepayment generally was permitted after fifteen to twenty years, at which point rent supplement or Section 8 subsidies would cease and the owner would have no legal obligation to retain the low-income character of the development. Similar problems arose with respect to Low Income Housing Tax Credit-supported developments, discussed *infra*, as well as privately owned, federally subsidized developments acquired by HUD upon default of the owners. *See, e.g., Cowherd v. Department of Hous & Urb. Dev.*, 827 F.2d 40 (7th Cir. 1987) (sale by HUD of foreclosed project without attaching rental subsidies was rational). For background on the prepayment problem, see Report By The National Low Income Housing Preservation Committee: Preventing The Disappearance of Low-Income Housing, *in Hearing before the Subcommittee on Housing and Community Development of the House Committee on Banking, Finance and Urban Affairs*, 100th Cong., 2d Sess. 78-120 (1988).

The "Mark to Market" Preservation Strategy

Fearing a loss of substantial numbers of housing units for low-income families through authorized prepayments, Congress began in 1987 a ten year effort to craft what is known as a "mark to market rents" low-income housing preservation program. The effort began with the Emergency Low-Income Housing Preservation Act of 1987 (ELIPHA), Pub. L. No. 100-242, §§201–03, 221–30, 232–35, 101 Stat. 1877–1886 (1988), that amounted to a two year moratorium on prepayments, followed by the Low-Income Housing Preservation and Resident Homeownership Act of 1990 (LIHPRHA), Pub. L. No. 101-625, 104 Stat. 4249 (*codified at* 12 U.S.C. §§4101–25), which established a three-part strategy for preserving section 221(d)(3) and section 236 developments as affordable housing: 1) encourage owners to remain in the 221(d)(3) and 236 programs in return for additional subsidies and financial incentives, 2) sell to a not-for-profit organization or other "qualified" buyer who agrees to keep the development in the affordable housing program, or 3) prepay upon meeting what many owners believed were onerous restrictions. Howard Cohen & Taylor Mattis, *Prepayment Rights: Abrogation by the Low Income Housing Preservation and Resident Homeownership Act of 1990*, 28 Real Prop. Prob. & Tr. J. 1 (1993). For an argument that the sale option to non-profits created "an extraordinary opportunity to achieve community control of affordable housing," see David Etezadi & Peter Manzo, *LIHPRA: Great Opportunity for Community Control*, 4 J. Affordable Housing & Community Dev. L. 67, 82 (1994–95). A more general limitation, which requires

HUD to find that a relocation plan is in effect before it can approve prepayment is codified at 12 U.S.C. § 1715z-15.

Over the next several years, Congress and HUD tinkered with a variety of approaches as the expiration date for hundreds of thousands of twenty-year Section 8 certificates approached. Adding to the sense of urgency was an increasing controversy in many communities over the fact that Section 8 rents had become much larger than comparable rents for unsubsidized housing units. If the contracts were renewed at the same rents, the controversy would increase in intensity. If the contracts were allowed to expire, the mortgages likely would go into default and the future of the units as housing for low-income families would become very much in doubt.

Multifamily Assisted Housing Reform and Affordability Act of 1997 (MAHRA)

In 1997 Congress enacted a permanent program, the Multifamily Assisted Housing Reform and Affordability Act of 1997 (MAHRA), Pub. L. No. 105-65, §§ 511–524, 111 Stat. 1385-1409 (*codified at* 42 U.S.C. § 1437f note), to restructure FHA-insured mortgages with Section 8 contracts to enable the mortgages to be amortized at market rents and the Section 8 contracts to be renewed at rents more in line with prevailing rents where the developments are located. In the legislative findings accompanying MAHRA, Congress estimated that the FHA insured multifamily housing portfolio consisted of 14,000 rental properties with an aggregate unpaid principal mortgage balance of $38 billion, with 10,000 of these properties receiving Section 8 project-based assistance. An estimated 2 million families lived in the 14,000 rental properties, 1.6 million of whom were in the Section 8-assisted units.

The restructuring is administered by participating administrative entities (PAEs), which may be state housing finance agencies, discussed *infra*, local housing agencies, and private entities in partnership with public purpose entities including HUD. The HUD Office of Multifamily Housing Assistance Restructuring (OMHAR) has overall supervisory responsibility.

MAHRA's basic restructuring strategy provides tools to refinance outstanding Section 8-supported notes and mortgages with two new notes and mortgages, a smaller first mortgage that can be amortized with rental payments approximating local prevailing rents, and a "soft" second mortgage for the remaining principle balance of the original note and mortgage. The second mortgage term is equal to that of the new first mortgage. Payments are deferred while the first mortgage is outstanding, unless the restructured project generates "excess project income" (profit), which is split 75–25% between payments on the second mortgage and payments to the project owner. The second note and mortgage may be forgiven if the project is acquired by "a tenant organization or a tenant-endorsed community-based nonprofit or public agency." MAHRA, §§ 514(g) (rent levels) and 517(a) (mortgage restructuring). A key element in the preservation strategy is the requirement that any restructuring plan include a "legally enforceable" promise by the owner to maintain affordability and use restrictions for an additional 30 years which is recorded in the public land records. MAHRA, § 514(e)(6). *See* Charles L. Edson, *HUD's Interim Mark to Market Regulations: A Work in Progress,* 8 J. Affordable Housing & Community Dev. L. 15, 15–23, 25 (1998) (discussing HUD's initial regulations implementing the restructuring program):

Tax Aspects of Restructuring

> A major concern with mark to market is that splitting the debt into a performing first mortgage and a non-performing second mortgage might cause the owner to be taxed on cancellation of indebtedness income in the amount of a second mortgage. One cause of such cancellation of indebtedness income is the fact

> that the second mortgage would be at a nominal interest rate, thus activating the Original Issue Discount (OID) rules. Under these rules, a below-interest debt, is reconfigured with a lower principal amount and a higher amount attributed to interest. Accordingly, the total debt after restructuring would be less than the pre-restructured debt, resulting in forgiveness of indebtedness income.
>
> Under Revenue Ruling 98-34, the Internal Revenue Service has held that the soft second in the case of a Section 8 mortgage restructuring would not produce Original Issue Discount. IRS ruled that such second mortgages fall under an exemption in IRS regulation Section 1.7872-5T(b)(5), exempting government-funded loans which are made available under a program of general applicability. The IRS held that MAHRAA was such a generally applicable program.
>
> The ruling did not address another crucial question as to whether the second mortgage is really debt that could reasonably be expected to be repaid. This is a fact and circumstances test that varies from project to project. However, as above noted MAHRAA limits the second mortgage to the amount likely to be repaid, which would be a positive factor in defending against any IRS challenge.
>
> Because the ruling was limited to the treatment of below market second mortgages under Section 7872, it did not address the applicability of Section 1274, which deals with debt issued for property. This might seem to be the case when a HUD-held loan is involved.
>
> Although the Revenue Ruling does not answer all of the questions, if provides a great impetus to the program in that it eliminates one significant tax issue.

Id. at 23. A HUD-financed study, RICHARD HILTON ET AL., EVALUATION OF THE MARK-TO-MARKET PROGRAM (2004), concluded that the mark-to-market ("M2M") process was effective in preserving affordable housing and that the retention of Section 8 subsidies, plus rehabilitation support that resulted in property improvements, provided substantial benefits to tenants in M2M-restricted developments. But the study also found that "direct tenant involvement in the process has been minimal." In one case cited, only 10 tenants came to a meeting that had been publicized extensively with flyers containing language that "was clear, precise, and free of jargon." And the study authors concluded that the M2M process was "ill-suited to address cases where key community stakeholders, including elected officials, oppose preservation of an affordable multifamily property," primarily because the statute and regulations did not address the question of who should take the lead in attempting to negotiate compromise solutions in such cases. The MAHRAA program has been extended through 2011.

Notes and Questions

1. The HUD study called attention to the difficulty of accomplishing a Section 8 project restructuring when "key community stakeholders" oppose retention of the low-income character of the development. In such circumstances, can neighboring residents and property owners, who have a statutory right to "participate effectively and on a timely basis in the restructuring process," MAHRA, § 514(f), effectively veto a restructuring plan that provides for demolition of a multi-family development and dispersal of Section 8 properties to other neighborhoods? *See Neighborhood Research Inst. v. Campus Partners,* 212 F.R.D. 364, 371–373 (S.D. Ohio 2002) (no express or implied private right of action exists under MAHRA). *See also Baker v. Property Investors of Connecticut,* 338 F. Supp 321 (D. Conn. 2004) (current and former Section 8 tenants' allegations that HUD's and pro-

ject owner's delay in making timely decisions regarding Section 8 restructuring proposal caused them "severe anxiety, emotional distress, and humiliation" did not rise to the required "injury in fact" for standing because no tenants were evicted or became homelessness as a result of the delays).

2. To what extent should owners of subsidized housing be required to retain the low-income character of their housing? Can and should they be required to retain that character after the original section 8 contracts expire but tenants continue to receive subsidies through the "enhanced" voucher program, 42 U.S.C. § 1437f(t), which is designed to cover increases in rent to "keep the tenants' portion of the rent stable at the pre-expiration rate." *People to End Homelessness, Inc. v. Develco Singles*, 339 F.3d 1, 3 (1st Cir. 2003). *See Feemster v. BSA Ltd. Partnership,* 548 F.3d 1063, 1069 (D.C. Cir. 2008) (lessor opting out of Section 8 assistance program following expiration of Housing Assistance Payments contract "may not ... refuse to accept payment by voucher and then contend that eviction is warranted for non payment of rent"). In *People to End Homelessness,* the court held that a non-profit organization seeking to preserve and expand housing for low-income households did not have standing to challenge the expiration of Section 8 contracts, even though HUD admittedly had failed to require the development owners to give the required one year notice of intention to terminate Section 8 contracts. The court concluded that the statutory remedy for breach of the notice requirements, a prohibition against eviction or rental increase until the proper notice is given, precluded the organization's action against HUD, and addressed any injury that may have been suffered by the non-profit organization.

3. If property is to be acquired by nonprofits, how should the sale price be established—what the market will bear? Appraised value? Owner's equity investment? Owner's exit taxes? Appraised value less some portion of the value of the subsidies received? *See* Michael Freedman, Comment, *In Search of Congressional Intent: Does LIHPRHA Restrict State and Local Governments from Preserving Affordable Housing?* 13 J. L. & Pol'y 741, 799–804 (2005) (recommending that state and local governments interested in preserving their privately owned, federally subsidized affordable housing enact preservation laws, such as the Illinois Assisted Housing Preservation Act, 310 Ill. Comp. Stat. 60/1–60/10.1, that enable and assist the transfer of such properties to non-speculative preservation owners, such as a tenant association, following the current owners' opting-out of federal affordable housing programs). Under the Illinois statute, if a tenant association desires to purchase a federally subsidized affordable housing development, it must present a "bona fide" offer to purchase within 90 days of giving notice of such intent to the owner. If the owner and the tenant association cannot agree on a price within 60 days of the notice of intent to purchase, the price is based on the property's "fair market value, based on its highest and best use, without affordability restrictions" as determined by a team of qualified appraisers, one selected by each party. If no agreement is reached then, the parties can jointly hire a third appraiser or agree to accept an average of the two appraisals. 310 Ill. Comp. Stat. 60/7. The student comment also discusses two conflicting circuit decisions, *Topa Equities, Ltd. v. City of Los Angeles,* 342 F.3d 1065 (9th Cir. 2003) (city's rent control ordinance, which prevented rent increases until existing tenancies were terminated, was not preempted by LIHPRHA) and *Forest Park II v. Hadley,* 336 F.3d 724 (8th Cir. 2003) (Minnesota statute imposing one-year notice requirement and other requirements in excess of federal requirements were expressly preempted by LIHPRHA). Expanding roles for not-for-profit housing corporations, and the potential tax consequences of such roles, are discussed *infra.*

4. The rent and renewal rules differ in the case of "exception" projects. Exception projects are those projects conventionally financed, financed by state or local tax-exempt

bonds, Section 202 or Section 515 projects, McKinney-Vento Homeless Assistance Act projects (discussed further in this Chapter in Section I *infra*), as well as those projects with rent above fair market rents but below comparable rents. In such cases, renewal would be on a project basis at the lesser of the existing rents adjusted by an operating cost adjustment factor or rents established on a budget basis with a budget-based rent adjustment if justified by increased operating expenses. In the case of moderate rehabilitation projects (except for McKinney-Vento Act projects), the rents would be the base rent adjusted by an OCAF [operating cost adjustment factor—Eds.]. Unlike restructured projects, exception projects would not have to accept renewal offers on a thirty-year basis. For discussion of renewal of expiring contracts for "exception" projects, see Charles L. Edson, *HUD's Interim Mark to Market Regulations: A Work in Progress*, 8 J. Affordable Housing & Community Dev. L. 15, 25 (1998).

E. Program Transformation: HOPE VI and Transformation of Rental Assistance

As illustrated by the Metro City problem at the beginning of this chapter, a major change in the focus of public housing authorities in urban centers was introduced following the 1992 study of severely distressed public housing. Beginning in 1993 as the Urban Revitalization Demonstration Program, 42 U.S.C. § 14371, a competitive grant program offered federal funds to public housing authorities owning severely distressed public housing units to enable them to transform those projects into more livable mixed-income neighborhoods. The program became known as HOPE VI (the acronym, HOPE, stands for Homeownership and Opportunity for People Everywhere, first introduced in the Cranston-Gonzalez National Affordable Housing Act of 1990, 42 U.S.C. § 12701 & ff, as a home ownership program). On the strength of a HUD General Counsel's opinion that nothing in the 1937 Housing Act prohibits private ownership of public housing so long as the units are occupied by public housing-eligible families, HUD promulgated a rule providing detailed regulatory guidance for local public housing authorities who wish to establish public-private partnerships for mixed income developments. 24 C.F.R. § 941.600. An interim rule, promulgated in 1997, is discussed in Paul Casey, *Real HOPE at HUD*, 7 J. Affordable Housing & Community Dev. L. 18 (1997).

Comprehensive housing legislation in 1998 established HOPE VI as a regular HUD program. The legislation authorized public housing authorities to "own, operate, assist, or otherwise participate in" mixed-finance projects, 42 U.S.C. § 1437z-7, and authorized HUD to provide grants to public housing authorities to enable them to participate in such developments in order to recast severely distressed urban public housing projects as mixed-income developments., 42 U.S.C. § 1437v. HOPE VI projects are public-private partnerships between public housing authorities and private developers. A typical HOPE VI development replaces concentrated, and isolated, usually high-rise, public housing units with mixed-income developments in which the units are allocated among three groups of families, those qualifying for traditional public housing, those qualifying for low-income housing tax credit (LIHTC) units (discussed *infra*), and those able to afford market rate rents.

The HOPE VI program is a competitive grant program. Any public housing authority owning severely distressed housing units is eligible to apply. Funds may be used for demolition, rehabilitation, reconfiguration, or replacement of obsolete public housing developments, revitalization of public housing sites and surrounding neighborhoods, development of housing to avoid or decrease concentration of very low-income families, and for the development of sustainable communities. The competitive nature of the program is illustrated by the 2009 Notice of Funding Availability announcing that $113 million was available and that HUD anticipated making only five or six grant awards, with a maximum grant of $22 million. HUD's Fiscal Year (FY) 2009 NOFA for the HOPE VI Revitalization Grants Program, FR-5300-N-23 (July 14, 2009), *available at* Grants.gov website. Selection criteria include the extent to which the grant will result in a revitalized site that will enhance the neighborhood, the capability of the applicant to manage large-scale redevelopment, and the extent of involvement of residents, State and local governments and private service providers, financing entities and developers in the revitalization process. 42 U.S.C. § 1437v. A 2003 amendment added a smaller grant program ($1,000,000 or less) for "Main Street" projects in smaller communities (50,000 population or under) to support affordable housing as a part of the revitalization or redevelopment of historic or traditional commercial areas. 42 U.S.C. § 1437v(n); BARRY G. JACOBS, HDR HANDBOOK OF HOUSING AND DEVELOPMENT LAW 109 (2008–2009).

HOPE VI projects make use of a variety of subsidy techniques discussed in this chapter, including mortgage insurance, direct capital grants, tax credits and deductions, state housing bonds, and housing trust funds. For a discussion of the real estate lawyer's role in a PHA-sponsored affordable housing partnership, see Jane Sheehan, *Mixed Finance; A Real Estate Lawyer's "Field of Dreams,"* 7 J. AFFORDABLE HOUSING & COMMUNITY DEV. L. 289 (1998). In the first ten years of the HOPE VI program, over $6 billion in federal funds "leveraged [more than $17.6 billion] in other public, private, and philanthropic investments," leading to the demolition of over 78,100 distressed public housing units. Margery Austin Turner et al., Estimating the Public Costs and Benefits of HOPE VI Investments: Methodological Report 1 (2007) (published by the Urban Institute). An additional 72,000 units had been approved for demolition by 2007, leading to speculation that the original estimate of 86,000 severely distressed units was low and that the problem continues to grow. *Id.* at 4.

Notes and Questions

1. In considering the appropriate blend of financing techniques for mixed income housing, developers start by estimating affordable rents for the target groups. As noted in the introductory readings in Chapter One, affordability estimates assume decent housing costs no more than 30% of family income for rents and utilities. Developers then estimate the cost to construct and operate the housing and the cost of financing the construction. From these estimates developers can identify "gaps" in the financing process which may or may not be able to be filled by one or more of the subsidy alternatives described in the matrix *supra*.

2. Other significant features of the 1998 legislative tilt toward public-private partnerships included new five year and annual planning requirements emphasizing "deconcentration of lower-income families" and "plans for conversion of existing public housing." 42 U.S.C. § 1437c-1. Perhaps most significantly, Congress reduced the requirement that public housing serve very-low-income persons (30% or less of area median income) from 75% of occupancy to 40% of occupancy. Pub. L. No. 105-276, § 513(a), 112 Stat. 2570 (1998) (*amending* 42 U.S.C. § 1437n). How do these changes affect your approach to the Metro City problem?

3. Public housing residents and their advocates have expressed fears that HOPE VI mixed income developments and other efforts to recast troubled public housing projects will result in a net loss of public housing units and corresponding displacement of low-income households. During the 1970s and 1980s, Congress mandated a "one-for-one"

replacement policy to guard against such losses. However, that rule was suspended in 1995 and replaced in 1998 by a provision requiring the housing authority to offer each displaced family "comparable housing" which may include Section 8 tenant-based or project-based assistance, discussed *infra,* or "occupancy in a unit operated or assisted" by the authority at a "comparable" rental rate. Pub. L. No. 105-276, § 531, 112 Stat. 2570 (1998) (*amending* 42 U.S.C. § 1437p). Advocates continue to press for reinstatement of the "one-for-one" rule, citing loss of housing for low-income people as mixed-income housing developments take precedence. *Waters Supports One-for-One Replacement Rule, Cites Loss of Units in Mixed-Income Housing,* 36 [Current Developments] Hous. & Dev. Rep. (Thomson-Reuters) 548 (Sept. 15, 2008).

4. Can housing vouchers pick up the slack? Would relocation of some low-income households to scattered-site suburban locations result in more economic and racial integration in both the old public housing and the new suburban locations? Would a solution to this issue in the Metro City problem be to give current residents of Grand Square and Laclede a choice of temporary relocation and returning to the proposed new housing, or permanent relocation with rental assistance to another part of the metropolitan area? Displacement and integration issues are discussed in Chapters 5 and 6 *infra.*

5. The relationship between PHAs and governmental entities becomes more complicated when private developers and property managers are involved. Developers and managers will rely upon federal money to support public housing units. What suggestions do you have for a regulatory and operating agreement between Metro City Housing Authority and private developers in the Metro City problem at the beginning of this chapter that would protect the private developers and managers from fluctuations in federal budgets? What do you think of the following approach?

Regulatory and Operating Agreement ("ROA")*

AGREEMENT made this 20th day of March, xxxx _____, by and between ___________ HOUSING AUTHORITY, a public body corporate and politic, organized and existing under the laws of the State of Missouri (the "Authority"), and ___________________ ASSOCIATES, L.P., a Missouri limited partnership ("Owner").

The Authority is the owner of certain real property located in the City of ____________ on which was located a public housing development known as ________________ Family Apartments. The Authority received approval by the United States Department of Housing and Urban Development ("HUD"), pursuant to Section 18 of the United States Housing Act of 1937, as amended (the "Act"), of its proposal to demolish the structures existing on the site, utilizing grant funds made available pursuant to Section 14 of the Act, and has received further HUD approval of its proposal to develop on the site of the former development, in partnership with third parties, a 400-unit mixed-income community, including 222 public housing replacement units, utilizing public housing development grant funds made available pursuant to Section 5 of the Act, in addition to other sources including private financing.

Development of the proposed mixed-income community on the former _____________ site will be implemented in two or more phases. Under the initial phase, following completion of demolition of existing structures and preparation of a developable

* Reprinted with permission of McCormack Baron Salazar, Inc., St. Louis, Missouri.

site, the Authority will lease a portion of the real property referred to above, consisting of approximately 12.56 acres, to the Owner pursuant to a 99-year lease (the "Ground Lease"). The site to be leased to the Owner pursuant to the Ground Lease comprises a portion of the site on which the ____________________ Family Apartments public housing development was located and a portion of certain additional property conveyed to the Authority by the City ______________ Pursuant to the Ground Lease, Owner will cause to be constructed on the leased property 53 separate structures containing, in the aggregate, 160 multifamily rental dwelling units known, collectively, as __________________________ (the "Development").

Owner and the Authority desire and intend that 93 units of the Development shall be set aside as "public housing" as defined in Section 3 (b) of the United States Housing Act of 1937, as amended (the "Act"), and eligible to receive to benefit of operating subsidies provided to the Authority by HUD pursuant to Section 9 of the Act for the term of the Ground Lease. Owner intends that 118 units of the Development (including the 93 units referred to above) will be operated and maintained as qualified low-income units under Section 42 of the Internal Revenue Code for a period of not less than the compliance period and any extended use period (as such terms are defined in said Section 42 of the Internal Revenue Code, as the same may be amended from time to time), and that the balance of the units of the Development will be operated and maintained as market-rate rental units. At the expiration of the term of the Ground Lease (or upon earlier termination thereof pursuant to its terms), all buildings and improvements located on the leased property will become the property of the Authority....

NOW, THEREFORE, The parties hereto agree as follows:....

2. *Authority Units.*

During the term of this Agreement, but subject to Section 6 hereof, Owner will continuously set aside 93 units of the Development, having a total of 257 bedrooms and having initially the units size distribution set forth below, for occupancy by public housing-eligible households at rents and subject to all other conditions operating the public housing units in accordance with the Act and the ACC, and in accordance with the terms of this Agreement, such units shall be eligible to receive the benefits of operating subsidies provided to the Authority by HUD pursuant to Section 9 of the Act or pursuant to any successor legislation providing for project-based or tenant based operating or rental assistance in respect of units in public housing developments or eligible occupants thereof (the units comprising such set-aside units from time to time being referred to herein collectively as the "Authority Units"). The Authority Units shall initially comprise the following mixture of unit sizes and descriptions:

2 Bedroom (walk-up)	5
2 Bedroom (townhouse)	34
3 Bedroom	42
4 Bedroom	8
5 Bedroom	3
6 Bedroom	1
Total	93

Consistent with the requirements currently applicable to public housing, a unit shall not lose its status as an Authority Unit solely because the income of the tenant residing therein rises above the applicable public housing income limit; any such unit shall be governed by rules generally applicable to units occupied by over-income tenants in the public housing program (subject to such modifications in lease and occupancy terms as are permitted hereunder). Owner may change the specific units designated as Authority Units at any time provided that (a) the number of bedrooms contained in the Authority Units remains 257, (b) if such change is to be made with respect to an occupied Authority Unit, the tenant of such unit shall have the same rights with respect to occupancy and rent as applied prior to removal of the unit's designation as an Authority Unit, and (c) the Authority Units shall at all times, to the extent feasible, be scattered evenly throughout the Development, and within structures within the Development, and shall not be concentrated in any particular area or areas within the Development or within structures within the Development. In the event of a Taking or Casualty (as such terms are defined in the Ground Lease) that diminishes the total number of residential units in the Development below 160, fifty-eight percent (58%) of the units remaining following such Taking or Casualty (and following any construction or reconstruction undertaken by reason thereof or necessitated thereby) shall be set aside as Authority Units.

3. *Operation of Authority Units.*

(a) Owner shall maintain and operate the Authority Units in compliance with all applicable requirements of the Act, HUD regulations thereunder, and the applicable regulations and policies of the Authority, and in accordance with the ACC (including any waivers granted pursuant thereto), the Ground Lease, the Consent Decree, and this Agreement. In the event of any conflict among the forgoing authorities, the ACC (including any waivers granted pursuant thereto) shall control (to the extent permitted by law). Notwithstanding the Owner's agreement to perform substantial obligations and responsibilities with regard to the Authority Units pursuant hereto, the Authority remains accountable to HUD for performance of such functions under and pursuant to the ACC and must monitor the performance of the Owner and the Management Agent to assure compliance therewith.

(b) Authority and Owner acknowledge that the goal of achieving long-term sustainability of the Development as a mixed-income community will be enhanced by administrative procedures and terms and conditions of occupancy which reduce discernible distinctions in maintenance and operation, and conditions of continued occupancy, between the Authority Units and other units in the Development to the greatest extent feasible while assuring that the Authority Units are available to house families who meet the occupancy objectives of the Authority. Subsections (c)–(g) of this Section 3 enumerate certain respects in which operating procedures and other requirements as to the Authority Units will differ from those in effect with respect to public housing units owned by the Authority. Authority and Owner agree that, if experience demonstrates a need for or the desirability to PHA-owned public housing, they will consult with each other regarding such further modifications and will take such further implementing steps as they agree to be advisable, including, as appropriate, requests to HUD for revision or waiver of regulations necessary to permit the Authority to undertake measures that enhance the long-term viability of the Development, or requests to implement statutory revisions made by Congress from time to time affecting either public housing in general or public housing located within privately-owned mixed-income communities in particular....

4. *Operating Subsidy Amount....*

(c) During each Authority Fiscal Year commencing with the Authority Fiscal year in which the first Authority Unit is available for occupancy, and subject to any limitations arising from application of Section 20 (e) of the Act, the Authority shall pay to the Owner a Development Operating Subsidy equal to (i) Estimated Authority Unit Expenses for such period, less (ii) Estimated Authority Unit Income for the period (such amount with respect to any period being referred to herein as the "Operating Subsidy Requirement").

The Authority shall pay to Owner, on the first day of each month of an Authority Fiscal Year, one-twelfth (1/12) of the Operating Subsidy Requirement for such Authority Fiscal year; provided, however, that Owner and the Authority may agree, upon determination of the Operating Budget and Operating Subsidy Requirement for any Authority Fiscal Year, to provide for unequal monthly payments for such year....

5. *Authority Reserve*

(a) Concurrently with its execution and delivery of the Ground Lease, the Authority will establish a separate trust account (the "Authority Reserve"), consisting of one or more separate accounts in a financial institution chosen by the Authority and acceptable to Owner whose deposits are insured by an agency of the Federal Government (the "Escrow Agent"), and shall deposit therein (from sources available to the Authority but in no event including operating subsidy funds or other public housing program funds), an amount not less than $372,000 (the "Initial Deposit").... Prior to the date which is the first anniversary of the first day of the month following the month in which the Development achieves 85% occupancy, the Authority shall make such further deposits (from sources available to the Authority including earned administrative fees or operating subsidy funds or other public housing program revenues available for operating expenses of the Authority but excluding funds made available under Sections 5 or 14 of the Act) to the Authority Reserve as shall be necessary in order that the amount held therein, including income earned thereon, shall be not less than three times the annualized amount of the Operating Subsidy Requirement determined pursuant to Section 4 hereof with respect to the Authority Fiscal Year in which first occupancy of the Development occurs. The Authority also shall cause all payments to it pursuant to Sections 3.4 and 3.5 of the Second Mortgage Loan Agreement of even date herewith between the Authority and the Owner to be deposited on its behalf by Owner into the Authority Reserve. Funds held in the Authority Reserve (including any additional amounts deposited therein from time to time pursuant to the terms hereof) shall remain funds of the Authority, shall be held in trust by the Escrow Agent, and shall be held and applied in accordance with the terms and conditions hereof....

(e) If at any time the Authority shall advise the Owner that, due to diminished appropriations of operating subsidy or similar cause, the Authority will be unable to make payments of Development Operating Subsidy in the full amount of the Operating Subsidy Requirement, Owner shall be entitled to institute the remedial steps described in Section 7(b) hereof, without prejudice to the Owner's additional rights under subsection (d) above....

6. *Public Housing Transformation*

(a) Subject to subsection (b) hereof, nothing contained herein shall prevent or diminish the full application to the Authority Units of any legislation enacted after the date hereof which provides for the termination of operating subsidies under Section 9 of the Act or of other Federal project-based assistance to public housing developments, including, without limitation, any provision thereof releasing or otherwise modifying occupancy or tenant restrictions previously applicable to units in such developments.

(b) It is of the essence of this Agreement that during the term of the Ground Lease, Owner will maintain and operate the number and type of dwelling units in the Development stated in Section 2 hereof as public housing units in accordance with all applicable requirements of the Act, the Consent Decree, and the ACC; provided, however, that if Authority Unit Income, plus any form of governmental operating or rental assistance received in respect of the Authority Units (including, without limitation, withdrawals from the Authority Reserve or other contributions by the Authority) shall be less than Authority Unit Expenses, the Owner shall at no time be required to contribute from its own funds (including funds derived from the operation of Development Units other than the Authority Units) toward Authority Unit Expenses in order to preserve the character of the number of units stated in Section 2 as public housing units. In the event that legislative changes or diminished appropriations significantly reduce the amount of operating subsidy provided by HUD to the Authority under Section 9 of the Act as in effect on the date hereof, the Authority shall remain obligated to pay Development Operating Subsidy to Owner in accordance with Section 4 hereof and Owner shall continue to maintain and operate the Authority Units as public housing units; provided, however, that if the aggregate of tenant rental contributions payable by occupants of such units (including, without limitation, Development Operating Subsidy, other project-based or tenant-based operating or rental assistance, withdrawals from the Authority Reserve, or other contributions by or on behalf of the Authority or with respect of Authority Units) are less than Authority Unit Expenses, Owner shall make any necessary withdrawals from the Authority Reserve in order to cover Authority Unit Expenses and to assure continued operation of the Authority Units as public housing units. If Owner and the Authority project that withdrawals from the Authority Reserve and future contributions from or on behalf of the Authority will not be sufficient to cover Authority Unit Expenses for a succeeding period of not less than two years, and without prejudice to Owner's right to institute the remedial actions described in Section 7 (b) hereof under the circumstances described therein, Owner shall take such steps as may be necessary and in accordance with the requirements of the Act, subject to continuing rights under law of existing tenants and subject, during the compliance period and any extended use period (as those terms are defined in Section 42 of the Internal Revenue Code), to occupancy and rent restrictions applicable to qualified low-income units under said Section 42, as amended from time to time, to increase the income level of tenants admitted to and occupying the Authority Units. In the further event that all such actions by the Owner and the Authority are insufficient to cover the Authority Units Expenses, the Owner may take all further actions necessary to increase the income from the Authority Units, including, without limitation, increases in rental payments from tenants and operating a portion of the Authority Units as market rate units to the extent necessary so that income from the Authority Units in the aggregate (including income from such converted units), plus all such public assistance as aforesaid, shall be not less than (but not substantially more than) Authority Unit Expenses; provided however, that any such actions must be consistent with the Act, as amended from time to time. If, subsequent to institution of remedial steps described above, the Authority shall reasonably demonstrate a capacity and commitment to provide assistance sufficient to support operation of the number of Authority Units operated as public housing prior to such action (and to restore any Reserve Shortfall in accordance with Section 5(f) hereof), the obligation of Owner to maintain such number of units as public housing in accordance with the terms hereof shall be reinstated, subject to continuing rights of existing tenants....

7. *Financial Statements and Reports; Remedies in Event of Deficit Operations; Annual Reconciliation....*

(b) If the quarterly statements of income and expenses for the Authority Units delivered pursuant to subsection (a) above shall indicate a cumulative operating loss over a period of two successive quarterly periods, taking into account all payments of Development Operating Subsidy made by the Authority during such period (exclusive of any withdrawals from the Authority Reserve), Owner shall have the right to seek to increase income from the Authority Units by leasing Authority Units, on turnover, to public housing-eligible families having higher income levels than the average incomes of the existing Authority Units residents and, if necessary (after reasonable opportunity to the Authority to agree to increase the amount of the Operating Subsidy Requirement), having higher income levels than would otherwise receive priority under the broad range of incomes local ranking preference applicable to the Development, provided that such admissions are in compliance with the requirements of the Act.

Owner shall not be required to seek to reduce maintenance and other operating expenses allocable to the Authority Units below the level of such expenses incurred for other units in the Development as a condition to, or as a preferred corrective action to, seeking to increase income from tenant rents in accordance with the foregoing sentence.

Notes and Questions

1. Who will own the land under the ROA? Who will own the public housing units? How would you describe the relationship between the PHA and the developer?

2. Note the impact of the operating subsidy. What remedies are available to the developer if Congress fails to appropriate sufficient funds to cover the operating subsidy commitment? Is your comfort level concerning the enforcement of the quoted ROA provisions increased by the following provision of the 1998 Act?:

> (h) *Effect of certain contract terms*—If an entity that owns or operates a mixed-finance project, that includes a significant number of units other than public housing units enters into a contract with a public housing agency, the terms of which obligate the entity to operate and maintain a specified number of units in the project as public housing units in accordance with the requirements of this Act for the period required by law, such contractual terms may provide that, if, as a result of a reduction in appropriations under section 9 or any other change in applicable law, the public housing agency is unable to fulfill its contractual obligations with respect to those public housing units, that entity may deviate, under procedures and requirements developed through regulations by the Secretary, from otherwise applicable restrictions under this Act regarding rents, income eligibility, and other areas of public housing management with respect to a portion or all of those public housing units, to the extent necessary to preserve the viability of those units while maintaining the low-income character of the units to the maximum extent practicable.

Pub. L. No. 105-276, § 539, 112 Stat. 2594 (1998) (*codified at* 42 U.S.C. § 1437z-7(h)).

3. In addition to the loss of public housing units issue, local housing authorities seeking to recast public housing to mixed income housing face questions regarding retention of control over land previously dedicated to public housing. Would an acceptable solution be for the Metro City Housing Authority to retain ownership of the entire tract and lease the land to a public-private development team structured as a limited partnership, and to execute reciprocal easements and restrictive covenants dedicating the housing to low income use?

In such an arrangement, do the following excerpts from a Memorandum of Ground Lease, together with the Regulatory and Operating Agreement excerpted *supra,* adequately protect the limited partnership entity from the effects of legislative changes or diminished appropriations? Do they adequately protect the housing authority's interest in providing housing for low income families, as well as the public's interest in proper use of public funds?

Memorandum of Ground Lease

THIS MEMORANDUM OF GROUND LEASE is made and entered into as of the ______ day of March, xxxx _______, by and between the ____________________ HOUSING AUTHORITY, a public body corporate and politic of the State of ___________ ("Lessor"); and ______________________ ASSOCIATES, L.P., a ________________ limited partnership ("Lessee").

WHEREAS, simultaneously herewith, Lessor and Lessee have entered into the certain Ground Lease Agreement (the "Lease"), pursuant to which Lessor has leased to Lessee those certain parcels of real property in the City of __________________, State of __________________ more particularly described on *Exhibit A* attached hereto and made a part hereof, together with the improvements, rights, easements, licenses, privileges and appurtenances thereunto attached or in any way belonging thereto; and

WHEREAS, the parties hereto desire to enter into this Memorandum of Lease in order to provide public record notice of the Lease and certain provisions, rights and obligations pertaining to the Leased Premises.

NOW, THEREFORE, for and in consideration of the foregoing premises, the sum of Ten and No/100 Dollars ($10.00), the covenants, representations, warranties and agreements set forth in the Lease, and other good and valuable consideration, the receipt and sufficiency of which are hereby acknowledged, the parties hereto do hereby agree as follows: ...

Section 3.6 *Restrictions Applicable to Public Housing Units.*

(a) Subject to the provisions of Subsections 3.6(c) and (d) below, during the Term or such lesser period as may be required by law or by the Annual Contributions Contract, Lessee will continuously set aside ninety-three (93) units of the residential units to be constructed on the Leased Premises, having a minimum aggregate total of two hundred fifty-seven (257) bedrooms, as Public Housing Units, for occupancy by Public Housing Eligible Households at rents and subject to all other conditions of the Act, the Regulatory and Operating Agreement and the Annual Contributions Contract.... [The omitted language tracks the language of Section 2 of the Regulatory and Operating Agreement reproduced *supra*—Eds.]

(b) During the period specified in Subsection 3.6(a) above, Lessee shall maintain and operate the Public Housing Units (i) in compliance with all applicable requirements of the Act, HUD regulations thereunder, and the regulations and policies of Lessor of which Lessee has been notified by Lessor; and (ii) in accordance with the Annual Contributions Contract, and the Regulatory and Operating Agreement, the Consent Decree, and this Lease. In the event of any conflict among the foregoing authorities, the Annual Contributions Contract shall control, to the extent permitted by law.

(c) Subject to Subsection 3.6(d) hereof (it being expressly acknowledged and agreed that Lessee at no time shall be required to contribute from its own funds toward Authority Unit Expenses in order to preserve the character of the Public Housing Units as such), nothing contained herein shall prevent or diminish the full application to the Public Housing Units of any legislation enacted after the date hereof which provides for the termination of operating subsidies under Section 9 of the Act or of other Federal project-based assistance to public housing developments, including, without limitation, any provision thereof releasing or otherwise modifying occupancy or tenant rent restrictions previously applicable to units such as the Public Housing Units.

(d) It is of the essence of Lessee's obligation under this Section 3.6 that during the Term or lesser period as may be required by law or by the Annual Contributions Contract,

Lessee will maintain and operate the number of dwelling units within the Leased Premises stated in Subsection 3.6(a) above as Public Housing Units in accordance with all applicable requirements of the Act and the Annual Contributions Contract ... [The omitted language tracks the language of Sec 6 (b) of the Regulatory and Operating Agreement reproduced *supra*—Eds.]

(e) The provisions of this Section 3.6 are intended to create a covenant running with the land encumbering the Leased Premises during the Term or such lesser period required by law or by the Annual Contributions Contract as described above, and binding upon Lessor, Lessee and each of their respective successors in title and assigns and all subsequent owners of the Leased Premises and the Improvements, including without limitation, any successor who acquires title to Lessee's Estate by foreclosure of a Leasehold Mortgage or instrument in lieu of foreclosure."

The transformation of severely distressed, high-rise urban public housing projects contemplated by the HOPE VI program is a complicated and often controversial endeavor, as the following case indicates.

Thompson v. United States Department of Housing and Urban Development

United States Court of Appeals
220 F.3d 241 (4th Cir. 2000)

TRAXLER, Circuit Judge:

In 1995, African-American public housing residents (the "Plaintiffs") filed a class action against the United States Department of Housing and Urban Development ("HUD"), HUD's then-Secretary Henry Cisneros, the Housing Authority of Baltimore City ("HABC"), and various Baltimore officials, seeking to eliminate racial segregation and discrimination in Baltimore's public housing system. In 1996, the parties entered into a Partial Consent Decree (the "Consent Decree") resolving some of the issues raised in the complaint. In 1998, HABC and the Baltimore officials (together, the "Local Defendants") filed a motion in the district court seeking to modify a portion of the Consent Decree. The district court granted the motion, and the Plaintiffs appeal. We reverse....

[T]he effect of Section XII of the Consent Decree is to require that new public housing financed with public funds be located in areas without high concentrations of minority residents or public housing. At issue in this case are the Local Defendants' current plans for Hollander Ridge and Cherry Hill, public housing developments located in impacted areas.

Built in the mid 1970s, Hollander Ridge is a 1,000-unit public housing development located on a 60-acre parcel of land on the eastern edge of Baltimore City. The site is cut off from the rest of the city by Interstate 95, and only one road provides access to the site. Hollander Ridge abuts the predominately white residential neighborhood of Rosedale. However, the relationship between Hollander Ridge and Rosedale residents has been so strained that, at the time of the hearing, the city was replacing a chain link fence with a wrought iron fence to completely surround Hollander Ridge, save for the lone entrance at the end of Hollander Ridge farthest away from Rosedale. The balance of the area surrounding Hollander Ridge is devoted to commercial and light industrial uses.

Hollander Ridge contains 522 family housing units located in 79 low-rise structures and 478 units of housing for the elderly located in a 19-story high-rise building. By the time the Consent Decree was entered into, the lack of regular maintenance and repair work had left Hollander Ridge in a shameful state of disrepair. When tenants moved out, routine repairs were not made and the units were generally allowed to remain vacant. The steeply-sloped topography of the site led to severe erosion problems, causing sanitary sewer lines to buckle and break, and exposing underground power lines. Many of the low-rise units were in need of substantial repair, including the replacement of heating and plumbing systems and upgrades of the electrical systems. Similar problems existed in the high-rise building, where many of the major systems needed to be replaced and the individual units needed significant updating. The high-rise building also suffered from structural problems that allowed water to leak into many units.

Shortly after entering into the Consent Decree, the Local Defendants, at the urging of HUD, applied for funds to rehabilitate Hollander Ridge under HUD's HOPE VI program. The Local Defendants' original plan was to modernize Hollander Ridge by, among other things, reducing the population density in the development through demolition and reconfiguration of existing units, and upgrading the housing units and amenities. This plan was consistent with the terms of the Consent Decree.

As part of its review of the HOPE VI application, HUD commissioned a viability assessment of Hollander Ridge conducted by Abt Associates, Inc. The September 1996 assessment report (the "Abt report") noted the poor physical condition of the development and concluded that the costs to rehabilitate it in accordance with the Local Defendants' plan were prohibitively high. The Abt report also questioned the viability and marketability of a modernized Hollander Ridge. The report noted, among other things, that the isolation of the site and the unavailability of nearby shopping and healthcare facilities made the location unattractive to those seeking family housing, and even more problematic for elderly residents. The Abt report recommended demolishing Hollander Ridge and acquiring or building replacement housing in other areas of the city, which would be a permissible use of HOPE VI funds.

After the Abt report was issued, HUD awarded the Local Defendants $20,000,000 for Hollander Ridge, one-half of the amount sought in the HOPE VI application....

The Local Defendants spent the year following the award of the HOPE VI grant attempting to finalize their plans for Hollander Ridge. They hired experts to determine how the site should be developed, and they expressed their disagreement with the findings of the Abt report. As late as November 1997, the Local Defendants assured HUD that a revitalized Hollander Ridge would be a viable site for family public housing.

However, around December 1997, in the wake of continued public opposition to the Hollander Ridge plan, the Local Defendants devised a completely new plan for Hollander Ridge. The new plan called for the demolition of all existing structures to make way for a "senior village," which would provide approximately 450 housing units for senior citizens only, with enhanced security, on site health care, and transportation services. The senior village was planned as a mixed-income community providing housing for low and moderate income seniors, including those who qualify for public housing.

The plans for the senior village at Hollander Ridge clearly violated Section XII of the Consent Decree. The Local Defendants therefore sought a modification of the Decree to allow them to seek federal funds for the plan.

The facts surrounding Cherry Hill are somewhat similar.... [Omitted—Eds.]

After conducting an evidentiary hearing, the district court believed that substantial changes in circumstances had occurred at Hollander Ridge and Cherry Hill since the entry of the Consent Decree. As to Hollander Ridge, the court decided that only after the Consent Decree did it become apparent that Hollander Ridge could not be modernized to provide family public housing, but that the site could be used to provide housing for the elderly.... The district court determined that these changes in circumstance rendered compliance with the Consent Decree detrimental to the public interest. Consequently, the district court amended the Consent Decree to allow the Local Defendants to proceed with their plans for Hollander Ridge and Cherry Hill....

To justify the modification of an institutional reform consent decree, the party seeking the modification "bears the burden of establishing that a significant change in circumstances warrants revision of the decree. If the movant cites significantly changed factual conditions, it must additionally show that the changed conditions make compliance with the consent decree 'more onerous,' 'unworkable,' or 'detrimental to the public interest.'" [*see Rufo v. Inmates of Suffolk County*, 502 U.S. 367, 384] A modification, however, should not ordinarily be granted "where a party relies upon events that actually were anticipated at the time it entered into a decree." *Id.* at 385.

A. *Hollander Ridge*

The district court believed that the circumstances surrounding Hollander Ridge had significantly changed because, after the Consent Decree, the Local Defendants realized that Hollander Ridge could not viably be rehabilitated to provide family housing, but that it could be used to provide housing for the elderly. Contrary to the district court's conclusion, however, the Local Defendants' post-Decree "discovery" that Hollander Ridge could not be rehabilitated as family housing cannot be considered a change of circumstance. The reasons that Hollander Ridge could not be rehabilitated, including the need for extensive repairs, the cost of those repairs, and the undesirability of Hollander Ridge because of its isolation, all existed before the entry of the Consent Decree. The only relevant post-Decree event was the issuance of the Abt report, which did not itself render Hollander Ridge unusable as a site for family public housing. Instead, the Abt report merely expressed an opinion that the conditions at Hollander Ridge made it unlikely that the Local Defendants' original modernization plan would be economically viable, an opinion with which the Local Defendants at first strongly disagreed. A modification of a consent decree must be based on a change in *facts*, not a change in opinion about the effect of unchanged facts. *See Id.* at 384 ("A party seeking modification of a consent decree may meet its initial burden by showing ... a significant change either in *factual conditions* or in law." (emphasis added)). Thus, the Local Defendants' changed opinion about the viability of Hollander Ridge as a site for family public housing simply cannot amount to a change of circumstance.

The only remaining justification for the modification as found by the district court, then, is the Local Defendants' present belief that the Hollander Ridge site is a viable location for the senior village. Although there is evidence in the record questioning the viability of the senior village plan, we will assume for the purposes of this opinion that it is in fact viable. However, the viability of the senior village is really beside the point.

The Local Defendants knowingly and voluntarily entered into the Consent Decree and agreed to Section XII, which provides that, until the other obligations under the Decree have been satisfied, any new construction of public housing built with public housing funds must be located in a non-impacted area. The very presence of Section XII makes it clear that the parties contemplated that new construction would be required or desired during the life of the Consent Decree. Given the allegations of the Plaintiffs' complaint—that HUD and the Local Defendants were continuing the formerly *de jure* segregated housing program through their tenant assignment and site selection policies—Section XII obviously provides an important means of furthering the Consent Decree's stated purpose of "provid[ing] enhanced desegregative housing opportunities for residents of Baltimore City public housing." By prohibiting the use of public housing funds for new public housing construction in impacted areas, Section XII ensures that Baltimore City public housing residents will be integrated throughout the city. Thus, the change of circumstance found by the district court—the need or desire for new construction—is a circumstance contemplated and anticipated by the parties at the time they entered into the Consent Decree. Indeed, the possibility that new construction would be needed is the very circumstance to which Section XII is specifically directed and the only circumstance that triggers its application. That the proposed housing is for the elderly is of no moment. Section XII prevents the Local Defendants from seeking public funding for the construction of new public housing in any impacted area until the other obligations under the Decree are satisfied; the provision does not limit its reach to the construction of family public housing, nor does it exempt from its reach the construction of public housing for the elderly....

We fully recognize that there is public support for the Local Defendants' plans for Hollander Ridge and Cherry Hill, particularly for the Cherry Hill project. And we also recognize that the planned projects would serve the needs of some residents of Baltimore's public housing system. Those facts, however, are insufficient to allow the Local Defendants to modify the Consent Decree. By prohibiting the use of public funds for new public housing construction in impacted areas, Section XII of the Consent Decree reflects a rational, negotiated-for allocation of scarce public housing funds that serves the needs of other residents of Baltimore's public housing system. The Local Defendants sought relief from Section XII based on changes in circumstances that were contemplated at the time of the Decree and that were the only circumstances that would trigger its application. Therefore, under *Rufo,* the Consent Decree could be modified only if the Local Defendants satisfied the "heavy burden" of establishing that they "made a reasonable effort to comply with the decree." *Id.* at 385. Because the Local Defendants did not establish that they made reasonable efforts to comply with Section XII before seeking its modification, they failed to carry their burden. The district court, therefore, abused its discretion by granting the motion to modify the Consent Decree. Accordingly, the district court's order modifying the Consent Decree is hereby reversed.

Notes and Questions

1. Most of the reported cases center on allegations of racial discrimination because of the displacement that often accompanies a Hope VI development. *See, e.g., Darst-Webbe Tenant Ass'n. Bd. v. St. Louis Hous. Auth.*, 417 F.3d 898 (8th Cir. 2005) (housing authority demonstrated legitimate, non-discriminatory policy objectives to support revitalization plan; HUD complied with its duty to affirmatively further fair housing in approving HOPE VI revitalization plan). Fair housing issues are discussed in Chapter 6 *infra.*

2. HOPE VI has been a controversial program for two major reasons: 1) the concern that transforming large urban public housing projects into mixed-income, mixed-use neighborhoods inevitably results in displacement of a substantial number of public housing tenants and a net loss of affordable housing units for very low income people, and 2) the large amount of money that is allocated to a small number of developments lessens the funds available for other public housing units in the HOPE VI grantee cities and in cities that do not succeed in obtaining HOPE VI grants. *See, e.g.,* Martin D. Abra-

VANEL, DIANE K. LEVY & MARGARET MCFARLAND, THE UNCHARTED, UNCERTAIN FUTURE OF HOPE VI REDEVELOPMENTS: THE CASE FOR ASSESSING PROJECT SUSTAINABILITY (2009) (recommending a comprehensive, third-party sustainability assessment of HOPE VI because, while its "model of mixed financing, ownership, management, income and tenure is very appealing from many perspectives," its sustainability is "not known"); URBAN INSTITUTE, A DECADE OF HOPE VI (2004) (evaluating projects in 166 cities and concluding that HOPE VI was an "ambitious effort to build economically integrated communities and give existing residents more choice in the private housing market." *Id.* at 2. *See also* Ethan Barlieb, *Hope VI Revitalization Grants: Weighing the Costs and Benefits, and Considering a Solution in the Context of Liberty City, Miami,* 15 U. MIAMI BUS. L. REV. 101 (2007) (arguing that cities seeking HOPE VI grants should be required to implement affordable housing policies, including inclusionary zoning, to reduce the negative impacts of HOPE VI); Matthew H. Greene, *The HOPE VI Paradox: Why Do HUD's Most Successful Housing Developments Fail to Benefit the Poorest of the Poor?* 17 J. L. & POL'Y 191, 229 (2008) (arguing that "funding developments that are built from grassroots movements will create a stronger foundation and self-interest among tenants in the success of their own development"); Jason Gubi, *Low Income Housing: HOPE VI and the Social Buy Program,* 10 T.M. COOLEY J. PRAC. & CLINICAL L. 417 (2008) (comparing HOPE VI to England's Social Buy program that offers financial assistance to housing project residents seeking to purchase homes); Danielle Pelfrey Duryea, *Comment: Gendering the Gentrification of Public Housing: HOPE VI's Disparate Impact on Lowest-Income African American Women,* 13 GEO J. ON POVERTY L. & POL'Y 567, 571 (2006) (arguing that HOPE VI "disproportionately destabilizes the economically-precarious, female-headed households who predominate in the severely-distressed public housing projects its grants have targeted").

3. Displacement of public housing residents in the wake of HOPE VI transformation efforts has been a serious problem for the program. (Displacement issues are discussed in Chapters 5 and 6 *infra*) For example, in Chicago "the largest redevelopment of public housing ever undertaken in the country" has stalled. According to an investigation by the Chicago Tribune, "only 30% of [a 10-year] plan's most ambitious element—tearing down entire housing projects and replacing them with new neighborhoods where poor, working-class and wealthier families would live side by side" had been completed by the end of the ninth year. Jason Grotto, Laurie Cohen & Sara Olkon, *Public Housing Limbo: Thousands of Families Displaced. Hundreds of Millions of Dollars Spent. Years Behind Schedule. What Went Wrong with Chicago's Grand Experiment,* CHI. TRIB., July 7, 2008, *available at* www.chicagotribune.com/news/nationworld/chi-cha-main-sunday-bd-06-jul06,0, 2989588.story.

The Tribune reporters characterized the Chicago plan as a "high-stakes wager: Upscale homes in the new developments would not only raise the aspirations of public housing families but also spur the construction of badly needed housing for the poor and affordable housing for working people struggling to buy a home. Instead, the market-rate homes have proven in some cases to be an albatross" as the collapse of the housing boom made it difficult "to sell high-priced homes amid a glut of new construction across the city." *Id.*

4. A number of HOPE VI projects have been successful in transforming whole neighborhoods. An article in Urban Land, the magazine of the Urban Land Institute, a developer-oriented organization, highlights four such projects in Baltimore, Cincinnati, Pittsburgh and Washington, D.C. Douglas Porter, *Designing HOPE,* URBAN LAND, Feb. 2008, at 112. In reviewing mixed-income residential developments near Johns Hopkins Medical Institute in Baltimore, Cincinnati's West End, the Hill District adjacent to down-

town Pittsburgh and the Capitol Hill area of Washington, D.C., Porter concluded that "design excellence can win supporters and influence investments in otherwise problematical locations and markets." *Id.*

5. But excellent design is not enough to guarantee long-term success. Not far from the Broadway Overlook HOPE VI near Johns Hopkins in Baltimore is the Reservoir Hill neighborhood which was a showcase of successful redevelopment in 2006, but in 2008 had become a showcase of the subprime mortgage meltdown as 95 properties were in foreclosure. "On one dismal street, three blocks of apartment buildings and row houses—many freshly renovated—stand vacant, their doors and windows boarded over to ward off thieves." Lori Montgomery, *Mortgage Crisis Reverses Tide of Urban Renewal*, WASH. POST, July 22, 2008, *available at* www.washingtonpost.com/wp-dyn/content/article/2008/07/21/AR2008072102490_pf.html. A $3.9 billion infusion of Community Development Block Grant (CDBG) funds (discussed in Chapter 5 *infra*), enacted as part of the Housing and Economic Recovery Act of 2008, is aimed at giving cities the ability to buy foreclosed residential units, make necessary repairs and sell them to nonprofit organizations as rental property for low-income families. Housing and Economy Recovery Act of 2008, Pub. L. No. 110-289, §§2401–02, 122 Stat. 2654.

A Note on Transforming Rental Assistance

Despite the substantial attention paid to the HOPE VI program, units converted under HOPE VI represent a very small segment (less than 10%) of the total public housing inventory. The remaining units face growing sustainability issues because of aging units, obsolescent designs and poor locations. HUD has estimated that public housing units not being converted through HOPE VI face a capital improvement backlog of between $20 and $30 billion.

HUD's proposed 2011 Budget, released February 1, 2010, includes a potentially fundamental change in its existing public housing program. The Budget "proposes long term fundamental reforms including launching a new initiative called Transforming Rental Assistance (TRA) to bring HUD's twentieth century rental assistance programs into the twenty-first century. TRA will preserve public housing by enabling its owners to address the current and future capital needs of their properties, especially by leveraging private capital, provide more choice to residents and begin to streamline the thirteen separate rental assistance programs run by HUD." [Proposed legislation authorizing the transformation plan was titled the Preservation, Enhancement and Transformation of Rental Housing Act (PETRA)—Eds.] The Proposed Budget of HUD identifies $350 million for this purpose. A summary statement in support of TRA released by HUD made the following points:

> Over the last 75 years, the Federal Government has invested billions in the development and maintenance of public and multifamily housing. This housing serves tremendously vulnerable people (extremely low-income families, seniors, and people with disabilities) who rely on it and will face few if any options in the event the housing is lost. Despite this sizable Federal investment and the great demand for deeply affordable rental housing, we continue to lose hard units. While some portion of these units has been lost due to their deteriorated physical condition, others—both publicly and privately owned—have left the affordable inventory out of their owners' frustration with HUD's administrative procedures or because HUD's preservation toolkit was lacking in resources and/or flexibility. Particularly for public housing, this trend shows no sign of slowing.

> HUD estimates that the public housing inventory faces a capital needs backlog ranging from $18 to $24 billion. Given the current Federal fiscal constraints, we cannot expect to meet this need from the Federal coffers. At the same time, the structure of the affordability covenants associated with the public housing program impedes private investment in the stock. To preserve the public housing stock and improve upon the multifamily programs, recognizing the investment of taxpayer dollars both programs represent, the President's Budget proposes to make available $350 million for phase one of an initiative called "Transforming Rental Assistance" (TRA).
>
> TRA will preserve public and assisted housing, enhance housing choice for residents, and increase administrative efficiency at all levels of program operations. For public and assisted housing owners, participation in the initiative will be voluntary and will involve conversion to an improved form of property-based rental assistance under section 8(o)(13) of the U.S. Housing Act of 1937. Conversion contracts will include a resident mobility feature. HUD intends through the conversion process to assure the physical and financial sustainability of properties, including through the implementation of energy-efficiency measures. Residents of converted properties, should they opt to move, will have access to tenant-based rental assistance as it becomes available, without reducing the number of units with property-based assistance. TRA also will streamline and improve the delivery and oversight of rental assistance and increase the share of housing choice vouchers used in lower poverty communities.

HUD Press Release No. 10-026, Feb. 1, 2010.

In a briefing on the proposed TRA program, HUD officials stressed three main goals: 1) preserve public and assisted housing, 2) streamline rental assistance programs, and 3) promote resident mobility. The 2011 budget request of $350 billion is estimated to cover the cost of a "voluntary"conversion of 300,000 public housing and privately-owned multifamily units to "long-term, property-based contracts." Through this process, owners would be put in "a position to address the immediate and long long-term capital needs of their properties and to prevent the future loss of units" (emphasis in original). Streamlining of the rental assistance programs is necessary because HUD currently provides "deep rental assistance to 4.6 million households through at least 13 different programs administered by 3 operating divisions ... [which is] delivered through an infrastructure that includes some 4,200 PHAs, 17,000 private owners, and hundreds of not-for-profit entities." Resident mobility will be enhanced through a provision in the new property-based contracts that a "unit will retain its assistance even if the tenant exercises mobility" and HUD promotion of "voluntary enlargement of geographical service areas for the Housing Choice Voucher program" and provision of "search assistance" for households possessing vouchers (emphasis in original). Investing in People and Places, HUD's FY2011 Budget: Stakeholder Briefing on the Transformation of Rental Assistance (Feb. 2, 2010).

Notes and Questions

1. Section 8(o)(13) (*codified at* 42 U.S.C. § 1437f(o)(13)), is a provision in the voucher program that authorizes PHAs to apply up to 20% of their ACC funds to a HAP contract tenant-based assistance program. Such a shift normally is designed to encourage residents to move out of public housing into privately-owned housing in other parts of the community. The TRA emphasis on voluntary action suggests that tenants might have a

choice to move or to stay, but in a unit governed by a long-term contract. Does this strategy strike you as a sound way to respond to the growing loss of public housing units? What type of tenants would you expect to take advantage of such a program? How might their choosing to leave affect the remaining public housing tenants?

2. In the TRA briefing, HUD officials emphasized that the TRA initiative was designed to preserve public housing "by enabling owners to address the current and capital needs of their properties," and that PHAs voluntarily converting units will receive "true bottom-line incentives" rather than "formula funding" as they "continue their move to 'asset management.'" "Asset management" is a form of project-based budgeting popular in the private sector. The following Note discusses the concept.

A Note on Project Based Budgeting (Asset Management)

Public housing authorities traditionally have received funds from HUD for operations and capital improvements based on evaluation of their entire portfolio of properties. Management of large urban PHAs often has been criticized for alleged failures to stay on top of repairs and maintenance requirements of particular buildings. In a large portfolio of projects, particular maintenance issues often would not be addressed to the satisfaction of affected residents, but it was difficult to determine accountability when looking at a report of the PHA's entire portfolio.

Following studies of the private sector model of *asset management*, in which business organizations evaluate individual projects or properties separately from other property they own, HUD issued new regulations in 2005 requiring PHA's owning 250 or more public housing units to convert to the asset management approach that is standard in the private rental market, 24 C.F.R. § 990.255 & ff. The regulations define project-based management ("PBM") as management services "tailored to the unique needs of each property, given the resources available to that property." Such services include "marketing, leasing, resident services, routine and preventive maintenance, lease enforcement, protective services, and other tasks associated with the day-to-day operation of rental housing," 24 C.F.R. § 990.275.

The key change is a requirement that PHAs "become accountable for each separate property they own" rather than lumping together all public housing projects owned by a particular PHA and reporting on a PHA level of generality. Meena S. Bavan & Shomon R. Shamsuddin, *The Transition to Asset Management in Housing*, 9 CITYSCAPE 185 (No. 2 2007), *available at* www.huduser.org/periodicals/cityscape.html. One of the reasons for the shift is the belief that segregating projects or properties in this manner will make it easier for PHAs to attract private investment through public-private partnerships for specific public housing redevelopment projects such as those authorized by the HOPE VI program, considered *supra*. But critics of the use of asset management in public housing "have expressed concern about increased administrative burdens, the potential for federal micromanagement, and inadequate funding levels." *Id.* at 191.

Notes and Questions

1. The 2005 asset management regulation requires that more attention be paid to the management of individual projects in a PHA's portfolio, rather than evaluating the entire portfolio as one unit. Consider the East St. Louis, Illinois Public Housing Authority, which manages over 2000 units housing with close to 5000 residents. The units are grouped

into 9 family developments, 6 high rise apartment buildings and a number of single family homes scattered throughout the city. East St. Louis Housing Authority Home Page, *available at* www.eslha.org. How would you describe the change in management responsibilities occasioned by the 2005 asset management regulation? For example, could you spend the authority's entire landscape budget on one garden apartment building, or would you be expected to spread it equally among all the developments? Would you be expected to hire an on-sight manager for each development, or could you use a centralized management staff? Does the change strike you as promoting efficiency and better accountability, or does it appear to be an example of the government tendency to impose mandates on subordinate governmental entities without providing the necessary funds to accomplish the new duties? In 2006, the public housing modernization budget had a deficit of $18 billion and was increasing at the rate of $2 billion per year. Bavan & Shamsudden *supra* at 189.

2. Review the asset management note *supra*. How will conversion of public housing units to "long-term, property-based contracts" facilitate asset management? Is such a move likely to enable PHAs to attract more private capital for the necessary preservation investments?

F. Interest Subsidy Programs

For a brief period between 1968 and 1973, two new federal programs featuring an interest subsidy became the cornerstones of federal housing policy.

1. Section 235 Homeownership Subsidy Program

The Section 235 program, 12 U.S.C. § 1715z, was designed to assist lower-income persons become homeowners by providing a deep subsidy in the form of interest reduction payments to mortgagees. The subsidy formula is calculated as the lesser of

> (A) the balance of the monthly payment of principal, interest, taxes, insurance, and mortgage insurance premium due under the mortgage remaining unpaid after applying 20 percentum of the mortgagor's income; or
>
> (B) the difference between the amount of the monthly payment for principal, interest, and mortgage insurance premium which the mortgagor is obligated to pay under the mortgage and the monthly payment for principal and interest which the mortgagor would be obligated to pay if the mortgage were to bear interest at the rate of 1 percentum per annum. 12 U.S.C. § 1715z(c)(1))

As noted previously, reference to the Matrix may be helpful in analyzing program elements.

For five years, the program was funded at a high level and provided mortgages in the $18,000–24,000 range to persons with incomes at 135% of local public housing authority limits. The income eligibility was later modified to 95% of area median income. Mortgages receiving 235 assistance also were eligible for FHA mortgage insurance under Section 221.

Controversies over the administration of Section 235 along with a change in direction regarding federal housing programs led to a sharp curtailment of the use of Section 235 after 1973. The program resulted in inflated, often fraudulent appraisals, and the sale of uninhabitable homes to families unable to maintain homes with defaults nearly bankrupting the FHA insurance fund. *See* Brian D. Boyer, Cities Destroyed for Cash: The FHA Scandal At HUD (1973). Total cost to the federal government in 1972 was estimated to be $1,051 per unit/year for an estimated eleven-year life, although contracts could extend as long as thirty years. U.S. Dep't of Housing and Urb. Dev, Housing in the Seventies 111 (1973). The 1987 Housing Act provided for a phase-out of the program after 1989.

2. Section 236 Rental Subsidy Program

The Section 236 program, 12 U.S.C. §1715z-1, was designed to assist lower-income renters and occupants of cooperatives through essentially the same interest subsidy scheme as Section 235. Two separate rental charges are used to calculate to the subsidy: (1) a "fair market rental charge" based on operation of the project with principal, interest, and mortgage insurance premium payments under the actual mortgage covering the project, and (2) a "basic rental charge," determined by calculating principal and interest payments under a 1% mortgage. The subsidy payment is the difference between the fair market rental charge and the basic rental charge, "or such greater amount, not exceeding the fair market rental charge, as represents 30 percentum of the tenant's adjusted income." 12 U.S.C. §1715z-1 (f)(1). Section 236 had approximately the same history and suffered the same fate as Section 235. Ultimately, rising interest rates threatened to inflate the subsidy and the HUD budget.

3. The Section 515 Rural Housing Program

The rural equivalent of the 236 program is the Section 515 program administered by the Rural Housing and Community Development Service (RHS) of the Department of Agriculture. Prior to 1994 the agency was called the Farmers Home Administration (FmHA). *See* 7 U.S.C. §6943. The Section 515 program is codified at 42 U.S.C. §1485 and remains active. RHS can operate its programs in rural areas, defined as open country or a town, village, or city with a population not in excess of 10,000 persons. RHS can operate in cities of up to 20,000 population if they are not contained within an SMSA and have a serious lack of mortgage credit. 42 U.S.C. §1490.

The Section 515 program is generally similar to the 236 program. However, where Section 515 operates without combination with other programs, there is no intervening loan from a private financial institution. The eligible sponsor secures a direct loan from RHS. Profit-oriented sponsors may develop Section 515 housing, but do not receive interest credits. Limited dividend and nonprofit sponsors may receive interest credits that reduce rentals to a 1% debt service level.

The Section 515 program may be used in tandem with the Section 8 program. HUD has established special procedures with RHS. 24 C.F.R. §§884.101–884.230.

In addition to the Section 515 program, RHS operates several other housing programs, including: 504 home rehabilitation (42 U.S.C. §1474); 514 and 516 farm labor housing (42 U.S.C. §§1484, 1486); 524 rural housing site loan program (42 U.S.C. §1490d); 523

mutual self-help housing program (42 U.S.C. § 1490c); and the 502 home loan and interest reduction program (42 U.S.C. § 1472).

G. Housing for the Elderly and Disabled (Sections 202 and 811)

The Section 202 program, enacted in 1959, 12 U.S.C. § 1701q, and its companion, the Section 811 program, enacted in 1990, 42 U.S.C. § 8013, are the principal programs which attempt to meet the housing needs of low-income elderly and persons with disabilities. Both programs provide grants to nonprofit sponsors to enable construction or substantial rehabilitation of supportive housing for their respective constituencies. Tenant eligibility is limited to persons and families who are elderly (at least 62 years of age) (202 program) or have disabilities as defined by law and regulations (811 program). For both programs, the term, "families," includes "2 or more ... persons living together, and 1 or more such persons living with 1 or more persons determined ... to be essential to their care or well being." 42 U.S.C. § 1437a(b). HUD requires sponsors, as in other programs, to meet development cost limitations, site approval criteria, sponsor's eligibility requirements, and to comply with HUD management regulations.

A HUD report, Barbara A. Haley & Robert W. Gray, Section 202 Supportive Housing for the Elderly: Program Status and Performance Measurement 17–24 (2008), *available at* www.huduser.org/Publications/pdf/sec_202_1.pdf, provides a summary of the Section 202 program. The authors identify five phases of the Section 202 program during its more than 50 years of existence. During the program's initial phase, from 1959–1974, HUD provided loans directly to nonprofit and limited dividend sponsors for 100% of the development cost of housing for moderate income elderly persons. The interest rate was fixed at the below-market rate of 3%. During this period, 335 projects were constructed totaling more than 45,000 units, most of which were efficiencies. During a five-year second phase, 1975–1980, project-based Section 8 rental assistance, with 20-year funding commitments, was added and the program emphasis shifted from moderate-income to low-income persons. Supportive services for frail elderly were added, and more one-bedroom units were constructed than efficiencies. More than 90,000 units were constructed in this five-year period.

Haley and Gray characterize a third phase during the 1980s as the "cost containment" phase, with services cut and fewer units constructed. A fourth phase began in 1990, as federal housing policy transitioned from the cost-containment emphasis of the 1980s to a new "project rental assistance contract" ("PRAC") strategy. During this time, a new program for persons with disabilities, Section 811 of the 1990 Cranston-Gonzalez National Affordable Housing Act, Pub. L. No. 101-625, 104 Stat. 4079 (1990), replaced the Section 202 program for persons with disabilities. Since 1993, Section 202's fifth phase has featured construction capital advances rather than direct loans. Since 1990, both programs have placed greater emphasis of the provision of supportive services as well as housing.

By 2006, approximately 6000 Section 202 developments provided housing for over 300,000 elderly and disabled households, 4000 of these in the older Section 202/8 direct loan program and 2000 in the Section 202/PRAC construction capital advance program. The study authors note "the potential of the Section 202 program to reduce Medicaid expenditures while providing a humane alternative to institutionalization.... [and that p]rogram efficiency could be increased if the Section 202 program were to provide more assistance to persons who are either at risk of institutionalization or already institutionalized." Haley and Gray at 12.

H. Direct Capital Grants

Modifications of the direct capital subsidy illustrated by Format VIII of the Matrix were added to private housing assistance programs in 1983 (42 U.S.C. § 1437o, repealed in 1990) to the public housing program in 1987 (42 U.S.C. § 1437c(a)(2)), and incorporated into a new targeted housing block grant program in 1990 (42 U.S.C. § 12721). Instead of financing capital subsidies through the issuance of low interest, tax exempt bonds, the 1983 and 1987 amendments provided for one-time, up-front grants of a fixed amount to cover part or all of the costs of development or rehabilitation. The private development subsidy, known as the housing development grant program, or HODAG, authorized grants of up to 50% of development cost. 42 U.S.C. § 1437o(d), repealed in 1990. The grants were required to be targeted to low-income areas and 20% of the units built with the grant assistance had to be set aside for low-income families with rents no higher than 15% of the area median family income. Because of the rent limitation requirement and the limits on the capital subsidy, developments in higher-cost localities would be feasible only if rents from the units not targeted to low-income families were skewed higher. Funding for the program was extremely limited and expired in October 1989.

A second use of the direct capital subsidy was authorized in 1987 as an alternative source of funding for public housing development. Development funds for new public housing would be available in up-front capital grants, but only under certain circumstances, including a showing of unmet demand for family housing, or that housing is required to replace units disposed of or demolished by the PHA or to comply with court orders. 42 U.S.C. §§ 1437c(a)(2), 1437c(j).

Housing Block Grants (HOME Investment Partnership Act of 1990)

In 1990, a targeted housing block grant program similar in concept to the Community Development Block Grant (CDBG) program discussed in Chapter 5 was enacted. 42 U.S.C. § 12741. States and local governments are eligible to receive housing block grants, but must develop comprehensive affordable housing strategies (CHAS) in order to receive the funds. 42 U.S.C. § 12746(5). One of the goals of this approach is to involve both public and private sectors in the planning process in order to be more responsive to the housing needs of the community.

Housing block grant funds are allocated through a "formula that reflects each jurisdiction's share of total need among eligible jurisdictions for an increased supply of affordable housing.... [A]llocation among units of general local government shall take into account the housing needs of metropolitan cities, urban counties, and approved consortia of units of general local government." 42 U.S.C. § 12747 (b)(1) (A).

A second significant feature is a specific statement of support for nonprofit community housing development organizations, including a requirement that 15% of each recipient's housing block grant be set aside for qualified nonprofits for 24 months after funds are made available. 42 U.S.C. § 12771.

Funds are made available to participating jurisdictions through a housing investment trust fund established by HUD, initially comprised of funds allocated to each participating jurisdiction, and thereafter augmented with subsequent allocations and repayments of funds drawn down from the trust fund—operating like a traditional line of credit, 42 U.S.C. § 12748.

States and local units of government receive direct federal grant money based upon an approved housing strategy. In general, states receive 40% and general local governments 60% of a formula-allocated housing block grant program for use in expanding the supply of affordable housing, 42 U.S.C. § 12747. Eligible expenditures are defined in 42 U.S.C. § 12742:

> (a) *Housing Uses*—Funds are available for most of the 'hard' costs associated with development activities that relate to the actual development costs such as acquisition of property, site preparation, relocation costs and constructions costs. Other 'soft' costs such as fees to developers, architects, contractors, etc. do not appear as eligible uses but are not specifically excluded as a prohibited use.
>
> Preference is given to the rehabilitation of substandard housing unless the jurisdiction can show that this is not cost effective. New construction is permitted, conditioned upon a showing that (i) an inadequate supply of housing is available at below fair market rental rates established by HUD, (ii) severe shortages exist of substandard buildings suitable for rehabilitation, (iii) construction of affordable housing is needed to facilitate a neighborhood revitalization effort by low-income and moderate-income families, and (iv) special needs housing requires new construction.
>
> (b) *Investments*—Funds can also be used by participating jurisdictions to provide equity investments, interest and non-interest-bearing loans and other forms of assistance not inconsistent with the purpose of HOP.
>
> (c) *Prohibited Uses*—Funds under the subtitle cannot be used to:
>
> (1) defray administrative costs of a particular jurisdiction;
>
> (2) provide tenant based rental assistance for replacement public housing or use in preserving units from expiring Section 8 contracts, etc.
>
> (3) provide non-federal matching contributions required under any other Federal program;
>
> (4) provide assistance under Section 9 of the United States Housing Act of 1937 (operating expenses for public housing);
>
> (5) provide assistance under Section 14 of the United States Housing Act of 1937 (improvements and maintenance of existing public housing units); and,
>
> (6) provide assistance to eligible low-income housing under the Emergency Low-Income Housing Preservation Act of 1987 or the Low-Income Housing Preservation Homeownership Act of 1990.

Notes and Questions

1. Viewed as a whole, do the HUD subsidy programs (including public housing and Section 8) reflect a thoughtful and ordered evolution of our national housing policy? Or

is it your impression that the programs represent a piecemeal *ad hoc* response to various problems and pressures?

2. For a study that describes how $3.1 billion of HOME funds were used to assist nearly 270,000 homebuyer units from 1992 to 2002 and examines the choices local governments are making in using the HOME program see the HUD report, STUDY OF HOMEBUYER ACTIVITY THROUGH THE HOME INVESTMENT PARTNERSHIPS PROGRAM (2004), available at http://www.huduser.org/Publications/pdf/Homebuy.pdf.

3. The insured loan programs have been a staple of federal housing policy since the 1930s. Losses resulting from faulty loan underwriting decisions or fraud have generally been minimal, but periodic scandals have called attention to an "uneasy partnership between the federal insurer and private enterprise ... [which] seesaws between the opposite dangers of insufficient incentive and unjust enrichment." CHARLES M. HAAR, LAND-USE PLANNING 866 (3d ed. 1977). A report prepared by the Department of Justice highlights what the report characterized as "known vulnerabilities" in the insurance programs:

> In order to obtain a VA-guaranteed or HUD-insured loan, a purchaser must process an application through a mortgagee approved to originate such loans. The mortgagee is then responsible for processing and submitting all paperwork to the agency in order to obtain the guaranty of insurance.
>
> The mortgagee earns his or her fees in several different ways. First, an origination fee is earned for the processing of the application; second, points are obtained for the loan; lastly, fees can be earned for the servicing of the loan. Many mortgagees simply originate the loan and subsequently sell the commercial paper for processing. The real estate company earns its fees from commissions in sales; therefore, it is motivated to sell as many houses as possible. Neither the realtor nor the mortgagee are particularly worried about potential foreclosures. The real estate company is not concerned even if the house goes into foreclosure immediately upon purchase, since it has already earned its commission. The lending institution is in the same position since it has already earned the origination fee and loan points. Since both the realtor and the lending institution earn their fees whether the loan is good or goes into foreclosure, there is little motivation on their part to ensure that the purchaser is qualified for the loan.
>
> Both HUD and VA utilize similar procedures in their home loan programs. Mortgagees, approved to originate insured mortgages, are required to obtain and verify information relative to a mortgagor's credit worthiness and ability to meet all monthly obligations. Both agencies rely on mortgagees to obtain factual data from the mortgagor, to verify and analyze the information obtained and to package the data and forward the application to the interested agency. Further, under the VA Automatic Approval Program and the HUD Direct Endorsement Program, the mortgagee underwrites and closes the mortgage loan without prior agency approval or review. In fact, the VA delegates such loan approval to the lenders on approximately half of their loan applications. Although quality control audits are supposed to be conducted on 5–10% of these pre-approved loans, it is obvious how such procedures can facilitate fraud by lenders.
>
> This dependence on the mortgagee, who is in fact a party to the transaction, with a direct financial interest in obtaining the insured loan and closing the deal, is a basic weakness in the system and subjects both VA and HUD to substantial exposure to loss or abuse in their home loan insurance programs. Home buyers

> and sellers, real estate salespersons, brokers and developers, as well as mortgagees, all can have a substantial interest in a real property transaction. As a result, any one or all of the parties to such a transaction could be involved in fraud in order to assure its completion. In addition, other parties to fraud could be fee appraisers, settlement attorneys, beneficiaries of the mortgagor or even VA or HUD employees.

U.S. Dep't of Justice, Investigation and Prosecution of Housing and Urban Development and Veterans Administration Frauds 6–8 (1987).

4. Is the Justice Department's criticism valid? What modifications to the insurance programs might be considered in light of the "known vulnerabilities?" Would a direct loan program be easier to police? In 1998, HUD opened a new Enforcement Center headed by a former member of the FBI's organized crime unit to step-up enforcement efforts against multi-family property owners and managers.

I. Federal Responses to Homelessness

As discussed in Chapter 1, since the 1980s the United States has experienced a series of upsurges in the number of persons and families who had no place to live except the streets or shelters for the homeless. While advocates, analysts and policy makers have disagreed sharply on the absolute number of homeless persons at any particular time and the locus of responsibility for the increases that have taken place, they generally have agreed that three categories of homeless persons exist: (1) traditional homeless—the "skid row bums," (2) mentally retarded persons who were no longer being institutionalized because of changes in state mental health programs, and (3) the "new homeless," persons and families who had lost jobs and then homes because of inability to make mortgage or rent payments.

After several years of often acrimonious public debate, Congress enacted in 1987 the Stewart B. McKinney Homeless Assistance Act, which purported to establish a comprehensive federal approach to an extremely complex problem. The Act was renamed the McKinney-Vento Homeless Assistance Act in 2000 and reauthorized in 2009 as part of the Helping Families Save Their Homes Act of 2009, Pub. L. No. 111-22, Div. B, § 1003(a), 123 Stat. 1632 (*amending* 42 U.S.C. § 11301 and ff and *codified at* 42 U.S.C. §§ 11301–11472)). The Act established a number of emergency aid programs to provide food, shelter, education, job training, and medical services to homeless people. A new and more comprehensive definition of homeless people was adopted in the 2009 reauthorization, as noted in Chapter 1 *supra.*

In general, the Act attempts to marshal the resources of existing programs and apply them to emergency homelessness situations, primarily through the work of the United States Interagency Council on the Homeless established by the Act. The 2009 reauthorization formalized the Interagency Council mission to "coordinate the Federal response to homelessness and to create a national partnership at every level of government and with the private sector to reduce and end homelessness...." Pub. L. No. 111-22, Div. B, § 1004(a)(1), 123 Stat. 1632 (*amending* 42 U.S.C. § 11311). The council is comprised of the agencies which are responsible for over 30 programs providing assistance to homeless persons.

HUD administers three competitive grant programs under the Continuum of Care aegis described in Chapter 1 *supra*: the Supportive Housing Program, the Shelter Plus

Care Program and the Single Room Occupancy Program. States, metropolitan cities (population over 50,000), and urban counties and supportive housing programs must first obtain approval from HUD of a current Comprehensive Housing Affordability Strategy (CHAS), discussed in Chapter 5 *infra*, or a Comprehensive Homeless Assistance Plan (CHAP). CHAPs must contain four components: (1) a description of the need for assistance, (2) a brief inventory of facilities and services available to homeless persons within the jurisdiction, (3) a two-part strategy to match needs with services and to recognize special needs of various categories of homeless persons, particularly families with children, the elderly, the mentally ill, and veterans, and (4) an explanation of how federal assistance "will complement and enhance" available services. 42 U.S.C. § 11361.

Emergency Shelter Grants

The Emergency Shelter Grants program provides funds to governmental agencies and nonprofit organizations for three types of expenditures: (1) renovation, major rehabilitation, or conversion of buildings for emergency shelters, (2) provisions of essential services in shelters, such as employment, health, drug abuse, or education, under carefully controlled limitations, and (3) costs of shelter maintenance, insurance, utilities, furnishings, and general operations. A 50% matching requirement is imposed, which may include in-kind services such as the value of donated buildings, volunteer time, or paid staff. 42 U.S.C. § 11374.

Supportive Housing

The Supportive Housing program seeks to ascertain innovative ways to provide transitional and permanent housing for homeless persons. Such housing must meet local code standards and offer supportive services as well as basic shelter. Supportive services are defined as assistance which meets the special needs of particular classes of homeless persons such as deinstitutionalized homeless persons and homeless families with children. Transitional housing is housing designed to facilitate the "movement of homeless individuals to independent living within a reasonable period of time." Group homes serving a maximum of eight handicapped homeless persons are eligible for assistance under the permanent housing component of the demonstration program.

Four types of assistance are available to project sponsors under the Supportive Housing program: (1) advances, not exceeding $200,000, for acquisition and rehabilitation of structures; (2) grants for moderate rehabilitation of existing structures; (3) annual payments of up to 75% of the operating costs of transitional housing; and (4) technical assistance. Fifty per cent matching is required to qualify for advances and grants for transitional housing. The limited funds available are awarded by HUD on a competitive basis upon the receipt of detailed applications. Standards for awards include ability of the sponsor, need, innovative quality, extent of matching funds, cost effectiveness, and extent to which needs will be met by the project. 42 U.S.C. §§ 11383–84.

Shelter Plus Care

Homeless service providers may apply for Section 8 funds to enable them to provide both housing and supportive services to homeless persons with disabilities and their families. Funds are available in four components: (1) Tenant-based Rental Assistance (TRA); (2) Sponsor-based Rental Assistance (SRA); (3) Project-based Rental Assistance (PRA); and (4) Single Room Occupancy-based Rental Assistance (SRO). TRA, SRA & PRA programs offer five year Section 8 contracts, although PRA programs may qualify for 10 year contracts if units are being rehabilitated with other funding. The SRO program requires moderate rehabilitation and offers 10 year Section 8 contracts. *See* U.S. Dep't of Hous. and Urb. Dev., 1997 Homeless Programs: Continuum of Care 13, 27, 41 (1997).

Regulations for the programs are: Emergency Shelter Grants, 24 C.F.R. § 576; Shelter Plus Care, 24 C.F.R. § 582, and Supportive Housing, 24 C.F.R. § 583.

Continuum of Care

HUD has been administering its homeless assistance programs through the Continuum of Care approach described in Chapter 1 *supra* since 1994. The Continuum of Care approach is described as a "community-based process that provides a comprehensive response to the different needs of homeless individuals and families." Homeless prevention is included, along with emergency, transitional, and permanent housing and services. The goal is to help homeless persons "make the critical transition from the streets to jobs and independent living." 1997 HOMELESS PROGRAMS, *supra* at 3. *See generally*, U.S. DEP'T OF HOUS. AND URB. DEV., BUILDING EFFECTIVE COALITIONS (2009), *available at* www.hudhre.info/documents/BuildingEffectiveCoalitions.pdf.

Use of Surplus Property

The original McKinney Act became mired in controversy over an important section that requires the federal government to identify underutilized public buildings that could be made available for facilities to assist the homeless. HUD has statutory responsibility for coordinating efforts to locate such properties and determine their suitability and availability for use. 42 U.S.C. § 11411. Delays in implementation led to lawsuits by advocates for the homeless, charging federal agencies with withholding vacant properties, particularly residential units that had been obtained by the government as a result of defaults on insured or guaranteed mortgages. 16 [Current Developments] Hous. & Dev. Rep. (WGL) 373 (1988).

One of the basic issues in the cases was the proper resolution of a policy conflict that has existed almost from the inception of the federal housing programs: how to square the government's responsibility to protect its investment in housing—in this case by selling foreclosed single-family homes to recoup losses in the housing insurance funds—with the congressional goal of a "decent home and suitable living environment for every American family." *Id.* at 414.

In 1994, Congress passed a law exempting military base closings from the McKinney Act provisions. Instead, the Department of Defense (DOD) is required to transfer such properties to local redevelopment agencies based on local redevelopment plans that are supposed to consider homeless needs along with economic development and job creation concerns. Base Closure Community Redevelopment and Homeless Assistance Act of 1994, Pub. L. No. 103-421, 108 Stat. 4346 (1994) (*codified at* 42 U. S. C. § 11301). DOD Regulations are codified at 32 C.F.R. § 176; HUD Regulations are codified at 24 C.F.R. § 586.

Notes and Questions

1. Other possible avenues for homeless assistance, principally under state statutory provisions, are discussed in Chapter 1 *supra* in connection with the right to housing.

2. For a number of years, Congress debated whether to modify the McKinney Act approach and fold it into a block grant. *See* 25 [Current Developments] Hous. & Dev Rep. (West) 614 (1998). Would a homeless assistance block grant, advocated by some housing supporters, in which funds were distributed by states and localities rather than Washington, resolve coordination problems that have plagued McKinney Act programs since their inception? The block grant concept is discussed in Chapter 5 *infra*.

3. For further discussion of homelessness, *see* NAT'L LAW CTR. ON HOMELESSNESS AND POVERTY, AN OUNCE OF PREVENTION: PROGRAMS TO PREVENT HOMELESSNESS IN

25 States (Feb. 2009), *available at* www.nlchp.org; U.S. Dep'ts of Health and Human Services and Hous. and Urb. Dev., Toward Understanding Homelessness: The 2007 Nat. Symposium of Homelessness Research (Sept. 2007), *available at* http://aspe.hhs.gov/hsp/homelessness/symposium07; U.S. Conf. of Mayors, Hunger and Homelessness Survey: A Status Report on Hunger and Homelessness in America's Cities (2009) (conducted annually); Jane B. Baron, *Homelessness as a Property Problem,* 36 Urb. Law. 273 (2004) (advocacy and policy issues); Nestor M. Davidson, *"Housing First" for the Chronically Homeless: Challenges of a New Service Model,* 15 J. Affordable Housing & Community Dev. L. 125 (2006); Jonathan L. Hafetz, *Homeless Legal Advocacy: New Challenges and Directions for the* Future, 30 Fordham Urb. L.J. 1215 (2003) (lawyer's role in helping the homeless); Symposium, *Representing the Poor and Homeless: Innovations in Advocacy,* 19 St. Louis U. Pub. L. Rev. 205 (2000).

J. Federal Tax Policy and Housing

The tax implications for the various program formats were discussed in connection with the Matrix, *supra.* This section looks more generally at major changes in tax policy enacted in the 1986 Tax Reform Act, which removed many of the popular tax shelter features of real estate investment such as accelerated depreciation, but retained the largest single shelter—the deductibility of interest paid on home mortgages.

1. The Low Income Housing Tax Credit (26 U.S.C. §42)

In order to forestall a predicted abandonment by the private sector of housing development for persons of low and moderate income, Congress enacted the Low-Income Housing Tax Credit (LIHTC) as a part of the Tax Reform Act. Since its enactment in 1986, the LIHTC has eclipsed all the other federal housing programs in size, with 1.67 million LIHTC housing units placed in service between 1987 and 2006. About 103,000 units have been added each year to the LIHTC portfolio. HUD National Low Income Housing Tax Credit (LIHTC) Database: Projects Placed in Service through 2006, *available at* www.huduser.org/databases/lihtc.html. The primary method by which LIHTC projects are developed is through syndicated limited partnerships, with approximately two-thirds of the portfolio controlled by the eight largest for-profit and nonprofit syndicators. Alex Schwartz and Edwin Meléndez, *After Year 15: Challenges to the Preservation of Housing Financed with Low-Income Housing Tax Credits,* 19 Housing Pol'y Debate 261, 261–62 (2008).

The LIHTC provides a dollar for dollar credit against a taxpayer's ordinary income tax obligations for a 10-year period beginning the year a "qualified low-income building" is placed in service or the following year, at the taxpayer's election, 26 U.S.C. §42(f). The credit amount is based on the "qualified basis" (the amount of the building that is devoted to low-income housing, computed as the lower of the percentage of units or floor space set aside for low-income housing), 26 U.S.C. §42(c). For newly constructed and substantially rehabilitated buildings, the credit equals 70% of the cost (present value) of low-income housing units that are not subsidized by any other federal housing program. This amounts to an annual credit of approximately 9% of the qualified building costs of the units. In the case of new or substantially rehabilitated buildings that are federally subsidized, as well as existing buildings that are acquired but not substantially rehabilitated, the credit amount is 30% of the cost of the units, which amounts to an annual credit of approximately 4% of the qualified building costs of the units, 26 U.S.C. § 42(b).

In order to qualify for the LIHTC, a building must satisfy three tests.

> (1) *Minimum set aside test.* At least 20% of the units must be "rent-restricted and occupied by" persons whose incomes are 50% or less of the area median gross income, or at least 40% of the units must be "rent-restricted and occupied by" persons whose incomes are 60% or less of the area median gross income, 26 U.S.C. § 42(g)(1).
>
> (2) *Rent restriction test.* The gross rent of a LIHTC unit may not exceed 30% of the applicable income limitation for the unit (50% or 60% of area median gross income. Gross rent includes any utility allowance under Section 8, but does not include any Section 8 payments or fees paid the unit owner for supportive services, 26 U.S.C. § 42(g)(2).
>
> (3) *Suitability for residential occupancy test.* Units must meet local health, safety, and building codes and provide permanent or transitional housing leading to permanent housing within 24 months. 26 U.S.C. § 42(i)(3)(B).

In return for the 10-year credit, building owners must continue to meet the qualified low-income building tests for a 15-year period, called the "compliance period." 26 U.S.C. § 42(i)(1). Failure to do so subjects holders of the tax credits to full or partial recapture of credits taken, along with an interest penalty, 26 U.S.C. § 42(j). Receipt of housing credits also is conditioned upon the execution, as a recordable restrictive covenant enforceable against subsequent owners, of an "extended low-income housing commitment" by the owner and the state housing credit agency which obligates the owner and subsequent owners to retain the low-income character of the building for an additional 15-year period, or longer if specified by the state housing credit agency. However, the extended use period will terminate if the building is acquired as a result to a bona fide foreclosure, or the state housing credit agency certifies that no prospective purchasers are willing to continue to operate the building as a qualified low-income building, 26 U.S.C. § 42(h)(6).

Administration of the LIHTC program is delegated to state housing agencies. Credits are allocated to states by a formula adjusted annually to account for inflation. The statutory figure is $1.75 multiplied by the State population, or $2 million, whichever is greater, supplemented by an annual cost-of-living adjustment. 26 U.S.C. § 42(h)(2)(C) & (H). In 2009, the allocation was the greater of $2.30 times the State population or $2.655 million. *States Will Have $716.8 Million in Tax Credits, $30.607 Billion in Tax-Exempt Bonds to Allocate in 2009*, 37 [Current Developments] Hous. & Dev. Rep. (West) 37 (Jan. 19, 2009). While the $716.8 million available in credits in 2009 was significant, it paled in comparison to the amount of taxes foregone, over $97 billion, by the mortgage interest tax deduction. U.S. Office of Management and Budget, Budget of the U.S., FY 2010, Analytical Perspectives, Table 19-1, at 300 (2009).

State housing credit agencies are responsible for allocating credits to developers and monitoring their use of the credits and compliance with the requirements of the statute.

Allocations are based on annual Qualified Allocation Plans (QAP), which must contain selection criteria based on housing priorities of the State, preferences for projects serving the lowest income tenants for the longest periods and in low-income census tracts

(50% of the residents have incomes below 60% of area median gross income, or a 25% poverty rate) and a procedure for monitoring compliance with the tax credit rules and notifying the Internal Revenue Service of noncompliance, as well as monitoring for noncompliance with habitability standards through regular site visits. 26 U.S.C. §42(m)(1)(B). A comparative analysis of all fifty states' Qualified Allocation Plans from 1990, 2000 and 2001 prepared by The Urban Institute for the Department of Housing and Urban Development identified the following preferences.

> [T]he most widely used preferences targeted projects that were in rural areas, contributed to community revitalization plans, leveraged funding from other governmental programs, served special needs residents, or extended affordability periods beyond minimum requirements. All of the states restricted developer and or builder fees, and several restricted the total tax credits any single project could receive. Other common state preferences were for projects that acquired and rehabilitated at-risk properties, had fewer and larger units, or were sponsored by non-profit organizations that were locally-based.

JEREMY GUSTAFSON & J. CHRISTOPHER WALKER, ANALYSIS OF STATE QUALIFIED ALLOCATION PLANS FOR THE LOW-INCOME HOUSING TAX CREDIT PROGRAM 19 (2002). By 2001, over forty states gave preference points for agreements to extend the affordability periods ranging from 40 to 60 years and even in perpetuity (Massachusetts, Michigan, and Vermont). *Id.* at 18–19.

Despite the popularity of the LIHTC, the housing collapse of 2007–2009 exposed the credit's dependence on the willingness of investors to purchase credits from housing developers. As credit markets dried up and investors retreated from real estate markets, prices which investors were willing to pay for housing tax credits dropped sharply. Many developers were unable to complete projects that had been started or were in the credit-approval pipeline. In response to the sudden drop in tax credit demand by investors, Congress established an emergency program enabling State LIHTC-allocation agencies to take a portion of their State housing credit ceiling for 2009 in the form of Section 1602 grants (named after the section of the American Recovery and Reinvestment Act of 2009 ("ARRA"), Pub. L. No. 111-5, 123 Stat. 115, which authorized the grants). Grants to developers could be made during 2010 for new construction or acquisition and rehabilitation of qualified housing units. Funds could continue to be disbursed through December 31, 2011, provided projects were at least 30% complete by the end of 2010. Department of the Treasury, Payments in Lieu of Low Income Housing Tax Credits, 74 Fed. Reg. 44751 (Aug. 31, 2009) (*codified at* 31 C.F.R. Pt. 32). In addition, $2.25 billion was made available to state credit allocation agencies to enable LIHTC-approved projects to fill financing gaps through a new program known as the Tax Credit Assistance Program ("TCAP"). For discussion of these emergency programs, *see* Michael J. Novogradac, Glenn A. Graff & Nicolo R. Pinoli, *Low Income Housing Tax Provisions of the Recovery Act of 2009: Tools to Close Financing Gaps in a Weak Tax Equity Market,* 18 J. AFFORDABLE HOUSING & COMMUNITY DEV. L. 465 (2009).

Notes and Questions

1. The Low-Income Housing Tax Credit (LIHTC) is a limited program designed to encourage equity investment in housing production activities. While it requires that tax credit investments be targeted to low-income persons, the value of the credit is insufficient by itself to enable rents to reach the payment capabilities of the low-income persons the tax credit program seeks to benefit. Developers of tax credit supported

projects have to confront sizable rental income gaps. The example of Format XIII illustrates the problem. With a market rent of $1,501 per month and a tenant rent of $750 for forty units set aside for persons in the 60% income range, participation in the tax credit program will produce a project rental income gap of up to $30,049 per month or $360,595 per year, requiring an upward skewing of the rent on the remaining eighty units approximately $501 per month, or some other form of subsidy. Necessary additional subsidies can be provided either by demand-based programs such as the Section 8 existing housing program or housing vouchers described above, or by supply-based programs such as the discontinued Section 8 new construction or substantial rehabilitation programs. State housing agencies have moved to fill the tax credit subsidy gap with monies generated by housing trust funds and special housing-related taxes described below.

The tax credit differs from previous housing tax benefits in that the credit applies only on a unit-by-unit basis rather than to the entire property. Under prior law, an entire building could be rapidly depreciated as long as the building contained at least 20% low-income units. Congress intended the new structure to provide a major incentive to include more low-income units since each additional unit will increase the investors' tax savings.

2. The LIHTC is structured in such a way to discourage other federal subsidies. The full 70% credit is awarded projects that do not receive other federal subsidies such as tax exempt financing and community development block grants, while projects securing such subsidies receive either a 30% credit or a 70% credit after the amount of the additional federal subsidy is subtracted from the project's basis. These provisions are designed to limit so-called "double-dipping" use of multiple subsidies. Does this policy make sense in light of the demonstrated gap between affordable rentals and development costs, particularly in areas other than those with relatively high median incomes and relatively low construction costs?

3. The tax credit is a complex program that is not without risk for developers and investors. For example, tax credits are granted only when projects are placed in service, even though tax credit allocations are made prior to the beginning of construction. In general, credits must be used in the year of allocation. Thus, if delays prevent a project from being placed in service during the year of the credit allocation, the developer may lose the allocated credits, thereby placing the project in jeopardy because of the potential loss of anticipated equity investment. The Technical Corrections Act of 1988 authorized a carryover of credit reservations for specific projects for up to twenty-four months, if at least 10% of the total estimated project development costs are expended in the year the credit allocation was received. 26 U.S.C. §42(h)(1)(E).

An element of risk for investors is contained in the requirement that low-income limitations be sustained for a fifteen-year period, even though the credit is taken over ten years. Projects can be penalized if during the fifteen years: (1) the level of low-income people occupying units declines below the level for which the tax credit was received; or (2) the level of low-income occupancy falls below the minimum initial eligibility threshold levels. If either of these two things occurs, the "accelerated" portion of the credit is recaptured, plus interest. The accelerated portion is the amount of the credit taken in prior years that exceeds the amount that would have been taken if the credit had been apportioned over the 15-year compliance period rather than the 10-year credit period. 26 U.S.C. §42(j)(3). This amounts to one-third of the credits taken in the 10-year period. During the last five years of the compliance period, the credit recapture percentage declines ratably each year (4/15, 3/15, 2/15, 1/15), Novogradac & Co., LLP, Low-Income Housing Tax Credit Handbook §3:211 (2009), citing the official ("Bluebook") explanation, General Explanation of the Tax Reform Act of 1986, prepared by the Staff of the Joint Committee on Taxation 165–166 (1987).

4. As noted above, the state-by-state per capita volume cap on use of the tax credit places a severe limitation on the potential effectiveness of the tax credit as a major contributor to national housing policy. The $700 million program represents a small fraction of the total federal allocation for Section 8 at the high point of that program, and an even smaller percentage of the amount of tax revenue forgone as a result of the continuing deductibility of interest on home mortgages, one of the few real estate tax preferences to survive the 1986 Tax Reform Act.

5. The 1986 Tax Reform Act limits the amount of tax credits that can be used by most taxpayers and eliminates their use altogether at very high income levels. With certain exceptions, losses from passive investments cannot be deducted against ordinary income. (*See* comment 2 following the Matrix *supra*) However, low-income housing investors with adjusted gross incomes under $200,000 can take a maximum credit of $7,500 per year, to reduce ordinary income. The credit begins to phase out as incomes increase over $200,000 and is eliminated altogether at $250,000.

The tax credit is similar to other passive losses in that it can be used to offset passive income without limitation. Wealthy taxpayers, however, often have sufficient passive losses to cover passive income. The 1986 restrictions severely reduced the profitability of tax shelter housing investments for these individuals who were the mainstay of the low-income housing syndication industry.

At the same time, the 1986 Tax Reform Act opened up new investment opportunities to most corporations since their passive loss limitations are exempt from the passive loss provisions. Qualified corporations are able to use an unlimited amount of depreciation deductions and tax credits to offset tax on business income. In many communities, non profit intermediaries have been established to recruit corporate investments and to review applications for support from non profit developers of LIHTC-qualified housing. As noted above, two of the largest syndicators of housing tax credits are non-profit organizations, Enterprise Social Investment Corporation and National Equity Fund.

6. In enacting the low-income tax credit, Congress attempted to create a direct relationship between the tax benefit and the housing benefit, the lack of which had been a major criticism of the tax shelter syndication format. However, in seeking to create this direct connection and to rationalize tax code housing production incentives, has Congress overcomplicated and excessively restricted the tax credit mechanism? A study of the first 20 years of the LIHTC program emphasized the benefits of the competitive nature of the program and the ability of state allocating agencies to "design their Qualified Allocation Plans so as to emphasize the factors on which they desire competition and select from among competing developers and projects accordingly." JILL KHADDURI & CHARLES WILKINS, DESIGNING SUBSIDIZED RENTAL HOUSING PROGRAMS: WHAT HAVE WE LEARNED? 19 (2007) (published by the Harvard University Joint Center for Housing Studies). Most states have adopted scoring systems to rate and rank applications for housing tax credits. *See, e.g.*, Ill. Housing Dev. Auth., 2008–2009 Qualified Allocation Plan, *available at* www.ihda.org/admin; N.C. Housing Fin. Agency, The 2007 Low-Income Housing Tax Credit Qualified Allocation Plan for the State of North Carolina 8–20 (2006), *available at* www.nchfa.com/Forms/QAP/2007/07QAPFinal.pdf.

Khadduri and Wilkins also note that the program has several built-in incentives for paying attention to quality of construction and management, particularly because the income range ($25,000–$40,000) of the households being served allows those households to choose conventional housing if the LIHTC housing is not up to the competition's standards. In addition, the strength of the compliance program and the fact that the LIHTC is not subject to annual appropriations are identified as strengths by the study authors. Khadduri and Wilkins *supra* at 19–21. Major shortcomings identified include the difficulty in reaching households with extremely low-income, and the fact that rental income typically doesn't fully fund operating costs and capital needs, *Id.* at 22–26. *See also* Alex Schwartz & Edwin Meléndez, *After Year 15: Challenges to the Preservation of Housing Financed with Low-Income Housing Tax Credits*, 19 Housing Pol'y Debate 261, 283 (2008) ("The most formidable challenge of all, at least for some projects, concerns the financing of necessary physical improvements. After 15 years, virtually any building will need replacement and upgrading of major systems").

7. Early criticisms of the LIHTC focused on the same reason that previous tax shelter provisions were criticized — inefficiency because of the high transaction costs associated with organizing and marketing the tax credit investment vehicle, see, *e.g.*, Janet Stearns, *Low-Income Housing Tax Credit: A Poor Solution to the Housing Crisis*, 6 Yale L. & Pol'y Rev. 203, 225–26 (1988). *See also* Florence Wagman Roisman, *Mandates Unsatisfied: The Low Income Housing Tax Credit Program and the Civil Rights Laws,* 52 U. Miami L. Rev. 1011 (1997–1998) (criticizing segregative site selection practices).

8. The impact of the 2007–2009 housing market collapse on the LIHTC raises questions about the future of the credit. Were the emergency programs enacted in 2009 "bail outs" of developers? Does the emergency funding suggest that Congress should subject the LIHTC to the regular budget review and approval process? Does it suggest that a direct subsidy program would be a more realistic alternative? For discussion of these issues, see Joint Center for Housing Studies of Harvard University, The Disruption of the Low-Income Housing Tax Credit Program: Causes, Consequences, Responses, and Proposed Correctives (2009) (stressing the long-term problem of restoring investor demand in the aftermath of the credit crisis which eliminated much of the after tax income that national banks, Fannie Mae and Freddie Mac had sheltered by investing in tax credit transactions and suggesting that tax credit duration (10 years) and recapture period (15 years) be shortened).

9. For other studies, see Michael J. Novogradac & Glen A. Graff, *Impact of the Housing and Economic Recovery Act of 2008 on Current and Future Low-Income Housing Tax Credit Properties,* 18 J. Affordable Housing & Community Dev. L. 47 (2008); Kirk McClure, *The Low-Income Housing Tax Credit Program Goes Mainstream and Moves to the Suburbs,* 17 Hous. Pol'y Debate 419 (2007); Roberta L. Rubin & Jonathan Klein, *Nonprofit Guarantees in Tax Credit Transactions: A New Era?* 15 J. Affordable Housing & Community Dev. L. 314 (2006); Brett D. Siglin, *Obstacles Encountered When Combining FHA and Other HUD Programs with Tax Credits,* 18 J. Affordable Housing & Community Dev. L. (2008); Adam McNeely, Comment, *Improving Low Income Housing: Eliminating the Conflict Between Property Taxes and the LIHTC Program*, 15 J. Affordable Housing & Community Dev. L. 324 (2006). A comprehensive reference manual that is updated annually is Novogradac & Company, LLP, Low-Income Housing Tax Credit Handbook (2009).

Metro City Problem (cont.)

The LIHTC is an extremely complex program, as noted above. How might the Metro City developer utilize the LIHTC most effectively? Given the lengthy compliance period (15 years) and the severe penalties for noncompliance (recapture of credits taken by investors), how might the parties establish a compliance process? Do the excerpts from the following Declaration of Land Use Restrictions for a companion state housing tax credit program suggest an effective method?

Declaration of Land Use Restriction Covenants for the State of Missouri Affordable Housing Tax Credits

THIS DECLARATION OF LAND USE RESTRICTION COVENANTS (this "Agreement"), dated as of the *7th* day of August XXXX______, by ____________ ASSOCIATES, L.P., a ________________ limited partnership, (hereinafter called the "Owner"), and by ____________ CORPORATION, a __________________ not for profit corporation, holding a ruling from Internal Revenue Service that it qualifies as tax exempt under IRC § 501(c) (3), (4) or (6), (hereinafter called the "Sponsor"), is hereby granted and declared as a condition precedent to the allocation of Missouri Affordable Housing Tax Credits by the MISSOURI HOUSING DEVELOPMENT COMMISSION, a governmental instrumentality of the State of Missouri or any successor to its rights, duties and obligations, whose officers are located at 3435 Broadway, Kansas City Missouri 64111 (hereinafter sometimes referred to as the "Commission" or as MHDC")....

NOW, THEREFORE, in consideration of the mutual premises and covenants hereinafter set forth, and other valuable consideration, the Owner, the Sponsor, and the Commission agree as follows:

SECTION 2—RECORDING AND FILING; COVENANTS TO RUN WITH THE LAND

(a) Upon execution and delivery by the Owner, the Owner shall cause this Agreement and all amendments hereto to be recorded and filed in the official public land deed records of the county in which the Property is located, and shall pay all fees and charges incurred in connection with such recording. The recording shall be after the recording of the First Mortgage in favor of MHDC, and the Second Mortgage in favor of ____________________ Housing Authority, and shall be subordinate thereto. In addition, this Agreement shall be subordinate to all other restrictions, easements, deeds of trust, encumbrances, rights-of-way, and other conditions of record existing as of *March 20, XXXX.*

(b) The Owner intends, declares and covenants, on behalf of itself and all future Owners and Operators of the Project during the term of this Agreement, with the exception of MHDC should MHDC become an Owner or Operator of the Project, that this Agreement and the covenants and restrictions set forth herein regulating and restricting the use, occupancy and transfer of the Project (i) shall be and are covenants running with the land and improvements, encumbering the Project for the term of this Agreement, binding upon the Owner's successors in title and all subsequent Owners and Operators of the Project, (ii) are not merely personal covenants of the Owner, and (iii) shall bind the Owner (and the benefits shall inure to the Commission and any past, present or prospective tenant of the Project) and its and their respective successors and assigns during the term of this Agreement. The Owner hereby agrees that any and all requirements of the laws of the State of Missouri to be satisfied in order for the provisions of this Agreement to constitute deed restrictions and covenants running with the land shall be deemed to be satisfied in full, and that any requirements or privileges of estate are intended to be satisfied, or in the alternate, that an equitable servitude has been created to insure that these restrictions run with the land. For the longer of the period that Affordable Housing Credits are claimed or the term of this

Agreement, each and every contract, deed, or other instrument hereafter executed conveying the Project or portion thereof shall expressly provide that such conveyance is subject to this Agreement, provided, however the covenants contained herein shall survive and be effective regardless of whether such contract, deed or other instrument hereafter executed conveying the Project or any portion thereof provides that such conveyance is subject to this Agreement.

(c) The Owner covenants to obtain the consent of the Second Mortgage Holder on the Project to this Agreement and such consent shall be a condition precedent to the issuance of Missouri Department of Revenue Form MOTC constituting final allocation of the Affordable Housing Credits....

SECTION 4—INCOME RESTRICTIONS; RENTAL RESTRICTIONS

The Owner represents, warrants and covenants throughout the term of this Agreement and in order to satisfy the requirements of the Act and Regulations that:

(a) Fifty percent (50%) of the residential units in the Project are an Affordable Housing Unit and will be occupied by individuals whose income is at or below the levels described in the Act and Regulations; and,

(b) Owner shall charge a gross rental rate on the Affordable Housing Units not to exceed fifty (50) percent of the maximum eligible household income of the Low-Income Tenant as defined in the Act and Regulations.

SECTION 5—TERM OF AGREEMENT

(a) Except as hereinafter provided, this Agreement, the Low-income use and rental restrictions specified herein shall commence with the first day of the initial ten (10) year compliance period in which any building which is part of the Project is placed in service and shall end on the last day of such initial ten (10) year compliance period. [The Missouri statute calls for a 10 year compliance period—Eds.] Tax Credits approved for qualified donors will be available for use any time after initial closing with the first mortgagee as defined in the First Mortgage Documents.

(b) Notwithstanding subsection (a), above, this Agreement, with respect to any building which is part of the Project, shall terminate on the date the building is acquired by foreclosure or instrument in lieu of foreclosure unless the Commission determines that such acquisition is part of an arrangement with the taxpayer, the purpose of which is to terminate such compliance or extended compliance period.

SECTION 6—ENFORCEMENT OF OCCUPANCY RESTRICTIONS

(a) The Owner shall permit, during normal business hours and upon reasonable notice, any duly authorized representative of the Commission, to inspect any books and records of the Owner regarding the Project which pertain to compliance with the Act and Regulations with respect to the income of Low-Income Tenants.

(b) The Owner shall submit a copy of the Certification of Continuing Program Compliance shown as *Exhibit B* to this Agreement to the Commission at least annually, or as requested by the Commission (but not more frequently than semi-annually) in order to monitor compliance with the provisions specified in the Agreement and the Act and Regulations.

(c) The determination of whether a tenant meets the Affordable Housing rental requirements shall be made by the Owner at least annually on the basis of the current income of each Low-Income Tenant. The Owner shall submit to MHDC the Income Certification for each low-income tenant on the form shown as *Exhibit C* to this Agreement, or on a substantially similar form approved by the Commission.

(d) The determination of whether a unit meets the Affordable Housing rental requirements shall be made by the Owner at least annually on the bass of the current rental information of such Affordable Housing Unit. The Owner shall submit to the Commission the unit certification for each Affordable Housing Unit on a form approved by the Commission.

(e) The Owner shall submit any other information, documents or certifications requested by the Commission which the Commission shall deem reasonably necessary to substantiate the Owner's continuing compliance with Act and Regulations.

(f) The Owner covenants that it will not knowingly take or permit any action that would result in a violation of the requirements of the Act and Regulations or this Agreement. Moreover, Owner covenants, subject to the provisions of the First Mortgage Documents, if any, to take any lawful action (including amendment of this Agreement as may be reasonably necessary, in the opinion of the Commission) to comply fully with the Act and Regulations or other official rules, rulings, policies, procedures or statements promulgated or proposed by the Missouri Department of Revenue, or the Commission, from time to time, pertaining to Owner's obligations under the Act and Regulations and affecting the Project but no such action shall alter the Owner's obligations under the First Mortgage Documents, if any.

(g) The Owner acknowledges that the primary purpose for requiring compliance by the Owner with the rent restrictions provided in this Agreement is to assure compliance of the Project and the Owner with the Act and Regulations.

Accordingly, the Owner in consideration for receiving Missouri affordable housing tax credits for this project for the qualified donors of the sponsor hereby agrees and consents, subject to the provisions of the first mortgage documents, that the commission, and to the extent permitted by law, any individual who meets the income limitation applicable under the act and regulations (whether prospective, present or former occupant) shall be entitled, for any breach of the provisions hereof, and in addition to all other remedies provided by law or in equity, to enforce by specific performance all of the obligations of owner under this agreement in a state court of competent jurisdiction. The Owner hereby further specifically acknowledges that the beneficiaries of the Owner's obligations hereunder cannot be adequately compensated by monetary damages in the event of any default hereunder....

(i) The Owner agrees that if at any point following execution of this Agreement, the Act and Regulations require the Commission to monitor the Project occupancy restrictions required by the Act and Regulations, the Owner will take, subject to the provision of the First Mortgage Documents, any and all actions reasonably necessary and required by the Commission to substantiate the Owner's compliance with the occupancy restrictions of the Act and Regulations, and will pay a reasonable fee to the Commission for such monitoring activities performed by the Commission....

Notes and Questions

1. Note the emphasis placed on compliance and compliance monitoring. What might "any and all actions reasonably necessary ... to substantiate the Owner's compliance" entail? Could the Commission revoke an award of tax credits for one project because of a failure to substantiate compliance on another project? *See Brademas v. Indiana Housing Finance Authority*, 354 F.3d 681 (7th Cir. 2004) (any cause of action for wrongful denial of federal housing tax credits would accrue on date denial was communicated, not a date two years later when bond financing was withdrawn for failure to obtain tax credits, thus two year statute of limitations had run before claim was filed).

2. A common source of litigation over the LIHTC program centers on the valuation of tax credit properties for state property tax purposes. Two questions commonly arise: First, whether market rents or actual, credit-induced reduced rents and corresponding use restrictions should be used in establishing value, and second, whether the tax credits should be considered in the valuation process. In *Town Square Limited Partnership v. Clay County Board of Equalization*, 704 N.W.2d 896, 900–903 (S.D. 2005), the Supreme Court of South Dakota held that both the restricted rental rates and the tax credits should be taken into consideration. Presumably the restricted rents would reduce the property value, but the tax credits would increase the value to prospective purchasers. The court noted that a solid majority of courts include the restricted rents but that other courts have split on the question of considering the tax credits when valuing property for tax purposes. The Supreme Court of Ohio, in *Woda Ivy Glen Limited Partnership v. Fayette County Board of Revision*, 902 N.E.2d 984 (Ohio 2009), agreed with the South Dakota court on the rent restriction question, but disagreed on the question of the tax credits. "As for the tax credits themselves, we discern ample reason to disregard them as constituting a part of the value of the realty to the extent that tax benefits are transferred apart from any transfer of the underlying fee interest in the property.... As a result, the tax credits qualify as intangible interests separable from the real property." *Id.* at 992 n.4. *See generally* George E. Jordan, *Appraising the Assets of Low-Income Housing Tax Credit Properties*, 67 Appraisal J., Jan. 1999, at 41; Jonathan Penna, *Fairness in Valuation of Low-Income Housing Tax Credit Properties: An Argument for Tax Exemption*, 11 J. Affordable Housing & Community Dev. L. 53 (2001); Joseph Rosenblum, *Assessing the Value of Affordability:* Ad Valorum *Taxation of Properties Participating in the Low Income Housing Tax Credit Program*, 2 J. Marshall L. Sch. Fair & Affordable Housing Legal Commentary 32 (2006).

K. State and Local Government Housing Programs

The major state and local housing initiative in the past half century has been the creation of housing finance agencies (HFAs). New York took the lead in 1960 and since then virtually all of the states, as well as a large number of cities and counties, have established housing finance agencies, The National Council of State Housing Agencies (NCHSA), www.ncsha.org, and the National Association of Local Housing Finance Agencies (NALHFA), www.nalhfa.org, provide advocacy, educational and research services to members.

The basic function of these agencies has been to generate interim and long-term financing through the issuance and sale of tax exempt, or, occasionally, taxable revenue bonds. A new generation of state and local activity emerged during the late 1980s, primarily in response to declines in federal housing activity, restrictions placed on the use of tax exempt bond financing, and delegation of the allocation and compliance monitoring responsibilities of the LIHTC program. Following the 1994 elections, the policies of the Clinton Administration and the Republican Congress of passing responsibilities to states and local governments—called "devolution"—accelerated the trend toward greater state activity. The new generation of state and local programs provide direct subsidies for housing through housing trust funds, use of unobligated housing bond program reserves, and enactment of special taxes such as real estate transfer taxes.

As housing finance agencies have matured, they have assumed responsibility for administering an increasing number of federally-sponsored housing programs, including the LIHTC program, the state's share of the HOME Investment Partnership housing block grant program, discussed *supra,* as well as "a variety of community and economic development programs and other programs, such as job training, weatherization, and low-income heating cost assistance, HFAs often further contribute to the supply of affordable housing by providing technical assistance, capacity building, and other program support to nonprofit housing providers." NAT'L COUNCIL OF STATE HFAS, STATE HFA FACTBOOK: 2008 NCSHA ANNUAL SURVEY RESULTS 3 (2010).

While administration of these federal programs, as well as housing trust funds, discussed *infra,* are important housing finance agency functions, the basic tool of housing finance agencies has been and continues to be bond financing. In 2008, total outstanding bonds issued by state HFAs amounted to $120 billion. *Id.* Additional billions were issued by local housing finance agencies. Most bonds are purchased by individual and institutional investors, although Federal Home Loan Banks have become important investors with state HFAs, by purchasing $4.6 billion in HFA bonds and providing an additional $5.6 billion in other financing to HFAs in the period from 1992–2008. *Id.* The attractiveness of HFA bonds derives in large part from their tax exempt feature. As a result of the federalism principle, derived from *McCulloch v. Maryland,* 4 Wheat. 316 (1819), that the federal government and state governments are separate sovereign entities, interest paid on state and local agency bonds normally is exempt from federal income taxes, I.R.C. § 103. States also typically exempt bond interest from state income taxes. As a result, the bonds can be sold at a lower interest rate than corporate bonds or bank investment accounts. The HFA combines its bond rate and its administrative costs and charges the housing owner an interest rate below that required in the commercial mortgage market. The tax system thus provides an indirect subsidy to the state agency interest rate. The monthly debt service on HFA financing is also less expensive because the typical loan period is forty years, while commercial lending terms rarely exceed thirty years.

State agency bonds are revenue obligations. They are repaid out of project revenues, and do not constitute an obligation of the state payable out of general tax revenue. These bonds are not backed by the full faith and credit of the state. Some state HFA bonds are referred to as moral obligation bonds. The moral obligation arises from the fact that the bonds are secured in part by a reserve fund, established by a state legislative financial appropriation or created out of the bond proceeds, to partially cover potential defaults. The state legislature may, but is not obligated to, maintain the reserve fund.

State agency bonds were widely used as a financing device for the Section 236 program as well as the Section 8 new construction and substantial rehabilitation program, and currently are an important source of funds for LIHTC projects. HFA financing reduces debt service and rentals, thus making many projects feasible.

Over the years, state HFAs have engaged in a variety of housing finance programs. These are described briefly below, and are summarized in the annual survey conducted by the National Council of State Housing Agencies, *supra:*

1. Multifamily direct loans to developers (construction, permanent, or both). Non-profit and limited dividend developers are eligible, depending on state law and regulation. Direct loans can be independent of federal subsidy or in combination with federal programs. Direct lending has been the most prevalent HFA activity.

2. Seed money loans. State agencies make interest-free or low-interest loans to nonprofit and public sponsors for initial development costs. These loans defray the sponsor's early development expenses, for which other funds may not be available, such as land options and fees for professional services. Seed money loans are generally repaid from the construction or permanent loan.

3. Single-family direct loans, typically as part of a "first time homebuyer" program. These loans are usually made directly to purchasers, through private mortgage lenders, which service the mortgages. They are normally insured by the FHA under the Section 203(b) single family mortgage insurance program described *supra* or by a private mortgage insurance company. The state program simply provides the loan funds. The programs usually limit the mortgage amount and the buyers' income to assure that they benefit low- and moderate-income families.

4. Single-family loans to lenders. This program provides an indirect single-family loan rather than a direct loan. The HFA lends low-interest money to lending institutions with the requirement that the proceeds be used for mortgages. The loan to the lender is collateralized by the financial institution's mortgage loans.

5. Single-family mortgage purchase. Under this indirect loan program, the state agency functions as a secondary mortgage market entity. It buys residential mortgages from lending institutions to assure that the lenders have sufficient funds available to make additional mortgage loans.

6. Insurance programs. HFA insurance programs allow lending under riskier circumstances than lenders normally accept since the loan is covered by state agency insurance. The programs are similar to federal mortgage insurance programs.

7. Development authority. Several HFAs have development powers to acquire and develop their own projects. The most sophisticated example is the New York Urban Development Corporation. Development powers are usually restricted to low- and moderate-income housing projects. Several HFAs operate as a state housing authority with the ability to construct, own, and manage public housing and Section 8 developments.

8. Subsidy programs. State subsidy programs generally take the form of interest reduction subsidies similar to the Section 236 subsidy, low-interest direct loans or grants to reduce the percentage of project development costs that must be financed by first mortgage loans, and rental subsidies to enable housing developments to reach lower-income families. Massachusetts, Maryland, Minnesota, and Virginia are examples of states with strong state subsidy programs. State subsidies come from direct appropriations from state general revenue funds (Florida and Minnesota), special taxes such as real estate transfer taxes (Maine),

unobligated housing agency reserves (Kentucky and Missouri), and special sources such as proceeds from successful environmental litigation (California). Many states are aggregating funds from a number of sources into housing trust funds, which are statutorily or administratively created special funds dedicated for housing programs and not subject to the annual state appropriation process. Proceeds are invested and the resulting income is used to make subsidy grants and loans.

Notes and Questions

1. As states and local governments have become more involved in housing issues, a question about their role remains. Are state and local housing finance agencies in a position to provide the kind of deep subsidies necessary to respond to the housing needs of very low- and extremely low-income households, or does their structure limit them to long term housing development financing and shallow subsidies designed to close "gaps" in such. *See generally* MICHAEL STEGMAN, STATE AND LOCAL AFFORDABLE HOUSING PROGRAMS: A RICH TAPESTRY (1999). For a description of the legal structure, financing, method of operation, and difficulties of first generation HFAs see Peter W. Salsich, Jr., *Housing Finance Agencies: Instruments of State Housing Policy or Confused Hybrids?*, 21 ST. LOUIS U. L.J. 595 (1978). *See also* PETER MORRIS, STATE HOUSING FINANCE AGENCIES (1974); *The State Role in Housing Finance and Development, in* HOUSING FOR ALL UNDER LAW 482–515 (Richard P. Fishman ed. 1978); Peter W. Salsich, Jr., *Urban Housing: A Strategic Role for the States*, 12 YALE L. & POL'Y REV. 3 (1994). For an early critique of state HFA performance, arguing that the state agencies have not sufficiently served the needs of lower-income housing groups, see Daniel Pearlman, *State Housing Finance Agencies and the Myth of Low-Income Housing*, 7 CLEARINGHOUSE REV. 649 (1974).

2. Can and should states do more than provide housing finance through municipal revenue bond proceeds, and the administration of federal programs such as the LIHTC? Would a general obligation bond issue backed up by the state's general taxing power, or a direct appropriation of state funds enable states to reach the housing needs of their poorest citizens? If so, would that be an appropriate use of the state taxing power? *See, e.g.*, Prop. 107, approved by the voters June 5, 1990 and entitled California Housing and Homeless Bond Act of 1990, CAL. HEALTH AND SAFETY CODE, §§ 53180–53209 (authorizing $300 million in general obligation bonds and appropriations from general revenue to pay annual principal and interest obligations on outstanding bonds). For a detailed summary of programs administered by state housing finance agencies, see National Council of State Housing Finance Agencies *supra.*

3. State and local HFAs also felt the impact of the 2008 credit crisis as investors shied away from their bond offerings. In response, HUD, Treasury and FHFA (the supervisor of Fannie Mae and Freddie Mac) provided temporary financing in 2009 to HFAs. Through the New Issue Bond Program (NIBP) Treasury offered to purchase securities from Fannie Mae and Freddie Mac that were backed by new state and local HFA bonds. Treasury also agreed to purchase participation interests in the Fannie Mae and Freddie Mac-administered Temporary Credit and Liquidity Program (TCLP). The TCLP was designed to provide temporary credit and liquidity to HFAs until normal credit markets could be restored. The bond program proved extremely popular, with 90 state and local HFAs from 49 states issuing over $15 billion in housing bonds in 2009. The credit and liquidity program provided twelve HFAs with $8.2 billion in credit and liquidity support in 2009. U.S. Dep't of Housing and Urban Development, Administration Completes Implementation of Initiative to Support State and Local Housing Finance Agencies, HUD No. 10-010 (Jan.

13, 2010), *available at* http://portal.hud.gov; NCSHA, Housing Bonds Fact Sheet 2010, *available at* www.ncsha.org/resource/housing-bonds-fact-sheet-2010.

State HFA legislation had to overcome state constitutional restrictions against creating public debt, lending state credit, and using public funds for private activities. The following case discusses these issues.

Utah Housing Finance Agency v. Smart

Supreme Court of Utah
561 P.2d 1052 (1977)

ELLETT, Chief Justice

In 1975 the Utah Legislature passed the Utah Housing Finance Agency Act. The Act creates the Utah Housing Finance Agency, a body corporate and politic of the State, Respondent herein (hereafter "Agency"). It has the power to sue and be sued. Generally, the Act creates an Agency composed of state officials and public members appointed by the Governor, upon whom are conferred powers to deal with the problems of an inadequate supply of decent, safe, sanitary housing for persons of low and moderate income in Utah by increasing the availability of mortgage funds for such housing.

The Act permits the Agency to obtain funds by the sale of notes and bonds and other obligations. Such notes and bonds, income therefrom, and payments thereon, together with all agency property, are exempt from taxation. The Agency is then commanded to make such tax exempt funds available on a low interest basis for the financing of the purchase, construction, or rehabilitation of housing for low and moderate income persons.

The Agency may adopt a number of techniques for making its funds available. It may make direct loans through qualified mortgage lenders to individuals for purchase, construction, or rehabilitation of housing. It may create a housing rehabilitation fund for direct loans for rehabilitation of low and moderate income housing. It may purchase loans from qualified mortgage lenders, providing that the funds paid the lender by the Agency will be used by the lender to make low interest mortgages to low- and moderate-income persons as defined by the Agency.

Presently, the Agency is in the process of finalizing rules and regulations for the implementation of its initial program. It desires to make an initial sale of bonds in order to obtain funds to be used to purchase mortgages, and has undertaken preparations for such a sale.

At the time of passage of the Act, the legislature appropriated to the Agency the sum of $200,000 to be used to establish a general operating fund and $300,000 to establish a capital reserve fund. The Agency has requested that this sum be disbursed to it from the State Treasury, to be used to cover initial expenses and to implement its initial program. The State Director of Finance and the State Auditor refused to take any steps to process the request of the Agency for funds because of substantial questions of the constitutionality of the Act.

The Agency filed an action for declaratory judgment and mandamus to have the Act declared constitutional and to require the appellants to take necessary steps for the disbursal of the funds. The Third Judicial District Court granted the Agency's requested relief and appellants brought this appeal. They claim that the Act and the appropriations thereunder are unconstitutional because no public purpose is served.

Many states with similar statutes have held that a public purpose is served by providing for low-income housing acts.

The Act contains a declaration of public purpose in Section 63-44a-2, U.C.A. 1953 (1975 Pocket Supp.). In that section, the legislature declares it the policy of the State to assist the provision of decent, safe, sanitary housing for the citizenry where private institutions fail to do so. There is then contained a statement that such a failure has occurred in that a lack of available financing has caused a decrease in housing starts and in the transferability of existing housing, with a resulting serious shortage of decent housing for persons of low- and moderate-income. Such a shortage, the legislature finds, leads to unemployment in the housing industry and to the creation of blight and slums. The legislature therefore specifically declares it a public purpose for the State to cooperate with private institutions to increase the amount of reasonably available financing for the construction, purchase, and rehabilitation of decent, low- and moderate-income housing. Such legislative findings are entitled to great weight and statutes should be sustained unless clearly in violation of fundamental law.

The matter of a serious shortage of safe, sanitary, decent housing for a large segment of the citizenry falls squarely within the police power of the legislature to deal with the health, safety, and morals of the populace. Courts which have discussed the matter indicate numerous ways in which making decent housing more readily available beneficially affects the health, safety and morals of the public.

Making it possible for a greater number of low- and middle-income persons to purchase homes gives a greater number a stake in society, and encouragement to be productive wage earners, and thus tends to stabilize society.

Increasing the transferability of low- and middle-income housing by increasing financing therefore, and increasing the availability of funds for home improvements on such housing, tends to prevent the creation of blight and slums and the consequent unsafe, overcrowded conditions which breed crime and disease. This Court has held that the redevelopment of blighted and slum areas is a public purpose for which funds may be spent.

It cannot be said that the finding of the legislature that a public purpose is served by increasing the availability of financing for construction, purchase, and rehabilitation of low- and moderate-income housing, is incorrect or unreasonable on its face. Regarding appellants' objection that the Act does not serve a public purpose, then, it remains only to be seen whether the method chosen by the legislature to remedy the problem defined is reasonably calculated to have the desired effect.

The general scheme chosen by the legislature is a common one. Stated briefly, the Agency is authorized to obtain tax free funds by the issuance of bonds and notes, which it uses to provide low interest financing for low- and moderate-income housing. Debt created by the sale of notes, bonds, and other obligations is payable only out of funds of the Agency, so that such obligations are self-liquidating. At least one court has specifically addressed the problem as to whether such a method is reasonably calculated to serve the public purpose of increasing financing for low- and moderate-income housing, holding that it is. [*West v. Tennessee Hous. Dev. Agency*, 512 S.W.2d 275 (Tenn. 1974)] Generally, the same method was employed by the agencies involved in all of the other sister state cases ... so that insofar as each finds that a public purpose is served by the legislation there involved, each implicitly finds that raising low interest funds for financing by sale of exempt self-liquidating bonds is an acceptably effective means of accomplishing the public purpose. The method is familiar in Utah where it has been approved for various public purposes.

The Housing Finance Agency Act serves a public purpose in that it is intended, and reasonably designed, to alleviate an actual and existing problem having a significant [effect] upon the public health, safety, and welfare.

Appellants assert that the Act is constitutionally offensive because its operation will confer certain private benefits. There is an obvious private benefit to persons who are able to obtain housing financing through the Agency who would not have been able to obtain it elsewhere. There is a less substantial benefit to mortgage lenders who participate in the Agency's mortgage transactions. These benefits, however, are merely incidental to the dominant purpose of the Act to alleviate a serious statewide shortage of decent low- and moderate-income housing, with its consequent ill effects. While it is improper to spend public funds for private purposes, such private benefits incidental to a dominant public purpose do not detract from the constitutionality of the legislation.

In *Tribe v. Salt Lake City Corporation*, [540 P.2d 499 (Utah 1975)], it was charged that urban renewal legislation was unconstitutional insofar as the proposed renewal projects would confer benefits upon adjoining private landowners. The Court held that these private benefits were incidental to the public purpose of clearing slums and blight, and thus not dispositive of the question of constitutionality. The legislation was held constitutional.

It is immaterial, of course, whether the incidental private benefits conferred by the legislation are viewed as particularly "personal." What could be more personal than the education provided by public universities, the food and clothing provided by public welfare subsidies, the medical attention underwritten by public Medicare programs, all of which have been found constitutionally proper?

The private benefits which may result from the operation of the Housing Finance Agency Act are not different in kind from those described in *Tribe*. They are equally incidental to the main public purpose of the Act, and do not affect its constitutionality. This question has been discussed and decided in favor of similar legislation in many of the sister states....

Appellants allege that the sale of bonds and notes by the Housing Finance Agency will result in the lending of state credit in favor of the Agency in violation of Article VI, Section 29 of the State Constitution and the creation of state debt in violation of Article XIV, Section 1 of the Utah State Constitution.

Debts and obligations of the Agency are payable solely out of funds of the Agency, ordinarily comprising proceeds from bonds and notes and payments on loans. The Act specifically provides that debts of the Agency cannot become debts of the state, that the credit of the state cannot be loaned in favor of the Agency, and that funds of the state cannot be obligated to pay debts of the Agency. All notes and bonds of the Agency must, by statute, bear a disclaimer to such effect. The Utah law is very plain that such self-liquidating notes and bonds of state agencies are not debts of the state and do not constitute a lending of the state's credit.

An agency which supports itself by the sale of self-liquidating notes and bonds in no way obligates the state to raise or spend tax revenues, and therefore creates no state debt. The Housing Finance Agency Act also provides, however, that the Agency must maintain a capital reserve fund sufficient to meet this requirement, an additional appropriation may be sought from the legislature to cover the deficit, and the legislature may make such an appropriation. In short, the legislature may make future appropriations to defray the obligations of the Agency. It has been charged in a number of the housing finance agency cases from sister states that such provisions constitute a lending of state credit and the creation of state debt because they indicate that recourse may be had to state funds to pay agency obligations where agency funds are insufficient. It does not appear that such provisions have been considered in a Utah case.

If the legislation requires future appropriations to defray the obligations of the Agency it would be invalid as lending the state's credit, but where, as here, it merely allows future appropriations without requiring such, it creates no binding obligation upon the state and therefore does not result in a debt of the state or the lending of the state's credit.

Other assignments of unconstitutionality of the Act have been considered, but we find them to be without merit. We hold the Act in question to be constitutional and thereof affirm the judgment of the trial court.

Notes and Questions

1. The so-called moral obligation bond (the state legislature "may" but is not legally obligated to make up any deficiencies in bond reserve accounts) has been a controversial part of state housing finance programs. Most courts that have considered challenges to moral obligation language, even when the legislative language is "shall" rather than "may," have refused to find such provisions invalid as creating an unconstitutional debt, reasoning that such a conclusion would conflict not only with standard statements in enabling legislation that bonds and other obligations of housing finance agencies do not create state debt, but also with the general principle that one legislature cannot commit succeeding legislatures to the appropriation of moneys. *See, e.g., Fults v. City of Coralville,* 666 N.W.2d 548, 558–559 (Iowa 2003) ("[T]he constitutional debt limitation ... applies to legally enforceable obligations, not to moral obligations.... The agreements are designed to give future city councils the flexibility to continue repayment, depending upon the city's budgetary needs in any given fiscal year"); *Schulz v. State,* 639 N.E.2d 1140, 1148 (N.Y. 1994) ("A moral obligation ... is not in and of itself 'debt'"); *In re Oklahoma Capitol Improvement Auth.,* 958 P.2d 759, 768 (Okla. 1998). Does the reserve fund make-up provision mean, as a practical matter, that the state will pay off the bonds if the underlying mortgages so into default? Are bondholders misled if they believe that, if mortgage repayments prove insufficient, a future legislature will appropriate funds to cure the default? If the statutory provision merely expresses an "expectation and aspiration," how does it secure the bondholders' interest? *See* Janice Griffith, *"Moral Obligation" Bonds: Illusion or Security?* 8 URB. LAW. 54 (1976); Peter W. Salsich, Jr., *Housing Finance Agencies: Instruments of State Housing Policy or Confused Hybrids?* 21 ST. LOUIS U. L.J. 595, 608–10 (1978).

If a state legislature appropriates funds to restore the reserve fund minimum, does such action violate state constitutional prohibitions against the lending of the state's credit? *See Massachusetts Hous. Fin. Agency v. New England Merchants Nat'l Bank,* 249 N.E.2d 599 (Mass. 1969); *Martin v. North Carolina Hous. Corp.,* 175 S.E.2d 665 (N.C. 1970). *But see Rich v. Georgia,* 227 S.E.2d 761 (Ga. 1976), holding the make-up provision an unconstitutional donation by the state to private parties. If investors believe that the state legislature will not appropriate the required funds, will they demand higher interest rates on the bonds, thus making HFAs less effective as a source of financing?

2. A statutory expansion of the North Carolina state housing program authorizing the sale of bonds to finance single-family and multifamily housing for persons of moderate incomes in response to skyrocketing interest rates in the early 1980s (17% for single-family mortgage loans and 19% for multifamily loans) was upheld in *In re Denial of Approval to Issue $30,000,000.00,* 296 S.E.2d 281, 286 (N.C. 1982):

> Any casual observer knows that the present economy is drastically different from that existing at the time the Act was originally enacted. Such an observer is equally

> aware of the serious problems facing those with moderate incomes who wish to acquire decent housing for their families. We agree with the appellee that issuance of the proposed bonds would benefit all the citizens of our State. The infusion of low interest mortgage money into the private construction industry should inevitably lead to more jobs, increased local and state tax revenues, more stable neighborhoods and an enhanced economy generally. The supply of available residential housing ultimately would be increased, thus generally improving the opportunities for our people to obtain better housing. Moreover ... the acquisition of houses by people otherwise unable to afford them provides those same people with a stake in the preservation of our society that they would not have were it not for the Agency's assistance.... A lack of adequate housing inevitably engenders slum-like conditions, a situation the legislature obviously sought to eliminate with its proposed bond proceeds.

3. In addition to public purpose and pledging of credit challenges, state housing programs also have been subjected to equal protection scrutiny, particularly when programs are broadened to include housing for moderate-income families and construction and employment preferences for lower-income persons in conjunction with housing development activities assisted by the state agency. *See, e.g., Steup v. Indiana Hous. Auth.*, 402 N.E.2d 1215 (Ind. 1980) (employment training and contract preferences for residents of area served by authority-assisted housing are rationally related to purposes of the state housing program).

4. One of the most active state housing programs has been the "first time home buyer affordable housing program," in which states use the proceeds from revenue bond issues to provide first mortgage loans at below market rates. Mortgage revenue bonds ("MRBs") are classified as private activity bonds by the Internal Revenue Code, 26 U.S.C. §§141, 143. Beginning in 1980, Congress has attached increasingly stringent restrictions to require targeting of such bonds to families of low and moderate income. In general, at least 95% of the net proceeds of a mortgage revenue bond issue must be used to finance the purchase of single-family residences by persons who did not have an ownership interest in their principal residence during the three years preceding the mortgage transactions, whose incomes do not exceed 115% of area median family incomes (140% for homes located in targeted areas of chronic economic distress or in which at least 70% of the families have incomes which are 80% or less of the statewide median income, 26 U.S.C. §143(j)), and who are purchasing homes costing no more than 90% of the average area purchase price for such homes (110% for targeted area residences). 26 U.S.C. §143(a), (c), (d), (e), and (f). Other restrictions include a statewide annual volume limitation on the total amount of bonds that can be issued, 26 U.S.C. §146 ($90 multiplied by the state's population in 2009), limitations on the amount of interest that can be earned by investment of bond proceeds ("arbitrage"), 26 U.S.C. §148, and a requirement that bonds be issued in registered form, 26 U.S.C. §149. Mortgage revenue bonds were targeted for extinction by legislative sunset provisions that were scheduled to be implemented after December 31, 1983, but which were extended on an almost annual basis until the program was authorized on a permanent basis in 1993. Since their inception, MRBs have helped 4 million lower-income persons obtain home ownership. In 2008 such buyers had average incomes of slightly over $39,000 and paid on average slightly less than $139,000 for their homes. Additional support for state housing bonds was provided by HERA in 2008, including exempting from the Alternative Minimum Tax interest earned by investors purchasing state housing bonds, and expanding tax-exempt housing bond issue authority. Pub. L. No. 110-289, 106 Stat. 3956–3964.

5. The standard penalty for noncompliance with the restrictions on private activity bonds is loss of tax exemption on interest income received by investors. 26 U.S.C.

§ 103(b)(1). Since investors have no direct control over the persons who obtain mortgage loans from a mortgage revenue bond issue, the risk of loss of tax exempt status can be substantial. State housing finance agencies have responded to this risk by requiring participating lenders to obtain affidavits of compliance from borrowers that they meet the income and purchase price limits, and to examine copies of federal income tax returns of borrowers for the three years prior to the execution of a mortgage. Is this a sufficient protection for the investor? Note that § 143(a)(2)(B) and (C) cushions the potential severity of investor risk by accepting "good faith" attempts to comply when coupled with corrections made within a "reasonable period" of discovery of noncompliance.

6. In addition to obtaining affidavits of compliance described above, state HFAs commonly require developers to enter into land use restriction agreements in which developers covenant to comply with provisions of the Internal Revenue Code preserving the tax exempt status of the bonds issued to fund their projects and the tax credit status of the equity investments in their projects. These restrictions are designed to run with the land and become an important enforcement tool for regulatory agencies. Excerpts from one in Missouri for a parallel Missouri housing tax credit are reproduced *supra* in connection with the discussion of the application of the LIHTC to the Metro City problem.

7. Multifamily housing bonds, except those issued to finance housing that will be owned by not-for-profit organizations holding tax exempt status under Section 501(c)(3) of the Code or by governmental units, are subject to the volume limitations and other restrictions of private activity bonds. 26 U.S.C. §§ 142(d), 145(a), and 146(g). To be tax exempt, such bonds must be used only to finance projects which meet the low-income standards of housing eligible for the low-income housing tax credit discussed earlier (20% of the units occupied by persons with incomes of 50% or less of area median gross income, or 40% with 60% of median income). 26 U.S.C. § 142(d). Note the preference given to ownership of rental housing by governmental or not-for-profit entities. What tax policy purpose is served by such preference? Why should there be a limit on the amount of housing bonds that may be issued to fund targeted low-income housing that will be owned by the private sector if a similar limit is not imposed on public or non-profit-owned housing? In 2008, the bond volume cap was amended to permit proceeds from one multifamily housing bond issue to be recycled as the bonds were retired and be used to finance a second qualified residential project without having the second financing transaction count against the bond volume cap. This amendment was expected to help cities and states who had exceeded their volume caps or faced that prospect to continue funding worthwhile housing developments. Housing and Economic Recovery Act of 2008, Pub. L. No. 110-289, Div. C., Title I, § 302(a), adding new subsection (6) to 26 U.S.C. § 146(i); Richard M. Froehlich, *"Recycled" Bond Program,* Practices & Perspectives, No. 1, 2009, at 9 (publication of the National Association of Local Housing Finance Agencies), *available at* www.nalhfa.org.

A Note on Taxable Bonds

Some states have authorized the use of taxable bonds to continue popular housing finance programs, particularly for situations in which the state does not want to limit housing assistance to comply with the stringent targeting standards of the Internal Revenue Code discussed earlier. In the Spring of 1998, the Delaware State Housing Authority (DSHA) funded a first-time home buyer mortgage assistance program through the sale of $3 million in zero coupon taxable bonds. Down payments and closing cost second mortgage loans of up to $10,000 dollars were made with the proceeds. Since there is no cap on taxable bonds, this program enabled DSHA to expand substantially its $500,000/per year tax exempt bond-financed mortgage assistance program. 26 [Current Developments] Hous. & Dev. Rep. (West) 54 (1998). Fact sheets for the Delaware programs are available at www.destatehousing.com/services/hb_sfmrb.shtml & hb_smal.shtml.

A number of states have responded to the mortgage foreclosure crisis by issuing taxable bonds and using the proceeds to assist families refinance adjustable rate mortgage loans with long-term fixed-rate loans. The bond proceeds typically are used for partial mortgage payments for 2–5 years on the borrowers' behalf to ease the transition to long-term, fixed rate loans. *See* Pew Charitable Trusts, Defaulting on the Dream: States Respond to America's Foreclosure Crisis (2008) For examples of specific statutory authorizations to issue taxable bonds, see Cal. Health & Safety Code §§ 51400 to 51403; Conn. Gen. Stat. § 3-20(s); N.J. Rev. Stat. § 55:14K-26. *See generally*, State and Local Government Debt Financing § 11:37 (M. David Gelfand ed. 2002 & Supp. 2008).

One of the more popular programs authorized by the American Recovery and Reinvestment Act of 2009 ("ARRA"—the "Stimulus" Act) is the Build America Bond program, 26 U.S.C., § 54AA, which authorizes states and local governments to issue taxable "tax credit" bonds providing a credit against federal income tax with respect to interest earned on the bonds. Three types of bonds, called BABs, may be issued: 1) Build America Bonds (Tax Credit), 26 U.S.C. § 54AA(d) (tax credits to investors), 2) Build America Bonds (Direct Payment), 26 U.S.C. § 54AA(g) (refundable tax credits to state and local government issuers), and 3) Recovery Zone Economic Development Bonds (Direct Payment) (deeper tax credits to state and local government issues). BABs are subject to the same requirements as tax-exempt bonds, 26 U.S.C. § 54AA and I.R.S. Notice 2009-26, Apr. 20, 2009. In the first few months of activity, over $50 million in BABS were sold. Stephen Gandel, *A Stimulus Success: Build America Bonds Are Working*, Time, Nov. 17, 2009, *available at* www.time.com/time/printout/0,8816,1939720,00.html.

Metro City Problem (cont.)

As advisor to the Metro City Housing Authority what role, if any, would you suggest for the state HFA? Should it provide a long term, first mortgage loan? If so, how would you determine the appropriate amount of the loan? Should the loan be insured by the FHA? If so, under what program? How would the debt financing relate to equity financing possibilities through the LIHTC?

L. Nonprofit Housing Associations

One of the major thrusts of housing policy designed to respond to the needs of low-income households in Western Europe, in countries such as Sweden, Denmark, Germany, Holland, and Britain, has been the utilization of the voluntary private, nonprofit sector. This trend is in stark contrast to the United States, where the profit-motivated investor has been a major participant in government-supported housing programs and nonprofit sponsors have played little part in our efforts until recently. While the governments in these European countries have undertaken to provide public housing, nonprofit housing associations have been given increasing responsibility for what is called social housing (also discussed in Chapter 1 *supra*).

1. Social Housing

The term, "social housing," has been given to the European practice of providing affordable housing through various types of private, nonprofit housing associations, as well as local public authorities. The term encompasses American concepts of "public," "subsidized," and "affordable" housing. Social housing emphasizes the cooperative or interdependent relationships that the term, "social," connotes (WEBSTER'S THIRD NEW INTERNATIONAL DICTIONARY (1993)). Security of tenure is a key feature of the concept. Rather than emphasizing the "public" or "private" nature of housing ownership and management, social housing emphasizes the community or "social" ownership of housing. *See generally* SOCIAL HOUSING IN EUROPE (Christine Whitehead & Kathleen Scanlon eds. 2007) (a publication of the London School of Economics and Political Science); Michael Stone, *Social Ownership, in* A RIGHT TO HOUSING: FOUNDATION FOR A NEW SOCIAL AGENDA 240 (Rachel G. Bratt, Michael E. Stone & Chester Hartman eds. 2006). According to Stone, housing is socially owned if "it is not owned or operated for profit; it cannot be sold for speculative gain, and it provides security of tenure for residents," *Id.* at 241. Social housing also has been called "non-market housing" or "community based housing," defined as "housing that is nonprofit and is produced and operated according to a national housing goal (a separate proposal that would make "adequate and affordable housing a universal national entitlement"). In community-based housing, "[t]he role of profit would be eliminated over time and the principal of community control would be substituted," JOHN GILDERBLOOM & RICHARD APPELBAUM, RETHINKING RENTAL HOUSING 181–183 (1988). *See also* DARINKA CZISCHKE & ALICE PITTINI: HOUSING EUROPE 2007: REVIEW OF SOCIAL, CO-OPERATIVE AND PUBLIC HOUSING IN THE 27 EU MEMBER STATES (2007); URBAN REGENERATION IN EUROPE: THE PLACE OF SOCIAL HOUSING IN INTEGRATED URBAN POLICIES (Darinka Czischke ed. 2009). Both reports were published by CECODHAS European Social Housing Observatory, www.cecodhas.org/observatory, with the assistance of BSHF Building and Social Housing foundation, www.bshf.org.

The voluntary housing sector as it has evolved in Great Britain is examined in J. BARRY CULLINGWORTH, ESSAYS IN HOUSING POLICY: THE BRITISH SCENE (1979); Christine Whitehead, *Social Housing in England, in* SOCIAL HOUSING IN EUROPE, *supra* at 54. According to Whitehead, the social rental sector peaked in 1979 at 5.5 million social rented units out of a total housing stock of 17.7 million units. Home ownership had been growing since the 1960s and by 2005 accounted for 70% of a larger total of 2.1 million units. The social rental sector had dropped to 4 million units, 18% of the total housing stock. Whitehead, *supra* at 54–55.

2. Nonprofit Housing Organizations in the U.S.

The idea of using the nonprofit sector to provide housing services as an alternative or complement to public and for profit providers first surfaced in the 1960s as part of the community action programs of the War on Poverty and the Great Society. Nonprofit community development corporations were organized and received funding for housing development through the federal subsidy programs discussed previously. But lack of resources and managerial experience caused many of them to fail, which in turn helped speed the decline of interest in and support for nonprofit housing efforts. The "Reagan Revolution" in 1980 "spelled an end to federal invocations of the 'neighborhood movement' and associated support for citizen participation." Susan S. Fainstein & Norman I. Fainstein, *Citizen Participation in Local Government, in* Public Policy Across States and Communities 223, 235 (1985).

The movement did not die, though. According to David J. Erickson, The Housing Policy Revolution: Networks and Neighborhoods (2009), nonprofits cobbled together funds from community development block grants, discussed in Chapter 5 *infra*, and low income housing tax credits, along with private donations and loans from state HFAs, to create a bottom-up housing development and management program that has grown into a decentralized housing network of considerable strength. A case in point is Beyond Housing, a nonprofit corporation in St, Louis, Missouri that began by acquiring one duplex in Richmond Heights, a first tier suburb of St. Louis, in the early 1980s and has grown to an organizations with a metropolitan reach, owning 250 single family units rented to Housing Choice Voucher holders, managing hundreds of multi-family units and engaging in community development with a loose consortium of 23 first tier suburban municipalities in the Normandy school district in St. Louis County. For a discussion of the evolution of Beyond Housing from a small nonprofit organization that renovated one or two houses at a time to a major provider of housing for low-income families in the St. Louis area, see Peter W. Salsich, Jr., *Beyond Housing: A Case Study of Combining Social Services and Affordable Housing,* 10 J. Affordable Housing & Community Dev. L. 20 (2000).

In 1987, Congress enacted a program, inspired by the achievements of a neighborhood-based program in Brooklyn, N.Y., called the Nehemiah Housing Opportunity Program after "the biblical leader who re-built the walls of Jerusalem." Nehemiah Corporation of America (Sacramento, California), The Nehemiah Story, *available at* www.nehemiahcorp.org/about.cfm. The statute authorized federal grants to nonprofit organizations to enable them to make loans to first-time buyers of "lower income." Title VI of the Housing and Community Development Act of 1987, Pub. L. No. 100-242, §§601 to 613, 101 Stat. 1951–1956 (1988). The program did not last long. It was repealed effective October 1, 1991. Pub. L. No. 101-625, §289(a)(3), (b), 104 Stat. 4128 (1990), except with respect to projects and programs for which binding commitments had been entered into prior to October 1, 1991. But the idea took hold. In 1994, the Nehemiah Corporation of America was founded in Sacramento, California with the assistance of a $5000 loan from a Baptist church. It has continued the home ownership focus with a down payment assistance grant program that had grown to $1.5 billion, serving 325,000 families, by 2008. The corporation also has been the managing partner in a number of affordable housing developments in California through the Nehemiah Progressive Housing Development Corporation and operates a community development financial institution, Nehemiah Community Reinvestment Fund, Inc., www.nehmiahcorp.org. In 2009, the corporation established a subsidiary, Nfinit Solutions, Inc., to provide counseling and educational services, as well as "sustainable home retention solutions" for homeowners threatened with foreclosure. "Workout solutions" listed on its website include loan modifications, repayment plans, reinstatement, forbearance, short-sale, deed-in-lieu and "cash for keys," www.homeretentionadvantage.com. The 2007–2009 foreclosure crisis is discussed in Chapter 1 *supra.*

An alternative model is illustrated by the Nehemiah Housing Corporation of Middletown, Connecticut, which provides transitional housing, permanent supportive housing and affordable rental housing for low-income households. *See* Nehemiah Housing Corporation, Connecticut Statewide LISC/Community Development Corporations, www.lisc.org/connecticut_statewide/partners/corporations.

For a case study of the potential for resident involvement in, and ownership of, housing developed with the financial assistance of the LIHTC program, see Michael Diamond, *Another Model of Low Income Housing Tax Credit Development: Building Housing and Building Capacity, in* AFFORDABLE HOUSING AND PUBLIC-PRIVATE PARTNERSHIPS 51 (Nestor M. Davidson & Robin Paul Malloy eds. 2009). Professor Diamond describes the negotiations between a non-profit developer and a newly-formed tenants association that led to a successful LIHTC housing rehabilitation development. A key factor in the negotiations was the presence of a local statute requiring that, as a condition to the sale of residential rental property, residents of that property be given a bona fide opportunity to purchase it. *See* District of Columbia Tenant Opportunity to Purchase Act, D.C. CODE §§42-3404.02 *et seq.*

As discussed in Clearinghouse Review, a survey by the National Economic Development and Law Center, of "trends in community-based development of low-income housing" identified two approaches being taken by urban areas in response to the sharp decline in direct federal assistance for housing in the 1980s: (1) creation of new state and local funding sources such as housing trust funds, linked development programs, and community loan programs, and (2) establishment of umbrella-type organizations to provide coordination, planning, and technical assistance to neighborhood-oriented developers, many of whom are not-for-profit organizations, who seek to use these new funds. David Kirkpatrick, Mary Ann Dillon & Susan Bloch, *Developments in Nonprofit Production of Low-Income Housing*, 20 CLEARINGHOUSE REV. 1227 (1987).

The authors summarize the work of several large, umbrella not-for-profit organizations: the Boston Housing Partnership, Inc., the Chicago Housing Partnership, the Enterprise Foundation, a national organization headquartered in Columbia, Maryland, that seeks to strengthen local nonprofit housing groups, Inter Faith Housing Task Force, Inc. of Wilmington, Delaware, Wisconsin Partnership for Housing Development, Inc., and the Low-Income Housing Fund of San Francisco. A common theme of these organizations is the establishment of a "city-wide nonprofit group with competent staff to assist local nonprofits with training, financing and direct development through joint ventures on specific projects. The board of the city-wide nonprofit is composed of people who are chosen for their ability to raise funds and to affect local policy development. This organization is then in a position to advocate for new policies, such as housing trust funds, linkage programs, or state tax credits." *Id* at 1230.

In 1990, a group of 37 large nonprofit housing providers formed the National Association of Housing Partnerships, later changed to the Housing Partnership Network (HPN). By 2007, HPN, which describes itself as "a business alliance of ... nonprofit development organizations" had grown to 95 members with a portfolio of 500,000 affordable homes developed or financed, 175,000 homes of lower-income families improved or repaired, and 400,000 families who had received homeownership counseling, Housing Partnership Network/Affordable Housing through Partnerships, www.housingpartnership.net. *See generally* NEIL MAYER & KENNETH TEMKEN, HOUSING PARTNERSHIPS: THE WORK OF LARGE-SCALE REGIONAL NONPROFITS IN AFFORDABLE HOUSING (2007) (publication of the Urban Institute 2007).

Nonprofit housing associations are included in the housing block grant program described *supra*. This involvement is accomplished in part by a 15% set-aside "formula allocation" of funds made available to participating jurisdictions that must be reserved for use by nonprofit organizations, 42 U.S.C.§12771. Their participation can take the form of developing, sponsoring or owning a development. The 15% set-aside provides nonprofit organizations with a bargaining tool in order to ensure involvement in the implementation of local housing policies and allows them to compete in sophisticated development negotiations.

Nonprofit set-aside funds must remain reserved for at least 24 months after which funds that have not been obligated may be recaptured for reallocation to other jurisdictions or may be used in the same jurisdiction as community organization support, 42 U.S.C. § 12771.

Local governments also are required to "make all reasonable efforts ... to maximize participation by the private sector, including nonprofit organizations and for-profit entities" in the implementation of the five-year comprehensive housing affordability strategies (CHAS) that communities must promulgate in order to receive block grant and other housing funds. 42 U.S.C. § 12751. Standards and procedures governing the CHAS process are found at 42 U.S.C. § 12705, and are discussed in Chapter 5 *infra*.

Notes and Questions

1. For a related discussion of models for funding some nonprofits, see Section L: Housing Trust Funds and Impact Fees *infra*.

2. In addition to the tax issues discussed *infra*, not-for-profit housing and community development corporations face important questions regarding long term sustainability. As the history of public housing and assisted housing discussed *supra* illustrates, a major test of not-for-profit strength will come when their housing developments are ten to fifteen years old. One study of thirty four developments owned by seventeen not-for-profit organizations in six cities concluded that "asset management"—conserving a building's long term financial and physical condition—was "the Achilles heel of the nonprofit housing sector." Rachel Bratt et al., *The Status of Nonprofit-Owned Affordable Housing*, 64 J. Am. Plan. Ass'n 39 (1998). In a paper presented nine years later, Dr. Bratt noted the continued growth of the nonprofit sector, and compared the strengths and weaknesses of for-profit and nonprofit housing developers and managers. She concluded that both sectors, as well as for-profit—nonprofit partnerships, which she supports, must pay attention to the "double bottom line," defined as "the simultaneous need for financial accountability *and* a commitment to social goals." Rachel G. Bratt, Should We Foster the Nonprofit Housing Sector as Developers and Owners of Subsidized Rental Housing? 44 (2007) (a publication of the Joint Center for Housing Studies, Harvard University), *available* at www.jchs.harvard.edu/publications/rental/revisiting_rental_symposium/papers/rr07-12_bratt.pdf. See *also* William M. Rohe et al., Sustainable Nonprofit Housing Development: An Analysis of the Maxwell Award Winners (1998) (a publication of the Fannie Mae Foundation) (concluding that organizational strength was crucial to a not-for-profit's long-term success in housing). An illustration of some of the potential problems is provided by the experience of the Cochran Gardens Tenant Management Corporation in St. Louis, a nonprofit resident housing corporation which managed a large public housing complex for over 20 years but lost its management contract when irregularities were discovered in the corporation's handling of housing modernization funds. Norm Parish, *Housing Authority Takes Over Cochran,* St. Louis Post-Dispatch, June 9, 1998, at A1.

3. Nonprofit housing organizations have used the community land trust ("CLT"), a format popular with open space and preservationist advocates, as a device for acquiring and holding land on which to develop both single-family and multi-family housing. In a CLT, a not-for-profit corporation whose members are drawn from a sponsoring community

or neighborhood takes title to land and then negotiates long-term ground leases (50 to 99 years) with housing developers and sponsors. Housing consumers, not having to purchase land enjoy lower rents and can use the land value towards their down payment. For discussion of the use of CLTs, *see* John Emmeus Davis & Rick Jacobus, The City—CLT Partnership: Municipal Support for Community Land Trusts (2008); David M. Abromowitz, *An Essay on Community Land Trusts: Toward Permanently Affordable Housing, in* Property and Values: Alternatives to Public and Private Ownership 213 (Charles Geisler & Gail Daneker eds. 2000); Julie Farrell Curtin & Lance Bocarsly, *CLTs: A Growing Trend in Affordable Home Ownership,* 17 J. Affordable Housing & Community Dev. L. 367 (2008).

4. For a review of legal and policy questions facing nonprofit housing organizations, *see* Megan J. Ballard, *Profiting from Poverty: The Competition between For-Profits and Nonprofit Developers for Low-Income Housing Tax Credits,* 55 Hastings L.J. 211 (2003); Rachel G. Bratt, *Viewing Housing Holistically: The Resident-Focused Component of the Housing-Plus Agenda,* 74 J. Am. Plan. Ass'n 100 (2008); Ingrid Gould Ellen & Ioan Voicu, *Nonprofit Housing and Neighborhood Spillovers,* 25 J. Pol'y Analysis & Mgmt. 31 (2006); Katherine M. O'Regan & John M. Quigley, *Federal Policy and the Rise of Nonprofit Housing Providers,* 11 J. Housing Res. 297 (2000).

3. Tax Issues for Nonprofit Housing Organizations

Not-for-profit organizations seeking to influence the housing markets in their communities face many difficulties, particularly if they desire to participate in the development or management processes. One of the most important questions that must be answered is what will be the attitude of federal and state taxing authorities from whom the not-for-profit organization may have received tax exempt status.

a. Exemption from Federal Income Taxes

Under Section 501(c)(3) of the Internal Revenue Code nonprofit entities organized and operated exclusively for charitable purposes may qualify for tax exempt status. Attaining tax exempt status can be critical to the success of a nonprofit housing organization because it provides a strong motivation for contributions from individuals and corporations seeking tax deductions for charitable contributions. The statutory requirement that an entity be organized exclusively for charitable purposes can be met by compliance with state statutory standards for nonprofit corporate formation. The operational standard is more nuanced. "The operational test requires both that an organization engage 'primarily' in activities that accomplish its exempt purpose and that not more than an 'insubstantial part of its activities' further a non-exempt purpose." *Arlie Foundation v. I.R.S.*, 283 F. Supp. 2d 58, 62 (D.D.C. 2003) (*citing* Treas. Reg. 26 C.F.R. § 1.501(c)(3)-1(c)(1) and concluding that a nonprofit organization that operated a conference center was not entitled to exempt status because of its extensive advertising and promotional budget and the fact that it competed with for-profit organizations for weddings and other special events).

Section 1.501(c)(3)-1(d)(2) of the same Treasury Regulations defines the term "charitable" as including the relief of the poor and distressed or of the underprivileged, and the promotion of social welfare by organizations designed to lessen neighborhood tensions, to eliminate prejudice and discrimination, or to combat community deterioration.

In a series of revenue rulings, which are interpretations of law based on specific factual situations, the Internal Revenue Service has held that programs to provide housing for low- and sometimes moderate-income persons can qualify for exempt status under Section 501 (c)(3) of the Code. In the leading ruling, Rev. Rul. 70-585, 1970-2 C.B. 115, the Service concluded that a nonprofit organization that was building or renovating houses for resale to low-income families who otherwise could not afford them qualified for tax exempt status because it was "relieving the poor and distressed," but that an organization formed to build new housing and rent it at cost to moderate-income families to alleviate a shortage of affordable housing in the community did not qualify for tax exempt status because it was "not designed to provide relief to the poor or to carry out any other charitable purpose under Section 501(c)(3)." A companion ruling concluded that, under Section 501(c)(4) of the Code (exemption from tax liability to the organization), a nonprofit organization providing management services for low- and moderate-income housing developments did not qualify because "its primary activity is carrying on a business with the general public in a manner similar to organizations that are operated for profit." Rev. Rul. 70-535, 1970-2 C.B. 117.

In 1980, The Tax Court issued an opinion, excerpted below, which established standards for not-for-profit organizations engaged in potentially profitable activities.

Plumstead Theatre Society, Inc. v. Commissioner

United States Tax Court
74 T.C. 1324 (1980)
aff'd, 675 F.2d 244 (9th Cir. 1982)

WILBUR, Judge:

Petitioner Plumstead Theatre Society was incorporated on January 18, 1977, as a nonprofit corporation under the laws of the State of California. Its principal place of business is in Los Angeles, Calif. It filed its application for recognition of exemption under section 501(c)(3) on June 17, 1977, with the Internal Revenue Service. On July 31, 1978, respondent issued to petitioner a final adverse ruling denying petitioner exempt status under section 501(c)(3). The reasons stated in the letter for denial are:

You are not operated exclusively for charitable or educational purposes within the meaning of section 501(c)(3) of the Code. A substantial purpose of your organization is a commercial purpose which is not an exempt purpose. Additionally, part of your net earnings will inure to the benefit of a private individual or shareholder. Furthermore, you are operated for private interests rather than public interests....

The issue for our decision is whether petitioner qualifies as a tax-exempt organization under section 501(c)(3). Respondent does not dispute that petitioner is organized for charitable and educational purposes, the first test an organization must pass in order to qualify for exemption. Rather, it argues that petitioner is not operated exclusively for charitable purposes within the meaning of section 501(c)(3), because petitioner has a substantial commercial purpose and is operated for the benefit of private, rather than public interests. Petitioner maintains that it is operated in a manner harmonious with the requirements of section 501(c)(3). We agree with petitioner that it is operated exclusively for charitable and educational purposes under section 501(c)(3).

Section 501(a) exempts from Federal income tax any organization which meets the criteria set forth in section 501(c). Section 501(c)(3) provides that a corporation which is organized and operated exclusively for charitable or educational purposes, among others, is an organization referred to in section 501(a), if no part of its net earnings inures to the benefit of any private individual or shareholder, and if it does not engage in other prohibited activity. It has long been recognized that the promotion and encouragement of the arts can be both charitable and educational....

Admittedly, the line between commercial enterprises which produce and present theatrical performances and nonprofit, tax-exempt organizations that do the same is not always easy to draw. Indeed, the theatre is the most prominent area of the performing arts in which commercial enterprises coexist, often in the same city, with nonprofit, tax-exempt charitable organizations that also sponsor professional presentations. *See* B. Hopkins, Law of Tax Exempt Organizations, sec. 6.9, p. 38 (3d ed. 1979).

However, there are differences. Commercial theatres are operated to make a profit. Thus, they choose plays having the greatest mass audience appeal. Generally, they run the plays so long as they can attract a crowd. They set ticket prices to pay the total costs of production and to return a profit. Since their focus is perennially on the box office, they do not generally organize other activities to educate the public and they do not encourage and instruct relatively unknown playwrights and actors.

Tax-exempt organizations are not operated to make a profit. They fulfill their artistic and community obligations by focusing on the highest possible standards of performance; by serving the community broadly; by developing new and original works; and by providing educational programs and opportunities for new talent. Thus, they keep the great classics of the theatre alive and are willing to experiment with new forms of dramatic writing, acting, and staging. Usually, nonprofit theatrical organizations present a number of plays during a season for relatively short specified time period. Because of a desired quality in acoustics and intimacy with the audience, many present their performances in halls of limited capacity. The combination of the shortness of the season, the limited seating capacity, the enormous costs of producing quality performances of new or experimental works, coupled with the desire to keep ticket prices at a level which is affordable to most of the community, means that, except in rare cases, box office receipts will never cover the costs of producing plays for nonprofit performing arts organizations. We feel that petitioner has shown that it is organized and operated similar to other nonprofit theatre organizations, rather than as a commercial theatre.

Respondent's last argument is that because of the partnership petitioner entered into with two private individuals and a corporation, whereby the limited partners provided capital in exchange for an interest in the profits and losses of First Monday [in October], petitioner is operated for private, rather than public interests. We do not agree. After entering into an agreement with Kennedy Center, petitioner discovered it was in need of funds for its share of the capitalization costs of First Monday. The record shows that in an arm's-length transaction, it obtained those funds by selling a portion of its interest in the play itself, for a reasonable price. Petitioner is not obligated for the return of any capital contribution made by the limited partners from its own funds, and the partnership has no interest in petitioner or in any other plays it is planning to produce. The limited partners have no control over the way petitioner operates or manages its affairs, and none of the limited partners nor any officer or director of Pantheon Pictures, Inc., is an officer or director of petitioner. We find this arrangement, limited to one play produced by petitioner, is no more intrusive or indicative of private interests than the contractual, percentage arrangement approved of in *Broadway Theatre League of Lynchburg, Va. v. United States,* 293 F. Supp. 346 (W.D. Va. 1968).

Therefore, we find that petitioner is organized and operated exclusively for charitable and educational purposes under section 501(c)(3).

Notes and Questions

1. The low-income housing tax credit discussed earlier includes provisions requiring that states reserve at least 10% of their tax credit allocations for use by nonprofit organizations. Would nonprofits jeopardize their tax exempt status by participating in the tax credit program? Recall that the tax credit is available to tax-paying investors. Participating nonprofits sell tax credits to qualified investors, usually by entering into partnerships with profit-motivated individuals or organizations. Should a for-profit subsidiary be formed to avoid the tax exempt status question? If so, does that requirement materially increase the complexity and resulting cost of nonprofit-sponsored housing? For a recommendation that the tax credit be made refundable (cash payment of the equivalent amount) to nonprofits in order to resolve uncertainties and conflicts of interest associated with the tax status of nonprofit organizations, see Janet Stearns, *The Low-Income Housing Tax Credit: A Poor Solution to the Housing Crisis*, 6 YALE L. & POL'Y REV. 203 (1988).

2. Enactment of the LIHTC raised new issues for not-for-profit housing corporations. Could, for example, a not-for-profit corporation form partnerships with profit-motivated individuals and organizations to enable the investors to gain the benefits of the LIHTC as well as state property tax exemptions afforded property owned by qualified not-for-profit organizations?

In *Housing Pioneers, Inc. v. Commissioner,* 49 F.3d 1395, *amended*, 58 F. 3d 401 (9th Cir. 1995) the court upheld a denial of 501(c)(3) status to such a corporation. The Court distinguished *Plumstead Theatre* because the investors who put up the capital for *Plumstead Theatre's* showing of "First Monday in October" were not shareholders, officers or directors of the not-for-profit corporation. In *Housing Pioneers,* two of the partners of a housing development (Grant Square Properties) also were partners of the not-for-profit corporation, Housing Pioneers, and Housing Pioneers evidenced no ability or reason to exist other than to channel the property tax exemption to its partners. 58 F. 3d at 404.

Housing Pioneers sent a shiver through the not-for-profit housing community. Was it simply a case of bad facts make bad law, or was the IRS signaling disapproval of not-for-profit participation in LIHTC developments? The IRS answered in May, 1996 with Revenue Procedure 96-32, establishing safe harbor guidelines.

Low-Income Housing Guidelines

Internal Revenue Service (1996), Rev. Proc. 96-32, 1996-1 C.B. 717
1996-20 I.R.B. 14, 1996 WL 211941 (I.R.S.)

Low-income housing guidelines. Guidance on qualification for tax-exemption under section 501(c)(3) is provided for organizations that provide low-income housing. The guidance includes a safe-harbor procedure to determine qualification....

SEC. 3. SAFE HARBOR FOR RELIEVING THE POOR AND DISTRESSED

.01 An organization will be considered charitable as described in § 501(c)(3) if it satisfies the following requirements:

(1) The organization establishes for each project that (a) at least 75% of the units are occupied by residents that qualify as low-income: and (b) either at least 20% of the units are occupied by residents that also meet the very low-income limit for the area or 40% of the units are occupied by residents that also do not ex-

ceed 120 percent of the area's very low-income limit. Up to 25% of the units may be provided at market rates to persons who have incomes in excess of the low-income limit.

(2) The project is actually occupied by poor and distressed residents. For projects requiring construction or rehabilitation, a reasonable transition period is allowed for an organization to place the project in service. Whether an organization's transition period is reasonable is determined by reference to all relevant facts and circumstances. For projects that do not require substantial construction or substantial rehabilitation, a one-year transition period to satisfy the actual occupancy requirement will generally be considered to be reasonable. If a project operates under a government program that allows a longer transition period, this longer period will be used to determine reasonableness.

(3) The housing is affordable to the charitable beneficiaries. In the case of rental housing, this requirement will ordinarily be satisfied by the adoption of a rental policy that complies with government-imposed rental restrictions or otherwise provides for the limitation of the tenant's portion of the rent charged to ensure that the housing is affordable to low-income and very low-income residents. In the case of homeownership programs, this requirement will ordinarily be satisfied by the adoption of a mortgage policy that complies with government-imposed mortgage limitations or otherwise makes the initial and continuing costs of purchasing a home affordable to low- and very low-income residents.

(4) If a project consists of multiple buildings and each building does not separately meet the requirements of sections 3.01 (1), (2) and (3), then the buildings must share the same grounds. The requirement does not apply to organizations that provide individual homes or individual apartment units located at scattered sites in the community exclusively to families with incomes at or below 80% of the area's median income.

.02 In applying this safe harbor, the Service will follow the provisions listed below:

(1) Low-income families and very low-income families will be identified in accordance with the income limits computed and published by the Department of Housing and Urban Development ("HUD") in Income Limits for Low and Very Low-Income Families Under the Housing Act of 1937. The term "very low-income" is defined by the relevant housing statute as 50% of an area's median income. The term "low-income" is defined by the same statute as 80% of an area's median income. However, these income limits may be adjusted by HUD to reflect economic differences, such as high housing costs, in each area. The income limits are then tailored to reflect different family sizes. If HUD's program terminates, the Service will use income limits computed under such program as is in effect immediately before such termination....

(2) The retention of the right to evict tenants for failure to pay rent or other misconduct, or the right to foreclose on homeowners for defaulting on loans will not, in and of itself, cause the organization to fail to meet the safe harbor.

(3) An organization originally meeting the safe harbor will continue to satisfy the requirements of the safe harbor if a resident's income increases and causes the organization to fail the safe harbor, provided that the resident's income does not exceed 140% of the applicable income limit under the safe harbor. If the resident's income exceeds 140% of the qualifying income limit, the organization

will not fail to meet the safe harbor if it rents the next comparable non-qualifying unit to someone under the income limits.

(4) To be considered charitable, an organization that provides assistance to the aged or physically handicapped who are not poor must satisfy the requirements set forth in Rev. Rul. 72-124, 1972-1 C.B. 145, Rev. Rul. 79-18, 1979-1 C.B. 194, and Rev. Rul. 79-19, 1979-1 C.B. 195. If an organization meets the safe harbor, then it does not need to meet the requirements of these rulings even if all of its residents are elderly or handicapped residents. However, an organization may not use a combination of elderly or handicapped persons and low-income persons to establish the 75-percent occupancy requirement of the safe harbor. An organization with a mix of elderly or handicapped residents and low-income residents may still qualify for tax-exempt status under the facts and circumstances test set forth in section 4.

SEC. 4. FACTS AND CIRCUMSTANCES TEST FOR RELIEVING THE POOR AND DISTRESSED

.01 If the safe harbor contained in section 3 is not satisfied, an organization may demonstrate that it relieves the poor and distressed by reference to all the surrounding facts and circumstances.

.02 Facts and circumstances that demonstrate relief of the poor may include, but are not limited to, the following:

(1) A substantially greater percentage of residents than required by the safe harbor with incomes up to 120 percent of the area's very low-income limit.

(2) Limited degree of deviation from the safe harbor percentages.

(3) Limitation of a resident's portion of rent or mortgage payment to ensure that the housing is affordable to low-income and very low-income residents.

(4) Participation in a government housing program designed to provide affordable housing.

(5) Operation through a community-based board of directors, particularly if the selection process demonstrates that community groups have input into the organization's operations.

(6) The provision of additional social services affordable to the poor residents.

(7) Relationship with an existing 501(c)(3) organization active in low-income housing for at least five years if the existing organization demonstrates control.

(8) Acceptance of residents who, when considered individually, have unusual burdens such as extremely high medical costs which cause them to be in a condition similar to persons within the qualifying income limits in spite of their higher incomes.

(9) Participation in a homeownership program designed to provide homeownership opportunities for families that cannot otherwise afford to purchase safe and decent housing.

(10) Existence of affordability covenants or restrictions running with the property....

Notes and Questions

1. Is the 10-part list included in the Safe Harbor Guidelines as an alternative "facts and circumstances" test helpful to not-for-profit organizations which are not in the safe har-

bor? Note that the list is not necessarily inclusive. What does the list tell you about correct application of the law? In commenting critically on the state of regulatory takings law, an experienced practitioner quoted a federal district judge at a takings seminar: "I know what a totality of circumstances determination is. But how was I supposed to reason in determining which factors are the important ones?" The practitioner lecturer responded that it was a good question for which he had no answer. Gideon Kanner, *Hunting the Snark, Not the Quark: Has the U.S. Supreme Court Been Competent in its Effort to Formulate Coherent Regulatory Takings Law?* 30 URB. LAW. 307, 317 n.37 (1998) (including references to 10-factor (or more) tests for regulatory takings claims adopted by a New Jersey appellate court in *East Cape May Assocs. v. Dep't of Environmental Preservation*, 693 A. 2d 114, 128–29 (N.J. Super Ct. App. Div. 1997) and the California Supreme Court in *Kavanau v. Santa Monica*, 941 P. 2d 851, 860 (Cal. 1997)).

2. For "precedential guidance" on joint ventures between exempt organizations and for-profit entities, using health care entities as examples, see Rev. Rul. 98-15, 1998-12 IRB 6, discussed in Rochelle Korman, *Joint Ventures with For-Profits after Revenue Ruling 98-15*, 27 Exempt Org. Tax Rev. 441 (2000).

3. The foreclosure crisis discussed earlier prompted a number of communities to encourage efforts to help people facing foreclosure remain in their homes. In a typical program, a nonprofit organization would purchase homes at or before foreclosure sales and rent the homes back to the previous owners at affordable rentals. Would you expect the organization in the following scenario to qualify for tax exempt status?

> A home inspection is done by a representative of M [the organization]. If the home is beyond repair or if the family will not be able to afford the home even if a short sale is done then M will not try to save it from foreclosure. If the clients and home meet the criteria set by M an attempt will be made to acquire the home through a short sale, for example if a home originally had a mortgage for 120,000 [it] would be purchased for $70,000. After the completion of your program the intent would be to sell the home back to the original owner for $80,000 plus closing costs. [M also would provide budget classes and assistance in finding alternative housing if a short sale is unsuccessful or if the family and/or home don't meet the program criteria.—Eds.] Once M acquires a home it will be rented back to the client. The business plan states the monthly rent of a lower value property, with a value range of $35,000–$100,000, will be $850. The monthly rent for a mid value property, with a value range of $100,000–$150,000, will be $1.200.... M plans to keep rent payment in the same range as the client's potential mortgage payment upon repurchase of the home. Clients will be given between twelve to fifteen months to clean up their credit and acquire financing to repurchase the home. As stated above [M expects] individuals to repurchase the homes at a minimum of $10,000 above the price ... [M] initially purchased the home for through the short sale.

In a Private Letter Ruling, I.R.S. Priv. Ltr. Rul. 2008-37-050 (June 16, 2008), the Internal Revenue Service rejected M's application for tax-exempt status because M "[had] not demonstrated [that M's] foreclosure program serves a charitable purpose. What was wrong with the plan? The relatively high rents, which would produce a 9–9.5% investment return, well above market rates at the time? Was it the fact that participants could be evicted from their homes if they became "unresponsive to the program?" Or the fact that virtually all of the organization's income would come from rents and sales of homes following participants' evictions?

4. Down payment assistance is another popular program for nonprofit organizations. Should tax exempt status be granted to a nonprofit corporation that solicits contributions from homebuilders and sellers, as well as other corporate and individual donors, to fund a down payment assistance program for HUD-qualified home buyers, and provides home buying seminars to such persons? The requested contributions from home builders and sellers equal $3% of a home's selling price. Qualified home buyers can expect down payment assistance up to 3% of a home's purchase price. *See* I.R.S. Priv. Ltr. Rul. 2007-04-041 (2006) (application for tax exempt status rejected; proposed program appeared to further a private business—home selling).

5. In Rev. Rul. 72-124, 1972-1 C.B. 145 cited in the Safe Harbor Guidelines, the Service opined that nonprofit organizations which operated homes for the aged could qualify for 501(c)(3) tax exempt status if their housing developments were "designed to satisfy the three primary needs of aged persons ... [1] housing ... designed to meet some combination of the physical, emotional, recreational, social, religious, and similar needs of aged persons ... [2] health care ... [by providing services] designed to maintain the physical, and if necessary, the mental well being of its residents ... [and 3] financial security ... [through a policy] of maintaining in residence any persons who become unable to pay their regular charges [with exceptions allowed for Federal or state assistance programs for persons of low- or moderate-income who are required to pay sufficient rent to enable the owner to recover operating costs] ... [and operating] so as to provide its services to the aged at the lowest feasible cost...." *Id.* at 146–47. In Rev. Rul. 79-18, 1979-1 C.B. 194, housing for the elderly was approved; in Rev. Rul. 79-19, 1979-1 C.B. 195 housing for physically handicapped was approved.

6. Does the increasing recognition of the link between social services and housing argue for a similar policy requiring nonprofit organizations to provide social services, such as day care and employment counseling, in addition to housing for non-elderly households in order to obtain tax exempt status? *See* John Ammann & Peter W. Salsich, Jr., *Non-Profit Housing Providers: Can They Survive The "Devolution Revolution?"* 16 St. Louis U. Pub. L. Rev. 321, 335–344 (1997) (reporting estimates of up to $2000/unit/year in costs for providing social services to help non-elderly tenants become self-sufficient). Or should provision of housing to those who cannot afford it, regardless of the age or status of the occupants, be sufficient ground for tax exemption as an organization operating exclusively for charitable purposes?

Metro City Problem (cont.)

Would a not-for-profit resident housing corporation participating as a co-general partner in a mixed housing development such as the one proposed in the Metro City problem, pages 158–59, *supra* qualify for tax-exempt status under the safe harbor guidelines? In the guidelines, the I.R.S. included the following examples:

> (2) Organization *O* will finance a housing project using tax-exempt bonds pursuant to § 145 (d). *O* will meet the 20–50 test under [26 U.S.C.] § 142(d)(1)(A). Another 45% of the residents will have incomes at or below 80% of the area's median income. The final 35% of the residents will have incomes above 80% of the area's median income. *O* will restrict rents charged to residents below the income limits to no more than 30% of the residents' incomes. *O* will provide social services to project residents and to other low-income residents in the neighborhood. Also, *O* will purchase its project through a government program designed to retain low-income housing stock. *O* does not meet the safe harbor. However, the facts and circumstances demonstrate that *O* relieves the poor and distressed....

(4) Organization *U* will purchase existing residential rental housing financed using tax-exempt bonds issued in accordance with [26 U.S.C.] § 145(d). *U* will meet the minimum requirements of the 40–60 test of [26 U.S.C.] § 142(d)(1)(B). It will provide the balance of its units to residents with incomes at or above area median income levels. *U* has a community-based board of directors. *U* does not satisfy the safe harbor. Moreover, the facts and circumstances do not demonstrate that *U* relieves the poor and distressed. *Id.* § 5.

Based on the guidelines and these examples, how would you structure a Metro City joint venture involving a not-for-profit resident housing corporation to maximize the corporation's chances of obtaining or retaining tax-exempt status?

---

b. Exemption from State Property Taxes

Similar problems of analysis arise with respect to the question whether nonprofit housing organizations should qualify for statutorily provided exemptions from state property taxes. In a leading case, the Missouri Supreme Court established an analytical structure for answering the question.

Franciscan Tertiary Province of Missouri, Inc. v. State Tax Commission of Missouri

Supreme Court of Missouri
566 S.W. 2d 213 (1978)

Finch, Judge.

[The court concluded that a nonprofit corporation organized to develop and own an apartment building for the elderly subsidized under Section 236 qualified for property tax exemption. The court reasoned as follows.—Eds.]

We hold that the word "used exclusively ... for purposes purely charitable, and not held for private or corporate profit" which appear in [Mo. Rev. Stat.] § 137.100 should and do have the same meaning whether applied to property used for a hospital, for training handicapped workers, for operating a YMCA type of program or for providing housing for the aged.

The first prerequisite for property to be exempt as charitable under § 137.100 is that it be owned and operated on a not-for-profit basis. It must be dedicated unconditionally to the charitable activity in such a way that there will be no profit, presently or prospectively, to individuals or corporations. Any gain achieved in use of the building must be devoted to attainment of the charitable objectives of the project.... [A]n exemption will not be granted covering property which houses a business operated for the purpose of gaining a profit, even though it is turned over to a parent organization to be used for what are admittedly independently religious or charitable purposes.

The requirement that the property must be operated as a not-for-profit activity does not mean that it is impermissible for the project at times or even fairly regularly to operate in the black rather than on a deficit basis, provided, of course, that any such excess of income over expense is achieved incidentally to accomplishment of the dominantly charitable objective and is not a primary goal of the project, and provided further that all of such gain is devoted to the charitable objectives of the project.

Another prerequisite for charitable exemption is that the dominant use of the property must be for the benefit of an indefinite number of people, for the purpose ... of "bringing their hearts under the influence of education or religion, by relieving their bodies from disease, suffering, or constraint, by assisting them to establish themselves for life, or be erecting or maintaining public buildings or works or otherwise lessening the burdens of government.... [through] humanitarian activities ... rendered at cost or less, which are intended to improve the physical, mental and moral condition of the recipients and make it less likely that they will become burdens on society and make it more likely that they will become useful citizens." *Salvation Army v. Hoehn*, 188 S.W.2d 826 (Mo. 1945) (*en banc*). Thus, it is required that there be the element of direct or indirect benefit to society in addition to and as a result of the benefit conferred on the persons directly served by the humanitarian activity....

A retirement center such as Chariton clearly serves an important social need. Such was expressly recognized by the Commission in its findings. Such projects are much more than a building with physical characteristics tailored to the often more limited mobility of its tenants. As the evidence in this case overwhelmingly suggests, such centers are designed and operated to encourage continued activity and further development. Through discussion groups, speakers, social activities, short trips, etc., plus periodic physical checkups, the continuing vitality and health of the residents is maintained. The Commission specifically found that the activities provided were extensive and worthwhile and were beneficial to the physical, spiritual, social and psychological needs of these elderly tenants. Such activity and the continued companionship available in such projects does help prolong life and health by reaffirming the sense that life is worth living, that society cares.

In its conclusions of law in support of its decision to deny a charitable exemption, the Commission ... expressed doubt that the tenants would consider themselves objects of charity and emphasized that they were not indigent. This is but further evidence of the inappropriate focus of such cases. In other areas, we have often reaffirmed the premise that charity is not limited to relief of the destitute.... Furthermore, we cannot believe that it is the intent of the people under 137.100 to withhold the financial assistance of a tax exemption until such time as our elderly are totally incapable of providing for themselves. The whole thrust of projects such as Chariton is to assist its tenants in avoiding such status by providing an atmosphere where they can remain self-sustaining as long as possible. The payment of monthly rent at Chariton and similar projects may for some be as important as the other valuable activities. Although federal or other assistance is obviously being provided, the sense of paying one's own way can be an important intangible which reaffirms continued vitality and dignity.

We do not believe that it may be said the benefits thus rendered to society are in any way less direct than those of ... the other residence halls cases. There was no assertion in the cases that the government was under any present duty to provide the type of facilities under review. Rather, such projects are said to build character and develop good citizenship, thereby contributing to the public welfare. In the present case, aside from furthering the moral well being of the tenants, the activities of the Chariton center are designed to reduce the likelihood that its residents will ever become public charges.

The fact that subsidization of part of the cost of furnishing such housing is by the government rather than private charitable contributions does not dictate a different result.... In this case, we actually have some substantial private charitable contributions in that Franciscan and affiliated organizations did contribute money and services, but the contribution to the project could have been solely from government funds....

The fact that rentals charged were to be applied in part to retirement of principal and interest incurred in acquiring or building the property in question does not dictate a denial of a charitable exemption if the facts otherwise support such an exemption, as they do here.... [T]he fact that rentals from tenants in Chariton were utilized in helping to retire principal and interest incurred in acquiring the building does not disqualify Franciscan from being granted a charitable exemption.

Notes and Questions

1. Should the age of the residents make a difference in the determination whether a development qualified for state property tax exempt status? Should an apartment complex that houses low- and moderate-income families be eligible for state property tax exempt status? *See Rio Vista Non-Profit Hous. Corp. v. County of Ramsey*, 277 N.W.2d 187 (Minn. 1979) (no to first question, yes to second); *Metropolitan Pittsburgh Non-Profit Hous. Corp. v. Board of Property Assessment*, 368 A.2d 837 (Pa. Commw. Ct. 1977) (yes to first question, no to second).

In *Partnership for Affordable Housing v. Board of Review for the City of Davenport*, 550 N.W. 2d 161, 165–67 (Iowa 1996), the Supreme Court of Iowa affirmed a denial of state property tax exemption for a limited partnership operating a LIHTC-supported development for low income, non-elderly single persons and families. In denying tax exempt status, the court stated:

> Partnership's sole corporate asset and function was the operation of Courtland as a low income housing facility within the framework of Partnership's certificate of limited partnership and Courtland's rental policies. Courtland was not established or operated as a food shelter or other form of retreat for the homeless or indigent. Through the Courtland project, Partnership provided its residents with nothing other than housing partly subsidized by the federal government....
>
> The rental policy of the Courtland Apartments is to rent the apartments to qualified low-income residents. Qualified low-income residents are defined as residents that meet the income restrictions for the Low Income Housing Tax Credit program as regulated by the Iowa Housing Finance Agency. Generally, residents' incomes are limited not to exceed 60% of the Scott County median income levels adjusted for family size.
>
> Notwithstanding the policy designating one rent-free apartment for abused women (that makes up 1/37th percent of all apartments at Courtland), Partnership does not have a policy for Courtland to accept residents for admission without regard to their ability to pay.... Partnership has introduced no evidence that it has ever waived rent for one of its residents.... Also, we conclude one rent-free apartment out of thirty-seven total apartments does not qualify the entire property for a charitable use exemption....
>
> There is no evidence in the present record to suggest Courtland is or has ever been operated or maintained by volunteers from the Davenport area. Furthermore, Partnership has identified no other way in which the operation of Courtland is aided through community support....
>
> Partnership claims its operation of Courtland benefits the Davenport community in many ways, including that Courtland provides affordable, low-rent housing for less fortunate members of the community and that one of Courtland's units

> is reversed for battered women in the community. We do not believe these admittedly laudable goals and purposes of Partnership's operation of Courtland rise to the level of charity.

Are the Iowa Supreme Court and the Internal Revenue Service on the same wave length? Should they be? Are there different policy considerations with respect to exemption from state property taxes and federal income taxes? *See* David A. Brennan, *The Commerciality Doctrine as Applied to the Charitable Tax Exemption for Homes for the Aged: State and Local Perspectives*, 76 FORDHAM L. REV. 833, 847 (2007) ("Tax-exempt law's commerciality doctrine provides that a charitable institution may conduct what looks like a commercial activity [e.g., a continuing care retirement center (CCRC)—Eds.] but still be entitled charitable income tax exemption under federal law so long as the activity is conducted in a manner that does not significantly advance non-charitable purposes"). In his essay, Prof. Brennan discusses cases from Georgia and Pennsylvania in which the courts treated CCRCs as complete integrated units even though the independent living section was profitable but the nursing home unit was not, *Board of Tax Assessors v. Baptist Village, Inc.*, 605 S.E.2d 436 (Ga. Ct. App. 2004); *Alliance Home v. Board of Assessment Appeals*, 919 A.2d 206 (Pa. 2007). Prof. Brennan cites Evelyn Brody, *The States' Growing Use of a Quid-Pro-Quo Rationale for the Charity Property Tax Exemption,* 56 EXEMPT ORG. TAX REV. 269, 270 (2007) for her analysis of "a growing divergence of federal and state policies and a growing acceptance by the states of a quid pro quo rationale for granting exemption," 76 FORDHAM L. REV at 835 n.6.

3. Do the following factors support the "social benefit" prerequisite spoken of in *Franciscan*: The presence of substantial, long-term government commitment to the elimination of blighted areas and the improvement of housing conditions, including the provision of housing subsidies such as existed in *Franciscan?* Would the lack of similar governmental support strengthen or weaken the case of a nonprofit housing provider?

Metro City Problem (cont.)

What safeguards would you build into the Metro City proposal, *supra*, to insure effective asset management? Management issues are discussed in Chapter 4 *infra*.

M. Housing Trust Funds and Impact Fees

Increased congressional pressure to limit the use of tax exempt bond financing, together with a decline in the extent of federal housing subsidy programs, has led states and the federal government to consider alternative sources of funds to support housing activities. However, concern that direct appropriations for housing programs could become a "bottomless pit" has made state legislatures reluctant to pick up the traditional federal support for housing development, and Congress wary of resuming open-ended direct funding of housing production.

1. State and Local Housing Trust Funds

One device that became popular in the 1980s is the housing trust fund (HTF), through which moneys from various sources are aggregated in a separate fund administered by the state treasurer or by a state housing or community development agency. The fund is invested and the resulting investment income is used to provide various types of housing subsidies such as rental assistance payments and capital grants.

The housing trust fund has become an attractive alternative because the legislature can seed the fund with a relatively small appropriation and then use the fund as a mechanism for aggregating contributions from local communities, impact fees exacted from developers, special taxes such as real estate transfer taxes, and un-obligated reserve funds generated by housing finance agencies. Supporters of the housing trust fund concept argue that a dedicated fund which is protected from the vagaries of the regular appropriations process will insure that housing programs receive their proper level of state support, and that special needs can be addressed with creative responses tailored to those needs. For examples of special state housing programs in which the trust fund concept is used see National Council of State Housing Agencies, State HFA Fact Book (2008).

HTFs have been established by numerous state and local governments to provide dedicated sources of revenue for affordable housing. Created by state legislation or local ordinance, HTFs have four characteristics: (1) providing an on-going source of revenue; (2) using this dedicated revenue for housing production; (3) targeting low- and moderate-income beneficiaries; and (4) establishing a permanent source of funding for affordable housing.

In addition some HTFs are created using special excise taxes, surplus funds, litigation settlements, and in some cases, general revenue appropriations. HTFs typically are authorized by state statute to receive and distribute monies for statutorily-authorized housing purposes such as seed money loans to non-profit housing organizations, rent subsidies, supportive social services, etc. *See, e.g.* Cal. Health & Safety § 50840; Fla. Stat. Ann. §§ 420.0005 (state housing trust fund), and 420.9079 (local housing trust fund); Mo. Rev. Stat. § 215.034 (state housing trust fund administered by Missouri Housing Development Commission).

The most popular state-level source of funds is a document transfer tax, which is a stamp tax on documents filed in the public land records evidencing transfers of property, as well as on certificates of stock, bonds, notes, and other evidences of indebtedness. *See, e.g.* Fla. Stat. Ann. §§ 201.01–201.09. The Housing Trust Fund Project, a special project of the Center for Community Change, tracks housing trust fund activities and advocates for their creation and growth. *See* Brooksm@commchange.org, *available at* www.communitychange.org.

Another source of revenue for local HTFs is derived from municipal "exactions" on large-scale private downtown commercial development projects. San Francisco led the way in 1981 with the creation of what is now known as the Affordable Office Housing Production Program. Downtown San Francisco commercial development projects must contribute approximately $5 per square foot to produce housing, most of which is targeted to low- and moderate-income housing. Boston followed suit with a similar program. These policies have become known as "linkage" programs. A variation of this approach adopted by cities like Miami and Seattle provides "density bonuses" for those large-scale downtown commercial development projects whose developers are willing to contribute to providing affordable housing (or similar amenities).

The rationale for the use of the police power by municipalities to exact development fees is the "nexus" between this type of development and its impact on the housing market. To prove this nexus, cities like San Francisco and Boston have demonstrated that the cumulative growth of downtown office and retail development have heightened housing demand. In tight housing markets with low rental vacancy rates and a shortage of below market housing, this threatens the further displacement of those unable to compete for market rate housing. By contributing linkage fees to assist in the development of affordable housing, private developers are thereby mitigating the negative impact of their development.

The "nexus" rationale is subject to legal challenge by developers who might argue that this cannot be demonstrated. They might also challenge the calculation of linkage fees as arbitrary and without a reasonable basis justifying the exercise of the police power. Since linkage policies have only covered new large-scale commercial projects and exempted small-scale and non-downtown projects, noncommercial projects, and existing businesses, equal protection arguments may also be raised. Finally, in some jurisdictions, developers have claimed that cities must have explicit state-enabling legislation authorizing linkage exactions. The following case discusses these issues.

Commercial Builders of Northern California v. City of Sacramento

United States Court of Appeals
941 F.2d 872 (9th Cir 1991)

SCHROEDER, Circuit Judge:

INTRODUCTION

Commercial Builders appeals the district court's grant of summary judgment in favor of the City of Sacramento in Commercial Builder's suit challenging a city ordinance to help expand available low-income housing. The Ordinance in question conditions certain types of nonresidential building permits upon the payment of a fee intended to offset the burdens on the city caused by low-income workers who move there to fill jobs created by the project in question. Appellants are a group of commercial developers who filed suit contending the ordinance constitutes a taking under the fifth and fourteenth amendments.

The district court granted summary judgment in favor of the city, holding that the Ordinance did not effect an unconstitutional taking. It specifically found that the Ordinance substantially advanced a legitimate interest and that the city had adequately supported its contribution requirement by showing a sufficient nexus between nonresidential development and the demand for low-income housing. The court therefore concluded that the ordinance was not infirm under *Nollan v. California Coastal Commission,* 483 U.S. 825 (1987), which requires such a nexus between land use restrictions and the articulated purpose behind them. Because we agree that the Ordinance here at issue does not amount to an unconstitutional taking, we affirm.

DISCUSSION

In 1987, the City and County of Sacramento commissioned a consulting firm, Keyser-Marston Associates, to study the need for low-income housing, the effect of nonresidential development on the demand for such housing, and the appropriateness of exacting fees in conjunction with such development to pay for such housing. Keyser-Marston submitted its report, estimating the percentage of new workers in the developments that would qualify as low-income workers and would require housing. As instructed, it also calculated fees for development based on a yearly subsidy of $12,000 per qualified household that would be connected to the development. This figure represented the difference between $42,000, the minimum cost of building a two-bedroom apartment, and $30,000, the maximum rental income expected from a low-income household. Also as instructed, however, in the interest of erring on the side of conservatism in exacting the fees, it reduced its final calculations by about one-half.

Based upon this study, the City of Sacramento enacted the Housing Trust Fund Ordinance on March 7, 1989. The Ordinance lists several city-wide findings, including the finding that nonresidential development is "a major factor in attracting new employees to the region" and that the influx of new employees "create[s] a need for additional housing in the City." Pursuant to these findings, the Ordinance imposes a fee in connection with the issuance of permits for nonresidential development of the type that will generate jobs. The fees, calculated using the Keyser-Marston formula, are to be paid into a fund to assist in the financing of low-income housing. The city projects that the fund will raise about $3.6 million annually, 9% of the projected annual cost of $42 million for the needed housing. Additional money will come from other sources, such as debt funding and general revenues.

Commercial Builders does not argue that the city lacks a legitimate interest in expanding low-income housing. Rather, it contends that this Ordinance constitutes an impermissible means to advance that interest, because it places a burden of paying for low-income housing on nonresidential development without a sufficient showing that nonresidential development contributes to the need for low-income housing in proportion to that burden. We affirm because we find the Ordinance sufficiently related to the legitimate purpose it seeks to achieve.

We have held that a condition placed upon the granting of a permit to develop land may constitute an impermissible taking, but we have done so only where the condition lacked any rational relationship to the project for which the permit was sought. In *Parks v. Watson,* 716 F.2d 646 (9th Cir. 1983), we held that where a developer seeking vacation of platted streets offered to pay for such vacation, a city could not insist that the developer dedicate its geothermal wells to the city as a precondition for such vacation. The dedication requirement, we held, "had no rational relationship to any purpose related to the vacation of the platted streets." 716 F.2d at 653. The condition therefore violated the fifth amendment....

The appellants contend that, even if the Ordinance would pass constitutional muster under these principles, it must be struck down because the Supreme Court has now articulated a more stringent standard under which courts must analyze the imposition of conditions upon development. The appellants point out that in *Nollan v. California Coastal Commission,* 483 U.S. 825 (1987), the Court held that such conditions must not only be ones that the government might "rationally have decided" to employ for a given legitimate public purpose; they must also substantially advance such a purpose. *See* 483 U.S. at 834 & n.4. They argue that under the standard articulated in *Nollan,* an ordinance that imposes an exaction on developers can be upheld only if it can be shown that the development in question is directly responsible for the social ill that the exaction is designed to alleviate.

As a threshold matter, we are not persuaded that *Nollan* materially changes the level of scrutiny we must apply to this Ordinance. The *Nollan* Court specifically stated that it did not have to decide "how close a 'fit' between the condition and the burden is required," because it found that the regulation in question "d[id] not meet even the most untailored standards." 483 U.S. at 838. It also noted that its holding was "consistent with the approach taken by every other court [which] has considered the question," Other circuits ...

have considered the constitutionality of ordinances that placed burdens on land use after *Nollan*. None have interpreted that case as changing the level of scrutiny to be applied to regulations that do not constitute a physical encroachment on land....

We therefore agree with the City that *Nollan* does not stand for the proposition that an exaction ordinance will be upheld only where it can be shown that the development is directly responsible for the social ill in question. Rather, *Nollan* holds that where there is no evidence of a nexus between the development and the problem that the exaction seeks to address, the exaction cannot be upheld. Where, as here, the Ordinance was implemented only after a detailed study revealed a substantial connection between development and the problem to be addressed, the Ordinance does not suffer from the infirmities that the Supreme Court disapproved in *Nollan*. We find that the nexus between the fee provision here at issue, designed to further the city's legitimate interest in housing, and the burdens caused by commercial development is sufficient to pass constitutional muster.

The appellants also place some significance on the fact that this Ordinance is a fee provision. They contend that the fee represents a transfer of property, i.e., the money paid over to the city. *See Webb's Fabulous Pharmacies, Inc. v. Beckwith,* 499 U.S. 155 (1980) (treating a purely financial exaction as a taking). In this respect, they argue, it more closely resembles a physical taking of property, which automatically falls within the purview of the fifth amendment, than a land use regulation, which is subject to a reasonableness analysis. Under appellants' theory, however, compensation would be required for every fee; therefore, every fee would be unconstitutional. We see no valid basis for such a rule.

Indeed, the only circuit to treat a fee provision as an unconstitutional taking under *Nollan* was ultimately reversed by the Supreme Court. In *Sperry Corp. v. United States,* 853 F.2d 904 (Fed. Cir. 1988), the Federal Circuit found unconstitutional a government exaction of a percentage of any award from the Iran Claims Commission. It treated the fee as a physical taking because it constituted a transfer of the possession of property. 853 F.2d at 906–07. It then invalidated it because if found the exaction arbitrary. The infirmity, the court held, was the assessment of the cost of the Iran hostage crisis only against those who successfully asserted claims associated with Iranian interests. Because that crisis was a national concern, the court concluded, the burden should instead have been borne equally by the whole nation.

The Supreme Court disagreed, holding that the exaction of a percentage of any award made by the Iran Claims Commission was a permissible means of collecting reimbursement for costs incurred in the operation of that Commission. *United States v. Sperry Corp.,* 493 U.S. 52 (1989). The Court expressed doubts as to the appropriateness of the Federal Circuit's analysis of the fee under principles applicable to physical takings, noting that "[i]t is artificial to view deductions of a percentage of a monetary award as physical appropriations of property. Unlike real or personal property, money is fungible." Under this reasoning, the Ordinance does not, as appellants suggest, constitute a taking per se.

In *Webb's Fabulous Pharmacies,* upon which these appellants have also relied, the Court struck down a Florida statute that confiscated all interest on interpleader funds deposited with the state courts. The Court there reasoned that the statute in question served no purpose, because another Florida statute required that parties make payments for the services rendered by court personnel in maintaining such funds. The appellants argue in this case that the Ordinance here at issue is similarly unrelated to a permissible purpose, contending that the mere desire to generate revenue for the public good cannot, after *Webb's Fabulous Pharmacies,* support the exaction.

The *Sperry* Court disposed of a similar argument. Its decision to uphold the deduction from awards was primarily based on the fact that the fee was used to pay for the operations of the tribunal that resolved the disputes of all of those from whom such a fee was collected; thus, a close nexus between the charge and the activity creating the cost was established. The Court indicated, however, that it would have been satisfied with an even looser nexus, stating that "Sperry may be required to pay a charge for the availability of the Tribunal even if it is made for the purpose of paying a social cost that is reasonably related to the activity against which the fee is assessed. Again, we conclude that the required nexus is present in this case.

Finally, the appellants contend that, regardless of the standard to be applied in assessing the validity of the Ordinance, they have raised an issue of material fact in their attack on the conclusions of the Keyser-Marston study. This attack came in the form of an affidavit from their planner, David Wade, suggesting that commercial development may be a less decisive factor in worker migration than the Keyser-Marston study indicates. Wade concluded that, in addition to employment opportunity, the availability of low-income housing is itself partly responsible for any influx of low-income employees to Sacramento. Wade also opined that it is at least as true that employers follow the work force as the converse. This affidavit, appellants argue, sufficiently calls into question the city's findings concerning the nexus between its Ordinance and the social ill it sought to cure to preclude summary judgment.

The appellants' argument lacks merit. Even viewing the Wade affidavit in the light most favorable to the developers, it does not rebut the Keyser-Marston conclusion that commercial development is related to an increase in the need for low-income housing. The Ordinance accounts for what the developers characterize as the indirectness of the connection between the creation of new jobs and the need for low-income housing by charging only a small percentage of what the Keyser-Marston study calculated to be the cost of meeting new low-income housing requirements. As we have already noted, nothing in *Nollan* or any other authority cited by the appellants requires the nexus to be more direct than that achieved through the legislative process that the city here employed. We therefore agree with the district court that the Wade affidavit is insufficient to preclude summary judgment.

CONCLUSION

The district court correctly found that, as a matter of law, Sacramento's Housing Trust Fund Ordinance does not work an unconstitutional taking. Summary judgment in favor of the city was therefore proper.

AFFIRMED

BEEZER, Circuit Judge, dissenting:

As Justice Scalia warned in *Nollan,* a state can leverage its police power to the point where a regulation of land use becomes an "out-and-out plan of extortion." *Nollan v. California Coastal Comm'n,* 483 U.S. 825, 837 (1987). Sacramento's ordinance is a transparent attempt to force commercial developers to underwrite social policy. Apparently, legislators find it politically more palatable to exact payments from developers than to tax their constituents. The Takings Clause prohibits singling out developers to bear this burden.

Historically, courts have upheld exactions when states were able to justify them as serving a public purpose related to burdens caused by development. For example, courts have sustained requirements that developers construct various on-site improvements, such as sewers, water mains, sidewalks, curbs, and gutters, storm drains, and landscaping. Requiring off-site improvements that serve a public purpose, such as roads, schools, parks and sewage treatment plants, may also be justified where the requirement alleviates a public burden or ameliorates harmful effects caused by the development. When the developer is asked to bear a fair share of the burden, such a requirement directly furthers the legitimate interest of the government. When the governmental exaction solves a problem actually created by the development (for example, requiring the developer to provide needed infrastructure), it is no coincidence that the exaction results in a benefit to the development as well as the community.

State and local governments face mounting budget deficits, attributable to decreased federal funding, recessionary pressures on tax collection and the growing popularity of "taxpayer revolts"—the most well-known example of which is California's Proposition 13. In response, state and local governments have begun to stretch the use of exactions to the breaking point. Sacramento would have developers pay not just for public improvements necessitated by development, but for private subsidies with little or no casual connection to development. Not surprisingly, under a scheme requiring no connection, no benefit accrues to the development in return....

Sacramento has commissioned a study that demonstrates at best a tenuous and theoretical connection between commercial development and housing needs. But the Takings Clause requires a cause-and-effect relationship between the two. In my view, Sacramento has not shown such a relationship. Even the study relied on by the city to support the ordinance states that its "nexus analysis does not make the case that building construction is responsible for growth."

The ordinance is nothing more than a convenient way to fund a system of transfer payments. Although Sacramento attempts to justify the ordinance as an exercise of its police power, the city actually is exercising its taxing power—free of the encumbrances generally thought to limit the exercise of that power....

The new workers attracted by the new jobs associated with the new development surely will increase the demand for all manner of goods and services. If Sacramento has shown a sufficient causal connection in this case, we can be expected next to uphold exactions imposed on developers to subsidize small business retailers, child-care programs, food services and health-care delivery systems.

Notes and Questions

1. For additional information on housing trust funds, see the Center for Community Change, Housing Trust Fund Project, http://www.communitychange.org/our-projects/htf. *See also* Mary Brooks, *Housing Trust Funds: A New Approach to Funding Affordable Housing, in* AFFORDABLE HOUSING AND URBAN REDEVELOPMENT IN THE UNITED STATES 229 (Willem Van Vliet ed. 1997).

2. For a discussion of municipal housing linkage programs, see William Merrill & Robert Lincoln, *Linkage Fees and Fair Share Regulations: Law and Method,* 25 URB. LAW. 23 (1993); W. Dennis Keating, *Linking Downtown Development to Broader Community Goals: An Analysis of Linkage Policy in Three Cities,* 52 J. AM. PLAN. ASS'N 133 (1986); Arthur C. Nelson, *Downtown Office Development and Housing Linkage Fees,* 54 J. AM. PLAN. ASS'N

197 (1988); Jane Schukoske, *Housing Linkage: Regulating Development Impact on Housing Costs*, 76 Iowa L. Rev. 1011 (1991).

3. In 1994, the Supreme Court added a second prong to the *Nollan* test by requiring that in addition to a nexus, the proposed exaction of land use concessions or impact/linkage fees must be "roughly proportional" to the impact of the proposed development on the public interest in question (in our case, affordable housing), as measured by an "individualized determination." *Dolan v. City of Tigard*, 512 U.S. 374, 391–395 (1994). The revised test now is called the *Nollan/Dolan* test.

In *Ehrlich v. City of Culver City*, 911 P.2d 429 (Cal. 1996), the Supreme Court of California extended the reach of *Nollan/Dolan* to individualized monetary exactions imposed as a condition to issuance of a development permit, but declined to apply the rule and its heightened scrutiny to a "generally applicable development fee or assessment." A concurring opinion stressed that "the taking of money is different, under the Fifth Amendment, from the taking of real or personal property." *Id.* at 451–55. Monetary exactions can have serious impact on the cost of producing affordable housing for low and moderate income households. The ordinance in *Commercial Builders* applied to nonresidential building permits. Can and should such fees be applied to residential builders? Do they amount to extortion because developers cannot proceed without the requisite permits? Should employers or contractors have to pay for affordable housing through such fees, considering that the compensation they pay in wages to employees or fees to independent contractors presumably takes into account some general understanding of the cost of shelter?

4. Inclusionary zoning as the antidote to exclusionary zoning can be closely related to the linkage question. Both are components of the broader question of land use control powers either to discourage or encourage the development of affordable housing. The topic of zoning is treated further in Chapter 6 *infra*.

2. National Housing Trust Fund Legislation

Following years of advocacy, Congress in 2008 tacked onto the Housing and Economic Recovery Act of 2008 two new housing development programs, the National Housing Trust Fund ("NHTF"), and the Capital Magnet Fund ("CMF"), HERA, §1131, adding §§1337–1339 to the Federal Housing Enterprises Financial Safety and Soundness Act of 1992, 12 U.S.C. §1301 *et seq.* The National Housing Trust Fund is a HUD-managed fund designed to provide funds for production, preservation, and rehabilitation of both rental housing and housing for homeownership for Very Low-Income ("VLI") households (50% or less of area median income) and Extremely Low-Income ("ELI") households (30% or less of area median income). The Capital Magnet Fund is a Treasury Secretary-managed fund designed to provide a competitive grant program to encourage private investment in affordable housing, as well as related economic development and community service activities.

After a three-year phase-in period, during which any funds appropriated to the NHTF were to be used to reimburse FHA for its costs in refinancing mortgages to prevent foreclosures, NHTF funds will be allocated as grants to states for redistribution to state housing finance agencies, state housing and community development entities and other "qualified instrumentalities." Seventy-five percent of the funds are to be earmarked for housing benefiting ELI households and the remaining 25% for VLI households.

The allocation and distribution process is described in the following excerpt.

Peter W. Salsich, Jr., National Affordable Housing Trust Fund Legislation: The Subprime Mortgage Crisis Also Hits Renters

16 Georgetown Journal on Poverty Law & Policy 11, 38–39, 41 (2009)

Distributions [from the NHTF to the states] will be made in accordance with a needs-based formula to be developed by HUD that includes the sum of four ratios: (i) the ratio of the shortage of standard rental units that are "affordable and available to extremely low-income renter households" in the state to the national shortage of such units, (ii) the ratio of the shortage of similar units for very low-income renter households, (iii) the ratio of extremely low-income renter households living with incomplete kitchen or plumbing facilities, or more than one person per room, or paying more than 50% of income for housing costs, and (iv) the ratio of very low-income renter households living with the same housing concerns, multiplied by the relative cost of construction in the state measured against national costs. [12 U.S.C. § 1338(c)(3)(b)]

5. State Allocation Plans

States or state-designated entities and grantees will be required to prepare allocation plans are based on "priority housing needs" [that conform to statutory and regulatory criteria—Eds.] and are consistent with established comprehensive housing affordability strategies ("CHAS"). [The CHAS process is discussed in Chapter 5 *infra*—Eds.] Allocation plans must provide that funding priority will be based on "geographic diversity," ability to undertake activities in a "timely manner," extent and duration of affordable rents for ELI families, extent to which other funds will be used and the merits of a particular proposal. "Geographic diversity" is not defined in this section, but in the Capital Magnet Fund section it is defined as including "those areas that meet objective criteria of economic distress as developed by the Secretary of the Treasury, which may include—

(i) the percentage of low-income families or the extent of poverty;

(ii) the rate of unemployment or underemployment;

(iii) extent of blight and disinvestment;

(iv) projects that target extremely low, very low, and low-income families in or outside a designated economic distress area; or

(v) any other criteria designated by the Secretary of the Treasury."

[12 U.S.C. § 1339(h)(2)(B)]

Presumably the Secretary of Housing and Urban Development will use the same or similar approach in defining "geographic diversity" for the Housing Trust Fund.

Eligible activities include "production, preservation, and rehabilitation," as well as operating costs, of rental housing, with at least 75% of the funds required to benefit extremely low-income (ELI) families and 25% very low-income (VLI) families, and homeownership opportunities for ELI and VLI first-time homebuyers who have completed a financial education and counseling program from an approved counseling agency, but only 10% of trust fund monies can be used for homeownership support. Eligible grant recipients include both for-profit and nonprofit organizations which demonstrate experience, financial and organizational capacity, ability, familiarity with the requirements of other housing programs, and provide assurances of compliance with program and statutory standards. [12 U.S.C. § 1338(c)(7),(9)& (10)....

Establishment of a national Housing Trust Fund with a dedicated source of funding pledged by law to support housing for the extremely low-income and very low-income cohorts accomplishes several things. The Federal Government becomes committed to providing predictable and regular financial support for additional housing production, primarily rental and affordable to the ELI and VLI cohorts. States and local entities that have gained valuable experience through the administration of their own housing programs over the last several decades will receive a substantial infusion of new monies. These funds will enable qualified state and local entities, both public and private, to respond to the increasingly severe housing needs of families least able to compete effectively for such housing in the private market.

Inclusion of the national Housing Trust Fund in the foreclosure relief legislation acknowledges the important point that renters as well as homeowners are affected by the foreclosure crisis. And while the focus of the Housing Trust Fund should remain on the housing needs of extremely low-income and very low-income renters, the allocation of Housing Trust Fund monies in the first years of operation to foreclosure relief programs represents a reasonable compromise and a recognition that enabling as many homeowners as possible to save their homes is a critical step toward stabilizing the overall housing market.

Notes and Questions

1. How should the NHTF and CMF be funded? Should their funding be subject to the annual appropriation process described in Chapter 2 *supra,* as is the direct-grant HOME program described *supra,* or should a funding mechanism be established that operates outside the regular appropriations process? The congressional plan outlined in HERA called for Fannie Mae and Freddie Mac to allocate "an amount equal to 4.2 basis points (0.042%) for each dollar of the unpaid principal balance of [each agency's] total new business purchases," with 65% of that amount set aside for the Housing Trust Fund and 35% for the Capital Magnet Fund. HERA, § 1131, adding § 1337(a)(1)(A)-(B), (a)(2)(A)-(B). This was expected to provide approximately $600 million per year. However, when the two agencies went into conservatorship, discussed *supra,* that funding source was shelved indefinitely. Advocates then sought and obtained support for a $1 billion appropriation from the Obama Administration. At press time, that request was still pending in Congress.

2. As noted above, the NHTF legislation requires HUD to develop a needs-based formula to allocate funds to states based on state-national ratios of the shortage of standard rental units "affordable and available" to ELI families and to VLI families, as well as the number of ELI and VLI renter households living with either "incomplete kitchen or plumbing facilities, more than 1 person per room or paying more than 50% of income for household costs," multiplied by the "relative cost of construction in the State." 12 U.S.C. §4568(c)(B). Proposed regulations promulgated by HUD call for an "allocation formula [that uses] a 50-12.5-25-12.5 weighting approach for the four factors." Housing Trust Fund; Allocation Formula; Proposed Rule, 74 Fed. Reg. 63938, 63940 (Dec. 4, 2009) (*to be codified at* 24 C.F.R. pt. 93). Note the tilt toward ELI households in both the statute and the regulations. Does this emphasis comport with housing needs identified in Chapter 1 *supra,* or does the allocation formula appear too narrow for a major new national housing production program?

3. For additional discussion of the trust fund legislative concept, see Frank Alexander, *Financing Affordable Housing in Georgia: The Possibility of a Dedicated Revenue Source,*

123 Ga. St. U. L. Rev. 363, 382 (1997) (discussing traditional opposition to dedicated sources of housing revenue); Winston Sale, *Effect of the Conservatorship of Fannie Mae and Freddie Mac on Affordable Housing,* 18 J. Affordable Housing & Community Dev. L. 287, 306–307 (2009); David Super, *Rethinking Fiscal Federalism,* 118 Harv. L. Rev 2544, 2620 (2005) (discussing the implications of diminished legislative control over budgetary matters); Laura Schwarz, Comment, *The 2007 National Affordable Housing Trust Fund Act: A National Fund for a National Need,* 17 J. Affordable Housing & Community Dev. L. 395 (2008); Beth Parr, Note, *Almost Home: Policy and Politics in the Campaign for a National Housing Trust Fund,* 11 Geo. J. on Poverty L. & Pol'y 321 (2004).

Chapter 4

Consumerism and the Management of Housing

This chapter explores the problems involved in allocating living space, particularly in urban settings and generally with respect to rental housing. Over the last half century, the evolution of the relationships between shelter providers (landlords or lessors) and shelter consumers (tenants or lessees) has been one of the most dramatic in the law. These developments can be seen in the roles undertaken by the legislatures (including the federal, state, and local governments), and the new doctrines originating in the courts. These developments have not come easily and the resolution has not been completed. This chapter explores that evolution.

This chapter opens with consideration of the relationships between housing consumers and providers in the private market. We examine the quests for quality, affordability, and availability of rental shelter. Next the chapter considers the relationships between public sector tenants and the governmental or quasi-governmental providers of housing and the quest for fairness, quality, security of tenure, and safety.

It makes for an interesting exercise to compare and contrast the different aspects of relationships and rights that exist between housing providers and housing consumers in the private market, on the one hand, and in the public sector, on the other hand. In which sector do tenants have the greatest protection? Are there rights in the private market that do not exist for public sector tenants? Do public-sector tenants have rights that private-sector tenants do not? Which tenants would seem to need the greatest protection? Are any aspects of a "right to housing," analyzed in Chapter 1, *supra,* recognized for tenants in either private or governmentally-provided or -assisted housing?

One issue that will be left for further analysis concerns impediments on access to private and governmentally-assisted housing attributable to various kinds of discrimination. This matter will be covered in Chapter 6, *infra.*

A. Private Market Tenants

Historically the common law offered little protection to tenants. As we shall see, today most jurisdictions treat residential leases much like any other consumer transactions, though some important legal and social differences persist.

In *Ingalls v. Hobbs,* 31 N.E. 286 (Mass. 1892), the Supreme Judicial Court of Massachusetts acknowledged that, under the doctrine of *caveat emptor,* the typical tenant had no remedy for leasing uninhabitable housing. Nor did the tenant or the tenant's guests have a right to recover from the landlord for personal injuries caused by a defect in any part of the building outside the areas used in common with other tenants. *Lawler v. Capital City Life Ins. Co.*, 68 F.2d 438 (D.C. Cir. 1933).

The warranty of habitability revolution replaced the harshness of the common law with the contemporary view of providers and consumers of housing. Now "landlords" (perhaps the term is anachronistic) are viewed like other retailers of goods, making fundamental guarantees about the product they place on the market. Some of the basic permutations of this struggle for a place to live follow, as we explore tenant remedies for breach of the developing warranties.

If fitness of the dwelling was the issue of the 1960s, surely rent control proved to be the most contentious struggle of the 1980s, a conflict that reached the dimensions of class warfare in many metropolitan areas. Major decisions on the legality of rent control and its historical and social context are the principal concern of the materials at this juncture. The flight from rental units to condominiums is considered along with some of its "ripple effects," including the displacement of lower-income by higher-income residents in the transformation and disruption of neighborhoods.

1. Tenant Protections in Private Housing: The Warranty of Habitability as a Shield

Javins, the case following, explores some of the underpinnings of the common law and traces the developments that culminated in the overthrow of the old order. Though the case was both seminal and far reaching, it raised more questions than it answered. The explanation for the traditional view of landlord responsibility may also be incomplete. Can you think of reasons not given in the opinion for the one-sided view of the law in the older decisions?

Javins v. First National Realty Corporation

United States Court of Appeals
428 F.2d 1071 (D.C. Cir. 1970)

J. Skelly WRIGHT, Circuit Judge:

These cases present the question whether housing code violations which arise during the term of a lease have any effect upon the tenant's obligations to pay rent. The Landlord and Tenant Branch of the District of Columbia Court of General Sessions ruled proof of such violations inadmissible when proffered as a defense to an eviction action for nonpayment of rent. The District of Columbia Court of Appeals upheld this ruling. *Saunders v. First National Realty Corp.*, 245 A.2d 836 (D.C. 1968).

I

By separate written leases, each of the appellants rented an apartment in a three building apartment complex in Northwest Washington known as Clifton Terrace. The landlord, First National Realty Corporation, filed separate actions in the Landlord and Tenant Branch of the Court of General Sessions on April 8, 1966, seeking possession on the ground that each of the appellants had defaulted in the payment of rent due for the month of April. The tenants, appellants here, admitted that they had not paid the landlord any rent for April. However, they alleged numerous violations of the Housing Regulations as "an equitable defense or [a] claim by way of recoupment or set-off in an amount equal to the rent claim," as provided in the rules of the Court of General Sessions. They offered to prove

> [t]hat there are approximately 1500 violations of the Housing Regulations of the District of Columbia in the building at Clifton Terrace, where Defendant resides, some affecting the premises of this Defendant directly, others indirectly, and all tending to establish a course of conduct of violation of the Housing Regulations to the damage of Defendants.

Appellants conceded at trial, however, that this offer of proof reached only violations which had arisen since the term of the lease had commenced. The Court of General Sessions refused appellant's offer of proof and entered judgment for the landlord. The District of Columbia Court of Appeals affirmed, rejecting the argument made by appellants that the landlord was under a contractual duty to maintain the premises in compliance with the Housing Regulations, *Saunders v. First National Realty Corp. supra*, 245 A.2d at 838.

II

Since, in traditional analysis, a lease was the conveyance of an interest in land, courts have usually utilized the special rules governing real property transactions to resolve controversies involving leases. However, as the Supreme Court has noted in another context, "the body of private property law ... more than almost any other branch of law, has been shaped by distinctions whose validity is largely historical." Courts have a duty to reappraise old doctrines in the light of the facts and values of contemporary life—particularly old common law doctrines which the courts themselves created and developed. As we have said before, "[T]he continued vitality of the common law ... depends upon its ability to reflect contemporary community values and ethics."

The assumption of landlord-tenant law, derived from feudal property law, that a lease primarily conveyed to the tenant an interest in land may have been reasonable in a rural, agrarian society; it may continue to be reasonable in some cases involving farming or commercial land. In these cases, the value of the lease to the tenant is the land itself. But in the case of the modern apartment dweller, the value of the lease is that it gives him a place to live. The City dweller who seeks to lease an apartment on the third floor of a tenement has little interest in the land 30 or 40 feet below, or even in the bare right to possession within the four walls of his apartment. When American city dwellers, both rich and poor, seek "shelter" today, they seek a well known package of goods and services—a package which includes not merely walls and ceilings, but also adequate heat, light and ventilation, serviceable plumbing facilities, secure windows and doors, proper sanitation, and proper maintenance.

Professor Powell summarizes the present state of the law:

> The complexities of city life, and the proliferated problems of modern society in general, have created new problems for lessors and lessees and these have been commonly handled by specific clauses inserted in leases. This growth in the number and detail of specific lease covenants has reintroduced into the law of estates for years a predominantly contractual ingredient. In practice, the law today concerning estates for years consists chiefly of rules determining the construction and effect of lease covenants.

Ironically, however, the rules governing the construction and interpretation of "predominantly contractual" obligations in leases have too often remained rooted in old property law.

Some courts have realized that certain of the old rules of property law governing leases are inappropriate for today's transactions. In order to reach results more in accord with the legitimate expectations of the parties and the standards of the community, courts have been gradually introducing more modern precepts of contract law in interpreting leases. Proceeding piecemeal has, however, led to confusion where "decisions are frequently conflicting, not because of a healthy disagreement on social policy, but because of the lingering impact of rules whose policies are long since dead."

In our judgment the trend toward leases as contracts is wise and well considered. Our holding in this case reflects a belief that leases of urban dwelling units should be interpreted and construed like any other contract.

III

Modern contract law has recognized that the buyer of goods and services in an industrialized society must rely upon the skill and honesty of the supplier to assure that goods and services purchased are of adequate quality. In interpreting most contracts, courts have sought to protect the legitimate expectations of the buyer and steadily widened the seller's responsibility for the quality of goods and services through implied warranties of fitness and merchantability Thus without any special agreement a merchant will be held to warrant that his goods are fit for the ordinary purposes for which such goods are used and that they are at least of reasonably average quality. Moreover, if the supplier has been notified that goods are required for a specific purpose, he will be held to warrant that any goods sold are fit for that purpose. These implied warranties have become widely accepted and well established features of the common law, supported by overwhelming body of case law. Today most states as well as the District of Columbia have codified and enacted these warranties into statute, as to the sale of goods in the Uniform Commercial Code.

Implied warranties of quality have not been limited to cases involving sales. The consumer renting a chattel, paying for services or buying a combination of goods and services must rely upon the skill and honesty of the supplier to at least the same extent as a purchaser of goods. Courts have not hesitated to find implied warranties of fitness and merchantability in such situations. In most areas product liability law has moved far beyond "mere" implied warranties running between two parties in privity with each other.

The rigid doctrines of real property law have tended to inhibit the application of implied warranties to transactions involving real estate. Now, however, courts have begun to hold sellers and developers of real property responsible for the quality of their product.

Despite this trend in the sale of real estate, many courts have been unwilling in imply warranties of quality, specifically a warranty of habitability, into leases of apartments. Recent decisions have offered no convincing explanation for their refusal, rather they have relied without discussion upon the old common law rule that the lessor is not obligated to repair unless he covenants to do so in the written lease contract. However, the Supreme Courts of at least two states, in recent and well reasoned opinions, have held landlords to implied warranties of quality in housing leases. *Lemle v. Breeden*, 462 P.2d 470 (Haw. 1969); *Reste Realty Corp. v. Cooper*, 251 A.2d 268 (N.J. 1969). *See also Pines v. Perssion*, 111 N.W.2d 409 (Wis. 1961). In our judgment, the old no-repair rule cannot coexist with the obligations imposed on the landlord by a typical modern building code, and must be abandoned in favor of an implied warranty of habitability. In the District of Columbia, the standards of this warranty are set out in the Housing Regulations.

IV

A. In our judgment the common law itself must recognize the landlord's obligation to keep his premises in a habitable condition. This conclusion is compelled by three separate considerations. First, we believe that the old rule was based on certain factual assumptions which are no longer true; on its own terms, it can no longer be justified. Second, we believe that the consumer protection cases discussed above require that the old rule be abandoned in order to bring residential landlord-tenant law into harmony with the principles on which those cases rest. Third, we think that the nature of today's urban housing market also dictates abandonment of the old rule.

The common law rule absolving the lessor of all obligation to repair originated in the early Middle Ages. Such a rule was perhaps well suited to an agrarian economy; the land was more important than whatever small living structure was included in the leasehold, and the tenant farmer was fully capable of making repairs himself. These historical facts were the basis on which the common law constructed its rule; they also provided the necessary prerequisites for its applications.

Court decisions in the late 1800's began to recognize that the factual assumptions of the common law were no longer accurate in some cases. For example, the common law since it assumed that the land was the most important part of the leasehold, required a tenant to pay rent even if any building on the land was destroyed. Faced with such a rule and the ludicrous results it produced, in 1863 the New York Court of Appeals declined to hold that an upper story tenant was obliged to continue paying rent after his apartment building burned down. The court simply pointed out that the urban tenant had no interest in the land, only in the attached building.

Another line of cases created an exception to the no-repair rule for short term leases of furnished dwellings....

These as well as other similar cases demonstrate that some courts began some time ago to question the common law's assumptions that the land was the most important feature of a leasehold and that the tenant could feasibly make any necessary repairs himself. Where those assumptions no longer reflect contemporary housing patterns, the courts have created exceptions to the general rule that landlords have no duty to keep their premises in repair.

It is overdue for courts to admit that these assumptions are no longer true with regard to all urban housing. Today's urban tenants, the vast majority of whom live in multiple dwelling houses, are interested, not in the land, but solely in "a house suitable for occupation." Furthermore, today's city dweller usually has a single, specialized skill unrelated to maintenance work; he is unable to make repairs like the "jack-of-all-trades" farmer who was the common law's model of the lessee. Further, unlike his agrarian predecessor who often remained on one piece of land for his entire life, urban tenants today are more mobile than ever before. A tenant's tenure in a specific apartment will often not be sufficient to justify efforts at repairs. In addition, the increasing complexity of today's dwellings renders them much more difficult to repair it than the structures of earlier times. In a multiple dwelling repair may require access to equipment and areas in the control of the landlord. Low and middle income tenants, even if they were interested in making repairs, would be unable to obtain any financing for major repairs since they have no long-term interest in the property.

Our approach to the common law of landlord and tenant ought to be aided by principles derived from the consumer protection cases referred to above. In a lease contract, a tenant seeks to purchase from his landlord shelter for a specified period of time. The landlord sells housing as a commercial businessman and has much greater opportunity, incentive and capacity to inspect and maintain the condition of his building. Moreover, the tenant must rely upon the skill and *bona fides* of his landlord at least as much as a car buyer must rely upon the car manufacturer. In dealing with major problems, such as heating, plumbing, electrical or structural defects, the tenant's position corresponds precisely with "the ordinary consumer who cannot be expected to have the knowledge or capacity or even the opportunity to make adequate inspection of mechanical instrumentalities, like automobiles, and to decide for himself whether they are reasonably fit for the designed purpose." *Henningson v. Bloomfield Motors, Inc.*, 161 A.2d 69, 78 (N.J. 1960).

Since a lease contract specifies a particular period of time during which the tenant has a right to use his apartment for shelter, he may legitimately expect that the apartment will be fit for habitation for the time period for which it is rented. We point out that in the present cases there is no allegation that appellants' apartments were in poor condition or in violation of the housing code at the commencement of the leases. Since the lessees continue to pay the same rent, they were entitled to expect that the landlord would continue to keep the premises in their beginning condition during the lease term. It is precisely such expectations that the law now recognizes as deserving of formal, legal protection.

Even beyond the rationale of traditional products liability law, the relationship of landlord and tenant suggests further compelling reasons for the law's protection of the tenants' legitimate expectations of quality. The inequality in bargaining power between landlord and tenant has been well documented. Tenants have very little leverage to enforce demands, for better housing. Various impediments to competition in the rental housing market, such as racial and class discrimination and standardized form leases mean that landlords place tenants in a take it or leave it situation. The increasingly severe shortage of adequate housing further increases the landlord's bargaining power and escalates the need for maintaining and improving the existing stock. Finally, the findings by various studies of the social impact of bad housing has led to the realization that poor housing is detrimental to the whole society, not merely to the unlucky ones who must suffer the daily indignity of living in a slum.

Thus we are led by our inspection of the relevant legal principles and precedents to the conclusion that the old common law rule imposing an obligation upon the lessee to repair during the lease term was really never intended to apply to residential urban leaseholds. Contract principles established in other areas of the law provide a more rational framework for the apportionment of landlord-tenant responsibilities: they strongly suggest that a warranty of habitability be implied into all contracts for urban dwellings.

B. We believe, in any event, that the District's housing code requires that a warranty of habitability be implied in the leases of all housing that it covers. The housing code—formally designated the Housing Regulations of the District of Columbia—was established and authorized by the Commissioners of the District of Columbia on August 11, 1955. Since that time, the code has been updated by numerous orders of the commissioners. The 75 pages of the Regulations provide a comprehensive regulatory scheme setting forth in some detail: (a) the standards which housing in the District of Columbia must meet; (b) which party, the lessor or the lessee, must meet each standard; and (c) a system of inspections, notification and criminal penalties. The Regulations themselves are silent on the question of private remedies.

Two previous decisions of this court, however, have held that the Housing Regulations create legal rights and duties enforceable in tort by private parties. In *Whetzel v. Jess Fisher*

Management Co., 282 F.2d 943 (D.C. Cir. 1960), we followed the leading case of *Altz v. Lieberson*, 134 N.E. 703 (N.Y. 1922), in holding (1) that the housing code altered the common law rule and imposed a duty to repair upon the landlord, and (2) that a right of action accrued to a tenant injured by the landlord's breach of this duty. As Judge Cardozo wrote in *Lieberson*:

> We may be sure that the framers of this statute, when regulating tenement life, had uppermost in thought the care of those who are unable to care for themselves. The Legislature must have known that unless repairs in the rooms of the poor were made by the landlord, they would not be made by anyone. The duty imposed became commensurate with the need. The right to seek redress is not limited to the city or its officers. The right extends to all whom there was a purpose to protect. 134 N.E. at 704.

Recently, in *Kanelos v. Kettler*, 406 F.2d 951, 953 (D.C. Cir. 1968), we reaffirmed our position in *Whetzel*, holding that "the Housing Regulations did impose maintenance obligations upon appellee [landlord] which he was not free to ignore."

The District of Columbia Court of Appeals gave further effect to the Housing Regulations in *Brown v. Southall Realty Co.*, 237 A.2d 834 (D.C. 1968). There the landlord knew at the time the lease was signed that housing code violations existed which rendered the apartment "unsafe and unsanitary." Viewing the lease as a contract, the District of Columbia Court of Appeals held that the premises were let in violation of Sections 2304[53] and 2501 of the Regulations and that the lease, therefore, was void as an illegal contract. In the light of *Brown*, it is clear not only that the housing code creates privately enforceable duties as held in *Whetzel*, but that the basic validity of every housing contract depends upon substantial compliance with the housing code at the beginning of the lease term. The *Brown* court relied particularly upon Section 2501 of the Regulations which provides:

> Every premises accommodating one or more habitations shall be maintained and kept in repair so as to provide decent living accommodations for the occupants. This part of this Code contemplates more than mere basic repairs and maintenance to keep out the elements; its purpose is to include repairs and maintenance designed to make a premises or neighborhood healthy and safe.

By its terms, this section applies to maintenance and repair during the lease term. Under the *Brown* holding, serious failure to comply with this section before the lease term begins renders the contract void. We think it untenable to find that this section has no effect on the contract after it has been signed. To the contrary, by signing the lease the landlord has undertaken a continuing obligation to the tenant, to maintain the premises in accordance with all applicable law.

This principle of implied warranty is well established. Courts often imply relevant law into contracts to provide a remedy for any damage caused by one party's illegal conduct. In a case closely analogous to the present ones, the Illinois Supreme Court held that a builder who constructed a house in violation of the Chicago building code had breached his contract with the buyer:

> [T]he law existing at the time and place of the making of the contract is deemed a part of the contract, as though expressly referred to or incorporated in it.... The

53. "No person shall rent or offer to rent any habitation, or the furnishings thereof, unless such habitation and its furnishings are in a clean, safe and sanitary condition, in repair, and free from rodents or vermin."

> rationale for this rule is that the parties to the contract would have expressed that which the law implies "had they not supposed that it was unnecessary to speak of it because the law provided for it...." Consequently, the courts, in construing the existing law as part of the express contract, are not reading into the contract provisions different from those expressed and intended by the parties, as defendants contend, but are merely construing the contract in accordance with the intent of the parties.

We follow the Illinois court in holding that the housing code must be read into housing contracts—a holding also required by the purposes and the structure of the code itself.[57] The duties imposed by the Housing Regulations may not be waived or shifted by agreement if the Regulations specifically place the duty upon the lessor. Criminal penalties are provided if these duties are ignored. This regulatory structure was established by the Commissioners because in their judgment, the grave conditions in the housing market required serious action. Yet official enforcement of the housing code has been far from uniformly effective. Innumerable studies have documented the desperate condition of rental housing in the District of Columbia and in the nation. In view of these circumstances, we think the conclusion reached by the Supreme Court of Wisconsin as to the effect of a housing code on the old common law rule cannot be avoided:

> [T]he legislature has made a policy judgment—that it is socially (and politically) desirable to impose these duties on a property owner—which has rendered the old common law rule obsolete. To follow the old rule of no implied warranty of habitability in leases would, in our opinion, be inconsistent with the current legislative policy concerning housing standards....

We therefore hold that the Housing Regulations imply a warranty of habitability, measured by the standards which they set out, into leases of all housing that they cover.

V

In the present cases, the landlord sued for possession for nonpayment of rent. Under contract principles,[61] however, the tenant's obligation to pay rent is dependent upon the landlord's performance of his obligations, including his warranty to maintain the premises in habitable condition. In order to determine whether any rent is owed to the landlord, the tenants must be given an opportunity to prove the housing code violations alleged as breach of the landlord's warranty.[62]

At trial, the finder of fact must make two findings: (1) whether the alleged violations[63] existed during the period for which past due rent is claimed, and (2) what portion, if any

57. "The housing and sanitary codes, especially in light of Congress' explicit direction for their enactment, indicate a strong and pervasive congressional concern to secure for the city's slum dwellers decent, or at least safe and sanitary, places to live." *Edwards v. Habib*, [397 F.2d 687, 700 (D.C. Cir. 1968)—Eds.]

61. In extending all contract remedies for breach to the parties to a lease, we include an action for specific performance of the landlord's implied warranty of habitability.

62. To be relevant, of course, the violations must affect the tenant's apartment or common areas which the tenant uses. Moreover, the contract principle that no one may benefit from his own wrong will allow the landlord to defend by providing the damage was caused by the tenant's wrongful action. However, violations resulting from inadequate repairs or materials which disintegrate under normal use would not be assignable to the tenant. Also we agree with the District of Columbia Court of Appeals that the tenant's private rights do not depend on official inspection or official finding of violation by the city government....

63. The jury should be instructed that one or two minor violations standing alone which do not affect habitability are de minimis and would not entitle the tenant to a reduction in rent.

or all, of the tenant's obligation to pay rent was suspended by the landlord's breach. If no part of the tenant's rental obligation is found to have been suspended, then a judgment for possession may issue forthwith. On the other hand, if the jury determines that the entire rental obligation has been extinguished by the landlord's total breach, then the action for possession on the ground of nonpayment must fail.[64]

The jury may find that part of the tenant's rental obligation has been suspended but that part of the unpaid back rent is indeed owed to the landlord. In these circumstances, no judgment for possession should issue if the tenant agrees to pay the partial rent found to be due. If the tenant refuses to pay the partial amount, a judgment for possession may then be entered.

The judgment of the District of Columbia Court of Appeals is reversed and the cases are remanded for further proceedings consistent with this opinion.

Notes and Questions

1. As Judge Wright suggested, the D.C. Circuit Court of Appeals did not write on a clean slate. One of the cases cited, *Lemle v. Breeden*, 462 P.2d 470 (Haw. 1969), expressly applied an "implied warranty of habitability" to affirm a judgment in favor of a lessee who had sued to recover his deposit and rent payment for premises which turned out to be overrun by rats. Where the defect in the premises existed at the time the lease was executed, and constituted a violation of the local housing code, a District of Columbia court had earlier used a theory of unlawful contract to deny a landlord possession and rent arrearage. *Brown v. Southall Realty Co.*, 237 A.2d 834 (D.C. 1968). More recently, a District of Columbia court held the void lease theory applies both to housing code violations that exist at the inception of the tenancy and to violations arising at a later point, voiding the contract during the course of the tenancy. *In re Stancil*, 2005 WL 3036647, 25 (Bankr. D.D.C. 2005). To establish a void lease claim, the tenant must show that 1) housing code violations exist at the premises; 2) the code violations make the premises unsafe or unsanitary; 3) the landlord knew or reasonably should have known of the conditions; 4) the tenant did not cause the conditions; and 5) the landlord failed to correct the violations in a timely manner. *Id.*

2. Though preceded by the cases discussed above, and decisions such as *Pines v. Persion*, 111 N.W.2d 409 (Wis. 1961), the visibility of the District of Columbia Circuit Court of Appeals, as well as the persuasiveness of *Javins* led to widespread adoption of the warranty of habitability. If not a revolution, the warranty of habitability by this time had at least reached the status of a movement. *See, e.g.*, *Green v. Superior Court*, 517 P.2d 1168 (Cal. 1974); *Jack Spring, Inc. v. Little*, 280 N.E.2d 208 (Ill. 1972); *Mease v. Fox*, 200 N.W.2d 791 (Iowa 1972); *Boston Hous. Auth. v. Hemingway*, 293 N.E.2d 831 (Mass. 1973). Eventually, the overwhelming majority of states, as well as The American Law Institute, adopted the rule of *Javins*. Only Alabama, Arkansas, Colorado, and Wyoming have yet to adopt the warranty by statute or court decision. Most jurisdictions adopted the rule by judicial fiat. *See* Jonathan M. Purver, Annotation, *Modern Status of Warranty of Habitability or Fitness*, 40 A.L.R.3d 646 (1971 & Supp. 1987). For a collection of some of the decisions recognizing the implied warranty of habitability. An authoritative article by a professor who participated in the *Green* litigation is Myron Moscovitz, *The Implied Warranty of Habit-*

---

64. As soon as the landlord made the necessary repairs rent would again become due. Our holding, of course, affects only eviction for nonpayment of rent. The landlord is free to seek eviction at the termination of the lease or on any other legal ground.

ability: A New Doctrine Raising New Issues, 62 CAL. L. REV. 1444 (1974). Most jurisdictions have now adopted the rule by statute. *See* Milton R. Friedman & Patrick A. Randolph, Jr., *Existence and Scope of Residential Implied Warranty of Habitability in Each Jurisdiction,* PLIREF-LEASES 10 App. 10A (2008).

3. The timing of the "revolution" in landlord-tenant law is worth considering. Why did the reforms occur in the sixties and seventies rather than in previous decades? At least one commentator has argued that the primary cause of the "revolution ... was the civil rights movement of the sixties." Edward H. Rabin, *The Revolution in Residential Landlord Tenant Law: Causes and Consequences,* 69 CORNELL L. REV. 517, 554 (1984). To support his thesis, Professor Rabin reprinted a letter from Judge Wright in which the judge candidly admitted that his concern for the living conditions of the mostly "poor and black" residents of Washington, D.C., slums "influenced" his decisions. *Id.* at 549. However, Professor Rabin's theory fails to adequately explain the rapid, widespread adoption of the landlord-tenant reforms, including the warranty of habitability. Professor Friedman noted that: "Although it is quite appropriate to point out the contribution of judges like Skelly Wright, liberal activism in the District of Columbia hardly explains why conservative Republican judges in Kansas or elsewhere should follow in his footsteps so slavishly. If the new law is so universally skewed toward tenants, something more fundamental must be afoot." Lawrence M. Friedman, *Comments on Edward H. Rabin, The Revolution in Residential Landlord-Tenant Law: Causes and Consequences,* 69 CORNELL L. REV. 585, 587 (1984). *See also* George M. Armstrong, Jr. & John C. LaMaster, *The Implied Innovation,* 46 LA. L. REV. 195 (1985), for a more balanced discussion of the causes of the "revolution."

4. Many states have adopted statutory versions of the implied warranty. Fifteen states have enacted some form of the Uniform Residential Landlord and Tenant Act (URLTA). *See* Robert D. Mercer-Falkoff, *The URLTA: The Impact of Existing States Laws,* 7 J. LEGIS. 159 (1980). *See also* Friedman & Randolph, Jr., *supra* note 2. At least one court has emphasized, somewhat ominously, that the warranty is purely statutory. *Doll v. Rapp,* 660 N.E.2d 542 (Ohio Mun. Ct. 1995). Yet another court was so strongly influenced by a state URLTA statute that had been passed, but was not yet in effect, that the court essentially made the statute retroactive by reading the implied warranty of habitability into the common law. *Foisy v. Wyman,* 515 P.2d 160 (Wash. 1973). Which warranty would you expect to prove more durable, one adopted by the legislature or one created by the courts?

2. The Implied Warranty Adopted as Sword or Shield

Hilder v. St. Peter

Supreme Court of Vermont
478 A.2d 202 (Vt. 1984)

BILLINGS, Chief Justice

Defendants appeal from a judgment rendered by the Rutland Superior Court. The court ordered defendants to pay plaintiff damages in the amount of $4,945.00, which represented "reimbursement of all rent paid and additional compensatory damages" for the rental of a residential apartment over a fourteen month period in defendants' Rutland apartment building. Defendants filed a motion for reconsideration on the issue of the amount of damages awarded to the plaintiff, and plaintiff filed a cross-motion for reconsideration of the court's denial of an award of punitive damages. The court denied both motions. On appeal, defendants raise three issues for our consideration: first, whether the court correctly calculated the amount of damages awarded the plaintiff; secondly, whether the court's award to plaintiff of the entire amount of rent paid to defendants was proper since the plaintiff remained in possession of the apartment for the entire fourteen month period; and finally, whether the court's finding that defendant Stuart St. Peter acted on his own behalf and with the apparent authority of defendant Patricia St. Peter was error.

The facts are uncontested. In October, 1974, plaintiff began occupying an apartment at defendants' 10-12 Church Street apartment building in Rutland with her three children and new-born grandson.[1] Plaintiff orally agreed to pay defendant Stuart St. Peter $140 a month and a damage deposit of $50; plaintiff paid defendant the first month's rent and the damage deposit prior to moving in. Plaintiff has paid all rent due under her tenancy. Because the previous tenants had left behind garbage and items of personal belongings, defendant offered to refund plaintiff's damage deposit if she would clean the apartment herself prior to taking possession. Plaintiff did clean the apartment, but never received her deposit back because the defendant denied ever receiving it. Upon moving into the apartment, plaintiff discovered a broken kitchen window. Defendant promised to repair it, but after waiting a week and fearing that her two year old child might cut herself on the shards of glass, plaintiff repaired the window at her own expense. Although defendant promised to provide a front door key, he never did. For a period of time, whenever plaintiff left the apartment, a member of her family would remain behind for security reasons. Eventually, plaintiff purchased and installed a padlock, again at her own expense. After moving in, plaintiff discovered that the bathroom toilet was clogged with paper and feces and would flush only by dumping pails of water into it. Although plaintiff repeatedly complained about the toilet, and defendant promised to have it repaired, the toilet remained clogged and mechanically inoperable throughout the period of plaintiff's tenancy. In addition, the bathroom light and wall outlet were inoperable. Again, the defendant agreed to repair the fixtures, but never did. In order to have light in the bathroom, plaintiff attached a fixture to the wall and connected it to an extension cord that was plugged into an adjoining room. Plaintiff also discovered that water leaked from the water pipes of the upstairs apartment down the ceilings and walls of both her kitchen and back bedroom. Again, defendant promised to fix the leakage, but never did. As a result of this leakage, a large section of plaster fell from the back bedroom ceiling onto her bed and her grandson's crib. Other sections of plaster remained dangling from the ceiling. This condition was brought to the attention of the defendant, but he never corrected it. Fearing that the remaining plaster might fall when the room was occupied, plaintiff moved her and her grandson's bedroom furniture into the living room and ceased using the back bedroom. During the summer months an odor of raw sewage permeated plaintiff's apartment. The odor was so strong that the plaintiff was ashamed to have company in her apartment. Responding to plaintiff's complaints, Rutland City workers unearthed a broken sewage pipe in the basement of defendants' building. Raw sewage littered the floor of the basement, but defendant failed to clean it up. Plaintiff also discovered that the electric service for her furnace was attached to her breaker box, although defendant had agreed, at the commencement of plaintiff's tenancy, to furnish heat.

In its conclusions of law, the court held that the state of disrepair of plaintiff's apartment, which was known to the defendants, substantially reduced the value of the leasehold from the agreed rental value, thus constituting a breach of the implied warranty of

1. Between October, 1974, and December, 1976, plaintiff rented apartment number 1 for $140.00 monthly for 18 months, and apartment number 50 for $125.00 monthly for 7 months.

habitability. The court based its award of damages on the breach of this warranty and on breach of an express contract. Defendant argues that the court misapplied the law of Vermont relating to habitability because the plaintiff never abandoned the demised premises and, therefore, it was error to award her the full amount of rent paid. Plaintiff counters that, while never expressly recognized by this Court, the trial court was correct in applying an implied warranty of habitability and that under this warranty, abandonment of the premises is not required. Plaintiff urges this Court to affirmatively adopt the implied warranty of habitability.

[The court's discussion of the historical relations between landlords and tenants based on the laws of property, the ruling of the *Javins* case, the changed nature of the modern urban tenants' needs and expectations discussed in *Javins,* and the developing modern views of courts that had examined the relationship and the changes is omitted.—Eds.]

Therefore, we now hold expressly that in the rental of any residential dwelling unit an implied warranty exists in the lease, whether oral or written, that the landlord will deliver over and maintain, throughout the period of the tenancy, premises that are safe, clean and fit for human habitation. This warranty of habitability is implied in tenancies for a specific period or at will. *Boston Hous. Auth. v. Hemingway,* [293 N.E.2d 831, 843 (Mass. 1973)]. Additionally, the implied warranty of habitability covers all latent and patent defects in the essential facilities of the residential unit.[2] Essential facilities are "facilities vital to the use of the premises for residential purposes ..." *Kline v. Burns,* 276 A.2d 248, 252 (N.H. 1971). This means that a tenant who enters into a lease agreement with knowledge of any defect in the essential facilities cannot be said to have assumed the risk, thereby losing the protection of the warranty. Nor can this implied warranty of habitability be waived by any written provision in the lease or by oral agreement.

In determining whether there has been a breach of the implied warranty of habitability, the courts may first look to any relevant local or municipal housing code; they may also make reference to the minimum housing code standards enunciated in 24 V.S.A. § 5003(c)(1)-5003(c)(5). A substantial violation of an applicable housing code shall constitute prima facie evidence that there has been a breach of the warranty of habitability. "[O]ne or two minor violations standing alone which do not affect" the health or safety of the tenant, shall be considered *de minimis* and not a breach of the warranty. [citing *Javins.*—Eds.] In addition, the landlord will not be liable for defects caused by the tenant. [citing *Javins.*—Eds.]

However, these codes and standards merely provide a starting point in determining whether there has been a breach. Not all towns and municipalities have housing codes; where there are codes, the particular problem complained of may not be addressed.... In determining whether there has been a breach of the implied warranty of habitability, courts should inquire whether the claimed defect has an impact on the safety or health of the tenant....

In order to bring a cause of action for breach of the implied warranty of habitability, the tenant must first show that he or she notified the landlord "of the deficiency or defect not known to the landlord and [allowed] a reasonable time for its correction...."

Because we hold that the lease of a residential dwelling creates a contractual relationship between the landlord and the tenant, the standard contract remedies of rescission,

2. The warranty also covers those facilities located in the common areas of an apartment building or duplex that may affect the health or safety of a tenant, such as common stairways, or porches. [citing *Javins.*—Eds.]

reformation and damages are available to the tenant when suing for breach of the implied warranty of habitability.... The measure of damages shall be the difference between the value of the dwelling as warranted and the value of the dwelling as it exists in its defective condition.... In determining the fair rental value of the dwelling as warranted, the court may look to the agreed upon rent as evidence on this issue...."[I]n residential lease disputes involving a breach of the implied warranty of habitability, public policy militates against requiring expert testimony" concerning the value of the defect.... The tenant will be liable only for "the reasonable rental value [if any] of the property in its imperfect condition during his period of occupancy...."

We also find persuasive the reasoning of some commentators that damages should be allowed for a tenant's discomfort and annoyance arising from the landlord's breach of the implied warranty of habitability. *See* Myron Moskovitz, *The Implied Warranty of Habitability: A New Doctrine Raising New Issues,* 62 Calif. L. Rev. 1444, 1470–73 (1974) (hereinafter cited as *A New Doctrine*); Comment, *The Implied Warranty of Habitability: A Dream Deferred,* 48 UMKC L. Rev. 237, 238, 250–251 (1980) (hereinafter cited as *A Dream Deferred*)]. Damages for annoyance and discomfort are reasonable in light of the fact that

> the residential tenant who has suffered a breach of the warranty cannot bathe as frequently as he would like or at all if there is inadequate hot water; he must worry about rodents harassing his children or spreading disease if the premises are infested; or he must avoid certain rooms or worry about catching a cold if there is inadequate weather protection or heat. Thus, discomfort and annoyance are the common injuries caused by each breach and hence the true nature of the general damages the tenant is claiming.

Moskovitz, *A New Doctrine, supra* at 1470–71.

Damages for discomfort and annoyance may be difficult to compute; however, "[t]he trier [of fact] is not to be deterred from this duty by the fact that the damages are not susceptible of reduction to an exact money standard....

Another remedy available to the tenant when there has been a breach of the implied warranty of habitability is to withhold the payment of future rent....[3] The burden and expense of bringing suit will then be on the landlord who can better afford to bring the action. In an action for ejectment for nonpayment of rent, 12 V.S.A. §4773, "[t]he trier of fact, upon evaluating the seriousness of the breach and the ramification of the defect upon the health and safety of the tenant, will abate the rent at the landlord's expense in accordance with its findings." *A Dream Deferred, supra,* at 248. The tenant must show that: (1) the landlord had notice of the previously unknown defect and failed, within a reasonable time, to repair it; and (2) the defect, affecting habitability, existed during the time for which rent was withheld. *See A Dream Deferred, supra,* at 248–50. Whether a portion, all or none of the rent will be awarded to the landlord will depend on the findings relative to the extent and duration of the breach.[4] *Javins, supra,* 428 F.2d at 1082–83. Of course, once the landlord corrects the defect, the tenant's obligation to pay rent becomes due again. *Id.* at 1083 n. 64.

---

3. Because we hold that the tenant's obligation to pay rent is contingent on the landlord's duty to provide and maintain a habitable dwelling, it is no longer necessary for the tenant to first abandon the premises ...; thus, the doctrine of constructive eviction is no longer a viable or needed defense in an action by the landlord for unpaid rent....

4. Some courts suggest that, during the period rent is withheld, the tenant should pay the rent, as it becomes due, into legal custody.... Such a procedure assures the availability of that portion, if any, of the rent which the court determines is due to the landlord....

Additionally, we hold that when the landlord is notified of the defect but fails to repair it within a reasonable amount of time, and the tenant subsequently repairs the defect, the tenant may deduct the expense of the repair from future rent. 11 Williston on Contracts § 1404 (3d ed. W. Jaeger 1968)....

In addition to general damages, we hold that punitive damages may be available to a tenant in the appropriate case. Although punitive damages are generally not recoverable in actions for breach of contract, there are cases in which the breach is of such a willful and wanton or fraudulent nature as to make appropriate the award of exemplary damages.... A willful and wanton or fraudulent breach may be shown "by conduct manifesting personal ill will, or carried out under circumstances of insult or oppression, or even by conduct manifesting a reckless or wanton disregard of [one's] rights.... When a landlord, after receiving notice of a defect, fails to repair the facility that is essential to the health and safety of his or her tenant, an award of punitive damages is proper....

> The purpose of punitive damages ... is to punish conduct which is morally culpable. Such an award serves to deter a wrongdoer ... from repetitions of the same or similar actions. And it tends to encourage prosecution of a claim by a victim who might not otherwise incur the expense or inconvenience of private action.... The public benefit and display of ethical indignation are among the ends of the policy to grant punitive damages.

In the instant case, the trial court's award of damages, based in part on a breach of the implied warranty of habitability, was not a misapplication of the law relative to habitability. Because of our holding in this case, the doctrine of constructive eviction, wherein the tenant must abandon in order to escape liability for rent, is no longer viable. When, as in the instant case, the tenant seeks, not to escape rent liability, but to receive compensatory damages in the amount of rent already paid, abandonment is similarly unnecessary.... Under our holding, when a landlord breaches the implied warranty of habitability, the tenant may withhold future rent, and may also seek damages in the amount of rent previously paid.

In its conclusions of law the trial court stated that the defendants' failure to make repairs was compensable by damages to the extent of reimbursement of all rent paid and additional compensatory damages. The court awarded plaintiff a total of $4,945.00; $3,445.00 represents the entire amount of rent plaintiff paid, plus the $50.00 deposit. This appears to leave $1500.00 as the "additional compensatory damages." However, although the court made findings which clearly demonstrate the appropriateness of an award of compensatory damages, there is no indication as to how the court reached a figure of $1500.00. It is "crucial that this Court and the parties be able to determine what was decided and how the decision was reached.

Additionally, the court denied an award to plaintiff of punitive damages on the ground that the evidence failed to support a finding of willful and wanton or fraudulent conduct.... The facts in this case, which defendants do not contest, evince a pattern of intentional conduct on the part of defendants for which the term "slumlord" surely was coined. Defendants' conduct was culpable and demeaning to plaintiff and clearly expressive of a wanton disregard of plaintiff's rights. The trial court found that defendants were aware of defects in the essential facilities of plaintiff's apartment, promised plaintiff that repairs would be made, but never fulfilled those promises. The court also found that plaintiff continued, throughout her tenancy, to pay her rent, often in the face of verbal threats made by defendant Stuart St. Peter. These findings point to the "bad spirit and wrong intention" of the defendants ... and would support a finding of willful and wanton or fraudulent conduct, contrary to the conclusions of law and judgment of the trial judge. However, the plaintiff did not appeal the courts' denial of punitive damages, and issues not appealed and briefed are waived....

We find that defendants' third claimed error, that the court erred in finding that both defendant Stuart St. Peter and defendant Patricia St. Peter were liable to plaintiff for the breach of the implied warranty of habitability, is meritless. Both defendants were named in the complaint as owners of the 10-12 Church Street apartment building. Plaintiff's complaint also alleged that defendant Stuart St. Peter acted as agent for defendant Patricia St. Peter. Defendants failed to deny these allegations; under V.R.C.P. 8(d) these averments stand as admitted.

Affirmed in part; reversed in part and remanded for hearing on additional compensable damages, consistent with the views herein.

Set forth below are selected provisions from a uniform act developed for adoption by states.

Uniform Residential Landlord and Tenant Act

§ 2.104. [Landlord to Maintain Premises]

(a) A landlord shall

(1) comply with the requirements of applicable building and housing codes materially affecting health and safety;

(2) make all repairs and do whatever is necessary to put and keep the premises in a fit and habitable condition;

(3) keep all common areas of the premises in a clean and safe condition;

(4) maintain in good and safe working order and condition all electrical, plumbing, sanitary, heating, ventilation, air-conditioning, and other facilities and appliances, including elevators, supplied or required to be supplied by him;

(5) provide and maintain appropriate receptacles and conveniences for the removal of ashes, garbage, rubbish, and other waste incidental to the occupancy of the dwelling unit and arrange for their removal; and

(6) supply running water and reasonable amounts of hot water at all times and reasonable heat [between [October 1] and [May 1]] except where the building that includes the dwelling unit is not required by law to be equipped for that purpose, or the dwelling unit is so constructed that heat or hot water is generated by an installation within the exclusive control of the tenant and supplied by a direct public utility connection.

If the duty imposed by paragraph (1) of subsection (a) is greater than any duty imposed by any other paragraph of that subsection, the landlord's duty shall be determined by reference to paragraph (1) of subsection (a)....

(d) The landlord and tenant of any dwelling unit other than a single family residence may agree that the tenant is to perform specified repairs, maintenance tasks, alterations, or remodeling only if

(1) the agreement of the parties is entered into in good faith and not for the purpose of evading the obligations of the landlord and is set forth in a separate writing signed by the parties and supported by adequate consideration;

(2) the work is not necessary to cure noncompliance with subsection (a)(1) of this section; and

(3) the agreement does not diminish or affect the obligation of the landlord to other tenants in the premises.

The landlord may not treat performance of the separate agreement described in subsection (d) as a condition to any obligation or performance of any rental agreement....

§ 3.101. [Tenant to Maintain Dwelling Unit]

A tenant shall

(1) comply with all obligations primarily imposed upon tenants by applicable provisions of building and housing codes materially affecting health and safety;

(2) keep that part of the premises that he occupies and uses as clean and safe as the condition of the premises permit;

(3) dispose from his dwelling unit all ashes, garbage, rubbish, and other waste in a clean and safe manner;

(4) keep all plumbing fixtures in the dwelling unit or used by the tenant as clear as their condition permits;

(5) use in a reasonable manner all electrical, plumbing, sanitary, heating, ventilating, air-conditioning, and other facilities and appliances including elevators in the premises;

(6) not deliberately or negligently destroy, deface, damage, impair, or remove any part of the premises or knowingly permit any person to do so; and

(7) conduct himself and require other persons on the premises with his consent to conduct themselves in a manner that will not disturb his neighbors' peaceful enjoyment of the premises.

Notes and Questions

1. Is URLTA § 2.104 (d), the provision allowing a tenant to partially waive the landlord's duty to repair, consistent with the reasoning of *Javins*? The URLTA specifically empowers courts to limit or refuse enforcement of unconscionable agreements. URLTA § 1.303. However, the comment to § 1.303 states that both landlords and tenants can take advantage of § 1.303. What does this comment suggest about the URLTA drafters' view of the relative bargaining power of landlords and tenants? Is it realistic to expect a residential tenant to be able to negotiate what is usually a contract of adhesion?

2. In contrast to the URLTA, the D.C. Court of Appeals invalidated exculpatory clauses which purported to waive the warranty of habitability in residential leases on a variety of grounds, including public policy. *George Washington Univ. v. Weintraub*, 458 A.2d 43 D.C. 1983). Most courts prohibit waiver. *Feldman v. Jasinski*, 2009 WL 3430287 (Mass. Ct. App. Oct. 20, 2009). For an even more aggressive approach, see *Leardi v. Brown*, 474 N.E.2d 1094 (Mass. 1985) (holding that the state's consumer protection act is violated by a lease provision reading, "[t]here is no implied warranty the premises are fit for human occupation (habitability) except so far as governmental regulation, legislation, or judicial enactment otherwise requires.")

3. Immediately following *Javins*, some commentators predicted that the adoption of the warranty of habitability would have dire economic consequences on the rental hous-

ing market and, eventually, on low-income tenants. *See e.g.*, Charles J. Meyers, *The Covenant of Habitability and the American Law Institute*, 27 STAN. L. REV. 879 (1975).

While Professor Meyers was bemoaning the marketplace implications of the new law, the Stanford Law Review undertook a study of court dockets to measure the effect of the doctrine. The inconclusive results are related in Ben H. Logan, III & John J. Sabl, Note, *The Great Green Hope: The Implied Warranty of Habitability in Practice*, 28 STAN. L. REV. 729 (1976). Urban planning professor and former poverty lawyer Alan Heskin subsequently studied the impact of the leading California case in the Los Angeles area and determined that no revolution in the relationship between landlords and tenants was apparent after the decision. Indeed, the judicial and economic systems seemed to digest the new rule without untoward effect—one way or the other. *See* Alan Heskin, *The Warranty of Habitability Debate: A California Case Study*, 66 CAL. L. REV. 37 (1978).

Though the rule's economic impact has concerned some courts (without deterring its adoption) elsewhere, there has been reluctance to impose a doctrine thought best left to the give-and-take of the legislative process. *See e.g., Ortega v. Flaim*, 902 P.2d 199 (Wyo. 1995). At least one legislature tailored the doctrine so that it did not apply to owners of less than seven units. *See* NEV. REV. STAT. § 118A.290. However, most judges have not hesitated to develop the common law, even in jurisdictions where the legislature has ventured to tinker with the relationship between owners and occupiers of rental property. *Compare* Joseph Grodin, *Justice Tobriner: Portrait of the Judge As An Artist*, 29 HASTINGS L.J. 7, 12–13 (1977) *with* Meyers, *supra*, at 897–901 *and* Irwin J. Nebron & Allan Ides, *Landlord Tenant Court in Los Angeles: Restructuring the Justice System*, 11 LOY. L.A. L. REV. 537 (1978).

Even critics of the recent "revolution" in landlord-tenant law must concede that succeeding decades have not borne out the earlier predictions of doom and gloom. *See e.g.*, Edward H. Rabin, *The Revolution in Residential Landlord-Tenant Law: Causes and Consequences*, 69 CORNELL L. REV. 517, 577 (1984). Professor Rabin indicated that:

> The legal developments of the seventies reduced the growth in supply of rental housing less than the inflation of that period reduced the growth in demand; supply grew faster than demand despite legal developments that discouraged some construction. Reduced demand, not changes in legal doctrine, caused reduced profits.

4. Two major problems that have absorbed the energies of the courts have been resolving what constitutes habitability and determining the complex question of remedies for breach of the warranty. The former has been usually resolved by holding landlords to standards imposed by health and safety codes. *See Scott v. Garfield*, 912 N.E.2d 1000 (Mass. 2009); Stoiber *v. Honeychuck*, 162 Cal. Rptr. 194 (Ct. App. 1980). Moskovitz, as discussed in *Hilder*, the principal case, *supra*, has suggested that the "housing codes should be viewed as a floor and not a ceiling. Threats to a tenant's health and safety, not simply or solely violations of the codes, should determine whether certain facilities are includable."

Far more difficult is the issue of what relief should be given for breach of the warranty. Two tests have emerged to establish a figure. The difference in value rule measures the damages "by the difference between the agreed upon rend and the fair rental value of the premises as they were during the tenant's occupancy in the unsafe, unsanitary or unfit condition." *Adams v. Woodlands of Nashua*, 864 A.2d 322 (N.H. 2005). The alternative test, percentage reduction of use, endorsed by *Green v. Superior Court*, 517 P.2d 1168, 1183 n.24 (Cal. 1974); *Linton v. Murray*, 2009 WL 4922481 (Cal. Ct. App. 1st Dist. Dec. 21, 2009) (unpublished and uncitable), reduces the tenant's rental obligation by a percentage corresponding to the relative reduction of use of the premises caused by the breach.

Moskovitz, critical of both tests as more suited to commercial rather than residential tenants, proposed yet a third test—"discomfort and annoyance." "Using the discomfort and annoyance approach, a court could assess damages at an amount equaling—or even exceeding—the contract rent." Moskovitz, *supra* at 1472. Since his article was written, however, the supreme court of Pennsylvania applied a percentage reduction of use formula to determine how much enjoyment of the premises had been diminished. *Pugh v. Holmes*, 405 A.2d 897 (Pa. 1979). The following excerpt from *Teller v. McCoy*, 253 S.E.2d 114 (W.Va. 1978) suggests that no one test is likely to be dispositive:

> We feel that neither [the difference in value or percentage reduction of use] approach should be the exclusive mode of assessing damages in such case. Of the two, the "difference in value approach" is far more widely accepted and we adopt it, in part, as the measure of damages in cases involving the breach of the implied warranty of habitability. But, money damages so assessed, while appropriate in the commercial cases, are inadequate in most residential landlord-tenant... cases, since the residential tenant who endures breach of the warranty of habitability morally does not actually lose only money. The typical residential tenant rents a dwelling for shelter, not profit. When the warranty is breached, he loses, instead, such intangibles as the ability to take a bath or use hot water as frequently as he would like, he may be forced to worry about the health of his children endangered by rats, roaches, or other undesirable pests, or he may be denied the use of certain rooms in the apartment because there is odor, severe water leakage, or no heat. "When [the measure of damages] is difficult to apply because the property in question is not used commercially, it may be necessary to formulate a measure of damages that is more uniquely adapted to the plaintiff's injury." [*Jarrett v. E.L. Harper & Son, Inc.*, 235 S.E.2d 362, 365 (W. Va. 1978).—Eds.]
>
> We recently addressed this precise issue in *Jarrett v. E.L. Harper & Son, Inc., supra*, where the plaintiff's water well was destroyed by the defendant, a contractor building a sewer for a public service district. The plaintiffs, without water for five weeks while a new well was being completed, sued for "annoyance, inconvenience, and 'general unpleasantness.'" We held in that case at syllabus point 3 that, "Annoyance and inconvenience can be considered as elements of proof in measuring damages for loss of use of real property."
>
> We feel that the true nature of the damages suffered by a tenant faced with a breach by the landlord of the warranty are not adequately measured by the exclusive use of the "difference in value" standard. Furthermore, the need for expert testimony under this approach could serve to deny the intended relief from a large number of low and middle income tenants who could not afford to litigate....
>
> Therefore, in response to the fourth certified question, we hold that when the warranty of habitability is breached, the tenant's damages are measured by the difference between the fair market value of the premises if they had been as warranted and the fair rental value of the premises as they were during the occupancy by the tenant in the unsafe and unsanitary condition. However, the tenant may additionally recover damages for annoyance and inconvenience proven to have resulted from the breach. *See also Vanlandingham v. Ivanow,* 615 N.E.2d

1361 (Ill. Ct. App. 1993); *Wade v. Jobe*, 818 P.2d 1006 (Utah 1991); Debra T. Landis, Annotation, *Damages Measure for Breach of the Warranty of Habitability*, 1 A.L.R.4th 1182 (1980).

What test was used by the court in the *Hilder* case, *supra*? How would the result differ with other measures of damages? Keep this issue in mind as you review the upcoming cases discussing contract and tort approaches to recovery.

5. If courts have been concerned about the measure of the tenant's damages, they have also sought to protect the landlord from the tenant's assertion of unfounded claims in an attempt to evade the rental obligation. Accordingly, from *Javins* on, courts have often required tenants to make future rent payments to the court clerk as they became due. *See Bell v. Tsintolas Realty Co.*, 430 F.2d 474, 479 (D.C. Cir. 1970) (protective orders are not favored and should be permitted "only in limited circumstances, only on motion of the landlord, and only after notice and opportunity for a hearing on such a motion."). *But see Bell v. Tsintolas Realty Co.*, 456 A.2d 820 (D.C. 1983) (protective orders are now the rule rather than the exception, and tenants who fail to make payments can be evicted before trial.)

3. The Warranty of Habitability as a Sword: Contract and Tort Theories

While many courts following *Javins* used the warranty of habitability to shield the tenants from the threat of eviction, the doctrine has served other tenants as a sword. Consider the following types of actions that a tenant can use to coerce a landlord into repairing rental property.

a. Tenant's Action for Debt

Berzito v. Gambino

Supreme Court of New Jersey
308 A.2d 17 (1973)

MOUNTAIN, J.

This case arises as the result of a dispute between a landlord and a tenant. It presents issues not previously passed upon by this Court.

The relief sought by the plaintiff-tenant was substantially granted by the Union County District Court, 274 A.2d 865 (1971), but that decision was reversed by the Appellate Division, 291 A.2d 577 (1972). We granted certification, 299 A.2d 67 (1972).

The opinions in the courts below reveal the factual situation, which we will briefly summarize here. In September 1968 the plaintiff rented from the defendant the second-floor, four-room furnished apartment at 608 Montgomery Street in Elizabeth for occupancy for herself and three minor children. There was no written lease; the rental for the apartment was fixed at $35 a week, with all utilities supplied. Plaintiff testified that at the time the terms of the arrangement were agreed upon the apartment was in a deplorable condition but the defendant promised he would make the premises "livable" and agreed to make certain specific repairs. The trial court found that these representations were in fact made, 274 A.2d 865, and the Appellate Division accepted this finding, 291 A.2d 577, as do we.

Testimony was submitted to the trial court that, at the time of the letting, screens and storm windows were either broken or missing, a number of windows were boarded up where the panes had been broken, several radiators were not to be found, there were holes in the floors and wall, plaster was falling, several electric fixtures were inoperable, there was a sewage backup in the cellar and the premises were infested with roaches and rodents. Much of the furniture was found unfit for use and was relegated to the basement. Plaintiff herself replaced the furniture as became necessary. During winter months there was sometimes no heat and at all times insufficient heat.

In addition to concluding that these conditions did in fact exist, the trial court further determined that the efforts of the landlord to correct these inadequacies were feeble and dilatory, and made only when prodded by the court and municipal authorities. 274 A.2d 865.

In June 1970 the landlord brought a summary dispossess action against the tenant alleging non-payment of rent. The court found that there had been a breach of the landlord's express warranty of habitability and reduced the rent to $75 a month retroactive to February 23, 1970, the date from which the tenant had paid no rent. This reduced sum was apparently forthcoming from the tenant at that time, but nothing was paid thereafter and on November 14, 1970 the tenant quit the premises.

In the present action the plaintiff seeks to recover the difference between the rent actually paid and an amount calculated at the rate of $75 a month for the period from the commencement of the tenant until February 23, 1970, pointing out that the landlord's default had continued throughout the entire term. The landlord counterclaimed for the rent remitted by the court. The trial judge determined that the landlord should fairly have been given one month from the date of the inception of the letting within which to undertake and complete the promised repairs. He rejected the defendant's contention that plaintiff has waived the failure to repair by continuing in possession and making full payment of the rent, pointing to the scarcity in the Elizabeth area of available housing for low-income families with children. The plaintiff had given the testimony to the same effect. He further concluded that since the repairs had never been adequately made, plaintiff was in fact entitled to the relief sought. Calculating the fair rental value at $75 per month, the landlord would have received a total of $1,200 for the period from November 1968 through February 1970. Since he had in fact received $2,380 during this period, it was determined that he should now return $1,180 and judgment for this amount was entered in the plaintiff's favor. 274 A.2d 865. The judgment was subsequently reduced to $973.75 to reflect a credit in defendant's favor of $206.25 as rent for the period from August 27, the time of judgment, to November 14, 1970. 291 A.2d 577.

The Appellate Division found that some of the defects might properly be classified as "amenities," that the tenant could have quit the premises had she wished but that she made no real effort to find other accommodations. It concluded that the diminution in rent which had been granted the tenant in the dispossess proceedings had achieved substantial justice between the parties and accordingly reversed the trial court judgment in plaintiff's favor.

In the case now before us the tenant did not vacate the premises claiming constructive eviction, nor did she undertake the needed repairs herself and then seek to offset the expense so incurred against her obligation to pay rent. Thus she did not seek either of the particular remedies afforded in [*Reste Realty Corp. v. Cooper*, 251 A.2d 268 (N.J. 1969), or *Marini v. Ireland*, 265 A.2d 526 (N.J. 1970)—Eds.]. The latter case held, however, as we have just noted, that in any residential lease, be it oral or written, there will be implied a covenant or warranty of habitability for the duration of the term. In this case the warranty happens to have been express, but for present purposes this makes no difference. A lessor becomes liable to a lessee for any breach of this covenant. Such a breach having occurred here, the question we are thus called upon to consider is what remedies are then available to a lessee. Are there remedies other than those granted in *Reste* and *Marini*? Were this an ordinary breach of contract, the most obvious remedy would be to award the tenant damages in an amount equal to the difference between the rent actually paid in accordance with the lease agreement and what would have been the fair rental value of the premises in their defective condition. The objection is made that, should we adopt this rule, it would drastically change the law, since traditionally most covenants in a lease—as opposed to those in an ordinary contract—are treated as being independent of one another so that while a tenant may have an action for damages against his landlord for the breach of the latter's express or implied covenant to repair, this right of the tenant in no way lessens his own obligation to make full and punctual payment of rent to the landlord.

This doctrine of independent covenants in leasehold arrangements is probably the most important single consequence of the traditional insistence of the law that because a lease may be said to convey an interest in property, most incidents of the landlord-tenant relationship are to be derived from principles drawn from the law of real property rather than from those to be found in the law of contracts. It has been persuasively argued that while the doctrine of independent covenants, and the strict application of the rule of caveat emptor historically so typical of leasing arrangements, may have resulted in fulfilling the reasonable needs and expectations of landlords and tenants in the agrarian society of medieval England, this is no longer true in modern urban and suburban society.

Today the tenant needs and expects more than the mere land itself. He generally needs and expects adequate shelter, heat, light, water, sanitation and maintenance. It is obviously unsatisfactory to tell him that he may sue his landlord for any failure to supply these necessities, but that at the same time he must make recurring rental payments as they fall due. *Marini* allowed the tenant, in effect, to apply rent monies to the making of necessary repairs. This was a clear departure from the traditional rule of independent covenants. But the opinion did go on to say that [t]he tenant has only the alternative remedies of making the repairs or removing from the premises upon such a constructive eviction.

The defendant here insists that this constituted a holding that no other remedy is available to a tenant, where the landlord is at fault, other than the two that are mentioned. This restrictive reading of *Marini* has been accepted elsewhere as well. *See* Restatement of the Law of Property, Second (Tent. draft No. 1, March 23, 1973) Section 5.4, page 213. Admittedly the sentence, read literally and apart from context, seems to support this position. But of course a casual dictum will not shackle the Court to prevent a later exercise of its creative powers in fashioning new remedies as need and occasion demand.

We now hold that the covenant on the part of a tenant to pay rent, and the covenant—whether express or implied—on the part of a landlord to maintain the demised premises in a habitable condition are for all purposes mutually dependent. Accordingly in an action by a landlord for unpaid rent a tenant may plead, by way of defense and set off, a breach by the landlord of his continuing obligation to maintain an adequate standard of habitability.

That such a breach may be availed of by way of defense in a summary dispossess proceeding has already been settled. *Marini v. Ireland, supra.*

Furthermore a tenant may initiate an action against his landlord to recover either part or all of a deposit paid upon the execution and delivery of the lease or part or all of the rent thereafter paid during the term, where he alleges that the lessor has broken his covenant to maintain the premises in a habitable condition. In such an action, if the alleged breach on the part of the landlord is proven, the tenant will be charged only with the reasonable rental value of the property in its imperfect condition during his period of occupancy. As a prerequisite to maintaining such a suit, the tenant must give the landlord positive and seasonable notice of the alleged defect, must request its correction and must allow the landlord a reasonable period of time to effect the repair or replacement. Not every defect or inconvenience will be deemed to constitute a breach of the covenant of habitability. The condition complained of must be such as truly to render the premises uninhabitable in the eyes of a reasonable person.

For the reasons set forth above the judgment of the Appellate Division is reversed and the judgment of the trial court, as amended, in the amount of $973.75 in favor of the plaintiff is herewith reinstated.

Notes and Questions

1. *Quevedo v. Braga*, 140 Cal. Rptr. 143 (Ct. App. 1977), held that a tenant could sue a landlord in contract for the breach of the implied warranty of habitability. The court, like that in *Berzito*, decided that a plaintiff could sue for retroactive rent abatement to compensate for overpayment of rent during the period the housing was uninhabitable. The *Quevedo* court further held that the action for a breach of the implied warranty sounded in contract and thus denied any compensation for the annoyance and discomfort allegedly caused by the defects in housing.

Should a tenant be compensated for the annoyance and discomfort caused by defects in his/her unit which render the unit uninhabitable? Does it matter whether the tenant knew of the defects before he/she moved in? The next case discusses some of these issues in detail.

b. Tenant's Action in Tort

Scott v. Garfield

Supreme Judicial Court of Massachusetts
912 N.E.2d 1000 (2009)

IRELAND, J.

We transferred this case from the Appeals Court to consider whether a lawful visitor may recover damages for personal injuries caused by a breach of the implied warranty of habitability. Charles M. Scott (Scott) suffered injuries while visiting an apartment leased by his friend from the defendants, Stuart and Ellen Garfield, when a railing on a second-floor porch gave way and he fell to the ground. Judgment entered for Scott on his claim of breach of the implied warranty of habitability, and the defendants appealed. Because we conclude that a lawful visitor may recover damages for personal injuries caused by a breach of the implied warranty of habitability, that the judge neither erred in finding that the loss of evidence by the defendants constituted spoliation nor abused his discretion in imposing sanctions therefore, and that the judge did not abuse his discretion in excluding from evidence the amounts of money paid by Scott's health insurer toward his medical bills, we affirm the judgment.

1. *Background.* We present the essential background and facts, reserving some details for our discussion of the issues raised.

In 1992, the defendants bought a three-story house in Lynn. The defendants resided on the first floor. In 1993, they let the second-floor apartment, which included a porch,[1] to the plaintiffs' friend, Sherry Baker.[2] Before the defendants leased the second-floor apartment to Baker, the department of public health of Lynn inspected it and issued a certificate of occupancy. The defendant Stuart Garfield was present on the second-floor porch on several occasions after 1993. He was a social guest of Baker at times, and he also had access to the porch annually in order to clean the gutters. In 1996, after being informed that a section of railing on one side of the porch was loose, Garfield repaired it. He made no repairs to the section of railing at the other side of the porch. In 2000, Garfield told Baker that he planned to repair the porches on the house, including the second-floor front porch. No repairs were made, however, before the date when Scott was injured. In 2002, Baker gave notice that she intended to terminate her lease and move out....

The plaintiffs commenced an action in the Superior Court, asserting claims for negligence and breach of the implied warranty of habitability, as well as a separate claim by Pamela Scott for loss of consortium. The defendants raised as a defense that, due to his alcohol consumption, Scott had been comparatively negligent. The case was tried to a jury.

The jury returned special verdicts in favor of Scott, on his claims of negligence and breach of the implied warranty of habitability, in favor of Pamela Scott, on her claim for loss of

consortium, and in favor of the Garfields on their comparative negligence defense, finding that Scott had been twenty per cent comparatively negligent. Mass. R. Civ. P. 49(a), 365 Mass. 812 (1974). Because judgment entered for Scott on his claim of breach of the implied warranty of habitability (rather than his claim for negligence), he recovered $450,000, the full amount of damages found by the jury with no reduction for the jury's finding of comparative negligence....

2. *Discussion.* a. *Implied warranty of habitability.* The defendants moved for a directed verdict, Mass. R. Civ. P. 50(a), 365 Mass. 814 (1974), and for judgment notwithstanding the verdict, or in the alternative for a new trial, Mass. R. Civ. P. 50(b), as amended, 428 Mass. 1402 (1998), on the breach of implied warranty of habitability claim, on the ground that Scott was a guest rather than a tenant and therefore could not recover under the implied warranty of habitability. The judge denied the motions.[3] The defendants contend that the judge erred in denying their motions because our case law has not recognized the right of a guest of a tenant to recover under the warranty. For the reasons that we now set forth, we conclude that a lawful visitor may recover for personal injuries caused by a breach of the implied warranty of habitability.

The implied warranty of habitability, as it has developed in our decisions, is a multifaceted legal concept that encompasses contract and tort principles, as well as the State building and sanitary codes. Although the warranty itself arises from the residential leasing contract between landlord and tenant, we have imposed a legal duty on the landlord,

---

1. The porch was located at the front of the house, directly above the first-floor porch, and was covered by a roof, which was held up by three columns. There were two sections of wooden railing, consisting of a top rail and a bottom rail, between which stood balusters. The sections of railing were attached to the columns at the far ends of the porch, and to either side of the column at the center of the porch.

2. Baker initially had a cotenant, who moved out in 1998.

3. The judge also denied a motion by the plaintiffs to set aside the jury's finding of comparative negligence.

in the form of an implied agreement, to ensure that the dwelling complies with the State building and sanitary codes throughout the term of the lease. (citing cases) ... "This warranty [insofar as it is based on the State Sanitary Code and local health regulations] cannot be waived by any provision in the lease or rental agreement"). To the extent that a residential lease is a contract between landlord and tenant, there is no question that only a tenant (and not a guest) can recover for economic loss caused by a breach of the implied warranty of habitability. See, e.g., *Cruz Mgt. Co. v. Thomas,* 417 Mass. 782, 787, 633 N.E.2d 390 (1994)....

Our conclusion that lawful visitors, like tenants, may recover for personal injuries caused by breach of the implied warranty of habitability rests, in part, on the expectation that a tenant might invite a guest into his home, and the concomitant expectation that the tenant's home must be safe for a guest to visit—which together go to the very heart of the landlord's contractual obligation to deliver and maintain habitable premises that comply with the building and sanitary codes. Our conclusion is consistent with the State sanitary code itself, which provides that the purposes of the minimum standards of fitness for human habitation are to "protect the health, safety and well-being of *the occupants of housing and of the general public*" (emphasis added). 105 Code Mass. Regs. § 410.001 (1997). A lawful visitor of an "occupant of housing" plainly comes within the scope of persons intended to be protected and therefore also within the ambit of the implied warranty of habitability while on the rented premises.

Moreover, we have long since eliminated much of the legal significance attached to the question of status in our tort law. See *Mounsey v. Ellard,* 297 N.E.2d 43 (Mass. 1973) (doing away with distinctions between categories of licensee and invitee and holding that landowner owes duty of reasonable care to all lawful visitors). A tenant's guest may recover damages from a landlord for personal injuries caused by negligent maintenance of the premises rented to the tenant. See *Young v. Garwacki,* 402 N.E.2d 1045 (Mass. 1980). Logic, therefore, compels our conclusion that a lawful visitor may also recover for personal injuries caused by a breach of the warranty of habitability. To decide otherwise would create or maintain a type of distinction based on status that we long ago rejected. It would not stand to reason that where a tenant and a lawful visitor both suffered injuries on the tenant's rented premises, caused by the same significant defect in violation of the sanitary code, the tenant might recover on a breach of warranty claim, while the tenant's guest could recover only in negligence, thus subjecting only the guest to a comparative negligence defense. See *Correia v. Firestone Tire & Rubber Co., supra* (comparative negligence statute, G.L. c. 231, § 85, not applicable to breach of warranty claim).[4]

Our holding also accords with the Restatement (Second) of Property (Landlord and Tenant) § 17.6 (1977), insofar as it provides:

> A landlord is subject to liability for physical harm caused to the tenant and others upon the leased property with the consent of the tenant or his subtenant by a dangerous condition existing before or arising after the tenant has taken possession ... and the existence of the condition is in violation of: (1) an implied warranty of habitability; or (2) a duty created by statute or administrative regulation.

4. We recognize that the inapplicability of comparative negligence as a defense to a breach of warranty of habitability claim may not relieve a tenant or a lawful visitor of his or her legal responsibility to act reasonably toward a defect on the premises. Cf. *Correia v. Firestone Tire & Rubber Co.,* 446 N.E.2d 1033 (Mass. 1983) (consumer's own negligence does not prevent recovery except where consumer unreasonably uses product that he knows to be defective and dangerous).

Turning to the issues in this case, there was no error in the denial of the defendants' motions for a directed verdict and for judgment notwithstanding the verdict. Based on the evidence, the jury reasonably could have found that the condition of the porch railing did not comply with the minimum standards required by the building and sanitary codes, in breach of the implied warranty of habitability, and that Scott suffered injuries as a result when the defective railing gave way....

The defendants further contend that the judge erred in failing to instruct the jury that they must find, as a threshold matter, that the porch was vital to the use of the demised premises in order to conclude that there was a breach of the implied warranty of habitability. This argument is unavailing where our decision in *Crowell v. McCaffrey*, 386 N.E.2d 1256 (Mass. 1979), stated that the implied agreement by a landlord to ensure that a rented unit complies with minimum standards prescribed by building and sanitary codes extends to a porch that is part of a rented unit.

3. *Conclusion.* For the foregoing reasons, we affirm the judgment entered in this case.

Notes and Questions

1. Some courts have considered expanding the breadth of the implied warranty of habitability's protection. In *Becker v. IRM Corp.*, 698 P.2d 116 (Cal. 1985), the California Supreme Court held a landlord "strictly liable in tort for injuries resulting from a latent defect in the premises when the defect existed at the time the premises were let to the tenant." However, ten years later California abandoned strict liability when it overruled *Becker. Peterson v. Superior Court*, 899 P.2d 905 (Cal. 1995) (*overruling Becker v. IRM Corp.*, 698 P.2d 116 (Cal. 1985)). So far, most states have not adopted the strict liability theory. *See* Francis M. Dougherty, Annotation, *Strict Liability of Landlord for Injury or Death of Tenant or Third Person Caused by Defect in Premises Leased for Residential Use*, 48 A.L.R.4th 638 (1986). *But see Johnson v. Scandia Associates, Inc.*, 641 N.E.2d 51 (Ind. Ct. App. 1994).

A related developing area is the landlord's liability for criminal acts on rented property. In *Trentacost v. Brussel*, 412 A.2d 436 (N.J. 1980), the court held the landlord liable for breaching the implied warranty of habitability when the tenant suffered a criminal assault due to the landlord's failure to secure the property. Accord *Brock* v. *Watts Realty Co.*, 582 So. 2d 438 (Ala. 1991); *Brownstein v. Edison*, 425 N.Y.S.2d 773 (Sup. Ct. 1980). *See also 111 E. 88 St. Partners v. Simon*, 434 N.Y.S.2d 886 (N.Y. Civ. Ct. 1980); Gary D. Spivey, Annotation, *Landlord's Obligation to Protect Tenant Against Criminal Activities of Third Persons*, 43 A.L.R.3d 331 (1972). *Cf. Bay Park One Co. v. Crosby*, 442 N.Y.S.2d 837 (Sup. Ct. 1981) (*contra*); *Doe v. New Bedford Hous. Auth.*, 630 N.E.2d 248 (Mass. 1994.) (landlord's duty under the warranty of habitability does not extend to providing security to prevent drug sales). Mac D. Heavener, III, *New Tort Liability for Residential Landlords in South Carolina*, 42 S.C. L. Rev. 241 (1990) (analyzing *Watson v. Sellers*, 385 S.E.2d 369 (S.C. Ct. App. 1989). *See also Ward v. Inshmaan Assocs. Ltd. Partnership*, 931 A.2d 1235 (N.H. 2007) (duty to protect tenants from criminal attack may only arise when a landlord has created, or is responsible for, a known defective condition that foreseeably enhances the risk of criminal activity); *Beato v. Cosmopolitan Assocs., LLC*, 893 N.Y.S.2d 578 (Sup. Ct. App. Div. 2d Dep't 2010).

2. The URLTA provides that the tenant can recover actual damages for the landlord's breach of his or her duties. One court has interpreted that provision to allow for the recovery of damages for emotional distress. The court declined to allow punitive damages

under the state's version of the URLTA. *Brewer v. Erwin*, 600 P.2d 398 (Or. 1979). *See* Wanda Ellen Wakefield, Annotation, *Emotional Distress Damages for Breach of the Implied Warranty of Habitability*, 6 A.L.R.4th 528 (1981).

3. As a result of *Javins* and its progeny, most jurisdictions have adopted new remedies for tenants. These remedies range from the most popular, a limited "repair and deduct" statutory remedy, to strong enforcement of tenant's rights under consumer protection statutes. Statutes permitting tenants to deduct the cost of repairs from rent may serve for minor repairs, but what relief do they afford a tenant who is without heat because the building's furnace needs to be replaced? Such statutes typically have complicated provisions for written notice and waiting periods before the tenant can attempt any repairs or rent deductions. For an example of a particularly exacting statutory scheme, requiring notice, waiting periods, written estimates delivered by certified mail, and limitations on the amount and frequency of deductions, see WASH. REV. CODE §§ 59.18.100 to 59.18.110. *Cf.* ARIZ. REV. STAT. § 33-1363; CAL. CIV. CODE § 1942. Another approach permits the tenant to deposit the rent into some form of escrow until the landlord completes the repairs. *See, e.g.*, OHIO REV. CODE ANN. §§ 5321.07 to 5321.10. Would this remedy be more effective for expensive work than a repair and deduct system? Do these schemes have advantage over the common-law rent withholding mechanism of *Javins?* Is an escrow account remedy better than the protective order system discussed in *Javins*? Which remedy potentially requires the tenant to deposit a larger payment? Which would more easily allow the tenant to seek a rent refund for the delay in making repairs?

Some states have gone beyond such limited remedies to apply consumer protection statutes to regulate the rental relationship. Consumer protection statutes such as state unfair business practices or "Mini-FTC" acts often provide for punitive or treble damages, a powerful enforcement tool. The tenant may have access to a state consumer protection agency to process complaints or the state's attorney general's office to bring suit for the tenant. The tenant can avoid the expense and delay of a private civil action and may be able to recover damages beyond the cost of repairs or a rent refund. Ironically, some states have refused to apply general consumer protection statutes because of the passage of a more specific (and limited) residential landlord and tenant scheme. *State v. Schwab*, 693 P.2d 108 (Wash. 1985). *But see Ethridge v. Hwang*, 20 P.3d 958 (Wash. Ct. App. Div. 1 2001) (extension of CPA to mobile home tenants). The applicability of consumer protection law in this area is still developing. *See, e.g., Wilson v. Parisi*, 549 F. Supp. 2d 637 (M.D. Pa. 2008); *Hardy v. Griffin*, 569 A.2d 49 (Conn. Ct. App. 1989); *Leardi v. Brown*, 474 N.E.2d 1094 (Mass. 1985); *Stanley v. Moore*, 454 S.E.2d 225 (N.C. 1995) (treble damages were recoverable under consumer protection statutes for utility shut off, despite ejectment statute's explicit provision that treble damages were not available); *Commonwealth v. Monumental Properties, Inc.*, 329 A.2d 812 (Pa. 1974). *See also Kingston Square Tenants' Ass'n v. Tuskegee Gardens, Ltd.*, 792 F. Supp. 1566 (S.D. Fla. 1992); James H. Backman, *The Tenant as a Consumer? A Comparison of Developments in Consumer Law and in Landlord Tenant Law*, 33 OKLA. L. REV. 1 (1980).

4. The development and application of housing codes as housing preservation measures is considered in Chapter 5. Excerpts from a typical housing code are set forth and some of the legal issues that arise in code enforcement are also considered.

Consumer protection could provide tenants with weapons beyond the sword and shield of habitability doctrine, but no weapon will be very useful unless the tenant is armored against retaliation.

4. Resisting Retaliatory Eviction

No matter the scope of remedies for "uninhabitable" apartments or homes, the landlord remains the owner and presumably can assert that interest so as to reclaim possession of the premises. Theoretically, a landlord can terminate a tenancy for no reason at all. But, as the following cases illustrate, a tenancy cannot be terminated for an improper motive. Tenants may not be evicted because they avail themselves of rights established by judicial decisions or legislative provision.

Edwards v. Habib

United States Court of Appeals
397 F.2d 687 (D.C. Cir. 1968)
cert. denied, 393 U.S. 1016 (1969)

J. Skelly WRIGHT, Circuit Judge:

In March 1965, the appellant, Mrs. Yvonne Edwards, rented housing property from the appellate, Nathan Habib, on a month-to-month basis. Shortly thereafter she complained to the Department of Licenses and Inspections of sanitary code violations which her landlord had failed to remedy. In the course of the ensuing inspection, more than 40 such violations were discovered which the Department ordered the landlord to correct. Habib then gave Mrs. Edwards a 30-day statutory notice to vacate and obtained a default judgment for possession of the premises. Mrs. Edwards promptly moved to reopen this judgment, alleging excusable neglect for the default and also alleging as a defense that the notice to quit was given in retaliation for her complaints to the housing authorities. Judge Greene, sitting on motions in the Court of General Sessions, set aside the default judgment and, in a very thoughtful opinion, concluded that a retaliatory motive, if proved, would constitute a defense to the action for possession. At the trial itself, however, a different judge apparently deemed evidence of retaliatory motive irrelevant and directed a verdict for the landlord.

Mrs. Edwards then appealed to this court for a stay pending her appeal to the District of Columbia Court of Appeals, and on December 3, 1965, we granted the stay, provided only that Mrs. Edwards continue to pay her rent. *Edwards v. Habib*, 366 F.2d 628 (D.C. Cir. 1965). She then appealed to the DCCA, which affirmed the judgment of the trial court. 227 A.2d 388 (D.C. 1967). In reaching its decision the DCCA relied on a series of its earlier decisions holding that a private landlord was not required, under the District of Columbia Code, to give a reason for evicting a month to month tenant and was free to do so for any reason or for no reason at all. The court acknowledged that the landlord's right to terminate a tenant is not absolute, but felt that any limitation on his prerogative had to be based on specific statutes or very special circumstances. Here, the court concluded, the tenant's right to report violations of law and to petition for redress of grievances was not protected by specific legislation and that any change in the relative rights of tenants and landlords should be undertaken by the legislature, not the courts. We granted appellant leave to appeal that decision to this court. We hold that the promulgation of the housing code by the District of Columbia Commissioners at the direction of Congress impliedly effected just such a change in the relative rights of landlords and tenants and that proof of a retaliatory motive does constitute a defense to an action of eviction. Accordingly, we reverse the decision of the DCCA with directions that it remand to the Court of General Sessions for a new trial where Mrs. Edwards will be permitted to try to prove to a jury that her landlord who seeks to evict her harbors a retaliatory intent.

I

Appellant has launched a constitutional challenge to the judicial implementation of 45 D.C. Code 902 and 910 in aid of a landlord who is evicting because his tenant has reported housing code violations on the premises. We do not, however, reach the question whether it is unconstitutional for the court to apply the statute in such circumstances because we think Congress never intended that it be so applied.

II

Appellant argues that, even if ... the concept of "state action" ... [is] interpreted narrowly, and the judicial implementation of the D.C. Code to effect a retaliatory eviction does not violate her First Amendment rights, her eviction would be unconstitutional nonetheless because the right to petition the government and to report violations of law is constitutionally protected against private as well as governmental interference.

III

But we need not decide whether judicial recognition of this constitutional defense is constitutionally compelled. We need not, in other words, decide whether 45 D.C. Code Section 910 could validly compel the court to assist the plaintiff in penalizing the defendant for exercising her constitutional right to inform the government of violations of the law, for we are confident that Congress did not intend it to entail such a result.

45 D.C. Code §910, in pertinent part, provides:

> Whenever ... any tenancy shall be terminated by notice as aforesaid [45 D.C. Code §902 ...], and the tenant shall fail or refuse to surrender possession of the leased premises, ... the landlord may bring an action to recover possession before the District of Columbia Court of General Sessions, as provided in sections 11-701 to 11-749.

And 16 D.C. Code §1501, in pertinent part, provides:

> When a person detains possession of real property ... after his right to possession has ceased, the District of Columbia Court of General Sessions ... may issue a summons to the party complained of to appear and show cause why judgment should not be given against him for restitution of possession.

These provisions are simply procedural. They neither say nor imply anything about whether evidence of retaliation or other improper motive should be unavailable as a defense to a possessory action brought under them. It is true that in making his affirmative case for possession the landlord need only show that his tenant has been given the 30-day statutory notice, and he need not assign any reason for evicting a tenant who does not occupy the premises under a lease. But while the landlord may evict for any legal reason or for no reason at all, he is not, we hold, free to evict in retaliation for his tenant's report of housing code violations to the authorities. As a matter of statutory construction and for reasons of public policy, such an eviction cannot be permitted.

The housing and sanitary codes, especially in light of Congress' explicit direction for their enactment, indicate a strong and pervasive congressional concern to secure for the city's slum dwellers decent, or at least safe and sanitary, places to live. Effective implementation and enforcement of the codes obviously depend in part on private initiative in the reporting of violations. Though there is no official procedure for the filing of such complaints, the bureaucratic structure of the Department of Licenses and Inspections establishes such a procedure, and for fiscal year 1966 nearly a third of the cases handled by the Department arose from private complaints. To permit retaliatory evictions, then, would clearly frustrate the effectiveness of the housing code as a means of upgrading the quality of housing in Washington.

As judges, "we cannot shut our eyes to matters of public notoriety and general cognizance. When we take our seats on the bench we are not struck with blindness, and forbidden to know as judges what we see as men." *Ho Ah Kow v. Nunan*, C.C.D. Cal., 12 Fed. Cas. 252, 255 (No. 6546) (1879). In trying to effect the will of Congress and as a court of equity we have the responsibility to consider the social context in which our decisions will have operational effect. In light of the appalling condition and shortage of housing in Washington, the expense of moving, the inequality of bargaining power between tenant and landlord, and the social and economic importance of assuring at least minimum standards in housing conditions, we do not hesitate to declare that retaliatory eviction cannot be tolerated. There can be no doubt that the slum dweller, even though his home be marred by housing code violations, will pause long before he complains of them if he fears eviction as a consequence. Hence an eviction under the circumstances of this case would not only punish appellant for making a complaint which she had a constitutional right to make, a result which we would not impute to the will of Congress simply on the basis of an essentially procedural enactment, but also would stand as a warning to others that they dare not be so bold, a result which, from the authorization of the housing code, we think Congress affirmatively sought to avoid.

The notion that the effectiveness of remedial legislation will be inhibited if those reporting violations of it can legally be intimidated is so fundamental that a presumption against the legality of such intimidation can be inferred as inherent in the legislation even if it is not expressed in the statute itself. Such an inference was recently drawn by the Supreme Court from the federal labor statutes to strike down under the supremacy clause a Florida statute denying unemployment insurance to workers discharged in retaliation for filing complaints of federally defined unfair labor practices. While we are not confronted with a possible conflict between federal policy and state law, we do have the task of reconciling and harmonizing two federal statutes so as to best effectuate the purposes of each. The proper balance can only be struck by interpreting 45 D.C. Code §§ 902 and 910 as inapplicable where the court's aid is invoked to effect an eviction in retaliation for reporting housing code violations.

This is not, of course, to say that even if the tenant can prove a retaliatory purpose she is entitled to remain in possession in perpetuity. If this illegal purpose is dissipated, the landlord can, in the absence of legislation or a binding contract, evict his tenants or raise their rents for economic or other legitimate reasons, or even for no reason at all. The question of permissible or impermissible purpose is one of fact for the court or jury, and while such a determination is not easy, it is not significantly different from problems with which the courts must deal in a host of other contexts, such as when they must decide whether the employer who discharged a worker has committed an unfair labor practice because he has done so on account of the employer's union activities. As Judge Greene said, "There is no reason why similar factual judgments cannot be made by courts and juries in the context of economic retaliation [against tenants by landlords] for providing information to the government." Reversed and remanded.

Notes and Questions

1. The sweep of the retaliatory eviction defense and the intractable nature of the struggle between urban landlords and tenants was revealed in *Robinson v. Diamond Hous.*

Corp., 463 F.2d 853 (D.C. Cir. 1972). The decision was a culminating chapter in what Judge J. Skelly Wright aptly characterized as a "saga."

In the first of three separate actions for possession, the tenant won under the doctrine of *Brown v. Southall Realty Co.*, 237 A.2d 834 (D.C. 1968), which holds that a lease purporting to convey property burdened with substantial housing code violations is illegal and void and that the lessor is not entitled to gain possession for rent due under the invalid lease. Mrs. Robinson had withheld rent when the lessor failed to repair the severely deteriorated premises. (Large pieces of plaster were missing throughout the residence, there was no step from the front walk to the front porch which was in turn shaky and unsafe, there was a wall in the rear bedroom unattached to the ceiling, there were nails protruding along the side of the stairway, glass was missing from a front window, and a kitchen window frame was so far out of position that the backyard was visible through the space between the window frame and the wall.)

The intrepid lessor then sued Mrs. Robinson for possession on the theory that she was a trespasser since the lease was void and she hence had no right to be on the premises. The landlord's theory was rejected, but in dicta, the court opined that Mrs. Robinson was a tenant at sufferance and could be evicted on thirty days' notice. The court added that District of Columbia housing regulations "do not compel an owner of housing property to rent his property. Where, as here, it has been determined that the property when rented was not habitable, that is, not safe and sanitary, and should not have been rented, and if the landlord is unwilling or unable to put the property in a habitable condition, he may and should promptly terminate the tenant and withdraw the property from the rental market, because the regulations forbid both the rental and the occupancy of such premises." *Diamond Hous. Corp. v. Robinson*, 257 A.2d 492, 495 (D.C. 1969).

Thereafter, the landlord filed yet a third action in which it declared that he was unwilling to make the repairs necessary to put the housing in compliance with the housing code and that he presently intended to take the unit off the rental market. Mrs. Robinson answered with the defense of retaliation, asserting that she was actually being evicted for having raised the *Southall Realty* defense in the original action.

In the course of holding that the retaliatory eviction defense was properly interposed and that the tenant could not be dispossessed unless the landlord could demonstrate a "legitimate business justification—other than the mere desire to get rid of a tenant exercising *Southall Realty* rights," the U.S. Court of Appeals for the D.C. Circuit suggested that:

> The landlord's mere allegation that he is removing the unit from the market because he cannot afford to make repairs does not mean that the jury will find that he is *in fact* unable to make the necessary repairs. Moreover, even if the jury makes such a finding, it still does not follow that judgment for the landlord is compelled. We must remember that we are dealing with a question of subjective motive, and that objective factors are relevant only as an indicia of motive. Thus the mere existence of a legitimate reason for the landlord's actions will not help him if the jury finds that he was in fact motivated by some illegitimate reason.... In cases of mixed motives, the jury will have the difficult task of weighing one against the other and determining which was the causative factor.

Robinson v. Diamond Hous. Corp., 463 F.2d 853 at 867. The court also spoke to the concerns raised by critics of the economic feasibility of tenant remedies such as warranty of habitability. (the excerpt from the Meyers article *supra* should be compared). The United States Court of Appeals for the D.C. Circuit has observed:

> In large measure, the scope and effectiveness of tenant remedies for substandard housing will be determined by the degree of protection given tenants against retaliatory actions by landlords. If a landlord is free to evict or otherwise harass a tenant who exercises his right to secure better housing conditions, few tenants will use the remedies for fear of being put out on the street.... Harley J. Daniels, *Judicial and Legislative Remedies for Substandard Housing: Landlord-Tenant Law Reform in the District of Columbia*, 59 Geo. L.J. 909, 943 (1971).
>
> The *Javins* and *Southall Realty* decisions—as well as the District of Columbia regulations patterned after them—were based on the express premise that private remedies for housing code violations would increase the stock of livable low-cost housing in the District. If exercise of those remedies leads instead to eviction of tenants and abandonment of what little low-cost housing remains in the District, the great goal of "a decent home and a suitable living environment for every American family." Section 1 of the Housing Act of 1937, 50 Stat. 888, as amended by the Housing Act of 1949, 63 Stat. 413, will be frustrated. *Cf.* Note, *Landlord's Violation of Housing Code During Lease Term*, 84 Harv. L. Rev. 729, 733–34 (1971).
>
> Of course, if the housing market is structured in such a way that it is impossible for landlords to absorb the cost of bringing their units into compliance with the housing code, there may be nothing a court can do to prevent vigorous code enforcement from driving low-cost housing off the market. But the most recent scholarship on the subject indicates this danger is largely imagined. In fact, it appears that vigorous code enforcement plays little or no role in the decrease in low-cost housing stock. When code enforcement is seriously pursued, market forces generally prevent landlords from passing on their increased costs through rent increases. *See generally* [Bruce] Ackerman, *Regulating Slum Housing Markets on Behalf of the Poor: Of Housing Codes, Housing Subsidies and Income Redistribution Policy*, 80 Yale. L.J. 1093 (1971). The danger stems not from the possibility that landlords might take low-cost units off the market altogether, but rather from the possibility that they will do so selectively in order to "make an example" of a troublesome tenant who has the temerity to assert his legal rights in court. We can be fairly confident that most landlords will find ownership of property sufficiently profitable—even with vigorous code enforcement—to remain in business. But it is undoubtedly true that the same landlords would be able to make a greater profit if the housing code were enforced laxly or not at all. There is thus a real danger that landlords may find it in their interest to sacrifice the profits derived from operation of a few units in order to intimidate the rest of their tenants.
>
> Fortunately, this is a danger with which the law is better equipped to deal. While the judiciary may be powerless to control landlords who no longer wish to remain landlords, it can prevent landlords from conducting their business in a way that chills the legally protected rights of tenants.

Robinson v. Diamond Hous. Corp., 463 F.2d at 860. The court based its economic conclusions on a controversial Yale Law Journal article which attracted a critical reply disputing its reasoning. *See* Neil K. Komesar, *Return to Slumville: A Critique of the Ackerman Analysis of Housing Code Enforcement and the Poor*, 82 Yale L.J. 1175 (1973). Neither did the court point out that Ackerman's analysis was based on an abstract model of the housing market, that it was not supported by empirical research, and that the avoidance of harmful effects on the poor from code enforcement required a subsidy payment. For more on the economics of housing code enforcement, see Chapter 5 *infra*. Do the weaknesses in the Ackerman analysis undercut the court's opinion?

2. Important in the reconciliation of the right to complain of housing violations with the right to select tenants in both *Edwards* and *Robinson* was the presence of housing and sanitary codes indicating "a strong and pervasive congressional concern to secure for the city's slum dwellers decent, or at least safe and sanitary, places to live." Toleration of retaliatory evictions would have undercut a legislative scheme which relied in significant measure on private initiative. In *Schweiger v. Superior Court*, 476 P.2d 97, 100 (Cal. 1970), the California Supreme Court followed the *Edwards* rule without the presence of the housing codes, declaring:

> [T]he *Edwards* court was faced with the problem of reconciling the apparently unlimited power of landlords to evict with the fundamental public policy underlying the housing and sanitation codes. The court held that landlords could not exercise their rights under the eviction statutes to retaliate against tenants invoking their rights under the housing and sanitation codes. Except for superficial distinctions, our problem is identical. If we fail to recognize a reasonable limitation on the punitive power of landlords to increase rents and evict tenants, the salutary purposes sought to be achieved by the Legislature in enacting Civil Code, sections 1941 and 1972 will be frustrated. If we deny tenants a defense against retaliatory eviction in unlawful detainer actions, we lend the exercise of the judicial process to aid landlords in punishing those tenants with the audacity to exercise their statutory rights. Thus sound statutory construction here, as *Edwards* held in comparable circumstances, requires that we reconcile sections 1942 and 1161 by recognizing existence of a defense in unlawful detainer actions when the landlord's motive is retaliation for the exercise of statutory rights under section 1942. Adoption of the alternative course would suggest a devious legislative intent to render section 1942 ineffective as a protective measure.
>
> Real party in interest Bonds urges us to distinguish *Edwards* on the ground that the policies underlying housing codes and sections 1941 and 1942 are not identical. Even if we concede that the protective policies inspiring housing codes are more pervasive than those underlying section 1942, the rationale of *Edwards* appears singularly appropriate to general statutory self-help remedies like section 1942. Whatever salutary legislative purpose induced the passage of section 1942, it cannot be achieved if tenants exercising the rights granted by the section may be punished with judicial approbation. Furthermore, the frustrating effect of landlord retaliation on the vitality of section 1942 is likely to be greater than it would be on the enforcement of housing codes, since section 1942 depends for its effectiveness exclusively on tenant initiative, as distinguished from governmental action.

Chief Justice Wright dissented, partly on grounds that judicial prohibition of retaliatory evictions and rent increases would raise a host of problems difficult to resolve consistently, but principally because the California legislature had provided a remedy (though inapplicable in *Schweiger*). *See* CAL. CIV. CODE §§ 1942, 1942.5.

The Uniform Residential Landlord and Tenant Act offers some protection to tenants from retaliatory evictions. The relevant provisions of the URLTA are set forth below.

Uniform Residential Landlord and Tenant Act

§5.101. [Retaliatory Conduct Prohibited]

(a) Except as provided in this Section, a landlord may not retaliate by increasing rent or decreasing services or by bringing or threatening to bring an action for possession after:

(1) the tenant has complained to a governmental agency charged with responsibility for enforcement of a building or housing code of violation applicable to the premises materially affecting health and safety; or

(2) the tenant has complained to the landlord of a violation under Section 2.104; or

(3) the tenant has organized or become a member of a tenant's union or similar organization.

(b) If the landlord acts in violation of subsection (a), the tenant is entitled to the remedies provided in Section 4.107 and has a defense in any retaliatory action against him for possession. In an action by or against the tenant, evidence of a complaint within [1] year before the alleged act of retaliation creates a presumption that the landlord's conduct was in retaliation. The presumption does not arise if the tenant made the complaint after notice of a proposed rent increase or diminution of services. "Presumption" means that the trier of fact must find the existence of the fact presumed unless and until evidence is introduced which would support a finding of its nonexistence.

(c) Notwithstanding subsections (a) and (b), a landlord may bring an action for possession if:

(1) the violation of the applicable building or housing code was caused primarily by lack or reasonable care by the tenant, a member of his family, or other person on the premises with his consent; or

(2) the tenant is in default in rent; or

(3) compliance with the applicable building or housing code requires alteration, remodeling, or demolition which would effectively deprive the tenant of use of the dwelling unit.

(d) The maintenance of an action under subsection (c) does not release the landlord from liability under Section 4.101(b).

Notes and Questions

1. As noted in the comment to *Javins*, *supra*, the notion that the legislature is the forum to work out the complexities of landlord-tenant conflict is a persistent, if minority, view. Comparison should be made between the attempt to work out a comprehensive solution in advance through URLTA 5.101 and the discussion in *Edwards* and *Robinson v. Diamond Hous. Corp.* Does the statute resolve all the possible permutations of the conflict or is there still need for judicial refinement of the retaliation doctrine? Or are statutes and judicial decisions mutually reinforcing approaches, especially since the court always has the last word on the resolution of inconsistencies between decisions and statutes?

2. Other courts have confronted the problem avoided by the U.S. Court of Appeals for the District of Columbia Circuit in the first two parts of the *Edwards* opinion. *See*

Hosey v. Club Van Cortlandt, 299 F. Supp. 501 (S.D.N.Y. 1969) (Landlord's use of the judicial process for retaliatory eviction is unconstitutional state action). *But see Stephanus v. Anderson*, 613 P.2d 533 (Wash. Ct. App. 1980) (No state action present in eviction action between private parties).

3. Reconsider Judge Wright's dictum in *Robinson v. Diamond Hous. Corp., supra*, about proof of retaliatory motive. How would a trier of fact distinguish between rent increases to pay for improvements to meet the requirements of the warranty of habitability (assuming even these raises would be legal) from rent increases to punish disagreeable tenants? What can a tenant do about a reduction in services, such as those imposed by a conservation-conscious landlord who sets back the thermostat in winter (and up in the summer)? The problem, so far as the tenant is concerned, is easier solved in jurisdictions like New Jersey which create a rebuttable presumption that illegal retaliation is the motive if action is commenced, for example, after a report of a building code violation by the tenant. *See* N.J. STAT. ANN. §§ 2A:42-10.10 and 2A:42-10.12. *Cf.* CAL. CIV. CODE § 1942.5, *supra; Building Monitoring Sys., Inc. v. Paxton*, 905 P.2d 1215 (Utah 1995).

4. While some tenants lease their apartments on a month-to-month basis, many tenants have fixed-term leases. Should a landlord be able to retaliate against a troublemaking tenant by refusing to renew such a fixed-term case? *See* Restatement (Second) of Property § 14.8 (1977). *Compare Frenchtown Villa v. Meadors*, 324 N.W.2d 133 (Mich. Ct. App. 1982) (reluctantly applying state law denying defense of retaliatory eviction in summary eviction proceeding based on nonrenewal of lease) *with Van Buren Apartments v. Adams*, 701 P.2d 538 (Ariz. Ct. App. 1984) (allowing the retaliatory eviction defense to nonrenewal of fixed-term lease). Could failure to renew a lease also be a violation of the covenant of good faith and fair dealing? *Cf. Stephanus v. Anderson*, 613 P.2d 533 (Wash. Ct. App. 1980); (state law exempting termination of month-to-month tenancies from prohibition against retaliation trumps covenant of good faith). The Washington legislature was shamed into plugging this statutory loophole by *Stephanus*. Brian T. McManus, Comment, *Retaliatory Evictions in Washington and Seattle: In Search of Public Policy*, 57 WASH. L. REV. 293 (1982). However, despite the extension to month-to-month tenants of protection against retaliation, local courts generally failed to notice or respect the new law. Interview with Alan Anderson, tenant advocate in Tacoma, Washington. For cases treating retaliation in a variety of contexts, *see* Annotation., *Retaliatory Eviction of Tenant for Reporting Landlord's Violation of Law*, 23 A.L.R. 5th 140 (1994).

5. Rent Control

a. Overview: Pros and Cons

The warranty of habitability and enforcement remedies such as the defense of retaliation are directed at the quality of the housing stock. Perhaps as part of the rising expectations of the 1960s and early 1970s, there was the hope that the free market should adjust itself to the new order and that the output would be not only an improvement in the quality of housing, but also an increase in the number of available habitable dwellings. Whatever the effect, however, of the warranty of habitability on housing quality, the issue of the late 1970s and of the 1980s turned out to be the *cost*, rather than the quality of housing. This issue of cost is, of course, directly tied to supply. As housing production has slowed, older housing has continued to deteriorate, while simultaneously the formulation of new households has been fueled by continued population growth as well as sociological causes such as divorce. The demand for shelter has far, far outstripped supply. This has led to a struggle for affordable living space that has reached the level of class warfare. At an immediate level, there is competition for living space between different groups within the population, between seniors and young families, or between urban blacks and urban pioneers, the young, professional offspring of the whites who fled to the suburbs in the 1950s and 1960s. But ultimately, the conflict is between those who own rental properties and those who rent. The battleground bears the term rent control.

A brief history and discussion of the essentials of this political and economic phenomenon appears in a report to the United States Department of Housing and Urban Planning on a study of three Los Angeles, California, neighborhoods (later published in a law review).

Donald C. Bryant and Henry W. McGee, Jr., Gentrification and the Law: Combating Urban Displacement

25 Washington University Journal of Urban & Contemporary Law 43, 120–26 (1983)

1. History of Rent Controls

Prior to the 1970's rent controls in the United States were limited to periods of war-generated "emergency" housing situations.

Rent controls were not adopted again until World War II. In 1942, Congress passed the Emergency Price Control Act, which authorized the Office of Price Administration to stabilize rents in areas which were designated as potential defense-rental areas. By October 1942, the entire nation had been so designated. After the war, the number of defense-rental areas was gradually decreased. Federal rent controls disappeared entirely by 1954....

Local rent controls have been adopted in a number of jurisdictions in recent years.[340] The first California rent control law was adopted by Berkeley through the initiative process in 1972. It prohibited across-the-board rent increases. Rather, the law provided that applications for rent increases had to be considered on a unit-by-unit basis. In *Birkenfeld v. City of Berkeley* [550 P.2d 1001 (1976), reprinted *infra*—Eds.], the California Supreme Court ruled that this mechanism was so unwieldy that it in effect would deny landlords rent increases for years and therefore constitute a denial of due process.

2. Specifics of Rent Controls

An effective rent control law is one which will provide tenants with the security of continuous occupancy free from rent increases which exceed owner's increases in operating costs.

a. Exemptions

Rent control laws typically exempt some units. A standard exemption is for owner-occupied buildings with fewer than a specified number of units. Rent control laws have

340. The one exception to this pattern is New York City, where rent controls have remained in effect continuously since World War II. *See* Monica R. Lett, Rent Control: Concepts, Realities, and Mechanisms 5 (1976). Starting in 1969, other localities have enacted rent controls. Boston and several of its suburbs adopted rent controls for varying periods. *See generally* George Sternlieb, The Realities of Rent Control in the Greater Boston Area (1975). In New Jersey, over 100 cities have enacted rent controls since 1973. *See* Kenneth K. Baar, *Rent Control in the 1970's: The Case of the New Jersey Tenants' Movement*, 28 Hastings L.J. 631 (1977).

also exempted single-family dwellings, buildings with fewer than a certain number of units, new construction, luxury units, and federally subsidized housing.

b. Vacancy Decontrol

The presence or absence of a vacancy decontrol provision in a rent control law is a critical determinant of its impact on gentrification. Decontrol allows a landlord to raise the rent without limit for a unit that becomes vacant. After the unit is rented to a new tenant, it again becomes subject to the rent control restrictions. However, the new rent may be much higher than the old rent.

It does not take much imagination to see that vacancy decontrol creates enormous incentives for landlords to evict tenants in order to charge higher rents. Vacancy decontrol may encourage landlords to act on breaches of leases that were previously ignored (typically a tenant has no bargaining power in setting the terms of a lease and the landlord can set terms which are difficult not to breach). Alternatively, landlords may refuse to maintain a unit, making continued occupancy undesirable. In neighborhoods that are undergoing rapid change and increases in rent, landlords can usually skirt the rent control laws because tenants are poor and not particularly knowledgeable. In a few years, vacancy decontrol can lead to substantial discrepancies in rental levels for comparable units in the same building. Therefore, successful rent control laws specifically exclude vacancy decontrol provisions.

c. Conversion and Demolition Regulation

In addition to substantial rent increases conversion or demolition of units may displace low income tenants. With rising home prices, property owners can profit more by converting their units for sale as condominiums than by maintaining them as rental units. In fact, condominiums are so valuable that it is often profitable to demolish rental buildings and build condominiums, especially when the number of units per lot can be increased. Thus, to be effective in preventing gentrification, rent control laws must regulate conversions and demolitions.

d. Fair Return Requirements

Due process requires that landlords subject to rent controls be permitted to receive a fair return on their investments. Rent control laws either provide for statutory increases for all landlords each year, or they grant discretion to determine what rent increases shall be allowed across the board based on general criteria, including increases in operating costs and fair return. These laws make provision for individual adjustments for landlords who are not receiving a fair return on their investment, who have made major capital improvements, or who for other reasons should receive an exceptional rent increase.

The standard definition of fair return is a return commensurate with returns on investments in other enterprises having comparable risks.[352] A problem arises when city planners attempt to translate this principle into a specific formula to determine a fair return for a particular building. Is a fair return a specific percentage of the fair market value of the property or of the cash investment made by the owner? Should mortgage interest

---

352. The two competing fair return standards are "return on value," favored by landlords, and "return on historical investment." The generally pro-tenant rent control boards in Berkeley and Santa Monica have since adopted a third formula, "maintenance of net operating income." The courts appear to be moving toward acceptance of this third standard as a formula midway between the value and investment standards. Owners are entitled to a rent increase if their net operating income is less than a designated percentage of gross rental income. Both the Berkeley and Santa Monica rent boards permit an additional inflation factor in this formula, although it is less than the actual rate of inflation. *See* Thomas Brom, *Courts Consider Limits on Landlords' Profits*, CAL. LAW., Sept. 1983, at 16.

rates, depreciation, and potential capital gains be taken into account? Despite substantial efforts, a precise formula has not been articulated for determining what is a fair return.

[In 1975, the New Jersey Supreme Court] indicated that a fair return was one which maintained owners at their same levels of net operating income prior to the implementation of rent controls. [*Helmsley v. Borough of Fort Lee*, 394 A.2d 65, 85–86 (1978)—Eds.]

The New Jersey approach is a reasonable and practical standard for determining fair return. Landlords held to a negative cash flow by this approach argue that it is unfair and confiscatory. When landlords purchase buildings at prices that will lead to negative cash flows, they are speculating that substantial profits will offset the risks and losses incurred in taking that flow position. Since they are speculating, it is not the role of rent control laws to protect them and award them individual rent increases not given to other landlords who do not have negative cash flows. Speculation necessarily implies the possibility of loss as well as profit.

Landlords argue that the net operating income standard is inherently inequitable because landlords who charged high rents and received substantial incomes before rent controls were adopted are rewarded, while landlords with relatively low rents are penalized.

Other definitions of fair return present problems. If fair market value is the standard to determine fair return, the result is tautological, because fair market value for property depends on its rental income. If return on cash investment is the standard, fair rent becomes a function of the purchase and financing terms of the building rather than the rent levels previously in effect for the building.

While fair return has eluded precise definition, the courts have indicated that the constitutional fair return standard does not require that every landlord make a profit or receive a positive cash flow. They have consistently held that calculating a landlord's cost need not include debt service. The emerging standard is that "efficient" landlords have a right to a net operating income equal to that amount which they had prior to the adoption of the controls.

Notes and Questions

1. For a discussion of historical matters; legal, legislative, and administrative issues; the economic, public policy, and political dimensions; and, case studies of rent control, see W. Dennis Keating, Michael B. Teitz, & Andrejs Skaburskis, Rent Control: Regulation and The Rental Housing Market (1998).

2. Rent control battles are waged within jurisdictions.

(a) For an excellent history of the fight for rent control in New Jersey, see Kenneth K. Baar, *Rent Control in the 1970's: The Case of the New Jersey Tenants' Movement*, 28 Hastings L.J. 631 (1977).

(b) The literature on New York City is substantial. *See generally* Peter Marcuse, Rental Housing in the City of New York (1979); Richard Chi-Cheng Hsia, *The ABC's of MBR: How to Spell Trouble in Landlord/Tenant Relations (Up Against the Crumbling Wall)*, 10 Colum. J. L. & Soc. Probs. 113 (1974); W. Dennis Keating, *Landlord Self-Regulation: New York City's Rent Stabilization System 1968–1985*, 31 J. Urb. & Contemp. L. 77 (1987); Guy McPherson, *It's the End of the World as We Know It (and I Feel Fine): Rent Regulation in New York City and the Unanswered Questions of Market and Society*, 72 Fordham L. Rev. 1125 (2004).

The New York Times Magazine presented the case for continuing regulation in 1997, condensed as follows: (1) Only 70,000 of the city's 1.1 million regulated apartments are subject to the strictest controls. About a million more apartments (those with more than six units built between 1947 and 1974 are rent stabilized—governed by somewhat looser regulations but with rent increases still subject to official guidelines. Nearly 600,000 other apartments are unregulated. (2) Arguably rent regulation is a predictable middle-class subsidy, like lower property taxes on single-family homes. Regulation is also about guaranteeing at least minimal building maintenance and services. Regulation—and the threat of mandatory rent reductions—offers great leverage over greedy landlords, managing agents and even co-op boards that might otherwise find means to force tenants out. (3) Rent regulation applies citywide, but the debate about prices largely concerns Manhattan. In poorer parts of the city market prices are about 25% less than the regulated rate. (4) Rent regulation would lapse if more than 5% of apartments were available. But has regulation really deterred developers from building more? Somewhat. But to build more, swaths of manufacturing and commercial districts would have to be rezoned for housing. Also, so-called affordable housing is hard to build without subsidies or tax abatements. Plenty of higher-priced apartments are being built anyway—and landlords may charge the first tenants whatever the market will bear. (5) Not all economists condemn rent regulation—even if the theoretical goal is to redistribute income. Writing a few years ago in the Journal of Economic Perspectives, Richard Arnott of Boston College concluded that "it is possible to design a set of rent regulations that result in an improvement in efficiency over the unrestricted market equilibrium." (6) Yes, but the truth is that the defenders of rent regulation aren't moved by economics, only politics. Cynics say that in repeatedly reviewing rent regulation, the Legislature has been guided by one equation: Tenants outnumber landlords. To which Bill Eimicke, a professor who served as State Housing Commissioner, replies, "If you're arguing that it's because the people want it, excuse me. This is a democracy." Sam Roberts, *The Case For Rent Regulation*, N.Y TIMES, May 4, 1997 (Magazine).

In 2003 New York extended rent regulations to the year 2011. Under "luxury" decontrol, vacated units renting for $2,000 or more monthly occupied by tenants with incomes of $175,000 or more the previous two years are permanently decontrolled. N.Y.C. ADMIN. CODE § 26-504.1-3. Luxury decontrol figured in the purchase of Stuyvesant Town and Peter Cooper Village in October, 2006. Developed on the east side of Manhattan after World War II by the Metropolitan Life Insurance Company, the two massive middle-income projects contain over 11,000 apartments housing around 25,000 tenants. The sale to Tishman Speyer for $5.6 billion (outbidding the tenants association) was called the most expensive residential real estate deal in American history. Almost 7,000 of the apartments were subject to rent stabilization. The buyer figured that a combination of luxury decontrol and forcing out occupants with illegal subleases would eventually allow it to charge market rents for most of these units. However, its plans soon ran afoul of tenant opposition. A class action lawsuit filed by the tenants association claimed that Tishman Speyer had illegally deregulated around 4,000 rent-stabilized apartments. Tenants claimed that the owners had received millions of tax breaks under the J-51 tax abatement program, which does not allow for deregulation for landlords claiming these benefits. They sued to have rent stabilization re-instated and rent overcharges returned. In March, 2009, an appellate court reversed the trial judge and ruled for the tenants. Sophia Hollander, *Behind an Outsize Court Case, Two Everyday Tenants.* N.Y TIMES, Mar. 15, 2009. This threatened the owners with eventual bankruptcy. Charles Bagli, *Buyers of Huge Manhattan Apartment Complex Risk Default.* N.Y. TIMES, Sept. 10, 2009. In October, 2009, New

York's highest court agreed with the tenants. *Roberts v. Tishman Speyer Properties*, 918 N.E.2d 900 (N.Y. 2009). The outcome depended upon an interpretation of the meaning of the legislation establishing luxury decontrol in 1993 (the Rent Regulation Reform Act, Chapter 253), and the exemption affecting apartments receiving J-51 benefits (N.Y.C. ADMIN. CODE § 26-504.1-2), taking into account its legislative history and its interpretation by the New York State Department of Housing and Community Renewal. The majority concluded that when landlords received the tax benefits, they forfeited their right to luxury decontrol. The dissent warned that "It will take years of litigation over many novel questions to deal with the fallout from today's decision." Charles Bagli, *Court Deals Blow to Owners of Apartment Complex*, N.Y. TIMES, Oct. 22, 2009.

(c) For discussions of rent control in Massachusetts, see HARBRIDGE HOUSE, INC., A STUDY OF RENT CONTROL AND EVICTION CONTROLS IN THE COMMONWEALTH OF MASSACHUSETTS (1974) and GEORGE STERNLIEB, THE REALITIES OF RENT CONTROL IN THE GREATER BOSTON AREA (1975). In Massachusetts, decontrol was enacted by state referendum in 1994.

(d) For early rent control developments in California, see W. Dennis Keating, *Rent Control in California: Responding to the Housing Crisis*, California Policy Seminar No. 16 (1983). California has state-mandated vacancy decontrol, enacted in 1995, that took full effect in 1999. CAL. CIVIL CODE § 1954.50 (Costa-Hawkins Rental Housing Act).

In addition to rent control conflicts in Santa Monica and the college town of Berkeley, the most contentious rent control battles in a major California city have occurred in San Francisco. CHESTER HARTMAN, CITY FOR SALE: THE TRANSFORMATION OF SAN FRANCISCO 341–361 (2002). For the current policies of San Francisco's Rent Board, see www.sfrb.org.

3. The "pros" and "cons" of rent control, as well as a comparative view, are presented in JOEL F. BRENNER & HERBERT M. FRANKLIN, RENT CONTROL IN NORTH AMERICA AND FOUR EUROPEAN COUNTRIES (1977). Also on the pros and cons, see Lawrence C. Becker, *Rent Control Is Not a Taking*, 54 BROOK. L. REV. 1215 (1989) and George W. Johnson, *Rent Control and the Theory of Efficient Regulation: Introduction: Is the United States Supreme Court Ready For the Question?*, 54 BROOK. L. REV. 729 (1988).

4. An advocate's view of rent control can be found in JOHN I. GILDERBLOOM ET AL., RENT CONTROL (1981) and JOHN I. GILDERBLOOM & RICHARD P. APPLEBAUM, RETHINKING RENTAL HOUSING (1988). A discussion of rent control as an economic and social policy is presented in EMILY ACHTENBERG, THE SOCIAL UTILITY OF RENT CONTROL (1971). Achtenberg points out that there is little evidence that rent control has deterred new construction, but that new construction without subsidies is not likely to benefit lower-income households. She believes that in order to facilitate housing maintenance, an effective rent control ordinance must balance both the rewards and the penalties, because low-income tenants will not benefit from ordinances that allow the landlord to pass automatically along operating and other costs to the tenants.

For other empirical studies reaching similar results, see David Bartelt & Ronald Lawson, *Rent Control and Abandonment in New York City: A Look at the Evidence*, *in* CRITICAL PERSPECTIVES ON HOUSING (Rachel G. Bratt, Chester Hartman, & Ann Meyerson eds. 1986) and John I. Gilderbloom, *Moderate Rent Control: Its Impact on the Quantity of the Housing Stock*, 17 URB. AFF. Q. 123–49 (1981).

5. A non-equivocal and decidedly hostile view of rent control is presented in Gerson Bakar, *Rent Control Decreases Housing Supply, Fails to Benefit the Poor*, 37 MORTGAGE BANKER, No. 8 1977, at 68:

It is important to note that rent control, in New York and elsewhere, is justified in the name of helping the poor. The U.S. Senate Banking, Housing and Urban Affairs committee, in a recent report looking at the reasons why the federal government had to bail out New York, says, "Interestingly enough, there is no evidence to show that rent control benefits the poor. Quite the contrary, it helps a small, privileged group of long-time residents, largely middle-class, while driving up rents in uncontrolled units."

The *Amsterdam News*, New York's leading black newspaper, has editorially stated that local rent control just does not help the poor: "We in minority areas are forced at times to live in rat-infested buildings that resemble bombed out war areas. And what is even more devastating is that the fact that this type of housing is rapidly increasing, instead of decreasing, and is unfortunately doing so *solely because of rent control*." (Emphasis added.)

There is a very good reason why local rent control harms the poor. For a variety of reasons, it leads to a shortage of housing; and whenever there is a shortage of anything in society, it is the poor who suffer.

From studies that are available, it seems obvious that the housing conditions of the poor are improved whenever there is a surge of new construction. The American tradition has always been to upgrade when better housing becomes available. That upgrading process inevitably allows new entrants on the housing ladder. As families upgrade into new units, structurally sound units become available for the poor. If we enact programs like rent control that inhibit new construction, the poor cannot get on the housing ladder.

None of this is meant to suggest that there is not a very real housing problem facing the poor, and particularly the elderly poor, in the United States at this time. But one is hard put to see how any program like rent control, which decreases the housing supply, will benefit the poor.

b. The Legal Status of Rent Control

1. The First Generation Ordinances

The "first generation" of rent control laws were temporary measures enacted in response to some local or national emergency. Initially, the "emergency" that the courts used to justify rent control was the exigent of economic problems generated by war and its aftermath. The leading United States Supreme Court case on the constitutionality of rent control ordinances was *Block v. Hirsch*, 256 U.S. 135, 156 (1921). In *Block*, Justice Holmes declared that landlord monopoly generated by housing shortages resulting from First World War economic dislocation justified a District of Columbia rent control ordinance:

> The space in Washington is necessarily monopolized in comparatively few hands, and letting portions of it is as much a business as any other. Housing is a necessity of life. All the elements of a public interest justifying some degree of public control are present.

Twenty years later in *Woods v. Cloyd Miller Co.*, 333 U.S. 138 (1948) and *Bowles v. Willingham*, 321 U.S. 502 (1944), the Supreme Court again rejected constitutional challenges to mandatory rent control by finding the statutes to be within the congressional war power. In doing so, the Court was able to find *explicit* constitutional authority to uphold the measures, and, therefore, rent increases could be constitutionally prescribed by Congress as a means to protect the populace from the economic and social pressures created by World War II. Thus, the Court established the precedent of upholding rent control laws as constitutional, if enacted in response to an emergency.

2. *The Second Generation Ordinances: Regulating the Cost of Habitation*

Although the early rent control laws were sustained due to the exigencies of war, it was not until the late 1960s and early 1970s that the first nonemergency rent control measures began to appear. These "second generation" rent control measures were, in most instances, the result of the initiative process and were an attempt by local communities to respond to economic and social changes within their communities. No longer were rent control ordinances tied to a perceived emergency.

Initially, the second generation ordinances were fairly limited in scope. The main focus was on protecting tenants from inflation by freezing rents and permitting increases under narrowly circumscribed conditions. In order for the ordinances to be constitutional, they had to provide the landowner a "fair net operating return." In most cases, this was accomplished not by establishing a "permissible" rent for the unit, but by calculating that amount which would assure the owner a fair return. The rent ceilings were calculated on the assumption that market rents at some previous time were reasonable, and this rate was then used as the starting point. While this formula attempted to equate rents with market forces, and since the baseline rent could be the rent charged at a date much earlier than the date of the ordinance, rents in some instances were actually decreased.

The decision by the California Supreme Court in the following case expresses the modern view on the constitutionality of second generation rent control ordinances.

Birkenfeld v. City of Berkeley

Supreme Court of California
550 P.2d 1001 (1976)

WRIGHT, C. J.

City's Power to Provide for Rent Control by Initiative Amendment to Its Charter

It is contended that the defendant city was barred from imposing rent controls by the conceded absence of any state statute authorizing local legislation on the subject. As will be hereinafter discussed, the regulation of rents is proper only insofar as it is a valid exercise of the police power. The Constitution itself confers upon all cities and counties the power to "make and enforce within [their] limits all local, police, sanitary, and other ordinances and regulations not in conflict with general laws." (Cal. Const., art. XI, §7.) A city's police power under this provision can be applied only within its own territory and is subject to displacement by general state law but otherwise is as broad as the police power exercisable by the Legislature itself.

The decisions cited in support of the contended necessity for statutory authorization of municipal rent control measures are all from other jurisdictions and make clear that the involved cities did not have any broad grant of police power such as that enjoyed by California cities.

Defendant and interveners properly concede that rent control is not a municipal affair as to which a charter provision would prevail over general state law under article XI, section 5 of the Constitution. Accordingly the charter amendment cannot be given effect to the extent that it conflicts with general laws either directly or by entering a field which general laws are intended to occupy to the exclusion of municipal regulation. The fact that the charter amendment prohibits landlords of residential units within the city from charging more than the maximum rents prescribed by a municipal rent control board under specified standards does not bring the amendment into conflict with general state law. California has no state rent control statute. There is of course extensive state legislation governing many aspects of landlord-tenant relationships, some of which pertain specifically to the determination or payment of rent. (*See e.g.*, Civ. Code § 827 (changing rent terms in tenancies of one month or less); Civ. Code § 1935 (apportionment of rent); Civ. Code § 1942 (right to deduct from rent for cost of repairs); Civ. Code § 1942.5 (restricting retaliatory rent increases); Civ. Code § 1947 (when rent is payable); Civ. Code § 1950.5 (advance payments of rent).) But neither the quantity nor the content of these statutes establishes or implies any legislative intent to exclude municipal regulation of the amount of rent based on local conditions. The charter amendment's purpose of preventing exploitation of a housing shortage through excessive rent charges is distinct from the purpose of any state legislation, and the imposition of rent ceilings does not materially interfere with any state legislative purpose. Whether the relevant field be deemed to be rent control as such or a broader aspect of landlord-tenant relations there is no legislative indication of "a paramount state concern [which] will not tolerate further or additional local action."

Regulation of Maximum Residential Rents in Berkeley as an Exercise of the Police Power

We have thus far concluded (1) that in the absence of conflicting or preemptive state law the defendant city's police power within its territorial limits is as broad as the police power exercisable by the Legislature and (2) that general state law does not preclude the defendant city from imposing maximum limits on residential rent within its territory or from restricting the grounds for evicting tenants for the purpose of enforcing those limits insofar as such control of rents and evictions is a proper exercise of the police power. We now consider whether defendant could rightfully exercise its police power in this manner under circumstances established by the record.

Thus, the Second Circuit Court of Appeals, in affirming dismissal of a landlord's action against a rent control official under the Civil Rights Act (42 U.S.C.A. § 1983) stated that "we have no doubt that it [the United States Supreme Court] would sustain the validity of rent control today.... The time when extraordinarily exigent circumstances were required to justify price control outside the traditional public utility areas passed on the day that *Nebbia v. New York*, 291 U.S. 502, 539 (1934), was decided. Whether, as some believe, rent control does not prolong the very condition that gave it birth, is a policy issue not appropriate for judicial concern." *Eisen v. Eastman*, 421 F.2d 560, 567 (2d Cir. 1969). Similarly the New Jersey Supreme Court in sustaining the validity of municipal rent control ordinances recently observed that "rent control is, of course, but one example of the larger and more pervasive phenomenon of governmental regulation of prices under the police power. For constitutional purposes, rent control is indistinguishable from other types of governmental price regulation." *Hutton Park Gardens v. Town Council*, 350 A.2d 1, 7 (N.J. 1975). Accordingly the New Jersey court concluded that the United States Supreme Court's abandonment of the emergency prerequisite for price regulation generally was fully applicable to rent control legislation. The same conclusion was reached by the Maryland Court of Appeals in *Westchester West No. 2 Ltd. Part v. Montgomery County*, 348 A.2d 856 (Md. 1975).

Before the present case California appellate courts have not been called upon to consider the validity of a rent control measure. However, the United States Supreme Court's previously described enlargement of its view of the scope of the police power to regulate prices and its consequent repudiation of any "emergency" prerequisite for price or rent controls find their parallels in our own decisions. It is now settled California law that legislation regulating prices or otherwise restricting contractual or property rights is within the police power if its operative provisions are reasonably related to the accomplishment of a legitimate governmental purpose and that the existence of an emergency is not a prerequisite to such legislation.

It is suggested that the existence of a serious public emergency should be constitutionally required for rent controls because they create uncertainty about returns from capital investment in rental housing and thereby discourage construction or improvement of rental units, exacerbate any rental housing shortage, and so adversely affect the community at large. Such considerations go to the wisdom of rent controls and not to their constitutionality. In determining the validity of a legislative measure under the police power our sole concern is with whether the measure reasonably relates to a legitimate governmental purpose and "[w]e must not confuse reasonableness in this context with wisdom."

We turn then to the question of whether the imposition of any form of residential rent controls for the purposes stated in the present charter amendment is within defendant's police power in that it is reasonably related to the accomplishment of an objective for which the power can be exercised. It has long been settled that the power extends to objectives in furtherance of the public peace, safety, morals, health and welfare and "is not a circumscribed prerogative, but is elastic and, in keeping with the growth of knowledge and the belief in the popular mind of the need for its application, capable of expansion to meet existing conditions of modern life." The charter amendment includes in its stated purposes for imposing rent control the alleviation of the ill effects of the exploitation of a housing shortage by the charging of exorbitant rents to the detriment of the public health and welfare of the city and particularly its underprivileged groups. (§ 1.) The amendment thus states on its face the existence of conditions in the city under which residential rent controls are reasonably related to promotion of the public health and welfare and are therefore within the police power.

However, the constitutionality of residential rent controls under the police power depends upon the actual existence of a housing shortage and its concomitant ill effects of sufficient seriousness to make rent control a rational curative measure. Although the existence of "constitutional facts" upon which the validity of an enactment depends is presumed in the absence of any showing to the contrary, their nonexistence can properly be established by proof.

In the present case the trial court received evidence presented by the parties from which it made findings concerning the existence of facts justifying the rent control provisions of the charter amendment and concluded that the emergency conditions that the court deemed constitutional required for rent control did not exist. As already stated no such emergency was constitutionally required. On this state of the record our task is to review the findings (there being no reporter's transcript) and to sustain the propriety of rent controls under the police power unless the findings establish a complete absence of even a debatable rational basis for the legislative determination by the Berkeley electorate that rent control is a reasonable means of counteracting harms and dangers to the public health and welfare emanating from a housing shortage. In reviewing the findings we also look to the trial court's memorandum opinion as an aid to their interpretation.

Far from dispelling any rational basis for rent control, the findings affirm the existence of housing problems that correspond in kind even if not in degree of gravity with the conditions described in section 1 of the charter amendment. A clause appearing at the outset of the findings on the "emergency" issue states that "whole segments of Berkeley's population suffer from a serious housing shortage."

Notes and Questions

1. In *Birkenfeld,* the California Supreme Court made the following comments on the confiscation issue:

> [T]he charter amendment drastically and unnecessarily restricts the rent control board's power to adjust rents, thereby making inevitable the arbitrary imposition of unreasonably low rent ceilings. It is clear that if the base rent for all controlled units were to remain as the maximum rent for an indefinite period many or most rent ceilings would be or become confiscatory. For such rent ceilings of indefinite duration an adjustment mechanism is constitutionally necessary to provide for changes in circumstances and also provide for previously mentioned situations in which the base rent cannot reasonably be deemed to reflect general market conditions. The mechanism is sufficient for the required purpose only if it is capable of providing adjustments in maximum rents without a substantially greater incidence and degree of delay than is practically necessary. "Property may be as effectively taken by a delay in declaring confiscatory laws unconstitutional as by an express affirmance of them...." *Smith v. Illinois Bell Tel. Co.,* 270 U.S. 587, 591 (1926) ... (enjoining enforcement of telephone rates because of unreasonable delay in acting upon application for rate increase). The charter amendment is constitutionally deficient in that it withholds powers by which the rent control board could adjust maximum rents without unreasonable delays and instead requires the Board to follow an adjustment procedure which would make such delays inevitable.

550 P.2d at 1029–30.

For other cases upholding rent control ordinances against attacks that the ordinances were confiscatory, see *Hutton Park Gardens v. Town Council,* 350 A.2d 1 (N.J. 1975) and *Hirschel v. City of New York,* 460 N.Y.S.2d 438 (Sup. Ct. 1983), the former holding that rent control ordinances are indistinguishable from other types of governmental price regulations and that a governmental price regulation need not be dependent on the existence of an "emergency" nor a determination that the industry regulated is "affected by a public interest" in order to withstand a constitutional challenge on substantive due process grounds. The court went on to say that in the context of price regulations, the question is whether the legislative body could have rationally concluded that restraint of the competitive market was in the public interest. Although historically in the area of rent control this conclusion was drawn from the existence of a serious housing shortage, the court acknowledged that the existence of other circumstances could rationally persuade a legislative body that the free housing market was not functioning in the public interest.

As to the issue that the West Orange and Wayne Township ordinances were confiscatory, the court held that a rent regulation that permits an "economically efficient" operator to obtain a "just and reasonable" return on his investment is not confiscatory. Additionally, the court held that it is not a valid objection to the "just and reasonable" requirement that the regulation may incidentally result in a decrease in the value of the property.

2. Proponents of rent control won a decisive victory—at least in principle—in *Birkenfeld.* Landlord and real estate industry interests were not content with the court's anti-confiscation requirements. Indeed, even before the decision was announced, efforts were underway to preempt the power of local jurisdictions to stabilize rents. According to Comment, Birkenfeld v. City of Berkeley, *Blueprint for Rent Control in California*, 7 Golden Gate L. Rev. 677, 679 n.5 (1977):

> Assembly members Campbell and Dixon of the California Legislature, apparently anticipating the *Birkenfeld* holding, introduced Assembly Bill 3788 on March 16, 1976. The bill was a declaration that the imposition of rent controls on private housing represented a matter of statewide concern; it prohibited local rent control without state authorization. Cal. A.B. 3788, Reg. Sess. 1975–76. The campaign to enact A.B. 3788 was marked by charges of massive spending by lobbyists acting on behalf of the California Housing Council, a group composed of some of California's "most influential apartment house developers, owners and managers...." The bill was passed on August 30, 1976, but was vetoed on Sept. 30, 1976, the day before it would have become effective, by Governor Edmund G. Brown.... Governor Brown claimed that the decision to adopt rent control should be made at the local level.

Following the passage of Proposition 13, which resulted in substantial tax cuts for landlords, there was a surge of support for rent control when it became evident that many landlords were not going to share their windfalls with their tenants. [Note that in *Rue-Ell Enterprises, Inc. v. City of Berkeley*, 194 Cal. Rptr. 919 (Ct. App. 1983), the court upheld an ordinance requiring a one-year reduction in rent increases for *commercial properties* measured by landlord's property tax savings under Proposition 13. (Emphasis added.)—Eds.] The clamor for controls was also fueled by the rise in real estate values and rents. The situation in Los Angeles was typical.

Between 1974 and 1979 single-family dwelling prices in Southern California increased by 185%, while for the nation as a whole, the increase was 80% during the same period. In some areas of Los Angeles, prices increased at the rate of 20% per year. At the same time, the sale prices of rental apartment units escalated sharply. The average sale price of units in buildings with twenty units or less in the City of Los Angeles, comprising about two-thirds of the city's rental stock, increased at a rate in excess of 15% per year from 1975 to 1978. At the same time, the vacancy rate for rental units was descending to the all-time low of under 2%.

Meanwhile rents were increasing at a substantial rate. Increases in rent were not apparently due to increases in operating costs, assuming debt service is not regarded as an operating cost. In most rental units, tenants paid for gas and electricity, which also increased substantially. While tenants' costs were increasing, the average Proposition 13 savings in the second half of 1978 was 57%, and many landlords were obtaining cuts of up to two-thirds of their previous tax bills. A study by the Santa Monica, California, Rent Control Board indicated that average landlord expenses for the period between April 1978 and July 1979 did not appreciably increase. Finally, the same study showed a very high rate of turnover in property ownership.

The situation in Los Angeles suggested a highly speculative market in which tenants were subjected to substantial rent increases far in excess of the cost of owning property. With single-family dwellings averaging well above $100,000, and a race between rent control proponents and apartment owners who wanted to convert to condominiums, the stage was set for heightened struggle in the conflict between owners and renters. As rent control ordinances began to spread from Beverly Hills to other California communities, Los Angeles passed a "Rent Stabilization Ordinance" on March 15, 1979, that was to last until April 30, 1980, but was thereafter extended.

Again landlord interests were not passive. A coalition of large landlords, bankers, and construction trade unions collected over a half million signatures and placed a so-called "Fair Rent Control Standards" article on the June 1980 ballot. Though advertised by its proponents as pro-tenant, even pro-rent control, the initiative would have nullified local rent control ordinances by preemption. The initiative exempted units from rent control when they were voluntarily vacated.

Despite a massive and well financed advertising campaign, the initiative was defeated. In 2006, a statewide California initiative, Proposition 90, would have repealed rent control (and limited the government's right to otherwise regulate private property) but it was narrowly defeated. In June, 2008, California voters overwhelmingly rejected another statewide initiative (Proposition 98) aimed at prohibiting rent control (and limiting the use of eminent domain).

Note that the Berkeley legislation was passed in a city-wide vote, but the defeated 1980 state-wide initiative forced the battle into city councils and county boards. Which strategy seems most likely to assure the most representative outcome and also the ordinance striking the best balance between lessor and lessee interests? For an excellent overview of the successes and failures of rent control ordinances, see Kenneth K. Baar, *Guidelines for Drafting Rent Control Laws: Lessons of a Decade*, 35 RUTGERS L. REV. 723 (1983).

3. The same day that *Hutton Park Gardens*, note 1 *supra*, was decided, the New Jersey Supreme Court also delivered opinions in *Brunetti v. Borough of New Milford*, 350 A.2d 19 (N.J. 1975), and *Troy Hills Village v. Parsippany-Troy Hills Twp. Council*, 350 A.2d 34 (N.J. 1975). The three cases developed the principles governing the facial validity of rent control ordinances, the court having previously determined that municipalities had the power to enact legislation in *Inganamort v. Borough of Fort Lee*, 303 A.2d 298 (N.J. 1973).

Though the power to regulate rents has been unequivocally affirmed, the details of rent control increase formulae remain a troublesome problem for the courts.

4. Rent control has also been attacked as an uncompensated "taking" in violation of the Fifth Amendment of the United States Constitution. But if the ordinance: (a) provides the landowner with a fair rate of return; (b) is neither arbitrary nor unreasonable; and (c) has a substantial relationship to public health, safety, morals, or general welfare, the ordinance is presumptively constitutional and will generally be upheld. Although the landowner may rebut this presumption by demonstrating that the ordinance infringes on a protected liberty or fundamental right, challenges on these grounds have been largely unsuccessful. *See Amberhill v. City of Berkeley*, 814 F.2d 1340 (9th Cir. 1987), holding that the use by the city of its regulatory powers to enact rent control measures could not be challenged before exhaustion of administrative remedies available to assure a fair return; *Gregory v. City of San Juan Capistrano*, 191 Cal. Rptr. 47 (Ct. App. 1983), upholding a rent control ordinance against an uncompensated taking attack where the formula calculating the fair rate of return was based on the actual property value assessed each year, taking into account inflation, capitalization, depreciation, and a number of other relevant economic factors, as well as the "value" of the property; *Santa Monica Beach Ltd. v. Superior Court*, 968 P.2d 993 (Cal. 1999) (alleged failure of rent control law to achieve goal of providing housing for poor, elderly, and young did not make the law invalid as a "taking" because

the law did advance legitimate state interest in preventing excessive and unreasonable rent increases).

Constitutional challenges to rent control ordinances on other grounds have met with varying results. *See Nash v. City of Santa Monica*, 688 P.2d 894 (Cal. 1984), *appeal dismissed*, 470 U.S. 1046 (1985) (dismissed for want of substantial federal question) (the California Supreme Court held that the city could restrict the demolition of rental units under its rent control laws) (legislatively overruled, Ellis Act, Cal. Gov't Code §§ 1760(a),7060.7; *Girard v. Town of Allenstown*, 428 A.2d 488 (N.H. 1981) (the New Hampshire Supreme Court held that locally enacted rent control ordinances were unconstitutional, as only the state legislature had the power to enact such laws). *See City of Santa Monica v. Yarmack*, 249 Cal. Rptr. 732 (Ct. App. 1988); *People v. H & H Properties*, 201 Cal. Rptr. 687 (Ct. App. 1984) (upholding a rent control law requiring relocation benefits be paid to displaced tenants prior to final map approval of a condominium conversion). *But see* Richard A. Epstein, *Rent Control and the Theory of Efficient Regulation*, 54 Brook. L. Rev. 741 (1988); and Jakob S. Harle, Comment, *Challenging Rent Control: Strategies for Attack*, 34 UCLA L. Rev. 149 (1986) (presenting a number of possible constitutional attacks to rent control, including challenges based on infringement on the right to travel, as violative of antitrust laws, and as an uncompensated taking).

5. After *Birkenfeld*, one of the major decisions considering fair rate of return was *Helmsley v. Borough of Fort Lee*, 394 A.2d 65 (N.J. 1978). The court held that the portion of a rent control ordinance that limited annual increases to 2.5% was unconstitutional, as the inadequacy of automatic increases, coupled with the Rent Leveling Board's inability to change base rents, made the ordinance confiscatory. The court concluded its opinion with the following observation:

> We have refrained deliberately from formulating a numerical test for confiscation. The concept of a minimum constitutional return is a theoretical tool, not a measurable quantity which can be fixed with precision. Judicial review of rent control measures is limited to determining whether the return permitted by an ordinance falls above or below this theoretical dividing point....
>
> Rent control implicates complex economic, social, and political issues. The state legislature is better equipped than most municipalities to formulate a comprehensive approach to this delicate problem....

Id. at 86.

The first paragraph throws the rent control back into the court of local jurisdiction. In view of the court's apparent facility with the mathematics of a fair rate of return, should it have attempted a formula? Is any possible? In the second paragraph, the court perhaps suggests some lack of confidence in local jurisdictions, though the suggestion is phrased in terms of a comprehensive approach. What are the values of a comprehensive approach? Are statewide bureaucracies likely to be sensitive to local economic conditions? Are local bodies likely to consistently have available the expertise to frame legislation to meet the court's anti-confiscation strictures? Does the following passage from the court's opinion disadvantage citizens of smaller communities:

> The foregoing analysis should make it clear that a municipality can constitutionally enact rent control ordinances with stringent controls like Fort Lee's. If it does so, however, it must be prepared to protect landlords' interests by providing prompt, fair, and efficacious administrative relief. Conversely, if a municipality is not prepared to support a sophisticated administrative relief system, it must adopt a more moderate rent control scheme, one which does not attempt to keep

> landlords' returns at the constitutional minimum. Obviously, such a scheme must at least be calculated to cover reasonable increases in landlord's operating costs without lengthy administrative proceedings.

Id. at 85.

In light of the decisions in *Birkenfeld* and *Helmsley*, consider the following questions: Is the ultimate fair rate of return that which will permit the landlord to remain in operation? Is this really a complex of economic, social, and psychological factors that defies measurement? Is the real test whether the landlord continues to own (or sells) the buildings? What if the high rate of return results in rents out of reach of the immediate tenants? *See Kirkpatrick v. City of Oceanside*, 283 Cal. Rptr. 191 (Ct. App. 1991) (whether a 2% rate of return is confiscatory presents a factual issue that cannot be resolved at the pleading stage of litigation).

6. Like many other states, California and Florida have both enacted statutes which protect mobile home park lessees from arbitrary eviction. *See* Cal. Civ. Code §§798.55–798.59; Fla. Stat. Ann. §§723.032, .061, .0615. The constitutionality of the prior Florida statute was upheld in *Stewart v. Green*, 300 So. 2d 889 (Fla. 1974). More than 100 California localities have enacted mobile home rent control.

One federal appellate court concluded that rent control for mobile home parks may present unique constitutional problems. *Hall v. City of Santa Barbara*, 813 F.2d 198 (9th Cir. 1987), *cert. denied*, 485 U.S. 940 (1988). In *Hall*, the plaintiffs alleged that state and local laws combined to give tenants the right to sell their mobile homes *with* the right to occupy the space on which the mobile home is located. Among other problems, plaintiffs claimed that tenants, rather than landlords, were being allowed to recognize a substantial profit, due to the artificially low space rent, by charging inflated prices for the space at time of sale.

Hall's innovation was to conclude that the rent control scheme might be unconstitutional because it transferred a marketable, possessory right from the landlords to the tenants without just compensation. The court used this alleged "transfer" to take the case out of the regulatory takings framework developed by the Supreme Court, and into that of "physical occupation." Thus, the *Hall* court concluded that the mobile home owners stated a valid claim even if they could not claim denial of a "fair rate of return." In support of the holding in *Hall*, see Werner Z. Hirsch & Joel G. Hirsch, *Legal—Economic Analysis of Rent Controls in a Mobile Home Context: Placement Values and Vacancy Controls*, 35 UCLA L. Rev. 399 (1988).

The *Hall* decision, however, was sharply criticized. *See Hall v. City of Santa Barbara*, 813 F.2d at 209 (Schroeder, J., dissenting from the denial of *en banc* hearing); Mary E. McAlister, Note, Hall v. City of Santa Barbara: *A New Look at California Rent Controls and the Taking Clause*, 17 Ecology L. Q. 179 (1990); Note, *The Constitutionality of Rent Control Restrictions on Property Owners' Dominion Interests*, 100 Harv. L. Rev. 1067 (1987). Eventually, the arguments made in *Hall* came before the Supreme Court and were rejected, for the most part. *Yee v. Escondido*, 503 U.S. 519 (1992). Although the Court did not address the regulatory takings or substantive due process claims, the idea that the regulatory "wealth transfer" could be a physical invasion or taking was rejected. The park owner argued that the rent control and limitations on evictions amounted to a "physical occupation" of the property and was thus a *per se* taking. The Court held that in the mobile home park context did not amount to a taking because the park owner voluntarily rented the property. The Court noted that the case would be different if the owner were compelled to rent or was forced to refrain in perpetuity from terminating a tenancy. The

Court noted the unique features of mobile home parks, acknowledging that "mobile" homes are in reality largely immobile (because of the cost of moving the home compared to the value of the home). *See* Kenneth K. Baar, *The Right to Sell the "Im"mobile Manufactured Home in Its Rent Controlled Space in the "Im"mobile Home Park: Valid Regulation or Unconstitutional Taking?* 24 Urb. Law. 157 (1992).

For argument that *Lingle v. Chevron, U.S.A., Inc.*, 544 U.S. 528 (2005), concerning the test for a regulatory taking *(infra)* can be invoked to find rent regulations unconstitutional, see Christina McDonough, *Rent Control and Rent Stabilization as Forms of Regulatory and Physical Takings*, 34 B.C. Envtl. Aff. L. Rev. 361 (2007). A challenge made originally under the *Agins* [*Agins v. Tiburon*, 447 U.S. 255 (1980)] test rejected in *Lingle* nevertheless succeeded under a *Penn Central* test analysis in *MHC Financing v. City of San Rafael*, 2008 WL 440282 (N.D. Cal. 2008). The city's mobile home rent control ordinance, as amended, limited annual rent increases for the space ("pad") to 75% of the annual CPI (Consumer Price Index) and also regulated vacancy rent increases. According to the park owner's expert witness, this created a "resale premium" favoring the mobile home owner/tenant who sold that reduced the market value of the 396-pad park from $140 million to only $23 million. The trial court held in favor of the owner in all three factors of the *Penn Central* test for a regulatory taking. *Penn Central Transportation Co. v. City of New York*, 438 U.S. 104 (1978).

This decision was reinforced in 2009 when a divided Ninth Circuit panel found that another California mobile home rent control ordinance also amounted to a regulatory taking under *Penn Central. Guggenheim v. Goleta*, 582 F.3d 996 (9th Cir. 2009), reh'g en banc granted, 598 F.3d 1061 (9th Cir. 2010), reversing the trial judge's decision. The majority found that a facial challenge to the ordinance (following a refiling after the *Lingle* decision undercut the basis of a ruling in favor of the owners) was viable and relied upon the park owners' expert's testimony that the "transfer premium" forced the owners to rent at close to an 80 percent discount below the market rate. The dissenting judge argued that these owners purchased a decade after the ordinance was enacted and the purchase price reflected any devaluation, thus not denying them their "investment-back expectations." The court was divided in its interpretation of the meaning of *Palazzolo v. Rhode Island*, 533 U.S. 606 (2001) as to whether notice of the below-market value of a rent-controlled mobile home park precluded a finding of a regulatory taking.

Should the U.S. Supreme Court review a mobile home rent control challenge under the three-part *Penn Central* test, these two decisions suggest that whether as-applied or facial, property owners may find a more favorable reception given their unique relationship to their tenants, who own their not so mobile homes.

In *Hacienda Valley Mobile Estates v. City of Morgan Hill*, 353 F.3d 651 (9th Cir. 2003), the Ninth Circuit ruled that the mobile home park owner failed to exhaust its state remedy and therefore failed the federal "ripeness" test. *See* also *Carson Harbor Village v. City of Carson*, 353 F.3d 824 (2004). In *Equity Lifestyle v. County of San Luis Obispo*, 548 F.3d 1184 (9th Cir. 2008), the Ninth Circuit rejected constitutional claims of violation of due process, equal protection and takings.

7. An additional measure giving tenants security of tenure has emerged along with rent control—just cause eviction. Though not nearly as widespread as rent control, this development must be seen as a logical consequence of rent control legislation, some of which has effectual just cause eviction protection. In most instances, the just cause eviction requirements in rent control ordinances are patterned after regulations prohibiting retaliatory evictions in privately owned government-subsidized housing. To compare the

regulations governing retaliatory evictions, see comments following *Edwards v. Habib*, *supra*, and *Joy v. Daniels* and accompanying text, *infra*. Security of tenure has also been part of British law for some time.

In Santa Monica, California, the rent control law forbids removal of a unit from the rental market unless the rent control board has found that the unit is not occupied by a person of low and moderate income, that it is not affordable by such a person, and that its removal will not adversely affect the supply of housing in the city.

Perhaps it will come as no surprise that New Jersey has an eviction for cause statute, described as "good cause." N.J. STAT. ANN. §2A:18-61.1. The statute enumerates a number of grounds for "good cause" eviction, including a failure to pay rent, destruction of the premises, and a desire on the part of the landlord to retire the dwelling unit from residential use. The landlord may also evict to convert the dwelling unit to a cooperative or condominium. Finally, the landlord may evict to remove health and safety violations affecting the tenants, if compliance without removal is infeasible. How much tenant protection does this statute afford? In the absence of a provision in a "just cause" eviction statute allowing eviction to carry out rehabilitation, one court has disallowed eviction for this reason. *Mayo v. Boston Rent Control Adm'r*, 314 N.E.2d 118 (Mass. 1974), noted, 11 URB. L. ANN. 319 (1976).

Although California and New Jersey are leaders in the advocacy of tenant protections, California failed to enact legislation similar to the New Jersey just cause eviction statute when the proposed legislation died in committee. Moreover, as noted earlier, California has now backtracked on the tenant-oriented thrust because of state-mandated vacancy decontrol enacted in 1995.

Would a "good cause eviction statute, if passed, stand the test of *Birkenfeld*? How might its statement of purpose read? *Cf. Sabato v. Sabato*, 342 A.2d 886 (N.J. Super. Ct. Law Div. 1975).

3. Rent Control: Due Process and Equal Protection

The Supreme Court in *Nebbia v. New York*, 291 U.S. 502 (1934), held that legislative ordinances regulating prices are subject to the same narrow scope of review under substantive due process as ordinances enacted under the police power. This scope of review is rational basis scrutiny. If the legislative body could have rationally concluded that the ordinance would serve the public interest without being arbitrary or discriminatory, then the court will uphold the ordinance.

In the area of rent control, the test as applied means that an ordinance regulating or limiting the use of real property for the public welfare does not violate due process provided the ordinance is reasonably related to the accomplishment of a legitimate government interest, and has a substantial relationship to public health, safety, general welfare, or morals.

The Supreme Court justified the notion that restrictions on the use of property are permissible in *Marsh v. Alabama*, 326 U.S. 501 (1946). In *Marsh* the Court stated that "ownership does not mean absolute dominion.... The more an owner, for his advantage, opens up his property for use by the public in general, the more do his rights become circumscribed by the statutory and constitutional rights of those who use it." *Id.* at 506. However, as rent control ordinances become more comprehensive in scope and begin to overly restrict a landowner's "dominion interests," it is possible that the traditional due process tests may no longer be valid. "Dominion rights" can be defined as a property interest premised on the right of the landowner to control the use of his property. *See* Note, *The Constitutionality of Rent Control Restrictions on Property Owner's Dominion Rights*, 100 HARV. L. REV. 1067 (1987).

Because housing shortages continue to be a national problem, the courts see rent control as a rationally related means to achieving the legitimate ends of arresting the depletion of housing stock and preventing the rapid escalation of rents. Although courts give great weight to the legislative determination that a housing shortage exists, this determination alone is not formally controlling. As the court said in *Birkenfeld v. City of Berkeley*, 550 P.2d 1001, 1024 (Cal. 1976):

> [O]ur task is to review the findings ... and to sustain the propriety of rent control under the police power unless the findings establish a complete absence of even a debatable rational basis for the legislative determination by the Berkeley electorate that rent control is a reasonable means of counteracting harms and dangers to the public health and welfare emanating from a housing shortage.

Constitutional challenges by landlords based on facial claims of violation of due process and equal protection have not generally fared well. For example, the U.S. Supreme Court rejected such claims in *Pennell v. City of San Jose*, 485 U.S. 1 (1988). This case also involved a claim of a regulatory taking because the city rent control ordinance allowed hearing officers to take tenant hardship into account if tenants objected to rent increases above the automatic level of eight percent.

Notes and Questions

1. Although the holding in *Pennell* appears to foreclose challenges to rent control based on the claims of "economic unfairness" or that rent control "forces private individuals to shoulder the public burden of subsidizing poor tenants," the opinion states that it was "premature" to consider the contention that rent control is an uncompensated taking. In *Pennell*, there was no evidence that the ordinance had been relied upon to reduce rent, or that the hearing officer was, in fact, "required" to reduce a proposed increase on the grounds of tenant hardship.

2. It is interesting to note that the holding in *Pennell* seems to contradict a Supreme Court decision of the 1987 term which recognized the "dominion rights" of the landowner. *See Nollan v. California Coastal Commission*, 483 U.S. 825 (1987) (conditioning a building permit on granting of a public easement was not a valid regulation of land use but an out-and-out plan of extortion, the condition would be lawful land-use regulation only if it *substantially* furthered a governmental purpose that would justify the denial of the permit); and *Loretto v. Teleprompter Manhattan CATV Corp.*, 458 U.S. 419 (1982) (holding that any government action that results in a "permanent physical occupation" is a taking regardless of the relative public benefit received or the minimal economic impact on the owner), compare *First Evangelical Lutheran Church of Glendale v. County of Los Angeles*, 482 U.S. 304 (1987) (a temporary regulatory taking that denies a landowner of all use of his property is not different in kind from a permanent taking and therefore requires compensation be paid to the landowner for the duration of the taking). Cf. *Yee v. Escondido*, discussed *supra*. For a discussion of an important New York decision employing the dominion rights theory in another context, see Suzanne K. Sleep, Comment, *Stonewalled by Seawall; New York Decision Imperils Legislative Solutions to Affordable Housing Shortage*, 45 U. MIAMI L. REV. 467 (1990–1991). *See also Dolan v. City of Tigard*, 512 U.S. 374 (1994).

Also, some state court decisions were resolved differently than *Pennell. See Hirschel v. City of New York*, 460 N.Y.S.2d 438 (Sup. Ct. 1983) (a statute enacting a rent freeze for senior citizens with annual incomes under $5,000 was confiscatory because tax abatements to landlords would not always offset the losses resulting in the landlords "subsidizing" the rent of some tenants without compensation), and *Property Owners Association v. Township of North Bergen*, 378 A.2d 25 (N.J. 1977) (invalidating an ordinance limiting rent increases greater than the annual 8% adjustment for senior citizens based on a "tenant hardship" provision). *See* Daniel M. Zupanec, Annotation, *Validity and Construction of Statute or Ordinance Establishing Rent Control Benefit or Rent Subsidy for Elderly Tenants*, 5 A.L.R. 4th 922 (1981).

3. The *Pennell* holding reasserts the Court's traditional view of regulations affecting purely "economic" interests of the landowner. If the regulation provides a "reasonable return" it will be upheld. *See Penn Central Transportation Co. v. City of New York*, 438 U.S. 104 (1978) (although landmark preservation law prevented owner from realizing a maximum profit, it was not a taking because it did not interfere with the owner's primary "investment-backed expectations" and did not prevent a reasonable return); *Village of Euclid v. Ambler Realty*, 272 U.S. 365 (1926) (holding that a change in zoning that resulted in losses of 75% of the value of the land was not unconstitutional as the rezoning was neither arbitrary nor discriminatory); *Hadecheck v. Sebastian*, 239 U.S. 394 (1915) (a land use regulation enacted for the health and safety of the community was not unconstitutional as a taking even though it resulted in a 90% reduction in the value of the petitioner's land). *See also MacCloud v. County of Santa Clara*, 749 F.2d 541 (9th Cir.), *cert. denied*, 472 U.S. 1009 (1985) (denial of the most profitable use of land is not a taking); *HFH Ltd. v. Superior Court*, 542 P.2d 237 (Cal. 1975) (mere reduction of market value as a result of a zoning action is not an uncompensated taking.) The United States Supreme Court has upheld this analysis. *Agins v. Tiburon*, 447 U.S. 255 (1980) (upholding open-space land zoning ordinances, which restricted five-acre tract of land to single-family residences and open-space use but did not prevent the best use of the land or extinguish a fundamental attribute of ownership). In *Lingle v. Chevron, U.S.A., Inc.*, 544 U.S. 528 (2005), the United States Supreme Court held that the "substantially advances" *Agins* test does not apply to regulatory takings,

4. But the "regulatory takings" problem when there is no "physical entry" has defied easy resolution. The Court has made clear, however, that when all economic value is destroyed by the state's regulatory act, a compensable taking under the Fifth Amendment to the Constitution of the United States has occurred. *Lucas v. South Carolina Coastal Council*, 505 U.S. 1003 (1992). What the "Takings Clause" applies to short of complete value destruction is not clear. The *Lucas* approach and its result on the facts have been critiqued unfavorably. *See* William W. Fisher III, *The Trouble with* Lucas, 45 STAN. L. REV. 1393 (1993) (arguing that Justice Scalia's *Lucas* analysis diverges from the originalist theory he purports to espouse in other contexts); John A. Humbach, *"Taking" the Imperial Judiciary Seriously: Segmenting Property Interests and Judicial Revision of Legislative Judgements*, 42 CATH U. L. REV. 771 (1993) (arguing that the Court's interpretation of the "Takings Clause" in cases like *Lucas* is, *inter alia*, inconsistent with the intentions of the of the Framers of the Constitution); William Michael Treanor, *The Original Understanding of the Takings Clause and the Political Process*, 95 COLUM. L. REV. 782 (1995); Donald H. Zeigler, *The New Activist Court*, 45 AM. U. L. REV. 1367 (1996) (ascribing the case to an "activist" view);

5. But the compensation objective has it proponents. *See e.g.* Richard A. Epstein, Lucas v. South Carolina Coastal Council: *A Tangled Web of Expectations*, 45 STAN. L. REV. 1369 (1993) (supporting compensation for takings apparently short of all value).

6. For a criticism of rent control as counterproductive to its stated goal of providing "adequate housing at a reasonable price," see Werner Z. Hirsch, *From "Food for Thought" to "Empirical Evidence" About Consequences of Landlord-Tenant Laws*, 69 CORNELL L. REV. 604, 609–11 (1984) (asserting that governmental interference with the operation of the market often results in conditions contrary to the original purpose and thereby aggravates the very condition the legislation was designed to alleviate. In fact, a number of economists have criticized rent control regulations on the grounds that they actually restrict, rather than expand, the supply of affordable rental housing). Courts have rejected such arguments as calling into question the wisdom, but not the constitutionality, of rent control. *See e.g., Schnuck v. City of Santa Monica*, 935 F.2d 171 (9th Cir. 1991).

7. Rent control continues to be the target of challenges. *See Rue-Ell Enterprises Inc. v. City of Berkeley*, 194 Cal. Rptr. 919 (Ct. App. 1983) (upholding an ordinance requiring a one-year reduction in rent increases for commercial properties measured by landlord's property tax savings under Proposition 13); *McHugh v. Santa Monica Rent Control Board*, 261 Cal. Rptr. 318 (Cal. 1991) (invalidating rent control agency's power to award treble damages); *Rent Stabilization Ass'n v. Higgins*, 630 N.E.2d 626 (N.Y. 1993) (upholding rent control administrative agency's extension of protection against eviction to larger class of family members). Though thus far surviving many constitutional challenges, rent control legislation has also been assailed, unsuccessfully as violative of the Sherman Act strictures prohibiting monopolies. *See Fisher v. City of Berkeley*, 575 U.S. 460 (1986).

8. For an excellent overview of the successes and failures of rent control ordinances, see Kenneth K. Baar, *Guidelines for Drafting Rent Control Laws: Lessons of a Decade*, 35 RUTGERS L. REV. 723 (1983).

c. *Multiple Dwelling Foreclosures*

An emerging source of concern is the foreclosure of apartment building with the resultant loss of habitation for non-mortgagee party tenants.

Vicki Been and Allegra Glashausser, Tenants: Innocent Victims of the Nation's Foreclosure Crisis

2 Albany Government Law Review 1 (2009)

Renters are innocent victims of the foreclosure crisis, losing their homes through no fault of their own when their landlord goes into foreclosure. Until lately, the national discussion on the foreclosure crisis largely focused on owner-occupied homes, but recent analysis reveals that the crisis is significantly impacting renters across the country. New York University's Furman Center for Real Estate and Urban Policy found that in New York City, well over half of all foreclosure filings in 2007 were on two to four family or multi-family buildings, and a growing body of data and anecdotal evidence indicates that the problem is not isolated to New York City; heart wrenching stories of renters losing their homes have appeared in newspapers nationwide. These renters often are completely unaware that their landlords are in default until utilities are shut off or an eviction notice appears on their door. Frequently, they lose not just their homes, but also their security deposits. Finding a new rental on short notice is often difficult, especially for low-income tenants who face increasing competition for fewer affordable apartments on the market. In the majority of states, purchasers at foreclosure sales are entirely within their rights to evict all existing tenants, but even when renters have the right to stay in their homes after foreclosure—when the tenant holds a Section 8 voucher, for example—they are frequently intimidated or improperly lured out of their homes with offers of "cash for keys." In addition, rental fraud has developed where landlords who know foreclosure is imminent, or non-owners posing as landlords, collect renters' money, then disappear. The actual owners can then evict the fraud victims.

A handful of states already protect tenants from foreclosure-related evictions by requiring a "just cause" for eviction, such as non-payment of rent. Around the country, local governments are debating stronger tenant protection laws to deal with the growing rental foreclosure crisis. These proposals include increased notice requirements, financial aid for moving expenses, and prohibitions against utility shut-offs.

This article aims to help inform the debate over these proposals. The first section reveals the scope of the crisis by describing what the available data tells us about the impact of foreclosures on renters and rental housing. The second section presents an overview of the rights tenants have when their landlord is foreclosed. It uses New York as an example, but highlights laws in other states that offer stronger tenant protection. The third section analyzes the debates taking place in state and local governments across the country, and reaches beyond the plight of the individual tenants to discuss the impact landlord foreclosure may have on the availability and quality of rental housing.

The displacement of renters due to foreclosure is not limited to a few heartrending tales scattered around the country. On the contrary, data demonstrates that the problem is widespread. In New York City, NYU's Furman Center for Real Estate and Urban Policy found that nearly 60% of the 15,000 notices of foreclosure filed in 2007 were on two to four family or multi-family buildings. Using a conservative estimate (assuming that an owner lives in one of the units in all two to four family buildings), the Center estimated that 15,000 renter households, or about 38,000 New Yorkers, were impacted by foreclosure.

Studies across the nation are uncovering similar trends. The Joint Center for Housing Studies of Harvard University found that in 2007, 20% of all foreclosure filings across the country were in non-owner occupied properties. The National Low Income Housing Coalition estimates that one third of all properties facing foreclosure across New England are in multi-unit buildings, and 45% of homes at the end of the foreclosure process in four New England states are rentals. In Chicago, the Woodstock Institute found that 35% of foreclosure filings were on two to six unit buildings, and other researchers are finding similar results in counties in Michigan, Minnesota, and North Carolina.

The scale of the foreclosure crisis is likely even greater for renters than these numbers indicate because of the emergence of new types of rental fraud. One type of fraud involves owners in default on their mortgage payments who know that their properties will soon enter foreclosure. The owners lease the properties out to unsuspecting renters, collect security deposits and rent, and disappear when the foreclosure process formally begins. Another fraud scheme involves individuals posing as landlords, and renting properties (often left vacant due to foreclosure) that they do not own. In this scam, the purported landlord collects security deposits and the first month's rent from tenants, even though the purported landlords have no legal possession of the property. When the real owner of the property (the mortgage holder or person who purchased the property at the foreclosure auction or from the bank's inventory) discovers the fraud, the tenants are evicted.

Tenants in rental housing that is foreclosed upon face the costs and disruption of having to find a new apartment and move, often with little notice, and are unlikely to be able to recover their security deposits. Even tenants who are legally protected from foreclosure-related eviction are at risk of losing their homes. Many tenants are unaware of their rights, so incentives such as "cash for keys" are attractive. "Cash for keys" is industry parlance for the practice some lenders who have acquired the property through foreclosure (or people who have purchased the property at a foreclosure auction or at another point in the foreclosure process) have of offering tenants money to vacate the home and drop any claims to possession. Generally, the new owner tells the tenant that if the tenant does not take advantage of the offer quickly (often within a week), they will still be evicted, but without any compensation. New owners have significant success in removing even tenants protected by federal or state laws....

Foreclosure laws do not generally mention renters. It is unsurprising, therefore, that tenants' rights in the foreclosure process usually are limited. Foreclosure laws vary state by state, but the effect of foreclosure on tenants is not significantly impacted by the state's theory of mortgages or the specifics of the state's foreclosure procedures. Therefore, rather than do an exhaustive fifty state survey, this section first will describe tenants' rights generally, using New York State law as an example, then will highlight a few states that have stronger tenant protections.

A. Tenants' Rights in Foreclosure: An Overview

To understand tenants' rights when their landlord's property is foreclosed upon, it is not necessary to have a detailed understanding of mortgage law, but a basic overview is helpful. In New York, as well as the majority of states, the mortgage creates a lien on the property that provides security for the debt. The borrower (the "mortgagor") grants a mortgage to the lender (the "mortgagee"), which gives the lender the right to force a sale of the property if the debt is not repaid. If the borrower defaults on the debt by failing to make scheduled mortgage payments, the lender may not take the property immediately. The lender must bring a foreclosure action, which is a legal proceeding to terminate the borrower's right to the property.

There are two main types of foreclosure: judicial foreclosure and non-judicial foreclosure. Judicial foreclosure in New York first requires the lender to serve the owner with notice that the lender has begun a legal action to force a sale of the property. The lender must file a notice of pendency (generally known as a lis pendens) with the county clerk, which provides constructive notice to the general public of the suit. Next, there is a judicial hearing to obtain a "judgment of sale," which, if the foreclosing lender prevails, directs the county sheriff, or other designated individual, to sell the property.

Non-judicial foreclosure is generally faster than judicial foreclosure, but, in New York, is permitted only in limited circumstances for residential buildings. For non-judicial foreclosure, the lender must publish a notice of sale in a local newspaper and serve a copy on the mortgagor, describing the property, mortgage, sum due, and time and place of the sale. The sale is then conducted at a public auction.

Under either judicial or non-judicial foreclosure, proceeds from the sale are applied to repayment of the debt secured by the foreclosed mortgage (after payment of any outstanding superior liens, such as property taxes), with any surplus paid to the homeowner. The foreclosing lender will acquire the property if there are no bids in excess of the amount set by the lender. Both types of foreclosures provide an opportunity for a defaulting mortgagor to pay off the remainder of the debt before the sale and maintain ownership of the property, which is called the "right of redemption." If borrowers do not exercise their right of redemption, all their rights to the property are extinguished by the foreclosure sale. When the defaulting mortgagor is a landlord, and that landlord fails to exercise the right of redemption and loses the property, tenants are at risk of having their leases terminated. Once leases are terminated, the purchaser has the option to evict the tenants.

Although the time required to complete foreclosure varies by state, judicial foreclosure generally entails a longer process. While non-judicial foreclosure ranges from three to eight months, judicial foreclosure generally takes over a year (for example, New York City judicial foreclosure typically lasts eighteen months).

Tenants' statutory rights in this process can be viewed at three points: (i) as of the signing of the lease (because the timing of the lease determines its priority compared to the mortgage), (ii) during the foreclosure process (when tenants have the right to be joined in a judicial foreclosure proceeding), and (iii) between the beginning of foreclosure and the time the tenant moves out (when tenants may have rights regarding notice of the foreclosure or before eviction)....

III. Mitigating Foreclosure's Impact on Tenants: Analysis of Local Proposals

Many state and local governments are debating proposals to shelter renters from the worst consequences of the foreclosure crisis. The next subsection assesses those proposals. But the fact that such proposals are seen as necessary raises questions about why tenants are being forced out of foreclosed properties, rather than being allowed to stay. Subsection B addresses that question.

A. Proposals to Increase the Protections Available to Tenants Whose Landlords Are Foreclosed

Some proposals seek to mitigate the impacts of the crisis with increased funding for outreach, and pro bono services to better inform tenants of the rights they already have, advise them about what they can do to protect themselves if their property enters foreclosure, and warn them against fraud by landlords or people posing as landlords. Others aim to enact laws that provide tenants more time to prepare for eviction by requiring notice to the tenant that the foreclosure process has started. Still others involve plans to mitigate post-foreclosure impacts on tenants that range from including emergency rental and moving assistance for tenants suddenly forced out of their homes to expunging foreclosure evictions from tenants' rental records.

States also are debating how best to prevent utility shut-offs and maintenance decline during foreclosure proceedings. Landlords in default often stop making utility payments, leaving renters without electricity, water or sewer service before the foreclosure is complete. Massachusetts already requires utility companies to notify tenants before shutting off utilities provided by the landlord. But because utility companies often lack information on which properties are not owner-occupied, shut downs still occur. Legislation pending in Rhode Island would require all foreclosure sale purchasers of properties with existing tenants to continue providing "essential services," including heat and water utility services. California debated requiring utility companies to notify tenants if their landlords were behind in payment, but Governor Schwarzenegger recently vetoed the legislation. That bill also would have addressed another harsh consequence of foreclosure for tenants: loss of the security deposit. Although the original landlords are required to return security deposits, tenants are often unaware of this right or are unable to locate their landlord, and have trouble recovering deposits after foreclosure. The California bill would have protected tenants from loss of security deposits by making new owners jointly and severely liable for the repayment. Finally, of course, existing "just cause" laws provide a model for states seeking to prevent eviction. A pending bill in Massachusetts, for example, would prohibit foreclosure as a cause for eviction, stating that "just cause" must be present in order to evict.

New tenant protections may bring unintended consequences. It is important, therefore, that this debate look beyond the individual tenants, and also consider how tenant protection laws might impact the availability and quality of rental housing more broadly. Municipalities considering whether to enact increased tenant protections should evaluate potential long-term consequences and be careful to avoid unintended negative impacts. The debated tenant protection proposals are clearly tenant-friendly, and they likely would provide some relief for individuals facing eviction after their landlord is foreclosed. There is also a possibility, however, that these proposals could negatively affect renters more broadly by driving up the cost of borrowing (and, as a result, driving up the rent), or by making renting more difficult. For example, if "just cause" eviction is required and foreclosure sale purchasers are responsible for continuing all prior lease agreements, buying a property at foreclosure could become (or be perceived as) more costly.

Frequently, buyers at foreclosure sales are the lenders themselves who are generally banks that lack the desire or expertise to serve as landlords. If foreclosure becomes more costly for the lending banks, those banks may be less likely to lend money to potential landlords, which would drive up the cost of borrowing, and consequently, increase the rent the landlord charges. Alternatively, the lenders could begin to prohibit the borrower from renting. Increased borrowing costs or anti-renting provisions could lead to a reduction in available rental housing. This would be especially problematic for low-income tenants in need of affordable housing.

New protections also could increase non-financing costs for landlords, which could similarly reduce the stock of affordable rental housing. If states adopt new eviction protections analogous to current "just cause" provisions (requiring "just cause" for any eviction, as opposed to adopting laws that only prohibit eviction due to foreclosure), it will become trickier for current landlords to evict tenants for a variety of reasons unrelated to foreclosure. Landlords may then be less inclined to rent, or require greater background checks, security deposits or qualifying incomes. This would likely disproportionately affect potential tenants who are low income, have bad credit, or any other characteristics the landlord considered risky. If eviction is more difficult or costly, landlords may fear renting to tenants they perceive as risky, which will reduce the options of renters searching for affordable housing.

Although these concerns are strongest for proposals that adopt "just cause" eviction statutes, they also are present for proposals increasing or requiring notice. Notice requirements provide tenants with greater opportunity to object throughout the foreclosure process, which could slow down foreclosure and thereby increase costs for foreclosing mortgagees. Landlords currently are able to convince tenants (even those who are protected by anti-eviction laws) to vacate through "cash for keys" or intimidation schemes. Notice to these tenants would allow them to become informed about their rights and to resist a landlord's pressure to vacate. Also, notice would allow them to insist that landlords go through the formal eviction processes, which would give the tenants an opportunity to raise defenses and cause delays. Increased time and cost of foreclosure could drive up the costs of borrowing, again reducing the supply, and raising the price, of affordable rentals. While these effects are uncertain, it is important for lawmakers to consider long term results so they don't negatively affect the same population they are aiming to protect....

Conclusion

Good tenants are innocent victims of the nation's foreclosure crisis. They do not have mortgages, they pay their rent on time, and think they have no reason to fear foreclosure. Then an eviction notice or "for sale" sign appears on their property and the foreclosure crisis ensnares them. In a handful of states, and in rent-regulated or Section 8 housing, "just cause" protects tenants from eviction. But in the vast majority of situations, tenants have no defense if their property is sold at a foreclosure sale and the new owner brings an eviction proceeding against them. These tenants must find new homes in an often increasingly competitive rental market, while their old homes often stay vacant, contributing to neighborhood decline.

As the significant impact the foreclosure crisis is having on tenants becomes clearer, state and local governments are debating how to mitigate the burden on renters. Proposals range from new "just cause" laws and prohibitions against utility shut-offs to notice requirements and moving assistance. The effect these new laws will have on the availability and quality of rental housing in the future is uncertain, as are the motivations of purchasers to continue evictions. Legislators should be mindful of the uncertainties, and consider the economic effects of proposed tenant protections on lenders and landlords in the public debate. In the end, it may be most effective for legislators to shift their focus towards working with lenders, banks, or other new owners to create incentives not to evict current tenants.

Notes and Questions

1. Many commentators speculate that the impact of the nation's foreclosure crisis is in its infancy. Most recently, evidence of the crisis can be found in the default of Tishman Speyer and BlackRock Realty on $4.4 billion in loans used to purchase the largest apartment complexes in Manhattan: Stuyvesant Town and Peter Cooper Village. While this record-breaking deal serves as the poster child for the entire housing bubble, what will happen to the tenants of the property's more than 11,000 apartments? Charles Bagli & Christine Haughney, *Wide Fallout in the Failed Deal for Stuyvesant Town*. N.Y. Times, Jan. 26, 2010.

2. Cook County Sheriff stopped evicting residents from foreclosed properties because an increasing number of tenants being evicted had been paying their rent, and many had no knowledge that their landlord was behind on the mortgage. Following the suspension, Chicago enacted a new law providing tenants' a 90-day grace period, starting from the time a foreclosure sale is confirmed, before they can be evicted. John Leland, *Sheriff in Chicago Ends Evictions in Foreclosures*. N.Y. Times, Oct. 8, 2008.

3. If rent control poses a risk of housing shortages, could there be other values advanced that justify the risk? The debate continues between the foes of rent control who condemn it as inefficient and a new generation of commentators who believe that rent control can preserve community values. *See* William H. Simon, *Social-Republic Property,* 38 UCLA L. Rev. 1355 (1991). *Cf.* Robert C. Ellickson, *Rent Control: A Comment on Olsen*, 67 Chi-Kent L. Rev. 947 (1991); Edgar O. Olsen, *Is Rent Control Good Social Policy,* 67 Chi-Kent L. Rev. 931 (1991). One commentator believes that rent control not only preserves important community values, but that in the unique situation of gentrification the dire predictions of economists are not borne out. Note, *Reassessing Rent Control: Its Economic Impact in a Gentrifying Housing Market,* 101 Harv. L. Rev. 1835 (1988).

4. Whatever the merits of the social policy debate, rent control appears to be declining, even in the holdout jurisdictions: California, New York, New Jersey, and the District of Columbia. Since 1994, most of these jurisdictions have legislatively decreased the extent of the control. Is this due to attacks by economists—or economics? Could the rise and decline of rent control be merely a function of the history of inflation in the United States? Or a more conservative political climate?

6. Condominium Conversion

One private market response to the shortage of housing has been the conversion of apartments to occupant-owned condominiums. In Charles M. Cobbe, Note, *Conversion of Apartments to Condominiums and Cooperatives: Protecting Tenants in New York*, 8 U. MICH. J.L. REF. 705, 706 (1975), the following reasons are suggested for conversions:

> The fundamental reason for the increase in conversions is that sale of buildings as condominiums or cooperatives is far more profitable in many areas than continued operation of the same buildings on a rental basis. Proceeds from the sale of a building as a condominium may amount to ten times the annual rental income from the building; in comparison, sale to another landlord may bring as little as six times the rent income. However, it remains uncertain whether the disparity between the profitability of maintaining rental housing and that of selling apartments as condominiums is the result of an unreasonably low rate of return from rental housing or, instead, of excessive profits from sales of apartments to occupant-owners.
>
> There is ample evidence to support the first of these two explanations. Landlords face increasing property taxes and maintenance costs, as well as high interest rates on loans necessary for renovation and improvements. Finally, it is asserted that demands by increasingly militant tenants for changes in landlords' maintenance practices not only increase financial costs but also make ownership of rental housing less attractive in personal, psychological terms.
>
> The opposite interpretation would emphasize that the demand for condominium and cooperative housing is increasing over the long run. Reasons for this are the psychological and financial benefits of homeownership which cooperative and condominium housing offer to those who cannot afford single-family houses. At the same time, high construction costs and municipal measures designed to limit population growth impede the construction of new multiple-unit housing, with the result that the brunt of increasing demand falls on a diminishing number of rental buildings still available for conversion. The inference is that the widening gap between quantities supplied and demanded makes possible excessive profits for landlords and sponsors who convert older buildings.

Donald C. Bryant and Henry W. McGee, Jr., Gentrification and the Law: Combating Urban Displacement

25 Washington University Journal of Urban and Contemporary Law 43, 62–65 (1983)

III. CAUSES OF GENTRIFICATION

A. Condominium Conversions

The conversion of apartments to condominiums and cooperatives is an urban phenomenon that depletes the supply of rental units and at the same time causes rental rates to rise in reaction to increased demand for the reduced pool of units. Although the wave of conversions does not appear to be racially motivated, it is class biased, driving out persons with low and moderate incomes. Minorities, the elderly, and handicapped suffer particular hardships when they are displaced.

Displacement results both directly and indirectly from conversions. Many formally undesirable neighborhoods have become very attractive due to downtown access or other locational attributes. Developers purchase buildings in these areas, displace lower income tenants, and then renovate the units for sale as condominiums to more affluent buyers. [I]indirect displacement can occur because of conversions in buildings located in "better" areas.... Middle income renters may be unable or unwilling to buy their converted units. They then seek housing in less expensive parts of town, bidding up rent levels in the dwindling rental stock. This in turn forces out lower income tenants who cannot afford the higher rents.

Condominium conversions severely test the traditional "trickle-down" theory that has been at the heart of housing development in the United States. The trickle-down theory maintains that each time occupancy of a unit changes, the new tenant will be from a lower income level. In effect, then, by meeting middle class housing needs, vacated rental units will trickle down to the poor. However, as one commentator observed, the trickle-down theory may work well for "the predominant majority of households ... [but] for the poorest urban households, especially poor minority-group members, this process is a social disaster. Using the trickle-down theory in support of conversions, many developers argue that condominium purchasers are former renters whose previous housing will become part of the rental supply for lower income tenants. This claim, however, does not address the absolute reduction in units caused by conversions and middle class in-migration. As market demand and inflation escalate the value of housing in low income areas, the filtering process cannot work. Displacement eventually results from the lack of alternative rental housing in the neighborhood. And a disproportionate number of those displaced are minorities.

Notes and Questions

1. Developers and other landlords often challenge municipal limitations on condominiums in the context of broader attacks on rent control ordinances. *See, e.g., Nash v. City of Santa Monica*, 688 P.2d 894 (Cal. 1984), *appeal dismissed for want of a substantial federal question*, 470 U.S. 1046 (1985) (the California Supreme Court held that the city could restrict the demolition of rental units under its rent control laws). In *Nash*, recall that the California Supreme Court upheld strict regulation of condominium conversions imposed by the city of Santa Monica. But recall that legislative action overruled the case. *See* discussion of *Nash* earlier in this chapter. Later challenges to a local ordinance on antitrust theories were also rejected, although in that case the court held that the plaintiff's taking claims were only unripe and not dismissible on the merits. *Traweek v. City and County of San Francisco,* 920 F.2d 589 (9th Cir. 1990). *See also G.D. Management Co. v. Negro*, 442 A.2d 611 (N.J. 1982) (upholding continuation of rent controls after condominium conversion); *AMN Inc. v. So. Brunswick Rent Leveling Bd.*, 461 A.2d 1138 (N.J. 1983) (undercutting *Negro* by exempting certain small-scale condominium owners). In general, condominium conversion regulation has been upheld by the courts in the same manner as rent control regulation. *See* Janet Boeth Jones, Annotation, *Validity and Construction of Law Regulating Conversion of Rental Units to Condominiums,* 21 A.L.R.4th 1083 (1983).

2. In addition to adopting conversion regulations as part of a rent control ordinance, some local governments have also implemented land-use controls to restrict condominium conversions. *See generally* Peter J. Macdonald, Note, *Displacement in Gentrifying Neighborhoods: Regulating Condominium Conversion Through Municipal Land Use Controls*, 63 B.U. L. Rev. 955 (1983). This approach, however, has not been entirely successful. Some

courts have concluded that because condominium conversions do not change the physical use of the land, the activity *is not* subject to local land-use regulations. *See, e.g., Griffin Dev. Co. v. City of Oxnard*, 199 Cal. Rptr. 739 (Ct. App. 1984), *vacated*, 703 P.2d 339 (Cal. 1985); *Miami Beach v. Arlen King Cole Condo Assn.*, 302 So. 2d 777 (Fla. Dist. Ct. App. 1974); *Wentworth Hotel, Inc. v. Town of Newcastle*, 287 A.2d 615 (N.H. 1972). However, given the Supreme Court decision in *Pennell, supra*, the reasoning of these cases may no longer be valid. *But see City of West Hollywood v. Beverly Towers,* 805 P. 2d 329 (Cal. 1991) (municipality could not enforce condominium conversion regulations enacted after real estate developer secured final subdivision map approval and permission from Department of Real Estate to sell individual apartments as condominium units although no units had been sold prior to the enactment of the regulations).

Donald C. Bryant and Henry W. McGee, Jr., Gentrification and the Law: Combating Urban Displacement

25 Washington University Journal of Urban and Contemporary Law 43, 75–81 (1983)

IV. REMEDIES FOR GENTRIFICATION

A. Condominium Conversions

1. Governmental Regulation

While state condominium regulation is generally not concerned with displacement of the poor, the California legislature has required localities to employ a variety of anti-displacement measures when regulating land use. These measures must be implemented when determining whether to issue subdivision maps for proposed conversions, and when monitoring conversions in California's coastal zone. In addition, all localities have broad authority under their police powers to provide supplemental protections. They can be applied to mitigate the two basic problems associated with conversions: reducing the supply of affordable rental housing and tenant displacement....

C. The Police Power....

i. Moratoriums

Temporary moratoriums prohibiting condominium conversions allow local jurisdictions time to assess and prepare appropriate legislation in light of an emergency conversion situation. For example, San Mateo County, California, imposed a one-year moratorium on conversions and then banned them altogether until the vacancy rate exceeds 4.85%.

Several other California cities have also employed longer moratoriums that prohibit conversions until vacancy rates exceed a prescribed level, usually 3 to 5 percent. While vacancy rate moratoriums have succeeded in stopping conversions, they may usually thwart the production of new rental units. Moratoria may have an unexpected side effect of discouraging rental development since the feasibility of many rental projects is based on their potential for conversion once the tax shelter benefits are exhausted.

ii. Tie-in with new construction or vacancy rates

Instead of prohibiting conversions altogether, localities may seek to maintain the existing level of rental stock by linking conversions to new rental construction.

iii. Low and moderate income housing requirements

Another approach to alleviating conversion and displacement focuses on low and moderate income units only.... [A]n ordinance enacted in [San Francisco] mandates that an applicant for conversion of a building with more than four units must satisfy a ten percent low to moderate income household occupancy requirement by providing such units either in the conversion project or within new construction elsewhere.

Converters can evade the purpose of such an ordinance by rapidly increasing rents, thereby forcing lower income tenants to vacate. A proposed subdivision ordinance in Los Angeles, California, would curb such evasion. The proposal calls for disapproval of a tentative map for a condominium conversion project if more than fifty percent of the units in the project at any time during the eighteen-month period prior to the map application were low or moderate cost housing, unless there are exceptional circumstances.

Another approach would assure that a percentage of converted units remain available to low and moderate income households. Local governments may require that a given percentage of units in each project be sold at below-market prices. Alternatively, the units could be sold to the locality for rental to lower-income persons.

iv. Tenant participation

In order to minimize displacement, a locality may require tenant participation in the conversion process. Some cities insist on tenant consent to the conversion. Under California law, tenants must be given notice of a proposed conversion....

v. Relocation assistance

When conversions are approved and displacement will occur, the converters may be required to pay tenant's moving expenses and to provide information about alternative housing. The quality of assistance required of developers varies. Some localities limit assistance to the posting of rental want ads. Several jurisdictions require that the developer find alternative, comparable housing for displaced tenants. Most jurisdictions, however, simply require monetary compensation. Many localities also provide special protections for tenants who are members of certain groups such as the elderly, the handicapped, or households with one or more children. Special protections range from increased relocation payments to lifetime leases. [For additional discussion of relocation and displacement problems, see Chapter 5, section D *infra*—Eds.]

Notes and Questions

1. For a full discussion of the condominium conversion problem and an analysis of federal, state, and local regulation of the condominium conversion process, see U.S. Dep't of Hous. & Urb. Dev., The Conversion of Rental Housing to Condominiums and Cooperatives (1980). *See also* Andrea L. Negroni, *Legal Status of Moratoriums on Condominium Conversions and Some Suggestions for Saluting Their Success*, 10 Current Mun. Probs. 129 (1983) and Perry J. Snyderman & Portia O. Morrison, *Rental Market Protection Through the Conversion Moratorium: Legal Limits and Alternatives*, 29 De Paul L. Rev. 973 (1980). Recent cases generally apply the conversion statutes strongly in favor of tenants. *See People v. Thomas Shelton Powers, M.D., Inc*, 3 Cal. Rptr. 2d 34 (Ct. App. 1992) (court requires landlord to disgorge excessive resale profits); *Daskel Investors, Inc. v. Rosenbloom*, 582 A.2d 854 (N.J. Super. 1990) (tenant was entitled to a second year of stay on eviction order because landlord failed to comply strictly with statute). *But see Resolution Trust Corp. v. Diamond*, 18 F.3d 111 (2d Cir. 1994) (using a taking analysis to reverse the

lower court's ruling that RTC couldn't repudiate statutory rent control tenancies to evict tenants after conversion). For further discussion on the phenomenon of gentrification, see James G. Durham & Dean E. Sheldon, III, *Mitigating the Effects of Private Revitalization on Housing for the Poor*, 70 MARQ. L. REV. 81 (1986).

2. It should also be noted that the gentrification controversy sometimes raises more than the issue of housing resources. For example, fears of racial/cultural domination can animate neighborhood resistance. As a minority graduate student concluded, "After years of being deprived of municipal services and virtually ignored by local government, it angers a displaced resident to witness white, middle-class pioneers enjoy the finer things of life in areas once considered home. Even if a 'native' manages to keep his/her inner-city home, the presence of white gentry and their material possessions is a constant reminder of his/her position in what may be the permanent underclass. The racial and class tension can be unbearable in situations where a gentrified area is bordered or surrounded by a sea of poverty and hopelessness." *See* Henry W. McGee, Jr., *Afro-American Resistance to Gentrification and the Demise of Integrationist Ideology in the United States,* 23 URB. LAW. 25, 45, (1991), *reprinted in* 23 LAND USE & ENVTL. L. REV. 215 (1992).

B. Public Sector Tenants

It may come as a surprise to some that tenants in publicly-owned housing initially had few recognized rights, and existed on month-to-month tenancies at the mercy of their public landlords. Tenant protections in public housing were won only after hard-fought court battles and pressures on the federal housing agency. Under pressure from the courts, HUD ultimately adopted regulations designating the content of public housing agency leases and providing protections for tenants evicted or otherwise aggrieved by actions taken by their housing authority. The battle between the public housing authorities and HUD over HUD's authority to adopt these regulations was resolved in *Housing Auth. of Omaha v. United States Hous. Auth.*, 468 F.2d. 1 (8th Cir. 1972) (upholding HUD regulatory authority). For further discussion of program relations, see Chapter 2 *supra.*

These battles had to be fought again when federal subsidies were extended to privately-owned housing, as in the Section 8 existing housing program. How long the tenant protections won in the public housing program will last and how far they extend to privately owned but federally subsidized housing is still not clear.

This section traces the development of tenant protections in publicly owned and in privately owned but federally assisted housing. It reviews the major court decisions and notes the development of HUD policy in response to judicial decisions conferring protections on tenants in subsidized housing.

1. The Government's Role in the Management of Subsidized Housing

Chapter 3 has outlined the major features of the subsidized housing programs and should be consulted at this point for a review of the major program features. As indicated there, both federal subsidy legislation and state-enabling legislation for public housing authorities place few restraints on local public housing rent and tenant policies. Local public housing authorities are free to determine their own rent, admission, and tenant policies, subject only to federal restrictions on income and rent limits. Rent limits established by local public housing authorities are subject to the federal government's 30% limitation on the proportion of income that can be spent for rent. See Chapter 3 for a discussion of this limitation and the exceptions that apply.

Court decisions on tenant evictions are better developed than the decisions on admissions. Major court decisions have established basic protections for tenants subject to eviction from public housing projects, and these protections are now reflected in federal regulations. The cases and materials that follow consider admission, eviction, and management practices in different types of subsidized housing, including conventional public housing owned and managed by local public housing authorities, project-based private subsidized housing, and the Section 8 Existing Housing certificate and voucher programs. Recall that in the Section 8 Existing Housing program, private landlords select the tenants from those provided with subsidy eligibility by the housing authority in the form of certificates or vouchers. Tenants can relocate from one home to another and take their subsidy with them. However, in project-based programs, the subsidy is tied to the landlord's unit and is not portable. The subsidy remains with the project, and the project owner assumes all maintenance and management responsibilities, including selection and eviction of tenants. The voucher program seems to be the future of subsidized housing, but the earlier programs developed the applicable law. Thus, it is appropriate to discuss the programs together, especially when they appear to be rapidly converging in their approach to management issues generally.

a. Admission Requirements

Holmes v. New York City Housing Authority

United States Court of Appeals
398 F.2d 262 (2d Cir. 1968)

Before HAYS, ANDERSON, and FEINBERG, Circuit Judges.

ANDERSON, Circuit Judge:

This class action was brought on September 9, 1966 by 31 named plaintiffs on behalf of themselves and all others similarly situated under the Civil Rights Act, 42 U.S.C. § 1983, and the Federal Constitution, challenging the procedures employed by the defendant New York City Housing Authority in the admission of tenants to low-rent public housing projects administered by it in New York City. The jurisdiction of the district court is predicated upon 28 U.S.C. § 1343(3).

The New York City Housing Authority is a public corporation created pursuant to the Public Housing Law of the State of New York for the purpose of implementing the State Constitution by providing "low-rent housing for persons of low income as defined by law...." New York State Constitution, Art. XVIII, Section 1. At the time of the complaint in this action, the Authority was providing housing facilities for more than 500,000 persons, in 152 public projects which it owned and administered in New York City. Approximately half of these were federal-aided projects, the remainder being supported by either State or local funds.

The eligibility requirements for prospective public housing tenants are set out in the Public Housing Law, and in resolutions adopted by the Authority pursuant to its rule-making power, Public Housing Law, § 37(1)(w). While these vary somewhat for federal, state, and local-aided projects two requirements common to all are that the applicant's annual income and total assets not exceed specified limits, and that, at the time of admission, the applicant ha[s] been a resident of New York City for not less than two years. In addition each candidate must be situated in an "unsafe, unsanitary, or overcrowded" dwelling, Resolution No. 62-7-473, Section 3 (federal aided projects), or living "under other substandard housing conditions," Resolution No. 56-8-433, Section 4 (state-aided projects). Each of the plaintiffs in the present action is alleged to meet these requirements.

Each year the Authority receives approximately 90,000 applicants out of which it is able to select an average of only 10,000 families for admission to its public housing projects. In doing so the Authority gives preference to certain specified classes of candidates, e.g., "site residents," families in "emergency need of housing," "split families," "doubled up and overcrowded families." Resolution No. 56-8-433, § 4.

In federal-aided projects the Authority is required to allocate the remaining apartments among non-preference candidates in accordance with "an objective scoring system" which is designed to facilitate comparison of the housing conditions of these applicants. Resolution No. 62-7-473, § 4(b). For state-aided projects, however, there is no similar regulation and we assume that this is also the case with local aided projects. The plaintiffs in this action are all non-preference candidates seeking admission to any of the public housing projects run by the defendant.

In the complaint the named plaintiffs allege that although they have filed with the Authority a total of 51 applications for admission to its housing facilities, 36 in 1965 or earlier, and some as long ago as 1961, none has been advised in writing at any time of his eligibility, or ineligibility, for public housing.

The complaint cites numerous claimed deficiencies in the admissions policies and practices of the Authority. Regulations on admissions (other than those pertaining to income level and residence) are not made available to prospective tenants either by publication or by posting in a conspicuous public place. Applications received by the Authority are not processed chronologically, or in accordance with ascertainable standards, or in any reasonable and systematic manner. All applications, whether or not considered and acted upon by the Authority, expire automatically at the end of two years. A renewed application is given no credit for time passed, or precedence over a first application of the same date. There is no waiting list or other device by which an applicant can gauge the progress of his case and the Authority refuses to divulge a candidate's status on request. Many applications are never considered by the Authority. If and when a determination of ineligibility is made (on any ground other than excessive income level), however, the candidate is not informed of the Authority's decision, or of the reasons therefore.

The complaint charges that these procedural defects increase the likelihood of favoritism, partiality, and arbitrariness on the part of the Authority, and deprive the plaintiff of a fair opportunity to petition for admission to public housing, and to obtain review of any action taken by the Authority. The deficiencies are alleged to deprive applicants of due process of law in violation of the Fourteenth Amendment to the Federal Constitution.

In the district court the defendant moved to dismiss the complaint for failure to state a claim within the court's civil rights jurisdiction. Alternatively it requested that the court refrain from the exercise of its jurisdiction under the doctrine of abstention.

On October 20, 1967, the motion was denied by the trial court which also refused abstention. Thereafter, permission was granted to the defendant to take this interlocutory appeal under 28 U.S.C. § 1292(b). The issues here are whether the plaintiffs have stated a federal claim, and, if so, whether the district court should proceed to the merits. We have concluded that the district judge was correct in answering each of these points in the affirmative and we, therefore, affirm his order.

Clearly there is sufficient [sic] in the complaint to state a claim for relief under § 1983 and the due process clause. One charge made against the defendant, which has merit at least in connection with state-aided projects where the Authority has adopted no standards for selection among non-preference candidates, is that it thereby failed to establish the fair and orderly procedure for allocating its scarce supply of housing which due process requires. It hardly need be said that the existence of an absolute and uncontrolled discretion in any agency of government vested with the administration of a vast program, such as public housing, would be an intolerable invitation to abuse. *See Hornsby v. Allen*, 326 F.2d 605, 609, 610 (5th Cir. 1964). For this reason alone due process requires that selections among applicants be made in accordance with "ascertainable standards," *id.* at 612, and, in cases where many candidates are equally qualified under these standards, that further selections be made in some reasonable manner such as "by lot or on the basis of the chronological order of application." *Hornsby v. Allen*, 330 F.2d 55, 56 (5th Cir. 1964) (on petition for rehearing). Due process is a flexible concept which would certainly also leave room for the employment of a scheme such as the "objective scoring system" suggested in the resolution adopted by the Authority for federal-aided projects.

[The court then held that plaintiffs had standing to raise the due process objection, and declined to abstain under federal abstention doctrine. The following comments by the court relevant to the federal abstention claim are of interest.—Eds.]

The Authority clearly does direct and control a complex administrative process, much of which is concerned with the establishment of standards and policies for the admission of tenants, a function which Congress has recognized that localities are "in a much better position than the Federal Government" to perform. S. Rep. No. 281, 87th Cong., 1st Sess. (1961) in 2 U.S. Code Cong. & Ad. News, pp. 1943–1944. But the complaint in this action wages only a very limited attack on that process, and in no sense does it seek to interpose the federal judiciary as the arbiter of purely local matters. Rather the plaintiffs assert a narrow group of constitutional rights based upon overriding federal policies, and ask federal involvement only to the limited extent necessary to assure that state administrative procedures comply with federal standards of due process.

The order of the district court is *Affirmed*.

Notes and Questions

1. Until 1974, the procedural process for resisting unjust evictions was somewhat clearer than the route for review of rejection of applications for admission to public housing. *Cf. Escalera v. New York Hous. Auth., infra.* As a matter of policy as well as constitutional law, should existing tenants receive greater protections than those persons who seek the subsidy in the first place? *See Sumpter v. White Plains Hous. Auth.*, 278 N.E.2d 892 (N.Y. 1972). "It has long been settled that a party aggrieved by loss of a pre-existing right or privilege may enjoy procedural rights not available to one denied the right of privilege in the first instance." Why should this be so?

In any event, as part of the amendment of the public housing statutes in 1974, Congress provided that housing authorities "shall promptly notify (1) any applicant determined to be ineligible for admission to the project of the basis for such determination and provide the applicant upon request, within a reasonable time after the determination is made, with an opportunity for an informal hearing on such determination, and (2) any applicant determined to be eligible for admission to the project of the approximate date of occupancy insofar as such date can be reasonably determined." 42 U.S.C. § 1437d(c)(3). The statute was implemented in HUD regulations. *See* 24 C.F.R. § 960.207.

The statute and regulations were construed in *Singleton v. Drew*, 485 F. Supp. 1020 (E.D. Wis. 1980), and in *Billington v. Underwood*, 613 F.2d 91 (5th Cir. 1980), the latter case holding that the housing authority "parroted" the HUD regulations but did not in fact afford the applicant the informal hearing mandated by federal law. *Singleton* also was critical of the crabbed interpretation of the HUD rules and suggested that they gave "protection to applicants for public housing that parallel those that would be required if the due process clause applied." 485 F. Supp. at 1023. In *Phelps v. Hous. Auth.*, 742 F.2d 816 (4th Cir. 1984), the Fourth Circuit criticized the *Holmes* court's generous interpretations of the Due Process Clause and of 42 U.S.C. § 1983. In denying the plaintiffs' due process claims, the *Phelps* court distinguished cases involving the eviction of public sector tenants from those involving the admission of such tenants. The court explained that the "claim ... of one who is already a tenant in a qualifying public housing project seems to us much more ascertainable and 'property-like' in character than plaintiffs' interest in any 'preference' [to earlier admission under 42 U.S.C. § 1437d (c)(4)(A)]." *Phelps*, 742 F.2d at 822 n.11. Furthermore, the court denied that the plaintiffs had an enforceable claim to the benefits of the procedures specified in 42 U.S.C. § 1437 under 42 U.S.C. § 1983.

If the need for low-income housing is greater than the supply, why should public policy be concerned with admission process issues? It is true that all available public housing units will be occupied by eligible families, and that due process in admissions requires a good deal of PHA time, trouble, and resources.

The Admission Procedure Regulations require an informal hearing. What makes a hearing informal? Does the informality result in a failure to protect the applicant's rights? If there is judicial review of admissions decisions, should there be a full due process hearing at the PHA level? Is there a basis to differentiate, on the issue of due process, between rejection of applicants and eviction of tenants? *See Escalera v. New York City Hous. Auth.*, *infra*, and comments following.

Do the statute and regulations require more or less procedural due process than does the Second Circuit in the *Holmes* opinion? What interest of the applicant is furthered? Of the public housing program?

2. Of more than passing concern to local communities is the problem of preference for admission based on residence in the community. In *Cole v. Hous. Auth.*, 435 F.2d 807, 813 (1st Cir. 1970), the court struck down, as violating the "right to travel" articulated in *Shapiro v. Thompson*, 394 U.S. 618 (1969), a Newport Rhode Island Housing Authority requirement restricting admission to those who had lived in the city for two years. Judge Coffin's opinion declared in part:

> Even by a standard of rational relationship to a permissible goal, we doubt that the justifications put forth by the Authority could withstand judicial scrutiny. The goal of preventing an influx of outsiders is constitutionally impermissible. The residence requirement is not rationally related to the goal of planning. The objective of achieving political support by discriminating means or by nourishing an illusion that means discriminate is not one which the Constitution recognizes. Nor do we believe the goal of promoting provincial prejudices toward long-time residents is cognizable under a Constitution which was written for the

> purpose of eradicating such provincialism. Certainly none of these interests counterbalances the fundamental right involved.

Despite Judge Coffin's appeal to the better angels of political sentiment, *Cole* was not followed in *Lane v. McGarry,* 320 F. Supp. 562, 564 (N.D.N.Y. 1970). The court decried

> as "far more theoretical than real" any construction of the right to travel to invalidate residence requirements as "anything other than insubstantial," and declared that an "inadequate supply of low income housing, unlike a limited amount of money, cannot be spread thin among the needy. Unless an absolute rule of first-come, first-serve is to prevail, some reasonable order can be maintained only by establishing reasonable preferences."

However, the year after *Lane*, the Second Circuit (which includes the state of New York) followed *Cole* in *King v. New Rochelle Municipal Housing Authority*, 442 F.2d 646 (2d Cir. 1971) and invalidated a five-year "durational" residency requirement. Presently, HUD regulations permit "actual" or "bona fide" residency requirements designed to exclude transient presence, but do not permit "durational" residency requirements based on length of time in the housing authority's sphere of operation. *See* 24 C.F.R. § 960.204(d) (conventional public housing); 24 C.F.R. §§ 980.613(e), 981.613(e), 986.132(e) (project-based programs); 24 C.F.R. § 982.208 (section 8 existing program). But see *Williams v. Town of Greenburgh*, 535 F.3d 71 (2d Cir. 2008). An individual housing authority's residence preference is still subject to challenge as violative of the Constitution or federal fair housing laws. *Comer v. Cisneros,* 37 F.3d 775 (2d Cir. 1994); *Vaughn v. Consumer Home Mortgage Co.,* 297 Fed. Appx. 23 (2d Cir. 2008). This may well be consistent with the requirements of *Shapiro v. Thompson, supra,* because in the housing context there may not be a "right to travel" that is recognized but rather a "right to migrate" which prohibits placing burdens on those who intend to make the new jurisdiction their residence (as distinguished from those who might desire transient—hotel-like—facilities while en route to some other jurisdiction).

What real difference is there between the forbidden durational requirements and the permissible actual residency requirements, since the latter effectually limit outsiders from meaningful access to public housing units? The ratio of vacancies to applicants in nearly every public housing jurisdiction means a wait of a year or more before housing is actually provided to an applicant. Why can't a housing authority simply close its list periodically for administrative reasons, thereby screening out new arrivals, at least until the list is reopened?

3. The problem of durational residency requirements is the beginning, not the end, of the problem of preferences for admission to public housing accommodations. What constitutional and policy problems might be presented by a state statute or local policy according a preference to the elderly or to veterans? *See Hess v. Ward*, 497 F. Supp. 786 (E.D. Pa. 1980) (approving such preferences but applying the HUD regulation to invalidate a durational residency requirement). What about state statute or local policy giving a preference to applicants who have resided in the jurisdiction of the authority for a stated time, but not making the preference absolute? Congress, in 1995, suspended the operation of federal preferences for homeless or poorly housed families, leaving local housing authorities great latitude in tenant selection. 42 U.S.C. §§ 1437d(c)(4)(A), 1437f(d)(1)(A). Local housing preferences, such as a preference for employed applicants, can seriously exacerbate discrimination problems. *See Davis v. New York City Hous. Auth.,* 1997 WL 407250 (S.D.N.Y. July 18, 1997), *vacated in part*, 166 F.3d 432 (2nd Cir. 1999) (injunction issued against implementation of employment preference in light of long-standing consent decrees against racial discrimination and steering; on appeal, the Second Circuit

vacated the substantive decision as the district judge failed to adequately explain the subsidiary facts and methodology underlying the ultimate finding that it was likely that plaintiffs would be able to show that preference would have a discriminatory effect by perpetuating segregation in certain developments).

4. The HUD Admission Procedure and Criteria Regulations set forth substantive guidelines for PHA admission criteria. The general policies appear in 24 C.F.R. § 960.204:

> (a) [E]ach PHA shall adopt and implement policies and procedures embodying standards and criteria for tenant selection which take into consideration the needs of individual families for low-income housing and the statutory purpose in developing and operating socially and financially sound low-income housing projects which provide a decent home and a suitable living environment and foster economic and social diversity in the tenant body as a whole.
>
> (b) Such policies and procedures shall be designed to: (1) Avoid concentrations of the most economically and socially deprived families in any one or all of the PHA's low-income housing projects; (2) preclude admission of applicants whose habits and practices reasonably may be expected to have a detrimental effect on the tenants or the project environment;....
>
> (c) Such policies and procedures shall: (1) Not automatically deny admission to a particular group or category of otherwise eligible applicants (e.g., unwed mothers or families with children born out of wedlock); (2) assure that selection by the PHA among otherwise eligible applicants is objective and reasonable; (3) be consistent with the PHA's responsibilities as a public body; and (4) be in compliance with State, local and Federal laws and regulations, including the nondiscriminatory requirements of Title VI of the Civil Rights Act of 1964, and the provisions of the ACC....

Specific guidelines are established in § 960.205:

> (a) The criteria to be established and information to be considered shall be reasonably related to individual attributes and behavior of an applicant and shall not be related to those which may be imputed to a particular group or category of persons of which an applicant may be a member....
>
> (b) The criteria to be established in relation to avoiding concentration of families with serious social problems in PHA projects and information to be considered shall be reasonably related to whether the conduct of the applicant in present or prior housing has been such as would not be likely to interfere with other tenants in such a manner as to diminish their enjoyment of the premises by adversely affecting their health, safety or welfare or to affect adversely the physical environment or the financial stability of the project if the applicant were admitted to the project. Relevant information respecting habits or practices to be considered may include, but is not limited to:
>
> (1) An applicant's past performance in meeting financial obligations, especially rent;
>
> (2) A record of disturbance of neighbors, destruction of property, or living or housekeeping habit at prior residences which may adversely affect the health, safety or welfare or other tenants; and
>
> (3) A history of criminal activity involving crimes of physical violence to persons or property and other criminal acts which would adversely affect the health, safety or welfare of other tenants....

(d) In the event of the receipt of unfavorable information with respect to an applicant, consideration shall be given to the time, nature, and extent of the applicant's conduct and to factors which might indicate a reasonable probability of favorable future conduct or financial prospects. For example:

(1) Evidence of rehabilitation;

(2) Evidence of the applicant family's participation in or willingness to participate in social service or other appropriate counseling service programs and the availability of such programs;

(3) Evidence of the applicant family's willingness to attempt to increase family income and the availability of training or employment programs in the locality.

Do these regulations represent an improper federal intrusion into the affairs of the PHA? What is the statutory basis for the regulations? *See* the discussion of federal PHA relations in Chapters 2 and 3, *supra*.

5. Do the HUD regulations violate any right an applicant may have to privacy? Do the regulations give PHAs and applicants sufficient guidance or are they too vague and subjective?

6. What substantive admission criteria should a PHA adopt? After the *Holmes* decision, the New York City Housing Authority adopted two categories for exclusion: ineligible and borderline. The ineligible category included families characterized as follows: presence of disease, illegal occupation, prone to violence, drug or alcohol addiction, sexual deviation, neighborhood disturbance, and destruction of property. The borderline category included those families evidencing lack of parental control, irregular work history, familial instability, or mental retardation of a family member. Are these categories and criteria rational? Do they comply with the HUD regulations? *See Floyd v. Hernandez-Pinero*, 603 N.Y.S.2d 847 (Sup. Ct. App. Div. 1993) (rejection based on past disturbances and destruction of property not borne out by evidence).

7. Do the above standards or the HUD guidelines limit the admission of people who need it most? Is there a justification for open admissions, that is, admission solely on the basis of financial need? If HUD or the courts restrict PHA freedom to choose, will public housing developments fill up with problem families, to the detriment of other residents and the program as a whole? Do the HUD regulations achieve an adequate balance between the housing need of the applicant and the community need or a financially and socially sound housing program? A forceful argument against open admissions is presented in Roger Starr, *Which of the Poor Shall Live in Public Housing*, 23 PUB. INT. 116 (1971). A response to Starr is found in Al Hirshen & Vivian Brown, *Too Poor for Public Housing: Roger Starr's Poverty Preferences*, 3 SOC. POL'Y 28–32 (May/June 1972).

The *Holmes* case served as a blueprint for admissions to project-based privately-owned subsidized housing as well, as can be seen from the following case.

Colon v. Tompkins Square Neighbors, Inc.

United States District Court
294 F. Supp. 134 (S.D.N.Y. 1968)

TENNY, District Judge.

This is a motion by defendants for an order dismissing the complaint herein for the following reasons: (1) that plaintiffs, pursuant to Rule 12(b) of the Federal Rules of Civil

Procedure, have failed to state a claim upon which relief can be granted; (2) that this Court lacks jurisdiction under 42 U.S.C. § 1983; and (3) that primary jurisdiction over the within cause of action lies with the appropriate administrative agencies. In the alternative, defendants seek a declaration pursuant to 28 U.S.C. § 1292(b) permitting their taking of an interlocutory appeal from the determination of the within motion and from the order of this Court dated June 26, 1968.

A brief review of the history of this cause of action from the time the complaint was filed on April 5, 1968, reveals that on April 15, 1968, Judge Tyler of this court denied plaintiffs' motion for a preliminary injunction, suggesting, however, that discovery proceedings be immediately commenced. Plaintiffs thereupon, within 20 days from the date the complaint was filed, brought on a motion pursuant to Rule 34 of the Federal Rules of Civil Procedure for discovery. This Court, *sua sponte* dismissed the complaint on the grounds that the Civil Rights Act, Pub. L. No. 90-284, 810(d) (April 11, 1968), required district courts to abstain from exercising jurisdiction in cases involving racial discrimination, where plaintiffs have not exhausted their state remedies, and where such remedies are as broad in scope as those offered by the statute.

On June 26, 1968, this Court granted plaintiff's motion for reargument and, upon reargument, adhered to its prior order of dismissal with respect to plaintiffs' claim of racial discrimination but reinstated the claims involving discrimination against welfare recipients and defendants' failure to publish a list of standards applicable to tenant eligibility, pending a determination by the Court of Appeals for the Second Circuit in *Holmes v. New York City Hous. Auth.*, 398 F.2d 262 (2d Cir., July 18, 1968)....

In the present case before this Court, plaintiffs complain not only of the existence of certain of the procedures found to be deficient, *Holmes, id.*, but also allege that applicants have been denied admission to the housing project *solely* on the basis of their status as welfare recipients.

Defendants contend, *inter alia*, (1) that no cause of action lies under 42 U.S.C. § 1983 or the Federal Constitution in that the necessary element of "state action" is not present herein ... and (3) that the proper administration of a housing project requires that the Management be permitted to exercise discretion in the selection of tenants.

Defendants attempt to distinguish the present case from *Holmes* inasmuch as that case involved state-aided public housing supervised directly by the Authority, whereas the instant case involves low-middle income housing which, although financed by an FHA-insured mortgage pursuant to Section 221 (d)(3) of the National Housing Act ... as well as other forms of City, State and Federal assistance, is directly managed on a day-to-day basis by defendant Tompkins Square Neighbors, Inc. (hereinafter referred to as "Tompkins Square"), a private corporation.

It appears, however, that defendants are attempting a distinction without a difference. The fact that Haven Plaza Apartments has been constructed on a designated urban renewal site, is financed by an FHA-insured mortgage, that the managing corporation, Tompkins Square, is a recipient of certain tax exemptions granted by the City as well as certain rent supplement subsidies and other forms of financial assistance from City, State and Federal authorities ... and that the daily operations are *ultimately* supervised by both New York City Housing and Development Administration and the Federal Housing Administration (hereafter referred to as the "FHA"), pursuant to Tompkins Square's Disposition Agreement with the City of New York and Regulatory Agreement with the FHA ... indicates that there exists sufficient and continuing government participation and involvement in the project so as to bring any discriminatory operational practices within the [ambit] of constitutional prohibition. *Burton v. Wilmington Parking Auth.*, 365 U.S. 715, 722 (1960); *Cooper v. Aaron*, 358 U.S. 1, 19 (1958). As clearly enunciated in *Cooper v. Aaron, supra*:

> State support ... through *any* agreement, management, funds or property cannot be squared with the Amendment's command that no State shall deny to any person within its jurisdiction the equal protection of the laws. (emphasis added)

Defendants' argument that the State does not breach its duty to protect the constitutional rights of its citizens until it fails to act upon specific complaints presented to it is without merit. By virtue of the State's election to put its property, power and prestige behind the housing project, in addition to its failure to affirmatively insure strict adherence to constitutional guarantees, it thereby becomes a party to the alleged discrimination. *Burton v. Wilmington Parking Auth., supra*, 365 U.S. at 725. Similarly, as evidenced by the cases cited herein, the generalization advanced by defendant Tompkins Square that State aid does not turn private enterprise into public activity is inappropriate as applied to the facts herein.

Turning to the complaint, plaintiffs first alleged that the refusal to admit applicants as tenants to Haven Plaza *solely* on the grounds that such applicants are recipients of welfare funds constitutes a violation of the Equal Protection Clause of the Fourteenth Amendment. With this, it is incumbent upon this Court to agree.

It is established in law that the Equal Protection Clause is only satisfied when classification rests "... upon some difference which bears a reasonable and just relation to the act in respect to which the classification is proposed...." *McLaughlin v. Florida*, 379 U.S. 184, 190 (1964).

The purpose of an effective means for the selection of tenants is clearly stated by the Rev. Paul Dano, Director and Chairman of the Renting Committee:

> If this project is to operate successfully and is to continue successfully over the years, it must have a stable group of tenants who will pay their agreed rentals and continue to pay their rentals, who will live together with minimum turnover, and who will cooperate among themselves and with the management in the maintenance and preservation of the property. Indifferent tenants, inconsiderate neighbors, uncooperative occupants, a high turnover rate-lead to an unhappy project, inevitably to higher cost of operation.

It is important, therefore, to determine whether the systematic excluding from the housing project of applicants solely because of their status as welfare recipients is a reasonable classification serving to effectuate the legitimate purpose of the Renting Committee. It appears clear to this Court that a welfare recipient need not be an uncooperative tenant, an indifferent occupant or an inconsiderate neighbor. Regarding the welfare recipients' reliability as to payment of the monthly rent, it would seem that some welfare recipients may have a history of delinquency in their payments whereas others may have been consistently dependable. Naturally, this Court would not require defendants to accept those recipients of welfare funds who would, of necessity, be required to devote an unreasonable portion of their income to the payment of their rent, thereby making nonpayment a likelihood. However, where the welfare recipient approved by the Department of Social Services as being compatible with his support budget, it would be an arbitrary classification in violation of the Equal Protection Clause of the Fourteenth Amendment to reject that applicant, despite status as a recipient of welfare funds. The day has passed when a citizen's right to participate in publicly-aided, publicly-supervised projects can be irrationally or arbitrarily withheld. *Rudder v. United States*, 226 F.2d 51, 53 (1955); *Thomas v. Hous. Auth.*, 282 F. Supp. 575, 580–581 (E.D. Ark. 1967); *see Holmes v. New York City Hous. Auth., supra.*

It generally follows, therefore, that since the allowance of absolute discretion in a government agency or private corporation acting as an arm of that agency invitation to the arbitrary exercise of power, "ascertainable standards" should be established and published so as to assure that worthy applicants are admitted to the project and unworthy applicants fairly rejected. *See Holmes v. New York City Hous. Auth., supra.* This is not to say that tenants must be selected on the basis of a "point system" or on the theory of "first come, first served." It is unquestionably beneficial to the apartment project as a whole if the element of human judgment and discretion is allowed to remain with the Rental Committee in the administration of its tenant selection procedure so long as that discretion is not permitted to transcend the boundaries established by the Fourteenth Amendment to the Constitution.

The "Tenant Selection Policy and Guidelines" submitted to this Court by defendant Tompkins Square is basically sound. However, the document, in its reference to the desirability of a "balanced tenant body", vaguely smacks of a quota system which, in the opinion of this Court, represents a constitutionally impermissible process requiring arbitrary rejection of applicants after a set quota has been met.

In order to avoid keeping applicants in a state of indefinite suspension pending a determination of their applications, a reasonable time limit should be agreed upon between the parties herein within which the Rental Committee should be required to complete its investigation of an applicant and notify the applicant as to the results thereof. Due to the steady inflow of application for low and middle income housing accommodations, the directors of Haven Plaza cannot be expected to process them with the same dispatch as would be anticipated from a private rental agent. Nevertheless, a time limit should be established by the parties herein which, although taking into account the amount of applications which steadily burdens the Rental Committee, primarily caters to the interest of the applicants in a prompt determination of their status and in having adequate time to obtain a review thereof.

Finally, a system should be created whereby a chronological waiting list is maintained, thereby affording the applicants an opportunity to gauge the progress of their cases as well as allowing both initial and renewed applications credit for time passed. *Holmes v. New York City Hous. Auth., id.*

Accordingly, after due consideration and for the reasons set forth herein, defendants' motion to dismiss is denied. However, due to the fact that certain of the controlling questions of law herein appear to be of first impression and could reasonably provoke a substantial difference of opinion, this Court ... permits an interlocutory appeal to be taken on the issues raised by the instant motion, and hereby amends the June 26, 1968 Order of this Court to similarly permit the taking of an interlocutory appeal from the issue disposed of therein.

Notes and Questions

1. The *Colon* court, without apparent hesitation, found that federally-subsidized landlords were required by the Due Process Clause to choose applicants in accordance with procedures similar to those imposed on PHAs by *Holmes, supra.* A split between the circuits has developed over the question of whether an application for Section 8 housing

rises to the level of a constitutionally protected property interest. For example, the Seventh Circuit in *Germain v. Recht-Goldin-Siegel Properties*, 745 F.2d 453 (7th Cir. 1984), held that applicants for subsidized housing did not have a constitutionally protected property interest. *Accord*, *Hill v. Group Three Hous. Dev. Corp.*, 799 F.2d 385 (8th Cir. 1986). *But see Ressler v. Pierce*, 692 F.2d 1212 (9th Cir. 1982) (applicant has a property interest because of the statutory purpose of the National Housing Act). *Accord Baldwin v. Housing Auth. of City of Camden*, 278 F. Supp. 2d 365 (D. N.J. 2003). Do the cases denying applicants for public or publicly subsidized housing mean that *Holmes*, *supra*, and *Colon*, *supra*, no longer are good law?

2. Recall that the Section 8 existing housing subsidy program provides for a Certificate of Family Participation for households eligible to participate in the program. In *Baker v. Cincinnati Metropolitan Housing Authority*, 490 F. Supp. 520 (S.D. Ohio 1980), applicants for Section 8 participation certificates challenged the informal post-denial hearing procedures made available by the authority. The court held that the applicants had a protectable constitutional interest in the certificates, but that the informal hearing procedures satisfied constitutional procedural due process. With this case, compare the eviction hearing procedure cases, *infra*. Consider the following:

> In subsidized housing, additional elements are present which weigh against providing a full hearing. The burden would fall on a private party likely to be less equipped to provide hearings. And if a PHA procedure were required, the resulting loss of landlord control over tenant selection could seriously discourage private participation in the subsidized housing programs, since it is widely recognized that tenant selection is one of the critical elements in the success of a housing project ... and is thus a matter with which potential landlords are likely to be intensely concerned.
>
> Furthermore, the balance of interests here as compared with that in the subsidized housing disputes previously considered—rent increases and evictions—also suggest that less protection may be required. The applicant has a substantially smaller interest in the housing than the current tenant. The burden on the landlord would be more substantial, since applications are likely to exceed greatly vacancies in successful subsidized projects. [HUD] policy recognizes that the decision to admit should involve a large element of discretion on the part of the landlord, rather than turning solely upon the resolution of particular disputes of fact.
>
> It would seem, therefore, that only an informal statement of reasons by the landlord to the applicant, followed by an opportunity for the applicant to explain and, if he wishes, to present informally evidence to the contrary, should be required. Courts could still review, as in *Colon*, claims that decisions were based on impermissible grounds.

Note, *Procedural Due Process in Government-Subsidized Housing*, 86 HARV. L. REV. 880, 911–12 (1973).

But see McNair v. New York City Hous. Auth., 613 F. Supp. 910 (1985); *Ferguson v. Metropolitan Dev. and Hous. Agency*, 485 F. Supp. 517 (1980). In *McNair*, the court held that where the PHA had a lengthy and cumbersome admissions process, requiring numerous visits to the PHA office interviews, home visits, and investigations in which the applicant was not allowed to participate, it was insufficient in terms of due process to deny admission without recounting the grounds or facts for ineligibility. The court also affirmed the HUD statutes and regulations that required the PHA to *promptly* notify rejected applicants of the basis of the determination and to provide the applicant, upon request, an opportunity within a "reasonable time" for an informal hearing to discuss the determination.

In *Ferguson*, the court found that the policy of the PHA of denying Section 8 benefits to applicants who owed money to the PHA was invalid on three grounds: (1) because this condition was not contained in Section 8 legislation enacted by Congress, the PHA could not add eligibility conditions; (2) that withholding Section 8 benefits was an unfair debt collection device that was in direct conflict with state law provisions providing exclusive remedies for collection of rent owed; and (3) as a matter of due process, the PHA could not withhold Section 8 benefits without affording the applicant notice and an opportunity to be heard on the issue of the validity of the debts.

b. Eviction and Management Issues

In *Rudder v. United States*, 226 F.2d 51 (D.C. Cir. 1955), appellants had refused to sign a certification form attesting that they were not members of a subversive organization as defined by a list prepared by the United States Attorney General. The loyalty document was mandated by Congress during the hysteria that swept the United States during the Cold War that ensued between the Soviet Union and the United States following World War II. The legislation was directed at employment, but its use was expanded to other governmental programs. The Attorney General gave the organizations and their members no hearings before he designated the organizations as subversive. Finally, the District of Columbia's Housing Authority gave the Rudder family no hearings before attempting the eviction.

Judge Edgerton's opinion was far reaching, anticipating developments more than a decade later. One sentence (here italicized) has been much quoted:

> The District of Columbia Code provides that a tenancy from month to month may be terminated on 30 days' notice, and that a landlord may recover possession in the Municipal Court. The Code does not require that a reason for termination be given. But those propositions do not decide this case. *The government as landlord is still the government.* It must not act arbitrarily, for, unlike private landlords, it is subject to the requirements of due process of law. Arbitrary action is not due process.
>
> In our opinion the United States acted arbitrarily in undertaking to evict the Rudders. Their refusal to deny that they were members of any organizations on the Consolidated List was not proof that they were members. Even proof that they were members of, e.g., a "totalitarian" organization, knowing nothing of its character, would be an arbitrary ground for an administrative decision to evict them from public housing.

Id. at 52 (emphasis added).

Early efforts by HUD to impose procedural requirements on local public housing authority (PHA) evictions were sustained in *Thorpe v. Housing Authority of the City of Durham*, 393 U.S. 268 (1969). Whether unreformed housing authority eviction procedures presented constitutional procedural due process problems was another story.

Despite the holding in *Escalera v. New York City Housing Authority*, *infra*, a leading case on the issue of due process right of public housing tenants, HUD regulations continued to vest the PHA with broad autonomy in determining eviction procedures and policies. This, coupled with disparate judicial definitions of due process in eviction cases, prompted HUD to promulgate the pre-eviction hearing procedures codified at 24 C.F.R. § 966.50.

1. Pre-Eviction Hearings

Prior to 1986, the right of tenants living in federally-subsidized housing not to be evicted from their place of residence except for good cause could be substantially undermined by landlords who abused state summary eviction proceedings. Although in theory the summary proceedings provided the tenants with "due process," the reality was that very few tenants contested the evictions, even in cases where they were evicted for reasons other than good cause. Because summary proceedings are formal and held after-the-fact, tenants who did contest their evictions were faced with substantial burdens: that of finding alternative housing and that of obtaining counsel for a legal proceeding in which the outcome was uncertain.

To respond to these realities, HUD adopted a pre-eviction hearing process for conventional public housing tenants in 1986. 24 C.F.R. §966.50. This process still provides the housing authorities with a means to evict, but, importantly, it provides the tenants with an informal, inexpensive forum in which the actions of their landlords can be challenged without forcing the tenants to secure alternative housing before they assert their rights. Additionally, this process also gives tenants who are successful at the hearing stage the incentive to secure legal representation and contest any subsequent unlawful detainer proceedings initiated by the landlords.

Escalera v. New York City Housing Authority

United States Court of Appeals
425 F.2d 853 (2d Cir. 1970)

Before MEDINA, WATERMAN, and SMITH, Circuit Judges.

J. Joseph SMITH, Circuit Judge.

Appellants are tenants in New York City public housing projects. They brought four suits in the United States District Court for the Southern District of New York against the New York City Housing Authority [hereinafter cited as "HA"] and certain individuals as officers of the HA in the form of class actions on behalf of themselves and all tenants similarly situated. The complaints invoked jurisdiction under the Civil Rights Act, 28 U.S.C. §1343(3) (1962), and alleged the deprivation of appellants' right to due process secured by the Fourteenth Amendment to the Constitution of their rights under the United States Housing Act of 1937.... They sought injunctive and declaratory relief against certain alleged practices of the HA, and in two instances (Haywood and Lockman) a money judgment for additional rents which had been paid.

Appellants sought a preliminary injunction by filing an order to show cause. Defendant then moved pursuant to Rule 12(b) of the Federal Rules of Civil Procedure to dismiss the actions for *inter alia*, failure to state a claim upon which relief could be granted, lack of jurisdiction, lack of substantial federal question, and failure to exhaust administrative remedies, and because the federal courts should abstain from considering these actions pending a determination by New York state courts in the first instance.

After the parties submitted affidavits, argument on the motions was heard before District Judge Sylvester J. Ryan. Thereafter by an opinion of October 31, 1968 ... and judgment of the next day, Judge Ryan granted defendants' motion, and dismissed the actions on the merits. We find error in the dismissal of these actions and remand to the district court to consider appellants' application for preliminary relief and to hold a trial on the merits.

The instant class actions challenge the constitutionality of the procedures used by the HA in three different types of actions: (1) termination of tenancy on the ground of non-desirability; (2) termination of tenancy for violation of HA rules and regulations; and (3) assessment of "additional rent" charges under the HA lease for undesirable acts by tenants. The HA, a corporate governmental agency financed by federal, state and city funds, administers the largest public housing program in the country, housing more than 144,000 families.

II

Appellants challenge the constitutionality of the HA procedures for terminating tenancies on the grounds of non-desirability and breach of the rules and regulations and for assessing "additional rent" charges, contending that these procedures deny members of their classes their rights to due process of law. Although the termination of tenancy procedures afforded by the HA in this case admittedly satisfy the requirements of the Department of Housing and Urban Development circular of February 7, 1967, considered by the Supreme Court in *Thorpe v. Hous. Auth. of City of Durham*, 393 U.S. 268 (1969) ... this is not dispositive of the question of whether the procedures satisfy the due process requirements of the Fourteenth Amendment.

Nor is it conclusive in the consideration of appellants' constitutional claims to argue that there is no constitutional right to continue living in public housing projects.... The government cannot deprive a private citizen of his continued tenancy, without affording him adequate procedural safeguards even if public housing could be deemed to be a privilege. *See Goldberg v. Kelly*, 397 U.S. 254, 262–63 (1970).

Since these actions were dismissed at the pleadings stage, we must view the allegations in the complaints and supporting affidavits in the light most favorable to the appellants ... in this light we find that appellants have a claim for relief. Certain aspects of the alleged present HA procedures cannot stand without a convincing showing at trial that the HA has compelling need for procedural expedition.

"The very nature of due process negates any concept of inflexible procedures universally applicable to every imaginable situation." *Cafeteria & Restaurant Workers Union, Local 473 v. McElroy*, 367 U.S. 866, 895 (1961). The minimum procedural safeguards required by due process in each situation depend on the nature of the governmental function involved and the substance of the private interest which is affected by the governmental action.... Since these competing interests have not been fully developed at the trial level, it is not now appropriate for this court to prescribe the minimum necessary procedural requirements. However, if appellants can show at trial the existence of certain of the pleaded HA procedures, we hold that they will have made out a *prima facie* case for relief; the exact nature and extent of that relief can only be determined after trial.

A

We consider first the procedures for terminating tenancies on the ground of nondesirability. We find this procedure may be deficient in four respects. First, summary notice such as that sent to the tenants here on the non-desirable conduct under consideration by the TRB [Tenant Review Board—Eds.] is inadequate. The one-sentence notices sent to the present appellants were insufficient to notify them even of the particular conduct thought by the TRB to be most serious. But since the TRB bases its decision on the tenant's entire folder, detailed notice as to the particular conduct thought to be most serious would be inadequate to give the tenant advance notice of all the items which might be considered against him so that he might challenge these items.

The purpose of requiring that notice be given to the tenant before the hearing is to insure that the tenant is adequately informed of the nature of the evidence against him so that he can effectively rebut that evidence. The instant one-sentence summary notices are inadequate for this purpose. Nor does the conference between the project manager and the tenant cure the deficiencies in the notice ... since the manager does not divulge all entries in the folder some of which may influence the TRB's decision.

Second, denying tenants access to the material in their folders, when the entire folder is considered by the TRB in its determination of eligibility, deprives the tenants of due process. A hearing at which the tenant can rebut evidence against him would be of little value if the TRB's ultimate decision can rest on items in the tenant's folder of which he has no knowledge and hence has had no opportunity to challenge.

If secrecy must be preserved as to some items in the tenant's folder, then these items may not be relied on in the decision of the HA. The decision must be based solely on the evidence adduced at the hearing.... Although it is unnecessary to write a full judicial opinion, the HA should "demonstrate compliance with this elementary requirement" and "state the reasons for [its] determination and indicate the evidence [it] relied on." [*Goldberg v. Kelly*, 397 U.S. at 271.—Eds.]

Third, denying the tenant the opportunity to confront and cross-examine persons who supplied information in the tenant's folder upon which HA action is grounded is improper...."In almost every setting where important decisions turn on questions of fact, due process requires an opportunity to confront and cross-examine adverse witnesses." *Goldberg v. Kelly, supra*, 397 U.S. at 269.

Under the present procedures, it appears that often the tenant is not even advised as to the source of many of the entries in his folder; preliminary disclosure of this information is, of course, necessary before the tenant can decide whether to confront the person supplying the damaging entry in his folder. If disclosure of the names of persons supplying information in the folder, or the subsequent confrontation at a hearing between the tenant and such persons, is deemed to be undesirable because of possible hostility amongst housing project neighbors, the HA may not base its determination on such information....

Finally, we find that the HA's failure to disclose the rules and regulations in the TRB Handbook governing the TRB panel at the hearing concerning termination for non-desirability may be found to be improper. *See Goldberg v. Kelly, supra*, 397 U.S. at 271 ("The decision maker's conclusion as ... must rely solely on the *legal rules* and evidence adduced at the hearing." [emphasis added]). Appellants allege that this information is necessary to adequate preparation of the tenant's substantive case before the TRB. If this is established at trial, these regulations must be made generally available prior to the hearing. The HA's argument, that the regulations contained in the Handbook are merely internal procedural guidelines, may be considered by the trial court in determining whether, in fact, the Handbook is necessary in preparing a tenant's case before the TRB.

B

Next, we consider the procedures for terminating tenancies on the ground of violation of rules and regulations and for assessing "additional rent" charges. Each procedure would seem to suffer the first three deficiencies of the TRB procedure. The tenant should be notified in advance of the complete grounds for the proposed action; should have access to all the information upon which any decision will be based, and should be afforded the right to confront and cross-examine witnesses in appropriate circumstances. In addition, it would seem that the tenant should be afforded the opportunity to present his side of the case in the presence of an impartial official, not merely to the project manager who instituted the proposed action against the tenant.

Although a full-fledged adversary hearing need not be afforded in all cases, the tenant must be adequately informed of the nature of the evidence against him and accorded an adequate opportunity to rebut the evidence. Indeed, in the cases of violations of rules and regulations and of "additional rent" charges, the evidence against the tenant is quite likely to come from third parties. In such cases, the tenant should be permitted to challenge the person supplying that evidence. The language of Mr. Justice Frankfurter ... is apt:

> The validity and moral authority of a conclusion largely depend on the mode by which it was reached. Secrecy is not congenial to truth-seeking and self-righteousness gives too slender an assurance of rightness. No better instrument has been devised for arriving at truth than to give a person in jeopardy of serious loss notice of the case against him and opportunity to meet it. Nor has a better way been found for generating the feeling, so important to a popular government, that justice has been done.

[*Joint Anti-Fascist Refugee Comm. v. McGrath*, 341 U.S. 123, 171–72 (1951) (concurring opinion).—Eds.]

Reversed and remanded for consideration of plaintiffs' motion for preliminary relief and for trial on the merits.

Notes and Questions

1. In a subsequent decision by the Eastern District of New York, the court upheld *Escalera* holding the following

> It remains to determine the type of notice and hearing which would be "appropriate to the nature" of *this* case. "The minimum procedural safeguards required by due process in each situation depend on the nature of the governmental function involved and the substance of the private interest which is affected by the governmental action," *Escalera*, 425 F.2d at 861, and requires the court to "use the three-factor balancing test articulated in *Mathews v. Eldridge* in deciding whether the demands of the Due Process Clause are satisfied," *Krimstock v. Kelly*, 464 F.3d 246, 253 (2d Cir. 2006): "First, the private interest that will be affected by the official action; second, the risk of an erroneous deprivation of such interest through the procedures used, and the probable value, if any, of additional or substitute procedural safeguards; and finally, the Government's interest, including the function involved and the fiscal and administrative burdens that the additional or substitute procedural requirement would entail." *Mathews v. Eldridge*, 424 U.S. 319, 335 (1976)....
>
> In doing so, the Court makes the following observations: First, it seems obvious that the process to be afforded should precede the initiation of eviction proceedings. This appears indicated because there is no immediate threat to the tenant's health or safety to warrant summary removal and because of HUD's position that a tenant would not be permitted to challenge the legitimacy of HUD's "substantial rehabilitation" determination in a summary eviction pro-

> ceeding under New York law. In any event, there is simply no warrant for subjecting a faultless tenant to the cost and burden of the summary eviction process applicable to those who have breached their leases as the price to pay for challenging the legitimacy of HUD's "substantial rehabilitation" decision.
>
> Second, the requisite notice should make it clear why the tenancy is being terminated, as well as the right and process to challenge that decision (to be determined by the Court after the hearing). In that latter regard, the Court is mindful of the salutary purpose of the MOU [memorandum of understanding between HUD and New York City's Department of Housing Preservation and Development governing the disposition of approximately 514 section 203(k) properties] to encourage the upgrading and sale of HUD's foreclosure housing stock by providing rehabilitation funding for prospective purchasers, and that an evidentiary hearing may not be warranted; however, as HUD itself has acknowledged, "[t]he right of management to make management decisions without the need to prove its case at an evidentiary hearing must be balanced against the countervailing consideration that persons receiving the benefits of subsidized housing not be denied these benefits arbitrarily." 41 Fed. Reg. at 43331. That consideration should require a process to ensure that "substantial rehabilitation" is not arbitrarily being employed as a pretext to evict a tenant from a perfectly decent home in order to sell it to a private developer. *See Escalera,* 425 F.2d at 863 ("Although a full-fledged adversary hearing need not be afforded in all cases, the tenant must be adequately informed of the nature of the evidence against him and accorded an adequate opportunity to rebut the evidence").
>
> Finally, the Court reemphasizes HUD's admission that the "substantial rehabilitation" notice exemption "highlights a fundamental problem." Tr. at 25. If a building was so in need of substantial rehabilitation that it posed a danger to the health or safety of its occupants, HUD would have to provide for substitute housing while the premises were being repaired, during which period tenants would only be temporarily displaced and not permanently evicted. There is, by contrast, no analogous protection when HUD uses substantial rehabilitation as a means to turn over housing stock to private developers. In other words, while effectuating the MOU may be a legitimate cause for non-renewal of a subsidized housing tenancy, it is somewhat ironic that tenants whose homes fall within the scope of the MOU—even those, like Clark and Linares, who have lived in their houses for many years—do not receive the same protection as low-income tenants whose homes are *truly* in need of rehabilitation. Assurances by HUD that these faultless tenants will not become homeless, either because HUD can undertake substantial rehabilitation without displacing them or because HUD will arrange substitute housing, would obviously bear on the Court's *Mathews* analysis, both in terms of the importance of the private interest at stake and the consequences of erroneous deprivations.

Linares v. Jackson, 531 F. Supp. 2d 460 (E.D.N.Y. 2008), *reconsideration partially denied*, 548 F. Supp. 2d 21 (E.D.N.Y. 2008).

2. *Caulder v. Durham Hous. Auth.*, 433 F.2d 998 (4th Cir. 1970), applied the balancing called for in *Goldberg v. Kelly*, 397 U.S. 254 (1970), and ordered *Escalera*-type procedures absent compelling reasons for summary eviction. Thereafter, in *Glover v. Hous. Auth.*, 444 F.2d 158 (5th Cir. 1971), the court of appeals upheld HUD Circular RGM 7465.9 (Feb. 22, 1971) which mandated hearings, impartial panels, right of cross-examination, right to the assistance of *privately* retained counsel, and findings of fact and law.

The failure of the court to require the appointment of counsel for tenants who could not afford lawyers may have stemmed more from economic than logical considerations. *Cf. Argersinger v. Hamlin*, 407 U.S. 25 (1972), which pursues a long tradition of compromise on this issue. The right of counsel was squarely confronted (and denied) in *Tyson v. New York City Hous. Auth.*, 369 F. Supp. 513 (S.D.N.Y. 1974). *See also* Steven Gunn, Note, *Eviction Defense for the Poor—Too Expensive or Justice*, 13 YALE L. & POL'Y REV. 385 (1995).

3. Other *Escalera* procedural problems remained for the courts. Specificity of the notice of the charges was considered in *Maeberry v. Housing & Redevelopment Authority*, 341 F. Supp. 643 (D. Minn. 1971), and in *Housing Authority v. Saylors*, 578 P.2d 76 (Wash. Ct. App. 1978). The latter case held the following to be inadequate notice: "You are in violation of your lease in section 6j: the tenant shall not commit or maintain a nuisance on or about the premises." Perhaps more importantly the impartiality of the decision maker remained to be defined. *See Lopez v. Henry Phipps Plaza South, Inc.*, 498 F.2d 937 (2d Cir. 1974).

A number of these procedural issues were resolved when HUD issued its Grievance Procedures in 1975, 24 C.F.R. §§966.50–966.57. These regulations apply to evictions as well as other complaints between the PHA and its tenants. 24 C.F.R. §966.4(1)(2). However, if the tenant threatens the health or safety of other tenants or PHA employees, the PHA can dispense with the procedure, provided the tenant is entitled to a judicial eviction hearing containing due process elements. 24 C.F.R. §966.51. Prior to a formal grievance hearing, the regulations require the parties to informally discuss and attempt to settle the grievance. A summary of the discussion must be made. 24 C.F.R. §966.54. If informal settlement fails, the tenant can request a formal hearing before an impartial, disinterested hearing officer or hearing panel selected jointly by the PHA and the tenant. 24 C.F.R. §966.55. Section 966.56 of the regulations sets out the hearing procedures:

> (b) The complainant shall be afforded a fair hearing providing the basic safeguards of due process which shall include:
>
> (1) The opportunity to examine before the hearing and, at the expense of the complainant, to copy all documents, records and regulations of the PHA that are relevant to the hearing. Any document not so made available after request therefore by the complainant may not be relied on by the PHA at the hearing;
>
> (2) The right to be represented by counsel or other person chosen as his or her representative;
>
> (3) The right to a private hearing unless the complainant requests a public hearing;
>
> (4) The right to present evidence and arguments in support of his or her complaint, to controvert evidence relied on by the PHA or project management, and to confront and cross-examine all witnesses on whose testimony or information the PHA or project management relies; and
>
> (5) A decision based solely and exclusively upon the has presented at the hearing....
>
> (e) At a hearing, the complainant must first make a showing of an entitlement to the relief sought and thereafter the PHA must sustain the burden of justifying the PHA action or failure to act against which the complaint is directed.

> (f) The hearing shall be conducted informally by the hearing officer or hearing panel and oral or documentary evidence pertinent to the facts and issues raised by the complainant may be received without regard to admissibility under the rules of evidence applicable to judicial proceedings....

Once the termination decision is made, the regulations prohibit the PHA from instituting a judicial eviction action until it has served a notice to vacate on the tenant. 24 C.F.R. §966.58.

HUD's attempt to expand the "threat" exception to the grievance requirement by issuing blanket determinations that state eviction procedures provided due process was extensively litigated. Washington state public housing tenants ultimately succeeded in challenging HUD's determination that the usual state eviction process was all that was due. *See Yesler Terrace Community Council v. Cisneros*, 37 F.3d 442 (9th Cir. 1994). After the tenants prevailed on the narrow ground that HUD had not followed proper notice and comment procedures in issuing the due process determination, HUD settled the case with an agreement that Washington PHAs would either provide a grievance hearing or set eviction cases for trial. Unless a grievance hearing was held, PHAs were prohibited from using the summary pretrial eviction show cause procedure that evicts most Washington tenants.

4. Beyond the question of procedural process lurks the question of what substantive reasons will justify expulsion from subsidized housing. The policy issues which inform answers to the complicated question of what behavior warrants eviction were discussed in Lawrence M. Friedman, *Public Housing and the Poor: An Overview*, 54 CAL. L. REV. 642, 644–69 (1966).

Friedman notes that one problem is that the goals of public housing have never been adequately defined. He asks whether it is the goal of the program to house the "respectable, unfortunate poor," or rehabilitate the "dependent" poor. Which goal is dominant will affect public housing eviction policies. *See also* Dean Heller, Comment, *Public Landlords and Private Tenants: The Evictions of "Undesirables" from Public Housing Projects*, 77 YALE L.J. 988 (1968).

Relatively early decisions held public housing authorities to some reasonable standards for eviction. For instance, *Sanders v. Cruise*, 173 N.Y.S.2d 871 (Sup. Ct. 1958), held that an eviction from a project on the ground that an adult son—not living in the project—was a narcotics addict exceeded any reasonable requirement for the peaceful occupancy of the projects. A decade later, another New York court said, in *Vinson v. Greenburgh Housing Authority*, 288 N.Y.S.2d 159, 163 (Sup. Ct. App. Div. 1968), *aff'd mem.*, 262 N.E.2d 211 (N.Y. 1970):

> We think that a housing authority cannot arbitrarily deprive a tenant of his right to continue occupancy through the exercise of a contractual provision to terminate the lease. In other words, the action of the housing authority must not rest on mere whim or caprice or an arbitrary reason.

Perhaps because of the paradox that tenants in the private sector had greater protection against eviction because of rent control, perhaps due to the political climate of the sixties, Massachusetts and Michigan passed statutes which required "just cause" before tenants could be evicted. (See the discussion of these issues in this chapter, *supra*). MASS. GEN. LAWS ANN. ch. 121B, §32, does not spell out just cause, but MICH. STAT. ANN. §125.694a, reads:

> (1) No tenancy or contract right to occupy housing in a project or facilities operated by any city, village, township or other unit of local government, as provided by this act, shall be terminated by the project management or the local housing commission except for just cause.
>
> (2) Just cause to terminate a tenancy or contract right to occupy housing includes, but is not limited to 1 [sic] or more of the following:

> (a) A failure to comply with the obligations of the lease or the lawful rules and regulations of the housing commission.
>
> (b) The use of a unit for any unlawful purpose, including any purpose for which the commission is entitled to recover possession of the premises by summary proceedings under section 5714(1)(b) of the revised judicature act of 1961, Act No. 236 of the Public Acts of 1961, being section 600.5714 of the Michigan Compiled Laws.
>
> (c) The maintenance of any unsafe, unsanitary, or unhealthful condition in any dwelling unit or in any of the common areas.

See also CAL. HEALTH & SAFETY CODE § 34331.

The enactment of state just or reasonable cause eviction legislation was arguably rendered unnecessary when HUD in 1975 adopted minimum public housing lease requirements. The regulations provide in part:

> That the PHA shall not terminate or refuse to renew the lease other than for serious or repeated violations of material terms of the lease such as failure to make payments due under the lease or to fulfill tenant obligations set forth ... [in the regulations] or for other good cause. 24 C.F.R. § 966.4(1)(1).

5. The HUD Lease Regulations also specify provisions that must be included in PHA leases, including those establishing the tenant's obligations to comply with PHA rules and refrain from abusing the property or disturbing neighbors. 24 C.F.R. § 966.4. The regulations also prohibit certain lease provisions, including confession of judgment, distraint for rent, PHA exculpatory provisions, and tenant waivers of notice, legal proceedings, jury trial, and appeal. 24 C.F.R. § 966.6.

c. The Special Issues of Drugs and Criminal Activity

Department of Housing and Urban Development v. Rucker

United States Supreme Court
535 U.S. 125 (2002)

Chief Justice REHNQUIST delivered the opinion of the Court.

With drug dealers "increasingly imposing a reign of terror on public and other federally assisted low-income housing tenants," Congress passed the Anti-Drug Abuse Act of 1988. § 5122, 102 Stat. 4301, 42 U.S.C. § 11901(3) (1994 ed.). The Act, as later amended, provides that each "public housing agency shall utilize leases which ... provide that any criminal activity that threatens the health, safety, or right to peaceful enjoyment of the premises by other tenants or any drug-related criminal activity on or off such premises, engaged in by a public housing tenant, any member of the tenant's household, or any guest or other person under the tenant's control, shall be cause for termination of tenancy." 42 U.S.C. § 1437d(*l*)(6) (1994 ed., Supp. V). Petitioners say that this statute requires lease terms that allow a local public housing authority to evict a tenant when a member of the tenant's household or a guest engages in drug-related criminal activity, regardless of whether the tenant knew, or had reason to know, of that activity. Respondents say it does not. We agree with petitioners.

Respondents are four public housing tenants of the Oakland Housing Authority (OHA). Paragraph 9(m) of respondents' leases, tracking the language of § 1437d(*l*)(6), obligates the tenants to "assure that the tenant, any member of the household, a guest, or another person under the tenant's control, shall not engage in ... [a]ny drug-related criminal activity on or near the premise[s]." Respondents also signed an agreement stating that the tenant "understand[s] that if I or any member of my household or guests should violate this lease provision, my tenancy may be terminated and I may be evicted."

In late 1997 and early 1998, OHA instituted eviction proceedings in state court against respondents, alleging violations of this lease provision. The complaint alleged: (1) that the respective grandsons of respondents William Lee and Barbara Hill, both of whom were listed as residents on the leases, were caught in the apartment complex parking lot smoking marijuana; (2) that the daughter of respondent Pearlie Rucker, who resides with her and is listed on the lease as a resident, was found with cocaine and a crack cocaine pipe three blocks from Rucker's apartment;[5] and (3) that on three instances within a 2-month period, respondent Herman Walker's caregiver and two others were found with cocaine in Walker's apartment. OHA had issued Walker notices of a lease violation on the first two occasions, before initiating the eviction action after the third violation.

United States Department of Housing and Urban Development (HUD) regulations administering § 1437d(*l*)(6) require lease terms authorizing evictions in these circumstances. The HUD regulations closely track the statutory language, and provide that "[i]n deciding to evict for criminal activity, the [public housing authority] shall have discretion to consider all of the circumstances of the case...." 24 C.F.R. § 966.4(*l*)(5)(i) (2001). The agency made clear that local public housing authorities' discretion to evict for drug-related activity includes those situations in which "[the] tenant did not know, could not foresee, or could not control behavior by other occupants of the unit." 56 Fed. Reg. 51560, 51567 (1991).

After OHA initiated the eviction proceedings in state court, respondents commenced actions against HUD, OHA, and OHA's director in United States District Court. They challenged HUD's interpretation of the statute under the Administrative Procedure Act, 5 U.S.C. § 706(2)(A), arguing that 42 U.S.C. § 1437d(*l*)(6) does not require lease terms authorizing the eviction of so-called "innocent" tenants, and, in the alternative, that if it does, then the statute is unconstitutional.[6] The District Court issued a preliminary injunction, enjoining OHA from "terminating the leases of tenants pursuant to paragraph 9(m) of the 'Tenant Lease' for drug-related criminal activity that does not occur within the tenant's apartment unit when the tenant did not know of and had no reason to know of, the drug-related criminal activity."

A panel of the Court of Appeals reversed, holding that § 1437d(*l*)(6) unambiguously permits the eviction of tenants who violate the lease provision, regardless of whether the tenant was personally aware of the drug activity, and that the statute is constitutional. An en banc panel of the Court of Appeals reversed and affirmed the District Court's grant of the preliminary injunction. That court held that HUD's interpretation permitting the eviction of so-called "innocent" tenants "is inconsistent with Congressional intent and must be rejected" under the first step of *Chevron U.S.A. Inc. v. Natural Resources Defense Council, Inc.*, 467 U.S. 837, 842–843 (1984).

We granted certiorari and now reverse, holding that 42 U.S.C. § 1437d(*l*)(6) unambiguously requires lease terms that vest local public housing authorities with the discre-

5. In February 1998, OHA dismissed the unlawful detainer action against Rucker, after her daughter was incarcerated, and thus no longer posed a threat to other tenants.

6. Respondents Rucker and Walker also raised Americans with Disabilities Act claims that are not before this Court. And all of the respondents raised state-law claims against OHA that are not before this Court.

tion to evict tenants for the drug-related activity of household members and guests whether or not the tenant knew, or should have known, about the activity.

That this is so seems evident from the plain language of the statute. It provides that "[e]ach public housing agency shall utilize leases which ... provide that ... any drug-related criminal activity on or off such premises, engaged in by a public housing tenant, any member of the tenant's household, or any guest or other person under the tenant's control, shall be cause for termination of tenancy." 42 U.S.C. § 1437d(*l*)(6) (1994 ed. Supp. V). The en banc Court of Appeals thought the statute did not address "the level of personal knowledge or fault that is required for eviction." Yet Congress' decision not to impose any qualification in the statute, combined with its use of the term "any" to modify "drug-related criminal activity," precludes any knowledge requirement. See *United States v. Monsanto*, 491 U.S. 600, 609 (1989). As we have explained, "the word 'any' has an expansive meaning, that is, 'one or some indiscriminately of whatever kind.'" Thus, *any* drug-related activity engaged in by the specified persons is grounds for termination, not just drug-related activity that the tenant knew, or should have known, about.

The en banc Court of Appeals also thought it possible that "under the tenant's control" modifies not just "other person," but also "member of the tenant's household" and "guest." The court ultimately adopted this reading, concluding that the statute prohibits eviction where the tenant, "for a lack of knowledge or other reason, could not realistically exercise control over the conduct of a household member or guest." But this interpretation runs counter to basic rules of grammar. The disjunctive "or" means that the qualification applies only to "other person." Indeed, the view that "under the tenant's control" modifies everything coming before it in the sentence would result in the nonsensical reading that the statute applies to "a public housing tenant ... under the tenant's control." HUD offers a convincing explanation for the grammatical imperative that "under the tenant's control" modifies only "other person": "by 'control,' the statute means control in the sense that the tenant has permitted access to the premises." 66 Fed. Reg. 28781 (2001). Implicit in the terms "household member" or "guest" is that access to the premises has been granted by the tenant. Thus, the plain language of § 1437d(*l*)(6) requires leases that grant public housing authorities the discretion to terminate tenancy without regard to the tenant's knowledge of the drug-related criminal activity.

The en banc Court of Appeals next resorted to legislative history. The Court of Appeals correctly recognized that reference to legislative history is inappropriate when the text of the statute is unambiguous. Given that the en banc Court of Appeals' finding of textual ambiguity is wrong, there is no need to consult legislative history.

A 1996 amendment to § 1437d(*l*)(6), enacted five years after HUD issued its interpretation of the statute, supports our holding. The 1996 amendment expanded the reach of § 1437d(*l*)(6), changing the language of the lease provision from applying to activity taking place "on or near" the public housing premises, to activity occurring "on or off" the public housing premises. See Housing Opportunity Program Extension Act of 1996, § 9(a)(2), 110 Stat. 836. But Congress, "presumed to be aware" of HUD's interpretation rejecting a knowledge requirement, made no other change to the statute.

Nor was the en banc Court of Appeals correct in concluding that this plain reading of the statute leads to absurd results.[7] The statute does not *require* the eviction of any ten-

7. For the reasons discussed above, no-fault eviction, which is specifically authorized under § 1437d(*l*)(6), does not violate § 1437d(*l*)(2), which prohibits public housing authorities from including "unreasonable terms and conditions [in their leases]." In addition, the general statutory pro-

ant who violated the lease provision. Instead, it entrusts that decision to the local public housing authorities, who are in the best position to take account of, among other things, the degree to which the housing project suffers from "rampant drug-related or violent crime," 42 U.S.C. § 11901(2) (1994 ed. and Supp. V), "the seriousness of the offending action," 66 Fed. Reg., at 28803, and "the extent to which the leaseholder has ... taken all reasonable steps to prevent or mitigate the offending action," *ibid.* It is not "absurd" that a local housing authority may sometimes evict a tenant who had no knowledge of the drug-related activity. Such "no-fault" eviction is a common "incident of tenant responsibility under normal landlord-tenant law and practice." 56 Fed. Reg., at 51567. Strict liability maximizes deterrence and eases enforcement difficulties. See *Pacific Mut. Life Ins. Co. v. Haslip,* 499 U.S. 1, 14 (1991).

And, of course, there is an obvious reason why Congress would have permitted local public housing authorities to conduct no-fault evictions: Regardless of knowledge, a tenant who "cannot control drug crime, or other criminal activities by a household member which threaten health or safety of other residents, is a threat to other residents and the project." 56 Fed. Reg., at 51567. With drugs leading to "murders, muggings, and other forms of violence against tenants," and to the "deterioration of the physical environment that requires substantial government expenditures," 42 U.S.C. § 11901(4) (1994 ed., Supp. V), it was reasonable for Congress to permit no-fault evictions in order to "provide public and other federally assisted low-income housing that is decent, safe, and free from illegal drugs," § 11901(1) (1994 ed.).

The en banc Court of Appeals held that HUD's interpretation "raise[s] serious questions under the Due Process Clause of the Fourteenth Amendment," because it permits "tenants to be deprived of their property interest without any relationship to individual wrongdoing." (citing *Scales v. United States,* 367 U.S. 203, 224–225 (1961); *Southwestern Telegraph & Telephone Co. v. Danaher,* 238 U.S. 482 (1915)). But both of these cases deal with the acts of government as sovereign. In *Scales,* the United States criminally charged the defendant with knowing membership in an organization that advocated the overthrow of the United States Government. In *Danaher,* an Arkansas statute forbade discrimination among customers of a telephone company. The situation in the present cases is entirely different. The government is not attempting to criminally punish or civilly regulate respondents as members of the general populace. It is instead acting as a landlord of property that it owns, invoking a clause in a lease to which respondents have agreed and which Congress has expressly required. *Scales* and *Danaher* cast no constitutional doubt on such actions.

The Court of Appeals sought to bolster its discussion of constitutional doubt by pointing to the fact that respondents have a property interest in their leasehold interest, citing *Greene v. Lindsey,* 456 U.S. 444 (1982). This is undoubtedly true, and *Greene* held that an effort to deprive a tenant of such a right without proper notice violated the Due Process Clause of the Fourteenth Amendment. But, in the present cases, such deprivation will occur in the state court where OHA brought the unlawful detainer action against respondents. There is no indication that notice has not been given by OHA in the past, or that it will not be given in the future. Any individual factual disputes about whether the lease provision was actually violated can, of course, be resolved in these proceedings.

We hold that "Congress has directly spoken to the precise question at issue." *Chevron U.S.A. Inc. v. Natural Resources Defense Council, Inc.,* 467 U.S. at 842. Section 1437d(*l*)(6)

---

vision in the latter section cannot trump the clear language of the more specific § 1437d(*l*)(6). See *Green v. Bock Laundry Machine Co.,* 490 U.S. 504, 524–526 (1989).

requires lease terms that give local public housing authorities the discretion to terminate the lease of a tenant when a member of the household or a guest engages in drug-related activity, regardless of whether the tenant knew, or should have known, of the drug-related activity.

Accordingly, the judgment of the Court of Appeals is reversed, and the cases are remanded for further proceedings consistent with this opinion.

It is so ordered.

[The Court was unanimous in its decision, with Breyer, J., taking no part in the consideration or decision of the cases.—Eds.]

Notes and Questions

1. In response to rising incidences of crime and drugs in America, particularly in association with the public housing, Congress enacted the Anti-Drug Abuse Act of 1988, Pub. L. No. 100-690, §5101, 102 Stat 4181, 4300. [The Anti-Drug Abuse Act is generally cited by its Public law number because it is codified in scattered sections of United States Code.—Eds.] For discussion of some of the problems, see Corinne A. Carey, *Crafting a Challenge to the Practice of Drug Testing Welfare Recipients: Federal Welfare Reform and the State Response as the Most Recent Chapter in the War on Drugs*, 46 BUFF. L. REV. 281 (1998).

2. With the ruling in *Rucker*, a clear precedent has been set with respect to innocent tenant evictions. *Rucker's* impact can be found in the recently decided *Housing Authority of Pittsburgh v. Fields*, 816 A.2d 1099 (Pa. 2003) (Pennsylvania Supreme Court relies for the most part on *Rucker*). Public Housing Authorities have been given *carte blanche* to evict tenants even in the presence of no fault eviction laws. Some observers have labeled tenants as bearing the burden of being "strictly liable" for the conduct of their relatives. The implications of *Rucker* for both *Escalera* and *Linares* remains to be seen. *See* this Chapter *supra*.

3. Is it possible for a state to retain its innocent tenant defense in the post-*Rucker* era? Looming just over the horizon, perhaps, is there a preemption battle. *See generally Rice v. Santa Fe Elevator Corp.*, 331 U.S. 218, 230–31 (1947). However, there is a presumption against finding preemption in areas traditionally regulated by the states. *California v. ARC Am. Corp.*, 490 U.S. 93, 101 (1989). Landlord-tenant law is one such area. Eric Wills Orts, *Tenants' Rights in Police Power Condemnations Under State Statutes and Procedural Due Process*, 23 U. MICH. J.L. REFORM 105 n.51 (1989).

In conferring discretion on state PHAs with respect to eviction, there is no evidence that Congress intended federal law to constitute the sole regulatory control over public housing. *General Motors Corp. v. Abrams*, 897 F.2d 34, 41 (2d Cir. 1990) (stating that federal law will not preempt state law in areas traditionally reserved for the states unless that was the "clear and manifest purpose of Congress").

The legislative history surrounding the 1990 Amendment of 42 U.S.C. §1437d(l)(6) indicates that "each case will be judged on its individual merits and will require the exercise of humane judgment by the PHA and the eviction court." S. Rep. No. 101-316, at 179 (1990). The Supreme Court stressed this in its holding in *Rucker* stating that the plain language of §1437d(l)(6) "unambiguously requires lease terms that vest local public housing authorities with the discretion to evict tenants for the drug-related activity of household members and guests." *Rucker*, 535 U.S. at 130. Under this scheme, state PHAs retain the discretion to take into account all circumstances relevant to a case, allowing them to evict when they deem it necessary. *Rucker*, 535 U.S. at 134. The innocent tenant defense, as codified in some states, would limit the discretion given to PHAs by 42 U.S.C. § 1437d(1)(6) and emphasized in *Rucker*. The current status of this possible improper limitation of discretion is to give deference to state regulations involving housing law issues, particularly where states give greater protections to tenants. *Kargman v. Sullivan*, 558 F.2d 612 (1st Cir. 1977) (dealing with Massachusetts rent control); *Rowe v. Pierce*, 622 F. Supp. 1030 (D.D.C. 1985) (dealing with eviction proceedings); *City of Everett v. Terry*, 789 P.2d 745 (Wash. 1990) (dealing with notice and cure provisions in an unlawful detainer action); *Franklin Tower One, L.L.C. v. N.M.*, 725 A.2d 1104 (N.J. 1999) (dealing with Section 8 vouchers). As such, a convincing argument could be made that an innocent tenant statute survives *Rucker*. *See* Sarah Clinton, *Evicting the Innocent: Can the Innocent Tenant Defense Survive a* Rucker *Preemption Challenge?*, 85 B.U. L. Rev. 293 (2005).

4. The *Rucker* decision's most lasting impact may be Rucker's implication for due process clause of the Fourteenth Amendment. In *Rucker*, the en banc Court of Appeals held that HUD's interpretation of § 1437d(l)(6) "raise[d] serious questions under the due process clause of the Fourteenth Amendment," because it permits "tenants to be deprived of their property interest without any relationship to individual wrongdoing." 237 F.3d, at 1124–1125 (*citing Scales v. United States*, 367 U.S. 203 (1961) (defendant charged with knowing membership in an organization that advocated the overthrow of the United States Government); *Southwestern Telegraph & Telephone Co. v. Danaher*, 238 U.S. 482 (1915) (an Arkansas statute forbade discrimination among customers of a telephone company)). Both of these cases deal with the acts of government as sovereign. In *Rucker*, however, the Supreme Court states that the government is acting as a landlord of property that it owns, invoking a clause in a lease to which respondents have agreed. As such, the government is not required to provide for due process concerns.

Should the government not be acting as sovereign in public housing cases but simply as a landlord, can the government evict for no good cause? Given one reading of *Rucker*, the government is no longer required to give cause when evicting a tenant. For purposes of public housing, the government possesses the same rights and privileges as any other landlord acting in the market. As such, cases such as *Joy v. Daniels* no longer govern due process concerns in public housing. The new precedent is that public housing tenants are no longer provided due process protection from innocent eviction or no cause eviction.

5. HUD has purported to determine that the "good cause" requirement does not apply to criminal activity evictions and that a conviction of criminal activity is not necessary. For a discussion of these and other provisions of the 1988 amendments to the National Housing Act, see Robert Hornstein, *Mean Things Happening in This Land: Defending Third Party Criminal Activity Public Housing Evictions*, 23 S.U. L. Rev. 257 (1996). *See also* 56 Fed. Reg. 51560 (Oct. 11, 1991) (comment § 3.3.5. Relation Between Civil Eviction Action and Criminal Proceeding, promulgating the lease and grievance procedure in which HUD purports to authorize eviction for drug or criminal activity regardless of whether formal criminal proceedings have been commenced or completed against tenants or their guests. One court appears to agree with HUD. In 1992, a New Jersey court held that criminal conviction was not necessary to evict a tenant, who was on probation for previous drug offenses, on grounds of alleged criminal activity because the eviction is considered a civil remedy, where landlord would only have to prove a preponderance of evidence supports cause for the eviction. *Housing Auth. of Newark v. Smith*, 624 A.2d 95 (N.J. Super. Ct. Law Div. 1992).

6. A related issue concerns information that a housing authority may request in considering an application for admission. The Eighth Circuit Court of Appeals has held that

a housing authority may require applicants to answer questions about drug and alcohol abuse, approving the question: "Have you *ever* been in a detoxification center or a chemical dependency program treatment?" The court held that provisions of the 1996 Housing Opportunity Program Extension Act, codified at 42 U.S.C. § 1437n(e)(1)(A), authorized the housing authority to ask the question. The court did not determine whether the statutory provision would permit the housing authority to deny all applicants who answered the question affirmatively. *Campbell v. Minneapolis Pub. Hous. Auth.*, 168 F.3d 1069 (8th Cir. 1999).

7. On the question of leases generally, prior to recent statutory, regulatory action, and *Rucker*, the cases were problematic about what could or could not constitute grounds for eviction. *See, e.g., Richmond Tenants Org. v. Richmond Redev. Auth.*, 751 F. Supp. 1204 (E.D. Va. 1990) (public housing lease must not contain unreasonable terms; may require tenant to refrain from illegal use, sale, or distribution and alcoholic beverages on the premises but not off; may not impose blanket possession prohibition of any weapon but may prohibit guns, firearms, nunchucks or similar instruments, blackjacks, and explosive devices thus allowing ceremonial swords or antique tomahawks; emergency eviction even of less than 24 hours valid; liability for certain activities of invitees sustained); *Spence v. O'Brien*, 446 N.E.2d 1070 (Mass. Ct. App 1983) (permitting illegal drug transactions on premises); *Zonner v. Heritage Hills, Ltd.*, 542 N.E.2d 697 (Ohio Ct. App. 1988) (may evict for growing marijuana, as cultivation is a felony and substantial breach of lease); *Housing Auth. v. Brown*, 349 S.E. 2d 501 (Ga. Ct. App. 1986) (marijuana possession fails to manifest creation or maintenance of threat to safety). *Cf. Kellner v. Cappellini*, 516 N.Y.S.2d 827 (Civ. Ct. 1986) (neighbors can petition for eviction "where drug activities [exist] despite landlord taking no action").

8. Commentators have critiqued the landlord's alleged right to evict an entire household due to alleged drug activities of one member as the attempt to impose a strict liability standard, on the basis of a "One Strike and You're Out" Policy. For discussion of the policy, including arguments against such a standard, see Jason Dzubow, *Fear-Free Public Housing?: An Evaluation of HUD's "One Strike and You're Out" Housing Policy*, 6 Temp. Pol. & Civ. Rts. L. Rev. 55 (1997); Ethan Breneman Lauer, *Housing and Domestic Abuse Victims: Three Proposals for Reform in Minnesota*, 15 Law & Ineq. 471, 483–505 (1997); Nelson H. Mock, *Punishing the Innocent: No-Fault Eviction of Public Housing Tenants For the Actions of Third Parties*, 76 Tex. L. Rev. 1495 (1998). For discussion of potential constitutional objections see Dean P. Cazenave, Comment, *Congress Steps Up War on Drugs in Public Housing—Has it Gone One Step Too Far?*, 36 Loy. L. Rev. 137 (1990). On the drug question generally, see Lawrence Shoffner & George Sumnik, *Controlling Drug-Related Activity in Residential Leaseholds*, 70 Mich. Bus. L.J. 168 (1991) (crack house problem, emphasizing Title VIII exemption for current drug addicts or those convicted of drug offenses); Kay Y. Young, *Handling a Drug-Related Eviction From Public Housing*, 25 Clearinghouse Rev. 793 (1991).

9. Families evicted for drug-related criminal activity may not be given a housing preference for three years unless they have successfully completed a rehabilitation program. *See* Cranston-Gonzalez National Affordable Housing Act, Pub. L. No. 101-625, § 501, 104 Stat. 4079, 4180–81 (1990) (*codified at* 42 U.S.C. § 12701 to 12912). The Cranston-Gonzalez provides for expedited grievance eviction proceedings for drug-related criminal activity, and authorizes eviction for such activities by household members or guests. § 503(a), 104 Stat 4184. The drug-related eviction provisions also apply to the low-income rental assistance program. § 546, 104 Stat 4220–21.

10. *See also HUD Presses Forward With Modified Program to Seize Leases of Drug Offenders*, 18 [Current Developments] Hous. & Dev. Rep. (WGL) 148 (1990) (now requir-

ing notice and hearing pre-eviction or notice without hearing at time of eviction if exigent circumstances, if tenant known as heavy trafficker, or has record of violence). *HUD to Seize Leases of Public Housing Tenants Implicated in Drug-Related Activity,* 18 [Current Developments] Hous. & Dev. Rep. (WGL) 59 (1990) (23 city joint enforcement with Justice Department).

For general background on drug forfeiture matters, see *United States v. James Daniel Good Real Property,* 510 U.S. 43 (1993) (real property cannot be seized under drug forfeiture statute until owner is given notice and hearing unless government proves exigent circumstances establishing need for immediate seizure); *United States v. 92 Buena Vista Ave,* 507 U.S. 111 (1993) ("innocent owner" defense may be raised when owner unaware home purchased with proceeds of illegal drug transaction under Comprehensive Drug Abuse Prevention and Control Act of 1970); *United States v. Robinson,* 721 F. Supp 1541 (D.R.I. 1989) (criminal forfeiture of lease for drug violation violates eighth amendment as excessive where public housing needed to provide shelter for children and forfeiture statute excludes public housing).

11. For a general discussion of the Fourth Amendment's protections and citing public housing search issues, see Scott E. Sundby, *"Everyman's" Fourth Amendment: Privacy or Mutual Trust Between Government and Citizen?,* 94 Colum. L. Rev. 1751 (1994).

12. Aside from enacting legislation to combat crime and drugs within public housing, public housing authorities adopted aggressive authority specific policing methods. Chicago Housing Authority ordered its police departments to sweep its residential buildings. *Pratt v. Chicago Hous. Auth.*, 848 F. Supp. 792 (N.D. Ill. 1994). The sweeps included searches of all residential units located within the buildings. Due to logistical difficulties, the sweeps normally took place several days after the emergency circumstances arose and never occurred earlier than forty-eight hours after the alleged criminal activity. Although the CHA obtained consent to search from many tenants, it conceded that consent was not obtained form some tenants, such as those who were not home when the searches occurred. The court held that CHA could not conduct warrantless searches of apartments without resident consent.

13. For a critical discussion of the crisis in public housing and the balance between due process and greater management flexibility, see Robyn Minter Smyers, *High Noon in Public Housing: The Showdown Between Due Process Rights and Good Management Practices in the War on Drugs and Crime*, 30 Urb. Law. 573 (1998). Ms. Smyers proposes that a "new consensus for change" can be distilled into "a few, broad-minded policy prescriptions for the courts, PHAs and HUD, and lawmakers." These include:

(1) That the courts avoid "heavy-handed intervention" into the management of public housing. "The courts rather should assume a more sensible and deferential role, like that of a 'friendly arbiter,' who helps PHAs meet their obligations to protect tenants' rights while still allowing them to respond to other economic and management demands."

(2) That reforms should focus on "the 'tried and true' good management practices of the past. The guideposts of successful public housing projects identified by the Urban Institute in the late 1960s and early 1970s—that include management strictness in enforcing rules, decentralization of decision-making authority, and tenant involvement in project operations—are a good place for PHAs to start."

(3) That "reforms should focus on protecting tenants' 'genuine' due process rights, not on the mechanics of PHA decision making. The past indicates clearly that people and not procedures are the best guarantees of decisions that enhance tenant autonomy, dignity, and responsibility."

(4) That "it must be recognized that some rights must be limited by competing demands and changed circumstances" rather than seeing rights in the public housing context as absolutes.

(5) That "the reforms must be driven and informed by tenants." We should "ask tenants who have lived through the last half century of changes in PHA management what they would do to make public housing better and safer."

Id. at 613–14.

2. Government-Assisted Rental Shelter: Tenant Protection in the Quasi-Private Sector

The dominant characteristic of public housing is that development, ownership, and operation of the projects is the responsibility of local governmental units. Rents are reduced through various federal and local subsidies. But as Henry Aaron suggests in Shelter and Subsidies 109 (1972), "The motives for public housing, as for much social legislation, have been mixed. The housing program established in 1937 expressed a desire to improve deplorable housing conditions and a concern over the depressed state of the economy and the construction industry." The twin aims of nurturing the economic order while providing shelter is also visible in the subsidized housing program which relies on private builders and developers, only in part because their political support is crucial to the growth of the program. More likely, the trend toward increased private sector participation in governmental programs reflects a recurrent and deeply held belief that profit, not public purpose, is the most dependable strategy to "get things done." According to Note, *Procedural Due Process in Government Subsidized Housing*, 86 Harv. L. Rev. 880, 881–87 (1973):

> Tenants in these publicly subsidized housing projects have sought due process protections comparable to those afforded to welfare recipients and conventional public housing tenants. Their claims have raised issues not present in the welfare and public housing cases, however, because of the use in the subsidized housing programs of private landlords as intermediaries in providing the government benefit. In evaluating these claims, for example, courts have had to consider the danger that imposing additional procedural constraints on the private operation of the housing would deter investment and thus undermine congressional efforts to involve private enterprise in meeting the current need for adequate housing.

Compare the procedural protections created for conventional public housing tenants with those crafted for privately-owned subsidized housing tenants in the following case.

Joy v. Daniels

United States Court of Appeals
479 F.2d 1236 (4th Cir. 1973)

Before CRAVEN, BUTZNER. and RUSSELL. Circuit Judges.

CRAVEN, Circuit Judge:

By this action for declaratory and injunctive relief under 42 U.S.C. § 1983, plaintiff challenges, as violative of the Fifth and Fourteenth Amendments, her threatened eviction from the Joseph Paul Apartments. The apartments are quasi-public, having been constructed and now being operated by defendant, Joseph Paul Apartments, Inc., under Section 221(d)(3) of the National Housing Act. The district court held that the plaintiff could properly be evicted since her tenant had expired under the terms of the lease, and that no other cause need be assigned for the eviction. We reverse.

I

The plaintiff, Thelma Joy, is the head of her household and with her four minor children constitutes a "family" within the statutory scheme. Her effective monthly income of $222.20 is a "low income" for purposes of the federal housing programs, and she thus qualifies for occupancy in the Joseph Paul Apartments. On September 2, 1970, plaintiff leased one of defendant's apartments. The standard form lease provided in relevant part:

> At the end of one year, lease is automatically renewed from month to month, rent to be payable in advance without demand on first day of each month. Either party may terminate lease at end of term or any successive term by giving 30 days' notice in advance to other party.

On September 11, 1971, the defendant gave plaintiff 30 days' notice to vacate, no cause being assigned. It appears that the plaintiff has continued to occupy her apartment on a month-to-month basis, with her tenant dependent on the outcome of this litigation.

Section 221(d)(3) of the National Housing Act, 12 U.S.C. § 1715(d)(3) (1971), is a statutory scheme for encouraging housing for low income families. To participate in this program, defendant was required to conform to a regulatory agreement with the Federal Housing Administration governing, *inter alia*, the construction, occupancy, and daily operations of the project. The FHA also grants defendant rent supplements for the plaintiff and other tenants.

II

Initially we must determine if the Fourteenth Amendment is applicable, *i.e.*, whether the action of defendant in seeking to evict plaintiff can be said to be "state action" since it is well settled the Fourteenth Amendment does not inhibit the conduct of purely private persons in their ordinary activities. The Supreme Court has never attempted to fashion a precise formula of what constitutes "state action" and the question frequently is difficult to determine. *Moose Lodge No. 107 v. Irvis*, 407 U.S. 163 (1972); *Burton v. Wilmington Parking Auth.*, 365 U.S. 715, 722 (1961). "State action" may result from administrative, regulatory, legislative, and judicial action. *Moose Lodge No. 107*, 407 U.S. at 179. The determination must be made on a case-by-case basis. "Only by sifting facts and weighing circumstances can the nonobvious involvement of the State in private conduct be attributed its true significance." *Burton*, 365 U.S. at 722.

In the present case the defendant receives mortgage benefits from the FHA and is thus subject to the attendant FHA regulations. Additionally, the defendant has undertaken to utilize the eviction procedures authorized by South Carolina. While these factors, either separately or combined, have been held insufficient to constitute "state action" they are relevant and material in the assessment of other evidence of state involvement.

The defendant receives rent supplements from the FHA. Prerequisite to obtaining these supplements, the defendant received specific authorization from the County Council. We view this involvement of the state (power delegated to local government) in this case as similar to the zoning power which, with state eviction proceedings, resulted in a holding of "state action" in *Lavoie v. Bigwood*, 457 F.2d 7 (1st Cir. 1972).

The participation of the federal government in such housing projects is conditioned upon state approval. The state is thus involved for there would otherwise be no federal direct funding through rent subsidies and indirect funding through mortgage benefits. We think that these factors coupled with utilization of state eviction procedure have "so far insinuated [the state] into a position of interdependence" with the defendant that the challenged activity "cannot be considered to have been so 'purely private' as to fall without the scope of the Fourteenth Amendment." *Burton*, 365 U.S. at 725. Accordingly, we hold there is sufficient state involvement to constitute "state action" for purposes of the Fourteenth Amendment. We also hold that the facts are sufficient to satisfy the "under color of" law clause of 42 U.S.C. § 1983. Accordingly, the district court had jurisdiction under 28 U.S.C. § 1343(3).

III

The district court concluded that plaintiff had no right of occupancy upon expiration of the term of the lease. Plaintiff contends that despite expiration of the term she may be evicted only for "good cause" and is entitled to the protection of procedural due process in the determination of whether cause exists. Since procedural due process applies only to the deprivation of interest protected by the Fourteenth Amendment, *i.e.*, liberty and property, we must first determine plaintiff's substantive rights. Thus we must now look at applicable statutes, governmental regulations, and the custom and understandings of public landlords in the operation of their apartments to determine if a public tenant has a "property interest" in a tenancy beyond the term of the lease except for cause.

[At this point, the court discusses the congressional goal of a decent home and suitable living environment, notes provisions of the federal Civil Rights Act prohibiting discrimination in federal programs, and quotes the Harvard Note, *supra*, on the point that subsidized housing tenants have a reasonable expectancy to stay on beyond the termination of a lease.—Eds.]

In view of the congressional policies of providing a decent home (with stability and security) for every American family, and of prohibiting arbitrary and discriminatory action, bolstered by the FHA regulations and custom, we find in the scheme of the National Housing Act and the Housing and Urban Development Act of 1965 a property right or entitlement to continue occupancy until there exists a cause to evict other than the mere expiration of the lease. We therefore hold that the case provision purporting to give the landlord power to terminate without cause at the expiration of affixed term is invalid.

In *Caulder v. Durham Hous. Auth.*, 433 F.2d 998 (4th Cir. 1970), *cert. denied*, 401 U.S. 1003 (1971), we stated:

> The "privilege" or the "right" to occupy publicly subsidized low-rent housing seems to us to be no less entitled to due process protection than entitlement to welfare benefits which were the subject of decision in *Goldberg* or the other right and privileges referred to in *Goldberg*.

433 F.2d at 1003. The court then held that tenants are entitled to notice, confrontation of witnesses, counsel, and a decision by an impartial decision maker based on evidence adduced at a hearing. As stated by the court below, it could be inferred that the plaintiff here was to be evicted for cause. If so, she would be entitled to the same procedural safeguards set forth in *Caulder*. To allow a quasi-public landlord to evict upon expiration of a fixed term is to enable secret and silent discrimination and would wholly emasculate the procedural safeguards of *Caulder*.

Indeed, the entitlement of plaintiff to continue occupancy of public housing, like the interest of a covered employee under the Social Security Act, is, we think, "of sufficient substance to fall within the protection from arbitrary governmental action afforded by the Due Process Clause." *Flemming v. Nestor*, 363 U.S. 603, 611 (1960). A position beyond that espoused in *Flemming* has been urged.

> But that under appropriate circumstances one's interest in his government job, his publicly financed home, his food stamp meals, or his state university educational opportunities may indeed be constitutional rights in the positive law sense ought no longer be denied. [Van Alstyne, *The Demise of the Right-Privilege Distinction in Constitutional Law*, 81 Harv. L. Rev. 1439, 1463–64 (1968)]

However, in view of our holding that the congressional scheme and custom give plaintiff a right to remain in her apartment we need not decide whether her claim is also protected by equal protection and "substantive" due process.

Finally we must determine what procedural due process requires by way of protection of plaintiff's right to tenancy except for cause. In *Johnson v. Tamsberg*, 430 F.2d 1125 (4th Cir. 1970), we noted that the South Carolina eviction scheme requires the landlord to prove in court his allegations, allows trial by jury, and we concluded that "public housing tenants are not actually ejected until basic due process requisites are satisfied." 430 F.2d at 1127. That is enough. A prior administrative hearing is not required so long as the tenant may at some stage receive a plenary judicial hearing. Since we now hold that a Section 221(d)(3) landlord must before eviction give his tenant a good-cause notice and prove such cause exists, and since the South Carolina eviction procedure is constitutionally adequate, we perceive no reason for retention of jurisdiction in the federal court to consider the question of good cause for eviction. Landlord-tenant law is traditionally the province of the states. State judges are bound as are we by the due process clause of the fourteenth amendment.

On remand the district will enter its decree invalidating the lease expiration clause and enjoining the defendant from attempting to evict the plaintiff except for cause under the procedural and substantive law of South Carolina.

Reversed and remanded.

Notes and Questions

1. Prior to *Joy v. Daniels*, courts had held that eviction in retaliation for associational activities or petitions to the FHA violated the First Amendment rights of assisted housing tenants. *See* Note, *supra*, 86 Harv. L. Rev. at 903–04. In *McQueen v. Druker*, 438 F.2d 781 (1st Cir. 1971), the court relied on the unconstitutionally of attaching conditions to governmental benefits which deprive citizens of rights protected by the Constitution. After *Joy v. Daniels*, HUD institutionalized "good cause" provisions in promulgating eviction procedures from privately owned, but governmentally subsidized housing projects. 41 Fed. Reg. 16924 (Apr. 22, 1976), and 41 Fed. Reg. 43329 (Sept. 30, 1976), codified at 24 C.F.R. §§ 247.1–247.10.

In part, the current regulations provide:

> (a) *General*. The landlord may not terminate any tenancy in a subsidized project except upon the following grounds:
>
> (1) Material noncompliance with the rental agreement,

(2) Material failure to carry out obligations under any state landlord and tenant act, or

(3) Other good cause....

(c) *Material noncompliance.* The term "material noncompliance with the rental agreement" shall include: (1) One or more substantial violations of the rental agreement, or to repeated minor violations of the rental agreement that disrupt the livability of the project, adversely affect the health or safety of any person or the right of any tenant to the quiet enjoyment of the leased premises and related project facilities, interfere with the management of the project or have an adverse financial effect on the project. Nonpayment of rent or any other financial obligation due under the rental agreement (including any portion thereof) beyond any grace period permitted under state law shall constitute a substantial violation of the rental agreement. The payment of rent or any other financial obligation due under the rental agreement after the due date but within the grace period permitted under state law shall constitute a minor violation.

24 C.F.R. § 247.3.

2. The procedural due process concerns were addressed in *Ferguson v. Metropolitan Dev. & Hous. Auth.*, 485 F. Supp. 517 (M.D. Tenn. 1980). The court applied *Goldberg v. Kelly* and its progeny to require a "pretermination hearing" before the authority could terminate Section 8 subsidies to a tenant in the authority's Section 8 existing housing program. The court did not require good or just cause for eviction, restricting its holding instead to invalidating a practice of terminating Section 8 tenants who owed the authority rent from a previous occupancy. The court found the policy unauthorized by statute and HUD requirements in the ACC. *See also Davis v. Mansfield Metro. Hous. Auth.*, 751 F.2d 180 (6th Cir. 1984) (holding that due process requires that a tenant for Section 8 housing who had been terminated or denied recertification based on outstanding claim for past due rent or property damage be able to request an informal hearing); *Simmons v. Drew*, 716 F.2d 1160 (7th Cir. 1983) (requiring pretermination hearing for Section 8 tenant who moved into subsidized unit too early for apparently good reason); *Green Park Assocs. v. Inman* 464 N.Y.S.2d 500 (Civ. Ct. 1983). *Contra*, on the back rent disqualification, *Vandermark v. Hous. Auth.*, 492 F. Supp. 359 (M.D. Pa. 1980).

The Eleventh Circuit held that tenants may not be evicted absent a showing of good cause in *Jeffries v. Georgia Residential Finance Auth.*, 678 F.2d 919 (11th Cir.), *cert. denied*, 459 U.S. 971 (1982), a case arising prior to Congress' legislative imposition of the good cause eviction standard.

3. *Swann v. Gastonia Hous. Auth.*, 675 F.2d 1342 (4th Cir. 1982) held that because a Section 8 existing housing tenant has an expectation of renewal, termination of a Section 8 lease is tantamount to an eviction. This conclusion was buttressed by *Mitchell v. HUD*, 569 F. Supp. 701 (N.D. Cal. 1983), which held that "termination" under the statute requiring good cause included both non-renewal and eviction. *Mitchell* and supporting cases forced HUD to rewrite its regulations governing termination of Section 8 leases; however, Congress amended the Act in 1996 to require good cause only for evictions during the term of the lease. 42 U.S.C. § 1437f(d)(1)(B)(ii). The amendments have been made for temporary periods in appropriation acts, but have been renewed for several years. Recall that legislation has been proposed that would eliminate the good cause requirement for all government housing programs. If the National Housing Act is amended to eliminate the good cause requirement, what becomes of the *Joy* court's view that a

property interest is created by the statutory policy of the Act? What arguments remain that good cause is constitutionally required to terminate a subsidized tenancy?

4. Even during the term of the lease, some cases have undermined the effectiveness of HUD regulations and their associated statutes by allowing landlords to evict Section 8 tenants despite failure to comply with the precise federal regulations. For example, the court in *Smith v. Hendrix*, 290 S.E.2d 504 (Ga. Ct. App. 1982), affirmed the eviction order and held that the landlord's failure to give the tenant proper notice did not prejudice the tenant. *Contra Central Brooklyn Urb. Dev. Corp. v. Copeland*, 471 N.Y.S.2d 989 (Civ. Ct. 1984); *Green Park Assocs. v. Inman*, 464 N.Y.S.2d 500 (Civ. Ct. 1983).

5. Was the court in *Joy v. Daniels* correct in its assumption that the tenant's due process rights could be protected in state court? What if the state eviction statute does not allow just cause defenses to be asserted in an eviction proceeding? There will be no successful equal protection objection to this omission. *See Lindsey v. Normet*, in Chapter 1 *supra*.

In *Anderson v. Denny*, 365 F. Supp. 1254 (W.D. Va. 1973), the court believed that the supremacy clause of the federal constitution provided an adequate basis for assertion of a tenant's procedural due process rights in a state court eviction proceeding. Do you agree? Some federal courts have required due process protections in subsidized housing evictions on the grounds that protections available in State court proceedings are inadequate. *See Caulder v. Durham Hous. Auth.*, 433 F.2d 998 (4th Cir.), *cert. denied*, 401 U.S. 1003 (1971). However, the trend seems to be to defer to the state courts. *See Perry v. Royal Arms Apartments*, 729 F.2d 1081 (6th Cir. 1984) (adequate due process provided by Tennessee eviction procedure for evictions under state law); *Swann v. Gastonia Hous. Auth.*, 675 F.2d 1342 (4th Cir. 1982) (holding that a state court eviction hearing obviated the need for a hearing before the PHA prior to termination of the tenant's Section 8 certificate); *Wiggins v. Department of Hous. & Urb. Dev.*, 523 F. Supp. 1170 (D. Md. 1981). *See* Martin J. McMahon, Annotation, *Tenant's Procedural Rights Prior to Eviction or Termination of Benefits Under Section Eight of the National Housing Act of 1937,* 81 A.L.R. Fed. 844 (1987).

6. Despite the plethora of cases allowing 42 U.S.C. § 1983 challenges to evictions by publicly subsidized landlords, the issue of whether such evictions are "under the color of state law" for purposes of Section 1983 remains controversial. *Compare Swann v. Gastonia Hous. Auth.*, 675 F.2d 1342 (4th Cir. 1982) (eviction from section 8 housing is "state action") *with Miller v. Hartwood Apartments, Ltd.*, 689 F.2d 1239 (5th Cir. 1982) (private entity operating section 8 development could not be sued under section 1983 even though tenants asserted that their evictions were "governmental action"). *See generally* Annotation, *When Is Eviction of Tenant by Private Landlord Conducted "Under Color of State Law" for Purposes of 42 U.S.C. § 1983*, 73 A.L.R. Fed. 78 (1985). If the voucher program is successful in privatizing the subsidized low-income housing market, the "color of state law" issue becomes more acute. *Id.* at 94.

7. Conventional public housing tenants can use the grievance procedure for disputes with a housing authority other than eviction, including the denial of the tenant's request to add a family member to the lease. *Saxton v. Housing Auth.*, 1 F.3d 881 (9th Cir. 1993). The housing authority in *Saxton* had argued that the rejected family member was entitled only to an informal hearing. Public housing tenants can request formal grievance hearings when the housing authority fails to make repairs and can be awarded rent abatements administratively. *Samuels v. District of Columbia,* 770 F.2d 184 (D.C. Cir. 1985). Some courts have been sympathetic to the argument that in other subsidized housing programs due process requires notice and a right to be heard before important actions are taken,

such as rent increases. *Geneva Towers Org. v. Federated Mortgage Investors,* 504 F.2d 483 (9th Cir. 1974). Other courts have been reluctant to impose such requirements on private landlords, and even the *Geneva* court held that a full-blown hearing was unnecessary in advance of the action. *See, e.g., Reiner v. West Village Assocs.,* 768 F.2d 31 (2d Cir. 1985) (tenants in 223(b) project opposing a rent increase do not have a property interest sufficient to invoke due process). It remains to be seen whether privatization will erode the procedural protections of public housing tenants or whether more enlightened times will again use these protections as models for all other housing programs.

A Concluding Note on Reform of the Landlord-Tenant Relationship

This chapter has highlighted the reform of the landlord-tenant relationship as a salient dimension of urban housing policy. This reform has concentrated on upgrading the quality of housing and on providing greater security for the tenant in rental housing accommodations. The cost of rental housing has been a secondary factor, except where rent control has attempted to place limits on tenant rents. Reformers have generally assumed that the legal reform of the landlord-tenant relationship can be secured without dramatic increases in rental housing costs.

Barring a political and economic upheaval of unprecedented magnitude, it is probable that a mixed private sector and governmental response will struggle with the persistent demand for affordable, safe, and sanitary shelter, designed and located to provide the complex of amenities meeting contemporary expectations. Alternative and more sweeping reforms, such as total public ownership of the rental housing stock, are not likely to occur within the limits of the present consensus about the permissible limits of government intervention in an avowedly free market economy. There has been a partial, not a total, revolution.

The priorities selected by the landlord-tenant reform struggle raise a number of questions. In an economy in which housing remains scarce and inflation continues to outstrip gains in income, consumer demand is likely to focus on the cost, not the quality, of housing. Housing subsidies are likely to support only a part of unsatisfied housing demand. If a better equilibrium between demand and supply returns, tenants are likely to be more selective in a market where there are affordable choices.

Questions also remain about the most effective strategy to achieve socially desirable housing goals. In both the private and public rental sectors, the abiding assumption has been that the conflict between landlords and tenants would improve the quality of housing in the marketplace. The prevailing hope has been that the judicial realignment of landlord and tenant demands for fair treatment would be satisfied by limitations on landlord autonomy in the private sector and the application of procedural due process limitations to the public landlord.

Reflection on the material in this chapter casts doubt on these assumptions, and raises questions about a widespread reliance on private conflict resolution to solve intractable social problems such as the shortage of housing and its impact on the quality of urban life. Is it clear that a sound housing policy should depend in any significant measures on private initiative alone? Do sometimes idiosyncratic shelter preferences really ensure a quality of housing that will guarantee healthy urban environments? At the level of simple justice, can individual needs be successfully met in the courtroom when economic issues are at the heart of the dispute?

At the level of interstitial legal problems, the courts are likely to remain the principal forum for adjusting shelter disputes. Class actions or not, judicial resolution of a case in court is also likely to have some impact on the fate of others not directly involved in the particular case. A strategy to create and sustain viable urban environments in which there is an adequate supply of housing will also require more than judicial intervention in the private housing market.

A long tradition of governmental intervention in housing markets has produced governmental programs designed to improve urban and neighborhood housing environments. The enactment of housing codes requiring the maintenance of housing is one example. Slum clearance is another. The next chapter turns to those governmental programs aimed explicitly at neighborhood revitalization and community rebuilding. They provide the material resources, technical expertise, and comprehensive social strategy that courts cannot supply.

Chapter 5

Community Development and Revitalization

Community development is a significant component of urban political life in the United States today. While 40 years ago the field consisted of a few organizations striving to improve the conditions and quality of life in a number of poor urban neighborhoods, today community development has developed into a field proffering a mainstream set of practices and institutions that build affordable housing, offer access to credit in low-wealth communities, provide education and other social services, and in a myriad of ways, seek to build the community's capacity to gain resources, deliver social goods, and participate effectively in the American economy. Community development is a complex field of practice that has only recently evolved into a distinct and recognized field of study. As a discipline, community development draws from the professional and academic fields of planning, sociology, economics, political science, geography, and more. Not the least of these is law.

The strategies, methods, and the major players in community development practice are wide-ranging, yet its aims are expressed as planned efforts to address the quality-of-life challenges facing communities. CD theory and practice are necessarily interdisciplinary, because community development connects the physical/geographic aspects with the economic, political, environmental, social and cultural aspects of each place where community development is undertaken. However, community development is necessarily practiced with reference to a wide framework of laws that apply to development projects.

Communities occupy a paradoxical "space" in U.S law and society: essential even in an economic view yet highly constrained in their ability to control what happens to them. Few communities in the usual usage of the word are coextensive with the legally constituted jurisdiction possessing law-making and enforcement powers such as cities, towns and counties. *Community* in its customary place-based sense refers to micro-local places where people live and work (though not necessarily doing both in the same locale). Communities are places of social, economic, and human interdependence. These are the sites of our housing, education, health care, daily convenience shopping, the places where we raise our children, and engage in the many other activities that sustain us physically, emotionally, socially, and psychologically. Thus, they are vital for the preservation of the larger society. Yet they are significantly constrained in what they can do to shape or control the larger economic and political forces that affect them.

The Legal Framework of Community Development. How land is used is an essential ingredient for communities as they develop or preserve their character and pursue shared purposes. Land use law is one of the primary ways that communities establish priorities, and address fiscal, aesthetic, service and lifestyle needs of their residents. Historically land use law has been a matter of state and local power, enacted by state and local governing bodies and implemented by locally elected or appointed boards, subject to requirements for publicized public hearings on proposed changes to the law.

Which laws apply to particular development plans and projects will vary to some extent by virtue of a project's proposed uses of land, the intended beneficiaries of the completed project, the mix of public and private finance; and the programmatic substance of the project once in operation. The physical dimensions of any built project invoke land use planning and zoning laws. Many projects require connections to the local infrastructure of roads, sewers and schools. Governmental powers including regulatory approvals, imposition of fees or the offer of financial incentives, must be exercised and decisions made.

Land use decisions have particular significance in the financial health of local governments. The real property tax remains the largest source of locally raised revenue for local governments, accounting for about 26% of local revenues, and increased nationally from 1980 to 1990 by 128%. David R. Berman, *State-Local Relations: Authority and Finances, in* MUNICIPAL YEAR BOOK 2007 (2007). Innovations in public and private financing of development projects also require the parties' careful attention. Local governments may expect developers of new private developments to contribute to the public costs of the infrastructure on which the project's buyers will depend, in the form of impact fees, or linkage fees imposed on commercial developers to offset the costs of additional public transportation or low- and moderate-income housing made necessary by the development. The interplay of local government resources and development practices provides one of the primary threads of the tapestry that is community development

Legal regulation also shapes many of the practitioners in the field of community development, by regulating the permissible activities and powers of the entity promoting the development as government, governmental instrumentality, private for-profit or not-for-profit organization, a community-based organization (CBO) or community development corporation (CDC) or a regional or national intermediary.

In the United States, the federal government has no department of national economic development to offer guidance to states or cities, nor is there a national development plan. Yet each of the 50 states has a department of economic development or its equivalent, as do most large cities and urban counties. The institutionalization of economic development, and the array of policy tools, has intensified since 1980. A wide-ranging examination is PETER K. EISINGER, THE RISE OF THE ENTREPRENEURIAL STATE: STATE AND LOCAL ECONOMIC DEVELOPMENT POLICY IN THE UNITED STATES (1988).

Federal laws that direct public money toward community development purposes direct local and state governments to engage citizens in public participation processes and to engage in comprehensive planning as a condition of the receipt of funds. Each of these domains of law has its genesis in the federal constitutional framework and related doctrines of federal, state and local governmental powers, as we shall see.

Outcomes and Processes. To many practitioners, community development connotes outcomes—some physical, social and economic improvement in a geographic community. The term also signifies a process by which members of communities are able to act together and to enhance their capacity to do so. This chapter embraces both the outcome and process meanings of community development and illuminates the relationships between the two.

Economic Development is treated in this chapter as an important auxiliary of community development. "Economic development" refers to state and local governments' efforts to attract and retain employers so as to create and retain employment and encourage new business investment in their locales, as well as public and private organizations' programs to prepare or retrain workers, create jobs, and increase income and standards of living. "Community economic development" is emerging as the rubric for non-governmental revitalization efforts to achieve more inclusive participation in economic growth. Both government-sponsored and citizen-directed economic development are addressed in this Chapter. *See generally* WILLIAM SIMON, THE COMMUNITY ECONOMIC DEVELOPMENT MOVEMENT (2001). See also BUILDING STRONGER COMMUNITIES: A GUIDE TO COMMUNITY ECONOMIC DEVELOPMENT FOR ADVOCATES, LAWYERS AND POLICYMAKERS (Roger A. Clay Jr. & Susan R. Jones eds. 2009) (publication of the American Bar Association).

Professor William Simon has described a "Community Economic Development Movement" of grass-roots efforts flourishing across the country, engaging "the most optimistic and innovative approaches to urban poverty on both the left and the right." Arising as support for traditional welfare rights and public housing programs has waned, the movement's participants exhibit "social entrepreneurialism" as they strive to channel the development of local markets in directions that promote social goals. Core elements of this approach to CED include: (1) objectives to develop housing, jobs or business opportunities for low-income people; (2) pursued by nonprofit, nongovernmental organizations (3) that are accountable to the residents of the community. The twin hallmarks of community development, in this perspective, are that the community is both beneficiary of the development, and its agent. This agency role is predominantly achieved through local non-business institutions known as community development corporations. WILLIAM H. SIMON, THE COMMUNITY ECONOMIC DEVELOPMENT MOVEMENT (2001).

Clay and Jones define community economic development as follows:

Roger A. Clay Jr. and Susan R. Jones, Building Stronger Communities: A Guide to Community Economic Development for Advocates, Lawyers and Policymakers

4–5 (Roger A. Clay Jr. & Susan R. Jones eds. 2009)

What Is CED?

CED emerged in the 1960s in response to calls by activists in low-income communities to incorporate local residents into the process of revitalizing their own communities. Supported primarily by the federal government and the Ford Foundation, the movement expanded in the 1970s to address further deterioration of urban and rural communities. The deindustrialization of the 1970s and 1980s intensified public antipoverty and social welfare efforts, and community organizations became the major vehicles for delivery of housing and job programs in low-income communities. The 1990s ushered in the demise of welfare, devolution from federal to state government, and a public policy emphasis on economic self-sufficiency.

While early legal representation focused primarily on such activities as workforce development, business development, manufacturing, and commercial and retail services, legal advocacy expanded to embrace the creation of affordable housing as well as microenterprises and worker-owned cooperatives, affordable child care and health care, and the creation of community development banks and credit unions. Market-based CED initiatives such as the Low Income Housing Tax Credit Program have spurred new programs such as the New Markets Tax Credit, one of the most recent economic development initiatives designed to stimulate investments in low-income rural and urban communities from commercial real estate to small business development using tax credits. At the same time, CED advocates promote economic justice tools such as living wages; equitable development; sector employment intervention; and other income and asset accumulation and wealth-building strategies, including individual development accounts. The contemporary CED movement also highlights human capital development; the importance of social networks; and creative, environmentally prudent employment options such as green jobs.

Throughout the evolution of the CED movement, lawyers have worked with community residents to provide a wide range of legal services from forming corporations for CDCs to serving as general counsel for public and private affordable housing developers.

Section A provides an overview of the sprawling field of community development, tracing its roots and dominant themes, and contemplating future directions of community development policy, programs and practices. Solving various problems in America's cities has been a focus of government policy and civic activism throughout the nation's industrial history, and intensifying in the post-industrial, increasingly global features of the national economy, with significant consequences for the communities in which Americans live. The legal framework in which community development takes place is a complex interplay of federal constitutional principles with state and local powers for regulating land use, safeguarding the general welfare, and taxing and spending public monies. The roles of public participation in the direction and benefit of community development initiatives, and of governmental accountability for the stewardship of public powers and resources, are important themes in community development law and practice.

Sections B and C frame contemporary public policy and programs of community development, and examine their theoretical underpinnings. These proceed from the early-twentieth century innovation of prescriptive housing codes, through the extensive possibilities facilitated by federal enactments and funding beginning mid-century, but then changed markedly by significant decentralization and shrinking federal financial aid for cities. The major policy objectives embodied in CD programs vary in the primacy of blight-removal, physical redevelopment, community building, or poverty alleviation and "equitable development."

Section B begins with one of the first urban revitalization techniques utilized—the municipal housing code, which has antecedents that go back to the early twentieth century. Building and housing codes today are garnering renewed attention as one strategy to induce resource-conserving construction and rehabilitation techniques. Now commonly used in most cities as a housing improvement measure, the housing code requires the minimum maintenance of existing housing, but generally provides neither subsidy nor compensation to owners of housing that is subject to its requirements.

In chronological terms, governmental support followed housing codes, primarily in the form of financing and grants for housing rehabilitation to assist owners in the improvement of the housing stock. These subsidies and grants initially were included in the slum clearance and redevelopment programs authorized by federal legislation enacted in 1949. The main legal tool of these slum clearance programs was to give municipalities power to acquire all of the land and structures in an area characterized as "blighted," clear the area, and sell the cleared land to a private entity for redevelopment. The availability of compulsory powers of land acquisition through eminent domain was a marked advance over establishing housing codes, which did not involve land acquisition. Substantial federal contributions were provided for the cost of acquisition, clearance, preparation of the infrastructure for sale, and administration of the project. The operations of redevelopment programs raise numerous legal and policy issues. The major issues are examined in Section B of this chapter.

The wide range of revitalization activities authorized by the Housing and Community Development Act of 1974 are discussed in Section C. This legislation terminated the slum clearance and several other federal urban revitalization programs, substituting a community development "block grant." Eligible local governments, under a formula contained in the federal legislation, can receive block grants that are available for a variety of revitalization techniques. These funds can finance housing construction and rehabilitation, public works, land acquisition, as well as slum clearance and local housing code programs, as well as and a number of activities considerably broader than the federal programs they replaced. Twenty years later, this central program was augmented through additional policy approaches to stimulate investment in economically distressed areas. These provide tax incentives, direct financial assistance, regulatory relief, or some combination of these approaches, with the objective to increase employment and promote economic activity, chiefly through tax benefits, to businesses in areas of high unemployment and pervasive poverty.

Section D traces the policy turn from "community development" to "economic development," and considers the wide range of players and practitioners of community development strategies. These include local governments, private for-profit developers and not-for-profit organizations that engage in development strategies, some based in the communities they serve, others acting regionally or nationally as intermediaries. Community development requires money and the mechanisms for financing community development initiatives also engage a set of public and private players, and an array of public finance mechanisms. Section D examines the forms of public and private development financial resources that are commonly assembled in order to accomplish development projects. Governments have taxing and spending powers, special debt tools, and credit quality that can be used to raise capital and direct resources for various types of economic development. Institutional resources of finance for real estate development include governments, banks, tax-credit syndication participants and private investors, venture capital funds and small business investment corporations, and a range of not-for-profit lenders and social investment vehicles, some of which are formed for the purpose of promoting community development.

Section E traces the legal evolution of the set of powers and programs which have dramatically remade American cities since the 1950s, beginning with the federal Urban Renewal program which authorized local governments to facilitate area-wide demolition and new construction. The "slum clearance" model of redevelopment has cast a long shadow over a variety of approaches to urban revitalization.

Community revitalization programs can also have secondary effects that require governmental intervention. One effect has been displacement of households and businesses by local public agencies or the private redevelopment approved by local jurisdictions, which occurs in the process of clearing land for redevelopment or carrying out housing rehabilitation and community development programs. Section F examines the protections and benefits, that are available to households and businesses displaced because of revitalization programs under the federal Uniform Relocation Act, and consider community-wide effects as well.

Section G concludes with a look at important issues emerging in "sustainable community development": equitable development and inclusive community benefit, the impacts of transportation choices on the character of urban redevelopment, and the potential for innovations in planning, transit policy and "green" building to integrate greater human health and wellbeing with environmental protection and community development.

The prevailing strategies leave some unanswered issues and may be too limited conceptually. Section G offers a brief survey of emerging alternative strategies and approaches to the problems of today's communities, including specifically an increasingly vigorous focus on coordinating development activities with transportation and sustainable planning, and a comparative perspective that draws on selected European examples.

A. Community Development's Origins

1. Responding to Substandard Housing Conditions and Neighborhood Decline

Neighborhood decline has long presented vexing and difficult challenges to strategists concerned with maintaining the vitality of cities. Neighborhood decline is one of the consequences of the major shift in the social and economic status of older cities that has occurred since World War II. The extensive suburban homebuilding that characterized the postwar period was accompanied by the rapid flight of upper-income and usually white residents from the inner cities to the suburbs. Their place was taken by lower-income groups, often minorities, who came to many of the northern industrial cities after the war. These changes in the character of the inner city placed special pressures on older urban neighborhoods that led to their decline and, in many cities, substantial clearance and redevelopment activities. For a discussion of foreclosures and vacancies cutting swaths through whole neighborhoods beginning in 2005, see Chapter 1 *supra*.

The intergovernmental character of housing and community development programs generally was examined in Chapter 2 of this course book, *supra*. In this chapter, it is important to understand the constitutional underpinnings of the differentiation between the levels of government as they allow, direct or accommodate the complex and interdisciplinary practices which comprise community development. Both the federal government and the fifty state governmental systems require separation of powers among their executive, legislative and judicial branches. Further, quasi-public and wholly-private sector entities are frequently used to implement government programs, especially at the state and local levels, and the private role is often encouraged or required by legislation. This produces a number of complicated arrangements: in the allocation of roles, in the formulation of priorities, and in coordination among the levels of governmental authority for policy, project approvals, and responsibility for outcomes.

Observers of American cities are familiar with the cyclical nature of urban decay. As older neighborhoods are occupied by less affluent residents, those neighborhoods simply do not have the resources needed to sustain the housing that exists there. Much of this housing is rented. As tenant incomes decline, landlords are unable to maintain their dwellings. The units decay, a new generation of even poorer tenants moves in, and the cycle continues until the neighborhood deterioration becomes irreversible. In recent years, the affluent have been abandoning neighborhoods when faced with the loss of home equity and finding their loans greatly in excess of the market value and making mortgage payments in excess of rents in superior properties. Similarly, foreclosures have hit the less affluent and landlords as jobs, credit, and savings are lost.

Housing must be maintained lest it decay, deteriorate, and become dysfunctional. While most governmental housing programs have concentrated on the production of new dwellings, one must not lose sight of the need to retain existing stock if housing production is ultimately to meet the demand for housing.

A number of factors limit the effectiveness of rehabilitation as a response to decaying housing and neighborhood blight. Economic incentives for developers—indeed virtually all systems for meeting housing needs—have been directed primarily toward developing new housing units. During the 1940s and 1950s, when problems of neighborhood deterioration became evident, the initial response was not rehabilitation but clearance and redevelopment. Older dwellings, especially nineteenth- and early twentieth-century (pre-World War I) units, were often considered inadequate for current tastes as to structure, aesthetics, and size. Even if repaired, these units would soon become totally obsolete. Architects, moreover, could build no monuments by redoing a predecessor's work. No rehabilitation industry existed, and contractors considered the work to be substantially different and more difficult than constructing on a clean site without having to deal with the present occupants. In total, the deck was stacked against retaining existing units and rehabilitating them.

Resistance to "urban removal," as renewal programs came to be known, forced a reappraisal of policy in the 1960s. In the 1970s, economic considerations and a shrinking federal governmental role coalesced, leading to the adoption of policies for rehabilitation and improvement as a somewhat less expensive alternative to clearance and redevelopment.

As neighborhoods age, the effects of "filtering" can be observed. As those with higher incomes move to more attractive areas, older neighborhoods become available to those with lower incomes. Neighborhoods containing roughly equivalent housing types tend to react to these pressures in generally similar ways. As filtering occurs, more persons with lower socio-economic (and usually minority racial) characteristics become residents.

As this process continues, those with the lowest incomes tend to be less able to effectively maintain their houses. Their incomes are more susceptible to economic downturns because of their job levels. Required maintenance is often deferred. Significant exterior—that is, visible—deterioration can result. To the extent that multiple-unit dwellings are situated in these areas, landlords who lose their original higher-income tenants find their market comprised increasingly of lower-income households, not able to pay higher rents. Management expenses increase, which is compounded by rent delinquencies and maintenance problems. The profitability of the housing investment then declines, and landlords often accelerate the process of decay by reducing maintenance expenditures. They decide to maximize short-term profitability rather than long-term returns on investment. Tax delinquencies are the next step, both in rental and owner-occupied dwellings.

Other neighborhood changes usually take place as the socio-economic characteristics of neighborhood residents change. Neighborhood commercial activities are often curtailed as existing businesses lose their client base. Changes in types of business activity occur and some commercial functions are lost to other areas, thus making the neighborhood less attractive.

Crime increases at the same time that these events are occurring. While perceptions may outdistance fact, insurance costs may also escalate and mortgage financing may become unavailable, or available only on onerous terms. Racial stereotypes may contribute to the neighborhood's decline. Allied with these changes in neighborhood characteristics is a reduction in political influence, resulting in lessened levels of city services, including police protection, public works, maintenance, and waste collection.

In many of the older cities, these problems are made worse because inner city areas originally lacked zoning controls. The housing stock tended to be on smaller parcels and had less square footage and a less desirable style than is acceptable under today's standards.

Finally, in the last stages of decay, patterns of housing abandonment occur. From an economic standpoint, abandonment reflects the decision of owners to walk away from an uneconomic investment. For landlords, it is the last stage of ownership; they have achieved the highest return possible without further investment in circumstances where additional investment would not be economic. For homeowners, a similar pattern evolves. Given existing indebtedness levels outstanding on their homes, homeowners conclude that further maintenance investments to bring units to acceptable standards will not be economically feasible. The cost of repairs and improvements on top of the existing debt burden would constitute an unrecoverable investment with no reasonable expectation of realizing these costs upon sale.

This syndrome of filtering, deferred housing maintenance, neighborhood deterioration, and abandonment is often accelerated by two factors. First, the changing racial composition of neighborhoods tends to expedite the process of decline as racial or ethnic minorities often with lower socio-economic status start to "tilt" the racial composition of the neighborhood. The potential category of new purchasers becomes more limited; often the area attracts only other minorities or "urban pioneers." Second, federal housing subsidy programs have contributed to neighborhood decline by extending homeownership to households not yet financially able to afford the cost of maintenance when the cost of repair, along with mortgage carrying costs, becomes higher than they can handle. These effects were especially observable in older cities such as Newark, Detroit, Philadelphia, and Cleveland.

When some abandonment takes place, the adjoining units are themselves affected. Abandoned units will be ravaged and vandalized if not maintained. Even if these units are quickly boarded up and their yards maintained, they still become a stigma for the block. One mark of a sickly neighborhood is the number of boarded-up structures. As the visual indicators of the neighborhood's deterioration accumulate—lack of exterior maintenance, boarded-up houses, and unclean, unrepaired streets—the blighting process accelerates. The neighborhood declines precipitously, and even the occupied, well-maintained homes on the same block begin to lose their value by association. Resident confidence wanes further, the neighborhood's housing market falls, and the area becomes irretrievable.

Rehabilitation and preservation techniques are an attempt to reverse this process before conditions become irreversible. Neighborhood revitalization strategies for neighborhoods in an incipient state of decline that have not yet reached terminal status make use of housing and building codes, which depend upon inspection and enforcement personnel as well as responsive owners. Where owners do not respond, and where the number of vacant or abandoned properties threaten to accelerate the decline of whole streets, blocks or neighborhoods, stronger remedies have been devised by cities, and advocated by community resident organizations. The exercise of governmental powers to demolish substandard properties, to place them under receivership and repair them, even to transfer ownership to willing buyers or hold them in a municipal land bank, raise important issues of the rights and responsibilities of property ownership and government stewardship. These will be taken up in section B2 *supra*.

2. The Legal Framework for Community Development Practice

Local Government in Community Development

Just as the federal government must look to the U.S. Constitution for the powers delegated to it by the states, so too are local governments created by their state and dependent upon delegation for all of their authority. States vary considerably in their forms of local government, and most have a combination of local entities variously called counties, towns, cities, villages or boroughs. In addition to general purpose local governments, there are many units of local government established to perform specific functions and provide specialized services: school districts, water and sewer districts, fire districts, economic development agencies, and special purpose districts which are important in the operation or regulation of specific services.

The source of authority for most local governments is to be found in their state charters. A majority of states have recognized some degree of home rule authority, continuing a commitment to the right of self-government that existed in England prior to the founding of this country, and is traced back in time to precede the Magna Charta. Sandra Stevenson, *Delegation of Home Rule Authority*, *in* LOCAL GOVERNMENT (2d ed. 2009). Usually there is an affirmative delegation of authority to the local government to adopt legislation, hold elections, and impose taxes to raise revenue for its activities, contract for services and supplies, manage property and acquire property through eminent domain. Some states limit home rule authority to their larger subdivisions. Be aware, however, that a minority of states adhere to Dillon's Rule, by which local governments hold only those powers which have been expressly granted them.

Authority delegated to a local government may usually be exercised only within its boundaries. However, extraterritorial authority is sometimes granted by a specific delegation of state authority to condemn land or impose regulatory conditions outside their jurisdictional boundaries, for example to provide needed utilities or services such as the maintenance of reservoirs or to condemn land needed for waste disposal facilities. Increasingly, local governments are included in regional or area planning beyond their own boundaries, through various forms of interlocal cooperation.

Local governments interact in numerous ways with federal and state governments, and other local governments as well, and these relationships are important in defining local powers, responsibilities and financial ability. Like states, local governments must comply with federal constitutional requirements of due process and equal protection when exercising their delegated authority. To comport with the Due Process clause, local regulation must be reasonable and reasonably related to the public health, safety and welfare. Citizens must be afforded reasonable opportunities to comply with or challenge regulatory action. A local enactment that conflicts with federal law will be preempted under the Supremacy Clause.

A local government generally cannot exercise its delegated powers to take federal land or regulate the activity of the federal government; but conversely, the federal government may exercise eminent domain powers to take local or state property, and may regulate state and local activity, as well as shape the relationship between states and their local governments. For example, Congress requires the states to engage local governments in transportation decisions in the Intermodal Surface Transportation Efficiency Act of 1991, 49 USC 101 (1996), and the Transformation Equity Act for the 21st Century, Pub. L. No. 105-178, 112 Stat. 164 (1998).

Land Use, Zoning and Planning

The role of local government in the planning, development and use of land is one of the most fundamental and highly valued exercises of local authority. Indeed it is one of the primary motivators for the voluntary creation of a local government. People who dislike the way their community is regulated (or unregulated) understand the importance of influencing the local decision makers. Developers who dislike the land use controls in one local government may seek accommodations in regulations, or annexation to another one deemed more amenable.

A local government's land use powers must be exercised in conformity with basic constitutional requirements in both federal and state constitutions. This means that all governmental regulation and action concerning land must protect individual liberties of freedom of speech, religion, equal protection and due process. Local government is empowered to regulate private property in order to benefit all members of the community, although it cannot make private owners to bear unreasonable public burdens. Where local regulation is so severe as to effect an unconstitutional taking of private property, it must pay just compensation.

Many local governments are required by their states to plan for the orderly future development of their community. Usually this is accomplished through preparation of a comprehensive plan. Some states require that local zoning be consistent with this plan. The terms "zoning" and "planning" are at times used interchangeably, and treated as a single concept. In reality the concepts are not synonymous. Zoning is concerned principally with the use of property, while planning is broader in scope and connotes the development of a community over time.

Master planning serves different purposes than zoning. While zoning addresses whether a particular area of a community may be used for a particular purpose, planning aims for the implementation of an overall design program for the present and future physical development as well as the services of an existing (or contemplated) municipality. Zoning is one end product of planning: it is through the mechanics of zoning regulations that the objectives of planning may be attained. A local government zones by dividing the land within its boundaries into districts, then defining the uses allowed within each. Basic types are residential, commercial and industrial. Often these are subdivided further, and further restrictions are applied such as building setbacks, height and area limits, and parking minimums.

Zoning and planning are complementary processes which serve common objectives: both are designed to direct and control the physical development of a community and its surrounding area in order to promote both immediate and ultimate social and economic well-being. Accordingly, there must be a direct and tangible link between comprehensive plans and zoning ordinances. The comprehensive plan is the policy statement of recommendations by the planning commission for the utilization and development of land. Only those provisions enacted through the jurisdiction's zoning ordinances have the force and effect of law—a city's zoning ordinance is the law, and its comprehensive development plan serves only as a guide to local government agencies charged with making zoning decisions. Nonetheless, zoning ordinances are required to conform to and implement development plans, and where a general plan is in effect when a zoning ordinance is passed, the ordinance may be invalid if it conflicts with the plan.

Unlike restrictive covenants or the common law of nuisance, enforcement of zoning regulations is not dependent upon the initiative of private landowners, and it does not rely primarily upon the courts to define permissible uses of land. Zoning regulations are drafted and enacted by legislative authority, and may be enforced by municipal action. *See, e.g.*, *Anderson House, LLC v. Mayor & City Council of Rockville*, 939 A.2d 116 (Md. 2008) (plans, which are the result of work done by planning commissions and adopted by ultimate zoning bodies, are advisory in nature and have no force of law absent statutes or local ordinances linking planning and zoning); *Schultz v. Pritts*, 432 A.2d 1319 (Md. 1981) (the very essence of zoning is the territorial division of land into use districts according to the character of the land and buildings, the suitability of land and buildings for particular uses, and uniformity of use).

Neighborhood Participation in Planning

Traditional participation by neighborhood organizations, while common, has been "highly informal and disorganized." *See* ALI Model Land Development Code, § 2-307, note (1974). Such participation may be narrowly focused on excluding perceived threats to the neighborhood, the extreme of which is the "not-in-my-backyard" (NIMBY) syndrome. It also may be part of a broader effort to improve or revitalize the neighborhood.

Neighborhood-based development corporations, organized as nonprofit legal entities under state law, provide a formal structure for citizen participation in neighborhood planning and development. The role of residents in making the decisions affecting their community weaves throughout CD law and practice, as the following brief history relates.

> For over thirty years neighborhood planning and development activities have played important roles in repeated efforts to combat poverty and decay in the American city. The current neighborhood collaborative planning movement has roots in three programs and activities of the 1960s: (1) the federal Community Action Program (CAP) of the Kennedy-Johnson War on Poverty,[1] (2) the Community Development Corporation (CDC) movement initiated in 1967 by the Bedford Stuyvesant Restoration Corporation of New York, and (3) the advocacy planning movement that was incorporated into the Federal model cities program.[2] A common denominator of these three programs and activities was the effort to involve directly the residents of low income communities in decisions affecting their neighborhoods. However, because the Federal programs providing the money for local planning and development efforts were top-down designed programs, and the officials in charge of these programs, as well as local elected officials, had little experience in collaborative decision-making with low income residents, the CAP agencies and the model cities program soon foundered on unrealistic expectations and insufficient resources. The ideal of resident participation in decisions affecting their neighborhoods, however, did not die. The CDC movement grew in fits and starts during the 1970s, 1980s, and 1990s. Neighborhood planning was reborn with the major decentralization of Federal programs begun in the Reagan Administration and carried forward in the Bush and Clinton Administrations, culminating in the Empowerment Zone, Hope VI, and TANF programs....

---

1. *See* Daniel P. Moynihan, Maximum Feasible Misunderstanding (1969) for a critical history of the CAP program.

2. The Demonstration Cities and Metropolitan Development Act of 1966, Pub. L. No. 89-754, 80 Stat. 1255. Model Cities was a short-lived program of the Johnson Administration that was superseded by the Community Development Block Grant (CDBG) program created in 1974 and codified at 42 U.S.C. § 5301ff.

> Neighborhood planning advocates found city officials increasingly receptive to their ideas as cities groped with the Federal decentralization movement.

Peter Salsich, *Grassroots Consensus Building and Collaborative Planning*, 3 WASH. U. J.L. & POL'Y 709, 712–714 (2000).

Notes and Questions

1. *Decentralization by Government in the 1980s.* The decentralization policy grew out of a major effort begun in the Reagan Administration to "privatize" domestic social programs. *See, e.g.*, PRESIDENT'S COMMISSION ON PRIVATIZATION, PRIVATIZATION: TOWARD MORE EFFECTIVE GOVERNMENT (1988); Peter W. Salsich, Jr., *Solutions to the Affordable Housing Crisis: Perspectives on Privatization*, 28 J. MARSHALL L. REV. 263, 275–88 (1995). *See also* U.S. DEP'T OF HOUS. & URB. DEV., EMPOWERMENT, A NEW COVENANT WITH AMERICA'S COMMUNITIES: PRESIDENT CLINTON'S NATIONAL URBAN POLICY REPORT (1995); U.S. DEP'T OF HOUS. & URB. DEV., BEYOND SHELTER: BUILDING COMMUNITIES OF OPPORTUNITY 18–22 (The United States Report For Habitat II) (1996).

A number of scholars have cautioned that economic development programs will not materially improve the lives of low-income inner city residents unless the structural realities of inner city life are addressed. *See, e.g.*, Audrey G. McFarlane, *Race, Space, and Place: The Geography of Economic Development*, 36 SAN DIEGO L. REV. 295 (1999).

The Federal Role in Community Development

All community development projects are "local" in a geographic sense, yet the federal government exerts a significant influence on the development activity across the nation. Since the 1930s, a variety of policies and programs have been created by Congress and federal agencies, to direct federal resources to serve an array of goals including neighborhood improvement, economic development, fair housing, and supportive social services. The legislative history of many of these enactments document Washington's concern to promote housing, for its intrinsic purpose of shelter as well as for the economic stimulus and job creation effects of housing production. The federal government has played a major role in the development of the modern residential mortgage market, including government-backed loans, conventional (nongovernmental) mortgage system, and the secondary market for loan products.

In general, the U.S. Department of Housing and Urban Development (HUD) is responsible for federal participation and programs in housing and urban development. 42 U.S.C. §§3531 to 3549. However, due to the economic stimulus potential of federal development policy, several other federal departments and agencies provide policy guidance as well as financial and technical assistance through programs that are important to the community development projects of states, localities, developers and community promoters. Complementing HUD, the Department of Veterans Affairs (formerly the Veterans Administration) and the Rural Housing Service (formerly the Farmers Home Administration) within the Department of Agriculture, make loan guarantees for home ownership by persons with military service or in rural areas, respectively.

Extending far beyond the production and availability of decent and affordable housing, the federal government promotes a wide array of community development activities that are important to state, local and nonprofit actors. These include job creation or retention, prevention or elimination of slums and blight, and the development of viable urban communities intended to provide a suitable living environment and expand economic opportunities, targeted to benefit low- and moderate-income families.

Over many years, the federal government has developed several programs to stimulate investment in economically distressed areas. These provide tax incentives, direct financial assistance, regulatory relief, or some combination of these approaches. Empowerment zones and enterprise communities, enacted in 1993, are designated to increase employment and promote economic activity through tax benefits for businesses, and eligibility is based on statutory criteria for rates of generalized economic distress, high unemployment, and pervasive poverty. Internal Revenue Code §§ 1391–1397D. The U.S. Treasury Department operates programs designed to direct private investment in the economic development of low-income communities, through the certification of Community Development Financial Institutions, IRC § 45D, as well as the New Markets tax credit and venture capital programs. Pub. L. No. 106-554, 114 Stat. 2763, 2763A-605, 2763A-653. The Internal Revenue Code provides tax incentives to depository institutions and to investors in support of housing and community development.

The Economic Development Administration, an agency within the U.S. Department of Commerce, was formed initially to promote economic development in rural areas, but since 1998, EDA programs have expanded to include urban areas as well. Pub. L. No. 105-393, 112 Stat. 3618 (*codified at* 42 U.S.C. § 3121 *et seq.*). EDA provides grants for public works, creation or expansion of industrial or commercial facilities, creation of long-term economic opportunities, trade adjustment assistance, or primarily benefit the long-term unemployed and low-income families. 42 U.S.C. §§ 3141, 3143, 3147, 3149; 13 C.F.R. Pt. 305.

The Small Business Administration also operates programs related to community development, chiefly, the 504 development company loan program for small business preservation and expansion, and targeted federal procurement rules of the HUBZone program.

NeighborWorks. The Neighborhood Reinvestment Corporation is a tax-exempt corporation created by Congress to mobilize public, private and community resources to revitalize older urban neighborhoods. The NRC is funded by federal appropriations but is not a federal department, agency or instrumentality. To accomplish its purpose, the NRC has established the NeighborWorks network, a nation-wide network of over 200 community-based organizations which help low- and moderate-income families to rent, own and maintain affordable housing.

Section 3. Employment and other economic opportunities generated by federal housing and community development programs are required, "to the greatest extent feasible," to be directed to low- and very-low income persons, particularly to residents of federally-assisted housing. 12 U.S.C. § 1701u(b), 24 C.F.R. Pt. 135. Youthbuild provides federal funding for employment and training for very-low-income individuals between 16 and 24 years old. Community-based nonprofit organizations, community development corporations, resident organizations and community action agencies are among the eligible applicants for Youthbuild program funding. 29 U.S.C. § 1513(b)(1)(B).

A Note on Rural Economic Development

The Census Bureau defines rural areas as "consisting of all territory, population, and housing units located outside of [urban areas or urban clusters]" and "comprise open country and settlements with fewer than 2,500 residents. "Urban areas" comprise larger places having a population of at least 50,000, with "densely settled areas around them."

USDA, Econ. Research Serv., *Measuring Rurality: What Is Rural?, available at* http://www.ers.usda.gov/briefing/rurality/WhatIsRural. The 2000 Census reported that non-urban America accounts for seventy-five percent of the nation's land, and is home to seventeen percent (49.2 million) of the U.S. population, in 2,052 counties. A new census term was introduced in 2000 for the built-up territory surrounding small towns and cities: those areas where the population is greater than 2,500 but less than 50,000 are considered "urban clusters" by the Census Bureau. According to the 2000 census, 11 percent of the U.S. population lived in 3,158 urban clusters.

Rural communities face a number of obstacles to community economic development. These include remote geographic location, limited financial and human resources, resource dependency, and eroded political power. *See generally* Joanna M. Wagner, *Improving Native American Access To Federal Funding For Economic Development Through Partnerships With Rural Communities*, 32 Am. Indian L. Rev. 525 (2008). It has been suggested that fully half of rural counties lack systematic plans for economic development due to lack of funding and staff resources. Instead, planning efforts in rural communities are reported as being driven by the availability of federal funds rather than a regular assessment of needs. While fifteen years ago there may have been less community-based development activity in rural areas than in cities, see Donald E. Voth, *A Brief History and Assessment of Federal Rural Development Programs and Policies*, 25 U. Mem. L. Rev. 1265, 1289 (1995) (arguing that rural people are unmobilized, unorganized, and unrepresented due to population migration), in 2010 numerous rural nonprofit organizations seeking to preserve and rejuvenate the economies of rural areas are networking vigorously on the World Wide Web.

At the federal level, policy and resources are directed to the renewal needs of rural areas through each of the extant community development programs. Typically, where the U.S. Department of Housing and Urban Development is the lead agency for urban communities, for rural communities the US Department of Agriculture (USDA) leads or assists in program administration and oversight, as is the case in the CDBG and Empowerment Zone/Enterprise Community programs. USDA operates its Office of Community and Economic Development (CED) which administers rural community and regional development programs, intended to demonstrate "how every rural community or region can achieve self-sufficiency through innovative and comprehensive strategic plans developed and implemented at a grassroots level." *See also* http://www.rurdev.usda.gov/rbs/cdp.html. For a useful introduction to USDA support for local rural revitalization, see Jacob R. Lofgren, *"I Miss Mayberry:" Revitalizing America's Rural Downtowns*, 13 Drake J. Agric. L. 419 (2008).

B. Historical Context: The Tools for Community Development Theory and Practice

1. Community Standards: Housing and Building Codes

a. Neighborhood Preservation through Building Demolition and Housing Codes

Municipalities have long used their police power authority to enact regulatory measures that achieve neighborhood preservation by requiring the maintenance of existing housing. The local housing code is the most important of these police power measures. In addition to requiring housing maintenance, codes mandate the provision and maintenance of necessary household facilities and the provision of minimum habitable space for each occupant of a dwelling. The origin of the housing code movement is discussed by Professor Friedman in an excerpt reprinted in Chapter 1 *supra*.

Because it is a police power measure, owners of housing do not receive compensation for their compliance with housing code requirements. They must make the required housing repairs at their own expense. The requirements enacted by local housing codes are usually the minimum necessary to provide and maintain adequate housing. Since code compliance is uncompensated, several constitutional problems must be considered. These constitutional issues as well as problems of housing code administration are examined in this section.

An important adjunct to the local housing code is the building demolition power, usually provided by state statute rather than by local ordinance. Municipalities are authorized by building demolition statutes to demolish buildings that are substandard, again without compensation to the owner of the building. Title to the land remains with the private owner once demolition has been carried out.

Building demolition statutes can provide an important legal tool in neighborhood revitalization programs by allowing municipalities to remove substandard dwellings without the need to use public funds for this purpose. Municipalities originally carried out building demolition under their common law nuisance powers, but legislatures at the close of the nineteenth century began enacting legislation that gave the building demolition power a statutory base.

There are two types of statutes. The first, based upon a model law drafted at the turn of the century, authorizes state fire marshals to demolish buildings in order to eliminate fire hazards. The second authorizes local agencies to demolish dangerous, unsafe, or unfit buildings.

1. The Constitutionality of Code Enforcement

The constitutional support for statutes authorizing demolition is mostly based on the nuisance rationale, which originated in equity, rather than the modern police power justification for municipal regulation of private property. Under equity principles, abatement is preferred over demolition because of the drastic nature of the remedy. As the following indicates, the repair test can influence a court's decision on the necessity for demolition:

Daniel R. Mandelker, Housing Codes, Building Demolition, and Just Compensation: A Rationale for the Exercise of Public Powers Over Slum Housing

67 Michigan Law Review 635, 649–52 (1968)

A corollary to equity's bias against the demolition remedy is a preference for repair as an alternative. Some of the legislation ... follows equity by explicitly providing a reasonable repair test as the basis for exercising the demolition power, but the equity bias survives in the cases even in the absence of such an explicit provision. This judicial interpretation is supported by the typical statutory authorization of repair or demolition as alternative remedies, even in the absence of an explicit repair test; similarly, statutes authorizing the removal of buildings as fire hazards force attention to the removal of the hazard rather than demolition of the building as the statutory objective. Some courts will order repair rather than demolition whenever repair can eliminate the fire or other danger.

Courts have isolated two other approaches to the alternative of repair as a test for demolition. One approach gives the owner an absolute election to make repairs, regardless of cost or of the relationship of cost to the value of the structure. Another approach places sufficient limitations on the right to repair to make the demolition remedy effective against a nonconsenting owner: repairs may not be made whenever the cost of repair is excessive. While judicial consideration of excessive cost is usually offhanded and casual, the cases have variously suggested that repairs will not be allowed when repair required exceeds the value of the building, or when repairs cannot be made at a reasonable cost. Even this attempt to distinguish judicially imposed cost limitations on the right to repair pushes the cases too far; the courts simply accept the repair test which was recognized in equity—repair is held to be the preferable alternative whenever it is practicable.

As indicated above, some statutes have codified the repair test for demolition, often by expressing it in comparative terms. These statutes commonly provide that demolition may be ordered whenever the needed repairs exceed a fixed percentage of building value. This standard is not only easy to administer, but is also easily translated into a measure of compensation. For example, when the repair ratio is exceeded, the building should be subject to acquisition without compensation because, alternatively, it could be demolished without compensation....

When the constitutionality of these repair ratios has been in issue, courts have approved them on the ground that legislation may, within reasonable limits, fix the level of deterioration which justifies demolition. Fifty, and even thirty percent ratios have been accepted. This rationale has been extended to cover a fifty percent repair ratio in a local demolition provision which was not part of a fire limits ordinance. Judicial acceptance of repair ratios as the basis for ordering demolition is surprising in view of the cases considering the constitutionality of demolition in the absence of such provisions. Even a fifty percent ratio would prohibit repair at a level well below the "substantial reconstruction" and similar tests which some courts have selected to measure an excessive repair burden. Most courts, however, have not noticed this problem.

Notes and Questions

1. The modern cases adopted the more modern police power theories to uphold building demolition ordinances. *See, e.g., Traylor v. City of Amarillo,* 492 F.2d 1156 (5th Cir. 1974). The nuisance origins of the building demolition power are still sometimes significant, as the housing code cases will illustrate. Neither are all courts receptive to building demolition requirements. *See Johnson v. City of Paducah,* 512 S.W.2d 514 (Ky. 1974), holding unconstitutional a local ordinance compelling demolition when the cost of repair exceeds 50% of the building's value.

2. The housing code and the demolition statutes presumably work in tandem. The demolition statute authorizes the demolition of dwellings that are substandard and not capable of repair. The housing code requires the minimum repair and maintenance of substandard dwellings. Dwellings not subject to demolition under demolition statutes presumably fall under the housing code and must be maintained and repaired by their owners without compensation.

3. Housing codes as a housing maintenance and neighborhood preservation strategy had fallen into disuse by the end of World War II. Only a few major cities had housing codes at that time. It was the federal housing agency, and ultimately Congress, that encouraged and then required the adoption of housing codes at the municipal level.

The enactment of housing codes was spurred by a community development strategy adopted in the early days of the federal urban redevelopment program—the Workable Program for Community Improvement. The purpose of the Workable Program was to encourage community efforts at neighborhood preservation to reduce the necessity for slum clearance programs that required the total clearance of substandard neighborhoods. The housing code was an important element of the Workable Program. Congress ultimately enacted the Workable Program requirement into law, and after 1964 required the local adoption and administration of housing codes in all cities participating in the federal urban redevelopment program. This requirement led to the widespread adoption of thousands of housing codes throughout the nation. The federal legislation that authorizes the present community development program does not require the adoption of housing codes. *See* Jane McGrew & John C. Bates, *Code Enforcement: The Federal Role*, 14 URB. LAW. 1 (1982) for a discussion of the relationship between federal housing programs and local code enforcement.

4. For a detailed account on the importance of rehabilitating single-room occupancy units for use by low-income households to aid the problem of homelessness, see Suzanne K. Sleep, *Stonewalled by* Seawall: *New York Decision Impedes Legislative Solutions to Affordable Housing Shortage*, 45 U. MIAMI L. REV. 467 (1991). SROs remain an element of the housing spectrum, although the federal policy approach to homelessness has moved since the 1990s from providing shelter, to ending homelessness by combining housing and complementary services. Federal support to communities seeking to address homeless persons' needs is made available to localities through the Continuum of Care, HUD's local planning process, which requires that government agencies, service providers and advocates meet to evaluate the needs of homeless persons in the community and plan to deliver housing and services to meet those needs. Local Continuums of Care submit their plans and apply to receive and administer federal funding under the McKinney-Vento Act for transitional housing, permanent housing and supportive services programs. In recent years, HUD has required Continuums to coordinate with local planning bodies that are preparing "10-Year Plans to End Homelessness" to leverage use of McKinney-Vento funds with other HUD sources such as Section 8, Community Development Block Grant, or HOME as well as other federal, state, and local funding.

The official federal definition of homelessness encompasses an individual who lacks a "fixed, regular, and adequate nighttime residence"; as well as individuals who primarily spend nights in a supervised temporary shelter (including welfare hotels, congregate shelters, and transitional housing), or "a public or private place not designed for, or ordinarily used as, a regular sleeping accommodation for human beings." 42 USC § 11302. A study of homelessness in 50 cities found that in virtually every city, the city's official estimated number of homeless people greatly exceeded the number of emergency shelter and transitional housing spaces. *See* National Law Center on Homelessness and Poverty, *Solutions through Alternative Remedies: Practical Models to Help End Homelessness* 3–4 (2004), *available at* http://www.nlchp.org/content/pubs/Solutions%20Through%20Alternative%20 Remedies1.pdf (describing the programs in Madison and Sacramento). About nine percent of the nation's homeless are in rural areas, according to The Council for Affordable and Rural Housing. In December 2008, an annual survey from the U.S. Conference of Mayors found that 12 major cities reported an increase in homelessness as a result of foreclosure, with renters of foreclosed properties being the victims most vulnerable to homelessness. The United States Conference of Mayors, *Hunger and Homelessness Survey* (Dec. 2008), *available at* http://www.usmayors.org/pressreleases/documents/hungerhomelessness report_121208.pdf.

5. While the primary function of housing and building codes is to set minimum standards and enforcement regulations related to physical safety, since their creation in the late nineteenth century, housing codes also have established occupancy limits. Occupancy limits specify the minimum size of bedrooms, or conversely, the maximum number of persons who can reside in a housing unit. The inclusion of occupancy limits implies that they are based in sound engineering concepts, or result from an empirical analysis of public health concerns, but this has not been demonstrated. If there is no scientific basis in safety, what justifies occupancy limits? Might they instead reflect social and cultural biases about how a family "should" live?

6. The interplay of housing regulations and the police power is explored in Karl Manheim, *Tenant Eviction Protection and the Takings Clause*, 1989 Wis. L. Rev. 925.

2. Housing Codes and Neighborhood Stabilization

Does code enforcement have renewed importance in preserving suburban neighborhoods, in light of the foreclosure epidemic discussed in Chapter 1? Consider:

> Much has been written about the macro-policy dimensions of our nation's housing and foreclosure crisis regarding such topics as the impacts of subprime lending, lax or nonexistent federal and/or state regulatory actions, cumbersome foreclosure processes and the crisis's long term repercussions on financial markets and the ultimate health of our nation's economy. Media reports dwell on the individual stories of families losing homes as direct targets of now bankrupt predatory lenders or inadvertent victims of so called exotic mortgage products. Examples abound of fraudulent real property schemes and overextended real property speculators who walked away from multiple mortgages leaving tenants and their families to fend for themselves.
>
> The picture throughout the country's cities and towns is not pretty, and if the economic and housing forecasters are right the crisis will likely deepen in severity, extend for several years and expand its reach. Only a handful of stories describe a foreclosure's impact on neighborhoods and the challenges that local governments face in containing the blighting influences of vacant properties.
>
> Working the frontlines of the foreclosure crisis are local government code enforcement departments as they attempt to maintain order and stabilize neighborhoods from the increasing social and economic harms of vacant and abandoned properties. When foreclosed homes become vacant, code departments are the first responders to citizen complaints often referred by mayors, city councilors, and county commissioners. Local code enforcement officials have the legal and policy responsibilities to enforce a wide array of building, housing, and property maintenance codes and to administer special nuisance abatement processes.
>
> The current foreclosure crisis, however, is draining department resources and testing the limits of code enforcement's legal authority and policy directives. With the constant rise in foreclosures, the meltdown in the mortgage industry and, now, the financial markets, the number of vacant and abandoned proper-

> ties will continue to grow for the foreseeable future. Classic research on the "Broken Windows Theory" documents that aggressive code enforcement can maintain a sense of community order, protect property values, and stabilize distressed neighborhoods. The challenge for communities and policymakers is whether the resources and capacity of their code enforcement programs can withstand the continuous wave of foreclosures and onslaught of vacant properties.

Joseph Schilling, *Code Enforcement and Community Stabilization: The Forgotten First Responders to Vacant and Foreclosed Homes,* 2 ALB. GOV'T L. REV. 101, 103–104 (2009).

Notes and Questions

1. To what extent is code enforcement a means to require private enterprise to shoulder an economic burden for improvements in housing quality that might reasonably be expected to be borne by the public? For discussion of the burdens imposed by code enforcement and land use regulation on entrepreneurship in center cities, see Stephen Clowney, *Invisible Businessman: Undermining Black Enterprise with Land Use Rules,* 2009 U. ILL. L. Rev. 1061.

An influential discussion of housing codes and code enforcement is contained in the Douglas Commission Report. REPORT OF THE NATIONAL COMMISSION ON URBAN PROBLEMS, BUILDING THE AMERICAN CITY 273–93 (1968). The Douglas Commission Report raised the question whether housing codes should be considered a "floor" or a "ceiling." The Commission argued that codes should be a floor, but that even higher standards should be required to fulfill the commitment of Congress to a decent home and a suitable living environment for every American family. What do you think of this strategy?

2. Should there be different code standards applicable to existing housing as compared to new housing? In what specific respects are differences acceptable? What are the implications for applying existing housing codes to rehabilitation activities? Consider the following:

> To the delight of many unlikely allies—builders, affordable housing experts, environmentalists, and preservationists—a few jurisdictions have begun designing codes that depart from traditional building codes and specifically encourage the renovation of older structures. These "rehabilitation codes" (or "smart codes") differ dramatically from traditional codes in that rehabilitation code standards are applied proportionately to the scope of construction efforts. If the work is minor—say, a repair—then only minimal requirements apply; if the work is major—a reconstruction or an addition—then stricter requirements apply. Moreover, rehabilitation codes contain clear guidelines that enable builders to accurately predict their expenses; by contrast, builders often cannot be sure how code officials will apply the traditional codes to older structures.
>
> The power to draft building codes has long resided with the states, the vast majority of which have assigned that power to local governments. The many jurisdictions that have adopted traditional codes have recognized that basic building regulations are essential because they reduce negative externalities that may be produced by substandard, nonregulated structures, and because they provide consumer protection. Without codes, builders have incentives to underinvest in safety features such as fire-resistant materials or plumbing, electrical, and heating equipment designed to prevent the spread of disease. With codes, builders are required to consider the external effects of their structures. Building codes also

> have the potential to combat crime and terrorism and to prevent widespread structural collapse and loss of life during earthquakes. This is because the technical requirements embodied in the codes, drafted by industry experts, ensure a minimum standard of quality. The guidance provided by codes is especially critical when individuals related to the construction project—such as buyers, owners, or occupants—lack independent technical expertise.
>
> While the rationale behind traditional codes is clear, few have recognized that we also need rehabilitation codes: Only a tiny fraction of the 10,000 jurisdictions with traditional building codes have adopted rehabilitation codes....
>
> Rehabilitation can help improve central cities, which have the highest concentration of older buildings.... [H]owever, cities are suffering from longstanding fiscal and social problems, including poor infrastructure, high unemployment, high tax burdens, broken educational systems, and impoverished governments. The failure of codes to encourage rehabilitation exacerbates these problems.
>
> Traditional building codes do little, for example, to encourage the rehabilitation of vacant and abandoned structures. The Census Bureau's 2003 American Housing Survey for the United States reported that eleven percent of all housing structures were vacant—including nearly four million central city structures. City by city, the numbers of vacant houses can be staggering. One recent study, surveying seventy metropolitan areas with populations of 100,000 or more, found that on average fifteen percent of urban land (both with and without buildings) sat empty. Vacant and abandoned buildings have many negative effects: They reduce potential tax revenues, encourage arson and accidental fires, lower values of surrounding property, harm neighborhood aesthetics, imperil public safety and health, and promote criminal activity. Despite these effects, property owners often conclude that the cost of retrofitting structures to meet current codes is too high and allow buildings to deteriorate further. While some of these buildings are beyond repair and must be demolished, many can—and should—be rehabilitated.
>
> Traditional codes also hurt central cities by giving suburban areas a competitive advantage. A federal commission investigating barriers to affordable housing estimated that building codes make rehabilitated projects in urban jurisdictions twenty-five percent more expensive than identical new construction projects in adjacent suburbs. As New Urbanist Andres Duany has argued, "[w]ithout [predictable] codes, older urban areas tend to suffer from disinvestment, as the market seeks stable environments. The competing private codes of the homeowners associations, the guidelines of office parks, and the rules of shopping centers create predictable outcomes that lure investment away from existing cities and towns."

Sara C. Galvin, *Rehabilitating Rehab through State Building Codes*, 115 Yale L. J. 1744, 1753 (2006).

3. The Douglas Commission made the point that poverty, either tenant poverty or the equivalent lack of return for landlords, is the primary inhibition on rigorous housing code enforcement. How can these two aspects of the problem be addressed and what approaches might be taken to overcome this facet of local government's resistance to enforcement? For a discussion on different theories of the efficacy of housing code enforcement, see Bruce Ackerman, *Regulating Slum Housing Markets On Behalf of the Poor: Of Housing Codes, Housing Subsidies and Income Redistribution Policy*, 80 Yale L.J.

1093 (1971); Neil K. Komesar, *Return to Slumville: A Critique of the Ackerman Analysis of Housing Code Enforcement and the Poor*, 82 YALE L.J. 1175 (1973); Edward H. Rabin, *The Revolution in Residential Landlord-Tenant Law: Causes and Consequences*, 69 CORNELL L. REV. 517 (1984).

4. What are the responsibilities of the locality concerning other activities necessary to enhance code enforcement? The Douglas Commission indicated that environmental degradation, principally through neglect of public works activities and public services, may obviate the efforts of private parties to adhere to housing codes. How should local government fulfill its responsibility in this respect? What factors should be considered in developing such companion activities? Given the overwhelming need of most cities for improvement of a large number of housing units and other building types, how can city actions best be structured to maintain and upgrade the city's physical fabric and infrastructure?

Might lax enforcement of codes in neighborhoods where owners or residents are racial minorities, constitute prohibited discrimination in the provision of municipal services as a violation of civil rights laws? The most generally relied upon guaranties of civil rights are found in the federal and state constitutions and civil rights statutes. State provisions prohibiting discrimination vary considerably. The small number of cases brought rely upon the Fourteenth Amendment. Where services or facilities are paid for out of public funds, courts have held that an injunction should be issued to rectify the violation of equal protection resulting from discriminatory practices in the provision of these items. One illustrative case is where 30% of streets in the black plaintiffs' community were unpaved compared with 18% in white neighborhoods, 90% of all street resurfacing work was done in white areas, and the storm drains in the black neighborhood were grossly inadequate compared to those in white parts of the city. On these facts the Eleventh Circuit ruled that the evidence strongly supported the inference of racial discrimination, and the city could be required to give priority to upgrading of street facilities in black areas. *Ammons v. Dade City*, 783 F.2d 982 (11th Cir. 1986).

Nonetheless, whether an injunction will be granted may turn on the method of financing for the disputed service or facility. Where the financing is by special assessment so that the residents of various areas may petition to receive the service and then must bear or share the cost to be incurred, several courts have refused to grant an injunction, on the ground that the service is available to all on the same basis even though some may be unable to afford it. The legal history and contemporary land use mechanisms that perpetuate inequality in municipal services is analyzed in John C. Dubin, *From Junkyards to Gentrification: Explicating a Right to Protective Zoning in Low-Income Communities of Color*, 77 MINN. L. REV. 739 (1993); Yale Rabin, *Expulsive Zoning: The Inequitable Legacy of* Euclid, *in* ZONING AND THE AMERICAN DREAM 101 (Charles M. Haar & Jerold S. Kayden eds. 1989).

5. Housing code enforcement varies by locality. Its administration depends upon such factors as the nature of the housing code, the funding and staffing of code enforcement agencies, and the policies of these agencies and the courts toward housing code enforcement. *See generally* Robin Powers Kinning, *Selective Housing Code Enforcement and Low-Income Housing Policy: Minneapolis Case Study*, 21 FORDHAM URB. L.J. 159 (1993); Symposium, *Code Enforcement: Issues and Answers for the '80s,* 60 U. DETROIT J. URB. L. 349 (1983).

6. In what respect is the housing standards issue a political question? In Britain, the government has found that standards have substantially increased since the end of the nineteenth century because of public expectations for acceptable dwelling conditions. As

a result, levels of housing amenity and minimum condition standards which were at one time acceptable are no longer in keeping with generally accepted concepts of living conditions. Similar changes have occurred in the United States during the last several decades. Given these circumstances, does this escalation in expectation argue for or against more vagueness in the definition of what constitutes a standard level of housing? Vague terms obviously can make enforcement more subjective and more difficult. What arguments are there for not adopting precise measurements for housing code standards?

7. By specifying minimum standards and conditions of repair for dwellings, the housing code also specifies the degree of repair required of dwelling owners. If the repair burden is too onerous, owners may object and may even bring an action in court challenging the application of the housing code to their dwelling as unconstitutional. Illustrating how the courts handle a constitutional challenge of this type, the New York Court of Appeals upheld the state Multiple Dwelling Law in *Adamec v. Post*, 7 N.E.2d 120 (N.Y. 1937). The code was challenged by the owner of a four story brick tenement built prior to 1901, twenty-five feet wide, which contained eight five-room apartments two to a floor, and two additional apartments in the basement.

> Under the provisions of the Multiple Dwelling Law (Consol. Laws, c. 61-a; Laws 1929, c. 713, as amended ... buildings used as multiple dwellings, though erected prior to 1901 in accordance with the requirements of the laws of the State which were then in force, must now comply with new requirements and higher standards enacted by the Legislature, for the protection of the safety and health of those who may live in these houses and, indirectly, of the people of the State. The plaintiff, claiming that the statute as amended is arbitrary and unreasonable and deprives him and others similarly situated of their property without due process of law, has brought this action, praying that the court declare the statute null and void in so far as it applies to buildings erected before 1901 and that an injunction issue against the Tenement House Commissioner restraining him from taking any steps to enforce the statute....
>
> The complaint alleges that the expense of all these "changes, additions, eliminations and alterations" would be "upwards of $5,000," although the plaintiff's property is assessed only "in the total sum of $13,500.00; the land being assessed at the sum of $5,000 and the building being assessed at the sum of $8,500.00."
>
> The imposition of the cost of the required alterations as a condition of the continued use of antiquated buildings for multiple dwellings may cause hardship to the plaintiff and other owners of "old law tenements" but, in proper case, the Legislature has the power to enact provisions reasonably calculated to promote the common good even though the result be hardship to the individual. "It is not the hardship of the individual case that determines the question, but rather the general scope and effect of the legislation as an exercise of the police power in protecting health and promoting the welfare of the community at large. It is a well-recognized principle in the decisions of the state and federal courts that the citizen holds his property subject not only to the exercise of the right of eminent domain by the state, but also subject to the lawful exercise of the police power by the legislature; in the one case property is taken by condemnation and due compensation; in the other the necessary and reasonable expenses and loss of property in making reasonable changes in existing structures, or in erecting additions thereto, are *damnum absque injuria*."

Tenement House Department of City of New York v. Moeschen, 72 N.E. 231, 232 (N.Y. 1904).

8. For a discussion of the origins of New York City's influential housing codes early in the Twentieth Century, see [excerpt from LAWRENCE M. FRIEDMAN, GOVERNMENT AND SLUM HOUSING (1968), reproduced in Chapter 1, *supra*.

9. *Adamec* represents a generous application of substantive due process doctrine to uphold the retroactive application of a housing code and was followed in *People v. Halpern*, 304 N.Y.S.2d 183 (City Ct. 1969), where the court held constitutional a requirement for the installation of an automatic sprinkler system in every non-fireproof hotel and rooming house and at least two exits for every multi-family building with four or more stories. *Accord, Kaukas v. City of Chicago*, 188 N.E.2d 700 (Ill.), *appeal dismissed*, 375 U.S. 8 (1963). Most courts have dismissed broadside attacks on housing codes. *See* Note, *Municipal Housing Codes*, 69 HARV. L. REV. 1115 (1956). Preserving codes against such attacks facilitated their extension as new issues in the safety of housing are identified. New York's Multiple Dwelling Law has been relied upon to establish requirements for various amenities such as locked doors and an intercom system to prevent unauthorized public access to a multiple dwelling, *Kazanoff v. U.S.*, 945 F.2d 32 (2nd Cir. 1991); the legalization of interim multiple dwellings, *Lower Manhattan Loft Tenants v. New York City Loft Bd.*, No. 96 Civ. 5516, 1997 WL 86404 (S.D.N.Y. Feb. 27, 1997) and the control of lead paint. *Chase Manhattan Bank v. T&N, PLC*, 905 F. Supp. 107 (S.D.N.Y. 1995). *See also Chang v. District of Columbia Dept. of Regulatory and Consumer Affairs*, 604 F. Supp. 2d 57 (D.D.C. 2009) (building code compliance); City of *Kansas City v. Jordan*, 174 S.W.3d 25 (Mo. Ct. App. W.D. 2005) (demolition of unsafe building); *Polakoff v. Turner*, 869 A.2d 837 (Md. 2005) (lead paint).

10. When a housing code sets requirements unrelated to life-threatening conditions, courts have sometimes held the application of the code unconstitutional. *See Gates v. Housing Appeals Bd.*, 225 N.E.2d 222 (Ohio 1967); Carol C. Friedman, Comment, *The Landlord's Economic Inability to Meet Housing Code Requirements: The "Hot Bath" Ordinance, An Illustration*, 23 ST. LOUIS U. L.J. 163 (1979). Housing code violations may be subject to criminal as well as civil sanctions. Housing codes also typically contain waiver provisions for economic hardship.

3. The Problem of Differential Enforcement Policy

One important characteristic of housing codes is the manner of their application. In the housing code excerpts included earlier, all requirements of the code appear equally important. Some municipalities have attempted to establish priorities in code administration by adopting differential code enforcement programs. Under this concept certain areas of the city and certain types of buildings are treated more stringently than others. The code enforcement agency may choose a complaint-based approach, an approach geared to occupancy changes, a city-wide or a zoned enforcement approach, or a combination of these. If the agency adopts a city-wide approach, full inspection of all dwelling units may not be possible in any one year. The city may then adopt a "cycle" inspection system in which different areas of the city are code-enforced in successive years until the entire housing stock has been inspected. The problems raised by this kind of code enforcement are discussed in Daniel R. Mandelker, Julie Gibb & Annette B. Kolis, *Differential Enforcement of Housing Codes—The Constitutional Dimensions*, 55 U. DET. J. URB. L. 517, 522–23 (1978).

> Gaining compliance is the most difficult aspect of code enforcement programs. Too lenient courts may render penalties for noncompliance ineffective as against code violators. The availability of technical and financial assistance also affects compliance. If violators cannot afford to pay for necessary repairs, imposition of a criminal fine aggravates the problem but does not solve it. The municipality may have to offer financial assistance to violators or to their tenants in order to avoid abandonment of the property or eviction of low-income tenants who cannot afford to pay for rent increases caused by improvements to the property.

Abuses may arise from the nature of the housing code standards. Code standards that stray too far from the necessary elimination of health and safety hazards, or that are obviously discriminatory, may be a burdensome application of the code on lower income and minority groups. An example is a code standard requiring lights in closets, or requiring screen doors and windows on all dwellings except those which are air-conditioned. Political abuses in code administration may also occur when code standards are general and uncertain, such as the customary "good repair" standard found in many codes.

The authors further observe:

> Housing codes and code enforcement are directed primarily to the maintenance of housing quality throughout the community. A differential enforcement program may be a reasonable method of implementing this goal, because the municipality recognizes the need to accommodate the enforcement of housing quality standards to variant housing conditions. At the same time, a differential program may prove burdensome to lower income and minority groups if the effect of that program reduces the mobility of these groups within the municipality.
>
> These conflicting pressures create policy dilemmas for the municipality and for the courts. One can argue that the implementation of a differential code enforcement program imposes unacceptable burdens on lower income and minority groups, but an effort to avoid these consequences may create pressures that make a responsive code enforcement program difficult, if not impossible to formulate.

Notes and Questions

1. At times, and in some jurisdictions, courts have shown more sensitivity to the economic impact of housing code enforcement. The leading case is *City of St. Louis v. Brune*, 515 S.W.2d 471 (Mo. 1974). In that case, the court considered the constitutionality of a housing code requirement that bathing facilities be connected to hot water. The circumstances of the case were compelling. The two buildings in the case were seventy years old and had a probable life of four or five years. They were located in a deteriorated and vandalized neighborhood that made the buildings practicably unrentable. There were no buyers for the buildings and they had no sale or loan value. Most of the tenants in the buildings were receiving social security or welfare assistance and could not afford the rent increase that compliance with the hot water provision would require. The cost of the improvements was substantial, and alterations necessary to provide them would reduce the kitchens in the buildings to the size of a closet. While noting that most courts had held housing codes constitutional as a valid police power regulation, the court in the *Brune* case held the code unconstitutional as applied. While not providing a comprehensive rationale for its decision, the court did note that "[t]he cost of the improvement

to the owners is not alone decisive ... but it may be a material element." What new elements does the *Brune* case introduce in cases considering the constitutionality of housing codes? The court noted the defendant's testimony that "he had been engaged in real estate ownership and management for 61 years," and that "his father and mother lived to the respective ages of 87 and 85 without having any baths connected to pipes and that he had none until he was 21." The court, thus, analyzed the issues, in part, as follows:

> The problem here is not actually one of public health; it is wholly different from those cases involving outside privies, sewage, etc. While the situation is by no means ideal, it really involves a matter of inconvenience to those tenants who choose to pay a minimum rent in return for incomplete facilities. The tenants may still bathe if they want to, and we are not convinced of any great danger that diseases will be spread.

Does the court mean to hold that the possibility of financial recoupment of the cost of repairs is a factor to consider? The physical condition or wealth of the neighborhood in which the dwellings are located? Does the *Brune* case implicitly support a strategy of differential code enforcement that would allow less stringent enforcement in badly deteriorated neighborhoods?

2. The Douglas Commission Report argued that housing code enforcement should be the mainstay of improving housing quality within cities. In *Brune,* the court seems to emphasize that the tenants in the unit under attack for not meeting housing codes were "living on welfare or social security." Given economic realities, how are necessary improvements to be financed? Having enacted the housing code, does government have an obligation to intervene to provide subsidies to support the tenant's contribution through housing allowances or to underwrite a portion of the owner's construction costs?

3. Should there be any limits to those housing matters that can be controlled by housing codes? How should the scope of "public safety and health" be measured? Is the lack of a bathtub sufficiently critical?

4. If repairs and, at times, improvements are forced on owners (and their tenants), won't abandonment and vandalism continue to spread? Should others who reside nearby or own adjacent property have any rights to enforcement of the codes to prevent the spread of blight? Would more rigid enforcement cause abandonment and displacement, additional neighborhood blighting and would that be an appropriate consideration in the mandate of health and safety? Can the same argument be made for food quality where standards enforcement could render food unaffordable at the markets for the poor?

5. What consideration should be given to the possibility that lower-income families who wish to expend minimal portions of their income for housing may be better accommodated in such blighted areas? Is it appropriate to enforce housing codes only in certain segments of the cities, for instance, those having the potential to be successfully rehabilitated, while leaving other areas without such a potential to slowly decay? Consider the following from Mandelker et al., *supra at* 555–56 n.196:

> The dilemma presents an interesting Catch-22 situation: housing code enforcement is most needed in areas with the shabbiest housing conditions. But the worst areas are completely exempted from enforcement under a successful due process-confiscation attack like that used in *Brune.* The only units sure to be enforced are those which already meet or approach the minimum standards. Enforcement of these units raises the overall "price" of living in them. Thus they drift farther out of range of those seeking to leave the worst areas.

6. Is there a better justification for exterior as contrasted to interior housing code enforcement? If interior deficiencies in housing also drive down prices, is this a sufficient basis to impose code enforcement on those who fail to maintain their units? Would such a justification be established by a showing of deleterious impact on the value of neighboring units? How can this be established? Does loss of value have a relationship to an owner's willingness to invest for purposes of improvements?

A court's determination that a confiscatory taking has occurred may be affected by the existence of a statute authorizing eminent domain in the circumstances. Where such a statute does not exist, will the same result be reached by holding the use of the police power unreasonable?

7. The *Brune* decision raises important questions of code enforcement economics. While housing codes do not establish repair and rehabilitation priorities, economists who study housing rehabilitation problems have developed criteria to determine when rehabilitation of housing is feasible as a housing strategy. Necessarily, these criteria compare rehabilitation with the option of demolition and the construction of a new dwelling unit. *See* William G. Grigsby & Louis Rosenberg, Urban Housing Policy (1975). *See also* Allan Mallach, Bringing Buildings Back: From Abandoned Properties To Community Assets 41–46 (2006) (discussing targeted code enforcement's role in effective local strategies to prevent abandonment).

8. Differential code enforcement is closely related to targeting strategies for neighborhood rehabilitation, which remain an accepted part of community development policy. The following brief excerpt reviews the elements of a targeting strategy and suggests criteria for selecting neighborhoods for code enforcement:

> The revitalization of deteriorating neighborhoods cannot be accomplished unless resources are concentrated in specific target areas. Although disinvestment and deterioration of housing is a problem when it occurs on a sporadic basis in sound neighborhoods due to the financial condition of a particular owner, the private housing market usually remedies the problem through sale and rehabilitation. A complaint code enforcement process can force owners to make a decision to reinvest or sell the property. Disinvestment is much more serious' however, when it is concentrated in a given location because housing conditions and the quality of life affect the decisions of other property owners and potential investors. Disinvestment breeds further disinvestment. This decline in neighborhood quality can also occur because public services and investments decrease relative to other areas. Therefore, programs aimed at upgrading a neighborhood must use a multi-dimensional approach that includes capital improvements, quality city services, social services, and housing improvements.
>
> In selecting neighborhoods for revitalization programs, a number of factors must be taken into account: (1) residents must exhibit a desire to stay in the neighborhood; (2) homeownership must be sufficient to give evidence of a stable population base; (3) the level of income in a large portion of the community must be high enough to support adequate property maintenance expenditures; and (4) neighborhood change in surrounding communities must be supportive of efforts to upgrade the area in question. Finally, prior to the development of any revitalization strategy, information describing the dynamics of the housing market must be examined. This data will give a more thorough understanding of the neighborhood's problems and it will provide the basis for evaluating the effectiveness of any strategy employed. In addition, it will provide hard, quan-

> tifiable data to use in dealing with private financial institutions and realtors and may be useful in obtaining their cooperation.

ROGER S. AHLBRANDT, JR. & PAUL C. BROPHY, NEIGHBORHOOD REVITALIZATION: THEORY AND PRACTICE 151–52 (1975).

9. There has been a spirited academic debate over the efficacy and impact of housing code enforcement on the poor, and particularly, about whether vigorous housing code enforcement raises the cost of housing. See Robin Powers Kinning, *Selective Housing Code Enforcement and Low-Income Housing Policy: Minneapolis Case Study*, 21 FORDHAM URB. L.J. 159 (1993) (arguing that selective code enforcement against repeat offenders and symbolically important buildings has a beneficial impact without a significant increase in rents). The academic literature to which Kinning's study pertains includes Bruce Ackerman, *More on Slum Housing and Redistribution Policy: A Reply to Professor Komesar*, 82 YALE L.J. 1194 (1973); Bruce Ackerman, *Regulating Slum Housing on Behalf of the Poor: Of Housing Codes, Housing Subsidies and Income Redistribution Policy*, 80 YALE L.J. 1093 (1971); Neil K. Komesar, *Return to Slumville: A Critique of the Ackerman Analysis of Housing Code Enforcement and the Poor*, 82 YALE L.J. 1175 (1973); Richard S. Markovits, *The Distributive Impact, Allocative Efficiency, and Overall Desirability of Ideal Housing Codes: Some Theoretical Clarifications*, 89 HARV. L. REV. 1815 (1976); Charles J. Meyers, *The Covenant of Habitability and the American Law Institute*, 27 STAN. L. REV. 879 (1975); Edward H. Rabin, *The Revolution in Residential Landlord-Tenant Law: Causes and Consequences*, 69 CORNELL L. REV. 517 (1984); Duncan Kennedy, *The Effect of the Warranty of Habitability on Low Income Housing: "Milking" and Class Violence*, 15 FLA. ST. U. L. REV. 485 (1987).

10. Constitutional challenges to differential code enforcement claiming violation of equal protection are not likely to be successful. *See, e.g., Maryland Mortgage & Inv. Co. v. State*, 332 A.2d 675 (Md. Ct. Spec. App. 1975).

11. *Housing Code Enforcement and the Taking Issue.* Historically, property owners may argue that enforcement of the housing codes resulting in the demolition of their buildings constitutes a taking requiring just compensation under the federal and state constitutions. This argument recurs in jurisdictions that provide a statutory procedure for transferring title to abandoned buildings, discussed *infra*.

12. In *Devines v. Maier*, 728 F.2d 867 (7th Cir.), *cert. denied*, 469 U.S. 836 (1984), tenants were ordered to temporarily vacate a building which the city ordered razed under a code enforcement program funded by a federal community development block grant. The tenants did not qualify for relocation benefits under relocation benefit guidelines adopted by the city. They argued that they should receive compensation under the taking clause because a taking had occurred.

The Seventh Circuit initially ruled in favor of the tenants but subsequently reversed itself in light of later decisions of the U.S. Supreme Court in *Texaco, Inc. v. Short*, 454 U.S. 516 (1982), and *Loretto v. Teleprompter Manhattan CATV Corp.*, 458 U.S. 419 (1982). In *Devines*, the court said "[I]t is a manifest injustice and contrary to the best interests of society to penalize the City of Milwaukee for properly enforcing its building code, designed in part, to reduce the incidence of substandard housing." 728 F.2d at 886. Is this interpretation of the taking doctrine really consistent with *Loretto*, which found a taking when government required landlords to accept TV cabling for tenants with only a "*de minimis*" compensation of one dollar? *Devines* arose because the displaced tenants were denied relocation benefits under the Uniform Relocation Act (URA). The district and circuit courts both upheld the city's denial of relocation benefits under the URA. For discussion of relocation eligibility, see F *infra*.

13. Most cities do not themselves pay any relocation benefits to tenants displaced by municipal code enforcement and do not require landlords to do so. Should the city or owners of slum property be compelled to pay for the relocation of these tenants when required to comply with the housing code?

14. In *Alger v. Department of Labor & Industry*, 917 A.2d 508 (Vt. 2006), tenants brought a class action against the Department of Labor and Industry for ordering closure of the apartment building where they lived and termination of utility services for housing code violations. Their legal theory was that they were entitled to recover for the taking of their property, i.e. their leaseholds, without due process or just compensation. Although the trial court dismissed the tenants' taking claim, the appellate court reversed on this issue. The Department had failed to enforce the housing code at the property until the conditions had engendered an emergency, thus while closure of the property without predetermination notice to the tenants was a necessary action, tenants stated a takings claim based on the Department's role in allowing the nuisance to continue unabated for so long. The Department's choice to enforce the housing code only as a last resort deprived them of all beneficial use of their homes.

4. Rehabilitation Codes

A growing number of states are considering or adopting codes to govern the rehabilitation of older buildings. One reason is the deterrence effect of conventional codes: buildings remain in disrepair because traditional codes make rehabilitation overly expensive. Estimates of this impact on new construction have ranged from 1% to 200%, and empirical research is thin. Another reason is the fact that rehabilitation is a powerful economic force. Although its impact is difficult to quantify—rehabilitation often occurs without building permits, and rehabilitation statistics are calculated in many different ways—the best estimates suggest that rehabilitation accounts for one-fifth of all construction. *See* Sara C. Galvin, *Rehabilitating Rehab Through State Building Codes*, 115 YALE L. J. 1744 (2006). In jurisdictions desiring to encourage rehab, the drawbacks of traditional codes include their inflexibility, the unpredictability and lack of uniformity in interpretation by code enforcers, and the need for uniform statewide training of code enforcement officials.

New Jersey pioneered the recent movement when it adopted a Rehabilitation Subcode in 1997. N.J. ADMIN. CODE tit. 5, § 5:23-6.1. New Jersey's Subcode establishes three types of projects—rehabilitation, change of use, and additions; and four categories of rehabilitation work—repair, renovation, alteration, and reconstruction. All the necessary codes are in one document, clearly separated from requirements for new construction.

Since New Jersey's adoption of a rehabilitation code, HUD issued a model rehab code based on it, the Nationally Applicable Recommended Rehabilitation Provisions. *See, e.g.*, *Smart Codes in Your Community: A Guide to Building Rehabilitation Codes* (2001) (published by Building Technology, Inc.), *available at* http://www.huduser.org/publications/pdf/smartcodes.pdf. In 2000 the International Code Council—a group created in 1994 to develop a single set of comprehensive, coordinated national model construction codes—adopted its own version of a model rehabilitation code, the International Existing Building Code. Rehab codes have been adopted in Rhode Island, Maryland, New Jersey, and Minnesota, among other states; and in Wichita, Kansas, and Wilmington, Delaware, among other cities.

Historic Structures. Special rules apply to the rehabilitation of historic structures; otherwise building or rehabilitation codes may require specified upgrades inconsistent with some of the historic structure requirements. Generally, substantial rehab is necessary in order for a building to qualify for historic preservation tax credits under various state or federal programs. However, state laws and local ordinances may restrict either the quantity or quality of rehabilitation, or both, in order to preserve the historic nature of the structure. For a useful toolkit, see NATIONAL TRUST FOR HISTORIC PRESERVATION, REBUILDING COMMUNITY, A BEST PRACTICES TOOLKIT FOR HISTORIC PRESERVATION AND REDEVELOPMENT, *available at* http://www.nationaltrust.org/issues/housing/Rebuilding_Community.pdf.

Green Building Codes. Other laws may affect rehabilitation as well. In a growing number of states and localities, new requirements for energy conservation may be imposed on almost any type of rehabilitation. These may involve passive solar energy efforts, water conservation, building and glass requirements, use of special appliances or components, and recycling requirements. Not surprisingly, these may add to construction costs. Some of these capital costs may be offset by public and private subsidy programs for energy conservation improvements made by the owner/developer; as well as reductions in operating or utility costs for residents. See the discussion of green building in the context of the discussion of sustainable development, *infra.*

Counsel should be aware that major rehabilitation of a structure with federal or state funds may trigger a variety of laws such as relocation obligations, discussed in Section F of this Chapter, *infra* and laws protecting rights of access for persons with disabling conditions, such as the Rehabilitation Act of 1973, discussed in Chapter 6 *infra.*

a. Housing Courts and Housing Code Remedies

Another reform in housing code administration frequently urged by housing professionals and housing activists is the municipal housing court. These advocates argue that housing code administration will suffer if the prosecution of code violations is consigned to local courts and judges who also try a large number of other cases. They will be unfamiliar with housing problems, unable to provide the expertise necessary to deal with complex housing issues, and unwilling because of their unfamiliarity with housing issues to levy the fines necessary to secure code compliance.

It is argued that a separate housing court can overcome all of these limitations, especially if the court is authorized to provide civil as well as criminal relief in housing code cases that can secure code compliance more effectively. Special housing courts have now been created in a number of municipalities throughout the nation. They provide an important test of the argument that a specialized court will improve housing code administration.

In 1980, Ohio's first housing court began to operate. Its origin and enabling statute are discussed in Frederic P. White, *The Cleveland Housing Court Act: New Answer to an Old Problem,* 30 CLEV. ST. L. REV. 41 (1981). The following article, based upon an evaluation of its first half-decade, discusses its impact on housing code enforcement in Cleveland.

W. Dennis Keating, Judicial Approaches to Urban Housing Problems: A Study of the Cleveland Housing Court

19 Urban Lawyer 345, 347–48, 351–57 (1987)

This court is a comprehensive housing court, the only such court in the state of Ohio. Its criminal jurisdiction included actions to enforce local building, housing, air pollution, sanitation, health, fire, and safety codes. Its civil jurisdiction included landlord and tenant claims (e.g., eviction actions for nonpayment of rent). Its equitable powers include injunctive remedies. In 1985, the court had a single judge and a staff of seven (including two housing specialists). Its annual budget was $227,000, provided by the City of Cleveland primarily through its Community Development Block Grant. The court's 1985 case load was 9,124.

A major criterion for the success of the housing court was said to be an increase in the processing of code violation cases. The number of code violation cases filed by the Cleveland Law Department, the city's prosecutor, did increase after 1980 but then leveled off. The great majority of the code violation cases in the housing court consisted of one- and two-family units. A majority were absentee-owned.

While the number of code enforcement cases comprised only a small percentage of the overall case load of the housing court, its handling of this important issue was said to be a key indicator of its acceptance and success.

A 1967–68 study of code enforcement in Cleveland found enforcement of housing codes through criminal prosecution to be ineffective. Criminal convictions resulting in small fines did not necessarily result in corrections of code violations. A 1981 analysis of the newly created housing court estimated that it typically took a year from the date of the initial code violation notice until the first court hearing and another year before existing violations were corrected.

The 1986 evaluation included an analysis of the court's code violation case load.... The data suggested that after the appointment of a judge, who finally lent stability to the court's operations, it began to process code violation cases more efficiently. From 1983 to 1984, the average period between the initial inspection request and the date of final judgment was reduced from 720 to 436 days. The period between the date the case was filed until the date of final judgment was reduced from 430 to 255 days. The average number of hearings fell from 10.4 to 7.4, as did the number of continuances granted from 6.2 to 3. The court has largely overcome the problem of delays caused by the nonappearance of defendants by instituting a bailiff service ensuring their appearance. This noticeable improvement in efficiency is one of the anticipated benefits of a housing court which is proficient and knowledgeable about this type of case.

Almost all defendants pleaded guilty or no contest. However, almost all the defendants had their fines suspended pending correction of the violations. This practice is the policy of the court, both to encourage compliance and to consider the stated inability of many defendant landlords and homeowners to pay for necessary repairs. There was no difference in the treatment of absentee landlords versus owner-occupants. In the sample the average reported initial fine in 1984 was $110. This compares with a 1969 figure of $70. However, virtually no data were available concerning the amount of the final fine ordered (whether or not the required repairs were made).

The City of Cleveland's Law Department reported average final fines of only $30 in 1984 (unchanged from 1983). It is probably safe to assume from this data that the housing court continues to levy nominal fines, preferring to suspend most fines to obtain compliance. Whether even small final fines were regularly paid was not ascertainable. To what extent fines include court costs is unknown.

The housing court judge's policy of reducing or suspending fines has been sharply criticized by the City of Cleveland's commissioner of building and housing, as well as some neighborhood groups. The commissioner supported severe and automatic fines, especially for repeat offenders and defendants who failed to make promised repairs after being granted a continuance to do so. The judge was also criticized by the commissioner, many housing inspectors and some neighborhood groups for having too liberal a policy toward granting continuances.

These are familiar issues in the long-standing debate over how best to enforce housing codes. Complicating the question in Cleveland is the economics of Cleveland's housing market. The 1980 income of both homeowners and renters is low compared to suburban Cleveland—$17,675 and $8,160, respectively. The median value of owner occupied housing was only $34,000 and rents were $145 monthly in 1980, both much lower than in suburban Cleveland. There is no data on landlords' incomes. What is known is that 21 percent of Cleveland's population is poor. This means that enforcement of the housing code is often difficult, if not impossible, either because the income of owner defendants is too low to qualify them for unsubsidized rehabilitation loans or because the tenants' income is too low to allow the owner to pass on repair costs through rent increases. Imposing severe penalties through fines to poor owners and landlords is unlikely to achieve the primary goal of improving housing quality.

Exacerbating the dilemma of the housing court judges and the court's housing specialists is the paucity of municipal programs to subsidize housing rehabilitation for lower income owners.

Notes and Questions

1. Code enforcement in older cities, including Cleveland, remains a challenging problem. Housing code enforcement as a system is more effective as a means of regulating new construction than it is in preventing or abating nuisance conditions in aging housing stock. Is the protection of neighborhoods from nuisance conditions properly seen as the first line of defense against the spread of blight, in a declining housing? The argument is that, especially in low-income neighborhoods with older structures, blight will surely overtake rehabilitation and restoration without a municipal system to uphold minimum standards.

2. The Keating evaluation of the Cleveland housing court concludes that it has had a positive but perhaps a limited impact on improving housing code enforcement. In 2007, the city's demolition budget was tripled, and the number of demolitions rose to 800, four times the number for any prior year. Advocates in that city view the Housing Court as the strongest institution in Cleveland's code enforcement system, which demonstrates that "a special purpose court with full jurisdiction over housing, building, and zoning matters can simultaneously protect the public health, safety, and welfare on the one hand and extract compliance from responsible parties on the other." Kermit Lind, *The Perfect Storm: An Eyewitness Account from Ground Zero in Cleveland's Neighborhoods*, 17 J. AFFORDABLE HOUSING & COMMUNITY DEV. L. 237, 243–244 (2008).

3. Other housing courts have claimed greater success. For example, the following excerpt summarizes the reasons for the success of the Pittsburgh housing court in the city's housing code enforcement program:

> Through the judicious use of fines, suspended fines, conditional sentences, extensions of time in appropriate cases, supervised probation, and the effective utilization of the services of and coordination with the many other governmental and private agencies in Pittsburgh, the housing court has achieved a remarkable level of success. For the recalcitrant offender, the imposition of a stiff fine may be the only remedy. In the case of the "good-faith" defendant who may need a little extra encouragement to comply within a reasonable time, a suspended fine may be the appropriate remedy under a sort of carrot and stick approach which often serves as an effective warning discouraging any future

> noncompliance. The conditional sentence is similar to the suspended fine approach but contains specific conditions with which the offender must comply in order to avoid paying the imposed fine.

Alan S. Penkower, *The Housing Court of Pittsburgh,* 17 URB. L. ANN. 141, 152 (1979).

4. Some housing courts have also appointed housing specialists to assist in housing code enforcement. Their function is to provide technical advice on code compliance and negotiate settlements in housing code compliance cases. *See* Paul G. Garrity, *The Boston Housing Court: An Encouraging Response to Complex Issues,* 17 URB. L. ANN. 15 (1979).

The Cleveland housing court article reviews the tenant remedies for housing code enforcement that have become common in many parts of the country. Many of these tenant remedies alter the traditional landlord-tenant relationship by allowing the tenant to withhold rent until a building is brought into code compliance, and by staying eviction while the building remains in violation of the code. This modification of the landlord-tenant relationship has prompted court challenges by owners of housing to the constitutionality of tenant remedies. How one court handled these challenges is indicated by the following case:

DePaul v. Kauffman

Supreme Court of Pennsylvania
272 A.2d 500 (1971)

ROBERTS, Justice.

This Court is urged by this appeal to hold unconstitutional the Pennsylvania Rent Withholding Act, Act of January 24, 1966, P.L. (1965) 1534, 1, as amended, 35 P.S. 1700-1 (Supp. 1970). We are unpersuaded and hold that Act to be a valid exercise of the Commonwealth's police power.

According to the terms of the Rent Withholding Act,[3] if a city certifies a dwelling as "unfit for human habitation," the tenant's rental obligation is suspended until the dwelling is re-certified as "fit" or until the tenancy is terminated for a reason other than the nonpayment of rent. During the period of rent suspension, rents due are to be deposited in an escrow account. If the dwelling is re-certified as fit within six months after the origi-

3. The Act reads....

Notwithstanding any other provision of the law, or of any agreement, whether oral or in writing, whenever the Department of Licenses and Inspections ... certifies a dwelling as unfit for human habitation, the duty of any tenant of such dwelling to pay, and the right of the landlord to collect rent shall be suspended without affecting any other terms or conditions of the landlord tenant relationship, until the dwelling is certified as fit for human habitation or until the tenancy is terminated for any reason other than nonpayment of rent. During any period when the duty to pay rent is suspended, and the tenant continues to occupy the dwelling, the rent withheld shall be deposited by the tenant in an escrow account in a bank or trust company approved by the city or county as the case may be and shall be paid to the landlord when the dwelling is certified as fit for human habitation at any time within six months from the date on which the dwelling was certified as unfit for human habitation. If, at the end of six months after the certification of the dwelling as unfit for human habitation, such dwelling has not been certified as fit for human habitation any moneys deposited in escrow on account of continued occupancy shall be payable to the depositor, except that any funds deposited in escrow may be used for the purpose of making such dwelling fit for human habitation and for the payment of utility services for which the landlord is obligated but which he refuses or is unable to pay. No tenant shall be evicted for any reason whatsoever while rent is deposited in escrow.

nal certification of unfitness, all funds in the escrow account are payable to the landlord. If, however, the dwelling remains unfit at the expiration of the six month period, all escrow funds are returnable to the tenant, except that such funds may be used to effect repairs needed to render the dwelling fit or to pay for utility services for which the landlord is obligated but unwilling or unable to pay. The Act further provides that no tenant shall be evicted for any reason during the rent suspension period.

Appellants, Peter, Eugene and Helen DePaul, are the owners of a nine-unit apartment building on East High Street in Philadelphia. On or about April 4, 1968, the City of Philadelphia certified that property "unfit for human habitation." Pursuant to the Rent Withholding Act and beginning on April 27, 1968, rents were withheld and paid to appellee, Samuel Kauffman, as escrow agent.

On October 17, 1968, appellants filed a complaint in equity seeking a declaration that the Rent Withholding Act is unconstitutional and an injunction restraining appellee from returning any of the escrow funds to the depositing tenants. In addition to the foregoing facts, appellants alleged that on some unspecified date they had applied for a loan to enable them to improve their East High Street property so as to make it "fit for human habitation." They asserted, however, that their loan application could not be processed before the expiration of the statutory six month period on October 27, 1968.

After the issuance of a preliminary injunction, appellee filed preliminary objections in the nature of a demurrer, alleging that he had complied fully with the provisions of the Rent Withholding Act. The court of common pleas sustained the preliminary objections and dissolved the preliminary injunction. The present appeal followed.

[The court then held that the act was not an unconstitutional delegation of legislative power.—Eds.]

Appellants further contend that the Rent Withholding Act works an arbitrary and unreasonable taking of their property without due process of law by denying them the right to collect rent and simultaneously protecting the tenant from eviction.

It has long been recognized that property rights are not absolute and that persons hold their property "subject to valid police regulation, made, and to be made, for the health and comfort of the people...." And among the legitimate objects of the regulation of property for the general welfare is an adequate supply of safe and decent housing. As put by Mr. Justice Holmes: "Housing is a necessary of life. All the elements of a public interest justifying some degree of public control are present." *Block v. Hirsh,* 256 U.S. 135 (1921). Of course, "a law which purports to be an exercise of the police power must not be unreasonable, unduly oppressive or patently beyond the necessities of the case, and the means which it employs must have a real and substantial relation to the objects sought to be attained." In light of these principles, the Rent Withholding Act does not offend due process.

It is evident that the sanctions imposed by the Act bear a real and substantial relationship to its objective of assuring decent and habitable rental property. "In *Reitmeyer v. Sprecher,* 243 A.2d 395 (Pa. 1968), we recognized that a severe housing shortage exists in many parts of the Commonwealth and that much of what housing does exist is in very poor condition. The legislature was obviously attempting [through the Rent Withholding Act] to improve this situation by giving tenants the power to put pressure on landlords to repair dilapidated, unsafe dwellings." It seems a matter of common sense that one in the business of renting real estate for profit who is faced with the temporary or permanent loss of rental income will, in some instances, take steps to avoid that loss. Indeed, appellants in this very case allege that after their property was declared unfit they sought to obtain a loan to enable them to make the necessary repairs.

Appellants' real complaint is that the Act is too severe, that it is "unduly oppressive or patently beyond the necessities of the case." In this regard, they note that under the terms of the Rent Withholding Act, a tenant may but need not necessarily employ the escrow funds to make the needed improvements and can avoid eviction during the period of rent suspension notwithstanding his mistreatment of the property or other violation of his lease, and the landlord may irretrievably lose rentals if, after making a good faith and reasonable effort, he cannot rehabilitate the property within six months after its certification as unfit. Appellants also construe the Act as allowing the tenant to remain in possession regardless of his payment of rent to the escrowee and as requiring the landlord to renew a lease which is set to expire during the statutory six month period. The foregoing features, however, do not render the Act unduly oppressive or otherwise unreasonable.

Preliminarily, we note that appellants' interpretation of the Act is erroneous in two respects. The Rent Withholding Act states expressly that "[d]uring any period when the duty to pay rent is suspended and the tenant continues to occupy the dwelling, the rent withheld *shall be deposited* by the tenant in an escrow account ..." (emphasis added). This language makes clear that a tenant may in no event remain in possession without paying the required rent to the escrowee. In addition, the Act does not, as appellants argue, require the renewal of a lease which is set to expire during the six month period of rent suspension. The Act provides that the duty to pay and the right to receive rent shall be suspended "without affecting any other terms or conditions of the landlord-tenant relationship." As the termination date of the lease is surely a term or condition of that relationship, the quoted language suggests that there is no requirement of involuntary lease renewal. On the other hand, the last sentence of the Act states: "No tenant shall be evicted for any reason whatsoever while rent is deposited in escrow." To give meaning to both of these portions of the Act, we conclude that the Act does not require the *renewal* of an existing lease but only an *extension* of the original lease so long as rent is in escrow.

This construction serves the intent of the Act. Undoubtedly, a portion of those who rent unfit dwellings are tenants from month to month or at will. With respect to this class of tenants, if the Act were construed to require no extension of the tenant's possessory right, the landlord could largely avoid the impact of the Act by giving notice to vacate as soon as the first rental payment was put in escrow. However, in the case of a tenancy from year to year or longer set to expire one or two months prior to the expiration of the rent withholding period, objectives of the Act would not be served and the landlord would be needlessly burdened, if he were required to renew the lease for an entire additional term.

That the Rent Withholding Act permits but does not require the necessary improvements to be made with the escrow funds is surely not unreasonable. A substantial and recurring part of a landlord's business is the maintenance of his property. Accordingly, it is to be expected that most landlords possess either the skills needed to make property repairs or, at least, the knowledge of whom to hire to make such repairs. Tenants, as a class are not likely to possess these skills and this knowledge in the same degree. Thus it is far from unreasonable to put the burden on the landlord rather than the tenant to make the needed repairs. Of course the Act imposes an additional burden upon the landlord in the sense that he will be out of pocket to the extent of the cost of the repairs until the repairs are completed and the rents released from escrow but we do not deem this unduly oppressive.

Neither are we persuaded by the example of a landlord who is unable to make the required improvements within six months notwithstanding his good faith efforts to do so. In the first place the Legislature had to set some cut off point in order to make meaningful the sanction of permanent rent loss. Otherwise, a landlord could procrastinate interminably. A half a year is surely not an unreasonably short time. Furthermore, there can be little sympathy for the landlord who despite diligence and good faith cannot repair his property within the allotted time. Landlords have a duty to maintain their properties in a condition fit for human habitation not only after that property has been certified as unfit but *at all times*. Section 7-104 of the Philadelphia Housing Code itself provides for fines of up to $300 or imprisonment for up to 90 days or both, for any violation for each day such violation continues after notice and opportunity to comply. Section 7-505 of the Code provides for direct abatement of the violation by the Department of Licenses and Inspections. Thus it is not unreasonable that a landlord suffer a financial penalty even if he cannot render his property fit within six months after its certification as unfit. This situation might have even been contemplated by the Act: the goal of good housing would be served not only by rehabilitating houses which are certified as unfit but also by *deterring* owners of rental property from allowing their property to degenerate into a condition of unfitness in the first place.

The provision of the Rent Withholding Act that insulates a tenant from eviction during the rent withholding period is not a constitutional deficiency. To be sure, this statutory right is a windfall to the tenant. However it serves as an additional deterrent inducing the landlord to maintain his property in a habitable condition. Furthermore one of the possibly beneficial effects of the Act is that it permits the aid of tenants in an effort to enforce health and housing codes. To enlist tenant initiative the Legislature might well have deemed it necessary to forestall tenant fear of landlord reprisal. And in the case where a tenant abuses the leased property while shielded from eviction by the statute the landlord is fully protected. He may sue the tenant for money damages for any destruction or, if monetary damages are inadequate, seek an injunction against the misuse of his property.

Finally, appellants assert that the Rent Withholding Act unconstitutionally impairs the obligation of contracts. This contention must also be rejected.

As applied to leases entered into or renewed after the effective date of the Act there can be no "impairment," for the laws in force when a contract is entered into become part of the obligation of contract "with the same effect as if expressly incorporated in its terms.

With regard to leases that predate the effective date of the Act it must be borne in mind that "'the interdiction of statutes impairing the obligation of contracts does not prevent the state from exercising such powers as ... are necessary for the general good of the public, though contracts previously entered into between individuals may thereby be affected.'" *Home Bldg. & Loan Ass'n v. Blaisdell,* 290 U.S. 398, 437 (1934). This Court has itself recognized that "'[t]he constitutional protection of the obligation of contracts is necessarily subject to the police power of the state, and therefore a statute passed in the legitimate exercise of the police power will be upheld by the courts, although it incidentally destroys existing contract rights....'" *Zeuger Milk Co. v. Pittsburgh School District,* 5 A.2d 885, 886 (Pa. 1939) (sustaining minimum price regulations modifying price term of existing contract).

We have already concluded that the Rent Withholding Act is a legitimate exercise of police power. In light of the paramount public interest in safe and decent housing, the landlord's pre-existing duty to comply with housing code standards, and the fact that in most instances there will be no permanent rent loss, we do not consider the Act to be an unconstitutional impairment of contract obligations.

Our conclusion today finds support in decisions of other jurisdictions which have upheld similar legislation.

The decree of the Philadelphia Court of Common Pleas is affirmed. Appellants pay costs.

BELL, Chief Justice (dissenting). [Omitted—Eds.]

Notes and Questions

1. Most courts have upheld the constitutionality of legislation of this type. The case of *Ten West 28th Street Realty Corp. v. Moerdler,* 275 N.Y.S.2d 144 (Sup. Ct. 1966) upheld New York's rent impairing violation law. *Farrell v. Drew,* 227 N.E.2d 824 (N.Y. 1967) upheld New York legislation authorizing the withholding of welfare recipient rents for substandard housing. Both cases are relied upon in the principal opinion [in parts that are omitted.—Eds.] *See* Jonathan M. Purver, Annotation, *Validity and Construction of Statute or Ordinance Authorizing Withholding or Payment into Escrow of Rent,* 40 A.L.R.3d 821 (1971). In a challenge to a rent withholding statute, the Seventh Circuit upheld the constitutionality of Chicago's Residential Landlord and Tenant Ordinance. *Chicago Bd. of Realtors v. City of Chicago,* 819 F.2d 732 (7th Cir. 1987). Judge Posner filed a detailed dissent. He is known as a leading proponent of the substantive due process argument against regulation of private property. The Sixth Circuit upheld the rent escrow provisions of Ohio's Landlord-Tenant Act in *Chernin v. Welchans,* 844 F.2d 322 (6th Cir. 1988).

2. An evaluation of the Pennsylvania rent withholding statute based on economic analysis, but not an empirical survey, indicated that the statute would improve housing conditions if it led to an expansion of the standard housing stock. The article predicted that abandonment would occur if rents were withheld on buildings in which landlords did not believe that additional investment was justified. Joseph R. Buckley & Gary N. Conley, Comment, *Housing Market Operations and the Pennsylvania Rent Withholding Act—An Economic Analysis,* 17 VILL. L. REV. 886 (1972). There is evidence that housing code enforcement has led to housing abandonment in some cities. William G. Grigsby, *Economic Aspects of Housing Code Enforcement,* 3 URB. LAW. 533 (1971). For a contrary view, see Duncan Kennedy, *The Effect of the Warranty of Habitability on Low Income Housing: "Milking" and Class Violence,* 15 FLA. ST. U.L. REV. 485 (1987). The comment above on "Housing Market Operations" in the Villanova Law Review also suggested that the distributive effects of rent withholding would be limited. Income would be redistributed from middle-income landlords to their poorer tenants. With this observation, contrast the findings in the classic study of the Newark slums, GEORGE STERNLIEB, THE TENEMENT LANDLORD (1966). Sternlieb found that minority, low-income owners increasingly dominated ownership in the Newark substandard housing stock. What does this finding say about the distributive effect of housing code enforcement techniques such as rent withholding? For a follow-up on the Sternlieb study, see GEORGE STERNLIEB & ROBERT W. BURCHEL, RESIDENTIAL ABANDONMENT: THE TENEMENT LANDLORD REVISITED (1973). The follow-up study documents an increase in minority ownership of substandard housing. *See also* MICHAEL A. STEGMAN, HOUSING INVESTMENT IN THE INNER CITY (1972). For a comprehensive review of housing code enforcement and tenant remedy problems, see Samuel Bassett Abbott, *Housing Policy, Housing Codes and Tenant Remedies: An Integration,* 56 B.U.L. REV. 1 (1976).

3. In *Orange Taxpayers Council, Inc. v. City of Orange,* 416 A.2d 353 (N.J. 1980), the court upheld the constitutionality of a local rent control ordinance requiring "substantial compliance" with local health and safety codes before a rent increase could be granted. The court held this provision of the ordinance constitutional. "No one would applaud the wisdom of lawmakers who by controlling the price of rental housing but not its qual-

ity, insured that their constituents could live in affordable dwellings that are unsafe, unsanitary and harmful to health."

4. Upholding the constitutionality of a tenant remedy statute is one matter. Effectiveness of such legal reforms is another. Why might tenant remedies have minimal effects on the rental housing market? One possibility is that the poor tenants who are likely to be evicted do not assert newly authorized actions in court, for any of several reasons. Six months after the Chicago ordinance was upheld in *Chicago Board of Realtors, Inc v. City of Chicago*, 819 F.2d 732 (7th Cir 1987), tenants were largely still oblivious to their newly acquired rights, despite a substantial publicity effort by the city. A study of Baltimore's housing court revealed that most tenants knew of their formal legal rights to challenge rent actions based on bad housing conditions, but did not assert their rights. Barbara Bezdek, *Silence in the Court: Participation and Subordination of Poor Tenants' Voices in Legal Process*, 20 Hofstra L. Rev. 533 (1992). Tenants and landlords may persist in following social norms, which in some sense are 'efficient,' regardless of what the law says. See Robert C. Ellickson, Order without Law: How Neighbors Settle Disputes 279 (1991) (arguing that the norm of "you are entitled to get what you pay for" governs landlord-tenant relations more than any legal regime). *See also* Lihor Jacob Strahilevitz, *Don't Try This at Home: Posner as Political Economist,* 74 U. Chi. L. Rev. 1873 (2007).

For some comparison of code enforcement in a specialized Housing Court, versus other municipal enforcement tools including nuisance abatement litigation, padlock laws and injunctions, criminal prosecution, and various administrative tribunals, see Gabriel Taussig, *City Code Enforcement: Tools For Building Better Communities*, 188 Practicing L. Inst. 495 (2001). For discussion of limitations in a system dependent on tenant enforcement of the warranty of habitability, see Bezdek, *supra.*

5. Some housing strategists have suggested the use of direct legal action against municipalities to compel enforcement of housing codes. The following report indicates how an action of this kind was carried out in the city of Chicago:

> [W]e have already mentioned mandamus in the context of securing enforcement of the housing codes. The remedy is also highly appropriate in other contexts, especially in cases where the city, in carrying out its code enforcement duties, encounters a recalcitrant landlord and, through judicial action, seeks either to compel the landlord to repair or to obtain a judicial order authorizing demolition. The landlord refuses to repair, contempt sanctions are not applied, and so the city seeks the easy way out—demolition. The scenario is then ripe for intervention by the tenants, as in *City of Chicago v. Chicago Title and Trust Co.,* No. 76 CH 56312 (Cir. Ct. of Cook Co., Chancery Div., filed November 23, 1976). There, the City of Chicago had sued the owners and trustee of the property for repair or demolition of certain unsafe residential premises. Prior to the institution of those proceedings, a group of tenants and former tenants of the building in question, together with a neighborhood council, had sued the same defendants in the same court, requesting injunctive relief ordering repairs and retroactive rent abatement for rents paid in excess of the defective premises' reasonable value. *Rivera v. Martin,* (76 CH 5464). After obtaining leave of court to intervene in the city's suit against the owners, the tenants voluntarily dismissed their action. As intervenors, they are now moving for (1) an order requiring the City of Chicago to repair the buildings; (2) leave to file a cross complaint against the City of Chicago; and (3) in the alternative, an order reappointing the previously dismissed receiver and

> requiring the public sale of the building to the highest bidder who presents a satisfactory plan for repairs.

The Expanding Role of the Municipality in Remedying Substandard Housing Conditions, L. Project Bull., June/July 1979, at 6.

Mandamus is available against a municipality only to compel the carrying out of a mandatory duty. Is a mandamus action against a municipality to enforce a housing code likely to be successful, given the highly discretionary nature of such codes?

6. This review of housing code and housing code enforcement problems suggests that code enforcement may not benefit lower-income households. A forceful presentation of this argument can be found in Chester W. Hartman, Robert F. Kessler & Richard T. LeGates, *Municipal Housing Code Enforcement and Low Income Tenants*, 40 J. Am. Inst. Plan. 90, 91 (1974). The authors conclude:

> As currently practiced, code enforcement can only occasionally aid low-income people and may in more cases than not actually bring harm to them.... In its present form, code enforcement, when pursued aggressively and mechanically, can harm the residents economically and socially, and can have detrimental effects on the low-rent housing stock.

Id. at 91.

You are left to conclude whether housing codes are a viable housing strategy, whether they implement the "right" to housing (*see* Chapter 1, *supra*), and whether they do or do not improve the housing conditions of lower-income households.

b. Reclaiming Vacant and Abandoned Buildings

In urban communities afflicted with widespread properties whose owners allow them to fall below code, and perhaps into a state of nuisance, persistent vacancy or legal abandonment, local governments and neighborhood residents struggle to devise strategic responses on a suitable scale. Consider this problem:

> On Homer Avenue on the east side of Cleveland, Ohio, vacant homes litter the landscape. Although fewer than twenty houses line this short, one-way street, seven of them sit empty and only two of those have been boarded and secured by the city. The vacant homes are in various states of disrepair. Their yards fill with weeds in the summer and a multiplicity of insects breed in the grass. Most of the houses have broken windows, chipped paint and dislodged gutters. One house draws a number of people who engage in illicit activities during the evening hours.
>
> In addition to the empty houses, three once vibrant commercial buildings sit empty as well. The factory at the end of the street provides one function for the neighborhood: teenagers amuse themselves from time to time by breaking the factory windows with rocks, leaving shattered glass strewn about the street. Two boarded school buildings dominate the other end of the street. Loose bricks occasionally cascade from the second stories, crashing to the street below. Although the current owner removed the rickety and rusty fire escapes that children previously climbed, poison oak plants still run the length of the building.

Matthew J. Samsa, *Reclaiming Abandoned Properties: Using Public Nuisance Suits and Land Banks To Pursue Economic Redevelopment*, 56 Clev. St. L. Rev. 189, 190 (2008).

An abandoned property is one for which the owner has stopped carrying out at least one of the significant responsibilities of property ownership, with the result that the property is vacant, or likely to become vacant in the immediate future. ALLAN MALLACH, BRINGING BUILDINGS BACK: FROM ABANDONED PROPERTIES TO COMMUNITY ASSETS, 1 (2005). The lack of minimal upkeep typically creates conditions which amount to a nuisance. Common law in the states generally defines abandonment as the owner's intent to relinquish rights to the property. Statutory definitions encompass a number of additional indicators of abandonment, such as the need for rehabilitation, tax delinquency, vacancy, or a finding of nuisance by a code official or court.

The burden of abandoned buildings falls heavily on cities. Neglected housing reduces property values and the tax base, and the enforcement of building and housing codes becomes increasingly difficult in neighborhoods where a great number of property owners allow the buildings to decline in condition. Cities facing spreading deterioration are hard-pressed to marshal the resources to redevelop neighborhoods.

All types of property fall into abandonment, ranging from single family homes to industrial complexes. *See* Michael A. Pagano & Ann O'M. Bowman, *Vacant Land in Cities: An Urban Resource* 1 (Dec. 2000) (Brookings Institution Survey Series), *available at* https://www.brookings.edu/dybdocroot/es/urban/pagano/paganofinal.pdf). Statistics show that declining cities with a population over 100,000 average about 10,000 abandoned structures. The City of Detroit holds title to more than 40,000 abandoned buildings, despite having demolished more than 28,000 structures since 1989. Id. at 49. Acquiring accurate statistics on abandonment poses significant difficulties, yet the data demonstrate clearly that in cities with declining populations, abandonment is widespread. The numbers of abandoned homes and vacant lots has increased dramatically in America's urban and suburban neighborhoods since the housing meltdown of 2006–2010. See the discussion in Chapter 1 *supra.*

Causes and Effects of Abandonment

Abandonment occurs for a variety of reasons, but economic factors are the dominant explanation. A faltering regional economy contributes heavily to abandonment. Where the costs of rehabilitating a property outweigh the potential return on such an investment, abandonment becomes an alternative. Because of this, abandonment is most pronounced in poorer urban areas with lower property values. Other factors that intensify the problem include changes in the real estate market caused by demographic shifts from urban to suburban living, and ill health or death resulting in a household transition. Predatory lending and real estate speculation add to the mix. The strategy of leaving a home vacant coupled with the caprices of real estate markets make speculation uniquely dangerous to urban neighborhoods. Speculation, in particular, contributes to abandonment because the speculator purposefully avoids investing capital in a vacant property while waiting for the real estate market to rise.

Abandoned and vacant homes pose significant dangers for urban neighborhoods. They drive down property values, create health hazards, threaten the safety of residents, and perpetuate an image of the neighborhood which promotes criminal behavior and discourages redevelopment. The "Broken Windows" theory asserts that the mere existence of abandoned housing detrimentally affects a neighborhood because it demonstrates to outsiders and residents that the neighborhood is of the type that supports crime and poverty, creating a vicious cycle that encourages additional abandonment. Owners of abandoned structures impose these externalities on neighborhood residents when they allow a vacant nuisance to persist. *See* NICOLE STELLE GARNETT, ORDERING THE CITY: LAND USE, POLICING, AND THE RESTORATION OF URBAN AMERICA (2010).

Many localities are deploying strategies to reclaim their residential communities and blighted commercial areas. Local governments commonly use tax foreclosure and building and housing codes as methods of abating nuisances, although neither procedure was designed for this purpose. Thus cities are devising new tools specifically to abate nuisances and control the disposition of nuisance properties for community-enhancing land uses. Widespread abandonment can generate land for parks, mixed use New Urbanist neighborhoods, or urban agriculture.

The decline of much urban realty in the 1970s and 1980s is captured in the following brief excerpt.

Eduardo Moisés Peñalver and Sonia K. Katyal, Property Outlaws

155 University of Pennsylvania Law Review 1095, 1122–29 (2007)

The decades after World War II saw a massive migration of capital and people out of America's cities and into its suburbs. Through its creation of the interstate highway system and the discriminatory policies of the Federal Housing Administration (FHA), which would not guarantee mortgages in urban or racially integrated neighborhoods, government policy both lured and pushed investment capital out of inner cities and into outlying areas. Following the path laid by the FHA, private mortgage lenders simply refused to lend money for the construction or upkeep of properties within many urban neighborhoods.

In some cases, the owners of urban residential properties did not respond to this capital drought by simply selling their real estate. In order to maximize the return on their investment, they engaged in a practice called "milking," taking advantage of favorable tax treatment and extracting rents from tenants while investing as little money as possible in the upkeep of their properties. In the most run-down neighborhoods, the final stage of this process was often either "arson-for-profit" or the sale of the property to speculators with little interest in rehabilitating the dilapidated buildings. In many cases, however, the owner simply abandoned his decrepit property, in which case it typically ended up in government hands after a tax foreclosure.

In the 1970s and 1980s, an epidemic of urban property abandonment led to a dramatic expansion of government-owned properties in cities across the country. By the 1980s, for example, New York City and Philadelphia each owned thousands of vacant buildings seized from delinquent taxpayers. These derelict properties became zones of criminality ... and blighted entire neighborhoods. Landlord abandonment therefore had the perverse effect of exacerbating the very urban ills on which subsequent abandonment was predicated. The result was an ever-widening zone of urban decay and dysfunction.

As the federal government did with its public lands in the nineteenth century, city governments attempted to quickly return this now publicly owned, abandoned property to the private sector by auctioning it to the highest bidder. In so doing, they hoped both to raise revenue and to foster private development that would, it was argued, increase the urban tax base. All too often, however, the highest bidder was a speculator who quickly allowed the property to fall back into tax arrears. In New York City, for example, in 1979 approximately ninety percent of auctioned properties were delinquent on property taxes within one year of their sale. When they were not auctioning it off to speculators, city governments seemed unable to figure out what to do with the property, often simply holding it in its dilapidated state, even in the face of strong local demand for low-income housing....

In the meantime, a consensus was forming among residents of blighted communities that absentee ownership was a source of neighborhood problems, and that conditions could be improved by transferring ownership from absentee landlords, the city, or speculators to local residents. Neighborhood activists and advocates for low-income housing in cities across the country organized protests aimed at pushing governmental owners of abandoned urban properties to seek ways to convert those properties into housing for the poor. In the late 1970s and early 1980s, when conventional protests proved ineffective, several groups, most prominent among them the Association of Community Organizations for Reform Now (ACORN), initiated squatting campaigns to attract attention to their demands. Unlike the squatters of the nineteenth century, who were motivated almost exclusively by a desire to acquire property for themselves, the urban squatters of the late twentieth century acted out of an amalgamation of motives, not least of which was a desire to express their opposition to the government's failure to provide adequate low-income housing in the cities.

a. Urban Homesteading: Recycling and Re-Titling Abandoned Housing

In today's large U.S. cities, the lack of low-income housing has generated a resurgence of interest in urban homesteading. The experience of squatters and New York City officials in forging a responsive urban homesteading program is detailed by Christine Wilson in *Urban Homesteading: A Compromise Between Squatters and the Law*, 35 N.Y.L. SCH. L. REV. 709 (1990). Wilson offers a sympathetic portrayal of squatting as a strategy used to overcome the market processes and policies which create both an excess of abandoned housing and a large number of unhoused people. That disjunction placed squatters who engaged in housing self-help in abandoned structures, into controversy with legal, political, and economic dimensions. Their position is controversial because (1) squatting violates traditional property law rights and norms; (2) squatters take over property at the expense of those who are on waiting lists for public housing; and (3) they antagonize neighborhood residents when acting without obtaining community support.

Throughout the 1980s, a bitter struggle unfolded between these two perspectives. Urban squatting movements garnered some success as a method of protest. News photos of squatters attempting to reclaim abandoned property through their own labor was appealing to American audiences, even in the general political conservatism of the early 1980s and its antipathy to poverty-relief programs. Urban squatters kept the need for low-income housing on the political agenda. Peñalver & Katyal, *supra* 155 U. PA. L. REV. at 1122–29.

After years and many arrests, The Association of Community Organizations for Reform Now (ACORN) persuaded squatters to give up squatting in favor of city-sanctioned homesteading. ACORN focused it's organized efforts on rehabilitating abandoned housing, in neighborhoods with high crime rates and low property values resulting from the dilapidation of the building stock.

Unlike squatters, homesteaders acquire their living quarters through legal channels. Federal homesteading laws use federally-owned housing stock to provide ownership and assist in the preservation and revitalization of selected neighborhoods. *See* 24 C.F.R. §§ 590.1–.31. Under these programs, federally owned property is provided with a fee simple title for no consideration. *Id.* § 590.7(b)(7). For the conveyance of property, the homesteader agrees to repair and continue to improve the property, to occupy for not less than five consecutive years, and to surrender the property upon any material breach of the agreement. *Id.* § 590.7(b)(5). *See also* 12 U.S.C. § 1706e(b)(6) (providing for the transfer of real property without payment as a "coordinated approach toward neighborhood improvement ... and the upgrading of community services and facilities"). New York City, Baltimore, and other large U.S. urban centers have offered similar programs. Legalizing homesteading can make it easier for homesteaders to get financial support from the city and other sources. In New York's program, the city provided homesteaders with buildings from its *in rem* (tax foreclosed) stock, with funds to rehabilitate the buildings. The homesteaders acquire the buildings for a nominal price, and covenant to renovate and not to make a profit on resale. The city retained title with the first right to repurchase at the cost/investment of the owners, rather than the market price, at such time as the homesteaders sell.

Such homesteading agreements benefit the city in at least three ways. First, facilitating "homesteading" encourages squatters to accomplish their goals through legal channels and alleviates neighborhood tensions caused by squatters. Importantly, providing homesteading groups with abandoned housing brings previously unusable housing units back into productive use for the cost of rehabilitation. Finally, neighborhoods with dilapidated, abandoned housing are relieved of the physical, social and economic drag of vacant houses, thereby reducing the negative externalities that often accompany vacant buildings.

Takings Versus Police Power

One problem underlying urban homesteading laws and vacant building receivership ordinances is whether the owner of the neglected or abandoned property is protected by the due process and just compensation requirements of the Fifth Amendment, or whether these provisions are exercises of the police power, in which case compensation need not be paid by the city. The eminent domain clause of the Fifth Amendment provides, "nor shall private property be taken for public use without just compensation." U.S. CONST. Amend. V. The United States Supreme Court has repeatedly held that the promotion of a city's interest in public welfare justifies the taking of private property, in a long line of cases throughout the Twentieth Century. *See, e.g., Penn Cent. Transp. Co. v. New York City,* 438 U.S. 104 (1978) (city may place restrictions on development of private property in order to preserve historical district); *Young v. American Mini Theatres*, 427 U.S. 50 (1976) (zoning restriction allowed because of city's interest in preserving the quality of urban life); *Berman v. Parker,* 348 U.S. 26 (1954) (upholding act providing for use of eminent domain power to develop slum areas and for possible resale of land to private); *Miller v. Schoene*, 276 U.S. 272 (1928) (court justified cutting down trees on one parcel of land as means of preventing spread of disease to other orchards in vicinity); *Euclid v. Ambler Realty Co.*, 272 U.S. 365 (1926) (zoning ordinance resulting in the reduction of private land value was justified by the promotion of health and security achieved by the diversion of the industrial flow from residential districts).

Arguably then, since the city has an interest in providing its residents with permanent housing, upgrading low-income neighborhoods, and ending friction between squatters and law enforcers, it may be within the city's power to seize vacant buildings in rundown neighborhoods that are rampant with drugs and crime, and utilize them in an urban homesteading program. Providing an orderly means for placing abandoned, dilapidated buildings under the control of responsible homesteaders or intermediary renovators would then be an instance where the health, safety, morals, or general welfare of the neighborhood and city would be promoted.

An early innovative approach to dealing with the problem of abandoned houses is a 1983 Detroit ordinance known as the "homesteaders" ordinance. It allowed individuals to identify "abandoned," tax-delinquent buildings, apply for a contract to repair and occupy them, following verification of the unit's status and repairability upon notice to the owner of record. The ordinance authorized individuals, without regard to income or repair skills, to repair and occupy the vacant residences. Applicants sign nuisance abatement contracts in which they agree to make necessary repairs within three years. The cost of these repairs becomes a lien on the property, redeemable by the owner or by purchasers at a tax foreclosure sale.

The city can foreclose for delinquent taxes (after three years) or can institute actions to quiet title even earlier, in order to allow the homesteader to become the owner of the rehabilitated property. The liens for the homesteader's "sweat equity" and for unpaid taxes are to be assessed upon foreclosure. The city of Detroit refused to implement the ordinance, asserting that it was unconstitutional and *ultra vires* of its charter, prompting a mandamus action by prospective homesteaders. The court of appeals sustained the ordinance ruling that the ordinance was a legitimate exercise of the city's police power. It rejected a claim that the ordinance was an invalid exercise of governmental eminent domain authority. The Michigan Supreme Court remanded on the issue of whether the ordinance operated to create a taking. The decision of the court of appeals follows. The state supreme court denied review of this decision in an order that apparently is unpublished.

Moore v. City of Detroit

Michigan Court of Appeals
406 N.W.2d 488 (1987)

M.J. KELLY, Judge.

[In 1983, Detroit amended its nuisance abatement ordinance to include a provision which grants occupancy to abandoned housing to which the city does not have title. Because the city process to take title by foreclosing its lien for unpaid real estate taxes often takes years, this ordinance was established to prevent losing these buildings to vandalism and decay, thus allowing for restoration before the city takes title.

Finding that the abundance of abandoned buildings scattered throughout the city created an unsafe and immoral atmosphere, the ordinance was enacted to eliminate the "public nuisance" and "blighting influence on the surrounding neighborhood" created by these buildings. The ordinance allows families to move into abandoned homes and repair them, thereby "preserv[ing] the residential housing stock of the city, increas[ing] neighborhood stability and provid[ing] needed homes for Detroit citizens." [Detroit Code § 12-11.—Eds.]

This case is before us on remand from the Supreme Court for a decision on whether Detroit City Ordinance No. 556-H "unconstitutionally deprives property owners of their property interests without due process of law or just compensation."

Defendants argue that Ord. 556-H authorizes the city to confiscate privately owned property for a public purpose and thus involves the exercise of the city's power of eminent domain rather than its police powers. [The court rejected this argument. It reviewed the purposes of the ordinance and found that they fell within the city's power to provide for the health and safety of its citizens.—Eds.] The court concluded:

> Although these goals, if achieved will no doubt benefit the public, we are not persuaded that the taking authorized under Ord. 556-H is for a "public purpose"

as that term has evolved under the law of eminent domain. Most significantly, Ord. 556-H does not impose upon the property owner a burden which should be borne by the public. In a disordered society, vacant houses develop into public nuisances, as that term is defined in Ord. 556-H, partly because of the action or inaction of their owners. It is neither unfair nor unjust for the city to impose the burden of abating these nuisances upon the public as a whole. Neighborhoods don't blight overnight.

[The court then added that to avoid a holding that the ordinance was a taking it must also find that the physical occupation of the property authorized by the ordinance was "reasonable under the surrounding circumstances." — Eds.] Before considering the reasonableness of the occupancy authorized under Ord. 556-H, we find it helpful to visit a few of its procedural provisions.

Since Ord. 556-H does not authorize permanent occupancy of private property by third persons, defendants' reliance on [*Loretto v. Teleprompter Manhattan CATV Corp.*, 458 U.S. 419 (1982) — Eds.] is not dispositive. The Supreme Court in *Loretto,* repeatedly emphasized that its decision is based upon the permanency of the government-authorized occupancy challenged therein. Defendants' reliance on *Loretto* stems from an erroneous interpretation of Ord. 556-H as authorizing the city to take title to real property.

Correctly interpreted, Ord. 556-H simply amends the city's original building code and creates an alternative to demolition or costly repairs by government or third persons who do not gain rights to occupy the property. Defendants agree that the city may authorize a third party to enter private property in order to demolish a building identified as a public nuisance and that the property owner has no right to just compensation for this taking. Defendants further admit that just compensation is not required where the city contracts with a third party to repair a building identified as a public nuisance. It is the nuisance abatement contractor's occupancy of the property while making repairs which defendants now challenge as unconstitutional.

Defendants, however, fail to adequately distinguish between a taking authorized under the original building code and the taking authorized under Ord. 556-H. Under both the original building code and Ord. 556-H, third parties are authorized by the city to enter onto private property for the purpose of abating a public nuisance. Although the entry and physical possession authorized under Ord. 556-H extends the duration of the physical occupancy and allows the third party to make general use of the property while abating the nuisance, obviously, such possession is not more intrusive than demolition.

In any event, the dispositive inquiry is whether this extended physical possession is reasonable under the circumstances. We believe that it is. As noted by Justice Stevens in *Young v. American Mini Theatres, Inc.,* 427 U.S. 50, 71 (1976), cities "must be allowed a reasonable opportunity to experiment with solutions to admittedly serious problems." After having determined that existing mechanisms were ineffective in attacking the perils of abandoned homes scarring its neighborhoods, the city's legislative body enacted Ord. 556-H as an alternative method of abating these public nuisances. Defendants have failed to carry their burden of proving that this alternative is unreasonable and, therefore, unconstitutional. *Van Slooten v. Larsen,* 299 N.W.2d 704 (Mich. 1980). Ord. 556-H authorizes only a temporary physical possession of property for the purpose of abating a public nuisance and relies upon other, well-established judicial processes in providing for the transfer of title to property. Built into the ordinance are ample notice and opportunity provisions which protect the right of the property owner to terminate the nuisance abatement contract at any point. Given the nature of the intrusion, the purpose sought to be accomplished and the ease with which a property owner may terminate a nuisance abatement contract, we cannot say that Ord. 556-H constitutes an unreasonable exercise of the city's police powers.

Notes and Questions

1. Historically, squatting in the United States occurred primarily in unsettled rural areas, with the motivation of settling and cultivating the land. A squatter is defined as one who settles on another's land, without legal title or authority. Much of the expansion of settlements across the United States was arguably accomplished through squatting. The first significant instances of urban squatting occurred during the California gold rush in San Francisco, and squatters inhabited major cities across the United States during the Depression of the 1930s. This history is recounted in Kenneth A. Manaster, *Squatters and the Law: The Relevance of the United States Experience to Current Problems in the Developing Countries,* 43 Tul. L. Rev. 94, 99 (1968). *See also* Brian Gardiner, Comment, *Squatters' Rights and Adverse Possession: A Search for Equitable Application of Property Laws,* 8 Ind. Int'l & Comp. L. Rev. 119 (2000) (comparative analysis).

Another common practice during the settlement of the continent was for the United States government to provide people with tracts of land to encourage development of the frontier. Through the Homesteading Act of 1862,[4] the federal government granted settlers up to 160 acres of public land, in exchange for a nominal fee and the promise to settle on and to cultivate the land for a specified time. After five years, provided the homesteader had not abandoned the land, the homesteader received the land free of charge. "In addition to the desire for western expansion, the purpose of homesteading, which is applicable to urban centers today, was to "reduce poverty, allay discontent in populated centers, and better distribute surplus population." Charles Abrams, Squatter Settlements: The Problem And The Opportunity 6 (1966).

2. The following excerpt describes some of the apparent shortcomings of urban homesteading programs:

> Advocates of homesteading argue that the gap between post-rehab market values and the cost of improvements can be closed by the elimination of middleman profits of developers and by donated labor of the homesteading families. The history of self-help housing, however, clearly demonstrates that this is impossible. Not more than a handful of families would have the requisite skills to enable them to make a substantial labor input. Moreover, even if they were able to do the work themselves, their loss would be no less real. Subsidies are obviously necessary to cover the losses which rehabilitation of abandoned structures in declining areas inevitably entails. These alone are not enough, however. Most of the neighborhoods in which cities own abandoned properties are simply not areas in which families should be encouraged to invest their financial resources, skills,

4. *See* Homestead Act of 1862, ch. 75, 12 Stat. 392 (*codified as* amended at 43 U.S.C. § 161) (repealed 1976); Homestead Act of 1891, ch. 561, 26 Stat. 1097 (repealed 1976); Homestead Act of 1908, ch. 19, 35 Stat. 6 (permitting second homestead if first homestead unsuccessful).

> and several years of their lives, unless collateral programs are developed to provide whatever additional resources are required to reverse downward market trends and upgrade the physical infra-structure and social environment. These programs do not now exist.
>
> Urban homesteading has been described as a brightly wrapped package with nothing inside. This characterization may be too charitable. There *is* something inside—a badly conceived program that totally ignores a large body of housing theory and experience. As this fact has become recognized by those who are attempting to make homesteading work, the content of the program has been altered, so much so in fact that it is now beginning to resemble prior conservation and renewal efforts, with only the name remaining unchanged.

William G. Grigsby & Louis Rosenberg, Urban Housing Policy 235–36 (1975).

3. The rise in home foreclosure associated with the Great Recession that began in 2007 (discussed in Chapter 1, *supra.*) induced a resurgence of interest in urban and suburban squatting. Across the country, non-profits such as the Poor People's Economic Human Rights Campaign (PPEHRC) and Miami's Take Back the Land, a program to assist newly homeless households to occupy foreclosed homes. If you were the City Solicitor advising the mayor of your city about ways to respond to an upsurge in squatting, which of these potential legal policies would you advocate: (a) increase housing code enforcement, including boarding up vacant residences; (b) penalize owners who stockpile vacant houses; (c) bolster municipal efforts to take control of vacant properties to return them to the stock of available housing; (d) implement or expand a city homesteading program?

In 2008, HUD allocated $3.92 billion to states and localities to acquire and redevelop foreclosed and abandoned properties, under the Neighborhood Stabilization Program created by the Housing and Economic Recovery Act of 2008 (HERA), Pub. L. No. 110-289, 122 Stat. 2654 (2008).

2. Receiverships

The remedy of receivership is an alternate approach that aids tenants living in substandard buildings as well as neighborhood groups concerned about vacant and abandoned buildings which threaten their safety and lead to further deterioration if they are not demolished. Many states have authorized their courts to appoint receivers to take over the management of abandoned and substandard residential property in order to rehabilitate them. In some cases, tenants have been appointed as receivers. An early example is New York City's community management program. *See generally* Lizabeth Allewelt, David Listokin & James J. Nemeth, *Housing Receivership: Self-Help Neighborhood Revitalization,* 27 Wash. U.J. Urb. & Contemp. L. 71 (1985).

James J. Kelly, Jr., Refreshing the Heart of the City: Vacant Building Receivership as a Tool for Neighborhood Revitalization and Community Empowerment

13-WTR Journal of Affordable Housing & Community Development Law 210 (2004)

[I]n the scenarios involving the bad faith speculator and the more innocent former community resident, conventional code enforcement faces limitations that flow directly from its emphasis on personal liability for code violations. In the speculator's case, the coercive and punitive aspects of conventional code enforcement necessitate a high level of process that hampers its effectiveness against those who know how to avoid discovery. For the former community resident, the failure of the personal accountability approach is more direct. Not all vacant houses come to be nuisances through the deliberate neglect of their owners; in certain cases, the properties fall into disrepair despite reasonable efforts by the owners. In these cases, bringing the owners to justice will not necessarily result in a renovated house.

In both the speculating investor and the former resident situations, renovation of the property appears to require a change in ownership. Yet tax foreclosure, as one promising method of redistribution, does not present itself as an immediate option. In the examples above, both the speculator and the former resident have kept the property taxes current, making tax foreclosure impossible for the time being.

Under Baltimore's vacant building receivership ordinance, the city, or its community nonprofit designee, has the power to ask a court to appoint a receiver for any property that has an outstanding vacant building violation notice. An owner, a mortgagee, or any other party with a preexisting interest in that property has to demonstrate the ability to rehabilitate the property without delay in order to avoid the appointment of the receiver. Once appointed, the vacant building receiver's administrative and rehabilitation expenses become a super-priority lien on the property. Other code enforcement receivership statutes have most of these elements, but the Baltimore ordinance adds something unique that makes it particularly effective in dealing with vacant rowhouses.

Most code enforcement receivership statutes require long waiting periods prior to a receiver's foreclosure on his or her special lien. For these statutes, oriented toward occupied buildings, foreclosure is a last-resort means of recouping the net expenses of renovating the tenant's houses. Baltimore's law, however, allows the court to have the receiver foreclose on this lien before rehabilitation work has even begun and auction the property off to a developer who has demonstrated the ability to rehabilitate the property immediately. Rather than require the receiver to go out and locate the monies necessary to make repairs, vacant building receivership, under the Baltimore code amendment, offers the court the option of privatized nuisance abatement.

Like tax foreclosure, vacant building receivership can be used to release delinquent properties from all manner of preexisting private claims that might cloud the title. As a whole, vacant building receivership addresses those vacant building problems unreachable by conventional means, thereby plugging a gap in a healthy urban community's defense against property abandonment.

Vacant Building Receivership As In Rem Code Enforcement

Because vacant building receivership focuses on fixing the vacant property itself rather than punishing its owner, speculators' attempts at evasion no longer pose a problem. Although the ultimate power of the court to induce compliance presupposes the owner's physical presence in the courtroom, the owner's attendance is not required for a receivership hearing to be effective. The focus of the proceeding is no longer the owner's culpability, but the termination of the owner's rights in the property.

Of course, to assert its jurisdiction, even in rem jurisdiction, the court must be satisfied as to the sufficiency of the notice provided to the defendant.... In *Mullane v. Central Hanover Bank & Trust Co.*, the U.S. Supreme Court found that the Due Process Clause required that notice of any court action affecting a person's rights be made in a manner "reasonably calculated" to give actual notice. This standard was not diminished by the fact that the rights in question might be limited to a particular piece of property located in the jurisdiction. As applied to public lien foreclosure proceedings, this rule invalidated procedures that involved notice only by publication with no attempt at more direct contact. But, once personal delivery has been attempted, in rem proceedings may be allowed to proceed by alternative service where in personam cases might need to wait for a showing that the defendant is deliberately evading service of process.

The speculating owner can no longer hide from his building code obligations with the satisfaction that no news is good news. If the owner's efforts at obscurity have been successful, the receiver can transfer the property without the owner even knowing it. The owner's anonymity, a strength in the arena of in personam code enforcement, becomes a weakness in this in rem context. If the owner wants to be notified of in rem proceedings like vacant building receivership, he will need to provide contact information that will allow him to be given notice. Whether or not the owner makes his whereabouts known, he will need to come forward and appear in the lawsuit to preserve his stake in the property. Faced with the unwelcome choice between repairing the property and seeing it transferred through judicial sale, our speculator could try to contest the allegations in the suit or even challenge the legitimacy of the vacant building receivership law itself.

Vacant Building Receivership As Privatized Nuisance Abatement

Unfortunately for the evasive speculator, the vacant building receivership law makes it simple to prove the need for judicial action. To establish a case for the appointment of a receiver, the petitioner need only show that a vacant building violation notice was properly issued and remains unabated because the property has not been rehabilitated. Under Baltimore's building code, a vacant building is defined as "an unoccupied structure that is unsafe or unfit for human habitation or other authorized use." The code declares such buildings to "be a fire hazard and a nuisance per se." The code also provides specific factual bases for the issuance of such a violation notice that are readily observable by a passerby and can be documented easily by photographs. Other states' receivership statutes, which deal with occupied buildings, generally require an additional finding that the code violations are sufficiently serious to constitute a nuisance or a threat to the health and safety of the residents. Because Baltimore's code provides such a clear and practical definition of the nuisance to be addressed, a petitioner in a vacant building receivership case can prepare for trial with confident ease.

Once the case has been established, the speculating owner, in order to avoid appointment of a receiver, will not only have to ask for a reasonable period of time to carry out the renovation but also have to post a completion bond to guarantee performance. If the property goes through the vacant building receivership auction process, even a fair judicial sale may leave the owner with nothing after the receiver's costs and expenses have been deducted from the proceeds.

[L]ike eminent domain, vacant building receivership can be useful for assembling dilapidated properties for redevelopment. The owner can avoid any interference with his rights simply by demonstrating his prospective ability to renovate the property. If the owner does not, the ordinance allows the court, in its discretion, to sell the property as a means of achieving code compliance. [T]he purpose of the sale is to transfer the property to a developer that will abate the nuisance.... Through a special auction at which only qualified, committed developers can bid, the government is bringing the resources of the market to bear on the vacant house problems that threaten to destroy those communities. Even though vacant building receivership can result in a forced sale that cannot be justified as a mere creditor's remedy, a vacant building receivership sale prior to rehabilitation to the property, does withstand constitutional review under the "nuisance exception."

With regard to vacant buildings, no owner has a property right to keep his or her house, even an unoccupied house, in a visibly uninhabitable condition. Vacant houses, at least as defined in Baltimore's building code, are nuisances per se and not merely because the building code explicitly declares them to be so. They are, as the code states, fire hazards. Because vacant rowhouses are involved in so many fires, adjacent homeowners find it difficult if not impossible to obtain casualty insurance as required by their mortgage agreements. Those vacant houses open to casual entry harbor all manner of illegal activity. The chronic interference with quiet enjoyment of neighboring property owners and the economic detriment to their interests go to the very heart of nuisance law. Vacant houses are properly classified among the very "noxious uses" that takings jurisprudence first embraced as preventable through harsh governmental action without compensation. Assured then that vacant building receivership meets this recently hardened standard for core police power objectives, we now examine the methods by which it achieves these crucial goals.

Vacant Building Receivership As Title-Clearing Mechanism

Sometimes the title to a vacant house is obscured by so many claims that receivership sale, or another title-clearing mechanism such as tax foreclosure, offers the only practicable way to transfer the property to a new owner. An interested purchaser would be unable to devote the time to negotiate releases from each and every person or entity with a lien on a particular vacant property of marginal value. Frequently, a vacant property can remain in limbo for a long time. The owner defaults on the mortgage payments, but the mortgagee does not act. The property's value, especially when weighed against the potential code enforcement liability, may not justify immediate foreclosure proceedings by a mortgagee.

If neither the owner nor the mortgagee keeps up the payments to the city, the vacant house might then be put up for tax sale. But, in healthy neighborhoods, investors purchase tax sale certificates, not with the intention of taking title to the property, but with the plan of waiting for someone to step forward and redeem the property by paying the back taxes and the high interest rate due the investor by law. In a vacant building receivership action, all of these stakeholders are given notice of their last chance to protect their interests in the property by seeing to its renovation. If they do not, they will be cleared out by the foreclosure sale along with the owner of the property.

Especially in complete default situations, the capacity to clear title effectively is defined by the availability of title insurance to the successful bidder at the receivership auction. Focusing on the unassailability of the court's jurisdiction, title insurance underwriters will want to know everything about how those with interests in the property were notified of the proceedings. Once they are satisfied, the receiver's grant of title will be just as marketable as a conventional bargain and sale deed.

By putting market forces to work in an effective in rem code enforcement proceeding, vacant building receivership has dealt with the bottom-line code enforcement goal of eradicating those vacant buildings not amenable to conventional solutions. The speculator can no longer expect to reap the benefits of community revitalization without keeping his own property up to code. Without punishing the former community resident for being in her predicament, vacant building receivership relieves her of responsibility for a property that she cannot maintain. Vacant building receivership supplements traditional code enforcement remedies in a manner that makes community organization central to the process of eradicating vacant houses. This multifaceted empowerment of neighborhood structures takes vacant building receivership beyond reactive problem solving and into the realm of market-based community building.

Empowering CDCs as Market Participants

[V]acant building receivership provides community-based housing developers with critical acquisition leverage for closing voluntary transfers and a mechanism for clearing title to properties that cannot be sold free and clear by their owners. Vacant building receivership also offers a means of gaining quick experience in the legal and financial realities of their business—the residential real estate market. Explanation of the basics about vacant building receivership includes valuable information about the land title system and the ways in which building codes are enforced. This education brings the personnel of a CDC into a world already well-known by its market competitors.

The true empowerment of CDCs, though, comes from negotiations with the owners of and other stakeholders in vacant properties in the neighborhood. Using the threat of a vacant building receivership sale, a CDC realizes the competitive advantage that it has from its willingness and ability to renovate vacant buildings and its strong relations with the community. After delivery of even the threat of receivership litigation, groups previously unable to establish contact with the owner of a vacant property will find that same owner calling them to make a deal. Most importantly, the negotiations need never end in failure. If the price demanded for a vacant property is extortionate, the receivership litigation moves to the next stage. Ultimately, the property must be rehabilitated, or it will be sold to someone who will rehabilitate it.

Notes and Questions

1. Similar to the approach of Baltimore City, New Jersey's Multifamily Housing Preservation and Receivership Act focuses on the problems blighted properties present for neighborhoods, and thus the New Jersey statute enhances the ability to use both public funds and receiverships to repair such buildings, and provides for the transfer of properties to responsible owners if the noncomplying owner does not reimburse the costs of repair. N.J. Stat. Ann. § 2A:42-114.

2. A major constitutional issue posed by the appointment of receivers who borrow funds to rehabilitate abandoned or substandard buildings is whether mortgage holders have a prior lien which supersedes the obligations incurred by the receiver. If the receiver must first pay outstanding taxes and prior mortgages, is it feasible to borrow additional funds for rehabilitation? If not, how can the receiver finance rehabilitation? *See Community Renewal Found. v. Chicago Title & Trust*, 255 N.E. 2d 908 (Ill. 1970).

3. Who is qualified to act as a receiver? The possible candidates include municipal code enforcement and housing agencies, attorneys, and neighborhood-based and tenant organizations.

4. This section has concentrated so far on legal responses to protect the public's interests in the minimal safety and sanitation of housing structures through code enforcement without subsidy. As we shall see, the public interests asserted in the condition and uses of private property can encompass considerably wider issues of neighborhood stabilization and change. We will explore these *infra*.

To what extent does government encourage compliance with its policies by paying some or all of the compliance costs incurred by private owners? Federal subsidies have been available for housing code enforcement since the mid-1960s, and municipalities have increasingly used subsidy programs to induce housing rehabilitation.

We now turn to an examination of neighborhood investment strategies and an analysis of housing rehabilitation subsidy programs.

3. The Neighborhood Investment Problem: Coordination of Private Investment and Public Subsidy in Residential and Commercial Redevelopment

In the conventional cycle of neighborhood decline and decay, the unwillingness of housing owners to invest in housing maintenance becomes a major problem. Housing codes attempt to compel investment in housing maintenance, but code enforcement will be ineffective if owners of housing perceive that investment is not a reasonable economic decision.

Housing strategists have recognized that housing code enforcement is rarely likely to reverse neighborhood decline. They have developed a number of neighborhood revitalization strategies that supplement the housing code enforcement effort, including strategies to speed the turnaround of vacant housing units and blocks. Additional investment-focused strategies deal with neighborhood investment problems at the source, through legislation that seeks to compel lending institutions to serve the credit needs of inner city residential areas and encourage private investment in low-income areas which historically have had limited access to credit. [access to capital for community development is discussed in this chapter *infra* and fair housing and credit laws are treated in Chapter 6 *infra*] Other strategies include federal and local subsidy programs for housing rehabilitation. In some communities, these subsidies are part of a concerted neighborhood revitalization program that includes the city, neighborhood residents, and the lending institutions. *See generally* Housing Rehabilitation: Economic, Social, And Policy Perspectives (David Listokin ed. 1983); Tim Iglesias & Rochelle E. Lento, The Legal Guide To Affordable Housing Development (2005).

a. Housing Rehabilitation

Since the 1980s, the policy tools have been shifting away from subsidy programs—although these still exist—toward investment incentives.

The Public Purpose Limitation and Local Expenditures. Constitutional issues also underlie housing subsidy programs for neighborhood revitalization. Congress has ample constitutional authority to make subsidies available for housing rehabilitation under the spending power of the General Welfare Clause found in Art. 1 § 8 of the federal constitution. At the state level, state and local rehabilitation subsidies may face constitutional problems under the constitutional doctrine, included in state constitutions or imposed by judicial decision, that public funds may be expended only for "public purposes." This public purpose limitation on public spending is similar to the comparable constitutional limitation on compulsory land acquisition exercised through eminent domain. The use of eminent domain must satisfy a "public use" test.

Under the public purpose limitation, state courts have had little difficulty in upholding public subsidies for housing when the subsidies serve lower-income households. The courts acknowledge that these households cannot satisfy their housing needs in the unsubsidized housing market, and that public subsidies to meet these needs serve an acceptable public purpose.

Housing subsidies directed to housing rehabilitation without reference to housing need can raise more difficult problems. In the case of California's innovative Residential Rehabilitation program, which provided below market loans financed through bonds, the courts upheld its constitutionality against a challenge that it served a private rather than a public purpose. *Board of Supervisors v. Dolan*, 119 Cal. Rptr. 347 (Ct. App. 1975). State legislation has also authorized state and local housing finance programs not limited to housing rehabilitation. This legislation usually authorized the issuance of revenue bonds by state or local authorities, which use the proceeds of the bonds to make direct loans to homebuyers or to purchase residential mortgages from lending institutions. Almost without exception, the courts have upheld the constitutionality of these programs. The cases usually rely on a shortage of housing or mortgage funds to find that the legislation serves a public purpose. *See State v. Housing Fin. Auth.*, 367 So. 2d 1156 (Fla. 1979); *State ex rel. Douglas v. Nebraska Mortgage Fin. Fund*, 283 N.W.2d 12 (Neb. 1979) (discussing some of the leading cases). Like the California law upheld in the *Dolan* case, some of this housing finance legislation also authorizes loans for housing rehabilitation. State housing finance agencies are discussed in Chapter 3, *supra*.

Federal Subsidy Programs. Beginning with the Housing Act of 1954 through which the federal government first funded code local enforcement programs and subsidized rehabilitation and conservation, as well as clearance, in the urban renewal program, the federal government has offered a variety of subsidy programs for the rehabilitation of housing, both owner-occupied and rental. The Community Development Block Grant (CDBG) program, discussed in section C *infra*, has been most used by recipient local governments for housing rehabilitation. *See generally* R. Allen Hays, The Federal Government and Urban Housing: Ideology and Change in Public Policy (1995). However, several of the best known programs—urban homesteading and the Sections 8 and 312 multi-family rehabilitation programs—have been terminated. The two major current vehicles for providing federal assistance to rehabilitate housing are the Community Development Block Grant (CDBG) Program and the Federal Housing Administration (FHA)'s Section 203(k) loan program for one-to-four family homes. 24 C.F.R. §§ 203.50, 440–494. The 203(k) program enables eligible homebuyers to obtain insured mortgage loans that cover both the costs of acquisition and rehabilitation. Two rationales support federal subsidies for rehabilitation: to save housing that might otherwise be lost and abandoned, and the usually lower costs to rehabilitate rather than to build new housing. The other major vehicle for federally subsidized housing rehabilitation has been the Section 8 program (now the Housing Choice Voucher program), discussed in Chapter 3, *supra*.

Federal economic stimulus legislation enacted in 2008 augments the current structure of subsidy for housing rehabilitation. Given the large-scale abandonment of housing due to the foreclosure crisis, discussed in Chapter 1, *supra*, it is likely that many localities will use their funds under the Neighborhood Stabilization Program (included in the Housing and Economic Recovery Act of 2008, Pub. L. No. 110-289, 122 Stat. 2654, 2850–54) to rehabilitate foreclosed and vacant housing, rather than see it deteriorate and require demolition. It is also possible that urban homesteading, discussed above, may be revived in an attempt to rehabilitate and preserve abandoned housing that can be saved.

The most recent federal initiative is the Rental Rehabilitation program created in 1984, 42 U.S.C. § 1437(o) and see also 42 U.S.C. § 1437(u), providing for vouchers for tenants who move on account of rehabilitation activities carried on under section 1437(o). The Rental Rehabilitation program has not been widely used.

One of the most significant federal programs involving financing of housing rehabilitation has been the Title I, Property Improvement Loan Insurance program. 12 U.S.C. § 1703. HUD works through private lenders to insure loans to individual homeowners who wish to make home improvements. Loans are at market rates and HUD insurance covers the lender for losses up to 90% of the loan. Loans can also be used for repairs to comply with code deficiencies and to bring units up to relevant federal rehabilitation standards.

While a very large number of loans have been insured through HUD under various programs, one can easily see that the program cannot be used by low-income families who cannot meet lender's eligibility criteria (even as the risk is reduced by insurance). Nor will such programs be available in areas in which lenders are concerned about declining property values.

b. *Taxation-Based Incentives for Investment in Community Revitalization*

Older jurisdictions dependent on property taxes and other locally collected taxes often feel compelled to raise property tax rates in order to have sufficient revenue to support existing infrastructure and services. This problem afflicts rural towns and counties, as well as cities, facing a declining population base. The resulting higher tax rates further penalize private rehabilitation and discourage reinvestment in these places. Adverse consequences may be to encourage further sprawl, and weaken the jurisdiction's competitive position for new construction, jobs, and homes. Local governments are developing an array of alternative tax policies designed to overcome these disadvantages and incentivize new investment in revitalization.

State and Local Property Tax Abatement

Property tax abatement is one of the most common strategies deployed by local governments to stimulate economic growth. Tax abatement is a temporary suspension or reduction of property tax payments, which local governments offer to businesses for policy-serving activities, for a specified length of time. A locality may utilize property tax abatement only to the extent of state-defined parameters on local taxation. Examples are housing rehabilitation, brownfields redevelopment and military base realignment. Localities frequently offer tax abatements to encouraging existing businesses to reinvest in the community, as well as to new businesses as an incentive to locate in a community.

It is often alleged that property taxation is an impediment to rehabilitation, since a dwelling's tax assessment and taxes will increase after it is rehabilitated. This problem is discussed in The Property Tax and Low-Income Housing Markets in Property Tax Reform 107 (George E. Peterson ed. 1973). Peterson points out that property tax assessment increases are more fear than reality since reassessment occurs infrequently as a result of upgrading.

Tax Abatements for Property Rehabilitation. A number of municipalities have attempted to deal with this problem by providing property tax abatements for rehabilitation. An abatement program of this kind has been in effect for some time in New York City. It provides twelve-year abatements on rehabilitated multifamily property. For discussion, see Janice C.

Griffith, *Revitalization of Inner City Housing Through Property Tax Exemption and Abatement: New York City's J-51 to the Rescue,* 18 URB. L. ANN. 153 (1980). The New York program has been quite controversial. When used in addition to subsidized or low-interest loans, it can provide a powerful inducement to housing rehabilitation. However, it has been severely criticized for being overly expensive, displacing low-income tenants, and eliminating low-rent units that were converted to market rate housing. *See* Debra S. Vorsanger, Note, *New York City's J-5I Program: Controversy and Revision,* 12 FORDHAM URB. L.J. 103 (1983–84).

Extensive use of a property tax abatement program throughout a city could be counterproductive. If widespread property tax abatement for rehabilitation were to lead to a general property tax increase, that could result in an increase in operating costs on housing not included in the abatement. Studies in New York indicate that the tax loss through property tax abatements is offset by increased revenue from other taxes generated by property tax rehabilitation. *See* Griffith, *supra* at 159–60. *See generally* GEORGE STERNLIEB, ELIZABETH ROISTACHER & JAMES W. HUGHES, TAX SUBSIDIES AND HOUSING INVESTMENT (1976).

Maryland offers a neighborhood stabilization state income tax credit, MD. CODE ANN., TAX-GEN. § 10-707, tied to the local property tax credit, and MD. CODE ANN., TAX-PROP. §§ 9-317(e), 318(d), 326, for older urban areas in Baltimore city, Baltimore County, and Prince George's and Montgomery Counties. It appears to be helpful in promoting homeownership and retention of housing value in older neighborhoods. Its policy premise is that slowing or reversing the loss of working homeowners in these urban areas is an essential part of assuring the continued vitality of these areas.

Maryland's refundable certified rehabilitation income tax credit for historic buildings and districts has stimulated substantial reinvestment in Baltimore City and older city centers. MD. CODE ANN., TAX-GEN. § 10-704.5; MD. CODE ANN., Art. 83B, § 5-801. It was a significant contributor to public and private financing packages for rehabilitation, until its expiration in 2004. Independent reviews of the program indicate substantial job creation and tax receipts as a result of developments supported in part by the credits. *See* HISTORICAL TAX CREDIT REPORT: ECONOMIC AND FISCAL IMPACTS Parts I–II, *available at* http://www.preservemd.org. The cost of the program has become an issue in difficult economic times, but given its substantial net benefits, using the program in key districts to accomplish re-use of old buildings is a strong public policy using state resources to promote private investments.

Virginia authorizes property tax credits for rehabilitation of residences with liens in excess of 50% of value, thereby providing a substantial tool for returning vacant and abandoned property to productive use. VA. CODE ANN. § 58.1-3220.01. Virginia law also grants authority to local governments to grant partial exemptions from real property taxes for rehabilitation of commercial and industrial buildings, VA. CODE ANN. § 58.1-3221, reflecting the significant potential impact of such properties on urban revitalization.

Pennsylvania authorizes split rate taxation by its cities and boroughs, which permits taxing buildings and land at differing rates. 24 PA. CONS. STAT. ANN. § 6-672(e); 53 PA. CONS. STAT. ANN. §§ 25894, 37531, 46302.1. The theory underlying taxation of land at a higher rate than buildings aids the reclamation of priority development areas by stimulating investment and reinvestment in improvements in these areas, thus forestalling reversion to vacant lots.

Pennsylvania's Local Economic Revitalization Tax Assistance Act (LERTA), 72 PA. CONS. STAT. ANN. § 4722, and its Deteriorating Real Property Act and Deteriorating Areas Improvement Act, 72 PA. CONS. STAT. ANN. §§ 4711-101, 4711-201, offer local governments flexibility to offer property tax inducements for rehabilitation and reinvestment in areas, dwellings, and commercial property.

Federal Tax and Regulatory Considerations

Brownfields Redevelopment: "Brownfields" are generally defined as abandoned, idle or underutilized industrial or commercial properties, where redevelopment is hindered due to the existence or suspicion of historical environmental contamination. Most but not all are in urban areas. Since the 1990s, both the federal and states' governments have been evolving a variety of policies, laws and regulations, to address the concerns of those seeking to undertake, or finance or invest in, such redevelopment projects, and to foster the recycling of older industrial sites rather than development of unsullied "greenfields."

This amalgamation of programs, legislation and initiatives has accelerated under the general rubric of "Brownfields Redevelopment," and the federal government and a majority of states have such programs. On an annual basis EPA awards a variety of project-specific grants and loans to encourage businesses and localities to redevelop Brownfield, including assessment and cleanup grants, revolving loan fund grants, and job training programs. In 2008, $74 million was awarded for a variety of grants and loans authorized by the 2002 Brownfields Revitalization Act, provided to 43 states, 2 U.S. territories and 2 tribal nations. David Farer, *Brownfields Redevelopment Initiatives: Federal and Selected State Programs, SP033 ALI-ABA 891(2008)*; James A. Kushner, *Brownfield Redevelopment Strategies in the United States*, 22 GA. ST. U. L. REV. 857 (2006).

Base Realignment and Closure (BRAC): "Base Realignment and Closure" is the process the U.S. Department of Defense (DoD) uses to reorganize its military installation infrastructure to support its forces more efficiently and effectively, increase operational readiness, and facilitate new ways of doing business. In 2002, Congress authorized a round of BRAC for 2005. The BRAC Commission approved the closure of 22 major installations and the realignment of another 33. Military installations often serve as economic engines for states and local communities. One military installation alone can generate thousands of jobs and billions of dollars in economic activity and tax revenue. For example, military installations are reported to provide a $44 billion annual economic benefit in Florida—9.8 percent of the gross state product, and in North Carolina, military base-related spending accounts for 7 percent ($18 billion) of total gross state product. Tara Butler, *State Financing Strategies To Address The Economic Impacts of Military Base Realignments and Closures*, SN005 ALI-ABA 1299 (2008). For a comparative analysis, see James A. Kushner, *Planning for Downsizing: A Comparison of the Economic Revitalization Initiatives in American Communities Facing Military Base Closure with the German Experience of Relocation the National Capital from Bonn to Berlin,* 33 URB. LAW. 119 (2001).

Federal Tax Credits. In addition to HUD's various subsidy programs, another major incentive for housing rehabilitation has been the provision of depreciation deductions in the Internal Revenue Code. The 1986 federal tax reform legislation replaced vaguely targeted tax benefits with a system of tax credits more carefully tailored to produce housing affordable to incomes below those served by the system of market based housing production. *See* Thomas A. Coughlin, *Using Historic Rehabilitation and Low-Income Housing Tax Credits,* 2 PRAC. TAX LAW. 25 (1988). The Low-Income Housing Tax Credit Program is widely recognized as the single biggest source of funds for producing and preserving affordable housing units in the U.S. today, providing over $13 billion annually to state and local housing finance agencies. Its operation and parameters are discussed in Chapter 3, *supra.* The Rehabilitation Tax Credit program encourages private investment in the rehabilitation of historic buildings in urban and rural communities. Pub. L. No. 94-455, §2124, 90 Stat. 1520, 1916 (1976). The credit's utility in community renewal was accelerated when the Tax Reform Act of 1986, Pub. L. 99-514, 101 Stat. 2189, created both a 20% tax credit for qualified rehab expenditures to restore a structure certified by the Secretary of the Interior as having historic significance. I.R.C. §47(a)(1)-(2). The 10% credit is allowable for qualified rehab of nonhistoric buildings built before 1936. Enhancements to the RTCs were enacted as part of the Housing Recovery Act of 2008, Pub. L. 110-289, 122 Stat. 2654. The federal RTCs can be used in combination with other federal and state tax credits, including the Low Income Housing Tax Credit under I.R.C. §42, the New Markets Tax Credit under I.R.C. §45D, and state-level tax credits.

c. Community-Based Organizations in Development: Policy and Program Supports

Community Development Corporations. Beginning in the late 1960s, neighborhood-based community development corporations (CDCs) have played an increasingly important role in the rehabilitation of substandard housing in low- and moderate-income neighborhoods. As of 2005, over 4,600 CDCs were operating throughout the United States, according to a census published by the National Congress for Community Economic Development (NCCED). The NCCED census was conducted by staff of the Urban Institute, and supported by dozens of charitable foundations. *See* Reaching New Heights, Trends and Achievements of Community-Based Development Organizations, available at http://www.ncced.org/documents/NCCEDCensus2005FINALReport.pdf (last visited November 4, 2009). These CDCs had developed 1,252,000 units of housing, 126 million square feet of commercial/industrial space, and created 774,000 jobs.

Conceptually, CDCs have their origins in the Civil Rights Era, and specifically, in the Economic Opportunity Act of 1964, which among other things authorized "community action agencies" whose underlying philosophy was the "maximum feasible participation" of community members in the decisions of local government so as to end racial exclusion and cronyism in the expenditure of public money. CDCs were often formed in response to local controversies, such as slum clearance and redlining by financial institutions. Many of the early CDCs received funds from the federal Office of Economic Opportunity, and philanthropies such as the Ford Foundation nurtured CDCs. Useful accounts of this period are Robert Halpern, Rebuilding The Inner City: A History of Neighborhood Initiatives To Address Poverty in the United States (1995) and Neal R. Peirce & Carol F. Steinbach, Corrective Capitalism: The Rise of America's Community Development Corporation, Report to the Ford Foundation 19–26 (1987).

A long-standing tenet of community-driven community development is that CDCs should be indigenous and locally-based, with governing boards comprised of area residents and business and civic leaders. Local groups, it was reasoned, would be more in tune with residents' needs and could give poor people more control over their communities. Two-thirds of CDCs in the 2005 census do have a distinctly local focus: They serve one city, several neighborhoods, or a single neighborhood. Yet the census also revealed organizations, especially in rural areas, that have much larger service areas. Aside from these local groups, a number of the national not-for-profit housing producers have local affiliates governed by local boards.

CDCs rely upon a combination of governmental, corporate and philanthropic funds for their community revitalization programs, including housing, economic development and social services. Some CDCs are fledgling groups, run by volunteers on a shoestring budget. Increasingly, however, this is the exception, not the rule. The median CDC, according to the NCCED census, has 10 paid employees. Twenty-five percent describe themselves as faith-based, although the majority of these explain that their explicit mission is not to foster a religious purpose. A significant share of CDCs generates housing for people with special needs, including disability, substance abuse and recovery, elderly, and homeless people. CDCs are increasingly being asked to develop community facilities by other local institutions, especially day care centers, health care centers, youth centers, arts programs, and other social service providers. It is not uncommon to find CDCs partnering with other nonprofits on such projects.

The vast majority of CDCs combine their physical and business development with other initiatives, which range from community organizing to prisoner re-entry programs. The most widespread community building activities in the 2005 NCCED census were those that focus on helping low-income residents to connect to opportunities in the larger economy: homeownership counseling (59%), budget and credit counseling (54%) and education/training (53%).

A growing number of CDCs have embraced microenterprise development as a poverty-fighting strategy. Micro lending seeks to encourage local entrepreneurship in low income communities, by providing small business loans, technical assistance or both to businesses with five or fewer employees. Microfinance blossomed in the U.S. in the mid-1980s in response to a need for better economic options for entrepreneurs who lack access to mainstream financial institutions. CDCs likely have a comparative advantage in identifying neighborhood-level lending opportunities and providing technical assistance to borrowers, because they can often connect better to prospective entrepreneurs than can banks or small business development agencies that comprise traditional business development.

Regulatory Definitions: Resident-Serving, Bank-Owned and Other "CDCs": Legally, CDCs are organized as not-for-profit corporations under state law, and apply for tax-exempt recognition as charitable organizations by the Internal Revenue Service under Section 501(c)(3). Not all "CDCs" are community-based or community controlled—a fact which can have important consequences for the human and geographical community in which the entity operates. "Community development corporation" is sometimes a defined term in federal housing, banking, and tax laws and regulations. The purposes of such provisions vary, and thus, so do the parameters of community control or benefit.

HUD programs in particular seek to direct public funds to economically distressed communities, through entities whose boards reflect a threshold of community participation and control of the organization, and presumably, its prioritization of development projects. One example is the availability of technical assistance and capacity building services within the HUD program for preservation of multifamily low-income housing, for community-based housing developers. To qualify, the applicant must be a "community development corporation" that "has a record of service to low and moderate income people in the community in which the project is located; [and] is organized at the neighborhood, city, county, or multi-county level," and in addition is a federally tax-exempt organization that has been in operation for two years or more. 24 C.F.R. § 248.420.

The community-service capacities of CDCs are also leveraged in programs of the Small Business Administration. For example, the HUBZone incentives for federal agencies to contract with small businesses expressly includes "nonprofit private locally initiated community development corporations" which "are directed to the solution of the critical problems existing in particular communities or neighborhoods" within urban and rural areas having concentrations or substantial numbers of low-income persons. 42 U.S.C. § 9805. For the purpose of this program a community development corporation is defined as "a nonprofit corporation responsible to the residents of the area it serves." 42 U.S.C. § 9802 (Community Economic Development Act of 1981, Title VI of Pub. L. No. 97-35, 95 Stat.

489 (as amended)). CDCs are allowable providers of Welfare-to-Work programs, under Department of Labor regulations, see 20 C.F.R. § 645.410.

Banks are permitted to form several types of subsidiary entities, including community development corporations provided no more than 5% of the parent corporation's capital is held therein. Riegle-Neal Interstate Banking and Branching Efficiency Act of 1994, Pub. L. No. 103-328, 108 Stat. 2339 (*amending* 12 U.S.C. § 24). CDCs are one of numerous types of approved community economic development entities in which banks may make qualified investments within the scope of the U.S. Treasury rules for assuring the safety and soundness of federally regulated financial institutions. Under 12 C.F.R. § 24.2 such an entity must make investments or conduct activities "that primarily benefit low- and moderate-income individuals, low- and moderate-income areas, or other areas targeted by a governmental entity for redevelopment." Regulation Y of the Federal Reserve System allows an array of investments by bank holding companies in corporations or projects "designed primarily to promote community welfare," 12 C.F.R. § 225.127.

Community Development Corporations are not to be confused with the similarly named "certified development companies," which are approved by the Small Business Administration to administer its 504 loan program. 13 C.F.R. §§ 120.800 *et seq.* A Certified Development Company is a nonprofit corporation set up to aid the economic development of its community, and works with SBA and private-sector lenders to provide growing businesses with long-term, fixed-rate financing for major fixed assets, such as land and buildings. Thus these operate with loan capital and collateral significantly greater than many community-based Community Development Corporations enjoy.

Notes and Questions

1. For an extensive report on community-based community development corporations, see Michael H. Schill, *Assessing the Role of Community Development Corporations in Inner City Economic Development*, 22 N.Y.U. Rev. L. & Soc. Change 753 (1996–97). Successful CDCs must assemble several kinds of capacities to engage in the complex work of community revitalization. These are analyzed in Ross J. Gittell & Margaret Wilder, *Community Development Corporations: Critical Factors that Influence Success*, 21 J. Urb. Aff. 341 (1999); Norman J. Glickman & Lisa J. Servon, *More than Bricks and Sticks: Five Components of Community Development Corporation Capacity*, 9 Housing Pol'y Debate 497 (1998).

2. *Additional Resources:* For a more specific look at the dynamics of community development corporations in Brooklyn, New York, see Brian Glick & Matthew J. Rossman, *Neighborhood Legal Services as House Counsel to Community-Based Efforts to Achieve Economic Justice: The East Brooklyn Experience*, 23 N.Y.U. Rev. L. & Soc. Change 105 (1997).

CDCs' origins, organizational development needs, and capital accumulation and management challenges are discussed in Nels J. Jackson, Lawrence H. Sharf & Robert M. Hager, *Community Development Corporations*, 83 Harv. L. Rev. 1558 (1970). For an evaluation of CDCs and their impact, see Neil Mayer, Neighborhood Organizations and Community Development: Making Revitalization Work (1984); Avis C. Vidal, Rebuilding Communities: A National Study of Urban Community Development Corporations (1992); Alexander Von Hoffman, House by House, Block by Block: The Rebirth of America's Urban Neighborhoods (2003) (describing CDCs efforts in revitalizing major American cities); Yael Krigman, *The Role of Community Development Corporations in Affordable Housing*, 19 J. Affordable Housing & Community Dev. L. 231(2010); Michael Kroopnick, *Affording Baltimore:*

Public-Private Approaches To Workforce Housing, 40 URB. LAW. 331, 342–348 (2008). For discussions of the issues facing "second generation" CDCs, see W. DENNIS KEATING, NORMAN KRUMHOLZ, & PHILIP STAR, REVITALIZING URBAN NEIGHBORHOODS (1996) and Langley C. Keyes, Alex Schwartz, Avis C. Vidal & Rachel Bratt, *Networks and Nonprofits: Opportunities and Challenges in an Era of Federal Devolution*, 7 HOUSING POL'Y DEBATE 201 (1996). For a discussion of nonprofit housing associations, see Chapter 3, *supra*.

C. The Federal Community Development Program

1. The Housing and Community Development Act

a. Purpose and National Objectives

Title I of the 1974 Housing and Community Development Act (HCDA) represented a new chapter in national community development policy. The primary statutory objective of the CDBG program is to develop viable communities by providing decent housing and a suitable living environment and by expanding economic opportunities, principally for persons of low- and moderate-income. The Act now requires that "not less than 70 percent of the aggregate of the federal assistance provided ... shall be used for the support of activities that benefit persons of low and moderate income...." 42 U.S.C. §5304(b)(3). This represents an increase from the 51% and 60% standards established in the 1983 and 1987 amendments, respectively. This general objective is achieved by granting "maximum feasible priority" to activities which benefit low- and moderate-income families or aid in the prevention or elimination of slums or blight. The emphasis on people with low incomes is reinforced by the formulas that determine how much money each entitlement jurisdiction and state receives. The formulas are based on factors heavily weighted by the degree of poverty and indicators of poor housing conditions in a jurisdiction.

In order to be eligible for funding, every CDBG-funded activity must qualify as meeting one of the *three national objectives* of the program. This requires that each activity, except those carried out under the basic eligibility categories of Program Administration and Planning and Capacity Building, meet specific tests for either: benefiting low- and moderate-income persons, preventing or eliminating slums or blight, or meeting other community development needs having a particular urgency because existing conditions pose a serious and immediate threat to the health or welfare of the community and other financial resources are not available to meet such needs. An activity that fails to meet one or more of the applicable tests for meeting a national objective is in noncompliance with CDBG rules. Criteria for determining relatedness to the three national objectives are elaborated in HUD rules at 24 C.F.R. §570.208.

Under current legislation, CDBG funds may be used for twenty-six separate eligible activities. As federal support for housing production has declined, limitations on the use of CDBG funds to support new construction have been relaxed. *See* 42 U.S.C. §5305(a). Under unique circumstances, States may also use their funds to meet urgent community development needs. A need is considered urgent if it poses a serious and immediate threat to the health or welfare of the community and has arisen in the past 18 months.

The most significant change from prior policy was a shift from single purpose or categorical grants to a more flexible concept of block grants, so that recipients may expend funds on a myriad of local activities according to locally developed priorities. Title I of the 1974 Act established the CDBG program as a replacement for a number of popular and controversial categorical grant programs, including urban renewal, model cities, neighborhood facilities, open space, water and sewer, and public facility loans. Instead of numerous separate programs with rigid national standards, the new CDBG program provided grants to cities and states to enable them to implement a variety of local public activities tailored to local conditions. The CDBG program has been extremely popular with local governments.

Two underlying considerations prompted this shift to the block grant format. First, under conventional urban renewal, recipient communities lacked flexibility to modify programs designed by HUD: projects that might work in Washington, D.C., or Baltimore, might not be the most appropriate strategies for the urban ills of Youngstown or Seattle. The related concern was that when cities merely implemented specific grant-in-aid programs, they had a tendency to look at the grant as free money, not subject to the traditional scrutiny and accountability given to the expenditure of locally raised revenues. The flexibility contained in HCDA shifted greater responsibility to recipient jurisdictions to address a broad range of problems and develop their own strategy, priorities, and programs. It was anticipated that greater responsibility for effectiveness, as well as programs tailored for local needs, would result in a more effective strategy. In any event, responsibility for program failures could no longer be fully attributed to HUD.

The other underlying theme that led to the passage of HCDA, one that is closely related to the former, is local autonomy. The Nixon administration campaigned for "states' rights" and freedom from Washington control, transferring power from across the Potomac back to the people through their state and local governments. Beginning with experiments in block grant funding under the Law Enforcement Assistance Administration (LEAA), the Comprehensive Employment Training Act (CETA), and the State and Local Fiscal Assistance Act of 1972 (General Revenue Sharing), the Nixon administration encouraged funding mechanisms that reduced the federal implementation role. *See* Kenneth Finegold, Laura Wherry & Stephanie Schardin, Block Grants: Historical Overview and Lessons Learned (2004) (publication of the Urban Institute New Federalism Program); Stephen J. Cole, *The Federal Spending Power and Unconditional and Block Grants to State and Local Governments*, 16 Clearinghouse Rev. 616 (1982). General Revenue Sharing was repealed as part of the 1986 tax reform package.

Under the HCDA's major funding component, the entitlement block grant, cities and other eligible government entities receive an amount based upon their proportionate need for urban aid. These funds can now be utilized to carry out a multitude of eligible projects. The CDBG recipient may but need not use the funds as previously directed by prior federal programs. Urban renewal grants covered the cost of administering a program, i.e. to plan, acquire, manage, clear, and make on-site improvements, including the difference between that cost and the market price sale to the redeveloper. Urban Renewal (James Q. Wilson ed. 1966). The later Model Cities program expanded projects to cover the full gamut of social and physical community needs. Demonstration Cities and Metropolitan Development Act of 1966, 42 U.S.C. §§ 3301–13. Both Model Cities and urban renewal have been subsumed by § 116(a) of the Housing and Community Development Act of 1974. 42 U.S.C. § 5316(a). For contemporaneous accounts and analysis, see Bernard J. Frieden & Marshall Kaplan, The Politics of Neglect (1975); Charles M. Haar, Between the Idea and the Reality (1975).

Consistent with the theme of increased local flexibility and control, CDBG also contained broad stipulations for community participation in priority setting. The program required municipalities applying for CDBG to (1) provide citizens with adequate information concerning proposed development and other important program requirements; (2) hold public hearings to get the views of citizens on community development and housing needs; and (3) provide citizens with an adequate opportunity to participate in the program. The federal legislation was not specific on how citizens should be engaged in CDBG. Many communities implement the requirement as communication rather than as actual power sharing. See LAWRENCE JOHNSON & ASSOC., U.S. DEP'T OF HOUS. & URB. DEV., CITIZEN PARTICIPATION IN COMMUNITY DEVELOPMENT: A CATALOG OF LOCAL APPROACHES 3 (1978).

The CDBG program is not a major program for production or service-delivery. Its annual appropriation of $4 billion pales in comparison to federal highway funding, Medicare, or Social Security. In 2010, Congress appropriated $73.2 billion to the Department of Transportation, $41.8 billion of which went to Federal Highway Administration. *See* http://www.dot.gov/budget/2010/bib2010.pdf. Just over $700 billion in appropriations were made to the Social Security Administration in discretionary and mandatory spending. *See* http://www.whitehouse.gov/omb/assets/fy2010_new_era/Summary_Tables2.pdf. Approximately $880 billion went to the Department of Health and Human Services, nearly a third of which went to Medicare. *See* http://www.hhs.gov/asrt/ob/docbudget/2010budgetinbrief.pdf. The CDBG program operates instead as a gap-filling incentive to encourage additional public and private investment in community development activities. CDBG block grants provide lump sums to states and cities to assist them to plug gaps in financing needed for major developments and public infrastructure, such as streets and utility lines, which serve them. Indeed one of the sources of CDBG's popularity is presumably its utility in facilitating private development through the construction or reconstruction of utilities, street improvements, and the creation of neighborhood amenities such as recreation centers, parks, and neighborhood facilities. Community Planning & Dev., U.S. Dep't of Hous. & Urban Dev., *Use of CDBG Funds in Support of Housing*, *available at* http://www.hud.gov/offices/cpd/communitydevelopment/rulesandregs/memoranda/cpd8914.cfm. Alternatively, CDBG funds may be allocated to smaller neighborhood improvement projects, again primarily as gap-financing or infrastructure-funding.

Throughout its forty-year life, the CDBG program has been an important but relatively small component of the total federal effort in housing and community development. For example, the 2002 CDBG appropriation of $5 billion was the high-water mark to date, yet it amounted to approximately 16 percent of HUD's discretionary spending authority for that year. *See* Peter Salsich, *Saving Our Cities: What Role Should the Federal Government Play?* 36 URB. LAW. 475, 484 (2004); URB. INST., FEDERAL FUNDS, LOCAL CHOICES: AN EVALUATION OF THE COMMUNITY DEVELOPMENT BLOCK GRANT PROGRAM 2-1 (1994). Adding the $157 billion in loan guarantees under the FHA mortgage insurance program and other housing guarantee programs, and the estimated $90 billion in mortgage interest and property tax deductions for owner-occupied houses and low-income housing tax credits to the total federal budget for housing and community development programs, the percentage allocated to the CDBG program drops to less than 2 percent. *Id.*

The CDBG program began with an appropriation of $2.5 billion for fiscal year 1975. Since that time, CDBG appropriation levels have gradually increased to the $4 billion range. Since its inception, real per capita spending for the CDBG has declined by almost three-quarters, from about $48 to about $13 per person, while the number of communities receiving funds directly from the federal government through the CDBG formula grant has nearly doubled from 606 in fiscal year 1975 to 1,128 in fiscal year 2006. U.S. General Accountability Office, *Community Development Block Grant Formula: Options for Improving the Targeting of Funds*, GAO-06-904T (June 27, 2006).

For FY09, CDBG formula grants received an appropriation of $3.642 billion. In addition, the American Recovery and Reinvestment Act of 2009 (ARRA), Pub. L. No. 111-5, 123 Stat. 115, created a one-time stimulus amount of $1 billion, directing states and entitlement jurisdictions to give priority to projects that can be awarded contracts based on bids within 120 days. The President's FY10 budget proposes $4.5 billion, along with recommendations to revise the allocation formula and to create a new Sustainable Communities Initiative.

Notes and Questions

1. *Distribution of Funds.* The Community Development Block Grant program is divided into two parts. The annual CDBG appropriation is allocated between States and local jurisdictions called "non-entitlement" and "entitlement" communities respectively. Most of the federal funds are distributed to cities over 50,000 and urban counties under a statutory formula. This is known as the "entitlement" program and is the program discussed in this chapter. The remaining federal funds are distributed to small cities through the states, unless the states decide not to administer the program. (The state-administered program has stayed closer to the block grant concept but is not discussed in this chapter.) Entitlement communities are comprised of the central cities of Metropolitan Statistical Areas (MSAs); metropolitan cities with populations of at least 50,000; and qualified urban counties with a population of 200,000 or more (excluding the populations of entitlement cities). HUD determines the amount of each grant by using a formula comprised of several measures of community need, including the extent of poverty, population, housing overcrowding, age of housing, and population growth lag in relationship to other metropolitan areas. States distribute CDBG funds to smaller units of general local government that carry out community development activities (known as the Small Cities program), unless the states decide not to administer the program.

2. Discussion of the 1974 Act should be placed in context. Six years prior to enactment, the National Advisory Commission on Civil Disorders (the "Kerner Commission") had issued its famous prophetic warning that the nation was heading toward division into two societies: "the haves and the have nots, the whites and the blacks." Report of the National Advisory Commission on Civil Disorders 1 (1968). In response, Congress passed landmark fair housing legislation in the Civil Rights Act of 1968, Pub. L. No. 90-284, § 801, 82 Stat. 73, 81 (*codified as amended at* 42 U.S.C. §§ 3601–19) and authorized major new housing production subsidies in the Housing and Urban Development Act of 1968, Pub. L. No. 90-448, §§ 101, 235, 236, 82 Stat. 476, 477, 498 (*codified as amended at* 12 U.S.C. §§ 1715z to 1715z-1). But just five years later, the new production programs were suspended by the Nixon Administration because of scandals in the administration of other housing subsidy programs and reports of low-income homeowners suffering foreclosures because of inability to afford maintenance and utilities costs. See Peter Salsich, *Saving Our Cities: What Role Should the Federal Government Play?* 36 Urb. Law. 475, 483 (2004).

3. As in all reform movements, the transfer of power has not been absolute. Congress and different administrations have battled back and forth over the amount of control HUD should exercise in the CDBG program. Tension among the wide-rang-

ing legislative objectives for which CDBG funds may properly be used—between eliminating slums and blight, preventing blighting influences, providing decent housing and a suitable living environment, and expanding economic opportunities, "principally for persons of low and moderate income," 42 U.S.C. § 1501(c)—has never been resolved satisfactorily. One likely implication of declining federal program control is that local politics tend to allocate funds according to political power rather than notions of neighborhood stress and need. Experience under state-administered community development grants indicates that there is much less targeting toward impacted and poverty neighborhoods than under federal allocation formulas, which tend to address regional and state equity considerations while permitting a targeting to urban needs. *See* Michael J. Rich, Federal Policymaking and the Poor: National Goals, Local Choices, and Distributional Outcomes (1993); James A. Kushner, *Non-Owner Rights in Real Property and Their Impact on Property Taxes,* 7 Urb. L. & Pol'y 333, 353 (1985).

4. *Devolution and Fiscal Retrenchment.* In the four decades of the CDBG program, the scale of government support for community developed has shrunk dramatically, and responsibility for community development has devolved from federal to local governments. Two processes which have been key in this restructuring, devolution and fiscal retrenchment, began under the Nixon administration. Block grants devolve responsibility for and much control over housing and social services for low income people and communities. As a consequence states and their subdivisions determine the priorities for spending federal funds for housing and community services under CDBG block grants, Low Income Housing Tax Credits, and social services for workforce development, childcare, and income assistance.

In the same period that devolution has restructured the federal-state relationship in the U.S., governmental resources for low income communities have shrunk markedly. In 1976 the budget for the US Department of Housing and Urban Development was 7% of the total federal budget, and shrank to 1% in 2005. National Low Income Housing Coalition, *Changing Priorities: The Federal Government and Housing Assistance: 1976–2005* (2004). Community Development Block Grants declined by 48% in real dollars. *Id.* Other examples pertaining to housing such as the elimination of project based Section 8 in 1983, and the enactment of the HOPE VI program which subsidizes demolition of public housing and disperses residents, are discussed in Chapter 3, *supra.* What consequences flow for community development from this structural shift? Does this help to explain the roles undertaken by community-based not-for-profits organizations, attempting to perform services once provided by government? The intensity of competition for local government resources with which to perform the devolved functions?

5. *UDAG: Early federal efforts to address root causes of urban distress.* The 1977 amendments, reflecting the Carter administration's pyrrhic attempt to increase urban spending and revitalization, added a new objective to the legislation, "the alleviation of physical and economic stress through the stimulation of private investment and community revitalization in areas with population outmigration or a stagnating or declining tax base." 42 U.S.C. § 5301(c)(8). Pursuant to this new objective, these amendments created the Urban Development Action Grant Program (UDAG), which emphasized economic development. Under UDAG, communities were eligible to seek HUD grants to attract private investment. Communities, under the UDAG program, could explicitly plan to include private developers to expand the economic base and to reclaim deteriorating neighborhoods. A city could also use HCDA money for almost any project that it determined to represent a unique opportunity for that city. UDAG was eliminated from funding in 1986.

The premise that strengthening the economic base through the creation of jobs is an important approach to curing urban ills recurs in the vigorous state and local economic development policies of the 1980s and 1990s. Whether the goals of dispersal and urban reclamation by industry and the middle class are inconsistent will be analyzed in the next sections of the text. The two Reagan terms produced no urban policy initiatives that can be characterized as such. But they did see a *de minimis* reduction in urban subsidies. *See* James A. Kushner, *The Reagan Urban Policy: Centrifugal Force in the Empire*, 2 UCLA J. Envtl. L. & Pol'y 209 (1982).

It is not necessary to conclude that housing and jobs must compete as the most appropriate community development concern. Both concerns can be addressed by community development programs, and attention must also be directed to strengthening the local tax base, which supports social and community services. The community development program clearly provides support for the retention of the central cities as viable governmental entities, an objective that might be considered foolhardy in light of the drift of jobs and population to the suburbs. Yet increasing housing, energy, and transportation costs may combine to make central cities more attractive as places in which to live and work.

6. The Housing and Community Development Act is codified in 42 U.S.C. §§5301–21. The conventional practice is to refer to sections of the act as it was enacted by Congress.

b. Community Development Block Grants

1. Eligible Activities

The first question that arises is what specific activities may be undertaken with HCDA funds. Certainly, the background of the legislation would suggest that the broad outline of eligible activities under the predecessor categorical grant programs would be permissible under the new law. You might list those activities that would be permissible under urban renewal, model cities, code enforcement, interim assistance, water and sewer facilities, neighborhood facilities, open space land, urban beautification, historic preservation, and rehabilitation grants. Compare your list with section 105(a), 42 U.S.C. §5305(a), which states that "[a]ctivities assisted under this title may include only" the two dozen activities enumerated. However, the watchword remains flexibility, and categorically ineligible activities are comparatively few. HUD regulations implementing the CDBG program have been revised significantly over the years. *See* 24 C.F.R. Part 570. Eligible activities may be grouped into categories, as related to housing, to real property generally, to public facilities, to public services, to economic development, and to assistance to Community Based Development Organizations (CBDOs).

The many activities related to housing eligible under the CDBG Program include housing services in connection with Home Investment Partnerships (HOME) funded projects, construction of housing by eligible Community Based Development Organizations (CBDOs) or as last resort housing, homeownership assistance (such as downpayment assistance and interest subsidies), and rehabilitation of residential buildings. Allowable rehabilitation activities can include acquisition for rehabilitation for residential purposes; labor and material, energy and water service improvements, removal of architectural barriers that restrict accessibility. Lead-based paint testing and abatement are eligible either as a stand alone program or included as rehabilitation.

In addition to the foregoing housing-related activities, many other real-property related activities are permitted, such as acquisition, clearance and demolition, site improvements, street improvements, code enforcement, historic preservation and property disposition. Activities related to public services are generally eligible: examples include job training and employment services, health care and substance abuse services, child care, crime prevention, and Fair Housing counseling.

Notes and Questions

1. Section 105, 42 U.S.C. § 5305, defines activities eligible for inclusion in a CD program. Which of the following are allowable activities:

a. Acquisition of an open site for development of a new town? Section 105(a)(1).

b. Construction of a new sewage or water treatment plant? § 105(a)(2). HUD approved St. Clair County, Illinois' use of HCDA grant funds to acquire land for a wastewater facility. 10 [Current Developments] Hous. & Dev. Rep. 139 (BNA) (1982).

c. Payment of enforcement expenses in a housing code receivership program? § 105(a)(3).

d. Urban renewal? § 105(a)(1).

e. Grants to homeowners for housing rehabilitation? § 105(a)(4).

f. Fair housing enforcement? § 105(a)(8).

g. May neighborhood organizations be funded? § 105(a)(15). Fair housing councils?

Note that CD funds may be used for relocation payments. § 105(a)(11). Why is this a "catch-22" for cities like St. Louis (or New York, Cleveland, and other older cities where redevelopment in poorer neighborhoods will be avoided due to the cost of acquisition and relocation)? The 1987 amendments also added substantial relocation planning and assistance requirements. For current requirements, see Housing Assistance Plans, Current Housing Affordability Strategies, and the Consolidated Plan, *infra*.

Block grant funds may be used to correct inferior rehabilitation work performed under block grant programs, but may not be used to perform work that should have been performed but was not. *CD Funds Can Be Used to Redo Poor CD Housing Rehab Work,* 10 [Current Developments] Hous. & Dev. Rep. (BNA) 284 (1982). What is the distinction? The 1987 amendments for the first time authorize a limited use of funds for housing construction. *See* § 105(a)(19), 42 U.S.C. § 5305(a) (19).

Block grant funds also may be used by a city to install a sculpture because HUD considers a work of art to be a public improvement. However, the sculpture must be installed in a low- or moderate-income area. *See Sculpture May be Installed as Public Improvement,* 25 [Current Developments] Hous. & Dev. Rep. (West) 589 (1998).

HUD published a final rule in 2006 that clearly allows the abatement of asbestos hazards and lead-based paint hazard evaluation and reduction as eligible rehabilitation activities in the CDBG program.

2. What activities are ineligible? The general rule is that any activity that is not authorized by HUD's regulations are not eligible. 24 C.F.R. § 570.207. Principally excluded from the use of CDBG funds are buildings, or portions thereof, used predominantly for the general conduct of government; general government expenses; political activities; the purchase of equipment, furnishings and personal property; operating and maintenance expenses such as maintenance and repair of streets, sidewalks, parks, playgrounds, lawn

mowing, water and sewer facilities, neighborhood facilities, senior centers, centers for the handicapped, parking and similar public facilities. Until the 1987 amendments, new housing construction and income or subsidy payments were also ineligible except for last resort relocation housing under 24 C.F.R. pt. 42. New housing construction can be assisted where it is housing of last resort for persons being displaced by government action or when it is carried out by a community-based development organization as part of a neighborhood revitalization project. 24 C.F.R. § 570.207(b). The last resort housing rules are included in 24 C.F.R. pt. 42.

CDBG funds cannot be used to directly assist a business to relocate from one labor market area (LMA) to another if the relocation is likely to result in a significant loss of jobs in the LMA from which the relocation occurs; all losses of 500 or more jobs, and no losses of 25 or fewer jobs, are "significant" for purposes of this rule. 24 C.F.R. §§ 570.210, 570.482(h).

3. In *Ulster County Community Action Committee v. Koenig*, 402 F. Supp. 986 (S.D.N.Y. 1975), the court refused to invalidate a proposed expenditure of CDBG funds for renovation of an auditorium. The application described the auditorium project as a conversion to a multipurpose community center, and therefore an authorized use because it was a reconstruction of neighborhood facilities under § 105(a)(2), 42 U.S.C. § 5305(a)(2). While the city produced no specific plans, the court adopted a presumption of regularity, finding it would be premature to rule that the proposed expenditure or construction was illegal. What would be the effect of a refusal to adopt such a presumption? What would be the effect on the "flexibility" aspect of HCDA? Does relaxed scrutiny on the issue of eligibility mean that allocation decisions are unreviewable?

4. How might recipients use block grants to shelter the homeless? Are emergency shelter programs eligible? Providing tax-foreclosed properties to local organizations? Rental of vacant schools? Funding to sheltering charities? *See HUD Suggests Ways For Cities to Use Programs to Shelter Homeless,* 10 [Current Developments] Hous. & Dev. Rep. (BNA) 830 (1983).

5. Can recipients use block grant funds to create a housing allowance or rent supplement program? Can recipients use their grant to construct low-cost housing? How about on-site improvements, interim financing, or leveraged lower interest rate mortgages for a new housing project? *See Counties Discuss Use of CD for Housing, Rehab, Economic Development,* 10 [Current Developments] Hous. & Dev. Rep. (BNA) 135 (1982). How about rehabilitation? Should there be a distinction?

Can recipients use block grants to eliminate slums and blight in a city? CD funds can be used to fund the acquisition and clearance of land only after a preliminary determination by HUD that the funded activity meets the objective of slum and blight elimination on an area basis. In addition, HUD must make a final determination on the end or actual use of the funds. *See Accurate Depiction of End Use Needed for Acquisition, Clearance to Qualify Under Blight Criterion*, 25 [Current Developments] Hous. & Dev. Rep. (West) 719 (1998).

6. Is relocation assistance to those displaced by community development activities eligible? What about displacement encouraged by the HCDA initiative and not directly funded by HCDA (e.g., private business expansion)? The 1987 amendments seek to conserve low-income housing by prohibiting displacement and requiring locally prepared anti-displacement and relocation assistance plans designed to minimize displacement. In addition, the 1987 amendments to the Uniform Relocation Assistance and Real Property Acquisition Policies Act of 1970 reach displacement by any activities receiving federal as-

sistance including the community development block grant program. The legislative modifications create a one-for-one replacement requirement, and relocation compensation must be sufficient to assure that for five years following displacement the displacees will not have to pay more than 30% of household income for housing costs. § 5304(d)(2)(A)(iii)(I). Previously, the Act only allowed assistance for direct displacement. *Anti-Displacement Rule Specifies Aid Required of CDBG, UDAG Grantees,* 16 [Current Developments] Hous. & Dev. Rep. (WGL) 238 (1988).

7. *Maintenance of Local Effort.* Is it possible that certain community development activities must be carried out by grant recipients? In its findings and purposes, Congress evidenced its intent that HCDA funds not be used to replace any previous locally provided resources. § 101(c) 42 U.S.C. § 5301(c). Would the placement of the restriction in the findings and purpose section, rather than in the substantive provisions, indicate that the limitation is unenforceable? If it cannot be enforced, what is there to prevent recipients from simply replacing previously locally-funded activities with HCDA funds and use the prior resources for tax reduction? What is the meaning of "substantially" reduce? Does it suggest a percentage of prior commitment as a standard for compliance? Since communities previously had to make a local contribution to match federal community development grants, should prior participating recipients have to continue funding community development at least to the extent of prior matching grants? Would reduction of simply the prior matching share or noncash credits constitute a "substantial reduction?" If a violation has occurred, what secretarial review provision would cover the noncompliance?

A maintenance of effort requirement is also contained in § 105(a)(8), 42 U.S.C. § 5305(a)(8). Communities may use their block grant funds for specified "soft" social services programs only if "such services have not been provided by the unit of general local government ... during any part of the twelve-month period immediately preceding the date of application submission." Failure to maintain prior local efforts at community development and using block grants to free up funds for ineligible activities may violate the Act. § 101(c), 42 U.S.C. § 5301(c). *See Blackshear Resident Org. v. City of Austin,* 659 F.2d 36 (5th Cir. 1981) (mootness on expenditure), *contra Davis v. HUD,* 627 F.2d 942 (9th Cir. 1980) (refusal to dismiss after expenditure). *See also NAACP-Santa Rosa-Sonoma County Branch v. Hills,* 412 F. Supp. 102 (N.D. Cal. 1976).

8. This discussion of the eligible activities problem underscores the wide range of discretion conferred on HUD by the HCDA. This Act probably gives more discretion to HUD than any of the other federal housing and community development legislation covered by this book. Consequently, HUD may use the administrative rule-making process to achieve substantial modification of program requirements without seeking new legislation. It was this use of HUD rule-making authority that prompted Congress to enact a legislative review of HUD regulations under the HCDA. *See* Chapter 2, *supra.*

9. *Waivers.* Any provision of the regulations covering the CDBG program that is not required by the statute may be waived by HUD. *See* 24 C.F.R. Pt. 5. The statute itself also provides that HUD may waive certain statutory provisions in the case of the use of CDBG funds to respond to a Federally-designated disaster. HCDA § 122. For example, waivers were announced for the use of nearly $3 billion in supplemental CDBG funds for New York City following the attacks on the World Trade Center, 29 [Current Developments] Hous. & Dev. Rep. 20 (WGL) (2002), and for the use of recovery funds by Louisiana and Mississippi following Hurricane Katrina, see 35 [Current Developments] Hous. & Dev. Rep. (West) 15 (November 2007). Waivers are published in the Federal Register. Waivers are

not authorized to set aside statutory fair housing, nondiscrimination, labor, or environmental requirements.

A Note on the Application and Review Process

The process of becoming eligible for funding in the community development block grant program might be expected to be pivotal to compliance with congressional goals and, more importantly, to the effectiveness of the program. Over time, Congress has gone in the opposite direction from an effective application and review process. Were sufficient resources allocated to post-application audits or reviews, the application process might not be central. However, heightened resource allocation for monitoring might be infeasible due to the myriad HCDA recipients and the limited funds available for program implementation. An effective application process could have the potential of encouraging the local recipient to engage in planning.

In the community development program, Congress initially established an application format that had the potential of encouraging better comprehensive planning on the part of recipients. The application process involved the identification of community development needs, their classification by priority into long-term goals and the creation of a short-term plan of action to achieve those goals. This incremental planning reflected the state of the art. In addition, and of greatest note, was that the application integrated housing goals and development. Overall housing needs had to be analyzed and similarly classified by priority and accompanied by short-range implementation plans. To receive approval, the community's development goals had to be consistent with housing goals.

In 1981, however, Congress eliminated any application requirement. Absent an application setting forth, in some detail, a development plan, not only is "front-end" review impossible but "post-funding" review is more difficult because the outcomes a development process is to foster are much more opaque. Indeed, the outcomes may be as broad as the general statutory language authorizing funding.

Would the design of an application process assure its implementation? Would communities fall into the old practice of "boilerplate" and avoid hard planning under HCDA? Could communities ignore the community development needs of lower-income neighborhoods, or the housing needs of its ill-housed? These are not easy questions to answer. Nevertheless, with the requirement of a substantial, not to mention, detailed application, several desirable outcomes might be postulated: first, HUD could have resolved to monitor and assure statutory compliance; second, if the judiciary were willing, HUD's efforts could have been augmented by the potential for citizen lawsuits to review planning under HCDA; and finally, should litigation and administrative review fail to achieve compliance, Congress might respond with enhanced restrictions or another change in program rules.

In 2006, significant modifications were made by HUD in the ConPlan process, reflected in final regulations at 24 C.F.R. Part 91.

Local Priority-Setting. To receive its annual CDBG entitlement grant, a grantee must develop and submit to HUD its Consolidated Plan, which is a jurisdiction's comprehensive planning document and application for funding under CDBG and related formula grant programs. The ConPlan, as it is popularly called, merges into one process and one document all the planning and application requirements of four HUD block grants: CDBG, HOME Investment Partnerships, Housing Opportunities for Persons with AIDS

(HOPWA), and Emergency Shelter Grants (ESG). In its Consolidated Plan, the jurisdiction must identify its goals for these programs as well as for housing programs. The goals will serve as the criteria against which HUD will evaluate a jurisdiction's Plan and its performance under the Plan.

The statutory basis for the ConPlan is the Comprehensive Housing Affordability Strategy (CHAS), a provision of the Cranston-Gonzalez National Affordable Housing Act, Pub. L. No. 101-625, tit. I, §§ 105–06, 104 Stat. 4079, 4088–91 (1990) (*codified at* 42 U.S.C. § 12705 (2000)). The CHAS established a local planning process that determined housing needs and assigned priorities to those needs. In 1995, HUD amended the CHAS regulations to create the ConPlan; there is no ConPlan statute. The ConPlan regulations merged the planning, application and performance reporting processes of the four block grants, resulting in one Strategic Plan, one 'application' document (the Annual Action Plan), and one set of performance reports (the CAPER, which incorporates CDBG's Grantee Performance Report). Jurisdictions develop ConPlans once every five years at a minimum, and are required to update them annually. *See* 24 C.F.R. pt. 91.

Public Notice, Comment and Review. The HDCA and Cranston-Gonzalez provisions for CDBG and CHAS require a public hearing to gather the public's ideas on the community development needs of the jurisdiction. Under HUD regulations this public hearing must precede the publication of a draft ConPlan. Notice of the availability the proposed ConPlan must be published and copies made available at no cost, such as at public libraries, and there must be at least one public hearing and 30 days to review and comment on the proposed Plan. The regulations require the jurisdiction to consider the public's comments on the Plan, include as an attachment to the final plan a summary of the comments received, and explain in the final ConPlan why public comments were not used.

Plan Elements. There are seven key elements of the ConPlan. (1) Housing and Community Development Needs: The jurisdiction must estimate housing needs for the upcoming five years, by income, family type, and tenure type (whether households rent or own. (2) Housing Market Analysis: description and analysis of the supply and demand for housing, condition and cost of available housing, distribution and concentration by income, race and ethnicity, and an inventory of housing facilities and services for people who are homeless, people with special needs, and people in need of supportive housing. Public housing, and the condition of public and assisted housing by income level, must be described. In addition, the ConPlan must account for units assisted with state or federal funds that might be lost from inventory for any reason. (3) The Strategic Plan: explains the jurisdiction's spending priorities for the block grant funding over the five years, stating specific objectives in measurable terms and estimating a timetable for achieving them. (4) The Anti-Poverty Strategy: The law calls for a description of goals, programs and policies for reducing the number of people with incomes below the poverty level. (5) Lead-Based Paint: The Strategic Plan must outline the jurisdiction's planned actions to find and reduce lead paint hazards. (6) Fair Housing: Each year the jurisdiction must certify that it is "affirmatively furthering fair housing." The jurisdiction must prepare an Analysis of Impediments (AI) to fair housing choice, although the AI is not required to be a part of the Strategic Plan or Annual Action Plan. (7) The Annual Action Plan: must describe the activities the jurisdiction will carry out in the upcoming year to address the Strategic Plan priorities, along with the jurisdiction's reasons for these allocation priorities. For uses of CDBG, there must be enough detail about each activity so that people can determine the degree to which they are affected. The ConPlan must include an estimate of the number and type of households that will benefit (does not apply to states).

States must describe how they will distribute funds to local governments and nonprofits, and there must be a description of all criteria used to select applications from localities. States must also describe how all CDBG money will be allocated among all funding categories (e.g., housing, economic development, public works, etc.).

Performance Reporting. Each jurisdiction that has an approved Consolidated Plan must annually review and report to HUD on the progress it has made in carrying out its strategic plan and its action plan. The purpose of the report is for the jurisdiction to show what it did to meet housing and community development needs, with particular emphasis on addressing the needs of households with incomes below 30% of the area median income (AMI). For each element of federal funding, the jurisdiction is required to describe the resources made available, the investment of available resources, the geographic distribution and location of investments, the families and persons assisted including the racial and ethnic status of persons assisted, actions taken by the jurisdiction to affirmatively further fair housing, and other actions indicated in the strategic plan and the action plan. HUD staff is required to review the Performance Evaluation Reports, and failure to submit a satisfactory report or to submit it on time is grounds for HUD to withdraw and reallocate a jurisdiction's funding. Performance measures are specified in instructions and guidelines published by HUD on its website, www.hud.gov. The Annual Performance Report contains a number of computer-based sets of records, four of which are explicitly available to the public. Annual performance reporting requirements are also merged into a set of documents called the CAPER. The CAPER is a general, aggregate picture of what the jurisdiction accomplished.

There are several public participation features related to the Annual Performance Report. There must be reasonable notice that the report is available, and the report must be available to the public. The public has only 15 days to review and comment on it; nevertheless, the jurisdiction must consider public comments and attach a summary of the comments.

Certifications. A jurisdiction's Consolidated Plan must include several required certifications. Foremost are the certification that not less than 70% of the CDBG funds received will be used for activities that benefit low- and moderate-income persons, over a one, two or three year period specified by the grantee; and the certification that the grantee will affirmatively further fair housing. HUD will approve a Consolidated Plan submission unless the Plan (or a portion of it) is inconsistent with the purposes of the National Affordable Housing Act or is substantially incomplete. HUD *can* disapprove the final ConPlan for several reasons, including failure to follow public participation requirements, failure to take appropriate actions to evaluate or overcome impediments to fair housing.

The federal categorical urban renewal program contained a requirement that urban renewal programs be related to a community plan. This requirement was never as effective as federal policy makers would have wished, and in most communities there was little attempt to analyze and establish a priority for community development needs. *See* Daniel R. Mandelker, *The Comprehensive Planning Requirement in Urban Renewal,* 116 U. Pa. L. Rev. 25 (1967), reporting case studies of renewal programs in St. Louis and Nashville.

Is the ConPlan process an advance over the application processes of CDBG's predecessor programs? Local urban renewal priorities were usually determined by powerful local constituencies, such as downtown merchants and chambers of commerce. They fought for and usually obtained local commitments for civic centers, sports stadia, and a variety of downtown redevelopment projects. Reinforcing political networks often developed at the local level gave local commercial interests a dominant role in the urban renewal decision-making process. HUD did not begin to emphasize housing objectives until late in the urban renewal program. The Model Cities program was a grand effort to carry out extensive community and neighborhood planning, but it was terminated before it could really be tested.

Notes and Questions

1. *Identification of Needs.* The original pre-1981 Act specified that the application was to set forth a "summary of a three-year community development plan which identified community development and housing needs." The proper identification of need was a critical step in designing a community development program which will achieve the HCDA's broad congressional goals. What was the potential for non-compliance with the needs assessment portion of the grant application? *See* James A. Kushner, *Litigation Strategies and Judicial Review Under Title I of the Housing and Community Development Act of* 1974, 11 Urb. L. Ann. 37, 41–42 (1976).

2. Does the elimination of the formal application encourage program noncompliance, poor planning, or planning that fails to address the needs of the poor and politically powerless? Can any such concerns be addressed through post-performance audits and administrative review?

3. Despite elimination of formal applications for entitlement grant communities, HUD retains both a pre-application and formal application for its small cities program. *Nickols v. Pierce,* 556 F. Supp. 1280 (S.D. Ohio 1982) (procedures validated). The general program has shifted from the application approach to a system of recipient certifications for program compliance followed by HUD administrative review.

4. *Prioritizing Among Eligible Activities.* One issue not directly addressed by the statute and regulations is the matter of priority. Should the program requirements mandate that certain activities are more important than others within the recipient jurisdiction? Assume a community with two neighborhoods, one rich, one poor. Assume a rich neighborhood proposes use of the block grant to preserve a fine old stand of trees that are infested with Dutch elm disease. The poor neighborhood wants a neighborhood library constructed. Who should prevail? The regulations allow expenditures for recreational projects. What priority should recreation projects have? How do communities measure or evaluate need? Might the measure be anticipated use? Would anticipated use be based upon present patterns of use of existing facilities? Would such a method carry a heavy middle-class bias because parks, libraries, and other public facilities located in wealthier neighborhoods tend to be more plentiful, of high quality, well maintained and more heavily used?

5. *Judicial Oversight.* Prior to 1981, when recipients were required to file an annual application together with a Housing Assistance Plan that assessed needs and proposed housing activity, the federal courts usually deferred to grant recipients in enforcing these requirements. *See Broaden v. Harris,* 451 F. Supp. 1215 (W.D. Pa. 1978). The 1981 Housing and Community Development Act Amendments, Omnibus Budget Reconciliation Act of 1981, Pub. L. No. 97-35, 95 Stat. 384, eliminated the requirement of a formally submitted application and, along with it, the approval standards of *inconsistency* and *inappropriateness,* no doubt reflecting the influence of the Reagan era deregulation movement. Instead, recipients are now required to submit to HUD an annual statement of program objectives and the projected use of funds. Accountability now shifted to HUD agency re-

view with substantive evaluation focused on activity eligibility and the satisfaction of statutory targeting and equal opportunity obligations.

The role of courts in overseeing consistency with the purposes of CDBG has thus diminished, as illustrated by cases such as *Grand Boulevard Improvement Ass'n v. City of Chicago*, 553 F. Supp. 1154 (N.D. Ill. 1982). In *Grand Boulevard* the court ruled that HUD failed to give consideration to the policies of housing preservation and avoidance of displacement when it reviewed the city's application proposing demolition of existing housing and the construction of new dwellings. The ruling did not challenge the ultimate policy or strategy choice, only the perfunctory and unconditional nature of HUD's application approval. It might appear that after the 1981 amendments eliminating the application and its review, the only basis for legal action would be for a violation of anti-discrimination, relocation, or environmental analysis statutes. *Cf. Alshuler v. HUD,* 686 F.2d 472 (7th Cir. 1982) (site selection challenge denied with dicta that a proposal based on distorted or inaccurate data when accurate information is readily available is subject to invalidation).

One reason for the broad deference accorded HUD in reviewing its supervision of HCDA is that, as an administrative agency, it is subject to the narrow review provided by the Administrative Procedure Act, 5 U.S.C. §706. *See Citizens to Preserve Overton Park v. Volpe,* 401 U.S. 402 (1971). Reviewability and other issues are examined in Chapter 2, *supra.*

6. *Certification and the Federal False Claims Act.* What could be the result if CDBG jurisdictions were to lapse into treating the certification requirement as boiler-plate, and HUD does not exercise its statutory oversight?

The Anti-Discrimination Center of Metro New York, Inc. brought suit as *qui tam* relator for the United States of America against Westchester County, New York, alleging that Westchester violated the False Claims Act, 31 U.S.C. §3729, *et seq.* ("FCA"), through certifications made to the Secretary of Housing and Urban Development ("HUD") between April 2000 and April 2006 to obtain over $52 million in federal funding for housing and community development.

ADC argued that the County made an implied false certification each time it submitted a payment request to HUD in connection with CDBG and other grants during the false claims period.

In order to impose liability under the FCA, the plaintiff must show that defendants (1) made a claim, (2) to the United States government, (3) that is false or fraudulent, (4) knowing of its falsity, and (5) seeking payment from the federal treasury.

United States *ex rel.* Anti-Discrimination Center of Metro New York, Inc. v. Westchester County

United States District Court
668 F. Supp. 2d 548 (S.D.N.Y. 2009)

The United States grants housing and community development-related funding to state and local entities. In order to receive certain federal funding, including CDBG funds, the County was required to certify that it would meet a variety of fair housing obligations, including that the County would AFFH [affirmatively further fair Housing—Eds.]. Specifically, grant recipients are required to make certifications to HUD that, *inter alia,* "the grant will be conducted and administered in conformity with the Civil Rights Act of 1964 and the Fair Housing Act, and the grantee will affirmatively further fair housing." 42 U.S.C. §5304(b)(2). To AFFH, the County was required to undertake three tasks: to "conduct an analysis of impediments to fair housing choice within the area, take appropriate actions to overcome the effects of any impediments identified through that analysis, and maintain records reflecting the analysis and actions in this regard." 24 C.F.R. §91.425(a)(1)(i), *see also id.* §570.601(a)(2). It is undisputed that the County was aware of its AFFH obligations during the false claims period, and that the County made claims for payments of grant funds from the United States during the period...."

The County's Consolidated Plans addressed housing and community development goals for four federal grant programs. Consolidated Plans serve four main functions: they are "[a] planning document for the jurisdiction," "[a] submission for federal funds under HUD's formula grant programs," "[a] strategy to be followed in carrying out HUD programs," and "[a] management tool for assessing performance and tracking results." 24 C.F.R. §91.1(b). Consolidated Plans are required to describe, *inter alia,* the jurisdiction's "general priorities for allocating investment geographically within the jurisdiction ... and among different activities and needs" for the following categories: affordable housing, public housing, homelessness, other special needs (including the elderly, disabled, persons with alcohol or drug addiction, persons with HIV/AIDS and their families, and public housing residents), and nonhousing development pursuant to the CDBG program. *Id.* §91.215....

The statutory and regulatory framework described above imposes no duty on the County to undertake any particular course of action to overcome an impediment to fair housing. After all, one course of action may be effective in one community and futile in another. The law does, however, require the recipient of the federal funds to certify that it will take "appropriate" actions to overcome the effect of the impediments to fair housing choice that its analysis has identified, and to maintain records reflecting both that analysis and those actions. *See* 24 C.F.R. §91.425(a)(1)(i). Because the County never did the required analysis of race-based impediments, it never created a contemporaneous record of how its management of the HUD-acquired funds or any other "appropriate" steps it could take would overcome the effects of those impediments. Thus, while the parties' evidence regarding the actions the County took and failed to take during the false claims period may be relevant at trial to issues like motive and knowledge, by pointing to its programs regarding affordable housing the County has failed to raise a question of fact as to whether its certifications to HUD were false when they represented that the County would take appropriate actions to overcome the effects of race-based impediments to fair housing choice that its analysis had identified....

In the instant case, 42 U.S.C. §5304(b)(2), pertaining to CDBG grants, expressly states that "*[a]ny grant* under section 5306 of this title *shall be made only if the grantee certifies* to the satisfaction of the Secretary that ... the grant will be conducted and administered in conformity with the Civil Rights Act of 1964 and the Fair Housing Act, and *the grantee will affirmatively further fair housing.*" (emphasis supplied).

[The District Court denied the County's motion to dismiss the action, yet also denied ADC's motion for summary judgment as to the knowledge element of an FCA claim—Eds.]

2. Targeting Benefits for the Poor

Perhaps the most controversial element of HCDA standards is the requirement that the program be targeted to benefit the poor. Most community development litigation has centered on the issue of targeting, with plaintiffs seeking more funds for the poor community or additional affordable housing in the suburbs.

Aid to poor neighborhoods is mandated by the 1981 version of the Act which provided that "the Community Development Program has been developed so as to give maximum feasible priority to activities which will benefit low- and moderate-income families or aid in the prevention or elimination of slums and blight." 42 U.S.C. § 5304(b)(2), *subsumed by* Pub. L. No. 97-35, 95 Stat. 384 (1981).

Congress has repeatedly reaffirmed and strengthened this targeting policy. In 1983 it passed the Domestic Housing and International Recovery and Financial Stability Act, Pub. L. No. 98-181, § 101(a)(2), 97 Stat. 1153, 1161 (1983) (*codified at* 42 U.S.C. §§ 5301(c), 5304(b)(3)), requiring that at least 51% of community development block grant funds over a three-year period must be used to benefit low- and moderate-income persons. Acquisition, construction, rehabilitation, or economic development projects come within the principal benefit standard if the activity is carried out in a majority low- or moderate-income neighborhood, provides services predominantly to that group or employs a majority of such persons. "Low- and moderate-income" is defined as 80% of area median income, while "very low income" is defined as 50% of the area median. Congress, in the Housing and Community Development Technical Amendments Act, Pub. L. No. 98-473, § 101(a)(9), 98 Stat. 2218 (1984), relaxed the rule where there are few low- or moderate-income households to allow projects of area-wide benefit to those persons. The minimum targeting standard was raised to 60% in 1987. *See also* House Conf. Rep. No 100-426, 100th Cong., 1st Sess., *reprinted in* 1987 U.S.C.C.A.N. 3458, 3520 (conferees intend 60% rule to apply to average spent over one-, two-, or three-year period, whichever the recipient selects for planning purposes). The Act now requires certification that 70% of the funds will be used for activities that principally benefit low- and moderate-income persons. 42 U.S.C. § 5304(b)(3) (with limited oversight and available waivers).

National Wildlife Federation v. Marsh

United States Court of Appeals
747 F.2d 616 (11th Cir. 1984)

KRAVITCH, Circuit Judge

[In a petition for panel rehearing, some of the appellants, namely individuals of low- or moderate-income, challenged the Eleventh Circuit's conclusion in *National Wildlife Federation v. Marsh*, 721 F.2d 767 (11th Cir. 1983), that section 5304(b)(3) of the "HCDA" 42 U.S.C. 5301 *et seq.* (1983), does not require a funded project principally to benefit low- and moderate-income persons.]

In 1968 the City of Alma formulated a plan [under the Model Cities Program] to revitalize the economy of the community and surrounding area. The plan featured four development projects: an air/rail industrial park, improved water and sewage treatment facilities, a modernized airport and the construction of a recreational lake, referred to as Lake Alma and the subject of over a decade of litigation. Lake Alma was considered the "urban shaper" of the four.

While funding for the lake under the Model Cities Program was being delayed by litigation over the environmental impact of the project, Congress enacted the HCDA in 1974. Alma sought funding under the Act and was awarded a $2.3 million block grant for fiscal years 1975 through 1977 and another $399,600 for fiscal years 1978 and 1979, but release of the money again was delayed by litigation over the environmental soundness of the proposed development. Finally, in 1982 the Department of Housing and Urban Development informed Alma it would release the funds if certain requirements were satisfied, including compliance with two 1978 HUD regulations, 24 C.F.R. § 570.302(b)(1) and (d), requiring that the project "principally" benefit low- and moderate-income individuals, i.e., that more than fifty percent of the benefiting public be persons of low or moderate income.

The data Alma submitted to HUD satisfied most of the criteria, but did not quite reach the fifty percent threshold of the principal benefit regulation. Notwithstanding the City's failure to comply with the regulation, the Deputy Secretary of HUD, exercising his authority under 24 C.F.R. § 570.4, waived the principal benefit regulation and released the funds on grounds that to do otherwise would result in undue hardship and would frustrate the purpose of the block grant statute.

Appellants requested a preliminary injunction to prevent the release of funds, which the district court denied.

On November 30, 1983, shortly before the opinion in this case was published, Congress amended 42 U.S.C. § 5304(b)(3) to require each grantee to certify that:

> [t]he projected use of funds has been developed so as to give maximum feasible priority to activities which will benefit low- and moderate-income families or aid in the prevention or elimination of slums or blight[;], and the projected use of funds may also include activities which the grantee certifies are designed to meet other community development needs having a particular urgency because existing conditions pose a serious and immediate threat to the health or welfare of the community where other financial resources are not available to meet such needs, *except that the aggregate use of funds received ... during a period specified by the grantee of not more than 3 years, shall principally benefit persons of low and moderate income in a manner that ensures that not less than 51 percent of such funds are used for activities that benefit such persons during such period....*

42 U.S.C. § 5304(b)(3) (Supp. 1984) (emphasis on 1983 amendment). Section 5304 previously required only that "maximum feasible priority" be given to activities that benefit low and moderate income individuals or aid in the prevention or elimination of slums or blight, and, based upon our review of the available legislative history to the HCDA, we held in *National Wildlife v. Marsh, supra,* that Congress rejected a strict percentage floor for use of funds and did not intend that at least fifty percent of the beneficiaries of every funded project should be lower income individuals. Petitioners contend that the 1983 amendments, which expressly require that fifty-one percent of the grantee's "aggregate use of funds received" principally benefit persons of low or moderate income, and accompanying legislative history, call for a different result than that reached by the panel.

[The Court considered whether to apply the new statute retrospectively, and concluded it should not, for several reasons, including the vested rights of the City in related CDBG grant funds.]

Although amended section 5304(b)(3) does not purport to govern the funding of individual activities within an overall program of wider scope, Congress, in the 1983 amendments, did enact statutory guidelines for determining when a particular activity, such as Lake Alma, qualifies as benefiting low and moderate income individuals. *See* 42 U.S.C. § 5305(c) (Supp. 1984). Significantly, however, the guidelines do not impose a rigid rule that to qualify as an activity benefiting persons of lower income the project must serve an area of at least fifty-one percent lower income residents. Under section

5305(c)(2), a project not satisfying a fifty-one percent benefit test will nonetheless qualify for funding if it serves an area comprised of a larger proportion of low and moderate income residents than seventy-five percent of the other areas in the jurisdiction of the recipient. 42 U.S.C. § 5305(c)(2) (Supp. 1984).This evidences the belief of the current Congress that each activity need not meet a rigid fifty-one percent principal benefit test.

It is not a simple task to divine the intended meaning of each provision in complex socio-economic legislation such as the HCDA. Our role as interpreters is made no less difficult, and correspondingly no less subject to criticism, when Congress employs ambiguous operative language in setting forth the criteria for obtaining the benefit of its programs. Our problem here is determining what Congress meant when it stated that "the projected use of funds [must be] developed so as to give maximum feasible priority to activities which will benefit low- and moderate-income families...." 42 U.S.C. § 5304(b)(3) (1983). When Congress enacted the HCDA in 1974, it considered and refused to adopt a Senate version that would have further defined "maximum feasible priority" by imposing a rigid percentage limiting the amount of funds available for activities that do not benefit low or moderate income individuals. We remain convinced that when it declined to enact a strict principal benefit provision, Congress intended to allow HUD to exercise its discretion in determining which projects were best suited for funding. Over the years, HUD has found it difficult but has used its best efforts to further the purposes of the Act and to predict the will of the majority of Congress. After a few years of experience, and prompted by HUD's 1982 proposed regulations, Congress decided to remove some of the agency's discretion and has now enacted more strict principal benefit requirements, but that does not affect our holding that there was no principal benefit requirement in the statute when HUD waived its regulation. If anything, it supports our reasoning that had Congress intended a rigid fifty-one percent test, it would have, as it now has, enacted one.

The motion for rehearing by the panel is denied.

Notes and Questions

1. HUD, under the Reagan administration, revised the methodology for determining lower-income benefit by allowing the value of assisted housing to be based on the total project cost rather than the cost of the units to be marketed to those of lower income. HUD claimed the measure is to encourage scattered sites and economic integration rather than pressuring recipients to have all units in the project planned for the poor in order to meet targeting obligations. The measure may, however, just be a clever bookkeeping device to attain the higher congressionally established target levels without additional effort. *Computation of Lower Income Benefit from CDBG Multifamily Activities to Be Revised,* 16 [Current Developments] Hous. & Dev. Rep. (WGL) 245 (1988). Although HUD is to audit a community's performance, recipients need only certify compliance with the targeting to principally benefit low- and moderate-income persons. 42 U.S.C. § 5304(b)(3). *See Grand Boulevard Improvement Ass'n v. City of Chicago,* 553 F. Supp. 1154 (N.D. Ill. 1982) (denial of fees following settlement in challenge to program failing to benefit the poor for failure to show HUD action unreasonable).

2. What *should* be community development policy? Does it make good sense to target the lion's share to ameliorate slums or benefit poorer city residents? Or should community development strategies take a different approach, one consistent with the apparent admissions of Congress in passing the law that it was badly split over the appropriate strategies for community development?

Note that the statute, in §§ 101(c), 42 U.S.C. § 5301(c), and 104(b), 42 U.S.C. § 5304(b)(3), in addition to the 70% rule, adopts an additional test for the eligibility of community development activities. They must either (1) benefit low- or moderate-income families, (2) aid in the prevention or elimination of blight, or (3) meet urgent community needs. Section 101(c) also makes the following statement of the purpose of the statute:

> The primary object of this chapter is the development of viable urban communities, by providing the decent housing and a suitable living environment and expanding economic opportunities, principally for persons of low- and moderate-income.

To what extent does the statutory "primary object" modify the three-pronged test? Would *Bradley v. HUD*, 648 F.2d 290 (5th Cir. 1981), ruling that there is no priority between aid to poor or elimination of blight, permitting the recipient to transfer 80% of rehabilitation funds to redevelopment planning, be different under the current legislation's 70% rule?

3. What of the decision not to fund activities in a very poor and deteriorated community that does not display a likelihood of stability and rejuvenation but rather to disperse limited resources to communities or neighborhoods likely to respond with increased maintenance and investment? Are triage and gentrification examples of policies that can hurt the poor, yet aid in stabilizing the physical neighborhood and, thus, possibly safeguard a tax base and employment base on which the poor in the wider community may also be critically dependent? *See also HUD Questions Use of Block Grant Funds for Integration Maintenance in Ohio,* 13 [Current Developments] Hous. & Dev. Rep. (BNA) 296 (1985); *90 Percent of CD Funds Used for Lower-Income Benefit, Report Says,* 12 [Current Developments] Hous. & Dev. Rep. (BNA) 996 (1985). This problem is discussed in Section F, *infra,* covering relocation and gentrification; and Chapter 3, *supra*, discussed the policy and effects of the HOPE VI program in public housing, which presents the parallel problem in the narrower context of distressed public housing projects.

4. A part of the history of the confrontation between HUD and Congress over targeting was the enactment of a requirement for congressional approval of HUD regulations. The one-house approval process is somewhat in doubt after *I.N.S. v. Chadha,* 462 U.S. 919 (1983) (invalidating scheme of one-house congressional disapproval for administrative deportation waivers, as the separation of powers doctrine allows Congress only the power to pass laws). *See Supreme Court Ban on Congressional Veto Unlikely to Have Major Effect on HUD Rules,* 11 [Current Developments] Hous. & Dev. Rep. (BNA) 87 (1983).

5. In communities lacking areas predominantly occupied by the poor, block grant activities must be targeted for projects that benefit the poor who do reside in the community, for the elimination of slums or blight, or toward meeting urgent community development needs. 10 [Current Developments] Hous. & Dev. Rep. (BNA) 56 (1982). Pursuant to the 1984 Technical Amendments, Pub. L. No. 98-479, 98 Stat. 2227, such communities may take on activities with area-wide benefits and neighborhood projects where the community's lower-income population concentration is reflected.

6. Citizens have long been recognized as having standing to challenge a recipient jurisdiction's use of CDBG funds as improper under HCDA. *See, e.g., Reese v. Miami-Dade County*, 210 F. Supp. 2d 1324, 1329–30 (S.D. Fla. 2002) (denying motion to dismiss claims based on 42 U.S.C. § 5304 alleging improper use of CDBG funds); *Winkler v. Chicago School Reform Bd. of Trustees*, No. 99 C 2424, 2001 WL 987883 (N.D. Ill. Aug. 29, 2001) (granting motion to dismiss against HUD and the U.S. Department of Defense and denying motion to dismiss against the Secretary of Defense and the Secretary of

Housing and Urban Development based on 42 U.S.C. §5303 et. seq. alleging improper use of CDBG funds); *DeRosa v. HUD*, 787 F.2d 840, 842 (2d Cir. 1986) (affirming district court's ruling that plaintiffs had standing to challenge CDBG grant as violating 24 C.F.R. Part 570); *Nat'l Wildlife Fed. v. Marsh*, 721 F.2d 767, 769 n.1, 770 (11th Cir. 1983) (district court held plaintiffs "had standing to challenge HUD's release of" CDBG funds as violative of 42 U.S.C. §5301 et seq. and 24 C.F.R. Pt. 570; defendants did not challenge this ruling); *N.A.A.C.P. v. Harris*, 607 F.2d 514, 516 n.1 (1st Cir. 1979) (district court held plaintiffs had standing to challenge legality of CDBG grants, defendants on appeal did not challenge this ruling); *Lower Moreland Homeowner's Ass'n v. HUD*, 479 F. Supp. 886, 896 (E.D. Pa. 1979) (plaintiffs had standing under 42 U.S.C. §5301 et seq. and 24 C.F.R. Pt. 570 to challenge CDBG grants); *Coalition for Block Grant Compliance v. HUD*, 450 F. Supp. 43, 50 (E.D. Mich. 1978) (plaintiffs had standing under 42 U.S.C. §5301 et seq. and 24 C.F.R. Pt. 570 to challenge block grants).

7. Given the flexibility accorded to recipient jurisdictions, it can be daunting for citizens to obtain federal court review of claims asserting inappropriate allocations of CDBG funds. A recent exception is *Iron Hawk v. Martinez*, No. 03-5038 (D.S.D. filed Apr. 29, 2003), in which low-income individuals challenged the intended expenditure by the city of South Bend, Indiana of $825,000 in federal CDBG funds of the $900,000 needed to build a shooting range. The city of South Bend argued that the use of CDBG funds was legal, despite the fact that internal e-mails produced in discovery stated, "There is no way to document the LMI [low and middle-income] benefit to meet the National Objective [required for use of CDBG funds]." Shortly after these emails were discovered, HUD wrote the State of South Dakota advising it that the CDBG award to the City of Sturgis for construction of the shooting range violated federal law. The *Iron Hawk* litigation is a part of a wider dispute concerning preservation of tribal religious uses of Bear Butte by several Cheyenne, Sioux and Lakota tribes, recounted by plaintiffs' counsel, James D. Leach, in *A Shooting Range at Bear Butte: Reconciliation or Racism?*, 50 S D. L. REV. 244 (2005). The legal claims under the federal Religious Land Use and Institutionalized Persons Act (RLUIPA), 42 U.S.C. §2000cc, are examined in Kristen A. Carpenter, *Old Ground and New Directions at Sacred Sites on the Western Landscape*, 83 DEN. U. L. REV. 981 (2006).

8. HUD may allow housing cooperatives to use CDBG funds on projects even if the 100% low- and moderate-income occupancy requirement has not been met. However, HUD has only waived the requirement when in support of its objective to decrease the spatial concentration of various income groups. *See Requirement for 100 Percent Low-, Moderate-Income Occupancy Waived for Mobile Home Co-Op*, 24 [Current Developments] Hous. & Dev. Rep. (WGL) 109 (1996).

3. Funding Allocation

The allocation of federal community development block grant funds is carried out under a rather complex if not byzantine formula, one that subjects community development to the vicissitudes of politics. Under the categorical grant programs, cities fared as well as their grantsmanship abilities allowed. A combination of good intergovernmental relationships, reasonable success with prior programs, resources to keep abreast of and carry out the application, planning, and local contribution requirements, and the support of strong congressional representation could guarantee a proportionately high level of federal aid. Under the 1949 national housing act, the bulk of federal aid was channeled to the older, Democratically controlled central cities. One of the principal changes in HCDA was the imposition of an allocation system allegedly designed to make the distribution scheme more equitable and more responsive to need.

The basic entitlement grant, as originally passed in 1974, was linked to population, wealth, and the extent of overcrowding in the housing supply, and appeared facially neutral. Cities automatically qualified for the grant if they met the requirements. However, an analysis of first-round participants disclosed that the Act had redistributed funds away from the central cities toward the medium-sized cities and the newer suburban population centers, away from older frostbelt cities that were losing population to the sunbelt, which tend to be Republican-dominated. The trauma of readjustment for those cities which had previously been funded at very high levels was partially delayed under "hold harmless" provisions, which allowed the phasing out of old program-funding levels during the initial program years. While central cities faced declining aid, suburban enclaves that never thought of applying to HUD for aid were now recipients of assistance. *See* Alvin Hirshen & Richard T. LeGates, *HUD's Bonanza for Suburbia,* 39 The Progressive 32 (1975).

The dire needs of the central cities, and the reality of HCDA as a suburban "tennis court" construction program, prompted Congress in the 1977 Act amendments to modify the prior plan. It legislated a dual formula to strengthen controls on how money was spent and to better serve communities with different types of problems. Formula A is based on poverty rate, population, and overcrowding, and tends to benefit rapidly growing cities with high poverty and insufficient affordable housing. Formula B is based on age of housing stock, poverty rate, and growth lag, factors which tend to benefit older cities with large stocks of old and deteriorating housing. 42 U.S.C. § 5306(b)(1). HUD calculates both formulas for all entitlement grantees and awards the larger amount. Now the extent of older pre-1940 housing stock and the community's growth trend are factored in. This growth trend or "growth lag," as the statute refers to it, is a relative measure of the number of persons who might have moved to the community had the community enjoyed a growth rate similar to the average for metropolitan areas. Section 106 of the 1981 Act reallocated block grant funds from a 20% rural to a 30% rural share. Eligibility of urban counties has further diluted the share of cities in ever-declining community development block grant appropriations. *See Urban Counties Using CDBG, Other Funds for Economic Projects, Study Says,* 14 [Current Developments] Hous. & Dev. Rep. (WGL) 806 (1987).

In addition to the basic entitlement grant, the HUD Secretary retains a fund for innovative and urgent projects; some funds are allocated to small cities and non-urban areas.

HCDA funds are not targeted to specific neighborhoods but can be used throughout the recipient community. Thus, while a city might be receiving the same size grant, it now faces more pressure to disperse that grant according to local political pressures. These political demands for the community-wide use of community development funds, together with the failure to increase the federal assistance available, mean declining resources for the neediest neighborhoods and low-income areas with the highest incidence of blight and the greatest rate of deterioration. Even when federal appropriations for community development have been relatively stable, the inherent "inflation tax" diminishes the real value of community development assistance available to recipient communities.

There is a long and substantive basis for associating deep and persistent poverty with central cities. Nonetheless, the burdens of poverty and thus the need for community development resources, is spreading. Analyses of the location of poverty in America show that by 2008, suburbs were home to the largest and fastest-growing poor population in the country. Between 2000 and 2008, the poor population in the suburbs of the country's largest metro areas grew by 25%. By 2008, "large suburbs were home to 1.5 million more poor than their primary cities and housed almost one-third of the nation's poor overall." ELIZABETH KNEEBONE & EMILY GARR, THE SUBURBANIZATION OF POVERTY: TRENDS IN METROPOLITAN AMERICA, 2000–2008 (Jan. 2010) (publication of the Brookings Institution). The largest increase was felt in Midwestern cities and suburbs. In 2008, 91.6 million people—more than 30% of the nation's population—fell below 200% of the federal poverty level. Of these, more individuals lived in families with incomes between 100% and 200% of poverty line (52.5 million) than below the poverty line (39.1 million) in 2008. *Id.*

Notes and Questions

1. Refer to the dual formula entitlement grant provisions. Are there additional factors that should be considered? Should the current factors be given different weight? May counties be recipients under HCDA? How does the formula relate to implicit policies of urban decentralization (housing dispersal and regional growth) and central city revitalization? Would taking a position on the policy debate conflict with the flexibility concept of HCDA?

2. The Brookings Institution study cited in the text predicts that this shift in the geography of American poverty is likely to continue as a result of the economic downturn that began in 2007, because of the faster pace of growth in suburban unemployment. The authors propose that effective response is likely to require regional-scale collaboration to effectively address the needs of a poor population that increasingly spills into the suburbs. How might the funding allocation criteria be modified to encourage or reward joint grant applications by city-urban county collaborations for CDBG projects?

4. Public Participation

Every CDBG-recipient jurisdiction is required to adopt a citizen participation plan that sets forth the jurisdiction's policies and procedures for citizen participation. 24 C.F.R. §91.105(a)(1). There must be adequate public notice to people who are likely to be affected by CDBG-funded projects, and people must be given reasonable and timely access to information. The citizen participation plan is explicitly required to provide for and encourage citizen participation in specified stages of the planning process. 24 C.F.R. §91.105(a)(2). Most significantly, the city must consider any comments of citizens received in writing, or orally at the public hearings, and attach a summary of these views, including those not accepted and the reasons therefore, to the final consolidated plan. 24 C.F.R. §91.105(b)(5).

In one sense, these changes to the CDBG requirements for public participation are a noteworthy advance, in that they compel cities to provide an explanation and justification for their funding decisions. Nevertheless, "they still only allow one-way communication of information to the public; any response of approval or disapproval by the community need not impact the final outcome of the decision." Audrey MacFarlane, *When Inclusion Leads to Exclusion*, 66 BROOK. L. REV. 861, 882 (2001).

A Note on CDBG in Disaster Recovery

Disaster Recovery Grants are authorized under Title I of the Housing and Community Development Act of 1974, *as amended*, Pub. L. No. 93-383, 88 Stat. 633 (*codified as amended at* 42 U.S.C. § 5301). *See also* Disaster Relief and Emergency Assistance Amendments of 1988, Pub. L. No. 100-707, § 105(e), 102 Stat. 4689, 4691; *Allocations and Common Applications and Reporting Waivers Granted to and Alternative Requirements for CDBG Disaster Recovery Guarantees*, 71 Fed. Reg. 7666 (Feb. 13, 2006). HUD provides flexible grants to help cities, counties, and States recover from Presidentially declared disasters, subject to availability of supplemental appropriations. HUD generally awards noncompetitive, nonrecurring Disaster Recovery grants by a formula that considers disaster recovery needs unmet by other Federal disaster assistance programs. These communities must have significant unmet recovery needs and the capacity to carry out a disaster recovery program. HUD notifies eligible governments, which must then develop and submit an Action Plan for Disaster Recovery, describing the needs, strategies, and projected uses of the funds, before receiving CDBG Disaster Recovery grants.

CDBG Disaster Recovery funds may be used for recovery efforts involving housing, economic development, infrastructure and prevention of further damage to affected areas, provided such use does not duplicate funding available from the Federal Emergency Management Agency, the Small Business Administration, and the US Army Corps of Engineers.

Congress has appropriated billions in disaster recovery CDBG grants in the last twenty years. The largest appropriation to date was the $16.5 billion to assist recovery following Hurricanes Katrina, Rita and Wilma in 2005; plus another $3 billion for Louisiana homeowner assistance. Hurricanes in 2007 prompted a $12.6 billion appropriation. Congress initially awarded $11.5 billion in CDBG funds to Mississippi and Louisiana recovery plans as states affected by Katrina and Rita through the Department of Defense Appropriations Act of 2006, Pub. L. No. 109-148, 119 Stat. 2680, 2779–80 (2005). That Appropriations Act precluded any single state from receiving more than 54% of its overall allocation. *See Allocations and Common Applications and Reporting Waivers Granted to and Alternative Requirements for CDBG Disaster Recovery Guarantees*, 71 Fed. Reg. 7666 (Feb. 13, 2006). Louisiana officials requested an additional $4.2 billion in CDBG funds to fully fund its housing assistance plan. In June 2006, Congress and President Bush agreed to provide the additional requested funds. New York City recovery post-September 11 was aided by over $3 billion in 2001 and 2002. Repeated flooding in the Midwest necessitated grants in 1993, 1997, and 2008 of $450 million, $500 million, and $300 million, respectively. Wildfires, earthquakes and mudslides have also prompted disaster grants.

Formally at least, CDBG Disaster Recovery grants are primarily to benefit low-income residents in and around communities that have experienced a natural disaster. Generally, grantees must use at least half of Disaster Recovery funds for activities that principally benefit low- and moderate-income persons. These can be either activities in which all or the majority of people who benefit have low or moderate incomes or activities that benefit an area or service group in which at least 51 percent of the populous are of low- and moderate-income.

Although CDBG requires that at least 70% of its funding be used for the benefit of low- and moderate-income persons, following Katrina the U.S. Congress authorized a general waiver of the CDBG's low- to moderate-income requirement. The result was to trim the mandatory minimum proportion of funding to be spent on low- to moderate-income people for all combined disaster recovery programs back down to 50%. 42 U.S.C. §§ 5301(c); 5304(b)(3)(A); *Allocations and Waivers Granted to and Alternative Requirements for CDBG Disaster Recovery Grantees*, 71 Fed. Reg. 7666-67 (Feb. 13, 2006).

Furthermore, the policy premise that informed the shift to the block grant model—that the government closest to the people is best able to respond to their needs—does not answer the persistent concern as to the equity or competence with which federal dollars are distributed at the local level. Several criticisms of state government failures in implementing Louisiana's Road Home program, which used CDBG funds to assist homeowners to rebuild after Hurricane Katrina, are marshaled in the following excerpt. Congress also held oversight hearings. *See Emergency CDBG Funds in the Gulf States: Uses, Challenges, and Lessons for the Future: Hearing Before the Subcomm. on Housing and Community Opportunity of the House Comm. on Fin. Servs.*, 110th Cong. 11, 68 (2008).

Davida Finger, Stranded and Squandered: Lost on the Road Home

7 Seattle Journal for Social Justice 59 (2008)

Louisiana's Privatization of Road Home

With statutory authority to contract with private parties, the State contracted with an ICF International subsidiary, ICF EMS, to manage the Road Home program in June 2006. The contract, initially valued at $756 million, had a stated term of three years.

Louisiana's selection of ICF to administer Road Home was controversial. Because ICF had an existing contract with OCD that included drafting the Road Home implementation plans, the Louisiana Board of Ethics stated that ICF should be disqualified from bidding on the Road Home contract. However, the Board of Ethics ultimately accepted ICF's position that ICF had sufficiently removed itself from discussion about solicitations for offers and concluded that ICF was eligible for the Road Home contract as long as it terminated its previous contract with OCD.

Prior to receiving the Road Home contract, ICF recognized the intricacies of the program, the importance of customer service, and the negative publicity it might face from failing. ICF identified many "performance and management risks" of the Road Home contract: "difficult deadlines;" "intense public scrutiny;" and "ensuring that the applications ... are processed and funds are disbursed in a timely fashion." But the risk ICF was most concerned about was "the adverse publicity associated with complaints from homeowners" because these complaints were likely to harm its reputation.

Even with this apparent understanding, ICF has experienced adverse publicity and complaints about its performance. In fact, ICF's own concerns proved to be accurate predictors of its large-scale failures. An Associated Press article about Road Home explained these broad failures: "ICF now stands accused of inflating its closing figures by deliberately using red tape, confusion and delays to get applicants to settle for low grant amounts."

One possible explanation for this systemic failure might be that the Road Home contract was of a much larger scope than any project ICF had ever undertaken, and it simply could not effectively handle the contract. Road Home accounted for 35 percent of ICF's 2006 revenue and 63 percent of its 2007 revenue. In 2005 and 2006, before Road Home's inception, no single contract accounted for more than 2 percent of ICF's total revenue. In 2007, no other single contract accounted for more than 1 percent.

Still, ICF increased profits after the Road Home contract award. Three months after winning the Road Home contract, ICF announced that it would sell its stock publicly, its first public offering in its thirty-seven years of existence. ICF's annual revenue increased fourfold between 2005 and 2007, and gross profit nearly tripled. For 2007, ICF's chief executive was awarded a $1.5 million "performance bonus." Indeed, the Road Home contract reportedly "sweetened [ICF's] initial public stock offering and helped it buy four other companies" with ICF now reaching into government contracting sectors such as national defense and the environment.

ICF's unsatisfactory implementation of Road Home has generated ample negative publicity. In December 2006, the Louisiana legislature called for an investigation of ICF's failures and unanimously expressed dissatisfaction with ICF, pointing to errors in "pre-storm property values, damage estimates, deductions for insurance proceeds, deductions for FEMA payments, and other numbers and calculations." In strongly worded resolutions, both the Louisiana House of Representatives and Senate called for ICF to be fired. Overall, ICF's dismal performance in implementing Road Home has been acknowledged by community organizations, mass media, think tanks, and government accountability organizations.

In December 2007, just prior to leaving office and despite continuing problems with ICF's performance, Governor Blanco increased the size of ICF's contract from $756 million to $912 million. This increase was made without disclosure to the legislature or the public. Thus, the State actually rewarded ICF when only one year prior the Legislature had wanted to fire ICF for broad programmatic failures. Just days before this turn of events, Governor Blanco's administration reported that it would not continue funding legal services intended to assist low-income homeowners move through Road Home application hurdles in order to receive their grants.

The LRA, under the new administration of Governor Bobby Jindal, called for an investigation. With ICF "widely questioned over bureaucratic delays and failures," Senator Mary Landrieu would later comment, "I remain concerned about the slow pace of grant awards and closings and question the contract award amount granted to ICF, especially in light of possible funding shortfalls in the Road Home. It is particularly disturbing that at the same time, ICF's executives were being rewarded with outrageous bonuses."

Months later, in July 2008, the State fined ICF $1 million for its failure to meet performance targets. This fine represents less than 1 percent of the $156 million increase that ICF received, an amount which even ICF's chief financial officer, Alan Stewart, referred to as "fairly nominal." Indeed, the "penalties in ICF's contract are too mild to be a real incentive for continued improvement." Most importantly for homeowners, the penalties imposed on ICF do not seem to have incentivized improvements. Problems with Road Home have persisted. A 2008 *Times-Picayune* opinion column noted that Road Home's failures have become so prevalent that only a "particularly egregious error [will] attract attention."

Notes and Questions

1. *Local Government Priority-Setting vs. Federal Control, Reprised.* At the end of 2009, as much as $1 billion of federal recovery funds earmarked for Louisiana remained unspent. Critics argue that is a consequence of the program priorities which denied equitable access by low- and moderate-income homeowners and renters, see, e.g. KALIMA ROSE, ANNIE CLARK & DOMINIQUE DUVAL-DIOP, POLICYLINK, A LONG WAY HOME: THE STATE OF HOUSING RECOVERY IN LOUISIANA 47 (2008), *available at* http://www.policylink.org/threeyearslater/equityatlas.pdf. as well as numerous technical program requirements. *See, e.g.* RICK EDEN & PATRICIA BOREN, RAND GULF STATE POLICY INSTITUTE, RAND CORPORATION, TIMELY ASSISTANCE: EVALUATING THE SPEED OF ROAD HOME GRANTMAKING 68 (2008), *available at* http://www.rand.org/pubs/documented_briefings/2008/RAND_DB557.pdf. Officials of the city of New Or-

leans sought to have the funds reallocated to it for the purposes of blight removal and infrastructure repair. *Federal Katrina Recovery Money Urged to Tackle N.O. Blight,* TIMES-PICAYUNE, Nov. 12, 2009.

2. CDBG funding was one of several sources of federal monies identified for reconstructing New Orleans, specifically for the acquisition of heavily flooded and damaged houses, demolition and site remediation, and repairing public transit. *See* BRING NEW ORLEANS BACK COMMISSION, URBAN PLANNING COMMITTEE, ACTION PLAN FOR NEW ORLEANS, WHAT WILL IT COST?, FINAL REPORT (Jan. 11, 2006).

3. There is political opposition to the use of eminent domain for private development, as we explore in Section C *supra*. Shortly after Hurricane Katrina, a member of Congress warned against its use to assemble land for new development in the low-lying and largely poor, minority neighborhoods of New Orleans. "We have to watch the redevelopment of New Orleans for a lot of reasons, and one of them is to make sure that the shadow government of the rich and powerful does not end up abusing eminent domain to take property that belongs to poor people in order to get them out of the city," said Congresswoman Maxine Waters. Carolyn Lochhead, *Lawmaker Cautions Against Eminent Domain in Rebuilding,* S.F. CHRON., Sept. 21, 2005.

4. If eminent domain is not used, how can the government assemble the parcels of land needed to accomplish redevelopment?

A Note on HUD's Statutory Supervisory Duties

In May 2009, two organizations and four low-income residents of Mississippi's Gulf Coast who were displaced from and suffered severe damage to their homes as a result of Hurricane Katrina, sued to challenge HUD's acceptance of a plan by the state of Mississippi to spend up to $570 million in CDBG disaster relief funds appropriated by Congress. Seeking declaratory and injunctive relief, plaintiffs characterized the state's proposed use as a diversion from critical housing needs that prompted Congress' action to spend them instead to finance the expansion and redevelopment of a commercial port in Gulfport (the "Port Project"). *Mississippi State Conference NAACP v. U.S. Dep't. HUD*, 677 F. Supp. 2d 311 (D.D.C. 2010). The suit turned on the meaning of HUD's duties under the CDBG statute to hold states to their certifications. To what extent is HUD's duty one of substantive review of state plans for the expenditure of the funds?

Plaintiffs' argument relied upon the statutory framework of HUD's oversight. HUD's regulations require that a "certification" must be an assertion "based on supporting evidence." 24 C.F.R. § 91.5. The regulations provide that HUD "will review" the "consolidated plan" in which the required certifications must appear, 24 C.F.R. § 91.500(a), and give HUD authority to "inspect" the evidence on which the certifications must be based. *See* 24 C.F.R. § 91.5. If there is evidence "that tends to challenge in a substantial manner the State's certification of future performance," HUD may determine that the certification is *not* "satisfactory to the Secretary." *See* 24 C.F.R. § 570.485(c). If HUD determines that a certification is not satisfactory, "the State may be required to submit further assurances as the Secretary may deem warranted or necessary to find the grantee's certification satisfactory." *Id.* HUD may "disapprove" any plan (or portion of a plan) that is substantially incomplete, 24 C.F.R. § 91.500(b), or that contains a certification that is not "satisfactory to the Secretary" within the meaning of 24 C.F.R. § 570.485(c). HUD is also authorized by 24 C.F.R. § 91.500(b) to disapprove a grantee's plan "if it is inconsistent with the purposes of the Cranston-Gonzalez National Affordable Housing Act, 42 U.S.C. § 12703."

With respect to the low-moderate income benefit requirement, as noted, the Department of Defense Appropriations Act of 2006, Pub. L. No. 109-148, 119 Stat. 2680, 2779–80 (2005), gave the agency more flexibility than 42 U.S.C. § 5321 would have: it said (a) that HUD could *generally* modify the requirement by requiring grantees to use their grants so that at least 50% of the money (rather than 70%) funded activities for the benefit of LMI persons, and (b) that HUD could in *specific* cases waive the LMI benefit requirement entirely, but only upon "a finding of compelling need." *Id.* While Congress said that HUD "shall waive, or specify alternative requirements for," any other statutory or regulatory requirement associated with the CDBG program, HUD could do so only upon (1) a request by the state that the waiver is required, (2) a finding by HUD that the waiver would not be inconsistent with the CDBG statute's overall purposes, and (3) advance publication of the waiver in the Federal Register. *Id.*

On January 8, 2010, the District Court granted HUD's motion to dismiss for lack of standing, ruling that the plaintiffs' claim of injury is not of injury to themselves, but rather, that Mississippi has not addressed "the unmet housing needs of Hurricane Katrina's poorest and neediest victims." *Mississippi State Conference NAACP v. U.S. Dep't. HUD*, 677 F. Supp. 2d 311 (D.D.C. 2010)."

Plaintiffs' principled objection to the diversion of $570 million to a Port Expansion Project when post-Katrina housing needs in Mississippi are still unmet may indeed be well-founded as a policy matter. Their lack of standing, however, deprives the court of subject matter jurisdiction." *Id.*

Notes and Questions

1. Where should plaintiffs take their important policy dispute if it cannot be heard in court?

2. Developing a governance structure to make sound rebuilding decisions is a challenge, both because of the necessity for federal, state and local coordination, and because so many of the affected residents were not currently residing in their Gulf Coast communities when critical decisions were being made. Can displaced residents have a meaningful role? International human rights law already offers a standard. The United Nations Guiding Principles on Internal Displacement, introduced into the United Nations in 1998, recognizes a right of internally displaced residents to return to their neighborhoods and contribute to the rebuilding process. "Internally displaced persons" are those who have been "forced or obliged to flee or to leave their homes or places of habitual residence" as a result of or to avoid conflict or "natural or human-made disasters" and who remain within their own country. UN Doc. E/CN.4/1998/53.Add.2 (1998). An illustrative application of these principles is offered by Charles Martel, *Bring it On Home: A Gulf Coast Marshall Plan Based on International Human Rights Standards,* 32 Vt. L. Rev. 57 (2007).

3. Within our federal system of governance, municipal authorities present the most immediate interface between a government and its citizens. What if local governments are overwhelmed by facing an emergency, or a long and daunting recovery? Legal authority to respond to emergencies is governed by the Stafford Act, which allocates the divided authority of federal and state governments and localities into a power-sharing arrangement that is intentional under long-standing principles of federalism. Federal power is constrained in the event of disasters so as to supplement but not to usurp state powers, which unless expressly granted are reserved to the States by the Tenth Amendment. The Stafford Act, 42 U.S.C. 5170 et seq. Natural disasters are events that, essentially by definition, are

beyond the capability of local governments. Indeed, following the terrorist attacks of September 11, 2001, the National Response Plan process was augmented by the addition of the catastrophic incident annex (NRP-CIA) so that the nation has a "push" system, in which federal authorities may take preventative and responsive measures under limited circumstances. This is in addition to the purely reactive "pull" system of the Stafford Act under which states must first request the President to make emergency or disaster declarations. U.S House of Representatives, A Failure of Initiative, Final Report of the Select Bipartisan Committee to Investigate the Preparation for and Response to Hurricane Katrina 131–132 (2006).

For a recent study revealing the comparatively limited capacity of county governments to provide the neighborhood habitability and political voice needed by millions of low-income households, see Michelle Wilde Anderson, *Cities Inside Out: Race, Poverty and Exclusion at the Urban Fringe*, 55 UCLA L. Rev. 1095 (2008).

4. Do the claims of the plaintiffs in *Mississippi NAACP v. HUD*, *supra*, gain any more force as denials of equal protection in delivery of municipal services for the preparation before and evacuation after the storm? As a form of exclusionary zoning? For commentary on these and related points, consider: Josephine Ross, *Still in Limbo: The Continuing Failed Response to Katrina*, 51 How. L. J. 565 (2008) (recounting a dismal degree of assistance to residents of a FEMA trailer camp by March 2007); Christine A. Klein & Sandra B. Zellmer, *Mississippi River Stories: Lessons from a Century of Unnatural Disasters*, 60 SMU L. Rev. 1471 (2007); (arguing that large-scale flood-plain developers are allowed to enjoy "double-takes" of taxpayer-funded subsidies, first in the form of flood-control levees and then as Fifth Amendment takings compensation after disaster strikes, whereas ordinary citizens do not enjoy parallel recovery aid). *See also* Michael Greenberger, *Preparing Vulnerable Populations for a Disaster: Inner-City Emergency Preparedness—Who Should Take The Lead?*, 10 DePaul J Health Care L. 251 (2007); Jonathan P. Hooks & Trisha B. Miller, *The Continuing Storm: How Disaster Recovery Excludes Those Most in Need*, 43 Cal. W. L. Rev. 21 (2006); Oliver A. Houck, Hurricane Katrina Symposium: *Reshaping the Legal Landscape of the Gulf, Retaking The Exam: How Environmental Law Failed New Orleans and the Gulf Coast South and How it Might Yet Succeed*, 81 Tul. L. Rev. 1059 (2007); Derrick Johnson, *The Accountability Gap: Unanswered Questions Two Years Later*, 16-Sum J. Affordable Housing Community Dev. L. 406 (2007).

5. In New Orleans, HUD announced in June 2006 that 5100 apartments in four major developments of public housing in New Orleans would be demolished, and many fewer apartments would be built by private developers. The demolition and private development would be financed by federal funds and federal tax breaks allocated by Congress to help Katrina victims. Roughly $80 million in Community Development Block Grant ("CDBG") funds were designated for private developers. William P. Quigley, *Obstacle to Opportunity: Housing That Working And Poor People Can Afford In New Orleans Since Katrina*, 42 Wake Forest L. Rev. 393, 404 (2007). A subsequent class action lawsuit sought to re-open 5000 public housing units closed since Katrina, alleging violations of the Fair Housing Act and due process. The district court in Louisiana held that claims under the Fair Housing Act could be enforced under 42 U.S.C. § 1983. However, the court held that there was no private right of action to enforce claims under the U.S. Housing Act and found that plaintiffs did not submit adequate evidence of discriminatory impact or intent. *Anderson v. Jackson*, No. CIV. A.06 3298, 2007 WL 458232 (E.D. La. Feb. 6, 2007), aff'd, 556 F.3d 351 (5th Cir. 2009). Plaintiffs alleged that since all of the residents of the developments were African-American, the decision to demolish necessarily had a discriminatory effect. The court determined that the appropriate legal standard is whether the agency decision

perpetuates segregation, and concluded that plaintiffs had not offered sufficient evidence to sustain a claim for disparate treatment or disparate impact under § 3604(a). The court granted summary judgment to the defendants on those discrimination claims, and also granted summary judgment on plaintiffs' equal protection claim. On appeal, the Fifth Circuit ruled that the section of United States Housing Act setting forth conditions for approval of application for demolition of federally-funded public housing did not create any private rights in public housing tenants to prevent demolition of public housing and affirmed, without discussion, the district court's denial of a preliminary injunction.

5. Federal Efforts to Mandate Local Strategic Plans

Under the original CDBG legislation (Section 104(c)) recipients had to submit to HUD an assessment of their lower-income housing needs and realistic annual goals. In 1981, the Reagan Administration eliminated the requirement for submission of a housing assistance plan (HAP). More recently, this has been superseded by the requirement that CDBG recipients have a current affordability strategy (CHAS), 42 U.S.C. § 5304. The CHAS requirement is now part of the requirement for a Consolidated Plan in which a CDBG recipient must identify its housing and community development needs and then identify a long-term strategy, including priorities to address them (Section 104[c]).

Over the history of the CDBG program, the most controversial aspect of this requirement was the original requirement of localities to identify lower-income persons "expected to reside" in the future. Several suburban communities resistant to the construction of low-income housing projects within their boundaries resisted complying with this when HAPs were still required. However, this did not lead to significant HUD intervention. Instead, exclusionary land use litigation often has been the only avenue to try to force such suburbs to permit the building of subsidized housing.

Notes and Questions

1. *Inconsistency data.* The failure to accurately identify existing housing needs and conditions presents a difficult issue of proof in litigation. Communities often lack the resources to compile meaningful data on existing housing conditions as published by the Census Bureau. The census no longer lists substandard dwellings, but instead is limited to compilations concerning overcrowding and the absence of plumbing facilities. To make matters worse, older cities and suburbs, aware of the nearly insurmountable problems of housing conditions, may be motivated to allocate CDBG funds to pet civic projects rather than make the mammoth commitment to housing preservation and rehabilitation that would be indicated by a realistic picture of housing needs in their CHAS and Consolidated Plan.

2. While the allocation of subsidies by HUD according to these requirements is salutary, it carries its own potentially adverse results when communities fail to seek subsidies aggressively. For example, a suburban community interested in avoiding its "fair share" of housing for low-income persons could underestimate need and thus assure that a diminished supply of subsidies will flow into the area. Consequently, those communities committed to the goals of HCDA, and in tune with the needs of the region's poor, will assume a disproportionate share of the lower-income housing burden, and thereby increase the potential for a concentration of such housing. For discussion of the impact of HAPs and successor requirements, see MARGERY AUSTIN TURNER ET AL., PLANNING TO MEET LOCAL

Housing Needs: The Role of HUD's Consolidated Planning Requirements in the 1990s 2–5 (2002) (a publication of the Urban Institute); Peter W. Salsich, Jr., *Toward a Policy of Heterogeneity: Overcoming a Long History of Socioeconomic Segregation in Housing*, 42 Wake Forest L. Rev. 459, 487–490 (2007).

3. What if a suburban community has a reasonable ConPlan, yet maintains exclusionary land-use controls that preclude the development of low-cost housing? These restrictions may take several forms, including exclusionary zoning through the use of large lot requirements or density limits, building restrictions in the form of minimum floor space, maximum limits on bedroom configurations and height limitations, and subdivision regulation in the form of setbacks or mandatory set-asides for such amenities as open space, parking, or public facilities. Other restrictive techniques include growth limitations linked to maximum annual starts, timed sequential growth programs, or regulation linking construction to the availability of supporting municipal services or schools. For discussion of exclusionary zoning, see Chapter 6.

In *Johnson v. County of Chester*, 413 F. Supp. 1299 (E.D. Pa. 1976), a challenge to the Williston Township community development grant, the court essentially found the dispute not to be ripe for review, preferring to allow HUD an opportunity to attain compliance with the standards of the Act. Note that the community was the site of the lawsuit which resulted in the Supreme Court of Pennsylvania's adopting its progressive approach condemning exclusionary zoning. *Township of Williston v. Chesterdale Farms, Inc.*, 341 A.2d 466 (Pa. 1975). *See also Surrick v. Zoning Hearing Bd.*, 382 A.2d 105 (Pa. 1977). For a general review of litigation issues in community development, see James A. Kushner, Fair Housing ch. 6, 8 (2d ed. 1995 & Supp. 2000); Otto J. Hetzel, *Remediation Techniques For Racial Housing Discrimination—An Introduction to the Symposium*, 51 Wayne L. Rev. 1461 (2005); Elizabeth K. Julian, *Fair Housing and Community Development: Time To Come Together*, 41 Ind. L. Rev. 555 (2008).

3. There was another side to the HAP requirements in that communities may attempt to use the requirements to impede the development of low-cost housing. HUD Section 8 project approval was upheld over city claims of HAP inconsistency in *City of Loveland v. Pierce*, 564 F. Supp. 76 (S.D. Ohio 1983) (HUD enjoys broad discretion). In *City of Lebanon v. HUD*, 422 F. Supp. 803 (M.D. Pa. 1976), the town attempted to stop a project for the elderly, alleging inconsistency with the HAP. However, the court upheld HUD's review of the project, which indicated that this was the only suitable site. Finding social need on the side of no relief, the court permitted the project to go ahead. Another version of the same story is found in *Rental Housing Association of Greater Lynn, Inc. v. Hills*, 548 F.2d 358 (1st Cir. 1977). A landlord organization attacked the plan to rehabilitate a factory into an elderly housing project, arguing inconsistency with the HAP and an already adequate supply of low- and moderate-income housing. In fascinating contrast to the Second Circuit in *City of Hartford v. Towns of Glastonbury*, 561 F.2d 1032 (2d Cir. 1977), *cert. denied*, 434 U.S. 1034 (1978) (denying city of Hartford standing to challenge an allegedly inadequate "expected to reside" figures submitted by suburban jurisdictions), the First Circuit, without reaching the merits, upheld the standing of the landlord organization. *Payne v. HUD*, 512 F. Supp. 1113 (S.D. Ohio 1982) (standing to challenge failure to develop subsidized housing but no relief as committed to HUD discretion); *Lower Moreland Homeowner's Ass'n v. HUD*, 479 F. Supp. 866 (E.D. Pa. 1979).

4. Title III of the Housing and Economic Recovery Act of 2008 (HERA), Pub. L. No. 110-289, 122 Stat. 2654 (2008), provided $4 billion to help state and local governments acquire and redevelop foreclosed properties. Administered in conjunction with the Community Development Block Grant Program (CDBG), the resulting Neighborhood Sta-

bilization Program (NSP1) allowed the Department of Housing and Urban Development to allocate federal assistance to states and local governments with high concentrations of foreclosed homes, subprime mortgage loans, and delinquent home mortgages. Under NSP1, non-profit entities could be a sub-recipient of federal assistance, but could not receive such funds directly. *See* www.hud.gov/nsp/. The American Recovery and Reinvestment Act of 2009 (ARRA), Pub. L. No. 111-5, 123 Stat. 115 included an additional $1 billion for NSP (NSP2), to tackle housing foreclosure and abandonment, and to provide for capacity building and support for NSP grantees. These funds were to be awarded competitively and directly to non-profit entities, in addition to state and local governments. HUD established procedures to expedite the use of these funds, including to reallocate cancelled or unused funds. Priority is for projects that can be awarded within 120 days from the date that the funds are made available to the recipients. To receive CDBG-R funding, each CDBG grantee must substantially amend its FY 2008 annual action plan.

6. Administrative Review

It should be clear from the foregoing that the commitment and aggressiveness of HUD in policing HCDA grantees for compliance with statutory directives is pivotal to HCDA enforcement, especially as it relates to funding priority for projects aiding low- and moderate-income households. While they assumed a "hands off" attitude, the Carter administration tightened up considerably. Grants were conditioned or denied in the face of noncompliance or a history of program defects, such as the failure to relocate displacees of prior programs or to take action in expanding the low-income housing supply. Nevertheless, a report by GAO concluded that HUD's CDBG monitoring practices were meaningless. General Accounting Office, *Report on the Management and Evaluation of the Community Development Block Grant Program Need to Be Strengthened,* CED-78-160 (Aug. 30, 1978). The Reagan and Bush I administrations were somewhere in between, perhaps motivated by fiscal concerns as much as program effectiveness.

HUD has considerable power to ensure compliance, for example, to condition or deny grants altogether to recipient jurisdictions with a history of program defects or noncompliance. HUD lacks the machinery to scrutinize every recipient's plan for its design and effects and so the next levels of inquiry are the level of response to citizen complaints and post-application monitoring. It must be recognized that HUD lacks the machinery to scrutinize every recipient's plan for its design and effects and so the next levels of inquiry are the level of response to citizen complaints and post-application monitoring.

To accomplish its CDBG mission, as well as HUD's significant other functions, HUD necessarily relies on the performance and integrity of thousands of others—mortgage lenders, contractors, property owners, public housing agencies, communities—to administer its programs. Strong oversight and management are critical to ensure that HUD's reliance on these third parties results in the effective stewardship of federal funds to achieve the federal programs' goals and objectives.

In the late 1980s, various management deficiencies led to a number of widely publicized instances of waste, fraud, abuse, and mismanagement at HUD. In 1994, the GAO designated all of HUD's major program areas as high risk because of department-wide deficiencies that undermined the integrity and accountability of HUD's programs. These deficiencies included weak systems for necessary data and management processes; poorly integrated, ineffective, and generally unreliable information and financial management systems; and ill-defined responsibilities and authorities between HUD headquarters and field offices, including a "fundamental lack of management accountability and responsibility." GAO, *Determining Performance and Accountability Challenges and High Risk* 6 (Nov. 2001) (GAO-01-159SP). HUD shed the 'high risk' label after implementing significant in-house reforms. *Id.* at 8.

In 2005, the Office of Management and Budget determined that the CDBG program was unable to demonstrate results at the national level. OMB, *Department of Housing and Urban Development PART Assessments* (Feb. 2005). OMB uses its Program Assessment Rating Tool (PART) to assess and improve program performance across the federal government. It looks at all factors that affect and reflect program performance including program purpose and design; performance measurement, evaluations, and strategic planning; program management; and program results. In response to OMB's analysis, HUD developed a new performance measurement system for the CDBG program, and in March 2006, published performance measures developed with a working group comprised of community development organizations. HUD's new outcome performance measurement system tracks outcome indicators that include the number of persons assisted by a public service activity, the number of housing units rehabilitated, and number and types of jobs created.

The statute, in Section 111, establishes an administrative procedure to deal with violations. This process can result in the loss of funds. In *City of Kansas City v. Department of Housing and Urban Development*, 923 F. 2d 188 (D.C. Cir. 1991), the court held HUD must provide CDBG entitlement cities with reasonable notice and opportunity for a hearing before conditioning, reducing, or terminating thier current grants as a sanction for past noncompliance. HUD has tried to condition future grants under Section 104(a) without providing an administrative hearing. Now, before taking any action to condition, reduce, or terminate grants, HUD follows Section 111 hearing procedures. The threat of having to provide a hearing has resulted in HUD negotiating with the recipient over specific restrictions.

The HCDA requires CDBG recipients to file annual performance reports. The review of these reports, along with audits by the HUD Inspector General, provide HUD with information on local performance and compliance with CDBG program objectives and the Consolidated Plan. These documents may also be useful to citizen groups challenging local programs. A combination of litigation and administrative enforcement might bring about greater compliance than has been achieved under prior programs.

7. Program Assurances and Responsibilities

Over the years, Congress has enacted a number of statutory requirements generally applicable to federal assistance programs. These include compliance with the federal civil rights acts and with the area-wide agency process for reviewing federal assistance applications. These requirements were discussed briefly in Chapter 2, Section B, *supra*.

The HCDA makes a number of these federal statutory requirements applicable to the community development program. To satisfy the National Environmental Policy Act (NEPA), an environmental review must be carried out under Section 104(f). An assurance that the community development program will be administered in conformity with federal civil rights legislation is required by Section 104(b)(2). The HCDA also requires an assurance that the community has provided a citizen participation program. § 104(a)(2). The community development program applicant may provide HUD with a "certification" that it has met the two requirements. § 104(b). This section reviews these program assurances and responsibilities.

a. Citizen Participation

Citizen participation in community development has had an erratic evolution. Beginning with early requirements for resident consultation in the urban renewal program, citizen participation has become an integral part of local community development efforts. The philosophy is that local residents should have a voice in the future of their neighborhoods, and that a partnership between local governments and their citizens will help guarantee program success.

Citizen participation has varied from consultation to the extensive citizen role in planning and program control in the War on Poverty and Model Cities programs. The War on Poverty was a collection of social programs initiated primarily in President Johnson's administration and intended to reduce poverty in this country. In some cities, citizen participation became advocacy planning. Each side generated its plan and proposal, and in many cases a citizen veto produced significant concessions. HCDA retains a role for citizens, though it is significantly less pronounced than in these earlier programs.

Participation in community development began with the modest commitment in the now repealed urban renewal program. There were essentially two procedures by which residents of a renewal area might express their views on a particular urban renewal program. The federal law contained a public hearing requirement, but residents of urban renewal project areas, in the early days, had rather mixed success at seeking court relief, or were denied effective relief. *See Gart v. Cole*, 263 F.2d 244 (2d Cir. 1959), *cert. denied*, 359 U.S. 978 (1959). Plaintiffs refused to be deterred. In two cases, which fairly may be described as "landmarks," they had a greater degree of success. *See Norwalk CORE v. Norwalk Redev. Agency*, 395 F.2d 920 (2d Cir. 1968); *Powelton Civic Home Hous. Ass'n v. HUD*, 284 F. Supp. 809 (E.D. Pa. 1968).

Responding to pressures from representatives of residents, poor and minority groups, HUD acted to remedy this deficiency by requiring the establishment of Project Area Committees (PACs) under the urban renewal program. The renewal agency was required to work closely with the PAC to ensure that project residents participated in the formulation and execution of plans for the renewal of the area. HUD required that the PAC have "clear and direct access to decision-making in all stages of the urban renewal process." PAC members had to have access to relevant decision-makers at appropriate points in the decision-making process so that the PAC's views could be presented before, not after, decisions were made.

The renewal agency was required to furnish the PAC with "sufficient information about the project" to enable the PAC members "to participate knowledgeably." It was also required to provide the PAC with necessary technical assistance, including administrative and secretarial staff, office space and equipment, and consulting assistants. Cost for such services could be recouped in the renewal grant.

Under the Model Cities program and the War on Poverty's Community Action program, communities experimented with processes that permitted even greater opportunities for citizen participation. These included the use of board membership quotas for citizens, community elections for governing bodies and the development of citizen vetoes over activities and policy decisions. As we examine the limited provisions for citizen participation under HCDA, it can be seen that the pendulum has swung away from the enthusiasm for participation of the 1960s. Furthermore, Congress would hardly have expanded flexibility for local control and local responsibility if it simply delegated its previous central control to community groups. The resulting scheme has allowed HCDA grant recipients to ignore citizen concern and input. The city-wide eligibility for HCDA funds also allows recipients to identify citizen input as multifaceted and often inconsistent as geographic neighborhoods compete for priority consideration. This is in stark contrast to the previous situation under the renewal programs, where poor neighborhoods could often identify common concerns and priorities and were the beneficiaries of a greater targeting of funds.

The limited requirements for hearings and consultation in the HCDA does little to encourage even the manipulation or co-opting of citizens that characterized much citizen participation under the predecessor programs. *See* National Urban League, Toward Effective Citizen Participation in Urban Renewal (1974). The HCDA sets out the citizen participation requirements in extremely general terms. The jurisdiction must provide information regarding proposed and possible activities, hold at least one public hearing, and give notice of, with opportunity to respond to, any program change. § 104(a)(2). Note also that neighborhood citizens' groups may be funded to carry out eligible community development activities under Section 105(a)(15).

For judicial review of similar requirements in the UDAG program, see the *DeRosa* case, *supra.* But note that the 1987 amendments strengthened the citizen participation requirements in the HCDA by requiring a citizen participation plan. *See* § 104(a)(3). This is part of the Consolidated Plan process.

Notes and Questions

1. For the general literature on citizen participation, see Alan A. Altshuler, Community Control (1970); Citizen Participation in Public Decision Making (Jack DeSario & Stuart Langton eds. 1987); Daniel Patrick Moynihan, Maximum Feasible Misunderstanding (1969); Ruth E. South, Citizen Action and the Neighborhood (CPL Bib. No. 188, 1987); Michael R. Williams, Neighborhood Organizations: Seeds of a New Urban Life (1985); Shery R. Arnstein, *A Ladder of Citizen Participation,* 35 J. Am. Inst. Plan. 216 (1969).

2. One of the more significant federal initiatives toward coordinated planning is contained in Section 204 of the Demonstration Cities and Metropolitan Development Act, 42 U.S.C. § 3302, later expanded by Title IV of the Intergovernmental Cooperation Act of 1968, 42 U.S.C. § 4201. Section 401(c) of the Intergovernmental Cooperation Act states that, to the "maximum extent possible, consistent with national objectives, all federal aid for development purposes shall be consistent with and further the objectives of state, regional and local planning." Pursuant to the President's rule-making authority under the law, the Office of Management and Budget promulgated what is referred to as OMB Circular A-95. This circular called for evaluation, review, and coordination of federally assisted projects. The circular, however, was repealed by President Reagan. Nevertheless, an alternative avenue for citizen input might be through the Intergovernmental Review of Federal Programs, Exec. Order No. 12,372, 3 C.F.R. 197 (1983), *reprinted in* 31 U.S.C. § 6506 (Supp. 1984) (state and local governments are to provide for the coordination and planning of federal grants; OMB Circular A-95 was authorized at 33 Fed. Reg. 16487 (Nov. 13, 1968)). HUD's regulations under the new order are published at 45 C.F.R. §§ 1233.1–1233.13. *See A-95 Replacement Rules Give States Broad Discretion in Reviewing HUD Programs,* 11 [Current Developments] Hous. & Dev. Rep. (BNA) 95 (1983).

3. *See also* William Ho, *Community Benefits Agreements: An Evolution in Public Benefits Negotiation Processes*, 17-WTR J. Affordable Housing & Community Dev. L. 7

(2008) (comparing the citizen participation mechanisms of federal community development policies and programs from Urban Renewal through Empowerment Zones); Audrey MacFarlane, *When Inclusion Leads to Exclusion: The Uncharted Terrain of Community Participation in Economic Development,* 66 Brook. L Rev. 861 (2001) (reviewing the public participation requirements and practices in the sequence of government urban redevelopment programs, and some of the resulting case law from 1949 to present).

b. Environmental Review

The National Environmental Policy Act (NEPA) created the requirement that "all proposals for ... major federal actions significantly affecting the human environment" be accompanied by a statement of the environmental impacts of a proposal and its alternatives. 42 U.S.C. § 4332. This statement is known as an environmental impact statement (EIS). Its purpose is to assure that decision makers are fully informed of environmental considerations. The Supreme Court has indicated that NEPA does not elevate environmental concerns over other considerations relevant to federal agency decision making in government programs. *Strycker's Bay Community Council v. Karlen,* 444 U.S. 223 (1980). Neither may a court nor a federal agency apparently rely on an EIS to disapprove a project otherwise authorized under federal program legislation. The EIS still remains valuable as a full disclosure document indicating the environmental impact of a proposed governmental action.

Section 104(g) of HCDA authorizes the delegation of EIS preparation responsibility to local governments receiving grants, and the courts have extended this delegation to the UDAG program. For discussion of this provision, see Daniel R. Mandelker, NEPA Law and Litigation, § 7.8 (2d ed. 1992 & Supp. 2010).

HUD is neither required to independently review impact statements submitted by local governments on their projects nor to prepare its own impact statement. *Crosby v. Young,* 512 F. Supp. 1363 (E.D. Mich. 1981). HUD's responsibilities are satisfied once a local government has certified that it has carried out its NEPA responsibilities. HUD's review is procedural. It need not review the adequacy of a local government's impact statement. *Brandon v. Pierce,* 725 F.2d 555 (10th Cir. 1984).

Notes and Questions

1. HCDA is subject to NEPA, and while some litigation has surfaced, many questions remain unresolved. Exactly what should be included in a study of the impacts and alternatives to community development activities is a changing subject. Certainly growth-inducing projects, such as highways and transit, water and sewer lines, new parking, or commercial facilities, should be assessed in terms of metropolitan development impacts and impacts on the poor and minorities. Air pollution from increased auto dependency must also be considered. What about displacement induced by redevelopment?

Although the EIS need not be prepared where there are solely social and economic impacts, *Hanley v. Mitchell,* 460 F.2d 640 (2d Cir.), *cert. denied,* 409 U.S. 990 (1972), where there are physical environmental impacts, the EIS must also assess social and economic impacts. *Olmsted Citizens for Better Community v. United States,* 793 F.2d 201 (8th Cir. 1986).

2. Should an environmental impact statement be prepared for the annual HCDA program itself rather than for the specific projects identified? HUD's position on this issue

is negative, and one federal court accepted it. *Ulster County Community Action Comm. v. Koenig*, 402 F. Supp. 968 (S.D.N.Y. 1975). However, the undertaking of a comprehensive program for community development would seem to call for such an overall evaluation of alternative strategies. To resolve this question, as in the case of many others that arise under the HCDA, it is essential to keep in mind the congressional goals of both NEPA and the HCDA. Would an EIS on a block grant activity be consistent with the apparent concern about red tape and bureaucratic delay? Such policy debates are likely to determine the outcome of these fundamental conflicts.

3. There is a negative side to environmental statutes, especially as they relate to the housing needs of the poor. In one leading case, *Nucleus of Chicago Homeowners Ass'n v. Lynn*, 372 F. Supp. 147 (N.D. Ill. 1973), *aff'd*, 524 F.2d 225 (7th Cir. 1975), residents of a Chicago neighborhood challenged the failure to prepare an EIS for a scattered site public housing project. Plaintiffs argued that the social characteristics of the project tenants would have an adverse impact on neighborhood quality. The district court held that "people pollution" was not an environmental impact covered by NEPA. On appeal, the court of appeals avoided this issue but held that the scattered, low density character of the project prevented any adverse environmental effects.

4. NEPA applies in urban areas, so creative litigants have used the EIS requirement to attack the impact of community development and UDAG programs and projects on urban areas, including their impact on low-cost housing. For a sampling of this litigation, see *National Wildlife Fed'n v. Marsh*, 721 F.2d 767 (11th Cir. 1983) (HCDA-assisted lake development); *Vieux Carré Property Owners, Residents & Assocs., Inc. v. Pierce*, 719 F.2d 1272 (5th Cir. 1983) (commercial center); *Morris County Trust for Historic Preservation v. Pierce*, 714 F.2d 271 (3d Cir. 1983), *subsequent proceedings*, 730 F.2d 94 (3d Cir. 1984) (historic building demolition); *Meija v. HUD*, 688 F.2d 529 (7th Cir. 1982) (deference); *Dickeyville Ass'n v. HUD*, 636 F. Supp. 362 (D. Md. 1986) (local certification for NEPA compliance removes HUD responsibility).

5. More recently, policy makers, practitioners of community economic development, and environmental justice proponents have begun to identify convergences between these disciplines, with important implications for public policy. In the arena of public health, evidence suggests that disparities in health between whites and people-of-color are "increasingly linked to the physical and social environments that fall under the traditional domains of housing, transportation, streetscapes, and community or social capital." Jason Corburn, *Confronting the Challenges in Reconnecting Urban Planning and Public Health*, 94 Am. J. Pub. Health 541, 543 (2004). *See also* Cal. Air Res. Bd., Air Quality and Land Use Handbook: A Community Health Perspective 1–3 (2005), http://www.arb.ca.gov/ch/handbook.pdf; Nat'l Acad. of Pub. Admin., Addressing Environmental Justice Concerns: How Environmental Justice Relates to Land Use Planning and Zoning 25 (2003); Patricia Salkin, *Environmental Justice and Land Use Planning and Zoning*, 32 Real Est. L.J. 429 (2004). An illustration of such convergence in local policy and practice is detailed by Charles Lee, *Warren County's Legacy for the Quest to Eliminate Health Disparities*, 1 Golden Gate U. Envtl. L.J. 53 (2007).

c. Equal Opportunity

Community development has been plagued with civil rights violations since its inception. Projects can be administered in a discriminatory manner, and program activities can be designed to destroy minority communities through demolition and displacement. Negative and passive forms of discrimination exist in addition to these examples of affirmative discrimination. The community development agency can fail to address the community development needs of minorities or minority neighborhoods. An example is a community development application addressing only the need for downtown commercial redevelopment.

This form of passive discrimination is all the more dramatic if the community has never sought federal funds for rehabilitation, renewal, or code enforcement activities in spite of a great need for housing improvement, but has used urban renewal funds for commercial needs. Such a program would eventually result in a high degree of deterioration in the affected neighborhoods. The eventual solution being abandonment or strict code enforcement, followed by orders to vacate, possibly forcing an exodus of poor and minority residents from the community. For examples of this problem, compare *English v. Town of Huntington,* 448 F.2d 319 (2d Cir. 1971) (no cause of action for alleged discriminatory code enforcement causing minorities to be displaced) with *Garrett v. City of Hamtramck,* 503 F.2d 1236 (6th Cir. 1974) (extensive remedial order to combat proven discriminatory displacement and nonrelocation). For a description of a new life for Hamtramck's Black community (the small city of Hamtramck, right in the middle of Detroit) that fought a court order to help rebuild an African-American enclave destroyed by neglect thanks to 200 new homes, see http://weekendamerica.publicradio.org/display/web/2008/04/17/hamtramck/.

More difficult to identify, and in many ways more destructive in result, are the secondary effects of community development policy. If policies encourage patterns of suburban sprawl so that jobs are relocated from the central city and dispersed to the suburban areas of the region, there will be decreased access to job opportunities for minorities residing in the segregated central city. The deteriorated inner city tax base will no longer be able to support needed social and educational services, and a reduced population density will mean a decrease in available public transit facilities.

A full exploration of constitutional and statutory civil rights protection will be undertaken in Chapter 6. They are briefly discussed here because these impacts are inherent in community development, and planning to alleviate these adverse influences and impacts must be undertaken. In addition, HCDA contains express civil rights requirements which include compliance with applicable federal civil rights statutes and compliance with the Act's own nondiscrimination provisions. These provisions are the functional equivalent to Title VI of the 1964 Civil Rights Act which prohibits discrimination in federally assisted programs. 42 U.S.C. § 2000(d). *See Guardians Ass'n v. Civil Serv. Comm'n,* 463 U.S. 582 (1983) (effects test for injunctive relief, intent test for damages). *Cf. NAACP v. Pierce,* 624 F. Supp. 1083, 1084 (D. Mass. 1985) (intent required under community development nondiscrimination provisions), *vacated on other grounds sub nom. NAACP v. Secretary of HUD,* 817 F.2d 149 (1st Cir. 1987). Section 109(a) of HCDA provides that "[n]o person in the United States shall on the ground of race, color, national origin, or sex, be excluded from participation in, be denied the benefits of, or, be subjected to discrimination under any program or activity funded in whole or in part with funds made available under this title." The Act on its face provides for the applicability of the 1964 and 1968 (Title VIII-Fair Housing) Civil Rights Acts. § 104(b)(2).

Notes and Questions

1. Are the civil rights requirements of the applicable statutes and Section 109 sufficient to protect against potential violations? In what way could provisions on violations and remedy or enforcement be enhanced? Do these laws protect against practices which

have a discriminatory "impact" on minorities or solely against practices which are "intentional"?

2. Cities without fair housing and programs to provide integrated housing opportunities may lose community development grants. *City of Norwood v. Harris,* 683 F.2d 150 (6th Cir. 1982) *(per curiam)* (upheld HUD's reduction of block grant entitlement to zero for failure to comply with fair housing commitment citing jurisdiction in the first instance to be in the district court); *United States v. City of Parma,* 494 F. Supp. 1049 (N.D. Ohio), *aff'd,* 661 F.2d 562 (6th Cir. 1980), *cert. denied,* 456 U.S. 926 (1982) (refusal to apply for block grant entitlement after housing assistance plan found invalid in prior funding year). *But see Latinos Unidos de Chelsea en Accion v. HUD,* 799 F.2d 774 (1st Cir. 1986) (aid to elderly rather than families under UDAG grant not racial discrimination and no private right of action to enforce HCDA nondiscrimination provisions or HUD's Title VIII obligations); *Angell v. Town of Manchester,* (D. Conn. Oct. 14, 1981), 3 Eq. Opportunity Hous. (P-H) ¶ 15,398 (upholding a community's right to withdraw from the HUD block grant program following a critical plebiscite). For an earlier suggestion to the contrary, see *Angell v. Zinsser,* 473 F. Supp. 488 (D. Conn. 1979) (suburb ordered to develop low-cost housing after withdrawal found to be racially motivated). The later *Manchester* opinion failed to adhere to the finding of racial motivation; the court eschewed an intent test, yet ruled that race was not the dominant motive of the community.

3. A cause of action may also be stated for the failure of a community to apply for available grants-in-aid that would aid in lessening regional segregation and local racial isolation or exclusion. The failure to apply for available block grant funds may be part of a pattern and practice to exclude minorities. *United States v. City of Parma, supra; Avery v. City of Chicago,* 501 F. Supp. 1 (N.D. Ill. 1978) (terminated subsidies and displaced minorities to make way for luxury hotel; standing denied to residents not evicted, but the case was not submitted on a theory that the action would end integration). *But see Angell v. Town of Manchester, supra.*

4. *Employment requirements.* The Davis-Bacon Act, 40 U.S.C. § 276(a), requires payment of wages at the prevailing rate and is applicable to construction projects and rehabilitation where more than eight units are involved. *See Universities Research Ass'n v. Coutu,* 450 U.S. 754 (1981) (rejecting a private right of action under the Act necessitating administrative enforcement). *See* 24 C.F.R. § 570.603.

There is also a requirement that federally assisted contractors, in their employment practices, comply with Executive Order 11,246 regarding nondiscrimination and affirmative action under government contracts. Exec. Order No. 11,246, 3 C.F.R. 39 (1965), *reprinted in* 42 U.S.C. 2000e app. at 1232–36. *Northeast Constr. Co. v. Romney,* 485 F.2d 752 (D.C. Cir. 1973) (HUD contract bid denied for failure to submit minority hiring goals); *M.C. West, Inc. v. Lewis,* 522 F. Supp. 338 (M.D. Tenn. 1981) (upholding minority business enterprise program with goals for minority participation on federal highway project). *But see Latinos Unidos de Chelsea en Accion v. HUD, supra* (mere underrepresentation of minorities in job or contract positions insufficient where significant number employed). James E. Jones, *Twenty-One Years of Affirmative Action: The Maturation of the Administrative Enforcement Process Under the Executive Order 11,246 as Amended,* 59 Chi.-Kent L. Rev. 67 (1982).

HCDA is also subject to Section 3 of the Housing and Urban Development Act of 1968, 12 U.S.C. § 1701(u), entitled "Employment Opportunities for Businesses and Lower Income Persons in Connection with Assisted Projects." Section 3 requirements have been reviewed and have been found to require affirmative action by the recipient to assure employment opportunities for area residents. *Ramirez, Leal & Co. v. C.D.A.*, 549 F.2d 97 (9th Cir. 1976), *modified*, 549 F.2d 156 (9th Cir. 1977). In the *Ramirez* case, an apparent violation of the Act was found despite the fact that the bid submitted exceeded those of competitors by 80%. *See* G. Kellam Scott, *Business Opportunities Through Contract Preference Under Section 3 of the Housing and Urban Development Act of* 1968, 14 RUTGERS L.J. 741 (1983).

5. *Avoidance of program assurances.* Avoidance occurs if a recipient uses devices to avoid arduous or costly responsibility under the Act. The potential for avoidance is perhaps greater under NEPA and the Uniform Relocation Act (URA). This is due to the huge costs involved that must be assumed, for the most part, by the recipient, and the distaste that agencies have for such red tape. The most overt example of avoidance would occur if a recipient undertook a strict area-wide code enforcement program in a deteriorated housing area prior to submitting an application calling for acquisition and clearance in the same area. The effect would, in many cases, result in displacement that would not be assisted under the URA due to the absence of acquisition and federal assistance. At the application approval stage, only demolition and inexpensive land acquisition would remain as an impediment to development and land marketing, thus greatly reducing the costs of the activity as well as the time required for execution. Such attempts at avoidance have, unfortunately, already proceeded beyond the hypothetical stage.

Another avoidance mechanism may emerge when a recipient negotiates with a private developer interested in acquiring occupied land for development activities. The city might urge the developer to acquire the property on the open market without relocation act benefits, with the city promising to condemn certain parcels if the developer is unable to secure the purchase of the desired land. This practice allegedly occurred in San Diego to avoid California Relocation Assistance Law requirements that are modeled on the federal law. The California legislature responded with an amendment to the state relocation law to cover such tactics. CAL. GOV'T CODE §§7260–74. The amendment covers acquisition "by a public entity or by any person having an agreement with or acting on behalf of a public entity." *Id.* at §7260.

Such practices clearly constitute an evasion of the law, and courts are unlikely to permit the observance of form over substance. *See La Raza Unida v. Volpe*, 488 F.2d 559 (9th Cir. 1973), *cert. denied*, 417 U.S. 968 (1974) (potential for utilizing federal funds required compliance with federal highway requirements). *But see Goolsby v. Blumenthal*, 597 F.2d 934 (5th Cir.), *cert. denied*, 444 *U.S.* 970 (1979).

What is the potential impact of local performance under the community development block grant approach in the areas of relocation, citizen participation, and project selection as it relates to programs to improve housing for the poor and projects to aid poverty-stricken communities? How might community development strategies be structured so as to serve the housing and community development needs of low-and moderate-income persons? What other goals should redevelopment play in the process of metropolitan redistribution of the economic and employment base, residency patterns, educational opportunities, and racial and economic isolation? For a comprehensive treatment of civil rights in community development, see JAMES A. KUSHNER, FAIR HOUSING ch. 6 (2d ed. 1995 & Supp. 2000).

6. *The Civil Rights Context for the 21st Century: The Geography of Opportunity.* To what extent do these legal provisions that seek to assure equal opportunity in the context of specific programs, reach the underlying dilemma of community development? Recall that

this course book treats "community development" as the endeavor to enhance the well-being and quality of life of American communities. Consider the extent to which, for many Americans, one's life chances are determined largely by where they happen to live: the quality of public primary education, access to employment, technology, credit for one's business or home purchase, as well as the built environment and municipal services. *See generally* Sherryl Cashin, *Civil Rights in the New Decade: The Geography of Opportunity*, 31 Cumb. L. Rev. 467, 468 (2001); James E. Rosenbaum & Stefanie DeLuca, *What Kinds of Neighborhoods Change Lives? The Chicago* Gautreaux *Housing Program and Recent Mobility Programs*, 41 IND. L. REV. 653 (2008); Michael H. Schill & Susan M. Wachter, *The Spatial Bias of Federal Housing Law and Policy: Concentrated Poverty in Urban America*, 143 U. PA. L. REV. 1285 (1995).

D. Economic Development: The Turn to Policies to Incentivize Private Market Investments for Community Development Purposes

Economic development has long been an element and goal of community development and, with devolution of the federal role in housing, has become central to federal community development policy. As urban planning has evolved, economic development has become the watchword for municipally directed community development planning and projects.

Community development practices by low-income communities that emerged in the 1960s responded to the felt importance of involving local residents in the processes of revitalizing their communities. This movement expanded in the 1970s as deindustrialization intensified public efforts to quell poverty and deliver social-welfare enhancing services to poor families. For these community-based campaigns for development, the linkage to economic opportunity has always been at the heart of the matter. Many focused primarily on securing what the policy landscape denominates workforce development, business development, as well as attracting manufacturing jobs, commercial and retail services. Community based development organizations expanded their work to encompass the creation of affordable housing, as well as employment innovations such as microenterprises and worker-owned cooperatives, and services that local markets did not provide their constituencies, including affordable child care and health care, access to credit, community development banks and credit unions.

> The 1980s witnessed a strong backlash against the public entitlement programs of earlier years, and the administrations of Ronald Reagan and George H.W. Bush significantly cut back government sponsored antipoverty programs. The efficacy of federal spending on AFDC and other means-tested public assistance programs was questioned given increases from $7.8 billion in 1960 to $40.7 billion in 1976. Fueled by a neoconservative agenda, under the Reagan administration, welfare cutbacks were the main target. Some of these benefits were reduced or dramatically terminated when Reagan signed the Omnibus Budget Reconciliation Act of 1981 during an economic recession. The administration's program of supply-side economics provided tax cuts to corporations and upper-income individuals. Privatization and fiscal conservatism, hallmarks of the Reagan years, created greater income disparities. Many other benefits to the

> poor such as food stamps, Medicaid, and housing assistance were also cut. At the same time, the decade witnessed structural shifts to the economy, the exodus of high-paying manufacturing jobs from urban areas, low-wage worker insecurity, and the resulting "spatial concentration of joblessness and poverty."

Roger Clay & Susan Jones, *A Brief History of Community Economic Development*, 18-SPG J. AFFORDABLE HOUSING & COMMUNITY DEV. 257, 263 (2009).

The 1990s ushered in the demise of welfare, devolution from federal to state government, and a public policy emphasis on economic self-sufficiency. Together with the evident success of the Low Income Housing Tax Credit Program in directing private investment toward the production of affordable housing, with little direct government subsidy, the policy turn has been to rely on market forces. This has spurred new programs intended to aid community development objectives: empowerment zones, an array of tax incentives, and the federal New Markets Tax Credits program, designed to stimulate investments in low-income rural and urban communities for business development, employment stimulus, and commercial real estate redevelopment.

To the tax credit approach, community-based advocates promote complementary approaches to deliver for more households in poor communities, a measure of inclusive participation in the prosperity that such business-focused development policies are intended to produce. These have included local ordinances for living wages; sectoral employment intervention; and other strategies for asset accumulation and wealth-building strategies, including financial education, counseling, sweat equity and shared-equity forms of home ownership and enterprise development. An extensive body of research and knowledge-sharing has accumulated. References to much of this appear throughout this chapter.

The federal role in economic development has long been to provide the banking, trade, and securities regulation to assure long-term growth. The actual planning for industrial and commercial development has been left to state and local regulation. In the mid-Twentieth century, the most direct programs of the federal government on local growth have been the development of the federal highway program, federal housing subsidies, and grants for community development and other infrastructure. The federal government has also administered programs to encourage small business development, including enterprises for minorities and poor communities. Although these programs have been supplemental and supportive of local planning, their impact on the nation has been profound.

1. Access to Capital for Community Development

The limited availability of credit in impoverished communities might seem at first blush to be an unremarkable consequence of their residents' poverty. Credit insufficiency has come to be viewed in urban policy as in part a cause, rather than solely a consequence, of poverty. The availability of credit in low income areas is impeded by three distinct problems.

The first, persistent, problem is race discrimination. The Fair Housing Act of 1968 and the Equal Credit Opportunity Act of 1975 were enacted to combat the practices of banks and government agencies which had openly restricted residential lending in minority neighborhoods ("redlining"). Studies continue to find that people who reside in predominantly minority neighborhoods and minority persons, have unequal success in applying for and getting loans, compared to white people or residents of white neighborhoods, even when their personal economic circumstances are the same. There have been few major enforcement actions against lenders under the civil rights statutes. *See* William H. Simon, The Community Economic Development Movement 26 (2001).

William Simon suggests a second problem as well: the inherent difficulty of coordination of redevelopment investments. Lenders appreciate that real estate investments tend to be mutually reinforcing, thus each lender has a material incentive to lend where others are lending and to avoid areas shunned by others. Where there is no mechanism for insuring complementary investments, poor impressions of a neighborhood can become self-reinforcing.

A third dimension of credit inaccessibility is the lack of information attendant to social distance. People with capital to lend tend to be socially distant from low and moderate income people and the neighborhoods they live in, and that social distance may make it harder for the lenders to assess the creditworthiness of these applicants and the value of their collateral. Lenders can invest in research to enhance their credit decision-making yet may be reluctant to do so for fear that the lender will not recover its costs, because of the coordination problem: others can observe the results of the lender's efforts, and hence get the benefit of them without contributing to the cost. *Id.* at 27–28. *See also* Michael S. Barr, *Credit Where it Counts: The Community Reinvestment Act and its Critics*, 80 NYU L. Rev. 513, 563–578 (2005) (reviewing recent empirical evidence on the generally positive effects of the CRA on market failures and discrimination); Kathleen C. Engel & Patricia A. McCoy, *A Tale of Three Markets: The Law and Economics of Predatory Lending*, 80 Tex. L. Rev. 1255, 1280–81 (2002) (describing opportunities that information asymmetries provide for predatory lenders and brokers).

Three significant legislative initiatives take important steps to respond to these problems of credit scarcity in poor communities, by encouraging lending, coordination of investments, and redressing the severe asymmetries of information that impede identification of creditworthiness in such communities. These are the Community Reinvestment Act (CRA), enacted by Congress in 1977 and strengthened by new implementing regulations in 1995, and the Community Development Banking and Financial Institutions Act (CDFI) of 1994, and the New Market Tax Credits program created by Congress by passage of the Community Renewal Tax Relief Act of 2000.

The Community Reinvestment Act

The CRA imposes on banks a "continuing and affirmative obligation to help meet the credit needs of the local communities in which they are chartered," 12 U.S.C. § 2901(a)(3), including low- and moderate-income ("LMI") neighborhoods. Id. at § 2903(a)(1). The purpose of the CRA is twofold. First, Congress intended the CRA to end the banking practice known as redlining, by which banks would refuse to lend in certain neighborhoods, especially older and inner-city neighborhoods and neighborhoods whose residents were predominantly minority or low-income. Second, the CRA was to encourage banks to lend more in redlined neighborhoods.

The CRA requires of any bank that receives federal deposit insurance a "continuing and affirmative obligation to help meet the credit needs of the local communities in which [it is] chartered." 12 U.S.C. § 4701 *et seq.* The obligation applies to the "entire community, including low- and moderate-income neighborhoods, consistent with the safe and sound operation of such institution." Banks must define an "assessment area" in which they conduct their major activities, and which does not gerrymander out minority or low income communities. Ratings of banks for CRA compliance are based on three types of activity—lending, investment, and service activities within the area—with lending activities weighted twice as much as the other two. Banks are reviewed periodically and receive an overall numerical score and one of five ratings, ranging from "outstanding" to "substantial noncompliance."[5] The "service test" evaluates factors such as the accessibility of branches and ATMs in low and moderate income neighborhoods, and the provision of specialized services such as credit counseling or homebuyer education, to low and moderate income customers. The "investment test" measures the bank's equity investments in or grants to institutions focused on the needs of low and moderate income residents of its assessment area, such as credit unions, small business loan funds, and affordable housing developers.

Two aspects of the CRA structure are most notable. First, the CRA creates an explicit duty to "local communities" and "neighborhoods," understood in precisely the CED sense to mean primarily the residents of small, geographically-bounded areas. Second, the vague and indirect enforcement structure of the Act creates a vital role for community-based organizations. Community groups organized around economic development issues are, the major source of pressure on the regulators in the ratings process. These groups can and do intervene in regulatory application proceedings to raise CRA issues. They also use low CRA ratings to generate bad public relations for local banks, and can generate bad public relations for local banks that score poorly in the CRA ratings. *See* Simon, *supra* at 30; Richard D. Marsico, *Democratizing Capital: The History, Law and Reform of the Community Reinvestment Act*, 49 N.Y.L. Sch. L. Rev. 717 (2005). For discussion of the utility of the CRA as prompting settlements connected to regulatory applications for mergers or acquisitions in which consortia of groups agree not to oppose the application in return for community development commitments, see Richard D. Marsico, *The New Community Reinvestment Act Regulations: An Attempt at Implementing Performance-Based Standards*, 49 Consumer Fin. L.Q. Rep. 47, 49–50 (1995). Such settlements can involve promises to lend specific amounts or to make loans on specified terms in low and moderate income neighborhoods, to open or refrain from closing branches or ATMs, to make investments or contributions to economic development projects, or to provide support to community-based organizations.

Community Development Financial Institutions

In 1994, the Congress created the CDFI Fund, housed within the Treasury Department, established by the Riegle Community Development and Regulatory Improvement Act of 1994, Pub. L. No. 103-325, 107 Stat. 2369. These organizations have loaned and invested billions of dollars in our nation's most distressed communities and have attracted many conventional investors into underserved areas. For small businesses in particular, CDFIs provide critical funding because many traditional creditors view such loans as too risky or, sometimes, too small to be profitable. In 2009, there were more than 1000 CDFIs certified by the Treasury Department, with collective assets of $25 billion. The Treasury recently estimated that the fund attracts $15 in nonfederal investments for every dollar it invests in a CDFI. U.S. Dep't of the Treasury, Office of Performance Budgeting and Strategic Planning (2009) (*FY 2010 Budget in Brief*).

---

5. Factors considered in assessing a bank's community-reinvestment lending include: the ratio of loans made within the assessment area to deposits (the "loan-to-deposit ratio"), the percentage of loans in the assessment area (the "concentration ratio"), the percentage of census tracts within the assessment area in which loans were made (the "penetration ratio"), the percentage of loans made to low and moderate income borrowers and to borrowers within census tracts with low or moderate average incomes.

CDFIs come in various forms. They may be banks, credit unions, nondepository and revolving loan funds, or venture funds. Generally, CDFIs strive to provide affordable and appropriate financial services to people and communities who traditionally lack access to such services. Responding to local needs, CDFIs may offer financing for homeownership, rental housing, commercial real estate, health care, small businesses, microenterprises, charter schools, and child care facilities, among other purposes. CDFIs often also work with traditional lenders to attract private capital for community development.

As a complement to lending, CDFIs offer training and technical assistance to their customers, directly or through partnerships, thus increasing borrower capacity and mitigating loan risk. Successful CDFI borrowers often graduate to conventional financing as their needs grow, thereby attracting the participation of mainstream lenders while freeing up CDFI resources to plant new seeds in the community. *See* Paul Weech, *Observations on the Effects of the Financial Crisis and Economic Downturn on the Community Development Finance Sector* (May 2009) (Federal Reserve Bank of San Francisco, Working Paper Series 2009-5).

New Market Tax Credits

The statutory purpose of the NMTC program is to encourage investments in low-income communities by providing a tax incentive for community development lenders and the capital markets to invest in communities that historically have had limited or no access to capital. The Treasury Department's Community Development Financial Institution Fund (CDFI Fund) regulates the investments allowable as "qualified low-income community investments." *See* Treasury Department Regulations § 1.45D-1, 26 C.F.R. § 1.

The "new markets" tax credit was modeled on the low-income housing tax credit program, which funds more than half of all affordable housing units created each year in the U.S. The NMTC is a substantial 39% tax credit, claimed over six years and one day, for qualifying investments. For an investment to qualify for NMTCs, it must be made through a special purpose entity, a Community Development Entity (CDE), certified by the CDFI Fund, or through an existing Community Development Financial Institution. Qualified Low-Income Community Investments must be made in one of four forms: (1) a loan or equity investment in a qualified business, which is active in a low-income community; (2) equity investments in or loans to another CDE; (3) purchase from another CDE of loans it has made to a qualified business; (4) or providing financial services, such as counseling, to businesses or residents of a low-income community.

The community-serving character of a CDE is prescribed by Congress in the three-part test set forth in Internal Revenue Code (26 U.S.C.) § 45D(c). The CDE must have as its primary mission to serve, or at least provide investment capital for, low-income communities or persons; and it must have either a governing or advisory board that maintains accountability to low-income communities. Finally, the CDFI Fund must certify the entity as a qualifying CDE. Similarly, a Qualified Business is generally required to be located in and to have a substantial connection to a low-income community. "Low income community" is also defined by law, generally as a census tract in which the poverty rate is at least 20%, or alternatively, where the median income is 80% or less of the area median income. The entire United States has been mapped to show all qualifying census tracts, on the CDFI Fund website, www.cdfifund.gov. Through fiscal year 2008, CDEs reported making about $12 billion in NMTC investments to about 2,111 projects located in all 50 states, the District of Columbia, and Puerto Rico.

In 2010 the General Accountability Office recommended to Congress that the NMTC Program be simplified. It reported that qualifying investments have been made in all 50 states, and that low-income communities appear to benefit from the projects supported by the tax credits; nonetheless, "the complexity of NMTC transaction structures appears to make it more difficult for CDEs to execute smaller transactions and results in less equity ending up in low-income community businesses" than would be the case with more straightforward transactions. GAO, *New Markets Tax Credit: The Credit Helps Fund A Variety of Projects in Low-Income Communities, But Could Be Simplified, GAO-10-334* (Jan. 2010).

2. Empowerment Zones and Enterprise Communities

Enterprise zones first became a topic in US urban policy during the Reagan administration. Conservatives promoted federal legislation to grant special status to depressed areas that would receive extraordinary employer tax benefits intended to stimulate investment and the employment of unemployed residents. The concept originated in England, where the Thatcher government implemented such a program. The Reagan proposal was stymied by opposition to the accompanying deregulation that was to accompany tax subsidies, in particular, waivers of environmental, occupational health and safety, and minimum wage requirements. *See* James A. Kushner, *The Reagan Urban Policy: Centrifugal Force in the Empire*, 2 UCLA J. ENVTL. L. & POL'Y 209 (1982).

While Reagan Administration proposals were never enacted by Congress, but enterprise zones were enacted by three-quarters of the states in the 1980s, which feature a variety of tax breaks for businesses located in these zones. Richard Briffault, *The Rise of Sublocal Structures in Urban Governance,* 82 MINN. L. REV. 503, 509 (1997) (noting the creation of at least five hundred zones). *See* ENTERPRISE ZONES: NEW DIRECTIONS IN ECONOMIC DEVELOPMENT (Roy E. Green ed. 1991); Michael Allan Wolf, *An Essay in Re-Plan: American Enterprise Zones in Practice,* 21 URB. LAW. 29 (1989).

Federally-supported enterprise zones re-emerged in the wake of the Los Angeles riots of 1992, following the Rodney King verdict. With the tentative support of the Bush administration, Congress enacted legislation authorizing the creation of 50 enterprise zones over four years with several tax incentives for zone employers. However, the day following his defeat in a bid for re-election that year, President Bush vetoed the legislation, which had been amended to include other unrelated tax reductions.

Successful candidate Bill Clinton supported enterprise zones. While his initial proposal was not fully enacted, Congress did pass its version in 1993 as part of the Omnibus Budget Reconciliation Act (OBRA), 26 U.S.C. § 1391. Following the Republican Congressional victory of 1994 and a competition involving hundreds of applicants, the Clinton administration named six urban and three rural enterprise zones, two supplemental enterprise zones, four enhanced enterprise communities, and 60 enterprise communities (urban and rural). *See* Audrey G. McFarlane, *Empowerment Zones: Urban Revitalization Through Collaborative Enterprise*, 5 J. AFFORDABLE HOUSING & COMMUNITY DEV. L. 35 (1995). The legislation specified the criteria for selection, including the population base. Recipients were eligible for expanded tax exempt financing, tax credits for eligible employers employing zone residents, and accelerated deductions for depreciable investments. *Id.* at 38–39. Unlike the Reagan and Bush proposals, the Clinton Administration proposal included Social Service Block Grants under Title XX of the Social Security Act: $100 million for each urban empowerment zone, $40 million for each rural empowerment zone, and approximately $3 million for each enterprise community. 42 U.S.C. § 1397f(a). These benefits have been made available over the ten-year period following the designation of the recipient communities. Each applicant had to prepare a strategic plan outlining their proposed use of federal benefits to promote economic development, community revitalization, and resident employment. *See* Marilyn Gittell, Kathe Newman, Janice Bockmeyer, & Robert Lindsay, *Expanding Civic Opportunity: Urban Empowerment Zones*, 33 Urb. Aff. Rev. 530 (1998).

The first round of Empowerment Zones generated $8 billion in additional private investment, with the Detroit zone attracting $2 billion, prompting President Clinton to call for a second round. *Clinton Calls for Second Empowerment Zone Round*, 23 [Current Developments] Hous. & Dev. Rep. (WGL) 643 (1996). The four main criteria for judging suitability for Zone designation have been the applicants' strategic planning for: (1) Economic Opportunity, (2) Sustainable Community Development, (3) Community-Based Partnerships, and (4) A Strategic Vision for Change. Economic Opportunity includes creating jobs within the community, attracting private investment, and expanding access for residents to jobs throughout the region.

Impressed by initial reports, Congress authorized a second round of designations in 1999, and the program expanded to include 15 new urban EZs, 5 new rural EZs, and 20 new rural ECs. Designation for Renewal Community status with a similar package of tax credits expanded the approach to rural communities. In December 2000, the Community Renewal Tax Relief Act of 2000, enacted as part of the The Omnibus Consolidation & Emergency Supplemental Appropriations Act for FY 2001 (Pub. L. No. 106-554, § 309(c), 114 Stat. 2763, 2763A-638 (2001)), expanded the initiative further by authorizing 40 Renewal Communities (RCs) and 9 more EZs. On December 31, 2001, HUD designated 28 RCs in urban areas and 12 in rural areas. Also, HUD designated 8 more urban EZs in a third round, and USDA designated 2 additional rural EZs. (HUD planned to designate just 7 Round III EZs, but one more designation opened because Atlanta, Georgia lost its EZ designation since the new RC designated in Atlanta shared Census tracts with the original Atlanta EZ).

All ECs designated in 1994 expired in 2004. The ECs that USDA designated in 1999, as well as all urban and rural RCs and EZs, expire at the end of 2009, although Congress is considering legislation to extend their designation periods. HUD's website maintains a portal for EZ/EC/RC management and evaluation materials. See *HUD's Initiative for Empowerment Zones and Renewal Communities (EZ/RC), available at* http://www.hud.gov/offices/cpd/economicdevelopment/programs/rc/. The U.S Department of Agriculture facilitated rural EZs and ECs. *See* http://www.ezec.gov/. At the time of publication both websites are active, and replete with maps and implementation resources.

HUD pegs the worth of the Empowerment Zone tax incentives and the Renewal Community tax incentives at approximately $11 billion of value to eligible businesses of all sizes in Empowerment Zones and Renewal Communities. The purpose of the incentives is to encourage businesses to open, expand, and to hire local residents. The incentives include employment credits, a 0% tax on capital gains, increased tax deductions on equipment, accelerated real property depreciation, and other incentives.

Notes and Questions

1. For a general discussion of the launch of the empowerment zones see Otto J. Hetzel, *Some Historical Lessons for Implementing the Clinton Administration's Empowerment*

Zones and Enterprise Communities Program: Experiences from the Model Cities Program, 26 URB. LAW. 6 (1994). For a comparative assessment, see Jennifer Forbes, *Using Economic Development Programs As Tools For Urban Revitalization: A Comparison of Empowerment Zones and New Markets Tax Credits*, 2006 U. ILL. L. REV. 177.

2. *What results?* The Community Renewal Tax Relief Act of 2000, *supra*, mandated that GAO report to Congress by January 31, 2004, 2007 and 2010 on the EZ, EC, and RC programs and their effect on poverty, unemployment, and economic growth in designated program areas. The 2010 report was summarized by GAO this way:

> While these programs initially offered a mix of grants and tax incentives for community and economic development, later rounds offered primarily tax incentives for business development. Grant funds in the early EZ and EC programs financed projects and activities to enhance community development. Further, the facility bond feature of the EZ and EC programs helped facilitate large business projects. More recently, the Commercial Revitalization Deduction (CRD) feature of the RC program helped to facilitate smaller business projects. Some information is available on the results of the EZ, EC, and RC programs. For instance, HUD collects data on utilization of facility bonds in EZs and the CRD in RCs. In addition, IRS provided data to HUD on EZ/RC employment credit use. However, data limitations make it difficult to accurately tie the use of the credits to specific designated communities. It is not clear how much businesses are using other EZ, EC, and RC tax incentives, because IRS forms do not associate these incentives with the programs or with specific designated communities. Going forward, the U.S. Census Bureau will begin releasing more frequent poverty and employment updates at the Census tract level than it has traditionally provided, and this information could be a useful tool in determining the effects of such programs on poverty and employment in designated Census tracts.

U.S. GOV'T ACCOUNTING OFFICE, REVITALIZATION PROGRAMS: EMPOWERMENT ZONES, ENTERPRISE COMMUNITIES, AND RENEWAL COMMUNITIES, GAO-10-464R (Mar. 12, 2010), *available at* http://www.gao.gov/products/GAO-10-464R. Should Congress renew the legislation? If so, what if any changes in the structure of grants, tax benefits, local priority-setting, or performance, should reauthorization include?

3. Urban Development Action Grant Program (UDAG). Prior to the federal and state embrace of the empowerment zone concept, Urban Development Action Grants evolved from a need to target more resources to relatively poor central cities and areas suffering fiscal distress, and a desire in HUD to establish a better linkage between community and economic development. While the UDAG program funding was terminated by Congress in 1986, it offers lessons in the issues raised by providing federal subsidies to private developers based upon the premise that this will promote job creation and retention for those in need of employment and in cities with declining commercial tax bases due to deindustrialization and disinvestment. There was also considerable debate over whether UDAG-subsidized development projects truly needed federal assistance and just how much employment they actually generated for poor or unemployed central city residents in distressed areas.

If there is a choice between transfer payments in the form of welfare or rent supplements, and the creation of jobs in the private sector through development that contributes to the local tax base, the latter is the more rational public policy, at least for that segment of the poor that potentially could join the labor force. However, the subsidy-jobs link must be carefully monitored if the poor are to be hired. The concepts underlying UDAG recur in successive economic development programs, which warrants a bit of further discussion.

(a) *Targeting Private Investment.* The UDAG was designed to inject a level of subsidy to provide sufficient incentive for local government and industry to cooperate in economic expansion. Criticism of the program came from advocates for the interests of the poor, who argued that many of the projects would have taken place without UDAG, that the recipients have been entities such as luxury hotel projects, and that there has been very little impact on the community development needs of the poor other than to provide some opportunities for the hiring of maids and maintenance workers at the minimum wage. *See UDAGs Inefficient, Poorly Targeted, OMB Director Charges in Senate Testimony,* 12 [Current Developments] Hous. & Dev. Rep. (BNA) 908 (1985) (leveraging only at 3.8 to 1, weighted too much to commercial rather than industrial, and not benefiting the poor while pirating jobs from other areas). HUD's position is that the historical experience has generated a 6.2 to 1 leveraging ratio, but the current experience is 5 to 1. *New Trends in UDAG Program Discussed by HUD Official,* 15 [Current Developments] Hous. & Dev. Rep. (WGL) 497 (1987). [Leveraging refers to the amount of private investment attracted compared to the UDAG or other government subsidy—Eds.]

(b) *Interjurisdictional Competition and Pirating.* One problem encountered under UDAG was competition between states to entice or pirate economic development projects from competing neighboring communities. The accelerating "economic war" among state and local governments seeking to lure businesses away from their existing locations is analyzed in, e.g., Kenneth P. Thomas, Competing for Capital 159 (2000) (estimating that total state and local government tax incentives and subsidies exceed $50 billion annually); Peter D. Enrich, *Saving the States from Themselves: Commerce Clause Constraints on State Tax Incentives for Business,* 110 Harv. L. Rev. 377, 382–89 (1997) (describing common tax incentives); Clayton P. Gillette, *The Law and Economics of Federalism: Business Incentives, Interstate Competition, and the Commerce Clause,* 82 Minn. L. Rev. 447, 479 (1997). For instances in the UDAG program, see *HUD, Jersey City Resolve Issues Holding Up $40 Million UDAG Award,* 11 [Current Developments] Hous. & Dev. Rep. (BNA) 1076 (1984) (in face of New York City's threatened lawsuit, waterfront project not to lease to New Yorkers; the pact raises unacknowledged problems of privileges and immunities). *But see City of New York v. Pierce,* 609 F. Supp. 798 (S.D.N.Y. 1985) (HUD's UDAG reconsideration rendered pirating challenge against New Jersey moot).

HUD's anti-pirating rules have been upheld. *New Jersey v. Pierce,* 669 F. Supp. 103 (D. N. J. 1987); *HUD Sets New Policy on UDAG Job Pirating; New York Drops Lawsuit Against Jersey City,* 12 [Current Developments] Hous. & Dev. Rep. (BNA) 627 (1985). *See also North Carolina UDAG Pirates Jobs from St. Paul, House Democrats Claim,* 12 [Current Developments] Hous. & Dev. Rep. (BNA) 757 (1985). The statutory anti-pirating provision is in § 119(h). How effective do you think it could be?

(c) For literature on the UDAG program, see Kenneth W. Ellison, *The Urban Development Action Grant Program: Using Federal Funds to Leverage Private Investment in Distressed Communities,* 11 Urb. Law. 424 (1979); Joseph P. Flanagan, *Bond Counsel Analysis of UDAG Projects,* 12 Urb. Law. 183 (1980); Special Report, *Leveraging of the Community Development Dollars: Ingredients of Success and Failure,* 5 [Current Developments] Hous. & Dev. Rep. (BNA) 277 (1977); Nancy Christopher, Lee Lawless & Jerry Simon, Comment, *Urban Redevelopment and the Fiscal Crisis of the Central City,* 21 St. Louis U. L.J. 820 (1978). *See also* Staughton Lynd, *Towards a Not-For-Profit Economy: Public Development Authorities for Acquisition and Use of Industrial Property,* 22 Harv. C.R.-C.L. L. Rev. 13 (1987).

4. *Model Cities*. The Clinton-era Enterprise Zone concept also owed something to the Model Cities initiative developed as part of the "Great Society" program in the 1960s. Demonstration Cities and Metropolitan Development Act of 1966, 42 U.S.C. §§ 3301–3313. *See* Bernard J. Frieden & Marshall Kaplan, The Politics of Neglect (1975); Charles M. Haar, Between the Idea and the Reality (1975). The Model Cities program was designed to expand revitalization programs to concentrate resources in selected neighborhoods, allowing funds to address the full gamut of social as well as physical community needs. Originally, the initiative called for a few experimental neighborhoods to receive all existing federal urban aid as well as funds to design new programs aimed at improving neighborhood stability. Often unfairly criticized as ineffective, the program was never launched as designed. Instead, funding was slashed while demand skyrocketed as most members of Congress wanted a handful of Model Neighborhoods for their constituents. The Politics of Neglect, *supra* at 214–217, 222–224. Indeed, toward the end of the program, cities were allowed to expand such neighborhoods to cover the entire inner-city, dissipating limited funding and frustrating unrealistic aspirations.

The Model Cities program was subsumed by § 116(a) of the Housing and Community Development Act of 1974, 42 U.S.C. § 5316. The Model Cities program is an example of excessively lofty objectives—legislative goals unattainable due to the legislative authorization, appropriations, and administrative implementation processes. Had the Model Cities experiments been allowed to occur as originally proposed, they may have resulted in urban successes deserving of replication and continued funding. Instead, the program was conveniently tossed into the failed programs hopper, thus justifying the conservative national agenda for reduced spending on transportation, housing, schools, employment, and justice. The failure of the Model Cities program presents an example of how many government programs have failed to generate their promised goals. This pattern has provided the justification for the conservative agenda of the past generation.

3. State and Local Economic Development Incentives

States and localities' economic development tools have included investment tax credits, job tax credits, property tax abatements, reduced financing rates (e.g., through tax breaks on the principal and interest paid on Industrial Revenue Bonds used to fund the project), sales tax refunds, training incentives, community development block grants, site preparation, and enterprise zone credits which typically include general income tax credits, job grants and credits, and income tax credits for real property improvements.

Most states have not attempted to evaluate the benefit of their economic development incentives, nor even to total their expenditures in the name of economic development. Sherry L. Jarrell, Gary Shoesmith, J. Neal Robbins, *Law And Economics of Regulating Local Economic Development Incentives,* 41 Wake Forest L. Rev. 805, 821–823 (2006) (reviewing the literature).

With Democrats and Republicans at the federal level competing to balance the national budget, encouragement and subsidy for community development, urban—suburban or rural—must come from the state and local government. Cities experienced with the renewal process developed renewal programs not dependent on federal subsidies. State and local enterprise zones, like the federal programs, may be tools to assist in encouraging economic development, particularly for less attractive areas seeking commercial or industrial development.

Tax increment financing of redevelopment uses the enhanced tax base to finance urban improvements. This becomes an additional tool added to the traditional use of both special assessments and below market municipal bonds paid off by annual property assessments. Tax increment financing can be successful, particularly in commercial and more affluent neighborhoods.

A recent trend in incentives is the increased use of "tax increment financing," which can be viewed as a financial incentive or infrastructure incentive. Under tax increment financing, the increased taxes on a developed parcel of land are not put in the general fund of the different taxing jurisdictions, but instead are devoted to special services related to the designated improvement district. For the sponsoring local government, one advantage of TIFs is that typically the TIF district captures all increased taxes that would have accrued to all the overlapping taxing districts, including school districts, the county government, and any special purpose governmental units.

TIFs have been authorized in 48 states. According to one survey, 50 percent of local communities have used TIFs. *See* Timothy J. Bartik, Local Economic Development Policies (2003) (a publication of the W.E. Upjohn Institute for Employment Research reviewing common strategies used by localities in the U.S. with observations on coordination with CDCs and across labor markets).

From the development point of view, under tax increment-financed redevelopment, municipal bonds can be sold to finance acquisition and when parcels are sold for redevelopment the taxes previously paid to taxing entities would be frozen. As development occurs enhancing the tax base and generating larger revenues, the increment—revenues in excess of the previous tax obligation—are used to pay off the bond indebtedness with the additional increment available for making public facility improvements within the project, even for rent or mortgage subsidies to generate affordable housing. The use of tax increment also subsidizes the project allowing a "write down" on the cost of the acquired land so as to make privately sponsored redevelopment more attractive. Similarly, in the renewal of downtowns, TIFs can be used to pay for infrastructure improvements upfront, to leverage other investment.

Tax increment financing has been sustained by the state courts that have reviewed the measure in light of state law. *E.g., In re Advisory Opinion*, 422 N.W.2d 186 (Mich. 1988); *State* ex rel. *Plaza Properties, Inc. v. Kansas City*, 687 S.W.2d 70 (Mo. 1985). *See also Castel Properties, Ltd. v. City of Marion*, 631 N.E.2d 459 (Ill. App. Ct. 1994) (scrutiny of blighting factors, finding project failed to comply with blight standards); *Tax Increment Fin. Comm'n v. J.E. Dunn Constr. Co.*, 781 S.W.2d 875 (Mo. 1989) (tax increment financed redevelopment does not involve an increase in tax requiring popular referendum).

While most states authorize locally-sponsored redevelopment with its opportunities for metropolitan entrepreneurship, some states may restrict direct involvement in private industry and development. *State v. Clay County Dev. Auth.*, 140 So. 2d 576 (Fla. 1962) (lack of power to issue bonds to construct industrial plant for lease to private corporation); *State* ex rel. *Beck v. City of York*, 82 N.W.2d 269 (Neb. 1957) (revenue bonds to construct and lease industrial buildings as either city credit extended or purchasers victims of delusion). For cases offering a broader interpretation of local attraction subsidies, see, e.g., *Gaylord v. Beckett*, 144 N.W.2d 460 (Mich. 1966) (authorizing revenue bonds to acquire industrial building in order to attract industry to the community as long as no public credit pledged); Dale F. Rubin, *Public Subsidies to Private Corporations: Are They Constitutional?*, 20 State & Local L. News, Winter, 1997, at 7 (publication of the American Bar Association).

Notes and Questions

1. *Anti-Competition and Interstate Commerce.* The U.S. Supreme Court recently restated and applied this long-established exception to the general rule of free competition among the states: a state's laws cannot discriminate against interstate commerce. *Granholm v. Heald*, 544 U.S. 460, 466 (2005) (invalidating state laws protecting in-state wineries). It does not matter whether the focus of the state incentive is on the benefited or the burdened party. State laws violate the Commerce Clause if they mandate "differential treatment of in-state and out-of-state economic interests that benefits the former and burdens the latter." *See also C & A Carbone, Inc. v. Town of Clarkstown*, 511 U.S. 383 (1994) (extending the reach of the commerce clause, authorizing courts to invalidate state and local regulation that carries an anticompetitive impact). The Court has ruled that state subsidies can generate a scheme that discriminates against interstate commerce. *West Lynn Creamery, Inc. v. Healy*, 512 U.S. 186 (1994) (effect of tax on all milk providers and subsidy to in-state dairy farmers constituted discrimination, while each component standing alone is apparently valid).

The Supreme Court took the *Granholm* case following intensive reaction to *Cuno v. DaimlerChrysler*, in which the Sixth Circuit Court of Appeals resolved a challenge to the validity of an Ohio state investment tax credit and a City of Toledo property tax exemption provided for the defendant manufacturer by state and local laws. The Sixth Circuit decided that the dormant commerce clause allows the property exemption but prohibits the tax credit. *Cuno*, 386 F.3d 738, 743 (6th Cir. 2004). The credit unconstitutionally discriminated because the effect was to prefer a local business that expands in Ohio over a local business that invests out of state. The Supreme Court granted certiorari, then vacated and remanded the Sixth Circuit's decision on procedural grounds, without reaching the merits. 547 U.S. 332 (2006).

2. *Targeting.* Communities sometimes fail to follow established standards. Courts, although giving broad deference to redevelopment planning, will step in when the deviation goes too far. For example, it has been held that using bonds secured by funds earmarked for low- and moderate-income housing to fund a use unrelated to providing affordable housing (such as building railroad overpasses) is invalid. *Lancaster Redev. Agency v. Dibley*, 25 Cal. Rptr. 2d 593 (Ct. App. 1993).

An important array of economic development activities are permitted under the federal Community Development Block Program. Yet as the following critical excerpt explains, the CDBG program is poorly designed for ameliorating the economic disinvestment which burden many urban areas.

Louise A. Howells, Looking for the Butterfly Effect: An Analysis of Urban Economic Development under the Community Development Block Grant Program

16 St. Louis University Public Law Review
383, 385, 389–90, 400–04, 406 (1997)

The CDBG program is the single largest source of funds available for urban economic development.... The CDBG program operates on the premise that the creation or retention of jobs for low- and moderate-income persons or the creation of jobs within certain low income areas will create expanded economic opportunity in urban areas....

Going down the list of frequently cited urban disadvantages, not a single one can be easily addressed under the CDBG program. A prime example, which is a substantial issue for older urban areas, is the difficulty in using CDBG funds to clean up brownfields (contaminated sites). Cities are frequently at a disadvantage to out-lying areas because of contamination from prior uses of property.

Recipients cannot use CDBG funds to clean up and redevelop brownfields unless the clean up fits into the current strictures of the "area basis" and "spot basis" rules.... The same is true for other infrastructure and public facilities improvements. Unless located in a residential area, an infrastructure or public facility project qualifies only if it is an economic development project that creates or retains jobs and meets the public benefit rule. A recipient cannot simply use funds to repair and replace infrastructure and water treatment facilities, to improve highway access to potential development sites, to redevelop sites containing obsolete buildings and improvements, or to develop sites for future development in areas that might be the most conducive to the attraction of business activity....

Recipients cannot use funds for general government expenses, and therefore cannot address the frequently cited social problems that inhibit development. Recipients cannot freely use CDBG funds for increased police protection. Likewise, recipients cannot use CDBG funds to improve the local school system.

The program design also ignores the dissipative nature of the economy and its tendency to change in irreversible ways, such as the de-industrialization of the urban economy experienced in this century. The program focus is upon the rehabilitation of urban neighborhoods, which assumes that the existing structures are viable. But, in some cases, the re-invention of urban areas will be necessary to address land uses made obsolete by de-industrialization and to alter the urban landscape to make it more attractive to investment.

Under the current program, a recipient cannot freely engage in site assemblage to create open space, a wildlife refuge, an industrial park or the like unless the project results in the direct creation or retention of jobs or somehow qualifies as a slum clearance or prevention project. The program also places its greatest faith in community-based development organizations, which concentrate upon isolated neighborhoods, and eschews reliance on mainstream institutions, such as banks, that may in fact be better equipped to pull off projects of significant impact when such projects are called for.

The program design also magnifies the impact of political dynamics on the selection and substance of individual projects. Because economic development projects must result in jobs, a recipient is likely to feel compelled to provide assistance to individual businesses in order to establish that jobs result from the activity. This set-up increases the likelihood that recipients will make concessions, or provide assistance, to businesses that might have engaged in the activity without CDBG assistance, or worse, to businesses that might not have otherwise engaged in the activity for good reason. In other words, the direct subsidy to businesses can distort the normal business decision process. The contracting process is also subject to the political influence that businesses may wield in seeking assistance.

To tie capital improvements to the direct creation or retention of jobs keeps urban communities hostage to the demands of private entities, which is both unnecessary and unjustified in light of the very clear need for such improvements. Moreover, local governments are arguably much better at infrastructure planning and development than they are at making decisions about the job creating potential and viability of particular businesses. Investing in infrastructure, public spaces, or site clean-up and redevelopment will provide continued benefit to the community, whereas investment in a business that fails is a waste of valuable resources.

Anecdotal evidence of the program's limitations arose during the 1992 congressional hearings. The Mayor of Bridgeport, Connecticut testified before the House Committee on Banking, Finance and Urban Affairs about his plans to address the serious economic problems facing his city. Among other things, his plan for revival included the development of Bridgeport's deep water harbor and an industrial corridor leading to it, which would capitalize on the fact that Bridgeport had the only significant waterfront acreage between Boston and Baltimore. He also cited the need for increased police protection and a better regional allocation of the cost of social and other services. During his testimony, a congressional representative complimented him on his lucid analysis of the problem, but commented that most of the items he had outlined did not come under CDBG. Bridgeport was not free to expend funds in creative ways that would create positive feedback in its economy or that would counterbalance the dynamics that created the imbalance between it and its wealthy suburban neighbors....

A related question is whether funding private businesses to create jobs in certain areas is an effective means of improving the economic lives of very low-income persons who are in most need. Recent experience in Chicago suggests that low-income persons may receive greater benefit from programs that enable them to move out of depressed urban areas.[148] The *Gautreaux* program, which was implemented as the result of a discrimination suit brought on behalf of Chicago public housing residents, permits public housing residents to receive Section 8 certificates and to move to private apartments in the city of Chicago or to apartments in wealthier suburbs. Studies of the program found that public housing residents who moved to an apartment in the suburbs were twenty-five percent more likely to have had a job than those who moved to an apartment in the city....

Notes and Questions

1. *Economic Development.* The focus of some cases has been discrimination against disfavored developers. Should the focus shift to interregional economic moves? What legal theories exist to challenge the pirating of "rust belt" companies by developing "sun belt" cities? In *Maready v. City of Winston-Salem*, 467 S.E.2d 615 (N.C. 1996), the North Carolina Supreme Court upheld a state statute authorizing local governments to make economic development incentive grants to private corporations. Designed to augment the local tax base and encourage economic development and job creation, the grants may have the effect of pirating employers from other communities. *Maready*, in sustaining the North Carolina Legislature's initiative, joined 46 other states in upholding the constitutionality of governmental expenditures and related assistance for economic development incentives. Is *Maready* an example of pirating or just good pro-active planning for economic development?

2. It is argued that the central strategy towards revitalizing America's cities is through economic development, job creation, and employment access by those seeking employment. Donald A. Hicks, *Revitalizing Our Cities or Restoring Ties to Them? Redirecting the Debate*, 27 U. Mich. J.L. Reform 813 (1995) (policies must avoid raising the business costs of existing enterprises in ways that are likely to diminish employment opportunities and opportunities offered by transforming new industrial cities are often irrelevant

---

148. James E. Rosenbaum et al., *Can the Kerner Commission's Housing Strategy Improve Employment, Education, and Social Integration for Low-Income Blacks?*, 71 N.C. L. Rev. 1519, 1521 (1993).

and inaccessible to legions of inner-city poor and policies must look to encouraging the poor to leave ghettos to find opportunity); Jack Sommer, *United States Urban Policy: What is Left? What is Right?*, 27 U. MICH. J.L. REFORM 661 (1995).

3. For a description of the Clinton Urban policy, embracing macro-level investment policies, a community development policy directed at improving the quality of life without new federal spending, productivity-enhancing capital investments, and relying on community-based organizations and independence, all as part of "Putting America First," see Michael A. Stegman, *National Urban Policy Revisited*, 71 N.C. L. REV. 1737 (1993). *See also* Margaret Beebe Held, *Developing Microbusinesses in Public Housing: Notes from the Field*, 31 HARV. C.R.-C.L. L. REV. 473 (1996); Louise A. Howells, *Looking for the Butterfly Effect: An Analysis of Urban Economic Development Under the Community Development Block Grant Program*, 16 ST. LOUIS U. PUB. L. REV. 383 (1997) (critical of block grant program approach to attract jobs and restrictive regulations prohibiting many critical capital investment expenditures); Michael H. Schill, *Assessing the Role of Community Development Corporations in Inner City Economic Development*, 22 N.Y.U. REV. L. & SOC. CHANGE 753 (1996–1997) (arguing such community-based businesses must be efficient competitors and conform to the reality of the market); David E. Steinglass, *Rebuilding the Inner City: A History of Neighborhood Initiatives to Address Poverty in the United States*, 22 N.Y.U. REV. L. & SOC. CHANGE 839 (1996–1997).

4. *UDAG Pirating.* Pirating problems arose under the short lived Urban Development Action Grant Program (UDAG), providing grants to cities to undertake public-private, typically, economic development projects. Cities attempting to lure employers to participate in the program led HUD to issue pirating regulations. *New Jersey v. Pierce*, 669 F. Supp. 103 (D. N. J. 1987) (anti-pirating rules sustained under authority of § 119(h) of the 1974 Housing and Community Development Act as amended in 1982). The UDAG experience demonstrates congressional power to regulate pirating.

5. *International Law.* The United States is a member of The World Trade Organization (WTO), whose requirements mirror the prior General Agreement on Tariffs and Trade ("GATT"), and is a signer of the Agreements on Subsidies and Countervailing Duties, known as the Uruguay Round Agreements. RALPH H. FOLSOM ET AL., INTERNATIONAL BUSINESS TRANSACTIONS ch. 7 (3d ed. 1995). Under the Uruguay Round Agreements covering subsidies, GATT was most concerned with imports and subsidies providing a competitive advantage. Terrence J. McCartin, *Red, Yellow or Green: GATT 1994's Traffic Light Subsidies Categories*, *in* PRACTICING LAW INSTITUTE, THE COMMERCE DEPARTMENT SPEAKS ON INTERNATIONAL TRADE AND INVESTMENT 611 (1994), *reprinted* in Folsom, *supra*, at 507 (such import impacting subsidies are "red light" and prohibited, while research and development is a permitted "green light" subsidy, with the remainder characterized as "yellow light" and actionable where a serious adverse impact is generated). *See also* Jennifer Gilbert, *Selling the City Without Selling Out: New Legislation on Development Incentives Emphasizes Accountability*, 27 URB. LAW. 427, 446 (1995) (arguing that subsidies are prohibited). Jennifer Gilbert argues effectively that recipients of economic development incentives must be made accountable. Other commentators argue that such incentives, primarily tax incentives, must be more efficient. *See* Scott Ziance, *Making Economic Development Incentives More Efficient*, 30 URB. LAW. 33 (1988). Do contemporary American urban boosterism and the pirating of employers or sports franchises through lucrative incentives arguably violate the WTO (formerly GATT)? Should urbanists and poverty lawyers as well as land use casebook authors take a course on international law and trade? *See also* Bennet Harrison & Sandra Kanter, *The Political Economy of States' Job Creation*, 44 AM. INST. PLAN. J. 424 (1978); Harold Wolman, *Local Economic Development Policy: What*

Explains the Divergence Between Policy Analysis and Political Behavior?, 10 J. Urb. Aff. 19 (1988).

6. *Government as Land Developer.* Professor George Lefcoe, in discussing public agency land developers, points to the potential danger to a community offering subsidies to industry or a developer:

> [P]rosperous firms are able to buy or lease their sites so cheaply that inquiries can be made about the good judgment or even integrity of local officials. Once a locality does grant land on "give-away" terms, other localities may feel obligated to follow its lead in order to preserve their industrial job bases. Not only do taxpayers suffer, but all the firms that had located in the jurisdiction earlier risk having to compete with newcomers whose rents they have, in effect, subsidized through their own taxes.

George Lefcoe, *When Governments Become Land Developers: Notes on the Public-Sector Experience in the Netherlands and California*, 51 S. Cal. L. Rev. 165, 169 (1978).

7. *The Kerner Commission Revisited.* Following the urban violence of 1967, President Johnson appointed a commission to study the links between racial discrimination and urban policy. John C. Boger, *Race and the American City: The Kerner Commission in Retrospect—An Introduction*, 71 N.C. L. Rev. 1289, 1292 (1993). The result was the Kerner Commission Report, Report of the Nat'l Advisory Comm'n on Civil Disorders (1968) [hereinafter cited as Report]. The Report made the now famous observation that "[o]ur nation is moving toward two societies, one black, one white—separate and unequal." Report at 1. The Report offered alternative strategies for urban policy, notably (1) doing nothing and leaving the cities to the free market, (2) enriching (or "gilding") the urban ghetto, primarily through grant-in-aid subsidies, or (3) pursuit of an integration strategy, opening all employment and residential neighborhoods to racial minorities. The Kerner Commission concluded that integration was the only viable urban strategy, albeit with the adjunct of ghetto enrichment. Report at 218–26. It is clear that America has neither enriched its cities nor integrated its residential communities. *See generally Symposium, The Urban Crisis: The Kerner Commission Report Revisited*, 71 N.C. L. Rev. 1283 (1993).

E. Re-Making Cities: Removal, Redevelopment, Regeneration

As we have seen in the preceding sections of this chapter, state and local government laws and procedures are invoked in virtually every effort of community development. What policy goals form the foundation for federal resources made available to states and localities? How—on what legal bases and through what forms of aid—has the federal government contributed to the tools for community development proponents? How are these resources made available, to whom, and under what conditions and constraints?

This section opens with consideration of the targeting of public resources to substandard neighborhoods within communities. It then considers the legal issues arising out of the urban blight concept and the use of eminent domain in urban redevelopment. The focus is on the use of eminent domain for clearance and redevelopment rather than the housing rehabilitation strategies later incorporated in the federal legislation.

1. From Federal "Urban Renewal" to Modern Redevelopment

A concern for substandard housing and interest in neighborhood redevelopment first surfaced in New York City before World War II. When neighborhood planners realized that new housing in cleared neighborhoods was not likely to be affordable by lower-income groups, they began to consider a number of subsidy possibilities that could accomplish this objective. From these beginnings, and the deliberations of a select committee convened during World War II by the national housing agency, the federally subsidized urban redevelopment program was born. Enacted by Congress in 1949, it was one of the major accomplishments of President Truman's administration. The legislation was extended in 1954 to include neighborhood rehabilitation, and the program was renamed "urban renewal," best-known for the slum clearance and redevelopment components of the program. The federal urban renewal program was replaced by the community development program authorized by the Housing and Community Development Act of 1974, yet slum clearance and redevelopment are also authorized under this legislation.

Blight eradication was central to the federal urban renewal program between 1949 and 1974. Federal urban renewal legislation provided federal subsidies for the cost of land acquired by local agencies in areas, locally designated as substandard and "blighted," and thus as suitable sites for urban renewal projects. Under the federal legislation, the federal housing agency had to approve each urban renewal project. After the urban renewal project was approved by the federal agency, a local agency, often a redevelopment agency established by state legislation, acquired and cleared the land in the project area and sold it for redevelopment to private redevelopers. The federal subsidy met the difference between the cost of acquiring the land and the cost to the private redeveloper on resale. Under the urban renewal program, cities could apply for federal grants to subsidize the cost of selling urban land to private redevelopers. The federal funds, in the form of a land write down, covered two-thirds of the difference between the local redevelopment agency's land costs—inclusive of costs of planning, administration, acquisition, demolition, and infrastructure—and the agency's resale price. This degree of subsidy was designed to make the targeted urban sites competitive with suburban green fields. Though directed primarily to the clearance and redevelopment of blighted residential neighborhoods, the federal program could also be used for clearance projects in blighted nonresidential areas. *See* George Lefcoe, *Redevelopment Takings After* Kelo*: What's Blight Got To Do With It?*, 17 S. Cal. Rev. L. & Soc. Just. 803 (2008). *See generally* Ashley A. Foard & Hilbert Fefferman, *Federal Urban Renewal Legislation, in* Urban Renewal: The Record and the Controversy 96 (James Q. Wilson ed. 1966); Charles J. Orlebeke, *The Evolution of Low-Income Housing Policy, 1949 to 1999*, 11 Housing Pol'y Debate 489 (2000).

The shift to the use of compulsory land acquisition powers, described in the Gordon excerpt that follows, created a new set of legal issues in community redevelopment programs, not least of these is the necessity to define urban residential blight. Another legal issue arose out of the use of compulsory land acquisition powers in urban redevelopment programs. Unlike housing codes which are enforced without compensation to owners of housing, compulsory land acquisition for urban redevelopment required the use of eminent domain and the payment of compensation to property owners whose land is acquired.

Eminent domain powers had historically been employed for clearly public uses, such as the construction of highways and public office buildings. In the urban redevelopment program, it was to be used for what some viewed as a private and constitutionally unacceptable purpose—the acquisition of land from one property owner and its transfer to another private entity for redevelopment and private gain. This new use of the eminent domain power raised important constitutional questions.

a. Blight as a Triggering Mechanism

Neither the original federal urban redevelopment legislation nor the present federal community development legislation defines blight. Blight must be defined by the state legislation authorizing local urban redevelopment programs. Local redevelopment agencies then apply the statutory blight definition to designate areas for urban redevelopment. Local agency application of the statutory blight definition is in turn subject to review in the state courts as a matter of state law.

The following statutory definition of blight is typical. It is patterned on a model law prepared by the federal housing agency:

> (11) "Slum area" means an area in which there is a predominance of buildings or improvements which by reason of dilapidation, deterioration, age or obsolescence, inadequate provision for ventilation, light, sanitation, or open spaces, high density of population and overcrowding, or any combination of such factors, are conductive to ill health, transmission of disease, infant mortality, juvenile delinquency and crime, injuriously affect the entire area, and are detrimental to the public health, safety, morals, or welfare.
>
> (12) "Blighted area" means an area (other than a slum area) where by reason of the predominance of defective or inadequate street layout, faulty lot layout in relation in size, adequacy, accessibility or usefulness, submergence of lots by water or other insanitary or unsafe conditions, deterioration of site improvements, failure to install public utilities, diversity of ownership, tax delinquency, defective or unusual conditions of title, improper subdivision or obsolete platting, or any combination of such factors, the development of such blighted area (which may include some incidental building or improvements) into predominantly housing uses is being prevented.

The blight designation is based on a generalized finding that the area is blighted. This determination is made by first assessing the physical condition of each dwelling unit in a residential area. The area as a whole can be blighted if a sufficient number of dwelling units in the area are found to be substandard.

Colin Gordon, Blighting the Way: Urban Renewal, Economic Development, and the Elusive Definition of Blight

31 Fordham Urban Law Journal 305, 306–319 (2004)

What is "blight"? Over half a century of federal and state urban renewal policy, and a slightly shorter history of local economic development policies, revolve around this question. These policies, ranging from the first stabs at federally-funded urban renewal in the 1940s to the contemporary fascination of local and state governments with tax increment financing ("TIF"), all involve, to some degree, public financing of private economic development or property transactions. In effect, such policies extend the public credit and the public power of eminent domain to private interests—a combination that has often incurred the opposition of both taxpayers and property owners displaced by urban renewal or redevelopment. The legal and political justification for such policies, as a result, leans heavily on an overarching public purpose: the elimination or prevention of blight. But "blight" is rarely defined with any precision in such statutes, and the courts have granted local interests almost carte blanche in their creative search for "blighted" areas eligible for federal funds or local tax breaks. This political and statutory confusion is rooted in a long history of local anxiety surrounding inner city housing, "slum clearance," and the fate of the central business district. A blighted area, as a Philadelphia planner proposed cryptically in 1918, "is a district which is not what it should be," and it is woven through recent history, economic development and urban redevelopment policies. The goals of such policies have always been to eradicate blight; however, as one California state legislator lamented in 1995, "Somewhere along the way ... defining blight became an art form...."

I. Fighting Blight: The Legal and Legislative Background

The modern statutory definition of blight is rooted in our first urban crisis, the Progressive-era response to the urbanization and industrialization in the late nineteenth and early twentieth century. Lamentable urban conditions, captured in the investigations of Jacob Riis and others, included the encroachment of commercial or industrial properties on residential neighborhoods, the inadequacy of basic public services, and the threat of moral decay, fire, and disease posed by tenement housing of urban working families. Cities, in the environmental determinism of urban reformers, had become "nurseries of crime, and of the vices and disorderly courses which lead to crime ... perpetrated by individuals who have either lost connection with home life, or never had any, or whose homes had ceased to be sufficiently separate, decent, and desirable to afford what are regarded as ordinary wholesome influences of home and family." Tenements, and substandard urban housing more generally, were considered "standing menaces to the family, to morality, to the public health, and to civic integrity."

The political response to such conditions ranged widely, and included urban beautification campaigns, the "model tenement" movement, "managerial" reform of urban governance, early efforts at urban planning and zoning, and [P]rohibition. But, despite the progress of home rule in many states, municipal powers to regulate or rehabilitate urban blight were quite limited. In part, this reflected political and fiscal constraints. Reformers increasingly understood "blight" as a condition of entire blocks or neighborhoods, but cities lacked the capacity to do much more than fine the occasional landlord or raze the occasional building. And in part, this reflected legal constraints on the local regulation of private property. Indeed, the only substantial legal footing for urban reform was the "police power" to safeguard the general welfare. For this reason, local efforts to address urban conditions leaned heavily on the threats to health or safety or moral order that animated local police powers. While efforts to eradicate blighted conditions were limited to land zoning and the authority of health departments and fire marshals, early definitions of "blight" did begin to crop up in local health and safety codes.

Political attention returned to urban conditions during the Great Depression, accompanied by the efforts of local, state, and federal officials to refine the definition of urban blight. Not surprisingly, such definitions drew largely on Progressive-era police powers. At a 1930 Housing Conference, the Hoover Administration defined "a slum" as "a residential area where the houses and conditions of life are of such a squalid and wretched character and which hence has become a social liability to the community." In 1937, the National Association of Housing Officials defined a slum, in language echoed in the second National Housing Act later that year, as

> an area in which predominate dwellings that either because of dilapidation, obsolescence, overcrowding, poor arrangement or design, lack of ventilation, light or sanitary facilities, or a combination of these factors, are detrimental to the safety, health, morals, and comfort of the inhabitants thereof.

Blight was defined more broadly, because most viewed it not as synonymous with "slum," but as a set of conditions often analogized as a disease or a cancer, which resulted in slums. At the 1930 Hoover Conference, blight was singled out as an "economic liability" whose demands upon the public purse outstripped its tax revenues. "Structures become shabby and obsolete," as one observer wrote in 1938, "[t]he entire district takes on a down-at-the-heel appearance. The exodus of the more prosperous groups is accelerated. Rents fall. Poorer classes move in. The poverty of the tenants contributes further to the general air of shabbiness. The realty owner becomes less and less inclined or able to make repairs."

Such efforts to define blight reflected not only the renewed urban crisis of the 1930s, but also the conviction, especially in the later New Deal, that urban conditions deserved federal and state political attention. New York in 1926 and New Jersey in 1929, led the way with laws granting eminent domain to private developers in exchange for rent controls and other regulatory conditions, but could not overcome the pervasive obstacles to redevelopment: private interests had no incentive to facilitate public policy, and public interests had no money to acquire or assemble private property. The National Housing Act of 1937 established a system of loans and grants-in-aid to local public housing authorities. As a compromise between real estate interests and housing advocates, the 1937 law made federal funds available for the construction of low-income housing, but also required the clearance of an equal number of "blighted" properties. Refined in 1941, the National Housing Act pressed state governments to pass enabling legislation—usually taking the form of sweeping urban redevelopment laws—under which municipalities could apply for federal funds. New York in 1941 was the first to follow the federal lead, and others followed as depression conditions were displaced by an equally troubling war-era housing shortage. By 1947, about half of the states had passed urban redevelopment laws that created quasi-public redevelopment corporations and endowed them with the power of eminent domain to clear and prepare "blighted areas" for redevelopment by private interests.

These redevelopment corporations were largely inactive until 1949, when a new Federal Housing Act made federal funds available for the redevelopment of large areas rather than merely the removal of discrete slum conditions. Under the new law, local redevelopment corporations could buy and clear blighted areas with federal money, sell the land to private developers, and use the proceeds to cover the redevelopment costs.

This expansive delegation of eminent domain did not go unchallenged, especially by private interests threatened or displaced by urban redevelopment plans. But state and federal courts persistently held that the broad public purpose of redevelopment over-rode the claims of individual property owners, and that resale of cleared properties to private developers amounted to an appropriate public use....

Federal law deferred the definition and determination of "blighted areas" to the state governments that enabled the redevelopment corporations and the local governments that administered them. Most states, in fact, stopped short of defining blight and instead offered a descriptive catalogue of blighted conditions—often pasted verbatim from Progressive-era health or safety statutes. In Missouri, for example, a blighted area was one in which:

> by reason of the predominance of defective or inadequate street layout, unsanitary or unsafe conditions, deterioration of site improvements, improper subdivision or obsolete platting, the existence of conditions which endanger life or property by fire and other causes, or any combination of such factors, retards the provision of housing accommodations or constitutes an economic or social liability or a menace to the public health, safety, morals, or welfare in its present condition and use.

In New Jersey, blight was defined as any one of a number of conditions, including buildings which were "substandard, unsafe, insanitary [sic], dilapidated, or obsolescent," discontinued industrial uses, unimproved vacant land "not likely to be developed through the instrumentality of private capital," and "lack of proper utilization." In California, a blighted area was characterized

> by the existence of buildings and structures ... which are unfit or unsafe to occupy for such purposes and are conducive to ill health, transmission of disease, infant mortality, juvenile delinquency, and crime because of any one or a combination of the following factors: [d]efective design and character of physical construction[; f]aulty interior arrangement and exterior spacing[; h]igh density of population and overcrowding [; i]nadequate provision for ventilation, light, sanitation, open spaces, and recreation facilities[; and a]ge, obsolescence, deterioration, dilapidation, mixed character, or shifting of uses.

While federal urban renewal was replaced in 1974 with the Community Development Block Grant program ("CDBG"), state redevelopment statutes and their Dickensian descriptions of "blight" persisted. More importantly, the blight language was grafted into new laws, including the profusion of TIF laws in the 1970s and 1980s.... [Tax Increment Financing is discussed *infra*—Eds.]

During the heyday of urban renewal, between 1949 and 1974, urban redevelopment corporations were established by state law, administered by local officials who were usually unelected, and funded largely with federal money. In more recent decades, state redevelopment statutes have been joined by a patchwork of state TIF laws; development is initiated by a combination of local officials, redevelopment corporations, and private developers; local projects are often effectively funded by other local tax entities, such as school districts and counties; and federal money and standards have largely evaporated. Local governments, under cover of vague state laws and beguiled by the prospect of capturing federal grants or a larger tax base, have every incentive to define blight expansively. And they have done so successfully, either by offering imaginative interpretations of older blight definitions, or by taking advantage of a more recent deregulation of those definitions....

From Housing to Economic Development

Through the first half of the twentieth century, blight was understood as a condition of substandard housing, and "eradicating blight" meant providing decent homes for urban working families. But even amidst the worries about a postwar housing crunch that animated state and federal efforts in the 1940s, urban housing policy was already adrift. Federal urban renewal was compromised by a raft of more generous federal policies, including highway spending, mortgage insurance, and accelerated depreciation for new developments, which subsidized and facilitated suburban flight. Federal housing policy, as we have seen, was already committed to improving the housing stock without increasing it. And, under constant pressure from local and real estate interests, Congress opened the door for the use of federal funds for non-residential development. While the Federal Housing Act of 1949 defined blighted areas as "predominantly residential," it did not require cities or developers to erect affordable housing on redeveloped districts. And Congress gradually amended the "residential threshold," allowing up to ten percent of federal funds to be spent on commercial development in 1954, and increasing this percentage to thirty-five in 1965.

As importantly, urban redevelopment policy was increasingly distracted by the concerns of realtors, developers, and business leaders representing the central business district ("CBD"). Between the [two World] wars, business interests had been wary of urban policy, especially given the threats to private interests posed by eminent domain and public housing. Increasingly however, urban business leaders saw urban redevelopment as a means of loosening the "dirty collar" of substandard housing that encircled most central business districts. These interests, however, had little patience with redevelopment plans that proposed to repopulate cleared slums with working families who neither shopped nor worked in the CBD. Instead, slum clearance would pave the way for CBD expansion or higher-end housing. At the same time, state and local politicians were leery of the costs of urban redevelopment and eager to reap its benefits. Accordingly, they tended to agree with CBD leaders that low-income and middle-income housing did not match the immense acquisition costs or economic potential of urban redevelopment. At the intersection of these private and public anxieties, urban redevelopment policies took a decisive turn. Slums were to be cleared not for better housing, but for a more abstract faith in local economic development and growth. Targeted areas were identified less by demonstrable need than by the willingness of private interests to invest in redevelopment. Redevelopment, in turn, rested on an increasingly elastic definition of "blight" that put the health of the CBD at the top of the urban agenda. Under state law, the drift from residential to commercial redevelopment was even more pronounced....

---

b. Takings of Private Property for Redevelopment Projects

When private property has been designated as "blighted" for purposes of redevelopment, condemnation proceedings may still be some years away. Has such property been "taken" for purposes of the Fifth Amendment's requirement that property be taken only for a public purpose, and then only if "just compensation" is paid? Most of the early urban redevelopment blight cases considered the designation for urban redevelopment of terminal, dead-end slums. The courts in these cases applied the usual deferential review standard even when sound buildings were included as part of a larger area in which blighting conditions prevailed.

Some courts no longer pay deferential respect to local blight determinations in urban redevelopment projects. This trend has been influenced by several factors. One is that many cities have redeveloped their terminal slums. Areas now included in urban redevelopment projects are more marginal.

Courts are also sensitive to the legal bind in which owners of property in urban redevelopment projects are placed. They are not entitled to a trial-type adjudication on the blight finding, and have no legal recourse until condemnation proceedings are filed. They may attack the blight finding at that time, but at that point the challenge may be too late. Blight designations often have a negative effect on the area covered, which may decline substantially by the time the condemnation action is filed. Tenants may leave rental housing, for example, which may then be vandalized and reduced to a practically valueless condition. A heightened judicial scrutiny of blight designations should encourage redevelopment agencies to exercise more caution before subjecting neighborhoods to the potential negative impacts of a blight designation.

Courts often rule that the mere designation of the urban redevelopment project is not a "taking" of property requiring compensation to the property owner. State courts also adhere to a rule that the value of property in condemnation actions is determined at the time of taking, which is usually when the eminent domain proceeding is filed. The owner of rental property that has been vandalized and made worthless in an urban redevelopment area prior to the time of taking will be out of luck in a state that follows this rule. Compensation will be paid based on the value of the property at the time of taking, not the value of the property at the time the property was blighted as part of the project designation.

The federal courts and a number of states have provided relief to the property owner in cases of this type. They either compensate the owner for the value of the property prior to any depreciation in value associated with the urban redevelopment project, or hold that the property was "taken" prior to the time any depreciation in value occurred. For discussion of these cases, see Gideon Kanner, *Condemnation Blight: How Just Is Just Compensation*? 48 NOTRE DAME L. REV. 765 (1973).

A Note on Berman v. Parker *and Blight Removal*

The landmark decision upholding the power of local urban redevelopment agencies to condemn slum areas, acquire and demolish on-site buildings (both sound and substandard), and then sell the cleared sites to developers (both private and public) to fulfill the goals of a redevelopment plan is *Berman v. Parker*, 348 U.S. 26 (1954). In this case, the local authority was the congressionally created District of Columbia Redevelopment Land Agency. As the following excerpt from Justice Douglas' opinion indicates, the court accepted the necessity to exercise eminent domain to clear a slum and declined to review the decisions of the planners regarding the choice of neighborhood, those buildings to be acquired, and post-clearance redevelopment priorities:

> Miserable and disreputable housing conditions may do more than spread disease and crime and immorality. They may also suffocate the spirit by reducing the people who live there to the status of cattle. They may indeed make living an almost insufferable burden. They may also be an ugly sore, a blight on the community which robs it of charm, which makes it a place from which men turn. The misery of housing may despoil a community as an open sewer may ruin a river.
>
> We do not sit to determine whether a particular housing project is or is not desirable. The concept of the public welfare is broad and inclusive....
>
> In the present case, Congress and its authorized agencies attack the problem of the blighted parts of the community on an area rather than on a structure-by-structure basis. That, too, is opposed by appellants. They maintain that since their building does not imperil health or safety nor contribute to the making of a slum or a blighted area, it cannot be swept into a redevelopment plan by the mere dictum of the Planning Commission or the Commissioners. The particular uses to be made of the land in the project were determined with regard to the needs of the particular community. The experts concluded that if the com-

> munity were to be healthy, if it were not to revert again to a blighted or slum area, as though possessed of a congenital disease, the area must be planned as a whole. It was not enough, they believed, to remove existing buildings that were unsanitary or unsightly. It was important to redesign the whole area so as to eliminate the conditions that cause slums—the overcrowding of dwellings, the lack of parks, the lack of adequate streets and alleys, the absence of recreational areas, the lack of light and air, the presence of outmoded street patterns. It was believed that the piecemeal approach, the removal of individual structures that were offensive, would be only a palliative. The entire area needed redesigning so that a balanced, integrated plan could be developed for the region, including not only new homes but also schools, churches, parks, streets, and shopping centers. In this way it was hoped that the cycle of decay of the area could be controlled and the birth of future slums prevented.... Such diversification in future use is plainly relevant to the maintenance of the desired housing standards and therefore within congressional power.

Id. at 32–35.

Notes and Questions

1. *Berman v. Parker* adopted a judicial attitude toward the constitutionality of urban redevelopment that was somewhat at variance with some state court decisions decided prior to that time that more restrictively interpreted "public use." The early state decisions are analyzed in Daniel R. Mandelker, *Public Purpose in Urban Renewal,* 28 Tul. L. Rev. 96 (1953).

The Supreme Court confirmed its deferential view of legislative findings of public purpose in *Hawaii Housing Authority v. Midkiff,* 467 U.S. 229 (1984). The Court upheld a Hawaii law that authorized a majority of the tenants holding leasehold estates of land to apply to the state housing agency for an order designating the land for acquisition by the tenants. In a sweeping decision, the Court held that the law reduced oligopoly in the holding of land, and left very little room for judicial review of public use. It held that "empirical debates" over the "wisdom of takings" are not to be carried out in federal courts when the legislative purpose is legitimate and the means not irrational. The Supreme Court did not revisit the question again until 2005, when it decided *Kelo,* excerpted and discussed below. In the intervening decades, tremendous changes took place in the fortunes of local jurisdictions, the availability of federal funding, political climate, and redevelopment practices—but not federal doctrine.

2. The problem of acquisition for conveyance to another private owner must be resolved under the doctrine of eminent domain, which limits governmental taking of private property for a public use, and is imposed either by the state constitution or court decision. This doctrine requires a use by the public, and if literally applied would invalidate urban redevelopment legislation that contemplates an ultimate use by a private developer.

Some state courts in the urban redevelopment cases have avoided this difficulty by dropping the *public use* test and requiring only that property acquired through eminent domain accomplish a *public benefit.* Other state courts clung to the public use test but held that it was satisfied by the public agency's acquisition and clearance of substandard property in urban renewal areas. Resale for private redevelopment was held to be "incidental" to the overriding public slum clearance use. In addition, the courts minimize the problem of private participation by emphasizing that redevelopment must be carried out in accordance with a redevelopment plan.

3. For further discussion of the evolving public use requirement, see Shaun A. Goho, *Process-Oriented Review and the Original Understanding of the Public Use Requirement*, 38 Sw. L. Rev. 37 (2008); Robert F. Manfredo, *Public Use & Public Benefit: The Battle for Upstate New York*, 71 Alb. L. Rev. 673 (2008). An early article suggested that the public use limitation on eminent domain no longer presented any serious obstacles to the implementation of public programs such as urban redevelopment plans. Comment, *The Public Use Limitation on Eminent Domain: An Advance Requiem*, 58 Yale L.J. 599 (1949).

4. For a compelling study of the rhetorical power of "blight" as a legal concept and of the property-rights-limitation it effected in Public Use Clause jurisprudence, see Wendell E. Pritchett, *The "Public Menace" of Blight: Urban Renewal and the Private Uses of Eminent Domain*, 21 Yale L. & Pol'y Rev. 1, 1–3 (2003). Pritchett recounts the strategies by which renewal advocates created a discourse of blight as a disease that endangers the future of the city, in order to secure public and judicial support for the expansive use of eminent domain that resulted in federal and state urban renewal programs. The role of the post-*Berman* cases in expanding eminent domain powers, which aided the urban renewal movement of the early twentieth century, is also examined.

A Note on The Holdout Problem and Eminent Domain

Governments have historically exercised eminent domain power to acquire land on which to build infrastructure and other projects used by or benefiting the public. This includes roads, sewers, municipal plants, hospitals and parks, and a host of other "public uses." The evolution of constitutional definition of "public use" is explored in the next section of this chapter. Often such projects require the assembly of many parcels to be feasible. Indeed, land assembly remains the most common controversy in public use litigation. Robert C. Ellickson & Vicki L. Been, Land Use Controls (3d ed. 2005).

Holdout landowners can be a significant impediment to land development. As a consequence, the use of eminent domain to acquire the holdout properties for projects benefiting the public may be the only way to allow development projects to continue. "Holdouts are endemic in public projects.... Preventing time-consuming strategic bargaining is an important justification for eminent domain." William A. Fischel, Regulatory Takings: Law, Economics, and Politics 68 (1995). Consider the complexity of site selection land acquisition necessary for local governments to assure such essential services as water, sewer, electricity, emergency preparedness and evacuation.

Now consider the obstacles to the acquisition of tracts needed for redevelopment of several blighted urban blocks or to construct public transit lines and stations. In essence, the identification of a particular tract of land necessary to the completion of a large-scale project permits the owner of that parcel to demand a higher price for the property than she would be able to otherwise, for example in a true competitive market. This gives such a holdout owner the power to veto the entire project if her demands are not met. Eminent domain can force the transfer at the price that would have prevailed in an actually competitive market. This helps to explain the constitutional principle that government must pay "just compensation" but not necessarily the price claimed by the owner.

Critics of the use of eminent domain for economic development suggest that this power is not really necessary, in view of the fact that some public projects are successfully undertaken without resort to the eminent domain power. This observation hardly eliminates the societal need or historical basis in the Constitution for the power of eminent domain.

First, projects in which private developers participate often achieve land assembly by relying on secret buying agents, in order to avoid "strategic bargaining" by owners of parcels who otherwise could attach a project premium to their price. Government actors are precluded from conducting business in a like manner, under a cloak of such secrecy. Thus public agencies are not able to operate just like their private counterparts to accumulate large tracts of land, and without the power of eminent domain, one or more holdout owners can thwart projects that nonetheless comply with the public use limitation. Furthermore, cited projects may not actually require the use of eminent domain, but that does not eliminate the importance of its threat role. Most transfers of property rights to accommodate redevelopment projects are technically voluntary transfers, but no doubt the prospect of the use of eminent domain weighs in owners' decisions to sell.

Brownfields. The inverse of the holdout problem is the return to productive use of contaminated properties, or "brownfields." Eminent domain plays an important role as communities develop strategies to clean up the brownfields of earlier economic innovation: to rehabilitate abandoned factories, reuse vacant industrial lots, clean up former petroleum storage sites, and cope with other relics of the industrial age. Mayor Anthony Williams of the District of Columbia, and past president of the National League of Cities, has called it "one of the most powerful tools city officials have to rejuvenate their neighborhoods." Charles Lane, *Justices Affirm Property Seizures*, WASH. POST, June 24, 2005, at A1. Former industrial sites are usually capable of more productive use, but traditional market forces are unlikely to prompt that use because of the high cost of cleanup, including liability of sellers under the Federal Comprehensive Environmental Response, Compensation and Liability Act (CERCLA) of 1980, 42 U.S.C. §§9601–75, or similar state statutes. For an updated compilation of state law governing brownfield remediation and cleanup liability, see National Conference of State Legislatures, http://www.ncsl.org/programs/environ/brownfields/brownfields.htm (Issue Area: Environmental Protection). Thus, condemnation is often the only practical way to redevelop contaminated urban properties. *See generally* Andrea L. Reed, Note, *Cleaning up Condemnation Proceedings*, 93 IOWA L. REV. 1135, 1143–44 (2008).

A Note on the Use of Eminent Domain for Economic Development

With the disappearance of the terminal slums, local urban redevelopment programs turned to different objectives. Local agencies used the eminent domain power to acquire property for housing rehabilitation and to implement commercial or industrial development programs. In some of these programs, the areas cleared were not blighted substandard areas in the conventional sense. State courts in recent years have faced new public use challenges to this new use of urban redevelopment powers.

Doctrinally, this sea change is manifested, albeit partially, in the "public use" cases of the last thirty years. While advocates have drawn sharp lines for or against the use of eminent domain to take private property for a publically beneficial project in which the end user will be a different private owner, courts are called on repeatedly to apply constitutional principles specific factual records and under varying state and local legislative enactments. This realm of contest over the meanings of public use or purpose versus the extent of private benefit from the taking, is pointedly illustrated by two influential cases a generation apart, each reviewing efforts of Michigan cities to use eminent domain to bolster their economic fortunes as their industrial base eroded: *Poletown Neighborhood Council v. City of Detroit*, 304 N.W.2d 455 (1981), and *County of Wayne v. Hathcock*, 684 N.W.2d 765 (Mich. 2004).

In *Poletown* the Michigan Supreme Court upheld the use of condemnation to achieve a plan by the Detroit Economic Development Corporation to acquire a large tract of land to be conveyed to General Motors Corporation as a site for construction of an assembly plant. A neighborhood association and several individual residents of the affected area known as Poletown, brought suit to challenge the project, claiming that the city had abused its discretion in deciding that condemnation of plaintiffs' property was necessary to complete the project. The supreme court upheld the trial court order dismissing the complaint. After noting that the Michigan constitution provides that property may only be taken for a public use, and that the Michigan cases used the terms "public use" and "public purpose" interchangeably, the court turned to a consideration of the statute.

The supreme court viewed the Economic Development Corporations Act as part of comprehensive legislation to address planning, housing and zoning, with the purpose to provide for the general health, safety, and welfare "through alleviating unemployment, providing economic assistance to industry, assisting the rehabilitation of blighted areas, and fostering urban redevelopment." To further the act's objective, the legislature had authorized municipalities to acquire property by condemnation in order to provide industrial and commercial sites and the means of transfer from the municipality to private users. Section 2 of the act provided:

> There exists in this state the continuing need for programs to alleviate and prevent conditions of unemployment, and that it is accordingly necessary to assist and retain local industries and commercial enterprises to strengthen and revitalize the economy of this state and its municipalities; that accordingly it is necessary to provide means and methods for encouragement and assistance of industrial and commercial enterprises in locating, purchasing, constructing, reconstructing, modernizing, improving, maintaining, repairing, furnishing, equipping, and expanding in this state and in its municipalities; and that it is also necessary to encourage the location and expansion of commercial enterprises to more conveniently provide needed services and facilities of the commercial enterprises to municipalities and the residents thereof. *Therefore, the powers granted in this act constitute the performance of essential public purposes and functions for this state and its municipalities.*" M.C.L. 125.1602; M.S.A. §5.3520(2). (emphasis added)

The neighborhood did not challenge the legislature's declaration that programs to alleviate conditions of unemployment and to preserve and develop industry are essential public purposes; nor contest the constitutionality of that general legislative power. Their challenge was directly to the constitutionality of using the power of eminent domain to condemn one person's property to convey it to another private person in order to bolster the economy.

> [Plaintiff-appellants] argue that whatever incidental benefit may accrue to the public, assembling land to General Motors' specifications for conveyance to General Motors for its uncontrolled use in profit making is really a taking for private use and not a public use because General Motors is the primary beneficiary of the condemnation. The defendants-appellees contend, on the other hand, that the controlling public purpose in taking this land is to create an industrial site which will be used to alleviate and prevent conditions of unemployment and fiscal distress. The fact that it will be conveyed to and ultimately used by a private manufacturer does not defeat this predominant public purpose.
>
> There is no dispute about the law. All agree that condemnation for a public use or purpose is permitted. All agree that condemnation for a private use or

> purpose is forbidden. Similarly, condemnation for a private use cannot be authorized whatever its incidental public benefit, and condemnation for a public purpose cannot be forbidden whatever the incidental private gain. The heart of this dispute is whether the proposed condemnation is for the primary benefit of the public or the private user.

The Michigan court applied deferential review to the legislature's determination that eminent domain "meets a public need and serves an essential public purpose," citing the United States Supreme Court holding in *Berman* that when a legislature speaks, the public interest has been declared in terms "well-nigh conclusive." *Berman v. Parker,* 348 U.S. 26, 32 (1954). Consequently, the court accepted Detroit's assessment of the project's public importance, concluding that,

> [T]he city presented substantial evidence of the severe economic conditions facing the residents of the city and state, the need for new industrial development to revitalize local industries, the economic boost the proposed project would provide, and the lack of other adequate available sites to implement the project.
>
> As Justice Cooley stated over a hundred years ago "the most important consideration in the case of eminent domain is the necessity of accomplishing some public good which is otherwise impracticable, and ... the law does not so much regard the means as the need." *People* ex rel. *Detroit Howell R. Co. v. Salem Twp. Board,* 20 Mich. 452, 480–481 (1870). When there is such public need, "[t]he abstract right [of an individual] to make use of his own property in his own way is compelled to yield to the general comfort and protection of community, and to a proper regard to relative rights, in others."
>
> In the instant case the benefit to be received by the municipality invoking the power of eminent domain is a clear and significant one and is sufficient to satisfy this Court that such a project was an intended and a legitimate object of the Legislature when it allowed municipalities to exercise condemnation powers even though a private party will also, ultimately, receive a benefit as an incident thereto.... If the public benefit was not so clear and significant, we would hesitate to sanction approval of such a project.

The *Poletown* court nevertheless articulated a "heightened scrutiny" standard, to be applied where the condemnation power as exercised benefits specific and identifiable private interests—as in the case before it.

> The power of eminent domain is restricted to furthering public uses and purposes and is not to be exercised without substantial proof that the public is primarily to be benefited.... Such public benefit cannot be speculative or marginal but must be clear and significant if it is to be within the legitimate purpose as stated by the Legislature. We hold this project is warranted on the basis that its significance for the people of Detroit and the state has been demonstrated.

Notes and Questions

1. *Judicial Review Standard.* What does the *Poletown* 'heightened scrutiny' standard require of the reviewing court? In *City of Center Line v. Chmelko*, 416 N.W.2d 401 (Mich. Ct. App. 1987), the state's intermediate court applied the "heightened" judicial scrutiny test enunciated in *Poletown* to invalidate a taking of land carried out by the city in order to protect its tax base and the economic viability of a commercial district. The court invalidated a city's exercise of eminent domain to condemn allegedly

"blighted" commercial buildings adjacent to a car dealership so the dealer could expand and not leave its location, as it had threatened to do. The court rejected the city's reasons for condemning the property as spurious. Although the city claimed that the condemned buildings were blighted, there was evidence in the case that they were well maintained.

What factors explain the different outcomes in these two decisions? Was it important that in *Center Line* the business planned to leave the city? In *Poletown* the project was carried out to make way for a new manufacturing plant in the city so GM's Cadillac division would not leave Detroit. How does the heightened scrutiny standard apply?

2. *"A Desperate City and a Giant Corporation."* Justice Fitzgerald filed a lengthy dissent which he concluded by stating:

> Eminent domain is an attribute of sovereignty. When individual citizens are forced to suffer great social dislocation to permit private corporations to construct plants where they deem it most profitable, one is left to wonder who the sovereign is.
>
> The sudden and fundamental change in established law effected by the Court in this case, entailing such a significant diminution of constitutional rights, cannot be justified as a function of judicial construction; the only proper vehicle for change of this dimension is a constitutional amendment. What has been done in this case can be explained by the overwhelming sense of inevitability that has attended this litigation from the beginning; a sense attributable to the combination and coincidence of the interests of a desperate city administration and a giant corporation willing and able to take advantage of the opportunity that presented itself. The justification for it, like the inevitability of it, has been made to seem more acceptable by the "team spirit" chorus of approval of the project which has been supplied by the voices of labor, business, industry, government, finance, and even the news media. Virtually the only discordant sounds of dissent have come from the minuscule minority of citizens most profoundly affected by this case, the Poletown residents whose neighborhood has been destroyed.
>
> With this case the Court has subordinated a constitutional right to private corporate interests. As demolition of existing structures on the future plant site goes forward, the best that can be hoped for, jurisprudentially, is that the precedential value of the case will be lost in the accumulating rubble.

Id. at 481–82.

3. *Poletown's Progeny.* The Michigan Supreme Court's *Poletown* decision was a pioneer in defining private economic development as "public use" under the eminent domain clause in that state's constitution, and several states followed its lead. According to a report issued in 2003, more than 10,000 properties were condemned or proposed for condemnation across the United States, for transfer to another private party. DANA BERLINER, PUBLIC POWER, PRIVATE GAIN 2 (2003) (publication of the Institute for Justice). Big box stores sought to obtain properties for commercial expansion through condemnation rather than through voluntary sales. *See* Adam Mossof, *The Death of Poletown: The Future of Eminent Domain and Urban Development after* County of Wayne v. Hathcock, 2004 MICH. ST. L. REV. 837, 841(2004).

4. *Relocation.* The *Poletown* project involved the demolition of residential (and nonresidential) property solely for a nonresidential project. While property owners received compensation and were relocated in accordance with the Uniform Relocation Act, the

demolished housing was not replaced. Legal rights and duties concerning displacement and relocation of homes and businesses are discussed in section F *infra*.

5. *Public Use and Public Purpose: Distinguished or Conflated?* (a) The modern cases tend to take a relaxed review of whether condemnation is for a public purpose when eminent domain is used as an adjunct to a development effort. *See, e.g., Shreveport v. Chanse Gas Corp.*, 794 So. 2d 962, 973 (La. Ct. App. 2001) (relying on *Berman*, *Midkiff*, and relevant legislative declarations to conclude that "economic development, in the form of a convention center and headquarters hotel, satisfies the public purposes and public necessity requirement of [state constitution]"); *Prince George's County v. Collington*, 339 A.2d 278 (Md. 1975) (county's acquisition by condemnation of lands to create industrial park to provide employment and general economic benefit was for a 'public use' rather than private use, even when the commercial land would be owned by private entities); *City of Duluth v. State*, 390 N.W.2d 757 (Minn. 1986) (condemnation of non-operating food processing plant to redevelop with a paper mill would be justified either to permit urban redevelopment of dilapidated property or to permit a development plan to go forward, even in face of landowners claim of a plan to reopen the food processing plant sometime in the future); *City of Kansas City v. Hon*, 972 S.W.2d 407 (Mo. Ct. App. 1998) (airport expansion to offer facilities for use of commercial or industrial, aviation-related developments); *Courtesy Sandwich Shop, Inc. v. Port of New York Auth.*, 190 N.E.2d 402 (N.Y. 1963) (World Trade Center is a public purpose because the use of the property sought to be condemned is functionally related to the centralizing of all port business even though private persons are to be the immediate lessees); *In re Fisher*, 730 N.Y.S.2d 516, 517 (Sup. Ct. App. Div. 1st Dep't 2001) (condemnation of property to expand the New York Stock Exchange's facilities, premised upon a finding of substantial public benefit from increased tax revenues, economic development and job opportunities, as well as preservation and enhancement of the city's prestigious position as a worldwide financial center); *City of Jamestown v. Leevers Supermarkets, Inc.*, 552 N.W.2d 365 (N.D. 1996) (stimulation of commercial growth and removal of economic stagnation satisfied "public use" requirement of United States and North Dakota's Constitutions, reversing and remanding on other grounds); *In Re Port of Grays Harbor*, 638 P.2d 633 (Wash. Ct. App. 1982) (proposed industrial development is for a public purpose and the Port's plan to eventually lease the property to private industry is statutorily authorized and is incidental to the main public purpose).

(b) The view is not without limits. *See, e.g., Wilmington Parking Auth. v. Land With Improvements*, 521 A.2d 227 (Del. 1987) (invalidating taking of land for parking facility); *City of Owensboro v. McCormick*, 581 S.W.2d 3 (Ky. 1979) (traditional public use test applied to invalidate statute authorizing acquisition of "any lands" for commercial or industrial development); *Mayor of Baltimore City v. Valsamaki*, 916 A.2d 324 (Md. 2007) (holding that, while urban renewal may be the basis for a government's taking of private property, a government entity must provide some assurance that the urban renewal will constitute a public use or public purpose for the property taken; it is not enough for the government entity to simply say that it is conducting urban renewal and leave it at that); *In re City of Seattle*, 638 P.2d 549 (Wash. 1981) (where primary purpose of municipal improvement, for which land was sought to be condemned, was to promote retail goals of the project and to forestall core city decay, such was not a "public use" for purpose of eminent domain, notwithstanding that part of project included a public square, park, museum and off-street parking, for which functions a city has eminent domain authority).

(c) The *Poletown* case attracted considerable negative academic commentary, foreshadowing more intensive scrutiny of public use/private benefit questions by scholars as well as courts. *See, e.g.*, Thomas S. Ulen, *Still Hazy After All These Years*, 22 Law & Soc.

INQUIRY 1011, 1035 (1997) (book review of WILLIAM A. FISCHEL, REGULATORY TAKINGS: LAW, ECONOMICS, AND POLITICS (1995)). For a sampling of the rejuvenated discussion of the public use requirement, see, e.g., Shaun A. Goho, *Process-Oriented Review and the Original Understanding of the Public Use Requirement*, 38 SW. L. REV. 37 (2008); John A. Humbach, *Constitutional Limits on the Power to Take Private Property: Public Purpose and Public Use*, 66 OR. L. REV. 547 (1987); David M. Lawrence, *Constitutional Limitations on Downtown Renewal Projects*, 35 VAND. L. REV. 277 (1980); Daniel R. Mandelker, *Public Entrepreneurship: A Legal Primer*, 15 REAL EST. L.J. 3 (1986); Robert F. Manfredo, *Public Use & Public Benefit: The Battle for Upstate New York*, 71 ALB. L. REV. 673 (2008); William J. Appel, Annotation, *Eminent Domain: Industrial Park or Similar Development as a Public Use Justifying Condemnation of Private Property*, 62 A.L.R. 4th 1183 (1989).

6. *County of Wayne v. Hathcock*. In 2004, the *Poletown* Court again faced the task of determining whether an economic development condemnation would constitute a "public use." The Michigan Supreme Court overruled its 1981 *Poletown* decision, in *County of Wayne v. Hathcock*, 684 N.W.2d 765 (Mich. 2004). In *Hathcock*, Wayne County sought to use the power of eminent domain to condemn the defendants' real property for the construction of a business and technology park. Wayne County argued that the new park would ultimately create jobs, increase tax revenue and broaden the County's tax base from predominately industrial to a mix of industrial, technology, and service. Overall, the new park would constitute a public use by revitalizing the county's economy, attracting new business to the area.

The court held that Wayne County intended to transfer "the condemned properties to private parties in a manner wholly inconsistent with the common understanding of 'public use,'" and as that requirement was understood when the Michigan Constitution was ratified. The transfer of condemned property to a private entity would be appropriate only in one of three contexts: "(1) where "public necessity of the extreme sort" requires collective action; (2) where the property remains subject to public oversight after transfer to a private entity; and (3) where the property is selected because of "facts of independent public significance," rather than the interests of the private entity to which the property is eventually transferred. The court held that Wayne County's business and technology park failed to fall into any of these three contexts of public use.

7. Scholarly commentary on the *Hathcock* decision has been largely laudatory. *See, e.g.*, M. Ryan Krirkham, County of Wayne v. Hathcock*: the Resurrection of the Public Use Limitation on the Power of Eminent Domain*, 32 N. KY. L. REV. 215, 236 (2005); Timothy Sandefur, *A Gleeful Obituary for* Poletown Neighborhood Council v. Detroit, 28 HARV. J.L. & PUB. POL'Y 651 (2005); Ilya Somin, *Overcoming* Poletown: County of Wayne v. Hathcock, *Economic Development Takings, and the Future of Public Use*, 2004 MICH. L. REV. 1005.

8. *The Property Rights "Movement" of the 1990s*. In the land-use arena, one of the most significant events of the last two decades has been the rise and impact of the so-called private property rights movement. Today it is a national coalition targeting land-use and environmental laws and policies, such as those for smart growth, farmland and wetland protection, and endangered species protection. This coalition argues that restricting private property is inefficient, ineffective, and un-American. The property rights movement has pursued a multilevel strategy to achieve its objectives—judicial, legislative, policy, and public relations. Since 1991, every state in the United States has considered state-based legislation in support of the policy position of the property rights movement, and twenty-seven states have passed such legislation. Compensation and taking-impact-assessment laws are the majority of the laws passed by the states. Harvey M. Jacobs, *New Actions or*

New Arguments Over Regulatory Takings?, 117 YALE L.J. SUPP. 65 (2007), *available at* http://thepocketpart.org/2007/09/16/jacobs.html. *See also* Steven J. Eagle, *The Birth of the Property Rights Movement (2001), available at* http://www.cato.org/pubs/pas/pa404.pdf (publication of the Cato Institute).

9. Debate continues over the degree to which these legal developments are rooted in a grassroots movement or produced by an industry-funded advocacy campaign to cripple environmental regulation. *See, e.g.*, DAVID HELVARG, THE WAR AGAINST THE GREENS: THE "WISE-USE" MOVEMENT, THE NEW RIGHT AND ANTI-ENVIRONMENTAL VIOLENCE (1994); LET THE PEOPLE JUDGE: WISE USE AND THE PRIVATE PROPERTY RIGHTS MOVEMENT (John D. Echeverria & Raymond Booth Eby eds. 1995); Jonathan H. Adler, *Back to the Future of Conservation: Changing Perceptions of Property Rights & Environmental Protection*, 1 NYU J. L. & LIBERTY 987 (2005); Robert H Nelson, *Federal Zoning: The New Era in Environmental Policy, in* LAND RIGHTS: THE 1990S PROPERTY RIGHTS REBELLION (Bruce Yandle ed. 1995).

Susette Kelo, the homeowner plaintiff in the case that follows, was represented by the Institute for Justice, self-described as the nation's only libertarian public interest law firm, which was founded in 1991 in Washington, D.C.

2. Redevelopment Purposes and Process in the Constitution's Crosshairs

In 2005, the U.S. Supreme Court decided three cases that rebuffed takings clause claims in federal court, and redirected private property owners to state courts and to state and local administrative and legislative processes for resolution. Taken together, the 2005 takings cases emphasize federalism's respect for the approaches of varied stated and local governments to property rights, land use regulation disputes, and the balances struck in light of local knowledge.

In *Kelo v. City of New London*, 545 U.S. 469 (2005), the Court broadly interpreted the "public use" phrase in the Takings Clause, holding that the public use clause permits governmental taking of private property for transfer to new private owners for the purpose of promoting "economic development." The Court declined to impose a heightened standard of judicial review on state and local government determinations of the public benefits anticipated from the use of eminent domain. Earlier in the term, the Court had reaffirmed the requirement that takings compensation claims against state and local governments must be litigated first in state rather than federal court, *San Remo Hotel v. City and County of San Francisco*, 545 U.S. 323, 339 (2005). Similarly, the Court steered challengers to state and local land use laws and environmental regulations into state legal and administrative remedies, in *Lingle v. Chevron USA Inc.,* 544 U.S. 528 (2005), refusing to recognize a more rigorous substantive due process challenge or any additional models to review regulatory takings. The concern for state and local decision making about land use halted the ascendancy of a nearly absolute view of property rights during the preceding two decades. One of the early and influential volleys in the rise of that modern property rights movement was RICHARD A. EPSTEIN, TAKINGS: PRIVATE PROPERTY AND THE POWER OF EMINENT DOMAIN (1985).

Read the following opinion excerpts, and consider the extent to which *Kelo* can be explained as a decision about the comparative institutional competence of courts and legislatures in discerning local public needs. The *Kelo* majority applied the principle that the role of courts is limited by "a longstanding policy of deference to legislative judgments" when reviewing public purpose. The case also serves as a touchstone in takings jurisprudence, and as a lens through which to consider persistent dilemmas of the interconnections of public and private money and influence in the redevelopment of U.S. cities at the turning of the twenty-first century. Several of these dilemmas are discussed in notes following the case.

Kelo v. City of New London, Connecticut

United States Supreme Court
545 U.S. 469 (2005)

Justice STEVENS delivered the opinion of the Court.

In 2000, the city of New London approved a development plan that, in the words of the Supreme Court of Connecticut, was "projected to create in excess of 1,000 jobs, to increase tax and other revenues, and to revitalize an economically distressed city, including its downtown and waterfront areas." In assembling the land needed for this project, the city's development agent has purchased property from willing sellers and proposes to use the power of eminent domain to acquire the remainder of the property from unwilling owners in exchange for just compensation. The question presented is whether the city's proposed disposition of this property qualifies as a "public use" within the meaning of the Takings Clause of the Fifth Amendment to the Constitution.

The city of New London (hereinafter City) sits at the junction of the Thames River and the Long Island Sound in southeastern Connecticut. Decades of economic decline led a state agency in 1990 to designate the City a "distressed municipality." In 1996, the Federal Government closed the Naval Undersea Warfare Center, which had been located in the Fort Trumbull area of the City and had employed over 1,500 people. In 1998, the City's unemployment rate was nearly double that of the State, and its population of just under 24,000 residents was at its lowest since 1920.

These conditions prompted state and local officials to target New London, and particularly its Fort Trumbull area, for economic revitalization. To this end, respondent New London Development Corporation (NLDC), a private nonprofit entity established some years earlier to assist the City in planning economic development, was reactivated. In January 1998, the State authorized a $5.35 million bond issue to support the NLDC's planning activities and a $10 million bond issue toward the creation of a Fort Trumbull State Park. In February, the pharmaceutical company Pfizer Inc. announced that it would build a $300 million research facility on a site immediately adjacent to Fort Trumbull; local planners hoped that Pfizer would draw new business to the area, thereby serving as a catalyst to the area's rejuvenation. After receiving initial approval from the city council, the NLDC continued its planning activities and held a series of neighborhood meetings to educate the public about the process. In May, the city council authorized the NLDC to formally submit its plans to the relevant state agencies for review. Upon obtaining state-level approval, the NLDC finalized an integrated development plan focused on 90 acres of the Fort Trumbull area.

The NLDC intended the development plan to capitalize on the arrival of the Pfizer facility and the new commerce it was expected to attract. In addition to creating jobs, generating tax revenue, and helping to "build momentum for the revitalization of downtown New London," *id.*, at 92, the plan was also designed to make the City more attractive and to create leisure and recreational opportunities on the waterfront and in the park. The city council approved the plan in January 2000, and designated the NLDC as its development agent in charge of implementation. The city council also authorized the NLDC to purchase property or to acquire property by exercising eminent domain in the City's name. The NLDC successfully negotiated the purchase of most of the real estate in the 90-acre area, but its negotiations with petitioners failed. As a consequence, in November 2000, the NLDC initiated the condemnation proceedings that gave rise to this case

Petitioner Susette Kelo has lived in the Fort Trumbull area since 1997. She has made extensive improvements to her house, which she prizes for its water view.... In all, the nine petitioners own 15 properties in Fort Trumbull—4 in parcel 3 of the development plan and 11 in parcel 4A. Ten of the parcels are occupied by the owner or a family member; the other five are held as investment properties. There is no allegation that any of these properties is blighted or otherwise in poor condition; rather, they were condemned only because they happen to be located in the development area.

We granted certiorari to determine whether a city's decision to take property for the purpose of economic development satisfies the "public use" requirement of the Fifth Amendment. Two polar propositions are perfectly clear. On the one hand, it has long been accepted that the sovereign may not take the property of *A* for the sole purpose of transferring it to another private party *B*, even though *A* is paid just compensation. On the other hand, it is equally clear that a State may transfer property from one private party to another if future "use by the public" is the purpose of the taking; the condemnation of land for a railroad with common-carrier duties is a familiar example. Neither of these propositions, however, determines the disposition of this case. As for the first proposition, the City would no doubt be forbidden from taking petitioners' land for the purpose of conferring a private benefit on a particular private party. Nor would the City be allowed to take property under the mere pretext of a public purpose, when its actual purpose was to bestow a private benefit. The takings before us, however, would be executed pursuant to a "carefully considered" development plan. The trial judge and all the members of the Supreme Court of Connecticut agreed that there was no evidence of an illegitimate purpose in this case. Therefore, the City's development plan was not adopted "to benefit a particular class of identifiable individuals."

On the other hand, this is not a case in which the City is planning to open the condemned land—at least not in its entirety—to use by the general public. Nor will the private lessees of the land in any sense be required to operate like common carriers, making their services available to all comers. But although such a projected use would be sufficient to satisfy the public use requirement, this "Court long ago rejected any literal requirement that condemned property be put into use for the general public." Indeed, while many state courts in the mid-19th century endorsed "use by the public" as the proper definition of public use, that narrow view steadily eroded over time. Not only was the "use by the public" test difficult to administer (*e.g.*, what proportion of the public need have access to the property? at what price?), but it proved to be impractical given the diverse and always evolving needs of society. Accordingly, when this Court began applying the Fifth Amendment to the States at the close of the 19th century, it embraced the broader and more natural interpretation of public use as "public purpose...." We have repeatedly and consistently rejected that narrow test ever since.

The disposition of this case therefore turns on the question whether the City's development plan serves a "public purpose." Without exception, our cases have defined that concept broadly, reflecting our longstanding policy of deference to legislative judgments in this field. In *Berman v. Parker*, this Court upheld a redevelopment plan targeting a blighted area of Washington, D.C., in which most of the housing for the area's 5,000 inhabitants was beyond repair. Under the plan, the area would be condemned and part of it utilized for the construction of streets, schools, and other public facilities. The remainder of the land would be leased or sold to private parties for the purpose of redevelopment, including the construction of low-cost housing. The owner of a department store located in the area challenged the condemnation, pointing out that his store was not itself blighted and arguing that the creation of a "better balanced, more attractive community" was not a valid public use. Writing for a unanimous Court, Justice Douglas refused to evaluate this claim in isolation, deferring instead to the legislative and agency judgment that the area "must be planned as a whole" for the plan to be successful. The Court explained that "community redevelopment programs need not, by force of the Constitution, be on a piecemeal basis—lot by lot, building by building." The public use underlying the taking was unequivocally affirmed:

> We do not sit to determine whether a particular housing project is or is not desirable. The concept of the public welfare is broad and inclusive.... The values it represents are spiritual as well as physical, aesthetic as well as monetary. It is within the power of the legislature to determine that the community should be beautiful as well as healthy, spacious as well as clean, well-balanced as well as carefully patrolled. In the present case, the Congress and its authorized agencies have made determinations that take into account a wide variety of values. It is not for us to reappraise them. If those who govern the District of Columbia decide that the Nation's Capital should be beautiful as well as sanitary, there is nothing in the Fifth Amendment that stands in the way.

In *Hawaii Housing Authority v. Midkiff*, the Court considered a Hawaii statute whereby fee title was taken from lessors and transferred to lessees (for just compensation) in order to reduce the concentration of land ownership. We unanimously upheld the statute and rejected the Ninth Circuit's view that it was "a naked attempt on the part of the state of Hawaii to take the property of A and transfer it to B solely for B's private use and benefit." Reaffirming *Berman's* deferential approach to legislative judgments in this field, we concluded that the State's purpose of eliminating the "social and economic evils of a land oligopoly" qualified as a valid public use. Our opinion also rejected the contention that the mere fact that the State immediately transferred the properties to private individuals upon condemnation somehow diminished the public character of the taking. "[I]t is only the taking's purpose, and not its mechanics," we explained, that matters in determining public use....

Viewed as a whole, our jurisprudence has recognized that the needs of society have varied between different parts of the Nation, just as they have evolved over time in response to changed circumstances. Our earliest cases in particular embodied a strong theme of federalism, emphasizing the "great respect" that we owe to state legislatures and state courts in discerning local public needs. For more than a century, our public use jurisprudence has wisely eschewed rigid formulas and intrusive scrutiny in favor of affording legislatures broad latitude in determining what public needs justify the use of the takings power.

Those who govern the City were not confronted with the need to remove blight in the Fort Trumbull area, but their determination that the area was sufficiently distressed to justify a program of economic rejuvenation is entitled to our deference. The City has carefully formulated an economic development plan that it believes will provide appreciable benefits to the community, including—but by no means limited to—new jobs and increased tax revenue. As with other exercises in urban planning and development, the City is endeavoring to coordinate a variety of commercial, residential, and recreational uses of land, with the hope that they will form a whole greater than the sum of its parts. To effectuate this plan, the City has invoked a state statute that specifically authorizes the use of eminent domain to promote economic development. Given the comprehensive character of the plan, the thorough deliberation that preceded its adoption, and the limited scope of our review, it is appropriate for us, as it was in *Berman*, to resolve the challenges of the individual owners, not on a piecemeal basis, but rather in light of the entire plan. Because that plan unquestionably serves a public purpose, the takings challenged here satisfy the public use requirement of the Fifth Amendment.

To avoid this result, petitioners urge us to adopt a new bright-line rule that economic development does not qualify as a public use. Putting aside the unpersuasive suggestion that the City's plan will provide only purely economic benefits, neither precedent nor logic supports petitioners' proposal. Promoting economic development is a traditional and long-accepted function of government. There is, moreover, no principled way of distinguishing economic development from the other public purposes that we have recognized.

Petitioners contend that using eminent domain for economic development impermissibly blurs the boundary between public and private takings. Again, our cases foreclose this objection. Quite simply, the government's pursuit of a public purpose will often benefit individual private parties. For example, in *Midkiff*, the forced transfer of property conferred a direct and significant benefit on those lessees who were previously unable to purchase their homes.... The owner of the department store in *Berman* objected to "taking from one businessman for the benefit of another businessman," referring to the fact that under the redevelopment plan land would be leased or sold to private developers for redevelopment. Our rejection of that contention has particular relevance to the instant case: "The public end may be as well or better served through an agency of private enterprise than through a department of government—or so the Congress might conclude. We cannot say that public ownership is the sole method of promoting the public purposes of community redevelopment projects."

It is further argued that without a bright-line rule nothing would stop a city from transferring citizen *A*'s property to citizen *B* for the sole reason that citizen *B* will put the property to a more productive use and thus pay more taxes. Such a one-to-one transfer of property, executed outside the confines of an integrated development plan, is not presented in this case. While such an unusual exercise of government power would certainly raise a suspicion that a private purpose was afoot, the hypothetical cases posited by petitioners can be confronted if and when they arise. They do not warrant the crafting of an artificial restriction on the concept of public use.

Alternatively, petitioners maintain that for takings of this kind we should require a "reasonable certainty" that the expected public benefits will actually accrue. Such a rule, however, would represent an even greater departure from our precedent. "When the legislature's purpose is legitimate and its means are not irrational, our cases make clear that empirical debates over the wisdom of takings—no less than debates over the wisdom of other kinds of socioeconomic legislation—are not to be carried out in the federal courts...." The disadvantages of a heightened form of review are especially pronounced in this type of case. Orderly implementation of a comprehensive redevelopment plan obviously requires that the legal rights of all interested parties be established before new construction can be commenced. A constitutional rule that required postponement of the judicial approval of every condemnation until the likelihood of success of the plan had been assured would unquestionably impose a significant impediment to the successful consummation of many such plans.

Just as we decline to second-guess the City's considered judgments about the efficacy of its development plan, we also decline to second-guess the City's determinations as to what lands it needs to acquire in order to effectuate the project. "It is not for the courts to oversee the choice of the boundary line nor to sit in review on the size of a particular project area. Once the question of the public purpose has been decided, the amount and character of land to be taken for the project and the need for a particular tract to complete the integrated plan rests in the discretion of the legislative branch."

In affirming the City's authority to take petitioners' properties, we do not minimize the hardship that condemnations may entail, notwithstanding the payment of just compensation. We emphasize that nothing in our opinion precludes any State from placing further restrictions on its exercise of the takings power. Indeed, many States already impose "public use" requirements that are stricter than the federal baseline. Some of these requirements have been established as a matter of state constitutional law [see, e.g., County of Wayne v. Hathcock, 684 N.W. 2d 765 (Mich. 2004)], while others are expressed in state eminent domain statutes that carefully limit the grounds upon which takings may be exercised. As the submissions of the parties and their *amici* make clear, the necessity and wisdom of using eminent domain to promote economic development are certainly matters of legitimate public debate. This Court's authority, however, extends only to determining whether the City's proposed condemnations are for a "public use" within the meaning of the Fifth Amendment to the Federal Constitution. Because over a century of our case law interpreting that provision dictates an affirmative answer to that question, we may not grant petitioners the relief that they seek.

Justice O'CONNOR, with whom THE CHIEF JUSTICE, Justice SCALIA, and Justice THOMAS join, dissenting....

Today the Court abandons this long-held, basic limitation on government power. Under the banner of economic development, all private property is now vulnerable to being taken and transferred to another private owner, so long as it might be upgraded—*i.e.,* given to an owner who will use it in a way that the legislature deems more beneficial to the public—in the process. To reason, as the Court does, that the incidental public benefits resulting from the subsequent ordinary use of private property render economic development takings "for public use" is to wash out any distinction between private and public use of property—and thereby effectively to delete the words "for public use" from the Takings Clause of the Fifth Amendment.... While the Takings Clause presupposes that government can take private property without the owner's consent, the just compensation requirement spreads the cost of condemnations and thus "prevents the public from loading upon one individual more than his just share of the burdens of government." The public use requirement, in turn, imposes a more basic limitation, circumscribing the very scope of the eminent domain power: Government may compel an individual to forfeit her property for the *public's* use, but not for the benefit of another private person. This requirement promotes fairness as well as security.

Where is the line between "public" and "private" property use? We give considerable deference to legislatures' determinations about what governmental activities will advantage the public. But were the political branches the sole arbiters of the public-private distinction, the Public Use Clause would amount to little more than hortatory fluff. An external, judicial check on how the public use requirement is interpreted, however limited, is necessary if this constraint on government power is to retain any meaning.

Our cases have generally identified three categories of takings that comply with the public use requirement, though it is in the nature of things that the boundaries between these categories are not always firm. Two are relatively straightforward and uncontroversial. First, the sovereign may transfer private property to public ownership—such as for a road, a hospital, or a military base. Second, the sovereign may transfer private property to private parties, often common carriers, who make the property available for the public's use—such as with a railroad, a public utility, or a stadium. But "public ownership" and "use-by-the-public" are sometimes too constricting and impractical ways to define the scope of the Public Use Clause. Thus we have allowed that, in certain circumstances and to meet certain exigencies, takings that serve a public purpose also satisfy the Constitution even if the property is destined for subsequent private use. See, *e.g.*, *Berman v. Parker*; *Hawaii Housing Authority v. Midkiff*.

This case returns us for the first time in over 20 years to the hard question of when a purportedly "public purpose" taking meets the public use requirement. It presents an issue of first impression: Are economic development takings constitutional? I would hold that they are not. We are guided by two precedents about the taking of real property by eminent domain. In *Berman*, we upheld takings within a blighted neighborhood of Washington, D.C. The neighborhood had so deteriorated that, for example, 64.3% of its dwellings were beyond repair. It had become burdened with "overcrowding of dwellings," "lack of adequate streets and alleys," and "lack of light and air." Congress had determined that the neighborhood had become "injurious to the public health, safety, morals, and welfare" and that it was necessary to "eliminat[e] all such injurious conditions by employing all means necessary and appropriate for the purpose," including eminent domain. Mr. Berman's department store was not itself blighted. Having approved of Congress' decision to eliminate the harm to the public emanating from the blighted neighborhood, however, we did not second-guess its decision to treat the neighborhood as a whole rather than lot-by-lot. In *Midkiff*, we upheld a land condemnation scheme in Hawaii whereby title in real property was taken from lessors and transferred to lessees. At that time, the State and Federal Governments owned nearly 49% of the State's land, and another 47% was in the hands of only 72 private landowners. Concentration of land ownership was so dramatic that on the State's most urbanized island, Oahu, 22 landowners owned 72.5% of the fee simple titles. The Hawaii Legislature had concluded that the oligopoly in land ownership was "skewing the State's residential fee simple market, inflating land prices, and injuring the public tranquility and welfare," and therefore enacted a condemnation scheme for redistributing title.

In those decisions, we emphasized the importance of deferring to legislative judgments about public purpose. Because courts are ill equipped to evaluate the efficacy of proposed legislative initiatives, we rejected as unworkable the idea of courts' "deciding on what is and is not a governmental function and ... invalidating legislation on the basis of their view on that question at the moment of decision, a practice which has proved impracticable in other fields." Likewise, we recognized our inability to evaluate whether, in a given case, eminent domain is a necessary means by which to pursue the legislature's ends.

Yet for all the emphasis on deference, *Berman* and *Midkiff* hewed to a bedrock principle without which our public use jurisprudence would collapse: "A purely private taking could not withstand the scrutiny of the public use requirement; it would serve no legitimate purpose of government and would thus be void." To protect that principle, those decisions reserved "a role for courts to play in reviewing a legislature's judgment of what constitutes a public use ... [though] the Court in *Berman* made clear that it is 'an extremely narrow' one." The Court's holdings in *Berman* and *Midkiff* were true to the principle underlying the Public Use Clause. In both those cases, the extraordinary, precondemnation use of the targeted property inflicted affirmative harm on society—in *Berman* through blight resulting from extreme poverty and in *Midkiff* through oligopoly resulting from extreme wealth. And in both cases, the relevant legislative body had found that eliminating the existing property use was necessary to remedy the harm. Thus a public purpose was realized when the harmful use was eliminated. Because each taking *directly* achieved a public benefit, it did not matter that the property was turned over to private use. Here, in contrast, New London does not claim that Susette Kelo's and Wilhelmina Dery's well-maintained homes are the source of any social harm. Indeed, it could not so claim without adopting the absurd argument that any single-family home that might be razed to make way for an apartment building, or any church that might be replaced with a retail store, or any small business that might be more lucrative if it were instead part of a national franchise, is inherently harmful to society and thus within the government's power to condemn.

In moving away from our decisions sanctioning the condemnation of harmful property use, the Court today significantly expands the meaning of public use. It holds that the sovereign may take private property currently put to ordinary private use, and give it over for new, ordinary private use, so long as the new use is predicted to generate some secondary benefit for the public—such as increased tax revenue, more jobs, maybe even esthetic pleasure. But nearly any lawful use of real private property can be said to generate some incidental benefit to the public. Thus, if predicted (or even guaranteed) positive side effects are enough to render transfer from one private party to another constitutional, then the words "for public use" do not realistically exclude *any* takings, and thus do not exert any constraint on the eminent domain power.

There is a sense in which this troubling result follows from errant language in *Berman* and *Midkiff*. In discussing whether takings within a blighted neighborhood were for a public use, *Berman* began by observing: "We deal, in other words, with what traditionally has been known as the police power." From there it declared that "[o]nce the object is within the authority of Congress, the right to realize it through the exercise of eminent domain is clear." Following up, we said in *Midkiff* that "[t]he 'public use' requirement is coterminous with the scope of a sovereign's police powers." This language was unnecessary to the specific holdings of those decisions. *Berman* and *Midkiff* simply did not put such language to the constitutional test, because the takings in those cases were within the police power but also for "public use" for the reasons I have described. The case before us now demonstrates why, when deciding if a taking's purpose is constitutional, the police power and "public use" cannot always be equated.

The trouble with economic development takings is that private benefit and incidental public benefit are, by definition, merged and mutually reinforcing. In this case, for example, any boon for Pfizer or the plan's developer is difficult to disaggregate from the promised public gains in taxes and jobs. Even if there were a practical way to isolate the motives behind a given taking, the gesture toward a purpose test is theoretically flawed. If it is true that incidental public benefits from new private use are enough to ensure the "public purpose" in a taking, why should it matter, as far as the Fifth Amendment is concerned, what inspired the taking in the first place? How much the government does or does not desire to benefit a favored private party has no bearing on whether an economic development taking will or will not generate secondary benefit for the public.

The Court rightfully admits, however, that the judiciary cannot get bogged down in predictive judgments about whether the public will actually be better off after a property transfer. In any event, this constraint has no realistic import. For who among us can say she already makes the most productive or attractive possible use of her property? The specter of condemnation hangs over all property. Nothing is to prevent the State from replacing any Motel 6 with a Ritz-Carlton, any home with a shopping mall, or any farm with a factory.

The Court also puts special emphasis on facts peculiar to this case: The NLDC's plan is the product of a relatively careful deliberative process; it proposes to use eminent domain for a multipart, integrated plan rather than for isolated property transfer; it promises an array of incidental benefits (even esthetic ones), not just increased tax revenue; it comes on the heels of a legislative determination that New London is a depressed municipality.... But none has legal significance to blunt the force of today's holding. If legislative prognostications about the secondary public benefits of a new use can legitimate a taking, there is nothing in the Court's rule or in Justice KENNEDY's gloss on that rule to prohibit property transfers generated with less care, that are less comprehensive, that happen to result from less elaborate process, whose only projected advantage is the incidence of higher taxes, or that hope to transform an already prosperous city into an even more prosperous one.

Finally, in a coda, the Court suggests that property owners should turn to the States, who may or may not choose to impose appropriate limits on economic development takings. This is an abdication of our responsibility. States play many important functions in our system of dual sovereignty, but compensating for our refusal to enforce properly the Federal Constitution (and a provision meant to curtail state action, no less) is not among them.... It was possible after *Berman* and *Midkiff* to imagine unconstitutional transfers from A to B. Those decisions endorsed government intervention when private property use had veered to such an extreme that the public was suffering as a consequence. Any property may now be taken for the benefit of another private party, but the fallout from this decision will not be random. The beneficiaries are likely to be those citizens with disproportionate influence and power in the political process, including large corporations and development firms. As for the victims, the government now has license to transfer property from those with fewer resources to those with more. The Founders cannot have intended this perverse result.

Justice THOMAS, dissenting....

If such "economic development" takings are for a "public use," any taking is, and the Court has erased the Public Use Clause from our Constitution.... If the Public Use Clause served no function other than to state that the government may take property through its eminent domain power—for public or private uses—then it would be surplusage.... The most natural reading of the Clause is that it allows the government to take property only if the government owns, or the public has a legal right to use, the property, as opposed to taking it for any public purpose or necessity whatsoever.... There is no justification for affording almost insurmountable deference to legislative conclusions that a use serves a "public use...." We would not defer to a legislature's determination of the various circumstances that establish, for example, when a search of a home would be reasonable or when a convicted double-murderer may be shackled during a sentencing proceeding ... or when state law creates a property interest protected by the Due Process Clause.... More fundamentally, *Berman* and *Midkiff* erred by equating eminent domain power with the police power of States....

The consequences of today's decision are not difficult to predict, and promise to be harmful. So-called "urban renewal" programs provide some compensation for the properties they take, but no compensation is possible for the subjective value of these lands to the individuals displaced and the indignity inflicted by uprooting them from their homes. Allowing the government to take property solely for public purposes is bad enough, but extending the concept of public purpose to encompass any economically beneficial goal guarantees that these losses will fall disproportionately on poor communities. Those communities are not only systematically less likely to put their lands to the highest and best social use, but are also the least politically powerful.... The deferential standard this Court has adopted for the Public Use Clause is therefore deeply perverse. It encourages "those citizens with disproportionate influence and power in the political process, including large corporations and development firms," to victimize the weak.... Public works projects in the 1950s and 1960s destroyed predominantly minority communities in St. Paul, Minnesota, and Baltimore, Maryland. In 1981, urban planners in Detroit, Michigan, uprooted the largely "lower-income and elderly" Poletown neighborhood for the benefit of the General Motors Corporation. Urban renewal projects have long been associated with the displacement of blacks; "[i]n cities across the country, urban renewal came to be known as 'Negro removal.'" Over 97 percent of the individuals forcibly removed from their homes by the "slum-clearance" project upheld by this Court in *Berman* were black. Regrettably, the predictable consequence of the Court's decision will be to exacerbate these effects.

Notes and Questions

1. *Protecting the Public from Pretexts.* Justice Kennedy, who voted with the majority, warned in a concurring opinion, "[a] court applying rational-basis review under the public use clause should strike down a taking that, by a clear showing, is intended to favor a particular private party, with only incidental or pretextual public benefits, just as a court applying rational-basis review under the equal protection clause must strike down a governmental classification that is clearly intended to injure a particular class of private parties, with only incidental or pretextual public justifications." Thus, while the scope of judicial scrutiny is narrow and the standard deferential, public use is not established as a matter of law whenever the legislative body acts. For an application of this principle, see *99 Cents Only Store v. Lancaster Redevelopment Agency*, 237 F. Supp. 2d 1123, 1129 (2001) (finding that the city's condemnation efforts "rest on nothing more than the desire to achieve the naked transfer of property from one private party to another").

2. *Transfers of Property to Private Parties.* Prior to its reiteration in *Kelo* of economic revitalization as a public purpose, the Supreme Court's cases demonstrate a breadth of permissible public purposes under the public use clause that involve transfers of property to private parties. For example, state and federal governments may validly transfer property from one private party to another to correct market failures. *Midkiff v. Hawaii*, 467 U.S. 229, at 243; *Ruckelshaus v. Monsanto Co.*, 467 U.S. 986, 1014–1015 (1984). The Court has also held that the government may take property from a party that fails to maintain it, and transfer the property to another private recipient who will provide appropriate upkeep, thereby enabling the government to use it for a proper purpose. *National R.R. Passenger Corp. v. Boston & Maine Corp.*, 503 U.S. 407, 422–23 (1992).

In *City of Norwood v. Horney*, 835 N.E. 2d 1115 (Ohio 2006), the Ohio Supreme Court unanimously invalidated a required blight finding for a redevelopment project in suburban Cincinnati on the ground that the standard of "deteriorating" conditions was void for vagueness. It also ruled that the intended transfer of the area to a private developer for economic development was not a "public use" as constitutionally required. The holdout property owners were represented by the Institute for Justice. Subsequently, the Ohio legislature adopted a more restrictive definition of "blight."

3. *"Promoting Economic Development" Rationale.* The *Kelo* case arose from the condemnation of ten residences and five other properties as part of a 2000 "development plan" in New London, Connecticut, that would transfer the property to private developers for the stated purpose of promoting economic growth in the town. None of the prop-

erties were alleged to be "blighted." Kelo's property, however, was within a blighted district and taken for right-of-way and not economic development. George Lefcoe, *Book Review, Jeff Benedict's Little Pink House: The Back Story of the* Kelo *Case*, 42 CONN. L. REV. 925, 931–32, 934 (2010). In 2005, when the Supreme Court finally addressed the question under the federal constitution, it held that the Public Use Clause permits governmental taking of private property for transfer to new private owners for the purpose of promoting "economic development" in *Kelo v. City of New London*, 545 U.S. 469 (2005). The majority appears to rely upon the extensive public planning process that preceded the condemnations. A number of cases decided following *Kelo* uphold the exercise of eminent domain in the service of important public values such as revitalization and tax revenue enhancement. *See, e.g., Rumber v. District of Columbia*, 598 F. Supp. 2d 97 (D.D.C. 2009) (condemnation of shopping center was for a valid public purpose, in light of testimony that the property was underused, neglected and poorly maintained, which conditions attracted crime; and that redevelopment would bring over 200 full-time jobs and $56 million in new sales taxes over 20 years); *Goldstein v. New York State Urb. Dev. Corp.*, 879 N.Y.S.2d 524 (Sup. Ct. App. Div. 2d Dep't 2009) (allowing condemnation of homes and businesses to make way for the Atlantic Yards project in Brooklyn, to include sports arena for a professional basketball team, offices and residences).

Does the Court's rationale allow the exercise of eminent domain by a town to take agricultural land (presumably unblighted) to further a public use of farmland preservation? Must the town have a legislatively adopted public policy to preserve farmland? What further action, if any, must the town take to satisfy *Kelo's* standard for a constitutional taking for economic development purposes? *See Aspen Creek Estates Ltd v. Town of Brookhaven*, 904 N.E.2d 816 (N.Y. 2009), *cert denied*, 130 S. Ct. 96 (2009).

4. *Does* Kelo *expect too much of local governments?* Does it impose a mandate for planning, through its reliance on the comprehensive redevelopment planning undertaken by New London for its legitimacy? Is this a process that courts can competently review? For one argument that municipal planning is both extremely complicated and highly political, and not within courts' expertise, see Brandon Simmons, Kelo's *Planning Mandate: Replacing Clarity with Complication*, 43 REAL PROP. PROB. & TR. J. 139 (2008). *See also* Nicole Stelle Garnett, *Planning as Public Use?* 34 ECOLOGY L.Q. 443 (2007); Mark B. Mihaly, *Living in the Past: The* Kelo *Court and Public-Private Economic Redevelopment,* 34 ECOLOGY L.Q. 1 (2007) (arguing that the *Kelo* dissenters and critics are decades out of date in their understanding of redevelopment and municipal finance). States and municipalities possess limited powers and resources, and yet land assembly will remain essential to accomplish public-serving projects such as infill and brownfield development and to avoid further sprawl development as the population grows. Arguments and evidence for development policies to densify and convert the cities to a transit-based society are examined in Section G *infra*.

5. *Does* Kelo *require enough of local governments* in exercising the eminent domain power on behalf of the public, in formulating a public use or purpose? *Kelo*, *Poletown* and numerous other economic-development takings cases offer a glimpse into the complexity of large-scale urban redevelopment projects desired by cities and their various constituencies—recall "the voices of labor, business, industry, government, finance, and even the news media" in Justice Fitzgerald's *Poletown* dissent, excerpted *supra*. Cities and their communities feel the need for economic renewal and adaptation to rapid and significant changes affecting them: in industry, technology, employment opportunities, workforce capabilities—whose interconnections require attention to urban redevelopment's considerable coordination demands. A dramatic example of the difficulties of ad-

dressing a city's public necessities is provided by New Orleans' faltering recovery from Hurricane Katrina and the breach of the levees in 2005; but U.S. cities generally struggle to maintain and enhance their urban systems. John J. Costonis, *New Orleans, Katrina and* Kelo*: American Cities in the Post-*Kelo *Era*, 83 TUL. L. REV. 395 (2008). Consider the efforts of U.S. communities to address the large, obviously systems-implicating, public purposes of curbing sprawl, reducing carbon emissions, slowing climate change, which are discussed *infra*.

Seen through this urban-systems lens, perhaps it is unhelpfully limiting to view the *Kelo* case as a tug of war over whether to employ a closed-ended twentieth-century definitional approach to ban "economic development" as a public use. Instead, should the public use requirement of the eminent domain power be coupled more closely to the solution of substantive urban-system problems? What results could this conception have for the land-use dimension of community development efforts, for struggling communities striving to provide healthier infrastructures that house, educate, employ and transport residents?

6. Kelo *Decision & Its Aftermath.* The *Kelo* ruling was denounced by many on both the right and the left sides of the political spectrum. At least forty-three states have enacted post-*Kelo* reform legislation to curb eminent domain, most through state legislation, and several by public referendum. Recent evaluations of the enactments characterize these as largely ineffective. *See, e.g.*, Alexandra B. Klass, *The Frontier of Eminent Domain*, 79 U. COLO. L. REV. 651 (2008); Ilya Somin, *The Limits of Backlash: Assessing the Political Response to* Kelo, 93 MINN. L. REV. 2100 (2009). Somin reports, furthermore, that citizen-initiated referendum initiatives have led to much stronger laws than those enacted through referenda initiated by state legislatures. Might the reason be that initiative propositions need not go through the political compromise process?

In its 5–4 decision, the Supreme Court upheld the New London takings and the economic development rationale for the condemnation. The *Kelo* majority mandated broad judicial deference to government decision making on public use issues, emphasizing that courts should not "second-guess the City's considered judgments about the efficacy of the development plan." The Court rejected the property owners' argument that the transfer of their property to private developers rather than to a public body required any heightened degree of judicial scrutiny. The majority also declined to require the City to provide any evidence that the takings were likely to achieve the economic benefits claimed in justification for the condemnations in the first place.

On the questions before the Court, the *Kelo* decision was consistent with federal 'public use' precedent, despite the crescendo of political discourse on property rights, and the radically changed urban redevelopment practices that tightened the mutual embrace of public officials and private participants in city-shaping projects. *Kelo* actually may have strengthened judicial scrutiny somewhat as compared to the earlier scant Supreme Court case law. *Hawaii Housing Authority v. Midkiff*, 467 U.S. 229, 241 (1984) held that the public use requirement is satisfied provided "the exercise of the eminent domain power is rationally related to a conceivable public purpose." Clearly, the judicial landscape on public use changed with *Kelo*—a fact underscored by the dissent of four Justices, who concluded that the economic development rationale should be categorically forbidden. *Kelo*, 545 U.S. at 499–505 (O'Conner, J., dissenting); *id.* at 519–23 (Thomas, J., dissenting). A fifth justice, Anthony Kennedy, signed on to the majority opinion, but in his concurring opinion argued that heightened scrutiny of eminent domain decisions should be used where there is evidence that a condemnation was undertaken as a result of "impermissible favoritism" toward a private party. *Id.* at 491 (Kennedy, J., concurring).

The conundrum of balancing public purpose, private property, and the proper exercise of legitimate constitutional authority is extremely complex. It should not be overlooked that a number of scholars view the Court's resolution as essentially correct. See, e.g., Abraham Bell & Gideon Parchomovsky, *The Uselessness of Public Use*, 106 COLUM. L. REV. 1412 (2006) (critical of *Kelo's* critics, finding compensation a sufficient brake on government abuse as compared to other forms of regulation and rights interference, and eminent domain an important governmental power); David L. Breau, *Justice Thomas'* Kelo *Dissent, or,"History as a Grab Bag of Principles,"* 38 MCGEORGE L. REV. 373 (2007) (questioning the historical conclusion that the public use provision was intended to impose a substantive limit on exercise of condemnation); Marcilynn A. Burke, *Much Ado About Nothing:* Kelo v. City of New London, Babbitt v. Sweet Home, *and Other Tales from the Supreme Court,* 75 U. CIN. L. REV. 663 (2006) (supporting the judicial restraint of *Kelo* and discussing the legislative aftermath); Daniel J. Curtin, Jr., *The Implications of* Kelo *in Land Use Law,* 46 SANTA CLARA L. REV. 787 (2006); Timothy J. Dowling, *How to Think About* Kelo *After the Shouting Stops,* 38 URB. LAW. 191 (2006) (correctly decided).

7. *Concerns of Unbounded, Unprincipled or Unaccountable Government Regard for Private Property Rights and the Public Welfare.* Although *Kelo* did not change the doctrinal landscape dramatically, the Court's narrow decision that the U.S. Constitution does not prohibit takings for economic development projects that transfer property from one private owner to another, was announced after decades of local redevelopment experience across the U.S.

8. *Who litigates?* Litigants in the takings cases are typically property owners, consequently their interests largely frame the case law in this complex and contentious debate. Several issues remain on the table which are highly consequential to non-owner households and to low-wealth communities as well. A growing body of scholarship documents the ways that both "blight" definitions and economic development takings disproportionately victimize the poor. *See, e.g.,* Wendell E. Pritchett, *The "Public Menace" of Blight: Urban Renewal and the Private Uses of Eminent Domain,* 21 YALE L. & POL'Y REV. 1 (2003); Ilya Somin, *Controlling the Grasping Hand: Economic Development Takings After* Kelo, 15 SUP. CT. ECON. REV. 183 (2007). *See also* David Dana, The *Law and Expressive Meaning of Condemning the Poor after* Kelo, 101 NW. U. L. REV. 365 (2007) (arguing that post-*Kelo* reform protects the middle class and the wealthy without protecting the poor).

In addition to the economic costs to communities and residents, economic development takings also inflict major nonpecuniary costs by destroying communities and forcing residents to relocate to less desired locations. Jane Jacobs observed this in her classic 1961 study:

> [P]eople who get marked with the planners' hex signs are pushed about, expropriated, and uprooted much as if they were the subjects of a conquering power. Thousands upon thousands of small businesses are destroyed.... Whole communities are torn apart and sown to the winds, with a reaping of cynicism, resentment and despair that must be seen to be believed.

JANE JACOBS, DEATH AND LIFE OF GREAT AMERICAN CITIES 5 (1961). *See also* MINDY FULLILOVE, ROOT SHOCK: HOW TEARING UP CITY NEIGHBORHOODS HURTS AMERICA, AND WHAT WE CAN DO ABOUT IT (2005); Barbara L. Bezdek, *To Attain "The Just Rewards of So Much Struggle:" Local-Resident Equity Participation in Urban Revitalization,* 35 HOFSTRA L. REV. 37 (2006); Marc Fried, *Grieving for a Lost Home: Psychological Costs of Relocation, in* URBAN RENEWAL: THE RECORD AND THE CONTROVERSY 359–61 (James Q. Wilson ed. 1966).

9. *Standard of Review: Judicial Deference to Legislation Action.* The condemnation upheld by the U.S. Supreme Court in *Berman* was the decision of Washington, D.C.'s rede-

velopment agency to condemn a department store and a hardware store, both functioning well and neither of them blighted. *Berman v. Parker*, 348 U.S. 26, 36 (1954). The agency argued that only through wholesale demolition and development could it restore the area and prevent the recurrence of slum conditions. Rather than determine whether the agency's claimed need for these properties was demonstrated or justified, the Court declared that the blight determination is one for the legislature to decide, subject only to rational basis judicial review. Once the Court determines that the project lies within the local government's police power, the means for attaining those goals—including taking private property through the exercise of eminent domain—is a matter of legislative choice. In *Hawaii Housing Authority v. Midkiff*, the Supreme Court held that condemnations and private-to-private transfers are permitted by the Takings Clause as public-use takings when they are "rationally related to a conceivable public purpose." Arguing in *Kelo* for a heightened standard of review in economic development cases, appellant's counsel characterized the rational basis standard as so permissive that it "invites powerful local businesses to persuade neutral public bodies to declare as 'blighted' the property they need for their own business expansion." Brief for the Cato Institute as Amicus Curiae supporting Petitioners, *Kelo v. City of New London*.

10. *Federal versus state constitutional standards.* The *Kelo* majority observed that "nothing in our opinion precludes any state from placing further restrictions on its exercise of the takings power." In the absence of an absolute federal prohibition on economic development takings, state courts can and sometimes do rule differently when interpreting state constitutions. For example, in a 2007 Colorado case, owners of property slated for condemnation resisted, arguing that the redevelopment project did not serve a legitimate public purpose under Colorado law because its purpose was to increase tax revenues, not to eliminate blight. *Sheridan Redev. Agency v. Knightsbridge Land Co.*, 166 P.3d 259, 261 (Colo. Ct. App. 2007). The trial court had deferred to the city's determination of blight, on the view that it could overturn the city's blight finding only if the city had made its finding in bad faith. However, the Colorado Constitution provides that the public use determination is judicial, to be made "without regard to any legislative assertion that the use is public." COLO. CONST. art. II, § 15. On this ground the court of appeals remanded for further findings as to public purpose. *Sheridan Redev. Agency*, 166 P.3d at 266–67.

11. *Defining Blight.* With three exceptions, every state allows condemnation for blight. Professor Ilya Somin has observed, "Early blight cases in the 1940s and 1950s upheld condemnations in areas that fit the layperson's intuitive notion of blight: dilapidated, dangerous, or disease-ridden neighborhoods. Somin, *supra* note 6 at 2120. For example, in *Berman v. Parker*, the well-known 1954 case in which the Supreme Court upheld the constitutionality of blight condemnations under the Federal Public Use Clause, the condemned neighborhood was characterized by "[m]iserable and disreputable housing conditions." According to the Court, "64.3% of the dwellings [in the area] were beyond repair, 18.4% needed major repairs, only 17.3% were satisfactory; 57.8% of the dwellings had outside toilets, 60.3% had no baths, 29.3% lacked electricity, 82.2% had no wash basins or laundry tubs, [and] 83.8% lacked central heating." *Berman v. Parker*, 348 U.S. 26, 32 (1954).

In the decades since *Berman v Parker*, many legislatures expanded state and local definitions of blight as broadly as the "underutilization" of real property, or areas posing obstacles to "sound growth" or "an economic or social liability." For example, New Jersey allows condemnation where an area suffers from:

> [a] growing lack or total lack of proper utilization of areas caused by the condition of the title, diverse ownership of the real property therein or other conditions, resulting in a stagnant or not fully productive condition of land potentially

> useful and valuable for contributing to and serving the public health, safety and welfare.

N.J. Stat. Ann. § 40A:12A-5e. Similarly broad powers are found in the redevelopment statutes of many states, including California, Delaware, Georgia, Illinois, Maine, Massachusetts, Minnesota, Pennsylvania, Rhode Island, and Virginia. Critics observe that virtually any property can be condemned as blighted under such broad definitions. For example, both Times Square in New York City and downtown Las Vegas were determined to be blighted, thereby justifying condemnations undertaken to acquire land for a new headquarters for the New York Times and parking lots for a consortium of local casinos, respectively. State courts upheld each determination. *See City of Las Vegas Downtown Redev. Agency v. Pappas*, 76 P.3d 1, 12–15 (Nev. 2003); *West 41st St. Realty, LLC v. State Urb. Dev. Corp.*, 744 N.Y.S.2d 121 (Sup. Ct. App. Div. 1st Dep't 2002), *cert. denied*, 537 U.S. 1191 (2003).

The *Kelo* decision did not alter this landscape. As of 2009, at least thirty-six states had enacted legislation responsive reforms in the wake of the Supreme Court's decision. A recent study of these enactments reports that the majority of these legislative efforts fail in their purported purpose, because they incorporated pre-*Kelo* definitions of "blight" or otherwise imposed no legal impediment to economic development takings and private-private transfers.

> [T]wenty-two of the thirty-six new state laws provide little or no protection for property owners against economic development takings. Only fourteen state legislatures have enacted laws that either ban economic development takings or significantly restrict them. The seventeen ineffective state laws are of several types. By far the most common are laws that forbid takings for economic development but in fact allow them to continue under another name, such as "blight" or "community development" condemnations. Other post-*Kelo* reforms lack teeth because they either forbid only those takings that are for "private" development (thus permitting localities to condemn under the standard theory that any such takings are really intended to promote "public" benefits) or are purely symbolic in nature.

Somin, *supra* note 6 at 2120.

The Michigan Supreme Court rejected the "economic development" rationale in *County of Wayne v. Hathcock*, *supra*, explaining:

> [The] "economic benefit" rationale would validate practically any exercise of the power of eminent domain on behalf of a private entity. After all, if one's ownership of private property is forever subject to the government's determination that another private party would put one's land to better use, then the ownership of real property is perpetually threatened by the expansion of plans of any large discount retailer, "megastore," or the like.

Hathcock, 684 N.W.2d at 786. Similarly, the Supreme Court of Illinois refused to allow a "contribu[tion] to economic growth in the region" to justify a taking on the ground that such a standard could justify virtually any condemnation that benefited private industry since "every lawful business" contributes to economic growth to some degree. *Southwestern Ill, Dev. Auth. v. National City Envtl., L.L.C.*, 768 N.E.2d 1, 9 (Ill. 2002), *cert. denied*, 537 U.S. 880 (2002).

12. *Public Power and Public-Private Development Partnerships.* Takings are but one particularly dramatic form of governmental facilitation of development. State and local governments also wield taxing and spending powers to provide direct grants and debt financing, and indirect assistance such as regulatory relief from zoning and building codes and gov-

ernment commitments to rent space. These powers, alone and in combination, offer significant cost savings to the private entities engaged in development projects, in that they profoundly alter the costs of land acquisition, land assembly and carrying costs necessary for redevelopment projects. This lengthy list of municipal tools underscores the fact that one of the thorniest problems courts face in resolving challenges to redevelopment takings is the intertwined character of much redevelopment as both private and public. How do private economic interests bear on the likelihood, or means by which, states may respond to Justice Stephens' admonition that states can further constrain economic development takings? Consider:

Barbara L. Bezdek, To Attain "The Just Rewards of So Much Struggle:" Local-Resident Equity Participation in Urban Revitalization

35 Hofstra Law Review 37 (2006)

Public-Private Redevelopment

Around the United States, cities are being remade through increasingly intricate and opaque "public/private partnerships" (PPPs), by which local government agencies trade essential infrastructure at low or no cost in exchange for a profit-sharing stake or other return on the city's investment. While this idea is not new, the scale of today's municipal reliance upon PPPs blurs the traditional separateness of the public and private sectors. Urban land is being reclaimed from low-wealth residents by local governments ... [a]ugmenting their traditional land use powers with new means of collaboration and exchange with private developers....

Today's public/private cooperation has its origins in the first federal revitalization programs. Congress designed its redevelopment programs to be federally funded and driven, but implemented at the local level.... Local jurisdictions realized it would give them the tools to clear away blighted eyesores and to build preferred developments in their place with the Federal Treasury footing the bill. Over the years, much redevelopment has been sharply criticized for its displacement of the poor people who lived where local officials yearned to rebuild....

In contemporary redevelopment, cities increasingly identify areas where they would like to support redevelopment in various ways ... [including] land banking or old-fashioned land assembly, then issue requests for development proposals (RFPs) or requests for qualifications (RFQs) for the development of desired uses on specific sites. Each of these processes contemplates an energetic level of communication and decisional participation between potential parties to the deal, but no more than statutorily required notice and participation by the public. Residents whose interests will be profoundly affected by the replacement of nearby row homes with a stadium or big box store have no more right to notice or participation than do taxpayers across town. Notice is achieved by formal publication, or on the redevelopment agency's website and by snail mail and email to those in the business who ask to be placed on the mailing list....

As project complexity has increased, participation policies have not kept pace. Community development projects are produced by a complex network—government policymakers, personnel in multiple departments, agencies, programs at federal, state and local levels, staff and directors of nonprofit organizations' foundations and their program managers, and an extensive array of for-profit and not-for-profit development partners—

as well as lawyers, planners, architects and builders. These players then typically relate to each other as participants in (1) direct physical development of housing or of facilities to be leased to existing for-profit businesses or to start-up local businesses, (2) technical and grant assistance or loans in connection with development projects, or (3) direct investments as partners in a joint venture.

The eclipse of traditional land use planning procedures by cities' wholehearted embrace of development agreements and similar bilateral negotiated approaches leaves next to no room for the public. State enabling statutes eliminate substantive restrictions that previously applied to negotiations between cities and developers, in order to provide exceptional bargaining flexibility. Public participation is perfunctory and futile: By design it is too little and too late, disproportionate to the complexity of the undertaking and to the preferential access of bidding developers.

The negotiated processes of most states utilizing development agreements are not covered by due process requirements of a public hearing, findings of fact, or prohibitions on ex parte communications between developer applicants and local officials. As a consequence, current procedures allow officials to relegate affected community members to after-the-fact comments, the timing of which precludes meaningful exchange of information between the public and local government officials. Conversely, the bilateral negotiation model accords to developers early, active and substantively significant opportunity for preliminary negotiation within the project approval process, wherein the developer applicant's input is both critical to the local government actors' decision-making, and analogous to the negotiation of private real estate deals.

The bilateral negotiation model grants to developers "wide latitude to pre-negotiate the extensive and intricate terms of their agreements outside of public forums, excluding affected third parties from the extensive information exchanges and substantive trading that occur during negotiations." It is little wonder, then, that "local officials often treat public participation as if it obstructs ... the decision process." No state statutes or local enabling ordinances allow, much less require, neighboring property owners or other concerned residents or community organizations to be parties to the agreement.

Not only do bilateral land deals evade constitutional due process requirements, but further, no other effective accountability mechanisms are available to those most impacted by the land use decision. Many states do not require their development agreements to be consistent with comprehensive plans or zoning codes. The American Planning Association's new Model Code takes this position, and allows development agreements to "address any issue that local land development regulations can cover," specifically allowing an agreement to depart from applicable zoning code regulations as long as it remains consistent with the broad policies of the comprehensive plan. Excluded third parties, seeking to gain judicial review of the agreements or the process by which they are negotiated, find that even lawsuits offer scant relief. Because "[development agreement acts] and other state laws governing [the] bilateral negotiated approaches afford substantial discretion to local governments, courts often are unable to scrutinize the substance of development agreements."

This depiction underscores the wildly lopsided terrain on which "public participation" is to take place when local governments engage in development agreements. The procedures on the books in most states omit community residents from the processes that fashion the [development] objectives [which are] instead forged by the profoundly asymmetric public/private development partnerships that predominate today. The bartering nature of the contemporary development process causes public officials to "behave like developers rather than guardians of the public interest." Not surprisingly, this profound asymmetry of access to official decision makers has produced widespread accounts of corruption and patterns of favoritism, and enervates the legitimacy of land use decision-making through negotiated development agreements.

Notes and Questions

1. *The Interest Group Capture Problem.* Political entities are potentially vulnerable to capture by the industries they regulate. This is a central tenet of an extensive interdisciplinary literature of the last four decades by legal scholars, economists and political scientists describing and analyzing interest group influence over government decision-making. According to this literature, not only are legislators disproportionately influenced by organized interest groups, agencies also are likely to be captured by the firms they regulate, even though agency decisions consequently may be inefficient and disadvantageous to the public interest. For a discussion of this literature, see, e.g., Einer R. Elhuage, *Does Interest Group Theory Justify More Intrusive Judicial Review?* 101 Yale L.J. 31 (1991). Development decisions made by agencies, whose heads are appointed by elected executives, are only very indirectly affected by voting or mobilizing voters.

2. Consider the relative abilities of development industry participants, on the one hand, and neighborhood residents on the other, to engage in any of the familiar forms of "demand-side" influence: influencing the information that reaches regulators, legislators, and the voting public; pressuring officials to support or oppose the appointment, removal or budget of top agency personnel; paying lawmakers in the form of supportive advertising, promises of future employment, speaking fees, campaign contributions, and so forth.

Planning and development authorities may be no more prone than other types of agencies to interest group capture, yet there are unique reasons for citizens to be concerned about capture in the redevelopment context. First, there are few if any practical limits on such takings. Charged to review legislative decisions, courts do not apply cost-benefit analysis in evaluating whether these projects *serve* a public use. *Kelo* clarified that the federal constitution only requires rational basis review by courts. States are free to set higher thresholds under their state constitutions, yet prescriptive definitions may pose little constraint on economic development takings.

3. Much redevelopment decision-making by local government since the 1980s has come to be the product of negotiated development agreements, bearing the hallmarks of private bargaining between parties to a deal, rather than agency planning subject to public participation rights and democratic oversight. This shift in the legal structures that shape much redevelopment is critically important to an understanding of the opportunities for communities to engage elected officials and potential partners in processes of "community development."

The potential consequences of the capture problem are described in the following excerpt, comparing *Poletown* and *Kelo*.

Ilya Somin, Controlling the Grasping Hand: Economic Development Takings after *Kelo*

15 Supreme Court Economic Review 183, 185–187, 193–197 (2007)

Kelo followed closely after *County of Wayne v. Hathcock*, in which the Michigan Supreme Court overruled *Poletown*, the most famous earlier decision justifying economic development takings. For years, *Poletown* stood as both the most infamous symbol of eminent domain abuse and a precedent justifying nearly unlimited power to condemn private property. *Poletown* held that condemnations transferring property from one private party to another satisfied the "public use" requirement even if the only claimed public benefit was that of "bolster[ing] the economy." While it was not the first decision upholding so-called "economic development" takings, *Poletown* was by far the most widely publicized. The notoriety stemmed from the massive scale of Detroit's use of eminent domain: destroying an entire neighborhood and condemning the homes of 4,200 people, as well as numerous businesses, churches, and schools, so the land could be transferred to General Motors for the construction of a new factory.

The *Poletown* court upheld the massive condemnations in Detroit primarily, if not solely, because of the "clear and significant" economic benefits that the GM factory was expected to provide for the city. Indeed, the majority suggested that if the expected benefits were not so great, "we would hesitate to sanction approval of the project." This fact renders all the more dubious the court's failure to require either the city or GM to ensure that the expected benefits would actually materialize.

Yet, as Justice Ryan emphasized in his dissenting opinion, the court failed to impose even minimal requirements of this kind. *City of Detroit v. Vavro*, [442 N.W.2d 730 (Mich. Ct. App. 1989), a 1989 Michigan Court of Appeals decision interpreting *Poletown*, confirmed Ryan's view, holding that "a careful reading of the *Poletown* decision reveals that ... a binding commitment [to provide the economic benefits used to justify condemnation] is unnecessary in order to allow the city to make use of eminent domain. Indeed, *Poletown* did not even require the new owner to proceed with the project that was initially used to justify the condemnation, much less proceed with it in a way that provided some predetermined level of economic benefit to the public....

Poletown's failure to impose any binding obligations on the new owners of property was not idiosyncratic. The same problem is evident in other states that permit economic development takings. The *Kelo* case is remarkably similar to *Poletown* in this respect. As the dissenting opinion in [the] Connecticut Supreme Court in *Kelo* pointed out, "[t]here are no assurances of a public use in the development plan [under which the owners' property was condemned]; there was no signed development agreement at the time of the takings; and all of the evidence suggests that the economic climate will not support the project so that the public benefits can be realized."

Notes and Questions

1. *Absence of Binding Obligations on the New Owner or on Government.* Just one year after the condemnations were upheld by the U.S. Supreme Court in *Kelo*, the New London development plan used to justify them appeared in jeopardy, due to contract issues and financial uncertainty, not the least of which was the unwillingness of investors to commit to the project. *See* William Yardley, *After Eminent Domain Victory, Disputed Project Goes Nowhere,* N.Y. Times, Nov. 21, 2005, at A1. In November 2009, Pfizer announced that it would leave New London altogether. Patrick McGeehan, *Pfizer to Leave City that Won Land-Use Case,* N.Y. Times, Nov. 13, 2009. The departure will take the city's largest taxpayer and 1,400 jobs out of New London, and leave behind the city's biggest office complex and an adjacent swath of barren land that was cleared of dozens of homes to make room for a hotel, stores and condominiums that were never built. *Id.*

Other states that allow economic development condemnations, like Connecticut, also fail to require either the government or the new owners to actually provide the promised public benefits. Thus, *Poletown* and *Kelo* highlight a systematic shortcoming of the economic development rationale generally. It is not an idiosyncratic problem confined to Connecticut and pre-*Hathcock* Michigan. Can New London and other redevelopment sponsors be held responsible for the effects of business cycles? For an inspiring tale of saving poor peoples' homes and their conversion into a cooperative when a Los Angeles freeway project in was abandoned after residents had been displaced but before the housing had been demolished, see ALLAN DAVID HESKIN, THE STRUGGLE FOR COMMUNITY (1991).

2. *Inflated Claims of Economic Benefit.* At the time of the Poletown taking controversy, GM projected that 6,000 jobs would be created. Ilya Somin, *Controlling the Grasping Hand: Economic Development Takings After Kelo,* 15 SUP. CT. ECON. REV. 183, 194 (2007). GM's estimate was embraced and reiterated by Detroit's mayor, even though GM had no legal obligation to provide the jobs or any other economic benefits promised. Opponents of the condemnations claimed that 9,000 jobs would be lost because of them. *See* John Bukowczyk, *The Decline and Fall of a Detroit Neighborhood: Poletown vs. GM and the City of Detroit,* 41 WASH & LEE L. REV. 49, 68 (1984). Both statements, by partisans in a bitter fight, might best be ingested with considerable salt. Data compiled by the city subsequently showed that one-third of the affected businesses closed down immediately, while two-thirds of the remainder (approximately 40 to 45 percent of the original total) relocated to other parts of Detroit. Somin, *supra* at 198 n. 66, *citing* BRYAN D. JONES ET AL., THE SUSTAINING HAND: COMMUNITY LEADERSHIP AND CORPORATE POWER 100 (1986).

> The danger inherent in this arrangement was apparent even at the time. As Justice Ryan warned in dissent, "there are no guarantees from General Motors about employment levels at the new assembly plant.... [O]nce [the condemned property] is sold to General Motors, there will be no public control whatsoever over the management, operation, or conduct of the plant to be built there." Ryan pointed out that "General Motors will be accountable not to the public, but to its stockholders;" it would therefore make decisions as to the use of the property based solely on stockholder interests, not the city's economic interests, which the condemnation was intended to further. "[O]ne thing is certain," Ryan emphasized, "[t]he level of employment at the new GM plant will be determined by private corporate managers primarily with reference, not to the rate of regional unemployment, but to profit." Justice Ryan's warning was prescient. The GM plant opened two years late; and by 1988—seven years after the Poletown condemnations—it employed "no more than 2,500 workers." Even in 1998, at the height of the 1990s economic boom, the plant "still employed only 3,600" workers, less than 60 percent of the promised 6,150.

Somin, *supra* at 194–95.

3. *What Happens When the Project Fails?* When an otherwise public project fails, valuable surplus land is left in the hands of the condemning agency. In response to *Kelo,* some states acted to preclude such a result by tightening their surplus property procedures. Would statutory provisions requiring the condemning authority to offer the unused property to the original property owner at the acquisition price, be an effective way to prevent such transfers of private property? In jurisdictions that have not enacted protections of this kind, is this an inevitable part of eminent domain law? *See* Jeffrey A. Beaver et al., *What Happens When the Project Fails?*, SM006 A.L.I.-A.B.A. 697, 708 (Jan. 4–6, 2007). *See also* Lynda J. Oswald, *Can the Condemnee Regain Its Property if the Condemnor Abandons the Public Use?,* 39 URB. LAW. 671, 680 (2007).

4. *Congressional Responses to the* Kelo *Decision.* Congress enacted the Bond Amendment on November 30, 2005, to forbid the use of funds allocated in the 2006 appropriations Act to "support" the use of eminent domain for "economic development that primarily benefits private entities" (amending the 2006 appropriation bill for the Transportation, Treasury, and Housing and Urban Development departments, and various independent agencies. Also in November, 2005, the U.S. House of Representatives passed the Private Property Rights Protection Act of 2005 ("PRPA") by a vote of 376 to 38. However, the 109th Congress ended without action by the Senate.

5. Some critics seek to limit the authority of government to use eminent domain for urban redevelopment, to shrink the opportunity for moneyed interests to leverage government power for their own projects. *See, e.g.*, Charles E. Cohen, *Eminent Domain After* Kelo v. City of New London*: An Argument for Banning Economic Development Takings*, 29 HARV. J.L. & PUB. POL'Y 491, 547–51 (2006) (discussing possible abuse by politically powerful groups and concluding that "ready availability of eminent domain for economic development projects poses grave risks of unfairness, inefficiency, and abuse"); Gideon Kanner, Kelo v. New London*: Bad Law, Bad Policy, and Bad Judgment*, 38 URB. LAW. 201, 233–35 (2006) (concluding that *Kelo* majority "surrendered the vital function of constitutional review to an unaccountable, self-serving business-government alliance").

Aside from the categorical ban on economic development takings sought by the Institute of Justice on behalf of the *Kelo* plaintiffs, or heightened scrutiny as adopted in Michigan but rejected by the U.S. Supreme Court in *Kelo*, what other rules might courts or legislatures develop in the quest to balance public need and private interests?

Improving the procedures required before the exercise of eminent domain, or changing the measure of "just compensation" are two additional approaches. *See, e.g.* J. Peter Byrne, *Condemnation of Low Income Residential Communities under the Takings Clause*, 23 UCLA J. ENVTL. L. & POL'Y 131 (2005); John Fee, *Eminent Domain and the Sanctity of the Home*, 81 NOTRE DAME L. REV. 783, 814–15 (2006) ("One reasonable approach to improving the valuation of homes [to take account of subjective value] would be to use a statutory formula to increase compensation as a percentage of market value"); Lee Ann Fennell, *Taking Eminent Domain Apart*, 2004 MICH. ST. L. REV. 957, 965–967; Michael Heller & Rick Hills, *Land Assembly Districts*, 121 HARV. L. REV. 1465, 1481–1483 (2008); James J. Kelly, Jr., *Taming Eminent Domain*, SHELTERFORCE, Mar. 22, 2008, *available at* http://ssrn.com/ abstract=1271223; Amnon Lehavi & Amir N. Licht, *Eminent Domain, Inc.*, 107 COLUM. L. REV. 1704, 1735–1743 (2007). Scholars who see current just compensation law as inadequate to limit government's eminent domain power have proposed a number of variations in the assessment of property value to achieve the justness of compensation. *See, e.g.*, Abraham Bell & Gideon Parchomovsky, *Taking Compensation Private*, 59 STAN. L. REV. 871 (2007) (proposing a means of setting compensation at subjective value); Lee Anne Fennell, *Revealing Options*, 118 HARV. L. REV. 1399, 1404 (2005) (noting the problem of false valuation statements); Michael A. Heller & James E. Krier, *Deterrence and Distribution in the Law of Takings*, 112 HARV. L. REV. 997 (1999) (criticizing as inefficient the costs of time and money to governments and private parties in the negotiations and litigation that attend eminent domain); Thomas Merrill, *The Economics of Public Use*, 72 CORNELL L. REV. 61, 90–93 (1986) (proposing to "increase costs in those situations where we wish to discourage the use of eminent domain" through the use of a surtax or bonus payment); Christopher Serkin, *The Meaning of Value: Assessing Just Compensation for Regulatory Takings*, 99 NW. U. L. REV. 677 (2005) (identifying valuation mechanisms for just compensation). For a proposed formula by which "just compensation" should incorporate the social contributions of poor homeowners and poor renters, see Michele

Alexandre, *"Love Don't Live Here Anymore:" Economic Incentive for a More Equitable Model of Urban Redevelopment*, 3 B.C. ENVTL. AFF. L. REV. 1, 5 (2008). Would much of the comdemnee complaints disappear if the purchase price reflected a portion of post-redevelopment land value?

6. As illustrated by the Poletown controversy over GM's promised jobs and Detroit's grant of tax abatement and infrastructure subsidies, local governments and their citizens may be better served by "clawback" provisions, which require repayment of subsidies if the promised performance by the benefited private developer do not materialize, or if the beneficiary ceases operation or relocates prior to the expiration of the subsidies. *See* Alan H. Peters, *Clawbacks and the Administration of Economic Development Policy in the Midwest*, 7 ECON. DEV. Q. 328 (1993). More recently, the developer of the massive Atlantic Yards redevelopment in Brooklyn decided to scale back considerably its promises of affordable housing in the project, after the courts had upheld the city's use of eminent domain on the project's behalf.

7. In a number of cities across the U.S., citizens have sought to directly accomplish public benefits not otherwise negotiated between their public representatives and private redevelopers. See the discussion of these "community benefit agreements," *infra*. An account of the Atlantic Yards redevelopment and controversy is included in Patricia Salkin, *Negotiating for Social Justice and the Promise of Community Benefits Agreements: Case Studies of Current Development Agreements*, 17 J. AFFORDABLE HOUSING & COMMUNITY DEV. L. 113 (2008).

A Note on the Commons and the AntiCommons in Community Development

As you may recall from the first-year property course, the tragedy of the commons refers to inefficient decisions regarding the allocation of property interests between the collectivity and one's personal stock in property that is openly accessible to many users. *See, e.g.*, Lee Ann Fennell, *Common Interest Tragedies*, 98 NW. U. L. REV. 907 (2004); Carol Rose, *The Comedy of the Commons: Custom, Commerce, and Inherently Public Property*, 53 U. CHI. L. REV. 711 (1986). A tragedy of the commons can occur when too many individuals have rights of exclusion in a scarce resource. The tragedy is that rational individuals, acting separately, may collectively waste the resource compared with a social optimum. Michael Heller, *The Tragedy of the Anticommons: Property in the Transition from Marx to Markets*, 111 HARV. L. REV. 621, 677 (1998). Tragedies of the commons result from two tendencies referred to as "overuse" and "underinvestment." A third, of "wasteful struggle" over the revenues or produce of a commons, has more recently been suggested. Hanoch Dagan & Michael Heller, *The Liberal Commons*, 110 YALE L J. 549 (2001) (describing a model of commons tailored to foster the social gains of collaboration while preserving participants' autonomous interests and right to exit).

How well does the overuse problem apply to the urban-form dilemma of sprawl, discussed *supra* in this chapter? Consider:

> The tendency towards overuse is typified by the example of grazing cattle [introduced by Garret Hardin in, *The Tragedy of the Commons*, 162 SCIENCE 1243 (1968)]; hence it is sometimes also termed an "overgrazing" problem. The basic idea is that grass is a replenishing resource that only can flourish when it is not constantly being trampled and eaten by cattle. Add too many cattle to a grazing field, and eventually the total amount of grass available for the entire group of cattle becomes

> depleted. Each additional head of cattle generates benefits that are wholly internalized by the animal's owner, but the owner internalizes only a fraction of the costs that the animal imposes on the grazing lands. Hence, the tendency is to add too many cattle.... [T]hese represent cases of negative externalities associated with resource use. Because the resource-appropriator is not taking all the costs of her appropriation into account, she is likely to do too much of it from the standpoint of allocative efficiency.

Fennell, *supra* at 914–915.

The problem of "underinvestment" is illustrated, to continue the agrarian metaphor, by shirking on a community farm, or property held by dispersed tenants-in-common. The person who cultivates crops internalizes all the costs, but where the land is open-access, each group member in a commons has the same ability to take the produce for himself. This arrangement dampens investment of effort by the members, since they cannot be confident of receiving the benefits of their initial investment, and the resulting underinvestment may lead to underuse of the resource. You may recognize this as the 'right to capture' problem presented in case *Pierson v. Post,* studied in many first year property courses.

Fennell, *Id.* at 921 adds to our understanding of commons problems by distinguishing the distributive aspect inherent in every commons tragedy:

> First, individual actors do not internalize all the externalities—costs or benefits—of a given action. This mismatch between internalized and actual costs and benefits undercuts the decision maker's assessment of whether the action is beneficial. Both overuse and underinvestment result from this failure. Second, the total return to the group members is larger in the case of cooperative action than in the case of defection. This requires more than a different distribution of the social good produced by the action; cooperation must actually increase the quantity of the good to be distributed.

In the context of real property, the total value of a tract of land will likely drop if it is broken up into pieces that are each too small to be of much use. In that situation, fragmentation itself can result in economic loss. Such fragmentation presents an anticommons: no one can use the property. Typically such loss results from boundary problems or the difficulty of coordination problems, or because economies of scale cannot be realized, or because additional transactions are necessary in order to aggregate a usable physical quantity of the resource. Problems of fragmentation are treated by a number of scholars including Eric Freyfogle, *The Tragedy of Fragmentation*, 36 Val. U. L. Rev. 307, 323–36 (2002) and Michael Heller, *The Tragedy of the Anticommons: Property in the Transition from Marx to Markets*, 111 Harv. L. Rev. 621 (1998).

The commons and anticommons concepts are illustrated by extractive industries. Consider oil and water, each of which constitutes a natural commons. The total amount that is available to be used by anyone is depleted by excessive or over-speedy extraction. Overdrafting of groundwater can lead to contamination, surface degradation, and more costly pumping in the case of water, see, e.g. Barton H. Thompson, Jr., *Tragically Difficult: The Obstacles to Governing the Commons*, 30 Envtl. L. 241, 250 (2000). Similarly, as property rights in petroleum evolved in the U.S., a period of "extractive anarchy" prevailed, resulting in fires, excessive drilling, and extraction problems. *See* Gary D. Libecap & James L. Smith, *The Economic Evolution of Petroleum Property Rights in the United States*, 31 J. Legal Stud. 589 (2002).

To what extent is this analysis applicable to the community development field, the purpose of which is to enhance the viability of neighborhoods, to grapple with issues of sustainability, presented in Section G of this chapter? Who are the members of the relevant commons: residents of the jurisdiction exercising powers of land use, taxing and spending, and building regulation? Residents of the region who share the carbon-based consequences of auto usage and other transit choices? Taxpayers—individuals and enterprises—who contribute to the costs of infrastructure expenditures? Does the tragedy of the commons model justify the use of code enforcement, urban redevelopment, and eminent domain?

F. Displacement and Relocation

1. The Problem of Displacement

a. The Problem

The displacement of households and their forced relocation to other areas of the community has long been the foreseeable and usually unfortunate outcome of community development and revitalization programs. Urban displacement was rampant in the days of large scale urban renewal and highway construction projects. One estimate indicates that over two million persons were displaced by urban renewal and highway programs between 1964 and 1972. Henry W. McGee Jr. & Donald C. Bryant Jr., *Gentrification and the Law: Combating Urban Displacement,* 25 Wash. U. J. Urb. & Contemp. L. 43(1983). Urban displacement has been reduced with the decline of urban renewal and highway building in urban areas, but displacement remains a serious problem in federally funded community development programs and housing rehabilitation projects. Urban displacement is also aggravated by the private housing rehabilitation efforts now under way in many cities, often on a significant scale. *See, e.g.,* Henry W. McGee, *Seattle's Central District, 1990–2006: Gentrification or Displacement?* 39 Urb. Law. 167 (2007). Purely private displacement is unaffected by federal relocation legislation.

The evidence on the impact of relocation caused by private rehabilitation is not yet complete, but earlier studies of relocation from urban renewal projects indicated, generally, that relocated households obtained improved housing conditions but at an increased cost. The effect of relocation on segregated housing patterns was mixed. Because urban renewal projects have a long association with the displacement of minority households, most often blacks, "[i]n cities across the country, urban renewal came to be known as 'Negro removal.'" Wendell Pritchett, *The "Public Menace" of Blight: Urban Renewal and the Private Uses of Eminent Domain,* 21 Yale L. & Pol'y Rev. 1, 47 (2003). *See also* Martin Anderson, The Federal Bulldozer: A Critical Analysis of Urban Renewal, 1949–1962 (1964). In many of the studies, displaced households suffered negative psychological and social effects. A number of the early studies are summarized in Chester W. Hartman, *Relocation: Illusory Promises and No Relief,* 57 Va. L. Rev. 745 (1971).

While the federal housing act of 1949 imposed relocation responsibilities on local urban renewal agencies, these public entities often did not carry out their relocation responsibilities either humanely or well. Federal legislation does not require the construction of new housing for displaced households, and relocation housing needs were met from the existing housing stock. Initially, no benefits were made available to displaced households. With their limited incomes, they were usually unable to acquire in the local housing market the "decent, safe and sanitary" housing the federal legislation required. Local agencies sometimes made public housing available to displacees, who then rejected this accommodation in significant numbers.

Federal assistance was gradually extended to displacees. This first occurred in 1961, with the enactment of the Section 221(d)(3) program for privately built, but federally subsidized, rental housing. Relocation benefits were added to the urban renewal and other federally-funded displacement causing legislation in the mid-1960s. These benefits were initially funded by 100% federal grants to local agencies. Congress also added other protection to the urban renewal legislation, such as a requirement that a designated amount of low- and moderate-income housing be provided in urban renewal project areas.

b. The Uniform Relocation Act

Relocation guarantees and benefits were established in a single piece of legislation when Congress enacted the Uniform Relocation Assistance and Real Property Acquisition Policies Act of 1970, 42 U.S.C. §§4601–55 (URA) (as amended by the Uniform Relocation Act Amendments of 1987, Pub. L. No. 100-17, 101 Stat. 246 [hereinafter the 1987 Act]). This legislation provided a uniform schedule of benefits and guarantees for all federal agencies and state and local agencies administering federally-assisted programs and projects, but carried impacts on the relocation problem that to some extent diminished statutory protection. Direct federal funding of relocation benefits was gradually phased out, and local agencies were required to meet relocation benefits out of project and block grants. The absolute guarantee of adequate housing contained in the early urban renewal legislation was replaced by a provision requiring "assurances" that adequate relocation housing would be provided. With the termination of the federal urban renewal program, the special protection built into that legislation was also eliminated.

Requirements to minimize displacement were enacted in 1987. The Housing and Community Development Act of 1987, Pub. L. No. 100-242, §509, 101 Stat. 1815, 1927 (1988), sought to conserve low-income housing by requiring locally prepared antidisplacement and relocation assistance plans designed to minimize displacement. In addition, the 1987 amendments to the Uniform Relocation Assistance and Real Property Acquisition Policies Act of 1970, 42 U.S.C. §§4601–55, reach displacement by any activities receiving federal assistance, including the Community Development Block Grant Program. The increased cost of local programs requiring relocation assistance has also resulted in retargeting aid to more affluent neighborhoods so as to avoid expensive displacement likely in the most blighted neighborhoods.

The 1987 legislation created a one-for-one replacement requirement of all lower-income dwelling units, whether vacant or occupied, that are demolished or converted to another use, and required that relocation compensation must be sufficient to assure that for five years following displacement, the displacee will not have to pay more than 30% of household income for housing costs. Previously, the Act only allowed assistance for direct displacement. The one-for-one replacement rule is promulgated at 24 C.F.R. §42.375. The tenant displacement assistance payment regulation is promulgated at 24 C.F.R. §42.350. The Department of Transportation, as the lead agency for URA implementation, has issued regulations which apply to HUD as well. 49 C.F.R. pt. 24 (DOT obligations under URA). The 30% of income provision was removed from the government-wide regulation when it was modified in 2005, in favor of a formulation as to rent of a comparable replacement dwelling "within the financial means" of the displaced person. 49 C.F.R. §24.2(a)(6).

Section 104(d) of the Housing and Community Development Act (HCDA) provides minimum requirements for HUD-funded projects under the CDBG, HOME and UDAG programs. The relocation assistance and payments for eligible persons under Section 104(d) are similar to those required for the URA but there are a number of differences. One significant difference between the laws is the period of time used to calculate a rental assistance payment; Section 104(d) uses 60 months versus 42 months for the URA. Section 104(d)-eligible displaced persons may also choose to receive relocation assistance under Section 104(d) or relocation assistance under the URA.

Congress eliminated HUD's limited one-for-one replacement policy in the "1995 Recession Act," Pub. L. No. 104-19, § 1002(a), 109 Stat. 194, 235–36 (*codified at* 42 U.S.C. § 1437(a)). In *Henry Horner Mothers Guild v. Chicago Housing Authority*, No. 91 C 3316, 1998 WL 111582 (N.D. Ill. Mar. 6, 1998), displacees of demolished public housing sought one-for-one replacement to which they were entitled under a preceding consent decree. The court rejected HUD's argument that the 1996 Appropriations Act, Omnibus Consolidated Rescissions and Appropriations Act of 1996, Pub. L. No. 104-134, § 201(b), 110 Stat. 1321, effectively repealed the savings provision, and extending the repeal to pre-1995 demolition, rendering the one-for-one decree requirement null and void. The court read the 1996 legislation as an *amendatory*, rather than a *repealing*, act. The court reasoned that a different interpretation would authorize HUD to unilaterally change the terms of negotiated agreements.

The remainder of this section considers the application of the URA to urban displacement problems. It covers applicability and benefit coverage problems, and problems of planning and implementation that have been endemic in the relocation effort. Much of the applicable case law and practice have arisen in the older contexts of urban renewal and highway building. They are applicable by extension in present-day community development efforts.

The Uniform Relocation Act governs the relocation and land acquisition programs of all Federal departments and agencies. It is codified at 42 U.S.C. §§ 4601–55. Statutory references to the Act in this section are to the section numbers of the Act as it was enacted by Congress. Uniformity in agency interpretation has been a problem under the URA. Section 213 (a) requires consultation among federal agencies to secure uniform administration. Each federal agency has issued its own URA regulations, and some supplement these with handbooks and manuals. Uniformity in the administration of the Act still remains a problem. Because federal and federally assisted programs differ significantly, uniformity in administration is difficult to achieve. A single government-wide rule implementing the Act was published in 1989. *See* 54 Fed. Reg. 8928 (1989), 68 Fed Reg. 70342 (2003). These regulations were substantially revised in 2005, principally to enhance interpretive uniformity. 49 C.F.R. § 24.2-24.

Notes and Questions

1. This discussion raises questions about the underlying statutory purpose of the URA. Is it intended to provide "restitution" to households displaced by federal programs, or is it intended to improve the housing conditions of these households? Or does the statute include both purposes? Review the statutory requirements closely. Is there a justification for improving the housing conditions of households in the relocation process?

2. The expiration of federal subsidies on privately owned low- and moderate-income housing also causes substantial displacement. Major legislation enacted in 1997 to ad-

dress the problem of loss of units due to subsidy expiration and conversion to market rentals is considered in Chapter 3. Nonetheless, the problem persists. To illustrate the scale of this residential displacement: by the end of 2006, more than a quarter (27%) of the 119,785 apartments in these subsidy programs in New York City had been lost since 1990, and another 18% were threatened with subsidy loss. Tom Waters & Victor Bach, *Closing the Door 2007: The Shape of Subsidized Housing Loss in New York City* (2007) (Community Service Society Policy Brief).

3. Congress, beginning in 1987, has made several legislative attempts to conserve low-income housing by regulating the sale and conversion of subsidized housing. Chapter 3, *supra* considers major legislation enacted to address this problem.

4. In *Price v. City of Stockton*, 394 F. Supp. 2d 1256 (E.D. Cal. 2005), the United States District Court for the Eastern District of California held that the plaintiffs, who included the Stockton Metro Ministry and other low-income Stockton residents, were entitled to an injunction against the defendant City to prevent it from tearing down single occupancy hotels in the downtown area. The plaintiffs alleged that the City had violated its statutory duties under the Housing and Community Development Act, the Uniform Relocation Act, and the comparable California statutes by tearing down the hotels and not providing the plaintiffs with alternate housing.

Faylor v. Szupper

United States District Court
No. Civ. A 08-996, 2009 WL 2982646
(W.D. Pa. Sept. 14, 2009)

The plaintiff, Cheryl Faylor, proceeding pro se, has filed an amended civil rights complaint pursuant to the Uniform Relocation Assistance and Real Property Acquisition Policies Act of 1970 ("URA"), 42 U.S.C. §§4601, et seq. The plaintiff contends that the defendants failed to comply with the URA during her relocation to other housing which violated her Fourteenth Amendment rights to equal protection (Count I) and due process (Count II) under 42 U.S.C. §1983. She also complains that the defendants engaged in a conspiracy to violate her rights under 42 U.S.C. §1985(3) (Count V) and are liable for breach of contract/unjust enrichment (Count III) and negligence (Count IV). The Court's federal question and supplemental jurisdiction are invoked....

The plaintiff alleges that she was a resident at 411 South 6th Street in Jeannette, PA for over five years; that she lived in a townhouse unit that was one of several units targeted for demolition to make way for a renovation project called the Jeannette 6th Street Project (the "Project"); and that the Project utilized federal funding through HUD's HOME Investment Partnership Program. In 2006 and 2007, HUD and Westmoreland County (the "County") entered into Agreements pursuant to the HOME Investment Partnerships Act, 42 U.S.C. §12701, et seq., whereby HUD agreed to make funds available in exchange for the County's agreement to develop affordable housing. The County disbursed HUD funds for the Project to HBH, which created WEM Housing to act as the general contractor on the Project. As general contractor, WEM Housing purchased the townhouse units on South 6th Street and hired PCC and Carlotta Paige to assist in relocating residents affected by the Project.

The plaintiff contends that on or about February 21, 2007, WEM Housing signed a purchase agreement with the owner of the building where she resided which was the "initiation of negotiations," at which time the agency was to notify her in writing of her eligibility for relocation assistance, but it failed to do so. In a letter dated March 2, 2007, HBH informed the plaintiff that her family may be displaced by the Project, and it provided her with information as to her potential rights as a displaced person under the URA. On or about April 2, 2007, employees from PCC met with the plaintiff to obtain information from her which would be used to complete her relocation assistance. However, the plaintiff avers that she received no further information or contact from HBH or PCC until August 2007, by which time her townhouse unit and other units in the building had fallen into disrepair. For instance, the plaintiff asserts that rotting trash and discarded mattresses accumulated in front of the building, grass and weeds grew taller than four feet high, abandoned units were not cleaned, and cockroaches, fleas and other vermin were present on the premises. plaintiff contends that on September 12, 2007, she saw Carlotta Paige and complained about her living conditions and inquired about relocation efforts, and Paige told her they were working on it; that on or about September 21, 2007, she received a letter from Chad Ruffner, informing her that she was eligible for relocation assistance and needed to relocate to a different residence upon 90 days notice, but the letter did not advise her how much rental assistance she would receive; and that on September 24, 2007, she wrote to Ruffner complaining about the vermin problem, after which HBH fumigated the vacant, uncleaned unit next to hers, and Ruffner inspected her premises and said he would talk to Carlotta Paige about it.

The plaintiff asserts that in October 2007, she witnessed two house fires within a four-day period just a block from her residence, and fearing increased vandalism from abandoned housing in the area, she informed HBH and HUD that she intended to move from her residence. In a letter dated October 12, 2007, HBH provided notice to the plaintiff that she had to vacate her unit within 90 days; this letter also informed the plaintiff that she was eligible for $1,450.00 for a moving allowance and $17,262.00 for rental assistance pursuant to the URA. On October 22, 2007, the plaintiff moved from her residence and signed a lease for a replacement dwelling. She received an advance for her security deposit and the first month of rent in the new dwelling. On November 29, 2007, PCC paid the rental assistance funds.

In a letter dated December 2, 2007, the plaintiff informed HBH and HUD of her intent to appeal her relocation assistance determination, as she believed she was entitled to $17,000 in additional funds. By letter dated February 1, 2008, Chad Ruffner informed the plaintiff that he needed additional information to assess her appeal. In a letter dated March 13, 2008, John Tolbert of HUD advised the plaintiff that after reviewing her appeal, it was determined that she and her family qualified for an additional $9,461.20 in rental assistance. The plaintiff wrote a letter to John Tolbert dated March 17, 2008, expressing her dissatisfaction with the recalculated amount of her rental assistance. Copies of this letter were sent to Michael Szupper of HUD and the County Commissioners. On March 31, 2008, the plaintiff received payment in connection with her appeal in the amount of $9,961.20, a sum which she believes is less than what she is entitled to under the URA.

The URA is designed to minimize the hardship of displacement on persons like the plaintiff who are displaced as a direct result of programs or projects undertaken by a federal agency or with federal financial assistance. 42 U.S.C. §4621(b). To that end, the URA provides relocation services and assistance to displaced persons. See, 42 U.S.C. §4625 and 49 C.F.R. Part 24. The parties agree that the plaintiff was eligible to receive several types of URA relocation services, including: relocation advisory services pursuant to 49 C.F.R. §24.205; relocation notices pursuant to 49 C.F.R. §24.203; reimbursement for moving expenses pursuant to 49 C.F.R. §§24.301 and 24.302; and payments for the added cost of replacement housing or rental assistance pursuant to 49 C.F.R. §§24.401–24.403.

The plaintiff contends that the defendants failed to comply with the URA in several respects—such as by failing to provide certain relocation services to her, not properly calculating her relocation rental assistance or making timely payment, and not promptly or properly determining her appeal—all of which deprived her of her Fourteenth Amendment rights to equal protection (Count I) and due process (Count II) under 42 U.S.C. § 1983.... [T]he plaintiff also complains that the defendants engaged in a conspiracy to violate her civil rights under 42 U.S.C. § 1985(3) (Count V) and are liable for breach of contract/unjust enrichment (Count III) and negligence (Count IV).

PCC and Carlotta Paige's motion to dismiss or for summary judgment, and HBH, WEM Housing and Chad Ruffner's motion to dismiss....

The Third Circuit Court of Appeals has held that a private cause of action exists against state officials for violations of § 4625 of the URA due to the absence of a comprehensive enforcement scheme under the Act. *Pietroniro v. Borough of Oceanport,* 764 F.2d 976, 980 (3d Cir. 1985), *cert. denied,* 474 U.S. 1020 (1985). *See also Munoz v. City of Philadelphia,* 2007 WL 2973837 (E.D. Pa., Oct. 10, 2007) ("a private cause of action exists under § 1983 for violations of § 4625(a) of the URA"), citing *Pietroniro.* The defendants do not argue otherwise.

Rather, in support of their pending motions, the defendants assert that the § 1983 claims against them fail, because they did not act under color of state law.... The United States Supreme Court has stated: "When Congress enacted § 1983 as the statutory remedy for violations of the Constitution, it specified that the conduct at issue must have occurred under color of state law; thus liability attaches only to those wrongdoers who carry a badge of authority of a State and represent it in some capacity." *National Collegiate Athletic Ass'n. v. Tarkanian,* 488 U.S. 179, 191 (1988). Thus, to state a viable § 1983 civil rights claim, the plaintiff must plead that the defendants, acting under color of state law, deprived her of a right secured by the Constitution or laws of the United States.... To determine if such private actors are subject to scrutiny under § 1983, we must assess whether their alleged conduct can be "fairly attributable to the state." *Lugar v. Edmondson Oil Co.,* 457 U.S. 922, 937 (1982). While there is no single or uniform test to determine if a private act may be attributable to the state, the Supreme Court has developed several frameworks for assessing this question, which it summarized as follows:

> [A] challenged activity may be state action when it results from the State's exercise of "coercive power," *Blum [v. Yaretsky,* 457 U.S. 991, 1004 (1982)], when the State provides "significant encouragement," either overt or covert, or when a private actor operates as a "willful participant in joint activity with the State or its agents," *Lugar* [457 U.S. at 941]. We have treated a nominally private entity as a state actor when it is controlled by an "agency of the State," *Pennsylvania v. Board of Directors of City Trusts of Philadelphia,* 353 U.S. 230, 231 (1957) (per curiam), when it has been delegated a public function by the State, *West v. Atkins,* [487 U.S. 42, 56 (1988)]; *Edmonson v. Leesville Concrete Co.,* 500 U.S. 614, 627–628 (1991), when it is "entwined with governmental policies" or when government is "entwined in [its] management or control." *Evans v. Newton,* 382 U.S. 296, 299, 301 (1966).

Brentwood Academy v. Tennessee Secondary School Athletic Ass'n., 531 U.S. 288, 296 (2001).

The Third Circuit Court of Appeals has stated that state action cases broadly divide into two factual categories: "The first category involves an *activity* that is significantly encouraged by the state or in which the state acts as a joint participant." Determining state action in these cases "requires tracing the activity to its source to see if that source fairly can be said to be the state. The question is whether the fingerprints of the state are on the activity itself." "The second category of cases involves an *actor* that is controlled by the state, performs a function delegated by the state, or is entwined with government policies or management." In these cases, determining state action "consists of asking whether the actor is so integrally related to the state that it is fair to impute to the state responsibility for the action. The question ... is whether the state so identifies with the individual (or entity) who took the challenged action that we deem the state's fingerprints to have been on the action."

In attempting to show state action here, the plaintiff points to the fact that HUD and the County entered into agreements pursuant to the Home Investment Partnerships Act, 42 U.S.C. §§ 12701, et seq., wherein HUD agreed to make funds available in exchange for the County's agreement to develop affordable housing. The plaintiff alleges, and the record shows that in order to receive HOME Investment partnership funding ("HOME funds"), the County provided certifications that it would comply with the URA and its implementing regulations and follow a residential anti-displacement and relocation assistance plan.

In order "to receive federal funds for projects ... state and local agencies must certify that they will provide relocation benefits under the URA to affected persons and businesses." *Supreme Oil Co. v. Metropolitan Transp. Auth.*, 157 F.3d 148, 150 (2d Cir. 1998), citing 42 U.S.C. § 4604. "The grantee agency [here, the County] may contract with another public or private agency to administer the relocation benefits, but the actual grantee remains at all times responsible for assuring that the federal funds are disbursed in compliance with the URA." Here, the County contracted with HBH to develop the Project at issue, and in connection therewith, it loaned HOME funds to HBH and WEM Housing. WEM Housing hired PCC and Carlotta Paige to assist in relocating persons displaced by the Project. In a letter agreement accepted on April 11, 2007, PCC agreed to provide comprehensive relocation services to HBH in connection with the Project.

It is clear that acts of private contractors do not become acts of the government by reason of their performing public contracts or public functions. *Rendell-Baker v. Kohn*, 457 U.S. 830, 841–42 (1981). However, state action may arise if private actors are delegated a "traditionally and exclusively" state function. *Jackson v. Metropolitan Edison Co.*, 419 U.S. 345, 352–53 (1974) (state action may be found "in the exercise by a private entity of powers traditionally exclusively reserved to the State."). Thus, in *West, supra,* the Supreme Court found that "[c]ontracting out prison medical care [did] not relieve the State of its constitutional duty to provide adequate medical treatment to those in its custody." The Court explained that the State bore an affirmative obligation to provide adequate medical care to prison inmates, notwithstanding that it delegated that function to a private doctor who voluntarily assumed such obligation by contract. Finding that the doctor was vested with authority to fulfill the State's medical obligations at the prison, the Court held that he was a state actor, and his medical treatment was "fairly attributable to the State."

Here, we must determine if the movants—in providing relocation benefits pursuant to the URA-engaged in acts "fairly attributable to the State." Importantly, "the relevant question is not simply whether a private group is serving a 'public function,'" but "whether the function performed has been 'traditionally the *exclusive* prerogative of the State.'"

Here, to receive federal funds for the Project, the County was required to give assurances that it would provide relocation benefits and services to displaced persons. See, 42

U.S.C. § 4630.[6] As mentioned above, the County provided such assurances and certifications to HUD. The County then contracted with HBH to develop the Project, it loaned HOME funds to HBH and WEM Housing, and WEM Housing hired PCC and Paige to assist in providing relocation services to persons displaced by the Project. All the while, the County remained responsible for ensuring that relocation benefits were disbursed in compliance with the URA. According to the plaintiff, the County delegated its responsibility for ensuring URA compliance to the movants, who improperly administered URA benefits

At this juncture, the parties have not addressed whether the function of providing relocation benefits to displaced persons under the URA is traditionally the exclusive prerogative of the state. "[T]he traditionally exclusive public function requirement is a rigorous standard that is rarely satisfied." However, liberally construing the plaintiff's allegations, as we must for pro se complaints, the movants may be said to have performed a traditionally exclusive governmental function in providing URA relocation benefits to her so as to be deemed state actors.

Still, we must assess whether the plaintiff has set forth a viable § 1983 claim against these defendants. "[T]he first step in evaluating a § 1983 claim is to identify the exact contours of the underlying right said to have been violated and to determine whether the plaintiff has alleged a deprivation of a constitutional right at all."

In Count I, the defendants are said to have violated the plaintiff's equal protection rights by failing to provide her with relocation assistance and services mandated by the URA. The United States Supreme Court has explained:

> The Equal Protection Clause of the Fourteenth Amendment commands that no State shall "deny to any person within its jurisdiction the equal protection of the laws," which is essentially a direction that all persons similarly situated should be treated alike. *City of Cleburne v. Cleburne Living Center,* 473 U.S. 432, 439 (1985). Here, the plaintiff has failed to plead a viable Fourteenth Amendment denial of equal protection claim. Where a plaintiff fails to allege membership in a protected class, as here, she may state a cognizable equal protection claim by asserting that she has been "intentionally treated differently from others similarly situated, and that there is no rational basis for the difference in treatment." *Village of Willowbrook v. Olech,* 528 U.S. 562, 564 (2000). Nowhere in the amended complaint does the plaintiff make such allegations. Rather, the plaintiff confirms that she "was not treated differently than the other displaced people of [her] building." As such, Count I is dismissed for failure to state a claim.

In Count II, the defendants are said to have violated the plaintiff's Fourteenth Amendment due process rights. The Due Process Clause of the Fourteenth Amendment provides that no state shall "deprive any person of life, liberty, or property, without due process of law." The Due Process Clause affords procedural and substantive safeguards, *Planned Parenthood of Southeastern PA. v. Casey,* 505 U.S. 833, 846–47 (1992); and the plaintiff complains that the defendants deprived her of both components of due process in the course of displacing and relocating her.

---

6. In part, 42 U.S.C. § 4630 provides: "Notwithstanding any other law, the head of a Federal agency shall not approve any grant to, or contract or agreement with, a displacing agency (other than a Federal agency), under which Federal financial assistance will be available to pay all or part of the cost of a program or project which will result in the displacement of any person on or after January 2, 1971, unless he receives satisfactory assurances from such displacing agency that—(1) fair and reasonable relocation payments and assistance shall be provided to or for displaced persons...."

To state a claim for deprivation of procedural due process under § 1983, a plaintiff must allege that (1) she was deprived of an individual interest that is encompassed within the Fourteenth Amendment, and (2) the procedures available to her did not provide due process of law. Construing the plaintiff's allegations in a light most favorable to her, she asserts that she has a protected property interest in relocation benefits which the defendants did not fully provide her.

The United States Supreme Court has recognized that certain benefits distributed by the government are a form of property protected by the due process clause. See *Mathews v. Eldridge*, 424 U.S. 319 (1976) (disability benefits); *Goldberg v. Kelly*, 397 U.S. 254 (1970) (welfare benefits). However, not every government benefits program creates constitutionally protected property interests. In order to have a property interest in a benefit, a person must "have a legitimate claim of entitlement to it." *Board of Regents of State Colleges v. Roth*, 408 U.S. 564, 577 (1972). In *Roth*, the Court explained that property interests are not created by the Constitution itself. Rather, they are created from an independent source—such as state law or a statute—which secures benefits and supports claims of entitlement to them.

The URA mandates that "[w]henever a program or project to be undertaken by a displacing agency will result in the displacement of any person ..." such person is entitled to relocation benefits, including moving and related expenses. 42 U.S.C. § 4622(a)-(b). The Act also provides that relocation assistance advisory services and programs are to be made available to displaced persons. 42 U.S.C. § 4625(b)-(c). It is not disputed that the plaintiff is a "displaced person" under the Act who is entitled to receive relocation benefits. Thus, it appears that she has a protected property interest in such benefits.

Nonetheless, to state a viable procedural due process claim, the plaintiff must allege that she received constitutionally inadequate process in connection with the deprivation of her benefits. "[T]o determine whether a constitutional violation has occurred, it is necessary to ask what process the State provided, and whether it was constitutionally adequate. This inquiry would examine the procedural safeguards built into the statutory or administrative procedure of effecting the deprivation, and any remedies for erroneous deprivations provided by statute or tort law." *Zinermon v. Burch*, 494 U.S. 113 (1990).

The URA does not provide a hearing for relocation benefit claims, and the plaintiff does not profess entitlement to a hearing. Rather, the Act authorizes the "head of the lead agency" (i.e., the Department of Transportation, see, 42 U.S.C. § 4601(12)) to issue regulations and establish procedures to assure that an aggrieved person may have her claim for benefits reviewed by the head of an agency having authority over the project. 42 U.S.C. § 4633(b). Under federal regulations implementing the URA, "[a]ny aggrieved person may file a written appeal with the Agency in any case in which the person believes that the Agency has failed to properly consider [her] application for assistance", including "a relocation payment". See, 49 C.F.R. § 24.10(b). The term "Agency" means: "the Federal Agency, State, State Agency, or person that acquires real property or displaces a person." 49 C.F.R. § 24.2(a)(1).

As gleaned from the amended complaint, the plaintiff contends that the defendants failed to promptly and adequately process and review her appeal of the relocation assistance determination as mandated in 49 C.F.R. § 24.10. Specifically, she asserts that the defendants failed to notify her of the proper agency in which to appeal; failed to provide her with access to her relocation file as she requested; failed to promptly review her appeal and consider its justification; failed to assign an authorized agency official to review her appeal; failed to properly recalculate her rental assistance payment; and failed to promptly notify her in writing of her appeal determination. To the extent she complains that deficiencies in the appeal process deprived her of procedural due process, the plaintiff has stated a viable claim against the movants, as they are said to have participated in the complained-of appeal procedures. As such, the procedural due process claim will not be dismissed against these defendants.

However, the plaintiff has failed to state a viable substantive due process claim. The Third Circuit Court of Appeals has explained that "the core of the concept of due process is protection against arbitrary action, and only the most egregious official conduct can be said to be arbitrary in the constitutional sense." An official's conduct violates the substantive component of the Due Process Clause when it "can properly be characterized as arbitrary, or conscience shocking". *County of Sacramento v. Lewis,* 523 U.S. 833, 846 (1998). Thus, for a substantive due process claim to lie, a plaintiff must have been deprived of a fundamental interest established by the Constitution under circumstances which "shocks the conscience."

Here, the defendants' alleged failure to properly calculate the plaintiff's relocation assistance and comply with the URA is not conscious shocking. The Third Circuit Court of Appeals has held that in a land-use controversy, official conduct will not be deemed to "shock the conscience" absent allegations of corruption or self-dealing, bias against an ethnic group, interference with constitutionally-protected activity or a virtual "taking" of property.... Based on the plaintiff's allegations of insufficient relocation assistance and failure to comply with the URA, none of which involve corruption, self-dealing, or bias against an ethnic group, her substantive due process claim fails.

In Count V, the plaintiff contends that the defendants conspired to deprive her of her Fourteenth Amendment due process and equal protection rights in violation of 42 U.S.C. § 1985. In pleading her conspiracy claim, the plaintiff cites to 42 U.S.C. § 1985(3). Under 42 U.S.C. § 1985(3), an action may be brought by a person injured by a conspiracy formed "for the purpose of depriving, either directly or indirectly, any person or class of persons of the equal protection of the laws, or of equal privileges and immunities under the laws." 42 U.S.C. § 1985(3). It is well settled that "because § 1985(3) requires the 'intent to deprive of *equal* protection, or *equal* privileges and immunities,' a claimant must allege 'some racial, *or perhaps otherwise class-based,* invidiously discriminatory animus behind the conspirators' action' in order to state a claim." *Griffin v. Breckenridge,* 403 U.S. 88, 102 (1971). Here, the plaintiff has failed to plead the requisites of a § 1985(3) conspiracy, as the amended complaint is devoid of allegations that the alleged conspiracy was motivated by a class-based, invidiously discriminatory animus. Hence, Count V is dismissed.

As for the plaintiff's state law claims, she purports to state a cause of action for breach of contract/unjust enrichment in Count III and negligence in Count IV. While the breach of contract/unjust enrichment claim fails against these defendants, the plaintiff has set forth a viable negligence claim against them....

[Plaintiff's contract claim was that the defendants created a contract or quasi-contract with her by using the URA to lure her into believing she would receive relocation assistance if she was displaced by the Project, but having failed to pay her the full amount of relocation assistance to which she was due, the movants were unjustly enriched at her expense. The court dismissed the claim under Pennsylvania contract law. Because there was no contract claim, her negligence claim was not barred by a "gist of the action" doctrine, thus her claim that defendants acted negligently in providing relocation services to the plaintiff, during which they were "callously indifferent" to her, survived defendants' motion to dismiss.—Eds.] While the plaintiff has pled a viable claim for denial of procedural due process against the County and the movants, and negligence against the movants, genuine issues of material fact exist on these claims. Accordingly, the plaintiff's motion for summary judgment will be denied.

Notes and Questions

1. The most extensive study conducted since the URA was enacted is U.S. Department of Transportation Relocation Retrospective Study in 1995. Nearly 90% of the homeowners surveyed indicated that they were "able to significantly upgrade" their housing, but over 50% of those surveyed were no longer living in their replacement housing a year after receiving the payment. U.S. DEP'T OF TRANSP., FED. HIGHWAY ADMIN., RELOCATION RETROSPECTIVE STUDY 2 (1996). For earlier studies, see Chester W. Hartman, *Relocation: Illusory Promises and No Relief*, 57 VA. L. REV. 745 (1971) (describing extensive uncompensated losses suffered by victims of urban renewal condemnations).

2. Forced displacement by development is a global problem of enormous dimensions and dire consequences for millions. Accordingly, in international development, numerous scholars track that displacement to distill knowledge of displacement's social costs for the displacees into patterns of predictable, cumulative dimensions of impoverishment, in order to devise successful resettlement practices for people involuntarily displaced by development. *See, e.g.*, Michael M. Cernea, *Impoverishment Risks, Risk Management, and Reconstruction: A Model for Population Displacement and Resettlement*, *available at* http://www.un.org/esa/sustdev/sdissues/energy/op/hydro_cernea_population_resettlement_background paper.pdf (last visited Oct. 20, 2008). There is an emerging principle based on international law of a right not to be displaced. *See generally* Ngai Pindell, *Is there Hope for HOPE VI?: Community Economic Development and Localism*, 35 CONN. L. REV. 385 (2002); Maria Stavropoulou, *The Right Not to be Displaced*, 9 Am. U.J. INT'L L. & POL'Y 689 (1994).

3. Book-length studies of "gentrification" include GENTRIFICATION, DISPLACEMENT, AND NEIGHBORHOOD REVITALIZATION (J. John Palin & Bruce London eds. 1984) (collected essays); LORETTA LEES, TOM SLATER & ERWIN WYLY, GENTRIFICATION (2008); KATH NELSON ET AL., GENTRIFICATION AND DISTRESSED CITIES: AN ASSESSMENT OF TRENDS IN INTRAMETROPOLITAN MIGRATION (1988). For a provocative view of the coalition of economic and governmental powers that often carry out public policy to the detriment of the central city poor, see the description of housing policy in Cambridge, Massachusetts, in John Mollenkopf & Jon Pynoos, *Boardwalk and Park Place: Property Ownership, Political Structure, and Housing Policy at the Local Level*, *in* HOUSING URBAN AMERICA 55 (Jon Pynoos et al. eds. 1973). For additional views see Keith Aoki, *Race, Space, and Place: The Relation Between Architectural Modernism, Post-Modernism, Urban Planning, and Gentrification*, 20 FORDHAM URB. L.J. 699 (1993) (aesthetic ideology, city planning, and architecture have generated segregation and gentrification); J. Peter Byrne, *Condemnation of Low Income Residential Communities under the Takings Clause*, 23 UCLA J. ENVTL. L. & POL'Y 131(2005); Matthew J. Parlow, *Unintended Consequences: Eminent Domain and Affordable Housing*, 46 SANTA CLARA L. REV. 841, 856–57 (2006) (by taking affordable housing units off the market, cities reduce the available housing stock for low-income residents, replacing them with new high-end commercial, residential, and mixed-use projects. *See also* CHESTER HARTMAN, W. DENNIS KEATING & RICHARD LEGATES, DISPLACEMENT: HOW TO FIGHT IT (1982); Donald C. Bryant & Henry W. McGee, *Gentrification and the Law: Combating Urban Displacement*, 25 WASH. U.J. URB. & CONTEMP. L. 43 (1983) [portions excerpted in Chapter 4, *supra*—Eds.]; James G. Dunham & Dean E. Sheldon, *Mitigating the Effects*

of Private Revitalization on Housing for the Poor, 70 MARQ. L. REV. 1 (1986); Lawrence Kolodney, *Eviction Free Zones: The Economics of Legal Bricolage in the Fight Against Displacement,* 18 FORDHAM URB. L.J. 507 (1991) (anti-gentrification strategy); Richard T. LeGates & Chester Hartman, *Gentrification-Caused Displacement,* 14 URB. LAW. 31 (1982); Peter Marcuse, *Gentrification, Abandonment and Displacement: Connections, Causes and Policy Responses in New York City,* 28 WASH U.J. URB. & CONTEMP. L. 195 (1985); Peter Marcuse, *To Control Gentrification: Antidisplacement Zoning and Planning for Stable Residential Districts,* 13 N.Y.U. REV. L. & SOC. CHANGE 931 (1985); Harold McDougall, *Gentrification: The Class Conflict Over Urban Space Moves into the Courts,* 10 FORDHAM URB. L.J. 177 (1982); Henry W. McGee, Jr., *Afro-American Resistance to Gentrification and the Demise of Integrationist Ideology in the United States,* 23 URB. LAW. 25 (1991).

4. On the psychological impacts of relocation, see generally MINDY THOMPSON FULLILOVE, ROOT SHOCK: HOW TEARING UP CITY NEIGHBORHOODS HURTS AMERICA, AND WHAT WE CAN DO ABOUT IT (2004); ALVIN L. SCHORR, SLUMS AND SOCIAL INSECURITY 17–25 (1964); Marc Fried, *Grieving for a Lost Home, in* THE URBAN CONDITION 151 (Leonard J. Duhl ed. 1963); Marc Fried & Peggy Gleicher, *Some Sources of Residential Satisfaction in an Urban Slum,* 27 J. AM. INST. PLAN. 305 (1961); Chester W. Hartman, *Social Values and Housing Orientations,* 19 J. SOC. ISSUES 113 (1963); Ray Telles, *Forgotten Voices: Gentrification and Its Victims,* 3 SCHOLAR 115 (2000). Displacement also has indirect effects on the housing market, as persons displaced by government programs may secure replacement housing by ousting other persons from housing they rent.

5. On centralized relocation services, see ROBERT P. GROBERG, CENTRALIZED RELOCATION: A NEW MUNICIPAL SERVICE (1969). Centralizing relocation services is no guarantee of adequate services. A review of the performance of the Philadelphia Centralized Relocation Bureau over a two-year period indicated that 77% of the legitimate needs of Bureau clients went unanswered. Among the benefits cited by advocates of a centralized relocation agency are increased influence in the structure of local government and the ability to sustain a relocation staff on a permanent basis, providing more skilled and experienced personnel.

6. Community development funds may be used to pay relocation benefits "when determined by the grantee to be appropriate to the community development program." § 105(a)(11). The URA is the principal federal legislation providing protection to displacees in housing and community development programs, but the 1987 amendments to the HCDA provide an alternative relocation program and compensation requirements, see HCDA § 104(d), 42 U.S.C. § 5304(d).

2. Coverage and Benefits under the Uniform Relocation Act

The congressional statement of purpose in the Uniform Relocation Act is sweeping: displacees are not to suffer "disproportionate injuries as a result of programs designed for the benefit of the public as a whole." § 201(b). In spite of this broad language, HUD and other federal agencies have not always given the URA a generous interpretation. The statute is complex, and the federal courts have cut back on its coverage. Note that we concentrate here on the relocation problems of tenants and homeowners, curtailing treatment of the relocation problems of businesses, which are litigated with more frequency.

a. Definitions

The definitions, Section 101, are critical to an understanding of the Act. Note that localities are included. Subsection (b)(3). Subsection (4) contains the triggering element that brings in federally assisted programs. Is community development (CD) covered? Public housing? Rehabilitation assisted with CD funds? The definition of "displaced person" in subsection (6) is essential to an understanding of eligibility. The original Act provided that "[t]he term 'displaced person' means any person who ... moves from real property, or moves his personal property from real property, as a result of the acquisition of such real property, in whole or in part, or as the result of the written order of the acquiring agency to vacate real property, for a program or project undertaken by a Federal agency, or with Federal financial assistance." The 1987 Act amended the provision to require notice of an *intent* to acquire. The provision contains both a timing and a substantive displacement requirement. Why? Note how the statute is acquisition oriented. What happens if an owner-occupant leaves a dwelling before the property is acquired in order to relocate more easily? Is such a displacee covered? Note the "program or project" phrase. How does that phrase apply in the CD program?

At the heart of housing advocates' concerns with the URA is the Act's apparent guarantee that a person may not be required to move from one's dwelling unless there is available a "comparable replacement dwelling." The criteria for the replacement dwelling are set out in Section 203(a)(10):

> The term "comparable replacement dwelling" means any dwelling that is (A) decent, safe, and sanitary; (B) adequate in size to accommodate the occupants; (C) within the financial means of the displaced person; (D) functionally equivalent; (E) in an area not subject to unreasonable adverse environmental conditions; and (F) in a location generally not less desirable than the location of the displaced person's dwelling with respect to public utilities, facilities, services, and the displaced person's place of employment.

The criteria are further delineated in the federal regulation at 49 C.F.R. § 24.2(a)(6), which includes an explanatory Appendix. Over the years, the regulatory definition and judicial interpretations have elaborated the meaning of "functional equivalence," and of "within the financial means" of the displaced person.

Local housing codes govern questions of how many bedrooms are needed for the number, gender and ages of individuals in the household. Lead-based paint safety is not in the 2005 rule but is in the Appendix thereto.

b. Moving Expenses and Homeowner's Payment

A significant benefit created by relocation law is the concept of the replacement housing payment. Section 202 provides for payment of actual and reasonable moving expenses as well as a dislocation allowance. Section 210 makes this and other provisions applicable to federally funded programs. Section 203 provides the homeowner's bonus payment of up to $22,500. What is the reason for the six-months' residency rule? *See also Nagi v. United States*, 751 F.2d 826 (6th Cir. 1985) (displacee eligible for benefits, despite failure to occupy house in one year, where misled by agency to believe family could temporarily split and reside in apartment during house search, as law requires fairness). *But see Kroger Co. v. Regional Airport Auth. of Louisville & Jefferson County*, 286 F.3d 382 (6th Cir. 2002) (disapproving the use of the substantial evidence standard of review in *Nagi* although not there dispositive).

If the agency acquires a substandard slum dwelling, is the occupant entitled to a standard dwelling? If the interest costs on the new mortgage are higher than they were on the old mortgage, is the displacee compensated for this increase up to the total benefit of $22,500? Is it likely that the generous 1960s' benefit cap of $15,000, even as modified by the 1987 cap of $22,500, will permit acquisition of a standard replacement dwelling in the twenty-first century by one displaced from substandard housing? Section 203(a) requires the displacee to obtain replacement housing within one year from final receipt of the acquisition payment.

The 2005 revised Regulation added a new provision prohibiting the solicitation of waivers of relocation assistance or benefits, 49 C.F.R. § 24.207(f), and augmented the relocation planning requirements to include displaced businesses as well as residences in relocation interviews and site assessment. *Id.* at § 24.205(a)(4).

c. Tenant Payments

Under Section 204, a displaced person who actually and lawfully occupied the dwelling for 90 days or more before the initiation of negotiation may receive *either* an amount up to $5,250 that will enable the displaced person to lease a comparable replacement dwelling for a period not to exceed 42 months, or to make a down payment on the purchase of a "decent, safe, and sanitary" dwelling. 42 U.S.C. § 4624; 49 C.F.R. § 24.402. The monetary caps established in 49 C.F.R. §§ 24.401(a) and 24.402(b) may be exceeded if comparable replacement property is not available within the monetary limits. 49 C.F.R. § 24.404(a).

Most agencies, in order to avoid administrative and monitoring problems, pay the tenant's adjustment payment in one lump sum at the time of displacement. Stories abound of tenants using the lump sum payment for nonhousing expenditures. Should agencies be compelled to disburse the tenant's payment monthly over the statutory payment period? This change would add additional costs to an already overloaded relocation process. Does the present lump sum payment method clearly subvert the statutory intent?

Are expenses incurred in searching for a replacement dwelling reimbursable? *See* 49 C.F.R. § 24.301(h)(9).

d. Federal Share

Prior to the 1970 Act, HUD or other displacement agencies assumed the total cost of displacement, and these were credited to the appropriate displacement program (e.g., urban renewal). Under the 1970 law federal agencies were to pay up to $25,000 of the cost for relocating each displacee until July 1, 1972. After that time, relocation costs were to be subject to the same matching treatment as other federal programs which displaced people, such as urban renewal.

Notes and Questions

1. Section 213(b)(3), providing for an administrative grievance procedure, was substituted for language which would have precluded judicial review of relocation benefits. May judicial review still be had? What effect does Section 102(a) have, which provides that Section 301, the acquisition policies portion of URA, creates no rights or liabilities and does not affect the validity of acquisition by purchase or condemnation, have on your answer to this question?

2. Some have argued for a change in the interest rate adjustment payment so that the monthly payment after purchase of a new dwelling would not exceed the monthly payment on the acquired dwelling. How would you amend the statute to provide for such a payment? Would you consider an amendment that would allow a mortgage on the new dwelling for a longer term than the unexpired term on the mortgage on the acquired dwelling? What if the mortgage on the acquired dwelling has been paid?

3. Some federal agencies, in order to remedy inadequacies in the homeowner's adjustment payment, make an additional payment to the homeowner under the "housing of last resort" provision. Is this additional payment justified by the language of that provision? A suggested amendment to the URA would remove the payment ceiling limitation and allow agencies to make whatever payment to homeowners as necessary to allow them to acquire new standard housing within their means. Would this amendment be desirable? *See* S. Lynn Martinez, *Protecting Low-Income Communities from the New "Urban Renewal:" Antidisplacement Advocacy and Relocation Rights Enforcement*, 37 Clearinghouse Rev. 304 (2003). *See generally* Sara E. Johnson, *A Survey of Federal Relocation Requirements and Antidisplacement Safeguards*, 17 Clearinghouse Rev. 818 (1983).

4. *Preprogram Activities.* The URA applies to federal and federally assisted acquisition. However, so simple a formula becomes complicated when applied to public works projects that may take decades to plan and execute. In *La Raza Unida v. Volpe*, 337 F. Supp. 221 (N.D. Cal. 1971), *aff'd*, 488 F.2d 559 (9th Cir. 1973), *cert. denied*, 417 U.S. 968 (1974), the state was engaging in right-of-way acquisition although it had yet to formally request federal highway construction funds. As the state's eventual options included pursuing federal funds, the court concluded that as long as that option remained realistic, compliance with the URA was necessary.

5. One problem no longer confronting displacees eligible for coverage under the URA is the question of judicial reviewability. The legislative history of the URA discloses a compromise to allow judicial review of disputes under the relocation provisions and a nonreview standard for the acquisition policies title. *Barnhart v. Brinegar*, 362 F. Supp. 464 (W.D. Mo. 1973). For a recent treatment reiterating that the URA does not provide a private right of action for monetary damages, see *Delancey v. City of Austin*, 570 F.3d 590 (5th Cir. 2009) (URA did not contain rights-creating language, and relevant URA provisions prescribing advisory services are directed at the "head of any displacing agency" rather than at individuals benefited by statute, construing § 205(b), (c), 42 U.S.C. § 4625(b), (c).

6. *Program Coverage—Housing Defaults.* In *Alexander v. HUD*, 441 U.S. 39 (1979), Justice Marshall wrote for a unanimous Court rejecting URA coverage for displacement from housing projects acquired by HUD after the projects' sponsors defaulted on federally insured loans despite a written order to vacate. Justice Marshall concluded that the legislative history of the written order clause reveals no congressional intent to extend relocation benefits beyond the acquisition context. Two causal requirements were identified. First, the written order to vacate must result directly from an actual or contemplated property acquisition. Second, and more fundamentally, that acquisition must be "for," or intended to further, a federal program or project. Therefore, a program developed after the agency procures property, such as demolition and reuse, will not suffice, even though it necessitates displacement, since that program could not have motivated the property acquisition. HUD's acquisitions occur as the result of the mortgage insurance programs' predictable, though unfortunate, failures, but the default acquisitions do not further the purpose of the particular programs.

Alexander is perhaps more understandable in the context of an involuntary project failure. Certainly the notion that every tenant in subsidized housing and every purchaser of an FHA- or VA-insured house receives, in addition to life tenure (subject to eviction for cause or foreclosure), a commitment for relocation benefits if they must ever involuntarily move seems beyond the intent of URA. The 1987 amendments to HCDA, the Housing and Community Development Act of 1987, Pub. L. No. 100-242, § 121(b)(3)(F),(G), 101 Stat. 1815, 1838 (1988) (*codified at* 42 U.S.C. § 1437p(b)(F), (G)), requires relocation expenses and satisfactory relocation in the demolition and disposition of HUD projects; §§ 201–263, 101 Stat. 1877 (*codified at* 12 U.S.C. § 1715l(d)(3) note) seeks to halt the sale and conversion of subsidized housing; and § 123, 101 Stat. 1842, 1846 (*codified at* 42 U.S.C. § 1437s(b)(4)), provides for a program of public housing homeownership, prohibits eviction, and provides for assistance to nonparticipating families.

In *Harris v. Lynn*, 555 F.2d 1357 (8th Cir.), *cert. denied*, 434 U.S. 927 (1977), the court ruled that public housing tenants relocated to other projects when a public housing project was demolished were not displaced under the meaning of the URA as there was no acquisition. The court found that financial considerations caused the relocation and that it did not matter that the relocation and demolition was funded by a federal grant. *See also Edwards v. District of Columbia*, 821 F.2d 651 (D.C. Cir. 1987) (no enforceable tenant rights against displacement from public housing due to HUD-approved demolition prompted by failure to maintain); *Frisby v. HUD*, 755 F.2d 1052 (3d Cir. 1985) (HUD may deny replacement or rehabilitation subsidies on sale of defaulted subsidized housing where not cost effective). The *Edwards* opinion has been superseded by statute. *See Dessin v. Housing Auth. of City of Fort Meyers*, 783 F. Supp. 587, 589 (M.D. Fla. 1990), *rev'd in part, remanded in part mem.*, 948 F.2d 730 (11th Cir. 1991). Subsection (d) was added by section 121(a) of the Housing and Community Development Act of 1987, Pub. L. No. 100-242, 101 Stat. 1815.

> to clarify that no PHA [public housing authority] shall take any steps toward demolition and disposition without having satisfied the statutory criteria. This provision is intended to correct an erroneous interpretation of the existing statute by the United States Court of Appeals for the D.C. Circuit in *Edwards v. District of Columbia and shall be fully enforceable by tenants of and applicants for* the housing that is threatened.

H. Conf. Rep. No. 100-426, 100th Congress, 1st Sess., *reprinted in* 1987 U.S.C.C.A.N. 3458, 3469. This congressional clarification has been interpreted to allow a cause of action by current or potential tenants where an authority has acted to constructively demolish public housing by failure to maintain. *See Tinsley v. Kemp,* 750 F. Supp. 1001 (W.D. Mo. 1990); *Concerned Tenants Ass'n of Father Panik Village v. Pierce,* 685 F. Supp. 316, 319–321 (D. Conn. 1988).

7. Enterprise Zone-generated displacement is not covered by the URA. 42 U.S.C. § 11503.

8. Would displacement by a HOPE VI project that reduces density and includes higher income residents in former public housing qualify? Would it matter if the displacees were in a structure to be demolished or one that was to be rehabilitated?

9. *Community Development Block Grants.* HUD regulations initially provided that any acquisition within three years prior to the filing of an application for community development funds was covered by the URA. Following the *Alexander* decision, HUD amended its regulation to conform with that decision and restricted URA coverage to acquisitions on or after the date of the application. HUD claimed that this change was necessary to conform with the "intent" requirement adopted in *Alexander*. Do you agree?

HUD then again amended its regulation to provide that with local agency and HUD agreement, an acquisition either before or after the application date could either be covered or not covered by URA. Why do you suppose HUD adopted this change? Is it consistent with *Alexander*? For discussion of these changes, see 44 Fed. Reg. 56324 (1979).

HUD regulations require a displacement strategy for those affected by private HUD-assisted rehabilitation activities or indirect displacement, which minimizes displacement and mitigates its adverse effects. *Cf. Dugger v. City of Missoula*, 676 F. Supp. 209 (D. Mont. 1987) (no URA coverage for lease termination of hamburger stand by lessor involved in block grant-funded redevelopment where specific leased property not acquired for the project with block grant funds).

10. *Rehabilitation*. The shift to an emphasis on rehabilitation in community development programs raised new problems of coverage under the URA. Often, rehabilitation projects are undertaken by private developers without federal assistance of any kind. This kind of rehabilitation is common in areas undergoing "gentrification"—the re-entry of upper-income households into lower-income neighborhoods. Rehabilitation in this situation usually leads to a substantial increase in housing costs and the displacement of lower-income residents previously living in the neighborhood. The 1987 housing legislation, the Housing and Community Development Act of 1987, Pub. L. No. 100-242, § 149, 101 Stat. 1815, 1853 (1988) (*codified at* 42 U.S.C. § 1437f(u)), provides for vouchers or Section 8 certificates for five years for those displaced by Section 8 rental rehabilitation activities.

In *Moorer v. HUD*, 561 F.2d 175 (8th Cir. 1975), *cert. denied*, 436 U.S. 919 (1978), the court ruled that persons displaced by private acquisitions of real property, aided by federal financial assistance through mortgage insurance and interest rate subsidy payments, were not "displaced persons" under URA. The question was whether the persons involved were displaced by governmental action either acquiring the property or issuing an order to vacate the property. *Accord Isham v. Pierce*, 694 F.2d 1196 (9th Cir. 1982) (federally subsidized rehabilitation of private residence hall not involving "acquisition"); *Dawson v. HUD*, 428 F. Supp. 328 (N.D. Ga. 1976), *aff'd per curiam*, 592 F.2d 1293 (11th Cir. 1979). *See* Note, 46 UMKC. L. Rev. 332 (1977). The 1987 Act in Section 101(6)(A)(i)(II) (*codified at* 42 U. S. C. § 4601(6)(A)(i)(II)) specifically covers direct displacement by federally assisted rehabilitation. Is *Moorer* legislatively overruled?

11. *Private Acquisition*. In *Young v. Harris*, 599 F.2d 870 (8th Cir.), *cert. denied*, 444 U.S. 993 (1979), the court ruled that displacees from a 106-acre project area were not covered by URA when the acquisition was financed under the state redevelopment law. The court reached this result notwithstanding that the project was to use community development block grant funds in its redevelopment activities and would use Section 8 subsidies for nearly a quarter of some 2,000 units of housing planed. The area was designated as a redevelopment area pursuant to the Missouri Urban Redevelopment Corporation Law, Mo. Rev. Stat., §§ 353.010–353.190.

Under the Urban Redevelopment Corporation Law, private corporations organized according to the statute with a public purpose of redeveloping blighted areas may be granted special privileges such as the power of eminent domain and property tax abatements on redeveloped property. The redevelopment plan financing consists of wholly private capital, with the only aspect of federal assistance in the form of mortgage insurance by the Department of Housing and Urban Development (HUD). Further city assistance included demolition of nine vacant buildings, street improvements, and the sale of land to the developer at extremely low cost by virtue of tax foreclosure sales.

The Missouri program in *Young* is unique to that state, but tax-increment-financed redevelopment programs are comparable and adopted through legislation in many states. *See* Alan Woolever, *Tax Increment Financing, Government Grants, and Developer Tax Consequences: An Analysis of Statutes, Regulations, Case Law and Related Policy Considerations*, 40 URB. LAW. 289 (2008).

12. *Code Enforcement. Devines v. Maier*, 665 F.2d 138 (7th Cir. 1981) (order to temporarily vacate is not covered "displacement"), *subsequent proceedings*, 728 F.2d 876 (7th Cir.), *cert. denied*, 469 U.S. 836 (1984); Steven R. Selsberg, Comment, *State Regulation of Substandard Housing and the Fifth Amendment Taking Clause:* Devines v. Maier, 29 WASH. U.J. URB. & CONTEMP. L. 263 (1985). See discussion of the *Devines* case in A Note on Housing Code Enforcement and the Taking Issue, *supra*, in this chapter.

13. With respect to farms, small businesses, and non-profit organizations, the Uniform Relocation Act provides for reasonable actual expenses for searching for and moving to a new site, and for re-establishing the enterprise in a replacement location up to $10,000. 42 U.S.C. § 4622(a)(1). Business or farm displacees may elect a lump sum payment in lieu of relocation costs, in an amount determined by the head of the agency, between $1,000 and $20,000. *Id* at § (c).

A Note on State Relocation Laws

As has been indicated before, there is no coverage under URA for persons displaced by purely state or local government activities, nor those displaced by purely private development. One HUD report indicated that 61% of the units removed from the housing supply of the city of Chicago between 1969 and 1971 were by local code enforcement and not covered by URA or other federal relocation requirements.

While the states were initially slow to develop relocation programs, states have passed statutes which provide benefits, including monetary assistance, to aid persons or businesses that are required to relocate, or discontinue business, by reason of some governmental activity such as redevelopment and housing code enforcement. Some states have passed laws which extend benefits, equivalent to URA benefits and requirements, to all government-caused displacement. *See, e.g.,* CAL. GOV'T. CODE §§ 7260–7277. Other states have passed relocation statutes that appear to grant additional protection, such as payment to homeowners greater than fair market value. *See* CAL. GOV'T. CODE §§ 7260–7277; Kan. Stat. Ann. §§ 58-3501–58-3508 (Relocation Assistance for Persons Displaced by Acquisition of Real Property); MD. CODE ANN., REAL PROP. §§ 12-201–12-212; MICH. COMP. LAWS §§ 213.321-332, 213.351-.361; N.Y. GEN. MUN. LAW § 74-b; OHIO REV. CODE ANN. § 163.51-62; VA. CODE ANN. §§ 25.1-400–25.1-421 (Relocation Assistance and Real Property Acquisition Policies).

Other states' acts merely authorize relocation payments when called for by the URA. *See, e.g., McKeon v. Hastings College of the Law*, 230 Cal. Rptr. 176 (Ct. App. 1986); *Auraria Businessman v. Denver Urb. Renewal Auth.*, 517 P.2d 845 (Colo. 1974); *Dukes v. Durante*, 471 A.2d 1368 (Conn. 1984) (city duty to relocate upon condemnation as unsafe, despite no acquisition); *City of Hartford v. Mejias*, 478 A.2d 269 (Conn. Ct. App. 1984) (code enforcement ordered); Bruce C. Fuchs, *Eviction of the Residential Tenant As a Result of Housing Code Enforcement: A Regulatory Taking Requiring Just Compensation?*, 12 CAP. U. L. REV. 481(1983). *Cf.* Marc Mihaly, *Living in the Past*, 34 ECOLOGY L Q 1, 2006 (opining that many states and cities go beyond the federal baseline requirements).

In *Baiza v. Southgate Recreation & Park Dist.*, 130 Cal. Rptr. 836 (Ct. App. 1976), benefits were denied to a tenant who moved following an eviction for nonpayment of rent. The *Baiza* case demonstrates the intricacies of relocation law. Should nonpayment of rent justify loss of displaced person status? What if the nonpayment was based upon uninhabitability of the dwelling?

Several state courts have held that the state relocation act requirement of acquisition of property as a precondition to recovery of benefits is met whether an "acquisition" is made by purchase or by condemnation. *But see Carr v. City of Pittsburgh*, 837 A.2d 655 (Pa. Commw. Ct. 2003), concluding that the City's purchase of a mobile home park from owner for purposes of building a community recreation center was not an "acquisition" within the meaning of Pennsylvania's Eminent Domain Code, and thus former residents of park were not displaced persons entitled to reimbursement for their relocation expenses. The sale of the park was an arms-length transaction, and there was no evidence that city would have exercised its power of eminent domain if owner had chosen not to sell park to city.

Some states provide that developers must provide relocation benefits or pay relocation fees where redevelopment displaces tenants. *See, e.g.*, WASH. REV. CODE § 59.18.440. Such laws must comply with the requirements of *Dolan v. Tigard*, 512 U.S. 374 (1994), demanding that exactions bear "rough proportionality" to the demand generated by the proposed project based on an individualized determination.

For an argument that the Washington law violates the Taking Clause and the rule of *Dolan*, see Joseph Lee, Note, *Sudden Impact: The Effect of* Dolan v. City of Tigard *on Impact Fees in Washington*, 71 WASH. L. REV. 205 (1996) (also arguing that relocation impact fees fail to meet the "essential nexus" test of *Nollan v. California Coastal Comm'n*, 483 U.S. 825 (1987), requiring that permit conditions substantially serve a legitimate state interest). Many states' courts have ruled that Dolan/Nollan scrutiny is inapplicable to impact fees that are legislatively created rather than based on ad hoc adjudicative rulings, perhaps in the expectation that legislative programs will achieve public purposes more uniformly and distribute fees in a more fair and transparent way. *Ehrlich v. Culver City*, 911 P.2d 429 (Cal.), *cert. denied*, 519 U.S. 929 (1996). *See also Golden Gate Hotel Ass'n v. City of San Francisco*, 836 F. Supp. 707 (N.D. Cal. 1993) (hotel conversion ordinance restricting conversion of residence hotels to other uses, through payment of in-lieu fee for displacees, construction of replacement units, rehabilitation of other units, or provision of emergency housing held not *per se* taking as not a total denial of economic use but a taking as too restrictive of investment backed expectations), *vacated on other grounds*, 18 F.3d 1482 (9th Cir. 1994); *Sintra, Inc. v. City of Seattle*, 829 P.2d 765 (Wash.), *cert. denied*, 506 U.S. 1028 (1992) (low income housing preservation ordinance requiring developer to either replace low-income housing eliminated or pay in-lieu fee into housing replacement fund where $218,000 fee to develop $670,000 piece of property violative of substantive due process and genuine issue of material fact of claim of damages based on city acting irrationally and invidiously, precluding summary judgment; taking violation possible as remand to determine economic effect as regulation appears to create a benefit for the government rather than abate a nuisance); Ronald H. Rosenberg, *The Changing Culture of American Land Use Law*, 56 SMU L. REV. 177, 258 (2006). *See also Venice Town Council v. City of Los Angeles*, 55 Cal. Rptr. 2d 465 (Ct. App. 1996) (sustaining Mello Act requiring local government to replace low or moderate income housing that is destroyed or converted as a result of a city permit or to pay an in-lieu fee).

State-mandated planning requirements can fall far short of the federal standards. In *Feagley v. Huntington County Planning Commission*, 330 A.2d 281 (Pa. Commw. Ct. 1974), the court held that while a statement of the extent of displacement and the effect on rehousing is required, no relocation plan need be available at the time of project approval. Ironically, such information probably exceeds the planning performance of most agencies under URA. Those planning requirements are the subject of the next section. Another indication of the liberality of state relocation programs is the California practice of covering voluntary moves in expectation of displacement and the state agency determinations.

While many states interpret their state relocation and acquisition acts to mirror the federal URA, this is not always so. The Supreme Court of Colorado, construing both the federal and the state URA, concluded that a regional transportation district's purchase of a railroad corridor for land-banking was not "for a program or project" for which federal financial assistance would be available, as it was a marketplace transaction in which the owner had elected to list the property for sale without coercion. At the time of the sale, the rail district did not know if it would develop a light rail system in the corridor, nor could it count on federal funding. Thus, the Colorado court held that neither the federal URA nor the state Relocation Assistance and Land Acquisition Policies Act applied to the acquisition of billboards in the corridor. *Regional Transp. Dist. v. Outdoor Systems, Inc.*, 34 P.3d 408 (Colo. 2001). The Minnesota Court of Appeals declined to construe Minnesota Uniform Relocation Act (MURA) to mirror the federal Uniform Relocation Assistance and Real Property Acquisition Policies for Federal and Federally Assisted Programs, which generally requires a displacement to be a direct result of an acquisition for a project or program, and thus MURA definition of "displaced person" should be construed to be broader than the federal act's definition, because the MURA definition does not include "direct result" and "project or program" requirements. *In re Relocation Benefits of Furniture, Inc.*, 642 N.W.2d 91 (Minn. Ct. App. 2002).

For early literature on state relocation programs, see generally Fairfax Leary, Jr. & Eric David Turner, *The Injustice of "Just Compensation" to Fixed Income Recipients—Does Recent Relocation Legislation Fill the Void?*, 48 Temp. L.Q. 1 (1974); Daniel R. Mandelker, *A Model State Relocation Law*, 1971 Urb. L. Ann. 117; Daniel D. Pearlman & Kenneth K. Baar, *Beyond the Uniform Relocation Act: Displacement by State and Local Government*, 10 Clearinghouse Rev. 329 (1976). *See also* John Fee, *Eminent Domain and the Sanctity of Home*, 81 Notre Dame L. Rev. 783, 818 (2006) (proposing a model statute requiring a government taking a personal residence by eminent domain to pay fair market value plus additional compensation for the nonpecuniary losses of "personal detachment from the home").

3. Relocation Planning Requirements

The URA, like its predecessor statutes and regulations, requires that agencies establish relocation assistance programs and administer the URA requirements. More specifically, the Act requires the making of "assurances" of available housing. The use of this vague term has resulted in the utter absence of credible relocation planning. Relocation planning is essential. If an adequate supply of decent affordable housing is not available, relocation agencies at eviction time will be forced to relocate displacees into overcrowded, unaffordable substandard housing. Yet, if agencies really did their homework and studied the available supply, it is likely that projects would be stalled, modified, or stopped because the resources were not there. The ultimate impact would be that the real costs of public improvement projects would be reflected in the project budget rather than being bidden in the form of housing deprivation to displacees and its ultimate destructive impact on the community. States may require prior approval of a Relocation Plan in advance of relocation activities. Under the federal requirements, relocation planning may include preparation of a study or survey of the relocation impacts of a project. However, it does not require approval of any plan by a federal entity prior to implementation.

Relocation planning is conceptually simple. *See generally* James A. Kushner & Frances E. Werner, *Illusory Promises Revisited: Relocation Planning and Judicial Review*, 8 Sw. U.L. Rev. 751 (1976). The basic requirements of a proper relocation plan are found in Section 205 of the URA. That section requires the displacing agency to determine:

(1) the displacees' needs and preferences;

(2) the availability of comparable decent, safe, and sanitary housing which meets the needs of displacees; and,

(3) coordination of relocation with work on the project.

If it is determined that comparable housing will not be available prior to displacement, the agency has the option of abandoning the project or utilizing the so-called "houser of last resort" provisions, 49 C.F.R. § 24.404(a), which allow the displacing agency to use project funds to construct or otherwise provide replacement housing, such as through increasing relocation payments. It is this last provision that can assure that federal displacement does not aggravate the already deteriorating lower-income housing supply. According to former United States Supreme Court Associate Justice Tom C. Clark, it is the provision of the URA that "put teeth" in the scheme. *Tullock v. State Highway Comm'n*, 507 F.2d 712 n.3 (8th Cir. 1974). Unfortunately, it has been implemented so infrequently that functionally it does not exist. Most agencies elect to make replacement housing payments in excess of the caps.

Notes and Questions

1. *Assurances.* Section 205(c)(3) contains what is left of the "duty" to provide relocation housing. The statute now talks in terms of an "assurance." What does this mean? Must the agency actually construct the relocation housing? The URA was enacted before the 1974 Housing Act, and consequently it is not keyed to the Housing Assistance Plan (HAP) requirement in the original CD program, nor the housing strategic plans required by the Cranston-Gonzalez National Affordable Housing Act of 1990, Pub. L. No. 101-625, tit. I, §§ 105–06, 104 Stat. 4079, 4088–91 (1990) (*codified at* 42 U.S.C. § 5304(c)(1)). The CHAS has now been replaced with the Consolidated Plan, adopted for local housing and community development programs. 24 C.F.R. pt. 91. See also the "assurance" requirement with the requirements included by the 1987 HCDA amendments in Section 104(d)(1).

2. *Substandard Housing.* When lower-cost central city housing is being used as a relocation resource, there is great danger that many "available" units will be substandard. What does the URA require in terms of the condition of replacement housing? Section 104(d)(1) of the HCDA? Are there techniques short of inspection of all claimed resources? Can a sampling technique be used? What should be the definition of "substandard"? Are there sources of data that can be used to determine the condition of the available housing stock? What problems should be anticipated in consulting census data? Vacancy studies?

What are the dangers in considering public housing units as replacement housing? Might the condition and location of certain public housing projects make their use as relocation resources questionable? What if there are long waiting lists for public housing? Do the same considerations apply to other HUD-assisted housing?

3. *New Construction.* Can relocation plans rely on new housing construction? Will such housing be too expensive to be affordable by displacees? Is there any danger in using new housing units to be subsidized under federal programs? Note that such housing may be subject to approval delays and lawsuits brought by objecting neighbors. Deficiencies in planning requirements under prior law are well illustrated by *TOOR v. HUD*, 406 F. Supp. 1024 (N.D. Cal. 1970).

4. *Property Maintenance.* Another problem associated with displacement is the maintenance of dwellings following acquisition and prior to demolition. As project execution can take many years, it makes sense to retain available shelter as long as possible. Yet maintenance tends to be deferred or nonexistent and neighborhood conditions can rapidly deteriorate. What steps or programs should be taken in project communities to stabilize neighborhood and housing conditions pending project execution? In *Jones v. District of Columbia Redev. Land Agency*, 499 F.2d 502 (D.C. Cir. 1974), the court held that the relocation agency was not required to maintain the units in compliance with the local housing code, but was required to comply with the "safe, decent and sanitary" requirement of the URA. Might such a standard induce displacing agencies to prematurely evict or demolish? Is this the same argument that is raised against housing codes and tenant remedies?

5. *Discrimination.* The displacing agency is required to make an affirmative showing that housing resources are available on a nondiscriminatory basis. HUD requires that "[r]eplacement housing for local agency listings and referrals must be demonstrated to be open to all." The mere existence of federal or state fair housing laws may not be used by the agency as evidence that relocation housing is "open." Is the displacing agency in violation of the URA if its relocation program places minorities in existing areas of racial concentration or in areas where their presence leads to racial concentration? Should relocation plans include consideration of the racial effects of the relocation program? If adverse racial effects are predicted, the plan should outline affirmative action to overcome them. The relocation agency is in a position to take such action if it has gathered data on displacee characteristics and needs and the available housing supply. "White flight" is almost certain to occur if the plan shows that many minority displacees are slated for relocation into an area undergoing rapid racial change. The neighborhood may then become racially concentrated. The planning process must foresee and guard against precisely this type of situation.

The overwhelming majority of persons displaced have been black. Several studies have documented the special plight of the displaced. *See, e.g.*, ADVISORY COMM'N ON INTERGOVERNMENTAL RELATIONS, RELOCATION: UNEQUAL TREATMENT OF PEOPLE AND BUSINESSES DISPLACED BY GOVERNMENT (1964). Relocation programs have attempted to remove minorities by community development activity. *Amen v. City of Dearborn*, 718 F.2d 789 (6th Cir. 1983), *cert. denied*, 465 U.S. 1101 (1984); *Garrett v. City of Hamtramck*, 335 F. Supp. 16 (E.D. Mich. 1971), *plan ordered*, 357 F. Supp. 925 (E.D. Mich. 1973), *rev'd in part*, 503 F.2d 1236 (6th Cir. 1974) (Title VI violation but excessive remedy); *Kankakee County Hous. Auth. v. Spurlock*, 120 N.E.2d 561 (I11. 1954); *Rowe v. Pittsgrove Township*, 379 A.2d 497 (N.J. Super. Ct. Law Div. 1977), *aff'd*, 411 A.2d 720 (N.J. Super. Ct. App. Div. 1980). African-American land ownership has declined by more than two-thirds since 1910. U.S. COMM'N ON CIVIL RIGHTS, THE DECLINE OF BLACK FARMING IN AMERICA (1982); David H. Harris, *The Battle for Black Land: Fighting Eminent Domain*, 9 NBA NAT'L B.A. MAG., Mar./Apr. 1995, at 12. *See also* NICHOLAS LEMANN, THE PROMISED LAND: THE GREAT BLACK MIGRATION AND HOW IT CHANGED AMERICA (1991).

Relocation programs seeking to displace into a nonexistent or racially segregated housing supply may be challenged. *Munoz-Mendoza v. Pierce*, 711 F.2d 421 (1st Cir. 1983) (HUD UDAG grant caused displacement, provided standing); *English v. Town of Huntington*, 448 F.2d 319 (2d Cir. 1971) (alleged only black-occupied buildings scheduled for code enforcement and displacement); *Garrett, supra. Cf.* Richard Lewis, Comment, *Destruction of Community*, 35 BUFF. L. REV. 365 (1986) (argued to be a tort).

Transit corridors can bisect minority neighborhoods. *Nashville 1-40 Steering Comm. v. Ellington*, 387 F.2d 179 (6th Cir. 1967), *cert. denied*, 390 U.S. 921 (1968); *Nashvillians Against 1-440 v. Lewis*, 524 F. Supp. 962 (M.D. Tenn. 1981) (upheld environmental analysis finding no proof of racial discrimination, only allegations of a barrier effect, the court refusing to speculate on future school attendance zones and potential segregative impact); *Harrisburg Coalition Against Ruining the Env't v. Volpe*, 330 F. Supp. 918 (M.D. Pa. 1971) (claims were not sustained for failure to prove intent).

6. *Expulsive Zoning.* Cites have been accused of using urban renewal or eminent domain to target the removal of racial minorities. *See Amen v. City of Dearborn*, 718 F.2d 789 (6th Cir. 1983), *cert. denied*, 465 U.S. 1101 (1984) (Arab-American removal); *Garrett v. City of Hamtramck*, 335 F. Supp. 16 (E.D. Mich. 1971), *plan ordered*, 357 F. Supp. 925 (E.D. Mich. 1973), *rev'd in part*, 503 F.2d 1236 (6th Cir. 1974) (alleged "Negro Removal" by a redevelopment plan targeting removal of all African-Americans from an area). *See also Hispanics United v. Village of Addison*, 988 F. Supp. 1130 (N.D. Ill. 1997) (approving consent decree). The suit alleged that city redevelopment plan was designed to eliminate Hispanic residential neighborhoods and that city displaced 44 families, intending to remove almost all 827 apartments Hispanics occupied. Under the decree, each of the 44 households would be paid compensation, relocation costs, and, in certain circumstances, increased sums. In addition, city would contribute money to a fair housing fund, pay damages to an organizational plaintiff, and make efforts designed to preserve and improve remaining community.

Expulsive designs also can be implemented through zoning designed to eliminate a minority neighborhood. Litigation challenging the rezoning of an historic African-American community in Cocoa, Florida resulted in a consent decree calling for the rehabilitation and preservation of an historic minority community. *Houston v. City of Cocoa*, No. 89-082-CIV-ORL-19 (M.D. Fla. Oct. 26, 1990) (consent decree) (funding rehabilitation with redevelopment and community development block grant funds), *earlier proceedings*, Fair Hous.-Fair Lending (P-H) ¶ 15,625 (M.D. Fla. Dec. 22, 1989) (denial of motion to dismiss).

On the topics discussed, see generally Judith E. Koons, *Fair Housing and Community Empowerment: Where the Roof Meets Redemption*, 4 GEO. J. ON FIGHTING POVERTY 75 (1996); Yale Rabin, *Expulsive Zoning: The Inequitable Legacy of Euclid, in* ZONING AND THE AMERICAN DREAM 122 (Charles M. Haar & Jerold S. Kayden eds. 1989). *Cf.* Jon C. Dubin, *From Junkyards to Gentrification: Explicating A Right to Protective Zoning in Low-Income Communities of Color*, 77 MINN. L. REV. 739 (1993) (advocating the protection and preservation of low-income minority communities through zoning, a variation on inclusionary zoning).

7. *Preferences for Former Site Residents.* Although former site residents displaced by redevelopment may often have contractual claims to preferences for new housing developed on the site of their former residence, courts have upheld policies that have denied such entitlements where promises were broken to achieve equal opportunity. For example, see *Raso v. Lago*, 135 F.3d 11 (1st Cir.), *cert. denied*, 525 U.S. 811 (1998) [reprinted in Chapter 6, *infra*—Eds.] In *Raso,* the First Circuit sustained the policy of refusing to

honor contractual and legal preferences enjoyed by former white residents of an urban renewal area in favor of an equal access policy adopted as part of developer's affirmative fair housing and marketing plan. The court distinguished affirmative action racial quota doctrine, despite the impact of negating preferences for former site residents that equal access policy would benefit racial minorities, over a dissent claiming that the policy should be treated as a racial classification as it was designed to benefit racial minorities and achieve integration. In *Otero v. New York City Housing Authority*, 484 F.2d 1122 (2d Cir. 1973), the Second Circuit sustained the denial of preferences for prior site residents who where racial minorities. In approving subsequent preference for elderly Hasidic Jews who sought housing to accommodate their need to walk to an historic synagogue in the neighborhood, the court stressed the integrative impact of the preferences and the segregative impact of honoring the preferences for prior site residents, the converse of *Raso*. Under earlier HUD regulations designed to provide CDBG displacees with the "reasonable opportunity" to relocate in their neighborhood, the obligation applied only where such opportunities actually existed. *Gomez v. Chody*, 867 F.2d 395 (7th Cir. 1989); *Mejia v. HUD*, 688 F.2d 529 (7th Cir. 1982).

8. *Houser of Last Resort.* Ultimately, if all else fails, federal agencies must make use of the "houser of last resort" provision of the URA. For a discussion of the creative and successful use of relocation resources. *See* Alice A. Ratliff & Michael D. Calhoun, *Use of Last Resort Housing Benefits and Redevelopment Powers to Preserve a Low-Income Community Threatened with Displacement: A Case History*, 22 Clearinghouse Rev. 442 (1988). One application of the houser of last resort requirement might be to deal with the problem of inflation. What should be the rule when the acquisition price plus the full payment of $22,500 is insufficient to find a replacement house? The 1987 Act specifically authorized such a payment in excess of the statutory cap in § 206(a). While the question has not reached the courts, the United States Comptroller General has ruled that all that need be done under the URA is to pay the rental subsidy. There is only a preference that homeowners remain homeowners, but there is no statutory right. Decision No. B148044, July 18, 1977 reported at 5 [Current Developments] Hous. & Dev. Rep. (BNA) 191 (1977). The houser of last resort provision requires the exhaustion of remedies in the form of a claim or request submitted and processed through the federal agency. *See TOOR v. HUD*, 406 F. Supp. 1024, 1054 (N.D. Cal. 1970).

California's so-called "Ralph Bill," enacted in 1968, permits the California Department of Public Works to build, rehabilitate, or purchase housing units and exchange such units for homes occupied by low-income families living on sites of proposed highways, if such sites are in economically depressed areas. Cal. Sts. & High. Code §§ 135.3–135.7. Such exchanges are at the option of the displacees and are an alternative to condemnation procedures and awards. The department is also authorized to contract with lending institutions to provide mortgage loans to displacees who have accepted such an exchange, in order to insure substitute financing at equivalent terms.

9. *Problem.* To work through some of the issues, consider the following problem: Greentown has received a block grant from HUD under HCDA. The block grant will be used to pave streets, acquire land, and make other public improvements. Part of the funds will be used to cover the costs of a "land write down" program in which land will be sold at less than the city's purchase price, to be redeveloped for a shopping center and office complex. Early in the planning phase of the project, there was discussion of the city's either purchasing or condemning some of the land occupied by deteriorating housing. Instead, Greentown decided that it would grant a diminishing ten-year tax abatement to properties developed on the land, but that developers would have to purchase any land on which occupied units were located. Two problems have been raised:

First, a small twenty-unit development is located on one of the sites needed for the complex. (a) If the owner, in contemplation of a sale to a developer, evicts the tenants and then sells to a developer, are tenants entitled to any relocation payments? (b) If the owner sells to a developer who then evicts the tenants, are the tenants entitled to relocation payments? (c) If Greentown uses part of its CDBG to initiate a code enforcement program and tenants' building is condemned, requiring tenants to vacate, are tenants entitled to relocation payments? (d) Does HUD have any relocation duties when it funds a CDBG recipient, duties which could be invoked by the tenants?

Second, one deteriorated house is owned by the occupant. Under what circumstances, if any, would the owner-occupant be entitled to relocation payments if the price for the house is less than 25% of the cost of any "standard" (no code violations, etc.) house in Greentown?

10. What happens if comparable replacement housing is "not available?" Because the standard of review under the Administrative Procedure Act is whether the agency action was arbitrary and capricious, HUD is not necessarily in breach of its obligations if some among the hundreds of displaced tenants fail to end up in comparable housing; the agency discharges its duty so long as it gives the tenants a "reasonable opportunity" to locate such housing using offered relocation services. *Dean v. Martinez*, 336 F. Supp. 2d 477, 490–491 (D. Md. 2004). Furthermore, "HUD's obligation is not—and could not possibly be—to identify housing opportunities for displaced tenants that are equivalent in all respects with the housing the tenants have lost." The URA requires only comparability, not equivalence, as between the prior apartment and the replacement housing. The statute defines a property as "comparable" if it is "functionally equivalent" and "generally not less desirable" as to location—terms that leave HUD discretion to consider the practical realities of the housing market in determining appropriate relocation sites for displaced tenants (citing with approval the observation by another district court that the URA entails no requirement that the comparable housing be located in the "immediate neighborhood," *Mejia v. HUD*, 518 F. Supp. 935, 938–939 (N.D. Ill. 1981), *aff'd*, 688 F.2d 529 (7th Cir. 1982). Factually, the plaintiffs supported their argument that HUD failed to meet its URA obligations to locate comparable replacement dwellings through affidavits of several tenants. The relocation office provided a list of old and unavailable units; relocation units necessitated plaintiffs to spend $30 a week on transit to work when they had been able to walk to work prior to relocation; to live far from school and an elderly parent's doctor. The court also noted the dearth of case law on agency compliance with the comparable replacement dwelling rule.

A Note on Acquisition Policies

The URA in Title III contains specific requirements for negotiations and acquisitions in land condemnation. Business and other nonresidential displacees are most often subject to abuses such as a refusal to negotiate or a low bid with a take it or leave it attitude. This approach often forces the property owner into litigation. Other abuses include offers below the very lowest appraisal received.

Residential displacees are affected to a lesser degree in that suitable comparable sales more often exist and a sense of the market can be readily obtained from real estate dealers or neighbors. The inefficiency of the Federal Housing Administration in regulating their appraisers has also resulted in the inflationary swelling of comparable housing prices. If appraisers give high appraisals to friendly speculators on properties that are substandard, these sales become comparable units to swell the values of subsequent appraisals which may be honest and accurate. Finally, should the agency give a lower bid, the difference in many cases is covered by a relocation payment (in the case of an owner-occupant), which could expand to cover the short fall of the appraisal. Of course, if the displacee is already eligible for the maximum grant, a low purchase price could result. With the inflation of housing prices occurring nationwide, relocation benefits may no longer subsidize improper agency acquisition tactics and homeowners will have to consider a condemnation action. Review Title III of the URA. What does it require in the acquisition process?

During congressional deliberation on the URA, a deadlock developed on the issue of judicial review of URA determinations. The resolution was the Muskie Compromise: there would be no judicial review of the acquisition policies in Title III in exchange for reviewability of the relocation title. *See Barnhart v. Brinegar*, 362 F. Supp. 464 (W.D. Mo. 1973). *See also State* ex rel. *State Highway Comm'n v. Anderson*, 735 S.W.2d 350 (Mo. 1987) (en banc) (as URA acquisitions unreviewable, no discovery or subpoenas available).

4. Exclusionary Displacement and Community Destruction

Compulsory displacements that occur for development reasons raise major questions of social justice because they inequitably distribute the losses and benefits of the redevelopment. In the paradigmatic context for the exercise of eminent domain power, for traditional public uses, forced displacement results from the need to build infrastructure—highways, hospitals, schools, and public transit. Such programs improve many people's lives, deliver indisputably important services, and proffer employment. Nonetheless, the interests of residents facing displacement differ in kind and quality from the general public's. Many of displacees' possessory and economic interests in the place of their community fall outside both the URA and the official costs of land assembly, despite their complete extinguishment. While local governments claim to advance the general welfare as they funnel public resources into the redesign of urban spaces, it is hard to avoid the unvarnished truth that municipalities are terminating the residency of some in order to construct shiny, new, private residences and shops for affluent in-movers. This presents us with ineluctable issues of social justice and equity. Outside the condemnation regime, it is low-income tenants who bear the greatest burden as cities court an increased tax base through gentrification.

A growing body of criticism decries cities' public/private redevelopment policies which continue to displace low-income households and raze their homes, but not to build more affordable housing. Herculean attempts by the private non-profit sector to staunch the loss of affordable housing, by community development corporations and intermediary non-profits, have been insufficient to replace lost affordable housing. Clearly the substantive and procedural requirements of existing relocation laws are inadequate to produce replacement housing for the displaced, and the private market and public housing policy fail in this as well, as detailed in Chapter 3, *supra*. Strands of the eminent domain scholarship recount the loss of housing and wholesale destruction of communities, particularly communities of color, during Urban Renewal and in the successive forms of redevelopment since, then as local governments have actively courted gentrification in inter-jurisdictional competitions for tax base. *See, e.g.*, Lynn E. Blais, *Urban Revitalization in the Post-*Kelo *Era*, 34 FORDHAM URB. L.J. 657, 674 (2007) (noting that, of the 34 states that enacted post-*Kelo* limitations on their eminent domain powers, two thirds of these retained exceptions for areas that could be shown to be blighted); Colin Gordon, *Blighting the Way: Urban Renewal, Economic Development, and the Elusive Definition of Blight*, 31

Fordham Urb. L.J. 305, 311–12 (2004); Chester W. Hartman, *Relocation: Illusory Promises and No Relief*, 57 Va. L. Rev. 745 (1971) (describing extensive uncompensated losses suffered by victims of urban renewal condemnations); George Lefcoe, *Redevelopment Takings after* Kelo: *What's Blight Got to Do with It?*, 17 S. Cal. Rev. L. & Soc. Just. 803, 815 (2008); Matthew J. Parlow, *Unintended Consequences: Eminent Domain and Affordable Housing*, 46 Santa Clara L. Rev. 841, 856–57 (2006) ("By taking such affordable housing units off the market by their exercise of eminent domain power, cities reduce the available housing stock for low-income residents as such units are usually replaced by new high-end commercial, residential, and mixed-use projects"); Wendell E. Pritchett, *The "Public Menace" of Blight: Urban Renewal and the Private Uses of Eminent Domain,* 21 Yale L. & Pol'y Rev. 1, 49 (2003).

But it would be erroneous to treat the problem as arising only from, or amenable to correction through, the narrow lens of eminent domain doctrine. The restructuring of urban space as cities experience economic change impacts the ability of low-income residents to stay put. Innovative strategies by citizens and communities seeking inclusive, equitable development models, are explored in the following section. They seek to address the following persistent problems of inequitable displacement: gentrification, and destruction of community through redevelopment.

The impact of gentrification on housing markets is discussed more fully in Chapter 4, *supra* of this text. The emphasis in this section is the potential for the body of laws address community development decision-making to plan for, minimize, and compensate for the displacement or total destruction of the human community where redevelopment is planned.

a. Displacement by Gentrification

Gentrification commonly refers to an upward shift in housing values, and in the income, education and occupational levels of new residents—the gentry—moving into the neighborhood. Moreover, "it almost always means increasing inequality and a widening gap between the more and the less successful." Henry W. McGee, *Seattle's Central District, 1990–2006: Gentrification or Displacement?* 39 Urb. Law. 167 (2007). This significant class shift is an important aspect that distinguishes "gentrification" from revitalization by the residents manifested in renewed pride and investment in a community, without the resentments occasioned by inmovers, documented by Professor McGee's study of Seattle's historically African-American, now gentrified, downtown district.

Disputes about whether gentrification causes displacement, and if so, whether that is a good thing for the poor among the public, have been at the heart of heated analytic and political debates over urban change for the last forty years. There can be no serious disagreement that the U.S. has seen 30 years of intense gentrification and sweeping public policy changes that impact the shape of our cities. These operate in contemporary housing market dynamics at the national, regional and city levels, and can be expected to create a variety of displacement pressures, intersecting in locally contingent ways on neighborhoods occupying desired redevelopment locales. Wholesale destruction of neighborhoods, of which Poletown is emblematic, is contrasted with gradual gentrification, as may occur when wealthier in-movers gradually repair and occupy low-income areas. Some suggest that, at least sometimes, gentrification also benefits the people who can stay put, rather than relocate. *See* J. Peter Byrne, *Two Cheers for Gentrification*, 46 How. L. J. 405 (2003); Andres Duany, *Three Cheers for Gentrification*, Am. Enterprise Mag., Apr./May 2001, at 36–39.

Residents may be displaced directly as a result of housing demolition, owners' conversion of rental units to condominiums, increased housing costs in the form of rent or taxes, landlord pressure, and eviction. Residents who manage to avoid these direct displacement pressures may nonetheless be displaced by rising housing expenses associated with gentrification. As affordable housing becomes scarce in gentrifying areas, neighborhoods become too pricey, requiring lower-income residents to search elsewhere for housing. Some may put off leaving the familiar neighborhood, at least for a time, by doubling or tripling up with family and friends; others however become homeless or move to city shelters; or move out of the city. Kathe Newman & Elvin K. Wyly, *The Right to Stay Put, Revisited: Gentrification and Resistance to Displacement in New York City*, 43 URB. STUD. 23, 45–46 (2006) (reviewing that literature, and presenting quantitative and qualitative analysis; concluding that while not all low-income residents are displaced by gentrification, because of New York City's "historically specific web of housing supports that developed ... from the 1920s to the 1970s," many are; reporting study results in Central Harlem, Lower Park Slope).

Where earlier research accepted displacement as a necessary part of the gentrification process, a few recent studies have suggested that disadvantaged renters in New York City were somewhat less likely to move out of gentrifying neighborhoods than out of non-gentrified neighborhoods. Lance Freeman & Frank Braconi, *Displacement or Succession? Residential Mobility in Gentrifying Neighborhoods*, 40 URB. AFF. 463 (2004); Lance Freeman & Frank Braconi, *Gentrification and Displacement*, 8 URB. PROSPECT 1 (2002); Jacob L. Vigdor, *Does Gentrification Harm the Poor?*, 2002 BROOKINGS-WHARTON PAPERS ON URB. AFF. 134. This evidence, while new and useful, is limited to one city and very like to conditions in rapidly gentrifying "hot-market" neighborhoods. In such markets, even those lower-income residents who manage to remain during initial economic transition may be forced out by subsequent rent hikes.

b. Community Destruction

But there is no denying the fact that entire viable communities have repeatedly been displaced, replaced by others' notion of higher, better use. Professor McGee has chronicled the displacement of African Americans from Seattle's Central District by gentrification in Henry W. McGee, *Seattle's Central District, 1990–2006: Gentrification or Displacement?* 39 URB. LAW. 167 (2007); Jon C. Teaford recounts the evisceration of an Italian enclave in Boston's West End; a Croatian-American community in the Vaughan Street area in Portland, Oregon; displacement of the residents of Philadelphia's Eastwick project; of the inhabitants of New York's West Village; of the Mexican American residents of Los Angeles' Bunker Hill; and the inhabitants of San Francisco's Western Addition. *See* John C. Teaford, *Urban Renewal and its Aftermath*, 11 HOUSING POL'Y DEBATE 443, 446–449 (2000). The stiff resistance put up by struggle of Boston's Chinese community in the face of highway extensions and hospital expansion is recounted in *The Struggle for Parcel C, in* PENDA D. HAIR, LOUDER THAN WORDS: LAWYERS, COMMUNITIES AND THE STRUGGLE FOR JUSTICE 120 (2001) (Report to the Rockefeller Foundation).

Are there distinct interests in community, or community claims on a place, to be considered in community development decision-making, in addition to the familiar claims of property entitlements? Consider the following excerpt:

> Invasive redevelopment projects destroy vital social and cultural ties crucial to residents' ability to meet their basic social and economic needs. Displacement spe-

> cialists working in international development call this "the resettlement effect," defined as the loss of physical and non-physical assets, including homes, communities, land, income-earning assets and sources, cultural sites, social structures, networks and ties, cultural identity and mutual help mechanisms. In the U.S., numerous studies document the significant economic and social welfare gains enjoyed by communities with strong social networks.[7] William Julius Wilson has described the social organization needed to realize and maintain common neighborhood goals, and has argued that communities unable to sustain the social networks that enable collective action, are made vulnerable to a range of urban problems, preventing the types of collaboration essential to community-building.[8]

Scholarly investigations of social capital feature its collective dimensions, and identify the forms of social capital within viable communities.[9] Social capital is what persons draw on when they enlist the aid of others to solve problems, seize opportunities, or accomplish objectives—or seek just to cope. Social capital is formed by informal networks of people (family, friends, neighbors) who can collaborate to address shared problems and gain access to city political power. One form, *coping capital,* is especially important for people who are chronically poor because it takes the place of services that money otherwise would buy. Two other forms include *social support*—which may come in myriad forms such as help with a flat tire, a ride, a small loan—and *social leverage* that helps one get ahead or improve one's opportunities, as through access to job information or scholarship recommendation.

The legal framework offered by property law recognizes numerous rights of persons residing in the path of municipality-assisted redevelopment, which currently are destroyed, without acknowledgement or compensation, in the exercise of urban redevelopment powers. Important community interests of persons and communities are similarly destroyed. Lee Ann Fennell has argued that spatial association should be treated as a distinct property entitlement, at least where patterns of exclusion combine to produce persistent spatial concentrations of poverty in urban areas, because of its character as a common resource that is vulnerable to problems of collective action.

> Neighborhood is a necessity for urban living. Urban renewal and gentrification, which clear out the old residents of stable yet poor neighborhoods, deprive poor residents of a vital support structure.

Barbara Bezdek, *Putting Community Equity in Community Development, in* Affordable Housing and Public-Private Partnerships ch. 6 (Nestor M. Davidson & Robin Paul Malloy eds. 2009).

Notes and Questions

1. Recognition of community interests in land use decisions comes chiefly in the form of nominal public participation rights by residents in the path of prospective redevelopment projects. Public notice and hearing processes, or consultation via charette, offer a veneer of inclusive deliberation yet exclude residents as stakeholders in the decision about

---

7. Several studies of social capital are reviewed in Sheila Foster, *The City as an Ecological Space: Social Capital and Urban Land Use,* 82 Notre Dame L. Rev. 527, 543–547 (2006).

8. William Julius Wilson, When Work Disappears: The World of the New Urban Poor (1997).

9. Elise M. Bright, Reviving America's Forgotten Neighborhoods: An Investigation of Inner City Revitalization Efforts 13 (2000).

community destruction. In practice, do these processes offer a means to shift the allocation of burden? For the argument that public hearings occur too late and address too little as a means to incorporate the community's interests into the project, see Alejandro E. Camacho, *Mustering the Missing Voices: A Collaborative Model for Fostering Equality, Community Involvement and Adaptive Planning in Land Use Decisions, Installment Two*, 24 Stan. Envtl. L.J. 269 (2005); Audrey G. McFarlane, *When Inclusion Leads to Exclusion: The Uncharted Terrain of Community Participation in Economic Development*, 66 Brook. L. Rev 861, 868–91 (2001) (reviewing resident participation requirements under various government programs for urban redevelopment from 1949 to the present).

2. Courts referee very few of these clashes between the interests of low-income residents—for continued residence, for the social capital accrued in their neighborhood, or adequate—replacement housing—and the interests of higher-earning and -spending denizens that cities aim to attract to the newly developed urban territories. What doctrinal reasons account for this?

G. Emerging Issues in Community Development: Equitable, Sustainable, Green Community Development

Prior sections of this chapter have explored the means by which community development and redevelopment proceeds in localities across the nation. One persistent procedural problem is endemic: whether due to the scale, pace, complexity, or use of public-private partnerships, many of the most impacting undertakings evade the ability of the locality's people to assure that their government is acting for the general welfare, rather than for other segments of the (present or hoped-for) populace.

1. Equitable Development and Community Benefit

A more particular application of this principle can be stated in the context of intensive redevelopment of deteriorated neighborhoods: local government should not callously jettison urban residents and scatter them for the gain of private developers and wealthier in-movers, without enabling the resident community members also to gain from the renewal of their neighborhood. In a well-functioning democracy, government's role is to responsibly assess the social welfare costs and benefits of its powers, without illegitimate favoritism or unjustifiable disparate impacts. Particularly in land use law, the central problem is to regulate the imposition of social costs onto others arising from a specific use of land. The law governing urban redevelopment is overdue for a corrective that will force the internalization of its true social costs.

The private contract model of development agreements and public/private partnerships tends to obscure the process that results in the inequitable allocation of the benefits and burdens of the deals that redistribute urban territories. The disfavored occupants of areas targeted for redevelopment garner no demonstrable share in the supposed gain to the general welfare which is the doctrinal justification for the city's exercise of governmental powers to condemn and re-title the residents' neighborhoods. Low-wealth communities are replaced by new upscale housing and shops and a brighter urban image. The displaced bear burdens which their compatriots do not: the destruction of their long-time neighborhoods and the social capital they have built up there. Local governments participating in the urban real estate market in this way are often frank about their purpose to engineer new urban territories and repopulate them with the wealthier classes. *See, e.g.* Audrey G. McFarlane, *The New Inner City: Class Transformation, Concentrated Affluence and the Obligations of The Police Power,* 8 U. Pa. J. Const. L. 1, 6–12 (2006) (citing numerous cities' development policies to encourage upper-middle class residential occupancy); Roberto G. Quercia & George C. Galster, *Threshold Effects and the Expected Benefits of Attracting Middle-Income Households to the Central City*, 8 Housing Pol'y Debate 409, 412–413 (1997) (anticipating fiscal and social benefits of revitalization). To a growing movement of concerned city-dwellers, the public policy to restructure the territories of the central city unfairly allocates the costs of revitalization to the current residents and distributes the benefits to others.

a. Equitable Development

This chapter began with the recognition that community development is a field of endeavor which in a myriad of ways, seeks to build communities' capacity to gain resources, deliver social goods, and participate effectively in the American economy.

The nascent movement for equitable development policies has sprung from two related insights. The first is that neighborhoods powerfully shape residents' access to social, political, and economic opportunities and resources. Residents of metropolitan regions are situated within a complex, interconnected web of opportunity structures (or lack thereof) that significantly shapes their quality of life. The term "opportunity structures" refers to those resources and services that contribute to individual and family stability and advancement. john a. powell, *Opportunity-Based Housing,* 12 J. Affordable Housing & Community Dev. L. 188, 191 (2003). Decades of social science research have confirmed that racially isolated and economically poor neighborhoods restrict employment options, house some of the lowest-performing schools, and expose children to high rates of crime and violence. The social opportunities of a community, and the advantages they confer, cluster and accumulate spatially.

The second animating insight is that the forces that limit opportunity work in combination with and reinforce each other. These forces include segregation in housing, discrimination in the labor market, and the fragmentation of metropolitan areas into many separate units of government. As explored in other chapters of this course book, most affordable housing is disconnected from significant educational, economic, social, and civic opportunities. This opportunity isolation and economic sorting of people in our metropolitan areas is not confined to U.S. cities. Many inner-suburban communities, particularly in the Northeast and Midwest regions, also experience opportunity isolation, such as an increase in foreclosure and vacant properties, fiscal distress, population decline, and spreading poverty. *See* Radhika K. Fox & Sarah Truehaft, *PolicyLink, in* Shared Prosperity, Stronger Regions: An Agenda for Rebuilding America's Older Core Cities 9 (2d ed. 2006), *available at* http://www.policylink.org/pdfs/CoreCities.pdf.

Furthermore, the opportunity structures are distributed geographically within a metropolitan region, with the very substantial aid of public policies and public money. Isolation from opportunity structures results from the concentration of scarce affordable housing in the central city and inner-ring suburbs. The relocation of opportunities to the outer-ring suburbs is subsidized largely by tax breaks and government grant programs. By one estimate, $250 billion in federal, state, and local funds have been invested in new water and sewer facilities between 1970 and 2000—a factor that favors ex-urban development for private real estate expansion. Daniel J. Hutch, *The Rationale for Including Disadvantaged Communities in the Smart Growth Metropolitan Development Framework*, 20 Yale L. & Pol'y Rev. 353, 359 (2002).

What about inclusive economic development that is not dependent upon land use decision-making? Anti-poverty advocates and policymakers have embraced asset-building strategies, prompted by the influential work of Michael Sherraden and colleagues who since 1991 have argued that modern welfare policy fails in its singular emphasis on income rather than a recognition of assets as a measure of economic well-being. Assets, argues Sherraden, properly understood, encompass less tangible resources including human capital, cultural capital, political capital and social capital, as well as tangible money savings, real property, stocks and bonds. Michael Sherraden, Assets and the Poor: A New American Welfare Policy (1991). The disparity in assets between the poor, middle class, and wealthy, is even greater than the gap in income, according to pioneers in the emerging field of asset-building as a poverty-alleviation strategy. The assets essential to economic security and opportunity include quality jobs, human capital, savings and investments—which at times have been aided by public policy such as 401(k) retirement savings vehicles and the GI Bill. The meaningful assets in the lives of many working yet poor urban residents in the U.S. consist of items far removed from our ordinary understandings of real property, or of "place," or of capital, but pivotal nonetheless in individuals' capacity to function—transportation, a telephone, a ladder, one's uniform. Kathryn Edin recounts the decision by one woman who resigned her job as a nurse's aide just months shy of earning her certificate, in order to work in retail at [a big box store] where she would have the opportunity, after 3 years, of a vested pension. Kathryn Edin, *More Than Money: The Role of Assets in the Survival Strategies & Material Well Being of the Poor*, *in* Sherraden, *supra* at 206.

b. Accountable Development: Community Benefits Agreements

In recent years, Community Benefits Agreements (CBAs) have garnered significant interest among communities and their advocates, precisely because they redress both this procedural insufficiency, and produce community-inclusive modifications to proposed redevelopment projects. Typically a community benefit agreement is a private contract negotiated between a prospective developer and representatives of affected communities. Several agreements have been reached whose terms and process show promise for this as one strategy to ameliorate many of the inequitable results of public/private redevelopments. Under a CBA, community parties gain promises modifying original development concepts, including affordable housing, employment participation, open space or other amenities, monitoring provisions, and potential remedies for breach. In cities around the U.S., CBAs include enforceable developer commitments to incorporate housing affordable to those who otherwise would be displaced, local and minority hiring, job training and wage provisions, and community facilities such as day care centers and parks. *See* Julian Gross et al., Community Benefits Agreements: Making Development Projects Accountable 9–10 (2005) (published by Good Jobs First & the California Partnership for Working Families), *available at* www.goodjobsfirst.org/pdf; Harold Meyerson, *No Justice, No Growth: How Los Angeles is Making Big-Time Developers Create Decent Jobs*, Am. Prospect, Oct. 22, 2006.

Patricia E. Salkin and Amy Lavine, Negotiating for Social Justice and the Promise of Community Benefits Agreements: Case Studies of Current and Developing Agreements

17 WTR-Journal of Affordable Housing & Community Development Law 113, 114–115 (2008)

The CBA is a relative newcomer to the toolbox of strategies that communities may utilize to ensure that development occurs consistent with the sometimes more narrow goals and desires of neighborhood residents, as opposed to the sometimes broader goals and desires of municipal and regional governing bodies....

CBAs are generally negotiated between coalitions of community groups that often include labor, environmental, and religious organizations. Many CBA provisions are inspired by social justice issues and may sometimes be viewed in context of community advocacy in support of environmental justice principles. Common CBA benefits provisions include living wage requirements, first source (i.e., local) hiring and job training programs, minority hiring minimums, guarantees that developments will include low-income and affordable housing, environmental remediation requirements, and funding for community services and programs. Since these agreements are negotiated between community coalitions and interested developers on a case-by-case basis, the benefits are typically tailored to provide specific desired community amenities such as parks, day care centers, youth facilities, and job training facilities.

The flexibility of the CBA begins with the process by which these agreements are negotiated. CBA discussions may be initiated by a project developer or by a community coalition, or in some cases they may be encouraged by city officials. The community is often represented by a coalition of community groups or organizations, and in some cases local government officials may be involved. Public input should play an important role in determining community goals and desires. The gathering of this input is a critical function of the community coalition so that the community is unified when negotiating with the project developer, and so that the developer can feel comfortable that the coalition is a legitimate community representative for purposes of negotiations.

Following the successful negotiation of a CBA, in states that authorize development agreements, it may be incorporated into this agreement made between the developer and the municipality as part of the planning process. Although this ensures a certain measure of transparency and also permits the government, as well as coalition members, to enforce the agreement, most states do not authorize local governments to enter into development agreements, many CBAs will be enforceable only by the contracting community groups....

Many advocates view CBAs as powerful tools for assuring that community needs and desires will not be neglected by large developers. Many developers support the voluntary negotiating process as a method by which to obtain community support and thereby avoid long government delays and perhaps ultimate denial of their project proposals. Although CBAs have been negotiated in relation to nearly fifty development projects in cities across the country, it is important to note that there is no specific statutory authority or regulations for these agreements and there are dozens of potential legal issues that might arise in litigation should these agreements be challenged in court. However, assuming there is equal bargaining power among the parties to a CBA negotiation, that there is full support of the community coalition from community members, and that the developer's assumptions about government approvals and project design are accurate enough to enable full compliance with the agreed to terms, CBAs can be an empowering social justice tool.

Notes and Questions

1. Are CBAs enforceable as contracts? Commentators have raised questions whether the community members have standing to enforce the terms in the event of breach. Doctrinally and factually the issue is one of actual consideration. If the community signatories assent, courts may treat CBAs as a bilateral agreement with beneficial promises to third parties. The CBA does not alter the legal structure of the public/private arrangement; it remains fundamentally contractual. It seeks to involve additional community parties who otherwise would be excluded from crafting the character and benefit of the proposed development, thus the bilateral negotiation becomes multi-lateral.

2. Practically speaking, is negotiation of a CBA limited to well-organized communities? For example, might communities already served by established organizations be better positioned to make their way to the bargaining table, before local officials and private developers have made the deal, or in sufficiently muscular coalition to effect modifications. In practice, a CBA may have particular utility in relation to very large projects affecting multiple neighborhoods, faith groups and unions; and conversely, require significant delegation by residents to community agents to navigate the coalition, negotiate and monitor the CBA. More worrisome, a few case studies of CBAs caution that some of those organizations that can muster themselves to the table may be insufficiently representative of the community facing displacement. *See, e.g.,* Patricia Salkin & Amy Lavine, *Negotiating for Social Justice and the Promise of Community Benefits Agreements: Case Studies of Current and Developing Agreements,* 17 J. Affordable Housing & Community Dev. 113 (2008). Several recent CBAs have come under stinging criticism for insufficiently inclusive representation. For example, the Bronx Terminal Market CBA, negotiated in 2006, involved no grassroots community organizations. Instead, eighteen community groups were handpicked by the borough president, and then were given just 30 days to draft an agreement. Heather Haddon, *Terminal Market Deal Criticized,* 19 Norwood News, Feb. 23, 2006–Mar. 8, 2006, at 4, *available at* http://www.bronxmall.com/norwoodnews/past/022306/news/N60223page1.html. They received no technical assistance. In the Bronx, however, the organizations did not see the completed CBA until the morning of the city council's vote to approve the development plans. At that point, seven of the organizations refused to sign, but the plan was approved nonetheless. The Yankee Stadium CBA lacked any pretense of being negotiated or signed by any community groups. Instead, it expressed the agreement between the Yankees, the Bronx borough president and the Bronx delegation of the New York City Council. Critics worry about the true representativeness of groups who step forward to participate. "Groups pop up and you're not sure who they represent," said Patricia A. Jones, the co-chairwoman of the Manhattan Community Board 9 task force on Columbia University's expansion in Manhattanville. Terry Pristin, *In Major Projects Agreeing Not to Disagree,* N.Y. Times, June 14, 2006, *available at* http://www.nytimes.com/2006/06/14/realestate/commercial/14agree.html.

3. A related concern by some observers is the capacity of community coalitions to participate constructively. Good Jobs First and Policy Link, two nonprofit think tanks in the forefront of promoting community benefit and equitable development, each advocate significant technical assistance as a necessary predicate to the effective bargaining position of community parties to CBAs. *See* Julian Gross et al., Community Benefits Agreements: Making Development Projects Accountable 9–10 (2005) (published

by Good Jobs First & the California Partnership for Working Families), *available at* www.goodjobsfirst.org/pdf; HEATHER McCULLOCH WITH LISA ROBINSON, SHARING THE WEALTH: RESIDENT OWNERSHIP MECHANISMS, A POLICYLINK REPORT (2001), *available at* http://www.policylink.org/pdfs/ROMS.pdf.

4. Accounts of the community negotiations, developer commitments, documents and monitoring materials are increasingly accessible. The Staples Center CBA was negotiated between the developer and the Figueroa Corridor Coalition for Economic Justice, which represented more than thirty community organizations, including environmental groups, church groups, health organizations, and immigrants' and tenants' rights supporters. Organizational and political support to the coalition and the community members was also provided by Strategic Action for a Just Economy (SAJE) and LAANE. View the Staples Center Community Benefits Agreement, at A-1, *available at* www.saje.net/atf/cf/{493B2790-DD4E-4ED0-8F4E-C78E8F3A7561}/communitybenefits.pdf. Additional community campaigns are discussed, and supporting documents referenced, at Community Benefits Agreement Handbook, supra note 3, and in the Salkin and Lavine article excerpted in the text.

c. Community-Based Joint Ventures*

If corporate capital vehicles are useful for upper income folks to build assets, then surely that can be true for low-wealth communities as well. Community enterprises that engage poor people as stakeholders can formulate cooperative relationships in ways that extend the social-capital of the collective undertaking. Community development corporations (CDCs) have been an important engine of community-based self-help for 30 years. While CDCs have sometimes been criticized as insufficiently accountable to the communities where they engage in revitalization, because of their dependence on funders' views than to their purported community base, numerous CDCs have managed to scrap their way further into market-based practices in service of their community stakeholders. [CDCs are discussed in this Chapter, *supra*—Eds.]

One particularly important path is the creation of enterprises formed with equity interests. Some CDCs are experimenting with issuing shares—to enable their stakeholders to be shareholders. Examples include the New Community CDC of Newark, New Jersey, which developed a supermarket, and the Kansas City CDC that owns a cement block factory. Other ventures include much-needed health care facilities or child care centers. Such enterprises combine the provision of much-needed services and employment with community ownership and control.

Innovations in resident-owned area-wide redevelopments are also underway, by which low-income residents of low-wealth areas where economic redevelopment is needed, participate as owners, with shared decision-making authority and financial stakes in the project's success. Two approaches on the horizon are discussed below.

(1) *The People's IPO: Market Creek Plaza.* The most robust model thus far for community equity shareholding is illustrated by Market Creek Plaza, an enterprise to revitalize a 20 acre industrial site in southeastern San Diego. The Market Creek Plaza enterprise was formed by a nonprofit organization and designed for the express purpose of engaging residents of the low-wealth Diamond Neighborhoods in the process and benefits of the

---

* This subsection is adapted from Barbara Bezdek, *Putting Community Equity in Community Development, in* AFFORDABLE HOUSING AND PUBLIC-PRIVATE PARTNERSHIPS ch. 6 (Nestor M. Davidson & Robin Paul Malloy eds. 2009).

project. In July 2006, Market Creek Partners offered 50,000 shares to local community residents at $10 a share, with a minimum investment of $200. At the time of the offering, Diamond Neighborhood residents had a median income of $32,800, and nearly one-third of the households earned less than $20,000 each year. Market Creek is now a thriving, $45 million commercial enterprise, making distributions to its investors. Its anchor tenant is a full service supermarket—the first major grocer to locate in the area in thirty years. The revitalization now includes a library and performing arts center, an elementary science center, a state-of-the-art high school, ethnic restaurants, and a conference center. In the next phase, more than 800 affordable housing units will be built on the site.

Purchasers become Diamond Community Investors and members of Market Creek Partners, LLC. As members, each purchaser is entitled to cast one vote, regardless of the number of units purchased, in the election of the company's advisory board. The minimum offering amount was $250,000, and the maximum offering amount was $500,000. These terms enabled local residents to own up to a 20% interest in the venture, while the Jacobs Center for Neighborhood Innovation (JCNI) retained a 60% interest, and the Neighborhood Unity Foundation (NUF), retained the remaining 20% interest. The project is intended to transfer complete ownership to local residents within 12 years.

Shareholder Qualification. Market Creek Partners established strict eligibility criteria for all purchasers. Most importantly, each purchaser was required to be a resident of the revitalization district as well as a state resident. The purchaser had either to reside currently or previously to have resided in one of eight designated "Diamond Neighborhoods." Shares' initial purchase and resale were limited to "Diamond Neighborhood Stakeholders" as defined by residency and investment intention.

To educate its prospective investors to make informed investment decisions in a commercial real estate venture, Market Creek Partners transformed its 200-page prospectus into a 20-page executive summary that included pictures and graphs to answer the investors' most frequently asked questions. The company's business model entailed involving Diamond Community residents to determine the types of businesses and services the residents hoped would be developed at Market Creek Plaza.

Community Benefit. The employment-related local-resident benefits of this joint venture model are similar to those sought under many CBAs: local hiring and minority contracting. Over 90% of the initial employees at the supermarket were hired from the community. These jobs are unionized and include living wages, health care, and pension plans. Some 69 percent of the construction contracts for Market Creek Plaza were awarded to local minority-owned enterprises, totaling $7.1 million.

Additional benefits are potentially still more transformative. As a catalyst for civic participation, the project involved 2,000 adults and over 1,000 youth, who have participated in land planning, leasing, marketing, research, advocacy, and ownership design. Extensive use of cross-cultural community teams has been a consistent feature of project implementation. In addition, the project provides for future neighborhood reinvestment, through the residents' locally controlled foundation, chartered to grant a portion of the profits from the development back into the neighborhood.

(2) *Homestead Stakes and Community Equity Shares.* Another approach in cooperative capitalism builds on the predicates within community-based development practices of community development corporations (CDCs), microlending, and community development financial institutions (CDFIs). A community enterprise whose shareholders include the residents when the development project is seeking municipal approvals, and

may grow to include incoming residents, is potentially an economic collaboration in which shareholders enjoy equal political and economic rights in the entity, more concretely and manageably than in the wider city polity.

Imagine that instead of the fiscal illusion of public benefit from the proliferation of public/private redevelopments that deplete the jurisdiction's affordable housing stock, it were possible to make those who bear the burdens of dislocation, direct beneficiaries of the new project. Imagine that local law directs or incentives the PPP to offer Equity Shares in the value-adding redevelopment to all the residents in the project impact area. This approach would provide much-needed modernization to the public comment practices of land use planning, and offer direct benefits to the affected city residents....

The fundamental premise of Community Equity Shareholding is that community members not lose their substantial investments in their place, nor have their residency terminated by local government land use practices that transfer public resources into largely private redevelopment of residences for others, *unless and until* residents have approved the redevelopment; and unless and until residents receive shares in the economic value of the project. Such approval might be accompanied by an agreement to exchange their community residency interests for an equity stake in the benefits generated by the new development. Such an equity stake could take the form of an alienable right to comparable replacement housing in the new development, or to shares in the increased economic value justifying the public participation in the project and generated by it over time, or both.

This set of property interests can be recognized through reforms of the redevelopment planning requirements of state enabling statutes. The result is a process that invests residents with rights to consent to development beforehand, and to a share in the benefits of the deal in which the locality partnered. Community equity shares make use of a familiar capital vehicle to render visible the residents' stakes in the community. Residents receive shares in the real estate venture—in effect, becoming members of the joint venture in urban redevelopment.

The Community Equity Shares concept offers a responsive framework to the inequitable allocations inherent in redevelopment theory and practice. It embodies three crucial principles missing from contemporary PPP practice: the principles of Fair Share—fair and inclusive shares in the wealth-creation facilitated by public investment; Governance—a right of residents of the targeted development zone to vote on the character of the planned redevelopment; and Collective Action—a framework to facilitate the recognition of the collective social capital of the community, and intentionality about exchanging it for the development sought by the public/private partnership.

1. *Fair Shares.* Most analyses of the inequitable development problem perpetuate the invisibility of community stakes, proposing to tweak eminent domain doctrine, but limiting redress to title owners of affected properties. One straightforward approach is to increase the payments made to displaced homeowners by monetizing the subjective value of property taken by eminent domain ("homeowner surplus") to deal with the obvious problem that forced sales at fair market value in severely disinvested neighborhoods fail to compensate displaced long-term owners for "the subjective element." While legal determinations of just compensation almost universally reject paying for the subjective value attributed by the owner, in some circumstances this seems particularly unjust. Some legal scholars have developed proposals for the award of supplemental damages to long-term owners according to a legislated schedule reflecting length of tenure; and programs for self-assessed valuation. These analytic developments are important for the subset of residents

in disinvested/development-targeted neighborhoods whom they reach. Yet the continued exclusion of non-title owners provides no remedy for substantial numbers of persons, households and their communal interests, which will be destroyed by redevelopment projects that uproot them.

2. *Governance.* The second element is the incorporation of a governance principle, to effect community consent and control regarding redevelopment decisions in their backyards. Recently, Michael Heller and Roderick Hills proposed to make land assembly the proper subject of the consent of the residents whose neighborhoods were in need of redevelopment, through Land Assembly Districts. The model of governance they envision is direct control by referendum. Pursuant to local legislation, the local government would construct consent to the land assembly by declaring a proposed Land Assembly District, and putting the detailed purchase proposal to a referendum of the intended condemnees.

3. *Collective Action.* Collective action and community consent could be fostered through voluntary land assembly, particularly if practiced by communities as a strategy to coordinate with, and benefit from, market-based redevelopment that threatens to overtake severely deteriorated, underinvested neighborhoods. Such an approach would go a long way to reconnect disinvested communities to thriving realty markets, by addressing the interrelated problems of land assembly and cost posed to development-seeking cities by fragmented and diversely held titles. Nonetheless, many communities targeted by PPPs do not have the political organization or technical support to see the development coming and to act in time. Where communities lack the leverage to negotiate meaningful promises from developers, their stakes in the urban space they share should be protected from expropriation.

2. Emerging Issues in Sustainable Redevelopment: Transportation and Green Building

As the twenty-first century proceeds, practices and principles for sustainable community redevelopment and revitalization focus with increasing urgency on the environmental sustainability of community design and construction. Environmental sustainability refers to the current generation protecting resources for use of subsequent generations, including water, air, and species protection. Given the huge projection of population increase, another one hundred million in the United States by 2040 and the aging of the American population, how should cities and citizens plan for the future? *See* Robert E. Lang & Arthur C. Nelson, *America 2040: The Rise of the Megapolitans*, PLAN., Jan. 2007. Global climate change indicates the necessity of a critical reduction in the emission of greenhouse gases such as carbon dioxide. How do concerns of sustainability intersect with practices and strategies of community development? How are poor and working people affected by a century of automobile-based urban design? How should transportation be planned and developed in the future to attain community sustainability objectives? What forms of urban design are currently encouraged and subsidized by government? These are some of the issues explored in this section.

Envisioning Sustainable Communities. According to a 1997 task force of the President's Council on Sustainable Development (PCSD), sustainable communities are "cities and towns that prosper because people work together to produce a high quality of life that they want to sustain and constantly improve. They are communities that flourish because they build a mutually supportive, dynamic balance between social well-being, economic opportunity, and environmental quality." SUSTAINABLE COMMUNITIES TASK FORCE, PRESIDENT'S COUNCIL ON SUSTAINABLE DEVELOPMENT, SUSTAINABLE COMMUNITIES TASK FORCE REPORT 2 (1997), *available at* http://clinton4.nara.gov/PCSD/Publications/suscomm/ind_suscom.html.

> The basic decision-making principle of sustainable development is the integration of environmental protection with conventional development. Instead of conventional development at the environment's expense, or environmental protection instead of development, the idea is to achieve both development and environmental protection at the same time. Conventional development embraces more than economic development; it also includes improvements in social well-being, peace, and security. The principle objectives of sustainable development are quality of life, freedom, and opportunity, for both present and future generations. The famous Brundtland Commission definition of sustainable development, "development that meets the needs of the present without compromising the ability of future generations to meet their own needs," indicates that future generations should not be burdened by today's shortsightedness.

John Dernbach & Scott Bernstein, *Pursuing Sustainable Communities: Looking Back, Looking Forward*, 35 URB. LAW. 495, 496 (2003) (*quoting* WORLD COMMISSION ON ENVIRONMENT AND DEVELOPMENT, OUR COMMON FUTURE 43 (1987)).

Sustainable development also encompasses the concept of economic supportability. A number of scholars and practitioners suggest that a fairer distribution of wealth, including economic assets as well environmental stewardship, is likely to be more politically supportable over the long-term and is morally necessary. *See* KENT E. PORTNEY, TAKING SUSTAINABLE CITIES SERIOUSLY: ECONOMIC DEVELOPMENT, THE ENVIRONMENT, AND QUALITY OF LIFE IN AMERICAN CITIES 177–219 (2003); AMARTYA SEN, DEVELOPMENT AS FREEDOM 36 (1999) (describing freedom as both "the primary end" and "the principle means of development"); On this view, communities will attain sustainable development their social and economic activity protects and restores the environment rather than degrades it, when development and environmental protection are mutually reinforcing rather than antagonistic, and when large-scale poverty no longer exists. John C. Dernbach, *Sustainable Development: Now More Than Ever, in* STUMBLING TOWARD SUSTAINABILITY 45 (John C. Dernbach ed. 2002). Until then, "sustainable development" is a calculated oxymoron which reminds us of the customarily obscured costs—social, economic, environmental, intergenerational—of conventional development.

a. Transportation in Urban Community Development

When Americans travel to European capitals they are struck by the clean, efficient, safe, and affordable public transit that seems to go everywhere, the wonderful public spaces devoted to pedestrians that can be enjoyed by walking, shopping, or sitting in a café. Europeans are more likely to walk, ride a bicycle, or take public transit for their transportation. Most Viennese own a transit pass purchased for a few hundred dollars a year; the average Viennese uses public transit 600 times a year. Most Americans rely solely on the automobile with dramatically fewer trips being made by walking or bicycle each year.

The United States has been going in the other direction from Asia, Latin America, and Europe. Between 1980 and 1990, 22 million new single occupant drivers were added to the commute (while only 19 million new workers joined the commute during the period), while transit lost 200,000 riders, four million stopped carpooling, and 650,000 stopped walking to work. DEPARTMENT OF TRANSPORTATION, TRANSPORTATION STATIS-

TICS: ANNUAL REPORT 1994 at 53. *See also* JANE JACOBS, THE DEATH AND LIFE OF GREAT AMERICAN CITIES 354 (1961) (95% of travel in Los Angeles by private automobile).

The fundamental reason for the difference in urban design is World War II. The United States, which emerged as victor with enormous industrial capacity and pent-up demand for consumer goods and housing, launched a program of sprawling suburbs all patterned on automobile travel and low-density single-family homes. Europe, decimated by war and in economic chaos, required public transportation and housing. Given limited land available for urban development and the lack of personal automobiles, the European nations' strategy was to build high-density apartment blocks linked by train, subway, or bus. The developed pattern became urban villages that were user-friendly to transit users, cyclists, and pedestrians. In contrast, U.S. cities feature urban sprawl, with far-flung roads and highways serving residential and commercial construction hopscotching over older towns once some distance from city centers. In many U.S. urban areas, it is no longer possible for a home seeker to find a better house in the outer suburbs for less money, because the cost of commuting downtown exceeds the higher cost of housing in close-in urban areas. Peter S. Goodman, *Fuel Prices Shift Math for Life in Far Suburbs*, N.Y. TIMES, June 25, 2008; Eric M. Weiss, *Around D.C., a Cheaper House May Cost You*, WASH. POST, Oct. 12, 2006.

The ultimate irony is not that the victors' dream was unworkable, inefficient, expensive, and polluting, while the vanquished developed the ideal model for urban design. Rather, it is that the pattern of decentralization and sprawl makes access by workers to jobs difficult, discourages urban job investment, and has created massive concentrations of the poor and ethnic minorities trapped in a metropolis that offers little opportunity to inhabitants and discourages investment. European communities are stable and attractive, in significant part because the developed infrastructure, including a unified transit system, is conducive to job creating investment. The 21st Century recession with its loss of employment and the destruction of American neighborhoods, particularly suburban subdivisions through abandonment and foreclosure, has underscored the failure of the U.S. model of urban design. The American style of city sprawl has dispersed employment centers throughout suburban rings, making suburban jobs inaccessible for those without a personal automobile. Highway oriented public policy in effect has financed the outward movement of corporate employers and the relocation of critical economic activity and services, and has left central cities with a depressed business and commercial environment and consequently, a declining economic base insufficient to support deteriorating public services. JAMES A KUSHNER, THE POST-AUTOMOBILE CITY 61–62 (2004).

Sustainable urban design requires integrating transit with housing, employment, and recreation. In addition, transit improvements can stimulate economic development. Transportation improvements can comprise central components of a revitalization scheme. Developments' ability to generate revenue supports the ability to pay fees to properly spread the costs. Around central bus line stops and transit or train stops, assessment districts and tax increment-financed development can stimulate redevelopment, capture the value increment for public improvements, and can reform community design to a community more pedestrian and transit user-friendly, one less dependent on automobile travel. The District of Columbia's Metro subway system has effectively generated dense developments at all of its stations and has established transit villages.

Of course, public transit is not always a sound economical investment in lower density sprawl-based communities. Typical suburban communities, like their rural counterparts, simply lack the density that can generate the ridership to support an efficient bus service that is within walking distance, a density that would discourage use. Furthermore, even successful transit village creation such as the D.C. Metro can cause negative impacts on some, particularly prior residents of lower income. The Adams-Morgan neighborhood before the construction of its Metro stop was a vibrant, ethnically diverse, modest income community that was gentrified by Metro access. As the community was reconfigured, it became home to more affluent in movers, and many of its prior residents displaced to make way for the Metro sought less pricey housing elsewhere.

The Los Angeles Metrolink commuter rail and the Metro light rail and subway system is a contrasting experiment for, unlike D.C., the Los Angeles system serves little more than the central business district and Universal Studios. The Los Angeles system serves none of the recreational beaches, sports stadia, parks, or museums outside the downtown and Pasadena areas, none of the major entertainment areas, none of the popular shopping and pedestrian-friendly streets, and only a very few residential "districts." It is only theoretically a means to get to Los Angeles International Airport, since to navigate the system to the airport requires multiple transfers between Metrolink train, subway, light rail and shuttle bus.

Similar to the Los Angeles experience, simply serving an area with a subway or other efficient transportation service does not guarantee revitalization and gentrification. Philadelphia's subway evidences this point. Its subway has long served the depressed areas on North Broad Street. Washington, D.C.'s comparative success is due to the density of job sites in the District, allowing many more residents of Maryland, the District, and Virginia to live car-free and rely on the subway for the journey to work as well as recreation, with links to most destinations. Banks and institutional lenders, however, are interested in upper income housing and prime office and commercial development and have not demonstrated interest in financing transit villages for those of lower income. Does this phenomenon require government to insure or directly finance transit-oriented development for neighborhoods containing primarily those of more modest income?

1. *Curbing Sprawl through Transit-Oriented Development*

Not all transit-related development is accurately characterized as "transit-oriented." Among theorists and practitioners, *transit village* refers to a community with transport opportunities other than personal automobile, and pedestrian access to housing, work, retail, and recreation. Some development at transit stops is merely transit-adjacent. *Transit-oriented development* refers to the richer, synergistic form encompassing higher-density housing, offices, and commercial development adjacent to transit stations or stops that are hoped to increase public transit ridership and reduce automobile vehicle miles traveled. While all transit villages constitute transit-oriented development, not all TODs are transit villages.

Michael Bernick and Robert Cervero, Transit Villages in the 21st Century

112, 224–226 (1997)

Rockridge

The Rockridge neighborhood of Oakland [California] is a prototypical transit-oriented community. Rockridge lies west of the hills in the older, more urbanized part of the East Bay. Rockridge blossomed around the turn of the [20th] Century as a major stop on the early Key System streetcar line and today retains many vestiges of a streetcar suburb. It is very compact, with mostly apartments and detached units with small yards and narrow sidelots. And it features a finely grained and integrated mixture of land uses....

[T]he influence of the early streetcar system is clearly expressed in Rockridge's somewhat rectilinear layout.

At the heart of the neighborhood is a retail district aligned along College Avenue, a street which once accommodated a cross-town streetcar line.... [a BART, San Francisco and the East Bay's subway and light rail system runs along and stops on College Avenue]. Retail shops form an unbroken streetwall that defines the avenue. Few blocks are interrupted by curbcuts, a legacy of Rockridge's streetcar days. Storefronts are scaled to the pedestrian, with shops typically 40 ft or less in width producing four or more shops on a typical block. Building entries open directly onto the sidewalk providing a nearly continuous sequence of showcase windows and shop entries. Many stores have loft apartments or offices above. Parking is accommodated on the street or behind buildings; few parking lots directly face College Avenue.

Like many streetcar suburbs which depended on trolleys for real estate speculation, Rockridge's residential areas feature regularity in lotting patterns and architecture. California bungalows, with porches facing the street and garages tucked behind, dominate residential streets. Small two-, three-, and four-unit residential buildings make up 22% of Rockridge's housing stock, and an estimated one-third of detached units have rear-lot accessory units. This mix of housing has created high average densities on many lots that do not disrupt the prevailing scale and grain of the neighborhood.

The entire Rockridge neighborhood is linked by an integrated network of sidewalks and pedestrian paths. Shade trees occupy the planting strip between most sidewalks and streets. In some locations, midblock pedestrian paths allow convenient access to transit lines. Overall, Rockridge is a very pedestrian-friendly neighborhood....

Rosslyn

When taking the Orange Line from downtown Washington to Arlington, Rosslyn is the first station one reaches upon crossing the Potomac.... Rosslyn blossomed as a major commercial center in the mid-1960s, and by the mid-1970s, it was packed with high-rise office towers. But with an auto-oriented built form, it was a far cry from being a transit-oriented center, much less a transit village. Rosslyn's 1960s building boom exposed the potential downside of rapid-pace, intensive development: mammoth buildings, absence of a pedestrian scale or streetlife, and a "sameness" about the built environment. In recent years, Arlington County has embarked on a concentrated effort to retrofit Rosslyn into a more balanced, mixed-use community focused around its Metrorail station....

Rosslyn's physical form reflected the state of planning practice at the time: widely spaced, rectangularly shaped buildings situated off of plaza's; a skywalk system to connect buildings and maintain the street level for automobiles; broad avenues, 70 to 80 ft wide, with narrow and sometimes discontinuous sidewalks.... In 1992, the Rosslyn Station Area Plan Addendum was adopted with the expressed goal of remaking Rosslyn into a transit village. The plan called for additional housing to complement office development, greater retail activity at all hours, and increased pedestrian access to an from the station. The plan addendum noted the tremendous growth of Rosslyn since 1962: Thirty years later, 7 million ft^2 of office space had been added (and another 312,000 ft^2 approved) along with 1654 hotel rooms and over 6,000 residences within a 10-min walk of the station....

It proposed the renovation and expansion of existing aging buildings in the core area, the development of a Central Place within a 3-block radius of the station, and the addition of amenities and microdesigns to enhance the walking environment. Renovations began in 1994 with the Commonwealth Building. This obsolete office structure was gutted, expanded, and refacaded. Three floors were added and the building was redesigned at ground level to provide for street-level retail, a small outdoor patio eating area, and an upgraded streetscape. The building's additional height and floor area were development bonuses provided in return for the street-level improvements.... Specific improvements that are planned include better lighting and public art within the station lobby, an upgrading of the Metrobus transfer facility adjacent to the station, and the planting of trees and greenery.

Notes and Questions

1. Rockridge is an example of new suburbanism, while Rosslyn shows a higher density city urbanism which might have been termed a suburb in the past. Rosslyn has achieved a superior jobs-housing balance which can result in a significant number of residents walking to work within the transit village. Transit-oriented development and transit villages may reflect a range of densities and designs around walkable, transit-served, mixed use communities.

2. Additional illustrative initiatives of Transit-Oriented Development are discussed in Robert Cervero, The Transit Metropolis: A Global Inquiry (1998). Connecticut has approved $1.65 million in grants to 35 communities, up to $50,000, to plan and create high density housing in town centers near public transit of at least 20 multifamily or 6 single-family homes per acre, with additional grants if 20% of the zone is for buyers earning no more than 80% of area's medium income. Lisa Prevost, *Towns Accommodate "Affordable,"* N.Y. Times, Aug. 30, 2009. California enacted Senate Bill 375 seeking to link land use and transportation planning around densified TODs through developer incentives. John Darakjian, Comment,. *SB 375: Promise, Compromise and the New Urban Landscape*, 27 UCLA J. Envtl. L. & Pol'y 371 (2009). *See also* George Galster et al., *Wrestling Sprawl to the Ground: Defining and Measuring an Elusive Concept*, 12 Housing Pol'y Debate 681 (2001) (noting that the definition of sprawl is elusive). *See generally* James A. Kushner Global Climate Change and the Road to Extinction: The Legal and Planning Response ch. 17 (2009); James A. Kushner, Healthy Cities: The Intersection of Urban Planning, Law and Health Ch. 21 (2007); James A. Kushner, The Post-Automobile City Ch. 4 (2004).

3. Densification should mean high density housing over shops, schools, and libraries, and offices. Decisions should be made to develop regional and local production of goods and food to reduce transportation-generated emissions. Although many cities are undertaking the development of new transit lines and embarking on transit-oriented development around stops, the housing developments are occupied by automobile users and very few transit patrons. The development of housing is actually dispersing employment locations away from transit-served areas. For example, at a transit-oriented project in Long Beach, California on the Blue Line trolley to Los Angeles, 6.3% of occupants use the line to commute while 78% have never used the line. Employment, recreation, shopping, and housing destinations must be linked by significantly expanded systems to capture riders away from their cars. Rents should be lowered for those using transit, parking significantly reduced, and a limited number of parking spaces located away from the building. Fares should be eliminated or transit passes provided to those who are carless and relying on transit. James A. Kushner, Global Climate Change and the Road to Extinction: The Legal and Planning Response 161–186 (2009).

4. Resistance to the development of transit-based development often comes from local reluctance to develop uses that generate the need for expensive services such as education and thus communities compete for the greatest generator of tax revenues: the big box re-

tail, commercial, or industrial use. Marlon Boarnet & Randall Crane, *L.A. Story—A Reality Check for Transit-Based Housing*, 63 J. Am. Plan. Ass'n 189 (1997) (explaining the lack of transit villages in the system of 232 existing and proposed Southern California rail transit stations as pressure on local government to generate sales and business taxes rather than property taxes, and to use transit primarily for economic development goals calling for the retention of industrial land uses).

5. One proposal to reduce local inter-jurisdictional competition for tax base is the proposal to share regional tax revenues. James A. Kushner, *The Reagan Urban Policy: Centrifugal Force in the Empire*, 2 UCLA J. Envtl. L. & Pol'y 209, 230 (1982) (describing the Minneapolis scheme which lowers tax burdens on firms in areas in need of an increased tax base by revenue sharing with wealthier areas, and would discourage the relocation of firms to areas with low taxes who receive excessive amounts of revenue in comparison to their required outlay for infrastructure and services); Note, *Making Mixed-Income Communities Possible: Tax Base and Class Desegregation,* 114 Harv. L. Rev. 1575 (2001); Rachel Weinberger, *The High Cost of Free Highways*, 43 Idaho L. Rev. 475 (2007).

6. *Bicycle Transit*: U.S. policy has not encouraged bicycle transit. For example, Mary Peters, the Secretary of Transportation in the Administration of George W. Bush, opposed spending federal money on bike paths. Indeed, on the August 17, 2007 PBS News Hour with Jim Lehrer, she said she did not consider bicycles to be transportation. A visit to the Netherlands where bicycles outnumber automobiles making the nation quite pleasant might have convinced her otherwise.

As of 1990, federal transportation funds for walking and cycling amounted to $2 million annually. Walking constitutes 0.7% and cycling 0.2% of person-miles of daily travel in the U.S. Half of all students go to school by car, but if just 6% of those driven walked or cycled, saving 1.5 million drop-offs and pickups, 60,000 gallons of gasoline would be saved daily. The 60,000 students, or 2.5% of U.S. students that cycle to school, save 100,000 gallons of gas daily. James A. Kushner, Global Climate Change and the Road to Extinction: The Legal and Planning Response 169–171 (2009).

7. Residents of European cities exercise more modal choices than their counterparts in the U.S. *See, e.g.*, Joel Walljasper, *Europeans Reclaim Their Cities from the Car*, Toronto Star, July 15, 1993, at A25 (Final ed.) (22% of nonpedestrian traffic in Heidelberg by bicycle; Bremen, Heidelberg, and L¸beck in Germany have designated bicycle-only streets); Jay Walljasper, Star Trib., Apr. 7, 1991, at 29A (in Amsterdam, 24% of all urban trips by public transit, 20% walking, and 20% bicycle; West Berlin tripled bicycle usage from 1986 to 1991, accounting for 6% of urban travel, with plans to increase to 12% with new exclusive lanes and traffic "calming" or slowing and reduction techniques). *See also* Jurgen Brunsing, *Public Transport and Cycling: Experience of Modal Integration in West Germany*, *in* The Greening of Urban Transport: Planning for Walking and Cycling in Western Cities 231, 232 (Rodney Tolley ed. 1990) (in Germany in 1982, 17.1% use bicycle as main means of transport for distances up to three kilometers, 6.8% by public transport, for distances longer than four kilometers, 6.1% use bicycle, and 17.3 use public transport); Wulf Hulsmann, *The 'Bicycle-Friendly Towns' Project in the Federal Republic of Germany, in* The Greening of Urban Transport, *supra* at 218 (bicycle accounts for eleven percent of all journeys in Germany where in some towns bicycles account 23 to 26% of all journeys, with 57% of trips on foot, bicycle, or public transit; suggesting that a proper bicycle promotion policy would cost about $300 million for the city and county of Los Angeles).

8. *Compact Communities for Health and Fuel Saving.* If just one in ten new home buyers selected a home site that cut the length of the work commute by one mile each way, 2.4

million gallons of gas could be saved each year, enough to fuel more than 10,000 road trips between Los Angeles and New York City, substantially reducing carbon emission ELIZABETH ROGERS & THOMAS KOSTIGEN, THE GREEN BOOK 136 (2007). Studies have shown that New Yorkers generate 7.1 metric tons of greenhouse gases annually compared to 24.5 generated by the average American and that miles driven dropped between 32 and 43% in Chicago, Los Angeles, and San Francisco as the density of neighborhoods doubled. John Norquist, *We Would Use Less Energy Living Closer Together: Cities Have Powerful Environmental Advantages: They Make it Easier to Walk and Use Public Transit*, PHILLY.COM, May 17, 2007. The larger and denser a city, the more sustainable its form and the fewer its carbon emissions. Lance Hosey, *Is Bigger Better?: New Research Supports Eco-Friendly Urbanism*, ARCHITECT MAG., Aug. 1, 2007 (reporting a study by Geoffrey Weast of the Santa Fe Institute). With walkable, more compact development, people drive 20 to 40% less and enjoy lower costs and improved health. REID EWING ET AL., GROWING COOLER 4 (2007).

Unfortunately, Americans are driving more as urban sprawl expands. Between 1950 and 1994, the number of miles driven annually in the U.S. increased by 140% while the population increased by only 50%. MATTHEW E. KAHN, GREEN CITIES 113 (2006). A study of Seattle, Washington found that residents of walkable communities drove 26 fewer miles daily than those residing in sprawling areas. Ewing, *supra* at 6. A meta-analysis of the collected studies on compact development disclose that households residing in developments at twice the density, diversity of uses, accessible destinations, and interconnected streets when compared to low-density sprawl areas drive about 33% less. *Id.* The average Atlanta household would drive 25% fewer miles if relocated to relatively compact Boston. Kahn, *supra* at 113. See Robert Cervero & Roger Gorham, *Commuting in Transit Versus Automobile Neighborhoods*, 61 J. AM. PLAN. ASS'N 210, 212 (1995) (in San Francisco neighborhoods originally designed pre-World War II around transit, 23% of trips made on foot, 22% by transit, while in newer auto-oriented neighborhoods only 9% on foot and 3% by transit).

A review of 23 studies comparing low density and compact communities found that residents of compact communities averaged 8% fewer total miles driven with a maximum reduction of 31.7%. Utilizing transportation models and the EPA's Smart Growth Index, research disclosed that infill locations would generate 35% less driving and emissions than traditional, low-density sites. Gasoline consumption would be reduced by 20 to 30% in sprawling cities like Houston and Phoenix if their urban structure more closely resembled Boston or Washington, D.C. The same family that consumes 1,407 gallons of gas annually in Houston, would use only 919 gallons if it resided in San Francisco.

An additional cause of sprawl and vehicle miles traveled is wealth accumulation: with each 10% rise in household income, annual household vehicle miles driven increases by 14%. In addition, 19.1% of suburban households own sport utility vehicles that get lower miles per gallon as compared to 12.1% of urban households.

9. *Does Sprawl Discourage Public Transport?* Sprawl not only reduces walking, cycling, it curbs public transport use. In 1960, 22% of workers took public transport or walked (while 64% drove); this number dropped by half by 1980, when just 6.4% took public transport, 5.6% walked, and 84% drove. Public transport use declined to 5.3% in 1990 and was down to 2.7% by 2000. In old transit cities, public transport use fell somewhat less, from 30% in 1970 to 23% in 1990; but in bus-only cities, transit users fell from 5% to 2%.

Transport service typically falls as communities sprawl. *See also* Ben Harder, *Road to Fat City Starts at Home*, L.A. TIMES, Nov. 6, 2006, reporting that living in sprawling suburbs leads to obesity as compared to living in walkable communities. *But see* Jean Eid et al., *Fat City: The Relationship Between Urban Sprawl and Obesity*, Oct. 19, 2006, *available at* http://diegopuga.org/papers/fatcity.pdf (arguing that changing the built environment would not counter the rise in obesity). The decline in public transport use also results in reduced public support for transport funding. Although the cost of gasoline and automobile transportation along with traffic congestion and awareness of global climate change are increasing popular support for public transport, in the 14 cities that have invested in rail systems over the past thirty years, the share of commuters taking public transport has actually dropped from 8% in 1970 to 6% in 2000. Rising suburban employment and rising inter-suburban commuting makes rails to the downtown less efficient and finds few drivers abandoning cars and bus riders may switch to automobiles resulting in lower bus use. Nevertheless, between 1994 and 2004, Boston and Washington, D.C. increased public transport ridership by 27%, suggesting that with an expanding demand for urban living, convenient transport, and densification around transit stops, a turnaround period for public transport has begun.

2. Why Is America so Automobile-Friendly?

When the affluent left the cities for the cleaner and quieter suburbs in the 1920s, a new pattern of consumer preference calling for single-family housing with spacious lawns and quiet streets in the suburbs emerged. Policies were established and pursued with suburbanization as a goal. The Federal Housing Administration, and later the Veterans Administration, made homeownership accessible and affordable and encouraged the development of large suburban subdivisions where land could be assembled cheaply in large tracts. In addition, generous tax shelters in the form of interest payment deductions guaranteed a virtually unlimited market for suburban homes. Decentralization was (and is) limited by the range of transportation. As transportation progressed from walking to the horse and later to the electric car lines of old, the perimeter of the city expanded to the capacity defined by each system.

Two events, inaugurated and supervised by the federal government, served to radically alter the pattern of limited New Deal sprawl. First, under the Public Utility Holding Act of 1935, the electric car lines, then owned and operated by the utility companies, were ordered to be divested. Following this divestiture, the General Motors Corporation, Firestone, Mack Truck, Phillips Petroleum, and Standard Oil of California, conspired to acquire and dismantle America's transit systems and replace them with inefficient G.M. and Mack Buses, which were fueled by Standard and Phillips and rolled along on Firestones. The industrial giants provided capital to the National Car Lines Company in exchange for exclusive purchase contracts. Before the Justice Department was able to stop the combination, forty-six cities' streetcar systems had been dismantled. Eventually the companies were convicted of criminal Sherman Act antitrust violations, yet the companies were slapped on the hand with $5,000 fines, and their culpable executives fined $1 apiece.

What the Justice Department could not or would not see was that urban boundaries were now nearly limitless and the public was forced to turn to automobiles for its transportation. Buses, though no longer limited to rails or electric cables, provided access to the most distant suburbs but failed to offer an efficient system to reach the sprawl of suburbia. The second event inaugurated and supervised by the federal government was the construction of the Interstate Highway System. Initially planned as a defense precaution, these highways provided highly-subsidized access to the outer city, thus stimulating additional sprawl. As the sprawl continued, industry moved to the suburbs, and shopping centers and malls arose to satisfy the needs of the decentralized metropolis. Diminished densities made mass transportation increasingly inefficient as the number of lines and the frequency of operation diminished with slackening demand. James A. Kushner, *The Reagan Urban Policy: Centrifugal Force in the Empire*, 2 UCLA J. Envtl. L. & Pol'y 209, 211–13 (1982). *See also* James A. Kushner, The Post-Automobile City Ch. 8–10 (2004); Michael Lewyn, *How Government Regulation Forces Americans into Their Cars: A Case Study*, 16 Widener L.J. 839 (2007).

A serious problem that inhibits rational transportation policy is that automobile-reliant sprawl is heavily subsidized, in at least three ways. The first is direct subsidy. The fossil fuel industry receives more than $210 billion in subsidy annually, having supported political campaigns with $181 million between 1990 and 2004. Worldwide, the annual subsidy for burning fossil fuel is $700 billion and $1.7 trillion is spent on purchasing oil annually. Second, U.S. drivers are underpaying local, state, and federal governments by $40 billion to $105 billion annually. Fuel taxes and fees underfund the costs of roads and highways by 20 to 70 cents per gallon of gasoline, excluding environmental and uncompensated crash costs, according to a study by Mark Delucchi at the U.C. Davis Institute for Transportation Studies. *Delucchi Study Finds that U.S. Motorists Do Not Pay Their Way*, Streetsblog, Sept. 20, 2007. General revenues and property taxes were required to cover road costs in the amount of $700 million annually in New Jersey, and $2 billion annually in New York. *Id.* Third, between $30 billion and $60 billion is spent annually for military expenditures protecting access to Middle Eastern oil while $257 billion, or roughly $2,000 per taxpayer annually, subsidizes automobile use. The Iraq war could cost between $1 trillion and $2 trillion. George Monbiot, Heat: How to Stop the Planet from Burning 56 (2007); Terry Tamminen, Lives Per Gallon: The True Cost of Our Oil Addiction 59 (2006).

Another way to view the gasoline subsidy is that the actual costs, including social costs, to the United States is $11 per gallon. One policy alternative proposed periodically is to use actual costs to establish a realistic gas tax. The federal gas tax has been at 18.4 cents a gallon since 1993. This is approximately 3.7 cents per mile for cars that get 13 miles per gallon and less than a penny per mile for a hybrid that gets 44 miles per gallon. This is not a perfect or permanent solution, because markedly improved gas mileage by most of the cars operated in the U.S. will at some point in the future deplete the federal Highway Trust Fund that funds highway infrastructure. Transit funding available from the federal gasoline tax is projected to decline from an $8.1 billion surplus in 2007 to a $1.7 billion deficit by 2009. This would explain why the government is encouraging toll roads, toll lanes, and congestion pricing (imposing charges for entering congested cities to discourage driving), as alternatives to a realistic carbon tax charged by the mile rather than the gallon. In 2008, the National Surface Transportation Policy and Revenue Commission proposed to increase the gas tax to 40 cents per gallon, but this was rejected by the second Bush Administration. While the Bush administration began to fund demonstration projects for toll roads and congestion pricing it also began a program to subsidize worker parking. *See generally* Andrew D. Appleby, *Pay at the Pump: How $11 Per Gallon Gasoline Can Solve the United States' Most Pressing Challenges*, 40 Cumb. L. Rev. 3 (2009–2010); Michael Lewyn, *Campaign of Sabotage: Big Government's War Against Public Transportation*, 26 Colum. J. Envtl. L. 259 (2001); Roberta F. Mann, *On the Road Again: How Tax Policy Drives Transportation Choice*, 24 Va. Tax Rev. 587 (2005).

Even with gas subsidies, drivers pay $34 per 100 miles to drive compared to $14 if they traveled by public transport. The total federal annual subsidy for trains equals less than the cost of replacing 1.5 miles of Interstate 880 damaged by the 1989 Loma Prieta earthquake. James A. Kushner, Global Climate Change and the Road to Extinction: The

LEGAL AND PLANNING RESPONSE 161–68 (2009); William Neuman, *Mixed Signals: Driving to Work as a Tax Break*, N.Y. TIMES, Aug. 16, 2007.

A Note on Transportation Planning

The Federal Regulatory Framework

Transportation Planning to Curb Air Pollution. The Clean Air Act requires the adoption of state implementation plans ("SIP") designed to reduce air pollution. The SIPs are specifically directed to reducing automobile usage and encouraging alternatives such as carpools and transit, with disincentives such as higher parking and toll costs. Philip Weinberg, *Public Transportation and Clean Air: Natural Allies*, 21 ENVTL. L. 1527 (1991). *See also Conservation Law Found. v. Federal Highway Admin.*, 24 F.3d 1465 (1st Cir. 1994) (citizen suits to enforce standards of performance under Clean Air Act, here in challenge to highway construction). Should the SIP include land use planning initiatives designed to reverse modal splits (referring to trends of alternative means of commuting) to encourage transit use, and discourage automobile dependency?

NEPA. The National Environmental Policy Act of 1969, 42 U.S.C. §§4321–4370(a), requires that proposals for major federal actions be accompanied by an environmental impact statement. *See generally* DANIEL R. MANDELKER, NEPA LAW AND LITIGATION (2d ed. 2009). NEPA, however, is a procedural statute; it does not require that agencies make environmentally protective decisions. *Robertson v Methow Valley Citizens Council*, 490 U.S. 332 (1989) (procedural requirement of disclosure, no substantive obligation of complete mitigation plan); *Stryker's Bay Community Council v. Karlen*, 444 U.S. 223 (1980) (environmental concerns not elevated over other considerations relevant to federal agency decisions and NEPA requires only full disclosure); *Strykers Bay Neighborhood Council v. City of New York*, 695 F. Supp. 1531 (S.D.N.Y. 1988) (NEPA creates only procedural rights, here refusing to halt development of luxury housing rather than affordable housing on urban renewal site). How should highway, housing, and transit projects be evaluated under NEPA? What impacts should be disclosed where housing or transportation proposals encourage and facilitate suburban sprawl single family development? What project alternatives or mitigation means should be considered? Must global climate change and greenhouse gas emissions be analyzed?

ISTEA, TEA-21 and SAFETEA-LU. The Intermodal Surface Transportation Efficiency Act of 1991, 23 U.S.C. §133, 49 U.S.C. §101, popularly referred to as "ISTEA," provided funds for anything from access to public transit, construction of bikeways, and improvement of pedestrian systems). Penny Mintz, *Transportation Alternatives Within the Clean Air Act: A History of Congressional Failure to Effectuate and Recommendations for the Future*, 3 N.Y.U. ENVTL. L.J. 156, 180–192 (1994). Efforts to utilize ISTEA as a litigation strategy to halt highway development, like the environmental assessment strategy were not effective. *Sierra Club v. Pena*, 915 F. Supp. 1381 (N.D. Ohio. 1996) (no private right of action under ISTEA and other challenges to urban corridor rejected); *Town of Secaucus v. Department of Transp.*, 889 F. Supp. 779 (D. N. J. 1995) (no private right of action; while funds could not be used to construct revenue-producing facility, could be used to strengthen foundation of supporting transportation hub); *Clairton Sportsmen's Club v. Pennsylvania Turnpike Comm'n*, 882 F. Supp. 455 (W.D. Pa. 1995). ISTEA expired at the end of 1997 and was readopted as the Transportation Equity Act for the 21st Century (TEA-21), Pub. L. No. 105-178, 112 Stat. 107 (1998) (*codified at* 23 U.S.C. §217), but allowed broad deference to local allocation between roads and transit. *See* Trip Pollard, *Follow the Money: Transportation Investments for Smarter Growth*, 22 TEMP. ENVTL. L. & TECH.

J. 155 (2004); Oliver A. Pollard, III, *Smart Growth: The Promise, Politics, and the Potential Pitfalls of Emerging Growth Management Strategies*, 19 VA. ENVTL. L.J. 247, 277 (2000). *See also* Dennis C. Gardner, *Transportation Reauthorization: A Summary of the Transportation Equity Act (TEA-21) for the Twenty-First Century*, 30 URB. LAW. 1097 (1998). Congress subsequently enacted The Safe, Accountable, Flexible, Efficient Transportation Equity Act: A Legacy for Users (SAFE-TEA-LU), Pub. L. No. 109-59, 119 Stat. 1144 (2005), as a further extension of the law from 2005 to 2009, offering additional subsidies but failing to define multimodalism. An earmark to the bill would have funded Alaska's bridge to nowhere Congress later enacted a technical corrections Act, the SAFETEA-LU Technical Corrections Act of 2008 (TCA). TEA-21, Pub. L. No. 102-240, 105 Stat. 1914 (1991). In 2009, the Obama Administration endorsed livability principles to achieve livable communities providing residents with transit assets for access to affordable housing and employment options. Lisa Caruso, NAT'L J., Oct. 5, 2009. *See* Statement of Secretary of Transportation Raymond H. LaHood before the Senate Comm. on Banking, Housing, and Urban Affairs, Mar. 12, 2009.

State and Local Initiatives

Transit Systems. Cities are recognizing the increased need for transit between the suburbs, and a decline in central city population, trip generation, as well as economic activity. ROBERT CERVERO, SUBURBAN GRIDLOCK (1986). In November, 2008, voters across the country approved 75% of the 34 referendums on the ballot, providing $75 billion for local transit projects. Statement of Parris N. Glendening, NAT'L J., Oct. 5, 2009. Paradoxically, following recent jumps in the gas prices and a worsening economy, mass transit ridership is climbing dramatically but at the same time state and local budgets are tighter and transit funding is being reduced. Michael Cooper, *Transit Use Hit Five-Decade High in 2008 as Gas Prices Rose*, N.Y. TIMES, Mar. 9, 2009); Richard Fausset, *A Mass Transit Dilemma: Ridership Up, Funds Down*, L.A. TIMES, Jan. 27, 2009.

Cities have often responded with a redistribution of transit subsidies to the outer city, often at the expense of higher urban bus and transit fares together with reduced service. *See New York Urban League v. State of New York*, 71 F.3d 1031 (2d Cir. 1995) (per curiam) (denial of preliminary injunction against city transit fare increase, the court deferring to government policymaking in the allocation of transportation subsidies and resources). The court overturned the district court's finding of a Title VI *prima facie* case as it was based on the disparate impact of fare box recovery ratios (bus and subway 12.2 percent increase as compared to 2.2 and 2.6 percent increases on suburban transit lines). Other costs of operation were not reflected and the record did not show suburban fare increases would generate adequate revenues. The court emphasized that central city residents benefitted from suburban transit subsidies in reduced traffic congestion and pollution, encouragement for central city business location, and provides additional fare-paying passengers for city subway and bus systems). *See also* Aaron Curtiss, *Rail System Ends 1st Year on Upswing*, L.A. TIMES, Oct. 27, 1993, at A3, A24 (noting that, while Los Angeles Metrolink commuter light rail train riders pay an average of $7.20 per trip, the public subsidy for each ride is another $12).

Equality in Public Transit Services. Transit systems often neglect bus riders as expensive subway and light rail projects are funded and designed to serve the more affluent suburban communities. *See* Kevin L. Siegel, *Discrimination in the Funding of Mass Transit Systems: Formulating a Title VI Challenge to the Subsidization of the Alameda Contra Costa Transit District as Compared to the Bay Area Rapid Transit District*, 4 HASTINGS WEST-NORTHWEST J. ENVTL. L. & POL'Y 107 (1997). Transit can operate much as a highway in bringing access to areas on the outskirts of metropolitan communities, enabling the development and marketing of single-family detached sprawl communities that generate more automobiles, more pollution, further reducing the density necessity to sustain an effective transit system, transit villages, or providing workers with efficient transit access to employment centers. Yale Rabin, *Highways as a Barrier to Equal Access*, 407 ANNALS 63 (1973). *See also* Patrick Moulding, *Fare or Unfair? The Importance of Mass Transit for America's Poor*, 12 GEO. J. ON POVERTY L. & POL'Y 155 (2005) (eschewing litigation and advocating creative policy formation).

Public transportation networks linking residents, employment, shopping, recreation and health care facilities and supported by high density mixed use communities can generate the revitalized metropolis. The American suburban family requires a fleet of very expensive cars requiring costly maintenance, insurance, and operation. Where families have two heads of household, they are likely to each be employed, leaving children both stranded in a subdivision far from community institutions and without supervision. Home purchase and maintenance is both more costly and more time-consuming than desired by modern suburban dwellers. Moreover, automobile use makes living in the suburbs more dangerous for its youth. In fact, the risk of early death is greater in the suburbs than in the central city. JANE JACOBS, THE DEATH AND LIFE OF GREAT AMERICAN CITIES 32–33 (1961); James Gerstenzang, *Cars Make Suburbs Riskier than Cities, Study Says,* L.A. TIMES, Apr. 15, 1996, at A1 (Valley ed.) (more deaths and injuries from cars in suburbs than from guns and drugs in urban settings in study of Pacific Northwest by Alan Thein Durning, titled "The Car and the City," disclosing that urban deaths occurred in 1995 at a rate of 16 per 1,000 residents, while the rate was 19.2 in the suburbs; although crime deaths were 10 per 1,000 in cities, and but 1 of 1,000 in suburbs, driving deaths were 18.2 per 1,000 in suburbs as compared to 6 of 1,000 in urban settings); Michael E. Lewyn, *Are Spread Out Cities Really Safer? (Or, is Atlanta Safer than New York?,* 41 CLEV. ST. L. REV. 279 (1993).

Comparative Perspectives on City-Level Policy. In Berlin, Germany, the community of Hellersdorf presents an interesting illustration of sustainable communities at the neighborhood level. Hellersdorf was a socialist suburban village of 130,000 on the northern political boundary of the city of Berlin within the former Eastern sector of the DDR. Hellersdorf was not a pretty village, although it was a transit village, lying at the end of a U-Bahn, or subway train line. There was a complete absence of color and foliage in a village of nearly uniform drab concrete apartment blocks, each building with at least one flat windowless wall. Hellersdorf also had no city services, not one telephone, and the apartment units were, like East Germany itself, deteriorating and in need of major rehabilitation. Undoubtedly, if Hellersdorf were located in an American city it would have become a slum and the market would have awaited its final decline when a developer would purchase the land at low cost, bulldoze the structures, and probably redevelop the community for upper income housing. Berlin never hesitated in immediately acting to stabilize one of its worst neighborhoods. The city planted 15,000 trees, modified building facades to introduce variation and color in the structures, and brought in top mural artists to paint beautiful varied mural designs on each building. The city, in public-private partnership with a large developer, rehabilitated the 130,000 units, commenced a program to privatize one quarter of the public housing, offering subsidies to purchasing tenants, and undertook a massive commercial mixed-use project to build a multi-screen entertainment complex with offices, shops and restaurants around and over the U-Bahn line. Hellersdorf demonstrates that through mixing different income groups within public housing, it is possible to bring about the de-stigmatization of neighborhoods. Hellersdorf has been transformed into a sustainable transit village. Berlin is now more stable and certainly presents an attractive site for private investment, secure that neighborhoods will not be abandoned or investment dishonored. James A. Kushner, *A Comparative Vision of the*

Ecology, Empowerment, and the Quest for a Just Society, 52 U. Miami L. Rev. 301, 309–315 (1998).

In the last decade, Los Angeles, by comparison, has spent billions of dollars on expensive transit improvements in subways, guideway trams, fixed rail trolleys, and light rail trains running on traditional rail corridors. Of nearly 200 transit stops, not one has been replanned as a transit village with shops, restaurants, housing, parks, offices, and pedestrian zones. Every heavy rail subway and Amtrak passenger train and every light rail commuter transit stop remains in a stark industrial district with a parking lot for transit users to switch from train to car for the final drive to a typically suburban single-family subdivision. It is time that federal transit subsidies be conditioned on integrated land use replanning around transit stops. A comprehensive plan amendment should include decisions on which stops should be high density designed around housing and commercial activity. Other stops should be set aside for lower density around new-urbanism-designed communities with single-family homes on small lots with front porches arranged around a New England village town center. Other stops should emphasize mixed-use industrial and office employment centers together with housing and shopping. Some communities are cooperating with the Federal National Mortgage Association and offering locational preference mortgages that permit higher loans for transit-accessible housing.

For areas unserved by fixed rail transit, transit villages can be planned around quality bus rapid transit running on rights-of-ways dedicated to bus use and express bus service that would provide superior service, as compared to other lower density areas that might be served by slower local busses or jitneys. In the inner city, transit villages could be linked with empowerment zones to provide industrial centers, and mixed use neighborhoods of varying densities, affording vibrant community centers containing collections of restaurants, cafes, stores, entertainment, and housing. It is time to abandon policies of triage, where neighborhoods containing concentrations of the poor are ignored in favor of more affluent communities. James A. Kushner, *The Reagan Urban Policy: Centrifugal Force in the Empire*, 2 UCLA J. of Envtl. L & Pol'y 209, 222 (1982). *See also* William C. Baer, *On the Death of Cities*, 45 Pub. Int. 3, 15–17 (1976), *reprinted in part in* Roger Montgomery & Daniel R. Mandelker, Housing in America 338 (2d ed. 1979).

Additional funding mechanisms available to most communities include redevelopment programs to assemble land, and financing techniques such as tax-increment financed redevelopment, that can both subsidize the redevelopment process and capture the enhanced tax revenues resulting from the increased property value following redevelopment. The tax increment can allow financing of neighborhood amenities and provide subsidies for generating affordable housing. In addition, impact fees imposed on unsubsidized housing and non-empowerment zone commercial, industrial, and residential development can fund additional affordable housing that could be integrated with moderate income housing to avoid restigmatization and resegregation of transit village development. Such fees may also be used to fund job training programs. Local government and Congress could also target community development block grant funding toward transit villages. In Los Angeles, the Blue, Gold, Green, Purple and Red subway, trolley, and guideway systems all have stops in lower income minority communities. With the state's empowerment zone legislation, those stops would be interesting sites for transit villages. Other nodes within African-American and Latino neighborhoods could be designated as empowerment zone transit villages, served by high quality express busses and linked to employment, entertainment, commercial, health, and housing centers. A transit village redevelopment strategy would be further advanced if states, counties, and local government would cooperate in restricting the continued development of inefficient and hyper-subsidized conversion of non-urbanized land to single-family sprawling traditional communities, while targeting infrastructure subsidies and programs such as Low Income Housing Tax Credit allocations, to transit village zones. Just as state and federal legislation should condition infrastructure and transit subsidies on planning that integrates land use and transit, communities should be obligated to establish urban growth boundaries and urban service districts that could restrict sprawl and encourage economic development within enterprise, empowerment, and transit village zones. 1 James A. Kushner, Subdivision Law and Growth Management §§ 2:12, 5:6 (2d ed. 2010). Such a redesigned community development pattern offers extraordinary opportunity for increased integration, reduced automobile use and dependency, enhanced employment access, the possibility of reconstruction of the city's tax base, and a realistic hope of extending sustainable communities throughout the region.

Notes and Questions

1. For a comparison with European community development policy, see James A. Kushner, *A Comparative Vision of the Ecology, Empowerment, and the Quest for a Just Society*, 52 U. Miami L. Rev. 301 (1998); James A. Kushner, *Growth for the Twenty-First Century: Tales from Bavaria and the Vienna Woods: Comparative Images of Planning in Munich, Salzburg, Vienna, and the United States*, 29 Urb. Law. 911 (1997); James A. Kushner, *A Tale of Three Cities: Land Development and Planning for Growth in Stockholm, Berlin, and Los Angeles*, 25 Urb. Law. 197 (1993). Virtually all development in Europe during the past generation has been infill, largely the redevelopment of brownfields and protecting scarce open spaces but with some notable exceptions. James A. Kushner, *Brownfield Redevelopment Strategies in the United States*, 22 Ga. St. U. L. Rev. 857 (2006); Richard G. Opper, *The Brownfield Manifesto*, 37 Urb. Law. 163 (2005); Anne Marie Pippin, Note, *Community Involvement in Brownfield Redevelopment Makes Cents: A Study of Brownfield Redevelopment Initiatives in the United States and Central and Eastern Europe*, 37 Ga. J. Int'l & Comp. L. 589 (2009). *But cf.* Michel van Eeten & Emery Rose, *When Fiction Conveys Truth and Authority: The Netherlands Green Heart Planning Controversy*, 66 J. Am. Plan. Ass'n 58 (2000) (noting that more development is occurring in the nation's revered Green Heart than in the urbanized cities surrounding it).

3. Emerging Strategies for Green Housing and Community Development

James A. Kushner, Global Climate Change and the Road to Extinction: The Legal and Planning Response

115–117, 141–143, 145–147, 181–182 (2009)

Housing policy has a great impact on carbon emissions. Construction can include green architecture or the use of materials that require less energy in production, such as recyclables rather than wood or steel, and green site planning. Passive solar heating and cooling through a heat exchange process involving water circulation through a ground piping system that heats in winter and cools in summer; south-facing, super-insulated, triple-glazed windows; organic or garden roofs, and limited external surfaces all require lower amounts of energy. Insulation made from recycled newspapers can significantly reduce energy consumption as can energy-saving systems and appliances. Solar or wind power can also be integrated into the production of houses and other buildings. For example, the technology exists to provide buildings with heating and air-conditioning that uses passive solar techniques rather than electricity but the solar industry is undercapitalized and the government is not supporting development.

Reuse of existing structures, particularly when made energy-efficient, will result in significant reduction of emissions as compared to demolition and new construction. It can dramatically reduce solid waste; Building demolition generates half of all land fill and other solid waste. Building a new home with recycled wood can save 3.2 acres of forest. Often, older homes are built using wood from old-growth forests which is four times more energy efficient than new growth lumber and will last 3 to 4 times as long. Through 2050, 89 million new or replacement homes and 190 billion square feet of new offices, institutions, stores, and other non-residential buildings will be constructed. Since two-thirds of all buildings projected to be constructed in the United States by 2050 have not yet been built, a great opportunity exists to reduce emissions and increase sustainability by changing building techniques and construction materials.

The United States ... trend [is] toward larger homes that demand more materials, more heating and cooling, more power for lighting and appliances, and often consume more land thereby making densification more difficult and costly. A 3,000 square-foot house over a 50-year lifetime generates 30 to 40 times the weight of the carbon contained in its frame or the equivalent of three 16-miles-per-gallon SUVs driven 12,000 miles per year for more than 50 years. The concrete production and transportation needed for the house generates 47 tons of carbon dioxide and the lumber laid end to end would extend more than four miles. Even if the 3,000 square-foot house utilizes green construction it consumes 50% more energy than a 1,500 [square-foot house built to] mediocre energy standards. The design of housing settlements has a profound effect on emissions since design can determine transport choices, e.g., the walkable community and the transit-served community compared to designs that depend on personal automobiles. During the next generation the population of the U.S. will increase by 100 million and jobs will swell by 60 million or a 40% increase in jobs in existence at the end of the 20th century. This will require increasing the housing stock by 25% together with another 20% due to disasters and redevelopment; 60% of non-residential development will be replaced. The new housing will equal one-half of all residential units existing at the end of the 20th century. The combined increase equals roughly 30 billion new square feet, an amount equal to all that existed at the end of the 20th century. Thus, America has the opportunity to rebuild in a more compact, sustainable, and economically efficient, egalitarian design, thereby elevating the very quality of life.

Global climate change mitigation requires a shift from fossil fuels and, along with conversion from coal and gas-fired electricity generation, transportation must change from automobiles. The suburban low-density urban form must be replaced with a higher density design that can be efficiently served by public transport. Smart growth describes more compact communities that are walkable and connected by public transport. Smart growth reflects an anti-sprawl strategy. One form of smart growth has been the establishment of urban growth boundaries to halt sprawl and protect open space, agriculture, and forest lands. Another variation is the use of urban service districts where infrastructure subsidies and development approval is directed to areas designated for urbanization. Really smart growth utilizes both methods but ties and defines urbanization areas to those served by public transport. Studies demonstrate that while urban containment in practice may raise housing prices, it also tends to preserve affordable rental housing stock and with adequate infill development, has no inflationary impact of housing price. [ARTHUR C. NELSON, CASEY J. DAWKINS & THOMAS W. SANCHEZ, THE SOCIAL IMPACTS OF URBAN CONTAINMENT 93–101(2007)]. Portland, Oregon is one example of these principles at work. What is extraordinary about Portland is that half of all development in the past decade has occurred within one block of a streetcar route, raising those property values between 35 and 40%. In light of the carbon emissions crisis, smart growth must be redefined to include sustainable planning and building with local agriculture, local waste management, water conservation, and energy independence through non-fossil-fuel, renewable resources such as solar or wind.

Curiously, outdated zoning schemes across America make it illegal to build classic communities such as Charleston, Savannah, Key West, or Alexandria as well as traditional neighborhoods. Walkable neighborhoods that allow the reduction of automobile use will require the overhaul of American zoning codes. Urban planning for real smart growth and sustainability will require expansion of expertise called for in the context of a legislature, planning commission or board. Greater understanding and sensitivity towards the environment should control regional as well as local planning. Shifting 60% of new growth to compact patterns would avoid 85 million metric tons of carbon dioxide emissions annually by 2030; the savings would equate to a 28% increase in federal vehicle efficiency standards to 32 miles per gallon by 2020. Reducing carbon emissions is linked to establishing compact high-density settlements, eliminating high carbon emitting internal combustion-fueled vehicles, and converting to renewable energy. Changes in transportation and how it integrates with jobs, housing, commercial, and recreation must drive the process to design the growing region. Current city design is one for automobiles rather than people.

Sprawl and suburbanization has also increased the urban footprint as suburban homeowners consume more space. Suburban homeowners have 35% more exterior space and 6% more interior space than central city homeowners. Between 1982 and 1992, the U.S. lost 4 million acres of farmland to suburbanization, an area equal to two-thirds the size of Vermont. Increasing residential density from four units per acre to five units per acre would reduce water consumption by 10%.

The American dream has shifted from the detached home in the suburbs with 55% indicating a preference for living in a smart growth community. Not only has the American dream shifted to smart growth, but a recent survey conducted by the National Association of Realtors and Smart Growth America disclosed that 75% of Americans believe that improving public transportation is a better long-term solution for reducing traffic congestion than building new roads; 26% of Americans believe developing communities that reduce the need to drive would be a better alternative. The same survey disclosed that the top three concerns of Americans regarding growth and development are loss of farmland to development (72%), increased traffic congestion and commute times (70%), and loss of open land such as fields and forests (70%). The immigrants to the United States will be searching for affordable homes in walkable neighborhoods with access by public transport to jobs. Twenty-one percent of Americans over the age of 65 do not drive and the aging population will increasingly require compact walkable communities with public transport or extensive programs of van service.

Healthy cities around the world, those that are consistently ranked as the most livable and act as a magnet for tourism and economic development, share some common attributes. Each has invested in modern public transport and provides user-friendly, inexpensive, safe and convenient access to destinations. Each has one or more attractive commercial centers which are car-free or traffic-reduced and allow walking from shop to shop with places to eat or a café, tavern, or film to enjoy. These centers can be designed to reflect community values, e.g., as around the proverbial small town model, around ethnic goods and restaurants, or more artistic or fanciful themes such as an Irish, German, Italian, or Korean theme, or one that reflects an historic period. This makes the most sense where a community has a particular type of architectural heritage that can be preserved and enhanced by being woven into to a living community.

Regardless of the science fiction-like scenario of a magical, technological solution to traffic congestion and global climate change, people and their elected representatives must demand that we pursue a policy of de-autofication. For, regardless of the pollution and energy issues, the increase in automobile and motor vehicle demand as the nation's population moves from 300 million to 400 million by 2040 will lead to using land to accommodate traffic that will prevent the development of walkable, pedestrian-friendly, low emissions communities. The space devoted to automobile infrastructure includes between seven and thirteen parking spaces for every vehicle, streets, parking lots, dealerships, repair, paint and body shops, service stations, parts and tire stores, and other car-related activity that could be converted to transit, bicycle, and pedestrian corridors and pedestrian infrastructure. One illustration of wasting space through dependency on automobiles is to consider that an underground metro can carry 70,000 passengers past a single point in a single lane in one hour, while surface rapid rail carries up to 50,000, a trolley or bus in a dedicated lane 30,000, while cars can carry only 8,000 people per hour. These automobile corridors and parking lots can become the high-density, transit-oriented developments to support public transport. With the elimination of automobiles and their infrastructure, more land will be available for parks, landscaped or tree-lined park-like walk and bikeways, urban agriculture, walking trails, dedicated bus routes, or other transit corridors.

Notes and Comments

1. Greening urban areas can have a significant effect. Planting two shade trees on the west side of a home or building and one on the east side can save 20% of the air conditioning bill. If shade trees were planted around 25% of air conditioned buildings, the energy saved would be enough to shut down three coal-fired power plants. Miami, Florida found that electricity bills were 10% lower in areas with more than 20% tree cover as compared to treeless areas. One tree can release 400 litres of water daily which can cool the air. If one in ten rural households planted a windbreak of evergreen shrubs and small trees, the energy savings could heat 57,000 Alaskan homes for a year. JAMES A. KUSHNER, GLOBAL CLIMATE CHANGE AND THE ROAD TO EXTINCTION 117 (2009). Vancouver, British Columbia has created a "green streets" program whereby streets are converted to partial or full pedestrian and bicycle access by converting the street to public gardens. The streets tend to be 100 to 500 feet long and serve as connectors between commercial and residential neighborhoods. Interview with Sandra James on Vancouver's Green Streets. THE DIRT, Oct. 2, 2009. From 1975 to 1992, Atlanta lost 380,000 acres of trees to development, a loss of 65% of the city's tree cover, creating a heat island. Asphalt, concrete, streets, and parking lots render the modern city five to eight degrees Fahrenheit hotter in summer than the surrounding countryside. James A. Kushner, *Urban Planning and the American Family*, 36 STETSON L. REV. 69 (2006).

2. For discussions of green architecture, see PETER BUCHANAN, TEN SHADES OF GREEN: ARCHITECTURE AND THE NATURAL WORLD (2005); BUILDING WITHOUT BORDERS: SUSTAINABLE CONSTRUCTION FOR THE GLOBAL VILLAGE (Joseph F. Kennedy ed. 2004) (emphasizing the use of straw); DEAN HAWKES & WAYNE FORSTER, ENERGY EFFICIENT BUILDINGS: ARCHITECTURE, ENGINEERING, AND ENVIRONMENT (2002); PETER F. SMITH, ARCHITECTURE IN A CLIMATE OF CHANGE: A GUIDE FOR SUSTAINABLE DESIGN (2001); JAMES STEELE, ECOLOGICAL ARCHITECTURE: A CRITICAL HISTORY (2005); BRENDA VALE

& ROBERT VALE, GREEN ARCHITECTURE: DESIGN FOR AN ENERGY-CONSCIOUS FUTURE (1991); Jason R. Busch et al., *Tax and Financial Incentives for Green Building*, 30 L.A. LAW. 15 (Jan. 2008); Keith J. Jones, *Being Green Doesn't Need to be Taxing: How New York State Law is a Vanguard for Using Green Infrastructure*, 29 PACE L. REV. 499 (2009) (describing state tax incentives for installing organic green roofs and encouraging more tax and subsidy incentives for green architecture); Charles J. Kibert & Kevin Grosskopf, *Envisioning Next-Generation Green Buildings*, 23 J. LAND USE & ENVTL. L. 145 (2007). Portland is proposing to green entire neighborhoods through an eco-district policy that will look at entire neighborhoods and develop improvements such as centralized heating plants that will pipe hot water underground to multiple buildings or reuse rainwater for neighboring structures. Linda Baker, *Green at City Scale*, GOVERNING, Aug. 2009, *available at* http://www.governing.com/article/green-city-scale; Vandana Sinha, *Critics Say New Green Rating Hurts Affordable Housing*, WASH. BUS. J., May 26, 2008. Communities such as Portland are looking to greening at the neighborhood rather than the structure level, and planning for centralized heating plants that pipe hot water to multiple buildings that would eliminate the need for chillers and boilers in individual buildings, rainwater reuse, with rainwater or greywater use in toilets. For a discussion of sustainability and the governance of cities, see Ileana Porras, *The City and International Law: in Pursuit of Sustainable Development*, 36 FORDHAM URB. L.J. 537 (2009).

3. The U.S., Leadership in Energy and Environmental Design ("LEED"), established by the United States Green Building Council, provides the most commonly used way of determining whether a building is more or less "green" or "sustainable." Green building awards, however, mask the fact that the average green building generates the need to increase automobile use for commuters and those traveling to the building by 137%, suggesting that sustainability ratings should include the reduction of automobile use and the increase in more sustainable forms of transport. LEED awards, offering better buildings with reduced energy use, better passive and sometimes active solar technology, recycled materials, and lowered water use have nevertheless been criticized for making limited improvements and carbon emissions reductions when the technology exists for far more significantly green materials and systems that can provide facades and roofs as solar generators and carbon sinks. Only about 1,000 buildings have been certified since 2000.

Some developers cherry-pick low-effort and low-cost LEED point strategies, e.g., installing bamboo flooring and bike racks, and that the cost of certification is relatively high (nearly $100,000). Even so, many developers are using the LEED checklist to build greener buildings without pursuing the costly certification making the program somewhat successful. JAMES A. KUSHNER, GLOBAL CLIMATE CHANGE AND THE ROAD TO EXTINCTION 117–118 (2009). Unfortunately, one quarter of new buildings receiving LEED certification fail to save much energy as their designs predicted and most do not track energy consumption once in use. Jacob Gordon, *The Good 100: Ending LEED's Monopoly*, GOOD 100, Oct. 7, 2009; Mireya Navarro, *Some Buildings Not Living Up to Green Label*, N.Y. TIMES, Aug. 31, 2009. *See also* Ajay Garde, *Sustainable by Design*, 75 JAPA 424 (2009) (only gold and platinum certified buildings are likely to incorporate green construction and technology criteria that improve the efficiency of their use of energy and water); Keith H. Hirokawa, *At Home with Nature: Early Reflections on Green Building Laws and the Transformation of the Built Environment*, 39 ENVTL. L. 507 (2009); Erin Burg Hupp, *Recent Trend in Green Buildings Laws: Potential Preemption of Green Building and Whether Retrofitting Existing Buildings Will Reduce Greenhouse Gases and Save the Economy*, 41 URB. LAW. 489, 496 (2009) (noting that green buildings cost but 1% of the project cost for large buildings and 5% for small buildings yet will reduce operation costs by 20% over a 20 year building life); Stephen T. Del Percio, Student Article, *The Creation of Uniform Sustainable Standards for the 21st Century or the Perpetuation of an Architectural Fiction?*, 28 ENVIRONS 117 (2004); Jennie Rothewnberg Gritz, *The Green Façade*, ATLANTIC, Nov. 24, 2009 (reporting studies that LEED buildings not performing well in energy conservation with one study finding LEED buildings but 5% better than non-LEED buildings and another finding 75% of LEED buildings failed to achieve expectations, and fewer than 30% of LEED-certified buildings qualify for the government's Energy Star label but that enhanced standards proposed). LEED certification has also been criticized for not addressing affordable housing and that cost factors have ruled out energy efficiency for those of lower income and as developers fail to develop affordable housing those in need travel further and aggravate sprawl.

4. *Parking and Sustainability.* In addition to fuel subsidies, most communities mandate that developers of residential, commercial, office, and industrial projects provide free parking. The area of land in the U.S. devoted to parking is 4,950 square miles, about the size of Connecticut and larger than Delaware and Rhode Island combined. The annualized capital and operating cost of off-street parking in the U.S. is between $79 billion and $226 billion. By comparison, the annual cost of operating roads and highways is between $98 billion and $177 billion. The average monthly cost of a parking space is $127, representing a $5.77 subsidy to the commuting worker. While drivers pay $3 billion annually for parking, the rest of the cost is bundled in the price of goods, services, and housing and thus 96 to 99% of the annual cost of parking is a subsidy. Drivers pay at most 4% of the cost of parking. When drivers paid 8.4¢ per mile in 1990 for automobile operation, the subsidy for free parking was as high as 11¢ a mile, as much as 131% of the costs of operation. The free parking subsidy, particularly when considering free parking at stores and at home where government mandated that the developer provide parking infrastructure as a condition of development, represents a subsidy that would be greater than if the government provided free gasoline. The total social cost of free off-street parking is between $127 and $374 billion annually, as much as the peacetime national defense or Medicare budgets. DONALD C. SHOUP, THE HIGH COST OF FREE PARKING 218 (2005). The author observes further, "[F]ree parking increases the demand for driving, which in turn increases the subsidy necessary to meet the peak parking demand. Minimum parking requirements are truly a great planning disaster—perhaps the greatest of all time. *Id.*

To offset the parking subsidy, gasoline taxes would have to be raised as much as $3.74 per gallon. The value of parking in the U.S. is more than the value of all vehicles and twice the value of all roads. Free parking reduces the cost of the commute by 71% or $5.77 daily. Removing the parking subsidy and adding it to the price of a gallon of gas through a parking tax would increase the price by $4.44. In addition, the cost of providing free parking has discouraged developers from constructing multi-family housing or redeveloping older buildings, due to the rent-inflating cost of parking regulations and is having an inflationary effect on the rents of the poor and working class. Minimum parking requirements add as much as 38% to the cost of apartment development.

The poor, the sector of society that lives most sustainably and often relies on public transport, must subsidize the drivers as the poor ultimately pay for free parking through higher prices for goods, services and rents. In cities other than Los Angeles, which typically offers occupants free parking, the amount of parking is being restricted and drivers must purchase a parking space that can cost as much as $225,000 in Manhattan. A New York City parking space exceeds not only the cost of the average American home, in cost per square foot it often exceeds the price of the owner's finished condominium. Allowing the market to set the price for parking and limiting parking availability will educate the public on the true cost of the automobile and swiftly shift travel preference to public transport, biking and walking.

Under the initiative established in 1997 legislation, U.S. employees can spend pre-tax wages up to $215 a month to pay for parking at work or at a commuter rail station, amounting to approximately a $1,000 annual subsidy designed to make driving to work more attractive. The provision also allows pre-tax dollars to be spent on transit but that provision is usable largely by suburban commuters using expensive rail travel. James A. Kushner, Global Climate Change and the Road to Extinction: The Legal and Planning Response 169–171 (2009).

One strategy would be to unbundle parking and housing. Required parking and automobile circulation infrastructure adds dramatically to the monthly rent. Tenants without cars should have a substantially reduced rent and those with automobiles should be sold or leased parking spaces and as well, pay a fee for the automobile infrastructure such as driveways. While Seattle has reduced its required parking to no more than 0.75%, a maximum of 1 space per unit in some San Francisco neighborhoods, Los Angeles requires a minimum of 2.25 spaces per unit. Linda Baker, *National Perspectives; No Parking: Condos Leave Out Cars*, N.Y. Times, Nov. 12, 2006 (reporting voluntary unbundling of parking in Seattle generates a market advantage). In addition to encouraging car-free living, affordable housing would be significantly more attainable. *See generally* Shoup, *supra*; Michael Lewyn & Shane Cralle, *Planners Gone Wild: The Overregulation of Parking*, 33 Wm. Mitchell L. Rev. 613 (2007). *See also* Rachel Weinberger, *The High Cost of Free Highways*, 43 Idaho L. Rev. 475 (2007). Regardless of the parking subsidy, as the nation proceeds toward another 100 million in population, there is no capacity to accommodate the vehicles that will be required at the present per capita rate. For example, in Los Angeles, the additional million population will generate the need for 675,000 cars, and at four to five parking spaces for each car currently provided the demand will be for 37 square miles of additional parking in the city. *Unhealthy by Design? Not if Cities Plan Liveable, Dense, Walkable Neighborhoods*, The Planning Report, June, 2006, *available at* http://www.planningreport.com/tpr/?module=displaystory_id=1174&format=html (reporting an interview with Gail Goldberg, Former Los Angeles Director of City Planning).

5. For a discussion of sustainable transport, see David Banister, Unsustainable Transport: City Transport in the New Century (2005). *See generally* Timothy Beatley, Green Urbanism: Learning from European Cities (2000).

6. *Transit-Oriented Development.* In its first year, the Obama Administration has endorsed transit-oriented development as the centerpiece of its housing, transportation, and urban policies. *See* Michael Cooper, *Administration Loosens Purse Strings for Transit Projects*, N.Y Times, Jan. 13, 2010. As of publication, although stimulus funds have been allocated for local transportation improvements, subsidies and guidance for transit-oriented development best practices are coming on line, while funds for transit operation and extension, are unavailable.

7. For discussions of smart growth and the halting of low density sprawl development to be replaced by walkable communities, see Robert H. Freilich, From Sprawl to Smart Growth: Successful Legal, Planning, and Environmental Systems (1999); James A. Kushner, The Post-Automobile City (2004); Arthur C. Nelson et al., The Social Impacts of Urban Containment (2007); Timothy Beatley & Richard Collins, *Smart Growth and Beyond: Transitioning to a Sustainable Society*, 19 Va. Envtl. L.J. 287 (2000); James A. Kushner, *Smart Growth, New Urbanism, and Diversity: Progressive Planning Movements in America and Their Impact on Poor and Minority Ethnic Populations*, 21 UCLA J.

ENVTL. L. & POL'Y 45 (2002/2003); James A. Kushner, *Smart Growth: Urban Growth Management and Land-Use Regulation Law in America,* 32 URB. LAW. 211 (2000); Michael Lewyn, *Sprawl, Growth Boundaries and the Rehnquist Court,* 2002 UTAH L. REV. 1.

8. For writings on car-free cities and housing, see J.H. CRAWFORD, CARFREE CITIES (2000); JAMES A. KUSHNER, THE POST-AUTOMOBILE CITY 76–84 (2004); James A. Kushner, *Car Free Housing Developments: Towards Sustainable Smart Growth and Urban Regeneration Through Car-Free Zoning, Car-Free Redevelopment, Pedestrian Improvement Districts, and New Urbanism,* 23 UCLA J. ENVTL. L. & POL'Y 1 (2005). *See also* Marcia D. Lowe, *Cars, Their Problems, and the Future, in* CITIES AND CARS 221 (Roger L. Kemp ed. 2007).

9. *Carbon Emissions and Health.* The air pollution and smog as well as carbon emissions from motor vehicles that exacerbate global climate change are also a public health hazard. Nationally, automobile pollution costs $24.3 billion annually. In the Los Angeles area, transportation sources account for between 60 and 90% of all air pollution. The annual cost in increased health care caused by the effects of petroleum just in California amounts to between $9 billion and $240 billion as compared to $8 billion in tobacco-related costs. Nationally, direct annual health care costs are between $54.7 billion and $672.3 billion. California's direct state health care payments related to petroleum pollution are between $500 million and $12 billion. Petroleum-based diseases in California result in 9,300 deaths, 16,000 hospital visits, 600,000 asthma attacks, and 5 million lost work days annually. In addition and in California alone, petroleum causes 1.7 million cases of respiratory illness and 1.3 million school absences. Is it time to declare both petroleum, internal combustion engines, and carbon a public nuisance, ban the use of fossil fuels, and bring private and public lawsuits for damages as in the case of tobacco? JAMES A. KUSHNER, GLOBAL CLIMATE CHANGE AND THE ROAD TO EXTINCTION: THE LEGAL AND PLANNING RESPONSE 173–174 (2009). As the average American is 20 pounds overweight and multiplying by 210 million adults traveling an average of 14,500 vehicle miles per year, a national diet could make a significant start towards energy independence by saving over a half a billion gallons of gas annually. Steven E. Polzin, *Time for Something Lighter: Obesity, Transportation and Energy Use,* PLANETIZEN, Oct. 30, 2006.

10. *Damages from Carbon Emissions.* Petroleum also generates $150 million in crop losses a year just in California's San Joaquin Valley, and statewide a loss of $300 million in farm income reflecting a loss of $54 million in federal income taxes that would have been paid. Nationally, crop losses from motor vehicle pollution is between $3 billion and $6 billion annually. Damage to buildings from motor vehicle pollution across the country is $1 billion to $8 billion annually. Annual forest damage from motor vehicle pollution is $2 million to $2 billion. Water pollution from leaking oil tanks, oil spills, and polluted runoff is between $4 million to $1.5 billion annually. In 1996, road congestion cost the United States $74 billion reflecting 4.6 billion lost hours and 6.7 billion wasted gallons of fuel. The Texas Transportation Institute in its 2007 Mobility Report conservatively estimates that Americans wasted 4.2 billion hours and 2.9 billion gallons of fuel while sitting in traffic in 2006. Anecdotally, congestion is much worse and far more costly today. A serious problem with congestion is the volume of traffic cruising in search of a cheap, on-street parking meter or free parking. Although raising parking meter fees will increase available spaces and reduce cruising, as long as parking is more than $1.20 per hour (the cost of operating a car), it will be cheaper to cruise than to park. JAMES A. KUSHNER, GLOBAL CLIMATE CHANGE AND THE ROAD TO EXTINCTION: THE LEGAL AND PLANNING RESPONSE 173–174 (2009).

Chapter 6

Fair Housing: Issues of Race, Class, and Status

In this chapter we turn to the problems of access to housing. The classic, and perhaps even today, paradigm cases involve discrimination against racial minorities, especially African Americans. Housing access limitations facing African Americans have received the most attention and have been the subject of a great number of corrective measures. Stopping racial discrimination has proved to be an extremely intractable task. But it should be emphasized that other groups face discrimination. The additional racial and ethnic groups include selected national origin or ethnic groups, especially Latina Americans (such as persons of Mexican and Puerto Rican origin), Indians and other native peoples, and persons of Asian origin (such as persons of Chinese, Indian, and Vietnamese origin).

Consideration of free access by minority groups frequently shades into the broader issue of access to housing by economic class. Some members of some minority groups are over-represented in the lower income classes. For example, class exclusions may apply to recipients of public assistance, persons who receive certain kinds of housing assistance (such as Section 8 vouchers or certificates), and effectively members of lower-income groups. The phenomenon of excluding lower economic classes represents what has been called economic segregation. Such segregation has the consequence of excluding members of lower-income classes not merely from housing opportunities but from an important, if not critical, host of opportunities including employment, education, governmental services, transportation, social outlets, political participation, and innumerable other public and private benefits.

In addition, discrimination exists against people who fall into certain status categories. Status discrimination imposes burdens or excludes women (especially unmarried heads of households), large families, families with children, persons with disabilities, gays and lesbians, the transgendered, and even college students.

In recent years, as we shall see, federal fair housing legislation has expanded the prohibited grounds of discrimination. It will be an instructive exercise to analyze the laws and cases to determine which groups are not or may not be protected. Thus, the title of this chapter—Fair Housing: Issues of Race, Class, and Status.

Section A begins the analysis by looking at the constitutional dimension of the free access issue. The exploration includes consideration of the doctrinal foundations that support the free access argument, principally the equal protection clause of the Fourteenth Amendment to the U. S. Constitution, and the limitations on the doctrinal and methodological approaches under constitutional analysis. One of the key questions to keep in mind is whether the constitutional basis for the free access argument is too limited and restricted to be an effective tool.

Sections B and C consider the statutory grounds upon which the free access question may be addressed. Here we look at the legislative basis (as distinct from the constitutional basis) for analyzing ways to provide freer access to housing. Two key questions arise in these sections. Does the legislation provide an adequate answer to the constitutional limits? What free access problems yet remain to be effectively addressed in the legislation, even after the amendment of the Civil Rights Act of 1968 by the Fair Housing Amendments Act of 1988?

Sections B and C represent functional divisions: Section B focuses on the responsibilities of the federal and state governments (and local governments as instrumentalities of the state governments) when these governments or their instrumentalities take actions that affect access to housing. Section C focuses on legislative proscriptions that apply to conduct in the private housing market that restricts free access or places special burdens on selected classes of housing consumers. Any division such as that made in Sections B and C cannot be discrete. Therefore, in some instances, as you will see, issues raised in one section could be raised in another. Moreover, in such cases the proper section in which to place a case or issue that overlaps both sections is at best debatable, if not arbitrary. Our goal in making divisions of the major issues and placing them in sections has been to facilitate analysis rather than to suggest fixed or rigid categories. Accordingly, Sections B and C focus on major themes of governmental and private action as organizational devices and not as doctrinally limiting categories.

There are two overarching issues to keep in view when analyzing the materials in this chapter. One issue is the extent to which the free access problem requires that housing needs be analyzed on a regional basis, rather than looking only within insular political entities. The other issue is whether new doctrines or laws are needed to provide free access to poor Americans who are not presently included in one of the statutorily protected groups (for example, conduct that excludes or that erects or fails to remove barriers that make housing unavailable to white persons who are in lower economic classes).

A Note on Fair Housing: Historical and Legal Contexts

It is now settled that America is a nation divided by residential living patterns according to race and income, and that, as foretold by the National Advisory Commission on Civil Disorders, the society is in many respects—"two societies, one black, one white—separate and unequal." The historical context and legal background are presented to illuminate several key issues that arise in the materials in this chapter.

I. Historical Context

Over the decades since the Civil War, powerful social, political, economic, and governmental forces have worked in tandem so that the overwhelming majority of blacks now reside in areas which are predominantly or solidly black. As rural blacks migrated in many cases from the South to urban centers and whites migrated to suburban locations, blacks became concentrated in older sections of central cities. Factors that combined to create this development clearly include racial prejudice, discrimination in the availability of housing, racial discrimination and disparate treatment in housing finance, economically exclusionary land use practices in suburban areas, and local, state, and federal governmental action and inaction buttressed by other social, economic, and political practices designed to exclude minorities and lower-income classes.

Racial prejudice is a fact of life in the United States. Scholars, social scientists, and governmental studies all confirm that it is so pervasive and so deep-rooted that it generates powerful forces which have influenced, probably determined, and certainly distorted the patterns of population distribution. These powerful forces led to the exclusion of blacks (and other ethnic minorities) from newer housing in central cities and from new, largely single-family developments in the suburbs. Exclusion from the wider housing markets created an artificial shortage of accessible housing and compounded actual shortages that already existed in many areas. Blacks, thus victimized, often "paid more for less," and were forced into overcrowded partitioned older units which were least able to withstand the higher intensity use. Much of the housing was in the hands of speculators who either could not or would not make adequate upkeep and repair. Housing quality rapidly deteriorated under such conditions.

Blacks could not do much to move outside the ghettos. Upwardly mobile blacks were excluded from other areas by intimidation, precluded from purchasing in white areas by restrictive covenants, steered away by the real estate industry, and unable to secure financing. Blacks who needed governmental subsidies were forced to live in units wherever the units were located. Typically, such units were located in already racially concentrated areas, having been excluded from non-impacted areas by refusals to rezone to permit higher densities required by governmental multifamily programs, rejection of units in white areas by referenda and governmental officials at all levels, deliberately segregative site and tenant selection practices, low density exclusionary zoning and cost-inflating development regulation in suburban areas, and outright opposition sometimes accompanied by violence and threats of violence.

Following World War II, the federal government played a major role in the maintenance and extension of residential segregation. Practices of the governmental agencies abetted those of the private real estate industry. In 1950, the National Association of Real Estate Brokers essentially enjoined its members from introducing "members of any race or nationality" into a neighborhood if such persons "will clearly be detrimental to property values." Although there is clear evidence that when blacks move into formerly white neighborhoods property values go up or remain stable (unless "blockbusting" or other scare tactics create "panic" selling by whites), it was clearly understood that the injunction of the Association precluded facilitating sale in white areas to blacks. The federal government played by the rules. The Federal Housing Administration's Underwriting Manual provided that "inharmonious racial groups" should not be infiltrated into neighborhoods with families of a different social group. Thus, subdivisions would be ineligible for federal mortgage insurance and loans in the absence of the execution of racial covenants that excluded Blacks and others who were permitted to purchase only in isolated all-minority subdivisions.

Other governmental programs facilitated the rise of the white suburbs. The interstate highway program, grants for developmental infrastructure (sewers, water systems, parks, school support), and the massive revolution in housing finance through the Veterans Administration (VA) and the Federal Housing Administration (FHA) were critically important as they subsidized the growth of the white-only suburbs. VA and FHA made widespread homeownership possible in America by authorizing or influencing the use of lower down payments (or no down payment in the case of the VA), longer mortgage payment periods, mortgage insurance, and direct loans or secondary market functions. These programs put builders to work and put financial institutions in the housing market. When these programs were at their initial apex of maximum impact, residential segregation was the standard business practice for the entire country. The central cities became increasingly poor, black, and deteriorated as suburbs drew off the successful white middle- and upper-income groups. In addition, the FHA and banks redlined the central cities, refusing to make loans to acquire businesses and housing or to undertake repairs and remodeling. The result was the decline of neighborhoods allotted to housing minorities and exclusion from the home equity building enjoyed by those in the suburbs.

The effect of housing discrimination is not isolated. It has multiple impacts on practically all phases of individual and community life. As the United States Civil Rights Commission has reported:

> A host of other social problems stems, at least in part, from discrimination in housing. Residential segregation has contributed to inequality in job opportunities, racially impacted and differentially endowed schools, greater tax burdens in central cities to support higher social service costs, and a distorted pattern of urban growth.... [H]ousing discrimination intensifies the critical problems of our cities: slums whose growth is abetted by the racial ghetto; loss of tax revenue [as high income individuals, businesses and even governmental employers move to suburban locations] ... through flight to the suburbs of those financially (and racially) able to leave—all this in face of growing city needs for transportation, welfare, and municipal services.

U.S. Civil Rights Comm., Twenty Years After Brown: Equal Opportunity in Housing 11 (1975).

II. Legal Context

A starting point for legal background on the fair housing question is probably the Thirteenth Amendment to the U.S. Constitution which, in 1865, abolished slavery. The following year Congress enacted the Civil Rights Act of 1866 (now codified as 42 U.S.C. §§ 1981, 1982). Section 1982 of that Act provided that: "All citizens of the United States shall have the same right, in every state and territory, as is enjoyed by the white citizens thereof to inherit, purchase, lease, sell, hold, and convey real and personal property." Two years later, in 1868, these provisions were buttressed by the adoption of the Fourteenth Amendment to the U.S. Constitution which made citizens of all persons born or naturalized in the United States and provided that: "No state shall ... deny to any person within its jurisdiction the equal protection of the laws."

Residential segregation was so entrenched by the time these provisions were interpreted to give them vitality that the question had become one of dismantling rigid patterns instead of preventing them. The first interpretation of the Fourteenth Amendment was a restricted one. In *The Civil Rights Cases*, 109 U.S. 3 (1883), the Supreme Court held that only discrimination by the state violated that amendment. Under municipal ordinances, therefore, entire city blocks were barred to occupancy or ownership by blacks if whites predominated on that block (and, at least theoretically, vice versa). This kind of segregation persisted legally until 1917, when the Court held in *Buchanan v. Warley*, 245 U.S. 60 (1917), that a white landowner's due process rights were violated by such ordinances. Until 1948, discriminating individuals could get judicial enforcement of restrictive covenants that forbade sale of property to African Americans and other minorities (frequently including Jews). They did so until the Supreme Court held in *Shelly v. Kraemer*, 334 U.S. 1 (1948), that state judicial enforcement of private racially restrictive covenants constituted "state action," and thus violated the Fourteenth Amendment.

These judicial developments were too limited and too late to forestall residential segregation. They were far too ineffective to combat residential segregation in a society legally committed to "separate but equal"—that is, segregation in all aspects of its national life. The "separate but equal" doctrine had sanctioned all forms of rigid segregation since just before the turn of the century. *See Plessy v. Ferguson*, 163 U.S. 537 (1896). The turning point, if there has been one, was more than half a century into the future. *Brown v. Board of Education*, 347 U.S. 483 (1954), ruled the doctrine inapplicable to schools and *Brown's* progeny, at last, recognized that "separate but equal" was anything but equal, in every aspect of American life, and was declared no longer permissible under the Constitution.

In 1962, President Kennedy promulgated Executive Order 11063. This order prohibited discrimination only in housing owned, operated, or assisted by the federal government. As implemented, the Executive Order was more limited than it appeared to be on its face. It was applied prospectively only, and FHA and VA by regulation exempted one- and two-family owner-occupied homes. Accordingly, it did nothing to dismantle existing segregation, which was widespread; it did nothing to forestall segregation in the single-family suburbs; and, of course, it did not apply to any conventional privately-financed multifamily or single-family homes. The Civil Rights Act of 1964 essentially enacted the Executive Order into congressional legislation and expanded "nondiscrimination" as national policy in public accommodations, federally funded programs, and employment. *See* 42 U.S.C. §§2000d–2000e.

In 1968, two major steps were taken. On April 11, 1968, President Johnson signed into law the Civil Rights Act of 1968, which contained Title VIII—a "fair housing" law for the nation (42 U.S.C. §§3601–3619, 3631). On June 17, 1968, the Supreme Court handed down its decision in *Jones v. Alfred H. Mayer Co.*, 392 U.S. 409 (1968), holding that the long dormant Civil Rights Act of 1866 (42 U.S.C. §1982) prohibited even private housing discrimination.

These were major new thrusts. But the problem of free access to housing has proved to be intractable. Segregation has remained a fact of life. Discrimination persists as a widespread public and private phenomenon. Blacks, Latinas and low-income groups continue to be segregated in declining urban centers and close-in older suburbs. The outer suburbs continue to be overwhelmingly white. In 1988, Congress responded to these continuing challenges by amending various provisions of the civil rights laws. First, Congress acted to clarify the interpretation of Title VI and related laws to apply nondiscrimination requirements to entire entities to which the provisions were otherwise applicable. Civil Rights Restoration Act of 1987, Pub. L. No. 100-259, 102 Stat. 28 (1988). Second, Congress amended Title VIII, *inter alia*, to broaden coverage and improve administrative remedies. Fair Housing Amendments Act of 1988, Pub. L. No. 100-430, 102 Stat. 1619 (1988).

Moreover, when the conduct of agencies of the federal government itself or recipients of federal funding is at issue (such as in Section B), other statutes may come into play. For example, Title VI of the Civil Rights Act of 1964, 42 U.S.C. §2000d prohibits discrimination by federal agencies and recipients of federal funds in terms that are broad enough to include some kinds of housing discrimination, although resort to Title VI will not often be necessary in the case of most housing-related discrimination. Antidiscrimination provisions are contained in the Housing and Community Development Act of 1974 governing community development funding. *See, e.g.*, 42 U.S.C. §5304(b) (entitlement areas); 42 U.S.C. §5306(d) (nonentitlement areas funded through states); and 42 U.S.C. §5307(e) (special purpose grants).

III. Remaining Problems and Issues

As already suggested, there are two basic sources of law in the fair housing area—constitutional and statutory. They raise two overriding issues. These are, first, how the courts have interpreted the substantive doctrines that govern fair housing issues, and second, whether the laws provide adequate and effective remedial tools. There are varied contexts in which these issues are presented. The contexts include the duties that devolve upon government and governmental agencies that have roles in the housing arena. More specifically, questions that arise include: the duties of HUD and the Rural Housing Service (formerly the Farmers Home Administration) when approving sites and the location of units and the criteria for selecting tenants for the units; the impact of various community development activities and projects that raise fair housing concerns; the consequences of participation or non-participation in various housing and development programs by suburban jurisdictions; and the deconcentration of racially impacted areas (generally central cities) by various kinds of dispersal activities that open up suburban areas to minority groups and lower-income families.

From the legal perspective, there are three key areas of problematic issues. The first area involves the question of how can advocates develop acceptable legal theories to get free access cases into court. Some of the specific issues in this area include: Exactly what are the fair housing rights that exist? What proof is required to make out a *prima facie* case of a fair housing violation? Whether and when must "intent" to discriminate be shown and, if so, what evidence will suffice to show such intent? Whether, at least under certain statutes, proof of "discriminatory effect" will make out a violation when intent cannot be proved, and, if so in what circumstances and upon what evidence?

A second key area concerns what Congress intended in certain statutes. Specific questions include: What happens assuming a *prima facie* case of discrimination can be shown? Does the plaintiff then win the case? If not, what evidence can legally justify such discrimination or otherwise rebut a *prima facie* case. What standard of proof is required to rebut a *prima facie* case? If the defendant offers evidence of rebuttal, does the defendant then win the case? If not, what must the plaintiff then do?

The third key issue assumes the existence of a fair housing violation, and then focuses on the remedy that is needed. There are many kinds of fair housing cases ranging from those involving governmental action at various levels of government to those of individuals. What are the strategies for getting the courts to grant effective workable remedies? What remedies will be an effective sanction for wrongdoing, will adequately compensate the victim, and will serve to deter others? Are the measures that are needed ones that a court can or should grant?

Notes and Questions

1. For further discussion of topics touched on here, see, e.g., the following: Elizabeth K. Julian, *Fair Housing and Community Development: Time to Come Together*, 41 Ind. L. Rev. 555 (2008). The author asserts that fair housing and community development are best advanced together. She believes that "at the intersection of race and poverty" the fair housing and community development movements have had their greatest challenges. Julian points out that neither movement has been individually successful in either creating open and inclusive communities of opportunity or making separate equal. The author observes that, "The fundamental principles of housing choice and equal opportunity appear to collide with the perceived need to focus those scarce resources, particularly federal housing dollars, on community revitalization work. However, this is a false dichotomy. Fair housing and community development are two sides of the same coin. They grew out of the need to address the twin evils of Jim Crow: separate and unequal." *Id.* at 557.

James A. Kushner, *Urban Neighborhood Regeneration and the Phases of Community Evolution After World War II in the United States*, 41 Ind. L. Rev. 575 (2008). The author sets out four phases of urban neighborhood change. He points out that in the fourth phase, although "[m]ore than one-third of African Americans—almost 12 million people—lived in suburbs.... African Americans [remain] the most residentially segregated group in the United States. Black suburbanization did little to desegregate metropolitan areas, for while the movement of blacks to the suburbs signaled the lifting of the suburban-urban barrier, any optimism about greater residential integration between whites and blacks was short-lived." *Id.* at 590.

john a. powell, *Reflections on the Past, Looking to the Future: The Fair Housing Act at 40*, 41 IND. L. REV. 605, 615 (2008), The author concludes that, "There is no longer a clear suburban-high opportunity/central city-low opportunity demarcation. The suburbs themselves are segregating into the "favored quarter" suburbs and poorer, resource-constrained suburbs. Increasingly, inner-ring or "first" suburbs are taking on the characteristics of their central city neighbors. Between 1999 and 2005, in the nation's 100 largest metro areas (which encompass two-thirds of the U.S. population), poverty rates rose, and "52[%] of metro residents living below the poverty line were found in [the] suburbs." This is the first time in modern history that more poor people are in the suburbs than the city. People (particularly new immigrants), jobs, and municipal distress are all suburbanizing. As a result, a suburban address does not necessarily indicate a neighborhood of "high opportunity," which casts doubt on the rosy glow of statistics indicating the increasing suburbanization of minorities. *Id.* at 609–610. *See also* David Villano, *Suburbs—Our New Slums?*, Pittsburgh Post-Gazette.com, Apr. 5, 2009, *available at* http://www.post-gazette.com/pg/09095/960370-109.stm. ("In 2005, as rising property values reduced affordable housing stock in inner-city neighborhoods, suburban poverty, in raw numbers, topped urban poverty for the first time").

Sheryll D. Cashin, *Drifting Apart: How Wealth and Racial Segregation are Reshaping the American Dream*, 47 VILL. L. REV. 595 (2002). The analysis in this article works from the premise that "Segregation is the natural tendency in America. And segregation, both racial and economic, breeds inequality." *Id.* at 596. In this article the author points out that although the minority population in America has grown rapidly over the last decade, some groups still remain highly segregated. Professor Cashin deploys the demographers' concept of a "dissimilarity index" in which the higher number represents a greater degree of segregation. A dissimilarity value of 60% or above is considered an extremely high level of segregation. The article points out that the national index for segregation for blacks is 65%. This means that 65% of black people would have to move in order to achieve an even distribution in America according to their proportion of the population. This figure is the national average, which means that it may be higher in some locations. One-half of all African Americans live in urban areas where the index is 75% or higher. The index for the Latino population is 52% and 42% for Asians. This article noted that while many African Americans live in urban areas, most whites, 71%, live in suburban communities, compared to 39% of African Americans. The article also discusses high levels of segregation among children. The national index for African American children is 68%. This causes a major problem because of how schools are funded. African American and Latino children are being taught in schools with a high level of poverty. The article highlights two complicating factors that work against higher degrees of residential integration: racial discrimination and the personal preferences of the American people.

Peter W. Salsich, Jr., *Toward a Policy of Heterogeneity: Overcoming a Long History of Socioeconomic Segregation in Housing*, 42 WAKE FOREST L. REV. 459 (2007. The author sets out four scenarios that might address some aspects of class exclusions, but finds that the proposals are probably unworkable in most jurisdictions. The proposals all involve purchasing:

a vacant 1950s vintage California ranch-style house on a 10,000 square foot lot that has been on the market for several weeks: (1) renovate and rent the house to a single person with three school-age children who is escaping a life in homeless shelters and transitional housing with the assistance of not-for-profit providers of "supportive housing"; (2) add a second story to the house and sell it to a large family (four or more children) that is eligible for or currently lives in public housing; (3) adopt the "tear down" philosophy driving the "McMansion" craze and replace the house with a new triplex that can be rented to three homeless persons or families who previously lived in a "big box" shelter; or (4) demolish the house, subdivide the lot into two smaller lots, and construct two small "Katrina Cottages" (600–800 square feet of living space, including two bedrooms) to be sold to welfare-to-work families graduating from a local home ownership and management course.

These four proposals represent newer ways of thinking about providing housing for low-income households. Instead of relying on the high rise and/or large tract urban public housing complexes of the 1950s and 1960s, the large privately owned subsidized apartment developments of the 1970s and 1980s, the homeless shelters of the 1990s and 2000s, and the FEMA trailers of 2005–2006, housing providers and advocates increasingly are emphasizing the importance of mixing assisted and/or supportive housing with market rate housing in stable residential neighborhoods, either in relatively large developments or in scattered site, single family, or duplex placements. The four hypothetical proposals are variations of the scattered site theme.

There is only one catch: in many such neighborhoods throughout the country, current land use regulations may not permit any of the four proposals to be implemented. For over eighty years, the particular form of land use regulation known as Euclidean zoning, which separates single family detached housing from all other forms of permissible land use has been the traditional favorite of local governments, particularly in the suburban areas of the nation's metropolitan areas. Justice Sutherland's derogatory reference to apartments (and by necessary implication, their occupants) as "mere parasite[s]" on residential neighborhoods in the Euclid decision has helped sustain an extreme reluctance of local governments, particularly in outlying suburbs, to permit the levels of density generally thought to be necessary to encourage developers to build housing for the lower half of the market, not to mention permitting scattered site deviations from the norm of single family-owned housing. As a result, restrictive local land use regulations increasingly are being identified as a major roadblock to affordable housing efforts throughout the country.

The question thus presents itself: is there a role for government, particularly the federal government, to play in enabling policies of the type being considered by our hypothetical not-for-profit client to be implemented in the face of local regulatory hostility? This Article answers "yes," with the recommendation that Congress enact legislation to authorize planning support for state and regional affordable housing initiatives and a federal override of local zoning laws when necessary to enable affordable housing developments receiving federal and state financial assistance to be scattered throughout residential neighborhoods.

Id. at 459–464.

Thaddeus J. Hackworth, Note, *The Ghetto Prison: Federal Policy Responses to Racial and Economic Segregation,* 12 Geo. J. Poverty Law & Pol'y 181 (2005). Using Washington, D.C. metropolitan area as an example of a larger-scale problem with segregation in America, the author points out that the increase of poverty concentration level for Black D.C. residents has risen from 1990 to 2000 by 19.3%. The author asserts that the Fair Housing Act had no teeth to enforce causes of action it had created and that affirmative action sometimes justified in education, employment, and voting rights, would have been a logical step for housing desegregation.

Lisa M. Krzewinski, *Section 8's Failure to Integrate: The Interaction of Class-Based and Racial Discrimination*, 21 B.C. Third World L.J. 315 (2001) (in a review of Stephen Grant Meyer, As Long as They Don't Move Next Door (2000), the reviewer examines the book's history of housing discrimination in roughly the century between the civil war and the passage of the Fair Housing Act. The book acknowledges institutionalized racism in America but argues that the cause of segregation in America today is not institutionalized racism on the part of lenders, real estate agents, or government action or inaction, but results from white homeowners, landlords, and tenants who are determined to keep their neighborhoods all white. The book discusses how economic bias creates or reinforces segregation using a case study approach, examines the history of Section 8 vouchers and examines the reasons vouchers do not address the dual implications of race and class. The book concludes with recommendations directed to long-term success: "In order to accomplish long-term change in housing desegregation, a three-prong attack is needed: (1) neighborhood revitalization in the inner city, (2) extensive counseling to section 8 recipients, and (3) a program of outreach to landlords." *Id.* at 329.

2. The National Advisory Commission on Civil Disorders was popularly known as the "Kerner Commission," having been named for Governor Otto Kerner of Illinois who served as chair of the commission. The commission was appointed by President Lyndon B. Johnson and issued its report in 1968. The "two societies" quote is taken from page one of the report Report Of The National Advisory Commission On Civil Disorders (1968). A book-length work, issued on the twenty-fifth anniversary of the Commission's report, contains a compendium of articles considering a broad range of issues touched on here. *Symposium, The Urban Crisis: The Kerner Commission Report Revisited*, 71 N.C. L. Rev. 1283 (1993).

3. For a critical discussion of the historical and legal aspects of residential segregation in the United States, which develops both the socio-political milieu as well as the legal and constitutional background necessary for complete appreciation of the topic addressed by the preceding note, see James A. Kushner, Apartheid in America (1980), originally published in 22 How. L.J. 547 (1979) and Douglas S. Massey & Nancy A. Denton, American Apartheid: Segregation and the Making of the Underclass (1993). For a treatment of fair housing from a litigation-oriented *prima facie* case approach, see James A. Kushner, Fair Housing: Discrimination in Real Estate Community Development and Revitalization (2d. ed. 1995 & Supp. 2000). For analysis of governmental duties and responsibilities, a basic work is James A. Kushner, Government Discrimination: Equal Protection Law and Litigation (2009–2010) (fully on-line in Westlaw treatises).

4. Related to racial segregation is concentrations of poverty and economic isolation which disproportionately affect poor minorities. One view of the role of federal housing policy in creating and sustaining geographic concentrations of poverty and of potential solutions to the problems of geographic concentrations is expressed in Michael H. Schill & Susan M. Wachter, *The Spatial Bias of Federal Housing Law and Policy: The Concentrated Poverty in Urban America*, 143 U. Pa. L. Rev. 1285 (1995) ("Throughout the twen-

tieth century, federal housing law and policy have exhibited a locational bias that has promoted the growth of large concentrations of poor people in the inner city.")

A longtime stalwart in the housing field takes issue with many of the conclusions drawn and the solutions proposed by Schill and Wachter. *See* Florence Wagman Roisman, *Intentional Racial Discrimination and Segregation by the Federal Government as a Principal Cause of Concentrated Poverty: A Response to Schill and Wachter*, 143 U. Pa. L. Rev. 1351 (1995). Professor Roisman points out, essentially: (1) that as critical as it is, fair housing enforcement alone is not necessarily a tool for deconcentrating poverty; (2) that increasing the availability of "affordable housing" through land use regulation will not deconcentrate poverty, because the subsidies are too shallow to offer opportunity to the poor; (3) that changes in the public housing program cannot solve poverty concentrations, but that rather deep subsidy programs—other than public housing—must be made available in areas outside of those with concentrated poverty; (4) that poverty should be ended, as that is the evil, rather than focusing exclusively on either housing or poverty concentration; and (5) that "mobility programs" need to be expanded and improved, such that more of the thirteen million persons in poverty will be enabled to escape both poverty and the limited geographic areas in which poor people can find housing.

For a gripping account of post-WWII segregation in the Philadelphia suburb of Levittown, Pennsylvania, built with Federal Housing Administration assistance, *see* David Kushner, Levittown: Two Families, One Tycoon, and the Fight for Civil Rights in America's Legendary Suburb (2009).

5. For an explanation of fair housing legal theories, see Robert G. Schwemm, *From* Washington *to* Arlington Heights *and Beyond: Discriminatory Purpose in Equal Protection Litigation*, 1977 U. Ill. L.F. 961 (1977). For the author's additional perspectives, see The Fair Housing Act After Twenty Years (Robert G. Schwemm ed. 1989). For an explanation of Title VIII, see Robert G. Schwemm, Housing Discrimination: Law and Litigation (1996 & Supp. 2009).

6. Additional references include: The Integration Debate: Competing Futures for American Cities (Chester Hartman & Gregory D. Squires eds. 2009); Report of the Bipartisan Millennial Housing Commission Appointed by the Congress of the United States 14 (2002) (prepared pursuant to Pub. L. No. 106-74, § 206(b), 113 Stat. 1047, 1070 (2000) and generally, though without significant attention to race as a variable, the state of the current housing affordability problem); Report of the National Commission on Fair Housing and Equal Opportunity: The Future of Fair Housing (2008) (sponsored by the Leadership Conference on Civil Rights, the Lawyers' Committee for Civil Rights Under Law, NAACP Legal Defense & Educational Fund, and the National Fair Housing Alliance to create a national, bipartisan fair housing commission to investigate the alarming state of U.S. housing in the wake of the subprime housing debacle); Segregation: The Rising Costs for America (James H. Carr & Nandinee K. Kutty eds. 2008), *reviewed by* W. Dennis Keating, 45 Urb. Aff. Rev. 568 (2010); Dolores Acevedo-Garcia et al., *Does Housing Mobility Policy Improve Health?*, 15 Housing Pol'y Debate 49 (2004); Robert D. Bullard, Glenn S. Johnson, & Angel O. Torres, *Race, Equity, and Smart Growth: Why People of Color Must Speak for Themselves*, *available at* www.ejrc.cau.edu/raceequitysmartgrowth.htm (compiling a massive volume of statistics and facts gathered in previous studies) (prepared by the Environmental Justice Resource Center) (last visited Jan. 8, 2010); Greg J. Duncan & Jens Ludwig, *Can Housing Vouchers Help Poor Children*? (July 2000) (The Brookings Institution Children's Roundtable No. 3); John Goering, Judith D. Feins & Todd M. Richardson, *A Cross-Site Analysis of Initial Moving to Opportunity Demonstration Results*, 13 J. Housing Res. 1 (2002);

Zhong Yi Tong, Special Report, Homeownership Affordability in Urban America: Past and Future (Apr. 2004) (published by the Fannie Mae Foundation), *available at* http://content.knowledgeplex.org/kp2/cache/kp/22736.pdf (last visited Feb. 27, 2010); *Paulette J. Williams, The Continuing Crisis in Affordable Housing: Systemic Issues Requiring Systemic Solutions*, 31 FORDHAM URB. L.J. 413 (2004). *See also Annotated Bibliography of Selected Fair Housing Issues* (1986) (Clearinghouse Publication No. 90), the *compilation of bibliographic references at* http://www.prrac.org/mobility/ (last visited Jan. 8, 2010), and three reports of the United States Civil Rights Commission, now somewhat dated, which provide helpful background on the social and legal dimensions of the fair housing quest. Equal Opportunity in Suburbia (1974), HOUSING DISCRIMINATION (1985) (U.S. Civil Rights Commission's publications Issues in 2 volumes), and Twenty Years After *Brown*: Equal Opportunity in Housing (1975).

7. On the question of race and property values, *see* LUIGI LAURENTI, PROPERTY VALUES AND RACE: STUDIES IN SEVEN CITIES (1960) (concluding that the entry of blacks into a neighborhood either had no effect on property values, or resulted in property values increasing) and HOWARD OPENSHAW, RACE AND RESIDENCE: AN ANALYSIS OF PROPERTY VALUES IN TRANSITIONAL AREAS (1973).

A. Constitutional Basis for Fair Housing: Equal Protection Theory, Methodology, and Limits

A Note on Equal Protection

In equal protection analysis, the touchstones are (1) governmental action or inaction, (2) which makes a classification or is tantamount to a classification (3) that adversely affects an interest of a person (*e.g.*, withholds a benefit, denies an advantage, or imposes a burden). Although of rather modern vintage, as generations of law students from the 1960s forward learned, the traditional analysis of equal protection questions involved a process of identifying the challenged conduct and determining whether the classification either (a) affected a "fundamental interest" or (b) made a "suspect classification." If it did either of these, the courts would give the classification "strict scrutiny." Strict scrutiny meant the government had to show a "compelling interest" or the classification would be struck down.

In stark contrast to classifications given strict scrutiny were those not falling in one of the strict scrutiny categories (essentially all other classifications), which would be upheld if the government could show that the classification had a "rational basis." A rational basis would be found if the court could divine, even on its own, practically any connection between the classification and a possibly legitimate activity or concern of the entity making the classification. "Rational basis" review provided virtually no scrutiny of challenged classifications. For a classic discussion of the matters touched on here, see Gerald Gunther, *Foreword: In Search of Evolving Doctrine on a Changing Court: A Model for a Newer Equal Protection*, 86 HARV. L. REV. 1 (1972). Professor Gunther noted that:

> Some situations evoked the aggressive "new" equal protection, with scrutiny that was "strict" in theory and fatal in fact; in other contexts, the deferential "old" equal protection reigned, with minimal scrutiny in theory and virtually none in fact." *Id.* at 8.

> The fundamental interests ingredient of the new equal protection was particularly open-ended. It was the element which bore the closest resemblance to freewheeling substantive due process, for it circumscribed legislative choices in the name of newly articulated values that lacked clear support in constitutional text and history. The list of interests identified as fundamental by the Warren Court was in fact—quite modest: voting, criminal appeals, and the right of interstate travel were the prime examples. But in the extraordinary amount commentary that followed, analysts searching for justifications for those enshrinements were understandably tempted to ponder analogous spheres that might similarly qualify. Welfare benefits, *exclusionary zoning, municipal services* and school financing came to be the most inviting frontiers. The expansiveness of the speculations derived special impetus from the fact that, to an unusual degree, litigation plans and doctrinal analyses came from the same hands. *Id.* at 8–9. [emphasis added]
>
> Some strategists recognized that the open-endedness of fundamental interests might prove a fatal flaw: if the claims extended beyond schools and *housing* to golf courses and sewers, the sheer magnitude of the enterprise might stifle the Court's egalitarian zeal. Yet even while some proponents of the new equal protection sought to reassure critics that inclusion of education among the preferred fundamental interests would not compel extension of that cherished status to municipal services generally, others engaged in ever more far-reaching exercises in advocacy and analysis. *Id.* at 10. [emphasis added]

Professor Gunther noted two developments as to which he proved to be a sage prognosticator. He foresaw a "mounting discontent with the rigid two-tier formulations of the Warren Court's equal protection doctrine" and that the "Court [was] prepared to use the clause as an interventionist tool without resorting to the strict scrutiny language of the new equal protection."

Notes and Questions

1. The traditional approach to equal protection analysis is reflected in *James v. Valtierra,* 402 U.S. 137 (1971), sustaining a referendum precondition to building public housing. [the case is reproduced in Chapter 1, *supra*—Eds.] The Court focuses on the rationality of the disparate treatment of classes of individuals in the absence of a suspect classification, for example, based on race or national origin, or a quasi-suspect classification, such as one based on gender, or a classification abridging a fundamental right. The Court has also applied equal protection analysis to instances of disparate treatment involving an individual, "as class of one" when an individual or entity is treated differently than those similarly situated regardless of any class membership. *Village of Willowbrook v. Olech*, 528 U.S. 562 (2000) (per curiam).

2. Article XXXIV was still presenting litigable issues nearly two decades after *Valtierra* was decided. *See Davis v. City of Berkeley*, 238 Cal. Rptr. 730 (Ct. App. 1987), *aff'd*, 794 P.2d 897 (Cal. 1990). The state trial court and court of appeals ruled that Article XXXIV did not require specific approval of each individual project. Rather its purpose was to permit the electorate to approve or disapprove, in general terms, proposed public housing development. The California Supreme Court held that the general approval was so "attenuated" from a seventy-five-unit project in question that it would render the approval process insignificant. But it denied a request for a new referendum because the project was virtually completed, 765 P.2d 46 (Cal. 1988), and on the merits, upheld the validity of the

referendum. 794 P.2d 897 (Cal. 1990). The passage of time between the challenged conduct and the conclusion of litigation challenging that conduct is frequently a problem of housing litigation in particular but institutional reform litigation in general. This topic is discussed in Chapter 2, *supra*.

3. Whether discriminatory "impact" (or "effect") would be sufficient to make out a constitutional violation or whether only intentional discrimination would be sufficient was not clear until *Washington v. Davis*, 426 U.S. 229 (1976). In that case the Court held in an employment testing case that discriminatory purpose or intent was required to make out a constitutional violation under the equal protection clause.

The *Arlington* case which follows addresses the applicability of *Washington v. Davis* to a housing context. Does the same analysis apply and, if so, what methodological approach is employed and upon what evidence?

Village of Arlington Heights v. Metropolitan Housing Dev. Corp. [Arlington I]

United States Supreme Court
429 U.S. 252 (1977)

[The Clerics of St. Viator, a religious order, owned a tract of land located in the Village of Arlington Heights, a suburb of Chicago. The village had a population of 64,000, of whom twenty-seven residents were black. In 1970, the order decided to use a portion of its land for construction of low- and moderate-income housing. They contacted Metropolitan Housing Development Corporation (MHDC). MHDC had experience in the building of developments using federal subsidies. The order and MHDC entered into a 99-year lease and an agreement of sale for a fifteen-acre site on the tract. The sales agreement was contingent upon MHDC's securing a zoning clearance from the Village of Arlington Heights and federal assistance under the Section 236 program.

[The site had been zoned for single-family housing since 1959. For MHDC to build the proposed project (to be known as Lincoln Green), the site would have to be rezoned from single-family to R-5 which was a multiple-family classification. To seek rezoning, MHDC filed a petition, as well as studies and other supporting materials in compliance with the village's procedural requirements. Three public hearings were held.

[At the Village Plan Commission public meetings, both supporters and opponents touched upon the so-called "social issue"—the desirability or undesirability of introducing at the proposed location lower-income housing that would probably be racially integrated. Opponents also stressed zoning factors that pointed toward denial of MHDC's application: The location had always been zoned single-family, and the Village's apartment policy called for limited use of R-5 zoning, primarily as a buffer between single-family development and commercial or manufacturing districts, none of which adjoined the project's proposed location.

[In June 1972, MHDC and several minority individuals brought suit against Arlington Heights, seeking declaratory and injunctive relief. The district court found for the defendant, stressing its inability to find either discriminatory effects or racially motivated intent. The court of appeals reversed, finding that the denial of rezoning had a discriminatory effect and had not been justified by a compelling interest. The refusal to rezone was held therefore to violate the Equal Protection Clause of the Fourteenth Amendment.

Mr. Justice POWELL, delivered the opinion of the court....

[After finding that the plaintiffs had standing, the Court, turned to the merits.—Eds.]:

III

Our decision last Term in *Washington v. Davis*, 426 U.S. 229 (1976), made it clear that official action will not be held unconstitutional solely because it results in a racially disproportionate impact. "Disproportionate impact is not irrelevant, but it is not the sole touchstone of an invidious racial discrimination." Proof of racially discriminatory intent or purpose is required to show a violation of the Equal Protection Clause. Although some contrary indications may be drawn from some of our cases, the holding in *Davis* reaffirmed a principle well established in a variety contexts.

Davis does not require a plaintiff to prove that the challenged action rested solely on racially discriminatory purposes. Rarely can it be said that a legislature or administrative body operating under a broad mandate made a decision motivated by a single concern, or even that a particular purpose was the "dominant" or "primary" one. In fact, it is because legislators and administrators are properly concerned with balancing numerous competing considerations that courts refrain from reviewing the merits of their decisions, absent a showing of arbitrariness or irrationality. But racial discrimination is not just another competing consideration. When there is a proof that a discriminatory purpose has been a motivating factor in the decision judicial deference is no longer justified.

Determining whether invidious discriminatory purpose was a motivating factor demands a sensitive inquiry into such circumstantial and direct evidence of intent as may be available. The impact of the official action—whether it "bears more heavily on one race than another," *Washington v. Davis*—may provide an important starting point. Sometimes a clear pattern, unexplainable on grounds other than race, emerges from the effect of the state action even when the governing legislation appears neutral on its face. *Yick Wo v. Hopkins*, 118 U.S. 356 (1886); *Gomillion v. Lightfoot*, 364 U.S. 339 (1960). The evidentiary inquiry is then relatively easy. But such cases are rare. Absent a pattern as stark as that in *Gomillion* or *Yick Wo*, impact alone is not determinative, and the Court must look to other evidence.

The historical background of the decision is one evidentiary source, particularly if it reveals a series of official actions taken for invidious purposes. The specific sequence of events leading up to the challenged decision also may shed some light on the decisionmaker's purposes. For example, if the property involved here always had zoned R-5 but suddenly was changed to R-3 when the town learned of MHDC's plans to erect integrated housing, we would have a far different case. Departures from the normal procedural sequence also might afford evidence that improper purposes are playing a role. Substantive departures too may be relevant, particularly factors usually considered important by the decisionmaker strongly favor a decision contrary to the one reached.

The legislative or administrative history may be highly relevant, especially where there are contemporary statements by members of the decisionmaking body, minutes of its meetings, or reports. In some extraordinary instances the members might be called to the stand at trial to testify concerning the purpose of the official action, although even then such testimony frequently will be barred by privilege.

The foregoing summary identifies, without purporting to be exhaustive, subjects of proper inquiry in determining whether racially discriminatory intent existed. With these in mind, we now address the case before us.

IV

This case was tried in the District Court and reviewed in the Court of Appeals before our decision in *Washington v. Davis, supra.* The respondents proceeded on the erroneous theory that the Village's refusal to rezone carried a racially discriminatory effect and was, without more, unconstitutional. But both courts below understood that at least part of their function was to examine the purpose underlying the decision. In making its findings on this issue, the District Court noted that some of the opponents of Lincoln Green who spoke at the various hearings might have been motivated by opposition to minority groups. The court held, however, that the evidence "does not warrant the conclusion that this motivated the defendants."

On appeal the Court of Appeals focused primarily on respondents' claim that the Village's buffer policy [requiring multifamily housing to be sited only where it serves as a buffer between single-family homes and traffic or commercial development—Eds.] had not been consistently applied and was being invoked with strictness here that could only demonstrate some other underlying motive. The court concluded that the buffer policy, though not always applied with perfect consistency, had on several occasions formed the basis for the Board's decision to deny other rezoning proposals. "The evidence does not necessitate a finding that Arlington Heights administered this policy in a discriminatory manner." 517 F.2d at 412. The Court of Appeals therefore approved the District Court's findings concerning the Village's purposes in denying rezoning to MHDC.

We also have reviewed the evidence. The impact of the Village's decision does arguably bear more heavily on racial minorities. Minorities constitute 18% of the Chicago area population, and 40% of the income groups said to be eligible for Lincoln Green. But there is little about the sequence of events leading up to the decision that would spark suspicion. The area around the Viatorian property has been zoned since 1959, the year when Arlington Heights first adopted a zoning map. Single-family homes surround the 80-acre site, and the Village is undeniably committed to single-family homes as its dominant residential land use. The rezoning request progressed according to the usual procedures. The Plan Commission even scheduled two additional hearings, at least in part to accommodate MHDC and permit it to supplement its presentation with answers to questions generated at the first hearing.

The statements by the Plan Commission and Village Board members, as reflected in the official minutes, focused almost exclusively on the zoning aspects of the MHDC petition, and the zoning factors on which they relied are not novel criteria in the Village's rezoning decisions. There is no reason to doubt that there has been reliance by some neighboring property owners on the maintenance of single-family zoning in the vicinity. The Village originally adopted its buffer policy long before MHDC entered the picture and has applied the policy too consistently for us to infer discriminatory purpose from its application in this case. Finally, MHDC called one member of the Village Board to the stand at trial. Nothing in her testimony supports an inference of invidious purpose.

In sum, the evidence does not warrant overturning the concurrent findings of both courts below. Respondents simply failed to carry their burden of proving that discriminatory purpose was a motivating factor in the Village's decision. This conclusion ends the constitutional inquiry. The Court of Appeals' further finding that the Village's decision carried a discriminatory "ultimate effect" is without independent constitutional significance.

V.

Respondents' complaint also alleged that the refusal to rezone violated the Fair Housing Act of 1968, 42 U.S.C. § 3601 *et. seq*. They continue to urge here that a zoning decision made by a public body may, and that petitioners' action did, violate § 3604 or § 3617. The Court of Appeals, however, proceeding in a somewhat unorthodox fashion, did not decide the statutory question. We remand the case for further consideration of respondents' statutory claims.

Reversed and remanded

Notes and Questions

1. As a preliminary matter you should note that, theoretically, there are various approaches to an analysis: (a) disproportionate impact is of itself sufficient to make out a *prima facie* case; (b) disproportionate impact may be sufficient but only in combination with some evidence of intent; (c) disproportionate impact can never be sufficient unless either the impact demonstrates intent or is itself so outrageous as to either permit an inference of intent or to be unjustifiable standing alone; (d) only intentional discrimination makes out a *prima facie* case and disproportionate impact may be some evidence, more or less probative, on the question of intent; or (e) only direct evidence of intent or strong circumstantial evidence from which intent can inferred will be sufficient. Where does *Arlington I* fall?

2. In footnote 21 of the *Arlington I* opinion, the Court discusses the "causation test" to be applied if there is proof that a decision was motivated in part by a racially discriminatory purpose. It concludes that such proof does not necessarily invalidate the decision, but merely shifts the burden to the decision-maker to establish that the same decision would have resulted even without the discriminatory motivation. In other words, the defendant may show that the discriminatory motivation is not the "cause" of the decision.

3. In its adoption of the "intent or purpose" test for the proof of prohibited discrimination, *Arlington I* treaded upon rather controversial territory. But, even before *Washington v. Davis,* the Court was tending away from expansionist equal protection theory.

For example, in *San Antonio Independent School District v. Rodriguez*, 411 U.S. 1 (1973), the Court held that relative economic deprivation did not violate equal protection at least when the benefit was not completely withheld. The Court rejected the argument that classifications premised on relative economic circumstances involved suspect classifications. Respecting the argument that housing is a fundamental right in the constitutional sense, we have already seen that there is no constitutionally protected right to housing. *Lindsey v. Normet*, Chapter 1, *supra*.

4. In *English v. Town of Huntington*, 448 F.2d 319 (2d Cir. 1971), minorities sued claiming that the town was dislocating minorities and not providing adequate relocation. Plaintiffs tried to make out an equal protection violation. There was no facial classification. The classification referred to condemnation of dilapidated houses. Based on "the dilapidated house classification," at the time of *English* there were at least four theories that might have been advanced to try to make out an equal protection violation:

> (a) Showing that only minorities who lived in dilapidated houses were being displaced, although nonminorities also lived in dilapidated houses. Such facts would bring the case within *Yick Wo v. Hopkins*, 118 U.S. 356 (1886) (municipal ordinance invalid which required all laundry owners not operating in brick

structures to secure a permit when permits are denied to all Chinese and granted to all whites, except one, who applied). Plaintiffs' facts would not support that theory, since some whites were displaced and no stark pattern of enforcement and non-relocation was shown.

(b) Showing that a "housing" classification was one that affected a "fundamental right." *But see Lindsey v. Normet*, *supra* (holding that housing is not a constitutionally protected fundamental right).

(c) Showing that the dilapidated house criterion was really one that created an "income" ("wealth" or "poverty") classification. But recall that the issue had been partially laid to rest in *Valtierra* and now perhaps has been definitely settled in *San Antonio School District v. Rodriguez.*

(d) Showing that the dilapidated house classification had a disproportionate impact on blacks and Puerto Ricans who were over-represented in the group of poor citizens who resided in dilapidated houses. The court in *English* recognized the point and dismissed it by noting that "it is an unpleasant fact of life that housing like this will be occupied by poor people, and still a more unpleasant one that black and Puerto Rican citizens are over-represented in that group." Was that a sufficient response?

5. The methodology of analyzing the equal protection issue is a subject of much discussion. Particularly troublesome has been the role of motivation, purpose, or intent, which the Supreme Court has now required to make out the equal protection violation. *See* Alan Brownstein, *Illicit Motive in the Municipal Land Use Regulation Process*, 57 U. Cin. L. Rev. (1988). *See generally* Laurence A. Alexander, *Introduction: Motivation and Constitutionality*, 15 San Diego L. Rev. 925 (1978); Paul Brest, Palmer v. Thompson: *An Approach to the Problem of Unconstitutional Legislative Motive*, 1971 Sup. Ct. Rev. 95; and John Hart Ely, *Legislative and Administrative Motivation in Constitutional Law*, 79 Yale L.J. 1205 (1970).

But there is not unanimous agreement that an inquiry into purpose or motive is necessary or helpful. *See* Kenneth L. Karst, *The Costs of Motive-Centered Inquiry*, 15 San Diego L. Rev. 1163 (1978); Arthur S. Miller, *If "The Devil Himself Knows Not the Mind of Man," How Possibly Can Judges Know the Motivation of Legislators?*, 15 San Diego L. Rev. 1167 (1978).

6. Various commentators have tried to work out the use of motive and theoretical foundations for its employment. *See* J. Morris Clark, *Legislative Motivation and Fundamental Rights in Constitutional Law*, 15 San Diego L. Rev. 953 (1978); Larry G. Simon, *Racially Prejudiced Governmental Actions: A Motivation Theory of the Constitutional Ban Against Racial Discrimination*, 15 San Diego L. Rev. 1041 (1978).

7. For a listing of five key problems posed by the intent test of *Washington v. Davis* as applied in *Arlington I,* see Charles E. Daye, *The Race, Class and Housing Conundrum: A Rationale and Proposal for a Legislative Policy of Suburban Inclusion*, 9 N.C. Cent. L.J. 37, 59–64 (1977). The proposal set forth was slightly reformulated and rationalized on different grounds in Charles E. Daye, Whither "Fair" Housing: Meditations on Wrong Paradigms, Ambivalent Answers, and a Legislative Proposal, 3 Wash. U. J.L. & Pol'y 241, 267–94 (2000).

8. Additional noteworthy insight about *Washington v. Davis* is provided in Theodore Eisenberg, *Disproportionate Impact and Illicit Motive: Theories of Constitutional Adjudication*, 52 N.Y.U. L. Rev. 36, 46–47 (1977):

> The Court's holding was motivated by its strong concern that a pure impact test "would raise serious questions about, and perhaps invalidate, a whole range

> of tax, welfare, public service, regulatory, and licensing statutes that may be more burdensome to the poor and to the average black man than to the more affluent white." The Court's concern is understandable; the specter of a judicially compelled proportionate society is a supportable reason for rejecting a pure impact test. But by imposing the additional requirement of intentional discrimination [*Washington v. Davis*] adopted a test which is simply unsatisfactory.
>
> [I]n summarily sweeping aside the many lower court cases that employed some form of impact test, the Court never paused to consider whether factors, other than intent, might justify relief under the equal protection clause. Nor did the Court explain why its rejection of a pure impact test inevitably led to a requirement that plaintiffs prove intentional discrimination. There are alternatives to the pure impact test short of requiring a showing of intentional discrimination. But the Court was so absorbed in advancing reasons for rejecting a pure impact test that it never considered these alternatives. [*Washington v. Davis*] seems to rest more on fear of a pure impact test than on the cogency of the standard it adopted.

9. The constitutional analysis is not the only perspective on *Arlington I*. There is the Court's reliance on the "zoning factors" present at the municipal level to sustain the village's refusal to rezone. For the argument that the Court's focus on the internal consistency of refusal to rezone was too narrow, and proposing that a broader community consistency and regional perspective should be employed, see Daniel R. Mandelker, *Racial Discrimination and Exclusionary Zoning: A Perspective on* Arlington Heights, 55 Tex. L. Rev. 1217 (1977).

10. Let's recapitulate: After *Arlington I*, what must a plaintiff show to make an equal protection case? Consider the following issues:

(a) What are the elements of the *prima facie* case?

(1) That plaintiff was excluded? *Query*: how can an excluded plaintiff be found to have standing? *See Warth v. Seldin*, 422 U.S. 490 (1975) (discussed in A Note on Standing in Federal Court, etc., in Chapter 2, *supra*).

(2) That plaintiff or members of plaintiff's class have been excluded?

(3) That there was a ready, willing, and able entity that would provide housing available to plaintiff but for the act of the defendant? *Query*: must plaintiff have made some contact or have some kind of preliminary commitment from the entity? How else to reckon "benefit"?

(4) That the challenged action was motivated, at least in part, by racial discrimination? *Query*: what if only one member of a multimember body can be shown to have had a racial motive? Does this mean there is no *prima facie* case, or does this go to the rebuttal of the case?

(b) Assuming plaintiff makes a *prima facie* case, how does defendant overcome it?

(1) Will the case be rebutted if defendant shows that the challenged action would have been taken even absent the discriminatory motivation?

(2) What burden of proof does defendant have to sustain to rebut the *prima facie* case? Is it a preponderance of the evidence, clear and convincing evidence, compelling reasons, or some other standard?

11. A good example of a finding of constitutionally prohibited discrimination in a housing context is *City of Cleburne v. Cleburne Living Center*, 473 U.S. 432 (1985). In

that case the city imposed a requirement that users of a dwelling as a home for persons with mental disabilities obtain a city permit, but required no permit for similar types of dwellings used for other purposes. The Supreme Court held that the requirement violated the Fourteenth Amendment's equal protection clause because the requirement reflected an irrational prejudice against mentally disabled persons and did not pose any special threat to the city's legitimate interests.

Note that *Cleburne* is really quite different from *Arlington I* in that *Cleburne* involves a classification made on the face of the statute, so the issue resolves into the question of whether the classification is permissible—a sort of one-step analysis (whether the discrimination is justified) where no issue of intent is presented since the terms of the statute express its intent. However, even with a rational basis review the court struck down the permit requirement because it could not find rational support for the special requirement applicable to the disability classification. Either this was "rational basis review with bite" or it was, in fact, the application of a standard that was more rigorous than traditional rational basis standards.

12. It is possible to assert constitutional issues, such as violation of the equal protection clause of the Fourteenth Amendment, only when governmental entities are involved or "state action" is otherwise present. *See generally Burton v. Wilmington Parking Auth.*, 365 U.S. 715 (1961), setting out reasons for the limitation to governmental action and discussing the test to be applied to determine when private parties become sufficiently involved with government to come under constitutional restrictions.

13. *See City of Cuyahoga Falls, Ohio v. Buckeye Community Hope Found.*, 538 U.S. 188 (2003). The City of Cuyahoga Falls passed an ordinance allowing Plaintiff—a non-profit developer—to build a proposed low-income housing development. But opposition developed and the city, under a provision of its Charter, submitted a referendum petition to voters that sought to repeal the ordinance. Under the City's Charter, the referendum petition stayed the site plan's implementation until its approval by the voters. Plaintiff sought, but was denied, an injunction against the petition, and the city engineer, on advice from the city law director, denied Plaintiff's request for building permits. The voters passed the referendum, thus repealing the ordinance but the Supreme Court of Ohio declared the referendum invalid under Ohio's Constitution. The City issued the building permits, and construction commenced. The low-income project was built despite the discriminatory citizen opposition. The Plaintiff, having been delayed in proceeding with construction, sued the City of Cuyahoga Falls to recover its costs caused by the delay alleging violations of equal protection based on the city's alleged complicity in the referendum. The Supreme Court cited *Arlington* in holding that neither the city's submission of the referendum petition to voters nor its refusal to issue building permits proved discriminatory intent required to sustain a claim on equal protection grounds.

14. *Alienage and Citizenship*. National origin, *Hernandez v. Texas*, 347 U.S. 475 (1954) and citizenship, *Bernal v. Fainter*, 467 U.S. 216 (1984) are deemed suspect classifications and generally subjected to strict scrutiny as in the case of race. But cf. *Ambach v. Norwick*, 441 U.S. 68 (1979) (allowing rational basis in matters touching on vital state interests such as public school teaching); *Hampton v. Mow Sun Wong*, 426 U.S. 88 (1976) (rational basis under federal legislation). While local ordinances or state law that would exclude aliens would violate equal protection as well as some federal and states civil rights legislation, the law is less clear on the issue of undocumented or illegal aliens. The federal government could arguably exclude the undocumented from federally-assisted housing, state and local government may be precluded from enacting laws that exclude or authorize housing providers to engage in discrimination. *See* Personal Responsibility and

Work Opportunity Reconciliation Act of 1996, Pub. L. No. 104-193, §§400–451, 110 Stat. 2105 (exempting certain aliens from exclusion from programs). In *Plyler v. Doe*, 457 U.S. 202 (1982), the Court invalidated the policy of Texas to exclude undocumented children from free public schooling, finding the policy irrational. The same reasoning might extend to public policies to exclude the undocumented from housing, both public and private. In addition to violating equal protection, such state and local authorization or obligation to exclude the undocumented may be preempted by the federal government's pervasive authority over immigration and naturalization under the supremacy clause. U.S. Const. Art. VI; Lozana v. City of Hazelton, 620 F.3d 170 (3d Cir. 2010) (invalidating local laws regulating access to housing and employment by undocumented under preemption); Garrett v. City of Escondido, 465 F. Supp. 2d 1043 (S.D. Cal. 2006) (preemption and due process). See generally 2 James A. Kushner, Government Discrimination: Equal Protection Law and Litigation §§5:6–5:10 (2009–2010) (fully on-line in Westlaw treatises).

You should keep in mind that we have looked only at the issue of a constitutional violation up to this point. We now turn to the issues of whether and, if so, when, there is a statutory basis for a claim, how that claim might be established, and how it may be defeated.

B. Legislative Fair Housing Policies: Governmental Duties

This is the first of two sections in which we consider statutory protections against discrimination. This section presents the development of duties placed on federal, state, and municipal entities when they act in the housing field. Of course, we have seen the many instances in which various governmental entities are involved: the federal government, principally as a provider of money for housing and community development assistance; the state government in a more limited role, principally as a conduit for selected federal money; and the local government, which acts—through its agencies—as developer and owner in the case of public housing, or as controller of location and as provider of essential services in the cases of all housing.

Fair housing implicates issues involving, for example, the problem of placement of assisted housing in a way that avoids creating geographic concentration within parts of a municipality; the problem of tenant selection which avoids racial concentration within developments; and the bigger problem of "dispersal" of assisted housing within geographic regions. In this section, the key problem is the interface of federal housing policy and the Civil Rights Acts of 1964 and 1968 together with various other sources of law such as Presidential Executive Orders. One problem that arises frequently concerns the role of the courts as instruments for both the interpretation of the duties the various levels of government have when they act in the housing area and the effective enforcement of rights which arise under the statutes as interpreted.

One cannot avoid the problems of federalism which arise when these issues are confronted. There are two major aspects of these problems. First, there is the generic issue of the effectiveness of judicial resolutions. Second, there is the practical problem of real or perceived limitations, which have shaped the development of the federal legislation. The ultimate questions, perhaps, are whether the legislation provides either clear commands or effective enforcement mechanisms; whether inherent ambiguity in the housing laws and the Civil Rights Acts can be resolved satisfactorily so as to make for sound housing and civil rights policies; whether the seeming conflicts between housing policies and civil rights policies are real or merely apparent; and finally whether new thrusts are needed to remedy deficiencies that may be discovered. There are thus four related tasks to be performed in working through this section (1) to analyze the housing laws and civil rights policies; (2) to understand the limits of the housing and civil rights laws, particularly from an effective enforcement standpoint; (3) to develop an appreciation for the difficulty of coordinating the housing and civil rights laws; and (4) to explore whether new or revised housing and civil rights laws or enforcement tools seem to be needed.

1. Federal Affirmative Duty to Promote Fair Housing

N.A.A.C.P., Boston Chapter v. Secretary of Housing and Community Development

United States Court of Appeals
817 F.2d 149 (1st Cir. 1987)

Before BOWNES, BREYER, and TORRUELLA, Circuit Judges.

BREYER, Circuit Judge.

The Federal Fair Housing Act (Title VIII of the Civil Rights Act of 1968) declares as its "policy" the provision of "fair housing throughout the United States." 42 U.S.C. § 3601. Its substantive provisions prohibit discrimination related to the rental or sale of places of dwelling. 42 U.S.C. §§ 3604–3606. In addition, it instructs the Secretary of Housing and Urban Development to "administer the programs and activities relating to housing and urban development in a manner affirmatively to further the policies of this [Fair Housing Act]...." 42 U.S.C. § 3608(e)(5). The specific question raised in this appeal is whether federal courts have the legal authority to review claims that the Secretary has failed to carry out this last instruction. The district court believed that, at least where the Secretary has not acted with a discriminatory purpose, the Secretary's compliance with § 3608(e)(5) is a matter that Congress has "committed to agency discretion by law." 5 U.S.C. § 701(a)(2). Accordingly, it held that it could not legally review the appellant's claims of violation and it dismissed the case. We believe, however, that the court has the power to review appellant's claim that the Secretary has not "administer[ed]" certain HUD programs "in a manner affirmatively to further" the Act's basic policy. Hence, we reverse the district court's dismissal and remand the case for further proceedings.

I

Nearly nine years ago, in April 1978, the NAACP sued the Secretary and other officials of the Department of Housing and Urban Development (collectively "HUD") claiming that HUD had failed "to enforce constitutional and statutory proscriptions against discrimination in Federally-assisted programs." Its complaint listed various acts and omissions related to HUD's administration of its Community Development Block Grant (CDBG) and Urban Development Action Grant (UDAG) programs in the City of Boston, which acts and omissions, it said, taken together, establish violations of various civil rights statutes, including HUD's duty "affirmatively to further" the Fair Housing Act's policies.

In 1983, the district court after trial found, as factual matters, that Boston has a history of racial discrimination in housing; that Boston suffers from a shortage of low-income family housing; that a higher proportion of black than white families are renters and a higher proportion of black than white renters are families with children (and thus that the housing shortage impacts more heavily on blacks than on whites); that Boston's neighborhoods are racially separate; and that "at least in part [as] the result of the lack of safe, desegregated housing in white neighborhoods" black families find it difficult to move out of black areas. *NAACP v. Harris*, 567 F. Supp. 637, 640–41 (D. Mass. 1983). The court also found that both city and federal officials were aware of these facts; that the city had not effectively enforced fair housing requirements; that neither the city nor HUD had sought to obtain or to provide UDAG funds for low-income housing; and that HUD had not obtained from the city the assessment of "any special needs of identifiable segments of the lower income population" that HUD regulations then required. *Id.* at 641–43.

In the court's view, these facts added up both to a violation of HUD's "minority housing needs" regulation and to a violation of HUD's Title VIII duty "affirmatively to further" the Act's policy. In particular, it wrote that HUD's failure to use its "immense leverage under UDAG" to provide "desegregated housing so that the housing stock is sufficiently large to give minority families a true choice of location," in the context of Boston's history and practices, violated HUD's Title VIII obligations. *Id.* at 644.

In late 1985, after the parties had submitted proposed forms of judgment, the district court decided that it could not enter an order granting relief from the legal violations that it had found. The court noted that in 1982 HUD had obtained from the city an acceptable "minority needs assessment," and held that HUD had thereby cured the violation of its own regulations, rendering further relief inappropriate. *NAACP v. Pierce*, 624 F. Supp. 1083, 1085 (D. Mass. 1985). The court also determined that it could not grant relief from the Title VIII violation because it did not have the legal authority to review the Secretary's compliance with the "affirmative furtherance" mandate. *Id.* at 1086–93. It held that Congress had not created any "private right of action" to enforce Title VIII's legal obligation, and that it could not review the Secretary's actions under the Administrative Procedure Act, 5 U.S.C. § 551 *et seq.*, because Congress had "committed" compliance with the obligation "to agency discretion," 5 U.S.C. § 701(a)(2). The court accordingly dismissed the NAACP's claims. The NAACP now appeals this dismissal.

[The court next discussed in part II of its opinion whether Title VIII bestowed a private right of action upon individuals against the federal government and found that there was no need for such an action. For discussion of that issue, *see* Chapter 2, *supra.*—Eds.]

III
The Substantive Claim

The government argues that § 3608(e)(5) imposes upon HUD only an obligation not to discriminate. It says that HUD's actions violate its obligations under Title VIII *only* when HUD engages in discriminatory conduct or when it funds a grantee who is engaged in such discriminatory conduct with the purpose of furthering the grantee's discrimination. [emphasis in original]. Since the district court found neither actual discrimination by HUD nor an effort purposely to further the discrimination of others, HUD, in the government's view, could not have violated § 3608(e)(5).

We do not agree that HUD's Title VIII obligations are as limited as the government claims. Rather, a statute that instructs HUD to administer its grant programs so as "affirmatively to further" the Act's fair housing policy requires something more of HUD than simply to refrain from discriminating itself or purposely aiding the discrimination of others. For one thing, as the government states its Title VIII obligation, it sounds very much like (and perhaps even less than) the obligation that the Fifth Amendment would impose upon HUD even in the absence of Title VIII. *See Washington v. Davis*, 426 U.S. 229 (1976). Yet, the history of Title VIII suggests that its framers meant to do more than simply restate HUD's existing legal obligations. *See* 114 Cong. Rec. 2281 (1968) (statement of Sen. Brooke) (a purpose of Title VIII is to remedy the "weak intentions" that have led to the federal government's "sanctioning discrimination in housing throughout this Nation"); *id.* at 2526–28 (statement of Sen. Brooke) (reviewing history of federal fair housing efforts); *id.* at 9577 (statement of Rep. Cohelan) (decrying historical "neglect" of minorities); *id.* at 9595 (statement of Rep. Pepper) (lamenting government's slowness in establishing truly "equal" rights); *see also, Clients' Council v. Pierce*, 711 F.2d 1406, 1425 (8th Cir. 1983) (holding that even if facts do not establish constitutional violation by HUD, they still establish violation of affirmative duty under Title VIII).

For another thing, as a matter of language and of logic, a statute that instructs an agency "affirmatively to further" a national policy of nondiscrimination would seem to impose an obligation to do more than simply not discriminate itself. If one assumes that many private persons and local governments have practiced discrimination for many years and that at least some of them might be tempted to continue to discriminate even though forbidden to do so by law, it is difficult to see how HUD's own nondiscrimination by itself could significantly "further" the ending of such discrimination by others.

Further, the legislative history does not support so constricted a reading of the statute. [The court reviewed statements of various members of Congress.—Eds.] This broader goal suggests an intent that HUD do more than simply not discriminate itself; it reflects the desire to have HUD use its grant programs to assist in ending discrimination and segregation, to the point where the supply of genuinely open housing increases. This view of the effect that Congress intended is at odds with the government's very narrow view of its obligation.

Finally, every court that has considered the question has held or stated that Title VIII imposes upon HUD an obligation to do more than simply refrain from discriminating (and from purposely aiding discrimination by others). Furthermore, the Supreme Court itself has identified the goal of Title VIII as "replace[ment of] ghettos 'by truly integrated and balanced living patterns.'" *Trafficante v. Metropolitan Life Insurance Co.*, 409 U.S. 205, 211 (1972) (quoting 114 Cong. Rec. 3422 (statement of Sen. Mondale)).

The government relies upon a recent Eleventh Circuit case, *Anderson v. City of Alpharetta*, 737 F.2d 1530 (11th Cir. 1984), as support for its narrow view of HUD's duties. In *Anderson*, a class of plaintiffs sued HUD, claiming that HUD had illegally failed to counteract "the deliberate footdragging of local governments" in constructing low-income public housing, which local delay the plaintiffs said was racially motivated. The Eleventh Circuit, in affirming dismissal for failure to state a claim, wrote that HUD itself is liable under Title VIII only

> first, when HUD has taken discriminatory action itself, such as approving federal assistance for a public housing project without considering its effect on the racial and socio-economic composition of the surrounding area; and second, when HUD is aware of a grantee's discriminatory practices and has made

> no effort to force it into compliance with the Fair Housing Act by cutting off existing federal financial assistance to the agency in question.

This formulation, even if overly narrow, still does not support the government's view of HUD's duties. It does not limit HUD's liability to purposive support of discrimination by others, nor does it limit HUD's "discriminatory action" to activity that itself forecloses housing opportunities on the basis of race. Rather, it includes within the scope of such action a failure to "consider [the] effect [of a HUD grant] on the racial and socio-economic composition of the surrounding area." And, the need for such consideration itself implies, at a minimum, an obligation to assess negatively those aspects of a proposed course of action that would further limit the supply of genuinely open housing and to assess positively those aspects of a proposed course of action that would increase that supply. If HUD is doing so in any meaningful way, one would expect to see, over time, if not in any individual case, HUD activity that tends to increase, or at least, that does not significantly diminish, the supply of open housing.

Having concluded that HUD's obligations under Title VIII extend beyond what the government claims, we must reject its request that we affirm the judgment below on the ground that HUD has not violated any legal obligation. The district court's opinions state a plausible case of a violation of HUD's obligations, even under the minimal standard set forth in the last paragraph. The district court stated, *inter alia*:

> 1) In the case of the City of Boston ... HUD's] efforts to ensure fair housing have been ineffective. It has accepted from the City cosmetic changes in the form of a Mayor's Office of Fair Housing and some public relations efforts instead of genuine enforcement.
>
> 2) [I]t had not required the City to establish an effective fair housing program in the face of knowledge of pervasive racial discrimination in the City.
>
> 3) The financing of desegregated housing so that the housing stock is sufficiently large to give minority families a true choice of location seems ... to be a[n] ... obligation of HUD under ... Title VIII.
>
> 4) [HUD] has not used any of its immense leverage under UDAG to provide adequate desegregated housing, except for Mission Park, which was not a project sponsored by the City.

These, and other roughly similar statements in the court's opinions, read as if the court had more in mind than a crude legal standard requiring HUD to provide housing for all those in need. We agree that HUD has no such obligation. *See* 114 Cong. Rec. 4975 (statement of Sen. Mondale) (policy "to provide ... for fair housing" is not a mandate to "provide housing" but only to "eliminate discrimination in the sale or rental of housing"). Rather, the court's statements read like an affirmative response to a claim that HUD's pattern of grant activity in Boston reflects a failure, over time, to take seriously its minimal Title VIII obligation to evaluate alternative courses of action in light of their direct effect upon housing.

Whether the district court's findings are adequately supported by the evidence, whether in context they make out a violation of law, whether and to what extent Title VIII obliges HUD to do even more than the minimum that we have stated in this opinion, all are legal questions that we do not—and indeed cannot—decide on this appeal. They are not squarely presented by the case in its present posture and the parties have not argued them. Given the nature of the record and the parties' arguments here, we find only the existence of a plausible claim of a Title VIII violation. We therefore decline the government's invitation to affirm on the alternative ground that HUD engaged only in legally permissible behavior.

IV

[In part IV of its opinion, the court discussed the reviewability of HUD's conduct under the federal Administrative Procedure Act. For discussion of that issue, see Chapter 2, *supra*. On the question of the federal agency's obligation for fair housing, the court continued.—Eds.]

Rather, here the court must decide whether, over time, HUD's pattern of activity reveals a failure to live up to its obligation. The standard for reviewing that pattern can be drawn directly from the statutory instruction to "administer" its programs "in a manner affirmatively to further the policies" of "fair housing." 42 U.S.C. §§ 3601 and 3608(e)(5). This standard, like many, may be difficult to apply to borderline instances, yet a court should be able to determine a clear failure to live up to the instruction over time. It should be able to determine whether the agency's practice, over time, in respect to this mandate has been "arbitrary, capricious, an abuse of discretion, or otherwise not in accordance with law." 5 U.S.C. § 706(2)(A). Doing so, in the context of a claim of serious failure over time to try to further Title VIII's goals, need not involve the court in "superintend[ing] economic and managerial decisions," or in reweighing matters that Congress has asked HUD to balance. Rather, this case seems to call for a more straightforward evaluation of whether agency activity over time has furthered the statutory goal, and, if not, for an explanation of why not and a determination of whether a given explanation, in light of the statute, is satisfactory. *See* 5 K. Davis, Administrative Law Treatise § 28.7, at 283 ("Courts that are unqualified to exercise particular discretion are often ... qualified to determine whether that discretion has been abused"). Such a case, obviously, is not easy to try, or to decide. Yet, we do not see how, or why, it is any more difficult than other civil rights cases in which courts have judged the lawfulness of agency behavior against roughly analogous standards.

Nor does it seem different, in principle, from other cases in which courts have reviewed agency activity for abuse of discretion granted by even more generally worded statutes. Of course, we do not mean to say that individual grant decisions are not reviewable under this statute—in appropriate cases they may be reviewable—but even if some, many, or all of them are not, nonetheless in the kind of "pattern or practice" case before us there is "law to apply." *Citizens to Preserve Overton Park v. Volpe*, 401 U.S. 402, 410 (1971). Third, and perhaps most important, we do not believe that judicial review of this kind of claim threatens unwarranted interference with HUD's ability to carry out its basic statutory missions. This is so for the reasons stated in the last paragraph. The legal claim before us is not that, in the case of any particular decision, HUD must promote desegregation. Rather, the NAACP asks for review of a series of decisions to determine whether, taken together, they violate the obligation to further the goals of Title VIII. To make this determination does not threaten a large number of legal challenges or otherwise impair HUD's ability to make grants. We do not see how a one-time review of HUD's practices under an "abuse of discretion" standard can pose a serious threat to the agency's effectiveness.

Fourth, it does not seem impossible here for the court to develop an appropriate remedy. Of course, the court faces the difficult task of avoiding both remedies that may be too intrusive, interfering with HUD's ability to carry out its basic grant awarding mission, and those that may prove to be ineffective. This difficulty is not, however, unsolvable. We do not see any reason why the court cannot effectively ensure HUD's future responsible exercise of discretion while at the same time preserving for the agency its discretionary options. In formulating its remedy, of course, the district court may, as it has already done, seek the advice and participation of HUD.

Just as we express no view now on the legal merits of the claims of violation, so we express no view on the remedies that may be appropriate. This task is to be undertaken by the district court in light of all the evidence, including any relevant events that may have occurred since the court rendered its initial decision. We state simply that the problems of devising a remedy do not seem insurmountable to the point where a conclusion of nonreviewability is warranted.

In sum, we do not believe the legal claims raised here fall within the APA's exception for "action committed to agency discretion by law."

V.

[The court discussed in part V whether the court had authority to grant relief upon reviewing HUD's conduct and whether it could compel HUD to take action. The court concluded that adequate power existed.—Eds.]

The decision of the district court is vacated and the case is remanded for further proceedings consistent with this opinion.

Notes and Questions

1. The portion of the case that deals with other procedural issues in the case is set forth in Chapter 2, *supra*.

2. Having found that there was a basis for review and a violation, the case was remanded. The following case is an excerpt from the District Court's Order in compliance with the remand for further consideration.

N.A.A.C.P., Boston Chapter v. Kemp

United States District Court
721 F. Supp. 361 (D. Mass. 1989)
clarified and amended, (Sept. 14, 1989)

MEMORANDUM AND ORDER FOR JUDGMENT

SKINNER, District Judge.

The plaintiff N.A.A.C.P., Boston Chapter ("NAACP") seeks injunctive and declaratory relief, on the grounds that the Secretary and other officials of the United States Department of Housing and Urban Development (collectively "HUD") have failed to administer certain programs in the City of Boston "in a manner affirmatively to further the policies of [the Federal Fair Housing Act, Title VIII of the Civil Rights Act of 1968]" ("the Act"), in violation of HUD's obligations under 42 U.S.C. § 3608(e)(5).

[The court discussed the background and developments that had transpired in the case, noted that a mediation effort had failed to produce any agreement between the parties, set forth and considered requests for relief the plaintiffs made and objections defendants advanced, and entered a declaratory judgment as to the nature of the violations, the defendant's liability, and the relief required to remedy the violations. It then entered an order which is excerpted below.—Eds.]

ORDER

A declaratory judgment and final decree shall enter forthwith in accordance with the foregoing.

DECLARATORY JUDGMENT AND FINAL DECREE

After a trial in this action for declaratory and injunctive relief, and after consideration of the parties' submissions with respect to remedies and in accordance with the memorandum filed herewith:

I. *Declaratory Relief*

It is Declared that:

A. During the period 1977 to 1982, in administering its programs and activities relating to housing and urban development in the City of Boston ("the City"), HUD did not satisfy minimum levels of compliance with Title VIII of the Civil Rights Act of 1968, 42 U.S.C. § 3608(e)(5), as amended, to administer its programs and activities in a manner affirmatively to further the policies of fair housing by:

1. Failing to promulgate regulations or guidelines which adequately set forth standards for HUD's administration and recipients' use of funds under HUD programs;

2. Failing to secure a minority needs assessment from the City in a timely manner;

3. Failing adequately to condition and monitor use of its funding by grantees and recipients, so as to assure the use of these monies to produce an adequate supply of affordable integrated family housing; and

4. Failing to require effective fair housing enforcement by the City.

B. In light of HUD's failure to comply with its statutory mandate, and the resultant lack of affordable desegregated housing, Metropolitan Area relief is appropriate under these circumstances, and to the extent provided in this Decree.

II. *Remedial Order*

It is Ordered that:

A. *Metropolitan Area Relief*

HUD shall require the owners and managers of any assisted public or private housing within any city or town within the Boston Metropolitan Statistical Area, including Boston ("the Metropolitan Area"), to participate fully in available programs designed to facilitate access to suburban housing opportunities for low-income minority households now living in the City. These programs shall include, without limitation, the listing requirements and affirmative marketing programs created pursuant to Section II.C.3 of this Decree.

The requirements of this Decree shall apply with equal force to all assisted housing in the Metropolitan Area. "Assisted Housing" means housing the cost of whose purchase, development, operation or rehabilitation is subsidized in whole or in part with public funds or other resources, whether such funds or resources derive from federal, state or local government.

In enforcing this Decree, HUD shall use any power it possesses to impose conditions on grantees, recipients, or beneficiaries, pursuant to any grant or any other program.

B. *Fair Housing Conditions Upon Funding to the Commonwealth of Massachusetts*

Following entry of this Decree, HUD shall include in any approval of an application for funding by the Commonwealth, under any grant or other program administered by

HUD pursuant to which it has the power to impose conditions upon grantees or recipients, the following conditions:

1. That the Commonwealth require owners and operators of any state-assisted public or private housing available for rental or sale in the Metropolitan Area to participate fully in programs designed to enhance access to low-income housing by Black households, including but not limited to, Section 8 rental subsidies and the listing and affirmative marketing programs created pursuant to Sections II.C.3 of this Decree.

2. That the Commonwealth promulgate legislation granting the Boston Fair Housing Commission ("the Commission") effective enforcement powers, including but not limited to, the power to issue subpoenas, levy fines and institute civil actions;

3. That the Commonwealth prepare and provide such reports and statements regarding assisted housing in the Metropolitan Area as are required from time to time by HUD. Such submissions shall include, without limitation, reports on the racial and family composition of state-assisted housing, and a statement of the projected use of funds and community development plan, as required by 42 U.S.C. § 5304.

C. *Fair Housing Conditions Upon Funding to the City*

Following entry of this Decree, HUD shall include in any approval of an application for funding by the City, under any grant or other program administered by HUD pursuant to which it has the power to impose conditions upon grantees or recipients, the following conditions:

1. That the City require the owners and operators of any City-assisted public or private housing available for rental or sale to participate fully in programs designed to enhance access to low-income housing by low-income Black households, including but not limited to Section 8 rental subsidies and the listing and affirmative marketing programs created pursuant to Section II.C.3 of this Decree.

2. That the City promulgate an amendment to its Fair Housing Ordinance eliminating the exemption of housing consisting of five or fewer units;

3. That within 60 days after HUD's approval of the application, the City design and submit to HUD and the plaintiff and, upon HUD's approval, implement a Fair Housing Program, to be administered by the Commission, including, without limitation, the following components:

a. *A Boston Housing Opportunity Clearing Center*, in which shall be listed all assisted public or private housing units available for sale or rental in the Metropolitan Area, which are required to be listed by this Decree or any other authority, or any private units which are offered for listing by their owners or operators;

b. *A Fair Housing Law Enforcement Program*, designed to identify and alleviate racially discriminatory practices in the sale and rental of housing in the City, which shall, without limitation:

(i) Hear and investigate complaints of discriminatory practices;

(ii) Bring administrative and judicial proceedings against persons engaging in discriminatory practices;

(iii) Assist victims of discrimination by providing information as to rights and available remedies, and referrals to legal services organizations and private attorneys available to assist in discrimination claims.

c. *An Affirmative Marketing Program* pursuant to 24 C.F.R. § 200.620, which requires the owners and operators of assisted housing in the City to pursue affirmative fair housing marketing policies in soliciting buyers and tenants, in determining their eligibility, and in concluding sales and rental transactions.

The Plan shall be designed to enhance the availability to persons of color of housing in neighborhoods which are now predominantly white. The goal of the Plan and its measure of success shall be to achieve a racial composition in assisted housing, in neighborhoods which are predominantly white, which reflects the racial composition of the City as a whole.

d. *A Fair Housing Public Education Program* designed to make use of various public forums, such as broadcast media, bill boards, and community and social service organizations, to inform the public of rights and available remedies under applicable fair housing and anti-discrimination laws and regulations, including but not limited to, the existence and functions of the Commission, the Clearing Center, and of the other components of the Fair Housing Program;

4.That the City prepare and submit to HUD such reports and statements regarding assisted housing as are required from time to time by HUD. Such submissions shall include, without limitation, a report on the racial and family composition of assisted housing, and a plan for the projected use of funds for community development, as required by 42 U.S.C. § 5304.

D. *Stock of Affordable Housing*

1. HUD shall use its best efforts and available resources to increase the supply of affordable integrated family housing in the City, whether public, public-assisted, or private.

2. HUD shall not agree to any disposition of HUD-assisted housing which has the effect of reducing the supply of affordable family housing in the City available as of the effective date of his Decree.

III. *Monitoring and Reports*

Commencing three months after the effective date of this Decree and every six months thereafter, HUD shall submit to the court and serve upon the plaintiff:

A. A report prepared by HUD or its grantees setting forth the current racial makeup, family composition and vacancy rate of HUD assisted housing projects or units in the City;

B. A report describing the activities carried out and the results achieved in implementing this Decree.

IV. *Retention of Jurisdiction*

A. Jurisdiction is retained by the court for the purpose of enabling the plaintiff and HUD to apply to the court at any time for such further orders as may be necessary or appropriate for the construction, implementation, modification or enforcement of this Decree.

B. At any time after the fifth anniversary of the effective date, either HUD or the plaintiff may request the court to review the progress made in implementing this Decree, and, based upon such review, to modify or terminate any and all rights or obligations provided therein.

C. If HUD is unable to comply with its obligations under this Decree, for lack of authorization or any other reason, the plaintiff may move for such comparable alternative relief as is appropriate.

Notes and Questions

1. Do you find the order to be "expansive?" Does it seem to be justified by the violations found? What do you imagine will happen to the degree of integration in housing over the course of years in the City of Boston? If one were to find that the level of housing availability and integration are essentially unchanged, what reason might explain those circumstances?

2. Finding an effective remedy in protracted, complex institutional reform litigation is problematic. This topic is discussed in depth in Chapter 2, *supra*.

3. *N.A.A.C.P., Boston Chapter* is a kind of institutional reform litigation. When does this kind of litigation reach a definitive conclusion? When are the courts finished with the litigation and its ramifications? In reflecting on this question you may wish to make a note to reconsider this question when you reach the *Gautreaux* cases *infra.* But for now, in the next case, let's take a look at the continuing issues and litigation in Boston.

Raso v. Lago

United States Court of Appeals
135 F.3d 11 (1st. Cir. 1998)
cert. denied, 525 U.S. 811 (1998)

Before SELYA, BOUDIN and STAHL, Circuit Judges.

BOUDIN, Circuit Judge.

[Plaintiffs are former residents of Boston's Old West End who were forced to relocate, pursuant to an urban renewal plan dating back to 1956, when their homes were taken by eminent domain in furtherance of that plan. They sue among others, HUD, the City of Boston, the Boston Redevelopment Authority ("the BRA"), and the developer of a new development called West End Place. Plaintiffs allege that they are being denied their statutory preference in West End Place because most former West Enders are white notwithstanding that former West Enders were to have first preference in the purchase or rental of residential units in West End Place, subject to applicable local, state, and federal laws.

In 1991, following the Order entered in *NAACP, Boston Chapter v. Kemp* above, HUD entered into a consent decree to end litigation over HUD's duties to foster integrated housing. The consent decree provided that all Boston area HUD affirmative fair housing marketing plans have as their goal the achievement of a racial composition, in HUD-assisted housing located in neighborhoods which are predominantly white, which reflects the racial composition of the City of Boston as a whole.

The developer, the government agencies, and the Old West End Housing Corporation, comprised *inter alia* of former West Enders, submitted the matter to mediation. The mediator, a former United States Attorney for Massachusetts, proposed that former West Enders receive a preference as to 55% of the units in West End Place, and all other applicants have equal access to the remaining 45%. The developer and the agencies agreed; the Old West End Housing Corporation, did not. Nevertheless, the mediator's solution was included in the developer's affirmative fair housing marketing plan, which HUD approved in 1996.

The plan operates as follows: West End Place contains 183 residential units that fall into three rent-based categories: 58 "low-income" units (subsidized by HUD funds), 48 "moderate-income units," and 77 units to be rented at market rates. Under the plan, the developer is to give former West Enders first preference as to 101 of 183 units, that is,

55% of the total. These 101 units are unevenly distributed over the three rent categories: former West Enders have a preference as to 19 low-income units (33%), 24 moderate-income units (50%), and 58 market-rate units (75%).

On September 26, 1996, the individual plaintiffs—four former West Enders—filed a complaint in the district court challenging the tenant selection process and the plan on numerous grounds; they purported to represent former West Enders as a class. The district court dismissed all claims with prejudice and entered judgment for the defendants.

The former West Enders appeal from the dismissal of only two of the numerous claims they made in the district court: first, a claim under 42 U.S.C. § 1983 that the plan violates equal protection principles because it comprises a forbidden racial classification, and second, a claim that section 49 creates a trust that subjects the BRA and developer to a trustee's fiduciary duties in favor of the former West Enders. Only the Court's discussion of the first claim is set forth.—Eds.]

We begin with section 1983, which pertinently provides that no person may deprive any person of his or her constitutional rights under color of state law. 42 U.S.C. § 1983. The City of Boston and the BRA are both "state actors," and the BRA played a central role in developing and fostering the plan challenged by plaintiffs. HUD is a federal entity not subject to section 1983, but its officials are directly constrained by equal protection principles.

In their complaint, the former West Enders allege that race was a motive for curtailing the statutory preference otherwise available to them. Specifically, the complaint cites the defendants' reliance upon the consent decree as comprising a racial purpose and goal and asserts that, as a result, the former West Enders were deprived of a benefit—a statutory preference for all of the apartments—based upon "a racial classification." In their appeal brief, plaintiffs' shorthand version is that the preference was curtailed "because" the former West Enders were predominantly white.

Factual assertions in a complaint are normally accepted as true for purposes of a motion to dismiss; in addition, the defendants do not dispute that racial concerns and the consent decree prompted their effort to cut back upon the statutory preference. The reason is apparent: the former West Enders are almost entirely white, and without some limitation on the preference rights of former West Enders, HUD would have been funding subsidized apartments from which minorities were effectively excluded.

HUD apparently thought that this outcome would violate the consent decree and its statutory obligation to promote fair housing. *See* 42 U.S.C. §§ 3601–3619 (1994); 24 C.F.R. §§ 200.600–200.640 (1997). HUD may have misunderstood both the consent decree and the federal statute, but whether it did or not, its purpose to increase minority opportunities for apartments in West End Place by curtailing the statutory preference is evident. To this end, it appears that HUD simply declined to authorize funding unless and until some of the apartments were made available to applicants other than former West Enders.

This undenied racial motive distinguishes the case from those others involving facially neutral actions—like a zoning law or employee qualification test—where the state actor denies any racial purpose or concern.[5] But the plaintiffs are mistaken in treating "racial

5. *See, e.g., Village of Arlington Heights v. Metropolitan Hous. Dev. Corp.*, 429 U.S. 252, 270–71 (1977) (upholding a refusal to rezone property to allow construction of multi-dwelling buildings); *Washington v. Davis*, 426 U.S. 229 (1976) (upholding a police department literacy exam that excluded mostly black applicants).

motive" as a synonym for a constitutional violation. Every antidiscrimination statute aimed at racial discrimination, and every enforcement measure taken under such a statute, reflect a concern with race. That does not make such enactments or actions unlawful or automatically "suspect" under the Equal Protection Clause.

It is quite true that government action taken out of hostility to a racial group can be condemned out of hand, *e.g. Yick Wo v. Hopkins,* 118 U.S. 356 (1886), but there is no allegation whatever in the complaint that the defendants were hostile to whites. Nor would any such motive be remotely plausible. Benign intentions do not immunize government action, but they substantially narrow the inquiry. The primary test is that any government action—regardless of benign intent—is suspect if it has been taken on the basis of a "racial classification"; in such cases, the classification must be justified by a compelling state interest and narrow tailoring. *See Adarand Constructors, Inc. v. Pena,* 515 U.S. 200 (1995).

Despite the use of the "racial classification" label, the complaint alleges no facts that would bring that label into play. The term normally refers to a governmental standard, preferentially favorable to one race or another, for the distribution of benefits. *E.g.,* [*Adarand Constructors, Inc. v. Pena,* 515 U.S. 200—Eds.] at 226–27; *City of Richmond v. J.A. Croson Co.,* 488 U.S. 469 (1989) (plurality opinion). Yet under the plan adopted in this case, the apartments freed from the statutory preference are made available to all applicants regardless of race.

West End Place was built with federal help and its apartments made especially desirable through federal subsidies. It might not seem remarkable that the government should insist, as a condition of this investment, that a fair number of the apartments should be effectively open to application by tenants of all races. Nor have we been able to find any case where the government has been required to show a compelling interest, or narrow tailoring of remedies, for a condition framed so as to secure equal treatment of applicants regardless of race.

Language in a few Supreme Court decisions could be taken to mean that any action in which race plays a role is constitutionally suspect. However, the governmental actions in those cases were fundamentally different and more provocative. In *Adarand,* the statute gave special incentives to government contractors to hire minority subcontractors.[6] The redistricting cases concern state voting districts designed to concentrate minority voters and effectively to reserve seats for minority candidates.[7]

Taken by itself, HUD's action in this case is almost the opposite of the racial preferences that the Court viewed as questionable in *Adarand* and the redistricting cases. Here, the government's condition on federal funds was that some of the apartments—which otherwise would have almost automatically been occupied by whites—be made available to all applicants on a race-blind basis. We cannot view this as a "racial classification" reserving benefits for a favored race, or as "an effort to segregate the races."

Several other equal protection arguments made by the former West Enders need no lengthy discussion, either because they have been essentially abandoned on appeal or because they are clearly unpersuasive. The former category includes the former West Enders' attack on HUD requirements that the apartments be publicized in minority communities;[8]

---

6. *See Adarand,* 515 U.S. at 205–06; *see also Croson,* 488 U.S. at 493–94; *Wygant v. Jackson Bd. of Educ.,* 476 U.S. 267, 279–80 (1986) (plurality opinion); R. Rotunda & J. Nowak, *Constitutional Law* § 18.10(a)(1) (2d ed. 1992 & Supp.1997).

7. *See Bush v. Vera,* 517 U.S. 952, 965–67 (1996) (plurality opinion); *Miller v. Johnson,* 515 U.S. 900, 906–09 (1995); *Shaw v. Reno,* 509 U.S. 630, 635–36 (1993).

8. HUD's regulations require affirmative outreach in both majority and minority communities, *see* 24 C.F.R. § 200.620(a); and in any case outreach efforts are not the real source of the plaintiffs' prob-

the latter includes the attempt to charge HUD with treating the consent decree's numerical "goal" as if it were a quota—a notion belied by the substantial preference retained for the former West Enders.

The story, however, is not quite over. It is one thing for HUD to insist that the apartments it subsidizes must effectively be open to all races; it would be quite another if HUD planned to impose this requirement only where the beneficiaries of the statutory preference were white. That, we think, would be government action based on a "racial classification" and would need to be narrowly tailored to serve a compelling government interest.

The difficulty is that we are dealing here with an ad hoc administrative action. Accepting the truth of the complaint's factual allegations, HUD's actions were prompted not by any general, racially skewed policy toward statutory preferences but by the peculiar interplay of Boston's consent decree, the Massachusetts statute, and the respective racial makeups of the Boston population and the former West Enders. What HUD would do in some other, hypothetical case is unknown, but it is certainly not precluded, either by the consent decree or anything else, from challenging statutory preferences that exclude whites. Cf. *Otero v. New York City Hous. Auth.*, 484 F.2d 1122, 1125 (2d Cir. 1973).

The plaintiffs have alleged no facts that, if proven, would reveal any secret discriminatory standard, pattern of past practice, or motive beyond the one HUD has admitted, namely HUD's concern that the preference in this instance, if unmodified, would restrict the apartments to whites and subject HUD to sanctions under the consent decree. Plaintiffs simply think that this purpose is enough to condemn HUD's action. For the reasons already given, we do not.

This is a case that stirs conflicting sympathies, for those ousted from their West End neighborhood by "urban renewal" many years ago no less than for minorities wrongly denied fair housing opportunities in Boston. But we have properly sought to decide this appeal based upon Supreme Court precedent, as best we can discern it, recognizing that the case is a difficult and unusual one on the edge of developing law.

Affirmed.

STAHL, Circuit Judge, dissenting in part.

There is for me considerable appeal in the majority's resolution of plaintiffs' equal protection claims. The governmental conduct these claims challenge involves a patently good faith and facially reasonable effort to accommodate the competing interests of two historic losers in Boston's housing wars: the racial and ethnic minorities entitled to invoke the protections of the consent decree in *NAACP v. Kemp* and federal fair housing laws, and the former West Enders, an ethnically diverse, lower middle class group which, in the name of "urban renewal," was forced from its neighborhood and could not afford to return.

Nonetheless, I cannot join the portion of the majority opinion that affirms the district court's pleadings-based dismissal of the equal protection claims. While I agree with the majority that reverse discrimination claims like the present one are "on the edge of developing law," I do think it settled that, when the government withdraws benefits from a class of citizens because of the race or ethnicity of the class, courts are to scrutinize strictly the government's conduct so as to ensure that it furthers a compelling governmental interest and is narrowly tailored to advance that interest. *See Adarand.* For the

---

lem—rather, it is the partial loss of their preference. The defendants are no less guilty of muddling the issue in their pretense that outreach efforts are all that are involved in this case.

reasons that follow, I believe plaintiffs' complaint fairly alleges such a withdrawal of benefits. And I do not see how we can, at this stage of the litigation, conclude that such a withdrawal of benefits passes strict scrutiny.

The complaint alleges that the governmental defendants curtailed plaintiffs' statutory preference in order to comply with the consent decree in *NAACP v. Kemp*. Because the purpose of that consent decree is "the achievement of a racial composition, in HUD-assisted housing located in neighborhoods which are predominantly white, which reflects the racial composition of the City of Boston as a whole," a reasonable inference to be drawn from plaintiffs' complaint, is that defendants acted as they did because the putative plaintiff class was predominantly white. The fact that defendants "do not dispute" this accusation, only underscores our obligation to subject defendants' conduct to strict scrutiny, *see Adarand*, ("[A]ny person, of whatever race, has the right to demand that any governmental actor subject to the Constitution justify any racial classification subjecting that person to unequal treatment under the strictest judicial scrutiny.").

The majority reaches a contrary conclusion—that strict scrutiny does not apply—because it regards the facts plaintiffs have pleaded in support of their equal protection claims insufficient to describe a "racial classification." In reaching its conclusion, the majority emphasizes the effect of curtailing the preference on non-parties to this litigation, ("[T]he apartments freed from the statutory preference are made available to all applicants regardless of race."), and the defendants' intent in enacting the curtailment, ("It might not seem remarkable that the government should insist ... that a fair number of the apartments should be effectively open to application by tenants of all races."). The majority also reads the complaint to allege only that defendants acted as they did because plaintiffs are racially identifiable; it does not read the complaint to allege that defendants acted as they did because plaintiffs are white.

Taking this last point first, I simply disagree with the majority's reading of the complaint. The complaint does not allege that the preference was curtailed because plaintiffs are racially monolithic; it alleges that the preference was curtailed because of the consent decree. And, as I have stated, because the consent decree operates only in favor of racial and ethnic minorities, it could not be read to require curtailment of the preference if the former West Enders were predominantly black. Thus, for purposes of evaluating defendants' Rule 12(b)(6) motion, I believe we must read into the complaint the allegation the majority believes necessary to trigger strict scrutiny: that defendants would not have acted as they did had the plaintiff class been predominantly of color.

Even if the majority has properly construed the complaint, I believe plaintiffs' equal protection claims are sufficient to withstand a Rule 12(b)(6) motion and to trigger strict scrutiny. In the redistricting cases, the Supreme Court has emphasized that government action which subordinates race neutral considerations to an overriding racial purpose is constitutionally suspect: "We recognized in *Shaw* [*v. Reno*, 509 U.S. 630 (1993)] that, outside the districting context, statutes are subject to strict scrutiny under the Equal Protection Clause not just when they contain express racial classifications, but also when, though race neutral on their face, they are motivated by a racial purpose or object." *Miller v. Johnson*, 515 U.S. 900 (1995) (affirming the invalidation, under equal protection principles, of a Georgia congressional redistricting plan designed to increase the number of majority black districts in Georgia). It remains to be seen whether the Court will press this principle to its outer limit and strictly scrutinize even governmental conduct which, though predominantly motivated by a racial purpose, would not appear to burden any person because of his or her race—*e.g.*, a public university's efforts at recruiting fully qualified applicants of color for its first year law school class. But it seems apparent that defendants' lack of hostility towards whites in particular does not shield their conduct—which has burdened plaintiffs because they are, as a group, racially identifiable—from the most searching judicial inquiry.

This leads to a final point. I think the majority runs afoul of *Adarand* in concentrating its focus so heavily on both defendants' intent and the effect of defendants' actions on non-parties to this case. The Supreme Court has squarely rejected the argument that classifications motivated by "benign" considerations should not be scrutinized strictly. And though this case does appear unique in that the government conduct at issue is more a withdrawal of a special benefit from whites than a giving of special benefits to members of minority groups,[9] the clear import of *Adarand* is that it is the plaintiff's "personal right to equal protection of the laws," and not some non-party's interest in competing for that which would be the plaintiff's but for his or her race, that is constitutionally safeguarded. Thus, in evaluating the constitutionality of defendants' conduct, we must not look to its effect and motivation with respect to others; we must look at its effect and motivation with respect to plaintiffs. And here, quite clearly, defendants' conduct has had the effect of depriving plaintiffs of a benefit and was prompted by the fact that plaintiffs are mostly white.

Because defendants' conduct should have been strictly scrutinized, their motion to dismiss plaintiffs' equal protection claim should have been denied and they should have been required to produce evidence that their conduct was narrowly tailored to advance a compelling governmental interest. *See Adarand* (reciting the components of the strict scrutiny inquiry); *see also Aiken v. City of Memphis*, 37 F.3d 1155, 1163 (6th Cir. 1994) ("When, as here, a race-based affirmative action plan is subjected to strict scrutiny, the party defending the plan bears the burden of producing evidence that the plan is constitutional"). Plaintiffs should then have been put to the burden of proving the unconstitutionality of defendants' conduct. *See Aiken* ("The party challenging [a racially-preferential] plan retains the ultimate burden of proving its unconstitutionality"). To the extent that the majority has reached a different conclusion, I most respectfully dissent.

Notes and Questions

1. The first case to expressly deal in depth with HUD's duties under the civil rights provisions was *Shannon v. Department of Hous. & Urb. Dev.*, 436 F.2d 809 (3d Cir. 1970). At the time of the decision, *Shannon* was a very important decision because it came when new construction was a major aspect of the federal housing and community development strategy. At this writing, new construction is not a major thrust of national policy. *Shannon* involved the issue of whether HUD had to take into account the possible racial impact on a recipient neighborhood of building low-income housing in the neighborhood. *Shannon* held that the Housing and Civil Rights Acts should be construed together:

> Read together, the Housing Act of 1949 and the Civil Rights Acts of 1964 and 1968 show a progression in the thinking of Congress as to what factors significantly contributed to urban blight and what steps must be taken to reverse the trend or to prevent the recurrence of such blight. In 1949 the Secretary, in examining whether a plan presented by an LPA included a workable program for community improvement, could not act unconstitutionally, but possibly could act neutrally on the issue of racial segregation. By 1964 [the Secretary] was di-

---

9. It is important to note that there is no indication that the benefit originally given (i.e., the full preference) was given to plaintiffs because they were predominantly white; rather, the preference was given because plaintiffs were ousted from their homes.

> rected, when considering whether a program of community development was workable, to look at the effects of local planning action and to prevent discrimination in resulting from such action. In 1968 [the Secretary] was directed to act affirmatively to achieve fair housing. Whatever were the most significant features of [a component of the program involved] for community improvement in 1949, by 1964 such a program had to be nondiscriminatory in its effects, and by 1968 the Secretary had to affirmatively promote fair housing.

Id. at 816. The court also confronted another vexing issue. Assuming the proposed housing is likely to be occupied primarily by low-income minorities, will enforcement of the civil rights policy against concentrating such housing in areas which are already characterized by such housing or which are minority areas conflict with the policy of fostering the development of housing? The court said

> Nor are we suggesting that desegregation of housing is the only goal of the national housing policy. There will be instances where a pressing case may be made for the rebuilding of a racial ghetto. We hold only that the agency's judgment must be an informed one; one which weighs the alternatives and finds that the need for physical rehabilitation or additional minority housing at the site in question clearly outweighs the disadvantage of increasing or perpetuating racial concentration.

Id. at 822. The means the court prescribed for implementation at the agency level was that the agency must have an "institutionalized method" for (a) knowing that there may be a policy conflict and (b) making a reasoned decision about the policy trade-offs.

2. In *Shannon*, the court stated that: "Increase or maintenance of racial concentration is *prima facie* likely to lead to urban blight and is thus *prima facie* at variance with the national housing policy." How do you interpret the meaning of this statement? In its implication, does the statement have a racist aspect?

3. One of the first cases to apply *Shannon* was *Croskey Street Concerned Citizens v. Romney*, 335 F. Supp. 1251 (E.D. Pa. 1971), *aff'd*, 459 F.2d 109 (3d Cir. 1972). *Croskey Street*, which involved public housing to be occupied by the elderly, came before Judge Joseph S. Lord, who was the district judge reversed in *Shannon* by the Third Circuit Court of Appeals. Judge Lord, applying *Shannon*, refused to enjoin the construction of a project of 100 units in a black area because it was part of a package of "balanced" sites, which included 313 units of housing in black areas and 360 in white areas. *See also Thompson v. Housing Auth.*, 251 F. Supp. 121 (S.D. Fla. 1966).

4. Does the site selection problem pose any intelligible legal issue without concurrent consideration of tenant selection policies? If so, what? Why? In thinking through your response to the preceding question, consider *Coffey v. Romney*, Equal Opportunity Hous. Rep. (P-H) ¶ 13,588 (M.D.N.C. 1972). *Coffey* involved not only the procedures HUD had to have, but also demonstrates the nature of the courts' limitations when reviewing a HUD decision which is being challenged as incorrect on the merits. In *Coffey*, HUD had decided administratively that the building of a particular development on a certain site would not cause or accelerate racial turnover from a white area in the immediate environs of the project. On judicial review, the court sustained HUD's decision. What is the issue before the court when it is reviewing a HUD decision on the merits?

The *Coffey* case was decided in May 1972. By September 1972, a local newspaper reported that the area around the proposed project had indeed become predominantly black. This meant that the prediction by expert witnesses and others had indeed come true, and HUD's decision (sustained by the court) that the project would not promote racial turnover was, in fact, wrong. The project, although marketed to be integrated, was virtually all black. Assuming this development, does it prove HUD's decision was wrong, that the *Coffey* decision was wrong, or some other point? In considering this, what was the legal issue the *Coffey* court had before it? Was the issue ever whether in fact racial turnover would be caused or accelerated? *See also King v. Harris*, 464 F. Supp. 827 (E.D.N.Y.) (another tipping case), *aff'd mem. sub nom. King v. Faymor Dev. Co.*, 614 F.2d 1288 (2d Cir. 1979), *rev'd and remanded on other grounds*, 446 U.S. 905 (1980) (in light of the Supreme Court's decision in *Strycker's Bay Neighborhood Council, Inc. v. Karlen*, 444 U.S. 223 (1980)), noted, 19 Urb. L. Ann. 303 (1980).

5. For further reading on the matters touched upon here, see generally Housing Desegregation and Federal Policy (John M. Goering ed. 1986) (broad-ranging coverage of topics from several perspectives). *See also* John O. Calmore, *Spatial Equality and the Kerner Commission Report: A Back-to-the-Future Essay*, 71 N.C. L. Rev. 1487 (1993).

6. Would there be a need for site selection regulations in a demand program, such as allowances or vouchers? Can you think of an explanation? Is it satisfactory? What if anything in nonconstruction programs could address the problem the site selection regulations are designed to combat? *See, e.g.*, 24 C.F.R. §§ 82.353 (where family can lease a unit with tenant-based assistance); 982.53 (equal opportunity requirements and protection for victims of domestic violence). It should also be noted that even though it is a construction program, the Low-Income Housing Tax Credit Program (discussed in Chapter 3, *supra*) does not appear to be subject to any similar requirements regarding site selection.

7. In 1980, Congress adopted the so-called "Brown Amendment," prohibiting HUD from disapproving subsidized housing projects solely because they are located in areas of racial concentration. 42 U.S.C. § 1436b. Language in the Conference Report states that current HUD site and neighborhood regulations are consistent with the amendment, but that the amendment addresses implementation of the regulations that arbitrarily denies assistance in areas of minority concentration. The Report also states that the amendment should not diminish HUD's efforts to promote equal opportunity and prevent racial discrimination. H.R. Rep. No. 1420, 96th Cong., 2d Sess. 112–13 (1980). What practical effect is this amendment likely to have on HUD project selection decisions? *See also Business Ass'n of Univ. City v. Landrieu*, 660 F.2d 867 (3d Cir. 1981). The district court interpreted the 1980 amendment to allow the placement of a housing project in a "racially impacted" area if justified by overwhelming need or some other aspect of national housing policy. The court of appeals distinguished between the requirements for projects located in racially impacted areas and those in areas in proximity to racially impacted areas. Is such a fine distinction likely to be practically workable?

8. A different manifestation of the failure to provide for fair housing arose in the case of Westchester County, New York. The Anti-Discrimination Center of Metro New York, Inc. (ADC) filed a Federal False Claims Act *qui tam* proceeding as Relator accusing Westchester County of obtaining funds from the United States by making false statements about the County's efforts to integrate housing on its applications for federal Community Development Block Grant funding. Specifically, the claim was that County officials knowingly and falsely certified that the County was affirmatively furthering fair housing. The United States intervened in the False Claims Act proceeding and all three parties entered into a two settlements. In one, the County agreed to pay the United States $30,000,000 in satisfaction of the allegations in the False Claims Act. The ADC was allocated $7,500,000 of this recovery by the United States in ADC's capacity of Relator in initiation of this action. In addition, ADC's attorneys were awarded $2,500,000 as attorneys' fees, expenses and costs to be paid by the County.

In the second settlement, the County agreed to submit to the oversight of a court-appointed monitor who will oversee expenditures of $50 million by the County over seven years for the purpose of building 750 homes in areas with low racial and ethnic diversity, i.e., in areas that are overwhelmingly white and affluent. The County also agreed to enact a (Bond) Act authorizing it to issue up to Thirty-Six Million Dollars ($36,000,000) in bonds to fund costs related to the settlement of the litigation and an additional Act setting forth policies and procedures which must be utilized in furtherance of the commitments established by the Stipulation and Order. *See U.S. ex rel. Anti-Discrimination Center of Metro New York v. Westchester County,* No. 6 Civ. 2860 (stipulation and order of settlement and dismissal Aug. 10, 2009). See also D. Kenneth Lange, Historic Settlement Reached in Desegregation Case Against Westchester County, 39 Housing L. Bull. 260 (2009); Peter Applebome, Integration Faces a New Test in the Suburbs, N.Y. Times, Aug. 23, 2009, at 3 (Sunday News of the Week).

A Note on the Special Federal Role in Fair Housing

The federal government has requirements and undertakes actions that affect fair housing strategies in a number of ways. HUD has numerous duties specified in particular laws and in general, it carries out its duties by promulgating regulations ranging from those governing tenant and site selection requirements to marketing requirements for federally assisted housing. *See generally* 24 C.F.R. §§ 100 to 180. Of course, HUD also has specific statutory duties under the Civil Rights Act of 1964, 42 U.S.C. § 2000d (prohibiting discrimination in federally assisted programs); the Civil Rights Act of 1968, 42 U.S.C. §§ 3601–3619, 3631 (fair housing and affirmative duties which we have already seen) and several Executive Orders, see Fair Hous.-Fair Lending (Aspen) ¶¶ 3981, 3991, and 4001.

In addition, specific statutes frequently set forth specific duties on HUD and other federal agencies. For example, the Housing and Community Development Act of 1974 imposes nondiscrimination requirements on HUD and recipients, 42 U.S.C. §§ 5306(d)(5)(B) and 5309, and upon HUD to enforce compliance. 42 U.S.C. § 5311. The Age Discrimination Act of 1975, 42 U.S.C. §§ 6101–6107, prohibits certain kinds of discrimination based on age in federally assisted programs. Moreover, many other federal agencies have housing-related civil rights duties. These include the Department of Agriculture administering housing programs for farmers and in rural areas, see 7 C.F.R. §§ 1901.201 to 1901.205, several regulatory agencies assessing financial institutions' records in making loans to low- and moderate-income neighborhoods under the Community Reinvestment Act of 1977, 12 U.S.C. §§ 2901–2903, and the Equal Credit Opportunity Act, 15 U.S.C. §§ 1691a–691e.

HUD has adopted general nondiscrimination regulations to implement its responsibilities under the 1964 Act, see 24 C.F.R. §§ 1.1 to 1.10 and its Affirmative Fair Housing Marketing Regulations to implement some of its duties under the 1968 Act. *See* 24 C.F.R. §§ 200.600 to 200.640. The regulations apply to HUD subsidized and unsubsidized single and multifamily developments. HUD's policy is stated as follows:

> It is the policy of the Department to administer its FHA housing programs affirmatively, as to achieve a condition in which individuals of similar income levels in the same housing market area have a like range of housing choices available to them regardless of their race, color, religion, sex, handicap, familial status or national origin. Each applicant for participation in FHA subsidized and unsubsidized housing programs shall pursue affirmative fair housing marketing policies in soliciting buyers and tenants, in determining their eligibility, and in concluding sales and rental transactions. 24 C.F.R. § 200.610.

To effectuate this policy, HUD requires project sponsors to submit an affirmative fair housing marketing plan that must be approved prior to construction of the development. The plan must establish a program to attract buyers or tenants on an equal opportunity basis by publicizing the development to minority families, including use of minority publications in the housing market area. All advertising must include the HUD equal opportunity slogan or logo, and must depict persons of minority as well as majority races, including both sexes. A nondiscriminatory hiring policy must be maintained for sales and rental staff, and all employees must be instructed concerning the nondiscrimination marketing policy. HUD local offices must inform fair housing organizations, including public housing authorities and local agencies responsible for providing relocation assistance, of any projects that have been approved for construction. *See, e.g.*, the Section 8 tenant based voucher program, 24 C.F.R. §§903.7(o), 982.53.

HUD also enters into agreements (previously called Voluntary Affirmative Marketing Agreements or VAMAs) with organizations involved in the sale or rental of dwellings or in other real estate-related transactions, such as lenders and hazard insurers. These agreements are designed to implement fair housing practices that allow all persons regardless of race, color, religion, sex, handicap, familial status or national origin to make free choice of housing location. For example, HUD first entered an agreement with the National Association of Realtors in the early 1970s, which it renewed in 1987. *See* 15 [Current Developments] Hous. & Dev. Rep. (WGL) 71 (1987). In 1995, HUD signed a new fair housing partnership agreement that replaced the 21-year-old agreement. The recent agreement no longer allows real estate professionals to create their own affirmative fair housing marketing plans. Instead, the members of the Association of Realtors will use a flexible model to satisfy HUD's requirement for the plans. 24 [Current Developments] Hous. & Dev. Rep. (WGL) 497 (1996). Similarly, in 1997, HUD also extended an agreement with the Mortgage Bankers Association of America to an additional three years. *See* 25 [Current Developments] Hous. & Dev. Rep. (West) 534 (1997).

In general, these are agreements to follow certain practices deemed to further fair housing goals. HUD has issued a Voluntary Affirmative Marketing Handbook in which HUD states that "This Handbook provides the background and authority for voluntary compliance activities, describes various kinds of voluntary plans and agreements that have been developed to promote HUD's equal opportunity goals, and specifies the procedure to be used in monitoring, evaluating, and reporting on these different kinds of voluntary instruments." available at http://www.hud.gov/offices/adm/hudclips/handbooks/fheh/80211/index.cfm (last visited 1/31/2010.)

HUD also provides assistance to two kinds of organizations that are involved in fair housing enforcement at the local and state levels. HUD provides funding to state and local governmental fair housing organizations (called the Fair Housing Assistance Program or FHAP). These funds are designed to enhance and build the capacity of state and local governmental agencies to combat housing discrimination. *See* 24 C.F.R. §115. Secondly, HUD also funds private, non-profit organizations that engage in whole or in part in fair housing enforcement (called the Fair Housing Initiatives Program or FHIP). The goal is to help private organizations that work to challenge and eliminate housing discrimination. *See* 24 C.F.R. §125.

Other federal attempts to foster nondiscriminatory housing practices in local jurisdictions involve the location of federal facilities. In 1971, HUD and the General Services Administration (the agency responsible for securing non-defense federal facilities, selecting locations and sites, and managing federal properties) entered into a Memorandum of Understanding designed

> to assure [for federal] employees the availability of low- and moderate-income housing without discrimination on the basis of race, color, religion or national origin, and to consider the need for development and redevelopment of areas ... and the impact on improving social and economic conditions of the area whenever Federal Government facilities locate or relocate at new sites, and to use its resources and authority to aid in the achievement of these objectives. Statement of Purpose.

Fair Housing-Fair Lending (P-H) ¶5101. A year later, HUD and GSA promulgated the procedures by which they would implement the Memorandum of Understanding. HUD would (1) make findings on the availability of housing for low- and moderate-income persons on a nondiscriminatory basis; (2) participate with GSA, the agency needing a facility, and the community involved in developing an affirmative action plan, if needed; and (3) give priority consideration to applications for assistance for housing proposed in accordance with the plan. GSA would advise HUD when it selected a site HUD had found unsuitable because it was not reasonably accessible on a nondiscriminatory basis to low- and moderate-income persons. *See* Fair Housing-Fair Lending (P-H) ¶5111.

You might be struck by the lack of teeth and authority in these measures. Can the federal government constitutionally impose more stringent conditions on the eligibility for federal funds or the location of federal facilities? For example, can it totally condition federal funds on a municipality's provision of a certain percentage of units for minorities?

Some of the issues posed by this discussion were raised in *Fullilove v. Klutznick*, 448 U.S. 448 (1980). That case involved the Public Works Employment Act of 1977, 42 U.S.C. §6705(f)(2), which provided that 10% of public works contracts should be set-aside for "minority business enterprises" (MBEs). MBEs were defined as businesses "at least 50% (or 51% of the stock in publicly held businesses) owned by Negroes, Spanish-speaking, Orientals, Indians, Eskimos, and Aleuts" who are United States citizens.

The Supreme Court, in a 6–3 decision, upheld the power of Congress to enact the provision in the face of claims by contractors that the set-aside violated the equal protection clause. Three Justices voted to sustain the provision as a remedial measure with the limited objective of opening up economic opportunity to minorities where the evidence demonstrated a marked disparity in the percentage of public contracts awarded to minorities. Justice Powell, concurring in a separate opinion, applied the test he enunciated in *Board of Regents v. Bakke*, 438 U.S. 265 (1978), and found that Congress had the authority to remedy effects of prior racial discrimination and had made appropriate findings as to the existence of such discrimination. Justices Marshall, Brennan, and Blackmun were willing to uphold the provision on the basis that a racial classification designed to further remedial purposes served important governmental objectives, which were substantially related to the achievement of the objective.

In other contexts, the Court has considered race-conscious plans and remedies, particularly in employment matters. The Court has considered cases that raised issues under Title VII of the Civil Rights Act of 1964, *e.g.*, voluntary plans, *United States v. Weber*, 443 U.S. 193 (1979); *Local No. 93, International Association of Firefighters v. City of Cleveland*, 478 U.S. 501 (1986); and *Johnson v. Transportation Agency*, 480 U.S. 616 (1987); as well as court-ordered plans, *e.g.*, *Firefighters Local Union No. 1784 v. Stotts*, 467 U.S. 561 (1984). In addition, the Court has considered the constitutionality of voluntary plans, *e.g.*, *Wygant v. Jackson Board of Education*, 476 U.S. 267 (1986), and court-ordered plans, *e.g.*, *United States v. Paradise*, 480 U.S. 149 (1987). The results have left considerable ambiguity as to the factual predicates necessary to the plans and the standards for considering the validity of race-conscious measures in the employment context. *See* Charles A. Shanor, *Affirmative Action in EEOC Litigation*, 21 Ga. L. Rev. 1059 (1987) (setting forth the classification of cases noted immediately above).

But because of retirements and replacement of Justices who decided the earlier cases, programs with race-based set-asides have been struck down or seriously curtailed by strict scrutiny requirements. In *City of Richmond v. J.A. Croson Co.*, 488 U.S. 469 (1989), the Court struck down a minority set-aside plan imposed by a municipality—the City of Richmond, Virginia—for city contracts. In *Adarand Constructors, Inc. v. Pena,* 515 U.S. 200 (1995) the Court held that a federal governmental set-aside program, *inter alia,* for minority businesses must meet the exacting test of strict scrutiny that state and local programs must meet, which practically dooms the programs, as they were originally enacted. In *Adarand,* the Court overruled *Metro Broadcasting, Inc. v. FCC,* 497 U.S. 547 (1990) to the extent it had suggested that a different standard (that was less fatal) might be applicable to actions of the federal government. *See also Shaw v. Reno*, 509 U.S. 630 (1993) (congressional redistricting with a racial objective must meet the virtually fatal strict scrutiny test).

Do all of these cases mean that a racial classification conditioning all federal assistance on the achievement of fair housing objectives could not be sustained? One key factor might be the existence of a prior history of racial discrimination in housing to be remedied. Is there such a history? *See, e.g,* James A. Kushner, *Apartheid in America: An Historical and Legal Analysis of Contemporary Racial Residential Segregation in the United States*, 22 How. L.J. 547, 548, 552ff (1979) (subsequently published as a monograph).

It has been proposed by one commentator that more stringent conditions be placed on the eligibility of jurisdictions to receive federal funds of any variety. *See* Charles E. Daye, *The Race, Class and Housing Conundrum: A Rationale and Proposal for a Legislative Policy of Suburban Inclusion*, 9 N.C. Cent. L.J. 37, 84 and Appendix (1977). The proposal would provide for "omnibus" conditioning of all federal funds on a nonexclusionary policy. Second, the proposal would address not merely nondiscrimination in its negative sense, but would require inclusionary policies as a condition of the receipt of any funds. Since the article was written prior to the restrictive Supreme Court cases, it is not clear whether the proposal would be regarded as "race-based" or more like a neutral requirement. In some ways the proposal might raise issues such as those considered in *Raso v. Lago, supra.*

Terms in the Civil Rights Act of 1964, § 602, 42 U.S.C. § 2000d-1 authorized refusal to fund or the termination for racially discriminatory conduct affecting federally funded programs, but provided that any "termination shall be limited in its effect to the particular program, or part thereof," which is found to be discriminatory. The scope of this provision was not clear. The matter came to a head in *Grove City College v. Bell,* 465 U.S. 555 (1984). The Supreme Court held that a termination of funding provision of Title IX of the Education Amendments of 1972 (which used the same "particular program, or part thereof" language in 20 U.S.C § 1682) applied only to a college's financial aid office and did not apply to the entire institution. In the Civil Rights Restoration Act of 1987, Congress rejected *Grove City* by broadly defining the language quoted to "mean all of the operations of" an institution, department, or agency, etc. Pub. L. 100-259 §6, 102 Stat. 31 (1988) (amending Title IX and the Civil Rights Act of 1964 and *codified at* 42 U.S.C. § 2000d-4a).

The implementation of integration objectives has proved to be both intractable and controversial. One of the more controversial matters concerns "managed occupancy" in public housing—generally the attempt to keep the number of minority persons in a given development from rising beyond a certain percentage of the total number. This idea can be expressed as a ceiling number of minorities or as a floor number of nonminorities. Unlike affirmative fair marketing which contemplates attempts to attract tenants through advertising and the like, the managed occupancy concept contemplates a more interventionist strategy, including, if necessary, assigning tenants to developments on the basis of race or, in extreme cases, holding units vacant until a tenant of the race that will maintain balance is available in order to maintain ratios or balance. HUD has declared both of these strategies to be unacceptable. *See e.g.*, 15 [Current Developments] Hous. & Dev. Rep. (WGL) 816 (1988) (Boston Housing Authority's plan to assign tenants by race unacceptable). *See also* 14 [Current Developments] Hous. & Dev. Rep. (BNA) 22 (1986) (HUD directs Louisville Housing Authority to remove race-conscious tenant assignment procedures). Courts have also declared some quotas to be illegal. *Burney v. Hous. Auth.*, 551 F. Supp. 746 (W.D. Pa. 1982) (permanent quota on minority occupants to maintain racial balance and prevent "tipping" held unconstitutional in the absence of proof that no alternative could be effective). *See also Shaker Heights v. Shaker Heights Hous. Assocs.*, Fair Hous.-Fair Lending (P-H) ¶ 15,533 (N.D. Ohio 1985). In cases of prior *de jure* segregation, however, the courts have approved nonpermanent, nonrigid quotas when necessary to effect a desegregation remedy. *See, e.g., Jaimes v. Lucas Metro. Hous. Auth.*, 758 F.2d 1036 (6th Cir. 1987).

Conversely, when inadequate steps are taken, the developments in a particular locality frequently are racially segregated by the action of tenants selecting projects that are racially identifiable with their race, or with the race that predominates in the neighborhood. HUD has been developing Guidelines to clarify the steps public housing authorities must take. *See* 15 [Current Developments] Hous. & Dev. Rep. (WGL) 434, 800, 979 (1988). The Guidelines are premised on prohibiting race-conscious assignments, the absence of free choice for tenants as to housing developments, the magnet development concept, and other measures. An example of the kind of plan that has been approved may be found in *Schmidt v. Boston Hous. Auth.*, 505 F. Supp. 988 (D. Mass 1981). In *Schmidt*, white plaintiffs filed constitutional and statutory challenges to a desegregation plan which accorded a "priority" to an applicant for a unit of housing if the unit was in a public housing development in which the applicant's race was in the minority. The plan had been implemented as part of the settlement of a state court suit in which the authority was required to develop a plan for the reduction of racial segregation and had been approved by HUD and the state court. The *Schmidt* court upheld the plan.

Notes and Questions

1. For analysis supporting at least some uses of "managed occupancy" as legal and constitutional, *see* Marc A. Kushner, Note, *The Legality of Race-Conscious Access Quotas Under the Fair Housing Act of 1968*, 9 CARDOZO L. REV. 1053 (1988). *See also* Robert C. Farrell, *Integrating By Discriminating: Affirmative Action that Disadvantages Minorities*, 62 U. DET. L. REV. 553 (1985); Bruce S. Gelber, *Race-Conscious Approaches to Ending Segregation in Housing: Some Pitfalls on the Road to Integration*, 37 RUTGERS L. REV. 921 (1985). For the view that "integration maintenance," no matter how well intentioned, is a violation of Title VIII and the Constitution, see Rodney A. Smolla, *In Pursuit of Racial Utopias: Fair Housing, Quotas and Goals in the 1980's*, 58 S. CAL. L. REV. 947 (1985).

2. A related question is managed occupancy in *private housing* that we explore in a subsequent section in this chapter *infra*, when we take up the *Starrett City* case. Are there

key differences in the permissibility of managed occupancy measures depending on whether the actor is a governmental entity, such as a public housing agency or a private entity operating private housing? This question and others will be examined in connection with consideration of the *Starrett City* case.

2. The General Duty of Nondiscrimination

a. Intentional Discrimination

A Note on the Gautreaux *Cases*

A study of governmental fair housing duties in selecting sites and tenants for housing would not be complete without analyzing "the *Gautreaux*" case[1]—a case which must be among the most protracted private litigation in the annals of recorded jurisprudence.

---

1. Judicial proceedings include thirty-four opinions as follows [District Court cases are in the Northern District of Illinois (N.D. Ill.) and Court of Appeals cases are in the Seventh Circuit (7th Cir.). These parts of the case citations will be omitted in this footnote.]

I. Pre-consolidation—the case against CHA: *Gautreaux v. Chicago Hous. Auth.*, 265 F. Supp. 582 (1967) (defendant's motion for summary judgment denied, issues as to motive of site selection and neighborhood racial composition remain); 296 F. Supp. 907 (1969) (CHA selected sites and assigned tenants on racially discriminatory basis); 304 F. Supp. 736 (1969) ("best efforts" order, CHA may not place housing in areas where nonwhite population exceeds 30% until 75% of total units are outside such areas of minority concentration); 436 F.2d 306 (1970) (affirming lower court's subsequent unreported order replacing "best efforts" order with a "timetable" order), *cert. denied*, 402 U.S. 922 (1971).

II. Pre-consolidation—the case against HUD: *Gautreaux v. Romney*, 448 F.2d 731 (1971) (reversing district court's dismissal of action against HUD, holding that HUD may be held liable for acquiescence in CHA's discriminatory conduct); *Gautreaux v. Romney*, 332 F. Supp. 366 (1971) (CHA intervenes as a defendant, and district court enjoins HUD from releasing $26 million to City of Chicago under Model Cities program until CHA and City comply with earlier court orders), *rev'd and remanded*, 457 F.2d 124 (1972) (district court exceeded its authority and abused its discretion in enjoining release of Model Cities funds); 342 F. Supp. 827 (1972) (district court suspends state law requiring approval of sites by Chicago City Council and orders CHA to submit sites directly to HUD), *aff'd sub nom. Gautreaux v. City of Chicago*, 480 F.2d 210 (1973), *cert. denied*, 414 U.S. 1144 (1974).

III. Post-consolidation: *Gautreaux v. Romney*, 363 F. Supp. 690 (1973) (plaintiffs' request for consideration of metro-area relief outside the City of Chicago denied), *rev'd sub nom. Gautreaux v. Chicago Hous. Auth.*, 503 F.2d 930 (1974) (district court erred in refusing to consider metro-area relief), *aff'd sub nom. Hills v. Gautreaux*, 425 U.S. 284 (1976) (metro-area relief in housing case will not exceed powers of district court to impose appropriate remedy); *Gautreaux v. Chicago Hous. Auth.*, 384 F. Supp. 37 (1974) (special master appointed to attempt to expedite compliance with court's orders); *Chicago Hous. Auth. v. Austin*, 511 F.2d 82 (1975) (defendant's petition for mandamus to set aside appointment of special master denied); *Gautreaux v. Landrieu*, 498 F. Supp. 1072 (1980) (plaintiffs' request for a receiver to administer CHA denied); 523 F. Supp. 665 (1981) (district court approves entry of a consent decree proposed by the parties), *aff'd sub nom. Gautreaux v. Pierce*, 690 F.2d 616 (1982); 523 F. Supp. 684 (1981) (granting plaintiffs' motion for award of attorney's fees), *aff'd sub nom. Gautreaux v. Chicago Hous. Auth.*, 690 F.2d 601 (1982), *cert. denied*, 461 U.S.961 (1983); *Gautreaux v. Pierce*, 524 F. Supp. 56 (1981) (HUD ordered to report on city's efforts to comply with housing production court orders); 535 F. Supp. 423 (1982) (plaintiffs' motion for modification of consent decree denied); 538 F. Supp. 1004 (1982) (plaintiffs' motion for modification of consent decree denied); 538 F. Supp l009 (1982) (plaintiffs' motion for modification of consent decree denied); 548 F. Supp. 1284 (1982) (at HUD's request density requirements of consent decree waived for a pending project), *aff'd*, 707 F.2d 265 (1983); 548 F. Supp. 1294 (1982) (plaintiffs' motion for modification of consent decree granted to reflect racial demographic shifts); 548 F. Supp. 1298 (1982) (HUD ordered to set aside units for the plaintiff class at the beginning of the fiscal cycle rather than during the cycle); 101

At the doctrinal level the *Gautreaux* litigation started out quite conventionally—as a case of intentional racial discrimination by the Chicago Housing Authority (CHA) in the selection of sites and the assignment of tenants. If the litigation had a novel portent, it might have been its theory that the Department of Housing and Urban Development (HUD) could be held liable for continuing to fund CHA with knowledge of CHA's discriminatory practices. But over the next twenty years, the cases would go through a series of proceedings in the district court, with frequent appeals to the court of appeals. One or more parties sought *certiorari* in the Supreme Court at least four times (denied three times and granted once).

The entire series of proceedings and opinions would make a complete case study of the judicial process in protracted housing litigation. But that would overburden this section. Accordingly, this note merely summarizes the major chronological and legal matters in the case.[2]

In 1966, the plaintiffs filed an action against CHA. That action charged, *inter alia*, that CHA had intentionally selected sites for public housing developments and pursued a tenant assignment policy for the purpose of maintaining patterns of residential segregation by race in public housing and in the City of Chicago. This action was styled *Gautreaux v. Chicago Housing Authority*, No. 66-C-1459 (N.D. Ill. 1966). A second companion action was filed simultaneously against HUD. This action was styled *Gautreaux v. Romney*, No. 66-C-1460 (N.D. Ill. 1966). It alleged that HUD had knowingly assisted CHA in carrying out a racially segregated public housing program by acquiescing in CHA's conduct and continuing to fund the public housing program with knowledge of CHA's conduct and that therefore HUD had sanctioned and assisted CHA's racially discriminatory housing practices. The complaint sought a declaratory judgment against HUD, an injunction to prohibit HUD from making any federal funds available to CHA which would support or further the racially discriminatory practices, and "such other and further relief as the Court may deem just and equitable." The district court dismissed the complaint against HUD, *inter alia*, for failure to state a claim.

In February of 1969, the court held that CHA had discriminated in site selection and tenant assignment. *Gautreaux v. Chicago Hous. Auth.*, 296 F. Supp 907 (N.D. Ill. 1969). In mid-1969, the court entered a Judgment Order setting out its decision on remedial actions required of CHA.

The 1969 Judgment Order against CHA contained a comprehensive plan designed to remedy the effects and prevent continuation of the discriminatory practices. The order

F.R.D. 704 (1984) (intervenors' motion for injunction to prevent HUD from implementing marketing plan denied), *aff'd*, 743 F.2d 526 (1984); *Gautreaux v. Chicago Hous. Auth.*, 610 F. Supp. 29 (1985) (granting plaintiffs' motion for award of attorneys fees); 15 [Current Developments] Hous. Dev. Rep. 24 (BNA) 24 (1987) (N.D. Ill. May 1987) (district court enters oral order giving CHA sixty days to put its scattered site operation under private management); *Gautreaux v. Pierce,* Nos. 66 C 1459, 66 C 1460, 1987 WL 13590 (N.D. Ill. July 9, 1987) (granting CHA's request for an evidentiary hearing on CHA conduct and capacity, which request was subsequently withdrawn).

2. The remaining discussion of the history of the litigation through 1976 (the first ten years) is adapted from Henry W. McGee, Jr., *Illusion and Contradiction in the Quest for a Desegregated Metropolis*, 1976 U. Ill. L.F. 948 App. The discussion of later proceedings through 1982 (years ten through sixteen) is adapted from Judge Pell's discussion in *Gautreaux v. Pierce*, 690 F.2d 616 (7th Cir. 1982). Changes inserted editorially are not noted in the text. For further details on the events since 1982, see 14 [Current Developments] Hous. Dev. Rep. (BNA) 1017 (1987); 15 [Current Developments] Hous. Dev. Rep. (BNA) 24 (1987); 15 [Current Developments] Hous. Dev. Rep. (BNA) 210 (1987); 15 [Current Developments] Hous. Dev. Rep. (BNA) 299 (1987); and 15 [Current Developments] Hous. Dev. Rep. (BNA) 368 (1987).

enjoined further construction of public housing in predominantly nonwhite areas without simultaneous construction in predominantly white areas. It mandated that CHA: (1) use its "best efforts" to increase the supply of family public housing units as rapidly as possible; (2) not commence construction of any family public housing units without first beginning construction of 700 units in the "General Public Housing Area" of Chicago (defined as census tracts which were both (a) 70% or more white as determined by the United States Bureau of the Census, and (b) not within one mile of a census tract 30% or more nonwhite—the criterion for the "Limited Public Housing Area") as determined by the United States Bureau of the Census; (3) locate 75% of all future family public housing units beyond the 700 units in the General Public Housing Area; (4) cease and desist discrimination on the basis of race; and (5) limit the size of new public housing projects and their concentration with other CHA projects. *Gautreaux v. Chicago Hous. Auth.*, 304 F. Supp. 736 (N.D. Ill. 1969).

In 1971, on plaintiffs' appeal from the dismissal of the action against HUD in *Gautreaux v. Romney*, the court of appeals reversed. It held that summary judgment was proper against HUD based upon findings and conclusions that HUD had knowingly acquiesced in CHA's discriminatory practices. The case was remanded to the district court for appropriate relief. *Gautreaux v. Romney*, 448 F.2d 731 (7th Cir. 1971). The district court ordered HUD to use its "best efforts" to increase the supply of dwelling units in conformity with the relevant federal statutes, rules, and regulations and with the provisions of a 1969 Judgment Order entered against CHA in the companion case of *Gautreaux v. Chicago Housing Authority*, 304 F. Supp. 736 (N.D. Ill. 1969).

However, the district court refused to order relief beyond the legal boundaries of the City of Chicago because it found the discriminatory practices to have been committed within those boundaries. *Gautreaux v. Romney*, 363 F. Supp. 690 (N.D. Ill. 1973). Shortly afterward, the case against HUD was consolidated with that against CHA.

In 1970, the district court modified the 1969 "best efforts" order because no units had been submitted to the Chicago City Council for approval under a state law, which required the council's approval. It imposed a "timetable" order that specified the number and date by which CHA must submit units to the city council for approval. The timetable order was affirmed in *Gautreaux v. Chicago Housing Authority*, 436 F.2d 306 (7th Cir. 1970), *cert. denied*, 402 U.S. 922 (1971).

A collateral attack on the placement of public housing units in a white area under the district court's order was initiated in 1972. The suit claimed that HUD had failed to file an environmental impact statement. The court of appeals affirmed a district court decision that the National Environmental Policy Act of 1969 did not require an impact statement. *Nucleus of Chicago Homeowners Ass'n v. Lynn*, 524 F.2d 225 (7th Cir. 1975), *cert. denied*, 424 U.S. 225 (1976).

Near the end of 1971, the district court enjoined HUD's release of $26 million under the Model Cities program to the City of Chicago until minimum compliance with the court's orders was achieved. *Gautreaux v. Romney*, 332 F. Supp 366 (N.D. Ill. 1971). The court of appeals reversed the injunction against release of the funds and remanded for further proceedings. *Gautreaux v. Romney*, 457 F.2d 124 (7th Cir. 1972).

The Chicago City Council persisted in its refusal to approve sites for public housing submitted by CHA. The district court suspended the application of the state law and ordered CHA to submit sites directly to HUD thus, of course, bypassing the city council. *Gautreaux v. Chicago Hous. Auth.*, 342 F. Supp. 827 (N.D. III. 1972), *aff'd sub nom. Gautreaux v. City of Chicago*, 480 F.2d 210 (7th Cir. 1973), *cert. denied*, 414 U.S. 1144 (1974).

A Special Master was appointed in 1974 to attempt to move the case and housing construction forward and to determine the causes of delay. *Gautreaux v. Chicago Hous. Auth.*, 384 F. Supp. 37 (N.D. Ill. 1974). A petition for mandamus to vacate reference to special master was denied in *Chicago Housing Authority v. Austin*, 511 F.2d 82 (7th Cir. 1975).

The court of appeals reversed the previously discussed district court decision in *Gautreaux v. Romney*, 363 F. Supp. 690 (N.D. III. 1973), in which the district court had refused to order metropolitan area relief, that is, relief beyond the legal boundaries of the City of Chicago. The court of appeals concluded that metropolitan area relief was not precluded simply because the wrongs had been committed within Chicago and against Chicago residents. It remanded the case to the district court for "the adoption of a comprehensive metropolitan area plan that will not only disestablish the segregated public housing system in the City of Chicago ... but will increase the supply of dwelling units as rapidly as possible." *Gautreaux v. Chicago Hous. Auth.*, 503 F.2d 930, 939 (7th Cir. 1974).

The court of appeals' decision was appealed to the U.S. Supreme Court on the permissibility of "inter-district relief for discrimination in public housing in the absence of a finding of an inter-district violation." *Hills v. Gautreaux*, 425 U.S. 284, 292 (1976). The Supreme Court affirmed the decision of the court of appeals. It remanded the case for further evidence and consideration on the issue of metropolitan area relief so that the district court could determine the nature and scope of relief.

On February 25, 1975, prior to the Supreme Court's decision, fourteen additional defendants, including the Illinois Housing Development Agency (IHDA), were added by the plaintiffs by way of a second supplemental complaint.

After the Supreme Court's remand on the metropolitan relief question, HUD and the plaintiffs voluntarily entered into a Letter of Understanding in June 1976. Plaintiffs agreed to postpone for one year any request for a metropolitan relief order in exchange for HUD's making a 400-unit allocation of Section 8 existing housing funds in the metropolitan area under a demonstration program. HUD also agreed to enter into a contract with a private organization for counseling prospective Section 8 tenants and to provide, in about one year, some 2,700 units of Section 8 existing in the metropolitan area outside Chicago and 1,500 Section 8 new construction and rehabilitation units in the Chicago area. In late 1977, this agreement was extended for an eighteen-month period through December 1978.

When progress proved to be negligible through December 1979, plaintiffs sought the appointment of a receiver for CHA to expedite compliance with the court orders. While noting that compliance with orders had been slow, the court believed that CHA was not entirely responsible and that major obstacles to compliance had been removed, with "great reservation" it denied, without prejudice, plaintiffs' motion seeking a receiver. *Gautreaux v. Landrieu*, 498 F. Supp. 1072 (N.D. Ill. 1980). Later, the agreement was extended into 1981.

In November 1980, the plaintiffs and HUD told the district court that they would soon have a draft settlement agreement between them, and the court set a December 1980 date for a preliminary hearing on the soon-to-be-proposed consent decree.

At the December 18 hearing, the district court determined that the proposed decree with exhibits was "within the range of possible approval." The court set a fairness hearing date of January 14, 1981, and approved the form of notice to be sent to the class members. This notice was mailed and published on December 25, 1980, *inter alia*, informing class members of the nature of the proposal.

In January 1981, IHDA filed a cross-claim seeking injunctive relief against implementation of the proposed decree alleging that the decree's requirements upon HUD went beyond the parameters of HUD's authority and restrictions imposed on HUD by its governing regulations. The court rejected the objections. *Gautreaux v. Landrieu*, 523 F. Supp. 665 (N.D. Ill. 1981). [the consent decree is an addendum to the court's opinion.—Eds.]

Following a contested hearing, in June 1981 the district court issued its memorandum opinion and order approving the consent decree. The decree was amended *sua sponte* and entered as a final order on June 30, 1981. An order changing a provision of the decree was entered in July 1981.

In an extensive opinion, the Seventh Circuit rejected arguments that the decree had not been adequately considered, conflicted with statutory provisions, and was unreasonable. The court also rejected objections of a member of the plaintiff class that the decree was illegal in that, in certain circumstances, the decree permitted placing assisted housing in racially "concentrated" and "mixed" areas. The court found that the decree's designation of "revitalizing" areas as suitable in general was not unreasonable, even if such areas contained "substantial" minority occupancy since they were undergoing physical development. Moreover, the court concluded that the potential "tipping" effects would have to be evaluated when a specific proposal had been made. *Gautreaux v. Pierce*, 690 F.2d 616 (7th Cir. 1982), *aff'g Gautreaux v. Landrieu, supra*.

The consent decree contained a provision that HUD would not approve any Section 8 new construction units in any census tract in which the new units would cause assisted housing to exceed 15% of the total number of apartments and residences in that census tract. A project was proposed and current census data showed that the project would raise assisted units in the census tract to 18.25%. HUD in making its initial assessment had used outdated census data. Without objection by plaintiffs' counsel, HUD applied for a waiver of the 15% limit that the court approved over objections of some of the parties. *Gautreaux v. Pierce*, 548 F. Supp. 1284 (N.D. Ill. 1982, *aff'd*, 707 F.2d 265 (7th Cir. 1983).

Residents of one of the "revitalizing" areas in which a project was to be located had been allowed to intervene in the action seeking waiver of the 15% limit. They were allowed, *inter alia*, to challenge HUD's involvement in the project, on the ground that the Consent Decree precluded HUD's involvement. After the court concluded that HUD's involvement was not in violation of the decree and that a waiver of the density requirement should be granted, these intervenors sought to challenge the project on the grounds that it would cause "tipping" in the area. The court held that, while the tipping issue could be raised in a separate suit, it could not be raised by way of intervention. *Gautreaux v. Pierce*, 743 F.2d 526 (7th Cir. 1984), *aff'g* 101 F.R.D. 704 (N.D. Ill. 1984).

In 1987, HUD released a report of its review of CHA's management operations between 1986 and 1987 and cited CHA for seventy-six violations of HUD rules, handbooks, and annual contribution contracts. In addition, progress toward compliance with court orders continued to be negligible. Only 438 scattered site units had been constructed by CHA to comply with *Gautreaux* court orders. Plaintiffs renewed in the district court what had become a periodic motion for the appointment of a receiver to manage CHA or parts of its operation. In May 1987, the district court in a bench ruling gave CHA sixty days to put its scattered site operation under private management or turn the operation over to a receiver. *See Gautreaux v. Pierce*, Nos. 66 C 1459, 66 C 1460, 1987 WL 13590 (N.D. Ill., July 9, 1987) (setting down discovery procedure and limits on evidentiary hearing requested by CHA in view of plaintiff's motion). CHA's request was subsequently withdrawn.

HUD also filed a motion to put CHA's entire operation in receivership because of, *inter alia*, pervasive mismanagement, violation of HUD policies, cost overruns, and excessive debts. In the meantime, the City of Chicago was trying to put together a package of assistance to CHA using community development block grants and other assistance, none of which was feasible without HUD's approval.

The district court on August 3, 1987, appointed a Receiver to run CHA's scattered site program because, as the court described it, "CHA proved inept at building housing on scattered-sites." CHA continued negotiations with HUD over whether CHA would be ousted from control of its entire operation. In September 1987 HUD and CHA reached an agreement in which the CHA Board of Commissioners would select an outside management team to run CHA's operations, in return for which HUD would not assert its right to what amounted to a "hostile takeover."

Additional proceedings dealing with the implementation of the judgment and Consent Decree in the case after 1987, as to which there have been many, are discussed in *Gautreaux v. Chicago Housing Authority*, 981 F. Supp. 1091 (N.D. Ill. 1997). Among matters of interest, the named plaintiff, Mrs. Dorothy Gautreaux, died. In 1997, HUD and the plaintiffs agreed to the termination of most elements of the consent decree because HUD, in October 1996, had met its obligation to place 7100 public housing residents outside of the largely minority "Limited Public Housing" areas as modified in various orders.

The next case reviews important aspects of the *Gautreaux* "saga" and shows that there are still important matters that remain to be addressed.

Gautreaux v. Chicago Housing Authority

United States District Court
4 F. Supp. 2d 757 (N.D. Ill. 1998)

MEMORANDUM OPINION AND ORDER

ASPEN, J.

Nearly thirty years ago, United States District Judge Richard B. Austin entered a judgment order against the Chicago Housing Authority (the CHA) with the hopes of correcting the effects of that agency's unconstitutional public housing site selection and tenant assignment procedures. *Gautreaux v. CHA*, 304 F. Supp. 736 (N.D. Ill. 1969). Blacks then made up 90% of the CHA's tenant base, but the CHA had deliberately restricted the number of blacks who could live in the four housing projects which were located in predominantly white areas, to the point where 93% to 99% of the tenants in those units were white. *Gautreaux v. CHA*, 296 F. Supp. 907, 909 (N.D. Ill. 1969). The other CHA units—the 99.5% which were located in predominantly black areas—housed the rest of the CHA's tenants, 99% of whom were black. *See id.* at 910. This arrangement, ruled Judge Austin, violated the Fourteenth Amendment. *See id.* at 914. And in a comment worth recalling here for its relevance today, he wrote:

> It is ... undenied that sites for the projects which have been constructed were chosen primarily to further the praiseworthy and urgent goals of low cost housing and urban renewal. Nevertheless, a deliberate policy to separate the races cannot be justified by the good intentions with which other laudable goals are pursued.

Id. (citing *Brown v. Board of Educ.*, 347 U.S. 483 (1954)) (emphasis added). The building block of Judge Austin's remedial judgment order was the Dwelling Unit, "an apartment or single family residence which is to be initially made available to and occupied by a low-income, non-elderly family, subsequent to the date hereof, directly or indirectly by or through CHA." *Gautreaux*, 304 F. Supp. at 737. He barred the CHA from "authoriz[ing], approv[ing], or implement[ing] any plan for Dwelling Units" or from "seek[ing] any approval or request or accept[ing] any assistance from any government agency with respect thereto" unless the plan's Dwelling Units were located in conformity with the order's requirements. *Id.* at 738. The order mandated that the CHA erect three Dwelling Units in a General Area (i.e. areas in Cook County with a white population of 70% or more) for every one Dwelling Unit it erected in a Limited Area (i.e. areas with a minority population of 30% or more), *Id.* at 738–39, though it did not require any new construction. This ratio was later changed from 3-to-1 to 1-to-1.

In 1993, the CHA applied for and received $50 million from the Department of Housing and Urban Development (HUD) under the auspices of the HOPE VI program (an acronym for Homeownership and Opportunity for People Everywhere). Congress created the HOPE VI program in 1992 with the goal of "empower[ing the] residents of severely distressed and obsolete public housing." S. Rep. 102-356, at 70 (1992). It intended to accomplish this via a three-part plan: (1) eliminating and (in some form) replacing dilapidated public housing structures, (2) providing residents of those structures with the skills necessary to achieve self-sufficiency, and (3) instilling a sense of community activism in residents of the blighted areas. *See id.* at 71.

It is the first part which is now at issue, as the CHA believes that it must spend its HOPE VI construction funds exclusively in the "3 separately defined areas containing the community's most severely distressed projects," to which the 1992 HOPE VI appropriation refers. *See* Pub. L. No. 102-389, 106 Stat. 1579 (codified as a Note to 42 U.S.C. § 1473*l*). This would mean, of course, that any construction of new public housing units[1] would take place in the distressed areas, which, by unfortunate circumstance, are also Limited Areas as defined by the judgment order. Recognizing that the judgment order requires equal construction in the General and Limited Areas, the CHA has asked that we "clarify" the judgment order and read it as not governing any use of HOPE VI funds.

The plaintiffs take issue with this request. They have previously pointed out to this Court that the construction of new public housing units is no longer in vogue, *see Gautreaux v. CHA*, 981 F. Supp. 1091, 1093 (N.D. Ill. 1997), and the HOPE VI money may be one of the few remaining funding sources for the construction of desegregated housing. Of course, if construction funds permanently dry up and if the plaintiffs do not succeed in convincing us to modify the judgment order, *see e.g., id.* at 1093–94, then this particular effort to desegregate public housing in Chicago will come to an end. We need not contemplate this possibility today, however, for the dilemma posed by the CHA—that the HOPE VI program compels spending only in Limited Areas while the judgment order compels equal spending in General Areas—rests on an illusion.

---

1. The CHA attempts to draw a distinction between replacement construction—construction which does not add to the agency's aggregate housing stock—and wholly new construction; the CHA argues that the injunction only governs the latter. This distinction may, as the CHA claims, have great significance to other housing decisions, but the judgment order does not differentiate between reconstruction and new construction: it speaks simply of Dwelling Units "initially make available to and occupied by a low-income, non-elderly family, subsequent to the date hereof." *Gautreaux*, 304 F. Supp. at 737. Housing units constructed with HOPE VI funds obviously qualify, and the use of such funds for the ends of desegregation is in keeping with the sweeping nature of the judgment order, the terms of which are as broad as the violation which it was designed to correct.

The 1992 HOPE VI authorization contemplates an "urban revitalization demonstration program involving major reconstruction of severely distressed or obsolete public housing projects," which is to be focused on "up to 3 separately defined areas, containing the community's most severely distressed projects." Pub. L. No. 102-389. This does not, however, amount to a requirement that all HOPE VI money must be spent physically within those distressed areas. One way to revitalize a distressed public housing neighborhood is to tear down some of the units there and rebuild them elsewhere, thereby lessening the concentration of public housing on the old site. *See* Pub. L. No. 104-134, 110 Stat. 1321 (the 1996 HOPE VI appropriation, providing funds for "replacement housing which will avoid or lessen concentration of very low-income families"); Pub. L. No. 104-204, 110 Stat. 2874 (the 1997 HOPE VI appropriation, providing for the same). HUD's HOPE VI Guidebook contemplates just such an approach, discussing "[p]ublic housing development (including on-site reconstruction as well as construction of off-site housing) funded by HOPE VI," and the legislative history is in agreement, *see* S. REP. 102-356, at 73 ("The balance of the [demolished] units could be replaced through ... traditional replacement means, including major reconstruction and scattered-site development...."). [emphasis added]...."). In a similar vein, the HOPE VI program also requires that some demolished public housing be replaced by Section 8 housing vouchers, *see* Pub. L. 103-124, which may be used without regard to the boundaries of the General or Limited Areas. *See* 42 U.S.C. § 1473f(r). We see no incompatibility between the HOPE VI program and the judgment order.

It is ironic that the CHA has chosen to argue that it must use the HOPE VI funds for urban renewal and to the exclusion of desegregation, for, as we observed earlier, in 1969 it attempted to characterize desegregation as a byproduct of urban renewal efforts. No matter: Congress and HUD, through HOPE VI, have afforded the CHA an opportunity both to revitalize distressed public housing neighborhoods and to desegregate public housing, and the CHA is duty-bound to vigorously pursue desegregation opportunities. *See Gautreaux*, 304 F. Supp. at 741 (judgment order Article VIII); *see also Gautreaux v. Landrieu*, 498 F. Supp. 1072, 1075 (N.D. Ill. 1980) ("Difficulty in attaining racially integrated public housing shall not be further condoned.... The CHA must have only one concern, housing in compliance with the repeated orders of this Court.").

We hold that the judgment order governs the CHA's use of HOPE VI funds, Accordingly, any construction of public housing in Cook County must conform to the judgment order's locational requirements. It is so ordered.

Notes and Questions

1. One of the decisions in the *Gautreaux* series which warrants further discussion is *Hills v. Gautreaux*, 425 U.S. 284 (1976). The district court's denial of any metropolitan relief encompassing areas outside the city limits of the City of Chicago was reversed. The court of appeals held that the district court must consider "the adoption of a comprehensive metropolitan area plan." *Gautreaux v. Chicago Hous. Auth.*, 503 F.2d 930 (7th Cir. 1974). HUD sought review in the Supreme Court, ostensibly to get a clarification of its authority, but HUD vigorously resisted any metropolitan relief, as the opinion makes clear.

A major issue the Court considered was the meaning of its decision in *Milliken v. Bradley*, 418 U.S. 717 (1974). *Milliken*, rendered after the district court's decision but before the court of appeals' decision, had disapproved an order "consolidating" school districts in the Detroit metropolitan area to remedy racial discrimination in the schools. In *Gautreaux*, the Court was called on to consider the metropolitan relief question in the housing context.

HUD contended that the *Milliken* decision barred a remedy affecting its conduct beyond the boundaries of Chicago for two reasons. First, HUD asserted that metropolitan relief would not be commensurate with the constitutional violation HUD committed. Second, HUD claimed that a decree regulating HUD's conduct beyond Chicago's boundaries would inevitably have the effect of "consolidat[ing] for remedial purposes" governmental units not implicated in HUD's and Chicago Housing Authority's violations.

The Court rejected both contentions and held that *Milliken* did not preclude an order against HUD affecting its conduct in the greater metropolitan area merely because HUD's constitutional and statutory violations were committed in Chicago. The Court distinguished *Milliken* on the ground that unlike the school districts in *Milliken,* HUD had been found to have violated the Constitution.

The Court also held that an order against HUD affecting its conduct beyond Chicago's boundaries would not impermissibly interfere with local governments and suburban housing authorities that were not implicated in HUD's unconstitutional conduct.

Its reasoning that no impermissible interference with local governments would be caused is particularly troublesome. The Court gave two reasons: first, that an order directed solely to HUD would not force unwilling localities to apply for assistance under programs requiring applications; and, second, that even in cases in which HUD could bypass local governments by contracting directly with housing owners (under the Section 8 program, for example), the local governmental units retained the right to comment on specific assistance proposals, to reject certain proposals that were inconsistent with their approved housing assistance plans, and to require that builders adhered to zoning and other land-use restrictions.

While the "no impermissible interference" rationale helped to answer HUD's coercion argument and thus, in that context, apparently supported a fair housing access principle, the decision took away as much as it gave. In recognizing local autonomy to impose land use requirements and to reject housing that might otherwise be needed to effectively remedy prior segregation, the Court left in place powerful impediments to free access. We have already seen in the *Arlington I* case, *supra,* the difficulty of making a constitutional case on equal protection grounds against exclusionary land use practices. When we take up the *Huntington* case, *infra,* we will look at whether land-use controls that frustrate freedom of access can be successfully challenged under the Fair Housing Act.

2. Literature on the *Gautreaux* cases and the remedial issues addressed in *Hills v. Gautreaux* is extensive.

(a) For views of plaintiffs' legal counsel, see Alexander Polikoff, Waiting for Gautreaux: A Story of Segregation, Housing and the Black Ghetto (2006); Alexander Polikoff, Gautreaux *and Institutional Litigation,* 64 Chi.-Kent L. Rev. 451 (1988). *See also* Pamela Bucy, Comment, Hills v. Gautreaux: *When a Federal Court May Grant a Inter-District Remedy in the Absence of an Inter-District Violation,* 13 J. Urb. L. 251 (1977); Charles E. Daye, *Role of the Judiciary in Community Development and Housing: Suggested Analytical Method,* 52 J. Urb. L. 689 (1975) (analyzing the *Gautreaux* remedy in the context of other major housing and development: cases and proposing a method of analysis); Jacqueline Leavitt, *The Use of Boundary Lines to Discriminate in the Provision of Housing by Race,* 54 J. Urb. L. 899 (1977); A. Dan Tarlock, *Remedying the Irremediable: The Lessons of* Gautreaux, 64 Chi.-Kent L. Rev. 573 (1988); Note, *The Role of the Judiciary in Desegregation: Permissible Remedies After* Hills v. Gautreaux, 54 J. Urb. L. 237 (1976).

(b) For Gautreaux demonstration program evaluations, see Xavier Briggs, Susan Popkin, & John Goering, Moving to Opportunity: The Story of an American Experiment to Fight Ghetto Poverty (2010); Leonard S. Rubinowitz & James E. Rosenbaum, Crossing the Class and Color Lines: From Public Housing to White Suburbia (2000); James Rosenbaum, Stefanie DeLuca & Tammy Tuck, *New Capabilities in New Places: Low-Income Black Families in Suburbia*, in The Geography of Opportunity: Race and Housing Choice in Metropolitan America (Xavier de Souza Briggs ed. 2005). For an early evaluation of the program under which some tenants in Chicago public housing were issued Section 8 certificates and enabled to move into suburban areas, see James E. Rosenbaum et al., *Can the Kerner Commission's Housing Strategy Improve Employment, Education, and Social Integration for Low-Income Blacks*, 71 N.C. L. Rev. 1519 (1993) (concluding that benefits included improved job prospects families and improved achievement levels for children of those who moved to the suburbs).

(c) For analysis of the problems of *Milliken* and *Hills v. Gautreaux*, see Gayle Binion, *Racial Discrimination by Alteration or Refusal to Alter School District Boundaries*, 54 U. Det. J. Urb. L. 811 (1977); Stephen B. Kanner, *Interdistrict Remedies for School Segregation After* Milliken v. Bradley *and* Hills v. Gautreaux, 48 Miss. L.J. 33 (1977); James A. Kushner & Frances E. Werner, *Metropolitan Desegregation After* Milliken v. Bradley*: The Case for Land Use Litigation Strategies*, 24 Cath. U. L. Rev. 187 (1975).

(d) For a general collection of the literature on the problem, see James A. Kushner, *Apartheid in America: An Historical and Legal Analysis of Contemporary Racial Residential Segregation in the United States*, 22 How. L.J. 547, 548 n.1, 620 nn. 165–75 (1975) (subsequently published as a monograph).

A Note on the Housing-Schools Nexus

Housing discrimination is but one element of a multifaceted social malaise. Consider the relationship between housing and educational opportunity. After the Supreme Court's decision in *Brown v. Board of Education*, 347 U.S. 483 (1954), it was clear that school attendance plans based on an intent to segregate were constitutionally impermissible. *Brown* did not reach a more difficult problem—the use of facially neutral school assignment criteria to produce a racially segregated system. The most common criterion is geography. Students are assigned to schools closest to their homes. As a result, segregated residential housing patterns produce segregated schools.

Inevitably, legal scholars mounted an attack on this form of racial separation. Owen M. Fiss, *Racial Imbalance in the Public Schools: The Constitutional Concepts*, 78 Harv. L. Rev. 564 (1965); Frank I. Goodman, *De Facto School Segregation: A Constitutional and Empirical Analysis*, 60 Cal. L. Rev. 275 (1972). The Supreme Court's response has not been entirely helpful. Broad remedies for school desegregation have been imposed in areas where geographical assignment reflects "a history of segregation." *Swann v. Charlotte-Mecklenburg Bd. of Educ.*, 402 U.S. 1, 26 (1971). The Court has been reluctant to break down racial barriers where segregation is not part of a "systematic program" and has not prohibited *de facto* segregation. *See Keyes v. School Dist. No. 1*, 413 U.S. 189, 201 (1973). The Court has severely restricted multidistrict school remedies. In *Milliken v. Bradley*, 418 U.S. 717 (1974) the lower courts found de jure illegal racial segregation in the Detroit public school system that had been committed by the school system and the State of Michigan. The lower courts also found that the only feasible desegregation plan for the Detroit schools required crossing the boundary lines between the Detroit School District and adjacent or nearby school districts for the limited purpose of providing effective desegregation. However, the Supreme Court held that the remedy could not include surrounding suburban school districts without a finding that the additional districts to be included did not operate unitary school systems or that they had committed acts that caused segregation. Even where residential patterns have shifted in response to a school desegregation order, the Court has held that the desired racial mix, once imposed, could not be maintained "in perpetuity." *Pasadena City Bd. of Educ. v. Spangler*, 427 U.S. 424, 436–37 (1976).

There are two major complex cases involving efforts to desegregate schools in the context of *both* school and housing remedies. One case is *Hart v. Community School Board*, 383 F. Supp. 699 (E.D.N.Y. 1974). Another, somewhat sensationalized, case is *United States v. Yonkers Board of Education*, 837 F.2d 1181 (2d Cir. 1987).

Hart, which arose out of litigation involving New York's Coney Island, was the first in which the court was lucid and thorough in its examination of the housing and schools nexus. Judge Weinstein examined the relationship between school attendance zones and government-assisted housing projects. State and federal housing authorities were found to be proper parties to the suit because "their actions help maintain segregated schools" and "no effective [remedy] is possible without a shift in the racial composition of the tenants in … public housing." 383 F. Supp. at 752–53. The housing agencies were held to be under a duty to "refertilize" the relevant geographical area with new families:

> There shall be accelerated reconstruction of the blocks south of the school. Renting and construction patterns shall be modified to encourage substantial numbers of whites and middle class families with children to move into buildings constructed with the aid of public funds. Plans should include advertising and inducements to encourage middle class persons to move into the area with their families in order to stabilize its population.

383 F. Supp. at 757–58. The scope of the anticipated remedy was so broad that the court appointed a special master, the late Curtis J. Berger a law professor from Columbia University, to formulate a comprehensive community plan "dealing not only with the elimination of segregation at [the school] but also with the housing, non-residential development, community welfare, recreational, transportation and protective facilities within the Coney Island neighborhood.…" 383 F. Supp. at 768. Three months were allotted for compilation of the report, a process which is detailed in Curtis J. Berger, *Away from the Court House and into the Field: The Odyssey of a Special Master*, 78 Colum. L. Rev. 707 (1978).

The plan ultimately approved by Judge Weinstein was far less extensive than the one originally envisioned. *Hart v. Community School Bd.*, 383 F. Supp. 769 (E.D.N.Y. 1974) (final order after submission of master's report), *aff'd*, 512 F.2d 37 (2d Cir. 1975). The court refused to impose an affirmative obligation upon housing authorities, in light of the "cooperative spirit" that had developed in regard to restructuring housing alternatives, and the unworkability of forcing such changes by judicial decree. 383 F. Supp. at 775.

In *Yonkers*, the court found that the city of Yonkers had intentionally segregated subsidized housing and public schools and that the board of education had intentionally segregated the public schools. The city's conduct consisted of confining subsidized housing to areas of high minority concentration that contributed to segregation of the schools. The board of education's conduct consisted of adherence to a neighborhood schools policy for the purpose of maintaining segregated schools.

Without the necessity of making any extension in the substantive law, the district court ordered the city to construct subsidized housing in nonminority areas and ordered the City and the board of education to implement a magnet school program. The court of appeals affirmed. *United States v. Yonkers Bd. of Education*, 837 F.2d 1181 (2d Cir. 1987), *cert. denied*, 486 U.S. 1055 (1988).

When a majority of the Yonkers City Council balked at approving the housing required by the court's remedial order, problems for the city arose, to say the least. The city council and school board moved to comply with the portion of the order that dealt with schools by adopting a magnet school and busing plan. As the council responded to growing community opposition, it declared a moratorium on public housing and refused to go forward with a plan for the building of 200 units of public housing and 800 units of low- and moderate-income housing. Although some revision of the order was being discussed by the parties, the district court judge refused to consider any changes until the council approved the original plan.

On August 1, 1988, the council by a 3–4 vote rejected a plan that would lead to compliance with the order. On August 2, 1988, the district court held the city and the four negative voting council members in contempt and imposed a $100 per day escalating fine, doubling each day. Everyone conceded that the fine would bankrupt the city. When the U.S. Supreme Court refused to suspend the running of the fines against the city (although suspending individual fines), two members of the council changed their vote after total fines had exceeded $800,000.00. *See* Hous. Aff. Letter, Sept. 16, 1988. *See also* 15 [Current Developments] Hous. & Dev. Rep. (WGL) 567, 681, 767 (1988) and 16 [Current Developments] Hous. & Dev. Rep. (WGL) 133 (1988). For a book that analyzes events in the battle over housing in Yonkers, see Lisa Belkin, Show Me a Hero (1999).

Other cases are of the traditional school desegregation variety. In this sort of case there is no attempt to impose a housing remedy as such, but there may be (1) a recognition that housing segregation has caused school segregation when school attendance is neighborhood based, or (b) there is a claim that the residential segregation has been reinforced or fostered by "white flight" because of the school desegregation order. Two major cases raising these considerations are *Board of Education of Oklahoma City Public School, Independent School District No. 89 v. Dowell,* 498 U.S. 237 (1991) and *Missouri v. Jenkins*, 515 U.S. 70 (1995).

Dowell, supra, involved thirty years of litigation. The district court, in prior proceedings, had found that Oklahoma City had intentionally segregated both schools and housing in the past, and that Oklahoma City was operating a "dual" school system that had been intentionally segregated by race. In additional proceedings, the district court found that the school board's attempt to desegregate by using neighborhood zoning failed to remedy past segregation because residential segregation resulted in one-race schools. Residential segregation had once been state imposed, and it lingered due to discrimination by some realtors and financial institutions. In those earlier proceedings, the district court held that school segregation had caused some housing segregation.

After operating under an injunction entered in 1972, the district court found, in 1977, that the school district had achieved "unitary" status. The court issued an order terminating the case. In 1985, the school board adopted a Student Reassignment Plan, under which a number of previously desegregated schools would return to primarily one-race status for the asserted purpose of alleviating greater busing burdens on young black children caused by demographic changes. The parents of black children challenged the assignment plan and sought to have the case reopened as to compliance with the desegregation order. The Supreme Court held, *inter alia*, that school desegregation decrees were not intended to operate in perpetuity, and that in determining whether to dissolve desegregation decree, the district court should consider whether school district had complied in good faith with the desegregation decree since it was entered and whether vestiges of past discrimination have been eliminated to the extent practicable.

In *Jenkins v. Missouri*, 807 F.2d 657 (8th Cir. 1986), *cert. denied*, 484 U.S. 816 (1987), HUD's conduct was expressly examined and HUD was exonerated from having caused housing segregation, and the court thus refused to impose an interdistrict busing order but granted aspects of relief that imposed on the state certain interdistrict funding requirements. In later proceedings in the case *sub nom Missouri v. Jenkins*, 515 U.S. 70 (1995), the Supreme Court rejected the district court's remedial order. In the part of the order dealing with racial demographic shifts affecting school desegregation, the court disapproved the *interdistrict* portion of the order designed to attract nonminority students from outside the school district into the school district on the grounds that the order went beyond the scope of *intradistrict* violation identified. In other aspects of the Supreme Court's decision, the Court disapproved the part of the district court order that required across-the-board salary increases for teachers and staff in pursuit of desegregative attractiveness as being beyond the scope of the court's remedial authority. It also disapproved the part of the order considering whether students in school district were at or below national norms on the grounds that such a consideration was not an appropriate test to determine whether previously segregated district had achieved partially unitary status.

In today's social and judicial climate, the grounds and issues have shifted. *Brown* prohibited conduct of school authorities that intentionally segregated public schools. How should the Court treat intentional conduct of school authorities designed to integrate or to maintain integrated schools?

Perhaps one could argue that we have come to a point at which the promise of *Brown* that schools would be integrated may prove to be increasingly difficult under the current Supreme Court's disposition. How can school districts create or maintain integrated schools when housing is segregated? Consider the case of *Parents Involved in Community Schools v. Seattle School Dist. No. 1*, 551 U.S. 701 (2007) set forth below.

Parents Involved in Community Schools v. Seattle School Dist. No. 1

United States Supreme Court
551 U.S. 701 (2007)

Chief Justice ROBERTS announced the judgment of the Court, and delivered the opinion of the Court with respect to Parts I, II, III-A, and III-C, and an opinion with respect to Parts III-B and IV, in which Justices SCALIA, THOMAS, and ALITO join.

The school districts in these cases voluntarily adopted student assignment plans that rely upon race to determine which public schools certain children may attend. The Seattle school district classifies children as white or nonwhite; the Jefferson County school district as black or "other." In Seattle, this racial classification is used to allocate slots in oversubscribed high schools. In Jefferson County, it is used to make certain elementary school assignments and to rule on transfer requests. In each case, the school district relies upon an individual student's race in assigning that student to a particular school, so that the racial balance at the school falls within a predetermined range based on the racial composition of the school district as a whole. Parents of students denied assignment to particular schools under these plans solely because of their race brought suit, contending that allocating children to different public schools on the basis of race violated the Fourteenth Amendment guarantee of equal protection. The Courts of Appeals below upheld the plans. We granted certiorari, and now reverse.

I

Both cases present the same underlying legal question—whether a public school that had not operated legally segregated schools or has been found to be unitary may choose to classify students by race and rely upon that classification in making school assignments. Although we examine the plans under the same legal framework, the specifics of the two plans, and the circumstances surrounding their adoption, are in some respects quite different.

A. ...

Seattle has never operated segregated schools—legally separate schools for students of different races—nor has it ever been subject to court-ordered desegregation. It nonetheless employs the racial tiebreaker in an attempt to address the effects of racially identifiable housing patterns on school assignments. Most white students live in the northern part of Seattle, most students of other racial backgrounds in the southern part....

B

Jefferson County Public Schools operates the public school system in metropolitan Louisville, Kentucky. In 1973 a federal court found that Jefferson County had maintained a segregated school system ... and in 1975 the District Court entered a desegregation decree.... Jefferson County operated under this decree until 2000, when the District Court dissolved the decree after finding that the district had achieved unitary status by eliminating "[t]o the greatest extent practicable" the vestiges of its prior policy of segregation.... In 2001, after the decree had been dissolved, Jefferson County adopted the voluntary student assignment plan at issue in this case....

III A

It is well established that when the government distributes burdens or benefits on the basis of individual racial classifications, that action is reviewed under strict scrutiny.... As the Court recently reaffirmed, "'racial classifications are simply too pernicious to permit any but the most exact connection between justification and classification....'" In order to satisfy this searching standard of review, the school districts must demonstrate that the use of individual racial classifications in the assignment plans here under review is "narrowly tailored" to achieve a "compelling" government interest.

Without attempting in these cases to set forth all the interests a school district might assert, it suffices to note that our prior cases, in evaluating the use of racial classifications in the school context, have recognized two interests that qualify as compelling. The first is the compelling interest of remedying the effects of past intentional discrimination.... Yet the Seattle public schools have not shown that they were ever segregated by law, and were not subject to court-ordered desegregation decrees. The Jefferson County public schools were previously segregated by law and were subject to a desegregation decree entered in 1975. In 2000, the District Court that entered that decree dissolved it, finding that Jefferson County had "eliminated the vestiges associated with the former policy of segregation and its pernicious effects," and thus had achieved "unitary" status.... Jefferson

County accordingly does not rely upon an interest in remedying the effects of past intentional discrimination in defending its present use of race in assigning students.

Nor could it. We have emphasized that the harm being remedied by mandatory desegregation plans is the harm that is traceable to segregation, and that "the Constitution is not violated by racial imbalance in the schools, without more." *Milliken v. Bradley*, 433 U.S. 267, 280, n. 14 (1977).... Once Jefferson County achieved unitary status, it had remedied the constitutional wrong that allowed race-based assignments. Any continued use of race must be justified on some other basis.

The second government interest we have recognized as compelling for purposes of strict scrutiny is the interest in diversity in higher education upheld in *Grutter v. Bollinger*, 539 U.S. 306, 328 (2003). The specific interest found compelling in *Grutter* was student body diversity "in the context of higher education." The diversity interest was not focused on race alone but encompassed "all factors that may contribute to student body diversity." We described the various types of diversity that the law school sought:

> [The law school's] policy makes clear there are many possible bases for diversity admissions, and provides examples of admittees who have lived or traveled widely abroad, are fluent in several languages, have overcome personal adversity and family hardship, have exceptional records of extensive community service, and have had successful careers in other fields....

The entire gist of the analysis in *Grutter* was that the admissions program at issue there focused on each applicant as an individual, and not simply as a member of a particular racial group. The classification of applicants by race upheld in *Grutter* was only as part of a "highly individualized, holistic review." As the Court explained, "[t]he importance of this individualized consideration in the context of a race-conscious admissions program is paramount." The point of the narrow tailoring analysis in which the *Grutter* Court engaged was to ensure that the use of racial classifications was indeed part of a broader assessment of diversity, and not simply an effort to achieve racial balance, which the Court explained would be "patently unconstitutional...."

In the present cases, by contrast, race is not considered as part of a broader effort to achieve "exposure to widely diverse people, cultures, ideas, and viewpoints ..." race, for some students, is determinative standing alone. The districts argue that other factors, such as student preferences, affect assignment decisions under their plans, but under each plan when race comes into play, it is decisive by itself. It is not simply one factor weighed with others in reaching a decision, as in *Grutter*; it is *the* factor. Like the University of Michigan undergraduate plan struck down in *Gratz v. Bollinger*, 539 U.S. 244 (2003), the plans here "do not provide for a meaningful individualized review of applicants" but instead rely on racial classifications in a "nonindividualized, mechanical" way.... [emphasis by the Court]

Even when it comes to race, the plans here employ only a limited notion of diversity, viewing race exclusively in white/nonwhite terms in Seattle and black/"other" terms in Jefferson County.... The Seattle "Board Statement Reaffirming Diversity Rationale" speaks of the "inherent educational value" in "[p]roviding students the opportunity to attend schools with diverse student enrollment...." But under the Seattle plan, a school with 50 percent Asian-American students and 50 percent white students but no African-American, Native-American, or Latino students would qualify as balanced, while a school with 30 percent Asian-American, 25 percent African-American, 25 percent Latino, and 20 percent white students would not. It is hard to understand how a plan that could allow these results can be viewed as being concerned with achieving enrollment that is "'broadly diverse.'" Citing *Grutter*.

Prior to *Grutter,* the courts of appeals rejected as unconstitutional attempts to implement race-based assignment plans—such as the plans at issue here—in primary and secondary schools. After *Grutter,* however, the two Courts of Appeals in these cases, and one other, found that race-based assignments were permissible at the elementary and secondary level, largely in reliance on that case.

In upholding the admissions plan in *Grutter,* though, this Court relied upon considerations unique to institutions of higher education, noting that in light of "the expansive freedoms of speech and thought associated with the university environment, universities occupy a special niche in our constitutional tradition...." The Court explained that "[c]ontext matters" in applying strict scrutiny, and repeatedly noted that it was addressing the use of race "in the context of higher education." The Court in *Grutter* expressly articulated key limitations on its holding—defining a specific type of broad-based diversity and noting the unique context of higher education—but these limitations were largely disregarded by the lower courts in extending *Grutter* to uphold race-based assignments in elementary and secondary schools. The present cases are not governed by *Grutter.*

B

Perhaps recognizing that reliance on *Grutter* cannot sustain their plans, both school districts assert additional interests, distinct from the interest upheld in *Grutter,* to justify their race-based assignments. In briefing and argument before this Court, Seattle contends that its use of race helps to reduce racial concentration in schools and *to ensure that racially concentrated housing patterns* do not prevent nonwhite students from having access to the most desirable schools.... Jefferson County has articulated a similar goal, phrasing its interest in terms of educating its students "in a racially integrated environment...." Each school district argues that educational and broader socialization benefits flow from a racially diverse learning environment, and each contends that because the diversity they seek is racial diversity—not the broader diversity at issue in *Grutter*—it makes sense to promote that interest directly by relying on race alone.... [emphasis added]

The Ninth Circuit below stated that it "share[d] in the hope" expressed in *Grutter* that in 25 years racial preferences would no longer be necessary to further the interest identified in that case. But in Seattle *the plans are defended as necessary to address the consequences of racially identifiable housing patterns.* [emphasis added.] The sweep of the mandate claimed by the district is contrary to our rulings that remedying past societal discrimination does not justify race-conscious government action....

The principle that racial balancing is not permitted is one of substance, not semantics. Racial balancing is not transformed from "patently unconstitutional" to a compelling state interest simply by relabeling it "racial diversity." While the school districts use various verbal formulations to describe the interest they seek to promote—racial diversity, avoidance of racial isolation, racial integration—they offer no definition of the interest that suggests it differs from racial balance....

C....

The parties and their *amici* debate which side is more faithful to the heritage of *Brown,* but the position of the plaintiffs in *Brown* was spelled out in their brief and could not have been clearer: "[T]he Fourteenth Amendment prevents states from according differential treatment to American children on the basis of their color or race...." What do the racial classifications at issue here do, if not accord differential treatment on the basis of race? As counsel who appeared before this Court for the plaintiffs in *Brown* put it: "We have one fundamental contention which we will seek to develop in the course of this argument, and that contention is that no State has any authority under the equal-protection clause of the Fourteenth Amendment to use race as a factor in affording educational opportunities among its citizens." There is no ambiguity in that statement. And it was that position that prevailed in this Court, which emphasized in its remedial opinion that what was "[a]t stake is the personal interest of the plaintiffs in admission to public schools as soon as practicable *on a nondiscriminatory basis*," and what was required was "determining admission to the public schools *on a nonracial basis*." *Brown v. Board of Educ.*, [349 U.S. 294, at 300–301 (1955) (*Brown II*) (emphasis by the Court)—Eds.] What do the racial classifications do in these cases, if not determine admission to a public school on a racial basis?....

Before *Brown*, school children were told where they could and could not go to school based on the color of their skin. The school districts in these cases have not carried the heavy burden of demonstrating that we should allow this once again—even for very different reasons. For schools that never segregated on the basis of race, such as Seattle, or that have removed the vestiges of past segregation, such as Jefferson County, the way "to achieve a system of determining admission to the public schools on a nonracial basis ..." is to stop assigning students on a racial basis. The way to stop discrimination on the basis of race is to stop discriminating on the basis of race.

The judgments of the Courts of Appeals for the Sixth and Ninth Circuits are reversed, and the cases are remanded for further proceedings.

It is so ordered.

Justice THOMAS, concurring. [Omitted—Eds.]

Justice KENNEDY, concurring in part and concurring in the judgment.

The Nation's schools strive to teach that our strength comes from people of different races, creeds, and cultures uniting in commitment to the freedom of all. In these cases two school districts in different parts of the country seek to teach that principle by having classrooms that reflect the racial makeup of the surrounding community. That the school districts consider these plans to be necessary should remind us our highest aspirations are yet unfulfilled. But the solutions mandated by these school districts must themselves be lawful. To make race matter now so that it might not matter later may entrench the very prejudices we seek to overcome. In my view the state-mandated racial classifications at issue, official labels proclaiming the race of all persons in a broad class of citizens—elementary school students in one case, high school students in another—are unconstitutional as the cases now come to us.

I agree with THE CHIEF JUSTICE that we have jurisdiction to decide the cases before us and join Parts I and II of the Court's opinion. I also join Parts III-A and III-C for reasons provided below....

I

The dissent finds that the school districts have identified a compelling interest in increasing diversity, including for the purpose of avoiding racial isolation. The plurality, by contrast, does not acknowledge that the school districts have identified a compelling interest here.... For this reason, among others, I do not join Parts III-B and IV. Diversity, depending on its meaning and definition, is a compelling educational goal a school district may pursue.

It is well established that when a governmental policy is subjected to strict scrutiny, "the government has the burden of proving that racial classifications 'are narrowly tailored measures that further compelling governmental interests....'" And the inquiry into less restrictive alternatives demanded by the narrow tailoring analysis requires in many cases a thorough understanding of how a plan works. The government bears the burden of justifying its use of individual racial classifications. As part of that burden it must establish, in detail, how decisions based on an individual student's race are made in a challenged governmental program. The Jefferson County Board of Education fails to meet this threshold mandate....

As for the Seattle case, the school district has gone further in describing the methods and criteria used to determine assignment decisions on the basis of individual racial classifications.... The district, nevertheless, has failed to make an adequate showing in at least one respect. It has failed to explain why, in a district composed of a diversity of races, with fewer than half of the students classified as "white," it has employed the crude racial categories of "white" and "non-white" as the basis for its assignment decisions....

As the district fails to account for the classification system it has chosen, despite what appears to be its ill fit, Seattle has not shown its plan to be narrowly tailored to achieve its own ends; and thus it fails to pass strict scrutiny.

II

Our Nation from the inception has sought to preserve and expand the promise of liberty and equality on which it was founded. Today we enjoy a society that is remarkable in its openness and opportunity. Yet our tradition is to go beyond present achievements, however significant, and to recognize and confront the flaws and injustices that remain. This is especially true when we seek assurance that opportunity is not denied on account of race. The enduring hope is that race should not matter; the reality is that too often it does.

This is by way of preface to my respectful submission that parts of the opinion by THE CHIEF JUSTICE imply an all-too-unyielding insistence that race cannot be a factor in instances when, in my view, it may be taken into account. The plurality opinion is too dismissive of the legitimate interest government has in ensuring all people have equal opportunity regardless of their race. The plurality's postulate that "[t]he way to stop discrimination on the basis of race is to stop discriminating on the basis of race," is not sufficient to decide these cases. Fifty years of experience since *Brown v. Board of Education,* 347 U.S. 483 (1954), should teach us that the problem before us defies so easy a solution. School districts can seek to reach *Brown*'s objective of equal educational opportunity. The plurality opinion is at least open to the interpretation that the Constitution requires school districts to ignore the problem of *de facto* resegregation in schooling. I cannot endorse that conclusion. To the extent the plurality opinion suggests the Constitution mandates that state and local school authorities must accept the status quo of racial isolation in schools, it is, in my view, profoundly mistaken.

The statement by Justice Harlan that "[o]ur Constitution is color-blind" was most certainly justified in the context of his dissent in *Plessy v. Ferguson,* 163 U.S. 537, 559 (1896). The Court's decision in that case was a grievous error it took far too long to overrule. *Plessy,* of course, concerned official classification by race applicable to all persons who sought to use railway carriages. And, as an aspiration, Justice Harlan's axiom must command our assent. In the real world, it is regrettable to say, it cannot be a universal constitutional principle.

In the administration of public schools by the state and local authorities it is permissible to consider the racial makeup of schools and to adopt general policies to encourage a diverse student body, one aspect of which is its racial composition. Cf. *Grutter v. Bollinger,*

539 U.S. 306 at 387–388 (2003) (KENNEDY, J., dissenting). If school authorities are concerned that the student-body compositions of certain schools interfere with the objective of offering an equal educational opportunity to all of their students, *they are free to devise race-conscious measures to address the problem in a general way and without treating each student in different fashion solely on the basis of a systematic, individual typing by race.*

School boards may pursue the goal of bringing together students of diverse backgrounds and races through other means, including *strategic site selection of new schools*; drawing attendance zones *with general recognition of the demographics of neighborhoods*; allocating resources for special programs; recruiting students and faculty in a targeted fashion; and tracking enrollments, performance, and other statistics by race. [emphasis added—Eds.] These mechanisms are race conscious but do not lead to different treatment based on a classification that tells each student he or she is to be defined by race, so it is unlikely any of them would demand strict scrutiny to be found permissible. *See Bush v. Vera*, 517 U.S. 952, 958 (1996) (plurality opinion) ("Strict scrutiny does not apply merely because redistricting is performed with consciousness of race.... Electoral district lines are 'facially race neutral' so a more searching inquiry is necessary before strict scrutiny can be found applicable in redistricting cases than in cases of 'classifications based explicitly on race'...." Executive and legislative branches, which for generations now have considered these types of policies and procedures, should be permitted to employ them with candor and with confidence that a constitutional violation does not occur whenever a decisionmaker considers the impact a given approach might have on students of different races. Assigning to each student a personal designation according to a crude system of individual racial classifications is quite a different matter; and the legal analysis changes accordingly.

Each respondent has asserted that its assignment of individual students by race is permissible because there is no other way to avoid racial isolation in the school districts. Yet, as explained, each has failed to provide the support necessary for that proposition. Cf. [*City of Richmond v. J.A. Croson Co.*, 488 U.S. 469, at 501 (1989)—Eds.] ("The history of racial classifications in this country suggests that blind judicial deference to legislative or executive pronouncements of necessity has no place in equal protection analysis"). And individual racial classifications employed in this manner may be considered legitimate only if they are a last resort to achieve a compelling interest. *See id.*, at 519 (KENNEDY, J., concurring in part and concurring in judgment).

In the cases before us it is noteworthy that the number of students whose assignment depends on express racial classifications is limited. I join Part III-C of the Court's opinion because I agree that in the context of these plans, the small number of assignments affected suggests that the schools could have achieved their stated ends through different means. These include the facially race-neutral means set forth above or, if necessary, a more nuanced, individual evaluation of school needs and student characteristics that might include race as a component. The latter approach would be informed by *Grutter*, though of course the criteria relevant to student placement would differ based on the age of the students, the needs of the parents, and the role of the schools.

III

The dissent rests on the assumptions that these sweeping race-based classifications of persons are permitted by existing precedents; that its confident endorsement of race categories for each child in a large segment of the community presents no danger to individual freedom in other, prospective realms of governmental regulation; and that the racial classifications used here cause no hurt or anger of the type the Constitution prevents. Each of these premises is, in my respectful view, incorrect.

A

The dissent's reliance on this Court's precedents to justify the explicit, sweeping, classwide racial classifications at issue here is a misreading of our authorities that, it appears to me, tends to undermine well-accepted principles needed to guard our freedom. And in his critique of that analysis, I am in many respects in agreement with THE CHIEF JUSTICE. The conclusions he has set forth in Part III-A of the Court's opinion are correct, in my view, because the compelling interests implicated in the cases before us are distinct from the interests the Court has recognized in remedying the effects of past intentional discrimination and in increasing diversity in higher education. As the Court notes, we recognized the compelling nature of the interest in remedying past intentional discrimination in *Freeman v. Pitts,* 503 U.S. 467, 494 (1992), and of the interest in diversity in higher education in *Grutter.* At the same time, these compelling interests, in my view, do help inform the present inquiry. And to the extent the plurality opinion can be interpreted to foreclose consideration of these interests, I disagree with that reasoning....

B

To uphold these programs the Court is asked to brush aside two concepts of central importance for determining the validity of laws and decrees designed to alleviate the hurt and adverse consequences resulting from race discrimination. The first is the difference between *de jure* and *de facto* segregation; the second, the presumptive invalidity of a State's use of racial classifications to differentiate its treatment of individuals.

In the immediate aftermath of *Brown* the Court addressed other instances where laws and practices enforced *de jure* segregation. *See, e.g., Loving v. Virginia,* 388 U.S. 1 (1967) (marriage); *New Orleans City Park Improvement Assn. v. Detiege,* 358 U.S. 54 (1958) *(per curiam)* (public parks); *Gayle v. Browder,* 352 U.S. 903 (1956) *(per curiam)* (buses); *Holmes v. Atlanta,* 350 U.S. 879 (1955) *(per curiam)* (golf courses); *Mayor and City Council of Baltimore v. Dawson,* 350 U.S. 877 (1955) *(per curiam)* (beaches). But with reference to schools, the effect of the legal wrong proved most difficult to correct. To remedy the wrong, school districts that had been segregated by law had no choice, whether under court supervision or pursuant to voluntary desegregation efforts, but to resort to extraordinary measures including individual student and teacher assignment to schools based on race. *See, e.g., Swann v. Charlotte-Mecklenburg Bd. of Ed.,* 402 U.S. 14 (1971); *see* also *Croson,* 488 U.S., at 519 (KENNEDY, J., concurring in part and concurring in judgment) (noting that racial classifications "may be the only adequate remedy after a judicial determination that a State or its instrumentality has violated the Equal Protection Clause"). So it was, as the dissent observes, that Louisville classified children by race in its school assignment and busing plan in the 1970's.

Our cases recognized a fundamental difference between those school districts that had engaged in *de jure* segregation and those whose segregation was the result of other factors. School districts that had engaged in *de jure* segregation had an affirmative constitutional duty to desegregate; those that were *de facto* segregated did not....

From the standpoint of the victim, it is true, an injury stemming from racial prejudice can hurt as much when the demeaning treatment based on race identity stems from bias masked deep within the social order as when it is imposed by law. The distinction between government and private action, furthermore, can be amorphous both as a historical matter and as a matter of present-day finding of fact. Laws arise from a culture and vice versa. Neither can assign to the other all responsibility for persisting injustices....

The cases here were argued upon the assumption, and come to us on the premise, that the discrimination in question did not result from *de jure* actions. And when *de facto* discrimination is at issue our tradition has been that the remedial rules are different. The State must seek alternatives to the classification and differential treatment of individuals by race, at least absent some extraordinary showing not present here.

C. ...

The idea that if race is the problem, race is the instrument with which to solve it cannot be accepted as an analytical leap forward. And if this is a frustrating duality of the Equal Protection Clause it simply reflects the duality of our history and our attempts to promote freedom in a world that sometimes seems set against it. Under our Constitution the individual, child or adult, can find his own identity, can define her own persona, without state intervention that classifies on the basis of his race or the color of her skin....

This Nation has a moral and ethical obligation to fulfill its historic commitment to creating an integrated society that ensures equal opportunity for all of its children. A compelling interest exists in avoiding racial isolation, an interest that a school district, in its discretion and expertise, may choose to pursue. Likewise, a district may consider it a compelling interest to achieve a diverse student population. Race may be one component of that diversity, but other demographic factors, plus special talents and needs, should also be considered. What the government is not permitted to do, absent a showing of necessity not made here, is to classify every student on the basis of race and to assign each of them to schools based on that classification. Crude measures of this sort threaten to reduce children to racial chits valued and traded according to one school's supply and another's demand.

That statement, to be sure, invites this response: A sense of stigma may already become the fate of those separated out by circumstances beyond their immediate control. But to this the replication must be: Even so, measures other than differential treatment based on racial typing of individuals first must be exhausted.

The decision today should not prevent school districts from continuing the important work of bringing together students of different racial, ethnic, and economic backgrounds. Due to a variety of factors—some influenced by government, some not—*neighborhoods in our communities do not reflect the diversity of our Nation as a whole.* [emphasis added—Eds.] Those entrusted with directing our public schools can bring to bear the creativity of experts, parents, administrators, and other concerned citizens to find a way to achieve the compelling interests they face without resorting to widespread governmental allocation of benefits and burdens on the basis of racial classifications.

With this explanation I concur in the judgment of the Court.

Justice STEVENS, dissenting.

While I join Justice BREYER's eloquent and unanswerable dissent in its entirety, it is appropriate to add these words.

There is a cruel irony in THE CHIEF JUSTICE's reliance on our decision in *Brown v. Board of Education,* 349 U.S. 294 (1955). The first sentence in the concluding paragraph of his opinion states: "Before *Brown,* schoolchildren were told where they could and could not go to school based on the color of their skin." This sentence reminds me of Anatole France's observation: "[T]he majestic equality of the la[w] ... forbid[s] rich and poor alike to sleep under the bridges, to beg in the streets, and to steal their bread." THE CHIEF JUSTICE fails to note that it was only black schoolchildren who were so ordered; indeed, the history books do not tell stories of white children struggling to attend black schools. In this and other ways, THE CHIEF JUSTICE rewrites the history of one of this Court's most important decisions. Compare *ante*, at 2767 ("history will be heard"), with *Brewer v. Quarterman*, 550 U.S. 286 (2007) (ROBERTS, C. J., dissenting) ("It is a familiar adage that history is written by the victors")....

Justice BREYER, with whom Justice STEVENS, Justice SOUTER, and Justice GINSBURG join, dissenting.

I describe those histories [of extended and extensive activities of the Seattle and Louisville school districts that preceded the current cases] at length in order to highlight three important features of these cases. First, the school districts' plans serve "compelling interests" and are "narrowly tailored" on any reasonable definition of those terms. Second, the distinction between *de jure* segregation (caused by school systems) and *de facto* segregation (caused, *e.g., by housing patterns* or generalized societal discrimination) is meaningless in the present context, thereby dooming the plurality's endeavor to find support for its views in that distinction. [emphasis added.] Third, real-world efforts to substitute racially diverse for racially segregated schools (however caused) are complex, to the point where the Constitution cannot plausibly be interpreted to rule out categorically all local efforts to use means that are "conscious" of the race of individuals....

Notes and Questions

1. Perhaps one could argue that we have come to a point at which the promise of *Brown* may not be fulfilled. Does the focus on the issue of race in isolation from its historical context work an injustice by treating communities in which segregation was not an openly declared policy different from communities which achieve the same segregated, unequal, poor educational outcome but there is no evidence that can be gleaned of a segregative intent? It has been suggested that:

> The issue before the Court [in *Brown*] was whether the states' intentional imposition of unequal education on the basis of race violated the equal protection clause. The issue thus had three distinct elements. First, the segregation was intentional. Second, it was unequal. Third, it was premised on race. Thus, the issue of unequal education in the absence of intentional state conduct was not presented. Nor was the issue of educational quality *qua* quality raised. Finally, the question of unequal education, even if intentionally imposed, but on some basis other than race—such as geography or family income—was not raised.
>
> In all of the cases I can find in which the Court has addressed education, but in which all three *Brown* elements were not present, the Court has refused to find a violation of equal protection.

Charles E. Daye, *Justice Byron R. White*, in *Symposium, Contributions of the Warren Court to Equal Protection*, 12 N. C. CENT. L. REV. 260, 266–67 (1980–81).

Thus, even when there is segregation but the state has not intentionally caused it there is no violation. *Keyes v. School District No. 1*, 413 U.S. 189 (1973). When there is unequal education but it is imposed on a non-racial basis (such as a property taxing system) there is no violation. *San Antonio Independent School District v. Rodriguez*, 411 U.S. (1973). When the segregation is caused by some factor other than race (such as geographic or housing patterns) there is no violation. *Pasadena City Bd. of Educ. v. Spangler*, 427 U.S. 424, 436–37 (1976).

2. Do cases like *Parents Involved and even Pasadena City Board of Education v. Spangler*, 427 U.S. 424 (1976), *supra note 1,* suggest that school remedies such as busing plans and school assignment plans are simply ineffective to break the segregation/resegregation cycle that is based on shifting housing occupancy patterns? Should district courts be required to periodically redraft school plans to override population shifts? Does it matter whether the shift can be proved, at least in part, to result from prior school desegregation plans? *See generally* Michael L. Wells, *Race-Conscious Student Assignment Plans After* Parents Involved*: Bringing State Action Principles to Bear on the De Jure/De Facto Distinction*, 112 Penn St. L. Rev. 1023 (2008) (examining the opinions of the Justices in *Parents Involved* and the difference between de jure segregation and de facto and raising questions about a bright-line de jure/de facto distinction of the plurality and the dissent's refusal to draw any distinction at all and proposing "a middle course" by arguing that a range of policy considerations should be brought to bear on the issue of whether the segregation in a given school district should be characterized as de jure or de facto). What is the compelling interest in *Parents Involved* that justifies a school integration plan? What sorts of voluntary plans are authorized by the majority of Justice Kennedy together with the dissenters?

3. At some point, are association freedoms infringed when a family that chooses a certain neighborhood for its excellent schools is required to send its children elsewhere? Or is that the right question? Suppose a significant number of families, black and white, choose neighborhoods because of their racial composition? Would it make a difference for either the school remedy or the housing remedy if it could be shown that middle- and upper-income black families (those with theoretical choice) voluntarily choose predominantly black neighborhoods because they want their children to be exposed to children who share their cultural background, or simply prefer their having neighborhood playmates of their racial background? Finally, would it make any difference if this "choice" were exercised because of a concern that their children might be exposed to ostracism or racial slurs on the neighborhood playground if black families try to integrate white neighborhoods? For a view questioning certain integration-premised assumptions, *see* Derrick A. Bell, *Serving Two Masters: Integration Ideals and Client Interests in School Desegregation Litigation*, 85 Yale L.J. 470 (1976).

4. The relationships between schools and housing are far too extensive to explore fully. Four key cases to analyze together are *Milliken v. Bradley*, *supra* (denying a metropolitan remedy for schools); *Hills v. Gautreaux*, *supra* (purportedly permitting metropolitan housing relief, but recognizing that housing is still subject to local governmental land-use controls); *Warth v. Seldin*, 422 U.S. 490 (1975) (denying standing to persons who do not reside in the jurisdiction); *Arlington I*, *supra* (holding that in a constitutional challenge to exclusionary zoning on equal protection grounds, plaintiffs must prove intent or purpose to discriminate). Together, these cases paint a less than bright picture for successful litigation about the housing-schools nexus. Do you *see* why this is so?

5. For further study on the data base problem, see Deirdre Pfeiffer, The Opportunity Illusion: Subsidized Housing and Failing Schools in California (2009) (published by The Civil Rights Project and critiquing the Low Income Housing Tax Credit Program as failing to meet civil rights and fair housing laws, as not lessening social, economic, or racial isolation, and as not offering opportunities to children to attend non-racially identifiable schools), available at www.civilrightsproject.ucla.edu (last visited Feb. 16, 2010).

See also Reynolds Farley, *Residential Segregation and Its Implications for School Integration*, 39 Law & Contemp. Probs. 164 (Winter 1975); Karl E. Taeuber, *Demographic Perspectives on Housing and School Segregation*, 21 Wayne L. Rev. 833 (1975).

6. Courts have considered an interdistrict remedy in housing cases other than *Hills v. Gautreaux*, see, *e.g.*, *Crow v. Brown*, 332 F. Supp. 382 (N.D. Ga. 1971), *aff'd per curiam*, 457 F.2d 788 (5th Cir. 1972) (imposing an interdistrict public housing desegregation order), and in school cases other than *Milliken v. Bradley*. Compare *Bradley v. School Board*, 462 F.2d 1058 (4th Cir. 1972), *aff'd by an equally divided Court sub nom. School Board v. State Bd. of Educ.*, 412 U.S. 92 (1973) (denying a metropolitan remedy) with *Evans v. Buchanan*, 393 F. Supp. 428 (D. Del. 1975), *summarily aff'd*, 423 U.S. 963 (1975) (considering interdistrict order). In *United States v. Board of School Commissioners*, 637 F.2d 1101 (7th Cir.), *cert. denied*, 449 U.S. 838 (1980) (generally referred to as "the Indianapolis case," where segregated public housing site selection was one factor the court considered in formulating a metropolitan remedy. *See also Little Rock School Dist. v. Pulaski County Special School Dist.*, 778 F.2d 404 (8th Dist. 1985) (en banc) (denying consolidation of school districts but imposing interdistrict remedies, in part, because of intentional segregation by local public agencies, with state authority, in public housing).

7. For commentary on the relationship between housing desegregation and school desegregation, see Erica Frankenberg, Leah C. Aden & Charles E. Daye, *Introduction, The Future is Now: Legal and Policy Options for Racially Integrated Education*, 88 N.C. L. Rev. 713 (2010) (introducing a series of articles dealing with education that propose solutions to problems presented by *Parents Involved*). The articles introduced are: Kristi L. Bowman, *Pursuing Educational Opportunities for Hispanic Students*, 88 N.C. L. Rev. 911 (2010) (suggesting, inter alia, that in light of the *Parents Involved* decision, the Supreme Court likely will evaluate the legality of integration policies based on whether districts' policies consider various minority groups outside of the "traditional," binary classification of race used in many court-ordered desegregation plans that were once, but are not now, reflective of many districts' student demographics.); William J. Glenn, *Altering Grade Configurations in Virginia Schools: Reducing School Segregation Without Necessarily Considering Race in Light of the* Parents Involved *Ruling*, 88 N.C. L. Rev. 1091 (2010) (suggesting that school districts consider grade reconfiguration as a method for educating all grade level students at the same school within a district); Danielle Holley-Walker, *After Unitary Status: Examining Voluntary Integration Strategies for Southern School Districts*, 88 N.C. L. Rev. 877 (2010) (providing empirical data to inform the scholarly debate about the extent to which courts are *not vehicles for* expanding education rights and looking at the important implications for the long-term impact of *Parents Involved*); Chinh Q. Le, *Racially Integrated Education and the Role of the Federal Government*, 88 N.C. L. Rev. 725 (2010) (positing that the political atmosphere is ripe to resurrect the federal government's commitments to civil rights in education under a new federal administration that prioritizes education reform); Roslyn Arlin Mickelson & Martha Bottia, *Integrated Education and Mathematics Outcomes: A Synthesis of Social Science Research*, 88 N.C. L. Rev. 993 (2010) (stressing the role integrated schools can play in remedying our national education crisis and evaluating high quality research from the past twenty years about the relationships between persistent gaps in mathematics achievement and the racial and socioeconomic composition of K-12 schools); Kimberly Jenkins Robinson, *Resurrecting the Promise of* Brown: *Understanding and Remedying How the Supreme Court Reconstitutionalized Segregated Schools*, 88 N.C. L. Rev. 787 (2010) (observing that courts may be of little help in pursuing integrated education in light of a review of decades-long judicial trends detrimental to integrating schools and recommending a series of executive

branch solutions for seeking integration); Stephen Samuel Smith, *Still Swimming Against the Resegregation Tide? A Suburban Southern School District in the Aftermath of* Parents Involved, 88 N.C. L. Rev. 1145 (2010) (describing the use of boundaries as a way to further integration, and illustrating the comprehensive approach needed today to pursue integration).

8. Other scholarship includes: Grover G. Hankins, *The Constitutional Implications of Residential Segregation and School Segregation*, 30 How. L.J. 773 (1987); Marjorie Heins, Comment, *Housing Remedies in School Desegregation Cases: The View from Indianapolis*, 12 Harv. C.R.-C.L. L. Rev. 649 (1977); Paul M. Ong & Jordan Rickles, *The Continued Nexus between School and Residential Segregation*, 15 Berkeley La Raza L.J. 51 (2004) (school segregation and residential segregation patterns differ depending on racial/ethnic compositions, but school segregation and residential segregation are strongly linked such that it is impossible to seek school integration without addressing residential segregation); Docia L. Rudley, *School Desegregation: Whose Responsibility?*, 12 T. Marshall L. Rev. 109 (1986); Robert R. Harding, Note, *Housing Discrimination as a Basis for Interdistrict School Desegregation Remedies*, 93 Yale L.J. 340 (1983).

9. Recall that *Hills v. Gautreaux* permits consideration of metro-area relief. How effective can the metropolitan housing order be even in the few rare cases in which it might be granted? One of the problems is that suburban areas and smaller municipalities may be committed to low density, single-family development. Such requirements, usually imposed through zoning and land-use regulation, can prevent or severely limit the placement of housing units under federal programs and housing units that might be privately built which could be used in demand programs such as Section 8 vouchers and housing allowances. These questions are analyzed in the next case in the following section.

b. Discriminatory Effects: The Prima Facie *Case Approach*

Huntington Branch, NAACP v. Town of Huntington

United States Court of Appeals
844 F.2d 926 (2d Cir.),
aff'd per curiam, 488 U.S. 15 (1988)

Before KAUFMAN, OAKES, and NEWMAN, Circuit Judges.

IRVING R. KAUFMAN, Circuit Judge:

Twenty years ago, widespread racial segregation threatened to rip civil society asunder. In response, Congress adopted broad remedial provisions to promote integration. One such statute, Title VIII of the Civil Rights Act of 1968 ("Fair Housing Act"), was enacted "to provide, within constitutional limitations, for fair housing throughout the United States." 42 U.S.C. § 3601. Today, we are called upon to decide whether an overwhelmingly white suburb's zoning regulation, which restricts private multi-family housing projects to a largely minority "urban renewal area," and the Town Board's refusal to amend that ordinance to allow construction of subsidized housing in a white neighborhood violates the Fair Housing Act.

The Huntington Branch of the National Association for the Advancement of Colored People (NAACP), Housing Help, Inc. (HHI), and two black, low-income residents of Huntington appeal from an adverse judgment of the United States District Court for the Eastern District of New York (Glasser, J.), following a bench trial, in their suit against the Town of Huntington (the Town) and members of its Town Board. Appellants allege that the Town violated Title VIII by restricting private construction multi-family housing to a narrow urban renewal area and by refusing to rezone the parcel outside this area where appellants wished to build multi-family housing. Specifically, appellants sought to construct an integrated, multi-family subsidized apartment complex in Greenlawn/East Northport, a virtually all-white neighborhood. The Town's zoning ordinance, however, prohibited private construction of multi-family housing outside a small urban renewal zone in the Huntington Station neighborhood which is 52% minority. Thus, appellants petitioned the Town to revise its code to accommodate the project. When the Town refused, appellants brought this class action to compel the change under Title VIII.

In the case currently appealed, *Huntington Branch, NAACP v. Huntington*, 668 F. Supp. 762 (E.D.N.Y. 1987), the district court refused to invalidate the zoning restriction. The district judge, however, incorrectly employed an intent-based standard for the disparate impact claim asserted here both in analyzing the showing of effect and in scrutinizing the validity of the Town's reasons for rejection. Accordingly, we reverse and, finding a Title VIII violation, grant appellants' request for site-specific relief. Although prior opinions exhaustively document the facts, a brief statement of the pertinent points will aid in the understanding of this case.

[Here the court discusses in detail factual findings that Huntington is a town of approximately 200,000 people; that in 1980, 95% of its residents were white; that blacks comprised only 3.35% of the town's population and were concentrated in areas known as Huntington Station and South Greenlawn; that the town has a shortage of affordable rental housing for low- and moderate-income households; that the town's Housing Assistance Plan (HAP) reveals that the impact of this shortage is three times greater on blacks than on the overall population; that a disproportionately large percentage of families in existing subsidized projects are minority; that, although a disproportionate number of minorities need low-cost housing, the town has attempted to limit minority occupancy in subsidized housing projects; that the town attempted to impose racial quotas on occupancy at a proposed 150-unit subsidized housing project in Huntington Station on the Melville Industrial Associates (MIA) site; and that HUD's area director wrote the town supervisor, that "limitations on minority occupancy of housing on the Huntington Station site are not justifiable and will not be permitted," in response to which the town board unanimously passed a resolution withdrawing its support for the project because they could not "ensure a particular ethnic mix." The court further found that under the town's zoning ordinance, multifamily housing is permitted only in an "R-3M Apartment District" and concluded that on its face the provision limited private construction of multifamily housing to the town's urban renewal area, where 52% of the residents are minority. Only one vacant parcel of land in Huntington was zoned R-3M and thus would be eligible for the appellants' proposed development: the MIA site. HHI determined that the project could foster racial integration only if it were located in a white neighborhood outside the Huntington Station and South Greenlawn areas. This decision eliminated consideration of the MIA site, the only vacant R-3M property located in the urban renewal area. The court further noted that HHI actively sought the assistance of town officials and that some of them assured HHI representatives that existing zoning should not impede their efforts because the town board would amend the zoning ordinance if it supported the organization's project. After a lengthy search, HHI determined that a 14.8-acre parcel located in the town was well suited for a 162-unit housing project because 98% of the population within a one-mile radius of the site was white. HHI set a goal of 25% minority occupants. The district court found that "a significant percentage of the tenants (at Matinecock Court) would have belonged to minority groups." HHI obtained its option to purchase the site and throughout 1980, HHI sought the approval of the town board to rezone the property to R-3M. When the proposal became public, substantial community opposition developed. The court's discussion continued—Eds.]

The district court based its refusal to order rezoning on three alternative grounds: (1) appellants never formally applied for rezoning; (2) even if they had applied, they failed to make the requisite *prima facie* showing of discriminatory effect; and (3) even if they had demonstrated discriminatory effect, the city had rebutted it by articulating legitimate, non-pretextual justifications. We now consider each ground separately. [The court found that the plaintiffs had made sufficient application and rejected the first ground—Eds.]

In its second holding, the court adopted the four-prong disparate impact test set out in *Metropolitan Housing Development Corporation v. Village of Arlington Heights*, 558 F.2d 1283, 1287–90 (7th Cir. 1977), *cert. denied*, 434 U.S. 1025 (1978) [hereinafter cited as *Arlington II*—Eds.], and concluded that, even if appellants applied for a rezoning change, they had failed to make out a *prima facie* case. The court considered:

> (1) how strong is the plaintiff's showing of discriminatory effect; (2) is there some evidence of discriminatory intent, though not enough to satisfy the constitutional standard of *Washington v. Davis*, [426 U.S. 229 (1976)]; (3) what is the defendant's interest in taking the action complained of; and (4) does the plaintiff seek to compel the defendant to affirmatively provide housing for members of minority groups or merely to restrain the defendant from interfering with individual property owners who wish to provide such housing.

Huntington, 668 F. Supp. at 781 (quoting *Arlington II*, 558 F.2d at 1290). On the first prong, the court found that the showing of discriminatory effect was "not particularly strong." Although the judge held that a shortage of rental housing existed, that a disproportionately large percentage of the households using subsidized rental units are minority, and, accordingly, that a "significant percentage" of Matinecock Court tenants would be minority, he compared the larger absolute number of white poor (22,160) with minority poor (3,671) and concluded that the beneficiaries "might not come disproportionately from minority groups." On the second factor, Judge Glasser found no proof of segregative intent, deeming this a plus in the Town's favor. In so holding, he determined that appellants had failed to prove that the Town was motivated by segregative intent when it confined subsidized housing to the urban renewal area. The third prong of *Arlington II*, he concluded, was satisfied by "legitimate, nondiscriminatory reasons for (the Town's) conduct." He deemed the fourth factor to cut in favor of appellants because they were not asking the Town to provide housing. Nevertheless, because the first three factors weighed in favor of appellees, he held that the appellants had failed to demonstrate a *prima facie* case.

In its third rationale, the court applied the test set forth in *McDonnell Douglas Corp. v. Green*, 411 U.S. 792 (1973), as a final determination on the merits for Title VII disparate treatment cases. According to this formula, if plaintiffs establish a *prima facie* case of disparate treatment, the "burden shifts to the defendant to articulate some legitimate, nondiscriminatory reason for the employee's rejection." If defendants meet this burden, plaintiffs must show that the legitimate justifications offered were pretextual and not the employer's true reasons. Applying this test, the court below found that, even if appellants had demonstrated a *prima facie* showing of discriminatory effect, the Town's justifications for rejecting the project were legitimate and nondiscriminatory reasons which "have not been exposed as pretextual."

We find it convenient to discuss Judge Glasser's second and third holdings together. In considering them, we start by pointing out that this case requires what has been called "disparate impact" or "disparate effects" analysis, not "disparate treatment" analysis. A disparate impact analysis examines a facially-neutral policy or practice such as a hiring test or zoning law, for its differential impact or effect on a particular group. Disparate treatment analysis, on the other hand, involves differential treatment of similarly situated persons or groups. The line is not always a bright one, but does adequately delineate two very different kinds of discrimination claims.

Here, appellees would collapse the distinction between disparate impact and disparate treatment by characterizing this as a "mixed" impact and treatment case. Thus, they argue, "treatment" analysis should be applied to the Town's refusal to rezone the Matinecock Court site, while "impact" analysis should be applied to the zoning ordinance's restriction of multi-family housing to the urban renewal area. Under appellees' methodology, however, every disparate impact case would include a disparate treatment component. This cannot be the case. There is always some discrete event (refusal to rezone property, refusal to hire someone because he did not graduate from high school) which touches off litigation challenging a neutral rule or policy.

The *prima facie* standard for Title VIII disparate impact cases involving public defendants is a question of first impression in this circuit. We have pointedly accepted the relevance of Title VII cases to Title VIII cases. The disparate impact approach of Title VII cases is fully applicable to this Title VIII case brought against a public defendant.

Under disparate impact analysis, as other circuits have recognized, a *prima facie* case is established by showing that the challenged practice of the defendant "actually or predictably results in racial discrimination; in other words that it has a discriminatory effect." The plaintiff need not show that the decision complained of was made with discriminatory intent. In determining whether discriminatory effect is sufficient, we look to congressional purpose, as gleaned from the legislative history of Title VIII, related Title VII jurisprudence, and practical concerns. Although none of these considerations is alone determinative, taken together they strongly suggest that discriminatory impact alone violates Title VIII.

The Act's stated purpose to end discrimination requires a discriminatory effect standard; an intent requirement would strip the statute of all impact on *de facto* segregation.... The two statutes are part of a coordinated scheme of federal civil rights laws enacted to end discrimination; the Supreme Court has held that both statutes must be construed expansively to implement that goal. Thus, just as the Supreme Court held that Title VII is violated by a showing of discriminatory effect, [*Griggs v. Duke Power Co.*, 401 U.S. 424 (1971) hereinafter cited as *Griggs*—Eds.] we hold that a Title VIII violation can be established without proof of discriminatory intent.

Practical concerns also militate against inclusion of intent in any disparate impact analysis. First, as this court noted in [*Robinson v. 12 Lofts Realty, Inc.*, 610 F.2d 1032 (2d Cir. 1979) reproduced *infra*—Eds.] "clever men may easily conceal their motivations." This is especially persuasive in disparate impact cases where a facially neutral rule is being challenged. Often, such rules bear no relation to discrimination upon passage, but develop into powerful discriminatory mechanisms when applied. Second, inclusion of intent undermines the trial judge's inquiry into the impact of an action. The lower court's insistence on probing the "pretextual" nature of appellees' justifications vividly demonstrates the extent to which an intent-based standard can infect an analysis and draw it away from its proper focus. Accordingly, we will not require proof of discriminatory intent to establish a *prima facie* disparate impact case under Title VIII.

Confusion concerning the content of a *prima facie* disparate impact case under Title VIII has been engendered by the tendency of some courts to consider factors normally advanced as part of a defendant's justification for its challenged action in assessing whether the plaintiff has established a *prima facie* case. That appears to have occurred in this case when Judge Glasser analyzed the factors set forth in *Arlington II* in the course of concluding that a *prima facie* case was not established. Though, as will shortly appear, we are not persuaded to adopt precisely the formulation of the *Arlington II* factors, we agree with the Third Circuit that factors such as those mentioned in *Arlington II* are to be considered in a final determination on the merits rather than as a requirement for a *prima facie* case.

Nothing in *Arlington II* indicates the court saw its test as anything but a final determination on the merits. Furthermore, treating the four factors as steps necessary to make out a *prima facie* case places too onerous a burden on appellants. The legislative history of the Fair Housing Act, although sparse, argues persuasively against so daunting a *prima facie* standard.

Moreover, both the majority and the thoughtful dissent in a recent Title VIII case in this circuit, [*United States v. Starrett City Associates*, reprinted *infra*—Eds.], agree: Congress intended that broad application of the anti-discrimination provisions would ultimately result in residential integration. Employing the test in *Arlington II* as a *prima facie* hurdle would cripple Title VIII.

Once a *prima facie* case of adverse impact is presented, as occurred here, the inquiry turns to the standard to be applied in determining whether the defendant can nonetheless avoid liability under Title VIII. The Third Circuit in [*Resident Advisory Board v. Rizzo*, 564 F.2d 125 (3d Cir. 1977)—Eds.] and the Seventh Circuit in *Arlington II* have both made useful contributions to this inquiry. Both circuits essentially recognize that in the end there must be a weighing of the adverse impact against the defendant's justification. As phrased by the Third Circuit, the defendant must prove that its actions furthered, in theory and in practice, a legitimate, bona fide governmental interest and that no alternative would serve that interest with less discriminatory effect. *Rizzo*. We agree with that formulation. Furthermore, according to the Third Circuit, "Title VIII criteria (would) emerge, then, on case-by-case basis." The Seventh Circuit adds two other factors that can affect the ultimate determination on the merits. One factor is whether there is any evidence of discriminatory intent on the part of the defendant. Though we have ruled that such intent is not a requirement of the plaintiff's *prima facie* case, there can be little doubt that if evidence of such intent is presented, that evidence would weigh heavily on the plaintiff's side of the ultimate balance. The other factor is whether the plaintiff is suing to compel a governmental defendant to build housing or only to require a governmental defendant to eliminate some obstacle to housing that the plaintiff itself will build. In the latter circumstance, a defendant would normally have to establish a somewhat more substantial justification for its adverse action that would be required if the defendant were defending its decision not to build.

In this case, we are obliged to refine the standard for assessing a Title VIII defendant's justification somewhat beyond what was said in either *Rizzo* or *Arlington II*. In *Rizzo*, two of the defendants offered no justification for the adverse decision, and the municipal defendant offered only the entire unacceptable apprehension of violence. The Third Circuit, therefore did not have anything of substance to weigh on the defendants' side. In *Arlington II*, the consideration of the defendant's justification scarcely moved past inquiring whether the municipal defendant was acting within the scope of zoning authority granted by state law.

In considering the defendant's justification, we start with the framework of Title VII analysis. When an employer's facially neutral rule is shown to have a racially disproportionate effect on job applicants, that rule must be shown to be substantially related to job performance. In a zoning case, the facially neutral rule is the provision of the zoning ordinance that bars the applicant and, in doing so, exerts a racially disproportionate effect on minorities. The difficulty, however, is that in Title VIII cases there is no single objective like job performance to which the legitimacy of the facially neutral rule may be related. A town's preference to maintain a particular zoning category for particular sections of the community is normally based on a variety of circumstances. The complexity of the considerations, however, does not relieve a court of the obligation to assess whatever justifications the town advances and weigh them carefully against the degree of adverse effect the plaintiff has shown. Though a town's interests in zoning requirements are substantial, they cannot, consistently with Title VIII, automatically outweigh significant disparate effects.

A district court's findings of fact may not be set aside "unless clearly erroneous." Fed. R. Civ. P. 52(a). But Rule 52(a), the Supreme Court has held, "does not inhibit an appellate court's power to correct errors of law, including those that may infect a so-called mixed finding of law, or a finding of fact that is predicated on a misunderstanding of the governing rule of law." With these principles in mind, we review Judge Glasser's findings in two areas: the strength of the discriminatory effect and the import of the Town's justifications.

The discriminatory effect of a rule arises in two contexts: adverse impact on a particular minority group and harm to the community generally by the perpetuation of segregation. *Arlington II*, 558 F.2d at 1290. In analyzing Huntington's restrictive zoning, however, the lower court concentrated on the harm to blacks as a group, and failed to consider the segregative effect of maintaining a zoning ordinance that restricts private multi-family housing to an area with a high minority concentration. Yet, recognizing this second form of effect advances the principal purpose of Title VIII to promote, "open, integrated residential housing patterns."

Seventy percent of Huntington's black population reside in Huntington Station and South Greenlawn. Matinecock Court, with its goal of 25% minorities, would begin desegregating a neighborhood which is currently 98% white. Indeed, the district court found that a "significant percentage of the tenants" at Matinecock Court would belong to minority groups. The court, however, failed to take the logical next step and find that the refusal to permit projects outside the urban renewal area with its high concentration of minorities reinforced racial segregation in housing. This was erroneous. Similarly, the district court found that the Town has a shortage of rental housing affordable for low- and moderate-income households, that a "disproportionately" large percentage of the households using subsidized rental units are minority citizens, and that a disproportionately large number of minorities are on the waiting lists for subsidized housing and existing Section 8 certificates. But it failed to recognize that Huntington's zoning ordinance, which restricts private construction of multi-family housing to the largely minority urban renewal area, impedes integration by restricting low-income housing needed by minorities to an area already 52% minority. We thus find that Huntington's refusal to amend the restrictive zoning ordinance to permit privately-built multi-family housing outside the urban renewal area significantly perpetuated segregation in the Town.

On the question of harm to blacks as a group, the district court emphasized that 22,160 whites and 3,671 minorities had incomes below 200% of the poverty line, a cutoff close to the Huntington Housing Authority's qualification standards. Thus, the district court focused on the greater absolute number of poor whites compared with indigent minorities in Huntington. The district court, however, did not analyze the disproportionate burden on minorities as required by *Griggs, supra.* By relying on absolute numbers rather than on proportional statistics, the district court significantly underestimated the disproportionate impact of the Town's policy. Thus, the district court perceived facts through a misapprehension of the applicable law and we must make our own findings at least as to the significance of the undisputed underlying facts.

The parties have stipulated that 28% of minorities in Huntington and 11% of whites have incomes below 200% of the poverty line. What they dispute is the meaning of these statistics. Judge Glasser found that, as the Town contends, there is no showing of discriminatory effect because a majority of the victims are white. We disagree for reasons analogous to those the Supreme Court enumerated in *Griggs.* The disparity is of a magnitude similar to that in *Griggs,* where the Court found discriminatory an employer's policy of hiring only high school graduates because 12% of black males in North Carolina had high school diplomas while 34% of white males were high school graduates. But the plaintiffs presented even stronger evidence reflecting the disparate impact of preventing the project from proceeding. Under the Huntington HAP for 1982–1985, 7% of all Huntington families needed subsidized housing, while 24% of the black families needed such housing. In addition, minorities constitute a far greater percentage of those currently occupying subsidized rental projects compared to their percentage in the Town's population. Similarly, a disproportionately high percentage (60%) of families holding Section 8 certificates from the Housing Authority to supplement their rents are minorities, and an equally disproportionate percentage (61%) of those on the waiting list for such certificates are minorities. Therefore, we conclude that the failure to rezone the Matinecock Court site had a substantial adverse impact on minorities.

In sum, we find that the disproportionate harm to blacks and the segregative impact on the entire community resulting from the refusal to rezone create a strong *prima facie* showing of discriminatory effect—far more than the *Rizzo* test would require. Thus, we must consider the Town's asserted justifications.

Once a plaintiff has made a *prima facie* showing of discriminatory effect, a defendant must present bona fide and legitimate justifications for its action with no less discriminatory alternatives available. Following *McDonnell Douglas,* a disparate treatment case, Judge Glasser held that if appellees articulate a legitimate, nondiscriminatory reason for their conduct, appellants must show that the reason is a "pretext." He went on to list the, seven reasons in Butterfield's October 14, 1980, letter to HUD and found then "legitimate, nondiscriminatory" reasons which "have not been exposed as pretextual." *Huntington,* 668 F. Supp. at 787. The *McDonnell Douglas* test, however, is an intent-based standard for disparate treatment cases inapposite to the disparate impact claim asserted here. No circuit, in an impact case, has required plaintiffs to prove that defendants' justifications were pretextual. In *Black Jack,* 508 F.2d at 1185, for example, the court required defendants to show that their conduct was necessary to promote a "compelling governmental interest." The Third Circuit in *Rizzo* rejected this standard for its own test of legitimate and bona fide concerns.

The *Rizzo* approach has two components: (1) whether the reasons are bona fide and legitimate; and (2) whether any less discriminatory alternative can serve those ends. For analytical ease, the second prong should be considered first. Concerns can usually be divided between "plan-specific" justifications and those which are "site-specific." "Plan-specific" problems can be resolved by the less discriminatory alternative of requiring reasonable design modifications. "Site-specific" justifications, however, would usually survive this prong of the test. Those remaining reasons are then scrutinized to determine if they are legitimate and bona fide. By that, we do not intend to devise a search for pretext. Rather, the inquiry is whether the proffered justification is of substantial concern such that it would justify a reasonable official in making this determination. Of course, a concern may be non-frivolous, but may not be sufficient because it is not reflected in the record.

Appellants challenge both the ordinance which restricts privately-built multi-family housing to the urban renewal area and the Town Board's decision to refuse to rezone the Elwood-Pulaski site. All the parties and the district court judge, however, focused on the latter issue. Indeed, appellees below simply relied on the existence of the Housing Assistance Plan and the zoning ordinance and failed to present any substantial evidence indicating a significant interest in limiting private developers to the urban renewal area. On appeal, appellees now contend that the ordinance is designed to encourage private developers to build in the deteriorated area of Huntington Station. Although we believe that the Town's failure to raise this argument below precludes its consideration here, we briefly address this contention. The Town asserts that limiting multi-family development to the urban renewal area will encourage restoration of the neighborhood because, otherwise, developers will choose to build in the outlying areas and will bypass the zone. The Town's goal, however, can be achieved by less discriminatory means, by encouraging development in the urban renewal area with tax incentives or abatements. The Town may assert that this is less effective, but it may actually be more so.

Developers are not wed to building in Huntington; they are filling a perceived economic void. Developments inside the urban renewal area and outside it are not fungible. Rather, developers prevented from building outside the urban renewal area will more likely build in another town, not the urban renewal area. Huntington incorrectly assumes that developers limit their area of interest by political subdivision. In fact, the decision where to build is much more complex. Hence, if the Town wishes to encourage growth in the urban renewal area, it should do so directly through incentives which would have a less discriminatory impact on the Town.

We turn next to the Town's reasons rejecting the Elwood-Pulaski site. The 1980 letter written by Town Supervisor Butterfield detailed seven justifications for the Town's refusal to rezone: (1) inconsistency with the Town's Housing Assistance Plan; (2) inconsistency with zoning; (3) traffic considerations; (4) parking and fire protection problems; (5) proximity to the railroad and Long Island Lighting Company substation; (6) inadequate recreation and play areas; and (7) undersized and unrealistic units. As the judge below noted, the first two beg the question because appellants are challenging the Town's zoning ordinance. More significantly, as we have already indicated, the Town simply relied on the existence of the Housing Assistance Plan and the zoning ordinance and failed to present any substantial evidence indicating why precluding plaintiff from building a multi-family housing project outside the urban renewal area would impair significant interests sought to be advanced by the HAP and the ordinance. The fourth, sixth and seventh problems are "plan-specific" issues which could presumably have been solved with reasonable design modifications at the time appellants applied for rezoning of the parcel. The fifth concern also is largely plan-specific because proper landscaping could shield the project from the railroad and substation.

Thus, only the traffic issue and health hazard from the substation are site-specific. At trial, however, none of Huntington's officials supported these objections. Butterfield, for example, was primarily concerned that the Matinecock Court project would "torpedo" the Town's plan to develop the site at Broadway and New York Avenue in the urban renewal area in Huntington Station. Moreover, Huntington's only expert, planner David Portman, set forth entirely different problems than were contained in Butterfield's letters. Specifically, he noted sewage concerns, lack of conformity with the low density of the surrounding neighborhood, and inaccessibility of the site to public transportation. Once during his testimony, he did mention "the relationship (of the site) to the power station." Never, however, did he raise any concern about a health hazard from the proximity to the substation. Indeed, appellees do not broach this issue in their brief to this court. Accordingly, we find the reasons asserted are entirely insubstantial.

The sewage problem was first raised at trial by appellees' expert Portman. Appellees now advance it as an additional concern. The district court, however, chose not to consider it. We agree. *Post hoc* rationalizations by administrative agencies should be afforded "little deference" by the courts, and therefore cannot be a bona fide reason for the Town's action. Moreover, the sewage concern could hardly have been significant if municipal officials only thought of it after the litigation began. If it did not impress itself on the Town Board at the time of rejection, it was obviously not a legitimate problem. In sum, the only factor in the Town's favor was that it was acting within the scope of its zoning authority, and thus we conclude that the Town's justifications were weak and inadequate.

In balancing the showing of discriminatory effect against the import of the Town's justifications, we note our agreement with the Seventh Circuit that the balance should be more readily struck in favor of the plaintiff when it is seeking only to enjoin a municipal defendant from interfering with its own plans rather than attempting to compel the defendant itself to build housing. As the *Arlington II* court explained, "courts are far more willing to prohibit even nonintentional action by the state which interferes with an individual's plan to use his own land to provide integrated housing." Bearing in mind that the plaintiffs in this case seek only the freedom to build their own project, we conclude that the strong showing of discriminatory effect resulting from the Town's adherence to its R-3M zoning category and its refusal to rezone the Matinecock Court site far outweigh the Town's weak justifications. Accordingly, to recapitulate, we find that the Town violated Title VIII by refusing to amend the zoning ordinance to permit private developers to build multi-family dwellings outside the urban renewal area. We also find that the Town violated Title VIII by refusing to rezone the Matinecock Court site. We thus reverse the district court and direct entry of judgment in appellants' favor. Appellees argue that we should deny site-specific relief because there are 64 "community development" sites available for low-cost multi-family housing in Huntington. They claim that a 1978 letter from Town Attorney Ronald Glickman to Michael Miness, Director of the Community Development Agency, established that any land within the community development areas can be rezoned as R-3M property. The record, however, makes clear that Glickman's interpretation of the zoning code was neither codified nor represents current Town policy. As late as 1983, Town Supervisor Butterfield stated that the ordinance restricted private developers to the urban renewal zone. The Town has maintained in its papers submitted to the district court and to the United States Supreme Court in its 1982 petition for *certiorari* in *Huntington I* that the R-3M district ..." provided for multiple dwellings in urban areas, or if owned by the Housing Authority, within or without such an area...." Moreover, not only are 63 of the "community development" parcels not presently zoned for multi-family housing, but most of the sites are not in fact vacant but are "under-developed." Therefore, there is only one site, not 64 sites, zoned and available for private low-cost multi-family housing. However, even as to the one site—the MIA site in Huntington Station—by the time of trial, HUD had determined it was in an area with a high concentration of minorities and therefore an inappropriate location for a federally subsidized housing development.

Ordinarily, HHI would not be automatically entitled to construct its project at its preferred site. The Town might well have legitimate reasons for preferring some alternative site to the one preferred by HHI. On the other hand, the Town would not be permitted to select a site that suits the Town's preference if that site imposed undue hardships on the applicant, such as distance from public transportation or other services. Thus, we would ordinarily remand this case to the district court to afford the appellees an opportunity to identify an alternative site, outside the urban renewal area, that would be appropriate for HHI's project and eligible for the same financial arrangements and assistance available at the Matinecock Court site. If the Town identified such a site, it would then have the burden of persuading the district court that there were substantial reasons for using its preferred site and that those reasons did not impose undue hardships on the appellants. If the district court was not persuaded on balance of the benefits of an alternative site, it would then enter an appropriate judgment to enable HHI to proceed with its project at the Matinecock Court site.

This case, however, is not ordinary. First, we recognize the protracted nature of this litigation, which has spanned over seven years. Further delay might well prove fatal to this private developer's plans. Second, other than its decision in December 1987 to build 50 units of low-income housing in the Melville section, the Town has demonstrated little good faith in assisting the development of low-income housing. After the Town began receiving federal community development funds, HUD found it necessary to pressure the Town continually to include commitments for construction of subsidized family housing in the Town's HAPs. Because of the Town's lack of progress in constructing such housing, HUD imposed special conditions on the Town's community development grants for the 1978 fiscal allocation. Thereafter, HUD continued to express its dissatisfaction with the Town's performance. This history, while it does not rise to a showing of discriminatory intent, clearly demonstrates a pattern of stalling efforts to build low-income housing.

Third, the other 63 parcels outside the urban renewal area are not presently zoned for multi-family housing and, indeed, the zoning ordinance presently forbids rezoning of these properties. Thus, this situation differs from *Arlington II*, where 6 tracts currently zoned for multi-family housing were available and, accordingly, the Seventh Circuit remanded the case to the district court to determine if one of those sites were suitable. Appellees cannot argue as they do now, that the zoning ordinance does not now limit private builders to the urban renewal area when the Town Board in its January 6, 1981, resolution refused to amend the ordinance to delete the restriction of such housing to the urban renewal area, and appellees throughout this litigation have defended that decision. We therefore refuse to remand this case to the district court to determine the suitability of the 6 sites outside the urban renewal area. Rather, we find that site-specific relief is appropriate in this case.

Accordingly, we direct the district court to include in its judgment provision ordering the Town to rezone the 14.8 acre Matinecock Court site located at the corner of Elwood and Pulaski Roads in Huntington Township to R-3M status. The judgment should also order the Town to strike from its R-3M zoning ordinance that portion which limits private multi-family housing projects to the urban renewal area.

Notes and Questions

1. The Supreme Court affirmed *per curiam*, stating:

> Since appellants conceded the applicability of the disparate-impact test for evaluating the zoning ordinance under Title VIII, we do not reach the question whether that test is the appropriate one. Without endorsing the precise analysis of the Court of Appeals, we are satisfied on this record that disparate impact was

shown, and that the sole justification proffered to rebut the prima facie case was inadequate. 488 U.S. 15, 18 (1988).

2. *Arlington II* was the first case to attempt to develop criteria for proving a Title VIII statutory violation after the Supreme Court's clarification in *Arlington I* that a constitutional violation required a showing of intent or purpose with respect to a refusal to rezone. The *Washington v. Davis* decision and its application to housing issues in *Arlington I* caused a renewed focus on the requirements of Title VIII.

3. *Arlington II* was ultimately settled by entry of a consent decree in April 1979. *Metropolitan Hous. Dev. Corp. v. Village of Arlington Heights*, 469 F. Supp. 836 (N.D. Ill. 1979), *aff'd*, 616 F.2d 1006 (7th Cir. 1980). Under its terms, the consent decree would be entered without finding of constitutional or statutory violations by the Village and the Village would annex and rezone an alternate site for housing development. Does the settlement suggest that the extensive litigation was ineffective? Can it be speculated whether absent the litigation a similar result might have been obtainable?

4. Obstruction of housing for low-income persons, especially when prospective residents will be minorities, is a frequent theme. The paradigm case is probably *Kennedy Park Homes Ass'n v. City of Lackawanna*, 318 F. Supp. 6 (W.D.N.Y.), *aff'd*, 436 F.2d 108 (2d Cir. 1970), *cert. denied*, 401 U.S. 1010 (1971). *See also Dailey v. City of Lawton*, 296 F. Supp. 266 (W.D. Okla. 1969), *aff'd*, 425 F.2d 1037 (10th Cir. 1970); *Crow v. Brown*, 332 F. Supp. 382 (N.D. Ga. 1971), *aff'd per curiam*, 457 F.2d 788 (5th Cir. 1972). In all of the cases above, the courts, after finding various forms of purposeful discriminatory conduct, ordered the municipality involved to cease its obstruction of housing.

Demonstrating that governmental action violates the Fair Housing Act can be difficult, particularly in the case of "sophisticated" conduct. Recall that the Fair Housing Act prohibits both intentional discrimination and conduct that has a discriminatory effect. For a case applying the *Arlington I* analytical methodology to find intentional discrimination, see *Greater New Orleans Fair Housing Action Center v. St. Bernard Parish*, 641 F. Supp. 2d 563 (E.D. La. 2009). The court invalidated, *inter alia*, for violating Title VIII, a municipal ordinance, that imposed a moratorium for twelve months or until the parish council enacted certain zoning updates on the development of multifamily housing of more than five units. The court considered in a detailed analysis the *Arlington I* factors for analyzing intent: *(1) the historical background of the decision, (2) the specific sequence of events leading up to the decision, (3) departures from the normal procedural sequence, (4) substantive departures and the defendant's justifications of the departures, and (5) legislative history of the defendant's conduct.*

In *Greater New Orleans Fair Housing Action Center* the court also found that the defendant's conduct had a discriminatory effect on minorities. After discussing the methodologies of *Arlington II* and *Huntington Branch*, the court continued:

(1) *strength of showing of disparate racial effect*

> As previously discussed, this Court has found that the moratorium would have a significant disparate racial effect. Particularly with regard to the impact on income-qualified African-American households and families, as compared to Caucasian households and families, African-Americans are at least 25%, and for some income groups, 86% more likely to be impacted by the moratorium than their Caucasian counterparts....
>
> The strength of that effect is further supported by the rigor of [Plaintiff's expert's] analysis. Statisticians test the likelihood of chance producing the same

> results that the moratorium produced by seeing if the analysis is "statistically significant...." Whether or not something is "significant" is assessed at different levels, such as 90%, 95%, and 99%. In the analysis performed in this case, all of figures cited in this opinion were statistically significant at the 99% confidence level. In plain language, this means that there is only a one percent likelihood that chance could have or would have produced the same type of disproportionate impact on African-Americans.
>
> (2) *some evidence of discriminatory intent*
>
> As this Court discussed previously, several aspects of this case provide evidence of discriminatory intent, in particular the historical background of events, the sequence of events leading up to the decision, and the departure from normal zoning procedure. Even if such evidence is not sufficient to support a finding of the moratorium's overall discriminatory intent, the preponderance of the evidence indicates at a minimum "some" evidence of discriminatory intent.
>
> (3) *defendant's interest in the moratorium*
>
> The Court has painstakingly identified six possible justifications or interests on behalf of the defendants earlier in this opinion discussing whether the moratorium was a "substantive departure." For each, the Court assessed the factual support for the justification, based on the evidence produced by each party and the testimony at trial. The Court does not find any of the six proffered interests persuasive.
>
> (4) *relief sought by the plaintiff*
>
> More fully stated, "does the plaintiff seek to compel the defendant to affirmatively provide housing for members of minority groups or merely to restrain the defendant from interfering with individual property owners who wish to provide such housing." This is clearly a case of the latter. In the Motion to Enforce, plaintiff does not seek an affirmative act from defendants. Rather, plaintiff and intervenor move this Court to rescind the moratorium such that Provident, a private developer, may proceed in the development process for the affordable housing sites.
>
> Based on the factual record and judged under a clear preponderance of the evidence, the Court finds that Ordinance # 905-09-08 has a discriminatory effect on African-Americans and therefore violates the Fair Housing Act, 42 U.S.C. § 3604(a)....

But Plaintiffs did not succeed on either the intentional discrimination claim or the discriminatory effects basis in *Artisan/American Corp. v. City of Alvin, Texas*, 588 F.3d 291 (5th Cir. 2009). As for intentional discrimination the Court noted that the Plaintiff's sole support for its intentional claim rested on the assertion of Plaintiff's co-owner that a former city council member told him that one or more other city council members uttered words to the effect that "we don't want those people here" and "we already have enough of those people here." The Court said that because no city council member confirmed this assertion, nor had any other person come forward who heard these remarks firsthand, there was insufficient evidence to draw a reasonable inference of racial animus that would violate Title VIII.

As to discriminatory effects the court noted that Plaintiff did not provide any analysis of the racial make-up of the relevant income pool who might have occupied the Tax Credit development while the defendant City presented unrefuted evidence that there are many other sites on which apartments may be constructed within the city, including sites next to the proposed site. The Court of Appeals upheld district court findings that most of the low-income housing within the county was already located in the defendant city. It distinguished cases in which disparate impact had been found noting that those cases involved a waiting list for affordable housing or a demonstrated shortage of affordable housing. Since Plaintiff did not present evidence of a waiting list and had not identified anyone affected by the denial of the building permit, the court held that Plaintiff's evidence failed to demonstrate that the defendant city's actions caused a significant discriminatory effect that would violate Title VIII.

5. The problem of sorting out private motivation and its effect on official decisions has been addressed in several cases. In *Smith v. Town of Clarkton,* 682 F. 2d 1055 (4th Cir. 1982) evidence showed that town officials withdrew from a multi-municipality housing authority in response to pressure from a racially discriminatory public sentiment. The Fourth Circuit held that such evidence was sufficient to establish discriminatory intent and discriminatory effect both of which violated Title VIII. But in *Malone v. Fenton,* 592 F. Supp. 1135 (E.D. Mo. 1984), *aff'd mem.*, 794 F.2d. 680 (8th Cir. 1986), the court found neither intent nor effects in the city of Fenton's refusal to rezone for multifamily subsidized housing. The district court held that there was no proof of intent under the *Arlington I* approach and insufficient proof of impact to make out a Title VIII claim.

In *Atkins v. Robinson*, 545 F. Supp. 852 (E.D. Va. 1982), *aff'd*, 733 F.2d 318 (4th Cir. 1984), the court held that a county's veto (under state statutes) of a housing project violated Title VIII. The court found that the veto (1) had a greater adverse effect on blacks and (2) perpetuated existing patterns of segregation. The court cited disproportionate need in the county among blacks as well as some evidence of racially discriminatory purpose which the court found to be "camouflaged" by statements that were purportedly directed to low-income housing. However, the county's veto was not found to have caused the loss of funding which led to the demise of the project, and the court denied relief to the plaintiffs.

The Sixth Circuit held in *United States v. City of Birmingham,* 727 F.2d 560 (6th Cir. 1984), that the city's interference with a proposed housing development violated Title VIII. Among other things, the plaintiffs proved that the city commission agreed to sell a former school site for a low-income housing project, that thereafter racially motivated public opposition arose, and that through a series of unusual events the commission pursued policies which appeased "those who expressed bigoted views." The unusual events included a decision to hold an advisory referendum on the proposed project and the defeat in subsequent elections of commissioners who favored the project.

6. When class issues arise, the cases have demonstrated the difficulty plaintiffs may expect to encounter. *See, e.g., Reinhart v. Lincoln County*, 482 F.3d 1225 (10th Cir. 2007). The plaintiffs, land developers, claimed a county's newly adopted land use plan and regulations had a discriminatory effect on certain specified classes of persons protected by the Fair Housing Act, including persons who were disproportionately racial minorities and female-headed, single-parent households because the new regulations would increase the cost of real estate in the County. Plaintiffs also provided statistics indicating that the demand for affordable housing in the County was increasing. Note that the Act does not protect any "economic classification" so the effect must be shown to be adverse by race or other named protected class. The District Court held that plaintiffs failed to show that the effect of the new regulations was discriminatory because the increased costs were imposed upon all residents of the county regardless of their race or family status. Plaintiffs appealed the court's ruling on their disparate impact claim. The Court of Appeals affirmed on the ground that plaintiffs failed to show that a specific policy caused a significant disparate effect on a protected group. Plaintiffs' disparate-impact claim was based upon the additional costs im-

posed by the new regulations. These costs, they argued, made it impossible for them to provide affordable housing, thereby injuring protected groups. However, the court stated it was not enough to show that the regulation would increase housing costs and members of a protected group tended to be less wealthy than others. It was essential to compare who could afford the housing before the new regulations went into effect with who could afford housing afterwards. Plaintiffs failed to provide evidence indicating before-and-after costs of dwellings and the percentages of protected and nonprotected persons who would have been priced out of the market as a result of an increase. The court cited, but did not reach or rely upon an apparently broader ruling set forth in *Hemisphere Building Co. v. Village of Richton Park*, 171 F.3d 437 (7th Cir. 1999) in which Judge Posner said that the neither the "reasonable accommodation" provision for the handicapped nor the disparate impact analysis required consideration of handicapped people's financial situation.

Similarly, in *Langslois v. Abington Housing*, 207 F. 3d 43 (1st Cir. 2000), Plaintiffs faced difficulties, even when the Court believed they had made out a prima facie case of disparate impact under the Fair Housing Act. Plaintiffs were low-income minorities and a coalition for the homeless who lived outside the jurisdictions of certain suburban public housing authorities (PHAs). Plaintiffs brought an action seeking an injunction to stop the PHAs from implementing a lottery system that gave a preference to local residents in allocating Section 8 certificates or vouchers. Plaintiffs alleged, in part, that the new system constituted unlawful racial discrimination under the Fair Housing Act, because it had a disparate racial impact. The Court of Appeals accepted the District Court's conclusion that the Plaintiffs' made out a prima facie case, but reversed that part of the lower court's decision in favor of Plaintiffs that engaged in "balancing" defendants' objective to give local preference against the harm to Plaintiffs caused by the disparate impact. The Court held that balancing was not appropriate in a case in which the defendants showed a valid justification for their decision. "In light of *Griggs* and the similarity of the statutes, it is a fair reading of the Fair Housing Act's "because of race" prohibition to ask that a demonstrated disparate impact in housing be justified by a legitimate and substantial goal of the measure in question; but beyond that, we do not think that the courts' job is to "balance" objectives, with individual judges deciding which seem to them more worthy."

7. In addition to the *Gautreaux* litigation, the courts have been called on to delineate the scope of HUD's responsibility in face of local obstruction. In *Client's Council v. Pierce*, 711 F.2d 1406 (8th Cir. 1983), the court held that HUD's continued funding of new public housing and modernization requests for the Texarkana (Arkansas) Housing Authority in face of more than a decade of racially discriminatory practices by the local authority showed a "discriminatory purpose" on the part of HUD. HUD was held liable under the Fifth Amendment and under Title VIII. The court specifically rejected HUD's purported "defense" that its continued funding was "the inevitable consequence of its legitimate desire to provide low income housing." In the aftermath of *Crow v. Brown*, *supra*, plaintiffs complained that HUD had failed to pressure a "footdragging" local authority within the area in which housing was to be built. HUD's failure was alleged to be a violation of HUD's duties to "affirmatively further" fair housing under Title VIII, 42 U.S.C. § 3608. But in *Anderson v. City of Alpharetta*, 737 F.2d 1530 (8th Cir. 1984), the court of appeals held that HUD's duty did not extend to "pressuring" a local authority to speed up its application, since HUD had not funded the authority or committed any discrimination itself.

8. Under the Fair Housing Act before the 1988 amendments, the United States Attorney General was authorized to bring suit only when a defendant engaged in a "pattern or practice" of discriminatory conduct. *See* the prior version of 42 U.S.C. § 3614 (1982). Although such cases raise the issue of standard of proof under Title VIII, there generally is

a course of conduct at issue, and the typical complaint alleges that the defendant's conduct "was for the purpose and had the effect of" racial discrimination. *See, e.g., United States v. City of Black Jack*, 508 F.2d 1179 (8th Cir. 1974), *cert. denied*, 422 U.S. 1042 (1975); *United States v. City of Parma*, 494 F. Supp. 1049 (N.D. Ohio 1980); *United States v. Northside Realty Associates*, 474 F.2d 1164 (5th Cir. 1973), *cert. denied*, 424 U.S. 977 (1976); and *United States v. West Peachtree Tenth Corp.*, 437 F.2d 221 (5th Cir. 1971).

The Fair Housing Amendments Act of 1988 broadened the authority granted to the United States Attorney General to bring suit. *See* A Note on Procedures, Remedies, Damages, and Attorney's Fees, *infra*.

A Note on Exclusionary Zoning

In addition to racial discrimination, distinct issues of class can be raised by the zoning problem. If zoning limitations and land use practices preclude low-income housing, there may be a racial issue because of the disproportionate impact analysis or "effects test" discussed in the previous section of this Chapter. When, however, racial impact cannot be proved or is not present, the matter cannot be viewed as a civil rights matter, and thus is not within the purview of either racial discrimination cases under the Fourteenth Amendment of the U.S. Constitution or the Federal Fair Housing Act, although the addition of "familial status" in the 1988 amendments may shade into class issues. Familial status is covered in Section C of this Chapter, *infra*. Instead the matter must be treated as a land-use problem, which is identified under the rubric of "exclusionary zoning." Zoning generally, with civil rights exceptions, has been seen historically as preeminently a province of state law. What would it require to reach the problem of exclusion by class either because racial impact cannot be proved or because the people excluded are white?

Peter W. Salsich, Jr. and Timothy J. Tryniecki, Land Use Regulation

336–341, 350–352 (1998)

The NIMBY Syndrome

Euclidean zoning, characterized by the territorial division of land into zones and the segregation of uses within each zone, has from the beginning had an exclusionary bias. One of the two main goals of the nation's first comprehensive zoning law, the New York City Zoning Ordinance of 1916, was to limit urban congestion. The means chosen to accomplish this goal—segregation of land activities, and the application of varying degrees of limitation on building height, size, and design—reflected a community value judgment that different types of land activity were inherently incompatible and should be kept separate.

Early legal objections to the discrimination inherent in the zoning approach were overcome by the requirements that district boundary lines be drawn on the basis of objective standards such as suitability of the land for particular uses, topography, existing patterns of development, and projected patterns of growth, and that all land within a particular zone be subject to the same set of regulations thus producing a rational classification under the Equal Protection Clause. The incompatibility of residential and industrial activity was considered to be obvious, thus separation of such activities made sense and the limitation on the use of private property that resulted was a reasonable exercise of the police power. Since all landowners within a given zone were permitted to make the same use of their property, no one was being treated unequally in the constitutional sense.

As long as the public interest justifying zoning was perceived as concern over inanimate sources of harm—such as noise, pestilence, fire, and other common forms of urban displeasure—zoning was not seen as posing a threat to other cherished American freedoms, including the right to associate, move about freely, and seek housing of one's choice. The Supreme Court, however, in its landmark decision *Village of Euclid v. Ambler Realty Co.*, 272 U.S. 365 (1921), upholding the comprehensive zoning concept, presaged a future in which all sorts of "different" types of people would be excluded from suburban American with a bit of ill-considered dicta concerning apartment buildings, and by necessary implication their occupants:

> With particular reference to apartment houses, it is pointed out that the development of detached house sections is greatly retarded by the coming of apartment houses, which has sometimes resulted in destroying the entire section for private house purposes; that in such sections very often the apartment house is a mere parasite, constructed in order to take advantage of the open spaces and attractive surroundings created by the residential character of the district. *Id.* at 394.

While it is unfair and a gross oversimplification to blame the Court for the housing problems of the poor, the disabled, and the elderly, the attitude reflected in that comment and the Court's relatively uncritical acceptance of the zoning concept gave the stamp of approval to an approach to land use control that awarded preferential treatment to the freestanding, relatively large lot, single-family housing development that dominated suburbia for the next half century....

Exclusionary Zoning

The term *exclusionary zoning* is derived from the phenomenon of "fiscal zoning"—zoning to attract activities such as commercial and light industrial uses that would increase the tax base, rather than activities that would drain the tax base through increased pressure on public schools, local welfare agencies, public transit systems, and the like. Fiscal zoning generally has been discredited when used to keep out lower-income people.

When zoning to improve fiscal ratables is combined with land use regulations that increase the required standard of housing quality beyond those necessary for health and safety and thereby "appear to interfere seriously with the availability of low- and moderate-cost housing where it is needed," a community is said to be engaged in exclusionary zoning.

In a now-classic study published in 1971 of the zoning practices of four New Jersey counties on the outskirts of New York City, Norman Williams and Thomas Norman identified six popular land use regulatory techniques that had particular impact on housing opportunities for low-and moderate-income persons:

> 1. *Minimum-Building-Size Requirements*—which are normally requirements for minimum floor space. Requirements for a larger house have the most obvious and direct influence on housing costs; for example, assuming average building costs of roughly $20 per square foot for tract housing (which may be optimistic), a requirement for a 1200-square-foot house has practically the same effect as a requirement for houses costing about $24,000. The cost of the lot and of site development must of course be added, so that the actual figure would probably be around $30,000.
>
> 2. *The Exclusion of Multiple Dwellings-Single-Family Restrictions.* Among those architects and planners who have a special interest in housing costs, there has

long been a widespread consensus that the most promising opportunity for good inexpensive housing is to be found in some form of multiple dwellings. With the recent sharp rise in housing costs, this is probably even more true nowadays. Such housing may take a variety of different forms, and more may be available in the future—garden apartments, "town houses," and various developments in "modular housing," which may be coming as a result of the hoped-for industrialization of the building industry.

3. *Restrictions on the Number of Bedrooms.* When multiple dwellings are permitted, the number of bedrooms is often restricted, either by the zoning ordinance or by informal pressure. The most frequent provision requires that 80 percent of the dwelling units shall have only one bedroom, and permits up to 20 percent with two bedrooms—and none with more. The fiscal motivation for such restrictions is obvious. Equally clearly, multiple dwellings subject to such restrictions do not provide the type of housing needed by most families of normal size.

4. *Prohibition of Mobile Homes.* Such homes now provided the only new inexpensive housing available in most areas, except for some public housing in the cities. They are efficient, readily available, and unnecessarily ugly.

5. *Frontage (i.e., Lot Width) Requirements.* The costs of site development, particularly for street paving and sewers, are fairly substantial, and so requirements for wide lots do affect the cost of housing noticeably. The impact of this factor depends of course on whether high standards for site development are imposed in subdivision control—and how high. Obviously, if curbs and storm sewers are also required the cost will go up substantially. Still, it is lot width, probably even more than lot size, which tends to preserve that much-desired semi-rural atmosphere.

6. *Lot Size Requirements.* While this device has attracted most of the attention, its actual impact is questionable.

Norman Williams, Jr. & Thomas Norman, *Exclusionary Land Use Controls: The Case of North-Eastern New Jersey*, 22 Syracuse L. Rev. 475, 481, 484 (1971).

In *Southern Burlington County N.A.A.C.P. v. Mount Laurel Tp.*, 336 A.2d 713 (N.J. 1975), *appeal dismissed & cert. denied*, 423 U.S. 808 (1975) [*Mt. Laurel I*] the Supreme Court of New Jersey held that a zoning ordinance that contravened the general welfare violated the state constitutional requirements of substantive due process and equal protection. The court articulated the principle of "fair share" housing and concluded that developing communities could not use their delegated police power to regulate land use in a manner that excluded housing for low-income persons. The constitutional obligation would be satisfied by "affirmatively affording a realistic opportunity" for the construction of a fair share of the present and prospective regional need for low- and moderate-income housing.

In *Southern Burlington County N.A.A.C.P. v. Mount Laurel Tp.*, 456 A.2d 390 (N.J. 1983) [*Mt. Laurel II*] the court returned to the original case after several intervening cases had fleshed out the law but failed to develop an effective remedy or means of administering the doctrine. In an eloquent opinion designed to "put some steel into that doctrine" and to emphasize that the *Mount Laurel* obligation is to provide a "realistic opportunity for housing, not litigation," the court reaffirmed the fair-share principle; concluded that it was applicable to all communities, whether developing or not, containing "growth areas" as shown on the concept maps of the New Jersey State Development Guide Plan; and held that municipalities' affirmative governmental obligation to provide a realistic opportunity for the construction of low- and moderate-income housing included the use of inclusionary devices, such as density bonuses and mandatory set-asides, as well as the elimination of unnecessary cost-producing land use requirements and restrictions....

The *Mount Laurel* cases have contributed two main points to housing and land use control jurisprudence. First, there is a clear recognition that the concepts of general welfare, on which zoning as well as all other exercises of the police power ultimately rest, includes "proper provision for adequate housing of all categories of people." *Mount Laurel I* contained extensive discussion of the importance of housing to individuals and the rationale for concluding that the term "general welfare" is broad enough in today's society to embrace notions of adequate housing. In *Mount Laurel II*, the court restated the constitutional principle as follows:

> [T]he State controls the use of land, *all* of the land. In exercising that control it cannot favor rich over poor. It cannot legislatively set aside dilapidated housing in urban ghettos for the poor and decent housing elsewhere for everyone else. The government that controls this land represents everyone. While the State may not have the ability to eliminate poverty, it cannot use that condition as the basis for imposing further disadvantages. And the same applies to the municipality to which this control over land has been constitutionally delegated.

Second, *Mount Laurel II* also recognized that certain planning and regulatory decisions will have an impact beyond the boundaries of the particular decision-maker's sphere of direct control. When the police power is delegated to local government, as in zoning, tax abatement, and eminent domain, the sphere of direct control and interest of the entity exercising the power is narrower than the sphere of control and interest of the delegating entity. The justification for the ultimate use of the police power, however, must relate to the general welfare of the people who are within the sphere of influence of the delegating agency. Thus, when the use of the police power will have an impact beyond the boundaries of the entity exercising the power, "the welfare of the state's citizens beyond the borders of the particular municipality cannot be disregarded and must be recognized and served."

Mount Laurel II acknowledges this point by reviewing the relationship of suburban exclusionary zoning to the continuing disintegration of cities and concluding that "[z]oning ordinances that either encourage this process or ratify its results are not promoting our general welfare, they are destroying it."

Courts in a number of other states have expressed disapproval of exclusionary zoning, but generally have declined to adopt the mathematical approach to determining appropriate remedies of the *Mount Laurel* cases. The Supreme Court of New Hampshire embraced the fair-share principle of *Mount Laurel* that requires all communities in a region to participate in efforts to accommodate affordable housing. Because the court's rationale was based on the state zoning enabling act, the decision has national significance. *Britton v. Town of Chester*, 595 A.2d 492 (N.H. 1991)....

A Note on Inclusionary Zoning Policies and Programs

In some high cost housing states and cities, a response to a reduction in federally-subsidized housing programs and limitations on their own ability to provide funding for low- and moderate-income housing led to the emergence of "inclusionary" zoning policies and programs. In the states of New Jersey and Massachusetts, this was adopted as one way to address the inequities caused by exclusionary zoning, *supra*. This approach relies upon private housing developers providing a percentage of below market units (usually ranging from 10–25%) in new developments of a certain size, either through mandated set-asides or voluntary programs.

Structure of Inclusionary Housing Programs

Localities that have adopted inclusionary policies, whether the policies are mandatory or voluntary, typically offer incentives to developers (in the absence of public subsidies) either to forestall developers' claims of regulatory takings or to encourage them to participate willingly. One major incentive is a density bonus, that allows the developer to exceed existing density limitations in order to offset the lower prices of below market units. Other typical incentives may include fast-track processing of applications and the waiver or reduction of planning requirements like the minimum number of parking spaces.

One aim of inclusionary programs can be "mixed income" housing, just like that being provided in HUD's HOPE VI program. However, some developers balk at providing below market rate units on-site for fear of jeopardizing sales, even though the market rate and below market rate units are to have similar designs, if not the same amenities. Therefore, many programs allow the developer to satisfy the affordable housing requirement off-site. If a developer does not want to build the below-market housing, many programs allow "in-lieu" alternatives. The developer can either "dedicate" land for below market rate housing units or make a payment to cover the cost of building such housing. In the latter case, either the government will itself build the housing or otherwise use the funds to subsidize affordable housing built by other developers. *See* Douglas R. Porter & Elizabeth B. Davison, *Evaluation of In-Lieu Fees and Offsite Construction as Incentives for Affordable Housing Production*, 11 Cityscape 27–60 (No. 2 2009). Some inclusionary zoning programs allow developers to appeal for an exemption based upon hardship or insufficient relationship to housing affordability.

Once the number of new housing units to be covered is set, the eligibility requirements for those occupying the units must be determined. The income limits for low- and moderate-income occupants are usually the federal and state standards. Often, the ratios for different groups (e.g., low- versus very low-income) within these ranges are set, as can be the mix of unit sizes (e.g., studios versus family units). In order to ensure that rental units remain affordable, the rent is controlled. For owner-occupied units, sales prices are controlled. In both cases, a period (e.g., 10–30 years) is chosen during which the controls apply. When controls expire, some localities reserve a right of first refusal to purchase at least some of the units, so that they may continue to be affordable for low- and moderate-income residents. Some communities wish to give priority or preference to current residents in need of affordable housing, including their own employees (e.g., teachers, police officers, and firefighters). For legal issues affecting such a policy, see Keaton Norquist, *Local Preferences in Affordable Housing: Special Treatment for Those Who Live or Work in a Municipality?* 36 B.C. Envtl. Aff. L. Rev. 207 (2009). Eligible occupants are chosen either in order of application or by lottery. Once the housing is built and occupied, there must be an agency to monitor continuing compliance during the period in which the rental or sales prices are controlled. Experience has shown that mandatory inclusionary zoning programs are more likely than voluntary ones to succeed at providing below market affordable housing. *See* Brian R. Lerman, *Mandatory Inclusionary Zoning-The Answer to the Affordable Housing Problem*, 33 B.C. Envtl. Aff. L. Rev. 383 (2006).

Selected Examples of Inclusionary Zoning Programs: County, State, Cities

County

Montgomery County, Maryland, outside Washington, D.C. is one of wealthiest counties in the United States. It is also one of the most expensive housing markets, leading to the adoption in 1973 of one of the first inclusionary zoning programs and arguably the most successful: the Moderately Priced Dwelling Unit (MPDU) Program. It was adopted over the veto of the County Executive, overridden by the County Council, and despite the threat of a lawsuit by homebuilders. *See* David Rusk, Inside Game, Outside Game: Winning Strategies for Saving Urban America ch. 9 (1999); Lerman, *supra*. Initially it imposed a mandatory requirement of the dedication of 15% (later changed to 12.5–15%) of the units in all new residential subdivisions of 50 or more units (later reduced to a threshold of 35 units and currently 20 units or more) with density bonuses of 20% (later increased to 22%). Initially, price controls lasted only 5 years but were later extended to 10 and then 20 years for rental units and 30 years for owner-occupied units. Upon the expiration of the required affordability period, the Montgomery County Housing Opportunities Commission (HOC) was given the first right of refusal to purchase up to one-third of the MPDUs, which it then rents to low-income households. The MPDU program allowed developers to provide affordable housing off-site and to make in lieu payments to make units affordable (e.g., in condominiums). The target population is households with incomes of 65% or less of median area income. As of 2007, Montgomery County cumulatively had produced a total of 12,500 MPDUs (71 percent owner-occupied and 29 percent rental). At that date, only 2,260 units were still under affordability controls. The HOC controlled another 1,700 units that it had purchased.

State

California leads the states in the adoption of inclusionary zoning by local governments. The impetus for inclusionary zoning in California was the 1978 passage of a constitutional amendment capping local property taxes (Proposition 13), which made it very difficult for most localities to provide financial support for affordable housing. By 2007, it was estimated in a study prepared by the California Rural Housing Coalition (CRHC) and the Non-Profit Housing Association of Northern California that about one-third (170) of California's cities and counties had inclusionary zoning programs. Affordable by Choice: Trends in California Inclusionary Housing Programs (2007). CRHC maintains a California Inclusionary Housing Policy Database: www.calruralhousing.org/inclusionary-housing-database. See also Nico Calavita et al., Inclusionary Zoning: The California Experience (2004); Antonio Bento et al., *Housing Market Effects of Inclusionary Zoning*, 11 Cityscape 7 (2009) (analyzing supply and price impacts in California during the period 1988–2005).

Cities

In addition to California cities of Sacramento, San Diego and San Francisco, other major U.S. cities with citywide inclusionary zoning programs are Baltimore, Boston, Denver, Seattle and Washington, D.C. *See, e.g.*, Jay Riffkin, *Responsible Development? The Need for Revision to Seattle's Inclusionary Housing Plan*, 32 Seattle U. L. Rev. 443 (2009). Chicago and New York have more limited inclusionary zoning policies.

Legal Challenges

Inclusionary zoning has been challenged facially and as applied on constitutional and statutory grounds. In one of the earliest challenges to inclusionary zoning, the Virginia Supreme Court found that the Fairfax County program was an unconstitutional taking.

Board of Supervisors v. DeGroff Enterprises, Inc., 198 S. E. 2d 600 (Va. 1973). However, its inclusionary zoning program was subsequently legitimized by state enabling legislation: Affordable Dwelling Unit (ADU) Program, www.fairfaxcounty.gov/rha/adu/aduprogram.htm. In *Mt. Laurel II*, the New Jersey Supreme Court specifically endorsed inclusionary zoning and mandatory set-asides as one method for New Jersey municipalities subject to its ruling to meet their fair share housing obligations and rejected the claim that it amounted to a regulatory taking. Lerman, *supra*, notes that inclusionary zoning can be implemented as a traditional land use ordinance, an exaction, or an impact fee:

> A land use ordinance is given substantial deference by the courts, and will most likely be upheld. However, an exaction does not receive the same judicial deference because exactions are based on adjudicative discretion. Courts require exactions to have a sufficient nexus or proportionality between the impact of the development and what is taken from the developer. Courts provide impact fees with more deference than exactions because they are legislative rather than adjudicative, and therefore apply to all developments (Lerman, *supra* at 394).

As long as mandatory set asides provide compensatory incentives, it is unlikely that developers' claims of a regulatory taking will succeed under prevailing U.S. Supreme Court precedents interpreting the Constitution's takings clause.

Local inclusionary zoning is best defensible if authorized by state enabling legislation and is general legislation. If it is applied only to individual projects on an *ad hoc* basis, it may be challenged under the *Nollan/Dolan* precedents. It is important that inclusionary zoning programs are justified by a housing analysis study that documents the need for affordable housing generated by the development. Equal protection challenges based on exempting smaller size housing developments are not likely to succeed as long as there is a rational basis for the choice of the threshold for coverage. However, statutory preemption may be an issue. For example, where state law requires enabling legislation to regulate rents and a municipality attempts to do this in an inclusionary housing program without such state authorization, the courts may invoke pre-emption to invalidate the local program as occurred in Wisconsin. *Apartment Ass'n of S. Cent. Wisconsin, Inc. v. City of Madison*, 722 N.W. 2d 614 (Wis. 2006). *See generally* Barbara Erlich Kautz, *In Defense of Inclusionary Zoning: Successfully Defending Affordable Housing*, 36 U.S.F. L. Rev. 971 (2002).

A leading case upholding inclusionary zoning as constitutional is *Home Builders Association v. City of Napa*, 108 Cal. Rptr. 2d 60 (Ct. App. 2001), *cert denied*, 535 U.S. 954 (2002). The city enacted a mandatory set-aside program of 10% affordable units for all new housing developments based upon a study of its affordable housing needs. While it did not provide incentives, it provided for off-site dedication of land or payment of fees in lieu of building alternatives and also a waiver provision if a developer sought relief. It was facially challenged as a regulatory taking. It is noteworthy that California localities must have a housing element as part of their required general plans that calculates their share of regional housing needs (Cal. Gov't Code §§65,580 to 65,589.8. Napa successfully argued that its inclusionary zoning fulfilled this statutory obligation. The court rejected the argument that the *Nollan/Dolan* exaction doctrines applied because this was not an exaction case. *See* Cecily T. Talbert & Nadia L. Costa, *Inclusionary Housing Programs: Local Governments Respond to California's Housing Crisis*, 30 B.C. Envtl. Aff. L. Rev. 567 (2003).

Two other notable challenges to inclusionary housing programs in two of the state's largest communities resulted in settlements. In San Diego, developers successfully challenged its ordinance in a 2006 state trial court ruling that it was a regulatory taking. *See San Diego's*

Affordable Housing Ordinance Declared Unconstitutional, 36 Housing L. Bull. 123 (June/July 2006). The city subsequently amended the ordinance to satisfy the developers' concerns about payment of fees and the basis for waivers. In 2004, Sacramento County adopted an inclusionary zoning program targeted at not only low-income households but also extremely low-income households (i.e., 30% or less of area median household income). The Building Industry Association (BIA) challenged the ordinance on nine statutory and constitutional grounds. A state trial court judge rejected all of these claims. *See Sacramento Inclusionary Housing Ordinance Survives Legal Challenge*, 36 Housing L. Bull. 153 (Aug. 2006). There was a subsequent mutual agreement to amend the ordinance to settle the BIA's appeal.

In *Action Apartment Association v. City of Santa Monica*, 82 Cal. Rptr. 3d 722 (Ct. App. 2d Dist. 2008), *cert. denied*, 129 S. Ct. 2387 (2009), the plaintiff landlords made a facial takings challenge to a 1990 initiative that required that 30% of all newly-constructed multi-family residential housing must be affordable to low- and moderate-income residents. They invoked the *Nollan/Dolan* exactions doctrine to argue that there was not a sufficient "nexus" between the construction of new residential housing and the need for affordable housing to justify the inclusionary requirement. *See* Chapter 3, § L, *supra*. The trial and appellate courts ruled that this doctrine did not apply to legislative policy (as opposed to judicial review of individual adjudicative land use decisions).

However, a more recent decision has caused concern about the legality of inclusionary zoning in California—*Palmer/Sixth Street Properties v. City of Los Angeles*, 96 Cal. Rptr. 3d 875 (Ct. App. 2009). In conditionally approving a mixed use redevelopment project plan that included 350 housing units on a parking lot, the city required that 15% of the rental housing be set aside for low income households (or an equivalent in-lieu fee must be paid). Rent restrictions would apply for 30 years or the life of the units. This condition was based on a city policy and an area housing needs study. An additional factor was that previously a hotel on the site with 60 low-income apartments had been demolished. The developer did not request a density bonus as authorized by Cal. Gov't Code §§ 65915 to 65918, where a developer voluntarily includes affordable units in a project. His application for a waiver was rejected by the planning agencies and the city council. The developer sued, claiming that this condition was pre-empted by the 1995 Costa-Hawkins Rental Housing Act (Cal. Civ. Code §§ 1954.50 to 1954.53, which allows residential landlords to set the initial rent levels at the time apartments are first rented. While the developer offered to pay the in-lieu fee if necessary rather than build the low-income apartments, this did not make the challenge moot.

The city argued that since this was not a local rent control ordinance, the Costa-Hawkins law did not apply. The city also cited as justification for its condition the state's Community Redevelopment Law, Cal. Health & Safety Code §§ 33000 to 33022, which requires redevelopment agencies to ensure that at least 15% of all new and substantially rehabilitated housing within a project area be affordable). The California Court of Appeal upheld the trial judge's decision in favor of the developer, holding that the Costa-Hawkins law pre-empted the city's rent restriction condition, as well as the in-lieu alternative. Supporters of inclusionary housing are expected to seek an amendment to the Costa-Hawkins law to exempt inclusionary housing from its reach. *See* Nadia I. El Mallakh, *Does the Costa-Hawkins Act Prohibit Local Inclusionary Zoning Programs?* 89 Cal. L. Rev. 1847 (2001).

Notes and Questions

1. The Santa Monica case was argued for landlords by, among others, James S. Burling, director of litigation for the Pacific Legal Foundation, which has long challenged

governmental regulation of private property: www.pacificlegal.org. His argument is published: James S. Burling & Graham Owen, *The Implications of* Lingle *on Inclusionary and Other Legislative and Monetary Exactions*, 28 Stan. Envtl. L.J. 397 (2009).

2. In addition to constitutional claims, opponents of inclusionary housing programs raise economic arguments against price controls, claiming that they negatively affect the supply of new housing. *See, e.g.,* Benjamin Powell & Edward Stringham, *"The Economics of Inclusionary Zoning Reclaimed:" How Effective Are Price Controls?* 33 Fla. St. U. L. Rev. 471 (2005). This is the same argument used by many economists against rent control.

3. In addition to its inclusionary housing program, Fairfax County, Virginia uses some of its local property taxes to provide subsidized, affordable housing (the "Penny for Affordable Housing Fund"): Derek Kravitz, *Fairfax County Supervisors Approve Affordable Housing Plan,*" Wash. Post, Jan. 27, 2010, at B4.

4. In *Mount Laurel II* the court called on the legislature to act and it responded with the enactment of a Fair Housing Act in 1985. The Act created a state Council on Affordable Housing to help municipalities meet their Mount Laurel obligations. For in depth analyses of *Mount Laurel* see Charles Haar, Suburbs Under Siege (1996); David Kirp *et al.*, Our Town (1996).

5. A major review of the *Mount Laurel* experience is found in *Mount Laurel Housing Symposium*, 27 Seton Hall L. Rev. 1268 (1997). Articles on housing discrimination, housing mobility, lessons learned from *Mount Laurel*, and affordable housing and social science are included. The authors of a major study on *Mount Laurel's* impact concluded that affordable housing has been built that "serves households who had genuine housing needs ... [but that] the judicial and legislative attempt to eliminate exclusionary zoning has not enabled previously urban residents to move to suburban municipalities and has not enabled Blacks and Latinos to move from heavily minority urban areas to the suburbs." Naomi Bailin Wish & Stephen Eisdorfer, *The Impact of Mount Laurel Initiatives: An Analysis of the Characteristics of Applicants and Occupants*, 27 Seton Hall L. Rev. 1268, 1305 (1997). Is a basic change of heart necessary? Do the fair housing remedies offer greater hope of success? *See* Affordable Housing Archive website covering Mount Laurel and its aftermath compiled by the late Professor John Payne: http://njlegallib.rutgers.edu/mtlaurel. (last visited Feb. 10, 2010). *See also* the New Jersey Department of Community Affairs website for the Council on Affordable Housing: www.state.nj.us/dca/affiliates/coah/index.html.

6. For additional discussion of *Mount Laurel,* see John Charles Boger, *Toward Ending Residential Segregation: A Fair Share Proposal for the Next Reconstruction,* 71 N.C. L. Rev. 1573 (1993); Paula A. Franzese, *Mount Laurel III: The New Jersey Supreme Court's Judicious Retreat,* 18 Seton Hall L. Rev. 30 (1988) (discussing the court as a catalyst for legislative action); John M. Payne, *Title VIII and Mount Laurel: Is Affordable Housing Fair Housing*, 6 Yale Law & Pol'y Rev. 361 (1988).

7. For two articles analyzing related broader issues, see Harold A. McDougall, *From Litigation to Legislation in Exclusionary Zoning Law*, 22 Harv. C.R.-C.L. L. Rev. 623 (1987) and Harold A. McDougall, *Regional Contribution Agreements: Compensation for Exclusionary Zoning*, 60 Temp L.Q. 665 (1987).

8. For the approach in New York, see *Berenson v. Town of New Castle*, 341 N.E. 2d 236 (N.Y. 1975) (adopting for New York a general welfare test under state statutory requirements to test zoning challenged as exclusionary).

9. For Pennsylvania's approach, see *Surrick v. Zoning Hearing Board*, 382 A.2d 105 (Pa. 1975) (to determine constitutionality in Pennsylvania partial exclusion of multifamily

development must be tested to determine whether the municipality is meeting its fair share of the present and prospective regional need for multifamily housing), and *Fernley v. Board of Supervisors*, 502 A.2d 585 (Pa. 1985) (total exclusion of multifamily development is presumptively invalid and burden shifts to municipality to establish that the zoning promotes public health, safety, morals, and general welfare). *See also* Todd J. Aschbacher, Comment, *A New Deference Towards Exclusionary Zoning in Pennsylvania: Appeal of* M.A. Kravitz Co., 28 Wash. U.J. Urb. & Contemp. L. 381 (1985).

10. The manifestations of exclusionary zoning can take many forms. *See, e.g.*, JoAnn Tracy, Comment, *Single-Family Zoning Ordinances: The Constitutionality of Suburban Barriers Against Nontraditional Households*, 31 St. Louis U. L.J. 1023 (1987). For a listing of types of land-use controls that might be exclusionary and proposing an inclusionary land-use federal statute—called the "One America Act"—together with a draft of such a statute, see Charles E. Daye, *The Race, Class and Housing Conundrum: A Rationale and Proposal for a Legislative Policy of Suburban Inclusion*, 9 N.C. Cent. L. Rev. 37, App. (1978).

11. For treatment of exclusionary zoning, as a municipal land use control issue, as well as jurisdiction-specific inclusionary zoning legislation, see generally Daniel R. Mandelker, Land Use Law (5th ed. 2003 & Supp. 2009). *See also* Douglas W. Kmiec, *Exclusionary Zoning and Purposeful Racial Segregation in Housing: Two Wrongs Deserving Separate Remedies*, 18 Urb. Law. 393 (1986).

12. An alternative approach is so-called "anti-snob" zoning override legislation. Massachusetts has pioneered this technique. Mass. Gen. Laws Ann. Ch. 40b, §§ 20–23. That approach is discussed in the following excerpt:

Peter W. Salsich, Jr. and Timothy J. Tryniecki, Land Use Regulation

352–354 (1998)

Zoning Override ("Anti-Snob") Legislation

One of the first states to respond legislatively to the exclusionary zoning phenomenon was Massachusetts when it enacted its celebrated "anti-snob" law in 1969. Rather than mandate affordable housing set-asides or authorize density bonuses, the anti-snob law established a housing appeals committee in the state Department of Community Affairs with authority to override local zoning decisions blocking low- or moderate-income housing developments, defined as housing subsidized by any federal or state housing production program.

Under the Act, public agencies and private organizations proposing to build low- and moderate-income housing may bypass local regulatory agencies by submitting a single application to the local zoning board of appeals, which is responsible for coordinating an analysis of the application by interested regulatory agencies, conducting a public hearing, and making a decision regarding the application. Comprehensive permits or approvals may be issued by the board of appeals, which must act within forty days after termination of the public hearing.

If the application is denied or approved with conditions that make the project "uneconomic," the developer may appeal to the state housing appeals committee, with the issues being whether the decision is "reasonable and consistent with local needs." The statute provides that requirements or regulations are "consistent with local needs" if they are imposed after a comprehensive hearing in one of the following two situations:

> 1) more than 10 percent of the housing units, or at least 1.5 percent of the total land area zoned for residential, commercial, or industrial use in the municipality is low- or moderate-income housing; or 2) the proposal would result in low- or moderate-income housing construction starts on more than three tenths of one percent of the land area, or ten acres, whichever is larger, in a calendar year.

If the state housing appeals committee concludes that the local zoning decision was not consistent with local needs, it vacates the decision and orders a comprehensive permit or approval to be issued provided that the proposed housing would not violate safety standards contained in federal or state building and site-plan requirements....

Twenty years after the Massachusetts statute was enacted, Connecticut followed suit with a similar zoning override procedure, although the override power was delegated to the judiciary rather than to a state administrative agency. Developers of affordable housing may appeal adverse land use regulatory decisions to the superior court of Hartford-New Britain. Affordable housing is defined as assisted housing or housing in which at least 20 percent of the dwelling units will be conveyed by deeds containing covenants or restrictions limiting sale prices or rents to levels enabling persons and families with median income or less to pay no more than 30 percent of their annual income for housing. Conn. Gen. Stat. Ann. § 8-30g.

Upon appeal, the burden shifts to the local agency to prove, based on the evidence in the record, that:

> (1) the decision from which such appeal is taken and the reasons cited for such decision are supported by sufficient evidence in the record; (2) the decision is necessary to protect substantial public interests in health, safety, or other matters which the commission may legally consider; (3) such public interests clearly outweigh the need for affordable housing; and (4) such public interests cannot be protected by reasonable changes to the affordable housing development. *Id.* at § 8-30q(c).

If the burden is not met, the court is directed to "revise, modify, remand, or reverse" the decision consistent with the evidence presented. Communities are exempt from the affordable housing override provisions if at least 10 percent of the existing housing units are affordable, or they have received a certificate of affordable housing project completion from the Connecticut commissioner of finance, which carries with it a one-year exemption.

Other states with zoning override programs include California and Rhode Island. California has enacted a series of provisions designed to improve the procedural posture of affordable housing development proposals, including limitations to adverse design criteria, requiring specific public health or safety reasons for disapproving or reducing densities of housing developments that are consistent with local zoning and general plans, and imposing the burden of proof on local government when a developer or other person appeals a permit denial or density reduction.

Notes and Questions

1. Does the burden-shifting aspect of zoning override laws offer a more effective approach to reconciling different interests?

2. For a discussion of the Massachusetts, New Jersey, Connecticut, and Rhode Island statutes that provide for a state override of local zoning decisions, see Sharon Perlman Krefetz, *The Impact and Evolution of the Massachusetts Comprehensive Permit and Zoning*

Appeals Act: Thirty Years of Experience with a State Legislative Effort to Overcome Exclusionary Zoning, 22 W. NEW ENG. L. REV. 381 (2001).

3. For further analysis of approaches to counteract local exclusion of affordable housing see 1 James A. Kushner, Subdivision Law and Growth Management §§ 3:8 to 3:25 (2nd ed. 2001 & Supp. 2010). This source cites judicial decisions and statutes on a state-by-state basis. It also contains comprehensive citation to references on legal limitations on growth management strategies.

3. Discrimination Based on Handicap

Marbrunak, Inc. v. City of Stow

United States Court of Appeals
974 F.2d 43 (6th Cir. 1992)

Before JONES and NORRIS, Circuit Judges; and WOODS, District Judge.

ALAN E. NORRIS, Circuit Judge.

Defendant, City of Stow, appeals from the district court's order granting the permanent injunction requested by plaintiff, Marbrunak, Inc., enjoining the city from enforcing a zoning ordinance imposing special safety requirements on a residence plaintiff sought to operate for four mentally [disabled] adult women. The injunction resulted from the court's conclusion that the city had violated the Fair Housing Amendments Act of 1988 ("FHAA"), 42 U.S.C. § 3601 *et seq*. The case was submitted to the court upon stipulated facts. Plaintiff cross-appeals the refusal of the district court to award attorney's fees.

Plaintiff is a non-profit corporation organized by the parents of the mentally [disabled] women. In February 1990, the Ohio Department of Mental Retardation and Developmental Disabilities awarded plaintiff a grant to establish a "family consortium" home. Under the rules of the department, a family consortium consists of individuals with mental retardation and developmental disabilities, and a group of their relatives who wish to provide for those individuals a home which is an extension of their family home. The department encourages families to combine their resources with public funds in order to provide these family-like homes. State licenses are not required for family consortium homes.

In April 1990, the parents signed a purchase contract for a house in a residential neighborhood in the city. The house previously had been used as a single-family residence, and was located in an area zoned for single-family dwellings. The parents were advised that they would need a conditional-use permit because the intended use made the home a boarding house, rather than a single-family dwelling. The city's law director also told them the home must satisfy section 153.149 of the city's zoning code, an ordinance which requires extensive safety protections for family homes housing individuals with developmental disabilities. These requirements are more rigorous than the state department's safety rules for family consortium homes, and are far more extensive than those required of single-family dwellings.[1]

1. The law director advised the parents that they would have to provide the home with a whole-house sprinkler system with alarms, fire retardant wall and floor coverings, lighted exit signs above all doorways, push bars on all doors, fire extinguishers every thirty feet, smoke alarms, and bring the unit into conformity with city codes. The only safety requirement imposed by the city on single-family homes not occupied by developmentally disabled persons is that smoke alarms be provided. The home already was equipped with smoke alarms. Each of the four women is fully ambulatory, able to hear, and is sighted. They will live with a house parent hired by their parents.

The parents were told that they could petition the city's Board of Zoning Appeals for a variance from the safety restrictions. Rather than seek the variance, plaintiff filed this lawsuit in the district court.

In arriving at its conclusion that the zoning ordinance as applied to plaintiff violated the FHAA, the district court noted that under the Act it is unlawful to discriminate in the sale of a dwelling to any person on the basis of handicap,[2] and that discrimination includes the refusal to make reasonable accommodations in rules when those accommodations may be necessary to afford a handicapped person equal opportunity to enjoy a dwelling. 42 U.S.C. § 3604(f)(3)(B). The Act defines "handicap" as a physical or mental impairment which substantially limits a person's major life activities. 42 U.S.C. § 3602(h). The court also noted legislative history indicating an intent that the prohibition against discrimination extend to zoning practices and enforcement of otherwise neutral safety regulations that have the effect of limiting the ability of handicapped individuals to live in the residence of their choice. The city does not dispute the court's conclusion that the zoning practices complained of by plaintiff are subject to federal court scrutiny pursuant to the FHAA.

The city ... repeats on appeal its hyper-technical argument that plaintiff lacks standing until it has suffered the required extent of injury, since it has not yet been subjected to actual enforcement of the zoning code. We agree with the district court's reasoning and conclusion that those arguments are not well-taken.

[W]e now turn to the issue which was focused upon in the district court. In oral argument, before this court, counsel for the city conceded that if the ordinance were enforced *in toto* against plaintiff, it would violate the FHAA since non-handicapped, single-family dwelling occupants were not required to comply with the ordinance. Accordingly, the issue boiled down to whether requiring plaintiff to seek a zoning variance was an unduly burdensome means of ascertaining the extent to which the ordinance would be enforced. According to the district court,

> Marbrunak's claims are that the City has enacted ordinances which unlawfully discriminate against developmentally disabled persons ... by imposing onerous safety and permit requirements on single-family residences occupied by developmentally disabled persons, whereas such restrictions are not applied to any other single-family use ... Marbrunak ... must either ... comply with safety restrictions applicable to licensed "family homes ..." or endure the arduous and time-consuming process of seeking a variance from the Board of Zoning Appeals.... The options given to Marbrunak by the City require it to choose between incurring needless expense in installing unnecessary safety devices or ... obtain unnecessary permits and variances before it can open the home.

The district court concluded that the zoning ordinance as applied to plaintiff violates the FHAA because it imposes safety requirements which are more stringent than safety requirements applied to other single-family residences, and the ordinance makes no effort to tailor the safety requirements to the particular disabilities of plaintiff's residents. According to the district court, the requirements

---

2. [I]t shall be unlawful ... (f)(1) To discriminate in the sale or rental, or to otherwise make unavailable or deny, a dwelling to any buyer or renter because of a handicap of ... (B) a person residing in or intending to reside in that dwelling after it is so sold, rented, or made available.... (3) For purposes of this subsection, discrimination includes.... (B) a refusal to make reasonable accommodations in rules, policies, practices, or services, when such accommodations may be necessary to afford such person equal opportunity to use and enjoy a dwelling.... 42 U.S.C. § 3604.

> are based on generalized perceptions about the inability of developmentally disabled persons to live safely in a "normal" home. The City would require that Marbrunak install an alarm system interconnected to a ceiling sprinkler system, yet it offers no evidence that any of the residents of the home are hearing impaired or otherwise unable to respond to the standard smoke alarms with which the home is already equipped.... The City requires Marbrunak to install doors with push-bars that swing outward with lighted exit signs posted above each door of the home without offering any evidence that the residents are or would be unable to use the types of doors already in the home, and without showing how the women would need lighted exit signs to find them. The City requires Marbrunak to install fire walls and flame retardant wall coverings without showing why such renovations are needed to ensure the safety of the residents. In sum, the requirements have little or no correlation to the actual abilities of the citizens upon whom they are imposed.... [T]he City's "blanket" fire and safety restrictions applied to all homes wherein developmentally disabled persons live, regardless of the individual abilities of the residents, are based on "false [and] overprotective assumptions about the needs of handicapped people, as well as unfounded fears of difficulties about the problems that their tenancies may pose ..." and ... the application of these restrictions to Marbrunak's family consortium home unreasonably limits its residents' opportunity to live in the community of their choice, a right guaranteed them by the FHAA....

We agree with the district court that the ordinance as applied to plaintiff violates the Act.

The city is correct in its contention that the FHAA does not prohibit the city from imposing *any* special safety standards for the protection of developmentally disabled persons. It may impose standards which are different from those to which it subjects the general population, so long as that protection is demonstrated to be warranted by the unique and specific needs and abilities of those handicapped persons.

However, as the district court noted, this ordinance makes no attempt at individualizing its requirements to the needs or abilities of particular kinds of developmental disabilities. The ordinance requires installation of protective safety devices in a residential facility for persons with developmental disabilities attributable to mental retardation, cerebral palsy, epilepsy, or autism. The safety measures include nearly every safety requirement that one might think of as desirable to protect persons handicapped by any disability—mental or physical; and all the requirements apply to all housing for developmentally disabled persons, regardless of the type of mental condition that causes their disabilities or of the ways in which the disabilities manifest themselves. The ordinance makes no effort, for example, to promulgate one set of safety standards tailored to the needs and abilities of developmentally disabled persons who are hearing impaired, another for those whose vision is impaired, another for those whose conditions impair their mobility, etc. Instead, the ordinance lumps all the requirements together and makes all of them applicable in the instance of every developmental disability. The expense that would result from complying with needless safety requirements amounts to an onerous burden which has the effect of limiting the ability of these handicapped individuals to live in the residence of their choice.

The question then becomes whether other provisions of the zoning code narrow application of the ordinance to only those safety requirements that are directed at the unique and specific needs and abilities of plaintiff's residents. The city argues that the narrowing is accomplished through its procedures for obtaining a zoning variance. However, the variance procedure provided by the city's zoning code cannot be said to save the ordinance by satisfactorily individualizing its safety requirements to the needs and abilities of the residents of plaintiff's home. The ordinance predates the FHAA and on its face violates that Act. No policy decision has been made by the city's legislative authority to conform the ordinance to the Act. It seems incongruous for the city to now argue that such legislative policy choices should be foisted on an ad hoc basis upon members of an administrative board and applicants for zoning variances. Manifestly, because the ordinance does not even mention the variance procedure, it cannot be argued that it is contemplated as part of a design that the safety requirements will always be tailored to the individual needs and abilities of handicapped applicants. Accordingly, in the absence of such a stated purpose and any standards for individualizing the requirements to applicants, resort to that procedure shifts to an applicant the burden of initially determining which safety requirements (if any) are appropriate to its particular situation, and then convincing the Board of Zoning Appeals that it should emasculate the ordinance by eliminating all but those requirements. Under the city's scenario, each applicant is required to persuade the Board to rewrite from the whole cloth particularized requirements, in order to customize an over-broad and over-inclusive ordinance to a handicapped applicant's needs. Subjecting developmentally disabled persons to such a standardless and unpredictable process is unwarranted and has the effect of limiting their ability to live in the residence of their choice.

Furthermore, as mentioned earlier, if one reads division (C) of the ordinance to say that it does not apply to plaintiff at all, then clearly an onerous and discriminatory burden would be placed upon plaintiff by requiring it to seek a variance that waives each and every safety requirement in order that plaintiff might be in the same position it would have been had the ordinance never been enforced!

Turning now to plaintiff's cross-appeal, we agree with its contention that the trial court abused its discretion by summarily denying its request for an award of attorney's fees and costs, without comment. Accordingly, that matter is remanded to the district court for further proceedings, since, upon the state of the record, we are unable to determine whether the denial of the request was warranted.

The city's appeal is found to be without merit and the judgment of the district court is affirmed in all regards except its denial of plaintiff's request for attorney's fees and costs, which matter is remanded to the district court for further consideration.

Notes and Questions

1. Are you able to determine whether the city may validly impose special safety or health requirements on those who provide housing for the handicapped? Or are all special requirements prohibited? If all requirements are not impermissible, what must the city demonstrate to impose special requirements?

2. Analyses of whether group homes have an effect on the values of neighboring properties have reached different conclusions. *See* Habitat for Humanity, Why Affordable Housing Does Not Lower Property Values, available at www.habitat.org/how/property values.aspx (citing data from eleven studies between 1982 and 1994 concluding that affordable housing, including residential care facilities and supportive housing, did not lower neighboring property values and based on research compiled by HomeBase/The Center For Common Concerns in San Francisco). *But see* Peter F. Colwell, Carolyn A. Dehring & Nicholas A. Lash, *The Effect of Group Homes on Neighborhood Property Val-*

ues, 76 LAND ECON. 615 (2000), available at http://www.jstor.org/stable/3146956?seq=1. The report concedes that the majority of studies show no adverse effect on neighborhood property values, but the authors conclude—based on a seven-neighborhood study conducted in DuPage County, Illinois—that "properties which are proximate to group homes experience a decline in value following the announcement of a group home's pending establishment."

3. There are some points about the handicapped that we should note at this point.

(a) Although *Marbrunak* is an example of discrimination by a governmental entity, discrimination based on handicap can and does take place in the private market. Thus, Title VIII violations based on handicap can and do arise under the next section of this chapter which deals with the private market.

(b) Substantial questions exist about the very nature of a handicap. One issue involved whether a person who was HIV-positive but who was asymptomatic for AIDS was "handicapped." In *Bragdon v. Abbott*, 524 U.S. 624 (1998), a patient infected with the human immunodeficiency virus (HIV) brought suit against dentist who refused to treat her in his office. The Supreme Court, in an opinion by Justice Kennedy, held that infection with HIV is a "disability" as defined in the Americans with Disabilities Act (ADA), 42 U.S.C. § 12102, even when the infection has not yet progressed to the so-called symptomatic phase, as a physical impairment which "substantially limits the major life activity" of reproduction. *See also Toyota Motor Mfg. Kentucky, Inc. v. Williams*, 534 U.S. 184 (2002) ("substantially limited in performing manual tasks" under the ADA addresses the question of whether the claimant is unable to perform the variety of tasks central to most people's daily lives, not whether the claimant is unable to perform the tasks associated with her specific job; thus carpel tunnel is not reached absent serious muscle atrophy); *Sutton v. United Air Lines, Inc.*, 527 U.S. 471 (1999) (not an impairment if it can be corrected by medication or corrective devices).

In the *Bragdon* decision the Court also pointed out that the ADA does not require another person to make an accommodation when to do so would pose a "direct threat" to the health or safety of others. *See* 42 U.S.C. § 12182(b) (3). The Court held that the existence or nonexistence of a significant health risk from treatment or accommodation of a disabled person must be determined from standpoint of the person who refused the treatment or accommodation, but the risk assessment must be based on medical or other objective evidence, and not simply on that person's good-faith belief that a significant risk existed.

(c) Is this decision relevant to the nondiscrimination on handicap provisions in the Fair Housing Act? In its opinion the Court noted that the ADA's definition of disability is drawn almost verbatim from the definition of "handicapped individual" included in the Rehabilitation Act of 1973, 29 U.S.C. § 706(8)(B), and the definition of "handicap" contained in the Fair Housing Amendments Act of 1988, 42 U.S.C. § 3602(h)(1).

The Court found it significant that HUD's implementing regulations construed handicap to include HIV infection. *See* 24 C.F.R. § 100.201(a)(2).The Court also cited several fair housing cases: *In re Williams*, 2A Fair Housing-Fair Lending (P-H) ¶ 25,007 at 25,111–25,113 (HUD Office of Admin. Law Judges Mar. 22, 1991) (adhering to this interpretation); *In re Elroy R. and Dorothy Burns Trust*, 2A Fair Housing-Fair Lending (P-H) ¶ 25,073 at 25,678 (HUD Office of Admin. Law Judges June 17, 1994) (adhering to this interpretation). The Court pointed out that the legislative record indicates that Congress intended to ratify HUD's interpretation when it reiterated the same definition in the ADA, citing H.R. Rep. No. 101-485, pt. 2, at 50, pt. 3, at 27, pt. 4, at 36 and S. Rep. No. 101-116, at 21.

It may be emphasized that issues of handicap can arise in many ways. What about a denial of rezoning that would permit a development for the "handicapped" to go forward? Many issues touched on in the preceding notes come together in the following case.

Budnick v. Town of Carefree

United States Court of Appeals
518 F.3d 1109 (9th Cir. 2008)

Before: WILLIAM C. CANBY, JR., DAVID R. THOMPSON, and MILAN D. SMITH, JR., Circuit Judges.

MILAN D. SMITH, JR., Circuit Judge:

Plaintiffs-Appellants, F.G. Budnick, and the development company of which he is the chief executive officer, Tempo, Inc. (collectively, Budnick), sued Defendants-Appellees, the Town of Carefree and four Town Council members (collectively, Carefree) after Carefree denied Budnick's request for a Special Use Permit (SUP) to build a multi-level continuing-care retirement community in Carefree. Budnick claimed that by denying the SUP, Carefree had violated the Fair Housing Amendments Act of 1988 (FHAA), the Americans with Disabilities Act (ADA), 42 U.S.C. § 1983, the Rehabilitation Act, and Budnick's rights to due process and equal protection under the Fourteenth Amendment. The district court granted summary judgment in Carefree's favor on all claims. Budnick now appeals the district court's grant of summary judgment on his FHAA claim. We affirm the decision of the district court.

I. FACTUAL AND PROCEDURAL BACKGROUND

In August 2003, Budnick filed an application for Site Plan Approval and a SUP with the Town of Carefree. Budnick sought the SUP to build the Residences at Carefree (RAC), which, according to Budnick, would be a "luxurious, age restricted, senior retirement residential community" that would "primarily serv[e] the active and independent discerning senior populace." The RAC was to be located on approximately forty-acres of property that was zoned for multiple-family residences (zone R-3) and detached single-family residences (zones R1-10 and R1-35). The proposed RAC did not comply with the applicable zoning ordinances because it would provide "healthcare, meal, laundry, housekeeping" and other services that constitute "special uses," and it was to include "attached dwelling units rather than detached" units and a two-story apartment building that would exceed height limitations in the zone. The RAC plans provided for a number of other amenities, including swimming pools, interior and exterior dining areas, a café, a library, a salon, and recreation areas.

Budnick's SUP application stated that the RAC would be a "village-like community" consisting of upscale apartments (83), exclusive casitas (60), and opulent single-family homes (18). The RAC would also include an "ancillary healthcare component" consisting of six assisted-care units (four beds per unit) and four skilled-nursing units (six beds per unit). Though the residents would not own their housing, Budnick's application explained that they would enter into life care contracts upon entry and would be guaranteed housing and care for the rest of their lives, including the provision of in-home healthcare, assisted living, and skilled-nursing care "if and when such assistance becomes necessary." The application also stated that potential residents would be evaluated before acceptance and only individuals capable of independent living upon entry into the community would be accepted.

On October 13, 2003, the Town of Carefree Planning and Zoning Commission held a hearing on Budnick's application. During this hearing, representatives of Budnick indicated that RAC residents would be "active, vibrant members of the community." Budnick made similar representations in a letter to the Mayor and Town Council members on November 26, 2003; in that letter, Budnick emphasized that RAC "entry [would be] *restricted* to healthy, active, independent seniors who will be impossible to tell apart from many of their neighbors throughout Carefree as they drive, walk, bike, shop, attend, participate, volunteer, teach, learn and enjoy life...." (emphasis in original) The letter further stated that the skilled nursing component "will be held in reserve for *temporary acute needs.*" (emphasis in original) The Commission voted four to one, with one abstention, to deny the SUP.

The Commission's denial of the SUP was appealed to the Town Council, which held a public hearing on the appeal on December 2, 2003. At that meeting, the Town's legal counsel explained that under his reading of Arizona Revised Statute § 9-462.04, the Town Council needed a supermajority vote to grant the SUP because at least 20% of the owners surrounding the proposed community had filed written protests. Budnick was informed of this supermajority requirement a few hours before the meeting. The Town Council voted four to three to deny the SUP.

On December 30, 2003, an attorney sent a letter on behalf of those developing the RAC and, for the first time, asserted that the RAC would serve "disabled residents" in the skilled-nursing and assisted-living units. The letter stated that the laundry, kitchen, healthcare, and restaurant facilities were necessary to provide services to those disabled residents and requested reasonable accommodation under 42 U.S.C. § 3604(f)(3)(B).

Carefree and Budnick met in January 2004, and Carefree offered a variety of options to Budnick so that the RAC might still be built, including: (1) helping Budnick to locate the project on a piece of land to be sold by the State Land Department that would be appropriately zoned; (2) reconsidering the application if commercial features were moved across the street to commercially zoned property; and (3) reconsidering the application if commercial features were scaled back to a size that would accommodate only the RAC's disabled residents. Budnick did not accept any of these alternatives and subsequently filed this lawsuit....

III. DISCUSSION

The FHAA forbids discrimination in the sale or rental of housing, which includes making unavailable or denying a dwelling to a buyer or renter "because of a handicap of ... a person residing in or intending to reside in that dwelling after it is sold, rented, or made available." 42 U.S.C. § 3604(f)(1)(B).[3] Title VII discrimination analysis is used to examine claims under the FHAA; thus, a plaintiff may establish discrimination in violation of the FHAA under a theory of disparate treatment or disparate impact.... Under § 3604(f)(3)(B) of Title 42, a plaintiff may also sue on the theory that a local municipality failed to make reasonable accommodations for housing for the disabled. Budnick asserted its discrimination claim under all three of these theories. We consider each theory in turn.

---

3. The FHAA extended the Fair Housing Act's protection against discrimination in the sale or rental of housing to those with disabilities. Fair Housing Amendments Act of 1988, Pub. L. No. 100-430, § 6(a), 102 Stat. 1619 (1988). Though the FHA and the FHAA use the term "handicap," 42 U.S.C. § 3604, we use the preferred term, "disabled," except when referring to the statutory language. *See Giebeler v. M & B Assocs.*, 343 F.3d 1143, 1146 n. 2 (9th Cir. 2003). We assign identical meanings to these terms.

A. Disparate Treatment

When disparate treatment is claimed as a result of the denial of a special use permit, the plaintiff must establish that: (1) the "plaintiff is a member of a protected class"; (2) the plaintiff "applied for a [special] use permit and was qualified to receive it;" (3) the permit was denied despite plaintiff's qualification; and (4) "defendant approved a [special] use permit for a similarly situated party during a period relatively near the time" it denied plaintiff's request.... The burden then shifts to the defendant to articulate "a legitimate, nondiscriminatory reason for its action ..." the plaintiff must then prove by a preponderance of the evidence that the defendant's asserted reason is a pretext for discrimination....

In lieu of satisfying the elements of a prima facie case, a plaintiff may also "simply produce direct or circumstantial evidence demonstrating that a discriminatory reason more likely than not motivated" the challenged decision.... Under either method, however, the plaintiff must counter the defendant's explanation with some evidence suggesting that the challenged action "was due in part or whole to discriminatory intent...."

Budnick cannot satisfy all the elements of a prima facie case for disparate treatment and has not pointed to direct or circumstantial evidence of discriminatory intent. Nor can Budnick rebut the non-discriminatory reasons Carefree has proffered to explain why it denied the SUP.

Though we agree with the district court that Budnick can meet the second and third elements of the prima facie case, we do not agree that Budnick has raised a genuine dispute of fact with respect to the first element: whether the RAC would house individuals with disabilities. Budnick suggests that the RAC would naturally house disabled individuals because the senior citizen residents of the RAC would have entered into life care contracts and would inevitably experience disabilities as they age. We hold that potential RAC residents do not presently qualify as disabled under the FHAA simply because some of them will become disabled as they age. To hold that they can currently be considered disabled under the FHAA would mean, in effect, that *every senior citizen* (indeed, *every person*) desiring to rent or buy housing could assert a present claim of discrimination based on inevitable disability due solely to the passage of time. Such a holding would also disregard the reality that even if many individuals become disabled as they age, many do not, and that being old is not, *per se*, equivalent to being disabled.

Bragdon v. Abbott, 524 U.S. 624 (1998), does not require a different construction of the FHAA. In *Bragdon*, the Court held that a person with HIV that had not progressed to the symptomatic phase was disabled within the meaning of the ADA. The *Bragdon* court noted, however, that, at that time, HIV followed "a predictable ... and unalterable course." ("In light of the immediacy with which the virus begins to damage the infected persons's white blood cells and the severity of the disease, we hold it is an impairment from the moment of infection.... HIV infection must be regarded as a physiological disorder with a constant and detrimental effect on the infected person's hemic and lymphatic systems from the moment of infection"). In contrast, the consequences of aging are entirely unpredictable, and are sometimes treatable.

Moreover, the undisputed facts confirm that Budnick repeatedly informed Carefree that the RAC's residents would be healthy and active, and that Budnick did not claim, prior to Carefree's denial of the SUP, that the RAC would house disabled residents. *See* 42 U.S.C. § 3604(f)(1)(B) (discrimination under FHAA must be "*because of a handicap* of ... a person residing in or intending to reside in that dwelling after it is sold, rented, or made available" (emphasis added)); *id.* § 3602(h)(1)-(3) (defining "handicap" as "a physical or mental impairment which substantially limits one or more of such person's major life activities; a record of having such an impairment; or being regarded as having such an impairment")....

Budnick's SUP application stated that the RAC would "primarily serv[e] the active and independent discerning senior populace," that the potential residents would be "evaluated" before acceptance, and that only individuals capable of independent living upon entry would be accepted as residents. In a letter dated November 26, 2003, Budnick made emphatic representations about the residents that would live at the RAC; Budnick wrote that "entry [would be] *restricted* to healthy, active, independent seniors who will be impossible to tell apart from many of their neighbors throughout Carefree as they drive, walk, bike, shop, attend, participate, volunteer, teach, learn and enjoy life...." (emphasis in original) It is not significant that Carefree was aware that healthcare service would be available to all RAC residents after entry; the mere availability of healthcare in no way suggests that the RAC's residents would be disabled within the meaning of the FHAA.

The fact that the RAC was to provide assisted-living and skilled-nursing units does not alter our analysis. Not only did Budnick represent in its SUP application that only individuals capable of independent living would be accepted, but Budnick also stated in its November letter, just before the December Town Council meeting, that the skilled-nursing component "will be held in reserve for temporary acute needs." Budnick did not assert that the assisted-living and skilled-nursing units would house the disabled until its December 30, 2003 letter, which Budnick sent after the Town Council had already denied the SUP.

Budnick also cannot satisfy the fourth element of the prima facie case.... [H]ere, Budnick has not set forth evidence to create a triable issue of fact as to whether Carefree has approved a SUP "for a similarly situated party during a period relatively near the time" it denied Budnick a SUP....

Carefree has set forth at least two reasons for denying the SUP: (1) to achieve its zoning goals, and (2) to preserve the character of the neighborhood. Both of these reasons were reflected in the comments of the zoning commissioners and Town Council members when they explained their votes against the SUP, and both of these reasons are legitimate and nondiscriminatory.... [We have] held that concern for the residential character of the neighborhood is a legitimate and nondiscriminatory goal.... Though Budnick made an effort to ensure that the RAC would aesthetically blend in with its surrounding neighborhood, Budnick nevertheless required a SUP because certain aspects of the RAC did not meet all of the requirements of the residential zones on which it would have been located. And, a city's interest in achieving its zoning goals has long been recognized as a legitimate governmental interest....

Budnick points to numerous pieces of evidence that, in its view, raise a triable issue of fact as to whether Carefree's reasons for denying the SUP were a pretext for discrimination against the disabled or are sufficient, in lieu of establishing a prima facie case, to demonstrate that a discriminatory reason more likely than not motivated Carefree's decision to deny Budnick a SUP. Even viewing the evidence in the light most favorable to Budnick, it does not support the conclusion that discrimination played a role in Carefree's decision.

Budnick suggests that "Carefree repeatedly rejected housing tailored for seniors with disabilities in residential neighborhoods," but Budnick admits that in both of the two cited instances, Carefree steered the projects into areas that were not zoned residential. Thus, this evidence demonstrates only that Carefree has consistently been concerned with maintaining the residential character of its neighborhood by adhering to its zoning ordinances....

Budnick suggests that discrimination can be inferred from the fact that Carefree's "General Plan" stated that Carefree was designed to cater to a retirement lifestyle. Nothing in the record suggests that the Planning and Zoning Commission or Town Council did not generally support RAC's location in Carefree; in fact, multiple commissioners and Town Council members stated that they thought the RAC was a good idea if located somewhere else in Carefree. Indeed, Carefree offered to assist Budnick in locating the RAC elsewhere in Carefree. Budnick suggests that the "frivolous" nature of the accommodations itself suggests a discriminatory intent. Given that Carefree offered three different options to Budnick on how the RAC might still be able to locate in Carefree, including reconsidering the application if commercial features were scaled back to a size that would accommodate only the RAC's disabled residents, we cannot infer a discriminatory intent....

The comments of neighbors also do not show any discriminatory motive on Carefree's part. Budnick claims that neighbors' comments at zoning hearings, for example, that they were concerned about the presence of ambulances, or that Carefree would be a place people came to die, evidence discriminatory intent. Carefree's zoning ordinance required the holding of a public hearing to determine whether granting the SUP would "serve the public health, safety, and welfare" and to allow the neighbors to comment on the RAC. Indeed, permitting town councils, planning commissions, and the like to hear the views of concerned citizens and other interested parties about proposed projects is the essence of all zoning hearings. There is no evidence in the record to suggest that the cited comments or similar ones, which were a small part of the total comments, motivated the commissioners or Town Council members to vote against the SUP, and we decline to make such an inference based solely on the fact that the comments were made....

Finally, we cannot infer a discriminatory intent from the fact that Carefree amended its zoning ordinance a few months after denying Budnick the SUP so that Continuing-Care Retirement Communities (CCRCs) such as the RAC would also need a SUP to locate in commercially-zoned areas. We decline to read into this requirement an intent to discriminate *against the disabled,* particularly in light of our conclusion that being old is not the equivalent of having a disability.

B. Disparate Impact

"To establish a prima facie case of disparate impact under the FHA, 'a plaintiff must show at least that the defendant's action had a discriminatory effect....'" [A] FHA plaintiff must establish "'(1) the occurrence of certain outwardly neutral ... practices, and (2) a significantly adverse or disproportionate impact on persons of a particular [type] produced by the [defendant's] facially neutral acts or practices ...' A plaintiff need not establish discriminatory intent but the discriminatory impact must be proven; an inference of discriminatory impact is not sufficient. Statistical analysis is admissible to establish disparate impact.... A defendant may rebut a plaintiff's proof of disparate impact by "supply[ing] a legally sufficient, nondiscriminatory reason...."

Budnick has set forth no evidence, statistical or otherwise, from which we can conclude that Carefree's permit practices have a disproportionate impact on the disabled or that there is a triable issue of fact as to the impact of Carefree's permit practices on the disabled. We have previously recognized the necessity of statistical evidence in disparate impact cases.... Though Budnick submitted national statistics to prove that the size of the proposal was necessary for the RAC to be financially viable, these statistics are not relevant to whether Carefree's permitting practices have a disparate impact on the disabled as compared to any other group of people....

C. Reasonable Accommodation

A municipality commits discrimination under the FHAA if it refuses "to make reasonable accommodations in rules, policies, practices, or services, when such accommodations may be necessary to afford [the physically disabled] equal opportunity to use and enjoy a dwelling." [S]*ee* 42 U.S.C. § 3604(f)(3)(B). To establish a claim of discrimination on a theory of failure to reasonably accommodate, "a plaintiff must demonstrate that (1) he suffers from a handicap as defined by the FHAA; (2) defendants knew or reasonably should have known of the plaintiff's handicap; (3) accommodation of the handicap 'may be necessary' to afford plaintiff an equal opportunity to use and enjoy the dwelling; and (4) defendants refused to make such accommodation."

For the reasons we have already discussed above, *see* Section III.A. *supra,* the undisputed facts do not support that the plaintiff (here, the potential RAC residents) suffer "from a handicap as defined by the FHAA." The undisputed facts also do not support that Carefree should have known that the RAC would house disabled individuals, particularly in light of the many representations that Budnick made to Carefree about the RAC residents, including that "entry [would be] *restricted* to healthy, active, independent seniors." (emphasis added)

Assuming, *arguendo,* that the SUP application was itself sufficient to request a reasonable accommodation, even though it did not explicitly do so, we nevertheless conclude that Budnick also cannot meet the third prima facie element. Budnick has not set forth sufficient evidence to establish that the RAC's amenities were necessary to house disabled seniors; in other words, that "but for the accommodation, [the disabled] will likely be denied an equal opportunity to enjoy the housing of their choice." To the extent Budnick suggests that the amenities requiring accommodation are "necessary to house the physically disabled," this suggestion is primarily based on Budnick's view that all of the RAC's residents may one day be disabled and, therefore, the amenities must have the capacity to serve all of the RAC's potential residents. Not only have we rejected this initial premise, but Budnick has also only summarily concluded that the RAC's amenities are necessary for the disabled and has not delineated for the court why each of the RAC's amenities are necessary in the first place. As a result, we need not discuss the reasonableness of the accommodations Carefree offered to Budnick after it denied Budnick's application for the SUP.

III. CONCLUSION

For these reasons, we AFFIRM the district court's grant of summary judgment.

Notes and Questions

1. There exist many issues of what constitutes reasonable accommodation, what an accommodation is, and how it is to be implemented. *See, e.g., Anast v. Commonwealth Apartments*, 956 F. Supp. 792, 801 (N.D. Ill. 1997). The *Anast* court stated:

> In determining what constitutes a reasonable accommodation, the court recognizes that "the requirement of reasonable accommodation does not entail an obligation to do everything humanly possible to accommodate a disabled person; cost (to the defendant) and benefit (to the plaintiff) merit consideration as

> well." [*Bronk v. Ineichen*, 54 F.3d 425, 428, 429 (7th Cir. 1995)—Eds.]. *See also Stephenson v. Ridgewood Village Apartments*, No. 1:93-CV-614, 1994 WL 792581 (W.D. Mich. Nov. 10, 1994) (citing *Southeastern Community College v. Davis*, 442 U.S. 397 (1979) ("An accommodation is reasonable if it neither requires a 'fundamental alteration in the nature of a program', nor imposes 'undue financial and administrative burdens.'"). Therefore, plaintiff must show that the desired accommodation will affirmatively improve a disabled plaintiff's quality of life by ameliorating the effects of the disability. *Bronk*, 54 F.3d at 429.

The Fourth Circuit has held that accommodations are required under the FHA if they are "(1) reasonable and (2) necessary (3) to afford handicapped persons equal opportunity to use and enjoy housing." *Bryant Woods Inn v. Howard County*, 124 F.3d 597, 602 (4th Cir. 1997). The plaintiff must prove all three elements by a preponderance of the evidence. Plaintiff operated a group home for 8 elderly persons who suffered from Alzheimers disease and other forms of dementia and disability. Plaintiff sought a zoning variance to expand to 15 residents. The Court held that the requested zoning variance to allow the expansion of a group home from eight to fifteen residents was not a request for a reasonable accommodation required by FHA.

2. In *Giebeler v. M & B Associates*, 343 F.3d 1143 (9th Cir. 2003), the Ninth Circuit Court of Appeals held that the Fair Housing Act required apartment owners to make a reasonable accommodation of a potential renter's AIDS-induced disability by assessing individually the risk of nonpayment created by Plaintiff's proposed financial arrangement in which Plaintiff's mother would rent the apartment and pay Plaintiff's rent, rather than inflexibly applying a rental policy that prohibited cosigners.

3. Under the Fair Housing Act if reasonable accommodations require modifications of structure the cost of modifications and of any restoration work must be borne by the handicapped person. 42 U.S.C. § 3604(f)(3)(A). Also, under Title VIII, prohibited discrimination includes a failure to design and construct certain "covered" multifamily dwellings in a manner that makes the dwelling accessible to and usable by handicapped persons. 42 U.S.C. § 3604(f)(3)(C). Plaintiffs filed an action against HUD alleging that the building industry nationwide was substantially out of compliance in some instances with construction requirements for making new rental properties accessible to the handicapped. The court dismissed the action. *American Disabled for Attendant Programs Today v. U.S. Dept. of Hous. & Urb. Dev.*, 170 F.3d 381 (3rd Cir. 1999) (holding that (1) plaintiffs failed to rebut presumption of unreviewability of HUD investigative and enforcement policies, and (2) judicial review was also foreclosed by lack of final agency action and availability of other adequate remedies).

4. Difficult problems can arise with timing of private civil actions seeking relief from an alleged failure to design and construct a covered multifamily dwelling to comply with accessibility standards that meet needs of handicapped persons. The Court of Appeals considered this question in *Garcia v. Brockway*, 503 F.3d 1092 (9th Cir. 2007), *panel opinion adopted en banc*, 526 F.3d 456 (9th Cir. 2008), *cert. denied*, 129 S. Ct. 724 (2008). The panel opinion adopted by the en banc court analyzed the issue as follows:

> [Title VIII provides that] "[a]n aggrieved person may commence a civil action in an appropriate United States district court or State court not later than 2 years after the occurrence or the termination of an alleged discriminatory housing practice." 42 U.S.C. § 3613(a)(1)(A). In other words, an aggrieved person must bring the lawsuit within two years of either "the occurrence ... of an alleged discriminatory housing practice" or "the termination of an alleged discriminatory housing practice." Here, the practice is the "failure to

> design and construct" a multifamily dwelling according to FHA standards. *Id.* § 3604(f)(3)(C). The statute of limitations is thus triggered at the conclusion of the design-and-construction phase, which occurs on the date the last certificate of occupancy is issued. In both cases, this triggering event occurred long before plaintiffs brought suit.

The Court rejected the Plaintiffs' claims that the statute of limitations was extended because the non-complying construction was a "continuing violation" of the Fair Housing Act. It also rejected the Plaintiffs' claims that the limitations period did not begin to run until plaintiffs "encountered" the Fair Housing Act violations by renting the dwelling and rejected the claim that the limitations period did not begin to run until plaintiffs visited the property seeking to rent it at which time they "discovered" the Fair Housing Act violations.

A Note on Fair Housing Enforcement and the First Amendment

The potential reach of some anti-discrimination measures has raised issues under the First Amendment to the United States Constitution. In 1977, the Supreme Court struck down a municipal ordinance that, in an effort to forestall panic selling and racial transition in neighborhoods, banned posting "For Sale" signs on front lawns. *Linmark Associates, Inc. v. Township of Willingboro*, 431 U.S. 85 (1977). The Court reasoned that the prohibition violated the First Amendment rights of potential home sellers.

A more politicized First Amendment flap arose about the Fair Housing Act as amended in 1988 to include the handicapped as a protected class. It appears that a HUD regional office, acting pursuant to a complaint, conducted an investigation in 1993 of three individuals from Berkeley, California who had protested against the conversion of a hotel into a homeless and substance abuser shelter in their neighborhood. 24 [Current Developments] Hous. & Dev. Rep. (WGL) 307 (1996). Their protest took the form of petitions and newsletters. In fact, after the investigation HUD dismissed the complaint, *inter alia*, on the ground that that activities engaged by the protesters were protected by the First Amendment.

When revealed in the media, criticism of the investigation was vociferous. Outrage was expressed that evidence of protests that used methods protected by the First Amendment might become the basis for asserting a violation of the Fair Housing Act, although nothing of the sort had actually transpired. Nevertheless, Congressional and other pressures arose arguing that even the potential of being investigated would have a "chilling effect" on the general public. *See* Nat Hentoff, *HUD's Attack on the First Amendment*, WASH. POST, Sept. 14, 1994, at A15; Heather MacDonald, *HUD Continues Its Assault on Free Speech*, WALL STREET J., Sept. 14, 1994, at A19; Kenneth Smith, *Halt That Criticism Housing Officials Imposed Speech Code*, WASH. TIMES, Dec. 21, 2000, at A23.

HUD's Assistant Secretary for Fair Housing and Equal Opportunity, at that time, Roberta Achtenberg, had to respond to these assertions. On September 2, 1994, she released a statement announcing that HUD could not and would not prosecute protesters for Fair Housing Act violations when the methods employed were protected by the First Amendment. She also asserted that "when confronted with a complaint that someone relentlessly harassed and intimidated a neighbor, HUD will stand up for the proposition that there is no place for such behavior in America."

The furor did not completely abate and in a further effort to quell the outcry HUD, on August 21, 1995, issued guidelines on Fair Housing Act enforcement and the protection of First Amendment rights. The revised Guidelines may be found at the following link: http://www.hud.gov/offices/adm/hudclips/notices/fheo/02-02fheo.doc (last visited March 4, 2010).

The guidelines, available at 1995 WL 908975, in part, provide that:

> [HUD] will not accept for filing or investigate any complaint under Section 818 [42 USC § 3617—Eds.] of the Fair Housing Act that involves public activities that:
>
> (1) are directed toward achieving action by a governmental entity or official; and
>
> (2) do not involve force, physical harm, or a clear threat of force or physical harm to one or more individuals.
>
> Examples of types of public activities that are "directed toward achieving action by a governmental entity or official" and are covered by these guidelines include:
>
> (a) distributing fliers, pamphlets, brochures, posters, or other written materials to the public at large;
>
> (b) holding open community or neighborhood meetings;
>
> (c) writing articles or letters to the editor or making statements in a newspaper;
>
> (d) conducting peaceful demonstrations;
>
> (e) testifying at public hearings; and
>
> (f) communicating directly with a governmental entity concerning official governmental matters.
>
> Moreover, in order to ensure that HUD's investigative process does not interfere with protected rights under the First Amendment, no complaint alleging a violation of Section 818 [42 USC § 3617] may be filed absent prior formal approval from the Washington Headquarters Office....

In its guidelines, HUD states that:

> It is clear that the Supreme Court has, in the civil rights context, determined that certain kinds of "speech" may constitutionally be prohibited because the speech is limited as part of a general prohibition against behavior which amounts to unlawful discrimination or interference with the exercise of civil rights. *See R.A.V. v. City of St. Paul,* [505 U.S. 377—Eds.] (1992); *Wisconsin v. Mitchell,* [508 U.S. 476, 487—Eds.] (1993) (citing *Roberts v. United States Jaycees*, 468 U.S. 609, 628 (1984); *Hishon v. King & Spalding*, 467 U.S. 69, 78 (1984); *Runyon v. McCrary,* 427 U.S. 160, 176 (1976).

The Fair Housing Act, therefore, constitutionally prohibits certain combinations of speech with behavior and speech itself that rises to the level of conduct. For example, where third parties, such as neighbors, engage in behavior, including speech, which is coercive, threatening, intimidating or harassing, the behavior may violate Section 818 [42 U.S.C. § 3617—Eds.] of the Act. *See, e.g., Sofarelli v. Pinellas County*, 931 F. 2d 718 (11th Cir. 1991*); People Helpers Foundation v. Richmond*, 781 F. Supp. 1132 (E.D. Va. 1992); *HUD v. Johnson*, [2A Fair Housing-Fair Lending (P-H) ¶ 25,076—Eds.] (HUD Office of Admin. Law Judges July 26, 1994); *HUD v. Williams* [2A Fair Housing-Fair Lending (P-H) ¶ 25,007—Eds.] (HUD Office of Admin. Law Judges Feb. 18, 1993); *HUD* *v. Weber*, [2A Fair Housing-Fair Lending (P-H) ¶ 25,041—Eds.] (HUD Office of Admin. Law Judges Feb. 18, 1993).

Notes and Questions

1. A legitimate question may well be raised as to the appropriate balance to strike between enforcing fair housing laws and protecting First Amendment rights. Clearly there is a balance to be struck, as in the case of using any evidence to establish a violation of law based on conduct or activities that might be constitutionally protected. But it is hard to see that the issue here is substantially different from other instances of such potential conflicts. Did HUD strike a proper balance or did it react to a political problem?

2. In the case of the HUD First Amendment flap, one can only wonder whether all of the outcry was motivated by egregiously overzealous enforcement of the Fair Housing Act by HUD or whether a different agenda was motivating some of the criticism. It may not be purely coincidental or surprising that Senator Faircloth was a consistent critic of HUD. In 1995, he introduced legislation to abolish HUD altogether. *See* Peter Drier, *Federal Housing Subsidies: Who Benefits and Why?*, *in* A Right To Housing: Foundation For A New Social Agenda 116 (Rachel G. Bratt, Michael E. Stone & Chester W. Hartman eds. 2006). *See also* S. 1145 introduced August 10, 1995 by Senator Faircloth proposing to abolish HUD, available at http://thomas.loc.gov/cgi-bin/bdquery/D?d104:8:./temp/~bdJyII::.

3. The episode became embroiled in litigation. Plaintiffs, who opposed the shelter, filed suit in Federal District Court represented, in part, by the Center for Individual Rights located in Washington, D.C. *See* the CIR website. http://www.cir-usa.org/cases/white_v_julian.html (last visited Feb. 26, 2010). Plaintiffs sought damages for the violation of their first amendment rights by reason of HUD's investigation. The district court held not only that the investigation by HUD was "itself ... violative of the plaintiffs' First Amendment rights," but also held that the defendants had no qualified immunity because a reasonable person in defendants' position could not have believed the investigation of the plaintiffs' activities was lawful. Nevertheless, the court held that defendants' liability for damages turned on a fact finding question on the "reasonableness" of their actions. *White v. Julian*, No. C 95-1757 MHP, 1996 WL 40192 (N.D. Cal. Jan. 5, 1996.) In a subsequent proceeding, the district court found that as a matter of fact a reasonable person in the position of the HUD employees would have recognized the "constitutional impropriety of investigating purely expressive activity" of the Berkeley objectors. *See White v. Lee*, 227 F.3d 1214 (9th Cir. 2000), *aff'g sub nom. White v. Julian*, No. C 95-1757 MHP (N.D. Cal. Dec. 18, 1998). Upon the filing of a complaint charging housing discrimination, is a HUD investigation to determine if neighbors or protesters are harassing or intimidating in violation of § 3617 or engaged in First Amendment protected activity itself a violation of the First Amendment. That, however, was all that the HUD office did in *White.*

4. An owner of rental housing is exempt from coverage under the Fair Housing Act if the property contains no more than four dwelling units and the owner resides in one of the four units (the "Mrs. Murphy" exemption). 42 USC § 3603(b). Thus, such an exempt owner is not prohibited from discriminating against a member of an otherwise protected class. An African American man brought a claim against an exempt rental property owner alleging a violation of the Fair Housing Act *because she told him she would not rent to him because he was black.* The Fourth Circuit, in an unpublished *per curiam* opinion, held that although the owner was renting one unit in a building of no more than four units

and resided in one of the units, nevertheless, she violated section 42 USC § 3604(c) of the Fair Housing Act *because she made a statement of her intent to discriminate on the basis of race. Racey v. Muir*, 112 F.3d 512 (Table), 1997 WL 226373 (4th Cir. May 7, 1997). The *per curiam* unpublished opinion also addressed First Amendment issues as follows:

> We find [defendant] Racey's assertion that her statements to [potential renter] Jackson were not commercial unpersuasive. While Racey did not explicitly propose a commercial transaction in the conversation itself, the purpose of Jackson's call was to respond to Racey's offer to rent property. Therefore, we find that the statements were made in the context of a potential commercial transaction.
>
> Since Racey's comments fall within the realm of commercial speech, we must balance the First Amendment interests at stake against the public interest served by the statute. We find that the public has an important interest in preventing discrimination in housing. Moreover, even though the owner of "an exempted dwelling is free to indulge his discriminatory preferences in selling or renting that dwelling, neither the [Fair Housing] Act nor the Constitution gives him a right to publicize his intent to so discriminate." Allowing discriminatory statements such as those here would undermine the purposes of the Fair Housing Act and would deter minorities from exercising their rights to fair housing. We further find that the statute here is narrowly tailored to accomplish this purpose. Racey's claims concerning overbreadth are unfounded since only aggrieved persons (i.e., persons who have been discriminated against in obtaining housing) can recover under the statute.

5. One rationale of the prohibition against making discriminatory statements might be that such statements, especially when embodied in printed or widely distributed media, "poison the atmosphere" and are therefore prohibited. Thus, in addition to the prohibition in the Mrs. Murphy context, the Fair Housing Act on its face prohibits discriminatory statements. Under the Act it is unlawful "To make, print, or publish, or cause to be made, printed, or published any notice, statement, or advertisement, with respect to the sale or rental of a dwelling that indicates any preference, limitation, or discrimination based on race, color, religion, sex, handicap, familial status, or national origin, or an intention to make any such preference, limitation, or discrimination," 42 U.S.C. § 3604(c), and the Act limits an otherwise exempt sale of a single family home without the use of brokers to only those sales made "without the publication, posting or mailing, after notice, of any advertisement or written notice in violation of section 3604(c) of this title." 42 U.S.C. § 3603(b)(1)(B).

If "poison atmosphere" is even in part the rationale, Congress left a hole in the prohibition when it provided immunity to internet service providers for posted notices. *Fair Housing Council of San Fernando Valley v. Roommates.com*, LLC, 521 F.3d 1157 (9th Cir. 2008), involved the interaction of the Fair Housing prohibition on discriminatory statements and the internet service provider exemption. The court analyzed that the Communications Decency Act of 1996, 47 U.S.C. § 230(c) grants immunity to providers of interactive computer services against liability arising from content created by third parties. The court noted that the immunity applied only if the interactive computer service provider did not also act as an "information content provider," which the Act defined as someone who was "responsible, in whole or in part, for the creation or development of" the offending content.

The Fair Housing Council Plaintiffs argued that the Defendant, Roommate.com, LLC operated a website designed to match people renting out spare rooms with people looking for a place to live and posed mandatory questions to prospective subscribers during the registration process that violated the Fair Housing Act and the analogous California law. Plaintiffs alleged that requiring subscribers to disclose their sex, family status and sexual orientation "indicates" an intent to discriminate against them, and thus violated the Fair Housing Act and state law. The court decided that the defendant created the questions and choice of answers, and designed its website registration process around them. Therefore, the court said that the defendant was undoubtedly the "information content provider" as to the questions and could not claim immunity for posting them on its website, or for forcing subscribers to answer them as a condition of using its services. *Id.* at 1164.

In addition, the court noted that the part of the profile that was alleged to offend the Fair Housing Act and state housing discrimination laws—the information about sex, family status and sexual orientation—was provided by subscribers in response to defendant's questions, which subscribers could not refuse to answer if they wanted to use defendant's services. The court thought that by requiring subscribers to provide the information as a condition of accessing its service, and by providing a limited set of prepopulated answers, defendant had become much more than a passive transmitter of information provided by others. But rather, it had become the developer, at least in part, of that information and that § 230 provided immunity only if the interactive computer service did not "creat[e] or develop" the information "in whole or in part." *See* 47 U.S.C. § 230(f)(3). Other issues in the case were remanded for trial in the District Court.

The finding that the defendant Roommates.com in *Fair Housing Councils* had become an "information content provider' and thus not exempt from liability for that part of its activities contrasts with *Chicago Lawyers' Committee for Civil Rights Under Law, Inc. v. Craigslist, Inc.*, 519 F.3d 666 (7th Cir. 2008). According to the court, "Some notices on craigslist proclaim 'NO MINORITIES' and 'No children,' along with multiple variations, bald or subtle." The court nevertheless found the popular craigslist internet site exempt because it was not a publisher or speaker of posted notices that offended Title VIII but a messenger and did not "cause" the posted notices. The court did point out, however that the Plaintiff Lawyers' Committee "Using the remarkably candid postings on Craigslist, can identify many targets to investigate. It can dispatch testers and collect damages from any landlord or owner who engages in discrimination." *See Havens Realty Corp. v. Coleman*, 455 U.S. 363 (1982); *Gladstone Realtors v. Bellwood,* 441 U.S. 91 (1979). It can assemble a list of names to send to the Attorney General for prosecution. But given § 230(c)(1) it cannot sue the messenger just because the message reveals a third party's plan to engage in unlawful discrimination."

6. In *New York State Association of Realtors, Inc. v. Shaffer,* 27 F.3d 834 (2d Cir 1994), an association of real estate brokers challenged the constitutionality of two regulations the New York Secretary of State issued under a state statute. The regulations (1) banned solicitation of residential property owners by brokers in designated geographic areas, and (2) prohibited brokers from making representations regarding entry or prospective entry into neighborhood of person or persons of particular race, color, religion or national origin.

On the first challenge, the court held that the Secretary did not establish a narrow fit between the regulation prohibiting all solicitations and the State's interest in regulating the brokers' commercial speech and did not show that other means (such as cease and desist orders on particular facts) would not be equally as effective while being less intrusive on First Amendment interests. On the second challenge, the court found that the State's interest in preventing "blockbusting" was sufficient to sustain the regulation, even as applied to truthful nonmisleading communications from brokers.

7. *Pearson v. Edgar*, 965 F. Supp. 1104 (N.D. Ill. 1997) is also a case raising First Amendment issues. An Illinois statute directed at preventing "panic peddling" and blockbusting (*see* discussion of blockbusting *infra*) prohibited real estate brokers and agencies from soliciting any persons who placed their names on an anti-solicitation list. Upon being found guilty of violating the anti-solicitation act real estate brokers sought injunctive relief and declaratory judgment that the statute was unconstitutional. In an extensive opinion, the District Court held that the statute prohibiting real estate brokers from soliciting an owner to list or sell his home if the owner has provided notice of his desire not to be solicited violated the First Amendment, and that the statute was unconstitutionally vague. It enjoined enforcement of the statute.

8. Of course, defendants who burned a cross on the property of a white family because it entertained blacks were not immune from conviction for violating 42 U.S.C. §3631(b), because such intimidation is not a protected activity even if symbolic speech is involved. *United States v. Hayward,* 6 F.3d 1241 (7th Cir 1993) (conviction affirmed). Similarly, a state's statutory ban on burning a cross with intent to intimidate does not violate the First Amendment. *Virginia v. Black,* 538 U.S. 343 (2003) (at least where such intent is presumed from the cross burning itself).

9. Questions of "freedom of religion" under the First Amendment have also been raised. First, under §807(a) the Fair Housing Act, 42 U.S.C. §3607(a), a religious group may limit or give preference in the sale, rental, or occupancy of dwellings "which it owns or operates for other than a commercial purpose to persons of the same religion ... unless membership in such religion is restricted on account of race, color, or national origin." *See United States v. Columbus Country Club,* 915 F.2d 877 (3d Cir. 1990) (country club's claim of religious exemption failed for lack of a sufficient connection to or control by a religious organization).

Second, because of the Fair Housing Act exemption, the freedom of religion issue arises indirectly. For example, in one case, the plaintiffs alleged that a defendant landlord, because of an agreement with Brigham Young University, segregated Mormon and non-Mormon students, in violation, *inter alia,* of the religious discrimination provisions of the Fair Housing Act. The district court held that the plaintiffs lacked standing to raise the religious discrimination issue. On appeal, on other grounds, the court of appeals vacated the district court's decision to render judgment on the merits of the case since it lacked jurisdiction because plaintiffs also lacked standing to raise the issue appealed. *Wilson v. Glenwood Intermountain Properties, Inc.*, 98 F.3d 590 (10th Cir. 1996), *rev'g* 876 F. Supp. 1231 (D. Utah. 1995).

Third, some state fair housing laws include a prohibition on discrimination based on "marital status," which has been interpreted to cover unmarried couples living together. In states with these interpretations the laws have raised the religious issue more directly.

For example, in *Smith v. Fair Employment & Housing Commission*, 913 P. 2d 909 (Cal. 1994), *cert. denied*, 521 U.S. 1129 (1997) a landlord, Mrs. Smith, claimed an exemption from the California fair housing law, *inter alia,* under the First Amendment as well as the federal Religious Freedom Restoration Act of 1993, 42 U.S.C. §2000bb to 2000bb-4. Smith had refused to rent to an unmarried couple on the grounds that the couple's cohabitation and sex outside of marriage were sins according to Smith's religious beliefs and her religion. She further argued that, under her religion, to rent the property to them would cause Smith to commit a sin. Smith, thus, claimed a right, based on the First Amendment's "free exercise" of religion clause, to an exemption from the California fair housing law's prohibition of marital status discrimination. The California Supreme Court held in *Smith* that enforcement of the marital status discrimination ban did not violate Smith's rights under either the First Amendment or under the Religious Freedom Restoration Act. *But see Thomas v. Anchorage Equal Rights Commission*, 165 F.3d 692 (9th Cir. 1999), vacated, 220 F.3d 1134 (9th Cir, 2000) (*en banc*), *cert. denied*, 531 U.S. 1143 (2001). The district court's ruling enjoining the enforcement of the nondiscrimination statute was vacated on the ground that the landlord's action challenging the constitutionality of the statute was not ripe for review before there was any enforcement of the statute and ordinance prohibiting marital status discrimination in rental decisions. The vacated decision of the Ninth Circuit panel in *Thomas* had reasoned that enforcement against Christian landlords of Alaska's fair housing laws prohibiting apartment owners from refusing to rent to unmarried couples infringed on the Christian landlords' rights under the free exercise clause of the First Amendment. That reasoning was based on a "hybrid claim" analysis in that under the Fifth Amendment the fair housing law amounted to a "taking" of the landlords' right to refuse to deal with unmarried couples, by forbidding landlords to refuse to sell, lease, or rent the real property to a person because of the person's marital status together with the religion-based claim met an exception recognized by a plurality of the United States Supreme Court. *See also Attorney General v. Desilets,* 636 N.E.2d 233 (Mass. 1994) (Massachusetts Supreme Judicial Court holding that Massachusetts Commission Against Discrimination, which had found probable cause to believe that landlords had violated antidiscrimination statute by declining to lease apartment to unmarried couple placed a burden on landlord's freedom of religion, but remanded for a determination of whether the Commonwealth could demonstrate a compelling state interest to justify the burden). In *State v. French,* 460 N.W.2d 2 (Minn. 1990), the Minnesota Supreme Court held that landlord did not violate Minnesota Human Rights Act's prohibition of marital status discrimination by refusal to rent house to tenant who intended to cohabitate with her fiancé prior to marriage and that the landlord's right to exercise his religion under Freedom of Conscience Provision of Minnesota Constitution outweighed any interest of tenant to cohabitate with her fiancé in rental property prior to her marriage.

For further analysis of the issues, see Keirsten G. Anderson, *Protecting Unmarried Cohabitants From the Religious Freedom Restoration Act*, 31 Val. U. L. Rev. 1017 (1997); Jerry DeMuth, *Not In My Apartment: When Landlords Mix Business and Religion,* 22 Hum. Rts 44 (Winter 1995); Maureen Markey, *The Price of Landlord's "Free" Exercise of Religion: Tenant's Right to Discrimination-Free Housing and Privacy,* 22 Fordham Urb. L.J. 699, 755–759 (1995).

4. Restrictions on Occupancy

City of Edmonds v. Oxford House, Inc.

Supreme Court of the United States
514 U.S. 725 (1995)

Justice GINSBURG delivered the opinion of the Court.

The Fair Housing Act (FHA or Act) prohibits discrimination in housing against, *inter alia*, persons with handicaps. Section 3607(b)(1) of the Act entirely exempts from the FHA's compass "any reasonable local, State, or Federal restrictions regarding the maximum number of occupants permitted to occupy a dwelling." 42 U.S.C. § 3607(b)(1). This case presents the question whether a provision in petitioner City of Edmonds' zoning code qualifies for § 3607(b)(1)'s complete exemption from FHA scrutiny. The provision, governing areas zoned for single-family dwelling units, defines "family" as "persons [without regard to number] related by genetics, adoption, or marriage, or a group of five or fewer [unrelated] persons." Edmonds Community Development Code (ECDC) § 21.30.010 (1991).

The defining provision at issue describes who may compose a family unit; it does not prescribe "the maximum number of occupants" a dwelling unit may house. We hold that § 3607(b)(1) does not exempt prescriptions of the family-defining kind, i.e., provisions designed to foster the family character of a neighborhood. Instead, § 3607(b)(1)'s absolute exemption removes from the FHA's scope only total occupancy limits, i.e., numerical ceilings that serve to prevent overcrowding in living quarters.

I

In the summer of 1990, respondent Oxford House opened a group home in the City of Edmonds, Washington for 10 to 12 adults recovering from alcoholism and drug addiction. The group home, called Oxford House-Edmonds, is located in a neighborhood zoned for single-family residences. Upon learning that Oxford House had leased and was operating a home in Edmonds, the City issued criminal citations to the owner and a resident of the house. The citations charged violation of the zoning code rule that defines who may live in single-family dwelling units. The occupants of such units must compose a "family," and family, under the City's defining rule, "means an individual or two or more persons related by genetics, adoption, or marriage, or a group of five or fewer persons who are not related by genetics, adoption, or marriage." Edmonds Community Development Code (ECDC) § 21.30.010. Oxford House-Edmonds houses more than five unrelated persons, and therefore does not conform to the code.

Oxford House asserted reliance on the Fair Housing Act, 102 Stat. 1619, 42 U.S.C. § 3601 *et seq.*, which declares it unlawful "[t]o discriminate in the sale or rental, or to otherwise make unavailable or deny, a dwelling to any buyer or renter because of a handicap of ... that buyer or a renter." § 3604(f)(1)(A). The parties have stipulated, for purposes of this litigation, that the residents of Oxford House-Edmonds "are recovering alcoholics and drug addicts and are handicapped persons within the meaning" of the Act.

Discrimination covered by the FHA includes "a refusal to make reasonable accommodations in rules, policies, practices, or services, when such accommodations may be necessary to afford [handicapped] person[s] equal opportunity to use and enjoy a dwelling." § 3604(f)(3)(B). Oxford House asked Edmonds to make a "reasonable accommodation" by allowing it to remain in the single-family dwelling it had leased. Group homes for recovering substance abusers, Oxford urged, need 8 to 12 residents to be financially and therapeutically viable. Edmonds declined to permit Oxford House to stay in a single-family residential zone, but passed an ordinance listing group homes as permitted uses in multifamily and general commercial zones.

Edmonds sued Oxford House in the United States District Court for the Western District of Washington seeking a declaration that the FHA does not constrain the City's zoning code family definition rule. Oxford House counterclaimed under the FHA, charging the City with failure to make a "reasonable accommodation" permitting maintenance of the group home in a single-family zone. The United States filed a separate action on the same FHA "reasonable accommodation" ground, and the two cases were consolidated. Edmonds suspended its criminal enforcement actions pending resolution of the federal litigation.

On cross-motions for summary judgment, the District Court held that ECDC § 21.30.010, defining "family," is exempt from the FHA under § 3607(b)(1) as a "reasonable ... restrictio[n] regarding the maximum number of occupants permitted to occupy a dwelling." The United States Court of Appeals for the Ninth Circuit reversed; holding § 3607(b)(1)'s absolute exemption inapplicable, the Court of Appeals remanded the cases for further consideration of the claims asserted by Oxford House and the United States. *Edmonds v. Washington State Building Code Council*, 18 F.3d 802 (1994).

The Ninth Circuit's decision conflicts with an Eleventh Circuit decision declaring exempt under § 3607(b)(1) a family definition provision similar to the Edmonds prescription. We granted *certiorari* to resolve the conflict and we now affirm the Ninth Circuit's judgment....

II

The sole question before the Court is whether Edmonds' family composition rule qualifies as a "restrictio[n] regarding the maximum number of occupants permitted to occupy a dwelling" within the meaning of the FHA's absolute exemption. 42 U.S.C. § 3607(b)(1). In answering this question, we are mindful of the Act's stated policy "to provide, within constitutional limitations, for fair housing throughout the United States." § 3601. We also note precedent recognizing the FHA's "broad and inclusive" compass, and therefore according a "generous construction" to the Act's complaint-filing provision.... Accordingly, we regard this case as an instance in which an exception to "a general statement of policy" is sensibly read "narrowly in order to preserve the primary operation of the [policy]...."

A

Congress enacted § 3607(b)(1) against the backdrop of an evident distinction between municipal land use restrictions and maximum occupancy restrictions.

Land use restrictions designate "districts in which only compatible uses are allowed and incompatible uses are excluded." [Daniel R. Mandelker, Land Use Law § 4.16, pp. 113–114 (3d ed. 1993)—Eds.] (hereinafter Mandelker). These restrictions typically categorize uses as single-family residential, multiple-family residential, commercial, or industrial. *See, e.g.*, E. Ziegler, Jr., Rathkopf's The Law of Zoning and Planning § 8.01, pp. 8-2 to 8-3 (4th ed. 1995); Mandelker § 1.03, p. 4; 1 E. Yokley, Zoning Law and Practice § 7-2, p. 252 (4th ed. 1978).

Land use restrictions aim to prevent problems caused by the "pig in the parlor instead of the barnyard." *Village of Euclid v. Ambler Realty Co.*, 272 U.S. 365, 388 (1926). In particular, reserving land for single-family residences preserves the character of neighborhoods, securing "zones where family values, youth values, and the blessings of quiet seclusion and clean air make the area a sanctuary for people." *Village of Belle Terre v. Boraas,* 416 U.S. 1, 9 (1974); *see also, Moore v. City of East Cleveland,* 431 U.S. 494, 521 (1977) (Burger, C.J., dissenting) (purpose of East Cleveland's single-family zoning ordinance "is the traditional one of preserving certain areas as family residential communities"). To limit land use to single-family residences, a municipality must define the term "family"; thus family composition rules are an essential component of single-family residential use restrictions.

Maximum occupancy restrictions, in contradistinction, cap the number of occupants per dwelling, typically in relation to available floor space or the number and type of rooms ... These restrictions ordinarily apply uniformly to all residents of all dwelling units. Their purpose is to protect health and safety by preventing dwelling overcrowding.

We recognized this distinction between maximum occupancy restrictions and land use restrictions in *Moore v. City of East Cleveland*, 431 U.S. 494 (1977). In *Moore*, the Court held unconstitutional the constricted definition of "family" contained in East Cleveland's housing ordinance. East Cleveland's ordinance "select[ed] certain categories of relatives who may live together and declare[d] that others may not;" in particular, East Cleveland's definition of "family" made "a crime of a grandmother's choice to live with her grandson." (plurality opinion). In response to East Cleveland's argument that its aim was to prevent overcrowded dwellings, streets, and schools, we observed that the municipality's restrictive definition of family served the asserted, and undeniably legitimate, goals "marginally, at best." (footnote omitted). Another East Cleveland ordinance, we noted, "specifically addressed ... the problem of overcrowding;" that ordinance tied "the maximum permissible occupancy of a dwelling to the habitable floor area." *Id.*, at 500, n. 7, accord, *id.*, at 520, n. 16, (Stevens, J., concurring in judgment). Justice Stewart, in dissent, also distinguished restrictions designed to "preserv[e] the character of a residential area," from prescription of "a minimum habitable floor area per person," in the interest of community health and safety.

Section 3607(b)(1)'s language—"restrictions regarding the maximum number of occupants permitted to occupy a dwelling"—surely encompasses maximum occupancy restrictions.[8] But the formulation does not fit family composition rules typically tied to land use restrictions. In sum, rules that cap the total number of occupants in order to prevent overcrowding of a dwelling "plainly and unmistakably ..." fall within § 3607(b)(1)'s absolute exemption from the FHA's governance; rules designed to preserve the family character of a neighborhood, fastening on the composition of households rather than on the total number of occupants living quarters can contain, do not.[9]

B

Turning specifically to the City's Community Development Code, we note that the provisions Edmonds invoked against Oxford House, ECDC §§ 16.20.010 and 21.30.010, are classic examples of a use restriction and complementing family composition rule.

---

8. The plain import of the statutory language is reinforced by the House Committee Report, which observes:

> A number of jurisdictions limit the number of occupants per unit based on a minimum number of square feet in the unit or the sleeping areas of the unit. Reasonable limitations by governments would be allowed to continue, as long as they were applied to all occupants, and did not operate to discriminate on the basis of race, color, religion, sex, national origin, handicap or familial status.

H.R. Rep. No. 100-711, p. 31 (1988).

9. Tellingly, Congress added the § 3607(b)(1) exemption for maximum occupancy restrictions at the same time it enlarged the FHA to include a ban on discrimination based on "familial status." *See supra*, at 1778, n. 1. The provision making it illegal to discriminate in housing against families with children under the age of 18 prompted fears that landlords would be forced to allow large families to crowd into small housing units. *See, e.g.*, Fair Housing Amendments Act of 1988: Hearings on H.R. 1158 before the Subcommittee on Civil and Constitutional Rights of the House Committee on the Judiciary, 100th Cong., 1st Sess., 656 (1987) (remarks of Rep. Edwards) (questioning whether a landlord must allow a family with 10 children to live in a two-bedroom apartment). Section 3607(b)(1) makes it plain that, pursuant to local prescriptions on maximum occupancy, landlords legitimately may refuse to stuff large families into small quarters. Congress further assured in § 3607(b)(1) that retirement communities would be exempt from the proscription of discrimination against families with minor children. In the sentence immediately following the maximum occupancy provision, § 3607(b)(1) states: "Nor does any provision in this subchapter regarding familial status apply with respect to housing for older persons."

These provisions do not cap the number of people who may live in a dwelling. In plain terms, they direct that dwellings be used only to house families. Captioned "USES," ECDC § 16.20.010 provides that the sole "Permitted Primary Us[e]" in a single-family residential zone is "[s]ingle-family dwelling units." Edmonds itself recognizes that this provision simply "defines those uses permitted in a single family residential zone."

A separate provision caps the number of occupants a dwelling may house, based on floor area:

> Floor Area. Every dwelling unit shall have at least one room which shall have not less than 120 square feet of floor area. Other habitable rooms, except kitchens, shall have an area of not less than 70 square feet. Where more than two persons occupy a room used for sleeping purposes, the required floor area shall be increased at the rate of 50 square feet for each occupant in excess of two. ECDC § 19.10.000 (adopting Uniform Housing Code § 503(b) (1988)).

This space and occupancy standard is a prototypical maximum occupancy restriction.

Edmonds nevertheless argues that its family composition rule, ECDC § 21.30.010, falls within § 3607(b)(1), the FHA exemption for maximum occupancy restrictions, because the rule caps at five the number of unrelated persons allowed to occupy a single-family dwelling. But Edmonds' family composition rule surely does not answer the question: "What is the maximum number of occupants permitted to occupy a house?" So long as they are related "by genetics, adoption, or marriage," any number of people can live in a house. Ten siblings, their parents and grandparents, for example, could dwell in a house in Edmonds' single-family residential zone without offending Edmonds' family composition rule.

Family living, not living space per occupant, is what ECDC § 21.30.010 describes. Defining family primarily by biological and legal relationships, the provision also accommodates another group association: five or fewer unrelated people are allowed to live together as though they were family. This accommodation is the peg on which Edmonds rests its plea for § 3607(b)(1) exemption. Had the City defined a family solely by biological and legal links, § 3607(b)(1) would not have been the ground on which Edmonds staked its case.... It is curious reasoning indeed that converts a family values preserver into a maximum occupancy restriction once a town adds to a related persons prescription "and also two unrelated persons."

Edmonds additionally contends that subjecting single-family zoning to FHA scrutiny will "overturn Euclidian zoning" and "destroy the effectiveness and purpose of single-family zoning...." This contention both ignores the limited scope of the issue before us and exaggerates the force of the FHA's antidiscrimination provisions. We address only whether Edmonds' family composition rule qualifies for § 3607(b)(1) exemption. Moreover, the FHA antidiscrimination provisions, when applicable, require only "reasonable" accommodations to afford persons with handicaps "equal opportunity to use and enjoy" housing. §§ 3604(f)(1)(A) and (f)(3)(B)....

The parties have presented, and we have decided, only a threshold question: Edmonds' zoning code provision describing who may compose a "family" is not a maximum occupancy restriction exempt from the FHA under § 3607(b)(1). It remains for the lower courts to decide whether Edmonds' actions against Oxford House violate the FHA's prohibitions against discrimination set out in §§ 3604(f)(1)(A) and (f)(3)(B). For the reasons stated, the judgment of the United States Court of Appeals for the Ninth Circuit is Affirmed.

Justice THOMAS, with whom Justice SCALIA and Justice KENNEDY join, dissenting.

Congress has exempted from the requirements of the Fair Housing Act (FHA) "*any* reasonable local, State, or Federal restrictions regarding the maximum number of occupants permitted to occupy a dwelling." 42 U.S.C. § 3607(b)(1) (emphasis added). In today's decision, the Court concludes that the challenged provisions of petitioner's zoning code do not qualify for this exemption, even though they establish a specific number—five—as the maximum number of unrelated persons permitted to occupy a dwelling in the single-family neighborhoods of Edmonds, Washington. Because the Court's conclusion fails to give effect to the plain language of the statute, I respectfully dissent.

I

Petitioner's zoning code reserves certain neighborhoods primarily for "[s]ingle-family dwelling units." Edmonds Community Development Code (ECDC) § 16.20.010(A)(1) (1991). To live together in such a dwelling, a group must constitute a "family," which may be either a traditional kind of family, comprising "two or more persons related by genetics, adoption, or marriage," or a nontraditional one, comprising "a group of five or fewer persons who are not [so] related." § 21.30.010. As respondent United States conceded at oral argument, the effect of these provisions is to establish a rule that "no house in [a single-family] area of the city shall have more than five occupants unless it is a [traditional kind of] family." In other words, petitioner's zoning code establishes for certain dwellings "a five-occupant limit, [with] an exception for [traditional] families."

To my mind, the rule that "no house ... shall have more than five occupants" (a "five-occupant limit") readily qualifies as a "restrictio[n] regarding the maximum number of occupants permitted to occupy a dwelling." In plain fashion, it "restrict[s]"—to five—"the maximum number of occupants permitted to occupy a dwelling." To be sure, as the majority observes, the restriction imposed by petitioner's zoning code is not an absolute one, because it does not apply to related persons.... But § 3607(b)(1) does not set forth a narrow exemption only for "absolute" or "unqualified" restrictions regarding the maximum number of occupants. Instead, it sweeps broadly to exempt *any* restrictions *regarding* such maximum number. It is difficult to imagine what broader terms Congress could have used to signify the categories or kinds of relevant governmental restrictions that are exempt from the FHA.

Consider a real estate agent who is assigned responsibility for the city of Edmonds. Desiring to learn all he can about his new territory, the agent inquires: "Does the city have *any* restrictions regarding the maximum number of occupants permitted to occupy a dwelling?" The accurate answer must surely be in the affirmative—yes, the maximum number of unrelated persons permitted to occupy a dwelling in a single-family neighborhood is five. Or consider a different example. Assume that the Federal Republic of Germany imposes no restrictions on the speed of "cars" that drive on the *Autobahn* but does cap the speed of "trucks" (which are defined as all other vehicles). If a conscientious visitor to Germany asks whether there are "*any* restrictions regarding the maximum speed of motor vehicles permitted to drive on the *Autobahn*," the accurate answer again is surely the affirmative one—yes, there is a restriction regarding the maximum speed of trucks on the *Autobahn*.

The majority does not ask whether petitioner's zoning code imposes any restrictions regarding the maximum number of occupants permitted to occupy a dwelling. Instead, observing that pursuant to ECDC § 21.30.010, "any number of people can live in a house," so long as they are "related 'by genetics, adoption, or marriage,'" the majority concludes that § 21.30.010 does not qualify for § 3607(b)(1)'s exemption because it "surely does not answer the question: 'What is the maximum number of occupants permitted to occupy a house? ...'" The majority's question, however, does not accord with the text of the statute. To take advantage of the exemption, a local, state, or federal law need not impose a restriction *establishing* an *absolute* maximum number of occupants; under § 3607(b)(1), it is necessary only that such law impose a restriction "regarding" the maximum number of occupants. Surely, a restriction can "regar[d]"—or "concern," "relate to," or "bear on"—the maximum number of occupants without establishing an absolute maximum number in all cases.

I would apply § 3607(b)(1) as it is written. Because petitioner's zoning code imposes a qualified "restrictio[n] regarding the maximum number of occupants permitted to occupy a dwelling," and because the statute exempts from the FHA "any" such restrictions, I would reverse the Ninth Circuit's holding that the exemption does not apply in this case....

Notes and Questions

1. In light of the Supreme Court's ruling, can you determine exactly what terms an ordinance must be that would fall within the exemption?

2. Maximum occupancy restrictions can also raise issues of discrimination based on "familial status." We defer that issue until we consider the "familial status" topic later in this chapter.

A Note on Municipal Services Equalization

In its 1974 Handbook on Nondiscrimination in Municipal Services, entitled *The Other Side of the Tracks*, the United States Civil Rights Commission, stated:

> At an earlier period in American life, "the other side of the tracks" referred to that part of town beyond the railroad, usually occupied by blacks and who daily confronted the oppression of discrimination. It was an area ignored by city officials and the townspeople they represented.
>
> Today, "the other side of the tracks" is often a ghetto, its residents denied the municipal services to which they are entitled, its boundaries demarked not by railroad tracks but by freeways over which suburbanites drive to and from jobs in the city.

U.S. Civil Rights Comm'n, The Other Side of the Tracks iii (1974)

The housing and the community development implications of inadequate municipal services are not hard to see. When differential services are provided between white and black neighborhoods, the equal opportunity issue is implicated.

Services typically provided by municipal governments include street upkeep and paving; installation and maintenance of water, sewer, and drainage facilities; installation and maintenance of street lights, traffic lights, and control devices; collection of garbage; provision of fire and police protection, libraries, public transportation system, and facilities; and medical care facilities.

In *Hawkins v. Town of Shaw*, 437 F.2d 1286 (5th Cir. 1971), *aff'd en banc*, 461 F.2d 1171 (5th Cir. 1972), black residents of the town proved that the town had provided a lower level of services to black neighborhoods in a grossly disparate manner compared to those provided in white neighborhoods. Some 99% of white residents were served by the town's sewer system but only about 80% of the black population had sewer service. Water drainage systems were provided in the white areas, but black areas had either inadequate drainage ditches or, on some streets, no system at all.

Suing under 42 U.S.C. § 1983, plaintiffs claimed that these disparities violated equal protection. Since the case was pre-*Washington v. Davis*, the Fifth Circuit panel decision was not clear in whether it grounded the case on discriminatory intent or discriminatory effects (or results), in holding that the evidence made out a case of racial discrimination. The *en banc* court's opinion stated that the facts supported a finding of "neglect involving clear overtones of racial discrimination ... resulting in the same evils which characterize an intentional and purposeful disregard of the principle of equal protection" and cited, *inter alia, Yick Wo v. Hopkins*, 118 U.S. 35 (1886). It has been noted that "the discriminatory purpose was overshadowed by the severity of the discriminatory effects." Henry W. McGee, Jr., *Illusion and Contradiction in the Quest for a Desegregated Metropolis*, 1976 U. Ill. L.F. 948, 977–78. Indeed, one commentator suggested that *Hawkins* was really a case of a suspect classification based on race, *id.* at 977 n. 151, citing Clark Waddeups, Note, Hawkins v. Town of Shaw—*Equal Protection and Municipal Services: A Small Leap for Minorities But a Giant Leap for the Commentators*, 1971 Utah L. Rev. 397, and thus did not make new law.

Hawkins was put to the test in *Beal v. Lindsey*, 468 F.2d 287 (2d Cir. 1972), and arguably came up short on the critical issue. In *Beal*, black and Puerto Rican residents living in areas around Crotona Park sued the city of New York and its officials. Plaintiffs claimed that the city assigned proportionately fewer recreational, maintenance, and supervisory personnel to Crotona Park than to other parks in the city. They further alleged that a higher proportion of minorities were served by Crotona Park than were served by other parks. As a consequence of such differential maintenance, they claimed that Crotona Park was littered with refuse, covered with broken glass, and had unusable benches, broken fences, and entranceways clogged with abandoned automobiles. This, they alleged, contrasted with the other parks, which were kept in "near spotless" condition.

In a battle of affidavits on defendants' motion to dismiss the complaint, defendants showed an equal or superior effort to maintain Crotona Park compared with other parks. The court sustained the district court's dismissal of the complaint on the grounds that it was premised on a theory that equal protection demanded the attainment of equal results. Instead, the court held that equal protection prohibited less state effort, and that the city satisfied its constitutional obligation by equal "inputs," even if equal results were not thereby obtained.

Notes and Questions

1. *Hawkins* is one of those cases which created a splash among the commentators and then virtually faded away. One area of problems involved the facts of *Hawkins*. A key *Hawkins* fact was that all of the services at issue were provided out of the town's general fund, and no assessments or special fees were involved.

(a) Financing from the Town's general fund created problems with litigation in municipalities, for example, in which street paving involved assessments of landowners for improvements on the basis of land footage fronting the street, or water and sewer installation involved fees and charges to be paid by the owner of the property served. Poor property owners would not be able to pay the cost, and landlords might pass the costs along to poor renters through rent increases.

(b) A second problem with applying *Hawkins* elsewhere could also arise. If improvements, such as street paving, were conditioned upon a petition filed by a certain proportion of owners whose property abutted a street, that could present a problem under *Hawkins*, because quite obviously, poor persons would not file such a petition and equally as obviously, absentee landlords would not be likely to petition unless they could anticipate rents to cover the assessments.

(c) A third problem applying *Hawkins* was that the Town of Hawkins at the time of the litigation, in fact, had a surplus. So, even where services were furnished out of the general fund, *Hawkins* did not implicate the municipal taxing power, at least not directly. The legal theory might work in these cases but the remedy would be problematic. *See Missouri v. Jenkins*, 495 U.S. 33 (1990) (a complicated case holding in part that a district court order directly imposing an increase in property taxes levied by a school district to insure funding to remedy unconstitutional segregation of district's schools violated principles of federal/state comity, but concluding that federal courts could require school district to levy taxes itself that were in excess of limits set by state statute in order to fund a school desegregation plan to remedy the constitutional violations found.)

(d) The other problems with *Hawkins* involve its legal theory. Was *Hawkins*, even before *Washington v. Davis*, limited to egregious cases? At least lawyers for potential plaintiffs could have had real doubts about making a case under *Hawkins* with less stark disparities.

(e) The final problem with *Hawkins* is its application in the equal inputs/unequal outputs cases, like *Beal*. Does *Beal* leave open the possibility of a qualitative analysis in light of intensity of usage? For example, can the input be measured in number of users, children, etc.? Or is it limited to quantitative inputs, such as x dollars per square foot of parks?

2. Often areas experiencing deterioration of services are those of high density land uses—for example, high-rise apartments with a high proportion of young children. Does *Beal's* "equal inputs" approach permit that to be taken into account, and must the municipality furnish proportionately greater services to accommodate more users to meet its equal protection duties?

3. Does the availability of funds under community development block grants help answer any of these problems? *See* regulation in 24 C.F.R. § 6.4(a)(3)(i) which provides that "In administering a program or activity in which the Recipient has discriminated on the grounds of race, color, national origin, religion or sex, the Recipient must take any necessary steps to overcome the effects of prior discrimination."

Does this regulation suggest a new function *Hawkins*-based litigation might serve? Does it at least give community groups additional bargaining leverage to compete for funds for their neighborhoods? But the leverage concept was not beneficial to the plaintiffs in *Dowdell v. City of Apoka*, 698 F.2d 1181 (11th Cir. 1983). However, upon proof under *Hawkins* standards of discriminatory provision of services, the court enjoined the city from initiating or constructing new municipal services in the white community until disparities in the black community were eliminated and "impounded" all of the city's general revenue sharing funds with the stipulation that the funds could be used only to pay for capital improvements in municipal services provided to the black community. The court found both intentional conduct that violated the Constitution and conduct which violated the nondiscrimination requirements of the State and Local Fiscal Assistance Act of 1972, 31 U.S.C. § 1242(a).

4. For additional analysis of municipal services issues, see Charles M. Haar & Daniel W. Fessler, The Wrong Side of the Tracks: A Revolutionary Rediscovery of the

COMMON LAW TRADITION OF FAIRNESS IN THE STRUGGLE AGAINST INEQUALITY (1986). For general background, see Ralph S. Abascal, *Municipal Services and Equal Protection: Variations on a Theme by* Griffin v. Illinois, 20 HASTINGS. L.J. 1367 (1969); Gershon M. Ratner, *Inter-Neighborhood Denials of Equal Protection in the Provision of Municipal Services*, 4 HARV. C.R.-C.L. L. REV. 1 (1968). For a more recent analysis of this subject, see Jon C. Dubin, *From Junkyards to Gentrification: Explicating a Right to Protective Zoning in Low-Income Communities of Color*, 77 MINN. L. REV. 739 (1993). For a global approach to municipal services equalization, see Jane E. Larson, *Free Markets Deep in the Heart of Texas*, 84 GEO. L.J. 179 (1995).

5. For other cases raising the equal services problem, see *Fire v. City of Winner*, 352 F. Supp. 925 (D.S.D. 1972) (finding no violation); *Hadnott v. City of Prattville*, 309 F. Supp. 967 (M.D. Ala. 1970) (ordering improvements in a park and its facilities); and *Selmont Improvements Assoc. v. Dallas County Comm'n*, 339 F. Supp. 477 (S.D. Ala. 1972) (ordering street paving).

6. A somewhat different manifestation of the services problem was presented in *Citizens for Underground Equality v. City of Seattle*, 492 P.2d 1071 (Wash. Ct. App. 1972). The city of Seattle, pursuant to a state enabling legislation, initiated a program to convert overhead utility wiring to an underground system. Costs of conversion on principal arterial streets and scenic points would be borne by the city. In residential neighborhoods, the conversion was to be financed by a combination of city funds and special assessments of real property which would benefit from the conversion.

Plaintiffs sued, challenging the program on its face, but did not claim racial discrimination. They claimed, *inter alia*, that the special assessments violated equal protection because only isolated neighborhoods which could afford the conversion program would be able to form local improvement districts which were necessary to secure the city's contribution. The court rejected the claim, holding that the assessments did not unconstitutionally discriminate against the poor because each neighborhood had an equal opportunity to seek the city's contribution upon equal terms.

7. Plaintiffs failed to state a claim in *Southend Neighborhood Improvement Corp. v. County of St. Clair*, 743 F.2d 1207 (7th Cir. 1984), upon alleging; that the city failed to keep tax-foreclosed property in black neighborhoods in good repair. The court held that Title VIII did not apply because the alleged conduct did not have the effect of making housing "unavailable" and Section 1982 did not apply because the alleged diminution in property values was "too tenuous" and indirect to make out a violation. *See also City of Memphis v. Greene*, 451 U.S. 100 (1981) (closing of a street through a white community traversed by black homeowners did not have sufficient relationship to black homeowners' property interests protected by Section 1982 to support an action).

C. Legislative Fair Housing Policies: Discrimination in the Marketplace

A Note on Coordination of Title VIII and Section 1982

Having examined in the previous section some of the key fair housing issues that arise when government is a housing actor, this section now shifts the focus to legislation that seeks to protect against discrimination in the private marketplace. There are two basic statutes that come into play, 42 U.S.C. § 1982 (known popularly as "Section 1982"), enacted as part of the 1866 post-Civil War legislative package, and Title VIII of the Civil Rights Act of 1968, 42 U.S.C. §§ 3601–3619, 3631.

Section 1982 deals only with property rights and is limited to racial discrimination. As interpreted, Section 1982 contains no exemptions and applies to private as well as public conduct. It was enacted pursuant to the Thirteenth Amendment of the U.S. Constitution.

Title VIII is designed to provide "fair housing"—presumably a broader concept than prohibiting discrimination. While it makes unlawful discrimination based on race, it also prohibits discrimination based on color, religion, sex,* familial status (families with children under 18),** handicap,** or national origin. Unlike Section 1982, which requires private enforcement, Title VIII also provides administrative remedies and authorizes federal suits.

Title VIII is not as broad as Section 1982, since it contains two principal exceptions to coverage. It exempts (a) single-family homes sold or rented by a private person who neither uses the services of a broker, nor places discriminatory advertisements, and (b) rooms or units in dwellings containing separate living quarters for no more than four families if the owner lives in one of the units. This section focuses on the forms of discriminatory conduct statutorily proscribed and analyzes the mode by which the legislation provides relief.

As will be noted more fully later, in addition to the federal legislation, a number of states and localities have enacted fair housing legislation. In some instances, the federal legislation requires that a complainant resort to state or local provisions when HUD has found that the state legislation or local ordinance is "substantially equivalent."

Notes and Questions

1. For further reading on housing discrimination see James A. Kushner, *Fair Housing: Discrimination in Real Estate, Community Development and Revitalization* (2nd ed. (1995 & Supp. 2000); Robert G. Schwemm, *Housing Discrimination: Law and Litigation* (2007 & Supp. 2009).

2. Prohibitions of discrimination exist in various kinds of other special contexts, which could involve housing, for example: (1) college dormitories (*e.g.*, Education Amendments Act of 1972, 20 U.S.C. § 1681); (2) handicapped access to housing (*e.g.*, Rehabilitation Act of 1973, 29 U.S.C. § 794); and (3) housing for various people by age group (*e.g.*, Age Discrimination Act of 1975, 42 U.S.C. § 6102).

3. If federal legislation can and does apply nationwide and generally offers uniformity of substantive and procedural provisions, what interests are served by the recognition of "substantially equivalent" state and local legislation, not to mention giving such legislation, in some respects, a priority?

4. HUD is authorized by Title VIII to establish by regulation, procedures and criteria governing the recognition of "Substantially Equivalent Laws." *See* 42 U.S.C. § 3610(f). A substantially equivalent fair housing law may be enacted by a state or local government.

* Added in 1974, 42 U.S.C. § 3604 (1982), as amended by Pub. L. No. 93-383, 88 Stat. 729 (1974).

** Added by Fair Housing Amendments Act of 1988, Pub. L. No. 100-430,102 Stat.1419 (1988).

In jurisdictions with recognized laws, all complaints filed with HUD will be referred to the state or local agency when the complaint is within the jurisdiction of that agency, 24 C.F.R. § 103.100 and no further action will be taken by HUD, except in specified circumstances. 24 C.F.R. § 115.204.

To give notice of the jurisdictions that have been certified a list of recognized jurisdictions is published periodically in the Federal Register. 24 C.F.R. § 115.102.

5. Even though the basis for a discrimination action may be a statute, constitutional issues may nevertheless be presented in determining (a) whether Congress had the power to adopt the provision in question and (b) the extent to which Congress may have been exercising all the power it was granted under the constitutional provision it relied upon to enact the statute in question. The power issue, among others, is analyzed in *Jones v. Alfred H. Mayer Co.*, 392 U.S. 409 (1968) (holding that 42 U.S.C. § 1982 prohibits private individuals as well as governmental agencies from discriminating on the basis of race in connection with real property transactions). The issue of power was not reached by the Court of Appeals when it decided that persons who purchased a property to prevent its use as home for the mentally disabled did not commit a violation of Title VIII on the grounds of either of having "made unavailable" or of having "interfered with rights" protected under Title VIII. The District Court however had reached the issue and held, *inter alia,* that to the extent Title VIII purported to prohibit discrimination based on handicap in purely private sale of a home Congress had attempted a regulation that could not be sustained under the commerce clause. *Michigan Protection and Advocacy Service, Inc. v. Babin* 18 F.3d 337 (6th Cir. 1994), *aff'g on other grounds,* 799 F. Supp. 695 (E.D. Mich. 1992).

6. Another significant question the Court addressed in *Jones v. Alfred H. Mayer Co.* was what effect, if any, the enactment of Title VIII of the 1968 Civil Rights Act had on Section 1982 and vice versa. The Court squarely held that Title VIII had no effect on Section 1982.

Jones v. Alfred H. Mayer Co. was argued in the Supreme Court on April 1 and 2, 1968. Title VIII was enacted on April 11, 1968. *Jones* was decided on June 17, 1968. The parties had addressed at oral argument the issue of the effect the then pending Civil Rights Act would have on Section 1982. Indeed, on April 22, 1968, the Court requested further views as to the effect of Title VIII on the *Jones* litigation.

This consideration led to the Court's detailed comparison and contrasting of Title VIII and Section 1982. The differences noted included the following: (1) Section 1982 was narrowly limited to race; Title VIII, as originally enacted, applied to race, color religion, or national origin; (2) Section 1982 was enforceable only at the instance of private persons, but Title VIII had a complex scheme of private enforcement and administrative enforcement and permitted the Attorney General to file enforcement actions; (3) Section 1982 by its terms appears to cover a narrow range of real and personal property matters, whereas Title VIII covered advertising, financial services, and other facilities and services connected with sales and rentals; and (4) Title VIII contained several exemptions from coverage, in contrast to Section 1982, which, as construed, covered all housing.

7. Note that Section 1982, as interpreted in *Jones*, covers all housing. This interpretation appears to raise an issue of statutory coordination with Title VIII. The essential problem is that Congress has enacted two statutes dealing with racial discrimination and housing. Both statutes, under the supremacy clause, are the "law of the land." But with respect to state laws on the same subject, one statute—Title VIII—clearly contemplates

the continued existence of such laws. The other—Section 1982—presumably should invalidate any state law on the same subject which is inconsistent with Section 1982, as interpreted (which, for example, contained exemptions of certain types of housing, thus invalidating, as to race, any and all such exemptions).

Now recall that Title VIII contains exemptions—for example, four-unit structures, one of which is occupied by owner—and that Title VIII specifically contemplates the continued validity of state laws. Indeed, Title VIII provides for referral by the Secretary of HUD to a state or local agency of a complaint in that jurisdiction which has a statute providing "substantially equivalent" rights and remedies. 42 U.S.C. § 3610(d). Indeed, in the 1988 amendments Congress gave such jurisdictions forty months to include the coverages added to the federal law in 1988. Moreover, Title VIII goes on to provide that it does not invalidate state and local laws that grant, guarantee, and protect the same rights as Title VIII. 42 U.S.C. § 3615.

Where does that leave the preemption issue? Congress, in amending Title VIII, anticipated the reverse argument that Title VIII might preempt other statutes and provided that Title VIII does not preempt other rights, procedures, or remedies available under the Constitution or "any other Act of Congress." (Section 12 of the Fair Housing Amendments Act of 1988, Pub. L. No. 100-430, 102 Stat. 1419.). The only case known to have raised the matter is *Richards v. Mangum*, 303 N.Y.S.2d 320 (Sup. Ct. 1969), *rev'd on other grounds*, 314 N.Y.S.2d 512 (Sup. Ct. App. Div. 1970). But the rulings did not reach the critical issue.

8. One other factor deserves mention. Section 1982 contains a normative referent as the benchmark against which discrimination is measured—rights enjoyed by white citizens. Title VIII contains a definitional referent as a benchmark—the prohibited acts defined in the statute.

9. Title VIII contains its own limitation of action provisions which were extended by the 1988 amendments from 180 days to one year to file an administrative complaint and two years to file a lawsuit. Section 1982 is silent on limitations. Courts have had to determine what law sets out limitations. It has been held that the statute of limitations of the state where the Section 1982 action arises governs Section 1982 actions. In *Wilson v. Garcia*, 471 U.S. 261 (1985), the Supreme Court held that actions under Section 1983 (another provision of the Civil Rights Act of which Section 1982 is a part) were governed by the state statute governing limitations for personal injury actions.

10. Although Section 1982 is silent on remedies, the courts in Section 1982 actions have power to grant damages and fashion equitable remedies. *See, e.g., Parker v. Shonfeld*, 409 F. Supp. 876 (D.C. Cal. 1976). This power also applies to state courts if they possess the general powers under state law. *Sullivan v. Little Hunting Park Inc.*, 396 U.S. 229 (1969).

11. Several commentators have analyzed *Jones*. Michelle Adams, *Subsidized Housing Program*, 71 Tul. L. Rev. 413 (1996); Gerhard Casper, Jones v. Mayer*: Clio, Bemused and Confused Muse*, 1968 Sup. Ct. Rev. 89; Douglas L. Colbert, *Liberating the Thirteenth Amendment*, 30 Harv. C.R.-C.L. L. Rev. 1 (1995); Robert L. Kohl, *The Civil Rights Act of 1866, Its Hour Come Round at Last:* Jones v. Alfred H. Mayer, Co., 55 Va. L. Rev. 272 (1969); Bernard Schwartz, *Rehnquist,* Runyon *and* Jones—*The Chief Justice, Civil Rights, and Stare Decisis*, 31 Tulsa L.J. 251 (1995).

12. Having examined some of the differences between Section 1982 and Title VIII what are the elements of an action under Title VIII? How does one make or rebut a *prima facie case*?

1. The Limits of Fair Housing Policy: "Managed Occupancy" and Integration Maintenance

Having looked at problems created by attempts to segregate and exclude on a racial basis, we turn now to the problem of an attempt arguably "to include or to maintain" on the basis of race. One extremely troublesome aspect of the problem involves how to draw a line between inclusion of one group and exclusion of another. Another involves how to rationalize whatever decision is made. Who, if anyone, is required to take or is prohibited from taking active management measures to obtain and maintain racial balance? What, if any, measures to maintain racial balance are permissible?

Does the Fair Housing Act mandate "efforts" or "results"? Does the act require nondiscriminatory "inputs" without regard to how the "outcome" is affected? Does the Act focus on "discrimination" from an "individual perspective" or does it focus on "integration" from a "group perspective"? Is there a distinction between prohibiting "discriminatory" conduct affecting access to housing and achieving "integrated" housing?

How can these questions be answered? Is there an answer in the statute? What view of these questions is taken by the *Starrett City* case, which is set forth next? What view is expressed by the government's argument in that case? Do you suppose Congress thought about all of, or even some of these questions? Suppose there is no substantial evidence that it did? How should courts go about addressing such matters?

There is a most fundamental matter to remember when trying to determine what is permissible and what is prohibited by the Fair Housing Act: the task is to determine what Congress intended. Ideally one might try to get empirical evidence of Congressional intent. But unfortunately, in enacting legislation Congress does not always enunciate its intent with unmistakable clarity. When the language does not fully answer the question one can then turn to other means—such as looking for legislative history. When that fails one must try to make an interpretation that accomplishes the policies it may be determined that Congress was attempting to effectuate. Even that, however, can be very difficult in some contexts. Consider the following case.

United States v. Starrett City Associates

United States Court of Appeals
840 F.2d 1096 (2d Cir.),
cert. denied, 488 U. S. 946 (1988)

Before NEWMAN, MINER, and ALTIMARI, Circuit Judges.

MINER, Circuit Judge:

The United States Attorney General, on behalf of the United States ("the government"), commenced this action under Title VIII of the Civil Rights Act of 1968 ("Fair Housing Act" or "the Act") against defendants-appellants Starrett City Associates, Starrett City, Inc. and Delmar Management Company (collectively, "Starrett") in the United States District Court for the Eastern District of New York (Neaher, J.). The government maintained that Starrett's practices of renting apartments in its Brooklyn housing complex solely on the basis of applicants' race or national origin, and of making apartments unavailable to black and hispanic applicants that are then made available to white applicants, violate section 804(a), (b), (c) and (d) of the Act, 42 U.S.C. § 3604(a)-(d) (1982).

The parties made cross-motions for summary judgment based on extensive documentary submissions. The district court granted summary judgment in favor of the government and permanently enjoined appellants from discriminating on the basis of race in the rental of apartments. Starrett appeals from this judgment.

Background

Appellants constructed, own and operate "Starrett City," the largest housing development in the nation, consisting of 46 high-rise buildings containing 5,881 apartments in Brooklyn, New York. [The complex had the benefit of state and federal assistance. During its development Starrett City's developer assured the city of New York it "intended to create a racially integrated community." Starrett sought to maintain a racial distribution by apartment of 64% white, 22% black and 8% hispanic at Starrett City. Starrett claims that these racial quotas are necessary to prevent the loss of white tenants, which would transform Starrett City into a predominantly minority complex. Starrett points to the difficulty it has had in attracting an integrated applicant pool from the time Starrett City opened, despite extensive advertising and promotional efforts. Because of these purported difficulties, Starrett adopted a tenanting procedure to promote and maintain the desired racial balance. This procedure has resulted in relatively stable percentages of whites and minorities living at Starrett City between 1975 and the present.

[Tenants that are found preliminarily eligible, based on family composition, income, employment and size of apartment sought, are placed in "the active file," in which separate records by race are maintained for apartment sizes and income levels. Applicants are told in an acknowledgment letter that no apartments are presently available, but that their applications have been placed in the active file and that they will be notified when a unit becomes available for them. When an apartment becomes available, applicants are selected from the active file for final processing, creating a processed applicant pool. As vacancies arise, applicants of a race or national origin similar to that of the departing tenants are selected from the pool and offered apartments.—Eds.]

In December 1979, a group of black applicants brought an action against Starrett in the United States District Court for the Eastern District of New York. Plaintiffs alleged that Starrett's tenanting procedures violated federal and state law by discriminating against them on the basis of race. The parties stipulated to a settlement in May 1984, and a consent decree was entered subsequently, *see Arthur v. Starrett City Assocs.*, No. 79-CV-3096, slip op. at 1 (E.D.N.Y. April 2,1985). The decree provided that Starrett would, depending on apartment availability, make an additional 35 units available each year for a five-year period to black and minority applicants.

Starrett maintained that the tenanting procedures "were adopted at the behest of the [s]tate solely to achieve and maintain integration and were not motivated by racial animus." To support their position, appellants submitted the written testimony of three housing experts. They described the "white flight" and "tipping" phenomena, in which white residents migrate out of a community as the community becomes poor and the minority population increases, resulting in the transition to a predominantly minority community. *See id.* at 674. Acknowledging that "'the tipping point for a particular housing development, depending as it does on numerous factors and the uncertainties of human behavior, is difficult to predict with precision,'" one expert stated that the point at which tipping occurs has been estimated at from 1% to 60% minority population, but that the consensus ranged between 10% and 20%. *Id.* Another expert, who had prepared a report in 1980 on integration at Starrett City for the New York State Division of Housing and Community Renewal, estimated the complex's tipping point at approximately 40%

black on a population basis. A third expert, who had been involved in integrated housing ventures since the 1950's, found that a 2:1 white-minority ratio produced successful integration.

The court, however, accepted the government's contention that Starrett's practices of making apartments unavailable for blacks, while reserving them for whites, and conditioning rental to minorities based on a "tipping formula" derived only from race or national origin are clear violations of the Fair Housing Act. The district court found that apartment opportunities for blacks and hispanic were far fewer "than would be expected if race and national origin were not taken into account," while opportunities for whites were substantially greater than what their application rates projected. Minority applicants waited up to ten times longer than the average white applicant before they were offered an apartment. Further, the court found that appellants' tipping argument was undercut by the "wide elasticity of that standard" and the lack of difficulty they had in increasing their black quota from 21% to 35% "when it became necessary to avoid litigating the private Arthur lawsuit which threatened their unlawful rental practices." The court also found that Starrett violated the Act by making untrue representations of apartment unavailability to qualified minority applicants in order to reserve units for whites. Finally, the court rejected Starrett's claim that the duty imposed upon government to achieve housing integration justified its actions, stating that "[d]efendant cannot arrogate to themselves the powers" of a public housing authority.

The court concluded that Starrett's obligation was "simply and solely to comply with the Fair Housing Act" by treating "black and other minority applicants ... on the same basis as whites in seeking available housing at Starrett City." The court noted that Starrett did not dispute any of the operative facts alleged to show violation of the Fair Housing Act. Accordingly, Judge Neaher granted summary judgment for the government, enjoining Starrett from discriminating against applicants on the basis of race and "[r]equiring [them] to adopt written, objective, uniform, nondiscriminatory tenant selection standards and procedures" subject to the court's approval. The court retained jurisdiction over the parties for three years.

Discussion

Starrett's allocation of public housing facilities on the basis of racial quotas, by denying an applicant access to a unit otherwise available solely because of race produces a "discriminatory effect ... [that] could hardly be clearer," *Burney v. Hous. Auth.*, 551 F. Supp. 746, 770 (W.D. Pa. 1982). Appellants do not contend that the plain language of section 3604 does not proscribe their practices. Rather, they claim to be "clothed with governmental authority" and thus obligated, under *Otero v. New York City Housing Authority*, 484 F.2d 1122 (2d Cir. 1973), to effectuate the purpose of the Fair Housing Act by affirmatively promoting integration and preventing "the reghettoization of a model integrated community." We need not decide whether Starrett is a state actor, however. Even if Starrett were a state actor with such a duty, the racial quotas and related practices employed at Starrett City to maintain integration violate the antidiscrimination provisions of the Act.

Starrett's use of ceiling quotas to maintain integration at Starrett City lacks [certain characteristics approved by the Supreme Court.—Eds.] First, Starrett City's practices have only the goal of integration maintenance. The quotas already have been in effect for ten years. Appellants predict that their race-conscious tenanting practices must continue for at least fifteen more years, but fail to explain adequately how that approximation was reached. In any event, these practices are far from temporary. Since the goal of integration maintenance is purportedly threatened by the potential for "white flight" on a continuing basis, no definite termination date for Starrett's quotas is perceivable. Second, appellants do not assert, and there is no evidence to show, the existence of prior racial discrimination or discriminatory imbalance adversely affecting whites within Starrett City or appellants' other complexes. On the contrary, Starrett City was initiated as an integrated complex, and Starrett's avowed purpose for employing race-based tenanting practices is to maintain that initial integration. Finally, Starrett's quotas do not provide minorities with access to Starrett City, but rather act as a ceiling to their access. Thus, the impact of appellants' practices falls squarely on minorities, for whom Title VIII was intended to open up housing opportunities. Starrett claims that its use of quotas serves to keep the numbers of minorities entering Starrett City low enough to avoid setting off a wave of "white flight." Although the "white flight" phenomenon may be a factor "take[n] into account in the integration equation," *Parent Ass'n of Andrew Jackson High School v. Ambach*, 598 F.2d 705, 720 (2d Cir. 1979), it cannot serve to justify attempts to maintain integration at Starrett City through inflexible racial quotas that are neither temporary in nature nor used to remedy past racial discrimination or imbalance within the complex.

Appellants' reliance on *Otero* is misplaced. In *Otero* the New York City Housing Authority ("NYCHA") relocated over 1800 families in the Lower East Side of Manhattan to make way for the construction of new apartment buildings. Pursuant to its regulations, NYCHA offered the former site occupants first priority of returning to any housing built within the urban renewal area. However, because the response by the largely minority former site residents seeking to return was nearly seven times greater than expected, NYCHA declined to follow its regulation in order to avoid creating a "pocket ghetto" that would 'tip" an integrated community towards a predominantly minority community. It instead rented up half of these apartments to non-former site occupants, 88% of whom were white.

In a suit brought by former site occupants who were denied the promised priority, the district court held as a matter of law that "affirmative action to achieve racially balanced communities was not permitted where it would result in depriving minority groups" of public housing, and thus granted summary judgment in favor of plaintiffs. This court reversed the grant of summary judgment, stating that public housing authorities had a federal constitutional and statutory duty "to fulfill, as much as possible, the goal of open, integrated residential housing patterns and to prevent the increase of segregation, in ghettos," but we recognized that "the effect in some instances might be to prevent some members of a racial minority from residing in publicly assisted housing in a particular location."

Otero does not, however, control in this case. The challenge in *Otero* did not involve procedures for the long-term maintenance of specified levels of integration, but rather, the rental of 171 of 360 new apartments to non-former site occupants, predominantly white, although former site residents, largely minority, sought those apartments and were entitled to priority under NYCHA's own regulation. The *Otero* court did not delineate the statutory or constitutional limits on permissible means of integration, but held only that NYCHA's rent-up practice could not be declared invalid as a matter of law under those limits. In fact, the court in *Otero* observed that the use of race conscious tenanting practices might allow landlords "to engage in social engineering, subject only to general undefined control through judicial supervision" and could "constitute a form of unlawful racial discrimination."

It is particularly important to note that the NYCHA action challenged in *Otero* only applied to a single event—the initial rent up of the new complexes—and determined tenancy in the first instance alone. NYCHA sought only to prevent the immediate creation of a "pocket ghetto" in the Lower East Side, which had experienced a steady loss of white population, that would tip the precarious racial balance there, resulting in increased white flight and inevitable "non-white ghettoization of the community." Further, the suspension of NYCHA's regulation did not operate as a strict racial quota, because the former site residents entitled to a rental priority were approximately 40% white. As a one-time measure in response to the special circumstances of the Lower East Side in the early 1970's, the action challenged in *Otero* had an impact on non-whites as a group far less burdensome or discriminatory than Starrett City's continuing practices.

Conclusion

We do not intend to imply that race is always an inappropriate consideration under Title VIII in efforts to promote integrated housing. We hold only that Title VIII does not allow appellants to use rigid racial quotas of indefinite duration to maintain a fixed level of integration at Starrett City by restricting minority access to scarce and desirable rental accommodations otherwise available to them. We therefore affirm the judgment of the district court.

JON O. NEWMAN, Circuit Judge, dissenting:

Congress enacted the Fair Housing Act to prohibit racial segregation in housing. Starrett City is one of the most successful examples in the nation of racial integration in housing. I respectfully dissent because I do not believe that Congress intended the Fair Housing Act to prohibit the maintenance of racial integration in private housing....

II.

In my view, the defendants are entitled to prevail simply on the statutory issue to which the Government has limited its lawsuit. Though the terms of the statute literally encompass the defendants' actions, the statute was never intended to apply to such actions. This statute was intended to bar perpetuation of segregation. To apply it to bar maintenance of integration is precisely contrary to the congressional policy "to provide, within constitutional limitations, for fair housing throughout the United States." 42 U.S.C. § 3601.

Title VIII bars discriminatory housing practices in order to end segregated housing. Starrett City is not promoting segregated housing. On the contrary, it is maintaining integrated housing. It is surely not within the spirit of the Fair Housing Act to enlist the Act to bar integrated housing. Nor is there any indication that application of the statute toward such a perverse end was within the intent of those who enacted the statute. It is true that there are some statements in the legislative history that broadly condemn discrimination for "any" reason. Senator Mondale, the principal sponsor of Title VIII, said that "we do not see any good reason or justification, in the first place, for permitting discrimination in the sale or rental of housing." 114 Cong. Rec. 5642 (1968). But his context, like that in which the entire debate occurred, concerned maintenance of segregation, not integration. His point was that there was no reason for discriminating against a Black who wished to live in a previously all white housing project. He explicitly decried the prospect that "we are going to live separately in white ghettos and Negro ghettos." The purpose of Title VIII, he said, was to replace the ghettos "by truly integrated and balanced living patterns." As he pointed out, "[o]ne of the biggest problems we face is the lack of experience in actually living next to Negroes." Starrett City is committed to the proposition that Blacks and Whites shall live next to each other. A law enacted to enhance the opportunity for people of all races to live next to each other should not be interpreted to prevent a landlord from maintaining one of the most successful integrated housing projects in America.

None of the legislators who enacted Title VIII ever expressed a view on whether they wished to prevent the maintenance of racially balanced housing. Most of those who passed this statute in 1968 probably could not even contemplate a private real estate owner who would deliberately set out to achieve a racially balanced tenant population. Had they thought of such an eventuality, there is not the slightest reason to believe that they would have raised their legislative hands against it.

The Court held [in *Otero*] that the Act was not violated simply because a race-conscious decision had been made in connection with rental policy:

> Congress' desire in providing fair housing throughout the United States was to stem the spread of urban ghettos and to promote open, integrated housing, even though the effect in some instances might be to prevent some members of a racial minority from residing in publicly assisted housing in a particular location.

Once the Court decided that a race-conscious rental policy did not necessarily violate the Act, it then faced the difficult issue in the case—whether the Act imposed an affirmative duty to promote integration of sufficient force to permit the authority to violate its own regulation. On that issue, the Court also ruled in favor of the authority, remanding for a trial at which the defendant could establish that its apprehension concerning a "tipping point" was well founded and that abandonment of its priority policy was necessary to promote integration.

Our case is much easier than *Otero*. Starrett City is not seeking to be released from a commitment it has previously made to any of the applicants for housing. To prevail it need not find in Title VIII some affirmative obligation compelling it to promote integration. It has freely chosen to promote integration and is entitled to prevail unless something in Title VIII forbids its voluntary policy. If anything in Title VIII prohibited race-conscious rental policies adopted to promote integration, *Otero* would have been summarily decided against the defendant.

But even if Title VIII can somehow be construed to make the lawfulness of a race-conscious rental policy that promotes integration turn on the duration of the policy, Starrett City is entitled to a trial so that it can prove its contention that its policy is still needed to maintain integration. In the District Court, the Government, though seeking summary judgment, contested Starrett City's factual contention that a race-conscious rental policy was currently needed to prevent the complex from passing the "tipping point" and becoming segregated. The Government relied on a brief affidavit of a HUD employee, who made primarily the unremarkable observation that it is difficult to predict with any certainty the precise "tipping point" in a particular neighborhood. In opposing summary judgment, Starrett City presented detailed affidavits providing abundant evidence to show that abandonment of its rental policies would cause the complex to pass the "tipping point" and soon become a segregated development. This evidence was solidly based on relevant experience. Several housing developments near Starrett City, operating without a policy of integration maintenance, have become racially segregated, including one across the street from Starrett City.

Until Congress acts, we should not lend our authority to the result this lawsuit will surely bring about. In the words of Dr. Clark:

> [I]t would be a tragedy of the highest magnitude if this litigation were to lead to the destruction of one of the model integrated communities in the United States.

Because the Fair Housing Act does not require this tragedy to occur, I respectfully dissent.

Notes and Questions

1. Starrett City officially changed its name to Spring Creek Towers. N.Y. Daily News, Sept. 26, 2002.

In late 2006, the owners of Starrett City proposed to sell the 46-tower apartment complex. According to canarsiecourier.com:

> More than two years after the "For Sale" sign went up for Starrett City, the owners last week [mid-February 2009.—Eds.] announced they gave up their plans to sell the 46-tower apartment complex east of Canarsie after a tentative deal with nonprofit groups and developers did not materialize.
>
> Owners of the largest federally subsidized housing complex in the nation, Starrett City Associates, said the property has been taken off the market due to the poor state of the economy and lack of financing that has drastically changed since the property was initially offered at the height of the real estate boom in December, 2006.
>
> According to media reports, the original billion-dollar price tag was beyond the reach of the only bidder left in the negotiations—a coalition of developers and nonprofit groups—that refused to budge from its top offer of $700 million that was made over two months ago.
>
> The coalition entered the bidding last March to maintain affordable rents for Starrett City residents, after housing officials rejected a second bid from Brooklyn-based realtor Clipper Equities, to purchase the development for a reported $1.3 billion.
>
> Starrett City Associates was forced to start a renewed effort to market the development last June when Senator Charles Schumer and Governor David Paterson told an anxious crowd of residents that the bidding process included a signed agreement that preserves the 5,800-apartment development as an affordable housing haven and allows eligible tenants to continue paying below-market rents for the next 20 years.
>
> The owners, the federal Department of Housing, and the state's and city's housing commissioners signed the agreement, formally called a Memorandum of Understanding. It not only included guidelines governing the sale of the 140-acre property, but strict restrictions on any future rent increases.
>
> Operating under the state's Mitchell-Lama program as subsidized federal housing, today about 90 percent of the tenants get direct federal rent subsidies or other types of government assistance from the city and state.
>
> Formally renamed Spring Creek Towers six years ago, Starrett City was originally a real estate investment for some 249 limited partners, including Donald Trump in one of his first major property ventures, who pooled $33 million in 1974 for a five percent down payment and received a one percent fixed mortgage.
>
> Investors risked their money on a low-income housing project in what was then a blighted Brooklyn community, but reportedly have reaped more than a 100 percent profit, not to mention generous tax breaks and low interest government loans they were granted over the years, according to media reports. Those investors hoped to cash out, which could possibly earn them at least $500 million.

http://www.canarsiecourier.com/news/2009-02-26/Top_Stories/Owners_Cancel_Starrett_City_Sale_Amid_Tough_Real_E.html (last visited Feb. 9, 2010).

2. How should a court respond to the "tipping" problem? It might be argued that "tipping" results from private expressions of racism and that any attempts to accommodate it by limiting the minority population inevitably tend to reinforce it.

3. In *Otero*, cited in *Starrett City*, the court approved the negation of dislocatee preferences which would have led to higher minority occupancy to be disregarded because enforcing it would negate the fair housing objective.

Is the problem in *Otero* qualitatively any different from the problem that would be presented if an all-white suburb dislocated persons for renewal purposes and desired to follow a dislocatee preference in new housing built on the renewal site? Recall that this is a similar problem to that addressed in *Raso v. Lago, supra*. Should a governmental agency have a wider latitude to engage in "managing occupancy" than a private entity? Does *Starrett City* suggest any approach to this question? Are *Starrett City, Otero*, and *Raso* consistent?

4. What of the argument that the intended beneficiaries of Title VIII are minorities and that enforcing the fair housing objective in *Otero* leads to the ironic result of depriving the minorities of both the dislocatee preference and the receipt of the housing benefit? *See Gladstone Realtors v. Village of Bellwood*, 441 U.S. 91 (1979), holding, that a municipality and individuals have standing to challenge racial "steering" on the grounds of "indirect" injuries they suffered when the practice occurred, although neither the municipality nor the individuals had been "steered." Doesn't this case suggest that the sweep of Title VIII is so broad that the primary beneficiary argument fails to carry persuasive force?

5. Does the *Starrett City* court close its eyes to the prospect that the development might be "tipped" to a minority community? Do you think the court doesn't care about that result? Or does the court think its options are limited by Title VIII (or the Constitution)? Or does the court think the evidence of tipping is insufficient? Or are there other considerations?

With respect to this last matter on the proof and nature of neighborhood change early research on the tipping process attempted to identify tipping points and ranges. The following excerpt summarizes some of this research:

> Investigators of the racial turnover process have attempted to identify tipping points and tipping ranges. In his 1960 study of benign quotas, Victor Navasky summarized the general experience with tipping points. He listed expert estimations of tipping points ranging from 25 percent black to 60 percent black. Eleanor P. Wolf, in a 1962 paper on the same subject, reached similar conclusions concerning the existence of the tipping process and the range of tipping points. Chester Rapkin, an expert on the subject of interracial housing, has remarked that in some situations, a single family can tip a neighborhood.
>
> Recognizing the existence of a tipping phenomenon, Grodzins pointed out that the "'tip point' varies from city to city and from neighborhood to neighborhood."
>
> If differing individual white tolerances for black neighbors and jittery white expectations are tipping's primary causes, then tipping points will vary according to the attitudinal composition of a given white population and the differing arrangements of environmental factors which could trigger uncontrolled white fears that an irrevocable chain of turnover has begun.
>
> A comparison of the histories of two Detroit neighborhoods illustrates how differing neighborhood circumstances can influence the tipping process. Lafayette

> Park is a high-cost housing development. When Eleanor Wolf studied this development in the early 1960's, its population was close to 10 percent nonwhite, and the development's low-rise units had a considerable number of vacancies. Wolf found that, to a great degree, the white tenants were confident of the development remaining predominantly white because this housing was considered too expensive for most black families. The Russell Woods neighborhood in 1955, when first studied by Wolf, housed only one or two black families. Although the approximately 700-household neighborhood was virtually all white at the time, Wolf reports that the researchers detected much concern about the area's racial future. By 1962, 75 percent of the neighborhood was black. Unlike Lafayette Park, the white families in Russel Woods could not rely, at least in part, on high housing costs to preserve the predominantly white composition of the neighborhood.

Bruce L. Ackerman, *Integration for Subsidized Housing and the Question of Racial Occupancy Controls*, 26 Stan. L. Rev., 245, 254–55 (1974).

The tipping phenomenon can also result from a high percentage of poverty. In one study it was noted that

> Studies have indicated that poverty concentrations start to create negative external effects when they exceed 5 to 20 percent. Regardless of what this precise point is (and it seems to vary depending on the outcome in question), the last decade saw a redistribution of metropolitan populations such that the share living in neighborhoods having 10–20 percent poverty rose one percentage point, and the share living in neighborhoods having 20–40 percent poverty also rose one percentage point. The result is that a larger fraction of the population may be living in neighborhoods with poverty rates that exceed the threshold for one or more social problem externalities, even though a smaller fraction reside in extreme-poverty neighborhoods.

George C. Galster, *Consequences from the Redistribution of Urban Poverty During the 1990s A Cautionary Tale*, Sept., 2003, 10–11, *available at* http://www.npc.umich.edu/publications/working_papers/paper9/03-09.pdf.

Do these studies support or undercut the court's treatment of the tipping problem? One theory is that institutional mechanisms produce segregation independent of individual preferences and interfere in the expansion of the housing supply for blacks. Another theory is that segregation results from individual preferences. Do either of the above theories support the results in *Starrett City* or *Otero*?

2. Disparate Treatment: The Prima Facie Case Approach

Robinson v. 12 Lofts Realty, Inc.

United States Court of Appeals
610 F.2d 1032 (2d Cir. 1979)

Before KAUFMAN, Chief Judge, and NEWMAN and KEARSE, Circuit Judges.

KEARSE, Circuit Judge:

This is an appeal by plaintiff Bennett Robinson from an order of the United States District Court for the Southern District of New York (Lee P. Gagliardi, Judge), denying an application for a preliminary and permanent injunction under the Fair Housing Act of 1968, 42 U.S.C. §§ 3601–3631 (1976), and the Civil Rights Act of 1866, 42 U.S.C. §§ 1981 and 1982 (1976), directing the defendant 12 Lofts Realty, Inc. (the "corporation") to permit him to purchase a cooperative apartment. For the reasons stated below, we reverse and remand for further proceedings.

I

The defendant corporation owns a twelve-story cooperative apartment building in Manhattan (the "building"). In January 1979, the corporation had ten shareholders; each shareholder owned ten shares and had a proprietary lease of one floor of the building. Defendant Paul Hanley is one of the shareholders of the corporation. He holds a proprietary lease of the seventh floor of the building. All of the building shareholders are White; there has never been a Black shareholder.

Plaintiff Bennett Robinson, who is Black, resides in a Manhattan rental apartment with his wife and two young daughters. Robinson holds a Ph.D. degree in physics from Stanford University and is employed as a research physicist by IBM. He earns a salary of $26,500 a year, plus $8,000 in benefits and stock options.

On January 22, 1979, Robinson entered into a written contract with Hanley to purchase, for $45,000, six and two-thirds of Hanley's shares and a proprietary lease of the south two-thirds of the seventh floor of the building. The contract made the sale conditional on Hanley's obtaining the consent of the corporation to the transfer.

On February 26, a meeting of the corporation's shareholders was convened to discuss the proposed sale to Robinson. At the meeting the building's manager reported that the second floor of the building was about to be sold to one Donald Kuspit, a White person. Thereafter, there was a "general discussion" of the proposed sale to Robinson. Following the discussion, the shareholders voted to amend the corporation's by-laws to establish a screening committee, which would meet with any prospective buyer and obtain a credit report, a resume, and a recommendation from his former landlord; the committee would then report to the shareholders at large for a final vote.

Following the February 26 meeting a screening committee was formed. The new procedure was not followed with respect to Kuspit, who soon became the corporation's eleventh shareholder. The committee eventually met with Robinson and his wife in early May. At the committee interview there was apparently a tenor to some of the committee's questions and comments that Robinson found offensive. The committee asked Robinson whether he had ever been convicted of a crime, whether he was involved in any "after-hours" club, and whether he had underworld connections. One committee member elaborated that they did not want criminal elements in the building, and stated that there had been a rumor floating around the building linking Robinson with criminal elements and an after-hours club. Despite his resentment at the questioning, Robinson answered all questions and assured the committee that he had never been convicted of a crime, had no underworld connections and had no involvement in any after-hours club, and that the space that he sought to purchase from Hanley was to be used as a residence for Robinson and his family.

The screening committee's written report, dated May 11, 1979, stated that Robinson's credit report, his resume, and a telephonic check with his landlord were all "satisfactory." The report also stated that the "Screening committees [sic] questions discussed that Dr. & Mrs. Robinson intended to use the space as their personal residence," and that at the interview the Robinsons had "answered all questions satisfactorily."

On May 17, a combined meeting of directors and shareholders was held to consider Robinson's proposed purchase. The first order of business, after correction and approval of the minutes of the previous meeting, was a review of the corporation's bylaws "to allow the agenda matter (7th fl. partial sale [to Robinson]) to take place with full understanding of the formal procedure required...." Following a "general discussion of the by-laws," the shareholders voted unanimously to increase the "51% Majority needed for approval" of a proposed resale of stock to 66 2/3%[4].... They then voted 10–1 to allow a secret ballot on all resale and sublet decisions. Then, after hearing a report of the screening committee, and receiving the committee's written report in which all matters were described as "satisfactory," the shareholders disapproved Robinson's purchase because only seven shareholders out of eleven (i.e., fewer than 2/3) voted in favor of it.

Robinson was thereafter notified of the rejection and brought this suit in the district court under 42 U.S.C. § 3601 *et seq.* and 42 U.S.C. §§ 1981 and 1982, seeking damages and injunctive relief....

Four of the corporation's shareholders, including Hanley, were called as witnesses for the defense. Richard Wengenroth, the corporation's president and a member of the screening committee, described the May 17 meeting at which Robinson's purchase was disapproved. He testified that he had reported to the shareholders that as to the objective questions considered by the screening committee, Robinson was "acceptable." He ascribed the rejection of Robinson to subjective reactions:

> At the same time, there were other questions that did not have to do with what I can only call objective matters, but had to do more with questions of personality exchanges that had been had between various people in the building with the applicant, and those were extended discussions....

Another shareholder, Joseph Russo, testified that "hours of discussion" were devoted to the question of Robinson's purchase, and that:

> Generally speaking, most of the people who had had any contact with him indicated to the rest of us that he had a personality that generally seemed counter to the personality that we were looking for. He was argumentative, he was caustic, he was sarcastic. In general, he did not get along with most of the people. It was as if he was demanding that space rather than asking, as everyone else had. That was the general tenor of almost all—in fact, of all of the comments, possibly with the exception of one that wasn't in that particular vein, but everyone that had met with him indicated that there was an acerbic quality to his personality that came out in every conversation with every member of the group thus far....

Russo also testified that it was reported at the May 17 meeting that Robinson had used profanity in a discussion with another shareholder.

Paul Waldman, the shareholder who owned the sixth floor, also supported the view that the shareholders found Robinson "disagreeable" and "did not like him personally:"

> Oh, the reasons were virtually unanimous, that they felt he was an extremely abrasive person. He was a person who was caustic and abrasive and would not fit into the personality of this family....

4. The corporation's by-laws did not expressly provide what consent was necessary for a transfer of shares; instead, they incorporated by reference provisions of the proprietary leases, which, according to the testimony of the president of the corporation, required 51% approval for a sale. The president also testified that although all of the initial sales of space had been handled informally, they had been made with the unanimous consent of the owners.

Waldman also indicated, as had Robinson in his testimony, that there had been sharp conflict between himself and Robinson with respect to Robinson's desire to install plumbing for the seventh floor by running a waste line through the floor and out along the ceiling of the sixth floor. However, Waldman testified that Robinson's desire to follow this procedure was not discussed at either the February 26 or the May 17 meeting. Robinson testified that he was aware prior to the May 17 meeting that Waldman would not permit this procedure and that Robinson was leaning toward use of an alternative procedure that had been adopted by Wengenroth....

The district court denied injunctive relief. It found that although Robinson had made out a *prima facie* case of housing discrimination, thus shifting to the defendant corporation the burden "to show in a convincing manner that there is a substantial justification for denying the plaintiff access to" the building, the corporation had met its burden:

> In the instant action, plaintiff has established his *prima facie* case by showing (1) that he belongs to a racial minority, (2) that he sought and could afford to purchase the south (sic) floor, and (3) that his application was denied. This court nonetheless concludes that no Section 3604 violation has been established because the defendant has come forward with evidence, as it has been described above, of legitimate, non-racial motivations for its change in voting procedures at the May 17, 1979 meeting and its subsequent denial of plaintiff's application to purchase shares in the defendant corporation.

The defense evidence credited by the district judge with respect to the corporation's change in voting procedures was testimony that the change was made because this was the first resale of stock in the building, as contrasted with an original sale.

The evidence adverted to by the court as to the reasons for the denial of Robinson's application fell into two categories: rumors and animosity. First the court found that "rumors with regard to the plaintiff had come to the attention of the various members of the defendant corporation"... that Robinson intended to use the premises for an after-hours club, that he intended to put plumbing lines through Waldman's ceiling, and that he had uttered vulgar language to another shareholder. The court expressly declined to assess the truth of these rumors, noting that Robinson denied them. Second, the court found that

> the steering committee, while it was indicated that the data supplied to it in response to the plaintiff being [sic] sufficient, nonetheless they had reported that in their opinion [plaintiff] had been abrasive in the interview that they had conducted for him, that he had resented certain questions that were asked of him, and others had indicated that in their opinion, the plaintiff had displayed an arrogant and uncooperative approach to the procedures that they had requested that he comply with before passing upon his application....

Based on these findings, the court concluded "that defendant cooperative denied plaintiff's application for reasons other than his race...."

The corporation denied Robinson's application because four shareholders voted against it. There was no evidence in the record, however, to show which shareholders cast the negative votes. Thus although the court found the above rumors to be "current" among the shareholders and credited the testimony that Robinson had appeared abrasive, it did not, and could not, make any finding of the actual motivation for the disapproval of Robinson's purchase.

Following the district court's denial of injunctive relief, Robinson took this appeal.

II

The Fair Housing Act, enacted as Title VIII of the Civil Rights Act of 1968, 42 U.S.C. §§ 3601–3631 (1976), makes it unlawful, with certain exceptions not pertinent here, for any person to refuse to sell or otherwise make unavailable a dwelling to any person because of race.[9] Section 3604(a) of 42 U.S.C. provides in pertinent part as follows:

> [I]t shall be unlawful—
>
> (a) To refuse to sell or rent after the making of a bona fide offer, *or to refuse to negotiate for the sale or rental of, or otherwise make unavailable or deny, dwelling to any person because of race*, color, religion, sex, or national origin. [emphasis added]

Section 3602(b) defines "dwelling" to include "any building, structure, or portion thereof which is occupied as, or designed or intended for occupancy as, a residence by one or more families," and clearly applies to cooperative apartment buildings such as that involved in the present action. Section 3612 gives a private right of action to a person who claims to have been denied housing on a basis prohibited by § 3604.

The threshold question in an action to enforce § 3604 is what the plaintiff must show in order to make out a *prima facie* case. The courts that have dealt with this question have concluded that in order to prove a *prima facie* case of race discrimination plaintiffs needed to show only that the action complained of had a racially discriminatory effect; they were not required to show that the defendants acted with racially discriminatory motivation. *E.g., Metropolitan Housing Development Corp. v. Village of Arlington Heights*, 558 F.2d 1283, 1287–90 (7th Cir. 1977), *cert. denied*, 434 U.S. 1025 (1978) [hereinafter "*Arlington II*"—Eds.]....

Thus, the Seventh Circuit, along with most other circuits, has held that discriminatory impact is the appropriate standard by which to determine whether a plaintiff has made out a *prima facie* case under § 3604(a).[10]

While most of the cases have pondered the nature of the *prima facie* case in the context of actions that affect a large group of people, the question has also been considered, and the effects test adopted, in suits brought to redress discrimination against individual plaintiffs. For example, in *Smith v. Anchor Bldg. Corp.*, [536 F.2d 233 (8th Cir. 1976)—Eds.], the Eighth Circuit stated as follows:

---

9. Robinson also sought injunctive relief under 42 U.S.C. § 1982, which provides that "All citizens of the United States shall have the same right, in every State and Territory, as is enjoyed by white citizens thereof to inherit, purchase, lease, sell, hold, and convey real and personal property." Since the record does not disclose whether or not Robinson is a United States citizen, we address only his Title VIII claim.

10. The decision of this Circuit in *Boyd v. Lefrak Organization*, 509 F.2d 1110 (2d Cir.), *cert. denied*, 423 U.S. 896 (1975), is not inconsistent. In *Boyd*, the majority rejected a challenge to a landlord's facially neutral requirements that may have had a racially discriminatory impact, stating as follows: "we will not impose an affirmative duty on the private landlord to accept low income tenants absent evidence that his motivation is racial rather than economic in origin." In dissent, Judge Mansfield stated "With due respect, the majority opinion seems to me to be grounded upon the erroneous concept that, in order to establish a violation of the Fair Housing Act, 42 U.S.C. § 3601 *et seq.*, direct evidence of a racially discriminatory motive or purpose on the part of the alleged violator must be adduced. In my view such proof is not required." However, these conclusions were drawn after a full trial of the case, in which the defendant had come forward with evidence as to why the criterion it adopted was used and why it was relevant to its decisions whether to rent the premises. The conclusion after a full trial that the plaintiffs have failed to show racial motivation does not imply that proof of motivation was required in order for the plaintiffs to establish a *prima facie* case.

> The concept of the *prima facie* case applies to an individual housing discrimination case.... Therefore, where a black rental applicant meets the objective requirements of a landlord, and the rental would likely have been consummated were he or she a white applicant, a *prima facie* inference of discrimination arises as a matter of law.

By analogy to the employment discrimination area, a plaintiff who claims that he as an individual has been the victim of a discriminatory denial of housing, may establish his *prima facie* case by proving the following facts:

(1) that he is Black;

(2) that he applied for and was qualified to rent or purchase the housing;

(3) that he was rejected; and

(4) that the housing opportunity remained available.

Consistent with the above authorities, the district court in the present case adopted the effects test as the proper standard. Finding that Robinson had established that he was a member of a minority, that he could afford to purchase the space sought, and that his application had been denied, the court held that Robinson had made out *prima facie* case.

Even if a motivation test were applied, Robinson would be found to have established his *prima facie* case, for the nature and timing of the corporation's actions with respect to Robinson's application readily permits an inference of racially discriminatory motivation. As Mr. Justice Stevens observed in his concurring opinion in *Washington v. Davis*, 426 U.S. 229 (1976), "[f]requently the most probative evidence of intent will be objective evidence of what actually happened rather than evidence describing the subjective state of mind of the actor." at 253. Similarly, the Supreme Court's opinion in *Village of Arlington Heights v. Metropolitan Housing Development, Corp.*, [*Arlington I*—Eds.] *supra*, points out:

> The specific sequence of events leading up to the challenged decision also may shed some light on the decisionmaker's purposes. For example, if the property involved here always had been zoned R-5 but suddenly was changed to R-3 when the town learned of MHDC's plans to erect integrated housing, we would have a far different case. Departures from the normal procedural sequence also might afford evidence that improper purposes are playing a role.

The evidence presented by Robinson as to the sequence of actions taken by the defendant corporation goes beyond establishing merely a discriminatory effect. When Robinson's proposed purchase came before the shareholders, the previous informal procedure was changed and a screening committee was created. Although it was said that the new procedure was to be followed with respect to "any" prospective purchaser, it was not followed with respect to Kuspit, the White prospective buyer who was then about to purchase the second floor; there is no indication that at that time there were any prospective purchasers other than Kuspit and Robinson. Following the determination by the newly established screening committee that Robinson's finances, recommendation, and all other "objective matters" were satisfactory, the corporation increased the percentage needed for approval of Robinson's purchase from 51% to 66 2/3%, and allowed the negative votes of four shareholders out of eleven to defeat the application. This sequence of events brings a conclusion of discriminatory motive well within the realm of legitimate inference.[12] It

12. The corporation's president testified that over the years some fifteen or sixteen Blacks, no more than one or two at a time, had been subtenants or guests in the building. It is not clear whether this estimate was for the period since August 1977 when the witness first moved into the building, or dated back to 1975 when the building first was converted to residential use. In any event, while this evidence has some relevance to whether or not the corporation's motivations were racial, the corpo-

is clear, therefore, that even were a motivation test to be applied, plaintiff has established a *prima facie* case.

III

The action under Title VIII does not normally end with the plaintiff's establishment of a *prima facie* case of race discrimination. The burden shifts to the defendant to come forward with evidence to show that his actions were not motivated by considerations of race. If the defendant does not present such evidence, the plaintiff will be entitled to relief.

> [W]here a black rental applicant meets the objective requirements of a landlord, and the rental would likely have been consummated were he or she a white applicant, a *prima facie* inference of discrimination arises as a matter of law. If the inference is not satisfactorily explained away, discrimination is established. *Williams v. Matthews* Co., [499 F. 2d 819, 826 (8th Cir.), *cert. denied*, 419 U.S. 1021, 1027 (1974).—Eds.]

In order to meet its burden, the defendant must offer evidence of the reasons its action was taken. Given the nature of the reasons proffered below, we do not believe this burden was satisfied in the present case. The corporation conceded that Robinson met all of the corporation's financial and objective criteria, and relied merely or possible subjective factors that could have induced votes against Robinson's purchase by four unidentified shareholders. Thus, although there was testimony that there were "rumors," there was no evidence that anyone believed the rumors to be true. There was no evidence as to which shareholders voted against Robinson, nor, perforce, any evidence as to their actual reasons. Without identification of and testimony by the persons who actually caused the denial of Robinson's application, it cannot be determined what motivated the rejection.

Our view that in the present case the corporation cannot successfully rebut plaintiff's *prima facie* case without the testimony of all of the stockholders who voted "no" does not suggest that such a requirement would be imposed in all cases. It is appropriate here because Robinson fell short of the required approval by just one vote. Thus, if any one of the four stockholders voted against Robinson because of his race, he was denied housing because of his race, regardless of the motives of the other three negative voters: the reversal of that one racially-motivated vote would have resulted in the approval of Robinson's purchase.

In the absence of testimony from the four negative voters, therefore, we find that the district court's conclusion that the corporation rejected Robinson's application "for reasons other than his race" is unsupported by the evidence. A *prima facie* case having been established, a Fair Housing Act claim cannot be defeated by a defendant which relies on merely hypothetical reasons for the plaintiff's rejection. To permit such a defense to prevail would effectively nullify the Act.

Because the trial was conducted initially as a hearing on the motion for a preliminary injunction and because the corporation may have been forestalled from coming forward with adequate justification for the denial of Robinson's application, we remand the case to the district court for further proceedings. If the shareholders who prevented Robinson's purchase do not come forward to testify in these proceedings, Robinson will be entitled to injunctive relief.

---

ration's willingness to have Blacks in the building on short-term basis does not dispose of the contention that the corporation was motivated by racial considerations in acting to prevent a sale.

IV

On remand, assuming that the four shareholders who voted against Robinson come forward to testify, the district court will be called upon to evaluate the sincerity of their stated reasons for voting against Robinson's purchase, and to determine whether the concerns they had negative any discriminatory intent that may be inferred from the sequence of events. To rebut Robinson's *prima facie* case, both issues must be decided in favor of the corporation.[13]

A

In evaluating the proposed justifications, the district court must carefully scrutinize suggested reasons that are not objective in nature. In cases in which discriminatory intent could be inferred from the sequence of events, the courts have generally viewed subjective explanations with considerable skepticism. The wisdom in such skepticism is obvious. "Any defendant can respond to a discriminatory effect with a claim of some subjective preference or prerogative and, if such assertions are accepted, prevail in virtually every case...." Thus, the courts have rejected defenses that a Black was denied housing because he would not "fit in" with the other tenants, *United States v. Youritan Construction Co.*, [370 F. Supp. 643, 650 (N.D. Cal. 1973)—Eds.] ("Prospective compatibility with other tenants is not an appropriate rental consideration where its application would have a discriminatory racial impact"); or because the applicant failed to comply with special procedures to show that he would be "a 'congenial' tenant," *United States v. Grooms*, 348 F. Supp. 1130, 1133 (M.D. Fla. 1972); or because he was a "belligerent appearing" applicant, *United States v. West Peachtree Tenth Corp.*, 437 F.2d 221, 223–24 (5th Cir. 1971) ("While such a [screening] procedure appears necessary and practical on the part of management in order to keep undesirables of any race out the building, it does create the 'opportunity' for discrimination in rentals"); or because the applicant was seen as "irritable and belligerent, more belligerent, and most belligerent," and was classified with potential "troublemakers," *Newbern v. Lake Lorelei, Inc.*, 308 F. Supp. 407, 413, 414 (S.D. Ohio 1968) (§ 1982 action); or because applicant was classified as a "troublemaker" on the strength of the defendant's belief that the applicant might bring a court challenge to certain subdivision building restrictions, *Williams v. Matthews Co.*, 499 F.2d 819, 828 n. 11 (8th Cir.), *cert. denied*, 419 U.S. 1021, 1027 (1974); or because the applicant may have had unclean clothing producing an offensive, or stale odor, *Stevens v. Dobs, Inc.*, 483 F.2d 82, 83 (4th 1973).

On remand, the court here should be similarly probing. The decision whether to credit the reasons advanced requires consideration of two questions: whether factors cited were actually believed by those who voted "no"; and if so, whether it was their belief in those factors that impelled them to vote "no." In making the latter determination, the logical relevance of the factor to the rejection is of significance. If the factor (whether subjective or objective) lacks relevance to the applicant's fit in the housing context, it becomes suspect. *See, e.g.*, *Bishop v. Pecsok*, 431 F. Supp. 34, 37 (N.D. Ohio 1976) ("Objective criteria cannot have the effect of excluding blacks from housing unless the criteria are demonstrably

---

13. If the district court concludes that the defendant corporation has rebutted Robinson's *prima facie* case, the hearing should not necessarily be ended there. Robinson must thereafter "be afforded a fair opportunity to show that [defendant's] stated reason for [Robinson's] rejection was in fact pretext." Of especial relevance would be evidence that the reasons advanced by the defendant for the rejection had not been considered sufficient by the defendant to reject White applicants. We have already adverted, for example, to the extent that some shareholders have run plumbing lines through the ceiling of the floor below. Robinson should be given the opportunity to demonstrate as fully as he can any pretextual character to the corporation's rebuttal.

a reasonable measure of the applicant's ability to be a 'successful tenant.' ") Thus, the court should consider whether it is credible that negative votes were cast because of a rumor that Robinson wanted to use the premises as an after-hours club, in light of his persistent denial of that rumor. Certainly the screening committee's report seemed to indicate a belief that Robinson wanted the premises for his residence. And the objective of preventing an after-hours club on the premises could have been achieved without discriminatory impact, simply by having all shareholders, old and new, covenant not to use premises for that purpose. Similarly, the court should consider whether it is credible that negative votes were cast because of a rumor that Robinson wanted to run plumbing lines through Waldman's ceiling. Assuming that the shareholders believed this rumor, the question remains whether their belief led them to vote against Robinson in light of the facts that such a desire on Robinson's part was not discussed at either of the shareholders meetings, and that some of the shareholders had in fact already used this type of procedure to meet their plumbing needs. Finally, in assessing explanation that depends on a rumor, the court must bear in mind that rumors are easily started and, although perhaps facially neutral, may easily be advanced with discriminatory intent.

The "animosity" defense also must be analyzed carefully, especially where predicated upon plaintiff's so-called "argumentative" or "caustic" reactions, which may well have been provoked intentionally by insistent and unprecedented question as to his possible underworld connections and the like.[14] *See, e.g., Newbern v. Lorelei, Inc., supra*, in which the defendant corporation attributed its rejection of a Black prospective buyer to his belligerency; the court rejected this defense, finding that the plaintiff had simply reacted to defendants' discourteous and stalling tactics, and that these tactics were "designed to cause what it described as a 'belligerency.' " In addition, in assessing testimony that the shareholders found Robinson too abrasive to "fit into" the "family," the court should consider the fact that seven out of eleven shareholders nevertheless voted to approve the purchase, and the fact that no shareholder, save Hanley, would even be on the same floor as Robinson. We note that Hanley, who had earlier rejected an offer from Robinson to buy the entire seventh floor for $70,000, chose to keep one-third of the floor and has remained willing to share that floor with Robinson.

B

If, after weighing all of the evidence, the court credits the reasons advanced as genuine, it must bear in mind that, despite occasional dicta to the contrary, race need not be the sole motivating factor in a denial that has a discriminatory effect in order for the plaintiff to succeed in a Title VIII claim. The denial violates § 3604(a) if race is even one of the motivating factors....

In sum, therefore, in order for the corporation to prevail, the district court must find that racial motivation did not play any role in the decision to deny Robinson's application. In its deliberations, the court must remember that "clever men may easily conceal their motivations." *United States v. City of Black Jack*, [508 F.2d 1179, 1185 (8th Cir. 1974), *cert. denied*, 422 U.S. 1042 (1975)—Eds.]. "As overtly bigoted behavior has become more unfashionable, evidence of intent has become harder to find. But this does not mean that racial discrimination has disappeared." *Arlington II, supra*, 558 F.2d at 1290. It means that when a discriminatory effect is present, the courts must be alert to recognize means that are subtle and explanations that are synthetic.

---

14. Apparently it was only Robinson who underwent questioning of this tenor. The testimony below was that Kuspit, for example, was asked merely where he worked and whether he afford the purchase.

In the final analysis, the court should bear in mind that throughout, Hanley has been willing to sell 2/3 of his floor to Robinson, only to be thwarted by the corporation. We should be especially chary of permitting a third party to prevent, on the basis of easily fabricated subjective factors, a sale of housing by a willing seller to an objectively acceptable buyer.

We reverse and remand for further proceedings consistent with this opinion. We trust that Judge Gagliardi's calendar will permit an expedited rehearing.

Notes and Questions

1. Upon remand the District Court conducted a hearing at which the four shareholders who voted against Robinson—Jon Jolcin, Donald Smith, Paul Waldman, and Donald Kuspit—testified. *See Robinson v. 12 Lofts Realty, Inc.*, 1980 U.S. Dist. LEXIS 11645. The court noted that under the decision of the Court of Appeals it was "called upon to evaluate the sincerity of their stated reasons for voting against Robinson's purchase, and to determine whether the concerns they had negate any discriminatory intent that may be inferred from the sequence of events. To rebut Robinson's prima facie case, both issues must be decided in favor of the corporation."

The court concluded that it should not grant Robinson's requested relief to order the defendant corporation to sell him shares because its refusal to sell did not violate Title VIII. The court explained:

The four shareholders collectively offered six reasons for voting against plaintiff. These reasons ... were (1) opposition to any transaction which would result in absentee ownership, (2) concern that plaintiff was involved in after-hours activities, (3) plaintiff's finances, (4) opposition to a sale involving less than ten shares, (5) the plumbing incident, and (6) plaintiff's personality. This court has evaluated each of these reasons and the testimony of each of the shareholders, bearing in mind that a Title VIII defendant's non-objective explanations for denying housing to an applicant must be meticulously scrutinized. After doing so, this court finds (1) that each shareholder "actually believed" the factors he cited, (2) that their belief in these factors "impelled" them to vote no, and thus (3) that racial motivation did not play any role in any of the shareholders decisions to cast negative votes. This court further finds that the reasons advanced by the shareholders negate any discriminatory intent that could be inferred from the sequence of events leading up to the defendant's consideration and rejection of plaintiff's application, as heretofore described.

Accordingly, this court holds that defendant has rebutted plaintiff's prima facie case of racial discrimination and that plaintiff's consolidated application for preliminary and permanent injunctive relief ... must be denied.

In reaching its conclusion the court said, apparently in response to the observation of the Court of Appeals on the question of "subjective" rebuttal reasons:

In assessing the credibility of the witnesses who testified that they were concerned about plaintiff's personality, this court has also considered "the fact that seven out of eleven shareholders nevertheless voted to approve the purchase, and the fact that no shareholder save Hanley, would even be on the same floor with Robinson...." If there is any testimony in the record which seems to sum up the sentiments of all the testifying shareholders, it is simply that "there was a high degree of ambivalence surrounding [Robinson's application] ..." The fact that some shareholders were more willing to take a "risk" than others does not mean that the more cautious members of the co-op did not actually believe the reasons they advanced and that these reasons did not cause them to cast their negative votes. Indeed, two of the three testifying shareholders who ultimately voted in favor of Robinson seemed to have reservations about plaintiff's personality ... Thus, after reviewing the record in its entirety, this court is convinced that the seven to four vote was the result of exactly what it should have been—the exercise of each shareholder's "own judgment ..." without any racial motivation on the part of any of the negative voters.

2. The *Robinson* case adopts the *prima facie* approach to Title VIII and shifts the burden to defendant to rebut the case with "evidence to show that [the challenged] actions were not motivated by considerations of race." Since, under the court's *prima facie* approach, motivation is not an element of the plaintiff's case, has the court mixed its apples and oranges? Or is there an adequate answer in the court's analysis which notes that plaintiff met the "financial and objective criteria" and calls on defendant to explain that the stated reasons were not mere pretexts for racial discrimination?

3. The *Robinson* court distinguished *Boyd v. Lefrak Organization*, 509 F.2d 1110 (2d Cir.), *cert. denied*, 423 U.S. 896 (1975). Can *Boyd* be distinguished, instead of being frankly overruled? In *Boyd*, plaintiffs alleged that defendant applied a rule that a rental applicant must have a net weekly income at least equal to 90%, of a month's rent (called the 90% rule). Plaintiffs alleged that the 90% rule violated Title VIII in that it disqualified all public assistance recipients (except a small number who could get acceptable co-signers), that a large majority of public assistance recipients were racial or ethnic minorities, and that, therefore, the 90% rule was racially discriminatory.

The court in *Boyd* thought the argument was merely *James v. Valtierra*, 402 U.S. 137 (1971) revisited, and rejected it. If *Boyd* was based on Title VIII, how could it be controlled by *Valtierra*, which was based on equal protection under the Constitution? The *Boyd* court concluded that the record would not support the contention that the facially neutral 90% rule was, in fact, *aimed* at excluding a racial minority. Is that the same test that the court employed in *Robinson*?

4. Is there, nevertheless, a key factual and theoretical difference between the across-the-board 90% rule in *Boyd* and the rejection of the plaintiff in *Robinson*? Can you articulate it?

5. Many housing cases can be classified as "disparate treatment" or "disparate impact"—terms that have been more fully explored in employment discrimination cases than in housing cases. Generally speaking, the treatment cases are those in which the plaintiff asserts that he or she was intentionally treated differently, for example, "because of race," than a similarly situated white person would have been. In the impact cases, the plaintiff asserts that a rule, policy, or practice, although neutral on its face, has a "disproportionate effect" on one of the classes protected against discrimination, and that plaintiff is a member of the class. *See generally* Frederic S. Schwartz, *The Fair Housing Act and "Discriminatory Effect:" A New Perspective*, 11 NOVA L. REV. 71 (1986) (reviewing the approaches and proposing an analytical model). *See also,* Christopher P. McCormack, Note, *Business Necessity in Title VIII Importing an Employment Discrimination Doctrine Into the Fair Housing Act*, 54 FORDHAM L. REV. 563 (1988).

6. Are the questions and distinctions suggested above adequately answered by the following statement the court made in *Boyd*?

> A businessman's differential treatment of different economic groups is not necessarily racial discrimination and is not made so because minorities are statistically overrepresented in the poorer economic groups.

If you think it is, then add to it the positive side of the *Valtierra* analysis. The logic would seem to suggest that the very same decision according differential treatment is unlawful, if it is "aimed" at a racial minority.

Consider the following hypothetical:

In Modern City there are three landlords—X, Y, and Z—who, with the exceptions noted below, are otherwise identically situated. Assume that each landlord adopts a rule limiting occupancy to persons earning $40,000 annually.

Landlord X has no knowledge of who does or does not earn $40,000 annually in Modern City.

Landlord Y knows that in Modern City (a) 10% of the black residents earn $40,000 annually and would be eligible under the rule and (b) 30% of the white residents earn $40,000 and would be eligible under the rule.

Landlord Z not only knows that in Modern City (a) 10% of the black residents earn $40,000 annually and would be eligible under the rule, and (b) 25% of the white residents earn $40,000 and would be eligible under the rule, but (c) announces that he adopted the rule for the purpose of trying to limit the number of blacks in his units.

Should X and Z be treated differently for purposes of the fair housing laws? If so, there are two questions. Assuming you conclude Z should not be able to enforce his rule, (a) how do you explain the difference and (b) how do you decide about Landlord Y?

In a homogeneous one-race society, what would be the basis for precluding a landlord from adopting as a management policy a $40,000 annual income policy? Does the analysis of this question shed any light on those in the preceding note? Assuming that you conclude that Landlords X, Y, and Z should not be treated differently, should all be able to apply the $40,000 annual income rule or none of them?

7. Assuming that at least you are willing to preclude Landlord Z from enforcing his $40,000 rule, note that the rule, in fact, will exclude some white persons (the 75% who do not earn $40,000 annually). What order should the court enter? (1) Enjoin the enforcement of the rule for blacks, or (2) enjoin the enforcement of the rule altogether for blacks and whites? How can remedy (2) be possible? Recall that 42 U.S.C. § 3604(a) of Title VIII applies only to "race, color, religion, sex, familial status, disability or national origin" and that Section 1982 applies solely to "race." If the rule is enjoined as applied to whites also, why isn't that simply overriding a management decision on a basis that amounts to unwarranted, and, presumably, statutorily unauthorized intrusion into management decisions?

Conversely, if the rule is enjoined as applied to blacks only, doesn't that create new problems? How can it be that blacks and whites excluded by the income rule do not have the same rights with respect to an injunction against that rule?

8. Other management practices can raise claims of discriminatory effects and issues of the rebuttal standard. In *Betsey v. Turtle Creek Associates*, 736 F.2d. 983 (4th Cir. 1984), the court applied a *prima facie* case approach to find a *prima facie* case upon proof by plaintiffs that defendant's plan to convert an apartment building to "all-adult" facility would have a disproportionate impact on minority tenants. Over 50% of the nonwhite tenants had children as opposed to only 14% of the white tenants. Counting the number of occupants, the court found that 75% of the nonwhite occupants but only 26% of the white occupants would be evicted.

The court remanded to the district court for consideration of the defendant's rebuttal evidence which the court said must be shown to be "a business necessity sufficiently compelling to justify the challenged practice."

The court stated that "The burden confronting defendants faced with a *prima facie* showing of discriminatory impact is different and more difficult than what they face when confronted with a showing of discriminatory intent." It noted that "some non-discriminatory reason" will rebut a *prima facie* case of discriminatory intent.

Why should there exist a different burden? If the burden differs, why should it be more difficult in an impact case than in an intent case? Is "some non-discriminatory reason" less difficult to show than "a business necessity"?

Note that under the Fair Housing Amendments Act of 1988, the plaintiffs in *Betsey* would be able to assert that the defendant's plans would violate the prohibition against discriminating on the basis of "familial status." *See* 42 U.S.C. § 3604(e).

9. In addition to the refusal to sell involved in *Robinson*, which might be classified generically as a species of (1) refusal to deal (which would include refusal to rent or negotiate, as examples), Title VIII covers (2) discrimination as to terms, conditions, services, or facilities; (3) false representations; (4) discriminatory advertising; (5) discrimination in financing, brokering, and appraising; (6) blockbusting and steering; and (7) a "catch-all" provision "to otherwise make unavailable or deny" a dwelling.

The prohibitions on discrimination against the handicapped are spelled out with more detail than the others. Note that sections 3604(a) and (b) do not specify the handicapped as a protected class. But note that the prohibitions in sections 3604(c) and (d) specify the handicapped and note the detail contained in section 3604(f). Does section 3604(f) contain, with respect to the handicapped, the same protections that are covered in sections 3604(a) and (b) for other protected classes?

10. A defendant charged with racial discrimination does have the opportunity to rebut a *prima facie* case, if one is made out. An example of this principle in operation is *Washington v. Sherwin Real Estate, Inc.*, 694 F.2d 1081 (7th Cir. 1982). The defendant's rebuttal evidence showed that the plaintiff husband was belligerent and rude in applying for an apartment. While it is certainly true that different courts will look at so-called "subjective factors" with varying degrees of scrutiny, the point is that such factors, when found credible by the finder of facts, as in *Sherwin Real Estate* and *Robinson*, will be sufficient to rebut a case. Is the error of *Boyd* that the disparate impact test under *Huntington* was met and the appropriate focus was the justification for the minimum income test?

A Note on Mixed Motives and "Partial" Discrimination

Sometimes a defendant may have had a "mixed motivation," or "multiple motives," or may have been influenced to make a decision only in part on prohibited discriminatory considerations. How should one deal with such issues?

Discrimination apparently may exist across a spectrum. Discrimination may be (1) the sole causal factor; (2) a dominant factor; (3) one among two or more coequal factors; (4) a significant factor; (5) a minor factor; (6) a minor factor, but other factors clearly predominate; or (7) a present, but not a causal, factor. There may be other points on the spectrum. What point on the spectrum should be sufficient to make out a violation of Section 1982 or Title VIII?

Although "partial discrimination" is addressed in *Robinson*, perhaps the leading case on the partial discrimination problem is *Smith v. Sol D. Adler*, 436 F.2d 344 (7th Cir. 1971). In *Smith*, the district judge as fact finder said in oral findings, "In my own judgment, my own sincere judgment, I think these people did not want to rent to her because she was colored." The district judge went on to say that the racial ground was not the sole reason for the discrimination nor was the total factor one of discrimination, but noted that the defendants were only too happy to find a valid excuse for denying the rental application of the black plaintiff. The cited valid reason was a purported refusal to rent to employed parents with infant children.

The court of appeals reversed on the ground that the district court's finding was clearly erroneous. The court held that

> [R]ace is an impermissible factor in an apartment rental decision and ... it cannot be brushed aside because it was neither the *sole* reason for discrimination nor the total factor of discrimination. We find no acceptable place in the law for partial racial discrimination....

It was clearly shown at trial from Adler's accepted applications for rental apartments by the two white employed married couples, each with an infant child to be cared for by some one [sic—Eds.] employed for that purpose, that his so-called uniformly applied policy was discriminatory as applied to [the plaintiff]. She was married, though separated from her husband, had an infant child, was employed and had another tenant in the same apartment building engaged to care for her child while she was at work. Thus, the "valid excuse" found by the trial court was in fact an invalid excuse.

Also in *United States v. Pelzer Realty Co.*, 484 F.2d 438, 443 (5th Cir. 1973), *cert. denied*, 416 U.S. 936 (1974), a district court denied injunctive relief in a Fair Housing case on the ground that a defendant had non-racial as well as racial motivations for his refusal to sell to Blacks on the same terms as Whites. The Court of Appeals for the Fifth Circuit reversed, stating that while it did not doubt that the defendant's "primary goal was to make money," "[w]e need not and do not find that racial prejudice dominated (defendant's) mind during the negotiations. It is enough that race was one significant factor he considered in his dealings with the men."

In *Woods-Drake v. Lundy*, 557 F.2d 1081 (7th Cir. 1982), the court held that a Title VIII violation can be made upon a showing that racial discrimination was a "significant factor" in the defendant's decision and that when race is found to be a significant factor the mere existence of other nonracial justifications for the challenged decision will be insufficient.

The partial discrimination problem has many manifestations. In *Bishop v. Pecsok*, 431 F. Supp. 34 (N.D. Ohio 1976), an inter-racial married couple brought suit against a landlord for racial discrimination. The court found that the landlord's educational and financial criteria were met, but that these criteria could not be used to exclude blacks unless the criteria were demonstrably a reasonable measure of the applicants' ability to be a successful tenant. In *Moore v. Townsend*, 525 F.2d 482 (7th Cir. 1975), the defendant changed her mind and decided not to sell her property when she became aware that the prospective buyers were black. The court held that race is an impermissible consideration in a real estate transaction, and that a plaintiff need only establish that race played some part in the refusal to deal.

Similarly in *Payne v. Bracher*, 582 F.2d 17 (5th Cir. 1978), the court found that, in the Fair Housing Act, Congress made clear its intent that the race of a tenant is not to be considered in any way when a tenant seeks to rent an apartment and that the presence of other factors also motivating refusal to rent cannot justify racial discrimination.

Contrast *Madison v. Jeffers*, 494 F.2d 114 (4th Cir. 1974). In *Madison*, the defendant refused to sell land, stating tax reasons. The court found that plaintiff did not prove that the seller was aware of the potential buyers' race and that prohibited factors had not been shown to have been considered. In ruling for the seller, the court opined that one who sells or leases real estate has a right to refuse approval on any honest basis unrelated to race of the prospective purchaser.

Notes and Questions

1. Is it possible to distinguish (a) discrimination as a causal factor from (b) discriminatory effects?

2. Is the issue discussed here of mixed motive and partial discrimination the same as that discussed in *Arlington I, supra,* as the "causation" problem?

3. Discrimination Based on Familial Status

Soules v. United States Department of Housing and Urban Development

United States Court of Appeals
967 F.2d 817 (2d Cir. 1992)

Before: TIMBERS, MESKILL and PRATT, Circuit Judges.

MESKILL, Circuit Judge:

This is a petition for review of an order of Administrative Law Judge William C. Cregar that became a final order of the Secretary of the United States Department of Housing and Urban Development (HUD) on October 21, 1991. Petitioners Soules and Housing Opportunities Made Equal, Inc. of Buffalo (HOME) argue that the Administrative Law Judge (ALJ) erred in dismissing discrimination claims brought under sections 3604(a) and (c) of the Fair Housing Act, 42 U.S.C. § 3601 *et seq.* (FHA). They argue that substantial evidence did not support the ALJ's decision and that the ALJ erred by inquiring into the respondents' intent on the section 3604(c) claim. We deny review.

BACKGROUND

The ALJ heard the following evidence. In April 1989, petitioner Sherry Soules was a single woman who lived with her mother and twelve year old daughter in a two bedroom apartment located on Richmond Avenue in Buffalo, New York.

Respondent Mary Jean Downs was a [real estate agent] and sole owner of Professional Realty Service (PRS), which she operated out of her residence in Buffalo. Downs listed, managed and rented properties.

Because of a New York State Health Department rule that required separate bedrooms for children of different sexes over five years old, the PRS lease application form asked the number and ages of children who would be occupying the premises. Although Downs employed a part-time worker, Eileen Anderson, to assist her in showing properties and taking lease applications, Downs herself conducted the actual selection of tenants.

When Downs conducted telephone interviews, she asked the same questions that appeared on the lease applications. During these conversations Downs generally declined to give out her last name; moreover, she did not reveal the addresses of listings to callers who appeared unlikely to qualify as lessees.

During March 1989, Downs signed an agreement with Robert Campise, the owner of a two family dwelling on Bird Avenue in Buffalo. Jeanette and Jerry D'Amaro, a couple who had helped Campise's mother prior to her entry into a nursing home, lived on the first floor. Because Mr. D'Amaro suffered from poor eyesight and possibly diabetes, Campise asked Downs to find a lessee who could "live harmoniously" with the D'Amaros.

During April 1989, Downs was caring for an elderly aunt who lived in Lima, New York, which is approximately an hour and fifteen minutes from Buffalo by car. During these trips, which extended overnight, Downs would take her aunt to doctors or to the hospital.

Also in April 1989, Downs placed ads in two Buffalo newspapers for apartments in the Richmond area. Dissatisfied with her housing at that time, Soules began to look for an apartment in the vicinity of Richmond Avenue, which was near her daughter's school and her mother's place of employment. The newspaper ad for the Bird Avenue apartment caught Soules' attention and she made several phone calls to Downs, leaving messages on an answering machine. Downs did not return the calls.

Soules finally reached Downs on or around April 20 and explained that she was interested in renting a three bedroom apartment in the Richmond area. Downs then asked her the number of persons who would live in the apartment and inquired how many of them would be adults. When Soules replied that two adults and a child would reside there, Downs inquired: "How old is your child?"

Rather than answering Downs' question, Soules demanded to know why Downs needed to know the child's age. Downs, who reacted negatively to Soules' questioning, replied that an elderly person lived in the first floor unit, and that she did not want an upstairs resident who would make too much noise. Although Soules continued to question her, Downs ceased volunteering information about the apartment. Downs, who at that point refused even to tell Soules her last name, told Soules that she would telephone her on the following Monday, April 24, if the apartment were available.

In her deposition, which the ALJ accepted as descriptive of her reaction to Soules, Downs portrayed her conversation with Soules as "unpleasant." She characterized Soules, whom she stated had "challenged" her on the phone, as having had "a very bad attitude."

After speaking to Downs, Soules contacted petitioner HOME. HOME is a non-profit membership organization that seeks to insure that all persons receive equal housing opportunities. Among its activities, it investigates allegations of discrimination and seeks legal redress for persons HOME believes have been aggrieved. To facilitate its investigations, HOME utilizes "testers," individuals who impersonate applicants, record the results of their tests and supply the results to HOME. Testers receive from HOME a profile based on the allegations being investigated, but HOME does not inform testers of the allegations' content.

When Soules called HOME, she was advised to wait until Monday, April 24, to see if Downs would return her call. In the meantime, HOME arranged for testers to contact Downs.

The first tester to make contact was Marjorie Murray. After Murray left messages on April 22 and 24, Downs returned the calls, leaving a message with Murray's secretary. When Murray returned the call, she spoke to Downs and explained that she was interested in a three bedroom apartment in the Richmond area. When Downs asked Murray how many people would live there, Murray replied that she would live there alone. Downs then described the apartment and told Murray that the apartment was on Bird Avenue in the Richmond area and that they could see it together the next day. Murray made an appointment and then, at HOME's request, cancelled it.

A second tester, Robin Barnes, also contacted Downs. When asked who would be living in the unit, Barnes told Downs that she, her seven year old son and her roommate would live there. Downs then asked Barnes if her son was quiet. When Barnes replied that he was, Downs stated that an elderly couple lived downstairs and that they "would probably not be able to take a noisy child running around." Although Downs did provide Barnes with the address of the apartment, she was apparently uncooperative. When Barnes asked to see the apartment, Downs told her that a Mrs. Anderson would call her to set up an appointment. Downs, however, never asked Anderson to show the apartment to Barnes, and no one contacted Barnes to arrange a showing. After Barnes made calls to Downs and left messages requesting to see the apartment, Downs called her and told her that the Bird Avenue apartment had been rented.

In the meantime, Soules finally did meet with Downs. Downs showed up twenty minutes late to the appointment and showed Soules not the Bird Avenue apartment, but instead a less appealing apartment on Lafayette Avenue. Downs told Soules that she had no apartments in the Richmond area. In fact, however, two such apartments were available.

Also during this time, the Perrys, a family that lived in another apartment managed by Downs, were forced to find another place to live. Even though they had children, Downs told them that the Bird Avenue apartment was available for rental. The ALJ noted in his opinion that he found Ms. Perry's testimony credible:

> Having observed her demeanor, I find Ms. Perry to be a credible witness. Since Ms. Downs ceased managing the Lafayette property in the summer of 1989, Ms. Perry no longer sees her. Ms. Perry lacks any apparent interest in the outcome of this proceeding.

Eventually the Bird Avenue apartment was rented to a single woman who had no children under the age of eighteen.

DISCUSSION

This case requires us to address the 1988 Amendments (Amendments) to the FHA. The Amendments, in part, extend to families with children the same protections that the FHA previously had afforded principally to minorities and members of religious groups.

Section 3604(a), as amended, makes it unlawful "[t]o refuse to sell or rent after the making of a bona fide offer, or to refuse to negotiate for the sale or rental of, or otherwise make unavailable or deny, a dwelling to any person because of race, color, religion, sex, *familial status*, or national origin." 42 U.S.C. § 3604(a) (Supp. 1991) (emphasis added). Section 3604(c) makes it unlawful

> [t]o make, print, or publish, or cause to be made, printed, or published any notice, statement, or advertisement, with respect to the sale or rental of a dwelling that indicates any preference, limitation, or discrimination based on race, color, religion, sex, handicap, *familial status*, or national origin, or an intention to make any such preference, limitation, or discrimination.

Id. § 3604(c) (emphasis added). Section 3602 defines "familial status" to include "one or more individuals (who have not attained the age of 18 years) being domiciled with" a parent or guardian. *Id.* § 3602(k). The FHA provides a private right of action to one who claims infringement of section 3604 rights, *see id.* §§ 3610, 3612(a), (b), and grants us appellate review, *see id.* § 3612(i).

A desire to solve a two-tiered problem provoked the Amendments. Congress' primary concern was to eliminate direct discrimination against families with children. H.R. Rep.

No. 711, 100th Cong., 2nd Sess. 19, reprinted in 1988 U.S. Code Cong. & Admin. News 2173, 2180 ("In many parts of the country families with children are refused housing despite their ability to pay for it."). Congress also was concerned that discrimination against children often camouflages racism or has an undesirable impact on minorities. *Id.* at 2182 ("[B]ecause predominantly white neighborhoods are more likely to have restrictive policies, racial segregation is exacerbated by the exclusion of children.").

However, the Amendments were not intended to place a straightjacket on landlords or unnecessarily to chill their speech. Accordingly, they were "carefully crafted to protect American families, without placing an undue burden on owners and landlords." 134 Cong. Rec. H4687 (daily ed. June 23, 1988) (remarks by Representative Pelosi). Significantly, the Amendments were not intended to "prevent a landlord from determining that a family is otherwise qualified before agreeing to rent to them." 134 Cong. Rec. H4681 (daily ed. June 23, 1988) (remarks by Representative Synar).

Petitioners argue that substantial evidence did not support rejection of their discriminatory denial claim under section 3604(a). They also claim that the ALJ erred when, in addressing their claim under section 3604(c) that the respondents made statements that indicated impermissible discriminatory preferences, he inquired into Downs' intent.

Congress grants us narrow review of agency decisions, and we will reverse one only if it is not in accordance with law or is unsupported by substantial evidence. *See* 5 U.S.C. § 706(2)(A), (E). Because petitioners appeal only from the ALJ's dismissal of the section 3604(a) and (c) claims, we address only the aspects of the ALJ's opinion that dealt with those statutory provisions.

A. Section 3604(a)

The burden shifting procedure employed in examining a section 3604(a) claim is well settled in this Circuit.... To make out a *prima facie* discriminatory housing refusal case, a plaintiff must show that he is a member of a statutorily protected class who applied for and was qualified to rent or purchase housing and was rejected although the housing remained available. A plaintiff in stating a claim under the FHA need allege "only discriminatory effect, and need not show that the decision complained of was made with discriminatory intent.

However, satisfying the requirements of a *prima facie* case does not guarantee recovery to a plaintiff. In part to ensure fairness, where a member of a protected group establishes that he was denied housing that remained available, we allow the defendant to explain whether his actions were motivated by impermissible considerations.... If, however, the defendant declines the opportunity to present evidence toward this end, the plaintiff is entitled to relief.

If the defendant does come forward with evidence in his defense, we allow a plaintiff an opportunity to show that a defendant's stated reason for denying the plaintiff's application for housing was pretextual. In examining the defendant's reason, we view skeptically subjective rationales concerning why he denied housing to members of protected groups. Our reasoning, in part, is that "clever men may easily conceal their motivations." ... There is less reason to be wary of subjective explanations, though, where a defendant provides objective evidence indicating that truth lies behind his assertions of nondiscriminatory conduct.

With these principles in mind, we turn to the specifics of the ALJ's rejection of the discriminatory denial claim.

The ALJ employed the ... burden shifting procedure in this case. Analyzing Soules' evidence, the ALJ concluded that a *prima facie* case had been established:

> [T]he record establishes that in April 1989, 1) Ms. Soules had a twelve year-old daughter; 2) she attempted to rent a three-bedroom apartment in the Richmond Area of Buffalo, and one of the apartments available at that time was the Bird apartment; 3) Respondents denied the Bird apartment to Ms. Soules, knowing of the familial status; and 4) the Bird apartment was rented to Diana Lennox, a person without a child under eighteen years of age.

In a footnote, the ALJ stated that a similar *prima facie* case had been made with regard to Barnes as well. Accordingly, the ALJ turned his attention to the defendants' allegedly legitimate, nondiscriminatory reasons for not renting the Bird apartment to Soules.

Downs, who admitted that she had no intention of renting the Bird Avenue apartment to Soules, insisted that her motives were nondiscriminatory. Rather, she argued that she had not been willing to rent it to Soules because of Soules' negative and combative attitude.

Analyzing the allegedly nondiscriminatory, legitimate reason, the ALJ noted that Soules took on her hostile tone after being asked her child's age. He concluded therefore that the reason for Downs' unwillingness to rent to Soules was legitimate only if the question leading to Soules' aggressive behavior was permissible. Because the question concerning the age of Soules' child was motivated by what the ALJ considered a legitimate reason—securing quiet neighbors for the D'Amaros—he shifted the burden to the petitioners to demonstrate that Downs' and PRS' allegedly legitimate reason for not renting Soules the apartment was pretextual.

The ALJ struggled to resolve both sides' arguments on the pretext issue. The main support in favor of the argument that Soules' negative attitude was a pretextual reason for Downs' not renting the Bird Avenue apartment to her was the disparate treatment of Soules and Barnes, the first tester, as compared to Murray, the second tester, and Lennox, the single woman who eventually rented the apartment. Less persuasive to the ALJ was that Downs had shown up late to her meeting with Soules and had been unwilling to provide information about apartments in the Richmond area.

As a legitimate reason for not renting to Barnes, Downs asserted that she was out of town a great deal caring for her aunt during the period in which Barnes was contacting her. Supporting this assertion was the testimony of Mr. Campise, the owner of the Bird Avenue apartment, who stated that he had difficulty reaching Downs at that time.

Attempting to balance the arguments concerning whether Downs' reasons for not renting to Soules and Barnes were pretextual, the ALJ focused on Ms. Perry's testimony. In the eyes of the ALJ, "the testimony of Ms. Perry conclusively establishes that Ms. Downs was willing and, in fact, attempted to rent the Bird apartment to a family with children under the age of eighteen.... [Downs] was ... as encouraging to Ms. Perry as she was to Ms. Murray and Ms. Lennox." Concluding therefore that the plaintiffs had not proven that Downs had acted as she did because she did not want to rent the Bird Avenue apartment to a family with children under eighteen, the ALJ rejected the section 3604(a) claim against Downs.

While Downs' questioning about children was probative on the issue of unlawful conduct, petitioners' evidence did not require the conclusion that impermissible denial of housing occurred. Where, as here, probative evidence also exists that a defendant denied housing to members of protected groups for legitimate, nondiscriminatory reasons, it remains for the trier of fact to determine whether a discriminatory denial of housing occurred.

Petitioners argue that the ALJ erred by accepting, as a deciding factor on the pretext issue, neutral testimony that Downs offered the Bird Avenue apartment to other members of petitioner's protected class. We disagree. Were we to require the ALJ to discredit Downs' professed reasons for not renting the Bird Avenue apartment to the petitioners or unnecessarily limit the weight that he could give that evidence, our decision effectively would render a nullity the burden shifting that we previously have endorsed. A case effectively would end once a plaintiff provided evidence sufficient to make out a *prima facie* claim, and some innocent defendants would be denied fair trials in discriminatory denial cases.

After reviewing the record and evaluating petitioners' contentions, the ALJ concluded that Soules' combative attitude and Downs' being out of town to aid a sick relative, rather than unlawful conduct, resulted in the housing denials at issue in this case. Substantial evidence supported this conclusion, and we need not decide whether we would reach this result were we to address the question de novo.

B. Section 3604(c)

The petitioners contest the ALJ's determination that respondents did not make statements indicating an impermissible preference, discrimination or limitation in violation of section 3604(c). Their principal argument in support of this position is that the ALJ erred by inquiring into the respondents' intent. We disagree.

In determining whether an ad or statement "indicates" impermissible racial discrimination, we ask whether "an ad for housing suggests to an ordinary reader [or listener] that a particular race is preferred or dispreferred for the housing in question...." The ordinary reader "is neither the most suspicious nor the most insensitive of our citizenry." Courts also have allowed parties to establish violations of section 3604(c) by proving an actual intent to discriminate.

Petitioners invoke an ordinary listener standard. Having concluded that this is an appropriate gauge for measuring compliance with the Amendments, we question whether the ordinary listener, in light of all the circumstances, would have interpreted [Downs'—Eds.] statements and questions to suggest an impermissible preference based on familial status.

In cases where ads are clearly discriminatory, a court may look at an ad and determine whether it indicates an impermissible preference to an ordinary reader, and inquiry into the author's professed intent is largely unnecessary.... [T]he Fourth Circuit [has] held that a rental ad specifying that an apartment was in a "white home" violated section 3604(c).

Openly discriminatory oral statements merit similarly straightforward treatment. In one case, for example, a landlord's statement to a white tenant that she should send her friends over to see a vacant apartment but to "make sure her friends are whites" was held to violate the FHA. [Also held to violate the Act are statements that black tenants were not allowed in a trailer park because white tenants would move out and statements that no blacks lived in development and were not allowed there even as guests—Eds.].

This section 3604(c) case presents more difficult problems. As the government points out in its papers, whereas "[t]here is simply no legitimate reason for considering an applicant's race ... there are situations in which it is legitimate to inquire about the number of individuals interested in occupying an apartment and their ages." Local zoning regulations, for example, might constitute a valid reason for asking whether and how many children a prospective tenant has. Conditions in the neighborhood known to be either ideally suited to or inherently dangerous to occupancy by families with children might well permit an inquiry about the ages of the family members. We agree with the respondents that, standing alone, an inquiry into whether a prospective tenant has a child does not constitute an FHA violation.

We next examine whether the FHA is necessarily violated when one asks whether a child is noisy. Respondents contend that when coupled with a question concerning children a question or statement about noise indicates an impermissible preference to an ordinary listener. This does not necessarily follow. One just as easily might conclude that if Downs had stereotyped all children as impermissibly noisy, then she would not have asked the second question.

That statements are not facially discriminatory, however, does not mean that they do not indicate an impermissible preference in the context in which they were made. In the context of printed ads, we have recognized that expression of a tacit preference not to provide housing to members of protected groups may violate section 3604(c). In *Ragin*, we held that a plaintiff had stated a section 3604(c) claim by alleging that the defendant had published housing ads over a twenty year period that featured thousands of human models of whom virtually none was black. The plaintiff claimed that "the repeated and continued depiction of white human models and the virtual absence of any black human models ... indicates a preference on the basis of race." Such a claim, we held, should not be dismissed.... Cf. *Saunders v. General Services Corp.*, 659 F. Supp. 1042, 1057–59 (E.D. Va. 1987) (finding violation of § 3604(c) where, in addition to a failure to use black models, substantial evidence existed that personnel of the corporation managing the properties in question were instructed to treat black tenants and prospective tenants less favorably than others and the corporation agreed to but did not in fact use an equal opportunity slogan or logo in its brochures). Dismissal of the claim at the posture it came to us in *Ragin* would have been unreasonable in light of the significant evidence from which the trier of fact could determine whether the ads indicated an impermissible preference....

Facially nondiscriminatory statements pose even greater difficulties than facially nondiscriminatory ads. The written content of questions and statements does not demonstrate the inflection of the speaker, and out of necessity courts must turn to other evidence in determining whether a violation of the FHA occurred. In this case, for example, Downs asked Barnes whether her child was noisy and later stated that an elderly tenant "would probably not be able to take a noisy child running around." Depending on the context and intent of the speaker, the latter question either could intimate an impermissible preference or simply might explain—to a desired tenant—why the first question had been asked. It also might send a message that a tenant with a noisy child will probably be confronted with regular complaints from the elderly tenant making the apartment less attractive to the prospective tenant. It is for this reason that factfinders may examine intent, not because a lack of design constitutes an affirmative defense to an FHA violation, but because it helps determine the manner in which a statement was made and the way an ordinary listener would have interpreted it. *See Ragin*, 923 F.2d at 1000 ("the intent of the creator of an ad may be relevant to a factual determination of the message conveyed."). We believe that such evidence may prove especially helpful where, as here, a court is charged with ascertaining the message sent by isolated words rather than a series of ads or an extended pattern of conduct.

In this case, after stating that the statements made by Downs facially did not indicate a limitation, preference or discrimination based on familial status, the ALJ inquired whether Downs' intent was discriminatory by examining whether her reasons for making her statements were legitimate and nondiscriminatory rather than pretextual. This procedure was not improper....

The respondents argued before the ALJ that the written questions on the application and Ms. Downs' oral questions regarding the numbers and ages of children were asked because a local health code precluded children older than five from sharing a bedroom with someone of a different sex. The ALJ determined that this reason was not pretextual.

As to the oral questions, the ALJ rejected the health code regulation as a satisfactory reason where, as here, only one child existed. However, the ALJ concluded that there was a non-pretextual reason for asking such questions:

> If sufficiently noisy, tenants can be deemed a nuisance and can be evicted. A housing provider is not precluded from attempting to ascertain whether prospective tenants will be noisy before the tenants move in. Nor is a housing provider precluded from advising prospective tenants that a quiet environment is desired by existing tenants.

In this case, the ALJ resolved that the reason for Downs' asking children's ages was to guarantee that the D'Amaros continued to live in a quiet environment. Evidencing this was that Downs did not ask a child's age as an isolated question but always coupled that query with either a follow-up question that specifically inquired whether the prospective tenant's child was noisy or a statement to the effect that the downstairs tenants were elderly and did not want those children who were noisy.

Having determined that the respondents' legitimate, nonpretextual reason for making their statements was to determine whether prospective tenants were noisy, the ALJ shifted the burden to the petitioner to demonstrate that this reason was a mere pretext for a desire to avoid renting to families with children under eighteen. Because Downs had in fact offered to rent the apartment to persons with children under the age of eighteen and other evidence failed to demonstrate that the respondents' objective of finding quiet neighbors for the D'Amaros was pretextual, the ALJ rejected the section 3604(c) claim.

As we stated in the context of the section 3604(a) claim, our role as an appellate court is not to embark anew in adjudicating the FHA claim before us, but only to determine whether substantial evidence supported the ALJ's determination. The facts of this case do not merit reversal in light of that standard.

CONCLUSION

The parties have raised other issues that do not affect our disposition of this appeal. We need not address them. The petition for review is denied.

Notes and Questions

1. Note in this case that an Administrative Law Judge heard the case. The ALJ decisionmaking vehicle was authorized in the 1988 Amendments to the Fair Housing Act. Today it appears that the ALJ procedure is being invoked for a large volume of cases. For further consideration of the various procedures available in a fair housing case, see *A Note on Procedures, Remedies, Damages, and Attorney's Fees, infra.*

2. In *Gilligan v. Jamco Dev. Co*, 108 F.3d 246 (9th Cir 1997), the court held that a complaint stated a claim under of familial status discrimination and thus survived a motion to dismiss in alleging that the defendant had a policy of refusing to rent to families who receive assistance under the federal program of Aid to Families with Dependent Children (AFDC). It was not clear whether plaintiffs would attempt to make out a disparate treat-

ment case or a disparate impact case. But the court noted that eligibility for AFDC was conditioned on having children in the household.

3. The *Soules* decision permits inquiry into whether the child was "quiet." If children are "inherently not quiet" is a quietness criterion one that at the least has a disparate impact on families with children? Is it tantamount to exclusion of children to require as a condition of rental that one have "quiet" children?

If a *prima facie* claim of disparate impact could be made that a quietness criterion disproportionately affected families with young children, and if the quietness criterion were not a pretext because it had some validity, would that necessarily mean a quietness criterion could not be enforced? What about the "no AFDC" criterion in *Gilligan*?

4. Ms. Soules became agitated by the questions Downs posed about children and for that reason Downs did not want to rent the property to her. Note that the court approved the ALJ's conclusion that Soules' hostility at the questions about children would be a legitimate reason for Downs' not renting to Soules if the questions about children were legitimate.

Is this the right approach? Maybe Soules became hostile because she was sensitized by prior experiences. So it might be argued that she reacted to the questions as a person with a child and not as just an ordinary listener who never experienced discrimination. In other words should the test be the "person with children who has experienced discrimination" or the "ordinary person?"

The "ordinary listener" test can be applied with a sensitive evaluation of the impact of words. *White v. U.S. Department of Housing and Urban Development*, 475 F.3d 898 (7th Cir. 2007) demonstrates how this can be the case. In *White*, the plaintiff called about renting an apartment in response to an advertisement. The defendant, who answered the phone, according to the plaintiff's testimony, asked the plaintiff, "How many in your family?" Plaintiff replied "One adult and two children." Whereupon the defendant asked plaintiff "Are you married?" When plaintiff says she responded, "No." Defendant said, "Well she can't rent to [me] because you have two children and no husband and this girl has to pay her mortgage."

The Court stated that the inquiry to be made under the objective standard is whether the alleged statement would suggest to an "ordinary listener" that a person with a particular familial status is preferred or disfavored for the housing in question. The Court noted that the Defendant's speaking about paying her mortgage was not an impermissible statement since it was about Plaintiff's ability pay the rent. The Court also noted that the Fair Housing Act does not include marital status among its protected classifications. The Court nevertheless concluded that Plaintiff demonstrated that the Defendant's statements indicated disfavor for Plaintiff's familial status because Defendant's statements would allow an "ordinary listener" to infer that Defendant had a preference against Plaintiff due to Plaintiff's familial status.

5. In determining whether an advertisement expresses a prohibited preference, the courts have generally employed an "ordinary reader" test to evaluate whether a particular advertisement conveys a discriminatory message. *Tyus v. Urban Search Management,* 102 F.3d 256 (7th Cir 1996), *cert. denied,* 520 U.S. 1251 (1997) (error to exclude expert testimony as to how an advertisement would affect an ordinary reader but not error to refuse to instruct jurors to evaluate the advertisements from the standpoint of "the ordinary African-American reader," rather than from standpoint of generic ordinary reader); *Jancik v. Department of Hous. & Urb. Dev.,* 44 F.3d 553 (7th Cir. 1995) (advertisement for "mature" persons held to indicate a preference based on familial status to the ordinary reader);

Housing Opportunities Made Equal, Inc. v. Cincinnati Enquirer, Inc., 943 F.2d 644 (6th Cir. 1991) (advertisements violate Title VIII if they indicate a preference to the ordinary reader making a natural interpretation of the ad), *citing United States v. Hunter*, 459 F.2d 205 (4th Cir. 1972) ("white home" in advertisement violates Title VIII); *Ragin v. New York Times Co.*, 923 F.2d 995, 999 (2d Cir.), *cert. denied*, 502 U.S. 821 (1991) (the ordinary reader is neither the most suspicious nor the most insensitive of our citizenry). *See generally* Mary A. Fiorino, Comment, *Advertising for Apartheid: The Use of All White Models in Marketing Real Estate as a Violation of the Fair Housing Act*, 56 U. Cin. L. Rev. 1429 (1988) (general treatment arguing for broad interpretation of Title VIII); Margot S. Rabin, Note, *Advertising and Title VIII: The Discriminatory Use of Models in Real Estate Advertisements*, 98 Yale L.J. 165 (1988) (arguing that intent to discriminate should not be required in the white-models cases and proposing an "ordinary reader" test to determine whether the ads are discriminatory). It may be useful to recall that the advertising area can raise First Amendment issues. *See A Note On Fair Housing Enforcement and the First Amendment, supra.*

6. As an example of the potential reach of some of the prohibitions, consider the prohibition on discriminatory advertising. In *Saunders v. General Services Corp.*, 659 F. Supp. 1042 (E.D. Va. 1986), the court held that the paucity of black models in an advertising brochure of which 134,000 were printed for a development conveyed a racial preference in violation of Title VIII, although black models proportionate to the racial composition of the housing market was not required. But the court distinguished *Saunders* on its facts in *Spann v. Colonial Village*, 662 F. Supp. 541 (D.D.C. 1987), *rev'd on other grounds* 899 F.2d 24 (D.C. Cir. 1990), *cert. denied*, 498 U.S. 980, 1046 (1991). *Spann* involved a defendant who placed ads in the Washington Post. Some of the ads contained only white models, others only black models, and some, models of both races; black models appeared in some 30–40% of the ads; and all ads carried the equal housing opportunity slogan and logo.

7. Certain housing for the elderly is exempt from the familial status requirements: (1) housing built under state or federal programs for elderly housing; (2) housing in which all residents are 62 or over; and (3) housing in which (a) at least 80% of the units are occupied by one person at least 55 years old and (b) as to which the owner publishes and adheres to policies and procedures that demonstrate intent to provide housing for persons 55 and older. 42 U.S.C. § 3607(b)(2)(C).

8. Note that in the *Soules* case part of the real estate agent's justification for asking about the number, ages, and gender of children was based on a New York State Health Department rule that required separate bedrooms for children of different sexes over five years old. Can such a rule itself be challenged as violating the Fair Housing Act? What evidence would a Plaintiff be likely to need, and what justifications, if any, could sustain a governmental requirement? These issues are considered in the following case.

Sierra v. City of New York

United States District Court
579 F. Supp. 2d 543 (S.D.N.Y. 2008)

OPINION AND ORDER

JED S. RAKOFF, District Judge.

Section 27-2076(b) of the New York City Housing Maintenance Code ("HMC") prohibits families with children under the age of sixteen from residing in single room occupancy units ("SROs"), which are defined in turn as "rooming units" that lack either an in-unit kitchen or an in-unit bathroom. Plaintiff Juana Sierra, a mother of two children who formerly occupied two units of that type, has challenged the restriction under the Fair Housing Act ("FHA"), 42 U.S.C. § 3604(a), arguing that it impermissibly discriminates on the basis of family status. Sierra asks the Court to declare the ordinance invalid and enjoin its future enforcement, as well as to award her damages. The City defendants—the City of New York, the N.Y.C. Department of Buildings ("DOB") and its Commissioner, and the N.Y.C. Department of Housing Preservation and Development ("HPD") and its Commissioner—oppose Sierra's request, defending section 27-2076(b) as a valid means of ensuring the safety of City residents. Each party contends that its respective position best protects the interests of families and children....

On September 3–5, 2008, the Court conducted an evidentiary hearing to resolve those factual disputes and so resolve plaintiff's requests for injunctive and declaratory relief....

Accordingly, the Court turns to the merits of the plaintiff's claims for injunctive and declaratory relief. HMC section 27-2076(b) provides, in relevant part:

> No rooming unit shall be occupied by a family with a child under the age of sixteen years, except that if a child is born to a family residing in such accommodations, the unlawful occupancy shall not commence until one year after the birth of such child.

The HMC further defines a "rooming unit" as "one or more living rooms arranged to be occupied as a unit separate from all other living rooms, and which does not have both lawful sanitary facilities and lawful cooking facilities for the exclusive use of the family residing in such unit." HMC § 2004(15). The City of New York enacted section 27-2076(b) in 1960 to protect children from what it deemed to be the inappropriate, unsafe, and unhealthy environments of SROs.

As the Court noted in its May 13 Order, the rationales cited by the City at the time the provision was enacted reflect a legitimate, bona fide governmental interest; however, the question now facing the Court is whether, today, the provision works "in practice" to further those interests. The burden of so proving falls on the City defendants, and the Court finds that the evidence adduced by the City defendants during the trial is sufficient to meet that burden.

The critical feature separating a rooming unit subject to HMC section 27-2076(b) from a unit not subject to that provision is that a rooming unit "does not have both lawful sanitary facilities and lawful cooking facilities for the exclusive use of the family residing in such unit," i.e., it lacks either a private kitchen or a private bathroom or both. Accordingly, the Court has considered *only* evidence pertaining to risks necessarily or very strongly associated with residences lacking such features....

Even disregarding arguments about substandard quality and demographic profiles, however, the City defendants have offered substantial evidence that the defining features of SRO housing are detrimental to children.

First, the fact that a bathroom is removed from a family's living space and shared with non-family members necessarily has impacts both on children's health and safety and on their privacy and development. Shared bathrooms expose children to dangers that their parents—no matter how conscientious—are unable to control: primarily, exposure to strangers and exposure to contagions.... The first may seriously compromise a child's safety; for example, Dr. Hart [Ph.D., an expert witness in environmental psychology—Eds.] estimated that a child might encounter as many as thirty or forty different individuals in and around a single bathroom ... and the Court heard anecdotal evidence that locking mechanisms on shared bathrooms are frequently either broken or inadequate.... As to risk of infection, while the Court received no conclusive evidence that SRO bathroom facilities are, as a rule, less hygienic than in-unit bathrooms, it is impossible, as a logical matter, for a parent to control the cleanliness of a shared bathroom in the way he or she might a private bathroom.... Additional problems stem from the fact that younger children cannot use an exterior bathroom without adult supervision; where it is lacking, they may endanger themselves by attempting to use the bathroom unassisted or by waiting, possibly risking medical consequences.... Furthermore, Dr. Hart presented research from psychology and social science literature concluding that shared, exterior bathrooms have negative impacts on children's development: for young children, for example, by thwarting toilet training, and for older children and adolescents by depriving them of privacy needed for healthy development....

Shared kitchens likewise pose health and safety risks for children. Kitchens are dangerous places for children, but it is difficult if not impossible for a parent to "child-proof" a shared kitchen; nor can a single parent leave a child unattended in the rooming unit while preparing meals.... Parents face additional obstacles to safe preparation of food; for example, many shared kitchens lack refrigerators, but even where refrigerators are present, parents may hesitate to use them because of concerns over food security.... It is also a particular challenge to keep shared kitchens clean for reasons similar to those related to shared bathrooms, and thus food preparation in shared kitchens carries greater health risks; there are, moreover, safety risks associated with bringing food back to eat in the living unit....

Finally, children's physical and psychological development is likely to be impeded by the nature of the living space within an SRO. The fact that SROs tend to be quite small is not, in and of itself, the problem, for lack of space is not indispensably linked to SRO housing: SROs, like regular apartments, can be small or large. By definition, however, only SROs may consist of a single room. (Any non-SRO housing would have, at the least, a separate bathroom). Dr. Hart cited research suggesting that living in a "single undifferentiated space," can delay development and deny children needed refuge....

In short, the essential elements of an SRO—lack of in-unit bathroom, lack of in-unit kitchen, and, usually, single-room living space—are detrimental in many respects to the welfare of children and inherently cannot be remedied by alternative measures. Moreover, as Dr. Hart repeatedly emphasized, these multiple harms cannot be considered independently, but rather have cumulative negative impacts....

In a perfect world, legislatures would always have scientific studies to guide and justify the measures they enact; however, such studies very rarely exist, and in any event, are in no way required to support a challenged statute—even one, like this one, that is facially discriminatory. To require such studies before finding that an ordinance "further[s] ... in practice, a legitimate, bona fide governmental interest" would be, in effect, to hold that no facially discriminatory statute ever could be upheld. Clearly, that is not the law, nor should it be.

As the legislative history of the FHA indicates, Congress intended to prohibit the exclusion of families with children from housing opportunities based on invidious discrimination and stereotypes. *See* Fair Housing Amendments Act of 1988 House Report, H.R. Rep. No. 100-711, at 19 (1988), *reprinted in* 1988 U.S.C.C.A.N. 2173. Such discrimination is a far cry from the City's rationales here, however—at least as limited by the Court.... [T]he City has produced extensive evidence demonstrating concrete physical and psychological effects of SRO living on children, rather than merely generalizations and conclusory assertions....

The plaintiff's second major challenge to the City's evidence is that, even if the Court finds the City's proof sufficient to establish that SRO housing has negative impacts on children, the City has failed to prove that those impacts are worse than any that children would suffer in feasible alternative housing situations. In other words, if children are excluded from SROs, the only available housing options their families can afford are likely to be just as problematic. This argument is a variation of the claim the plaintiff advanced at the summary judgment stage, which was that to the extent section 27-2076(b) drives families from SROs, it delivers them into homeless shelters or onto the streets.

Yet the Court heard no material evidence supporting this hypothesis. As an initial matter, the only displaced family of which the Court is specifically aware—Sierra's own family—is in neither situation. Rather, Sierra and her children now live with her sister and her sister's family. While the Court in no way suggests that this situation is idea—on the contrary, the "doubled up" conditions are undoubtedly crowded—it is a far cry from living on the streets; moreover, there is a strong argument to be made that because Sierra and her children now share kitchen and sanitary facilities with family members only, this arrangement is safer for her family than the typical SRO....

Likewise, the Court heard no material evidence tending to support the plaintiff's other primary argument at summary judgment: that section 27-2076(b) is enforced primarily by landlords seeking to evict families with children so that they can rent to higher-paying tenants....

In sum, the Court concludes that the City has carried its burden of demonstrating that HMC section 27-7076(b) furthers, in theory and in practice, legitimate government interests in the health, safety and welfare of children that cannot be achieved through other alternatives, and that HMC section 27-2076(b) does not violate the Fair Housing Act. The Court therefore denies Sierra's requests for injunctive and declaratory relief. Moreover, the above conclusion also moots, as a matter of law, Sierra's claim for damages against the City defendants, which presupposed their enforcement of an invalid regulation. Accordingly, the Clerk of the Court is directed to enter judgment dismissing the Complaint with prejudice.

4. Discrimination Based on Sex and Sexual Harassment

Krueger v. Cuomo

United States Court of Appeals
115 F.3d 487 (7th Cir. 1997)

Before FLAUM, KANNE, and ROVNER, Circuit Judges.

FLAUM, Circuit Judge.

Lyle Krueger petitions for review of a decision and order of the Secretary of the Department of Housing and Urban Development ("HUD") concluding that Krueger violated the Fair Housing Act, 42 U.S.C. § 3601 *et seq.*, by sexually harassing one of his tenants. We affirm.

I.

In April 1992, Debbie Maze was living in Kenosha, Wisconsin with her two children, ages four and three, in her sister's two-bedroom apartment, also home to the sister's boyfriend and four children. Maze had been searching for an apartment for three months, and her section 8 housing voucher was due to expire in late May. So when she saw a "for rent" sign on an apartment owned by Lyle Krueger, she inquired within and found Krueger, who gave her a rental application and suggested they meet the next morning for breakfast.

At the breakfast meeting, it became apparent that Maze could not afford the three-bedroom, $547-a-month apartment, for her housing voucher provided only $395 for a two-bedroom apartment, to which she was expected to add a personal contribution of $52 per month [for a total rent of $447 per month—Eds.] Although Krueger initially refused to rent the apartment to Maze, he soon changed his mind. He located Maze through her sister, a former tenant, and arranged for another breakfast meeting. At this second meeting, Krueger told Maze that she could pay money on the side or "fool around or something" to make up the $100 shortfall. She declined this payment scheme, but Krueger nevertheless agreed to rent her the apartment. Maze did not own a car, and Krueger gave her a ride home from their meeting. In his car, Krueger rubbed Maze's thigh and predicted, "we're going to be close." Maze asked Krueger not to touch her.

On May 11, Krueger and Maze went to the Kenosha Housing Authority to sign a rental agreement. In the elevator on the way to the office, Krueger touched Maze, rubbed her, and tried to kiss her. She told him to stop, a request he greeted with laughter. After the two had signed the lease, an undaunted Krueger once again prophesied that he and Maze "were going to be real close." Maze was so disturbed by Krueger's behavior that, later the same day, she returned alone to the Housing Authority. There, she reported Krueger's advances to a Housing Authority official, Paula Lattergrass, who urged her not to take the apartment. Maze felt that she had few alternatives other than to move into the apartment, but she did, at the suggestion of Lattergrass, file complaints against Krueger with the Urban League and HUD.

Krueger's unwelcome advances continued after Maze moved into the apartment on May 13. He made a habit (three to four times a week, Maze recalled) of arriving unannounced; he would knock on the first-floor doorway, enter before Maze could respond, and climb the internal staircase to her apartment. Once inside, he would grab and touch Maze, doing so on at least one occasion in front of her children. He suggested that she send the children to her mother's so that she and Krueger could go away together. On another occasion, he repeated his hope that they would be "real close" and asked if they were "going to do good in bed." When Maze demurred, he told Maze that he was losing money because of her and reminded her that he could have rented the apartment to someone else. Krueger also asked Maze out for drinks. Maze, who is black, told Krueger, who is white, that she did not date white men. Four or five times, she observed him parked outside her home watching her apartment. Maze began to seek ways to minimize contact with Krueger. In order to do so, she brought her rent checks to Lattergrass, who forwarded them to Krueger.

Under these circumstances, it would be inapt to speak of a deterioration in the relationship between Krueger and Maze; but from Krueger's perspective at least, matters did take a turn for the worse after he learned that Maze had filed harassment charges against him. In a series of letters written during the summer of 1992, Krueger expressed his dissatisfaction with Maze as a tenant. These letters explicitly linked the perceived decline in their relations to Maze's filing of harassment charges against Krueger ("Before you moved in you were very friendly ... you were a pleasure to be with and then you filed sexual harassment charges"), informed Maze that Krueger would be willing to break the year-long lease, and repeatedly suggested that Maze "think about moving." The letters also referred to a ten-dollar fee, imposed as a result of the Housing Authority's purported delay in forwarding Maze's rent check, and to the cost of repairs made to the apartment, both of which Krueger intended to deduct from Maze's rent payments. In October, the letters became more official in tone. On October 20, Krueger informed Maze that, because lead had been detected in her children's blood, she would have to vacate the apartment and remove all of her belongings, including furniture, in order for him to take "corrective action." (In fact, Krueger only painted over the lead-based paint; Maze and her children were able to spend daytime hours at her mother's for the two or three days required to complete the painting.) The most recent letter in the record, dated October 22, 1992, came from Krueger's lawyer, who instructed Maze that she must either pay "unpaid rent" or vacate her apartment within five days.

As Krueger indicated in his letters, the "unpaid rent" represented the cost of repairs that he had deducted from Maze's rent payments, as well as the ten-dollar late fee. The repairs in question were the unclogging of Maze's toilet and sink and the replacement of her apartment door, which she had forced open after one of her children locked himself inside the apartment. Prior to Krueger's attempt to evict Maze, the landlord and tenant had met at the Housing Authority in an attempt to resolve the payment dispute, and Lattergrass had presented a compromise solution, under which Maze would pay for a portion of the repairs. Based on her inspection of the apartment, Lattergrass believed that Maze was only partly responsible for the plumbing difficulties and that the broken door had needed only a new lock, not complete replacement. Nevertheless, Krueger refused to accept any money from Maze.

Krueger continued to sexually harass Maze after she became pregnant in October 1992. In February 1993, Maze moved out of her apartment and into her mother's home, a two-bedroom unit shared by Maze's stepfather and her brother. She did not find another apartment until May 1993.

Maze's complaint against Krueger came before an administrative law judge ("ALJ") in December 1995. After hearing testimony from Krueger, Maze, her sister Barbara Maze, Lattergrass, and a HUD investigator, the ALJ ruled in favor of Maze. In his decision and order, dated June 7, 1996, the ALJ noted that, in contrast to Debbie Maze's "straightforward, consistent, and credible" testimony, which was corroborated by Lattergrass and Barbara Maze, Krueger's testimony was "riddled with inconsistencies" and, in places, "simply ... not believable." Significantly, the ALJ found that Krueger's conduct had caused Maze to move out of her apartment. Krueger "made Maze's tenancy untenable," in the ALJ's view; "Eventually the tenancy became so miserable that she felt compelled to move out." The ALJ also rejected Krueger's proffered explanations for his attempts to evict Maze (her hostility toward him, her failure to pay rent) and found that Krueger's actions were a direct response to her refusal to submit to his demands and to her filing of harassment charges. Because Maze's rejection of Krueger's advances resulted in an adverse consequence (i.e., being forced out of her apartment), the ALJ concluded that Krueger had engaged in *quid pro quo* sexual harassment. Accordingly, the ALJ held that Krueger had violated 42 U.S.C. § 3604(b), which forbids discrimination on the basis of sex "in the terms, conditions, or privileges of sale or rental of a dwelling, or in the provision of services or facilities in connection therewith...." The ALJ also held that Krueger's continued campaign of harassment—an interference with Maze's right to quiet enjoyment of her tenancy—and his retaliation against Maze for her filing a complaint each independently violated 42 U.S.C. § 3617, which makes it "unlawful to coerce, intimidate, threaten, or interfere with any person in the exercise or enjoyment of, or on account of his having exercised or enjoyed ... any right granted or protected by section ... 3604 ... of [Title 42]." Krueger was enjoined from committing future acts of discrimination, assessed a civil penalty of $10,000, and ordered to pay Maze $622 for alternative housing costs, $2,000 to compensate for the inconvenience occasioned by her loss of the apartment, and $20,000 for Maze's emotional distress. On July 7, 1996, the ALJ's ruling became the final order of the Secretary pursuant to 42 U.S.C. § 3612(h)(1). Krueger now appeals the agency's liability determination and argues that the damages and civil penalty are excessive.

II.

Krueger's challenge to HUD's conclusion that he violated sections 3604(b) and 3617 warrants little discussion. This court has recognized that sexual harassment in the housing context can violate the Fair Housing Act, *see DiCenso v. Cisneros*, 96 F.3d 1004, 1008 (7th Cir. 1996), and Krueger does not argue otherwise. Moreover, although he purports to raise legal issues subject to our plenary review, the legal standards Krueger proposes do nothing to undermine the agency's analysis. Krueger's arguments ultimately rest on the assertion that he attempted to evict Maze for "legitimate business reasons" and that there was "no causal connection between Krueger's alleged sexual advances and her moving out of the apartment"—a view of the evidence directly in conflict with the ALJ's findings. From our perspective, those findings need only be supported by substantial evidence: "we may not decide the facts anew, reweigh the evidence, or substitute our own judgment for that of the Secretary." *Jancik v. Department of Housing and Urban Development*, 44 F.3d 553, 556 (7th Cir. 1995) (citations and internal quotations omitted). "'[A]n ALJ's credibility determinations,'" we have explained, "'will be overturned ... only when extraordinary circumstances so require.'" Certainly, no such "extraordinary circumstances" are present in this case, in which Maze buttressed her convincing testimony with the testimony of a disinterested witness (Lattergrass) to whom she had promptly reported the misconduct at issue. On this record, we have no basis for upsetting the agency's findings.

III.

Krueger also argues that the civil fine assessed against him ($10,000) and the damages awarded Maze ($622 in alternative housing costs and $22,000 for emotional distress and inconvenience) were excessive.

The ALJ based his award of alternative housing costs on Maze's estimate of her moving expenses and the rent she paid for three months to her mother and for one month to her new landlord, less the amount she would have had to contribute during this period under her lease with Krueger. On appeal, Krueger complains that Maze introduced no corroborating testimony or documentation and that the money Maze furnished her mother was not rent but went to pay the cable or phone bill. We, however, agree with HUD that the relevant inquiry is not how Maze's mother chose to apply the funds Maze contributed. Rather, it is enough that Maze paid this money in consideration of her being permitted to live in her mother's apartment. Further, Krueger has cited to us no authority for the proposition that Maze was required to document her alternative housing costs with exacting specificity, and we have not uncovered any. To the contrary, we believe that the ALJ was entitled to make a reasonable estimate, based on all of the evidence before him, of Maze's alternative housing costs.

Similarly, the evidence was sufficient to support the award of damages for emotional distress. Krueger observes that the direct evidence of Maze's emotional distress was limited almost entirely to her own testimony. He argues that because the ALJ's decision focused primarily upon Krueger's behavior, rather than Maze's reaction to that behavior, the award constitutes an unrequested, and therefore improper, punitive sanction. What Krueger neglects, however, is that the ALJ was obligated to "look at both the direct evidence of emotional distress and the circumstances of the act that allegedly caused the distress." *United States v. Balistrieri*, 981 F.2d 916, 932 (7th Cir. 1992). "The more inherently degrading or humiliating the defendant's action is, the more reasonable it is to infer that a person would suffer humiliation or distress from that action; consequently, somewhat more conclusory evidence of emotional distress will be acceptable to support an award for emotional damages." It demands little in the way of either empathy or imagination to appreciate the predicament of a woman who is harassed in full view of her children, whose home becomes not a sanctuary but the situs of her torment, and who concludes that she has no alternative but to leave a long sought-for apartment. Maze testified that Krueger made her feel "real dirty," "like a bad person," and "scared" her. She was not required, as Krueger appears to believe, to call an expert witness.

Also without merit is Krueger's appeal of the Secretary's award of $2,000 to compensate Maze for her inconvenience. In ordering this relief, the ALJ noted that Maze had to search for new housing during the winter, to live for three months in crowded conditions in her mother's apartment, and eventually to accept a smaller, less well-heated apartment. Krueger's argument to this court—that Maze could have moved during the summer, when Krueger "actually tried to evict her" and that she "did not have to move in with her mother," but "could have waited and moved into a new apartment"—contradicts itself. Worse, it ignores both the limited options available to Maze and the egregiousness of Krueger's misconduct. From all that appears, Maze dealt as well as could be expected with an intolerable situation.

Finally, we are not persuaded that the $10,000 civil fine—the maximum penalty authorized under the governing statute, *see* 42 U.S.C. § 3612(g)(3)(A)—was excessive. In opposition to this fine, Krueger contends that "to pay this civil penalty, he would have to sell one of [his four] properties, which is too severe a penalty for [his] alleged conduct." Yet difficulty paying is not inability to pay, and a painless sanction would have little deterrent effect. In arriving at the $10,000 figure, the ALJ did consider Krueger's financial resources, as well as the seriousness of his misconduct and the need to deter him and other landlords from repeating the harassment that Maze experienced. Section 3612(g)(3) of Title 42 authorizes civil penalties "to vindicate the public interest," and the ALJ acted well within his authority in imposing the maximum fine available.

The order of the Secretary is AFFIRMED.

Notes and Questions

1. The classic case of gender discrimination most likely arises when a landowner refuses to rent to a male or female person, as the case may be. In this kind of case the landowner refuses, for example, to rent to males on the basis of his experience that "males did not keep a clean house." *See HUD v. Baumgardner*, No 05-89-0306-1, 2A Fair Housing-Fair Lending (P-H) ¶ 25,006 (HUD Office of Admin. Law Judges Nov. 15, 1990) (sex discrimination violation found).

2. A court might find against a tenant with a less clear case of sexual harassment or an incident that is alleged to create a "hostile housing environment." *DiCenso v. Cisneros,* 96 F.3d 1004 (7th Cir 1996) (male landlord came to apartment, and standing just outside of door, asked female tenant about the rent, simultaneously began caressing her arm and back, and said to her words to the effect that if she could not pay the rent, she could take care of it in other ways).

3. *Honce v. Vigil,* 1 F.3d 1085 (10th Cir. 1993), is a case in which the court held that the plaintiff female failed to make out a *prima facie* case of a violation of Title VIII. The landlord asked plaintiff out on dates three times before she leased a lot in his mobile home park. Each time she declined. Thereafter a series of disputes arose and plaintiff moved. The court held that the plaintiff did not demonstrate (1) "disparate treatment" based on gender because the landlord offered all services of the park to plaintiff, (2) *quid pro quo* sexual harassment because no service was conditioned on sexual favors, (3) "hostile housing environment" even though the landlord's behavior was "eccentric, and probably unwarranted," it was not directed solely at plaintiff, nor was the hostile conduct sexual or directed solely at women. The case contains a good summary of the relevant cases.

4. *See also* Michelle Adams, *Knowing Your Place: Theorizing Sexual Harassment at Home,* 40 ARIZ. L. REV. 17 (1998); Regina Cahan, Comment, *Home is No Haven: An Analysis of Sexual Harassment in Housing,* 1987 WIS. L. REV. 1061.

5. In *Krueger,* note the limitations the court places on the scope of review since it is considering the ruling of the ALJ. How does this affect the appellant?

6. The ALJ applied a fairly "liberal" measure of damages and the court upholds the damages awarded. The ALJ awarded a $10,000 "civil penalty" which was the maximum that could be awarded for a first offense. *See A Note on Procedures, Remedies, Damages, and Attorney's Fees, infra.*

A Note on Post-Acquisition Discriminatory Conduct: Harassment and Denial of Services

In *Krueger v. Cuomo* the ALJ held that the owner's continued campaign of harassment—an interference with the tenant's right to quiet enjoyment of her tenancy—and his retaliation against the tenant for her filing a complaint each independently violated 42 U.S.C. § 3617, which makes it "unlawful to coerce, intimidate, threaten, or interfere with any person in the exercise or enjoyment of, or on account of his having exercised or enjoyed ... any right granted or protected by section ... 3604 ... of [Title 42]."

This fact pattern raises the issue of whether a violation may be based on conduct that occurs after the complainant's occupancy or purchase of a dwelling—i.e. on "post acquisition conduct." In *Krueger* the owner's conduct made the environment so intolerable that the plaintiff moved out—and in that sense the discriminatory conduct "made the housing unavailable" as set forth in 42 U.S.C. § 3604.

Does the Fair Housing Act apply to post-acquisition or post-occupancy conduct of an actor that is claimed to violate the protections accorded under the Act?

Halprin v. Prairie Single Family Homes of Dearborn Park Ass'n, 388 F.3d 327 (7th Cir. 2004), involved homeowners in a suburban subdivision who filed suit under the Fair Housing Act, 42 U.S.C. §§ 3604 and 3617. The principal defendant was the homeowners' association that managed the subdivision and provided various services to the homeowners. Other defendants were a corporation and its president that also provided services and was alleged to have acted in cahoots with the association in harassing the plaintiffs and some of the plaintiffs' neighbors.

Judge Posner's decision for the Seventh Circuit panel included the following:

> The complaint—our only source of facts, because the suit was dismissed for failure to state a claim—alleges the following: One of the plaintiffs is Jewish. The president of the association wrote "H-town property" on a wall of the plaintiffs' property, "H-town" being short for "Hymie Town," and he further vandalized the property by damaging trees and plants and cutting down strings of holiday lights. When the plaintiffs posted flyers offering a reward for identifying the vandal, the president destroyed or removed the flyers. To further thwart the plaintiffs' efforts to investigate the vandalizing of their property, the association destroyed minutes of its board meetings and erased a tape recording of a meeting at which the president had threatened to "make an example" of the plaintiffs. The defendants applied chemicals to the plaintiffs' yard against the plaintiffs' wishes and with adverse effects on their health and peace of mind and adopted rules restricting the plaintiffs' lawful use of their property. The entire campaign of harassment was caused or at least influenced by the religion of the Jewish plaintiff. Of course we do not vouch for any of these allegations, but for purposes of this appeal we must assume that they are true.
>
> A section of the Fair Housing Act makes it unlawful "to coerce, intimidate, threaten, or interfere with any person in the exercise or enjoyment of, or on account of his having exercised or enjoyed, or on account of his having aided or encouraged any other person in the exercise or enjoyment of, any right granted or protected by section 3603, 3604, 3605, or 3606 of this title." 42 U.S.C. § 3617. The only one of the enumerated sections that is possibly relevant here is section 3604, which makes it unlawful "(a) To refuse to sell or rent after the making of a bona fide offer, or to refuse to negotiate for the sale or rental of, or otherwise make unavailable or deny, a dwelling to any person because of race, color, religion, sex, familial status, or national origin," or "(b) To discriminate against any person in the terms, conditions, or privileges of sale or rental of a dwelling, or in the provision of services or facilities in connection therewith, because of race, color, religion, sex, familial status, or national origin." The language indicates concern with activities, such as redlining, that prevent people from acquiring property.... Our plaintiffs, however, are complaining not about being prevented from acquiring property but about being harassed by other property owners. So it is difficult to see how they can have been interfered with in the enjoyment of any right conferred on them by section 3604.
>
> As a purely semantic matter the statutory language might be stretched far enough to reach a case of "constructive eviction," which is one way to describe the present case (more precisely, "attempted constructive eviction"). If you burn down someone's house you make it "unavailable" to him, and "privileges of sale or rental" might conceivably be thought to include the privilege of inhabiting the premises. Acts of post-sale discrimination have been litigated successfully under the Act in two reported cases, *Trafficante v. Metropolitan Life Ins. Co.*, [409 U.S. 205 (1972)]; *Krueger v. Cuomo*, 115 F.3d 487 (7th Cir. 1997), but in neither was the Act's applicability to such discrimination discussed—apparently the issue hadn't been raised. In several other cases the Act has been held to forbid harassment amounting to constructive eviction by analogy to "constructive discharge," a form of dis-

crimination recognized in Title VII cases.... But in none of these cases did the court consider the difference in language between the two statutes. None of the five cases contains a *considered* holding on the scope of the Fair Housing Act in general or its application to a case like the present one in particular.

Title VII protects the job holder as well as the job applicant, so an employer who resorts to harassment to force an employee to quit is engaged in job discrimination within the meaning of the Act.... The Fair Housing Act contains no hint either in its language or its legislative history of a concern with anything but *access* to housing. Bernard Schwartz, *Statutory History of the United States: Civil Rights Part II* 1709-17, 1742-51, 1762, 1769 (1970); *Hearings before the Subcomm. on Housing & Urban Affairs of the S. Comm. on Banking & Currency on S. 1358, S. 2114, and S. 2280,* 90th Cong., 1st Sess. (1967), *passim;* 114 Cong. Rec. S2274 (daily ed. Feb. 6, 1968) (statement of Sen. Mondale). Behind the Act lay the widespread practice of refusing to sell or rent homes in desirable residential areas to members of minority groups. Since the focus was on their exclusion, the problem of how they were treated when they were included, that is, when they were allowed to own or rent homes in such areas, was not at the forefront of congressional thinking. *That* problem—the problem not of exclusion but of expulsion—would become acute only when the law forced unwanted associations that might provoke efforts at harassment, and so it would tend not to arise until the Act was enacted and enforced. There is nothing to suggest that Congress was trying to solve that future problem, an endeavor that would have required careful drafting in order to make sure that quarrels between neighbors did not become a routine basis for federal litigation.

Reference to legislative history is criticized when it is used to give a statute a reach that exceeds what its words suggest. Our use here is the opposite; it is to confirm that the words mean what they seem to mean.

So the plaintiffs have no claim under section 3604. And this might seem to doom their claim under section 3617 as well, because that section provides legal protection only against acts that interfere with one or more of the other sections of the Act that are referred to in section 3617, of which the only one even remotely relevant to this case is section 3604.

But this conclusion reckons without a regulation issued by the Department of Housing and Urban Development that in the name of section 3617 forbids among other things "threatening, intimidating or interfering with persons in their enjoyment of a dwelling because of the race, color, religion, sex, handicap, familial status, or national origin of such persons, or of visitors or associates of such persons." 24 C.F.R. § 100.400(c)(2). The regulation cuts section 3617 loose from section 3604, contrary to the language of section 3617. Interference with "enjoyment of a dwelling," forbidden by the regulation, is something that can take place after the dwelling has been acquired, though we know that section 3604 is not addressed to post-acquisition discrimination. The regulation may stray too far from section 3617 (which remember is tied, so far as bears on the issues in this case, to section 3604) to be valid, though *Gonzalez v. Lee County Housing Authority,* 161 F.3d 1290, 1304–05 and n. 43 (11th Cir. 1998), the only appellate decision to address the issue, holds that it is valid. But the defendants have not challenged the regulation's validity and so its possible invalidity has been forfeited as a ground upon which we might affirm the district court. The defendants quote the regulation, but only to observe, quite mistakenly, that it "simply reiterates the language of section 3617." The entire point is that it does not. If it did, the defendants would be home free.

The remaining question is whether the conduct alleged in the complaint amounts to "threatening, intimidating or interfering" within the meaning of the statute and the regulation. The defendants argue that it does not, because it is far less ominous, frightening, or hurtful than burning a cross in a neighbor's front yard or assaulting the neighbor physically. But that cannot be the test. There are other, less violent but still effective, methods by which a person can be driven from his home and thus "interfered" with in his enjoyment of it. See, e.g., *Krueger v. Cuomo, supra,* 115 F.3d at 490–91 (sexual harassment); *Regional Economic Community Action Program, Inc. v. City of Middletown,* 294 F.3d 35, 43–44 (2d Cir. 2002) (economic pressure); *Walker v. City of Lakewood,* 272 F.3d 1114, 1126–31 (9th Cir. 2001) (same). Of course, to repeat an earlier point, we do not want, and we do not think Congress wanted, to convert every quarrel among neighbors in which a racial or religious slur is hurled into a federal case. But what is alleged in this case (as in the factually similar case of *Ohana v. 180 Prospect Place Realty Corp.,* 996 F. Supp. 238, 239 (E.D.N.Y. 1998)) is a *pattern* of harassment, invidiously motivated, and, because backed by the homeowners' association to which the plaintiffs belong, a matter of the neighbors' ganging up on them. We are far from a simple quarrel between two neighbors or the isolated act of harassment committed by the landlord in *DiCenso v. Cisneros, supra,* 96 F.3d at 1006.

The case is affirmed in part, but for the reasons just explained it is reversed with regard to the section 3617 charge, which we direct the district court to reinstate along with the state law claims, which the court dismissed only because it mistakenly believed that the complaint failed to state a federal claim.

The Ninth Circuit has disagreed with the Halprin analysis and expressly held in *Committee Concerning Community Improvement v. City of Modesto, California*, 583 F.3d 690, 713–14 (9th Cir. 2009) that Title VIII extends to events after a dwelling is acquired. The court reasoned as follows:

For the reasons that follow, we conclude that the FHA reaches post-acquisition discrimination:

First, the statutory language does not preclude all post-acquisition claims. The statute prohibits discrimination "in the terms, conditions, or privileges of sale or rental of a dwelling, or in provision of services or facilities in connection therewith." 42 U.S.C. § 3604(b). The inclusion of the word "privileges" implicates continuing rights, such as the privilege of quiet enjoyment of the dwelling. While defendants argue that "the provision of services or facilities in connection therewith" refers only to services or facilities provided at the moment of acquisition in connection with the sale or the rental, this is hardly a necessary reading. There are few "services or facilities" provided at the moment of sale, but there are many "services or facilities" provided to the dwelling associated with the occupancy of the dwelling. Under this natural reading, the reach of the statute encompasses claims regarding services or facilities perceived to be wanting after the owner or tenant has acquired possession of the dwelling.

Second, the regulations implementing the FHA, promulgated by the Department of Housing and Urban Development, also support permitting post-acquisition claims. 24 C.F.R. § 100.65, entitled "Discrimination in terms, conditions and privileges and in services and facilities," provides, in pertinent part:

> (a) It shall be unlawful, because of race, color, religion, sex, handicap, familial status, or national origin, to impose different terms, conditions or privileges relating to the sale or rental of a dwelling or to deny or limit services or facilities in connection with the sale or rental of a dwelling.
>
> (b) Prohibited actions under this section include, but are not limited to....
>
> > (2) Failing or delaying maintenance or repairs of sale or rental dwellings because of race, color, religion, sex, handicap, familial status, or national origin ...
> >
> > (4) Limiting the use of privileges, services or facilities associated with a dwelling because of race, color, religion, sex, handicap, familial status, or national origin of an owner, tenant or a person associated with him or her.

The sections prohibiting "[f]ailing or delaying maintenance or repairs of sale or rental dwellings" and "[l]imiting the use of privileges, services or facilities associated with a dwelling" appear to embrace claims about problems arising after the tenant or owner has acquired the property. In common parlance, issues relating to "maintenance or repairs" or "services or facilities associated with a dwelling" tend to be issues arising after the tenant or owner has come into possession of the dwelling and sought out maintenance, repair, or services. *See, e.g.,* [*Landesman v. Keys Condo. Owners Ass'n,* No. C 04-2685 PJH, 2004 WL 2370638 (N.D. Cal. Oct. 19, 2004), aff'd, 125 Fed. Appx. 146 (9th Cir. Mar. 30, 2005)—Eds.] (discussing regulation in the context of challenge to condominium association rules placing restrictions on use of the swimming pool by children).

Additionally, limiting the FHA to claims brought at the point of acquisition would limit the act from reaching a whole host of situations that, while perhaps not amounting to constructive eviction, would constitute discrimination in the enjoyment of residence in a dwelling or in the provision of services associated with that dwelling. Under so limited a reading of the statute ...

> it would not violate § 3604(b) for a condominium owners' association to prevent a disabled person from using the laundry facilities or for a landlord to refuse to provide maintenance to his Hispanic tenants. Similarly, it would not violate § 3604(b) for a landlord to sexually harass a tenant or to raise the rent of only Jewish tenants. It would not violate § 3604(c) for a landlord to use racial slurs to or about existing tenants or to spray-paint such a slur on an occupant's door. Nor would it violate § 3604(c) for a homeowners association to print up flyers denigrating a particular resident due to her religious faith and post them throughout the neighborhood. All of these behaviors would be beyond the law's purview solely because of when they occurred.

Rigel Oliveri, *Is Acquisition Everything? Protecting the Rights of Occupants Under the Fair Housing Act,* 43 Harv. C.R.-C.L. Rev. 1, 32–33 (2008) (asserting that pre-*Halprin* case law found post-acquisition claims under § 3604 permissible, criticizing the *Halprin* decision, and proposing a framework that "focuses less on the point of acquisition and more on the identity of the defendant and the relationship between the parties"). *See also* [*Bloch v. Frischholz,* No. 06-3376, 2009 WL 601419 (7th Cir. Jan. 16, 2009).] (Wood, J., dissenting) (noting that permitting post-acquisition claims "will ensure that member of protected groups

> do not win the battle (to purchase or rent housing) but lose the war (to live in their new home free from invidious discrimination)").
>
> In our view, the [Fair Housing Act] does apply to post-acquisition discrimination, and the District Court erred in deciding otherwise....

Another case has raised even more poignantly the post-acquisition problem which can only occur after occupancy—the refusal to provide services, such as water and sewer. Kennedy v. City of Zanesville, *Ohio*, 505 F. Supp. 2d 456, 463 (S.D. Ohio 2007) (Zanesville). Excerpts from the *Zanesville follow:*

Sixty-eight individual plaintiffs, the Fair Housing Advocates Association ("FHAA"), and the Ohio Civil Rights Commission ("OCRC") (collectively, "Plaintiffs"), filed this civil rights action against the City of Zanesville ("City"), Muskingum County ("County"), Washington Township ("Township") and individual elected officials from the County and Township, (collectively, "Defendants"). Plaintiffs claim that Defendants' had a policy, pattern, and practice of denying public water service to the individual Plaintiffs during the last fifty years because they are African-American and/or because they reside in a predominantly African-American neighborhood.

The individual Plaintiffs lived, at various times, in the Coal Run neighborhood located within the County and Township, and just outside the Zanesville city limits. The neighborhood includes approximately twenty-five homes, and historically the residents of Coal Run have been African-American. Currently, approximately eighty-five percent of the Coal Run neighborhood residents are African-American, while the County and Township both are over ninety-five percent white. Contaminated by years of mining in the area, the ground water in the Coal Run neighborhood is not safe for residential purposes. Prior to receiving public water service in 2004, Plaintiffs, therefore, used wells, hauled water, had water delivered to their homes, and even collected rain water and melted snow in order to have safe, usable water for drinking, cooking, and bathing.

A. The Facts Presented by Plaintiffs

According to Plaintiffs, the residents of Coal Run suffered under a decades-long discriminatory government policy of refusing to provide clean water to their neighborhood due to its racial makeup. Plaintiffs claim that Coal Run was surrounded by waterlines going to predominately white areas and Plaintiffs, despite repeated requests, were not permitted to connect to the adjacent lines. Plaintiffs contend that the City, County, and Township are all responsible for the waterlines that run through the County, and even though Defendants had the power and ability to bring water to Coal Run, they engaged in three broad forms of discrimination to deny the neighborhood water. First, Plaintiffs claim that Defendants regularly passed over the Coal Run neighborhood in favor of funding and constructing waterlines for, often more distant, white areas. Second, Plaintiffs state that Defendants rejected or disregarded the numerous requests for waterlines to be extended into Coal Run, while at the same time pursuing projects in response to requests from white areas. Third, Plaintiffs claim that Defendants denied individual requests from Coal Run residents to connect to an existing line—the Old Adamsville Road line—while letting white homes connect.

1. Defendants' General Roles in Providing Water to Coal Run

Plaintiffs assert that all Defendants had a responsibility to provide water to Coal Run residents. First, Plaintiffs state that the City supplied water in two ways: (1) since the 1930s, the City regularly constructed water projects in various areas adjoining the City; and (2) from

1956 until 2004, the City operated and controlled the Old Adamsville Road line, which served white residences on Adamsville Road and down Langan Lane, both of which border the Coal Run neighborhood. Plaintiffs state that, for the first forty-two years of the Adamsville line's existence, the City partnered with the Washington Rural Water Authority ("WRWA") in the operation of the line, and obtained exclusive control over it in 1998 when WRWA dissolved.

Second, Plaintiffs assert that the County was also responsible for providing residential water services. Plaintiffs state that in 1967, the County created the East Muskingum Water Authority ("EMWA") as an independent water authority, and the EMWA constructed water projects throughout its jurisdiction over the following thirty-six years. The County advocated for water services for various predominantly white areas since at least 1978, and the County began funding and constructing water projects throughout the County in 1990. In 2000, the County acquired a portion of the EMWA and began increasing efforts to bring water to County residents. Plaintiffs assert that in 2003, the County acquired the EMWA in its entirety and, by doing so, expressly assumed the EMWA's liabilities as part of the acquisition.

Finally, Plaintiffs state that Washington Township encompasses the Coal Run area. Plaintiffs claim that, starting in approximately 1995, the Township began making substantial efforts, including through legislation and advocacy, to obtain water for some of the predominantly white areas of the Township, while at the same time ignoring Plaintiffs' requests.

After Plaintiffs filed their discrimination charges with the Ohio Civil Rights Commission and their federal suit alleging, inter alia, a violation of Title VIII the authorities ran water lines to plaintiffs' community. Nevertheless, Plaintiffs sought damages "for fifty years of monetary loss, humiliation, and deprivation of civil rights suffered as a result of the local governments' discriminatory actions and to ensure that no other residents are denied water because of their race." Relman and Dane website: http://www.relmanlaw.com/cases.html (last visited Feb. 8, 2010.)

After ruling upon a number of procedural issues, the court found that material issues of fact existed warranting a trial. The case went to trial before a jury which, on July 10, 2008, returned a verdict in favor of Plaintiffs totaling nearly $11 million. *Kennedy v. City of Zanesville*, Ohio, 505 F. Supp. 2d 456 (S.D. Ohio 2007), 2008 WL 2714071 verdict, agreement and settlement July 10, 2008). On March 5, 2009, it was reported that the case had been settled. http://www.dispatch.com/live/content/local_news/stories/2009/03/05/azanes.html (last visited Feb. 26 2010.) Therefore, no appeal will be taken. Thus, the issue of after-acquired discriminatory conduct will await another case on another day.

Notes and Questions

1. The Fifth Circuit, purporting to follow Halprin, has said that § 3604(b) dealing with discrimination "in the terms, conditions, or privileges of sale or rental of a dwelling, or in the provision of services or facilities in connection therewith" applies only to discrimination that "precludes" the sale or rental of housing. *Cox v. City of Dallas*, 430 F.3d 734 (5th Cir. 2005), *cert. denied*, 547 U.S. 1130 (2006).

2. For a discussion of the post-acquisition question see Robert G. Schwemm, Cox, Halprin *and Discriminatory Municipal Services Under the Fair Housing Act*, 41 Ind. L. Rev. 717 (2008); and Aric Short, *Post-Acquisition Harassment and the Scope of the Fair Housing Act*, 58 Ala. L. Rev. 203 (2006).

5. Discriminatory Mortgage Lending and Mortgage Redlining

Latimore v. Citibank, F.S.B.

United States District Court
979 F. Supp. 662 (N.D. Ill. 1997),
aff'd, 151 F.3d 712 (7th Cir. 1998)

MEMORANDUM OPINION AND ORDER

BUCKLO, District Judge.

The plaintiff, Helen Latimore, sued Citibank, F.S.B. ("Citibank") and two of its employees, Marcia Lundberg and Ed Kernbauer, for racial discrimination in denying a mortgage loan application. The defendants have moved for summary judgment. For the following reasons, the motion is granted.

I.

On August 16, 1993, Ms. Latimore, an African-American, submitted an application for a mortgage loan to Citibank. She sought $51,000, using her residence at 6150 South Ingleside, Chicago, Illinois as collateral. The racial population of Ms. Latimore's neighborhood was and is over 90 percent African-American. Citibank assigned Mr. Kernbauer, its in-house appraiser, to prepare an appraisal of [Ms.—Eds.] Latimore's house. On August 26, 1993, Mr. Kernbauer prepared an appraisal report valuing the plaintiff's property at $45,000, yielding a loan-to-value ratio of 113 percent. For the type of loan Ms. Latimore was seeking, Citibank's lending criteria required a loan-to-value ratio of, at most, 75 percent.

There followed several telephone conversations between the plaintiff and Ms. Lundberg, the Citibank's account executive responsible for Ms. Latimore's application. Ms. Lundberg informed the plaintiff that the appraisal value of her property would not support the loan. Upon learning that Ms. Latimore had higher appraisals of her home, Ms. Lundberg asked that they be forwarded. Ms. Lundberg received an appraisal report, dated October 8, 1992 and reflecting a value of $82,000 ("October 1992 appraisal"), and submitted it, along with Mr. Kernbauer's appraisal, to the Citibank's Appraisal Review Department.

Having reviewed Ms. Latimore's file, the Appraisal Review Department concluded that no change was warranted to Mr. Kernbauer's initial appraisal of $45,000. After informing Ms. Latimore of that decision, Ms. Lundberg submitted the plaintiff's application to Underwriting, which denied the loan. As an African-American, Ms. Latimore was entitled to another level of review by the Community Reinvestment Act ("CRA") Committee. The CRA Committee examined the plaintiff's file and concluded that the denial of her loan application was consistent with the Citibank's underwriting criteria. Citibank mailed an adverse action notice to Ms. Latimore on October 12, 1993. On January 23, 1995, Ms. Latimore filed suit.

In Counts I through IV, Ms. Latimore alleges that the defendants discriminated against her on the basis of her race or the racial composition of her neighborhood by denying her a loan, in violation of Sections 1981 and 1982 of the Civil Rights Act, 42 U.S.C. §§ 1981, 1982, the Fair Housing Act ("FHA"), 42 U.S.C. § 3605, and the Equal Credit Opportunity Act ("ECOA"). 15 U.S.C. § 1691(a)(1). In Count V, Ms. Latimore alleges a violation of the Illinois Consumer Fraud and Deceptive Business Practices Act ("Illinois Consumer Fraud Act"). 815 ILCS 505/1 *et seq.* (1993). The defendants move for summary judgment.

II.

To prevail on a claim under Sections 1981[4] and 1982,[5] the plaintiff must prove intentional discrimination by the defendants. In contrast, under the FHA[6] and the ECOA,[7] the plaintiff "must show that 'race was a motivating consideration in the [defendants'] decision' not to make the loan."

Thus, in a case where the plaintiff alleges that her loan application was discriminatorily denied, she must prove (1) that she is a member of a protected class, (2) that she applied for and was qualified for a loan, (3) that the loan was rejected despite her qualifications, and (4) that the defendants continued to approve loans for applicants with qualifications similar to those of the plaintiff.[8]

There is no dispute that Ms. Latimore, an African-American, satisfies element one. The remaining elements are disputed. The defendants maintain that, although Ms. Latimore's credit history met the Citibank's underwriting guidelines, she was ultimately not qualified for a loan because she did not satisfy the Citibank's loan-to-value ratio of, at most, 75 percent. Ms. Latimore maintains that, due to race considerations, Mr. Kernbauer's appraisal did not reflect her home's true value, and that Ms. Lundberg assisted white applicants but not African-Americans during the appraisal review process.

To withstand summary judgment, Ms. Latimore must provide evidence from which a reasonable factfinder could conclude that she meets the elements of the *prima facie* case. Because the last three elements are intertwined, Ms. Latimore's task is essentially to show that the defendants treated her materially differently than similarly situated white loan applicants or loan applicants from non-minority neighborhoods.

Mr. Kernbauer's Appraisal

Mr. Kernbauer appraised Ms. Latimore's home at $45,000. Ms. Latimore offers the October 1992 appraisal of $82,000, which she forwarded to Ms. Lundberg; her expert's "reconstructive" appraisal of $62,000; and a 1994 appraisal of $79,000, performed in connection with the plaintiff's receipt of a mortgage loan from the Household Bank. A townhouse similar to Ms. Latimore's, but with four additional rooms, sold for $50,000 several months after Mr. Kernbauer's appraisal.

Although Ms. Latimore's expert, Russell Hume, selected different comparable sales and made different adjustments to those sales than Mr. Kernbauer, Mr. Hume admitted

4. 42 U.S.C. § 1981(a) provides, in part, that "[a]ll persons within the jurisdiction of the United States shall have the same right in every State and Territory to make and enforce contracts."

5. 42 U.S.C. § 1982 provides that "[a]ll citizens of the United States shall have the same right, in every State and Territory, as is enjoyed by white citizens thereof to inherit, purchase, lease, sell, hold, and convey real and personal property."

6. This statute makes it "unlawful for any person or other entity whose business includes engaging in residential real estate-related transactions to discriminate against any person in making available such a transaction, or in the terms or conditions of such a transaction, because of race [or] color." 42 U.S.C. § 3605(a).

7. This statute makes it "unlawful for any creditor to discriminate against any applicant, with respect to any aspect of a credit transaction ... on the basis of race [or] color." 15 U.S.C. § 1691(a)(1). FHA and ECOA encompass "disparate impact"/"discriminatory effect" claims, as well as "discriminatory intent" claims. The former arise "when a facially neutral policy or action has an unequal impact on different subgroups in the housing market."

8. If the plaintiff makes out a *prima facie* case, the burden of production shifts to the defendant to articulate a non-discriminatory reason for declining the loan application. If the defendant satisfies his burden, the plaintiff must prove that the defendant's reasons are not the true reasons for the decision, but a pretext for discrimination.

that the selection of comparable sales is an art, not a science, that adjustments are judgment-driven, and that he could support the adjustments Mr. Kernbauer made. The question, however, is whether there is evidence from which a reasonable factfinder could conclude that Mr. Kernbauer was inconsistent in his appraisal methods depending on "the race or neighborhood of the homeowners."

It is undisputed that in 1993, Mr. Kernbauer's appraisals supported the loan amounts of other African-American residents of Ms. Latimore's Woodlawn neighborhood. In addition, John March, Citibank's then Chief Community Reinvestment Act Underwriter for U.S. Operations, affirms that in 1993, Mr. Kernbauer appraised the property of 69 African-American applicants. Only three of those applications, including the plaintiff's, were declined because of the appraised value of the property.

Ms. Latimore argues that under [*Watson v. Pathway Financial*, 702 F. Supp. 186 (N.D. Ill. 1988)—Eds.], *Steptoe v. Savings of America*, 800 F. Supp. 1542 (N.D. Ohio 1992), and *Old West End Ass'n v. Buckeye Fed. Sav. & Loan*, 675 F. Supp. 1100 (N.D. Ohio 1987), she has presented a triable case. In *Watson*, the defendant claimed that he rejected the plaintiffs' application because they had a history of late payments. The plaintiffs countered with evidence that "other applicants with late payments did receive loans from [the defendant]." The court held that, for the purposes of the FHA, the plaintiffs made out a *prima facie* case, because they created a factual issue as to whether they were qualified for the loans and whether the defendant approved the loan applications of persons with similar qualifications. In the present case there is no evidence that Mr. Kernbauer appraised Ms. Latimore's house using a different method than similarly situated houses owned by non-minorities or houses in non-minority neighborhoods. There is likewise no evidence that his appraisals consistently caused denials of loans to minorities or persons residing in minority neighborhoods, while resulting in approvals for non-minorities or people in non-minority neighborhoods.

Ms. Latimore's reliance on *Old West End Ass'n* and *Steptoe* is based on the courts' holdings that a plaintiff claiming racial discrimination in appraisal practices under the FHA makes out a *prima facie* case by showing that (1) the property was in a minority neighborhood, (2) an application for a loan secured by this property was made, (3) an independent appraisal concluded that the value of the property was sufficient to secure the loan, (4) the applicant was otherwise credit worthy, and (5) the loan application was rejected. However, this particular formulation of the *prima facie* case has not been used anywhere besides the Northern District of Ohio. In addition, both cases involved materially different facts.

In *Old West End Ass'n,* the plaintiffs sought to sell a house in a minority neighborhood. They agreed with the buyers on a purchase price of $78,500. The firm that prepared mortgage applications ordered an appraisal, which valued the house at the sale price and noted that the predominant value of the properties in the area was $70,000. The firm forwarded the application, along with the appraisal, to the lender. The lender denied the buyers' loan application for $78,500. The court concluded that the plaintiffs made out a *prima facie* case of an FHA violation because there was evidence that defendant's alleged reason for denial was untrue as well as evidence that the lender's underwriting practices differed depending upon the racial composition of the neighborhood.

In *Steptoe*, the minority plaintiffs sought to buy a house in a racially mixed neighborhood. The house they found was advertised at $129,900, but the sellers agreed to accept $115,000. The plaintiffs applied for a loan to the defendant, who ordered an appraisal. The defendant's staff appraiser concluded that the house was worth $115,000. The defendant's chief appraiser disagreed and ordered a new appraisal, which was lower and on the basis of which the plaintiffs' application for a $103,500 loan was denied. The *Steptoe* court found an inference of racially motivated behavior from the facts that, despite the downward revision of the appraisal, the defendant continued to carry the property on its comparable sales card as valued at $115,000, and the chief appraiser failed to follow the defendant's policies regarding reappraisals. Moreover, the plaintiff's expert testified that the defendant's second appraisal was defective, and the plaintiffs proffered statistical evidence supporting their theory that the defendant's lending practices resulted in a racially discriminatory effect in the neighborhood in which the plaintiffs sought to reside.

In the present case, by contrast, there is no evidence of the sort present in *Old West End Ass'n* or *Steptoe*, or any other evidence which would allow a reasonable factfinder to conclude that Mr. Kernbauer appraised Ms. Latimore's house as he did because of her race or the racial composition of her neighborhood. The uncontradicted evidence shows that his appraisals consistently supported mortgage loans for other African-Americans and in the same neighborhood. A meaningful *prima facie* case must bear a logical relationship to the illegal discrimination for which it establishes a legally mandatory, rebuttable presumption. It must, in short, allow a jury to infer a violation. Here, the *prima facie* case must allow a factfinder to infer that the defendants acted because of racial considerations.

Ms. Lundberg & the Appraisal Review Process

Ms. Latimore contends that, during the appraisal review process, Citibank treated her differently than similarly situated white applicants. In support of this contention, Ms. Latimore offers the following undisputed evidence. An appraisal of a home of one of Ms. Lundberg's white clients done during 1993 was too low to support a loan. Ms. Lundberg and the applicant's [real estate agent] discussed getting "comparables" for the review process. The applicant provided such "comparables" and Ms. Lundberg forwarded them to Gary Schlittler of the Citibank's Appraisal Review Department. Mr. Schlittler sent the "comparables" to the appraiser. The appraiser refused to revise the appraisal and the client's loan application was therefore denied. Ms. Latimore provides evidence that other Citibank's account executives were able to assist their white clients in increasing their appraisals on the basis of additional "comparables."

Ms. Latimore argues that Ms. Lundberg treated her differently than the white applicant because she never specifically requested "comparables." However, Ms. Lundberg's purpose for requesting the October 1992 appraisal was to obtain "comparables" and, undisputedly, such was her practice in cases similar to Ms. Latimore's. The plaintiff does not argue that she did not know or understand that a real estate appraisal is based on "comparables." Ms. Latimore offers no evidence that Ms. Lundberg asked her white client for "comparables" in addition to, or instead of, an available appraisal. Significantly, when the "comparables" provided by Ms. Lundberg's white client failed to result in an upward reevaluation of the original appraisal, Ms. Lundberg did not request additional "comparables." When Ms. Latimore insists that Ms. Lundberg should have informed her that her appraisal's "comparables" were unacceptable,[17] she is asking for an additional step which Ms. Lundberg did not take with respect to a similarly situated white client.

Ms. Latimore has not presented sufficient evidence for a reasonable factfinder to conclude that Ms. Lundberg treated the plaintiff differently than the white loan applicants by

17. Stating that Mr. Kernbauer's comparables were 6 blocks away, while those in Ms. Latimore's October 1992 appraisal were further than 13 blocks away from the plaintiff's residence, Mr. Schlittler wrote in Ms. Latimore's file that absent any other data, no change of Mr. Kernbauer's appraisal was warranted.

not specifically requesting additional "comparables" to challenge Mr. Kernbauer's appraisal. Therefore, summary judgment is granted as to Ms. Lundberg on Counts I through IV. Ms. Latimore does not claim that any other agents of Citibank acted discriminatorily towards her. Since Citibank can only act through its agents, summary judgment is granted as to Citibank on Counts I through IV.... For the reasons stated above, defendants' motion for summary judgment is granted.

Notes and Questions

1. A major part of Ms. Latimore's claim was that the appraiser used differential appraisal standards that undervalued the plaintiff's home because it was located in a minority neighborhood. Although this claim could not be sustained on the facts shown, the issue can be troublesome. If location of the property is a legitimate factor that may be considered in making an appraisal, how can location be differentiated from race when the location can be identified by race? *See* 42 U.S.C. § 3605(c) as amended by the 1988 amendments which contains an "appraisal exemption" and provides that appraisers may "take into consideration factors other than" race and other prohibited factors. Does this solve the problem?

2. David Listokin and Stephen Casey in their book, Mortgage Lending and Race 9–11 (1980) point out aspects of racial bias in financing:

> Two forms of racial bias, neighborhood and individual, are cited as possibly contributing to the urban financing problem for both may be factors and it is difficult to dissociate the neighborhood versus individual influence. The black homebuyer will usually purchase, rehabilitate, or refinance a property in a black neighborhood. The financing difficulty encountered, a difficulty which is a distinct feature of the current urban financing dilemma, may result from lender discrimination against the minority homebuyer himself, or the surrounding neighborhood, or a combination of the two.

The book continues by discussing two models of behavior:

> The economic and eco-race models do not attempt to explain all possible causes of the urban financing problem but recognize the multidimensional catalysts which shape the credit shortfall. The two models focus on two major facets of the problem—the influence of economic and racial criteria. The economic model stresses the former's influence; financial institutions are guided by neutral economic forces. Lenders, the strongest proponents of this model, admit there are distinctions in the availability of credit by neighborhood but argue that these differentiations are due to market forces. Urban areas may receive few loans because demand is weak—a function of older resident age, lower income, and other characteristics. Urban applicants, properties and neighborhoods may additionally pose a greater economic risk ... for such reasons as lower resident affluence, heightened property obsolescence and marginal neighborhood public utilities. The eco-race model admits that lenders are influenced by economic considerations, but stresses the addition of racial discriminatory policies against minority areas and individuals.

3. A path-breaking four-part study tracked lending patterns of Atlanta lenders for home purchase and home improvement from 1981 through 1986 showed that discrimination is a major problem for blacks seeking home loan funds. Bill Dedman, *The Color of Money*, Atlanta J.-Constitution, May 1, 1988, through May 4, 1988.

The study found (1) that white borrowers received five times as many home loans as blacks with the same income and that the disparity had been widening each year; (2) because of difficulties of getting loans from banks and savings and loan companies, blacks more frequently went to unregulated mortgage companies, finance companies, and other sources and secured loans at much higher interest rates; (3) appraisers, mostly white, devalued black-owned homes, causing them to be valued at less than the purchase price with the consequence that the buyers' loan applications would be rejected; and (4) that the major lenders' denial of redlining and offer of economic reasons for the disparities were particularly suspect in face of federal records that a black-owned Atlanta bank which lent almost exclusively to blacks in black neighborhoods had a lower real estate default rate than the six largest banks in the city and the lowest default rate on real estate of any bank its size in the United States in 1986.

4. The Home Mortgage Disclosure Act of 1975, 12 U.S.C. §2801-2810 (popularly called "HMDA") and the Community Reinvestment Act of 1977, 12 U.S.C. §2901-2906 (popularly called "CRA") have imposed data keeping and disclosure obligations on financial institutions that make possible the kind of study done by the Atlanta Journal-Constitution. What effect, if any, can be given to the 1988 amendments' imposition of duties on federal agencies having regulatory or supervisory authority over financial institutions to "affirmatively further" fair housing? *See* 42 U.S.C. §3608(d).

The two statutes cited do not have very effective, if any, adequate enforcement mechanisms. The major effect of the acts may be that community advocates and activists can analyze the HMDA data and disseminate information to pressure the financial institutions in the public forum. Also under CRA, advocates can resist a financial institution's merger, expansion, and opening of new branches since a financial institution's seeking a new "deposit facility" triggers CRA scrutiny. *See* Penny Loeb et al., *The New Redlining*, U.S. News & World Rep., Apr. 17, 1995, at 51, *available at* 1995 WL 3113665 (discussing the prevalence of lending and insurance redlining based on an extensive study and pointing out that under CRA regulators between 1977 and 1995 had denied only 20 of 77,000 bank requests to expand or merge).

For further discussion of these issues, see Keith N. Hylton & Vincent D. Rougeau, *Lending Discrimination: Economic Theory, Econometric Evidence and the Community Reinvestment Act*, 85 Geo. L.J. 237 (1996) and Anthony D. Taibi, *Banking, Finance, and Community Economic Empowerment: Structural Economic Theory, Procedural Rights, and Substantive Racial Justice*, 107 Harv. L. Rev. 1463 (1994).

5. In 1992, the Federal Reserve Bank of Boston completed a study, familiarly termed the "Boston Fed Study." The study focused on mortgage discrimination and found that "blacks were … turned down almost sixty percent more often than similarly qualified whites." Alicia H. Munnell *et al.*, *Mortgage Lending in Boston: Interpreting the HMDA Data* 2 (Federal Reserve Bank of Boston, Working Paper No. 92-7, 1992). The Boston Fed Study showed that minorities receive fewer loans because of racial discrimination. However, the results are controversial because of debate about the methods the researchers used. *See* Peter P. Swire, *The Persistent Problem of Lending Discrimination: A Law and Economics Analysis*, 73 Tex. L. Rev. 787, 789 (1995).

6. Discussions of research on discriminatory mortgage lending patterns and practices are extensive. (a) For a fairly broad perspective, see Organizing Access to Capital: Advocacy and Democratization of Financial Solutions (Gregory D. Squires ed. 2003) and Symposium: *The Community Reinvestment Act: Still Relevant at 30?*, 53 N.Y.U. L. Rev. (2008–2009). *See also* Pierre Clavel, *From Redlining to Reinvestment: Community Responses to Urban Disinvestment*, Int'l J. Urb. & Regional Res., 1997, at 167; Gregory D. Squires & William Velez, *Neighborhood Racial Composition and Mort-*

gage Lending: City and Suburban Differences, 9 J. URB. AFF. 217 (1987) (containing a list of references).

(b) For a critical and specific look into the effectiveness of governmental regulatory practices concerning mortgage discrimination, see Michael S. Little, *A Citizen's Guide to Attacking Mortgage Discrimination: The Lack of Judicial Relief*, 15 B.C. THIRD WORLD L.J. 323 (1995) and Willy E. Rice, *Race, Gender, "Redlining," and the Discriminating Access to Loans, Credit, and Insurance: A Historical and Empirical Analysis of Consumers Who Sued Lenders and Insurers in Federal and State Courts, 1950–1995*, 33 SAN DIEGO L. REV. 583 (1996).

(c) For a case study of one institution, see Andrew Holmes & Paul Horvitz, *Lending Discrimination Claims and the Issue of Redlining: Analysis of Lending Patterns for an Individual Institution*, 10 J. FORENSIC ECON. 51 (Jan. 1, 1997).

(d) For two city-specific examinations, see THOMAS W. POGGE ET AL., PARTNERS IN NEED: A FOUR YEAR ANALYSIS OF RESIDENTIAL LENDING IN CHICAGO AND ITS SUBURBS (1986) (pamphlet published by the Woodstock Institute) and Steven R. Holloway, *Exploring the Neighborhood Contingency of Race Discrimination in Mortgage Lending in Columbus, Ohio*, 88 ANNALS OF ASS'N AM. GEOGRAPHERS 252 (1998).

(e) Other articles of interest on this subject include Kathleen E. Keest, *Residential Mortgage Litigation: Credit Discrimination*, 989 PLI/Corp. 569 (Apr. 1997); Stanley D. Longhofer, *Discrimination in Mortgage Lending: What Have We Learned?*, 1996 ECON. COMMENT. 5 (Quarter 4 1996) (publication of the Cleveland Federal Reserve Bank discussing the broad problem of mortgage discrimination based on race), *available at* http://www.clevelandfed.org/Research/Commentary/1996/081596.htm; David E. Runck, *An Analysis of the Community Development Banking and Financial Institutions Act and the Problem of "Rational Redlining" Facing Low-Income Communities*, 15 Ann. Rev. Banking L. 517 (1996) (discussing problems of securing mortgages); Gregory D. Squires, *Policies of Prejudice: Risky Encounters With the Property Insurance Business,* 39 CHALLENGE 45–50 (No. 4, July/Aug. 1996) (examining the slow recognition of mortgage discrimination).

7. A broad analysis of the relationship between access to property ownership and the nation's interest in liberty and citizenship is set forth in Phyliss Craig-Taylor, *To Be Free: Liberty, Citizenship, Property, and Race,* 14 HARV. BLACKLETTER L. J. 45 (1998). Professor Craig-Taylor argues, inter alia, that discrimination in mortgage lending undercuts aspects of citizenship such that "anti-discrimination laws in the areas of lending and real estate are necessary to the protection of citizen liberty and independence." *Id.* at 87.

8. Although far from resolved, the litigation filed in Federal Court by the City of Baltimore against Wells Fargo Bank alleges, based in part on allegations from former employees of Wells Fargo, that the bank had a program that pushed predatory loans on hapless buyers that, inter alia, led to rampant foreclosures and consequent damages to the City of Baltimore, including decreased property tax revenues, increased police and fire department costs, and the cost of boarding up and managing vacant properties. Allegations include claims that Wells Fargo loan officers sought blacks in Baltimore to market them high-interest subprime mortgages and targeted black churches. These alleged practices are claimed to violate the Fair Housing Act. *See Mayor and City Council of Baltimore v. Wells Fargo Bank, N.A.*, 631 F. Supp. 2d 702 (D. Md. 2009). (city is entitled to discovery and Bank's motion to dismiss denied). *See* Michael Powell, *Bank Accused of Pushing Mortgage Deals on Blacks*, N.Y. TIMES, June 6, 2009, *available at* http://www.nytimes.com/2009/06/07/us/07baltimore.html (last visited Feb. 16, 2010). The District Court dismissed the action. *Mayor and City Council of Baltimore v. Wells Fargo Bank, N.A.*, 677 F. Supp. 2d

847 (D. Md. 2010) (action dismissed with leave to plaintiffs to file an amended complaint by February 3, 2010). *See also* Jonathan Stempel, *Wells Fargo Mortgage Case in Baltimore Dismissed*, Reuters, Jan. 7, 2010, *available at* http://www.reuters.com/article/idUSN07 19660920100107 (last visited Feb. 16, 2010).

A Note on the "Exploitation" Theory

In an action filed under Section 1982, plaintiffs in *Clark v. Universal Builders, Inc.*, 501 F.2d 324 (7th Cir.), *cert. denied*, 419 U.S. 1070 (1974), advanced, *inter alia*, an "exploitation theory," asserting that defendants took advantage of racial discrimination which they did not necessarily create. The exploitation theory was premised on the existence of "dual markets" in the Chicago housing market area—one for blacks and one for whites—as a result of intense racial discrimination and a supply of housing in the black market that was insufficient to meet the demand. The defendants were charged with having entered into the black housing market and with building and selling homes (a) far in excess of their fair market value; (b) far in excess of the prices which whites paid for comparable homes in the white market; and (c) on more onerous terms than similarly situated whites encountered.

The district court denied defendants' motion to dismiss the complaint. *Contract Buyers League v. F & F Investment*, 300 F. Supp. 210 (N.D. Ill. 1969), *aff'd on other grounds*, 420 F.2d 1191 (7th Cir.), *cert. denied*, 400 U.S. 821 (1970). The case then went before a different district court judge who rejected the exploitation theory and held that plaintiffs could prevail only if they proved the "traditional theory" of discrimination—that *defendants* refused to sell to black buyers or that *defendants* sold the same or similar housing to whites for more favorable prices or terms. The district court granted defendants' motion for a directed verdict. Plaintiffs appealed.

On this appeal, the court of appeals confronted the issue of whether Section 1982 would sustain the exploitation theory. The court said that,

> Contrary to the trial court's stance [in the second hearing], the shortage of housing here was triggered not by an economic phenomenon but by a pattern of discrimination that has no place in our society. Accordingly, neither prices nor profits—whether derived through well-intentioned, good-faith efforts or predatory and unethical practices—may reflect or perpetuate discrimination against black citizens. We agree with Judge Will's statement [after the first hearing] that "there cannot in this country be markets or profits based on the color of a man's skin.

Clark v. Universal Builders, Inc., 501 F.2d at 332.

The court remanded for a new trial. On remand, after a sixteen-day nonjury trial the district court found that plaintiffs had failed to meet their burden of proof and entered judgment for the defendants. The Seventh Circuit affirmed. *Clark v. Universal Builders, Inc.*, 706 F.2d 204 (7th Cir. 1983).

Exactly what happened to the promise of the exploitation theory? The 1974 decision sustaining the exploitation theory was a limited one in view of the procedural posture of the case. The district court had granted defendants' motion for a directed verdict in a case tried before a jury. On appeal the court of appeals asked "whether the evidence, both the admitted evidence and erroneously excluded evidence, when viewed in the light most favorable to plaintiffs, together with all inferences that may be reasonably drawn there from, is such that it can be found that plaintiffs have made out a *prima facie* case." 501 F.2d at 328.

In a trial on the merits (before the judge or to a jury), the court does not take such a view of the evidence, but asks whether the plaintiffs have sustained their allegation "by a preponderance of the evidence." With respect to proof the role of the court of appeals is limited. Findings of fact will be overturned, as the court stated in *Clark,* only if they are "clearly erroneous"—the appellate court is left with a "definite and firm conviction that a mistake has been committed." 706 F.2d at 206.

The court of appeals recognized that the 1974 *Clark* opinion had established the governing law which gave plaintiffs two alternate approaches: (1) the traditional theory—that defendants treated black persons less favorably than it treated similarly situated white persons; and (2) the exploitation theory—that defendant took advantage of racial dual markets by demanding unreasonable terms and prices of black buyers. As to the traditional theory, the court sustained district court findings that the homes plaintiffs sought to compare were not comparable and thus that theory was not sustained.

As to the exploitation theory, the trial court credited much of plaintiffs' testimony and evidence as proving that during the relevant period the black population was increasing, thus creating greater demands for housing, and that there was a "pent-up" demand for single-family homes due to the historical pattern of racial discrimination in the Chicago housing market. But the court of appeals agreed with the district court that the plaintiffs' proof did not establish how the defendant could have obtained the market power to have carried out the exploitation claimed. Defendants' market share was not sufficient, according to the court, to show market dominance because of competition as well as the existence of the rental and existing housing markets. Thus the court held that plaintiffs had not established how defendants could have charged "unreasonable" prices in face of a housing market which showed "no indicia of being monopolized or uncompetitive." 706 F.2d at 211.

Notes and Questions

1. For further analysis of the contract buyers process see Beryl Satter, Family Properties: Race, Real Estate, and the Exploitation of Black Urban America (2009).

It was established in *Clark* that "relatively" comparable housing was more expensive in the black market. If plaintiffs could afford and were paying higher prices for housing in the black market, the argument that economic forces precluded their purchasing in the white market is not present. What forces could account for the dual markets in this situation? True, a black market might exist in the sense that there existed areas in which white home seekers would not purchase homes. But what of the white market, that is, why wasn't there a black market and an "integrated" market?

Would the legal analysis vary if defendants could have shown a genuine preference among blacks, even those who by definition could afford to live elsewhere, to live in the black area? Is there any evil to be addressed in this situation? *See* Wilhelmina A. Leigh & James D. McGhee, *A Minority Perspective on Residential Racial Integration*, in Housing Desegregation and Federal Policy 30 (John M. Goering ed. 1986) (discussing reasons blacks might favor or disfavor residential integration).

2. *Clark* was a Section 1982 action. Would a similar action lie under Title VIII? What language, if any, can be cited?

For an analysis of *Clark*, which synthesizes the major cases bearing on the dual markets problem, see James A. Kushner & Frances E. Werner, *Metropolitan Desegregation After* Milliken v. Bradley*: The Case for Land Use Litigation Strategies*, 24 Cath. U.L. Rev. 187 (1975) (advocating shared liability for a discriminatory result on the part of all who participate in effectuating it).

3. In *Love v. De Carlo Homes, Inc.*, 482 F.2d 613 (5th Cir.), *cert. denied*, 414 U.S. 1115 (1973), the Fifth Circuit rejected an "exploitation" theory for plaintiff's Section 1982 action. Plaintiff alleged that defendant had developed a residential subdivision and sold homes in the subdivision to blacks on "onerous" terms. The court recognized that dual markets existed, but held that for that reason the plaintiff's comparison with another subdivision developed for whites were not probative. Thus, said the court, plaintiffs could not show disparity of treatment as between whites and blacks which fell within "equal protection concepts." For a comparative analysis of *Clark* and *Love*, see William E. Martin, Note, *Housing and Section 1982: The Advisability of Extending Statutory Mandate Beyond Acts of Traditional Discrimination*, 1975 DUKE L.J. 781.

4. Although not employing an "exploitation analysis" as such, a court used the "dual markets" analysis (combined with numerous other factors) to find a pattern and practice of racial discrimination on the part of a local government in *United States v. City of Parma*, 494 F. Supp. 1049 (N.D. Ohio 1980). *See also* W. Dennis Keating, *The* Parma *Racial Discrimination Remedy Revisited*, 45 CLEV. ST. L. REV. 235 (1997) (providing an in-depth analysis of the remedial problems in the case).

5. Notwithstanding the *Clark* setback, there is still litigation advancing, *inter alia*, the "exploitation theory." *Honorable v. The Easy Life Real Estate System, Inc.*, 182 F.R.D. 553 (N.D. Ill. 1998) (certifying a class of purchasers of "renovated" properties targeted for sale to low-income minority buyers who alleged that the seller made cosmetic repairs, concealed major structural defects, falsely certified to HUD and lenders facts basic to the transaction, promised to remedy defects and did not do so). *See also Class Action Certified In Suit Alleging Exploitation of Minority Homebuyers*, 26 [Current Developments] Hous. & Dev. Rep. (West) 410 (1998) (discussing *Honorable)*.

6. The disadvantageous home financing offered to blacks was an important fact in *Clark*. It is an aspect of the phenomena known as "redlining"—the refusal of financial institutions to lend in neighborhood considered undesirable. Redlining also includes the practice of making loans on disadvantageous terms in redlined neighborhoods. If loans from major financial institutions are not available, buyers must turn to other sources—specialty mortgage lenders, mortgage brokers, finance companies, etc.—and almost always must pay higher interest or confront other terms less favorable to the purchaser.

7. Violations of Title VIII and Section 1982 have been catalogued by various writers. A comprehensive catalogue is contained in JAMES A. KUSHNER, FAIR HOUSING: DISCRIMINATION IN REAL ESTATE, COMMUNITY DEVELOPMENT, AND REVITALIZATION (2d ed. 1995 & Supp 2000).

6. Discriminatory Insurance Practices and Insurance Redlining

Nationwide Mutual Insurance Company v. Cisneros

United States Court of Appeals
52 F.3d 1351 (6th Cir. 1995)
cert. denied, 516 U.S. 1140 (1996)

Before: KENNEDY and MILBURN, Circuit Judges; WISEMAN, District Judge.

MILBURN, Circuit Judge.

Plaintiffs Nationwide Mutual Insurance Company and Nationwide Mutual Fire Insurance Company appeal the district court's grant of summary judgment to defendants

Henry Cisneros, Secretary of the United States Department of Housing and Urban Development; Jerald L. Steed and Charles W. Brown, Executive Director and Chairperson, respectively, of the Dayton, Ohio Human Relations Council; and the City of Dayton, Ohio, in this action for declaratory judgment and injunctive relief in which plaintiffs challenged defendants' authority to regulate the issuance and cancellation of homeowner's insurance policies under the Fair Housing Act. On appeal, the issues are (1) whether the district court erred in finding that the Fair Housing Act governs the business of property insurance, (2) whether the district court erred in finding that the McCarran-Ferguson Act does not preempt the regulation of the business of insurance under the Fair Housing Act, and (3) whether the district court erred in dismissing plaintiffs' state law claims. For the reasons that follow, we affirm.

I. A.

Plaintiffs Nationwide Mutual Insurance Company and Nationwide Mutual Fire Insurance Company (collectively "Nationwide"), Ohio corporations, seek declaratory and injunctive relief from attempts by the Department of Housing and Urban Development ("HUD") to regulate plaintiffs' property insurance underwriting practices under the Fair Housing Act ("the Act"), 42 U.S.C. § 3601, *et seq*. The insurance underwriting practices in question involve "redlining," in which the insurer charges higher rates or declines to write insurance for people who live in particular areas. Defendant HUD is responsible for the administration of the Fair Housing Act. Plaintiffs also seek declaratory and injunctive relief from attempts by defendants Jerald L. Steed, Charles Brown, and the City of Dayton ("the Dayton defendants") to regulate plaintiffs' property insurance underwriting practices under Ohio state law and Dayton municipal law. As earlier stated, Jerald L. Steed and Charles Brown are the Executive Director and the Chairperson, respectively, of the Dayton Human Relations Council ("DHRC"). In addition to enforcing fair housing provisions of Dayton ordinances, DHRC also assists HUD in the local administration of housing discrimination complaints under the Fair Housing Act.

Under the Fair Housing Act, HUD is responsible for receiving and investigating charges of discrimination in housing. Because mortgage lenders require borrowers to obtain and maintain property and hazard insurance on mortgaged property as a condition of obtaining a loan, HUD has interpreted the Fair Housing Act as prohibiting discriminatory practices relating to property and hazard insurance. HUD has adhered to this interpretation of the Act since at least 1978, when HUD's General Counsel wrote in a memorandum to the Assistant Secretary for Equal Opportunity:

> Adequate insurance coverage is often a prerequisite to obtaining financing. Insurance redlining, by denying or impeding coverage makes mortgage money unavailable, rendering dwellings "unavailable" as effectively as the denial of financial assistance on other grounds[.]

Memorandum to the Assistant Secretary for Equal Opportunity (Aug. 25, 1978).

Furthermore, in 1988, the Fair Housing Act was amended to authorize HUD to issue rules to implement the Act. 42 U.S.C. § 3614a. At that time, HUD issued a regulation reflecting its interpretation of the Act and its application to insurance companies. This regulation defined "other prohibited sale and rental conduct" to include:

> Refusing to provide municipal services or property or hazard insurance for dwellings or providing such services or insurance differently because of race, color, religion, sex, handicap, familial status, or national origin.

24 C.F.R. § 100.70(d)(4).

In May 1990, HUD received a complaint from Steven and Jennifer Beavers alleging that Nationwide had cancelled their homeowner's insurance because of their race and/or place of residence. HUD referred this complaint to the DHRC, which determined that it was "probable" that Nationwide had violated the City of Dayton's fair housing ordinances. In addition, on September 28, 1990, Sarah Wilson filed a housing discrimination complaint with HUD, alleging that Nationwide had refused, because of her sex, race, and the racial make-up of the area, to reinstate her insurance policy on a residential building that was located in a predominantly black area of Toledo, Ohio. HUD and the DHRC were in the process of investigating these complaints when Nationwide filed this action. Both investigations have been held in abeyance pending the conclusion of this case....

II. A....

Plaintiffs argue that the district court erred in finding that defendants have delegated authority, under the Fair Housing Act, or under "substantially equivalent" local ordinances, to regulate plaintiffs' property insurance underwriting practices. Specifically, plaintiffs assert that the plain language, structure, and legislative history of § 3604(a) and (b) of the Fair Housing Act preclude this finding. Section 3604(a) and (b) of the Fair Housing Act state that it shall be unlawful:

> (a) To refuse to sell or rent after the making of a bona fide offer, or to refuse to negotiate for the sale or rental of, *or otherwise make unavailable or deny*, a dwelling to any person because of race, color, religion, sex, familial status, or national origin.
>
> (b) To discriminate against any person in the terms, conditions, or privileges of sale or rental of a dwelling, or *in the provision of services* or facilities in connection therewith, because of race, color, religion, sex, familial status, or national origin.

42 U.S.C. § 3604(a) and (b) (emphasis added). HUD has interpreted these provisions of the Fair Housing Act to prohibit "[r]efusing to provide ... property or hazard insurance for dwellings or providing such ... insurance differently because of race...." 24 C.F.R. § 100.70(d)(4). Plaintiffs argue that HUD, in promulgating this regulation, has exceeded the authority delegated to it by Congress under the Fair Housing Act, and therefore the Dayton defendants lack the authority to investigate claims of discriminatory insurance underwriting practices. The district court rejected plaintiffs' argument and adopted the reasoning of the magistrate judge in his report and recommendation, which concluded that HUD had "not exceeded its statutory authority in enacting its regulations because the interpretation of the Fair Housing Act embodied in that regulation is one to which judicial deference is to be accorded under [*Chevron, U.S.A., Inc. v. Natural Resources Defense Council, Inc.*, 467 U.S. 837 (1984)]. Furthermore, even in the absence of *Chevron* deference, HUD's interpretation of the Fair Housing Act is correct."

We are confronted with two questions when we review an agency's construction of a statute. In *Lansing Dairy, Inc. v. Espy*, 39 F.3d 1339 (6th Cir. 1994), we stated:

> First and foremost is the question whether Congress has directly spoken to the matter at hand. "If the intent of Congress is clear, that is the end of the matter; for the court, as well as the agency, must give effect to the unambiguously expressed intent of Congress." If, however, the court decides that Congress has not directly addressed the precise question at issue, the court may not simply impose its own construction of the statute. "Rather, if the statute is silent or ambiguous with

> respect to the specific issue, the question for the court is whether the agency's answer is based on a permissible construction of the statute."

In *Chevron*, the Court also stated that in determining whether an agency's answer is based on a permissible construction of a statute, a reviewing "court need not conclude that the agency construction was the only one it permissibly could have adopted to uphold the construction, or even the reading the court would have reached if the question initially had arisen in a judicial proceeding." However, the Court also noted that "[t]he judiciary is the final authority on issues of statutory construction and must reject administrative constructions which are contrary to clear congressional intent." Thus, we must first determine whether the text of the Fair Housing Act addresses the precise issue in this case, i.e., whether § 3604(a) and/or (b) govern the issuance and cancellation of property insurance policies.

In *N.A.A.C.P. v. American Family Mut. Ins. Co.*, 978 F.2d 287, 298 (7th Cir. 1992), *cert. denied*, 508 U.S. 907 (1993), the Seventh Circuit held that Congressional intent regarding the application of § 3604 of the Fair Housing Act to insurance practices is unclear:

> The Fair Housing Act does not define key terms such as "service" and "make unavailable." [sic] By writing its statute in the passive voice—banning an outcome while not saying *who* the actor is, or *how* such actors bring about the forbidden consequence—Congress created ambiguity.

On the other hand, plaintiffs argue that the plain language and structure of § 3604(a) preclude its application to insurance providers. Specifically, plaintiffs rely on the canons of statutory interpretation of "ejusdem generis" and "expressio unius est exclusio alterius" in support of their contention that insurance underwriting practices are not governed by the Fair Housing Act. First, plaintiffs argue that HUD's interpretation of § 3604 conflicts with the principle of "ejusdem generis," which states that where general words follow specific words in a statutory enumeration, the general words are construed to embrace only objects similar in nature to those objects enumerated by the preceding specific words.... Thus, plaintiffs argue that in § 3604(a), because the general phrase "otherwise make unavailable or deny" follows the specific examples of failure "to sell or rent" or refusal "to negotiate for the sale or rental" of a dwelling, the phrase "otherwise make unavailable or deny" does not include any activities that do not directly affect the availability of a dwelling. We disagree. Plaintiffs' argument that the phrase "otherwise make unavailable or deny" must only include activities that directly affect the availability of a dwelling does not clarify Congressional intent as to whether the availability of property insurance falls within this category. Therefore, we conclude that the canon of "ejusdem generis" does not preclude HUD's interpretation of § 3604(a).

Second, plaintiffs argue that the maxim "expressio unius est exclusio alterius," which states that the mention of one thing implies exclusion of another, also precludes HUD's interpretation of § 3604. Specifically, plaintiffs note that § 3604(b) proscribes discrimination in the "terms, conditions, or privileges of sale or rental of a dwelling, or in the provision of services or facilities in connection therewith," and that § 3605 bars discrimination in mortgage financing. Therefore, plaintiffs assert that the fact that the statute proscribes some conduct that indirectly affects housing, i.e., services and mortgage financing, suggests that property insurance is not covered by the Act. Relying on the Fourth Circuit's decision in *Mackey v. Nationwide Ins. Cos.*, 724 F.2d 419 (4th Cir. 1984), plaintiffs argue that this result is necessary to avoid rendering §§ 3604(b) and 3605 of the Act superfluous. In *Mackey*, the Fourth Circuit concluded § 3605 shows that § 3604 must be read narrowly. "If § 804 [§ 3604] was designed to reach every discriminatory act that might conceivably affect the availability of housing, § 805's [§ 3605] specific prohibition of discrimination in the provision of financing would have been superfluous." The Seventh Circuit rejected this argument in *American Family*, holding that §§ 3604 and 3605 overlap and that

> [c]onveying meaning to diverse interpreters for an uncertain future is a difficult business. A wise drafter may state a principle in one section and list some applications of that principle in another, to make pellucid what ought to be apparent but which some judges (and many lay persons) will miss unless spelled out. Using the instance to restrict the principle would gum up the process of communication, inverting every effort to clarify.

We agree with the conclusion in *American Family* that §§ 3604 and 3605 overlap and are not mutually exclusive. We note that many courts have applied § 3604 to a number of parties and practices not mentioned in §§ 3604(b) and 3605. *See United States v. City of Parma*, 661 F.2d 562 (6th Cir. 1981) (imposition of building height limitations), *cert. denied*, 456 U.S. 926 (1982); *Metropolitan Hous. Dev. Corp. v. Village of Arlington Heights*, 558 F.2d 1283 (7th Cir. 1977) (issuance of zoning permits), *cert. denied*, 434 U.S. 1025 (1978); *Kennedy Park Homes Ass'n, Inc. v. City of Lackawanna*, 436 F.2d 108 (2d Cir. 1970) (rezoning property plaintiff picked for low-income housing project and denying sewer hookups), *cert. denied*, 401 U.S. 1010 (1971). Furthermore, plaintiffs' argument seems confused. Plaintiffs assert that the phrase "otherwise makes unavailable or denies" is "a catch-all for other activities which, like selling or renting, directly affect the availability of a dwelling. The fact that Congress did not expressly identify each of those other activities does not render § 3604(a) "vague." This argument seems to contradict plaintiffs' argument that by listing proscribed behavior in § 3604(b) and 3605, Congress intended for all other activity affecting the availability of housing to be outside the [ambit—Eds.] of the Fair Housing Act. Therefore, we conclude that the principle of "expressio unius est exclusio alterius" does not preclude HUD's interpretation of the Act.

Plaintiffs further argue that the legislative history of the Fair Housing Act reflects the Congressional intent that the Fair Housing Act not govern insurance underwriting practices. Relying on *Mackey*, plaintiffs argue that although Congress did not directly address the Act's application to insurance practices, it is implausible that Congress intended the Fair Housing Act to reach insurance practices in light of the fact that (1) Congress enacted the Urban Property Protection and Reinsurance Act of 1968 ("UPPRA"), *see* 12 U.S.C. § 1749bbb, *et seq.*, in the same year it enacted the Fair Housing Act, and (2) subsequent attempts to amend the Fair Housing Act to expressly prohibit discrimination in insurance have failed.

Plaintiffs assert that "[t]he fact that hazard insurance was not mentioned in the [Fair Housing Act] or its legislative history strongly indicates that [Congress did not intend to proscribe discrimination in hazard insurance]." Plaintiffs note that Congress enacted UPPRA in 1968, the same year the Fair Housing Act was enacted, to handle the problem of the unavailability of hazard insurance in some urban areas. However, in *Dunn v. Midwestern Indem. Mid-American Fire & Casualty Co.*, 472 F. Supp. 1106, 1111 (S.D. Ohio 1979), the court found that the purposes of the Fair Housing Act and UPPRA were different. The court noted that UPPRA "was enacted to protect private insurance companies from the risk of catastrophic losses which resulted from riots or civil disorders[,]" but did not "expressly address the issue of discriminatory insurance redlining based on race." We agree that the purposes of the two acts are different and that the enactment of UPPRA does not shed light on Congress' intent regarding the application of the Fair Housing Act to insurance underwriting practices. In *American Family*, the Seventh Circuit noted:

> Silence in the legislative history could imply that Members of Congress did not anticipate that the law would apply to insurers. Silence equally could imply that the debate was about the principle of nondiscrimination, leaving details to the future. The backwards phraseology of § 3604 suggests the latter possibility.

Therefore, we conclude that the legislative history of the Fair Housing Act does not preclude HUD's interpretation of the Act.

Next, plaintiffs argue that the failure of subsequent attempts by Congress to amend the Fair Housing Act to expressly prohibit discrimination in insurance supports their contention that Congress did not intend for the Act to govern insurance underwriting practices. Plaintiffs stress that attempts to amend the Act failed after the Fourth Circuit's decision in *Mackey*, which squarely rejected the proposition that §§ 3604(a) or (b) implicitly encompassed the regulation of insurance. However, in *American Family*, the Seventh Circuit held that *Mackey*'s conclusion that unsuccessful attempts to amend the Fair Housing Act to explicitly address discriminatory insurance practices reflected Congress' disapproval of this reading was unwarranted. Seventh Circuit explained:

> Proposed legislation can fail for many reasons. Some Members of Congress may oppose the proposal on the merits; others may think it unnecessary and therefore not worth the political capital needed to write the "clarification" into the statute over opposition; still others may be indifferent, or seek to use the bill as a vehicle for some unrelated change. Congress may run out of time, as a noncontroversial bill sits in a queue while a contentious proposal is debated. No surprise, therefore, that the Supreme Court repeatedly reminds us that unsuccessful proposals to amend a law, in the years following its passage, carry no significance.

Thus, we conclude that subsequent failed attempts to amend the Fair Housing Act are not helpful in determining the intent of the Congress that enacted the Act. Furthermore, Congress gave HUD the authority to promulgate regulations knowing that HUD had consistently interpreted the Act as governing insurance underwriting practices. Therefore, we conclude that plaintiffs have failed to show any evidence of Congressional intent to preclude the application of the Fair Housing Act to insurance underwriting practices.

We next turn to the second question under a *Chevron* analysis—whether the agency's interpretation of the Fair Housing Act is reasonable. Under *Chevron*, "if the statute is silent or ambiguous with respect to the specific issue, the question for the court is whether the agency's answer is based on a permissible construction of the statute." "However, this deference does have its limits. Courts may invalidate agency adjudication or rulemaking which is 'inconsistent with the statutory mandate or that frustrate[s] the policy that Congress sought to implement.'" "Similarly," where the court determines that, given the intention of Congress to achieve some goal, '"there are compelling reasons that [the agency interpretation] is wrong,"' "the court may invalidate the agency's action."

In *American Family*, the court found that "Section 3604 is sufficiently pliable that its text can bear the Secretary's construction [interpreting § 3604 as prohibiting insurance redlining]." We agree. The purpose of the Fair Housing Act as a whole is "to eliminate the discriminatory business practices which might prevent a person economically able to do so from purchasing a house regardless of his race...." Moreover, "[t]he language of the Act is broad and inclusive...." Thus, we conclude that HUD's interpretation of the Fair Housing Act is reasonable in light of the direct connection of availability of property insurance and ability to purchase a house.

Plaintiffs argue, however, that the "[d]enial of property insurance, even if discriminatory, is simply not akin to denying or making unavailable a dwelling." Therefore, plaintiffs argue that the provision of insurance is too attenuated to the availability of housing for insurance providers to be governed by the Fair Housing Act. Plaintiffs rely on *Babin*, in which we addressed the question of the extent to which "the phrase 'otherwise make unavailable' reaches out to make unlawful actions that are removed from the central event of purchasing or leasing a dwelling but nonetheless have some effect on a person's ability to acquire housing" in interpreting a similar provision of the Fair Housing Act that prohibits discrimination on the basis of a person's handicap. In *Babin*, the plaintiffs alleged that neighbors who bought a house to prevent its use as a group home for mentally handicapped adults violated the Fair Housing Act by making housing "unavailable" to a protected class of people. In holding that the Fair Housing Act could not be read so broadly so as to encompass "normal economic competition," we refused to interpret the Act to prohibit "any action that results in the unavailability of housing for protected classes." However, in *Babin*, we also acknowledged that the phrase "otherwise make unavailable" might extend to "other actors who, though not owners or agents, are in a position directly to deny a member of a protected group housing rights."

Babin is distinguishable from the present case. Unlike *Babin*, the availability of property insurance has a direct and immediate affect on a person's ability to obtain housing. Accordingly, we conclude that HUD's interpretation of the Fair Housing Act is consistent with goals of the Fair Housing Act and a reasonable interpretation of the statute.

[The court's discussion of several other issues is omitted. Points the court addressed which are omitted include *inter alia*: that the scope of the *Chevron* decision was not limited to its facts; that other federal statutes did not preempt state-regulated insurance companies from HUD regulations under the Fair Housing Act; and that HUD was correct in its claim that the application of its regulation under a disparate impact approach was not ripe for review since HUD had never applied the regulation to insurance practices under a disparate impact analysis.—Eds.]

III.

For the reasons stated, the judgment of the district court is AFFIRMED.

KENNEDY, Circuit Judge, dissented.

Notes and Questions

1. Insurance redlining has been documented. While the discrimination today may not be based as readily on explicit racial criteria as in the past, reliance on stereotypes and subjective factors produces an identifiably racially correlated result. Gregory D. Squires & William Velez, *Insurance Redlining and the Transformation of an Urban Metropolis*, 23 URB. AFF. Q. 63 (1987). Without the availability of mortgage insurance, title insurance, and hazard insurance, loans for purchasing or rehabilitating property in the affected community cannot be secured. Decline is virtually inevitable. *See* Willy E. Rice, *Race, Gender, "Redlining," and the Discriminating Access to Loans, Credit, and Insurance: A Historical and Empirical Analysis of Consumers Who Sued Lenders and Insurers in Federal and State Courts, 1950–1995*, 33 SAN DIEGO L. REV. 583 (1996) (substantial discussion of insurance discrimination and ineffective state and federal regulatory enforcement).

2. In response to allegations that Nationwide Insurance Company did not make insurance available to homeowners in minority communities, Nationwide signed an

agreement with the U.S. Department of Justice on March 10, 1997. Highlights on the agreement include Nationwide's pledge of a $13.2 million investment into 10 cities' minority neighborhoods. Nationwide also agreed to re-train its employees, among other things, to disregard race as a factor for affecting applicants for insurance with the company. In addition, Nationwide will use the media to promote its new image of its participation in urban markets. *See* 24 [Current Developments] Hous. & Dev. Rep. (WGL) 720 (1997).

7. Steering and Blockbusting

Heights Community Congress v. Hilltop Realty

United States Court of Appeals
774 F.2d 135 (6th Cir. 1985),
cert. denied, 475 U.S. 1019 (1986)

Before MERRITT and KENNEDY, Circuit Judges; and PHILLIPS, Senior Circuit Judge.

Cornelia G. KENNEDY, Circuit Judge.

Defendants appeal the District Court's declaratory judgment that they engaged in racial steering on eight occasions in violation of ... the Fair Housing Act, 42 U.S.C. § 3604(a) (otherwise denying housing because of race), and on one occasion in violation of § 3604(c) (making statement indicating racial preference in housing); and blockbusting by mail solicitation on one occasion in violation of § 3604(e) (inducing sale for profit by representation involving race). Plaintiffs are the City of Cleveland Heights (City or Cleveland Heights) and the Heights Community Congress (HCC), an umbrella organization of civic groups that monitors compliance with the fair housing laws. In addition to declaratory relief, the District Court awarded HCC $1 in nominal damages, but declined to grant injunctive relief. Defendants Hilltop Realty, Inc. (Hilltop) and Bruce Johanns, a Hilltop agent, appeal the court's findings that they violated the Fair Housing Act and the awarding of nominal damages; plaintiffs appeal from the court's denial of injunctive relief. We reverse the District Court's finding that defendants violated § 3604(e); in all other respects, we affirm.

I

Cleveland Heights ... is a suburb of the City of Cleveland. The City had a population of 57,767 in 1970 and 56,438 in 1980. Black residents comprised 2.5% of its population in 1970 and 24.9% in 1980, with greater concentrations of blacks in areas adjacent to East Cleveland, which had a black population of 58.6% in 1970 and 86.5% in 1980. Most of the overall increase of black residents in Cleveland Heights occurred from 1970–76.

In 1965 and again in 1972, the homes of black residents who had recently moved into the community were bombed, and around the same time several areas of the City were the subject of heavy real estate solicitation. Among the actions of the City in response was a proclamation in 1965 declaring Cleveland Heights to be a racially open community, a 1967 ordinance forbidding "for sale" signs on private residences, a 1972 anti-telephone solicitation ordinance, and adoption in 1976 of a comprehensive real estate program, including an ordinance forbidding discrimination in housing, blockbusting, steering, and solicitation of homeowners who have filed no solicitation notices.

HCC was founded in 1972. It is a not-for-profit corporation under Ohio law, which has as its primary objective the promotion and maintenance of Cleveland Heights as an open and integrated community. Its membership includes governmental representatives; school board, library, religious and other community-wide groupings; businesses and merchants; and neighborhood organizations. Two of its major programs have been periodic new homebuyer questionnaire surveys and audits of realty companies and agents, including a 1978 audit contracted for by the City. Auditing was carried out through the use of "checkers"—paired black and white volunteers who represented to real estate agents that they were seeking housing and presented the agents with similar needs and circumstances. The results of that audit led to filing of the instant lawsuit.

II

[The court first held that the City and HCC had standing to sue, after which it addressed the merits of the action.—Eds.]

III

The District Court found that five Hilltop agents violated § 3604(a) on eight occasions between 1976 and 1978 by engaging in "racial steering," which the court determined "otherwise made unavailable" housing on account of race. These violations were imputed to Hilltop. Only one of the violations occurred within the 180 day limitations period prior to the date this suit was filed. The District Court held that the complaint was timely as to all violations alleged based upon its finding that they constituted a continuing pattern and practice of unlawful conduct.

In [*Havens Realty Corp. v. Coleman*, 455 U.S. 363, 366 n.1 (1982)—Eds.], the Court adopted plaintiffs' definition of "racial steering" as:

> a "practice by which real estate brokers and agents preserve and encourage patterns of racial segregation in available housing by steering members of racial and ethnic groups to buildings occupied primarily by members of such racial and ethnic groups and away from buildings and neighborhoods inhabited primarily by members of other races or groups."

Although in [*Gladstone, Realtors v. Village of Bellwood*, 441 U.S. 91 (1979)—Eds.] and *Havens* the Court did not specifically address whether the racial steering violates Title VIII, *see Bellwood*, 441 U.S. at 116 n. 32, the District Court held that in the absence of significant discriminatory effect, which it found was not present in this case, an incident of racial steering would violate § 3604(a) upon a showing of intent. Defendants do not directly dispute this interpretation of the law. Rather, they argue that truthful informational statements with racial content, failure to show homes in a particular location absent a specific request, and lack of service, do not violate the Act. The District Court was correct in holding that to violate § 3604(a), one looks to whether the statement or conduct would have an untoward effect on reasonable person under the circumstances who is seeking housing, and behind the statement or conduct to the intent of the agent. If a statement or act would have a discriminatory effect and is made with the intent to steer, it violates § 3604(a). *See Zuch v. Hussy*, 394 F. Supp. 1028, 1045–46 (E.D. Mich. 1975), *aff'd and remanded,* 547 F.2d 1168 (6th Cir. 1977).

The District Judge painstakingly reviewed the facts of each alleged § 3604(a) violation and applied the above principles of law to his findings. In several instances he found that plaintiffs had failed to establish either an act that would constitute steering, or the requisite intent. The essence of defendants' objections to the court's findings is that they were unsupported by the record. Discriminatory intent is a question of fact subject to the clearly erroneous standard of review.

Of particular importance, since it constitutes the linchpin supporting the remaining violations found by the District Court, is the violation which occurred within that limitations period. In [sic] October 26, 1978, Hortense Johnson, a black checker, began an audit of Hilltop agent Elayne Liff. After Johnson had described her needs to Liff, Liff attempted to contact the owner of one home, who was black, that met Johnson's description. After determining that the home had been taken off the market Liff suggested no other homes to Johnson, either at that time or in the days following. Four days later, in a call in response to Johnson's follow-up call, Liff stated that she was busy preparing for a vacation trip to Hawaii and would contact Johnson upon her return. She did not offer to arrange for another agent to assist Johnson.

The District Judge carefully reviewed the testimony of Johnson and Liff. He found that Liff's normal practice would have been to suggest additional listings to Johnson during her initial visit besides the single black-owned home about which Liff inquired and to refer Johnson to another agent if Liff was unavailable to help her. The court observed that although Liff claimed she was suspicious of Johnson, these suspicion were irrelevant to whether, in departing from her normal procedure, Liff denied Johnson the opportunity to see available homes on the basis of race, because Liff also testified that despite her suspicions, she "'still went about (her) business in that usual manner.'" The court concluded that Liff's failure to provide service to Johnson violated § 3604(a).

[W]e cannot say that the District Court's finding that Liff committed a violation of § 3604(a) is clearly erroneous. Nor were the court's findings clearly erroneous respecting the other § 3604(a) violations, or the § 3604(c) violation....

Defendants also object that the District Court erred in finding that Hilltop had "the power to control the acts" of its agents ... and hence was liable for the violations committed by those agents. It argues that its agents were independent contractors, over whom under common law it has no control. This argument has consistently been rejected in Fair Housing Act cases. The court did not err in holding Hilltop liable for the violations of its agents.

IV.

The District Court also found that Hilltop and its agent Bruce Johanns had violated 3604(e), when Johanns mailed solicitation cards to 40 to 60 residents in a two block area of Census Tract 1401 in northeast Cleveland Heights. Johanns worked as a painting contractor in the area between 1974 and 1977, during which time he solicited painting jobs by mail. Upon becoming a Hilltop agent in 1977, he sent an announcement card to the residents of the area. In August 1978, he sent a card to residents announcing that a home in the neighborhood had been listed with him, which said: "If you have a friend or relative who would like to live near you, please have them give me a call, and I will be pleased to give them all the details and arrange for them to see it." The listed home, which had a black owner, was sold to a white buyer. In September 1978, he sent out another post card, which stated that the listed home had been sold, and represented: "In selling this property, we came into contact with other families who wish to buy in your neighborhood. Are you interested in selling your property? We would welcome the opportunity of consulting with you without obligation." Johanns admitted that there were no other families that had contacted him wishing to buy in the neighborhood. It is the September mailing that the District Court found violated § 3604(e).

In *Zuch*, Judge Keith held that:

> Section 3604(e) ... is aimed at both overt "blockbusting" and other uninvited solicitations in racially transitional neighborhoods where it can be established (1) that the solicitations are made for profit, (2) that the solicitations are intended to induce the sale of a dwelling, and (3) that the solicitations would convey to a reasonable man, under the circumstances, the idea that members of a particular race are, or may be, entering the neighborhood.

There is no question that Johanns' September mailing was made for profit and intended to induce the sale of a dwelling. However, an inducement to sell only violates § 3604(e) if, as provided in the statute, it includes "representations regarding the entry or prospective entry into the neighborhood of a person or persons of a particular race." Such representations may be obvious or subtle, but a representation respecting race must be made. The third part of the test stated by Judge Keith in *Zuch* merely restates the representation requirement in a way that encompasses both direct and subtle references to race. Thus, the critical question in the instant case is whether the post card sent by Johanns contained a representation that would convey to reasonable persons in the solicited area that blacks were seeking to move into the neighborhood.

In resolving this question in any given case, "[t]he concept of a racially transitional neighborhood is critically important to this litigation, because it is within this context that the activities of the real estate industry, in general, and the defendants, in particular, must be scrutinized." The court found the solicited area to be a "racially transitional neighborhood."[4] It found that Johanns was warned by one resident, Mr. Hollis, after his first mailing that the resident had filed a no solicitation card with the City and that Johanns had violated the City's no-solicitation ordinance by mailing the card to him, and that another resident, Mr. Ciocia, had complained to Hilltop after the August and September mailings. The court credited the testimony of Mr. Ciocia that he was fearful of the effect of the post cards, and that of another witness, Mr. Russo, a person with experience in real estate who lived near the solicited area, who testified that if he lived in the solicited area and received one of the cards, he would have been concerned. The court concluded that Johanns was aware of the racial composition of the neighborhood, and that to have continued to solicit "in a neighborhood that he knew was racially transitional and, therefore subject to the fears of panic selling, rendered his acts of solicitation at least reckless." Thus, although the card sent by Johanns was completely neutral on its face,[5] the court found that it contained a representation respecting race because he knew that any form of solicitation would be likely to excite the fears of neighborhood residents and trigger panic selling.

The statute does not prescribe that a § 3604(e) violation may only occur when a prohibited representation is made in a transitional neighborhood. Whether a neighborhood

---

4. The record shows that the two block area solicited by Johanns was virtually an all-white enclave in an otherwise integrated neighborhood. Census Tract 1401 had an estimated nonwhite population of 22% in 1978, 29% in 1979 and 37% in 1980, although the census statistic of 1980 was 30.7% nonwhite. Neighboring census tracts contained census blocks with black populations substantially higher than the 24.9% overall figure for Cleveland Heights. On the basis of these figures, the District Court determined that the solicited area was transitional, quoting language from *Zuch* to the effect that a "racially transitional neighborhood" or "changing neighborhood" "[t]o the layman ... is used and understood to mean that blacks are moving into an area."

5. There were no subtle representations by Johanns of the sort present in *Zuch*—salespersons showing houses to black persons at night with lights on and windows unobstructed, flyers picturing or in-person visits by black agents, or literature containing thinly veiled reference to neighborhood safety and other concerns foremost in the minds of white residents in neighborhoods undergoing change.

is in transition is significant only to the extent that its residents become more susceptible to the exploitative tactics of blockbusting.

> It is a well known fact that racial tensions and anxieties are generated when blacks move into previously all-white neighborhoods. It is also well known that many real estate agencies attempt to exploit such a situation by making repeated, uninvited solicitations for the sale of homes. In most instances, this activity (commonly referred to as "blockbusting") has proven to be an effective means of stimulating the sale of homes in racially transitional neighborhoods. It does so by capitalizing upon the racial fears of whites, reminding them that blacks are moving into the area. The process was articulated quite clearly in *United States v. Mitchell*, 335 F. Supp. 1004, 1005–1006 (N.D. Ga. 1971), where the United States District Court for the Northern District of Georgia stated:
>
> > The evidence at the trial disclosed many illuminating things about what happens in a residential neighborhood when it becomes racially transitional. For example, if these cases are typical—and the court believes they are—the following consequences can be predicted as inevitable, and beyond dispute: First, a sense of panic and urgency immediately grips the neighborhood and rumors circulate and recirculate about the extent of the intrusion (real or fancied), the effect on property values and the quality of education. Second, there are sales and rumors of sales, some true, some false. Third, the frenzied listing and sale of houses attracts real estate agents like flies to a leaking jug of honey. Fourth, even those owners who do not sell are sorely tempted as their neighbors move away, and hence those who remain are particularly vulnerable. Fifth, the names of successful agents are exchanged and recommended between homeowners and frequently the agents are called by the owners themselves, if not to make a listing then at least to get an up-to-date appraisal. Constant solicitation of listings goes on by all agents either by house-to-house calls and/or by mail and/or by telephone, to the point where owners and residents are driven almost to distraction.
> >
> > In this maelstrom the atmosphere is necessarily charged with *race*, whether mentioned or not, and as a result there is very little cause or necessity for an agent to make direct representations as to race or as to what is going on. On the contrary both sides already know, all too well, what is going on. In short, for an agent to get a listing or make a sale *because* of racial tensions in such an area is relatively easy, whereas the direct mention of race in making the sale is superfluous and wholly unnecessary." [Emphasis by the Court.—Eds.]

Zuch, 394 F. Supp. at 1049–50.

A racially neutral form of solicitation may very well contain an obvious representation respecting race in a highly charged atmosphere such as that described above. Such an atmosphere was not, however present in the instant case. Although the solicited neighborhood could fairly be described as transitional, in the sense that residents perceived that blacks were moving into it or adjacent areas, its residents were not in the grip of panic. The neighborhood was not the subject of frenzied real estate activity. Johanns was a white real estate agent who sent a racially neutral card to the residents of a small area, many of whom were former painting customers and knew Johanns, following up a sale of a black-owned home to a white buyer. While we do not suggest that real estate agents are "entitled to one bite" in transitional neighborhoods before panic has set in, the essence of the District Court's reasoning is that any form of solicitation in any area into which blacks have moved or are moving is a *per se* violation of § 3604(e). We have serious doubts that such a sweeping restriction on commercial speech would be constitutional, *see Linmark Associates Inc. v. Township of Willingboro*, 431 U.S. 85 (1977), and do not believe that Congress intended the statute to be so applied. *See Zuch*, 394 F. Supp. at 1046 ("Fair Housing Act ... was designed to provide, within constitutional limit, for fair housing throughout the United States"). We do not agree with plaintiffs that the difference between the instant case and *Zuch*, *Mitchell*, and other cases finding § 3604(e) violations merely one of degree. In the absence of evidence of panic selling or other incident of a racially charged atmosphere that would impute to any real estate solicitation a racial connotation, or evidence of an actual representation respecting race, whether suggestive or direct, there simply has not been a prohibited representation within the meaning of § 3604(e). Since neither was proven in the instant case, we reverse the District Court's finding that the mailing violated § 3604(e).

VI.

We reverse the judgment of the District Court finding that Hilltop and its agent Bruce Johanns violated § 3604(e). In all other respects, the judgment of the District Court is *affirmed*.

Notes and Questions

1. Notice that the court held the defendant Hilltop Agency liable for the discriminatory conduct of agent Liff. The Supreme Court has subsequently held, as found in *Heights Community Congress*, that the Fair Housing Act imposes vicarious liability on a principal or an employer in accordance with traditional agency rules for conduct that occurs in the scope of the agent's employment. It rejected a theory that the Fair Housing Act also imposed liability on corporate owners and officers for the unlawful acts of a corporate employee simply on the basis that the owner or officer controlled (or had the right to control) the actions of that employee. *Meyer v. Holley*, 537 U.S. 280 (2003).

2. What are the evils of blockbusting?

> In the classic blockbusting pattern, homes are purchased at panic depressed prices by the speculator and resold at inflated rates to Negroes who have limited access to the housing market. Both white seller and black purchaser lose in the exchange: the former by selling in an artificially unfavorable market, the latter by paying an exorbitant sum for the "privilege" of unconsciously abetting segregation in housing. In addition, blockbusting results in social alarm through the fears engendered in white homeowners and the Negroes' resentment of the white exodus which follows the arrival of blacks in the neighborhood. The blockbuster utilizes techniques of direct personal contact with the white homeowner. By means of telephone and door-to-door solicitation, he forecasts an influx of blacks and a resulting deterioration of schools and increase in crime. Many homeowners may initially resist these scare tactics, but the appearance of large "for sale" and, "sold" signs and large numbers of prospective Negro purchasers often confirm their latent fears; such signs and reports of sales to Negro buyers may be fabricated or exaggerated by the blockbuster. Further pressure may be applied in the form of advice that property values are dropping rapidly and that every day's delay is costly. The speculator then offers quick cash to clinch the deal. When this scenario is repeated a sufficient number of times to induce a neighborhood panic, an all white or lightly integrated area rapidly becomes all black or even ghettoized.

> The modern blockbuster has apparently refined these traditional techniques. Possibly influenced by high interest rates, he does not specialize in purchasing homes for resale at great price differentials. Instead, he serves as an agent in panic sales from white owners to black buyers and profits from the numerous commissions attendant to transforming a neighborhood. In lieu of blunt statements that Negroes are "taking over the neighborhood," he makes subtle references to changing neighborhoods, to the expansion of neighboring ghettoes, to his personal fear of crime in the area, and to the increasing difficulty of finding purchasers for homes in the neighborhood. Mass solicitation of sellers through mail and personal contact remains part of his brand of panic peddling.

Note, *Blockbusting*, 59 GEO. L.J. 170 (1970).

3. The cause of action for blockbusting raises a number of issues. First, what is the nature of the offense? The offense consists of: (1) making uninvited solicitations to sell property; (2) when the solicitations are made for profit; (3) with intent to induce sale; and (4) the statements of solicitation would convey to a reasonable person, under the circumstances, the idea that members of a particular race are, or may be, entering the neighborhood. *See Zuch v. Hussey*, 394 F. Supp. 1028 (W.D. Mich. 1975). But answering a good faith question asked by the seller regarding race of a home buyer is not a *per se* violation. *United States v. Saroff*, 377 F. Supp. 352 (E.D. Tenn.), *aff'd*, 516 F.2d 902 (6th Cir. 1975). However, no actual sale need take place, and the profit may be in the form of real estate brokerage commissions. *Brown v. State Realty*, 304 F. Supp. 1236 (N.D. Ga. 1969).

4. You may have noticed in *Heights Community Congress v. Hilltop Realty* that Cleveland Heights in 1967 adopted an ordinance forbidding "For Sale" signs on private residences. Communities took such actions in an attempt to forestall panic selling generated by the display of "For Sale" and "Sold" signs in neighborhoods. Such ordinances raised issues under the First Amendment. The matter of completely banning "For Sale" and "Sold" signs reached resolution in *Linmark Associates, Inc. v. Township of Willingboro*, 431 U.S. 85 (1977), when the Supreme Court held that such prohibitions violated the First Amendment rights of potential home sellers. The ruling left open the question of the limits of content-neutral signs that purported to regulate "time, place and manner."

The Town of Euclid, Ohio enacted ordinances that imposed strict limits on size and placement of any signs, including real estate sales signs. In a suit brought by an association of real estate agents, the City of Euclid defended the limitations as "time, place, and manner" restrictions on signs that were justified on the basis of aesthetics without reference to content of signs making the restrictions content-neutral. The court agreed that the requirement was content-neutral, irrespective of alleged motives of council members who enacted ordinance to limit real property "For Sale" signs. But the court held that the restrictions were not narrowly tailored to serve significant government interest in aesthetics; and that the restrictions did not leave open ample alternative channels for communication of information, and thus violated the First Amendment. *Cleveland Area Board of Realtors v. City of Euclid*, 833 F. Supp. 1253 (N.D. Ohio 1993), *aff'd*, 88 F. 3d 382 (6th Cir. 1996). Cleveland Heights subsequently dropped its ban on for sale signs about the time that neighboring Euclid's real estate sign restrictions were invalidated.

For discussion of the problem of fair housing enforcement and the First Amendment, see A Note on Fair Housing Enforcement and the First Amendment, *supra*.

5. For other aspects of the blockbusting problem, see *United States v. Bob Lawrence Realty, Inc.*, 474 F.2d 115 (5th Cir.), *cert. denied*, 414 U.S. 826 (1973), and *United States*

v. Mintzes, 304 F. Supp. 1305 (D. Md. 1969). For textual discussion on blockbusting generally, see Susan S. Glassberg, *Legal Control of Blockbusting*, 1972 URB. L. ANN. 145; Joseph G. Bisceglia, Comment, *Blockbusting: Judicial and Legislative Response to Real Estate Dealer's Excesses*, 22 DE PAUL L. REV. 818 (1973); *Blockbusting: A Novel Statutory Approach to an Increasingly Serious Problem*, 7 COLUM. J.L. & SOC. PROB. 538 (1971).

6. The following description of steering may provide perspective on the problem posed in the principal case:

> Racial steering is a generic term for a variety of long-standing and ubiquitous practices by which a real estate broker directs buyers toward or away from particular houses or neighborhoods according to the buyer's race. These practices may be divided into two broad classes of conduct: (1) advising customers to purchase homes in particular neighborhoods on the basis of race; and (2) failing, on the basis of race, to show, or to inform buyers of, homes that meet their specifications.
>
> Brokers steer for a variety of reasons. Sellers may instruct brokers not to show their homes to members of a particular race. Where the broker steers on his own initiative, he tends to justify the practice by relying on traditional industry values. Until 1950, the Code of Ethics of the real estate brokerage industry encouraged racial steering. The National Association of Realtors (NAR) and its constituent local boards have in the past been vocal opponents of fair housing legislation.
>
> While the industry has recently adopted an official policy of nondiscrimination, this change in industry norm is not likely to eliminate steering. One sociologist has identified a pervasive "broker ideology" which fosters the practice of racial steering. Brokers generally assume that white home owners and home buyers desire segregated communities. Accordingly, a broker may steer white buyers toward white neighborhoods in the belief that he is satisfying their preferences, and steer black buyers away from such areas in order to preserve the values and standards of the white areas in which he operates. If the broker assumes that buyers prefer to live with persons of their own race, he may not view his practices as discriminatory or their segregative effects as pernicious. Rather, both the practices and effects may be seen as consistent with the segregative tendencies of the society at large.

T. Alexander Aleinikoff, Note, *Racial Steering: The Real Estate Broker and Title VIII*, 85 YALE L.J. 808, 809–12 (1976).

7. A steering violation is particularly subtle and evanescent. However, steering has been found in *United States v. Mitchell*, 580 F.2d 789 (5th Cir. 1978) (steering to one section of a large apartment complex); *United States v. Real Estate One*, 433 F. Supp. 1140 (E.D. Mich. 1977) (real estate agent's newspaper ads, use and assignment of sales force, and attitudes of sales staff found to have a "steering effect"). *See also Wheatley Heights Neighborhood Coalition v. Jenna Resales Co.*, 447 F. Supp. 838 (E.D.N.Y. 1978) (multiple listing service not liable for alleged racial steering practiced by member brokers); and *Gladstone Realtors v. Village of Bellwood*, 441 U.S. 91 (1979) (holding that persons or entities injured by acts of steering may sue even if they were not "steered"). The Court discusses the effects of steering at 109–111, noting that steering "manipulates the housing market in the described area of the village."

8. If steering consists of market manipulation, how is a decree prohibiting steering to be enforced? Consider the commentary that follows from Alexander Aleinikoff's Note in the Yale Law Journal, *supra* Note 6.

> Liability for racial steering will alter substantially the ordinary business practices of the broker and may inflict significant costs on his operations. To comply with Title VIII, the broker would not be able to limit the customer's choice of housing to neighborhoods with a particular racial composition. Thus, he might have to show homes in several different neighborhoods. However, this cost may not be substantial, because the broker need not show more homes than is his custom. Compliance with Title VIII will also prevent the broker from excluding black buyers from white areas. Since residents of white areas may prefer to list their homes with brokers who will steer black buyers away from their neighborhoods, brokers who comply with the law are likely to be at a competitive disadvantage relative to brokers who do not comply. Vigorous enforcement of the statute could prevent any disadvantage to law-abiding brokers, but might lead sellers who wish to discriminate to do without brokerage services altogether. However, sellers as well as brokers are prohibited from discriminating in the sale of housing; therefore, the incentive to avoid brokered transactions would exist primarily in those situations where a home owner believes he can locate an "acceptable" buyer without having to refuse to sell to others on the basis of race.

85 Yale L.J. at 824. How would you draft a decree to achieve these effects?

9. In the *Gladstone Realtors v. Village of Bellwood*, 441 U.S. 91 (1979), the Supreme Court left open the question of standing for testers who investigate racial steering. One federal court held that testers falsely advised on the basis of race as to the availability of housing had standing as testers to sue under the Fair Housing Act. *Coles v. Havens Realty Corp.*, 633 F.2d 384 (4th Cir. 1980). The court noted that the breadth of congressional protection from housing discrimination is apparent from the Act. It said that if the broker had truthfully advised the testers on the availability of units in the integrated apartment dwelling, the social reform legislated by Congress would have been advanced without legal action. While not purporting to formulate a general rule for tester standing, the court noted that these plaintiffs "occupy a narrow island limited to areas fundamentally necessary for access to the federal courts."

The Supreme Court reversed. *Havens Realty Corp. v. Coleman*, 455 U.S. 363 (1982), *rev'g* 633 F.2d 384 (4th Cir 1980). The Court held that a white tester, as a tester, did not have standing because the white tester would have been given truthful information—a unit was available. Title VIII, in 42 U.S.C. § 3604(d), reasoned the Court, makes it unlawful to represent that a unit is not available when a unit is in fact available. Conversely, a black tester was held to have standing because the defendant will be charged by that tester with falsely representing a unit is not available. It should be noted that the Court distinguished between standing as a tester and standing as an individual. Both black and white testers were held to have standing when asserting "distinct and palpable injuries." In *Havens*, which was a steering case, the plaintiffs alleged that defendants' conduct deprived them of "the right to the important social, professional, business and economic, political and aesthetic benefits of interracial associations that arise from living in integrated communities free from discriminatory housing practices." In remanding to the district court, the Court required plaintiffs to amend their complaint to more particularly allege their injury, since it did not think that the allegation that they were injured as citizens of the City of Richmond was sufficient. Plaintiffs would be required to state the neighborhoods in which they lived and their proximity to defendants' alleged steering.

Additionally, a nonprofit corporation—HOME (Housing Opportunities Made Equal)—was found to have standing to challenge alleged steering on the grounds that defendants' conduct frustrated the organization's efforts to assist equal access through counseling and referral and that the organization had found it necessary to devote "significant resources to counteract" defendants' conduct.

10. What about the use of tester evidence in conventional cases of housing discrimination? Assume a newspaper carries an advertisement for a vacant apartment. A white tester applies for the apartment and is told the apartment is available. One hour later a black applicant applies and is told falsely the apartment is not available. The white tester, of course, did not intend to rent the apartment. Is her evidence admissible in a Title VIII court proceeding brought by the black applicant? Is there any problem with the timing or order of the testing? Do testers need to go before the black applicant and then return after the black applicant to make an airtight case?

The admissibility and value of "tester" evidence has been explicitly affirmed. *Richardson v. Howard*, 712 F.2d 319 (7th Cir. 1983). The court stated that tester evidence may be not only indispensable but may be more reliable than that of the alleged victim of discrimination. Testers, the court reasoned, were more likely to be dispassionate observers of events. The court also recognized that testers could quickly dispel false claims of discrimination to the benefit of innocent parties. Otto J. Hetzel, Symposium, *Introductory Comments on the Fair Housing Testing Conference and the Importance of Testing to Achieve Compliance with the Fair Housing Act*, 41 URB. LAW. 229 (2009); Otto J. Hetzel, Symposium, *Remediation Techniques For Racial Housing Discrimination—An Introduction To The Symposium*, 51 WAYNE L. REV. 1461 (2005).

8. Enforcement Procedures, Options, Damages, and Remedies

The report on the House version of the 1988 amendments notes major problems that existed with the 1968 Fair Housing Act:

> [Prior law] has been ineffective because it lacks an effective enforcement mechanism. Private persons and fair housing organizations are burdened with the primary enforcement responsibility. Although private enforcement has achieved some success, it is restricted by the limited financial resources of litigants and the bar, and by disincentives in the law itself. The federal enforcement role is severely limited.
>
> Under [previous] law, although HUD investigates housing discrimination complaints, it can use only "informal methods of conference, conciliation, and persuasion" in an attempt to resolve them. HUD can do no more than this and lacks the power even to bring the parties to the conciliation table. HUD cannot sue violators to enforce the law, as in other civil rights laws.
>
> The Justice Department can sue, but only in cases of a "pattern or practice" of discrimination. In order to redress the ordinary individual case of discrimination, the victim of discrimination must bring a lawsuit in court. Although private enforcement has achieved success in a limited number of cases, its impact is restricted by lack of private resources, and is hampered by a short statute of limitations, and disadvantageous limitations on punitive damages and attorney's fees.

H.R. Rep. 100-711, 100th Cong. 2d Sess. 16 (1988).

Damages

In general, an injured person may be awarded compensatory damages, injunctive relief, civil penalties, and attorney's fees, subject to certain limitations, discussed below. Damages include out-of-pocket expenses; damages for embarrassment, emotional distress, and humiliation; and, in appropriate cases, punitive damages, subject to the limitations contained in the act on the amount of "civil penalties" that may be imposed.

Procedures and Remedies

The 1988 amendments provide five avenues to enforcement. First, under an administrative enforcement scheme, there are two mechanisms. A complainant can file a complaint with HUD. The statute of limitations has been extended to one year (from 180 days under the old law). 42 U.S.C. § 3610(a). If the complaint filed with HUD involves a jurisdiction with a certified substantially equivalent law, HUD refers the matter for disposition to the agency in that jurisdiction which administers the fair housing law. *Id.* at § 3610(f). Prior to final disposition of a complaint, the act provides that, if the Secretary of HUD concludes that prompt judicial action is necessary, HUD may authorize a civil action and the Attorney General will commence an action for temporary or preliminary relief. *Id.* at § 3610(e).

In addition, if the Secretary determines that the matter involves the legality of any State or local zoning ordinance the Secretary, instead of issuing a charge "shall immediately" refer the matter to the Attorney General for enforcement under § 3614 (the fifth method discussed below). *Id.* at § 3610(g)(2)(C).

Second, under the administrative method, HUD may itself file a complaint on its own initiative, may investigate, and may make conciliation efforts. Following the investigation, HUD must dismiss the complaint or issue a charge. If a charge is issued the matter will be decided in a hearing before an Administrative Law Judge (ALJ) unless, within twenty days, the parties, including the complainant, the respondent, or an aggrieved person, make an election to have the charge decided in a civil action in court. *Id.* at § 3612(a), (b).

Under this second mechanism before an ALJ, the proceedings must commence within 120 days after the issuance of the Secretary's charge and must conclude within 60 days after commencement (unless it is impracticable to do so). The parties may be represented by counsel, obtain subpoenas and discovery, and present evidence. The ALJ is empowered to issue orders for "such relief as may be appropriate," including actual damages, injunctive and other equitable relief, as well as "civil penalties." *Id.* at § 3612(g). Civil penalties which appear to be in the nature of punitive damages, however, are limited to $10,000 for a first discriminatory housing practice, up to $25,000 for a second discriminatory housing practice within a 5-year period, and up to $50,000 for two or more discriminatory housing practices within a 7-year period. The ALJ's order is subject to review by the Secretary of HUD (or his or her designee) and to judicial review. In addition, HUD may petition the United States Court of Appeals for the circuit in which the violation occurred for enforcement of an order.

The third enforcement mechanism involves a party's election to have a judicial proceeding. If an election is made for a court proceeding after HUD's filing of a charge, the Secretary is required to authorize a civil action in a United States district court, and within thirty days after the election for a court proceeding is made, the Attorney General is required to commence the civil action "on behalf of" the aggrieved person. The court may grant such relief as it could grant in a private enforcement action, *Id.* at § 3612(o), which is discussed below.

The fourth enforcement mechanism is a private civil action brought by an aggrieved person. An aggrieved person may file an action for appropriate relief within two years after an alleged discriminatory housing practice or the breach of a conciliation agreement entered into under Title VIII. The action may be filed notwithstanding the filing of a complaint with HUD, but the private civil action is barred if an ALJ has commenced a hearing on the charge. In a judicial civil action the court may award actual and punitive damages without limitation, and may grant injunctive and other affirmative relief. *Id.* at § 3613. In addition, the Attorney General may intervene in the action by certifying that the case is of "general public importance." *Id.* at § 3613(e).

Fifth, the original act authorized the Attorney General to sue only in "pattern or practice" cases. The 1988 amendments broaden the enforcement power by authorizing the Attorney General to sue not merely when there is reasonable cause to believe persons are engaged in patterns or practices of discrimination, but also when "any group of persons has been denied rights granted [in Title VIII] and such denial raises an issue of *general public importance*." *Id.* at § 3614. [emphasis added]

In judicial actions brought by the Attorney General (a) on the ground that the defendant is engaged in a "pattern or practice" or (b) because the case is of "general public importance" and in actions that the Attorney General brings (c) on referral from HUD or (d) for breach of a conciliation agreement, the relief that may be granted includes injunctions, other relief including monetary damages without limitation, and "civil penalties" to "vindicate the public interest" limited to $50,000 for a first violation and to $100,000 for any subsequent violation. *Id.* at § 3614.

Attorney's Fees

The amendments authorize attorney's fees in the discretion of the judge or ALJ under the first four enforcement mechanisms discussed above. *Id.* at § 3612(p) (administrative proceedings before an ALJ and court proceedings arising from administrative proceedings, including elections after the filing of a charge by the Secretary. *Id.* at § 3613(c)(2) (civil actions for private enforcement). In addition, when civil action is commenced for private enforcement—the fourth mechanism—the court upon application may appoint an attorney for the complainant or the party charged with a violation. *Id.* at § 3613(b). The amendments thus change the limitation contained in the original Title VIII under which attorney's fees could be awarded only when the plaintiff was unable to obtain representation otherwise for financial reasons.

Notes and Questions

1. The statutory language does not make clear what role a private attorney will play in the action when, pursuant to an aggrieved person's election, the Attorney General commences an action on behalf of that person. Could the Justice Department and the private attorney represent the plaintiff? If true representation had been intended, why is the language used that the action shall be filed "on behalf of the aggrieved party"?

Conversely, suppose there comes a point when the complainant's interest and the interest of the government diverge? Which interest then predominates with the government attorneys? *See* Eugene R. Gaetke & Robert G. Schwemm, *Government Lawyers and Their Private "Clients" Under the Fair Housing Act*, 65 Geo. Wash. L. Rev. 329 (1997) (discussing among other cases, the *Soules* case, *supra.* In the *Soules* case the government attorneys first represented Soules, the claimant. But when she decided to appeal the ALJ's adverse ruling these attorneys abandoned her on the ground that the government could not appeal an adverse decision of the ALJ. Finally, to make matters worse, other government attorneys actually *opposed* Soules on the merits of her appeal in the Second Circuit by arguing that questions about whether she had a child or whether the child was noisy were permissible and did not constitute familial status discrimination.)

2. For an empirical comparative analysis between public and private attorneys' effectiveness in pursuing fair housing claims concluding that enforcement with private attorneys is more effective, see Michael Selmi, *Public vs. Private Enforcement of Civil Rights: The Case of Housing and Employment*, 45 UCLA L. Rev. 1401 (1998).

3. For general consideration of relief and damages see James A. Kushner, Fair Housing (2d ed. 1995 & Supp. 2000). For discussion of enforcement problems under the Fair Housing Act prior to the 1988 amendments, see James A. Kushner, *An Unfinished Agenda: The Federal Fair Housing Enforcement Effort*, 6 Yale L. & Pol'y Rev. 348 (1988), and Alexander M. Waldrop, *Enforcement of the Fair Housing Act: What Role Should the Federal Government Play?*, 74 Ky. L.J. 201 (1985–86). For discussion of the 1988 Amendments Act generally, see James A. Kushner, *The Fair Housing Amendments Act of 1988: The Second Generation of Fair Housing*, 42 Vand. L. Rev. 1049 (1989).

Index